UNDERSTANDING & MANAGING

ORGANIZATIONAL BEHAVIOR

Jennifer M. George and Gareth R. Jones
A CUSTOM EDITION

Taken from:

Understanding and Managing Organizational Behavior, Fourth Edition
by Jennifer M. George and Gareth R. Jones

PEARSON CUSTOM PUBLISHING
75 Arlington Street, Suite 300, Boston, MA 02116
A Pearson Education Company

For Nicholas and Julia

brief contents

table of contents

---

4 PERCEPTION, ATTRIBUTION, AND THE MANAGEMENT OF DIVERSITY   103

---

5 LEARNING AND CREATIVITY   139

14   COMMUNICATION IN ORGANIZATIONS   435

preface

We have substantially revised the organization and content of the fourth edition of our book, *Understanding and Managing Organizational Behavior,* to reflect the changes that are taking place in the world of work and organizations.

First, the ways in which continuing advances in information technology are affecting all aspects of behavior in organizations has received increased attention in this new edition. We have expanded our already extensive coverage of the ways in which digital and wireless communication are transforming how people perform their jobs, how teams function, and how organizations achieve their goals.

Second, the increasing globalization of business and diversity of the workforce have led us to change the way we discuss and present the many opportunities and challenges globalization and diversity pose for understanding and managing organizational behavior.

Third, recent ethical controversies and scandals that have involved a growing number of well-known companies such as WorldCom, Enron, and Boeing and managers such as Bernard Ebbers and Kenneth Lay, have led us to rethink our treatment of ethics and ethical behavior.

Finally, the continuing advances made by organizational behavior scholars and researchers as they develop new and improved theories and models to explain why and how people and teams behave as they do has led us to modify, update, and refine our coverage of many different aspects of organizational behavior. Concepts like *personality, trust, creativity, mood, emotion, continuous learning, virtual teams, telecommuting, outsourcing, and knowledge management* are now found in all the central research areas of organizational behavior such as learning, motivation, leadership, group behavior, and communication.

A MAJOR REVISION

Our challenge in revising *Understanding and Managing Organizational Behavior* has been to incorporate and integrate the latest advances in theorizing and research and provide a thorough and contemporary account of the factors that influence organizational behavior. Most importantly, we strived to convey this knowledge to students in a very readable, applied, hands-on format to increase their understanding and enjoyment of the learning process.

To provide the most current coverage of organizational behavior in a way that enhances student interest, learning, and retention, we have reorganized the chapters in our book. **We have made major changes to Chapter 1 to reflect contemporary organizational behavior issues and challenges**; in Chapter 1, we provide a new approach to understanding and managing organizational behavior that sets the scene for the rest of the book.

In Part One, *Individuals in Organizations*, we have made major changes to underscore the many ways in which people can contribute to organizations and how an understanding of factors such as **personality, emotional intelligence, creativity, and motivation** can help organizations and their members channel effort and behavior in ways that promote the achievement of organizational objectives and the well-being of all organizational stakeholders, including employees. **In Chapters 2, 3, and 4, we have expanded our coverage of personality, emotional intelligence, mood and emotion, values and ethics, and the proactive management of diversity**; additionally, we link these factors to important behaviors and determinants of organizational effectiveness. We have refocused **Chapter 5** to convey the variety of ways in which organizational members can and do learn with a **new emphasis on continuous learning through creativity**. Our treatment of work motivation has been revamped. In Chapter 6, we provide an integrated account of work motivation and the latest development in motivation theory and research. Chapter 7 focuses on how to create a motivating work environment through job design, organizational objectives, and goal setting. **Chapter 8** addresses **the changing nature of the employment relationship and the implications of factors such as outsourcing, pay differentials, boundaryless careers**, and values for motivation and performance. Lastly, in Chapter 9, we focus on the very real stressors people face, how they can be effectively managed, and finding a balance between work and other aspects of life. Overall,

Part I has been substantially revised to reflect both contemporary theorizing and research and the very real challenges and opportunities facing organizations and their members.

In Part Two, *Group and Team Processes*, we bring together the many ways in which organizational members work together to achieve organizational objectives, the challenges they face, and how to achieve real synergies. Chapters 10 and 11 have been revised to focus on the key factors that lead to effective work groups and teams. **Chapter 12 provides an updated treatment of leadership in organizations.** We have moved our discussion of power, politics, conflict and negotiation to Chapter 13 of this part. In Chapter 14, we discuss how the latest developments in information technology have changed the nature of communication in and between organizations. In the final chapter in this part, **Chapter 15**, we provide updated coverage of **decision-making, knowledge management, and innovation**.

Part Three, *Organizational Processes*, has also undergone major changes in this new edition. In order to provide an integrated treatment of organizational culture and to underscore the importance of ethics in all organizations, **we have separated our treatment of organizational structure and organizational culture.** Chapter 16 focuses on organizational design, structure, and control; in this chapter, we discuss the factors that affect important organizational design choices and the consequences of these choices. **Chapter 17** is devoted to an **integrated treatment of organizational culture and ethical behavior.** In this new chapter, we provide an expanded account of the informal and formal social processes in organizations that affect the way people behave, the sources of organizational culture including organizational ethics, and the nature, causes, and consequences of ethical behavior. We also discuss the factors that can lead to unethical behavior. **Rather than having global issues presented in a separate chapter towards the end of the book as in the prior edition, in this edition, we provide integrated, up-to-date coverage of current global issues**, challenges, and opportunities in each of our chapters in a content-driven fashion. Finally, we have updated our coverage of **organizational change** and development to reflect current realities in the very dynamic environment in which organizations operate.

The combined result of all these changes to the content and organization of our book is a fresh approach that continues and builds off of our leading-edge coverage of organizational behavior topics and issues that our adopters have so appreciated in our prior editions. We have also continued our commitment to providing a treatment of organizational behavior that (1) is comprehensive, integrated, and makes important theories and research findings accessible and interesting to students; (2) is current, up-to-date, and contains expanded coverage of significant contemporary issues including ethics, diversity, globalization, and information technology; (3) uses rich, real-life examples of people and organizations to bring key concepts to life and provide clear managerial implications; and, (4) is experiential and applied. Our end of chapter experiential exercises contained in *Exercises in Understanding and Managing Organizational Behavior* give students the opportunity to catch the excitement of organizational behavior as a fluid, many-faceted discipline with multiple levels of analysis and develop and practice their own skills.

PEDAGOGICAL STRUCTURE

We believe that no other organizational behavior textbook has the sheer range of learning features for students that our book has. These features—some integrated into the text and some at the end of each chapter or part—engage students' interest and facilitate their learning of organizational behavior. The overall objective of these features is to help instructors actively involve their students in the chapter content.

Opening Case

Students enter the chapter via an in-depth, real-world example of people and organizations that focuses attention on the upcoming chapter issues.

Running Glossary

To help students assimilate organizational behavior terminology, we have included a running glossary that provides a definition for every key term in the book.

In-Text Features

Understanding and Managing Organizational Behavior reflects all the current and pressing concerns facing organizations, managers, and employees today. In four different types of in-text boxes (*OB Today, Managing Ethically, Focus on Diversity, and Global View*), we provide up-to-date, real-world examples that bring the content of each chapter to life and engage students to actively think about what they are learning. These boxes are not mere summaries of academic studies or contrived situations; they are real-life stories from the frontline of today's businesses. They are different from similar features in most other textbooks in that they are directly integrated into the text material to highlight and illustrate significant points. We have deliberately presented these features this way because our experience has shown that students are more likely to read material that is seamlessly woven into the fabric of the chapter rather than set apart.

In-Text Exercise

Each chapter includes an in-text exercise, *You're the Management Expert*, which calls upon students to use what they have learned in the chapter thus far and develop and practice their skills. This exercise presents students with a realistic problem an employee in an organization encounters; students apply what they have learned by developing a solution to the problem.

End of Chapter Exercises

The unit entitled *Exercises in Understanding and Managing Organizational Behavior* found at the end of each chapter includes a wide range of activities to help students solidify their knowledge and build and practice their skills. We have carefully developed these exercises to provide instructors with both flexibility and variety for use in large and small classes, as in-class exercises and out-of-class assignments, and to be done individually and in groups. An overriding goal of these exercises is to help students appreciate that there are often no absolute answers to organizational behavior issues and that they must use what they have learned to understand and analyze particular situations, develop and compare alternative courses of action, and generate options for solutions.

Questions for Discussion and Review

In this section, we provide a set of specific questions to stimulate class discussion and help students review chapter material.

Building People Skills

This exercise challenges students to analyze experiences from their own lives and the lives of those they interact with based on the chapter content. It shows students how very applicable the chapter content is to everyday life in and around organizations and how it can help them interpret and understand what they encounter. It builds their perceptual skills—seeing and understanding things at a deeper level now that they have mastered the material in the chapter.

A Question of Ethics

This exercise presents students with a fundamental ethical challenge or dilemma that directly relates to the chapter content. It pushes them to think about ethical implications of different OB topics that ordinarily might not have occurred to them. It also encourages them to develop their own perspective and develop their ethical reasoning skills. This exercise also works well for an in-class discussion after students have worked through it individually.

Small Group Breakout Exercise

This is an in-class exercise to be completed in small groups of 2-5 students. The exercise challenges students to examine, reflect, and share their own experiences vis-à-vis a specific, key question related to the chapter content. They then analyze their collective experiences and come away with conclusions/lessons-learned that they share with the class as a whole.

Topic for Debate

This exercise forces students to actively think about what they have learned and approach it from an informed and critical perspective. Student teams are assigned one side of a fundamental debate in the substantive area of the chapter and develop and present arguments to support it. This exercise makes students think about chapter content at a deeper level, whether or not they personally agree with the side they are taking in the debate. Debates, rebuttals, and questions from the audience fire up students' involvement and spark a high level of class participation.

Experiential Exercise

This is an in-depth team-based exercise that presents students with a real-life problem in organizational behavior that they address based on the chapter content. It challenges students to apply what they have leaned to a specific kind of challenge in organizational behavior. By doing this first in a team, and then hearing other teams' solutions, students are enlightened about multiple issues and perspectives.

Making the Connection

This is an exercise conducted outside the classroom whereby students find real-life mini-cases from the popular and business press that directly illustrate chapter content. These cases can then be used for student-led class discussions of important organizational behavior challenges.

New York Times Cases in the News

These are very recent articles from the *New York Times* that illustrate chapter content, show chapter content in a different and very relevant light, and illuminate some of the challenges and opportunities for OB related to the chapter content. They are excellent active-learning cases both for individual reflection and critical thinking and meaningful class discussion.

TEACHING SUPPORT

OneKey Online Courses

OneKey offers the best teaching and learning online resources all in one place.

OneKey is all instructors need to plan and administer their course. OneKey is all students need for anytime, anywhere access to online course material. Conveniently organized by textbook chapter, these compiled resources help save time and help students reinforce and apply what they have learned. OneKey for convenience, simplicity, and success. *OneKey is available in three course management platforms: Blackboard, CourseCompass and WebCT.*

For the student

- **Learning Modules** which include section reviews, learning activities and pre- and post-tests
- **Student PowerPoints**
- **Research Navigator**–four exclusive databases of reliable source content to help students understand the research process and complete assignments

Instructor's Resource Center available online, in OneKey or CD-ROM

The Instructor's Resource Center, available on CD or at www.prenhall.com, or in your OneKey online course, provides presentation and other classroom resources. Instructors can collect the materials, edit them to create powerful class lectures, and upload them to an online course management system. Using the Instructor's Resource Center on CD-ROM, instructors can easily create custom presentations. Desired files can be exported to the instructor's hard drive for use in classroom presentations and online courses.

With the Instructor's Resource Center, you will find the following faculty supplements:

- **PowerPoints:** Two PowerPoint packages are available with this text. The first is a fully developed, non-interactive set of instructor's PowerPoints. The second is an enhanced, interactive version of the first with video clips and Web links. Both versions contain teaching notes.
- **TestGen test-generating software:** The printed test bank contains approximately 100-120 questions per chapter including multiple-choice, true/false, essay questions. Each test question is ranked by level of difficulty (recall, understanding, and analysis), and contains page references to give the instructor a quick and easy way to balance the exams. (*Print version also available.*)
- **Instructor's Manual:** This Instructor's Manual includes everything you expect including a wealth of additional experiential exercises and teaching tips. The Video Guide is also available. (*Print version also available.*)
- **Test Item File:** (*Word File*)
- **Art files from the text**

Video

21 videos are included to complement your lectures. Companies represented include American Apparel, WNBA, Boeing Satellite Systems, and Creative Age Publications.

Companion Web site

The text Web site (www.prenhall.com/george) features chapter quizzes and student PowerPoints, which are available for review or can be conveniently printed three-to-a-page for in-class note taking.

ACKNOWLEDGMENTS

Finding a way to coordinate and integrate the rich and diverse organizational behavior literature is no easy task. Neither is it easy to present the material in a way that students can easily understand and enjoy, given the plethora of concepts, theories, and research findings. In writing *Understanding and Managing Organizational Behavior*, we have been fortunate to have the assistance of several people who have contributed greatly to the book's final form. We are very grateful to David Parker, our editor, and Melissa Yu, assistant editor, for providing us with timely feedback and information from professors and reviewers that have allowed us to shape the book to meet the needs of its intended market, and to Marcela Boos for ably coordinating the book's progress. We also appreciate the word-processing and administrative support of Elaine Morris, and the research assistance of Alexander Ruiz, both of Rice University.

We are very grateful to the many reviewers and colleagues who provided us with detailed feedback on the chapters and for their perceptive comments and suggestions for improving the manuscript.

A special thank you to the following professors who reviewed this fourth edition multiple times over the past two years:
Rosemary Maellero, University of Dallas
Jeanne McNett, Assumption College
James Schmidtke, California State University–Fresno
Dave Hennessy, Mount Mercy College
Stewart Edwards, Marymount University and NVCC
Dean Frear, Wilkes University
Regina Bento, University of Baltimore
Christina Stamper, Western Michigan University
Alicia Boisnier, University of Buffalo
Robert Whitcomb, University of Wisconsin–Eau Claire
Dave Day, Columbia College

Additional reviewers of this fourth edition:
Courtney Hunt, Northern Illinois University
Robert Augelli, University of Kansas
Betty Velthouse, University of Michigan–Flint
Mary Hogue, Kent State University Stark Campus
Jeanette Davy, Wright State University
Deborah Litvin, Merrimack College
LaVelle Mills, West Texas A&M University
Peggy Brewer, Eastern Kentucky University
Phyllis Harris, University of Central Florida
Eli Kass, Saint Joseph's University
Sean Valentine, University of Wyoming
Cheryl Adkins, Longwood University
Asha Rao, California State University–Hayward
John Klocinski, Lourdes College
Angela Miles, Old Dominion University

Shane Spiller, Morehead State University
Margaret Padgett, Butler University
Nancy Powell, Florida International University
Brian Usilaner, University of Maryland University College
Elena Capella, University of San Francisco
Ronald Humphrey, Virginia Commonwealth University

Reviewers of Previous Editions
Cheryl Adkins, Louisiana State University
Deborah Arvanites, Villanova University
Robert Bontempo, Columbia University
W. Randy Boxx, University of Mississippi
Dan Brass, Pennsylvania State University
Diane Caggiano, Fitchburg State University
Russell Coff, Washington University
Lucinda Doran, The Hay Group
Mark Fearing, University of Houston
Dave Fearon, Central Connecticut State University
Steve Grover, University of Otago
Bob Gulbro, Jacksonville State University
Jennifer Halpern, Cornell University
Sandra Hartman, University of New Orleans
Bruce Johnson, Gustavus Adolphus College
Mary Kernan, University of Delaware
Karen Maher, University of Missouri–St. Louis
Stephen Markham, North Carolina State University
Gary McMahan, University of Texas–Arlington
Janet Near, Indiana University

Tim Peterson, University of Tulsa
Allayne Pizzolatto, Nicholls State University
Peter Poole, Lehigh University
Elizabeth Ravlin, University of South Carolina
Diana Reed, Drake University
Sandra Robinson, University of British Columbia
Chris Scheck, Northern Illinois University
William Sharbrough, The Citadel
Eric Stephan, Brigham Young University
Charlotte Sutton, Auburn University
Susan Washburn, Stephen F. Austin State University
Frank Wiebe, University of Mississippi

Thanks are also due to Ken Bettenhausen, University of Colorado at Denver; David Bowen, Thunderbird; and Art Brief, Tulane University.

Finally, we are grateful to two incredibly wonderful children, Nicholas and Julia, for being all that they are and the joy they bring to all who know them.

— Jennifer M. George
Jesse H. Jones Graduate School of Management
Rice University

— Gareth R. Jones
Lowry Mays College and Graduate School of Business
Texas A & M University

about the authors

 **Jennifer M. George** is the Mary Gibbs Jones Professor of Management and Professor of Psychology in the Jesse H. Jones Graduate School of Management at Rice University. She received her B.A. in Psychology/Sociology from Wesleyan University, her M.B.A. in Finance from New York University, and her Ph.D. in Management and Organizational Behavior from New York University. Prior to joining the faculty at Rice University, she was a Professor in the Department of Management at Texas A&M University.

Professor George specializes in Organizational Behavior and is well known for her research on mood and emotion in the workplace, their determinants, and their effects on various individual and group-level work outcomes. She is the author of many articles in leading peer-reviewed journals such as the *Academy of Management Journal*, the *Academy of Management Review*, the *Journal of Applied Psychology*, *Organizational Behavior and Human Decision Processes*, *Journal of Personality and Social Psychology*, and *Psychological Bulletin*. One of her papers won the Academy of Management's Organizational Behavior Division Outstanding Competitive Paper Award and another paper won the *Human Relations* Best Paper Award. She is, or has been, on the editorial review boards of the *Journal of Applied Psychology*, *Academy of Management Journal*, *Academy of Management Review, Journal of Management*, *Organizational Behavior and Human Decision Processes*, *International Journal of Selection and Assessment,* and *Journal of Managerial Issues*, was a consulting editor for the *Journal of Organizational Behavior*, and was a member of the SIOP *Organizational Frontiers Series* editorial board. She is a Fellow in the American Psychological Association, the American Psychological Society, and the Society for Industrial and Organizational Psychology and a member of the Society for Organizational Behavior. Professor George is currently an Associate Editor for the *Journal of Applied Psychology*. She also has co-authored a leading textbook on *Contemporary Management*.

 **Gareth Jones** received both his B.A. and Ph.D. from the University of Lancaster, U.K. He previously held teaching and research appointments at the University of Warwick, Michigan State University, and the University of Illinois at Urbana-Champaign. Professor Jones specializes in both organizational behavior and organizational theory and is well known for his research on socialization, culture, and applying transaction cost analysis to explain many forms of intraorganizational and interorganizational behavior.

He also has published many articles in leading journals of the field and is one of the most prolific authors in the *Academy of Management Review*. One of his articles won the Academy of *Management Journal* Best Paper Award. He is, or has been, on the editorial review boards of the *Academy of Management Review*, the *Journal of Management*, and *Management Inquiry*.

Professor Jones is a professor of Management at Lowry Mays College and Graduate School of Business at Texas A&M University, where he is actively involved in teaching and research in Organizational Behavior and related fields.

Introduction to Organizational Behavior

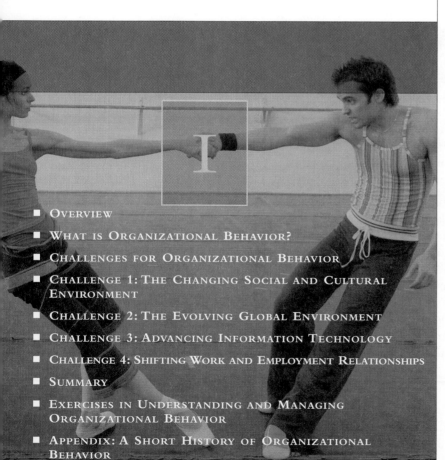

I

LEARNING OBJECTIVES

After reading this chapter, you should be able to:

■

Define organizational behavior and explain how and why it determines the effectiveness of an organization.

▩

Appreciate why the study of organizational behavior improves a person's ability to understand and respond to events that take place in a work setting.

■

Differentiate among the three levels at which organizational behavior is examined.

▩

Appreciate the way changes in an organization's external environment continually create challenges for organizational behavior.

▩

Describe the four main kinds of forces in the environment that pose the most opportunities and problems for organizations today.

OPENING CASE

IKEA Has a Global Approach to OB

What Are the Keys to IKEA's Success?

IKEA is the largest furniture chain in the world. In 2003, the Swedish company operated over 160 stores in 22 countries.[1] IKEA has 20 percent of the global furniture market, but to its managers and employees this is just the tip of the iceberg. They believe IKEA is poised for massive growth throughout the world in the coming decade because it can provide what the average customer wants: well-designed contemporary furniture at an affordable price. IKEA's ability to provide customers with affordable furniture is very much the result of its approach to organizational behavior (OB)—the way it treats its employees and operates its stores throughout the world. In a nutshell, IKEA's OB approach revolves around simplicity, attention to detail, cost-consciousness, and responsiveness in every aspect of its actions and behavior.

The origins of IKEA's successful approach derive from the personal values and beliefs of its founder, Ingvar Kamprad, about how organizations should treat their employees and customers.[2] Kamprad, who is now in his seventies, was born in Smaland, a poor Swedish province whose citizens are well known for being entrepreneurial, frugal, and hardworking. Kamprad definitely absorbed these values, for when he entered the furniture business he made them the core of his approach to OB. He preaches to his store managers and employees about the need to operate in a no-frills, cost-conscious way and that they are all in business "together," meaning that every person in the company plays an important role and has an obligation to each other.

What does Kamprad's frugal, cost-conscious approach mean in practice? All IKEA's members fly coach class on business, stay in inexpensive hotels, and work to keep traveling expenses to a minimum. It also means that IKEA stores operate with the simplest set of rules and procedures possible and that employees are expected to work together to solve problems on an ongoing basis to get the job done. Many famous stories exist about how the frugal Kamprad also always flies coach class and about how, when he takes a can of soda from the minibar in a hotel room, he replaces it with one bought in a store. Kamprad also makes a point of carrying customers' bags to their car—despite the fact that he is a multibillionaire ranked in the top 20 on *Forbes* list of the world's richest people![3]

IKEA's employees see what his approach to OB means as soon as they are recruited to work in one its stores. Starting at the bottom of the ladder, they are quickly trained to perform all the various jobs involved in operating its stores. They also learn the importance IKEA attaches to them taking the initiative and responsibility for solving problems and for focusing on the customer. Employees are rotated between departments and sometimes stores, and rapid promotion is possible for those who demonstrate the enthusiasm and "togetherness" signifying they have bought into IKEA's approach. Everyone who works at IKEA dresses casually (Kamprad has always worn an open-neck shirt), and there are no marks of status such as executive dining rooms or private parking places.

Most of IKEA's top executives and store managers rose from its ranks. To make sure executives are constantly in touch with what's going on along the front lines, once a year the company holds a "breaking the bureaucracy week" during which time executives are required to do store and warehouse work.

IKEA's employees believe if they buy into the company's work values, keep its operations simple and streamlined, and focus on being one step ahead of potential problems, they will share in its success. Promotion, training, above-average pay, a generous store bonus system, and also the personal well-being that comes from working in a place where people are valued by their co-workers are some of the rewards that Kamprad pioneered to build and strengthen IKEA's global OB approach.

Whenever IKEA enters a new country or opens a new store in a new city, it sends its most experienced store managers there to establish its global OB approach. When IKEA first entered the United States, the attitude of U.S. employees puzzled the company's managers. Despite their obvious drive to succeed and good education, employees seemed reluctant to take the initiative and assume responsibility. IKEA's managers discovered that their U.S. employees were afraid mistakes would result in the loss of their jobs. They strived to teach employees the "IKEA way," and its approach to OB has prevailed. Today the United States has become one of IKEA's best markets, and it plans to open many more U.S. stores over the next decade.

Overview

KEA has found a way to create a set of organizational behaviors that lead to a cooperative, win-win situation for the company and its employees. IKEA's employees work hard, are happy working for their company, and are less inclined to leave their jobs than employees in many other kinds of retailing companies. This favorable work situation has been created because IKEA:

- Strives to increase employees' skills and knowledge and encourages them to take responsibility and to work in ways that lead to fast, helpful customer service.

- Provides employees with rewards that encourage high performance and ensure employees' contributions are recognized.

- Creates a work setting in which employees develop a long-term commitment to the organization and are willing to cooperate and work hard to further its goals.

As IKEA's approach suggests, creating a favorable work situation in which people at all levels want to behave in ways that result in customers receiving a high-quality product does not happen by chance. It is the result of careful planning and a solid understanding and appreciation of *how* people behave in organizations and *what* kinds of things cause them to behave the way they do. The best way to gain such an understanding of people at work, and the forces that shape their work behavior, is to study *organizational behavior*, the subject of this book.

In this chapter, we first define organizational behavior and discuss how having a working knowledge of it is essential in today's complex, global world. We then examine how changes taking place *outside* an organization in the global, social, technological, and work or employment environment are changing the way people work together and cooperate *inside* an organization. We will focus on how rapid environmental changes pose behavioral challenges for all the people who work inside the organization. By the end of this chapter, you will understand the central role that organizational behavior plays in determining how effective an organization and its members are in achieving their goals.

What is Organizational Behavior?

To arrive at a useful and meaningful definition of organizational behavior, let's first look at what an organization is. An **organization** is a collection of people who work together to achieve a wide variety of goals. Individual goals are what people are trying to accomplish for themselves—earning a lot of money, helping promote a worthy cause, achieving certain levels of power and prestige, enjoying a satisfying work experience, and so on. Organizational goals are what the organization as a whole is trying to accomplish, such as providing innovative goods and services that customers want, getting candidates elected, raising money for medical research, making a profit to reward stockholders, managers, and employees, and so on. An effective organization is one that achieves both individual and organizational goals.

Police forces, for example, are formed to provide security for law-abiding citizens and a secure, rewarding career for police officers while they perform their valuable service. Paramount Pictures was formed to achieve the goal of providing people with entertainment while making a profit, and in the process, actors, directors, writers, and musicians are employed to do well-paid and interesting work.

Organizations exist to provide goods and services that people want. The amount and quality of these goods and services are the result of the behaviors and performance of the organization's employees—its managers, highly skilled employees in sales or research and development, and the people who actually produce or provide the goods and services. Today, most people make their living by working for some kind of organization. Thus, nearly everyone can benefit from studying organizational behavior. Even people who volunteer to work in nonprofit or charitable organizations can benefit by

Organization A collection of people who work together to achieve individual and organizational goals.

learning the principles of organizational behavior. Like most employees today, volunteers also attend training courses to help them understand the many issues and challenges facing people who work together to aid, for example, the ill, the distressed, or the homeless.

THE NATURE OF ORGANIZATIONAL BEHAVIOR

Organizational behavior
The study of factors that affect how individuals and groups act in organizations and how organizations respond to their environments.

Organizational behavior (OB) is the study of the many factors that have an impact on how people and groups act, think, feel, and respond to work and organizations and how organizations respond to their environments. Understanding how people behave in an organization is important because most people will work for one at some point in their lives and are affected both positively and negatively by their experiences in it. An understanding of OB can help people enhance the positive and reduce the negative effects of working in organizations.

Most of us think we have a basic, intuitive, common-sense understanding of human behavior in organizations because we all are human and have been exposed to different work experiences. Often, however, our intuition and common sense are wrong. We do not really understand why people act and react the way they do. For example, many people assume that happy employees are productive employees—that is, that high job satisfaction causes high job performance—or that punishing someone who performs consistently at a low level is a good way to increase performance, or that it is best to keep pay levels secret. As we will see in later chapters, all these beliefs are either false or are true only under very specific conditions. Applying these principles indiscriminately can, therefore, have negative consequences for employees and organizations.

The study of organizational behavior provides a framework for understanding and appreciating the many forces that affect behavior in organizations. It allows employees at all levels in an organization to make correct decisions about how to behave and work with other people to achieve organizational goals. OB replaces intuition and gut feeling with a well-researched body of theories and systematic guidelines for managing behavior in organizations. The study of OB provides a set of tools—concepts and theories—that help people to understand, analyze, and describe what goes on in organizations and why. OB helps people understand, for example, why they and others are motivated to join an organization, why they feel good or bad about their jobs or about being part of the organization, why some people do a good job and others don't, why some people stay with the same organization for 30 years and others seem to be constantly dissatisfied and change jobs every two years. In essence, OB concepts and theories allow people to correctly understand, describe, and analyze how the characteristics of individuals, groups, work situations, and the organization itself affect how members feel about and act within their organization (see Figure 1.1).

FIGURE 1.1

What Is Organizational Behavior?

Organizational behavior
Provides a set of tools that allow:

People to understand, analyze, and describe behavior in organizations

Managers to improve, enhance, or change work behaviors so that individuals, groups, and the whole organization can achieve their goals

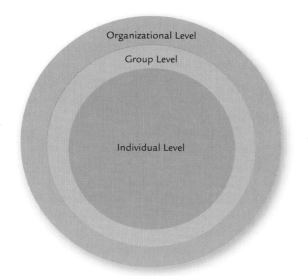

FIGURE **1.2**
Levels of Analysis in Organizational Behavior

LEVELS OF ANALYSIS

In practice, there are three main levels at which organizational behavior is examined: the individual, the group, and the organization as a whole. A full understanding of OB is impossible without a thorough examination of the factors that affect behavior at each level (see Figure 1.2).

Much of the research in OB has focused on the way in which employees' personalities, feelings, and motivation affect how well they do their jobs—whether they like what they do, whether they get along with co-workers, and so on. In Chapters 2 through 9, we examine individual characteristics that are critical for understanding and managing behavior in organizations: personality and ability, attitudes, values, moods, perception and attribution, learning, motivation, and stress and work-life linkages (see Figure 1.3).

The effects of group or team characteristics and processes (such as communication and decision making) on organizational behavior also need to be understood. A **group** is two or more people who interact to achieve their goals. A **team** is a group in which members

Group Two or more people who interact to achieve their goals.

Team A group in which members work together intensively to achieve a common group goal.

FIGURE **1.3**
Components of Organizational Behavior

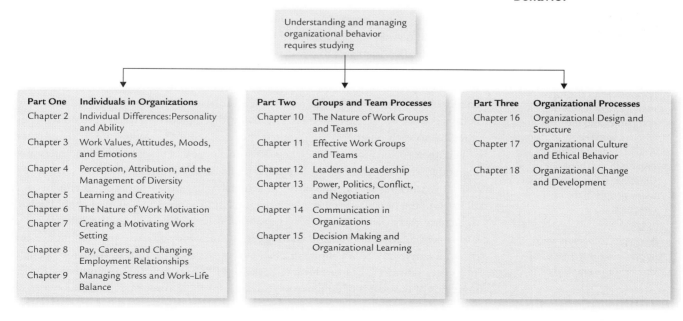

Part One	Individuals in Organizations	Part Two	Groups and Team Processes	Part Three	Organizational Processes
Chapter 2	Individual Differences: Personality and Ability	Chapter 10	The Nature of Work Groups and Teams	Chapter 16	Organizational Design and Structure
Chapter 3	Work Values, Attitudes, Moods, and Emotions	Chapter 11	Effective Work Groups and Teams	Chapter 17	Organizational Culture and Ethical Behavior
Chapter 4	Perception, Attribution, and the Management of Diversity	Chapter 12	Leaders and Leadership	Chapter 18	Organizational Change and Development
Chapter 5	Learning and Creativity	Chapter 13	Power, Politics, Conflict, and Negotiation		
Chapter 6	The Nature of Work Motivation	Chapter 14	Communication in Organizations		
Chapter 7	Creating a Motivating Work Setting	Chapter 15	Decision Making and Organizational Learning		
Chapter 8	Pay, Careers, and Changing Employment Relationships				
Chapter 9	Managing Stress and Work-Life Balance				

Understanding and managing organizational behavior requires studying

Virtual team A group whose members work together intensively via electronic means and who may never actually meet.

work together intensively to achieve a common group goal. A **virtual team** is a group whose members work together intensively via electronic means and who may never actually meet. The number of members in a group, the type and diversity of team members, the tasks they perform, and the attractiveness of a group to its members all influence not just the behavior of the group as a whole but also the behaviors of individuals within the group. For example, a team can influence its members' decisions on how diligently they should do their jobs or how often they are absent from work. Chapters 10 through 15 examine the ways in which groups affect their individual members and the processes involved in group interactions such as leadership, communication, and decision making.

Many studies have found that characteristics of the organization as a whole (such as its culture and structural design) have important effects on the behavior of individuals and groups. The values and beliefs in an organization's culture influence how people, groups, and managers interact with each other and with people outside the organization, such as customers and suppliers. Organizational culture also shapes and controls the attitudes and behavior of people and groups within an organization and influences their desire to work toward achieving organizational goals. An organization's structure controls how people and groups cooperate and interact to achieve organizational goals. The principal task of organizational structure is to encourage people to work hard and coordinate their efforts to ensure high levels of organizational performance. Chapters 16 through 18 examine the way organizational structure and culture affect performance and also examine how factors such as the changing global environment, technology, and ethics impact work attitudes and behavior.

CEOs like Carly Fiorino of Hewlett-Packard are responsible for the top management teams of their companies and the thousands workers who report to them. A solid understanding of organizational behavior helps CEOs like Fiorino steer these many people in the right direction.

Manager A person who supervises the activities of one or more employees.

ORGANIZATIONAL BEHAVIOR AND MANAGEMENT

The ability to use the tools of OB to *understand* behavior in organizations is one reason for studying this topic. A second reason is to learn how to *use* and *apply* these concepts, theories, and techniques to improve, enhance, or change behavior so that employees, groups, and the whole organization can better achieve their goals. For example, a salesperson working in Neiman Marcus in Houston has the individual goal, set by his supervisor, of selling $5,000 worth of men's clothing per week. In addition, he and the other members of the men's clothing department have the group goal of keeping the department looking neat and attractive and of never keeping customers waiting. The store as a whole (along with all the other stores in the nationwide Neiman Marcus chain) has the goals of being profitable by selling customers unique, high-quality clothes and accessories and providing them with excellent service. If all these different goals are met, employees receive a large yearly pay bonus, and Neiman Marcus makes a profit.

A knowledge of organizational behavior can help Neiman Marcus employees earn their bonuses. For example, OB research has found that organizations whose employees have been taught how to work as a team and to take pains to be helpful, courteous, and agreeable to each other and to customers will be more effective than those organizations whose employees do not behave in this way. At Neiman Marcus, employees know what kinds of behaviors result in satisfied customers. They know that if they work hard to be courteous and agreeable to each other and to customers they will sell more clothes and so they (1) will achieve their personal sales goal, (2) their department's goal of never keeping customers waiting, and (3) the organization's goals of being profitable and providing excellent service.

A working knowledge of organizational behavior is important to employees at all levels in the organization because it helps them to appreciate how they should behave to achieve their own goals, such as a promotion or higher income. But knowledge of OB is particularly important to **managers**, people who supervise the activities of one or more employees. Sam Palmisano, chief executive officer (CEO) of IBM, for example, and Carly Fiorino, CEO of Hewlett-Packard (HP), bear ultimate responsibility for the hundreds of thousands of employees who work for these companies. The sales managers of IBM's or HP's southern region, who control hundreds of salespeople, are also managers, as are the managers (or supervisors) in charge of the companies' computer service centers, who supervise only a handful of service technicians.

Managers at all levels confront the problem of understanding the behavior of their subordinates and responding appropriately. Palmisano and Fiorino have to manage their companies' **top-management teams**, high-ranking executives who jointly plan the companies' strategy so that they can achieve their goals. The sales managers have to manage their sales forces so that they sell the mix of computer hardware, software, and services that best meets customers' information-processing needs. The service managers have to manage computer technicians so that they respond promptly and courteously to customers' appeals for help and quickly solve their problems. (And IBM and HP compete vigorously to provide customers with high-quality customer service.)

Each of these managers faces the common challenge of finding ways to help the organization achieve its goals. A manager who understands how individual, group, and organizational characteristics affect work attitudes and behavior can begin to experiment to see whether changing one or more of these characteristics might increase the effectiveness of the organization and its individuals and groups. **Organizational effectiveness** is the ability of an organization to achieve its goals. The study of organizational behavior helps managers meet the challenge of improving organizational effectiveness by providing them with a set of tools:

♦ A manager can work to raise an employee's self-esteem or beliefs about his or her ability to accomplish a certain task in order to increase the employee's productivity or job satisfaction.

♦ A manager can revise the reward system to change employees' beliefs about the extent to which their rewards depend on their performance.

♦ A manager can change the design of a person's job or the rules and procedures for doing the job to reduce costs, make the task more enjoyable, or make the task easier to perform.

Recall from the chapter-opening case that IKEA's goal is to attract customers by providing them with high-quality, affordable furniture. To achieve this goal, IKEA's founder created a work setting in which employees were taught what kinds of organizational behaviors result in economical, cost-conscious store operations. IKEA succeeded because it chose a way to motivate and reward employees that encourages them to work hard and well and behave in a way that benefits everyone. A key challenge for all organizations, and one that we address throughout this book, is how to encourage organizational members to work effectively for their own benefit, the benefit of their work groups, and the benefit of their organization.

MANAGERIAL FUNCTIONS

The four principal functions or duties of **management** are the processes of planning, organizing, leading, and controlling an organization's human, financial, material, and other resources to increase its effectiveness.[4] And, as our preceding examples showed, managers knowledgeable about organizational behavior are in a good position to improve their ability to perform these functions (see Figure 1.4).

Planning. In **planning**, managers establish their organization's strategy—that is, they decide how best to allocate and use resources to achieve organizational goals. At Southwest Airlines, for example, Chairman Herb Kelleher's strategy is based on the goal of providing customers with low-priced air travel.[5] To accomplish this goal, Southwest uses its resources efficiently. For example, Southwest uses only one kind of plane, the Boeing 737, to keep down operating, training, and maintenance costs. Employees

Top-management team
High-ranking executives who plan a company's strategy so that the company can achieve its goals.

Organizational effectiveness
The ability of an organization to achieve its goals.

Management The process of planning, organizing, leading, and controlling an organization's human, financial, material, and other resources to increase its effectiveness.

Planning Deciding how best to allocate and use resources to achieve organizational goals.

FIGURE 1.4

Four Functions of Management

cooperate and share jobs when necessary to keep costs down, and the company's use of the Internet is state of the art and one of the easiest to use in the industry.

Planning is a complex and difficult task because a lot of uncertainty normally surrounds the decisions managers need to make. Because of this uncertainty, they face risks when deciding what actions to take. A knowledge of organizational behavior can help improve the quality of their decision making, increase the chances of success, and lessen the risks inherent in planning and decision making. First, the study of organizational behavior reveals how decisions get made in organizations and how politics and conflict affect the planning process. Second, the way in which group decision making affects planning and the biases that can influence decisions are revealed. Third, the theories and concepts of organizational behavior show how the composition of an organization's top-management team can affect the planning process. The study of organizational behavior, then, can improve a manager's planning abilities and enhance organizational performance.

Organizing. In **organizing**, managers establish a structure of relationships that dictates how members of an organization work together to achieve organizational goals. Organizing involves grouping workers into groups, teams, or departments according to the kinds of tasks they perform. At IBM, for example, service technicians are grouped into a service operation department, and salespeople are grouped into the sales department.

Organizational behavior offers many guidelines on how to organize employees to make the best use of their skills and capabilities. In later chapters, we discuss various methods of grouping workers to enhance communication and coordination while avoiding conflict or politics. At Southwest Airlines, for example, although employees such as pilots, flight attendants, and baggage handlers are members of particular departments, they are expected to perform one another's nontechnical jobs when needed.

Leading. In **leading**, managers encourage workers to do a good job (work hard, produce high-quality products) and coordinate individuals and groups so that everyone is working to achieve the organization's goals. The study of different leadership methods and of how to match leadership styles to the characteristics of the organization and all its components is a major concern of organizational behavior. Today, the way managers lead employees is changing because millions of employees work in **self-managed teams**, groups of employees who are given both the authority and responsibility to manage many different aspects of their own organizational behavior. These groups, for example, are often responsible for interviewing job applicants and for selecting new team members. Team members then train new recruits as well as help each other improve their own level of job skills and knowledge. They also work together to develop new work methods and procedures that can increase their effectiveness.

Organizing Establishing a structure of relationships that dictates how members of an organization work together to achieve organizational goals.

Leading Encouraging and coordinating individuals and groups so that all organizational members are working to achieve organizational goals.

Self-managed teams Groups of employees who are given the authority and responsibility to manage many different aspects of their *own* organizational behavior.

Managers who used to actively supervise the team now play a different role—that of coach or mentor. Their new role is to provide advice or support as needed and to champion the team and help it to obtain additional resources that will allow it to perform at a higher level and earn greater rewards as well. The way in which a small company, Dick's Drive-In Restaurants, chose and followed this approach to managing organizational behavior illustrates many of these issues, as the accompanying OB Today suggests.

ob today

Dick's Restaurants Understands Its Employees

Dick's Drive-In Restaurants is a five-store, family-owned hamburger chain based in Seattle, Washington. Founded in 1954, its owners have pursued an innovative approach to retaining hardworking employees in the fast-food industry—one known for its high level of employee turnover.[6] From the beginning, Dick's decided to pay its employees well above the industry average and offer them many benefits too. Dick's pays its 110 part-time employees $8.75 an hour. It also covers 100 percent of the cost of its employees' health insurance and offers employees who have worked at Dick's for six months up to $10,000 toward the cost of their four-year college tuition! Dick's even pays its employees their regular wage if they perform four hours of voluntary work each month in the local community.

Dick's competitors, on the other hand, national hamburger chains such as Wendy's and McDonald's, pay their part-time employees at the minimum wage of $5.85 an hour and offer them no health insurance and few other benefits—certainly nothing that can compare to Dick's. When asked why Dick's adopts this approach, Jim Spady, Dick's vice president, answered, "We've been around since 1954, and one thing we've always believed is that there is nothing more important than finding and training and keeping the best people you possibly can."[7]

Dick's approach to organizational behavior begins when it recruits new hires straight from high school. Its managers emphasize that they are looking for hard work and a long-term commitment from employees. In return, Dick's will help and support employees by providing them with above-average pay, health care insurance, and tuition money while they work their way through school. Dick's expects its employees to perform to the best of their ability to get its burgers, and its customers, out the door as fast as they can. Employees are expected to be able to perform any of the tasks that have to be done in the restaurant such as taking orders, cooking the food, and cleaning up the premises. When performing their work, Dick's employees don't wait to be asked to do something; they know what to do to provide customers with the freshest burgers Seattle has to offer.

Dick's does not expect its employees to remain with the company *after* they have graduated; however, it does want them to stay with the company until they graduate. And here lies the reason why Dick's can afford to reward its employees with such generous salary and benefits compared to its competitors. Employee turnover at large national burger chains is frequently more than 100 percent a year, meaning a typical burger restaurant has to replace all its employees at least once a year. As a result, large chains have to recruit and train new employees continually, which is very expensive and greatly increases the costs of operating a restaurant. High employee turnover also makes it difficult for managers to develop close working relationships with employees and find ways to encourage them to perform at a high level.

Dick's approach to organizational behavior that leads to high performance and low turnover keeps operating costs low. Dick's managers have discovered that if employees stay for at least six months its lower operating costs more than compensate for the extra pay and benefits employees receive. Dick's approach has, therefore, created a win-win situation for the company and its employees. If a person has to work his or her way through college, then Dick's seems to be a good place to do it.

Controlling Monitoring and evaluating individual, group, and organizational performance to see whether organizational goals are being achieved.

Role A set of behaviors or tasks a person is expected to perform because of the position he or she holds in a group or organization.

Skill An ability to act in a way that allows a person to perform well in his or her role.

Conceptual skills The ability to analyze and diagnose a situation and to distinguish between cause and effect.

Human skills The ability to understand, work with, lead, and control the behavior of other people and groups.

Technical skills Job-specific knowledge and techniques.

Controlling. Finally, in **controlling**, managers monitor and evaluate individual, group, and organizational performance to see whether organizational goals are being achieved. If goals are being met, managers can take action to maintain and improve performance; if goals are not being met, managers must take corrective action. The controlling function also allows managers to evaluate how well they are performing their planning, organizing, and leading functions.

Once again, the theories and concepts of organizational behavior allow managers to understand and accurately diagnose work situations in order to pinpoint where corrective action may be needed. Suppose the members of a group are not working effectively together. The problem might be due to personality conflicts between individual members of the group, to the faulty leadership approach of a supervisor, or to poor job design. Organizational behavior provides managers tools they can use to diagnose the source of the problem and make an informed decision about how to correct it. Control at all levels of the organization is impossible if managers do not possess the necessary organizational behavior tools.

MANAGERIAL ROLES

Managers perform their four functions by assuming specific roles in organizations. A **role** is a set of behaviors or tasks a person is expected to perform because of the position he or she holds in a group or organization. One researcher, Henry Mintzberg, has identified 10 roles that managers play as they manage the behavior of people inside and outside the organization.[8] (See Table 1.1.)

MANAGERIAL SKILLS

Just as the study of organizational behavior provides tools that managers can use to increase their ability to perform their functions and roles, it can also help managers improve their skills in managing organizational behavior. A **skill** is an ability to act in a way that allows a person to perform well in his or her role. Managers need three principal kinds of skills in order to perform their organizational functions and roles effectively: conceptual, human, and technical skills.[9]

Conceptual skills allow a manager to analyze and diagnose a situation and to distinguish between cause and effect. Planning and organizing require a high level of conceptual skill, as do the decisional roles discussed previously. The study of organizational behavior provides managers with many of the conceptual tools they need to analyze organizational settings and to identify and diagnose the dynamics of individual and group behavior in these settings.

Human skills enable a manager to understand, work with, lead, and control the behavior of other people and groups. The study of how managers can influence behavior is a principal focus of organizational behavior, and the ability to learn and acquire the skills that are needed to coordinate and motivate people is a principal difference between effective and ineffective managers.

Technical skills are the job-specific knowledge and techniques that a manager needs to perform a specific organizational role—for example, in manufacturing, accounting, or marketing. The specific technical skills a manager needs depend on the organization the manager is in and on his or her position in the organization. The manager of a restaurant, for example, needs cooking skills to fill in for an absent cook, accounting and bookkeeping skills to keep track of receipts and costs and to administer the payroll, and artistic skills to keep the restaurant looking attractive for customers.

Effective managers need all three kinds of skills—conceptual, human, and technical. The lack of one or more of these skills can lead to a manager's downfall. One of

TABLE I.I

Types of Managerial Roles

Type of Role	Examples of Role Activities
Figurehead	Give speech to workforce about future organizational goals and objectives; open a new corporate headquarters building; state the organization's ethical guidelines and principles of behavior that employees are to follow in their dealings with customers and suppliers.
Leader	Give direct commands and orders to subordinates; make decisions concerning the use of human and financial organizational resources; mobilize employee commitment to organizational goals.
Liaison	Coordinate the work of managers in different departments or even in different parts of the world; establish alliances between different organizations to share resources to produce new products.
Monitor	Evaluate the performance of different managers and departments and take corrective action to improve their performance; watch for changes occurring in the industry or in society that may affect the organization.
Disseminator	Inform organizational members about changes taking place both inside and outside the organization that will affect them and the organization; communicate to employees the organization's cultural and ethical values.
Spokesperson	Launch a new organizational advertising campaign to promote a new product; give a speech to inform the general public about the organization's future goals.
Entrepreneur	Commit organizational resources to a new project to develop new products; decide to expand the organization globally in order to obtain new customers.
Disturbance handler	Move quickly to mobilize organizational resources to deal with external problems facing the organization, such as an environmental crisis, or internal problems facing the organization, such as strikes.
Resource allocator	Allocate organizational resources between different departments and divisions of the organization; set budgets and salaries of managers and employees.
Negotiator	Work with suppliers, distributors, labor unions, or employees in conflict to solve disputes or to reach a long-term contract or agreement; work with other organizations to establish an agreement to share resources.

the biggest problems that entrepreneurs who found their own businesses confront—a problem that is often responsible for their failure—is lack of appropriate conceptual and human skills. Similarly, one of the biggest problems that scientists and engineers transitioning into management confront is their lack of effective human skills. Management functions, roles, and skills are intimately related, and in the long run the ability to understand and manage behavior in organizations is indispensable to any actual or prospective manager.

Challenges for Organizational Behavior

In the last few decades, the challenges facing organizations to effectively utilize and develop the skills, knowledge, and "human capital" of their employees have been increasing. As we noted earlier, among these challenges, those stemming from changing pressures or forces in the social and cultural, global, technological, and work environments stand out. To appreciate the way changes in the environment affect behavior in organizations it is useful to model an organization from an open-system perspective. In an **open system**, an organization takes in resources from its external environment and

Open system Organizations that take in resources from their external environment and convert or transform them into goods and services that are sent back to their environments where customers buy them.

FIGURE 1.5

An Open-System View of Organizational Behavior

ENVIRONMENT

The activities of most organizations can be modeled using the open-system view. At the *input stage*, companies such as Ford, General Electric, Ralph Lauren, IKEA, and Dick's Drive-In Restaurants acquire resources such as raw materials, component parts, skilled employees, robots, and computer-controlled manufacturing equipment. The challenge is to create a set of organizational behaviors and procedures that allows employees to identify and purchase high-quality resources at a favorable price. An **organizational procedure** is a rule or routine an employee follows to perform some task in the most effective way.

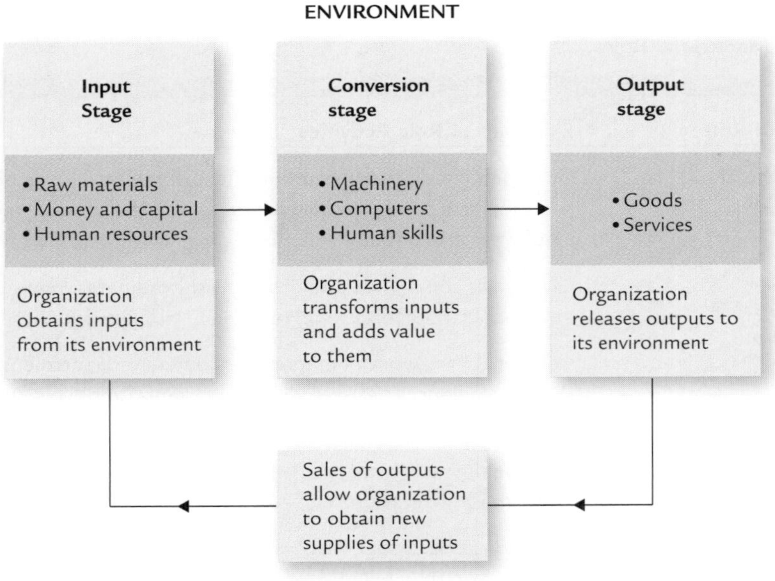

converts or transforms them into goods and services that are sent back to that environment, where they are then bought by customers (see Figure 1.5).

Once the organization has gathered the necessary resources, conversion begins. At the *conversion stage*, the organization's workforce, using appropriate skills, tools, techniques, machinery, and equipment, transforms the inputs into outputs of finished goods and services such as cars, appliances, clothing, and hamburgers. The challenge in this case is to develop the set of organizational behaviors and procedures that results in high-quality goods and services produced at the lowest possible cost.

At the *output stage*, the organization releases finished goods and services to its external environment, where customers purchase and use them to satisfy their needs. The challenge at this stage is to develop the set of organizational behaviors and procedures that entices customers to buy a company's products and become loyal customers. The money the organization generates from sales enables it to acquire more resources so the cycle can begin again.

The system just described is said to be "open" because the organization draws from and interacts with the external environment to secure resources, transform them, and then sell the products created to customers. Only by continually altering and improving its organizational behaviors and procedures to respond to changing environmental forces can an organization adapt and prosper over time. Organizations that fail to recognize the many changing forces in the environment lose their ability to acquire resources, sell their products, and often disintegrate and disappear.

In the next sections, we introduce the four major organizational behavior challenges facing firms when the environment in which they operate changes. We then examine these challenges in more depth throughout the rest of the book to reveal the many dramatic ways in which organizational behavior and procedures are changing today enabling organizations to adapt and prosper.

Organizational procedure
A rule or routine an employee follows to perform some task in the most effective way.

Challenge 1: The Changing Social and Cultural Environment

Forces in the social and cultural environment are those that are due to changes in the way people live and work—changes in values, attitudes, and beliefs brought about by changes in a nation's culture and the characteristics of its people. **National culture** is the set of values or beliefs that a society considers important and the norms of behavior that are approved or sanctioned in that society. Over time, the culture of a nation changes, and this affects the values and beliefs of its members. In the United States, for example, beliefs about the roles and rights of women, minorities, gays, people with disabilities, love, sex, marriage, war, and work have changed in each passing decade.

Organizations must be responsive to the changes that take place in a society, for these changes affect all aspects of their operations. They affect hiring and promotion practices, for example, and the forms of organizational behaviors and procedures that are seen as appropriate in the work setting. For example, in the last 10 years the number of women and minorities assuming managerial positions in the workforce has increased by over 25 percent. As we discuss in detail in later chapters, organizations have had to make enormous strides to prevent their employees from discriminating against others on the basis of age, gender, or ethnicity and also have had to work to prevent sexual harassment. Two major challenges of importance to organizational behavior today are those that derive from a breakdown in ethical values and from the increasing diversity of the workforce.

National culture The set of values or beliefs that a society considers important and the norms of behavior that are approved or sanctioned in that society.

DEVELOPING ORGANIZATIONAL ETHICS AND WELL-BEING

Recently, huge ethical scandals have plagued hundreds of U.S. companies such as Worldcom, Tyco, Adelphia, Enron, and Arthur Andersen, whose top managers put personal gain ahead of their responsibility toward their employees, customers, and investors. Many of these companies' stock prices have collapsed, and ordinary Americans have seen the value of their pension plans and investments plunge in value as a result. In light of these scandals, the effect of ethics, an important component of a nation's social and cultural values, on the behavior of organizations and their members has taken center stage.[10]

An organization's **ethics** are the values, beliefs, and moral rules its managers and employees should use to analyze or interpret a situation and then decide what is the "right," or appropriate, way to behave.[11] The ethical problem is to decide how a particular organizational behavior will help or harm people or groups—both inside and outside the organization—who will be affected by it.[12] Ethical organizational behavior is important because it can enhance or reduce the **well-being** (happiness, health, and prosperity) of a nation, an organization, citizens, and employees in several ways.[13]

Ethics The values, beliefs, and moral rules that managers and employees should use to analyze or interpret a situation and then decide what is the "right" or appropriate way to behave.

First, ethics help managers establish the goals that organizations should pursue and the way in which people inside organizations should behave to achieve them.[14] For example, one goal of an organization is to make a profit so that it can pay the managers, employees, suppliers, shareholders, and others who have contributed their skills and resources to the company. Ethics specify what actions an organization should engage in to make a profit. Should an organization be allowed to harm its competitors by recruiting their skilled employees or preventing them from obtaining access to vital inputs? Should an organization be allowed to produce inferior goods that may endanger the safety of customers? Should an organization be allowed to send U.S. jobs abroad where wages are $5 per day? What limits should be put on making a profit, and who should determine those limits?[15] The devastating effect of a lack of ethics is illustrated by the example of Metabolife, which makes and sells the drug ephedra.

Well-being The condition of being happy, healthy, and prosperous.

managing ethically

Ephedra Is a Dangerous Drug

Metabolife International is one of largest companies making and selling ephedra, a widely used supplement by young people for weight loss or body building purposes. Although fears about this drug's side effects have been around for years, Metabolife had resisted attempts by the Food and Drug Administration (FDA) to obtain a list of customer reports about the effects they had experienced from using its pills. Once the FDA asked the Justice Department to open a criminal investigation, Metabolife released over 16,000 customer reports about its ephedra products that listed nearly 2,000 adverse reactions, including 3 deaths, 20 heart attacks, 24 strokes, and 40 seizures.[16]

Why hadn't U.S. food and safety laws mandated Metabolife reveal this information earlier? Unlike drugs only available by prescription, the FDA does not regulate over-the-counter vitamin supplements even though such drugs can have life-threatening effects. Because no laws existed to force Metabolife to disclose evidence of adverse side effects—something all pharmaceutical companies are required to do by law—it chose to hide this information. Its actions might be legal but they are unethical, and those who have suffered adverse reactions from using its pills have begun to sue the company.

In 2003, Metabolife was ordered by an Alabama court to pay $4.1 million to four people who had a stroke or seizure after taking its diet pills.[17] If all its victims sue Metabolife, it seems likely that the company will be put out of business. In the meantime, the huge lobbying campaign that began in 2003 to ban ephedra from the market was successful in 2004. The FDA gained the power to ban the drug and did so. The FDA can also now police vitamin companies and force them to disclose any adverse reactions experienced by their customers.

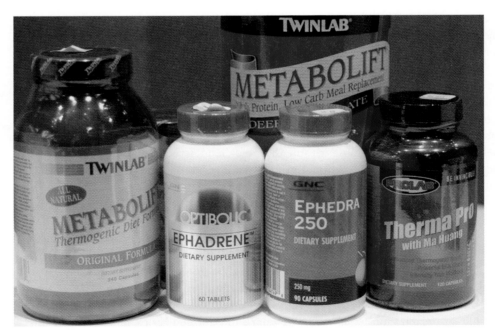

The ultimate goal of the firm is to make a profit. Suppose you were on the board of directors for Metabolife International: Would you have advised the company to warn consumers about the adverse effect of the company's diet pills if it weren't required by law?

In addition to defining right and wrong behavior for employees, ethics also define an organization's **social responsibility**, its obligations toward people or groups outside the organization that are directly affected by its actions.[18] Organizations and their managers must establish an ethical code that describes acceptable behaviors and then create a system of rewards and punishments to enforce ethical codes.

Different organizations have different views about social responsibility.[19] To some organizations, being socially responsible means performing any action, as long as it is legal. Other organizations do more than the law requires and work to advance the well-being of their employees, customers, and society in general.[20] Target, UPS, and Ben & Jerry's, for example, contribute a significant percentage of their profits to support charities and community needs, and they expect their employees to be socially active and responsible. Starbucks and Green Mountain Coffee Roasters seek out coffee-growing farmers and cooperatives that do not use herbicides and pesticides on their crops, that control soil erosion, and that treat their employees fairly and with respect in terms of safety and benefits. Starbucks also signs contracts with small coffee growers abroad to ensure they receive a fair price for their coffee crop. Even if world prices for coffee plunge, Starbucks want its growers to remain honest and loyal.

Not all organizations are willing or able to undertake such programs, but they still need codes of conduct that spell out fair and equitable behavior if they want to avoid doing harm to people and other organizations. Developing a code of ethics helps organizations protect their reputation and maintain the goodwill of their customers and employees.

The challenge is to create an organization whose members resist the temptation to behave in illegal and unethical ways that promote their own interests at the expense of the organization or promote the organization's interests at the expense of people and groups outside the organization. Employees and managers have to recognize that their behavior has important effects not only on other people and groups inside and outside the organization but also on the organization itself.[21] The well-being of organizations and the well-being of the society of which they are a part are closely linked and are the responsibility of everyone.[22] Therefore, the challenge of creating an ethical organization is an issue that we will take up throughout the text. With this in mind, take a look at the ethical exercise in "A Question of Ethics," which is found in Exercise in Understanding and Managing Organizational Behavior, a collection of experiential exercises located at the end of every chapter of this book.

> **Social responsibility** An organization's obligations toward people or groups that are directly affected by its actions.

DEALING WITH A DIVERSE WORKFORCE

A second social and cultural challenge is to understand how the diversity of a workforce affects organizational behavior. **Diversity** results from differences in age, gender, race, ethnicity, religion, sexual orientation, socioeconomic background, and capabilities or disabilities. If an organization or group is composed of people who are all of the same gender, ethnicity, age, religion, and so on, the attitudes and behavior of its members are likely to be very similar. Members are likely to share the same attitudes or values and will tend to respond to work situations (projects, conflicts, new tasks) in similar ways. By contrast, if the members of a group differ in age, ethnicity, and other characteristics, their attitudes, behavior, and responses are likely to differ as well.

In the last 20 years, the demographic makeup of employees entering the workforce and advancing to higher-level positions in organizations has been changing rapidly. Partly because of affirmative action and equal employment opportunity legislation, the number of minority employees entering and being promoted to higher-level positions has increased.[23] By the year 2005, African American and Hispanic employees are expected to make up over 25 percent of the workforce, and the percentage of white males is expected to decrease from 51 percent to 44 percent.[24] At the same time, the number of women entering the workforce has also been increasing dramatically, and they are ascending to higher and higher positions in management.[25] Finally, the diversity of the U.S. population is increasing rapidly because of the large numbers of people immigrating to the United States to live and work.

> **Diversity** Differences resulting from age, gender, race, ethnicity, religion, sexual orientation, and socioeconomic background.

FIGURE **1.6**
The Challenge Posed
by Diverse Workplace

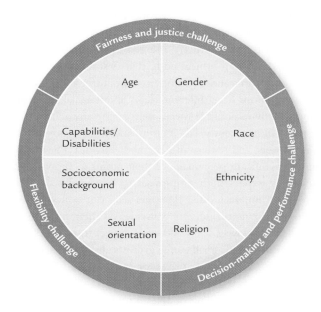

The increasing diversity of the workforce presents three challenges for organizations and their managers: a fairness and justice challenge, a decision-making and performance challenge, and a flexibility challenge (see Figure 1.6).

Fairness and Justice Challenge. Jobs in organizations are scarce. As a result, getting a job and being promoted is a competitive process. Managers are challenged to allocate jobs, promotions, and rewards in a fair and equitable manner. As diversity increases, achieving fairness can be difficult, at least in the short run, because many organizations have traditionally appointed white male employees to higher organizational positions. Also, seniority plays a role, and many minorities are recent hires.[26] Rectifying this imbalance by actively recruiting and promoting more women and minorities can lead to difficult equity issues because attempting to rectify the imbalance reduces the prospects for white males.[27] A goal to increase diversity can, therefore, strain an organization's ability to satisfy the aspirations of at least part of its workforce. This, in turn, can directly affect the workforce's well-being and performance.[28] Organizations must learn to manage diversity in a way that increases the well-being of all employees, but clearly this is difficult.[29]

Decision-Making and Performance Challenge. Another important challenge posed by a diverse workforce is how to take advantage of differences in the attitudes and perspectives of people of different ages, genders, or races, in order to improve decision making and raise organizational performance.[30] Many organizations have found that tapping into diversity and taking advantage of the potential of diverse employees will lead to new and improved organizational behaviors and procedures.[31] Union Bank of California (UBC) is one example of a company that has enjoyed huge success because of the way it has developed an approach to diversity that reflects the needs of its employees, its customers, and its environment.[32]

With assets of over $35 billion, UBC, based in San Francisco, is the third largest commercial bank in California and among the 30 largest banks in the United States.[33] California is one of the most diverse states in the nation. Over half the population is Asian, black, Hispanic, or gay. Recognizing this fact, the bank has always tried to recruit a diverse set of employees. However, UBC recently realized it could use the diversity of its employees to build its customer base. The process started when George Ramirez, a UBC vice president, suggested that the bank should create a marketing group to develop a plan to attract customers who were Hispanic like himself. So successful was this venture that a group of African American employees decided that they should create a marketing group to develop a marketing campaign to attract new African American customers. It was soon clear to UBC that it should capitalize on its diversity to improve customer service as well, so that, for example, a customer entering a branch in a predominantly Latino neighborhood would be greeted by a substantial number of Latino employees.[34]

UBC, like many other organizations, also discovered that as its reputation for being a good place for minorities to work increased, it could attract highly skilled and motivated minority applicants. As Takahiro Moriguchi, its former CEO, said when he accepted a diversity award for the company: "By searching for talent from among the disabled, both genders, veterans, all ethnic groups and all nationalities, we gain access to a pool of ideas, energy, and creativity as wide and varied as the human race itself. I expect diversity will become even more important as the world gradually becomes a truly global marketplace."[35]

Flexibility Challenge. A third diversity challenge is to be sensitive to the needs of different kinds of employees and to try to develop flexible employment approaches that increase their well-being. Examples of some of these approaches include the following:

♦ New benefits packages customized to the needs of different groups of employees, such as single employees with no children as well as families, gays in long-term committed relationships, and employees caring for aged parents.

♦ Flexible employment conditions such as "flextime" that give employees input into the length and scheduling of their workweek.

♦ Arrangements that allow for job sharing so that employees are better able to care for their children or aged parents, for example.

♦ Designing jobs and the buildings that house organizations to accommodate the needs of employees and customers with disabilities.

♦ Creating management programs designed to provide constructive feedback to employees about their personal styles of dealing with minority employees.[36]

♦ Establishing mentoring relationships to support minority employees.[37]

♦ Establishing informal networks among minority employees to provide social support.[38]

Managing diversity is an ongoing activity that has many important implications for organizations. We discuss diversity in depth in Chapter 4.

Challenge 2: The Evolving Global Environment

The challenge of responding to social and cultural forces increases as organizations expand their operations globally. **Global organizations**, such as GM, Toyota, IKEA, Nokia, PepsiCo, and Sony, are companies that produce or sell their products in countries and regions throughout the world. Because each country has a different culture, when companies expand their operations abroad, they encounter vastly different social values, beliefs, and attitudes.[39] Two important challenges facing global organizations are to appreciate the differences between countries and then to benefit from this knowledge to improve an organization's behaviors and procedures.[40]

Global organizations Companies that produce or sell their products in countries and regions throughout the world.

UNDERSTANDING GLOBAL DIFFERENCES

Companies must learn about many different kinds of factors when they operate globally.[41] First, there are the problems related to understanding organizational behavior in different global settings.[42] Evidence shows that people in different countries have different values, beliefs, and attitudes about the very nature of work itself. It has been argued, for example, that Americans have an individualistic orientation toward work and Japanese people have a collectivist orientation. These different orientations toward work reflect cultural differences, which affect people's behavior in groups, commitment, and organizational loyalty.[43]

Organizational behavior becomes especially complex at a global level because the attitudes, aspirations, and values of the workforce also differ by country. For example, most U.S. employees are astonished to learn that in Europe the average employee receives from four to six weeks paid vacation a year. In the United States, a comparable employee receives only one or two weeks. Similarly, in some countries, promotion by seniority is the norm, but in others, level of performance is the main determinant of promotion and reward. Understanding the differences between national cultures is important in any attempt to manage behavior in a global organization.[44]

Second, problems of coordinating the activities of an organization to match its environment become much more complex as an organization's activities expand across the globe.[45] Decision making, for example, must be coordinated between managers at home and those in countries abroad who are likely to have different views about what goals an organization should pursue. The way managers organize the company and decide how to allocate decision-making authority and responsibility between managers at home and abroad is one of the most significant functions of global managers.[46]

Third, in many cases, global organizations locate in a particular country abroad because this allows them to operate more effectively, but doing so also has major effects on their home operations. Today, for example, the need to reduce the costs of making and selling goods to stay competitive with companies from around the world has pushed many United States companies to make most of their products abroad. They contract with manufacturers in countries where labor costs are low to make their products, which are then shipped back to the United States for sale. In the last decade, for example, over 10 million jobs have been lost in the U.S. garment-making industry. Companies such as Levi Strauss, which made all its clothing in the United States 20 years ago, now contract with foreign manufacturers. Today, virtually all Levi's products are made abroad. Because the company has been losing billions of dollars, it has been forced to change the way it operates to cut costs.

In the global environment, however, conditions are constantly changing. Increasingly, those countries that gained the jobs lost by American workers are experiencing the same problem themselves because some other country uses still lower costs to compete for manufacturing contracts, as the accompanying organizational insight suggests.

GLOBAL LEARNING

Global learning The process of acquiring and learning the skills, knowledge, and organizational behaviors and procedures in countries overseas.

Although the changing global environment has been a major threat to U.S. organizations and workers, it also offers them many opportunities to improve the way they operate. By fostering **global learning**, the process of acquiring and learning the skills, knowledge, and organizational behaviors and procedures that have helped companies abroad become major global competitors, U.S. companies have also prospered.[47] For example, U.S. companies have been able to gain access to many kinds of valuable resources that have long been present in companies abroad. Ford and General Motors have been able to acquire the design skills of Italian companies such as Ferrari and Lamborghini, electronic components from

global view

What Goes Around Comes Around

If you look at the label inside some of your clothing, you will probably find that it was made in Mauritius, a tiny island off the southeastern coast of Africa famous for its white sand beaches. In the 1980s, to alleviate its enormous poverty, Mauritius created a low-tax export zone to encourage foreign clothing companies to locate there and employ its citizens, who at that time, worked for 10 cents an hour or less. For many years, this worked well for the island. The average income of its people climbed steeply, and it became one of the most prosperous countries in Africa. More and more companies such as Gap and The Limited had their clothing made in Mauritius. By 2000, the country was exporting over $1 billion of low-cost clothing to the United States every year. Meanwhile, the jobs of U.S. garment industry workers were disappearing.

However, the information technology and service industries in the United States were growing rapidly and creating new jobs for American workers. Despite the loss in manufacturing jobs to third world countries, the number of people employed in the United States rose to record levels during this same time period. By 2000, however, the picture was not so rosy on Mauritius because its labor costs had increased, and billions of people in countries such as India and China (who are paid some of the lowest wages in the world) could do the same work for less. U.S. clothing companies shifted their business to India and China, and unemployment increased dramatically in Mauritius to almost 10 percent. To compete against China and India, factories on Mauritius laid off their own citizens and began hiring temporary workers from India and China willing to work for lower wages.

Mauritius learned the hard way that global competition is a fierce process. And, unlike the United States whose vibrant economy creates new jobs, its people are struggling to cope with the new reality of a lower–cost global economy that can go elsewhere. Mauritius is now trying to create more jobs by focusing on tourism. Unfortunately, it is a long way from the United States, making it far off the beaten trail for Americans, who spend more on tourism than any other country in the world.

Free-trade around the globe cuts both ways, as the people of Mauritius, a tiny island off the coast of Africa, discovered. For two decades, Mauritius' citizens manufactured clothing for U.S. clothing labels outsourcing the work. But the country's prosperity unraveled when lower-cost producers like China and Vietnam captured much of the business.

Japanese companies such as NEC and Matsushita (well known for their quality), and machine tools and manufacturing equipment from German companies such as DaimlerChrysler and BASF (well known for their excellent engineering skills). Companies also learn how to better serve the needs of their customers and, of course, then they can attract more customers. For example, the potential size of the U.S. market for hamburgers is 265 million people, but there are 3 billion potential burger-eaters in Asia alone. Thus, it is not surprising that McDonald's has expanded globally, opening restaurants throughout Asia and the rest of the world to take advantage of the huge global appetite for fast food.[48]

Expatriate employees The people who work for a company overseas and are responsible for developing relationships with organizations in countries around the globe.

To respond to the global challenge more and more companies are rotating their employees to their overseas operations so they can learn firsthand the problems and opportunities that lie abroad. **Expatriate employees** who live and work for companies located abroad can help their companies develop improved organizational behaviors and procedures in many ways. First, expatriate managers can learn about the sources of low-cost inputs and the best places to assemble their products throughout the world. Second, expatriate managers in functions such as research and development, manufacturing, and sales can take advantage of their presence in a foreign country to learn the skills and techniques those companies have to offer. They can apply this knowledge to improve the performance not only of their operations abroad but also of their domestic or home operations. Many companies also use global virtual teams to augment global learning.[49]

After World War II, for example, many of Toyota's manufacturing managers visited the U.S. car plants of GM and Ford to learn how these companies assembled cars. They then took that manufacturing knowledge back to Japan, where they improved on the American techniques and developed the "lean" manufacturing technology that gave Toyota and other Japanese automakers a competitive advantage over U.S. companies in the 1980s. Recognizing that Japanese companies had improved their quality, in the 1980s and 1990s, GM, Ford, Xerox, Motorola, and many other U.S. companies sent their managers to Japan to learn about *their* new techniques. By 2000, companies like Ford had become almost as efficient as their Japanese competitors. In this way, global learning continually takes place as organizations compete with one another worldwide for customers. Organizational effectiveness increases because all global companies are forced to keep abreast of the most recent technological advances and adopt the best organizational behaviors and procedures if they are to survive and prosper.

Challenge 3: Advancing Information Technology

One kind of technology that is posing a major challenge for organizations today is information technology (IT). Just decades ago, science fiction writers such as Robert Heinlein and Isaac Asimov imagined devices like wrist-held videophones, virtual reality machines, and speech-programmed, handheld computers. Today, companies such as Palm, HP, Nokia, Sony, and Microsoft are offering these devices to their customers. Even science fiction writers did not imagine the development of the **World Wide Web**. We live in a different world than just a decade ago; advances in IT have changed the way people think and the very nature of OB. To understand how IT has changed OB and the way companies operate, it is necessary to first understand what information is.

World Wide Web A global store of information that contains the products of most kinds of human knowledge such as writing, music, and art.

Suppose you add up the value of the coins in your pocket and find you have $1.36 in change. You have been mentally manipulating the basic data—the numerical value of each individual coin—to obtain information about the total value your change can buy. You need to know, for example, if you have enough change to buy a soda and a candy bar. **Information** is a set of data, facts, numbers, and words that has been organized in such a way that it provides its users with knowledge. **Knowledge** is what a person perceives, recognizes, identifies, or discovers from analyzing data and information. Over time, the result of acquiring more and better information and knowledge is learning. In an organization, the issue is to use and develop IT that allows employees to acquire more and better information that increases an organization's ability to learn and respond to its environment.

Information technology (IT) consists of the many different kinds of computer and communications hardware and software and the skills that designers, programmers, managers, and technicians bring to it. IT is used to acquire, define, input, arrange, organize, manipulate, store, and transmit facts, data, and information to create knowledge and promote organizational learning. **Organizational learning** occurs when members can manage information and knowledge to achieve a better fit between the organization and its environment. Later, we examine the effect IT has on two important kinds of organizational behaviors—first, those behaviors that increase effectiveness by helping an organization improve the quality of its products and lower its costs; second, those behaviors that increase effectiveness by promoting creativity and organizational learning and innovation.

IT AND ORGANIZATIONAL EFFECTIVENESS

The Internet and the growth of **intranets**, a network of information technology inside an organization that links its members, have dramatically changed organizational behavior and procedures. With information more accurate, plentiful, and freely available, IT allows for the easy exchange of know-how and facilitates problem solving.[50] And as computers increasingly take over routine work tasks, employees have more time to engage in constructive, work-expanding kinds of activities such as developing new products, finding better ways of performing tasks, and giving customers better service.[51]

Consider what happened at the textile fibers division of Du Pont, the giant chemical company. To reduce costs, Du Pont offered early retirement incentives to reduce its workforce, and over half its middle managers decided to take the early retirement package. At first, the division's top managers panicked, wondering how work could get done if everyone left at the same time. But the division had recently installed an e-mail system and a corporate intranet that supplied its remaining employees with most of the information they needed to perform their tasks. Employees began to use it heavily and learned to make their own decisions. Over time, the intranet actually speeded communication and decision making, and Du Pont was able to cope with the exodus of early retirees.[52]

IT has allowed organizations to become much more responsive to the needs of their customers, too. Organizations such as retail stores, banks, and hospitals depend entirely on their employees for high-quality service at reasonable cost. As the United States has moved to a service-based economy (in part because of the loss of manufacturing jobs abroad), advances in IT have made many kinds of service organizations more effective.[53] Sometimes, however, IT actually can reduce effectiveness, as the use of telemarketing discussed in the accompanying OB Today suggests.

Information A set of data, facts, numbers, and words that has been organized in such a way that it provides its users with knowledge.

Knowledge What a person perceives, recognizes, identifies, or discovers from analyzing data and information.

Information technology The many different kinds of computer and communications hardware and software, and the skills of their designers, programmers, managers, and technicians.

Organizational learning The process of managing information and knowledge to achieve a better fit between the organization and its environment.

Intranets A network of information technology linkages inside an organization that connects all its members.

ob today

Telemarketing Turns Off Customers

In the 1990s, telemarketing by companies peddling telephone service and credit cards increased dramatically. Improvements in IT made it possible for telemarketers to target customers and then automatically dial their phone numbers repeatedly until they answered. At this point, a sales rep would come on the line to sell the company's product to the customer. To prevent such unwelcome intrusions, customers began to use services such as caller ID and gadgets such as the TeleZapper to block these calls. Finally, in 2003, national legislation was passed that allows customers to register with the Federal Trade Commission and be put on a "do not call" list.

This has forced companies to rethink their approach to selling. Surprisingly, despite the fact we are living in a "wired world," some organizations have gone back to the old-fashioned method of door-to-door selling. Hundreds of companies such as telephone providers AT&T and SBC, cable TV providers such as Comcast, and countless regional utility companies are sending out thousands of door-to-door sales reps to "connect" with people in the evenings at their homes.

Many people think it is their friends and neighbors knocking at their doors—but no—it's sales reps determined to get them to switch their phone, cable, or utility service provider. People reluctant to slam the door in a sales rep's face versus slamming down the phone have been switching service providers only to regret it later. Just as complaints about phone selling soared in the 1990s, so now, too, are complaints against door-to-door salespeople. It seems this kind of organizational behavior is not leading to increased effectiveness either.

Finally, integrating and connecting a company's employees through electronic means such as video teleconferencing, e-mail, and intranets is becoming increasingly important in global organizations. Because the success of a global company depends on communication between employees in its various business operations both at home and abroad, teleconferencing has grown. Teleconferencing allows managers in different countries to meet face-to-face through television hookups. It reduces communication problems, allows decisions to be made quickly, and facilitates learning when managers in foreign and domestic divisions meet to confront important issues and to solve mutual problems. For example, Hitachi uses an online teleconferencing system to coordinate its 28 R&D laboratories worldwide, and Ford uses one to coordinate the activities of its worldwide car design activities.

IT, CREATIVITY, AND ORGANIZATIONAL LEARNING

Today, using new information technology to help people, groups, and organizations be creative and innovative is a major challenge. *Creativity* is the generation of novel and useful ideas. One of its outcomes is *innovation*, an organization's ability to make new or improved goods and services or improvements in the way they are produced. The United States has some of the most innovative companies in the world, and innovation is the direct result or outcome of the level of creativity in an organization.

IT plays a major role in fostering creativity and innovation because it changes organizational behaviors and procedures. Innovation is an activity that requires the constant updating of knowledge and the constant search for new ideas and technological developments that can be used to improve a product over time. Typically, innovation takes place in small groups or teams. IT can be used to create virtual teams that can enhance creativity and cooperation between employees. Developing an IT system that allows scientists and engineers from all parts of a company to cooperate by way of bulletin boards, chat rooms, or teleconferencing are also ways IT can enhance creativity and speed innovation. One good example of a company using IT to promote creativity and innovation is IBM.

IBM's thousands of consultants are experts in particular industries such as the car, financial services, or retail industries. They have a deep understanding of the particular problems facing companies in those industries and how to solve them. CEO Palmisano asked IBM's consultants to work closely with its software engineers to find ways to incorporate their knowledge into advanced software that can be implanted into a customer's IT system. Toward that end, IBM is developing 17 industry "expert systems," which are industry-specific, problem-solving software organizations that researchers and scientists can use to improve their ability to create new products. One of these expert systems is being developed in the pharmaceutical industry. Using IBM's new software, a company can simulate and model the potential success of its new drugs under development. Currently only 5 to 10 percent of new drugs make it to the market. IBM's new software will help scientists make better decisions about which drugs to develop and how to develop them.

As all these examples suggest, there are many, many ways IT can be used at all levels in the organization, between departments and between global divisions, to enhance learning, speed decision making, and promote creativity and innovation. Throughout this book, you will find many more examples that underscore the importance of facilitating learning, creativity, and organizational behavior today.

Challenge 4: Shifting Work and Employment Relationships

In the last few decades, the relationship between an organization and its members has been changing because of increasing globalization and the emergence of new information technologies.[54] The effects of these changes on organizational behavior have taken many forms, and important developments include a shortening employment relationship because of downsizing, the growth in the number of contingent or temporary employees, and increasing use of outsourcing.[55]

In the past it was quite common for many people to spend their whole careers at a large company such as IBM, Microsoft, or Ford, often moving up the organizational hierarchy over time to more senior and better-paying jobs. Throughout the 1990s, most companies were pressured by global competition to find ways to reduce operating costs. The result was that tens of millions of employees found themselves laid off by their companies and forced to search for new jobs.

Downsizing is the process by which organizations lay off managers and workers to reduce costs. The size and scope of downsizing have been enormous. It is estimated that in the last few decades, *Fortune* 500 companies have downsized so much that they now employ about 15 to 20 percent fewer employees than previously. The drive to reduce costs is often a response to increasing competitive pressures in the global environment.[56]

Although companies often realize considerable cost savings by downsizing, the remaining employees in downsized organizations often work under stress, both because they fear they might be the next employees to be let go and because they are forced to do the work that was previously performed by other employees—work that often they cannot cope with.[57]

The increasing tendency of companies to lay off hardworking, loyal employees when the need arises seems to be changing the employee–employer relationship.[58] Today, employees realize that to keep their jobs and to advance to better ones they need to invest more in themselves and make sure that they keep their job skills and knowledge up-to-date. They also need to be on the lookout for possible new job opportunities. Some experts argue that a person starting a career today can expect to make at least

Downsizing The process by which organizations lay off managers and workers to reduce costs.

U.S. companies are saving millions by downsizing workers and outsourcing jobs in unprecedented numbers. The companies contend it's necessary to stay competitive, and most economists agree. But what effect do you think it has on organizational behavior?

six to eight job and changes over the course of his or her working life—some by choice and some due to layoffs.[59]

Other important trends that go hand in hand with downsizing are the increasing use of empowered self-managed teams, contingent or temporary workers, and outsourcing. **Empowerment** is the process of giving employees throughout an organization the authority to make important decisions and to be responsible for their outcomes. Self-managed teams are work groups that have been empowered and given the responsibility for leading themselves and ensuring that they accomplish their goals.[60]

As organizations have downsized, they also have increased their use of contingent workers to keep costs down. **Contingent workers** are people who are employed for temporary periods by an organization and who receive no benefits such as health insurance or pensions. Contingent workers may work by the day, week, or month performing some functional task, or they may contract with the organization for a fee to perform a specific service to the organization. Thus, for example, an organization might employ 10 temporary accountants to "do the books" when it is time to close them, or it

Empowerment The process of giving employees throughout an organization the authority to make important decisions and to be responsible for their outcomes.

Contingent workers People employed for temporary periods by an organization and who receive no benefits such as health insurance or pensions.

you're the management expert

Moving to Self-Managed Teams

Tony Norris is the owner of a large building products supply company. He has decided that he could operate more effectively if he organizes his 30 employees into three self-managed work teams. Previously his employees worked separately to stock the shelves, answer customer questions, and check out customers under the supervision of five department managers. Norris believes this system did not encourage employees to find ways to improve operating procedures

and also raised costs. He believes he can offer better customer service if he changes to team-based organizational behaviors and procedures.

Norris has asked you, one of his best managers, to think about the kinds of opportunities and problems this shift to teams might cause. He also wants your frank opinion of his idea and whether you think it will increase the effectiveness of the company. When you meet him tomorrow, what will be your response to his ideas? Why?

may contract with a software programmer to write code for a specialized software program for a fixed fee.

Contingent workers cost less to employ because they receive no benefits and they can be let go easily when their services are no longer needed. It has been estimated that 20 percent of the U.S workforce today consists of part-time employees who work by the day, week, month, or even year for their former employers. Part-time employees pose a new organizational behavior challenge because they cannot be motivated by the prospect of rewards such as job security, promotion, or a career within an organization.

Organizations are also increasing the amount of outsourcing they do. **Outsourcing** is the process of employing people and groups outside the organization, or other organizations, to perform specific jobs or types of work activities that used to be performed by the organization itself. For example, jobs such as bookkeeping, computer support, and Web site design are performed not within the organization but by **freelancers**— independent individuals who contract with an organization to perform specific tasks. They often work from their homes and are connected to an organization by computer, phone, fax, and express package delivery. Sometimes an organization will outsource an entire activity such as manufacturing, marketing, or the management of its information systems to a company that can do it at a lower cost than the organization itself.

Downsizing, empowered self-managed teams, the employment of part-time contingent workers, and outsourcing are ways in which organizations are changing organizational behaviors and procedures to compete effectively against domestic and global competitors. Several OB researchers believe that organizations in the future will increasingly become composed of a "core" of organizational employees who are highly trained and rewarded by an organization and a "periphery" of part-time employees or freelancers who are employed when needed but will never become true "organizational employees." The challenge facing people today is to continually improve their skills and knowledge so that they can secure well-paying and satisfying employment either inside or outside an organization.

> **Outsourcing** The process of employing people and groups outside the organization, or other organizations, to perform specific jobs or types of work activities that used to be performed by the organization itself.
>
> **Freelancer** A person who contracts with an organization to perform specific services.

Summary

Organizational behavior is a developing field of study. Changes in the environment constantly challenge the ability of organizations and their owners, managers, and employees to adapt and change work behaviors and procedures to increase the effectiveness with which they operate. In this chapter, we make the following major points:

1. Organizations exist to provide goods and services that people want, and the amount and quality of these goods and services are products of the behaviors and performance of an organization's employees.

2. Organizational behavior is the study of the many factors that have an impact on how people and groups act, think, feel, and respond to work and organizations and how organizations respond to their environments. Organizational behavior provides a set of tools—theories and concepts—to understand, analyze, describe, and manage attitudes and behavior in organizations.

3. The study of organizational behavior can improve and change individual, group, and organizational

behavior to attain individual, group, and organizational goals.

4. Organizational behavior can be analyzed at three levels: the individual, the group, and the organization as a whole. A full understanding is impossible without an examination of the factors that affect behavior at each level.

5. A significant task for an organization's managers and employees is to use the tools of organizational behavior to increase organizational effectiveness, that is, an organization's ability to achieve its goals.

6. The activities of most organizations can be modeled as an open system in which an organization takes in resources from its external environment and converts or transforms them into goods and

services that are sent back to that environment, where customers buy them.

7. Changing pressures or forces in the social and cultural, global, technological, and employment or work environment pose many challenges for organizational behavior, and organizations must respond effectively to those challenges if they are to survive and prosper.

8. Two major challenges of importance to organizational behavior today from the social and cultural environment are those that derive from a breakdown in ethical values and from the increasing diversity of the workforce.

9. Two important challenges facing organizations from the global environment are to appreciate the differences that exist between countries and then to benefit from this new global knowledge to improve organizational behaviors and procedures.

10. Changes in the technological environment, and particularly advances in information technology, are also having important effects on organizational behavior and procedures. IT has improved effectiveness by helping an organization improve the quality of its products, lower their cost, and by promoting creativity and organizational learning and innovation.

11. Many changes have also been taking place in the employment or work environment and important developments that have affected organizational behavior include a shortening employment relationship because of downsizing, the growth in the number of contingent or temporary employees, and outsourcing.

Exercises in Understanding and Managing Organizational Behavior

Questions for Discussion and Review

1. Why is a working knowledge of organizational behavior important to organizations and their employees?

2. Why is it important to analyze the behavior of individuals, groups, and the organization as a whole to understand organizational behavior in work settings?

3. What is an open system and why is it important for an organization to be open to its environment?

4. Select a restaurant, supermarket, church, or some other familiar organization, and think about how which kinds of organizational behaviors and pro-

cedures are the most important determinant of its effectiveness.

5. What are organizational ethics, and why are ethics such an important issue facing organizations today?

6. Why is diversity an important challenge facing organizations today?

7. What special challenges does managing behavior on a global scale pose for organizations?

8. In what ways does IT change organizational behaviors and procedures?

9. Why has the employment relationship been shortening?

Building People Skills

Behavior in Organizations

Think of an organization—a place of employment, a club, a sports team, a musical group, an academic society—that provided you with a significant work experience, and answer the following questions.

1. What are your attitudes and feelings toward the organization? Why do you think you have these attitudes and feelings?

2. Indicate, on a scale from 1 to 10, how hard you worked for this organization or how intensively you participated in the organization's activities. Explain the reasons for your level of participation.

3. How did the organization communicate its performance expectations to you, and how did the organization monitor your performance to evaluate whether you met those expectations? Did you receive more rewards when you performed at a higher level? What happened when your performance was not as high as it should have been?

4. How concerned was your organization with your well-being? How was this concern reflected? Do you think this level of concern was appropriate? Why or why not?

5. Think of your direct supervisor or leader. How did this person's leadership style affect your attitudes and behaviors?

6. How did the attitudes and behavior of your co-workers affect yours, particularly your level of performance?

7. Given your answers to these questions, how would you change organizational behaviors and procedures to make this organization more effective?

A Question of Ethics

Ethical Versus Unethical Behavior

What factors determine whether behavior in organizations is ethical or unethical? Divide up into small groups and think of some unethical behaviors or incidents that you have observed in organizations. The incidents could be something you experienced as an employee, a customer, or a client, or something you observed informally.

Discuss these incidents with other group members. Then identify three important criteria to use to determine whether a particular action or behavior is ethical. These criteria need to differentiate between ethical and unethical organizational behavior. Be ready to describe the incidents of unethical behavior and criteria with the rest of the class.

Small Group Break-Out Exercise

Identifying an Open System

Form groups of three or four people and appoint one member as the spokesperson who will communicate your conclusions to the rest of the class.

1. Think of an organization you are all familiar with such as a local restaurant, store, or bank. Once you have chosen an organization, model it from an open systems perspective. For example, identify its input, conversion, and output processes.

2. Identify the specific forces in the environment that have the greatest opportunity to help or hurt this organization's ability to obtain resources and dispose of its goods or services.

3. Using the three views of effectiveness discussed in the chapter, discuss which specific measures are most useful to managers in evaluating this organization's effectiveness.

Topic for Debate

Now that you understand the nature of organizational behavior and management and the kinds of issues they address, debate the following topic:

Team A. The best way to increase organizational effectiveness is to clearly specify each employee's job responsibilities and then to closely supervise his or her work behavior.

Team B. The best way to increase organizational effectiveness is to put employees in teams and allow them to work out their own job responsibilities and supervise each other.

Experiential Exercise

Ethical Issues in Globalization

There are many laws governing the way companies in the United States should act to protect their employees and to treat them in a fair and equitable manner. However, many countries abroad do not have similar laws and treat employees in ways that would be seen as unacceptable and unethical in the United States.

Either individually or in small groups think about the following issues and answer the questions they raise.

1. In Pakistan and India it is common for children as young as 8 years old to weave the handmade carpets and rugs that are exported to Western countries. Many of these children work for a pittance and are losing their eyesight

because of the close attention they have to devote to their task, often for 12 hours a day. Do you think these children should be employed in such occupations? Do you think it is ethical to buy these rugs?

2. Millions of U.S. workers in manufacturing industries have lost their jobs because companies have moved their operations to low-wage countries overseas. In other countries, many women and children work long hours a day for low wages performing the jobs that used to be done by workers in the United States. Do you think it is ethical for multinationals to operate on the basis of where they can obtain low-cost resources? Do you think laws should be passed to prevent global companies from locating abroad to protect the relatively high-paying jobs of U.S. workers?

Making the Connection

At the end of most chapters is a "Making the Connection" exercise that requires you to search newspapers or magazines in the library for an example of a real company that is dealing with some of the issues, concepts, challenges, questions, and problems dealt with in the chapter. The purpose of the exercise for this chapter is to familiarize you with the way in which managers make use of organizational behavior to increase organizational effectiveness.

Find an example of an organization that is currently facing one of the four challenges discussed in the chapter. What problem is it facing? What effects is it having on the organization? How is the organization responding to the challenge?

New York Times Cases in the News

The New York Times

For Many, Full-Time Work Means Part-Time Benefits

BY ABBY ELLIN

LIKE many new college graduates, Kellie Lee was thrilled when she finally got a serious job. It was actually her dream job, a position as an admissions counselor at an acting school and career center in Longwood, Fla.

"The owner had the most wonderful spirit," said Ms. Lee, 23, who lives in Orlando.

She quit three days later—after she was told she would not be given any benefits by Ashley Camille's Modeling, Acting and Career Center, even though she was a full-time employee.

"When I asked about benefits she said we would talk about the logistics when I got there," said Ms. Lee. "I expected to get them. If you're doing your job for the company, I feel that it's acceptable to ask for benefits." She added: "Healthcare, 401(k)—I see what my parents are dealing with and they're stressed out over whether Social Security is going to exist for them. It's scary."

The school disputed Ms. Lee's account. Sonya Callender, the head of the school, said that it first gives benefits after employees have worked six months.

Growing numbers of job applicants are finding that positions with benefits are scarce. And unlike Ms. Lee, many young college graduates—and even some older workers wishing to make career changes—are taking jobs without health insurance or retirement plans because, they say, they cannot find anything with more security.

Andrew Nolin, 23, is another new employee without benefits. He took a full-time job last year at the Microtel Inns and Suites in Seneca Falls, N.Y., as a night auditor. He does not receive health or retirement benefits, he said. But, he added, "I had been looking for a job for a while and that was the first one that hired me." He said he has one more year before he will be removed from his parents' policy. After that, he doesn't know what he will do. "I am kind of worried, that's why I'm looking for another job right now," he said. "Hopefully, I won't get sick."

Employers say they are not happy to be cutting back on benefits. But faced with a sluggish economy and rising health care costs, they say they have little choice but to slash benefits packages, whether that means requiring a waiting period before benefits kick in, or offering no benefits at all.

Few employers were willing to speak publicly about any cutbacks they are making in employee benefits. But Bob Schleizer, executive vice president and chief financial officer of Xponential Inc, which runs a chain of 26 pawnshops in the Southeast, said his company had pared back.

In the past, the company offered full benefits for full-time employees, plus stock options. But in 2001, the company went through financial difficulties, and last year the package changed. "We no longer offer benefits to anyone except full-time managerial staff," said Mr. Schleizer, who came as a turnaround specialist from Tatum CFO Partners. "Out of our 180 employees, only 40 are eligible for benefits." To partly offset the change, the company increased pay by about 50 cents an hour for employees no longer receiving benefits.

Steven Rothberg, president and founder of CollegeRecruiter.com, in Minneapolis, said: "It's not a new strategy, but it's one that when the labor market is strong it wasn't used very much because in order to attract talented people, employees had to provide benefits. Now we're back to the old way, to a more traditional employment model: the power rests with the employer."

In the past, most companies offered benefits to their full-time, permanent employees, and it was only part-time workers or outside contractors who would be excluded. "Companies used to staff with freelancers who are flexible but don't get benefits," said Sara Horowitz, the founder of Working Today, which offers inexpensive insurance plans for freelancers and other independent contractors. "Now, companies are scaling back their benefits for their permanent work force making the distinction between freelancers and employees, in effect, meaningless."

Still, many young people, at least, say they are not especially concerned by the shift. "One of the challenges if you're hiring entry-level folks, Generation X types, is they think they're going to live forever," said John W. Robinson IV, an employment lawyer with Fowler White Boggs Banker, a firm in Tampa, Fla. "They're not interested in a pension or even a substantial medical plan. They'd rather have cash."

"In our law firm, it wasn't as critical to entry level lawyers to get pension and other fringe benefits as it was to just get cash, in part because they had to pay student loans from school and law school," he said. "They said they would worry about pensions in 40 years."

That is how Kevin Lister feels. He was hired a year and half ago, when he was 25, at Mindbridge Software, outside of Philadelphia. Six months after he started working there he was given benefits. "I was unemployed for three or four months before I got the job and I was just happy to work," said Mr. Lister, who is now a sales executive there. "My mother was worried that I didn't get benefits, but that's her being a mother. I was just in a bad situation at that time—I needed to get a job. Every job that I talked to there was a minimum of three months to get benefits anyway."

Scott Testa, the director of human resources at Mindbridge, said the 120-person software company generally hires employees right out of college without offering them benefits when they start.

"It sounds terrible, but it's kind of like a supply and demand," he said. Employees undergo a probationary period for six to nine months. After that, the company evaluates them, he said. "Benefits are expensive to the company and to the new hires benefits weren't important—it was more important getting a job with a new company in a good industry," he said.

Job seekers determined to get benefits are most likely to find them at large companies. According to a 2002 study by the Kaiser Family Foundation, 99 percent of large companies, defined as those with 200 or more employees, offer health benefits. (A percentage unchanged from the year before.)

Only 61 percent of firms with 3 to 199 employees offered benefits in 2002, down from 67 percent in 2000. And a 2003 study by the Employer Benefit Research Institute found that 58 percent of full-time employees in medium to large businesses—over 100 employees—participate in an employee based retirement plan, compared with only 27.8 percent of small firms.

"Smaller firms have a hard time because of the rising costs of health care," said Carol Lachnit, the editor of *Workforce Management,* a magazine in Costa Mesa, Calif., about employment issues. "Bigger firms realize that you get better employees when you can offer them a more comprehensive package of salary and benefits, and it's important to them to make those benefits available to employees."

Some companies increase salaries "in an effort to soften the blow," said Robert Kneip, president and chief executive of the Oasis Group, a company in West Palm Beach, Fla., that provides professional services such as benefits management to other companies. "A lot of employees these days are making their own risk-benefit decisions—do I really need benefits or is that as important to me as a higher wage or job flexibility? More companies are evaluating the costs of benefits and are being forced to cut back or eliminate their benefits programs."

"Firms don't like to eliminate benefits programs," he added. "I don't know of anybody who has happily or gladly or willingly cut back on benefits. It's a real unfortunate economic imperative."

Ms. Lee, for one, has not devised a plan for obtaining benefits once they run out; for now, she is on her parents' health insurance policy. "I am hoping to be a student forever so I'll get insurance," she said. "Otherwise, I don't know what I'll do."

SOURCE: "For Many, Full-Time Work Means Part-Time Benefits," Abby Ellin, *New York Times,* August 17, 2003, 10.1.

Questions for Discussions

1. How do the changes taking place in the kinds of benefits workers receive affect the employment relationship?

2. What implications do these changes have for employee motivation and involvement in an organization?

3. What lessons should people seeking jobs learn from the experiences of these employees?

The New York Times

As Levi's Work Is Exported, Stress Stays Home

BY RALPH BLUMENTHAL

Clara Flores once thought she had the job of a lifetime, even, perhaps, the most solid job in America.

She made blue jeans. Not just any blue jeans.

Levi's.

"It was the original," Ms. Flores said. "Wherever you went, it was the same Levi's blue jeans."

The $4.2 billion company, founded 150 years ago by Levi Strauss, a Bavarian immigrant who settled in San Francisco to outfit the gold miners, has turned out more than 3.5 billion pairs of the sturdy denim jeans with their trademark rivets at the seams and little red pocket tab, becoming an American icon right up there with Coca-Cola, Hollywood, baseball and the Colt .45.

But by the end of the year, the last pair of Levi's made in America will roll off the sewing and finishing lines at the factory here, another casualty of the shrinking homegrown apparel industry that since 1995 has halved its domestic work force in favor of cheaper foreign labor. It will be a setback, too, for San Antonio, the Alamo city, thronged with tourists but suffering from a string of factory closings, although Toyota is building an $800 million plant to open in 2006.

Levi Strauss & Company's last three Canadian plants will close next March, the company announced last month, part of a restructuring that will cut its payroll from a height of 37,000 employees in 1996 to 9,750 by next year and leave none of its jeans production in North America.

The steps follow the closing of its original plant in Valencia, Calif., last year, and of many plants in the 90's, when revenues began dropping from a peak of $7 billion. In Texas, Levi Strauss closed eight plants in El Paso and others in Brownsville and the Rio Grande valley, one of the country's poorest areas.

The work will be contracted to suppliers in 50 countries, from the Caribbean to Latin America and Asia, where competitors, with few exceptions, have also shifted manufacturing or made jeans all along.

But those companies' jeans are not Levi's, perhaps the most distinctive garment of the 20th century and a mainstay of the vintage clothing market, with about 200 listings Saturday on eBay. (Levi Strauss itself two years ago bought a pair of rediscovered 1880's overalls for $46,532.) Levi's also spawned a fiercely competitive jeans industry. In the last 10 years, 200 new brands have entered the market, Levi Strauss says.

"Levi's are so identified with America," said Bruce Raynor, president of Unite, the apparel workers' union, who laid the job losses to American trade policy and the might of merchandising behemoths like Wal-Mart, which set the pace of the industry and scour the world for low-cost labor. Levi's themselves are now sold at Wal-Mart.

Philip A. Marineau, who left PepsiCo in 1999 to lead the family-owned Levi Strauss Company as president and chief executive, said he saw little symbolism in the company's American production shutdown.

"Consumers are used to buying products from all over the world," Mr. Marineau said on the telephone from company headquarters in San Francisco. "The issue is not where they're made. For most people that's not gut-wrenching anymore."

But it is for employees like Ms. Flores, 54, an $18-an-hour hem sewer and Unite's local president. Ms. Flores, who has worked for the company for 24 years, will soon join 819 fellow employees in San Antonio lining up for severance benefits, retraining classes and grants to start their own businesses. Workers said the company had a progressive record of providing for its laid-off employees, but Ms. Flores, noting the four weeks of annual paid vacation and family medical and dental benefits for $24 a week, asked, "Where are we ever going to find something like this?"

Marivel Gutierez, 43, a side-seam operator and union secretary, who also has 24 years of service, acknowledged that workers in Mexico and elsewhere would benefit. "There still probably is an American dream," she said of the boon to those workers. "But what about us? What happens to our American dream?"

The union officers attributed the workers' plight to the North American Free Trade Agreement and to consumers who no longer seem to care where products are made as long as the price is low.

After Nafta took effect in 1994, Mr. Raynor of Unite said, the country lost 785,000 apparel jobs, with 700,000 remaining. He said that despite the dominance of Wal-Mart, the country's largest company with revenues of $250 billion and a work force of 1.2 million, Americans would willingly pay more for domestic products.

Josephine Rosales, 55, a sewing machine mechanic and worker at the San Antonio plant for 26 years, agreed. "If only more people would pay attention to what they buy and where it was made," she said.

But Mr. Marineau said marketing research did not show that consumers were ready to spend more to support American industries.

"Consumers desire to spend less on necessities and more on luxuries," he said. Besides, he said, Levi's were already premium-priced compared with many other brands.

Levi Strauss prides itself on its production agreements with foreign suppliers that, it says, rule out partnerships with sweatshops. While other major retailers settled a lawsuit on sweatshop labor on Saipan in the Pacific, Levi Strauss has chosen to fight it, arguing that the company had ceased operations there.

Through its Levi Strauss Foundation and other charitable efforts, the company has contributed to community groups providing retraining and other services to displaced workers.

"Levi Strauss has always been better—I'm not going to say great, but better," said Mr. Raynor. "Levi's has the best pay and benefits in the industry."

So its exodus from San Antonio is all the more painful, a reminder of the furor after the closing of the company's Zarzamora Street plant here in 1990 threw 1,400 people out of work. The company had little experience in easing the blow, and "everything went wrong," Ms. Flora recalled. "People came in black and said it was closing. They were wearing suits, but that's how people saw it—they were men in black."

Some workers fainted from shock. With union leaders caught off guard and the company unprepared to offer immediate assistance programs, an advocacy group led protests.

Levi Strauss learned from the experience, said Olga Kauffman, a community organizer and consultant hired by the company to help steer relocation services to the workers. But the overriding problem, Ms. Kauffman said, was that the jobs available were largely in lower-paying service industries. One exception, she said, was health care, which, unlike apparel manufacturing, cannot be shipped out of the country.

But Ms. Gutierez said she was in a panic: "What's waiting for me out there?"

SOURCE: "As Levi's Work Is Exported, Stress Stays Home," Ralph Blumenthal, *New York Times*, October 19, 2003, 1.24.

Questions for Discussion

1. What are the sources of Levi-Strauss's problems?

2. What steps has Levi's taken to manage them?

3. Is it ethical for Levi's to close down all its U.S. factories and transfer jobs overseas?

CHAPTER APPENDIX

A Short History of Organizational Behavior Research

The systematic study of organizational behavior began in the closing decades of the nineteenth century, after the industrial revolution had swept through Europe and America. In the new economic climate, managers of all types of organizations—political, educational, and economic—were increasingly turning their focus toward finding better ways to satisfy customers' needs. Many major economic, technical, and cultural changes were taking place at this time. With the introduction of steam power and the development of sophisticated machinery and equipment, the industrial revolution changed the way goods were produced, particularly in the weaving and clothing industries. Small workshops run by skilled employees who produced hand-manufactured products (a system called crafts production) were being replaced by large factories in which sophisticated machines controlled by hundreds or even thousands of unskilled or semiskilled employees made products. For example, raw cotton and wool, which in the past families or whole villages working together had spun into yarn, were now shipped to factories where employees operated machines that spun and wove large quantities of yarn into cloth.

Owners and managers of the new factories found themselves unprepared for the challenges accompanying the change from small-scale crafts production to large-scale mechanized manufacturing. Moreover, many of the managers and supervisors in these workshops and factories were engineers who had only a technical orientation. They were unprepared for the social problems that occur when people work together in large groups (as in a factory or shop system). Managers began to search for new techniques to manage their organizations' resources, and soon they began to focus on ways to increase the efficiency of the employee–task mix. They found help from Frederick W. Taylor.

F. W. TAYLOR AND SCIENTIFIC MANAGEMENT

Frederick W. Taylor (1856–1915) is best known for defining the techniques of scientific management, the systematic study of relationships between people and tasks for the purpose of redesigning the work process to increase efficiency. Taylor was a manufacturing manager who eventually became a consultant and taught other managers how to apply his scientific management techniques. Taylor believed that if the amount of time and effort that each employee expends to produce a unit of output (a finished good or service) can be reduced by increasing specialization and the division of labor, the production process will become more efficient. Taylor believed the way to create the most efficient division of labor could best be determined using scientific management techniques rather than intuitive or informal rule-of-thumb knowledge. Based on his experiments and observations as a manufacturing manager in a variety of settings, he developed four principles to increase efficiency in the workplace:[61]

- *Principle 1: Study the way employees perform their tasks, gather all the informal job knowledge that employees possess, and experiment with ways of improving the way tasks are performed.*

  To discover the most efficient method of performing specific tasks, Taylor studied in great detail and measured the ways different employees went about performing their tasks. One of the main tools he used was a time and motion study, which involves the careful timing and recording of the actions taken to perform a particular task. Once Taylor understood the existing method of performing a task, he then experimented to increase specialization; he tried different methods of dividing up and coordinating the various tasks necessary to produce a finished product. Usually this meant simplifying jobs and having each employee perform fewer, more routine tasks, as at the pin factory or on Ford's car assembly line. Taylor also sought to find ways to improve each employee's ability to perform a particular task— for example, by reducing the number of motions employees made to complete the task, by changing the layout of the work area or the type of tool employees used, or by experimenting with tools of different sizes.

- *Principle 2: Codify the new methods of performing tasks into written rules and standard operating procedures.*

  Once the best method of performing a particular task was determined, Taylor specified that it should be recorded so that the procedures could be taught to all employees performing the same task. These rules could be used to further standardize and simplify jobs—essentially, making jobs even more routine. In this way efficiency could be increased throughout an organization.

◆ *Principle 3: Carefully select employees who possess skills and abilities that match the needs of the task and train them to perform the task according to the established rules and procedures.*

To increase specialization, Taylor believed employees had to understand the tasks that were required and be thoroughly trained in order to perform the task at the required level. Employees who could not be trained to this level were to be transferred to a job in which they were able to reach the minimum required level of proficiency.[62]

◆ *Principle 4: Establish a fair or acceptable level of performance for a task and then develop a pay system that provides a reward for performance above the acceptable level.*

To encourage employees to perform at a high level of efficiency, and to provide them with an incentive to reveal the most efficient techniques for performing a task, Taylor advocated that employees benefit from any gains in performance. They should be paid a bonus and receive some percentage of the performance gains achieved through the more efficient work process.

By 1910, Taylor's system of scientific management had become nationally known and in many instances faithfully and fully practiced.[63] However, managers in many organizations chose to implement the new principles of scientific management selectively. This decision ultimately resulted in problems. For example, some managers using scientific management obtained increases in performance, but rather than sharing performance gains with employees through bonuses as Taylor had advocated, they simply increased the amount of work that each employee was expected to do. Many employees experiencing the reorganized work system found that as their performance increased, managers required them to do more work for the same pay. Employees also learned that increases in performance often meant fewer jobs and a greater threat of layoffs because fewer employees were needed. In addition, the specialized, simplified jobs were often very monotonous and repetitive, and many employees became dissatisfied with their jobs.

From a performance perspective, the combination of the two management practices of (1) achieving the right mix of employee–task specialization and (2) linking people and tasks by the speed of the production line resulted in the huge savings in cost and huge increases in output that occur in large, organized work settings. For example, in 1908, managers at the Franklin Motor Company using scientific management principles redesigned the work process, and the output of cars increased from 100 cars a month to 45 cars a day; employees' wages, however, increased by only 90 percent.[64]

Taylor's work has had an enduring effect on the management of production systems. Managers in every organization, whether it produces goods or services, now carefully analyze the basic tasks that employees must perform and try to create a work environment that will allow their organizations to operate most efficiently. We discuss this important issue in Chapters 6 and 7.

THE WORK OF MARY PARKER FOLLETT

Much of Mary Parker Follett's (1868–1933) writing about management, and the way managers should behave toward employees, was a response to her concern that Taylor was ignoring the human side of the organization.[65] She pointed out that management often overlooks the multitude of ways in which employees can contribute to the organization when managers allow them to participate and exercise initiative in their everyday work lives.[66] Taylor, for example, never proposed that managers should involve employees in analyzing their jobs to identify better ways to perform tasks or even ask employees how they felt about their jobs. Instead, he used time and motion experts to analyze employees' jobs for them. Follett, in contrast, argued that because employees know the most about their jobs, they should be involved in job analysis and managers should allow them to participate in the work development process.

Follett proposed that "Authority should go with knowledge . . . whether it is up the line or down." In other words, if employees have the relevant knowledge, then employees, rather than managers, should be in control of the work process itself, and managers should behave as coaches and facilitators—not as monitors and supervisors. In making this statement, Follett anticipated the current interest in self-managed teams and empowerment. She also recognized the importance of having managers in different departments communicate directly with each other to speed decision making. She advocated what she called "cross-functioning": members of different departments working together in cross-departmental teams to accomplish projects—an approach that is increasingly utilized today.[67] She proposed that knowledge and expertise, and not managers' formal authority deriving from their position in the hierarchy, should decide who would lead at any particular moment. She believed, as do many OB researchers today, that power is fluid and should flow to the person who can best help the organization achieve its goals. Follett took a horizontal view of power and authority, rather than viewing the vertical chain of command as being more essential to effective management. Thus, Follett's approach was very radical for its time.

THE HAWTHORNE STUDIES AND HUMAN RELATIONS

Probably because of its radical nature, Follett's work went unappreciated by managers and researchers until quite recently. Most continued to follow in the footsteps of Taylor and, to increase efficiency, they studied ways to improve various characteristics of the work setting, such as job specialization or the kinds of tools employees used. One series of studies was conducted from 1924 to 1932 at the Hawthorne Works of the Western Electric Company.[68] This research, now known as the Hawthorne studies, was initiated as an attempt to investigate how characteristics of the work setting—specifically the levels of lighting or illumination—affect employee fatigue and performance. The researchers conducted an experiment in which they systematically measured employee productivity at various levels of illumination.

The experiment produced some unexpected results. The researchers found that regardless of whether they raised or lowered the level of illumination, productivity increased. In fact, productivity began to fall only when the level of illumination dropped to the level of moonlight, a level at which presumably employees could no longer see well enough to do their work efficiently.

As you can imagine, the researchers found these results very puzzling. They invited a noted Harvard psychologist, Elton Mayo, to help them. Mayo proposed another series of experiments to solve the mystery. These experiments, known as the relay assembly test experiments, were designed to investigate the effects of other aspects of the work context on job performance, such as the effect of the number and length of rest periods and hours of work on fatigue and monotony.[69] The goal was to raise productivity.

During a two-year study of a small group of female employees, the researchers again observed that productivity increased over time, but the increases could not be solely attributed to the effects of changes in the work setting. Gradually, the researchers discovered that, to some degree, the results they were obtaining were influenced by the fact that the researchers themselves had become part of the experiment. In other words, the presence of the researchers was affecting the results because the employees enjoyed receiving attention and being the subject of study and were willing to cooperate with the researchers to produce the results they believed the researchers desired.

Subsequently, it was found that many other factors also influence employee behavior, and it was not clear what was actually influencing Hawthorne employees' behavior. However, this particular effect—which became known as the Hawthorne effect—seemed to suggest that the attitude of employees toward their managers affects the level of employees' performance. In particular, the significant finding was that a manager's behavior or leadership approach can affect performance. This finding led many researchers to turn their attention to managerial behavior and leadership. If supervisors could be trained to behave in ways that would elicit cooperative behavior from their subordinates, then productivity could be increased. From this view emerged the human relations movement, which advocates that supervisors be behaviorally trained to manage subordinates in ways that elicit their cooperation and increase their productivity.

The importance of behavioral or human relations training became even clearer to its supporters after another series of experiments—the bank wiring room experiments. In a study of employees making telephone switching equipment, researchers Elton Mayo and F. J. Roethlisberger discovered that the employees, as a group, had deliberately adopted a norm of output restriction to protect their jobs. Other group members subjected employees who violated this informal production norm to sanctions. Those who violated group performance norms and performed above the norm were called "ratebusters"; those who performed below the norm were called "chisellers."

The experimenters concluded that both types of employees threaten the group as a whole. Ratebusters threaten group members because they reveal to managers how fast the work can be done. Chisellers are looked down on because they are not doing their share of the work. Work-group members discipline both ratebusters and chisellers in order to create a pace of work that the employees (not the managers) think is fair. Thus, the work group's influence over output can be as great as the supervisors' influence. Since the work group can influence the behavior of its members, some management theorists argue that supervisors should be trained to behave in ways that gain the goodwill and cooperation of employees so that supervisors, not employees, control the level of work-group performance.

One of the main implications of the Hawthorne studies was that the behavior of managers and employees in the work setting is as important in explaining the level of performance as the technical aspects of the task.

Managers must understand the workings of the informal organization, the system of behavioral rules and norms that emerges in a group, when they try to manage or change behavior in organizations. Many studies have found that, as time passes, groups often develop elaborate procedures and norms that bond members together, allowing unified action either to cooperate with management in order to raise performance or to restrict output and thwart the attainment of organizational goals.[70] The Hawthorne studies demonstrated the importance of understanding how the feelings, thoughts, and behavior of work-group members and managers affect performance. It was becoming increasingly clear to researchers that understanding behavior in organizations is a complex process that is critical to increasing performance.[71] Indeed, the increasing interest in the area of management known as organizational behavior, the study of the factors that have an impact on how individuals and groups respond to and act in organizations, dates from these early studies.

THEORY X AND THEORY Y

Several studies after World War II revealed how assumptions about employees' attitudes and behavior affect managers' behavior. Perhaps the most influential approach was developed by Douglas McGregor. He proposed that two different sets of assumptions about work attitudes and behaviors dominate the way managers think and affect how they behave in organizations. McGregor named these two contrasting sets of assumptions Theory X and Theory Y.[72]

Theory X

According to the assumptions of Theory X, the average employee is lazy, dislikes work, and tries to do as little as possible. Moreover, employees have little ambition and wish to avoid responsibility. Thus, the manager's task is to counteract employees' natural tendencies to avoid work. To keep employees' performance at a high level, the manager must supervise them closely and control their behavior by means of "the carrot and stick," that is, rewards and punishments.

Managers who accept the assumptions of Theory X design and shape the work setting to maximize their control over employees' behaviors and minimize employees' control over the pace of work. These managers believe that employees must be made to do what is necessary for the success of the organization, and they focus on developing rules, standard operating procedures, and a well-defined system of rewards and punishments to control behavior. They see little point in giving employees autonomy to solve their own problems because they think that the workforce neither expects nor desires cooperation. Theory X managers see their role as closely monitoring employees to ensure that they contribute to the production process and do not threaten product quality. Henry Ford, who closely supervised and managed his workforce, fits McGregor's description of a manager who holds Theory X assumptions.

Theory Y

In contrast, Theory Y assumes that employees are not inherently lazy, do not naturally dislike work, and, if given the opportunity, will do what is good for the organization. According to Theory Y, the characteristics of the work setting determine whether employees consider work to be a source of satisfaction or punishment. Managers do not need to closely control employees' behavior in order to make them perform at a high level, because employees will exercise self-control when they are committed to organizational goals. The implication of Theory Y, according to McGregor, is that "the limits of collaboration in the organizational setting are not limits of human nature but of management's ingenuity in discovering how to realize the potential represented by its human resources."[73] It is the manager's task to create a work setting that encourages commitment to organizational goals and provides opportunities for employees to be imaginative and to exercise initiative and self-direction.

When managers design the organizational setting to reflect the assumptions about attitudes and behavior suggested by Theory Y, the characteristics of the organization are quite different from those of an organizational setting based on Theory X. Managers who believe that employees are motivated to help the organization reach its goals can decentralize authority and give more control over the job to employees, both as individuals and in groups. In this setting, individuals and groups are still accountable for their activities, but the manager's role is not to control employees but to provide support and advice, to make sure they have the resources they need to perform their jobs, and to evaluate them on their ability to help the organization meet its goals.

Individual Differences: Personality and Ability

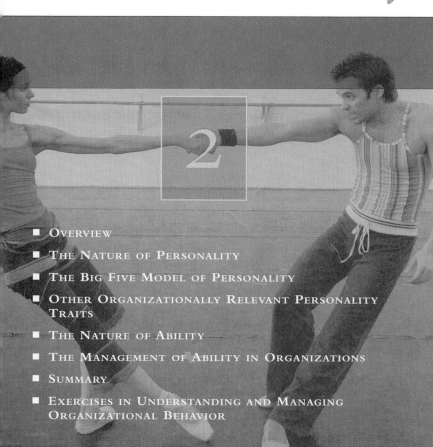

2

LEARNING OBJECTIVES

After studying this chapter, you should be able to:

■

Understand the nature of personality and how it is determined by both nature and nuture.

■

Describe the Big Five personality traits and their implications for understanding behavior in organizations.

■

Appreciate the ways in which other personality traits, in addition to the Big Five, influence employees' behaviors in organizations.

■

Describe the different kinds of abilities that employees use to perform their jobs.

■

Appreciate how organizations manage ability through selection, placement, and training.

OPENING CASE

Weldon's Determination

What Does It Take to Lead One of the Largest Pharmaceutical Companies in the World in a Changing and Highly Competitive Environment?

William Weldon, two years into his position as CEO of Johnson & Johnson (J&J), faces a daunting task—leading a 118-year-old company made up of 204 separate businesses organized into three divisions (drugs, medical devices and diagnostics, and consumer products) in a competitive and turbulent environment. To carry on J&J's history of growth into the future, Weldon will need to build or acquire a new $4 billion business on an annual basis.[1] Moreover, he will need to perform a delicate balancing act—allowing J&J's businesses the autonomy that has enabled them to operate in a nimble and entrepreneurial fashion while at the same time encouraging them to cooperate and exchange information to achieve the real synergies only a large, multibusiness company can achieve in this complex industry.[2]

Weldon has met this challenge with conscientiousness, determination, enthusiasm, openness to new ideas, and a healthy respect for what has made J&J a corporate success story for over 100 years.[3] Weldon's persistence and determination landed him his first job at J&J as a sales representative straight out of college in the early 1970s; Howard Klick hired Weldon to sell pharmaceuticals after a single interview because his drive and ambition were so readily apparent. Weldon proceeded to rise through the ranks and headed up the drug division in 1998.[4]

While setting difficult goals and striving to achieve them has always been a driving influence for Weldon, he also appreciates the more human side of managing people. For example, when Dr. Per A. Peterson, head of pharmaceutical research and development, told Weldon he was considering leaving J&J because of personnel problems, Weldon invited Peterson over to his house and made him breakfast. The two then spent the day discussing the problems that were frustrating Peterson. Within a week, Weldon had made the changes that Peterson sought and Peterson decided to stay at J&J. As Peterson puts it, "What else can you say to a guy that makes you an omelet at six in the morning? . . . You say yes."[5] Weldon's high self-esteem contributes to his ability to influence others such as Peterson. And his conscientiousness ensures that he stands by his word.

Influencing those around him while remaining open to new ideas has served Weldon well and should help him meet the challenge of leading J&J in the current era. Weldon and other industry experts believe that future advances in the industry lie in combining insights and innovations from J&J's different businesses and divisions. For example, medical devices such as stents and sutures are being coated with drugs to help unclog arteries and ward off infections.[6] Different J&J businesses that were accustomed to operating autonomously to make medical devices or drugs have to learn to cooperate and work together to take advantage of these cross-discipline advances. Thus, Weldon is encouraging employees in J&J's different businesses to cooperate with each other and work together as new product development teams.[7]

Weldon's discipline has led him to recognize the need for J&J to cut costs to remain competitive. Thus, he is centralizing certain administrative functions and purchasing to lower duplication of functions across businesses. Over 1,000 of J&J's 112,000 employees have been offered early retirement packages as another cost-cutting move. Although cutting costs might not be popular with employees, cost savings are needed to fund R&D efforts for developing new pharmaceuticals.[8]

Weldon faces many challenges, especially because J&J's next major new product isn't due out until 2006 and competitors are making inroads into some of J&J's existing markets.[9] Although time will tell if Weldon is successful in making needed changes at J&J while retaining its core strengths, Weldon certainly seems to have the intelligence, determination, persistence, openness to new ideas, and ability to influence others needed for the job.

Overview

Each member of an organization has his or her own style and ways of behaving. Effectively working with others requires an understanding and appreciation of how people differ from one another. William Weldon, for example, is persistent and determined, qualities that have contributed to his success at J&J. In order to effectively work with Weldon, it is important that Weldon's subordinates and colleagues understand what he is like and what is important to him.

In this chapter, we focus on individual differences, the ways in which people differ from each other. Managers need to understand individual differences because they have an impact on the feelings, thoughts, and behaviors of each member of an organization. Individual differences affect, for example, job satisfaction, job performance, job stress, and leadership. Organizational members interact with each other on a daily basis, and only if they understand each other are their interactions likely to result in high levels of satisfaction and performance.

Individual differences may be grouped into two categories: personality differences and differences in ability. We focus on the nature, meaning, and determinants of personality and on the ways that personality and situational factors combine to influence feelings, thoughts, and behavior in organizations. We discuss specific personality traits that are particularly relevant to organizational behavior. We then turn our attention to differences in ability. After describing various types of ability, we discuss the key issue for managers: how ability can be managed to ensure that employees can effectively perform their jobs.

> **Individual differences** The ways in which people differ from each other.

The Nature of Personality

People's personalities can be described in a variety of ways. Some people seem to be perfectionists; they can be critical, impatient, demanding, and intense. Other kinds of people are more relaxed and easygoing. You may have friends or co-workers who always seem to have something to smile about and are fun to be around. Or perhaps you have friends or co-workers who are shy and quiet; they are hard to get to know and may sometimes seem dull. In each of these examples, we are describing what people are generally like without referring to their specific feelings, thoughts, and behaviors in any given situation. In formulating a general description of someone, we try to pinpoint something that is relatively enduring about the person, something that seems to explain the regularities or patterns we observe in the way the person thinks, feels, and behaves.

Personality is the pattern of relatively enduring ways that a person feels, thinks, and behaves. Personality is an important factor in accounting for why employees act the way they do in organizations and why they have favorable or unfavorable attitudes toward their jobs and organizations.[10] Personality has been shown to influence career choice, job satisfaction, stress, leadership, and some aspects of job performance.

> **Personality** The pattern of relatively enduring ways that a person feels, thinks, and behaves.

DETERMINANTS OF PERSONALITY: NATURE AND NURTURE

Why are some employees happy and easygoing and others intense and critical? An answer to this question can be found by examining the determinants of personality: nature and nurture.

Personality is partially determined by **nature**, or biological heritage. The genes that you inherited from your parents influence how your personality has unfolded.[11] Although specific genes for personality have not yet been identified, psychologists have studied identical twins in an attempt to discover the extent to which personality is inherited.[12]

> **Nature** Biological heritage, genetic makeup.

Because identical twins possess identical genes, they have the same genetic determinants of personality. Identical twins who grow up together in the same family have the same permissive or strict parents and similar life experiences. If the twins have similar personalities, it is impossible to identify the source of the similarity because they have not only the same genetic makeup but also similar life experiences.

FIGURE **2.1**

Nature and Nurture: The Determinants of Personality

Nurture Life experiences.

In contrast, identical twins who are separated at birth and raised in different settings (perhaps because they are adopted by different families) share the same genetic material but often have very different life experiences. Evidence from research on separated identical twins and other studies suggests that approximately 50 percent of the variation we observe in people's personalities can be attributed to nature—to genetic factors (see Figure 2.1).[13] Thus, about half of the variation we observe in employees' personalities in organizations reflects the distinctive ways of thinking, feeling, and behaving they inherited from their parents. The other 50 percent reflects the influence of **nurture**, or life experiences.

Personality develops over time, responding to the experiences people have as children and as adults. Factors such as the strictness or permissiveness of a child's parents, the number of other children in the family, the extent to which parents and teachers demand a lot from a child, success or lack of success at making friends or getting and keeping a job, and even the culture in which a person is raised and lives as an adult are shapers of personality.

Because about half of the variation in people's personalities is inherited from their parents and, thus, is basically fixed at birth, it comes as no surprise that personality is quite stable over periods of time ranging from 5 to 10 years. This does not mean that personality cannot change; it means that personality is likely to change only over many years. Thus, the impact of any specific work situation or crisis on an employee's personality is likely to be felt only if the situation continues for many years. An important outcome of this fact is that managers should not expect to change employees' personalities. In fact, for all practical purposes, managers should view employees' personalities as relatively fixed in the short run.

Personality, nevertheless, is an important individual difference that managers and other organizational members need to take into account in order to understand why people feel, think, and act as they do in organizations. For example, realizing that an employee complains a lot and often gets upset because of his or her personality will help a manager deal with this type of employee, especially if the employee's job performance is acceptable.

PERSONALITY AND THE SITUATION

Because personality accounts for observable regularities in people's attitudes and behaviors, it would seem reasonable to assert that it would account for such regularities at work. A substantial body of literature in psychology and a growing set of studies in organizational behavior suggest that personality *is* useful for explaining and predicting how employees generally feel, think, and behave on the job.[14] Personality has been shown to influence several work-related attitudes and behaviors, including job satisfaction (see Chapter 3), the ability to handle work-related stress (see Chapter 8), the choice of a career (see Chapter 8), and leadership (see Chapter 12).[15] Because of personality, some people, like William Weldon in the opening case, are very conscientious about most things they do and, thus, perform at a higher level than do those who are not so conscientious, as we discuss later in this chapter.[16]

However, in addition to personality, the organizational situation also affects work attitudes and behaviors. In some organizations, there are strong situational constraints and pressures (such as job requirements or strict rules and regulations) that force people to behave in a certain way, regardless of their personalities.[17] For example, an employee on an assembly line manufacturing bicycles must put handlebars on each bicycle that passes by. A bike passes by every 75 seconds, and the employee has to be sure that the handlebars are properly attached to each bicycle within that time frame. It doesn't matter whether the employee is shy or outgoing; regardless of his or her personality, the employee has a specific task to perform day in and day out in the same manner. Because the employee is not free to vary his or her behavior, personality is not useful for understanding or predicting job performance in this situation.

Consider another example. Employees at McDonald's and other fast-food restaurants follow clearly specified procedures for preparing large quantities of burgers, fries, and shakes and serving them to large numbers of customers. Because each employee knows exactly what the procedures are and how to carry them out (they are spelled out in a detailed manual), the food is always prepared in the same manner, regardless of the employees' personalities.

As those two examples show, in organizations in which situational pressures on employees' behavior are strong, personality may not be a good predictor of on-the-job behavior. When situational pressures are weak, however, and employees have more choice about how to perform a job, personality plays a more important role, and what a person can put into his or her job performance will sometimes depend on the kind of person he or she is. For instance, a statewide English curriculum requires English teachers to teach Shakespeare's *Macbeth* to high school seniors, but the curriculum does not specify exactly how the play is to be taught. A teacher who is outgoing and has a flair for the dramatic may bring the play and its themes to life by dressing up in period costumes and acting out scenes. A teacher who is less outgoing may simply ask students to take turns reading aloud from the play or ask them to write a paper on how Shakespeare reveals a certain theme through the play's dialogue and action.

By now it should be clear to you that both personality and situational factors affect organizational behavior.[18] It is the interaction of personality and situational factors that determines how people think, feel, and behave in general and, specifically, how they do so within an organization (see Figure 2.2). Robert Greene, for example, is an executive in an advertising agency who is responsible for coming up with advertising campaigns and presenting them to the agency's clients. Greene is a creative, achievement-oriented person who has good ideas and has developed the agency's most successful and lucrative campaigns. But Greene is also shy and quiet and cannot always effectively communicate his ideas to clients. Greene's personality and the situation combine or interact to determine his overall performance. He performs well when working on his own or with his team to develop advertising campaigns, but in interpersonal situations, such as when he presents his campaigns to clients, he performs poorly. A manager who understands this interaction can capitalize on the personality strengths (creativity and achievement orientation) that propel Greene to develop successful advertising campaigns. The manager can also guard against the possibility of clients having a negative reaction to Greene's shyness by teaming him up for presentations with a gregarious executive whose strong suit is pitching campaigns to clients. If Greene's manager did not understand how Greene's personality and the situation interacted to shape Greene's performance, the advertising agency might lose clients because of Greene's inability to relate to them effectively and convince them of the merits of his campaigns.

FIGURE 2.2

The Interaction of Personality and Situational Factors

Effective managers recognize that the various situations and personality types interact to determine feelings, thoughts, attitudes, and behaviors at work. An understanding of employees' personalities and the situations in which they perform best enables a manager to help employees perform at a high level and feel good about the work they are doing. Furthermore, when employees at all levels in an organization understand how personality and the situation interact, good working relationships and organizational effectiveness are promoted.

PERSONALITY: A DETERMINANT OF THE NATURE OF ORGANIZATIONS

Attraction-selection-attrition (ASA) framework The idea that an organization attracts and selects individuals with similar personalities and loses individuals with other types of personalities.

Ben Schneider, a prominent organizational researcher at the University of Maryland, has come up with an interesting view of the way in which personality determines the nature of whole organizations. He calls his schema the **attraction-selection-attrition (ASA) framework**.[19] Schneider proposes that the "personality" of a whole organization is largely a product of the personalities of its employees. He suggests that individuals with similar personalities tend to be attracted to an organization (*attraction*) and hired by it (*selection*), and individuals with other types of personalities tend to leave the organization (*attrition*). As a result of the interplay of attraction, selection, and attrition, there is some consistency or similarity of personalities within an organization, and this "typical" personality determines the nature of the organization itself.[20]

ASA processes operate in numerous ways. When organizations hire new employees, they implicitly size up the extent to which prospective hires fit in with the organization—that is, the extent to which their personalities match the personalities of current members. This sizing up is especially likely to occur in small organizations. Larry Pliska, who heads up Planterra, a Michigan company that sells plants and trees, hires all new managers himself so that he can be sure they relate to and support his philosophy for the company. John Schaeffer, founder of the California company Real Goods Trading, conducts most of the final interviewing and does most of the hiring for his company in an attempt to find what he calls "even-tempered" employees.[21]

What are the implications of the ASA framework? We would expect, for example, that people who are creative and like to take risks would be attracted to entrepreneurial organizations and would be likely to be hired by such organizations. Individuals who do not have this orientation either would not seek jobs with these organizations or would be likely to leave them. Over time, ASA processes may result in these organizations being composed of large numbers of creative risk takers who, in turn, give the organization its entrepreneurial nature. The entrepreneurial nature of the organization, in turn, influences employees' feelings, thoughts, and behavior and reinforces their own propensity for risk taking. It is important to realize that although ASA processes can strengthen an organization, they can also lead an organization to perform poorly or fail. This negative outcome occurs when most members of the organization view opportunities and problems in the same way and, as a result of their shared point of view, are resistant to different points of view and making needed changes.

The Big Five Model of Personality

When people describe other people, they often say things like "She's got a lot of personality," meaning that the person is fun loving, friendly, and outgoing, or "He's got no personality," meaning that the person is dull and boring. In fact, there is no such thing as a lot of personality or no personality; everyone has a specific type of personality.

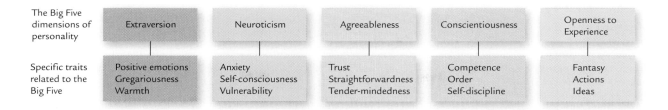

FIGURE **2.3**

The Hierarchical Organization of Personality

Source: Adapted from R. R. McCrae and P. T. Costa, "Discriminant Validity of NEO-PIR Facet Scales." *Educational and Psychological Measurement* 52: 229–237. Copyright 1992. Reprinted by permission of Sage Publications, Inc.

Trait A specific component of personality.

Because personality is an important determinant of how a person thinks, feels, and behaves, it is helpful to distinguish between different types of personality. Researchers have spent considerable time and effort trying to identify personality types. One of the most important ways that researchers have found to describe a personality is in terms of traits. A **trait** is a specific component of personality that describes the particular tendencies a person has to feel, think, and act in certain ways, such as in a shy or outgoing, critical or accepting, compulsive or easygoing manner. In the opening case, William Weldon of J&J was described as being conscientious and open to new experiences; as you will learn, conscientiousness and openness to experience are actually two personality traits. Thus, when we speak of a person's personality, we are really referring to a collection of traits that describes how the person generally tends to feel, think, and behave.

Researchers have identified many personality traits, and most psychologists agree that the traits that make up a person's personality can be organized in a hierarchy.[22] The Big Five model of personality places five general personality traits at the top of the trait hierarchy: extraversion, neuroticism, agreeableness, conscientiousness, and openness to experience (see Figure 2.3).[23] Each of the Big Five traits is composed of various specific traits. Extraversion (the tendency to have a positive outlook on life), for example, consists of specific traits such as positive emotions, gregariousness, and warmth. The Big Five and the specific traits lower in the hierarchy are universal. They can be used to describe the personalities of people regardless of their age, gender, race, ethnicity, religion, socioeconomic background, or country of origin.

Each of the general and specific traits represents a continuum along which a certain aspect or dimension of personality can be placed. A person can be high, low, average, or anywhere in between on the continuum for each trait. Figure 2.4 shows a profile of a person who is low on extraversion, high on neuroticism, about average on agreeableness and conscientiousness, and relatively high on openness to experience. To help you understand what a Big Five personality profile means, we describe the extremes of each trait next. Keep in mind that a person's standing on the trait could be anywhere along the continuum (as in Figure 2.4).

Extraversion

Low	High

Neuroticism

Low	High

Agreeableness

Low	High

Conscientiousness

Low	High

Openness to experience

Low	High

FIGURE **2.4**

A Big Five Personality Profile

This is the profile of a person who is low on extraversion, high on neuroticism, about average on agreeableness and conscientiousness, and relatively high on openness to experience.

FIGURE **2.5**

A Measure of Extraversion or Positive Affectivity

Source: A. Tellegen, "Brief Manual for the Differential Personality Questionnaire," unpublished manuscript, University of Minnesota, 1982. Reprinted with permission.

Instructions: Listed below is a series of statements a person might use to describe her or his attitudes, opinions, interests, and other characteristics. If a statement is true or largely true, put a "T" in the space next to the item. If the statement is false or largely false, mark an "F" in the space.

Please answer *every statement*, even if you are not completely sure of the answer. Read each statement carefully, but don't spend too much time deciding on the answer.

_____ 1. It is easy for me to become enthusiastic about things I am doing.

_____ 2. I often feel happy and satisfied for no particular reason.

_____ 3. I live a very interesting life.

_____ 4. Every day I do some things that are fun.

_____ 5. I usually find ways to liven up my day.

_____ 6. Most days I have moments of real fun or joy.

_____ 7. I often feel sort of lucky for no special reason.

_____ 8. Every day interesting and exciting things happen to me.

_____ 9. In my spare time I usually find something interesting to do.

_____ 10. For me life is a great adventure.

_____ 11. I always seem to have something pleasant to look forward to.

Scoring: Level of extraversion or positive affectivity is equal to the number of items answered "True."

EXTRAVERSION

Extraversion The tendency to experience positive emotional states and feel good about oneself and the world around one; also called positive affectivity.

Extraversion, or **positive affectivity**, is a personality trait that predisposes individuals to experience positive emotional states and feel good about themselves and about the world around them. Extraverts—people high on the extraversion scale—tend to be sociable, affectionate, and friendly. Introverts—people low on the extraversion scale—are less likely to experience positive emotional states and have fewer social interactions with others. At work, extraverts are more likely than introverts to experience positive moods, be satisfied with their jobs, and generally feel good about the organization and those around them. Extraverts also are more likely to enjoy socializing with their co-workers. They may do particularly well in jobs requiring frequent social interaction, such as in sales and customer relations positions.

Of course, people who are low on extraversion can succeed in a variety of occupations. For example, Steve Case, former chairman and CEO of America Online and AOL Time Warner, is often described as not being high on extraversion.[24] An example of a personality scale that measures a person's level of extraversion is provided in Figure 2.5.

NEUROTICISM

Neuroticism The tendency to experience negative emotional states and view oneself and the world around one negatively; also called negative affectivity.

In contrast to extraversion, **neuroticism**, or **negative affectivity**, reflects people's tendency to experience negative emotional states, feel distressed, and generally view themselves and the world around them negatively. Individuals high on neuroticism are more likely than individuals low on neuroticism to experience negative emotions and stress over time and across situations. Individuals who are high on neuroticism are more likely to experience negative moods at work, feel stressed, and generally have a negative orientation toward the work situation.[25] Often, the term *neurotic* is used in the media and popular press to describe a person who has a psychological problem. Neuroticism, however, is a trait that all normal, psychologically healthy individuals possess to a certain degree.

Instructions: Listed below is a series of statements a person might use to describe her or his attitudes, opinions, interests, and other characteristics. If a statement is true or largely true, put a "T" in the space next to the item. If the statement is false or largely false, mark an "F" in the space.

Please answer *every statement*, even if you are not completely sure of the answer. Read each statement carefully, but don't spend too much time deciding on the answer.

_____ 1. I often find myself worrying about something.

_____ 2. My feelings are hurt rather easily.

_____ 3. Often I get irritated at little annoyances.

_____ 4. I suffer from nervousness.

_____ 5. My mood often goes up and down.

_____ 6. I sometimes feel "just miserable" for no good reason.

_____ 7. Often I experience strong emotions—anxiety, anger—without really knowing what causes them.

_____ 8. I am easily startled by things that happen unexpectedly.

_____ 9. I sometimes get myself into a state of tension and turmoil as I think of the day's events.

_____ 10. Minor setbacks sometimes irritate me too much.

_____ 11. I often lose sleep over my worries.

_____ 12. There are days when I'm "on edge" all of the time.

_____ 13. I am too sensitive for my own good.

_____ 14. I sometimes change from happy to sad, or vice versa, without good reason.

Scoring: Level of neuroticism or negative affectivity is equal to the number of items answered "True."

FIGURE **2.6**

A Measure of Neuroticism or Negative Affectivity

Source: A. Tellegen, "Brief Manual for the Differential Personality Questionnaire," unpublished manuscript, University of Minnesota, 1982. Reprinted with permission.

Individuals high on neuroticism are sometimes more critical of themselves and their performance than are people low on neuroticism. That tendency may propel them to improve their performance. As a result, they may be particularly proficient in certain situations, such as ones that require a high degree of quality control, critical thinking, and evaluation. Individuals high on neuroticism may also exert a needed "sobering" influence during group decision making by playing devil's advocate and pointing out the negative aspects of a proposed decision. Individuals low on neuroticism do not tend to experience negative emotions and are not as critical and pessimistic as their high-neuroticism counterparts. An example of a personality scale that measures neuroticism is provided in Figure 2.6.

AGREEABLENESS

Agreeableness is the trait that captures the distinction between individuals who get along well with other people and those who do not. Likability in general and the ability to care for others and to be affectionate characterize individuals who are high on agreeableness. Individuals low on agreeableness are antagonistic, mistrustful, unsympathetic, uncooperative, and rude. A low level of agreeableness might be an advantage in jobs that require a person to be somewhat antagonistic, such as a bill collector or a drill sergeant. Agreeable individuals generally are easy to get along with and are team players. Agreeableness can be an asset in jobs that hinge on developing good relationships with other people. An example of a scale that measures agreeableness is provided in Figure 2.7.

Agreeableness The tendency to get along well with others.

Listed below are phrases describing people's behaviors. Please use the rating scale below to describe how accurately each statement describes **you**. Describe yourself as you generally are now, not as you wish to be in the future. Describe yourself as you honestly see yourself, in relation to other people you know of the same sex as you are, and roughly your same age.

1	2	3	4	5
Very inaccurate	Moderately inaccurate	Neither inaccurate nor accurate	Moderately accurate	Very accurate

_____ 1. Am interested in people.

_____ 2. Have a rich vocabulary.

_____ 3. Am always prepared.

_____ 4. Am not really interested in others.*

_____ 5. Leave my belongings around.*

_____ 6. Have difficulty understanding abstract ideas.*

_____ 7. Sympathize with others' feelings.

_____ 8. Pay attention to details.

_____ 9. Have a vivid imagination.

_____ 10. Insult people.*

_____ 11. Make a mess of things.*

_____ 12. Am not interested in abstract ideas.*

_____ 13. Have a soft heart.

_____ 14. Get chores done right away.

_____ 15. Have excellent ideas.

_____ 16. Am not interested in other people's problems.*

_____ 17. Often forget to put things back in their proper place.*

_____ 18. Do not have a good imagination.*

_____ 19. Take time out for others.

_____ 20. Like order.

_____ 21. Am quick to understand things.

_____ 22. Feel little concern for others.*

_____ 23. Shirk my duties.*

_____ 24. Use difficult words.

_____ 25. Feel others' emotions.

_____ 26. Follow a schedule.

_____ 27. Spend time reflecting on things.

_____ 28. Make people feel at ease.

_____ 29. Am exacting in my work.

_____ 30. Am full of ideas.

*Items reverse scored: 1=5; 2=4; 4=2, 5=1

Scoring: Sum responses to items for an overall scale.

Agreeableness = Sum of items 1, 4, 7, 10, 13, 16, 19, 22, 25, 28

Conscientiousness = Sum of items 3, 5, 8, 11, 14, 17, 20, 23, 26, 29

Openness to experience = Sum of items 2, 6, 9, 12, 15, 18, 21, 24, 27, 30

FIGURE 2.7

Measures of Agreeableness, Conscientiousness, and Openness to Experience

Source: http://ipip.ori.org/ipip/, Lewis R. Goldberg, Oregon Research Institute.

CONSCIENTIOUSNESS

Conscientiousness The extent to which a person is careful, scrupulous, and persevering.

Conscientiousness is the extent to which an individual is careful, scrupulous, and persevering. Individuals high on conscientiousness are organized and have a lot of self-discipline.[26] Individuals low on conscientiousness may lack direction and self-discipline. Conscientiousness is important in many organizational situations and has been found to be a good predictor of performance in many jobs in a wide variety of organizations.[27] Roger Salquist, entrepreneur and CEO of the successful Calgene Inc. (now part of Monsanto Corporation), is known for his attention to details. When trying to win U.S. Food and Drug Administration (FDA) approval for his genetically altered tomato, for instance, Salquist made over 25 trips to Washington, DC, and was relentless in his efforts to provide the FDA and other agencies with all the scientific data he could in support of the safety of his tomato. Salquist's conscientiousness paid off because the FDA agreed that no special labeling or testing would be necessary for genetically engineered foods such as Calgene's new tomato.[28] In the opening case, it is also clear that William Weldon of J&J is high on conscientiousness.

Of course, in order for conscientiousness to result in high performance, employees need to have the capabilities or skills needed to be high performers. For example, a recent study found that when job performance depends on being effective interpersonally, conscientiousness was only positively related to performance among those employees who had high social skills.[29] An example of a scale that measures conscientiousness is provided in Figure 2.7.

OPENNESS TO EXPERIENCE

The last of the Big Five personality traits, **openness to experience**, captures the extent to which an individual is original, open to a wide variety of stimuli, has broad interests, and is willing to take risks as opposed to being narrow-minded and cautious. Recall William Weldon's openness to new ideas in the opening case. For jobs that change frequently, require innovation, or involve considerable risk, individuals who are high on openness to experience may have an advantage. For openness to experience to be translated into creative and innovative behavior in organizations, however, the organization must remove obstacles to innovation. Moreover, jobs and tasks must not be too closely defined so that job holders are able to use their openness to experience to come up with new ideas.[30] Entrepreneurs, who are often characterized as risk takers,[31] frequently start their own businesses because the large organizations that employed them placed too many restrictions on them and gave them too little reward for innovation and risk taking. Although openness to experience clearly is an advantage for entrepreneurs and performing jobs that require innovation, organizations also need people to perform jobs that do not allow much opportunity for originality. In addition, organizations are sometimes afraid to take the risks that employees high on openness to experience may thrive on. An example of a personality scale that measures openness to experience is provided in Figure 2.7.

Sometimes the combination of high openness to experience and high conscientiousness can be beneficial when employees need to make difficult decisions in uncertain times. This has proven to be the case for Fujio Mitarai, CEO of Canon, Inc., as profiled in the accompanying Global View.

Openness to experience
The extent to which a person is original, has broad interests, and is willing to take risks.

global view

Fujio Mitarai Cuts Costs and Takes Risks at Canon

Fujio Mitarai, president and CEO of Canon, Inc., has turned around Canon's fortunes and tripled its net profits since assuming the top post at this global camera, printer, fax, and copier maker in 1997. Mitarai has made many changes at Canon—changes that reflect his high levels of conscientiousness and openness to experience. Mitarai realized that to revitalize Canon he needed to cut costs and boost profitability. His conscientiousness helped him to take the steps needed to make this happen—shutting down weak businesses and divisions, pushing employees to always be on the lookout for ways to cut costs, and rewarding employees for increasing sales and profitability.[32]

Whereas Mitarai's discipline has served Canon well, so has his high level of openness to experience. Mitarai's openness to experience has influenced him throughout his life. As a child who only knew the Japanese language and culture, he longed to go overseas. After a few years at Canon in Japan, in 1966 he transferred to the company's New York office, where he remained for 23 years, building the camera and copier business for Canon in the United States. In 1989, he returned to Japan as managing director prior to assuming the CEO position.[33]

Mitarai's openness to both the Japanese and the American ways of managing has led him to become somewhat of a role model for other executives, and he was recently named one of *Business Week*'s "Best Managers."[34] For example, consistent with American practices, he believes in merit pay to reward high performers; consistent with Japanese practices, he values loyalty and, thus, is an advocate of lifetime employment. Rather than appoint outsiders to the board of directors to keep top management on track, he prefers the value-added contributions insiders on the board can make. However, he also recognizes the need for the oversight of management that is accomplished by empowering auditors to play a more active role in corporate governance.[35]

Mitarai's openness to experience has even changed the way that Canon manufactures its cameras and copiers. In Japan, Mitarai replaced its traditional assembly lines used for production with a "cell" system. Each cell is made up of six workers who assemble products in a small area rather than on a long assembly line. Cell production has proven to be much more efficient than assembly lines in Japan, and Canon is now implementing the new method in its production facilities outside of Japan. Looking to the future, Mitarai has increased Canon's spending on research and development to take advantage of the latest scientific developments in technology to create new and better products.[36] Clearly, high levels of conscientiousness and openness to experience have helped Mitarai get Canon back on track.

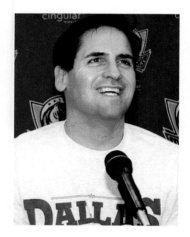

Being open to new experiences and willing to take risks has paid off handsomely for billionaire Mark Cuban, the colorful owner of the Dallas Mavericks. Cuban made his first million founding a computer company after college—without ever having taken an information systems class.

CONCLUSIONS

Research suggests that the Big Five traits are important for understanding work-related attitudes and behaviors and, thus, our understanding of organizational behavior. As we discuss in more detail in Chapter 9, for example, neuroticism or negative affectivity is useful in understanding stress in the workplace.[37] Researchers have found that individuals high on negative affectivity are more likely to indicate that there are significant stressors in the workplace and to experience stress at work. Research has also shown that individuals high on extraversion or positive affectivity are more likely to feel good at work and be satisfied with their jobs. These people are likely to perform well in jobs such as sales and management, which require social interaction.[38]

As you have undoubtedly recognized from our discussion of the Big Five traits, there is no such thing as a good or bad personality profile. Each person is unique and has a different type of personality that may be suited to different kinds of organizational situations. Good managers need to understand and learn to deal with people of all personality types.

Other Organizationally Relevant Personality Traits

Several other specific personality traits are relevant to understanding and managing behavior in organizations (see Figure 2.8).

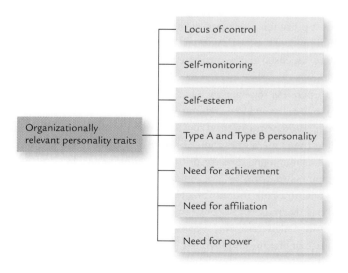

FIGURE 2.8

Personality Traits Specifically Relevant to Organizations

you're the management expert

LOCUS OF CONTROL

People differ in how much control they believe they have over the situation they are in and over what happens to them. Some people think they have relatively little impact on their surroundings and little control over important things that happen in their lives. Others believe that they can have a considerable impact on the world around them and on the path their lives take. The locus of control trait captures this difference among individuals.[39]

"Externals," or individuals with an **external locus of control**, tend to believe that outside forces are largely responsible for their fate, and they see little connection between their own actions and what happens to them. "Internals," or individuals with an **internal locus of control**, think that their own actions and behaviors have an impact on what happens to them. When people with an internal locus of control perform well, they are likely to attribute their performance to qualities within themselves, such as their own ability or effort. When people with an external locus of control perform well, they are likely to attribute their performance to external forces such as luck, the effects of powerful people, or simply the fact that the task was easy. In organizations, internals are more easily motivated than externals. Internals do not need as much direct supervision because they tend to believe their work behaviors influence important outcomes such as how well they perform their jobs and the pay increases, praise, job security, and promotions they receive.

External locus of control Describes people who believe that fate, luck, or outside forces are responsible for what happens to them.

Internal locus of control Describes people who believe that ability, effort, or their own actions determine what happens to them.

SELF-MONITORING

Self-monitoring is the extent to which people try to control the way they present themselves to others.[40] High self-monitors want their behavior to be socially acceptable and are attuned to any social cues that signal appropriate or inappropriate behavior. They strive to behave in a situationally appropriate manner. For

Self-monitoring The extent to which people try to control the way they present themselves to others.

example, if they are in a meeting and see others making suggestions, they will try to make suggestions as well. They are also good at managing the impressions that others have of them. In contrast, low self-monitors are not particularly sensitive to cues indicating acceptable behavior, nor are they overly concerned about behaving in a situationally appropriate manner. For example, they may act bored in a meeting with the president of an organization or voice their concerns in a job interview about working long hours. People who are low self-monitors are guided by their own attitudes, beliefs, feelings, and principles and are not too concerned about what others think of their behavior.

High self-monitors are more likely than low self-monitors to tailor their behavior to fit a given situation. Thus, high self-monitors may perform especially well in jobs such as sales or consulting, which require employees to interact with different types of people on a regular basis. In addition, because high self-monitors can modify their behavior to approximate what individuals or groups expect of them, they are particularly effective when an organization needs someone to communicate with an outside group whose support is being sought, such as when a nonprofit organization tries to secure donations from wealthy individuals, for example.

Low self-monitors are more likely than high self-monitors to say what they think is true or correct and are not overly concerned about how others will react to them. Thus, low self-monitors may be especially adept at providing organizational members with open, honest feedback (particularly when it's negative) and playing devil's advocate in decision-making groups. A scale that measures self-monitoring is provided in Figure 2.9.

FIGURE **2.9**

A Measure of Self-Monitoring

Source: S. Gangestad and M. Snyder, "'To Carve Nature at Its Joints': On the Existence of Discrete Classes in Personality," *Psychological Review* 92 (1985): 317–49. Copyright 1985 by the American Psychological Association. Reprinted with permission.

Instructions: Please indicate the extent to which each of the following statements is true or false for you personally.

_____ 1. I find it hard to imitate the behavior of other people.

_____ 2. At parties and social gatherings. I do not attempt to do or say things that others will like.

_____ 3. I can only argue for ideas that I already believe.

_____ 4. I can make impromptu speeches even on topics about which I have almost no information.

_____ 5. I guess I put on a show to impress or entertain others.

_____ 6. I would probably make a good actor.

_____ 7. In a group of people, I am rarely the center of attention.

_____ 8. In different situations and with different people, I often act like very different persons.

_____ 9. I am not particularly good at making other people like me.

_____ 10. I'm not always the person I appear to be.

_____ 11. I would not change my opinions (or the way I do things) in order to please someone or win their favor.

_____ 12. I have considered being an entertainer.

_____ 13. I have never been good at games like charades or improvisational acting.

_____ 14. I have trouble changing my behavior to suit different people and different situations.

_____ 15. At a party I let others keep the jokes and stories going.

_____ 16. I feel a bit awkward in public and do not show up quite as well as I should.

_____ 17. I can look anyone in the eye and tell a lie with a straight face (if for a right end).

_____ 18. I may deceive people by being friendly when I really dislike them.

Scoring: Individuals high on self-monitoring tend to indicate that questions 4, 5, 6, 8, 10, 12, 17, and 18 are *true* and that questions 1, 2, 3, 7, 9, 11, 13, 14, 15, and 16 are *false*.

SELF–ESTEEM

Self-esteem is the extent to which people have pride in themselves and their capabilities.[41] Individuals with high self-esteem think they are generally capable and worthy people who can deal with most situations. Individuals with low self-esteem question their self-worth, doubt their capabilities, and are apprehensive about their ability to succeed in different endeavors.

Self-esteem has several implications for understanding behavior in organizations.[42] Self-esteem influences people's choices of activities and jobs. Individuals with high self-esteem are more likely than individuals with low self-esteem to choose challenging careers and jobs. Once they are on the job, individuals with high self-esteem may set higher goals for themselves and be more likely to tackle difficult tasks. High self-esteem also has a positive impact on motivation and job satisfaction. Clearly, William Weldon's high self-esteem has contributed to his success at J&J. It must be kept in mind, however, that people with low self-esteem can be just as capable as those with high self-esteem in spite of their self-doubts.

Self-esteem The extent to which people have pride in themselves and their capabilities.

TYPE **A** AND TYPE **B** PERSONALITIES

In the popular press, you will often hear someone referred to as a "Type A" or read that "Type A personalities" are prone to high blood pressure. Individuals who are **Type A** have an intense desire to achieve, are extremely competitive, have a sense of urgency, are impatient, and can be hostile.[43] Such individuals have a strong need to get a lot done in a short time period and can be difficult to get along with because they are so driven. They often interrupt other people and sometimes finish their sentences for them because they are so impatient. More relaxed and easygoing individuals are labeled **Type B**.

Because they are able to accomplish so much, Type A's would seem to be ideal employees from the organization's perspective, especially in situations in which a lot of work needs to be done in a short amount of time. However, because they can be difficult to get along with, Type A's may not be effective in situations that require a lot of interaction with others. Consistent with this observation, one study found that Type A managers were more likely to have conflicts with their subordinates and with co-workers than were Type B managers.[44] Type A employees are not particularly good team players and often work best alone. In addition, Type A's may get frustrated in long-term situations or projects because they like to see results quickly.

Another important difference between Type A and Type B individuals has received a lot of attention in the popular press. Type A individuals are more likely than Type B's to have coronary heart disease. In fact, two heart doctors identified this trait after they realized that many of their heart attack patients were very impatient, sometimes hostile, and always in a hurry and watching the clock. Some research suggests that a tendency toward hostility is particularly responsible for Type A's heart problems.

Type A A person who has an intense desire to achieve, is extremely competitive, and has a strong sense of urgency.

Type B A person who tends to be easygoing and relaxed.

NEEDS FOR ACHIEVEMENT, AFFILIATION, AND POWER

David McClelland has done extensive research on three traits that are present in all people to varying degrees: the need for achievement, the need for affiliation, and the need for power.[45] Individuals with a high **need for achievement** have a special desire to perform challenging tasks well and to meet their own personal standards for excellence. They like to be in situations in which they are personally responsible for what happens, like to set clear goals for themselves, are willing to take personal

Need for achievement The desire to perform challenging tasks well and to meet one's own high standards.

responsibility for outcomes, and like to receive performance feedback. Not surprisingly, such individuals are often found in jobs that help them to satisfy their strong desire to excel. Indeed, McClelland has found that entrepreneurs and managers are especially likely to have a high need for achievement. In one study, for example, McClelland found that 10 years after graduation, undergraduates who had shown a high need for achievement were more likely to be found in entrepreneurial occupations than were those who had shown a low need for achievement.[46] In addition, effective managers often have a strong goal orientation and tend to take moderate risks, a finding that is consistent with the profile of an individual with a high need for achievement. It is not surprising, therefore, that a high need for achievement often goes hand in hand with career success. This has been the case for Flight Operations Vice President Captain Deborah McCoy, who oversees more than 8,700 flight attendants and 5,200 pilots at Continental Airlines.[47] As a teenager, McCoy worked at a grocery store to earn money to take flying lessons. She joined Continental as a pilot in 1978 and has since been promoted many times, leading up to her current high-ranking position.[48]

Need for affiliation The desire to establish and maintain good relations with others.

Individuals with a high **need for affiliation** are especially concerned about establishing and maintaining good relations with other people. They not only want to be liked by others but also want everyone to get along with everyone else. As you might expect, they like working in groups, tend to be sensitive to other people's feelings, and avoid taking actions that would result in interpersonal conflict. In organizations, individuals with a high need for affiliation are especially likely to be found in jobs that require a lot of social interaction. Although they make good team players, a manager might not want a group to be composed primarily of individuals with a high need for affiliation because the group might be more concerned about maintaining good interpersonal relations than about actually accomplishing its tasks. Individuals with a high need for affiliation may also be less effective in situations in which they need to evaluate others because it may be hard for them to give negative feedback to a co-worker or a subordinate—a task that might disrupt interpersonal relations.

Need for power The desire to exert emotional and behavioral control or influence over others.

Individuals with a high **need for power** have a strong desire to exert emotional and behavioral control or influence over others.[49] These individuals are especially likely to be found in managerial jobs and leadership positions, which require one person to exert influence over others. Individuals with a high need for power may actually be more effective as leaders than those with a low need for power. In a study of the effectiveness of former presidents of the United States, for example, Robert House of the University of Pennsylvania and his colleagues found that a president's need for power was a good predictor of his performance and effectiveness in office.[50] The power-level needs of a president were assessed by analyzing his inaugural speeches for thoughts and ideas indicative of the need for power. From the opening case, it is clear that William Weldon has a high need for power, which contributes to his effectiveness as CEO of J&J.

What combination of the needs for achievement, affiliation, and power results in higher managerial motivation and performance? Although it might seem that high levels of all three are important for managerial effectiveness, research by Michael Stahl suggests that managers should have a high need for achievement and power.[51] A high need for affiliation might not necessarily be a good quality in managers because they may try too hard to be liked by their subordinates instead of trying to lead them to higher performance levels. Stahl's findings on managerial effectiveness primarily apply to lower- and middle-level managers.[52] For top executives and managers, the need for power appears to be the need that dominates all others in determining their success.[53]

HOW PERSONALITY IS MEASURED

We have been discussing the various traits that make up an individual's personality without much mention of how to determine an individual's standing on any of these traits. By far the most common and cost-effective means of assessing the personality traits of adults is through scales developed to measure personality. To complete these scales, individuals answer a series of questions about themselves.[54] Figures 2.5, 2.6, 2.7, and 2.9 provide examples of scales that measure the Big Five personality traits and self-monitoring. Personality scales like these are often used for research purposes, for example, to determine how people who vary on these traits respond to different work situations. Although the use of such scales always runs the risk of respondents intentionally distorting their answers to portray themselves in a desirable fashion, research suggests that this is not a significant problem.[55]

The Nature of Ability

When looking at individual differences and the way they affect the attitudes and behaviors of employees, we must look not only at each employee's personality but also at the *abilities*, *aptitudes*, and *skills* the employee possesses. Those terms are often used interchangeably. In our discussion, however, we focus on **ability**, which has been defined as "what a person is capable of doing."[56] Ability has important implications for understanding and managing organizational behavior. It determines the level of performance an employee can achieve and, because the effectiveness of an organization as a whole depends on the performance levels of all individual employees—from janitors and clerks to upper managers and the CEO—ability is an important determinant of organizational performance. Two basic types of ability affect performance: cognitive or mental ability and physical ability.

Ability The mental or physical capacity to do something.

COGNITIVE ABILITY

Psychologists have identified many types of cognitive ability and grouped them in a hierarchy. The most general dimension of cognitive ability is *general intelligence*.[57] Below general intelligence are specific types of cognitive ability that reflect competence in different areas of mental functioning (see Figure 2.10). Eight types of cognitive ability identified and described by psychologist Jum Nunnally, whose work was based in part on the pioneering work of L. L. and T. G. Thurstone in the 1940s, are described in Table 2.1.[58]

Research suggests that cognitive ability predicts performance on the job, as long as the ability in question is relied on in performing the job.[59] For example, numerical ability is unlikely to predict how well a writer or comedian will perform on the job. To understand the relation between cognitive ability and job performance, one needs to identify the abilities that are required to effectively perform the job.[60] In the previous example, verbal

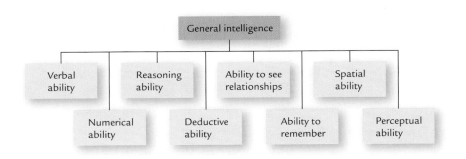

FIGURE 2.10
Types of Cognitive Ability

TABLE 2.1

Cognitive Abilities

Ability	Description	Examples of jobs in which the ability is especially important
Verbal ability	Ability to understand and use written and spoken language	Comedians, teachers, lawyers, writers
Numerical ability	Ability to solve arithmetic problems and deal with numbers	Waiters, investment bankers, engineers, accountants
Reasoning ability	Ability to come up with solutions for problems and understand the principles by which different problems can be solved	Therapists, interior designers, car mechanics, computer software designers
Deductive ability	Ability to reach appropriate conclusions from an array of observations or evaluate the implications of a series of facts	Medical researchers, detectives, scientists, investigative reporters
Ability to see relationships	The ability to see how two things are related to each other and then apply this knowledge to other relationships and solutions	Anthropologists, travel agents, consultants, wedding planners
Ability to remember	Ability to recall things ranging from simple associations to complex groups of statements or sentences	Translators, salespeople, managers, researchers
Spatial ability	Ability to determine the location or arrangement of objects in relation to one's own position and to imagine how an object would appear if its position in space were altered	Air traffic controllers, architects, clothing designers, astronauts
Perceptual	Ability to uncover visual patterns and see relationships within and across patterns	Professional photographers, airplane pilots, cruise ship captains, landscape designers

Source: Based, in part, on J. C. Nunnally, *Psychometric Theory*, 2nd ed. (New York: McGraw-Hill, 1978).

Surgeons like those who separated Ahmed and Mohamed Ibrahim—Egyptian twins conjoined at the head—need both cognitive and physical skills. The delicate, intricate procedure, required a year of planning and 26 hours of surgery prior to complete. The twins were separated in 2003.

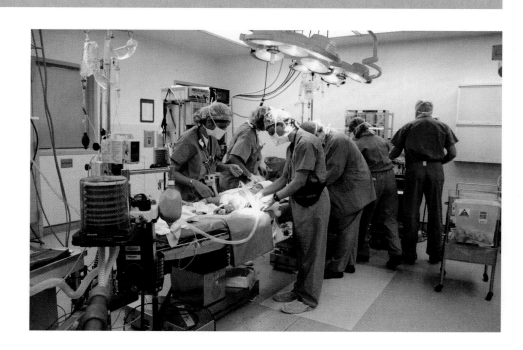

ability is especially likely to be important for a writer or comedian. Thus, this is the cognitive ability most likely to predict success in these jobs.[61] Cognitive ability also is an important contributor to group or team performance.[62] It is important to keep in mind, however, that other things determine performance in addition to cognitive ability.

PHYSICAL ABILITY

People differ not only in cognitive ability but also in physical ability. Two types of physical abilities are motor and physical skills.[63] A *motor skill* is the ability to physically manipulate objects in an environment. A *physical skill* is a person's fitness and strength. E. A. Fleishman has devoted considerable attention to identifying and studying physical ability and has concluded that there are 11 basic motor skills (such as reaction time, manual dexterity, and speed of arm movement) and nine physical skills (such as static strength, which includes the ability to lift weights and stamina).[64]

WHERE DO ABILITIES COME FROM AND HOW ARE THEY MEASURED?

Like personality, both cognitive ability and physical ability are determined by nature and nurture (see Figure 2.11). General intelligence is determined by the genes we inherit from our parents (nature)[65] and by situational factors (nurture). Standardized tests such as the GMAT (General Management Aptitude Test) or the SAT (Scholastic Aptitude Test) are designed to measure certain basic aptitudes and abilities that people are probably born with, but we know that people's scores on these tests change over time and that situational changes such as repeated training on practice exams can improve performance. Moreover, an individual may be genetically endowed with superior intelligence, but if that person grows up in a severely impoverished environment (characterized by poor nutrition, irregular school attendance, or parents who are drug abusers), his or her scores on standard intelligence tests will probably suffer.

Both nature and nurture also determine physical ability. Height, bone structure, limb length, and relative proportions are genetically determined and cannot be changed. Through practice and training such as weight lifting and aerobic exercise, however, people can enhance some of their physical and motor skills.

Researchers have developed many accurate paper-and-pencil measures of cognitive ability; managers can often rely on the results of these tests as useful indicators of the underlying ability they are measuring. The tests can be used to ensure that prospective employees have the types of ability necessary to perform a job, to place existing employees in different jobs in an organization, to identify individuals who might need additional training, and to evaluate how successful training programs are in raising ability levels (we discuss each of these issues in the next section). Before using any of these tests, however, managers have to make sure that the tests are ethical and do not unfairly discriminate against different kinds of employees. Some tests of cognitive ability have been criticized for being culturally biased. Critics say that they ask questions that, because of differences in the test takers' ethnic backgrounds, may be relatively easy for members of certain groups to answer and more difficult for members of other groups to answer.

Physical ability can be measured by having a person engage in the activity he or she would have to do on the job. For example, managers who need to see whether a

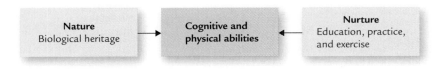

FIGURE 2.11

Nature and Nurture: The Determinants of Cognitive and Physical Abilities

prospective employee is strong enough to deliver, unpack, and set up heavy appliances could ask the individual to lift progressively heavier weights to determine the level of his or her static strength. New York City Sanitation Department evaluates the physical ability of prospective employees by having them pick up trash bags and toss them into garbage trucks.

Although organizations spend considerable time and effort to ensure the people they hire have the abilities they need to be effective in their jobs, sometimes people are not given the opportunity to use their abilities on the job. A recent study of over 600 managers and 700 hourly employees found that two thirds of the managers and employees surveyed thought that their companies used only about 50 percent of their employees' cognitive abilities.[66] Even some IT professionals believe that their abilities are not being effectively utilized. A recent study of over 200 IT professionals found that over 40 percent of them were so bored at work that they thought about quitting their current jobs.[67] Hence, in addition to ensuring that employees have the abilities needed to perform at a high level, organizations should also strive to give them the opportunity to use them.

Cognitive and physical abilities can degenerate or become impaired because of disease, drug or alcohol abuse, excessive levels of stress, or fatigue. In many organizations, it is important to accurately assess the ability level of an employee to know what he or she is capable of doing, but it is also necessary to know when and why that ability may become impaired. Organizations have traditionally responded to impairment by testing employees for substance abuse. This has, indeed, been found to reduce illegal drug use.[68]

Drug testing can detect the presence of drugs and alcohol, but it does not tap into impairment due to other factors like excessive fatigue or disease. Another problem with conducting a drug test is that it usually takes at least two to three days to get the results back. In response to those problems, some firms have developed "fitness for duty" performance tests to determine whether employees can safely perform their jobs. Some of these tests involve the use of computer terminals and games that measure accuracy and reaction time against an employee's baseline score.[69]

EMOTIONAL INTELLIGENCE: A NEW KIND OF ABILITY

Emotional intelligence The ability to understand and manage one's own feelings and emotions and the feelings and emotions of other people.

Psychologists have identified a new kind of ability that is not so much concerned with cognitive or physical capabilities but rather with emotional capabilities. **Emotional intelligence** is the ability to understand and manage one's own feelings and emotions and the feelings and emotions of others.[70] People differ in terms of the extent to which they know how they are feeling, why they are feeling that way, and their ability to manage those feelings. Similarly, they differ in their ability to understand what other people are feeling and why and their ability to influence or manage the feelings of others. Emotional intelligence describes these individual differences[71] and helps promote effective functioning and well-being among employees. An example of a scale that measures emotional intelligence is provided in Figure 2.12.

Research on emotional intelligence is in its early stages. However, it is plausible that emotional intelligence may facilitate job performance in a number of ways and a low level of emotional intelligence may actually impair performance. For example, psychologist Martin Seligman found that salespeople at Metropolitan Life who were high on optimism (an aspect of emotional intelligence) sold considerably more insurance policies than salespeople who were less able to manage their feelings and think positively.[72] As another example, a recent study conducted by Kenneth Law and colleagues found that emotional intelligence predicted levels of life satisfaction among students and levels of job performance among employees in Hong Kong and the People's Republic of China.[73]

Recent theorizing and research suggest that emotional intelligence is an especially important ability for leaders and managers, enabling them to understand and relate well to others as well as understand themselves.[74] Emotional intelligence also helps leaders and managers maintain their enthusiasm and confidence and communicate a vision to followers that will energize them to work toward organizational goals.[75] Jing Zhou and Jennifer George, professors at Rice University, have theorized that leaders' emotional intelligence might be especially important for awakening employee creativity.[76] For Sir Rocco Forte, CEO of Forte Hotels, the ability to understand how customers feel and determine what they want is the key to excellent customer service.[77]

Emotional intelligence sometimes plays a subtle but important role in effective workplace behaviors. For example, consider the case of Jane, who was hired by George McCown of McCown Dee Leeuw, a buyout company in Menlo Park, California, to help determine which companies are good purchase opportunities. Jane was highly intelligent with excellent numerical skills and a top-notch educational background. McCown sent Jane to visit a company he was interested in purchasing. After visiting the company and performing various calculations, Jane advised McCown to buy the company because the numbers looked good. McCown, however, decided to visit the company himself, and he was glad he did. As he puts it, "I could tell in the first two minutes of talking to the CEO that he was experiencing serious burnout. The guy was being

FIGURE **2.12**

A Measure of Emotional Intelligence

Source: K. Law, C. Wong, and L. Song, "The Construct and Criterion Validity of Emotional Intelligence and Its Potential Utility for Management Studies," *Journal of Applied Psychology*, 2004, 89(3), p. 496; C. S. Wong and K. S. Law, "The Effects of Leader and Follower Emotional Intelligence on Performance and Attitude: An Exploratory Study," *Leadership Quarterly*, 2002, 13, pp. 243–274.

Please indicate the extent to which you agree or disagree with each of the following items using the 1–7 scale below.

1	2	3	4	5	6	7
Totally Disagree	Disagree	Somewhat Disagree	Neither Agree Nor Disagree	Somewhat Agree	Agree	Totally Agree

_____ 1. I have a good sense of why I have certain feelings most of the time.

_____ 2. I always know my friends' emotions from their behavior.

_____ 3. I always set goals for myself and then try my best to achieve them.

_____ 4. I am able to control my temper so that I can handle difficulties rationally.

_____ 5. I have good understanding of my own emotions.

_____ 6. I am a good observer of others' emotions.

_____ 7. I always tell myself I am a competent person.

_____ 8. I am quite capable of controlling my own emotions.

_____ 9. I really understand what I feel.

_____ 10. I am sensitive to the feelings and emotions of others.

_____ 11. I am a self-motivating person.

_____ 12. I can always calm down quickly when I am very angry.

_____ 13. I always know whether or not I am happy.

_____ 14. I have good understanding of the emotions of people around me.

_____ 15. I would always encourage myself to try my best.

_____ 16. I have good control of my own emotions.

Scoring: Self-Emotions Appraisal = sum of items 1, 5, 9, 13
Others-Emotions Appraisal = sum of items 2, 6, 10, 14
Use of Emotion = sum of items 3, 7, 11, 15
Regulation of Emotion = sum of items 4, 8, 12, 16

overwhelmed by problems. On paper, things looked great. But he knew what was coming down the line. Jane had missed those cues completely."[78] Evidently, Jane's low level of emotional intelligence prevented her from understanding how the CEO of the targeted company was feeling and why—cues her boss was able to pick up on. Jane is no longer with McCown Dee Leeuw.[79]

Andrea Jung, CEO and chair of Avon Products, is a firm believer in the importance of emotional intelligence. As she puts it, "Emotional intelligence is in our DNA here at Avon because relationships are critical at every stage of our business."[80] Understanding people and relationships clearly has paid off for Christine Poon, head of worldwide pharmaceuticals at Johnson & Johnson (J&J), as profiled in the accompanying Focus on Diversity.

The Management of Ability in Organizations

Although we have mentioned the many types of ability that people possess, only a few abilities are likely to be relevant for the performance of any particular job. Managerial work, for example, requires cognitive ability, not very many physical abilities, and some degree of emotional intelligence, whereas being a grocery store shelf stocker or a car washer requires mainly physical ability. A brain surgeon, for instance, must rely on cognitive and physical abilities when performing highly complicated and delicate operations.

focus on diversity

Christine Poon Understands People at J&J

In the opening case, we profiled William Weldon, CEO of J&J.[81] Christine Poon, head of J&J's largest business segment, worldwide pharmaceuticals, sits on his executive committee and has about 39,000 employees in her unit.[82] Poon, who grew up in the midwesternern United States, was one of the few Chinese American children in her elementary school. Later on, when she first began her career, she stood out as a Chinese American woman manager. Now she stands out for having achieved one of the highest-ranking positions in J&J. Interestingly, Poon doesn't act like a "celebrity manager"; she believes that all employees make a company successful, not just those at the very top.[83] Poon's high level of emotional intelligence is reflected in her philosophy, management style, and how she interacts with people.

Poon has an easygoing demeanor and seems down to earth, yet she is a careful and deliberate decision maker. Equally important to her is fostering a work environment where respect for employees, customers, and the general public is valued.[84] She has the confidence and emotional stamina to take on what might seem to be insurmountable challenges and conquers them in an easygoing manner.

Poon's management style also attests to her emotional intelligence. She is friendly and open, but she can also be direct and insistent. She is intelligent and creative and encourages those around her to be equally inquisitive and ask questions.[85] Poon respects people, whether they are her subordinates or her superiors, which gives her the ability to be humble and effective at the same time.[86] She is results oriented and wants to succeed, but she also realizes that it is her employees who drive that success, so she treats them as equal members of her team.[87] All in all, Poon's emotional intelligence has enabled her to capitalize on her own strengths and the strengths of those around her.

Emotional intelligence led Sir Rocco Forte to create a leading luxury hotel management company in Europe by helping him understand what customers want. Despite his expertise and success, Forte says the real asset of his hotels is its employees.

For managers, the key issue regarding ability is to make sure that employees have the abilities they need to perform their jobs effectively. There are three fundamental ways to manage ability in organizations to ensure that this match-up happens: selection, placement, and training.

SELECTION

Managers can control ability in organizations by selecting individuals who have the abilities they need. This first involves identifying the tasks they want the employees to accomplish and the abilities they need to do them. Once these abilities are identified, managers then have to develop accurate measures of them. The key question at this point is whether a person's score on an ability measure is actually a good predictor of the task that needs to be performed. If it isn't, there is no point in using it as a selection device. Furthermore, it would be unethical to do so. An organization that uses an inappropriate measure and rejects capable applicants leaves itself open to potential lawsuits for unfair hiring practices. But if the ability measure does predict task performance, then managers can use it as a selection tool to ensure that the organization has the mix of abilities it needs to accomplish its goals.

PLACEMENT

Once individuals are selected and become part of an organization, managers must accurately match each employee to a job that will capitalize on his or her abilities. Again, managers need to identify the ability requirements of the jobs to be filled, and they need accurate measures of these abilities. Once these measures are available, the aim is to place employees in positions that match their abilities. Placement, however, involves more than just assigning new employees to appropriate positions. It is also becomes an issue in horizontal moves or promotions within the organization. Obviously, an organization wants to promote only its most able employees to higher-level positions.

TRAINING

Selection and placement relate to the *nature* aspects of ability. Training relates to the *nurture* aspects of ability. Training can be an effective means of enhancing employees' abilities. We often think that the goal of training is to improve employees' abilities beyond the minimum level required. Frequently, however, organizations use training to bring employees' skills up to some minimum required level. Extensive research suggests that job-appropriate training is effective in increasing employees' skills and abilities and, ultimately, their performance.[88]

To gain a competitive advantage, organizations often need to use new and advanced technology to lower costs and increase quality, efficiency, and performance. Companies that use advanced technology often find that their employees' abilities and skills are deficient in a number of ways. In the factories of the past, most employees could get by with sheer physical strength and stamina, but those days are largely gone. In today's technical world, higher levels of skill are generally needed.

The need for training became obvious at Collins & Aikman, a carpet firm, when it computerized its factory to remain competitive.[89] Employees started to tell managers that they couldn't work with computers. Managers soon realized that they had significantly underestimated the number of employees needed to keep the factory running—employees who could read and perform necessary calculations were covering for those who could not. A little probing indicated that about a third of the factory's workforce had not completed high school.

Rather than resorting to drastic measures such as abandoning the new technology or moving production overseas where labor costs are cheaper, Collins & Aikman decided to equip the employees with the skills they needed to be competitive. An adult education instructor was hired to teach classes two days a week on every shift. The classes covered reading, writing, science, social studies, and math. Employees, some of them older, were at first apprehensive about taking classes, but the instructor's warmth and agreeableness soon overcame their misgivings and embarrassment over their own shortcomings.

Collins & Aikman's investment paid off. Productivity increased, returns due to poor quality decreased, and employees felt more confident about their new jobs. Employee morale and even health seem to have improved, judging by the number of sick days taken. The children of Collins & Aikman's employees have benefited as well because their parents are now encouraging them to stay in school.[90] The company's commitment to its employees was recently acknowledged by the Michigan Business & Professional Association when it was named one of Metro Detroit's "Best and Brightest Companies to Work For" in 2003. Firms are chosen for this award based on the extent to which they value their employees as their most important asset.[91]

Training can also be used to increase the emotional intelligence of employees. In order for emotional intelligence training to succeed, however, employees must recognize the importance of emotional intelligence and be motivated to improve their own emotional capabilities. Emotional intelligence training typically begins with an accurate assessment of the employee's strengths and weaknesses. Someone who is very familiar with the employee's on-the-job behaviors and is trusted by the employee should provide this assessment. Employees then need to practice handling different situations and reflect on what went well and what didn't. Throughout the process, the support of a trusted confidant or coach can help them realistically analyze their own feelings and behaviors and the feelings and behaviors of others. Over time, as employees begin to develop more effective ways of interacting with others, their emotional intelligence has the potential to increase. Today, emotional intelligence training is becoming more commonplace. Avon and Metropolitan Life are among the many companies that offer emotional intelligence training to their employees.

Summary

The two main types of individual differences are personality differences and ability differences. Understanding the nature, determinants, and consequences of individual differences is essential for managing organizational behavior. Because people differ so much from each other, an appreciation of the nature of individual differences is necessary to understand why people act the way they do in organizations. In this chapter, we made the following major points:

1. Personality is the pattern of relatively enduring ways that a person feels, thinks, and behaves. Personality is determined both by nature (biological heritage) and nurture (situational factors). Organizational outcomes that have been shown to be predicted by personality include job satisfaction, work stress, and leadership effectiveness. Personality is not a useful predictor of organizational outcomes when there are strong situational constraints. Because personality tends to be stable over time, managers should not expect to change personality in the short run. Managers should accept employees' personalities as they are and develop effective ways to deal with people.

2. Feelings, thoughts, attitudes, and behaviors in an organization are determined by the interaction of personality and the situation.

3. The Big Five personality traits are extraversion (or positive affectivity), neuroticism (or negative affectivity), agreeableness, conscientiousness, and openness to experience. Other personality traits particularly relevant to organizational behavior include locus of control, self-monitoring, self-esteem, Type A and Type B personalities, and the needs for achievement, affiliation, and power.

4. In addition to possessing different personalities, employees also differ in their abilities, or what they are capable of doing. The two major types of ability are cognitive ability and physical ability.

5. Types of cognitive ability can be arranged in a hierarchy with general intelligence at the top. Specific types of cognitive ability are verbal ability, numerical ability, reasoning ability, deductive ability, ability to see relationships, ability to remember, spatial ability, and perceptual ability.

6. There are two types of physical ability: motor skills (the ability to manipulate objects) and physical skills (a person's fitness and strength).

7. Both nature and nurture contribute to determining physical ability and cognitive ability. A third, recently identified, ability is emotional intelligence.

8. In organizations, ability can be managed by selecting individuals who have the abilities needed to accomplish tasks, placing employees in jobs that capitalize on their abilities, and training employees to enhance their ability levels.

Exercises in Understanding and Managing Organizational Behavior

Questions for Discussion and Review

1. Why is it important to understand that both nature and nurture shape an employee's personality?

2. What are some situations in which you would *not* expect employees' personalities to influence their behavior?

3. What are some situations in which you would expect employees' personalities to influence their behavior?

4. Is it good for organizations to be composed of individuals with similar personalities? Why or why not?

5. A lawyer needs to score high on which of the Big Five personality traits? Why?

6. What are some jobs or situations in which employees who are high on agreeableness would be especially effective?

7. When might self-monitoring be dysfunctional in an organization?

8. What levels of the needs for achievement, power, and affiliation might be desirable for an elementary school teacher?

9. What types of cognitive ability are especially important for an upper-level manager (such as the president of a division) to possess? Why?

10. Think of a job for which emotional intelligence might be an especially important ability for the jobholder to possess. Find someone in your local community who has this kind of job. In an interview, determine the extent to which the person actively tries to manage his or her own emotions or the emotions of others at work.

Building People Skills

Characteristics of People and Jobs

Choose a job that you are very familiar with—a job that you currently have, a job that you used to have, or the job of a close family member or friend. Or the job could be one that you have been able to observe closely during your interaction with an organization as a customer, client, or patient. For the job of your choosing, respond to the following items.

1. Describe the job, including all the tasks that the jobholder must perform.

2. Choose two of the Big Five personality traits that you think would have the most impact on the jobholder's feelings, thoughts, attitudes, and behaviors. Explain why you think these traits might be particularly important for understanding the jobholder's reactions.

3. Identify three of the organizationally relevant personality traits that you think would affect perfor-

mance on this job and explain why you think they are likely to be important.

4. Which of the jobholder's behaviors are primarily determined by the situation and not personality?

5. What cognitive abilities must the jobholder possess?

6. What physical abilities must the jobholder possess?

7. How can selection and placement be used to ensure that prospective jobholders have these abilities?

8. How can an organization train jobholders to raise levels of these abilities?

A Question of Ethics

Emotional intelligence, the ability to understand and manage one's own and other people's moods and emotions, can be increased through training. When people are high on emotional intelligence, they are better able to understand and use emotions to influence others. However, people can be influenced in positive and negative ways. As an example of the latter, historical atrocities and cult tragedies have been attributed to the ability of certain individuals to have high levels of influence over others.

Questions

1. What are the ethical implications of emotional intelligence training?
2. What steps can organizations take to ensure that employees' emotional intelligence is put to good use and not used for personal gain or unethical purposes?

Small Group Break-Out Exercise

Understanding Situational Influences

Form groups of three or four people and appoint one member as the spokesperson who will communicate your conclusions to the rest of the class.

1. Take a few minutes to think about a recent incident in which you behaved in a manner that was inconsistent with your personality and/or abilities.
2. Take turns describing these situations and why you behaved the way you did.
3. As a group, develop a list of the characteristics of situations in which people's behavior is primarily determined by the context or situation and in which individual differences play a very minor role.
4. Think of reasons why it is important for employees and managers to be aware of situational influences on work behavior.

Topic for Debate

Personality and ability have major implications for how people feel, think, and behave in organizations. Now that you have a good understanding of these individual differences, debate the following issue.

Team A. Organizations should select or hire prospective employees on the basis of their personality traits.

Team B. Organizations should *not* select or hire prospective employees on the basis of their personality traits.

Experiential Exercise

Individual Differences in Teams

Objective

In organizations like Merck & Co., the pharmaceuticals giant, and Microsoft Corporation, the leading producer of computer software, research scientists or computer programmers often work together in small teams on complex, pathbreaking projects to create new drugs or computer software. Team members interact closely, often over long time periods, in order to complete their projects. Individual differences in personality and ability provide teams not only with valued resources needed to complete their projects but also with potential sources of conflict and problems. Your objective is to understand how individual differences in personality and ability affect people's behavior in teams.

Procedure

The class divides into groups of three to five people, and each group appoints one member as spokesperson to present the group's findings to the whole class. Each group discusses how the personalities and abilities of team members may affect team performance and may cause conflict and problems. Using the knowledge of personality and ability gained in this chapter, each group answers the following questions.

1. Do certain personality traits make people good team members? If so, what are they and why are they important? If not, why not?
2. Is it more effective for teams to be composed of members who have different personality types or similar personality types?
3. What kinds of abilities make people good team members?
4. Should team members have similar or different kinds and levels of abilities?

When all the groups are finished discussing these issues, the spokespersons take turns presenting their groups' findings to the rest of the class, and the instructor lists the findings on the board.

Making the Connection

Find an example of a manager who has helped or hurt his or her organization in an important way. For example, the manager may have helped the organization to develop new and successful products or find new customers, or the manager may have behaved in an unethical fashion or driven customers away. What personality traits may have influenced this manager's behavior? What abilities may have contributed to this manager's success or failure?

New York Times Cases in the News

The New York Times

Getting to Know You Is as Easy as A, B, C or D

BY EILENE ZIMMERMAN

After a long interview process during the summer. Dionne Glenn was told she had to do one more thing before learning whether she would be hired as a branch manager for Central Bank of Houston: take a simple multiple-choice test online. "They told me it was a management test," Ms. Glenn, 34, said.

It didn't take her long to realize that it was actually a personality test. "It threw me off," she said. "I was expecting questions about how I would handle myself in a variety of situations." Instead, she said, she was asked to choose from a list of personal attributes that best described herself. In dealing with others, for instance, was she "co-operative, agreeable," or "sweet, pleasing" or "stubborn, unyielding"?

Although she knew there were no wrong answers, she said she worried that her responses would not accurately reflect her personality. Ultimately, Ms. Glenn, who has 13 years of experience in the banking industry, was hired. The company allowed her to view a report assessing her personality, work style and abilities, and Ms. Glenn said it was uncannily accurate. "It really works; my profile was exactly me," she said.

The use of pre-employment tests has been increasing as businesses look for ways to the rising pool of candidates in this tight job market. Companies of all sizes and across all industries—like Toyota, Bank of America, Sonesta International Hotels and Subway, to name a few—use them routinely. For employment testing companies, this has meant an increase in business of 10 percent to 15 percent a year, on average, for the last three years, said William G. Harris, executive director of the Association of Test Publishers.

These psychometric tests, as they are known in the industry, measure psychological attributes—"measuring the psyche," explained Debra Condren, president of Business Psychology Solutions, an executive coaching firm with offices in New York and San Francisco. Under this umbrella fall personality tests, intelligence quotient tests, ability testing and aptitude tests. Some are geared for specific industries or jobs. "Business needs some tool for qualifying," said William Byham, founder of Development Dimensions International, a company, in Costa Mesa, Calif., that helps with selection, promotion and training of employees. "You can press a key and send your resume out to 2,000 organizations."

Another factor is cost. Employee turnover is often expensive: the Society for Human Resource Management estimates the cost of replacing supervisory, technical and management personnel at 50 percent to several times the departing employee's annual salary. Testing experts say psychometric tests can greatly improve the chances of finding the right person for a particular job or corporate environment; the tests can be relatively inexpensive to administer, often less than $50 a candidate, although the cost can go as high as $10,000 for senior executive positions like chief executive.

Employers generally use more than just one test to make a decision; in many cases, several tests are used in conjunction with interviews.

Many tests now on the market measure what people in the industry call "the big five": conscientiousness, agreeableness, emotional stability, openness and extroversion. Steven Lorenzet, a professor of human resource management at Rider University in Lawrenceville, N.J., said studies show that psychometric tests are accurate predictors of how someone will behave at work.

Dave Ratner, founder and president of Dave's Soda and Pet City in Agawam, Mass., a small chain of stores selling pet food and a variety of sodas, said he learned that the hard way. When he experimented with testing three years ago, he said, he was warned that a candidate he wanted to hire would not be right for the job. "I went against the advice of the tester and hired the guy," he said. "Two months later, after I invested all this time and money training him, he up and bolted."

In the two years since he made the testing of job candidates routine, turnover has been lower and personnel problems have been rare, Mr. Ratner says, adding that he now pays close attention to the test results.

Stephen Henson, a vice president at Kelly Blue Book in Irvine, Calif., a resource for car buyers, said the company tests job candidates to find employees with "a specific set of skills" or traits for certain positions.

"We had a couple of really strong candidates for this data analyst spot," he recalled, "but after they took the personality profile test we found their personality made them 'inspirational and charming,' someone you would like as a person.

"Although those are great attributes, this particular job doesn't call for someone who is social," he said. "We need someone who is a great critical thinker; accuracy is important to them."

For job applicants, pre-employment tests often add anxiety to an already stressful process. "I knew there was a lot of competition for this position, and I wanted it," said Ms. Glenn, the bank manager from Texas. On the day of her test, she said, three other candidates also were waiting to be tested.

Kelly Wright, recently hired as an account manager at Hetrick Communication a marketing and public relations firm in Indianapolis, was given a personality test at the end of a five-week period that included several interviews and a take-home writing assignment. Ms. Wright, 37 has 17 years of experience in public relations. But Pamela Klein chief operating officer of Hetrick said that because it had only 24 employees, it could not afford any mistakes in hiring.

Ms. Wright, of Lebanon, Ind., said her reaction to having to take the test was "both surprise and terror."

"I felt like I was already a good fit for the company and had gotten positive feedback from my interviews," she said.

So what should job candidates do? Just answer the questions candidly, authorities on testing say, and treat the tests as another recruiting tool. Besides, they say, the tests could prove just as useful for the job seeker as for the potential employer "Yes, you may lose the job, but then again, it may have not been the right place for you," said Mel Kleiman, managing partner at the Hire Tough Group in Houston, which devises recruiting programs.

Employers who administer tests are generally looking for candidates who can fit into the corporate culture and handle the demands of the job. Some want to weed out candidates with traits that may be deemed undesirable, like aggressiveness.

"We've had a lot more interest in what we do in just the last three or four months," said Michael D. McIntyre, an assistant professor at the University of Tennessee College of Business, who helped develop a multiple-choice test for hostility. He uses the test in his consulting work.

"We look at underlying personality traits to assess the risk of a person acting in a hostile way," Mr. McIntyre said.

He says his test includes reasoning problems that ask test takers to draw conclusions. "Other tests ask someone if they have a bad temper, things like that," he said. "No one is going to admit they are a powder keg waiting to explode."

He says that 5 percent to 10 percent of the people tested will score high enough to be considered a risk for aggressive behavior.

Screening also can assess integrity and leadership qualities. Because of recent scandals across corporate America, some companies are scrambling for tests to screen out people who are unsuitable for top executive spots.

Steven Berglas, an executive coach and adjunct professor at the Marshall School of Business at the University of Southern California, says he has developed a test to identify narcissistic character traits and people who cannot adapt to change. "You want leadership to be responsive to change, like market shifts," Dr. Berglas said.

His test, conducted orally, asks executive candidates questions like these: "When you made the biggest mistake in your professional life, what did you learn?" and "Who do you give most credit for your career success?" He said the ability to share success and acknowledge failure provide insight into how someone might function in a powerful role. Dr. Berglas says he is converting the interview into a written test.

Although some job applicants may dread a pre-employment test, it may help to motivate them after their hiring. "Testing gives the impression that a company wants the best people it can get, that it is very selective, that you are special," said Aurelio Prifitera, president of the Psychological Corporation in San Antonio, which sells human resources-related tests.

Jerry Velasco, 50, the new director of training for managers and supervisors at El Taco Tote, a chain of Mexican restaurants, said that before he was hired in October, he had to take a 50-question Wonderlic Personnel Test, which measured I.Q. At first, Mr. Velasco said, he wondered if it was truly necessary: after all, he had considerable experience in the hospitality industry, having spent 18 years working for Marriott. But in hindsight, he said, he found the test to be a good evaluation tool.

"I definitely can see how it could be very useful," he said. "I feel now like I know I'm a good fit for this job."

Thuy Pham, 26, a newly hired data analyst at Kelly Blue Book, said she found it reassuring that the company cared enough about its employees to go to such lengths. "I have worked at other companies where they only wanted me to perform a function, and as long as I could do that, it was enough," she said. "I want to stay in this job a long time, so I'm actually glad they care enough to determine if I am a good match."

Sample Questions for Job Candidates

To place job candidates in the appropriate positions, many employers test cognitive ability and intelligence quotient.

"Generally, the higher the I.Q., the quicker and more thoroughly a person will learn anything," said Charlie Wonderlic, president of Wonderlic Inc. of Libertyville, Ill., the creator of the 50-question Wonderlic Personnel Test, which has been used by companies for more than six decades. Mr. Wonderlic says the test helps to predict a person's success on the job. The company says that only four people have received a perfect score of 50 and that the national average is 21.6.

Wonderlic has calculated what it considers minimum scores for nearly every job in the economy. The minimum score for mechanical engineers is 30, while the minimum for corporate executives and sales managers is 28. For nurses, it is 26; bank tellers, 23; telemarketers, 22; cashiers, 20; and factory workers, 17. Although not the actual questions, here is a sampling of the types of questions used in the Wonderlic Personnel Test:

1. Assume the first two statements are true. Is the final one true, false or not certain?

> *The boy plays baseball.*
> *All baseball players wear hats.*
> *The boy wears a hat.*

2. Paper sells for 21 cents a pad. What will four pads cost?

3. How many of the five pairs of names listed below are exact duplicates?

a. *Nieman, K.M. Neiman, K.M.*
b. *Thomas, G.K. Thomas, C.K.*
c. *Hoff, J.P. Hoff, J.P.*
d. *Pino, L.R. Pina, L.R.*
e. *Warner, T.S. Wanner, T.S.*

4. "Resent" and "reserve." Do these words:

a. *Have similar meanings*
b. *Have contradictory meanings*
c. *Mean neither the same nor opposite*

5. A train travels 20 feet in one-fifth of a second. At this same speed, how many feet will it travel in three seconds?

6. When rope is selling at $.10 a foot, how many feet can you buy for 60 cents?

7. The ninth month of the year is:

a. *October*
b. *January*
c. *June*
d. *September*
e. *May*

8. Which number in the following group represents the smallest amount?

a. *7*
b. *.8*
c. *31*
d. *.33*
e. *2*

9. In printing an article of 48,000 words, a printer decides to use two sizes of type. Using the larger type, a printed page contains 1,800 words. Using smaller type, a page contains 2,400 words. The article is allotted 21 full pages in a magazine. How many pages must be in smaller type?

10. Three individuals form a partnership and agree to divide the profits equally. X invests $9,000, Y invests $7,000, Z invests $4,000. If the profits are $4,800, how much less does X receive than if the profits were divided in proportion to the amount invested?

11. Assume the first two statements are true. Is the final one true, false or not certain?

> *Tom greeted Beth.*
> *Beth greeted Dawn.*
> *Tom did not greet Dawn.*

12. A boy is 17 years old and his sister is twice as old. When the boy is 23 years old, what will be the age of his sister?

ANSWERS

1. True	7. d.
2. 84 cents	8. d.
3. One	9. 17
4. c.	10. $540
5. 300 feet	11. Not certain
6. 6 feet	12. 40 years old

SOURCE: "Getting to Know You Is as Easy as A, B, C or D," by E. Zimmerman, *New York Times*, November 23, 2003, BU2.

Questions for Discussion

1. What are the pros and cons of using personality tests in selection decisions?

2. Is the use of personality tests appropriate for hiring for jobs that depend primarily on cognitive ability?

3. Why is it important to use multiple tests and sources of information when making hiring decisions?

4. How would you feel if you needed to take a personality test or an honesty test to be considered for a job you really wanted to obtain?

The New York Times

Taking On the Tyco Challenge

BY CLAUDIA H. DEUTSCH

Laurie Siegel, the senior vice president for human resources at Tyco International, went to a management meeting last month. She and her fellow executives talked about international business, procurement, compensation programs, all sorts of nitty-gritty business subjects. Good ideas were floated, but what struck her was something else: "It felt like such a wonderfully normal thing to do," she recalled, a smile spreading across her face.

Ms. Siegel's enthusiasm for the ordinary can be forgiven. At Tyco, it is something to strive for, not take for granted. This is the company, remember, that was swept up in an accounting scandal and whose former chief executive and former chief financial officer are on trial, accused of things like granting unauthorized bonuses and using the company coffers as personal piggybanks. Its entire board and much of its executive staff have been with the company less than a year.

Ms. Siegel, 47, has never met L. Dennis Kozlowski, the former chief executive, or Patricia Prue, her predecessor in the human resources job and an important prosecution witness in the trial. Nor does she particularly want to. They are Tyco's past. She is concerned with its future.

"From the minute I heard about this job, I said, 'This has my name on it,'" Ms. Siegel recalled in her spacious but sparsely decorated office in Tyco's new headquarters in Princeton, N. J. "I want to drive change, and when you've got a burning platform like this, you can drive it so much faster."

In the 11 months since she was recruited from Honeywell International to help rebuild Tyco, she has barely applied the brakes. Tyco, whose revenue grew to $36.8 billion for fiscal 2003, primarily through acquisitions, has never had a companywide computer system, a central procurement function or even an intranet. Far more troubling, it did not have a strong corporate governance function or a bonus system that made any real sense. "There was no question that the rules of the road had to be first on the plate," she said.

Ms. Siegel did not write Tyco's new ethics policy. But she hires the people who enforce it (100 internal auditors so far), coordinates ethics training (all Tyco employees attended a one-day ethics seminar in May, and its 25,000 managers will get more detailed programs), disseminates and explains the ethics code to 260,000 employees in more than 100 nations (remember, without an intranet) and recommends disciplinary action against anyone violating it.

She says she has also replaced a system that awarded huge bonuses to anyone who "somehow drove the numbers up" with one based on assessments of how managers set and meet goals. Tyco's bonus budget for the fiscal year that ended on Sept. 30 will be reduced by $90 million, or 25 percent, from the payouts last year.

Lots of employees squawked, but she makes no apologies. "The stock had fallen from $60 to $10, the bonus program was a major use of cash, and it was something the financial community was watching," she said.

That sounds much more like line-management-speak than human resources patois, but those who know Ms. Siegel are not surprised. "Laurie has always been more like a general manager who happens to have human resources expertise," said Julian Kaufman, a former Honeywell colleague who is now president of a consulting firm, the JDK Group.

Ms. Siegel has masterminded a China Council, composed of the heads of all of Tyco's Asian businesses, to make sure they do not compete with one another for talent, inundate customers with duplicate sales calls or build capacity when a sibling company has excess space. She has hired a new information technology chief to help install a companywide communications system, as well as a procurement specialist to centralize buying systems and identify services to farm out to contractors.

No to the big bonuses, yes to the ethics courses.

She has revamped her department to make it more than just an office for administering benefits and payroll and analyzing compensation plans at target companies. "There was no talent development under the old regime because Dennis Kozlowski did not consider it a priority," recalled R. Hal Johnson, vice president for leadership development. He and Ms. Siegel are creating a database of employee skills to make it easier to promote people into other divisions or to know what training they need.

It has been a hectic year, and making sure that neither her family nor Tyco gets short shrift is a neverending battle. She rarely comes in on weekends. When she travels overseas, an alarm clock set to New Jersey time goes off when she should call her daughters to say goodnight.

"Laurie is one of those rare executives who can successfully balance more than a full-time job with being a great mom," said Donald J. Redlinger, her former boss at Honeywell.

It helps that her husband, who runs his own business, has picked up many of the parental duties. Still, she has developed her own fail-safe technique to make sure that no important task is overlooked.

"I have a one-list rule," she said. "Anything that's important to get done that day, be it getting data to the compensation committee or helping Julia prepare for her bat mitzvah, it all goes on the same list."

Human resources was a late entry on the young Ms. Siegel's career to-do list. As a child in Chicago, she wanted to be an architect. But after discovering how long it takes to get projects off the ground, her enthusiasm waned. At 28, she received a business degree from Harvard, then became a compensation consultant. In 1990, she married Joseph Nosofsky; two years later, Julia was born.

Suddenly, her frequent traveling felt burdensome, not glamorous. She took an in-house human resources job at Avon Products. She felt bored, so two years later, despite being pregnant with her second daughter, Emma, she jumped at an offer to help shake up some of the compensation systems at AlliedSignal, the corporate name before Allied and Honeywell merged in 1999.

In her nine years there, Ms. Siegel rotated though many businesses.

"Some were great, some were in turn-around, some needed total reinventing—it was exactly the type of environment she faces at Tyco," said Richard F. Wallman, who recently retired as

Honeywell's chief financial officer. At Honeywell, Ms. Siegel also got a grounding in Six Sigma, a statistical method of quality control that she is putting into effect at Tyco. And she learned to be a strong advocate for employees, particularly when raises were not forthcoming. She started services to help employees cope with dependent care and elder care, and began sending them annual statements quantifying the value of fringe benefits and training.

At Tyco, said Eric M. Pillmore, senior vice president for corporate governance, she almost single-handedly persuaded management to give all employees free access to the fitness center being built in Princeton.

Ms. Siegel knows that it will take more than a free gym to make Tyco an employer of choice. "I've interviewed lots of people who can't stand up to the "soccer game' test," she said. "They're not going to be comfortable wearing a Tyco T-shirt to their kids' sporting events"

But she believes that the reluctant ones are fewer and farther between. "Our stock is climbing back up," she said— it is now at $21.57, up more than 160 percent from its low of $8.25 on July 25, 2002. "And every month the perception of Tyco as a company in trouble is lessened."

SOURCE: "Taking on the Tyco Challenge," by C. H. Deutsch, *New York Times,* November 23, 2003, BU2.

Questions for Discussion

1. What personality traits do you think Laurie Siegel would be high on?

2. What personality traits do you think Laurie Siegel would be low on?

3. In what ways might her behavior and actions at Tyco be both a function of her personality and the situation?

4. What abilities do you think she is calling on in her role as senior vice president for human resources at Tyco?

Work Values, Attitudes, and Moods and Emotions

3

LEARNING OBJECTIVES

After studying this chapter,
you should be able to:

■

Describe the nature of work values and
ethical values and why they are of critical
importance in organizations.

■

Understand why it is important to
understand employees' moods and
emotions on the job.

■

Appreciate when and why emotional labor
occurs in organizations.

■

Describe the nature, causes, theories, and
consequences of job satisfaction.

■

Appreciate the distinction between affective
commitment and continuance commitment
and their implications for understanding
organizational behavior.

OPENING CASE

Richard Branson Is Never Bored

Is it Possible to Have Fun While Performing a Very High Stakes Job?

Richard Branson, the maverick founder and chief executive of Virgin Group Ltd., describes his own experience of work as follows, "I don't think of work as work and play as play. It's all living . . . I'm living and learning every day."[1] Living and learning for Branson means indulging his endless curiosity, being adventuresome, having fun, and filling each day with a seamless integration of work and family life.

Branson, a high school dropout, has grown the Virgin Group into a $7 billion collection of 224 companies, each with its own CEO and board of directors. These companies are truly a diverse lot ranging from records (Virgin Records) and airlines (Virgin Atlantic) to retail goods, cell phones, and consumer electronics. Some of his companies are very successful and others not so successful, but Branson clearly has had enough success to continue to pursue new businesses that strike his fancy; his net worth is estimated to be over $2.5 billion.[2]

Branson's accomplishments are pretty impressive for someone who didn't finish high school, let alone go to college and, by his own admission, did not set out to make a lot of money and become a CEO. Rather, Branson's love of adventure drove him to get involved in a variety of ventures at an early age. Branson was born in Britain and, after quitting high school, wanted to start his own youth-oriented magazine called *Student* (sort of like a British version of *Rolling Stone Magazine*). But Branson lacked funding to get the magazine going. In order to raise capital for the magazine, he started a record company based on mail orders. The record company eventually opened a recording studio and

Virgin Records took off.[3] From records, Branson branched out into airlines (Virgin Atlantic, Virgin Express, and Virgin Blue) and a wide range of other kinds of businesses.[4]

Branson thrives on adventure, taking risks, and enjoying life to its fullest. He can't stand being bored and always likes to be doing something. In terms of his career, that means building new businesses. Of course, he wants these businesses to be successful but not so much for financial gain as to enable him to keep doing what he loves—learning about new businesses and diving in headfirst.[5] When he launched a joint venture with Sprint PCS to provide a prepaid phone plan that would be hip and appeal to customers in their late teens and early twenties, he propelled himself into New York's Times Square wearing little more than a cell phone.[6] Publicity stunts like this one have built the Virgin brand and made Branson recognizable around the world.

Branson also values his family time and often works from home when he is not traveling. He typically wakes up early in the morning and does some work, then has time with his family, then works some more; work and family life are often intertwined. Eschewing computers and the Internet, he writes down everything in a daily journal and communicates by cell phone. He seems to thrive on a relentless stream of activity including hot air ballooning and tennis.[7]

For all his love of adventure and fun, Branson also keeps a close eye on his businesses. For example, when his cellular phone business was launched in the United Kingdom, he called the executive in charge four times on a Sunday morning between 6 and 7 A.M. Branson didn't like the voice instructions on the customer service line and, before the hour was up, had rewritten the script.[8] Perhaps it is the combination of intense involvement and commitment with a love of surprise and adventure that explains Branson's accomplishments. One thing is certain—he has enjoyed every minute of it.

Overview

What people think and feel about work in general, and about their jobs and organizations in particular, affects not only how they behave at work but also their overall well-being—how happy, healthy, and prosperous they are. From the opening case, it is clear that the way that Richard Branson experiences his work has led to personnel fulfillment, enjoyment, and satisfaction and great success for

Virgin Group Ltd. In this chapter, we focus on the thoughts and feelings that determine how people experience work and the ways in which these thoughts and feelings affect organizational behavior. We discuss values, attitudes, and moods and emotions—the different types of thoughts and feelings people have about work in general and about their jobs and organizations in particular. We describe the nature and consequences of two of the most widely studied work attitudes: job satisfaction and organizational commitment. By the end of this chapter, you will have a good appreciation of the range of thoughts and feelings central to the experience of work and the implications of these thoughts and feelings for understanding and managing organizational behavior.

Values, Attitudes, and Moods and Emotions

The thoughts and feelings people have about work, their jobs, and their organizations determine how they experience work. Some thoughts and feelings are fundamental and broad; they are concerned not so much with aspects of a particular job or organization but more with the meaning and nature of work itself. These thoughts and feelings, called *values*, are relatively long lasting. Other thoughts and feelings are more specific. Those that are focused directly on a person's current job or organization, called *work attitudes*, are not as long lasting as values. *Work moods and emotions*—that is, how people feel while they are performing their jobs from day to day, hour to hour, and even minute to minute—also determine how they experience work. Next we describe each of these determinants of how people experience work.

THE NATURE OF VALUES

Values are one's personal convictions about what one should strive for in life and how one should behave.[9] While researchers have identified multiple values ranging from a world at peace and a world of beauty to a comfortable life and social recognition, two kinds of values that are especially relevant to organizational behavior are work values and ethical values (see Figure 3.1; in Chapter 17, we describe another type of important values, national values).

Work Values. **Work values** are an employee's personal convictions about what outcomes one should expect from work and how one should behave at work. Outcomes that people might expect to obtain through work include a comfortable

Values One's personal convictions about what one should strive for in life and how one should behave.

Work values An employee's personal convictions about what outcomes one should expect from work and how one should behave at work.

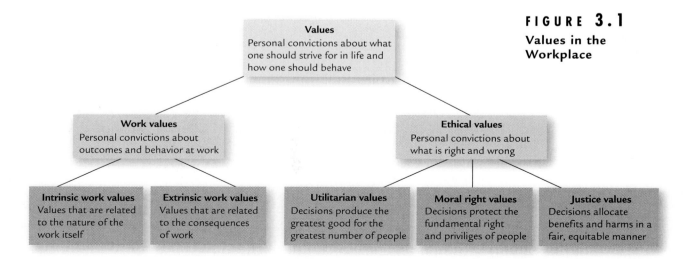

FIGURE 3.1

Values in the Workplace

Values
Personal convictions about what one should strive for in life and how one should behave

Work values	Ethical values
Personal convictions about outcomes and behavior at work	Personal convictions about what is right and wrong

Intrinsic work values	Extrinsic work values	Utilitarian values	Moral right values	Justice values
Values that are related to the nature of the work itself	Values that are related to the consequences of work	Decisions produce the greatest good for the greatest number of people	Decisions protect the fundamental right and priviliges of people	Decisions allocate benefits and harms in a fair, equitable manner

existence with family security, a sense of accomplishment and self-respect, social recognition, and an exciting life.[10] Ways people think they should behave at work include being ambitious, imaginative, obedient, self-controlled, and respectful to others.[11] Work values are general and long-lasting feelings and beliefs people have that contribute to how they experience work.

Why are work values important for understanding and managing organizational behavior? They reflect what people are trying to achieve through and at work. An employee who thinks that he should learn new things on the job, for example, will be unhappy working as a cashier in a supermarket because, once he has learned how to use the cash register, there will be little opportunity for any further learning. His unhappiness may, in turn, cause him to be less helpful to customers or more likely to look for another job.

The work values that researchers in organizational behavior have identified generally fall into two broad categories: intrinsic work values and extrinsic work values (see Table 3.1).[12]

Intrinsic work values are values that are related to the nature of the work itself. Employees who desire to be challenged, learn new things, make important contributions, and reach their full potential on their jobs have intrinsic work values. These employees want challenging jobs that use all of their skills and abilities and provide them with responsibility and autonomy (the ability to make decisions) while at the same time giving them opportunities for personal growth. Employees who desire adventure, being creative, or helping other people also are satisfying intrinsic work values as the work they perform, whether it be building new businesses, composing a new symphony, or helping a troubled teen, is what is important to them. From the opening case it is clear that Richard Branson strives to satisfy his own intrinsic work values.

Rather than valuing features of the work itself, some employees have **extrinsic work values**, values that are related to the consequences of work. Employees whose primary reason for working is to earn money, for example, have extrinsic work values. They see work primarily as means of providing economic security for themselves and their families. These employees value their work not for its own sake but for its consequences. Other extrinsic work values include a job's status in the organization and in the wider community, social contacts provided by the job, and the extent to which a job enables an employee to spend time with his or her family, pursue a hobby, or volunteer for a worthy cause.

Intrinsic work values Work values that are related to the nature of work itself.

Extrinsic work values Work values that are related to the consequences of work.

TABLE 3.1

A Comparison of Intrinsic and Extrinsic Work Values

Intrinsic Work Values	Extrinsic Work Values
Interesting work	High pay
Challenging work	Job security
Learning new things	Job benefits
Making important contributions	Status in wider community
Reaching full potential at work	Social contacts
Responsibility and autonomy	Time with family
Being creative	Time for hobbies

Because working is the way most people make a living, there is an extrinsic element to most people's work values, but many people have both extrinsic and intrinsic work values. Extrinsic and intrinsic work values differ in their relative importance from one person to another. An elementary schoolteacher who likes teaching but quits her job to take a higher-paying position as a sales representative for a computer company has stronger extrinsic than intrinsic work values. A social worker who puts up with low pay and little thanks because he feels that he is doing something important by helping disadvantaged families and their children has stronger intrinsic than extrinsic work values.

When making changes in the workplace, managers need to take into account employees' values. Managers may try to increase employees' motivation by making their work more interesting, giving them more freedom to make their own decisions, or expanding the number of activities they perform (see Chapters 6, 7, and 8 for details on motivation). A manager might try to increase the motivation of a computer sales representative by requiring her to call on different types of customers and by giving her the responsibility for setting up the equipment a customer purchases.

The success of such approaches to increasing motivation, however, depends on the extent to which the change in an employee's job relates to the employee's values. Making the work of the computer sales representative more interesting and challenging may do little to increase her motivation if her strong extrinsic work values result in her being motivated primarily by the money she earns. Indeed, these efforts may actually backfire if the sales representative thinks she is working harder on her job but not receiving any additional financial compensation. Employees who are extrinsically motivated may be much more responsive to financial incentives (such as bonuses) and job security than to changes in the work itself.

Because work values reflect what employees are trying to achieve through working, they hold the key to understanding how employees will react to different events in the workplace and to understanding and managing organizational behavior. Managers need to be especially sensitive to the work values of their subordinates when making changes in jobs, working hours, or other aspects of the work situation.

Ethical Values. **Ethical values** are one's personal convictions about what is right and wrong. Ethical values help employees decide on the right course of action and guide their decision making and behavior.[13] Especially in situations in which the proper course of action is unclear, ethical values help employees make moral decisions. Some ethical values are focused on an individual's conduct and whether it is right or wrong, such as being honest or trustworthy.[14]

Other kinds of ethical values come into play when a person must decide how to make decisions that have the potential to benefit or harm other individuals or groups. These ethical values are especially important guides for behavior when a decision may benefit one individual or group to the detriment of another.[15] For example, Eastman Kodak recently announced that because of lower demand for camera film due to the popularity of digital cameras, it would be eliminating close to 15,000 jobs around the world over the next three years.[16] This means that close to 20 percent of Kodak's employees will lose their jobs. When the workforce reductions were announced, the price of Kodak stock rose over $3 per share.[17] Fewer employees means fewer costs and greater profitability. The workforce reduction benefits shareholders of the corporation because the value of their stock has increased, but it hurts those employees whose jobs have been or will be cut.

Utilitarian, moral rights, and justice values are complementary guides for decision making and behavior when a decision or action has the potential to benefit or harm others.[18] **Utilitarian values** dictate that decisions should be made that generate the greatest good for the greatest number of people. **Moral rights values**

Ethical values One's personal convictions about what is right and wrong.

Utilitarian values Values that dictate that decisions should be made so that the decisions produce the greatest good for the greatest number of people.

Moral rights values Values that dictate that decisions should be made in ways that protect the fundamental rights and privileges of people affected by the decisions.

Managers like Andrew Fastow of Enron were rewarded for delivering bottom line results—even if it meant crossing ethical and legal boundaries. "You do it, it works, and you do it again," commented one former employee of the illicit activities occurring at the company. "It doesn't take long for the lines to blur between what's legal and what's not."

Justice values Values that dictate that decisions should be made in ways that allocate benefits and harms among those affected by the decisions in a fair, equitable, or impartial manner.

Code of ethics A set of formal rules and standards, based on ethical values and beliefs about what is right and wrong, that employees can use to make appropriate decisions when the interests of other individuals or groups are at stake.

Whistleblower A person who informs people in positions of authority and/or the public of instances of wrongdoing, illegal behavior, or unethical behavior in an organization.

indicate that decisions should be made in ways that protect the fundamental rights and privileges of people affected by the decisions, such as their freedom, safety, and privacy. **Justice values** dictate that decisions should be made in ways that allocate benefit and harm among those affected by the decisions in a fair, equitable, or impartial manner.[19]

Each of these kinds of ethical values should be taken into account when evaluating whether or not a course of action is an ethical one. Even with these values as guides, employees are often faced with ethical dilemmas because the interests of those who might be affected by the decision are often in conflict and it is not always clear how to determine, for example, how to weigh the benefits and costs of different groups to determine the greatest good, which rights and privileges must be safeguarded, and what is a fair or ethical decision.[20] For example, what sort of job security do loyal and hardworking employees deserve? What does the corporation owe its shareholders in terms of profits?

People develop their own individual ethical values over time based on influences from family, peers, schooling, religious institutions, and other groups.[21] As employees, these ethical values guide their behavior in the workplace. Sometimes different groups of employees or people holding certain kinds of jobs or professions develop what are called professional ethics.[22] Physicians, lawyers, and university professors have professional ethics that dictate appropriate and inappropriate behaviors. Societal ethics, embodied in laws, customs, practices, and values, apply to a society as a whole.

Individual ethics, professional ethics, and societal ethics all contribute to an organization's code of ethics. A **code of ethics** is the set of formal rules and standards, based on ethical values and beliefs about what is right and wrong, that employees can use to make appropriate decisions when the interests of other individuals or groups are at stake.[23] Recent corporate scandals, allegations of wrongdoing, and fraud at companies such as WorldCom, Enron, Tyco, Adelphia, and ImClone[24] have resulted in many organizations taking active steps to ensure that employees behave in an ethical manner and their codes of ethics are followed. However, some of the organizations in which the most egregious instances of fraud have recently occurred actually did have codes of ethics.[25] The problem was that they were not followed, and outside parties such as auditors, bankers, analysts, and lenders did not intervene when they should have. Rather, as in the case of Enron, it took the courageous action of a whistleblower (Sherron Watkins) to bring the wrongdoing to light.[26] A **whistleblower** is a person who informs people in positions of authority and/or the public of instances of wrongdoing, illegal behavior, or unethical behavior in an organization.[27] As the accompanying Managing Ethically feature illustrates, having a code of ethics only results in ethical behavior when it is followed and enforced.

THE NATURE OF WORK ATTITUDES

Work attitudes are collections of feelings, beliefs, and thoughts about how to behave that people currently hold about their jobs and organizations. Work attitudes are more specific than values and not as long lasting because the way people experience their jobs often changes over time. For example, a person's work situation might be altered due to a job transfer or being given or denied a promotion. As a result, his or her work attitudes might change, too. Values, in contrast, can and often do remain constant from job to job and organization to organization. Two work attitudes that have especially important implications for organizational behavior are job satisfaction and organizational commitment.

managing ethically

When Codes of Ethics Fail

Enron had a code of ethics and a conflict-of-interest policy that, if followed, should have prevented the downfall of this once high-flying company. However, its board of directors waived the code and policy to allow Enron managers to form the off-balance-sheet partnerships that destroyed the company.[28] At Tyco, one of the lawyers in charge of compliance with ethics policies has been accused of falsifying records. Arthur Andersen LLP, Enron's auditing firm, was convicted of obstruction of justice for destruction of documents pertaining to Enron's audits. Ironically, prior to the conviction, Arthur Andersen routinely performed ethics consulting services for clients.[29]

"Ethical failures usually are not the result of people not knowing the law or regulations. It is because they felt a variety of other pressures . . ." explains Barbara Lee Toffler, an ethics expert and professor at Columbia University's business school.[30] It is because of these pressures that the federal government passed the Sarbanes-Oxley Act of 2002, which has dramatically increased the reporting and accountability obligations of public companies and also requires independence on the part of a company's audit committees.[31] The act also provides protections for whistleblowers and has increased the criminal penalties for those engaging in white-collar crime. The act has been called, "the most dramatic change to federal securities laws since the 1930s."[32]

Does passage of the the Sarbanes-Oxley Act override the need for an organization to have a code of ethics? Absolutely not. Rather, the act not only requires a code of ethics be enacted, but it also mandates strict adherence to it. It also requires that organizations have ethics programs in place.[33] If a company is convicted of fraud, the penalties might be reduced if the firm can document it had implemented programs to encourage ethical behavior and detect fraud. Many organizations such as Ford Motor Co. and Johnson & Johnson are stepping up their ethics training for all employees through the use of Web-based programs offered by companies such as Integrity Interactive Corp. and the Legal Knowledge Co.[34] A number of nonprofit organizations, such as the National Whistleblower Association, formed in 1988, provide assistance to would-be whistleblowers.[35] Hopefully, heightened public awareness of the potential for corporate wrongdoing, penalties for those convicted of white-collar crimes, enforcement of the Sarbanes-Oxley Act, and protection for would-be whistleblowers will reduce the incidence of unethical behavior in organizations.

Job satisfaction is the collection of feelings and beliefs that people have about their current jobs. People's levels or degrees of job satisfaction can range from extreme satisfaction to extreme dissatisfaction. In addition to having attitudes about their jobs as a whole, people also can have attitudes about various aspects of their jobs such as the kind of work they do; their co-workers, supervisors, or subordinates; and their pay.

Organizational commitment is the collection of feelings and beliefs that people have about their organization as a whole. Levels of commitment can range from being extremely high to extremely low, and people can have attitudes about various aspects of their organization such as the organization's promotion practices, the quality of the organization's products, and the organization's stance on ethical issues.

Work attitudes, like job satisfaction and organizational commitment, are made up of three components: feelings, the affective component; beliefs, the cognitive component; and thoughts about how to behave, the behavioral component (see Figure 3.2).[36] For example, the *affective component* of an employee's attitude is the employee's *feelings* about his or her job or organization. The *cognitive component* is the employee's *beliefs* about the job or organization—that is, whether or not he or she believes the job is

Work attitudes Collections of feelings, beliefs, and thoughts about how to behave in one's job and organization.

Job satisfaction The collection of feelings and beliefs that people have about their current jobs.

Organizational commitment The collection of feelings and beliefs that people have about their organization as a whole.

FIGURE 3.2
Components of Work Attitudes

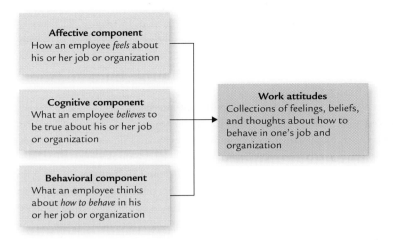

Affective component
How an employee *feels* about his or her job or organization

Cognitive component
What an employee *believes* to be true about his or her job or organization

Behavioral component
What an employee thinks about *how to behave* in his or her job or organization

Work attitudes
Collections of feelings, beliefs, and thoughts about how to behave in one's job and organization

meaningful and important. The *behavioral component* is the employee's *thoughts* about how to behave in his or her job or organization. Each component of a work attitude influences and tends to be consistent with the other components.

Because job satisfaction and organizational commitment are key determinants of the experience of work and central to understanding and managing organizational behavior, we explore these two work attitudes in depth later in the chapter.

THE NATURE OF MOODS AND EMOTIONS

Work moods How people feel at the time they actually perform their jobs.

Work mood describes how people feel at the time they actually perform their jobs. Some employees tend to feel excited and enthusiastic at work, whereas others feel anxious and nervous, and still others feel sleepy and sluggish. Much more transitory than values and attitudes, work moods can change from hour to hour, day to day, and sometimes minute to minute. Think about how your own moods have varied since you woke up today or about how your moods today differ from how you felt yesterday. Then you will have some idea about the fluctuating nature of work moods.

Although people can experience many different moods at work, moods can be categorized generally as positive or negative. When employees are in *positive moods*, they feel excited, enthusiastic, active, strong, peppy, or elated.[37] When employees are in *negative moods*, they feel distressed, fearful, scornful, hostile, jittery, or nervous.[38] Sometimes employees' feelings are neither strongly positive nor negative; they may simply experience less intense feelings such as being drowsy, dull, and sluggish or calm, placid, and relaxed.[39] The extent to which employees experience positive, negative, and less intense moods at work is determined by both their personalities and the situation.

Recall from Chapter 2 that employees who are high on the personality trait of *positive affectivity* are more likely than other employees to experience positive moods at work, and employees who are high on the trait of *negative affectivity* are more likely to experience negative moods at work. A wide range of situational factors also affects work mood—major events and conditions, such as receiving a promotion (or a demotion) and getting along well with one's co-workers, and relatively minor conditions, such as how pleasant the physical surroundings are.[40] If you stop and think a minute about the different factors that influence your own moods—weather, pressures of school or family life, your love life, and so on—you will see that many of them, though unrelated to work, nonetheless have the potential to influence an employee's mood on the job. Getting engaged, for example, may put an employee in a very good mood both on and off the job, but having a big argument with one's spouse may put an employee in a very bad mood.

Research suggests that mood at work has important consequences for understanding and managing organizational behavior.[41] Employees in positive moods at work, for example, are more likely to be helpful to each other and those around them, including clients and customers, and they may also be less likely to be absent from their jobs.[42] One study found that salespeople who were in positive moods at work provided higher-quality service to customers in a department store than did salespeople who were not in positive moods.[43] Another study found that the extent to which leaders (in this case, managers of small retail stores) experienced positive moods was related to the performance levels of their subordinates (the salespeople in the stores). (Leadership is the subject of Chapter 12.)[44] Research has also found that moods influence important behaviors such as creativity, decision making, and the accuracy of judgments.[45]

Recent studies suggest that the influence that moods have on behaviors is likely to depend on the situation or context, too.[46] For example, some studies have found that people in positive moods are more likely to come up with unusual word associations, which has been used to index creativity.[47] The reasoning in these studies is that positive moods result in people thinking more broadly or expansively. However, other studies have found that being in a negative mood sometimes fosters creativity. For example, when employees are striving to be creative on the job, and have to determine for themselves how well they are doing or when they have to come up with a creative idea under pressure, people in negative moods tend to demand more of themselves and put forth more effort to be creative.[48] Whether positive moods, negative moods, or both lead to creativity appears to depend on situational factors such as the goals or objectives that are being sought, the extent to which people receive clear feedback about how they are doing, and the nature of the tasks they are working on.[49] Similarly, we know that positive and negative moods influence decision making. Again, however, the exact nature of that influence depends on situational factors such as the kind of decision being made, the goals of the decision maker, and the kinds of information available to the decision maker.

Clearly, work moods can have important effects on organizational behavior. Moreover, because managers and organizations can do many things to promote positive moods—for example, giving people attractive offices to work in, giving praise when it is deserved, providing employees with opportunities for social interaction, and incorporating fun and humor into the workplace—work moods are receiving additional attention from researchers and managers alike. From the opening case, it is clear that Richard Branson believes that work should be a source of enjoyment and positive feelings. Additionally, because all employees are likely to experience negative moods at some time or another on the job, it is important to understand the consequences of those bad feelings and how they might be channeled into effective behaviors. (For more on understanding and managing moods, see the discussion of emotional intelligence in Chapter 2.)

Moods tend to be general and pervasive feelings that do not interrupt employees' thoughts or behaviors. Emotions, by contrast, are much more intense than moods. **Emotions** are intense, short-lived feelings that are linked to a specific cause or antecedent. Over time, emotions can feed into moods.[50] Take the case of Mary and Paul Putnam, a dual-career couple who work in different states and have been commuting on weekends to see each other. Both of the Putnams have been trying to relocate to eliminate their long-distance marriage, and they have agreed that whoever finds an acceptable position first will make the move. Recently, Paul received a phone call indicating that he was offered a position in a company close to where Mary is working. It is just what he has been looking for. Paul is ecstatic and puts what he has been working on aside. He is thrilled and calls Mary, and the two count their blessings for their good fortune. A short while later, Paul realizes he must get back to work and finish a report that is due to his boss the following day; throughout the day, Paul is in a great mood, even when he is not thinking about his new job.

On certain kinds of jobs, it is important that employees express certain kinds of moods and emotions and refrain from expressing other kinds. For example, waiters, flight attendants, and cheerleaders are expected to display positive moods and emotions like enthusiasm and pleasure and refrain from expressing negative moods and emotions like anger and hostility. Thus, no matter how distressed these employees might be for a variety of reasons—say, being

Emotions Intense short-lived feelings that are linked to a specific cause or antecedent.

Emotional labor The work that employees perform to control their experience and expression of moods and emotions on the job.

forced to deal with a difficult customer, experiencing flight delays, or having problems at home—they are expected to be cheerful and pleasant. Sometimes this is very hard to do and quite stressful. We have all been in situations in which we tried to hide how we really felt and express an emotion other than our true feelings. This can be quite challenging on occasion. Now imagine having to do this day in and day out as part of your job. **Emotional labor** is the work that employees perform to control their experience and expression of moods and emotions on the job.[51]

Emotional labor is governed by *display rules*.[52] There are two types of display rules: feeling rules and expression rules. *Feeling rules* dictate appropriate and inappropriate feelings for a particular setting.[53] For example, funeral directors are not supposed to feel delighted in the presence of grieving families, and managers are not supposed to feel angry when letting subordinates know that they have just received promotions. As another example, professors are expected to be enthusiastic when they teach classes and not be bored. *Expression rules* dictate what emotions should be expressed and how they should be expressed in a particular setting.[54] For example, professors are expected to be enthusiastic via their facial expressions and tone of voice, but they are not expected to jump up and down and hoot and holler. Employees who are high on emotional intelligence (see Chapter 2) are likely to be better able to follow feeling and expression rules.

Emotional labor takes place in many organizations and in a variety of kinds of jobs. For example, many employees believe that they should not cry in the workplace in front of co-workers, no matter how badly they might be feeling. However, jobs do differ in terms of the extent to which emotional labor is required on a day-to-day basis. Jobs that involve high levels of interpersonal interaction (whether with the public, students, co-workers, clients, customers, or patients) typically require more emotional labor than jobs that entail less frequent interactions with others.

Emotional dissonance An internal state that exists when employees are expected to express feelings that are at odds with how the employees are actually feeling.

Emotional dissonance occurs when employees are expected to express feelings that are at odds with how the employees are actually feeling.[55] For example, a waiter who is angry after dealing with a particularly difficult customer is nonetheless expected to act pleasant and helpful. Emotional dissonance can be a significant source of stress for employees,[56] especially when it occurs frequently or on a day-to-day basis. (We discuss stress in more detail in Chapter 9.)

Emotional labor is part and parcel of high-quality customer service, as indicated in the accompanying OB Today.

Although he doesn't have to, Professor Dennis Minechella holds study sessions in residence hall lounges and the student union to personally help freshman biology students at Purdue University. Minechella frequently visits as many as three different residence halls in a single evening.

ob today

Inn at Little Washington Takes Emotional Labor One Step Further

The restaurant at the Inn at Little Washington is famous for its exceptional food and perhaps even more famous for its high-quality customer service.[57] The Inn's hotel and restaurant were founded by Patrick O'Connell (the chef) and Reinhardt Lynch (the business manager) in picturesque Washington, Virginia, in 1978.[58] O'Connell, who manages the restaurant, believes it is his obligation and the obligation of his staff to provide such a superior dining experience that people leave the restaurant feeling much better than when they entered it. Not only is the staff expected to manage their own emotions, but they are also expected to manage the emotions of their customers.

When a dining party enters the restaurant, the captain assigns the party a mood rating gauging their current state of mind from a low of 1 to a high of 10. Ratings of 7 and lower suggest that the party seems unhappy or displeased. The mood ratings are placed on the table's order and also hung in the kitchen. O'Connell insists that guests leave his restaurant with a mood rating of 9 or 10, and staff members are encouraged to do whatever they can to see that this happens. Tours of the kitchen, tableside visits from the chef, and complimentary drinks or desserts all are used to try to ensure that everyone leaves the restaurant feeling great.[59] And it is up to the staff to figure out how to improve the moods of customers who might have just gotten into an argument or had a very rough day.

The restaurant staff also is required to be very knowledgeable about a variety of topics ranging from different kinds of foods and wines to the likes and dislikes of important food and restaurant critics. Staff members are admonished never to say "no" or "I don't know."[60] O'Connell provides them with training and experience before they actually begin serving customers, so they never need to plead ignorance. New waitstaff receive several months of training, which includes being asked every kind of question that a customer might pose to them. Only when they are able to satisfactorily answer these questions do they receive their portion of the tip pool. O'Connell indicates that his almost fanatical approach to providing high-quality customer service essentially reflects his gratitude to his customers, without whom the restaurant would cease to exist. And employees seem to like the emphasis on customer service; turnover at the Inn is much lower than at many other restaurants.[61]

RELATIONSHIPS BETWEEN VALUES, ATTITUDES, AND MOODS AND EMOTIONS

Values, attitudes, and moods and emotions capture the range of thoughts and feelings that make up the experience of work. Each one of these determinants of the experience of work has the potential to affect the other two (see Figure 3.3). Because work values are the most stable and long lasting, they can strongly affect work attitudes, moods, and emotions. A person whose work values emphasize the importance of being ambitious, for example, may have negative work attitudes toward a job that offers no possibility of promotion.

Work attitudes can affect work moods and emotions in a similar fashion. A salesperson who is very satisfied with his or her job and loves interacting with customers may often be in a good mood at work. In this case, work attitudes (job satisfaction) affect work moods and emotions (positive feelings).

In the long run—over the course of a few years—a person's work values might change in response to his or her more fleeting attitudes, moods, and emotions toward work. A person who values work as merely a way to make a living and not as a source of personal fulfillment might find a nursing job so rewarding and exciting that he or

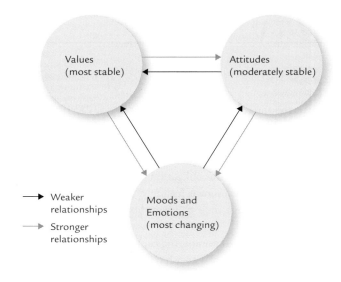

she is usually in a good mood while on the job and finds it satisfying. Eventually, the person's work values may change to include the importance of doing something to help other people. By contrast, an employee who frequently experiences bad moods at work and often feels angry (perhaps because of a dishonest or unpleasant supervisor) may be less satisfied and decide the job isn't meeting his or her expectations. Persistent moods and emotions, in other words, can have an impact on long-held attitudes and values.[62]

When members of an organization share important values, have positive attitudes, and experience positive moods, they may be more likely to trust each other.[63] **Trust** is an expression of confidence in another person or group of people that you will not be put at risk, harmed, or injured by their actions.[64] Trust, in turn, can enhance cooperation and the sharing of information necessary for creativity and innovation. A lack of trust between employees and managers is often symptomatic of more widespread problems in an organization.[65] At a minimum, managers must ensure that employees can be confident that their well-being will not be jeopardized by their jobs. Unfortunately, this is not always the case.

Trust An expression of confidence in another person or group of people that you will not be put at risk, harmed, or injured by their actions.

Job Satisfaction

Job satisfaction (the collection of feelings and beliefs that people have about their current jobs) is one of the most important and well-researched work attitudes in organizational behavior. Why do managers and researchers think it's so important? Job satisfaction has the potential to affect a wide range of behaviors in organizations and contribute to employees' levels of well-being. Interestingly enough, research suggests that levels of job satisfaction in the United States actually declined from 1995 to 2003.[66] According to a Conference Board survey conducted both years, in 1995, 58 percent of those surveyed indicated that they were satisfied with their jobs. This number dropped to 49 percent satisfied in 2003. Only about 20 percent of those surveyed in 2003 were satisfied with their organization's promotion and bonus practices, and only about 33 percent were satisfied with their pay.[67] The researchers speculate that perhaps the declines in satisfaction are due to many organizations downsizing and raising their expectations about what employees who remain on the job should be capable of accomplishing.[68]

DETERMINANTS OF JOB SATISFACTION

What causes different employees to be satisfied or dissatisfied with their jobs? Four factors affect the level of job satisfaction a person experiences: personality, values, the work situation, and social influence (see Figure 3.4).

Personality. Personality, the enduring ways a person has of feeling, thinking, and behaving (see Chapter 2), is the first determinant of how people think and feel about their jobs or job satisfaction.[69] An individual's personality influences the extent to which thoughts and feelings about a job are positive or negative. A person who is high on the Big Five trait of extraversion, for instance, is likely to have a higher level of job satisfaction than a person who is low on this trait.[70]

Given that personality helps to determine job satisfaction and that personality is, in part, genetically determined, researchers have wondered whether genetics influence job satisfaction. Richard Arvey of the University of Minnesota and his colleagues explored the extent to which employees' levels of job satisfaction were inherited from their parents.[71] They studied 34 identical twins who were raised apart from an early age. The twins shared the same genetic makeup but were exposed to different situational influences in their developmental years and later in life. For each pair of twins, the researchers measured the degree to which one twin's level of job satisfaction was the same as the other twin's level.

The researchers found that genetic factors accounted for about 30 percent of the differences in levels of job satisfaction across the twins in their study. Another interesting finding was that the twins tended to hold jobs that were similar in complexity, motor skills needed, and physical demands required. This suggests that people seek out jobs that are suited to their genetic makeup. In other words, people's personalities (which are partially inherited) predispose them to choose certain kinds of jobs.

What do these findings mean for managers? Essentially, they suggest that part of job satisfaction is determined by employees' personalities, which an organization or manager cannot change in the short run. Does this mean that managers should not worry about the job satisfaction levels of their subordinates or that it is pointless to try

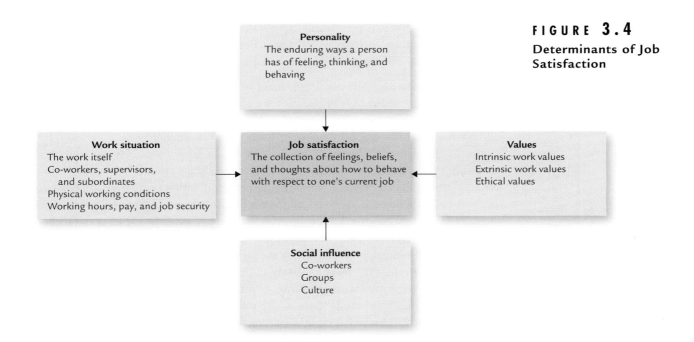

FIGURE 3.4
Determinants of Job Satisfaction

to improve levels of job satisfaction? Definitely not. Although it certainly is impressive that genetic factors account for 30 percent of the differences in levels of job satisfaction, 70 percent of the variation in job satisfaction remains to be explained. It is this 70 percent that managers can influence. Thus, managers should be concerned about job satisfaction because it is something that is within their power to influence and change.

Values. Values have an impact on levels of job satisfaction because they reflect employees' convictions about the outcomes that work should lead to and how one should behave at work. A person with strong intrinsic work values (those related to the nature of the work itself), for example, is more likely than a person with weak intrinsic work values to be satisfied with a job that is interesting and personally meaningful (such as social work) but that also requires long working hours and doesn't pay well. A person with strong extrinsic work values (those related to the consequences of work) is more likely than a person with weak extrinsic work values to be satisfied with a job that pays well but is monotonous.

The Work Situation. Perhaps the most important source of job satisfaction is the **work situation** itself—the tasks a person performs (for example, how interesting or boring they are), the people a jobholder interacts with (customers, subordinates, and supervisors), the surroundings in which a person works (noise level, crowdedness, and temperature), and the way the organization treats its employees (such as the job security it offers them and whether the pay and benefits are fair). Any aspect of the job and the employing organization is part of the work situation and can affect job satisfaction.[72] According to *Working Mother* magazine, which publishes a list of the top 100 companies for working mothers, flexibility is a very important contributor to the job satisfaction levels of working mothers.[73] Flexibility can take many forms ranging from compressed workweeks and flexible working hours to the ability to take an extended leave of absence to attend to a sick child. For Cindy Clark, an employee at the IKEA furniture store in Plymouth Meeting, Pennsylvania, IKEA's flexibility has been a blessing. When her son Ryan was born, she was able to switch to a three-day workweek.[74] When Ryan was recently diagnosed with leukemia, Clark took a six-month leave of absence to take care of him, knowing that her job would be waiting for her when Ryan recovered and she could get back to work.[75]

Most people would be more satisfied with a job that pays well and is very secure than with a job that pays poorly and exposes the employee to the ever-present threat of a layoff. Some of the theories of job satisfaction that we consider later in the chapter focus on the way in which specific situational factors affect job satisfaction.

Social Influence. The last determinant of job satisfaction is **social influence**, or the influence that individuals or groups have on a person's attitudes and behavior. Co-workers, the groups a person belongs to, and the culture a person grows up and lives in all have the potential to affect employees' levels of job satisfaction.

Social influence from *co-workers* can be an important determinant of an employee's job satisfaction because co-workers are always around, often have similar types of jobs, and often have certain things in common with an employee (such as educational background). Co-workers can have a particularly potent influence on the job satisfaction levels of new hires. New hires are still likely to be forming an opinion about the organization and the job. They might not yet know what to make of it or whether or not they will ultimately like it. If they are surrounded by co-workers who are dissatisfied with their jobs, they are more likely to be dissatisfied themselves than if they are surrounded by employees who enjoy and are satisfied with their jobs.

The groups he or she belongs to also influences an employee's level of job satisfaction. The family in which a child grows up, for example, can affect how satisfied the child is with his or her job as an adult. An employee who grows up in a wealthy family might be dissatisfied with a job as an elementary schoolteacher because the salary places

Work situation The work itself, working conditions, and all other aspects of the job and the employing organization.

Social influence The influence that individuals or groups have on a person's attitudes and behavior.

the high standard of living he or she enjoyed while growing up out of reach. A teacher raised under more modest circumstances might also desire a higher salary but might not be dissatisfied with his or her teaching job because of its pay level.

A wide variety of groups can affect job satisfaction. Employees who belong to certain religious groups are likely to be dissatisfied with jobs that require working on Saturdays or Sundays. Unions can have powerful effects on the job satisfaction levels of their members. Belonging to a union that believes managers are not treating employees as well as they should be, for example, might cause an employee to be dissatisfied with a job.

The *culture* a person grows up and lives in may also affect an employee's level of job satisfaction. Employees who grow up in cultures (such as the American culture) that emphasize the importance of individual achievement and accomplishment are more likely to be satisfied with jobs that stress individual accomplishment and provide bonuses and pay raises for individual achievement. Employees who grow up in cultures (such as the Japanese culture) that emphasize the importance of doing what is good for everyone may be less satisfied with jobs that stress individual competition and achievement. (We discuss national culture in more depth in Chapter 17.)

In fact, cultural influences may shape not just job satisfaction but also the attitudes employees have about themselves. An American may introduce a lecture with a joke that displays both his knowledge and his wit, but a Japanese lecturer in the same position would more likely start off apologizing for his lack of expertise. According to Dr. Hazel Markus of the University of Michigan and Dr. Shinobu Kitayama of the University of Oregon, these two contrasting styles reflect how Americans and Japanese view themselves, which is, in turn, based on the values of their respective cultures.[76]

Consistent with American culture, the American lecturer views and portrays himself as independent, autonomous, and striving to achieve; this makes him feel good and makes his American audience comfortable. In contrast, Japanese culture stresses the interdependence of the self with others; the goal is to fit in, meet one's obligations, and have good interpersonal relations. The Japanese lecturer's more self-effacing style reflects these values; it demonstrates that he is but one part of a larger system and emphasizes the connection between himself and the audience.

Markus and her colleagues have been conducting some interesting research that further illuminates the effects of culture on attitudes about the self. They have asked Japanese and American students to describe themselves using what the researchers call the "Who Am I" scale. Americans tend to respond to the scale by describing personal characteristics (such as being athletic or smart). Japanese students, however, tend to describe themselves in terms of their roles (such as being the second son). These responses again illustrate that Americans view themselves in terms of personal characteristics, and Japanese view themselves in terms of social characteristics such as their position in their family.[77] This is a simple yet powerful demonstration of how the culture and society we grow up in influences our attitudes, even attitudes as fundamental as our attitudes about ourselves!

Theories of Job Satisfaction

There are many theories or models of job satisfaction. Each of them takes into account one or more of the four main determinants of job satisfaction (personality, values, the work situation, and social influence) and specifies, in more detail, exactly what causes one employee to be satisfied with a job and another employee to be dissatisfied. Here, we discuss four of the most influential theories: the facet model, Herzberg's motivator-hygiene theory, the discrepancy model, and the steady-state theory. These different theoretical approaches to job satisfaction are complementary. Each helps us understand the various aspects of job satisfaction by highlighting the factors and issues managers need to consider in order to enhance the satisfaction levels of their subordinates.

THE FACET MODEL OF JOB SATISFACTION

Job facet One of numerous components of a job.

The facet model of job satisfaction focuses primarily on work situation factors by breaking a job into its component elements, or **job facets**, and looking at how satisfied employees are with each facet. Many of the job facets that researchers have investigated are listed and defined in Table 3.2. An employee's overall job satisfaction is determined by summing his or her satisfaction with each facet of the job.

As Table 3.2 indicates, employees can take into account numerous aspects of their jobs when thinking about their levels of job satisfaction. The facet model is useful because it forces managers and researchers to recognize that jobs affect employees in multiple ways. However, managers who use this model to evaluate the work situation's effect on job satisfaction always need to be aware that, for any particular job, they might inadvertently exclude an important facet that strongly influences an employee's job satisfaction.

The extent to which an employing organization is "family friendly," for example, is an important job facet for many employees. Given the increasing diversity of the workforce and the increasing numbers of women, dual-career couples, and single parents who

TABLE 3.2

Job Facets That Play a Part in Determining Job Satisfaction

Job Facet	Description
Ability utilization	The extent to which the job allows one to use one's abilities
Achievement	The extent to which an employee gets a feeling of accomplishment from the job
Activity	Being able to keep busy on the job
Advancement	Having promotion opportunities
Authority	Having control over others
Company policies and practices	The extent to which they are pleasing to an employee
Compensation	The pay an employee receives for the job
Co-workers	How well one gets along with others in the workplace
Creativity	Being free to come up with new ideas
Independence	Being able to work alone
Moral values	Not having to do things that go against one's conscience
Recognition	Praise for doing a good job
Responsibility	Being accountable for decisions and actions
Security	Having a secure or steady job
Social service	Being able to do things for other people
Social status	The recognition in the wider community that goes along with the job
Human relations supervision	The interpersonal skills of one's boss
Technical supervision	The work-related skills of one's boss
Variety	Doing different things on the job
Working conditions	Working hours, temperature, furnishings, office location and layout, and so forth

Source: D. J. Weiss et al., *Manual for the Minnesota Satisfaction Questionnaire,* 1967. Minnesota Studies in Vocational Rehabilitation: XXII. © 1967 University of Minnesota. Reproduced by permission of Vocational Psychology Research.

need to balance their responsibilities on the job and at home, family-friendly organizational policies and benefits are becoming important to more and more employees.[78]

Amgen, a biotechnology company and drugmaker, was listed in *Fortune* magazine's 100 Best Companies to Work for in 2004.[79] Amgen recently opened one of the biggest on-site child care facilities in the United States. The child care center can accommodate up to 430 children ranging in age from 6 weeks to 5 years old. Although employees must pay for their children to come to the center, it is less expensive than other child care facilities and provides a safe and educational environment. Bright Horizons, headquarted in Massachusetts, manages the center for Amgen. Before the new center opened, Amgen had a much smaller on-site facility with a long waiting list.[80]

Another issue that must be considered by managers using facet models of job satisfaction is that some job facets may be more important than others for any given employee.[81] Family-friendly policies, for example, are generally valued by employees with dependents, but they clearly are less important for employees who are single and intend to remain so. Telecommuting (see Chapter 9) and work-at-home arrangements might be facets that appeal to working parents and those with long commutes, but they might not appeal to younger employees who enjoy social interaction with their co-workers. Compensation and security might be key job satisfaction facets for a single woman who has strong extrinsic work values. At the other end of the spectrum, a high-ranking military retiree receiving a generous pension might have strong intrinsic work values; he might be more satisfied with a postretirement job offering high levels of ability utilization, achievement, and creativity.

Frank Courtney, a Harvard University graduate, was the butt of jokes when he accepted a position with U.S. Steel while many of his classmates were accepting positions with more prestigious and glamorous companies.[82] Working in heavy industry, however, provided Courtney with a job facet he truly desired: responsibility. At U.S. Steel, he was responsible for overseeing the production and shipping of hundreds of tons of steel while his buddies in the more glamorous legal and financial industries were spending a lot of their time making photocopies.[83]

HERZBERG'S MOTIVATOR–HYGIENE THEORY OF JOB SATISFACTION

One of the earliest theories of job satisfaction, Frederick Herzberg's motivator-hygiene theory, focuses on the effects of certain types of job facets on job satisfaction. Herzberg's theory proposes that every employee has two sets of needs or requirements: motivator needs and hygiene needs.[84] *Motivator needs* are associated with the actual work itself and how challenging it is. Job facets such as how interesting the work is, autonomy on the job, and the responsibility it affords satisfy motivator needs. *Hygiene needs* are associated with the physical and psychological context in which the work is performed. Job facets such as the physical working conditions (for example, the temperature and pleasantness of the surroundings), the nature of supervision, amount of pay, and job security satisfy hygiene needs.

Herzberg proposed the following theoretical relationships between motivator needs, hygiene needs, and job satisfaction:

1. When motivator needs are met, employees will be satisfied; when these needs are not met, employees will not be satisfied.

2. When hygiene needs are met, employees will not be dissatisfied; when these needs are not met, employees will be dissatisfied.

According to Herzberg, an employee could experience job satisfaction and job dissatisfaction at the same time. An employee could be *satisfied* because *motivator needs* are being met by. For example, the employee might find the work interesting and challenging yet be *dissatisfied* because his or her *hygiene needs* are not being met. (Perhaps the position offers little job security.) According to the traditional view of job satisfaction, satisfaction and dissatisfaction are at opposite ends of a single continuum, and employees are either satisfied or dissatisfied with their jobs. Figure 3.5(a) illustrates the traditional view. Herzberg proposed that dissatisfaction and satisfaction are two *separate dimensions*, one ranging from satisfaction to no satisfaction and the other ranging from dissatisfaction to no dissatisfaction. Figure 3.5(b) illustrates Herzberg's view. An employee's location on the satisfaction continuum depends on the extent to which motivator needs are met, and an employee's location on the dissatisfaction continuum depends on the extent to which hygiene needs are met.

Many research studies have tested Herzberg's formulations. Herzberg himself conducted some of the early studies that supported the theory. He relied on the *critical incidents technique* to collect his data. Herzberg and his colleagues interviewed employees and asked them to describe a time when they felt particularly good about their jobs and a time when they felt particularly bad about their jobs. After collating responses from many employees, they made the following discovery: Whenever employees related an instance when they felt good about their job, the incident had to do with the work itself (it was related to their *motivator needs*). Whenever they described an instance when they felt bad about their job, the incident had to do with the working conditions (it was related to their *hygiene needs*). These results certainly seemed to support Herzberg's theory.

When other researchers used different methods to test Herzberg's theory, however, the theory failed to receive support.[85] Why did studies using the critical incidents technique support the theory? As you will learn in Chapter 4, people have a tendency to want to take credit for the good things that happen to them and blame others or outside forces for the bad things. This basic tendency probably accounts for employees' describing good things that happened to them as being related to the work itself, because the work itself is something an employee can take direct credit for. Conversely, working conditions are mostly outside the control of an employee, and it is human nature to try to attribute bad things to situations beyond one's control.

Even though research does *not* support Herzberg's theory, the attention Herzberg paid to motivator needs and to work itself as determinants of satisfaction helped to focus researchers' and managers' attention on the important topic of job design and its effects on organizational behavior (discussed in detail in Chapter 7). Nevertheless, managers need to be aware of the lack of research support for the theoretical relationships Herzberg proposed.

FIGURE 3.5
Two Views of Job Satisfaction

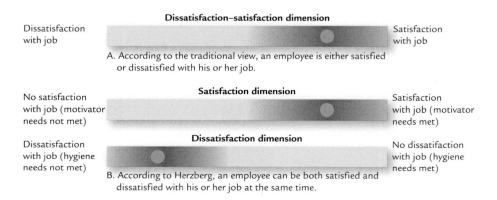

Dissatisfaction–satisfaction dimension

Dissatisfaction with job

Satisfaction with job

A. According to the traditional view, an employee is either satisfied or dissatisfied with his or her job.

Satisfaction dimension

No satisfaction with job (motivator needs not met)

Satisfaction with job (motivator needs met)

Dissatisfaction dimension

Dissatisfaction with job (hygiene needs not met)

No dissatisfaction with job (hygiene needs met)

B. According to Herzberg, an employee can be both satisfied and dissatisfied with his or her job at the same time.

THE DISCREPANCY MODEL OF JOB SATISFACTION

The discrepancy model of job satisfaction is based on a simple idea: To determine how satisfied they are with their jobs, employees compare their job to some "ideal job."[86] This ideal job could be what one thinks the job should be like, what one expected the job to be like, what one wants from a job, or what one's former job was like. According to the discrepancy model of job satisfaction, when employees' expectations about their ideal job are high, and when these expectations are not met, employees will be dissatisfied. New college graduates may be particularly prone to having overly high expectations for their first jobs.[87] According to discrepancy models of job satisfaction, they are bound to experience some job dissatisfaction when their new positions fail to meet their high hopes.

Some researchers have combined the facet and discrepancy models of job satisfaction.[88] For each of the job facets described in Table 3.2, for example, we could ask employees "how much" of the facet they currently have on the job compared to what they think their jobs should have. The difference between these two quantities would be the employees' level of satisfaction with the facet. For example, an employee who indicates that she thinks she should have a lot of autonomy on her job but reports that she currently has limited autonomy would be dissatisfied with the autonomy facet of her job. After determining satisfaction levels for each of the job facets in this manner, the total of all of the responses would yield an overall satisfaction score.

Discrepancy models are useful because they take into account that people often take a comparative approach to evaluation. It is not so much the presence or absence of job facets that is important but rather how a job stacks up against an employee's "ideal job." Managers need to recognize this comparative approach and should ask employees what they want their jobs to be like. This information can help them make meaningful changes to increase the level of job satisfaction their subordinates are experiencing.

THE STEADY-STATE THEORY OF JOB SATISFACTION

The steady-state theory suggests that each employee has a typical, or characteristic, level of job satisfaction, called the steady state or equilibrium level. Different situational factors or events at work may move an employee temporarily from this steady state, but the employee will return eventually to his or her equilibrium level[89] (see Figure 3.6). For example, receiving a promotion and raise may temporarily boost an employee's level of job satisfaction, but it eventually will return to the equilibrium level. The finding that job satisfaction tends to be somewhat stable over time[90] supports the steady-state view. The influence of personality on job satisfaction also is

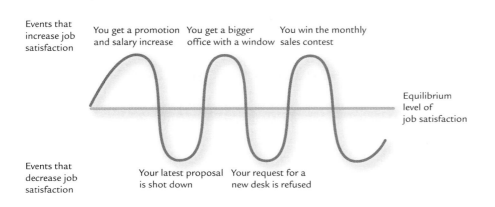

Events that increase job satisfaction

You get a promotion and salary increase

You get a bigger office with a window

You win the monthly sales contest

Equilibrium level of job satisfaction

Events that decrease job satisfaction

Your latest proposal is shot down

Your request for a new desk is refused

FIGURE 3.6

Job Satisfaction as a Steady State
An employee's level of job satisfaction fluctuates above and below the equilibrium level as events increase or decrease job satisfaction.

FIGURE **3.7**

Sample Items from Popular Measures of Job Satisfaction

Source: (A) D. J. Weiss et al., *Manual for the Minnesota Satisfaction Questionnaire,* 1967. Minnesota Studies in Vocational Rehabilitation: XXII. Copyright 1967 University of Minnesota. Reproduced by permission of Vocational Psychology Research. (B) R. B. Dunham and J. B. Herman, "Development of a Female Faces Scale for Measuring Job Satisfaction." *Journal of Applied Psychology* 60 (1975): 629–31. Copyright 1975 by the American Psychology Association. Reprinted with permission.

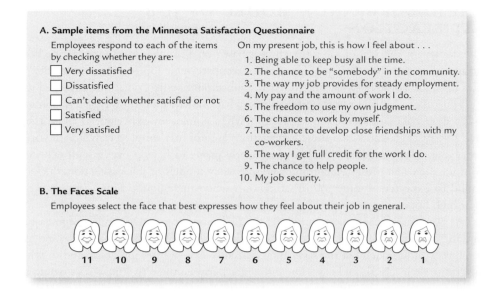

consistent with the steady-state approach. Because personality, one of the determinants of job satisfaction, is stable over time, we would expect job satisfaction to exhibit some stability over time.

The steady-state theory suggests that when managers make changes in the work situation in an effort to enhance job satisfaction levels, they need to determine whether the resulting increases in satisfaction are temporary or long lasting. Some researchers have found, for example, that when changes are made in the nature of the work itself (such as making jobs more interesting), levels of job satisfaction increase temporarily (e.g., for six months) but then return to their former levels.[91] To decide on the most effective ways to sustain an increase in job satisfaction, it is also important for managers to determine *how long* it takes employees to return to their equilibrium levels. Changes in some job facets, for example, may lead to longer-lasting changes in job satisfaction than changes in other facets.

MEASURING JOB SATISFACTION

There are several measures of job satisfaction that managers can use to determine job satisfaction levels. A manager who discovers that most employees are dissatisfied with the same few job facets and that overall levels of job satisfaction are low as a result can use this information to determine where to make changes in the work situation. Researchers can also use these measures to learn more about the causes and consequences of job satisfaction. Most of these measures ask employees to respond to a series of questions or statements about their jobs. Among the most popular scales are the Minnesota Satisfaction Questionnaire (based on a facet approach),[92] the Faces Scale,[93] and the Job Descriptive Index.[94] Sample items from the first two of these scales appear in Figure 3.7.

Potential Consequences of Job Satisfaction

Earlier, we said that job satisfaction is one of the most important and most studied attitudes in organizational behavior. One reason for the interest in job satisfaction is that whether or not an employee is satisfied with his or her job has consequences not just for the employee but also for co-workers, managers, groups, teams, and the organization as a whole. In this section, we consider several potential consequences of job satisfaction: job performance, absenteeism, turnover, organizational citizenship behavior, and employee well-being.

DOES JOB SATISFACTION AFFECT JOB PERFORMANCE?

Intuitively, most people (including managers) believe that job satisfaction is positively associated with job performance—that is, that employees who are more satisfied with their jobs will perform at a higher level than those who are less satisfied. Many studies have been conducted to see whether this piece of conventional wisdom holds true. Surprisingly, the results indicate that job satisfaction is *not* strongly related to job performance; at best, there is a very weak positive relationship. One recent review of the many studies conducted in this area concluded that levels of job satisfaction accounted for only about 2 percent of the differences in performance levels across employees in the studies reviewed.[95] Another recent review found somewhat similar results; job satisfaction accounted for, on average, about 3 percent of the differences in performance levels across employees.[96] For all practical purposes, then, we can conclude that job satisfaction is *not* meaningfully associated with job performance.

Although this finding goes against the intuition of many managers, it is not that surprising if we consider when work attitudes such as job satisfaction *do* affect work behaviors. Research indicates that work attitudes (such as job satisfaction) affect work behaviors only when employees are free to vary their behaviors and when an employee's attitude is relevant to the behavior in question.

Are most employees free to vary their levels of job performance to reflect how satisfied they are with their jobs? Probably not. Organizations spend considerable time and effort to ensure that members perform assigned duties dependably regardless of whether they like their jobs or not. As you will see in later chapters, organizations develop rules and procedures that employees are expected to follow. To ensure the rules are followed, they reward employees who perform at acceptable levels and punish or dismiss employees who do not. Such rules, procedures, rewards, and punishments are situational pressures that compel employees to perform at acceptable levels.

If chefs in a restaurant, for example, lower the quality of the meals they prepare because they are dissatisfied, customers will stop coming to the restaurant, and the restaurant will either go out of business or the owners will replace the chefs. Similarly, firefighters will not keep their jobs if, because of their levels of job satisfaction, they vary the number of emergencies they respond to. And a secretary who, because of dissatisfaction, cuts back on the quality or quantity of letters he or she types is likely to be reprimanded or even fired and certainly will not be offered a promotion.

In order for a work attitude (job satisfaction) to influence behavior, the attitude must be relevant to the behavior in question (job performance). Sometimes employees' levels of job satisfaction are not relevant to their job performance. Suppose a security guard is satisfied with his job because it is not very demanding and allows him to do a lot of outside reading while on the job. Clearly, this employee's job satisfaction is not going to result in higher levels of performance because the reason for his satisfaction is that the job is not very demanding.

Because of strong situational pressures in organizations to behave in certain ways and because an employee's level of job satisfaction may not be relevant to his or her job performance, job satisfaction is *not* strongly related to job performance. Some research, however, suggests that the direction of influence between these two factors (satisfaction and performance) may be reversed: Job performance may lead to job satisfaction if employees are fairly rewarded for a good performance. The relationship between job performance and rewards, the importance of equity or fairness, and the implications of these issues for understanding and managing organizational behavior are covered in more detail in Chapters 6, 7, and 8.

TABLE 3.3
Determinants of Absence from Work

Motivation to Attend Work Is Affected by	Ability to Attend Work Is Affected by
Job satisfaction	Illness and accidents
Organization's absence policy	Transportation problems
Other factors	Family responsibilities

ABSENTEEISM

Absenteeism can be very costly for organizations. It is estimated that approximately a million employees a day are absent from their jobs. In a year, absenteeism costs companies in the United States approximately $40 billion.[97] Not surprisingly, in an effort to reduce absenteeism, many researchers have studied its relationship to job satisfaction. Research focusing on this question has indicated that job satisfaction has a weak negative relationship with absenteeism: Employees who are satisfied with their jobs are somewhat less likely to be absent.[98]

Richard Steers and Susan Rhodes have provided a model of absenteeism that helps explain these results.[99] They propose that employee attendance is a function not only of their motivation to go to work but also of their ability to attend (see Table 3.3). An employee's *ability* to go to work is influenced by illness and accidents, transportation problems, and family responsibilities. Because of the variety of situations and factors that affect work absences, it's not surprising that the relationship between satisfaction and absenteeism is relatively weak. Job satisfaction is just one of many factors that affect the *motivation* to attend.[100]

Absenteeism is a behavior that organizations can never eliminate, but they can control and manage it. Attendance policies should not be so restrictive, however, that they literally force employees to come to work even if they are ill. A certain level of absenteeism—perhaps from a high-stress job—can be functional. Many companies, such as General Foods Corporation, have acknowledged this possibility by including "mental health days" or "personal days" in their absence policies. General Foods employees can take a mental health or personal day at their discretion. They aren't penalized for these absences, and the absences don't count toward the number of sick and vacation days they're allowed.

TURNOVER

Turnover The permanent withdrawal of an employee from the employing organization.

Turnover is the permanent withdrawal of an employee from the employing organization. Job satisfaction shows a weak-to-moderate negative relationship to turnover—that is, high job satisfaction leads to low turnover. Why is this relationship observed? Employees who are satisfied with their jobs are less likely to quit than those who are dissatisfied, but some dissatisfied employees never leave, and others who are satisfied with their jobs eventually move on to another organization. Moreover, unlike absenteeism, which is a *temporary* form of withdrawal from the organization, turnover is *permanent* and can have a major impact on an employee's life. Thus, the decision to quit a job is not usually made lightly but is instead the result of a carefully thought-out process.

When, in the turnover process, does job satisfaction play an important role? According to a model of the turnover process developed by Bill Mobley, job satisfaction triggers the whole turnover process (see Figure 3.8).[101] Employees who are very satisfied with their jobs may never even think about quitting; for those who are dissatisfied, it is the dissatisfaction that starts them thinking about quitting.

As indicated in Figure 3.8, job dissatisfaction will cause an employee to begin thinking about quitting. At this point, the individual evaluates the benefits of searching for a new job versus the costs of quitting. These costs could include any corporate

FIGURE 3.8

Mobley's Model of the Turnover Process

Source: Adapted from W. H. Mobley, "Intermediate Linkages in the Relationship Between Job Satisfaction and Employee Turnover," *Journal of Applied Psychology* 6 (1977): 237–40. Copyright 1977 by the American Psychological Association. Reprinted with permission.

benefits that are linked to seniority (such as vacation time and bonuses), the loss of pension and medical plans, and a reduced level of job security (which is often based on seniority in the organization). On the basis of this cost/benefit evaluation, the individual may decide to search for alternative jobs. The person evaluates and compares these alternatives to the current job and then develops an intention to quit or stay. The intention to quit eventually leads to turnover behavior. Hence, although job satisfaction or dissatisfaction is an important factor to consider because it may trigger the whole turnover process and start an employee thinking about quitting, other factors come into play to determine whether or not an employee actually quits. (Mobley's model applies neither to employees who impulsively quit their jobs nor to employees who quit their jobs before even looking for alternatives.)

Just as in the case of absenteeism, managers often think of turnover as a costly behavior that must be kept to a minimum. There are certainly costs to turnover, such as the costs of hiring and training replacement employees. In addition, turnover often causes disruptions for existing members of an organization; it may result in delays on important projects; and it can cause problems when employees who quit are members of teams.

Although these and other costs of turnover can be significant, turnover can also have certain benefits for organizations. First, whether turnover is a cost or benefit depends on who is leaving. If poor performers are quitting and good performers are staying, this is an ideal situation, and managers may not want to reduce levels of turnover. Second, turnover can result in the introduction of new ideas and approaches if

Staples Canada employees go the extra mile to demonstrate their commitment. Each year the company holds a 100 kilometer stationary bike race in the company's home office to raise money for the United Way. The event is webcast to all Staples stores across Canada on the company intranet.

the organization hires newcomers with new ideas to replace employees who have left. Third, turnover can be a relatively painless and natural way to reduce the size of the work-force through *attrition*, the process through which people leave an organization of their own free will. Attrition can be an important benefit of turnover in lean economic times because it reduces the need for organizations to downsize their workforces. Finally, for organizations that promote from within, turnover in the upper ranks of the organization frees up some positions for promotions of lower-level members. Like absenteeism, turnover is a behavior that needs to be managed but not necessarily reduced or eliminated.

ORGANIZATIONAL CITIZENSHIP BEHAVIOR

Organizational citizenship behavior Behavior that is not required but is necessary for organizational survival and effectiveness.

Although job satisfaction is not related to job performance, research suggests that it is related to work behaviors that are of a more voluntary nature and not specifically required of employees. **Organizational citizenship behavior** (OCB) is behavior that is above and beyond the call of duty—that is, behavior that is not required of organizational members but is nonetheless necessary for organizational survival and effectiveness.[102] Examples of OCB include helping co-workers; protecting the organization from fire, theft, vandalism, and other misfortunes; making constructive suggestions; developing one's skills and capabilities; and spreading goodwill in the larger community. These behaviors are seldom required of organizational members, but they are important in all organizations. Helping co-workers is an especially important form of OCB when it comes to computing in the workplace and learning new information technologies.

Employees have considerable discretion over whether or not they engage in acts of organizational citizenship behavior. Most employees' job descriptions do not require them to come up with innovative suggestions to improve the functioning of their departments. Nevertheless, employees often make valuable innovative suggestions, and it may be that employees who are most satisfied with their jobs are most likely to do so. Once again, because these behaviors are voluntary—that is, there are no strong situational pressures to perform them—it is likely that they are influenced by attitudes such as job satisfaction. As we saw earlier, work moods are also likely to have some impact on these behaviors. Employees who are in positive moods are especially likely to perform forms of OCB, such as helping customers or suggesting new ideas.[103]

Dennis Organ of Indiana University suggests that satisfied employees may be likely to perform these behaviors because they seek to give something back to an organization that has treated them well.[104] Organ notes that most people like to have fair exchanges with the people and organizations for which they work. Because of this desire, employees who are satisfied may seek to reciprocate or give something back to the organization by engaging in various forms of OCB.

Because the various forms of organizational citizenship behavior are not formally required of employees, they may not be formally recognized by the organization's reward and incentive systems. Often managers may not even be aware of these behaviors or may underestimate their occurrence (as in the case of employees helping others with their PC problems). This lack of awareness does not mean, however, that managers cannot recognize and acknowledge OCB that does occur.

John Brady, president of John Brady Design Consultants, developed a simple yet innovative method to acknowledge OCB. At the start of each year he gives each of his 18 employees a jar containing 12 marbles. Throughout the year, employees give marbles to others who have helped them in some way or have accomplished some out-of-the-ordinary feat. In this way, employees are recognized for the OCB that occurs and are proud of the marbles they accumulate over the year, even though they may receive no more tangible rewards (such as a bonus) for performing these behaviors.[105]

Similarly, Texas A&M University recognizes OCB by publishing accounts of OCB in the *Human Resources Newsletter* distributed periodically to all employees of the university. A special section of the newsletter titled "We Caught You Doing Something Right" chronicles instances of OCB that have taken place during the past few months. Here is a sample entry: "Michael Jackson, who works in the Library, was caught coming in on his own time to review work for a cooperative grant-funded project involving 18 Texas academic libraries. By voluntarily contributing his time, Michael has enabled the Texas Documents to the People Project to stay on schedule."[106]

EMPLOYEE WELL-BEING

Employee well-being—how happy, healthy, and prosperous employees are—is the last potential consequence of job satisfaction we consider. Unlike absenteeism and turnover, this consequence focuses on the employee rather than the organization. If you count the number of hours of their adult lives that employees spend on the job, the number is truly mind-boggling: An employee who puts in an eight-hour day, works five days a week, and has two weeks off a year for vacation works approximately 2,000 hours a year. Over a 40-year period (from age 25 to 65), this employee clocks in some 80,000 hours on the job. (These figures don't even touch on the amount of time employees spend thinking about their jobs during their time off.) Being dissatisfied with one's job for a major portion of one's working life almost certainly adversely affects well-being and general happiness. Consistent with this observation, research suggests that job satisfaction contributes to overall well-being in life.[107] According to Benjamin Amick, a professor at the University of Texas, "More satisfaction leads to improved physical and mental health and saves money through reduced health-care costs and improved productive time at work."[108]

Employee well-being How happy, healthy, and prosperous employees are.

Organizational Commitment

Whereas job satisfaction relates to feelings and beliefs that individuals have about specific jobs, organizational commitment relates to feelings and beliefs about the employing organization as a whole. Researchers have identified two distinct types of organizational commitment, affective commitment and continuance commitment.[109] **Affective commitment** exists when employees are happy to be members of an organization, believe in and feel good about the organization and what it stands for, are attached to the organization, and intend to do what is good for the organization. **Continuance commitment** exists when employees are committed not so much because they want to be but because they have to be when the costs of leaving the organization (loss of seniority, job security, pensions, medical benefits, and so on) are too great.[110] As you might imagine, affective commitment generally has more positive consequences for employees and organizations than continuance commitment.

Affective commitment The commitment that exists when employees are happy to be members of an organization, believe in and feel good about the organization and what it stands for, are attached to the organization, and intend to do what is good for the organization.

Continuance commitment The commitment that exists when it is very costly for employees to leave an organization.

DETERMINANTS OF AFFECTIVE COMMITMENT

A wide range of personality and situational factors has the potential to affect levels of affective commitment. For example, employees may be more committed to organizations that behave in a socially responsible manner and contribute to society at large. It is easier to believe in and be committed to an organization that is doing good things for society rather than causing harm, such as polluting the atmosphere. Ben & Jerry's Homemade, the ice cream company, encourages employee commitment through socially responsible corporate policies and programs that support the community and protect the environment.[111] The Body Shop, which manufactures and sells organic beauty products, engenders commitment in its employees by supporting the protection of the environment and animal rights. Employees may also be more likely to be committed to an organization that shows that it cares about its employees and values them as individuals. Managers cannot expect employees to be committed to an organization if the organization is not committed to employees and society as a whole.

you're the management expert

Increasing Affective Commitment

Juan Quintero is a division manager in a large consumer products firm. Quintero's division recently underwent a restructuring, which resulted in 10 percent of the division's employees being laid off. Quintero did everything he could to help those employees who were laid off find other positions by, for example, giving them advance notice of the layoff, enabling them to use office space at the company until they found a new job, hiring career counselors to help them figure out their best options and prepare résumés, and so forth. He also honestly explained to all employees why the restructuring and resulting layoffs were a business necessity. Prior to the layoff, Quintero felt pretty good about satisfaction and commitment levels in his division. On prior annual surveys the company had conducted, Quintero's division always came out on top in terms of employee satisfaction and commitment. However, he is beginning to worry that things might have changed, and he has data to support his fears. After informal chats with some of the division's employees, Quintero sensed diminished levels of job satisfaction and affective commitment to the company. On the latest annual survey conducted one month ago, Quintero's division scored in the lowest quartile in affective commitment. Quintero is concerned, to say the least. He cannot understand why attitudes have changed so much over the year. Even more worrisome, he does not know how to address this problem. Looking for an expert in organizational behavior, Quintero has come to you for help. Why have levels of affective commitment deteriorated in this division, and how can he bring them back up to their prior highs?

POTENTIAL CONSEQUENCES OF AFFECTIVE COMMITMENT

Managers intuitively believe that employees who are committed to an organization will work harder, and research has found affective commitment to have a weak positive relationship with job performance.[112] However, affective commitment (like job satisfaction) may be more highly related to organizational citizenship behavior (OCB). Because these behaviors are voluntary, they tend to be more directly related to employees' attitudes toward an organization. When affective commitment is high, employees are likely to want to do what is good for the organization and, thus, perform OCBs.[113] However, when continuance commitment is high, employees are not expected to go above and beyond the call of duty because their commitment is based more on necessity than a belief in what the organization stands for.

Affective commitment also shows a weak, negative relationship to absenteeism and tardiness.[114] A stronger negative relationship exists between affective commitment and turnover. Employees who are committed to an organization are less likely to quit; their positive attitude toward the organization itself makes them reluctant to leave.[115]

Summary

Values, attitudes, and moods and emotions have important effects on organizational behavior. Values (an employee's personal convictions about what one should strive for in life and how one should behave) are an important determinant of on-the-job behavior. Job satisfaction and organizational commitment are two key work attitudes with important implications for understanding and managing behaviors such as organizational citizenship behavior, absenteeism, and turnover. Work moods and emotions also are important determinants of behavior in organizations. In this chapter, we made the following major points:

1. Two important kinds of values that influence organizational behavior are work values and ethical values. Work attitudes, more specific and less long lasting than values, are collections of feelings, beliefs, and thoughts that people have about how to behave in their current jobs and organizations. Work moods and emotions, more transitory than both values and attitudes, are people's feelings at the time they actually perform their jobs. Values, attitudes, and moods and emotions all have the potential to influence each other.

2. Work values are employees' personal convictions about what outcomes they should expect from work and how they should behave at work. There are two broad types of work values, intrinsic work values and extrinsic work values. Intrinsic work values are values related to the work itself, such as doing something that is interesting and challenging or having a sense of accomplishment. Extrinsic work values are values related to the consequences of work, such as having family security or status in the community.

3. Ethical values are an employees' personal convictions about what is right or wrong. Three types of ethical values are utilitarian values, moral rights values, and justice values. Utilitarian values dictate that decisions should be made so that the decision produces the greatest good for the greatest number of people. Moral rights values indicate that decisions should be made in ways that protect the fundamental rights and privileges of people affected by the decision. Justice values dictate that decisions should be made in ways that allocate benefits and harms among those affected by the decision in a fair, equitable, or impartial manner.

4. Two important work attitudes are job satisfaction and organizational commitment. Job satisfaction is the collection of feelings and beliefs that people have about their current jobs. Organizational commitment is the collection of feelings and beliefs that people have about their organization as a whole. Work attitudes have three components: an affective component (how a person feels about his or her job), a cognitive component (what a person believes about his or her job), and a behavioral component (what a person thinks about how to behave in his or her job). People can have work attitudes about specific aspects of their jobs and organizations and about their jobs and organizations as a whole.

5. People experience many different moods at work. These moods can be categorized generally as positive or negative. When employees are in positive moods, they feel excited, enthusiastic, active, strong, peppy, or elated. When employees are in negative moods, they feel distressed, fearful, scornful, hostile, jittery, or nervous. Employees also experience less intense moods at work, such as feeling sleepy or calm. Work moods are determined by both personality and situation and have the potential to influence organizational behaviors ranging from absence to being helpful to customers and coworkers to creativity to leadership. Emotions are intense, short-lived feelings that are linked to a specific cause or antecedent. Emotional labor is the work that employees perform to control their experience and expression of moods and emotions on the job.

6. Job satisfaction is one of the most important and well-researched attitudes in organizational behavior. Job satisfaction is determined by personality, values, the work situation, and social influence. Facet, discrepancy, and steady-state models of job satisfaction are useful for understanding and managing this important attitude.

7. Job satisfaction is not strongly related to job performance because employees are often not free to vary their levels of job performance and because sometimes job satisfaction is not relevant to job performance. Job satisfaction has a weak negative relationship to absenteeism. Job satisfaction influences turnover; employees who are satisfied with their jobs are less likely to quit them. Furthermore, employees who are satisfied with their jobs are more likely to perform voluntary behaviors, known as organizational citizenship behavior, that contribute to organizational effectiveness. Job satisfaction also has a positive effect on employee well-being.

8. Organizational commitment is the collection of feelings and beliefs that people have about their organization as a whole. Affective commitment exists when employees are happy to be members of an organization and believe in what it stands for. Continuance commitment exists when employees are committed to the organization because it is too costly for them to leave. Affective commitment has more positive consequences for organizations and their members than continuance commitment. Affective commitment is more likely when organizations are socially responsible and demonstrate that they are committed to employees. Employees with high levels of affective commitment are less likely to quit and may be more likely to perform organizational citizenship behavior.

Exercises in Understanding and Managing Organizational Behavior

Questions for Discussion and Review

1. How would you describe a person you know who has strong intrinsic and extrinsic work values?

2. Why might two employees with the same job develop different attitudes toward it?

3. On what kinds of jobs might the moods that employees experience be particularly important for understanding why they behave as they do?

4. Why are attitudes less long lasting than values, and why are moods more transitory than attitudes?

5. What specific standards might people use to determine their satisfaction with different facets of their jobs?

6. Why is job satisfaction not strongly related to job performance?

7. Should managers always try to reduce absenteeism and turnover as much as possible? Why or why not?

8. In what kinds of organizations might organizational citizenship behaviors be especially important?

9. What specific things can an organization do to raise levels of affective commitment?

10. In what kinds of organizations might affective commitment be especially important?

Building People Skills

Understanding Your Own Experience of Work

1. Describe your work values. Are they predominantly extrinsic or intrinsic?

2. How would your work values affect your reactions to each of these events at work?

   A. Getting promoted

   B. Being reassigned to a position with more responsibility but receiving no increase in pay

   C. Having to work late at night and travel one week a month on a job you find quite interesting

   D. Having a stressful job that pays well

   E. Having an exciting job with low job security

3. Describe your mood over the past week or two. Why have you felt this way? How has your mood affected your behavior?

4. What facets of a job are particularly important determinants of your level of job satisfaction? What standards do you (or would you) use to evaluate your job on these dimensions?

5. Toward what kind of organization are you most likely to have affective commitment? Toward what kind of organization are you most likely to have continuance commitment?

6. How might your affective commitment to an organization affect your behavior?

7. What forms of organizational citizenship behavior are you especially likely to perform and why? What forms of organizational citizenship behavior are you least likely to perform and why?

A Question of Ethics

On some jobs, employees are expected to perform emotional labor most of the time. Salespeople, for example, are often required to be cheerful and polite, even to the most unpleasant customers. However, this can create high levels of stress for employees to the extent that they often have to hide their true feelings. Additionally, to the extent that a customer is rude or abusive, demands for emotional labor might be questionable on ethical grounds.

Questions

1. Are there limits to the extent to which an employer should require employees to perform emotional labor? If so, what are these limits? If not, why not?
2. Under what condition do you think it would be unethical to require emotional labor from employees? Be specific.

Small Group Break-Out Exercise

Identifying Unethical Behavior

Form groups of three or four people, and appoint one member as the spokesperson who will communicate your conclusions to the rest of the class:

1. Take a few minutes to think about instances in which you observed unethical behavior taking place in an organization (as an employee, customer, client, or observer).
2. Take turns describing these instances.
3. Each person then should take a few minutes to write down criteria that help to distinguish ethical behavior from unethical behavior.
4. Using input from Step 3, as a group, come up with the key criteria that you think should be used to determine whether behavior is ethical or unethical.

Topic for Debate

Values, attitudes, and moods and emotions have important implications for understanding and managing organizational behavior. Now that you have a good understanding of values, attitudes, and moods and emotions, debate the following issue.

Team A. Because job satisfaction is not related to job performance, managers do not need to be concerned about it.

Team B. Managers *do* need to be concerned about job satisfaction even though it is not related to performance.

Experiential Exercise

Promoting Organizational Citizenship Behavior

Objective

Organizations work most effectively when their members voluntarily engage in organizational citizenship behaviors. It is likely that you have witnessed some kind of organizational citizenship behavior. You may have seen this behavior performed by a co-worker or supervisor where you work. You may have seen this behavior when you were interacting with an organization as a customer or client. Or someone in your university (a faculty or staff member or a student) may have gone above and beyond the call of duty to help another person or the university as a whole. Your objective is to identify instances of OCB and think about how managers can promote such behavior.

Procedure

Each member of the class takes a few minutes to think about instances of organizational citizenship behavior that he or she has observed and makes a list of them. The class then divides into groups of three to five people, and each group appoints one member as spokesperson to present the group's conclusions to the whole class. Group members do the following:

1. Take turns describing instances of organizational citizenship behavior they have observed.
2. Discuss the similarities and differences between each of these instances of organizational citizenship behavior and suggest some reasons why they may have occurred.
3. Compile a list of steps that managers can take to promote organizational citizenship behavior.

Spokespersons from each group report the following back to the class: four examples of organizational citizenship behavior that group members have observed and three steps that managers can take to try to promote OCB.

Making the Connection

Find an example of an organization that recently made some changes that have the potential to improve employees' attitudes or moods. Why did this organization make these changes? Why do you think these changes might improve employees' attitudes or moods?

New York Times Cases in the News

The New York Times

This Mayor's a Workhorse, and She Does It for Nothing

BY SARAH KERSHAW

SALEM, Oregon

AT 60, Janet Taylor was contemplating retirement. But there was the nagging question of what she could do for Salem, the city she describes as her "salvation."

Salem is the city where Mrs. Taylor's mother, who was raising her four children alone, nearly deaf and suffering from other health problems that made it difficult for her to work, moved the family in 1956. It was then a small town, the slow-moving Oregon state capital in the Willamette River Valley.

The children, born in Portland, 47 miles north of here, were raised on welfare in a blue-collar neighborhood in northeast Salem. Which is all the more reason Mrs. Taylor still sounds awed and tickled when she talks about being the new mayor of Salem.

"I feel like this is really, truly a way that maybe I can give some good back again," said Mrs. Taylor, who won the mayoral primary in May 2002 with such a high percentage of the vote, 63 percent, that she was declared the winner and allowed, under Oregon law, to bypass the general election, although she did not take office until last January.

"When people say to me, 'I can't believe you're doing it,' I say, 'I can't believe that I wouldn't have tried,'" she said. "Truthfully, I needed to say thank you."

When the previous mayor decided not to run, Mrs. Taylor, who is 61, received a lot of encouragement to jump into the race. She had been managing a successful metal roofing company that she and her husband, Duane, started in the early 1980's, but had been involved in Salem politics, first through her local neighborhood association, and later as the chairwoman of the board of Salem's economic development corporation. She was also vice president of the Chamber of Commerce. All these positions provided her with a raw look at an economically depressed city, she said, that was in dire need of new, pro-business leadership.

But she was also discouraged from running—by Duane, for one, who had retired in 1995—and other friends and associates who advised her that becoming mayor of Salem, the second largest city in Oregon with a population of 142,000, when the city was struggling would wear her out.

"Knowing her as a business associate and as a friend, I told her I thought she should be enjoying the fruits of her labor," said Larry Glassock, the president of the Strategic Economic Development Corporation of the mid-Willamette Valley, the board of which Mrs. Taylor was chairwoman. "Being mayor was going to interfere with that. We had a heart-to-heart and I had her convinced for about 30 days."

Salem has a long history of volunteerism. Dozens clean the parks, staff the libraries and patrol the city's neighborhoods, and volunteerism is an ethic that Mrs. Taylor, as mayor, often mentions. So it was fitting, she said, that she would take on the challenge for no compensation. Technically, the job pays $274 a month, but

Mrs. Taylor declined the stipend, saying she thought the money could go to better uses.

In July, six months after she took office, the Taylors sold their metal roofing business, Taylor Metal Products. Although they are still receiving some income from it, Mrs. Taylor is making a lot less money.

In Salem, the city manager, who draws a salary, runs the daily operations, and the mayor and city councilors set policy. The job of mayor could, potentially, be mostly ceremonious, presiding over the Monday night City Council meetings and attending the occasional ribbon cutting or ground-breaking.

But Mrs. Taylor, who has the demeanor of a chipper school principal and often describes things, particularly the various new development projects she has spearheaded in Salem, as just wonderful, has made her tenure as hands-on as possible. She works 40 to 50 hours a week and has already declared she will run for a second two-year term. She had no plans to become a career politician at the outset, she said, but she was not ruling out running for other offices later on.

"If you'd asked me three or four months ago, I would have said no," Mrs. Taylor said, referring to the possibility of making a career of politics. "But I think I'd like to see what opportunities are there and make that assessment down the road."

She said the two-year mayoral term seemed too short, since she took office. "I'd like to accomplish some things here before I make any decisions. It was never about going into politics, it was that I wanted to head this ship in a positive direction and change the political climate."

Mrs. Taylor is a registered Republican, although she was a Democrat for 20 years, and said she defied political pigeonholing.

Her days are a whirl of activity, usually beginning by 7:30 with meetings—on what to do about the huge waste-water fees being imposed on Salem by the federal government, or about the silicon-chip company that is threatening to leave town with hundreds of jobs because it can receive much better tax breaks in Ohio.

What Mrs. Taylor says she loves about the job are the little and big victories that make her feel that she is making a difference. For instance, the $32 million convention center downtown, which the city was planning to build for 40 years, was stalled until last summer, when Mrs. Taylor and other city officials got involved and helped cut through the red tape. Construction began in August and the center is scheduled for completion in 2005.

Then there was the Puentes Brothers tortilla factory, whose owner, George Puentes,

was so frustrated by the city bureaucracy standing between him and a new plant that he was also planning to leave Salem.

But Mr. Puentes, who knew Mrs. Taylor as a member of the Chamber of Commerce, was receptive to her hard selling of Salem, and decided he would stay. And Mrs. Taylor promised him she would help streamline the permit process for building a new tortilla factory. He employs 110 people and the city, Mrs. Taylor said, could ill afford to lose those jobs.

"We knew we had to grow, but we weren't going to do it blindly," Mr. Puentes said, during a recent tour with Mrs. Taylor of the new plant, which opened in October in the northeast part of the city. "And then Janet got elected and I said, 'I think we'll stay.'"

Mrs. Taylor smiled and said: "Thank you, George. I really appreciate it."

Mrs. Taylor acknowledged that she was not entirely prepared for the pressure-cooker atmosphere that comes with being mayor of a city plagued by unemployment, fiercely fighting to keep businesses, create new jobs and revitalize its slowly recovering historic downtown district.

"People say I'm thriving on it, that it has energized me," Mrs. Taylor said. "Both are true. It has challenged me at times. It has exhausted me. But it feels so wonderful to me, it truly does."

SOURCE: "This Mayor's a Workhorse, and She Does It for Nothing," by S. Kershaw, *New York Times*, November 17, 2003, 23.

Questions for Discussion

1. What values are important to Janet Taylor?

2. How would you characterize her attitudes about her job as mayor?

3. What kinds of emotions and moods do you think she experiences on the job?

4. Why, at age 60, has she agreed to be mayor of Salem, Oregon (and not get paid for it)?

The New York Times

<u>Youthful Attitudes, Sobering Realities</u>

A Tough Labor Market Hasn't Shaken Priorities Of Younger Workers

BY JULIE CONNELLY

Patrick Keyes, a senior partner and director for business development at Ogilvy & Mather Worldwide, the advertising agency in New York, enjoys acting as a mentor to his young staff members. Mr. Keyes, 40, says it is a powerful substitute when he cannot agree to their demands for raises or bonuses.

"After we complete a pitch for new business," he said, "there are always opportunities to tell them what they did right, or explain how they might have done it better."

Mr. Keyes's coaching can be quite specific, particularly when young people are too casual in communicating with senior executives. "I had to explain," he said, "that it wasn't the best idea for a junior person to conclude an e-mail to the president of Ogilvy with, 'Thoughts?'"

In many ways, his comments capture the attitudes of America's newest labor force, 30-something workers—the so-called Generation X—and their 20-something counterparts, Generation Y, who are old enough to be starting careers. This group, ages 20 to 34, makes up roughly a third of the working population, according to the Bureau of Labor Statistics.

These younger workers are often viewed as demanding, self-absorbed and presumptuous, but also as ambitious, free-thinking and eager to learn. They form "a dramatically different labor market that is changing not just the way people are hired and fired, but also how they view their jobs, their employers and their careers," said Peter Cappelli, the author of "The New Deal at Work: Managing the Market-Driven Workforce" and a professor of management at the Wharton School of the Business at University of Pennsylvania.

They think of themselves as free agents and want to rewrite the rules. But for now, they just need a job.

Because of an unsettled economy and an employment market that has not been kind to these workers, they think there is no reward for loyalty and are reluctant to make longterm commitments. Though they have been called disloyal and unwilling to pay their dues, the reality is that they are adapting to a workplace in which "corporations broke the old arrangement unilaterally," Professor Cappelli said. "They've seen what's gone on with their parents' generation, and a lack of trust in the corporation is a perfectly rational response to that."

This lack of trust is giving rise to another phenomenon, a sense of free agency among young workers who expect to create lifetime careers not with one or two companies, but as independent contractors, selling their services on a project basis to many employers. Each new job is a new negotiation—for pay, obviously, but also for control of the working environment, balance between work and private life and training for the next job.

According to Bruce Tulgan, the founder of RainmakerThinking, a consulting firm in New Haven that studies young workers: "Free agency has swept across the entire work force. Skilled workers of all ages are trading stability for mobility."

The strain is most developed in the 30-something workers who have never known a stable workplace and grew up mainly as self-reliant latchkey children. "As a result," Mr. Tulgan, 36, said, "X'ers are used to facing problems on our own and have great confidence in our ability to fend for ourselves."

That may explain why young workers seem to be self-centered in their approach. "The things they ask us about are benefits, rewards and career opportunities—the things that impact 'me'—rather than where are we going to be as a company in 10 to 15 years," said John Lankford, the director for management education and leadership development at Oakwood Healthcare in Dearborn, Mich., who recruits young workers.

Mr. Tulgan views this as a sophisticated response to a workplace that operates without the myth of job security. In the last two decades, businesses have embraced large layoffs in the name of cost cutting while reducing benefits for those employees who somehow escaped the scythe. "They don't want to be suckers," he said of younger workers. "They look around and say: 'Don't tell me about the long-term. Do you think I'm a fool?'"

The current economy is putting the concept of free agency to the test. Unemployment is higher among younger workers than in the general population. As of September 2003, the national unemployment rate was 6.1 percent, but it was 10.9 percent for those 20 to 24 and 6.3 percent for those 25 to 34, according to the Bureau of Labor Statistics.

Jeff Taylor, the chairman and founder of the Internet bulletin board Monster.com, said that "of the college class of 2003, 93 percent are still looking for full-time employment." Monster.com, which is aimed at workers of all ages, is popular with young people. On Oct. 21, an online poll of 4,570 visitors to the site revealed that when finding a job, 71 percent planned to stay put, 14 percent expected to move on within two months and 14 percent planned to leave within six months.

These numbers, while reflecting the state of the job market, also highlight the mixed message that many young workers send out: though leery of company loyalty, they long for a stable and comfortable work environment.

Though a better economy might encourage David Wallsh to start looking around, he plans to stay in his current job. At 25, he is a customercare consultant for LendingTree.com, an Internet lending service in Charlotte, N.C. He was hired in July 2001, and it is his fourth job since he graduated from Muhlenberg College in Allentown, Pa. A psychology major who wanted to go into human resources, Mr. Wallsh received no job offers after he graduated, so he took jobs as a desk clerk in two hotels and then answered phones at a bank's call center.

He found out about LendingTree at a job fair, and his first position was working the night shift answering e-mail messages from customers. It took him more than six months to be hired permanently, but now he has been promoted and is working days.

At this point, he said: "My seniority is more important than a paycheck. I might want to become a loan officer."

Another young person who finds herself driven by the economy into doing work she never expected to do is Keeley Canning Luhnow, 28. She graduated from Wake Forest University School of Law in Winston-Salem, N.C. in May 2002, expecting to practice hospitality law. Though her husband had a job in San Diego, she was willing to relocate for an opportunity to join a big law firm. But she received no offers from firms in any of the cities she and her husband were willing to move to, so she accepted a position as an associate in a one-person firm in La Mesa, Calif., specializing in elder law.

"I wasn't very keen on elder law when I took the job," she said, "but I've grown to like it. My future depends on what happens with the job market, but my employer hopes I'll inherit her practice."

Experts predict that although young workers are glad to have jobs now, they will grow restless once the economy improves. And when employers start vying for these young workers again, experts say, they will have to make an effort to overcome the young people's cynicism and deal with their contradictory behavior.

"These young people have moved a lot and they come from broken marriages," said Chris Widener, the president of Made for Success, a leadership consulting firm in Issaquah, Wash. "They look for stability, community, security in the workplace, and if they don't get it they'll move on to another employer."

Regina Richardson, 26, a senior sales manager at the Millennium Hotel in Cincinnati, has been with the company for four years. What keeps her there, she said, is a boss who "pushes me to achieve what is seemingly unattainable, so I can move ahead with my career." Plus, she said: "It's a friendly place. We all know each other's kids' names and dogs' names."

Even so, Ms. Richardson is not sure she will stay with the company for the long haul. She was raised by a single mother, whom she is proud of and who has worked in the registrar's office at Pennsylvania State University for nearly 18 years. "She's very happy where she is," Ms. Richardson said. "But where the older generation considers it stability, I consider it being stuck."

Christian Reyes, 28, a senior quality assurance engineer at Electronic Arts, an entertainment software developer in Redwood City, Calif., is equally wary. "We all have these hopes that there will be opportunities for us to build loyalty to the job, though we're cynical," he said. Mr. Reyes has had three jobs since graduating from college. Most of his friends, he said, did the dot-com hopscotch, and most have settled for pay cuts and temporary jobs in the aftermath of the Internet bust.

Complicating life for many employers is that with Gen X'ers, everything is apparently open for negotiation. "This is a generation that is used to asserting itself," said Jeff Chambers, the vice president for human resources at SAS, a software company in Cary, N.C. "They know they are mobile; they know they have opportunities."

Judith Gerberg, the director of Gerberg & Company, a career counseling service in New York, said that many young workers were used to negotiating with their parents "and they bring this behavior into the office."

Mr. Lankford, the health care recruiter, said that young workers often challenged company policies on matters like tuition reimbursement. "Their attitude is, 'Why won't you pay for this?'" he said. "Instead of accepting that these are our policies, they'll say: 'Let's talk about making an exception.' Or, 'Let's change the policies.'"

Mr. Lankford, 52, said he was inclined to extend himself not only because the health care industry is in a ferocious bidding war for talent but also because "these people think out of the box."

A frequent point of negotiation is the work-life balance. "No matter how bad the economy gets, these workers won't work in an environment they don't like," said Ann A. Fishman, president of Generational Targeted Marketing, a research company in New Orleans. "They are willing to give up salaries to have quality of life in the workplace."

Young workers are turned off by having to put in "face time." For instance, they think, why can't we tote our laptops to the wireless cafe and log in from there?

"The old 40-hour workweek just doesn't apply," said Conrad Sam, 29, director for sales and marketing at Smashing Ideas, a Web site developer in Seattle. "The average age here is 27 or 28, and people come in when they want. If there's work to be done, you'll stay and do it. No one I know would ever work for anyone where there's a premium on face time."

Education and training are other negotiating matters: free agents quickly discover that survival depends on keeping their skills current. "They want to learn constantly because once they stop learning, they stop being viable," said Heather Neely, a consultant at Rainmaker-Thinking.

Ultimately, many experts think that negotiation as a model is unsustainable because it causes each employee to focus on his or her own needs instead of the task at hand. "But what does work is giving people latitude around their working conditions," said Rebecca Ryan, the founder of Next Generation Consulting, a company in Jackson, Wis., that advises businesses on how to attract young talent.

Managing younger workers can be challenging. Bosses sometimes complain about these employees' short attention spans and habits like talking to friends via cellphone or by instant messaging or downloading music while engaged in job-related tasks.

"Multitasking is a myth," said Jennifer B. Kahnweiler, the founder of About You, a career counseling company in Dunwoody, Ga. "I watch my daughters talking on the phone while instant-messaging someone else, watching television and reading a book. You can't transfer that to the business environment. It won't work—you lose something important if you don't pay attention."

Yet the appeal of young workers springs from many of the traits that drive their bosses crazy, especially their independence and belief that they should be given special projects, rather than dues-paying chores.

"They are willing to take on tasks they have no knowledge about and they fearlessly march ahead," Mr. Keyes said. "I like that."

SOURCE: "Youthful Attitudes, Sobering Realities," by J. Connelly, *New York Times,* October 28, 2003, E1, E6.

Questions for Discussion

1. What are members of Generation X and Generation Y trying to obtain out of life and working?

2. How do they believe one should behave at work?

3. What role do loyalty and commitment play in the workplace today?

4. How might the values and attitudes of members of Generations X and Y lead to changes in the workplace?

Perception, Attribution, and the Management of Diversity

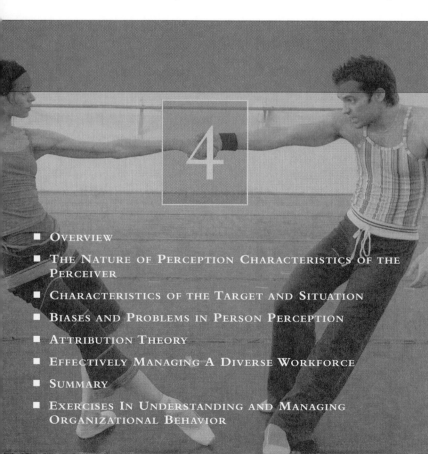

4

LEARNING OBJECTIVES

After studying this chapter, you should be able to:

■

Describe how perception is inherently subjective and how characteristics of the perceiver, the target, and the situation can influence perceptions.

■

Understand how the use of schemas can both aid and detract from accurate perceptions.

■

Be aware of biases that can influence person perception.

■

Understand why attributions are so important and how they can sometimes be faulty.

■

Appreciate why the effective management of diversity is an imperative for all kinds of organizations and the steps that organizations can take to effectively manage diversity.

■

Describe the two major forms of sexual harassment and the steps organizations can take to combat sexual harassment.

OPENING CASE

Proactively Managing Diversity

Why Do Organizations Need to Guard Against Discrimination and Proactively Manage Diversity?

Many people believe that discrimination is a thing of the past. They acknowledge that discrimination in the workplace was a serious problem in earlier times but feel that today, heightened awareness of the problem, as well as the significant legal and financial consequences that can result from it, have eliminated most forms of discrimination.

Unfortunately, discrimination is not a thing of the past. Class-action discrimination lawsuits are still being settled every day to the tune of millions of dollars. For example, over the past 10 years, the Adam's Mark chain of luxury hotels agreed to pay $8 million to settle a racial discrimination lawsuit;[1] Texaco settled a $176.1 million racial discrimination lawsuit involving 1,400 employees;[2] Ford Motor Company agreed to pay $3 million to settle allegations that women and minority applicants were discriminated against in the hiring process at several Ford plants;[3] and Coca-Cola settled a racial discrimination lawsuit for $192.5 million.[4] Currently, unsettled suits alleging workplace discrimination are pending at organizations ranging from Johnson & Johnson and BellSouth to the National Football League.[5]

When managers become aware of evidence of potential discrimination, they need to pay immediate attention and act proactively to address the potential problem and perhaps change the organization's policies and practices. How problems were addressed at General Motors when its minority dealership program was in trouble is a case in point. Problems with the program became apparent in a report prepared by civil rights attorney Weldon Latham. The report addressed alleged problems ranging from minority dealers being overcharged for their dealerships and given undesirable locations to being inadequately trained and having their life savings depleted as a result. GM's program was originally designed to eliminate discrimination, but it seemed to be hurting rather than helping minority dealers.

Eric Peterson, who had recently become head of the minority dealership program when Latham's report came out, took quick, proactive steps and implemented 213 of Latham's 215 recommendations to solve the problems he had docu-

mented. General Motors now responds to minority dealers' complaints within 30 days; 80 percent of minority dealers are now earning a profit compared to only 50 percent before the changes, and approximately 16 percent of minority dealerships are earning more than $1 million, which compares favorably with statistics for GM dealerships overall.[6]

Cyrus Mehri, a well-known attorney who specializes in discrimination lawsuits, not only seeks financial compensation for the victims of discrimination, but he also seeks to proactively change the organizations accused of it. For example, Mehri was involved in the Texaco and Coca-Cola lawsuits. As part of the settlements he helped to negotiate, both companies were required to have seven-person diversity task forces, appointed from outside the company, that have the authority to investigate, monitor, and make changes to company policies and practices. The goal is to ensure that minorities are fairly treated.

This is one of the many ways Mehri proactively looks for innovative ways to help victims and organizations resolve discrimination suits and, equally important, improve the functioning of organizations for everyone's betterment. For example, Mehri recently represented African-American employees who filed a class-action lawsuit alleging racial discrimination at the Nashville automobile-glass plant of Visteon Corporation. The suit couldn't have come at a worse time, given that the plant was already losing money. Working with Bob Poppell, an attorney representing Visteon, Mehri negotiated a settlement whereby Visteon would publicly issue a report card twice a year breaking down salaries, raises, and promotions by race and gender.[7]

When minorities and women are discriminated against, not only do the victims suffer, but so too do other employees and the organization as a whole. Diverse employees are valuable contributors to organizational effectiveness. When they are unfairly treated, the organization suffers by not being able to fully realize all they have to offer. Ironically, sometimes discrimination goes undetected and even its victims do not realize the injustices they are experiencing. For this reason, Mehri advocates the kind of openness and transparency that now exists at Visteon due to the initiation of the semiannual diversity report cards. As Mehri says, "Transparency acts like a Pentium chip to bring about change. . . . It's better than litigation . . . Once you go from secrecy to disclosure, you can change a company overnight."[8]

Often two people in an organization with the same qualifications are viewed differently. One may be seen as much more capable than another, even though there is no objective basis for this distinction—the "more capable" person doesn't perform at a higher level. The opening case shows, for example, that African Americans and other minorities in business settings are sometimes seen as less capable and competent than nonminority employees, even when they have identical qualifications.

As another example of the way people can view things differently, think of the last group meeting you attended and the different ways in which people in the group interpreted what went on in the meeting. One person might have seen the final decision as the result of an impartial consideration of all alternatives, but another person might have seen it as the result of a powerful member imposing her or his will. Similarly, what might have appeared to be a reasonable, lively discussion to one person was a noisy, incomprehensible free-for-all to a second, and deeply offensive to a third. The fact is that each of us sees and interprets the same people, objects, and events differently.

In this chapter, we look at how perception and attribution help people organize, make sense of, and interpret what they observe. We discuss why equally qualified members of an organization or equally well-intentioned customers are perceived differently, why people who attend the same meeting might have different interpretations of what went on, and even why two people who watch the same movie might come away with very different opinions about it. A major focus of this chapter is the role of perception and attribution in the effective management of diverse employees. Throughout the chapter, we give examples of how managers can enhance their ability to manage diverse employees by paying attention to the way they perceive and judge other people.

Perception and attribution are of fundamental importance in understanding and managing organizational behavior because all decisions and behaviors in organizations, such as the management of diversity, are influenced by how its members interpret and make sense of the people and events around them. Decisions about who should be hired, fired, transferred, or promoted and decisions about how to encourage organizational members to be more productive, to be more helpful to co-workers, or to perform otherwise desirable organizational behaviors are all based on managers' interpretations of the situations they face. Managers at all levels of an organization who understand how perception and attribution shape such interpretations are in a good position to try to ensure that their decisions help rather than harm the organization and its members. Understanding perception and attribution can actually help people at all levels of an organization interact with others and be more effective in their jobs.

The Nature of Perception

Perception is the process by which individuals select, organize, and interpret the input from their senses (vision, hearing, touch, smell, and taste) to give meaning and order to the world around them.[9] Through perception, people try to make sense of their environment and the objects, events, and other people in it. Perception has three components (see Figure 4.1):

Perception The process by which individuals select, organize, and interpret the input from their senses.

1. The *perceiver* is the person trying to interpret some observation that he or she has just made or the input from his or her senses.

2. The *target of perception* is whatever the perceiver is trying to make sense of. The target can be another person, a group of people, an event, a situation, an idea, a noise, or anything else the perceiver focuses on. In organizational behavior, we are often concerned with *person perception*, or another person as the target of perception.

FIGURE 4.1

Components of Perception: Perceiver, Target, and Situation

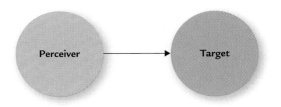

Situation or context in which perception takes place

3. The *situation* is the context in which perception takes place—a committee meeting, the hallway, in front of the office coffee machine, and so on.

Characteristics of all three components influence what is actually perceived.

People tend to think that perception is a simple phenomenon. They believe that there is an objective reality—a reality that exists independent of who observes or describes it—and that as long as their senses are not impaired (as long as they see clearly, hear well, are not intoxicated, and so forth), perception is simply the understanding of this objective reality. People who believe in objective reality tend to believe that their own perceptions are accurate depictions of that reality. They believe that they perceive the true nature of the target (see Figure 4.1) and behave as if this were the case.

The perceptual process, however, does not always yield **accurate perceptions**—perceptions that are as close as possible to the true or objective nature of the target. Even people who are trying to be totally "objective" often base their decisions and act on an interpretation of reality that is subjective—that is, one that is based on their own thoughts, feelings, and experiences. As a result, interpretations of reality vary among individuals. What is seen depends on who is doing the looking.

The fact that perception is not always accurate has significant implications for understanding and managing organizational behavior. Virtually every decision that a manager makes—whether it be about hiring, firing, compensating organizational members, and so on—depends on the perceptions of the decision maker, so accurate perceptions are the prerequisite for good decisions. When perceptions are inaccurate, managers and other members of an organization make faulty decisions that hurt not only the employees involved but also the organization. Why are accurate perceptions of such fundamental importance in organizational behavior in general and in managing diverse employees in particular? The answer to this question touches on issues of motivation and performance, fairness and equity, and ethical action.

Motivation and Performance. Recall from Chapter 1 that a major responsibility of managers at all levels is to encourage organization members to perform to the best of their abilities in ways that help the organization achieve its goals. In essence, managers need to make sure that subordinates are motivated to perform at a high level. Because motivation and performance are of such fundamental importance in organizations, in Chapters 6 and 7 we discuss them in detail and the organizational behavior tools that managers can use. However, in order to use these tools and motivate their subordinates, managers need to first have an understanding of their diverse subordinates and see them as they really are. The more accurately managers perceive subordinates, the better able they are to motivate them. For example, a manager who accurately perceives that a subordinate is independent and resents close supervision will be more likely to give the subordinate the breathing room he or she needs. Similarly, if a manager accurately perceives that a subordinate who shies away from difficult tasks has the ability to do them but suffers from low self-esteem (one of the personality traits discussed in Chapter 2), the manager will be more likely to assign to the subordinate tasks of an appropriate level of difficulty while at the same time providing the

Accurate perceptions
Perceptions that are as close as possible to the true nature of the target of perception.

encouragement and support the subordinate needs. Accurate perceptions also help managers relate to each other and enable members at all levels to work together to achieve organizational goals.

Fairness and Equity. Suppose a manager supervises a diverse group of 20 subordinates and every six months the manager has to decide how well each subordinate performed and how big a bonus each deserves. When the manager makes these decisions, it is extremely important that his or her perceptions of each subordinate's performance are as accurate as possible. If the manager's perceptions are inaccurate, the wrong decisions will be made, and some employees are likely to believe they are not being fairly treated and perhaps even being discriminated against. If some of the high performers receive lower bonuses than some of the mediocre performers, for example, the high performers might feel they are not being treated fairly. As you will see in Chapter 6, fair and equitable treatment is important when it comes to motivating employees. Consequently, inaccurate perceptions on the part of the supervisors of these high performers may breed resentment and and cause them to minimize their efforts: Why should they bother to try so hard when their efforts are not being recognized? Similarly, as suggested by the opening case, if African Americans are passed up for promotions because they are mistakenly perceived to be less competent, this unfair treatment hurts not only these employees but also the organization as a whole because it won't fully be utilizing the talents of all of its members. Ultimately, some minority employees may leave the organization to seek fairer treatment elsewhere; this turnover will further weaken the organization. It is, therefore, extremely important that managers' perceptions be accurate because their decision making and ultimate effectiveness depend on it.[10]

Ethical Action. We mentioned in Chapter 1 that the workforce is becoming increasingly diverse and members of an organization often interact with others who may be different from them in age, race, gender, ethnicity, and other characteristics. Accurately perceiving diverse members of an organization and their abilities, skills, and performance levels is not only a legal requirement but also an ethical necessity. To give these individuals the opportunities and rewards they deserve, avoid illegal discrimination, and act in an ethical manner, a manager's perceptions must, therefore, be accurate. Managers and others who understand what perceptions are, how they are formed, and what influences them are in a better position to ensure this happens and that the organization benefits from it.

Characteristics of the Perceiver

Have you noticed that several people can observe the same person or event and come away with different interpretations of what they saw? That suggests that something about the perceiver may influence his or her perception.

Perceivers do not passively process information. Their experience or knowledge (*schemas*), their needs and desires (*motivational states*), and their feelings (*moods*) filter information into their perceptions of reality (see Figure 4.2). We now consider the way each of these characteristics of the perceiver affects perception.

FIGURE 4.2

Characteristics of the Perceiver That Affect Perception

SCHEMAS: THE PERCEIVER'S KNOWLEDGE BASE

When John Cunningham, a project manager at the engineering firm Tri-Systems Inc., was assigned to a new supervisor (a retired Air Force colonel), he did not gather a lot of information before forming an impression of him. Instead, he took whatever information was at hand (however incomplete) and developed his own view or perception of his new boss. Simply knowing that his new supervisor used to be in the military was enough to convince Cunningham that he had a pretty good handle on what the retired colonel was like. Cunningham's supervisor in his last position had served in the armed forces, and Cunningham had found him bossy and opinionated. To a neutral observer, such limited information (the supervisor's military background) hardly seems sufficient to support an assessment. But for Cunningham, the equation was simple: His new ex-military supervisor would be opinionated and bossy just as his other one had been.

Like Cunningham, we all interpret the world around us on the basis of limited information. In large part, we rely on past experience and the knowledge we have gathered from a variety of sources to interpret and make sense of any new person or situation (the *target of perception*) we encounter. Our past experiences are organized into **schemas**, abstract knowledge structures that are stored in memory and allow people to organize and interpret information about a given target of perception.[11] Once an individual develops a schema for a target of perception (such as a former military person), any new target related to the schema activates it, and information about the target is processed in a way consistent with information stored in the schema. Thus, schemas determine the way a target is perceived.

Schemas help people interpret the world around them by using their past experiences and knowledge. Think about the last time you went to a party where there were many people you didn't know. How did you decide whom to talk to and whom to try to avoid? Without realizing you were doing so, you probably relied on your schemas about what different types of people are like to form your perceptions and then decided with whom you wanted to spend some time.

John Cunningham's schema for "ex-military supervisor" indicates that "ex-military supervisors are bossy and opinionated." Because his new boss was in the military, Cunningham perceives him as bossy and opinionated. All perceivers actively interpret reality so that it is consistent with their expectations, which are, in turn, determined by their schemas.[12]

Schemas also influence the sensory input we pay attention to and the input we ignore. Once a schema is activated, we tend to notice information that is consistent with the schema and ignore or discount information that is inconsistent. Because of his schema, Cunningham is especially attuned to any information that indicates that his new supervisor is bossy and opinionated (the boss has already rearranged the office layout), but Cunningham tends to ignore information to the contrary (the boss solicits and listens to other people's suggestions).

By selecting sensory input consistent with existing schemas and discounting or ignoring inconsistent input, schemas are reinforced and strengthened. It is not surprising, then, that schemas are resistant to change.[13] Resistance does not indicate that schemas are immutable; if they were, people would be unable adapt to changes in their environment. Schemas are, however, slow to change. A considerable amount of contradictory information must be encountered before a person's schemas are altered and he or she is able to perceive a target differently.

Are Schemas Functional? Many times we jump to the wrong conclusions and form inaccurate perceptions of other people based on our schemas, especially when we have limited information about the target. Schemas, nevertheless, are functional for perceivers. We are continually bombarded with so much sensory input, so many potential

Schema An abstract knowledge structure that is stored in memory and makes possible the organization and interpretation of information about a target of perception.

targets of perception, that we cannot possibly take them all in and make sense of each one. Schemas help us make sense of this confusing array of sensory input, help us choose what information to pay attention to and what to ignore, and guide our perception of often ambiguous information. In this way, schemas help members of an organization learn about and adapt to the complex environment inside and outside the organization.

Schemas can be dysfunctional, however, if they result in inaccurate perceptions. Cunningham's new supervisor may not be at all bossy or opinionated but may instead be an accessible, competent, and talented manager. Cunningham's schema for "ex-military supervisor," however, causes him to perceive his boss in a different, and negative, light. Thus, Cunningham's schema is dysfunctional because his inaccurate perceptions color his interactions with his new boss.

Inaccurate perceptions can also be dysfunctional for the target of perception. Some men in business have schemas that fit successful female professionals into a pigeonhole marked "wife, mother, daughter."[14] When a man with such a schema encounters a woman in an organization, the schema is activated, and the man perceives the woman as less competent and capable in a business context than she actually is. This incorrect perception can hurt the woman's future prospects when she is passed up for promotion or denied access to financing to start her own business.

Schemas can guide perceptions in a functional way, but we have to guard against the common tendency to jump to incorrect conclusions based on our past experiences.[15] John Cunningham clearly did not have enough information to have an accurate perception of his supervisor, and he should have refrained from making a judgment until he saw how his supervisor actually behaved on the job.

Stereotypes: An Example of a Dysfunctional Schema.

A **stereotype** is a set of overly simplified and often inaccurate beliefs about the typical characteristics of a particular group. We all are familiar with stereotypes based on highly visible characteristics such as race, gender, nationality, or age, and we are aware of the damage they can do.[16] Stereotypes are dysfunctional schemas because they are often based on inaccurate information about individuals' interests, beliefs, capabilities, behaviors, and so on. Stereotyped individuals are assigned to the schema only because they possess a single distinguishing characteristic.

As soon as a person is encountered and stereotyped, the perceiver assumes that the person has the characteristics associated with the stereotype.[17] The perceiver pays attention to information consistent with the stereotype and ignores inconsistent information. Because objective reality (what the person is really like) rarely matches subjective reality (what the perceiver *thinks* the person is like), stereotypes can be dysfunctional and damaging to the perceiver, the target, and the organization.

Stereotypes based on race, gender, and age have been responsible for discrimination in society in general and in the workplace in particular. As a result of the negative effects of such stereotypes, it is illegal to discriminate against people because of their race, gender, or age, and organizations that do so may face lawsuits, as indicated in the opening case.

Employees have to guard against thinking stereotypically about different types of organizational members. One way to do so is to encourage members of an organization to think about the characteristics that really affect job performance and not irrelevant characteristics like age, race, or gender. Discriminating against or treating employees differently because of their gender, age, or race is not only illegal but also unethical. Moreover, it is unethical to discriminate against employees based on any characteristic unrelated to performance whether it is sexual orientation, religion, disabilities, or country of origin. In the years since the fateful September 11 terrorist attacks. Arab Americans and others of Middle Eastern descent have been victims of discrimination in the workplace as indicated in the accompanying OB Today.

Stereotype A set of overly simplified and often inaccurate beliefs about the typical characteristics of a particular group.

People have a natural tendency to gravitate towards those like themselves. Employees and firms need to actively guard against stereotyping by concentrating on an individual's personal strengths and weaknesses and how well they match up with the job—not their age, race, or gender.

ob today

When Appearance Takes on a Totally New Meaning

Chirinjeev Kathuria is a successful American entrepreneur. With dual M.B.A. and M.D. degrees, he has co-founded numerous global telecommunications companies and local broad-band companies. Kathuria is also a Sikh, has a beard, and wears a turban. His appearance was never an issue until September 11, 2001. Since that time, however, he has experienced firsthand the toll that discrimination takes on its victims on a day-to-day basis. Air travel has become a nightmare, passersby on the street sometimes shout derogatory comments at him, and investment bankers seem more skeptical about his ventures. Ruefully, Kathuria empathizes with African Americans who sometimes still experience discrimination inside and outside the workplace.[18]

Kathuria's experience resonates with Fawaz Ismail, founder and CEO of Alamo Flags, the largest U.S. retail supplier of flags. After September 11, Ismail, a Palestinian American, and his employees have been treated with suspicion and derision, even by some customers as they purchase U.S. flags. For example, Alamo's chief financial officer, Aladdin Cherkaoui, who is of Morrocan descent, recalls a customer asking him if the money he just paid for some flags would be going to Osama bin Laden. And another of his employees of Jordanian descent, who went to an emergency room in Brooklyn, New York, for medical treatment, was beaten and robbed by security guards.[19]

Some Arab Americans have lost their jobs due to post–September 11 discrimination and are having a hard time finding new ones. Osama Sweilan lost his job at Federal Express after suspicions were raised about why he was visiting the flight simulator room. And Mamdouh Bayoumy claims that a company reneged on a job offer he had previously accepted.[20] Of course, heightened concerns over security and safety are justified and have made life more complicated for everyone. However, rather than discriminating against and alienating Arab Americans and immigrants from Arab countries, perhaps their help should be solicited in fighting terrorism. As *BusinessWeek* editor Alex Salkever suggests of Middle Eastern immigrants: "With their cultural sensibilities and understanding of Farsi and Arabic, they are better able to spot signs of terrorist activity than some Arabist desk jockey buried by reams of mostly meaningless communications intercepts."[21]

THE PERCEIVER'S MOTIVATIONAL STATE

Perceiver's motivational state The needs, values, and desires of a perceiver at the time of perception.

The **perceiver's motivational state**—the perceiver's needs, values, and desires at the time of perception—influences his or her perception of the target. Perceivers see what they want to see, hear what they want to hear, and believe what they want to believe because of their motivational state. A simple yet ingenious experiment has demonstrated the effects of the perceiver's motivational state. Participants are shown a series of meaningless abstract pictures and are asked what objects and shapes they perceive in them. The images they see depend on their motivational states. Those who are hungry, for example, are motivated to see food and actually do indicate that they perceive images of food in the abstract pictures.[22]

Like schemas, motivational states can result in inaccurate perceptions and faulty decision making. Suppose a manager does not get along with a hardworking, productive subordinate. The subordinate is a thorn in the manager's side, and the manager would welcome any opportunity to justify recommending that the subordinate be transferred to another position or even dismissed. What is likely to happen when the manager must evaluate the subordinate's performance on some relatively subjective dimensions such as cooperation and being a good team player? Even if the subordinate actually deserves to score high, the manager may rate the person low.

Organizational members need to be aware that their own needs and desires influence their perceptions and can result in faulty decisions that have negative consequences for the organization. One way managers can guard against this outcome is to base perceptions on actual behaviors they have observed a person performing. In sum, managers need to be aware of their own motives, concentrate on perceiving how people actually perform, and refrain from assuming how someone probably behaved when they did not directly observe his or her behavior.

THE PERCEIVER'S MOOD

The **perceiver's mood**—how the perceiver feels at the time of perception—can also influence perception of the target. In Chapter 3, we discussed how work moods (people's feelings at the time they perform their jobs) influence organizational behavior. People's moods also affect their perception of a target.[23]

Marie Flanagan, a fashion designer for a clothing manufacturer, was so excited about the new line of women's suits she finished designing late one afternoon that she could hardly wait to show her sketches to her supervisor Phil Kraus the next day. But when Flanagan saw Kraus in the hallway the next morning, he barely grunted "hello," and later that morning his secretary told Flanagan that Kraus was in a terrible mood. Despite her eagerness to find out what Kraus thought of her new line, Flanagan decided to wait until he was in a better mood before showing him her sketches. She reasoned that even if the new line was a potential winner, Kraus was likely to find fault with it because of his bad mood. She realized that people's moods influence their perceptions and judgments. When employees are in a positive mood, they are likely to perceive their co-workers, supervisors, subordinates, and even their jobs in a more positive light than they would when they are in a negative mood.[24]

Perceiver's mood How a perceiver feels at the time of perception.

Characteristics of the Target and Situation

We defined *perception* as the process whereby people select, organize, and interpret the input from their senses to give meaning and order to the world around them. This input comes from the targets of perception in the situations in which they are perceived. Thus, just as characteristics of the perceiver influence perceptions, so, too, do the characteristics of the target and the situation (see Table 4.1).

How do characteristics of the target influence perception? Consider two job applicants (the targets of perception) who have similar qualifications and are equally capable. An interviewer (the perceiver), however, perceived one applicant much more positively than the other because of the way each acted during the interview. One applicant tried to make a good impression by volunteering information about his past accomplishments and achievements and behaving in a confident and businesslike fashion. The other was low key and mentioned his achievements only when he was specifically asked about them. The difference in behavior caused the interviewer to perceive one applicant as more capable than the other.

Here is an example of how the situation influences perception. Suppose you (the perceiver) see one of your friends (the target) wearing a bathing suit at the beach (the situation). You might perceive that he is relaxed and enjoying himself. Now suppose you see the same friend wearing a bathing suit at work (another situation). You perceive that he is psychologically disturbed.

In this section, we consider the ambiguity and social status of the target and impression management by the target. We then discuss how characteristics of the situation influence perception by providing additional information for the perceiver to use to interpret the target. Managers and other members of an organization who are aware

TABLE 4.1

Factors That Influence Perception

Characteristics of the Perceiver	Characteristics of the Target	Characteristics of the Situation
Schemas: The perceiver's knowledge base	Ambiguity: A lack of clearness or definiteness that makes it difficult to determine what a person, place, or thing is really like	Additional information: Situational information that the perceiver uses to interpret the target
Motivational state: The perceiver's needs, values, and desires at the time of perception	Social status: A person's real or perceived position in society or an organization	Salience: The extent to which a target stands out among a group of people or things
Mood: The perceiver's feelings at the time of perception	Use of impression management: A person's efforts to control others' perceptions of him or her	

of the ways in which various target- and situation-related factors influence perception are well positioned to ensure that their perceptions of people, things, and events are as accurate as possible.

AMBIGUITY OF THE TARGET

The word *ambiguity* refers to a lack of clearness or definiteness. It is difficult for a perceiver to determine what an ambiguous target is really like. As the ambiguity of a target increases, it becomes increasingly difficult for perceivers to form accurate perceptions. It is also more likely that different perceivers will differ in their perceptions of the target.

Consider the case of four managers who are jointly responsible for choosing new locations for fast-food restaurants for a national chain. Certain locations (for example, those across the street from a large university) are sure winners and others (for example, those difficult to enter and leave because of traffic congestion) are sure losers. Such locations are relatively unambiguous targets of perception. Each of the four managers perceives them accurately, and they agree with each other about the desirability of those locations.

When the nature of a target is clear, different perceivers have little difficulty forming similar perceptions of the target that are close to its real nature. But when a target is ambiguous, the perceiver needs to engage in a lot more interpretation and active construction of reality to form a perception of the target. The suitability of some of the locations that the four managers must evaluate is ambiguous. Will a restaurant located in a once prosperous but now failing shopping mall that is being renovated do well? Will a restaurant located on the outskirts of a small town in a rural area attract enough customers to earn a profit? The managers' perceptions of the desirability of such locations tend to be less certain than their perceptions of less ambiguous locations, and they often find themselves disagreeing with each other.

The more ambiguous a target is, the more potential there is for errors in perception. Thus, when targets are ambiguous, members of an organization should not be overly confident about the accuracy of their perceptions, and they should acquire as much additional information as they can to help them form an accurate perception. When looking at ambiguous restaurant locations (to continue our example), the four managers should collect a lot of information—estimates of the performance levels of other fast-food restaurants in the vicinity, traffic patterns at mealtimes, population growth in the area, spending patterns of likely patrons, and so on—to be sure their perceptions are accurate before they make a decision.

SOCIAL STATUS OF THE TARGET

Social status is a person's real or perceived position in society or in an organization. In the minds of many people, targets with a relatively high status are perceived to be smarter, more credible, more knowledgeable, and more responsible for their actions than lower-status targets. Organizations often use a high-status member to make an important announcement to other members of the organization or to the public at large because the audience is likely to perceive the announcer as credible. A lower-status member of the organization who is more knowledgeable than anyone else about the issue at hand is likely to lack credibility because of his or her status.

To ensure that women and members of minority groups enjoy equal footing with white men and have the social status they deserve in an organization and to conform to legal requirements, many organizations have adopted affirmative action programs. These programs, however, sometimes perpetuate the perception problems and stereotypes they were meant to overcome. Women and minority group members are sometimes perceived as having relatively low status in the organization because they were affirmative action hires—people hired not because of their own merits but because of their gender or minority status. Their affirmative action status causes other members of the organization to perceive and treat them as second-class citizens.

U.S. courts have been increasingly restricting affirmative action programs in universities on the grounds that they are unconstitutional. The Business-Higher Education Forum, a recently formed cooperative consisting of 25 corporations, 36 universities, and 7 nonprofit organizations is nonetheless seeking to promote diversity in the college admissions process. CEOs of major corporations support the Forum because in the years to come they want to be able to hire and maintain a diverse workforce reflecting the broader diversity of their customer bases.[25]

IMPRESSION MANAGEMENT BY THE TARGET

Impression management is an attempt to control the perceptions or impressions of others.[26] Just as a perceiver actively constructs reality through his or her perceptions, a target of perception can also play an active role in managing the perceptions that others have of him or her.

People in organizations use several impression management tactics to affect how others perceive them. They are especially likely to use these tactics when interacting with perceivers who have power over them and on whom they are dependent for evaluations, raises, and promotions.[27] Subordinates, for example, use impression management tactics on their supervisors to a greater extent than supervisors use them on subordinates. Nevertheless, impression management is a two-way street engaged in by people at all organizational levels as they interact with superiors, peers, and subordinates as well as with suppliers, customers, and other people outside the organization. Table 4.2 describes five common impression management tactics: behavioral matching, self-promotion, conforming to situational norms, appreciating or flattering others, and being consistent.

Conforming to situational norms—the informal rules of behavior that most members of an organization follow—is a particularly important impression management tactic.[28] Situational norms can pertain to working past the traditional 5 P.M. quitting time to impress the boss, disagreeing with others in meetings to be seen as important, or even dressing to make a good impression.

People differ in the extent to which they conform to situational norms and engage in other forms of impression management. In Chapter 2, we discussed how people who are high on the trait of self-monitoring are especially concerned about behaving appropriately. It is likely, therefore, that people who are high on self-monitoring are more likely than individuals who are low on self-monitoring to engage in impression management tactics such as conforming to situational norms.

Social status A person's real or perceived position in society or in an organization.

Impression management An attempt to control the perceptions or impressions of others.

TABLE 4.2

Impression Management Tactics

Tactic	Description	Example
Behavioral matching	The target of perception matches his or her behavior to that of the perceiver.	A subordinate tries to imitate her boss's behavior by being modest and soft-spoken because her boss is modest and soft-spoken.
Self-promotion	The target tries to present herself or himself in as positive a light as possible.	An employee reminds his boss about his past accomplishments and associates with co-workers who are evaluated highly.
Conforming to situational norms	The target follows agreed-upon rules for behavior in the organization.	An employee stays late every night even if she has completed all of her assignments because staying late is one of the norms of her organization.
Appreciating or flattering others	The target compliments the perceiver. This tactic works best when flattery is not extreme and when it involves a dimension important to the perceiver.	A co-worker compliments a manager on his excellent handling of a troublesome employee.
Being consistent	The target's beliefs and behaviors are consistent. There is agreement between the target's verbal and nonverbal behaviors.	A subordinate whose views on diversity are well known flatters her boss for her handling of a conflict between two co-workers of different racial backgrounds. When speaking to her boss, the target looks her boss straight in the eye and has a sincere expression on her face.

Source: C. N. Alexander, Jr., and G. W. Knight, "Situated Identities and Social Psychological Experimentation," *Sociometry* 34 (1971): 65–82; S. T. Fiske and S. E. Taylor, *Social Cognition* (Reading, MA: Addison-Wesley, 1984); K. J. Gergen and M. G. Taylor, "Social Expectancy and Self-Presentation in a Status Hierarchy," *Journal of Experimental Social Psychology* 5 (1969): 79–92; D. Newston and T. Czerlinsky, "Adjustment of Attitude Communications for Contrasts by Extreme Audiences," *Journal of Personality and Social Psychology* 30 (1974); 829–37; B. R. Schenkler, *Impression Management: The Self-Concept, Social Identity, and Interpersonal Relations* (Monterey, CA: Brooks/Cole, 1980); M. Snyder, "Impression Management," in L. S. Wrightsman (Ed.), *Social Psychology in the Seventies* (New York: Wiley, 1977).

Conforming to situational norms can often be difficult for people operating in the international arena. Common courtesies and gestures that are taken for granted in one culture or country may be frowned on or downright insulting in another. The common hand signal for "OK" that is used in the United States, for example, is considered obscene in Brazil, Ghana, Greece, and Turkey and means "zero" or "worthless" in France and Belgium. As another example, in the United States it is considered polite to ask a man how his wife is, but in Arab countries this inquiry is considered indiscreet.[29]

Outright deceit can be used in impression management but is probably not very common. Ingrained moral or ethical codes prevent most people from deliberately misrepresenting themselves or lying.[30] In addition, the chances of being found out are often pretty high. Claiming on an employment application, for example, that you attended a certain school or worked for a company though you never did is neither honest nor smart. Most impression management is an attempt to convey as positive an impression as possible without lying about one's capabilities, achievements, and experiences. People are especially likely to engage in impression management when they are likely to benefit from it. The reward may be desirable job assignments, promotions, raises, or the good opinions of others.

INFORMATION PROVIDED BY THE SITUATION

The situation—the context or environment surrounding the perceiver and the target—provides the perceiver with additional information to use in interpreting the target. Consider the situation Marci Sloan was in when she started a new job as supervisor of salespeople in a large department store. The department store had just begun a push to increase the quality of customer service, and Sloan's boss impressed on her that improved service to customers should be a major priority for her department. On her first day on the job, Sloan decided to spend as much time as she could unobtrusively observing her salespeople in action so she could get a good idea of the level of service they were routinely providing.

The levels of service offered by the four salespeople she was able to observe varied considerably. In forming her perceptions of these salespeople, however, she relied not only on the behavior she observed but also on the situation in which the behavior occurred. One key factor was how busy the department was when she observed each salesperson. She observed two of them in the morning when business was slow. Each person handled only two customers, but one salesperson provided significantly more service than the other. She observed the other two salespeople in the late afternoon, the busiest time of day for the department. Both had a continual stream of customers. One salesperson handled more customers than the other, but the slower salesperson gave each customer more personal attention. Clearly, Sloan could not rely solely on the behavior of the salespeople in forming her impression of the customer service they were providing. She also had to consider all the additional information that the situation provided.

STANDING OUT IN THE CROWD: THE EFFECTS OF SALIENCE IN A SITUATION

In considering how the situation affects perception, we need to focus on one factor that is particularly important: the **salience** of the target in the situation—that is, the extent to which the target stands out in a group of people or things. We have all experienced the effects of salience. Have you ever been the only student in a room full of professors, the only man in a group of women, or the only African American person in a room full of white people? A salient individual is very conspicuous and often feels self-conscious. He or she believes that everyone is watching his or her every move. That assessment is pretty accurate too. The other people in the group or room do pay more attention to the salient person, for he or she indeed does stand out. Salience, in and of itself, *should not affect* how a target is perceived. After all, a man is the same person regardless of whether he is in a room full of men or women. But remember that perception is a subjective process and, because of that subjectivity, salience *does affect* how a target is perceived. Table 4.3 lists some situational factors that cause a target to stand out.

Salience The extent to which a target of perception stands out in a group of people or things.

TABLE 4.3

Causes of Salience

Cause	Description	Examples
Being novel	Anything that makes a target unique in a situation	Being the only person of a particular age, sex, or race in a situation; wearing jeans when everyone else is dressed in business clothes
Being figural	Standing out from the background by virtue of being bright or illuminated, changing, moving, sitting or standing in a prominent place, or seeming to be complex	Being in a spotlight; moving more than others in a group; sitting at the head of the table; wearing bright clothes
Being inconsistent with other people's expectations	Behaving or looking in a way that is out of the ordinary	A normally shy person who is the life of the party; a salesperson who insults a customer; a man or woman who is exceptionally attractive

Source: S. T. Fiske and S. E. Taylor, *Social Cognition* (Reading, MA: Addison-Wesley, 1984); R. M. Kanter, *Men and Women of the Corporation* (New York: Basic Books, 1977); L. Z. McArthur and E. Ginsberg, "Causal Attribution to Salient Stimuli: An Investigation of Visual Fixation Mediators," *Personality and Social Psychology Bulletin* 7 (1981); 547–53; L. Z. McArthur and D. L. Post, "Figural Emphasis and Person Perception," *Journal of Experimental Social Psychology* 13 (1977); 520–35; C. Wolman and H. Frank, "The Solo Woman in a Professional Peer Group," *American Journal of Orthopsychiatry* 45 (1975): 164–71.

What are the consequences of salience for perception in organizations? Consider the experiences Mary Schwartz has had as the only female partner in a small consulting firm. Her male colleagues treat her as their equal, and she gets along well with each of them, but she still feels the effects of her salience. These effects take the form of extreme evaluations and stereotyping.

Extreme Evaluations. Schwartz noticed that her male colleagues' reactions to her various accomplishments and mishaps on the job seemed to be extreme. She recently landed a major new account for the firm and received such lavish praise that she became embarrassed. Likewise, when she was unable to attend an important meeting because of a family problem, it was made clear to her that she had lost favor in everyone's eyes.

Schwartz's experience is not unique. Individuals who are salient are often perceived in more extreme terms (positive or negative) than inconspicuous members of a group. They are also seen as being especially influential or responsible for what happens to them and to the groups they belong to.[31]

Stereotyping. On several occasions Schwartz felt that her male colleagues were unintentionally stereotyping her as a "typical woman." They frequently called on her to enlighten them about the "woman's point of view" on various matters such as how to deal with a female client or subordinate. On several occasions, Schwartz was tempted to tell her colleagues that all women are not alike and to point out that she had more in common with them even though they were men than she had in common with their female subordinates or clients.

Individuals who are salient, like Schwartz, are often perceived in terms of whatever is causing their salience: They are stereotyped.[32] Perceivers consider the thoughts, feelings, and behaviors of salient individuals to be more consistent with their distinguishing feature than would be the case if they were not salient. Perceivers often also view them as being representative of all people who are like them with regard to the salient characteristic.

Being salient and stereotyped in a situation can actually result in a target's performance being adversely affected.[33] Research by Claude Steele, a psychologist at Stanford University, has found that when people who are salient think about stereotypes that are relevant to task performance, their performance might actually be impaired.[34] Performance impairment occurs because salient, stereotyped individuals become concerned that others will perceive them based on the stereotype, which distracts them and diverts some of their attention away from task performance.[35] This phenomenon, called *stereotype threat,* can affect the performance of individuals who are salient for a variety of reasons.[36]

The decisions of Justice Sandra Day O'Connor, the first woman to serve on the U.S. Supreme Court were closely watched following her appointment in 1981 by President Ronald Reagan. Justice O'Connor's first major case came in 1982. She wrote an opinion holding that a male student could not be rejected from a nursing school because of his gender.

Salience due to race has particularly powerful effects on perception. Although there are more African Americans and minorities in management positions today than there were several years ago, African American managers still experience the effects of their relative salience and stereotyping. A recent study found that 45 percent of minority senior executives had been the butt of cultural or racial jokes while on the job, and 44 percent reported that they had to control their anger resulting from differential treatment at work. More than half of the executives felt that their organizations gave less challenging assignments to minorities.[37] Other research suggests that a little less than half of minority employees believe that their organizations are not trying hard enough to provide opportunities for nonwhite employees. Thus, it may not be surprising that African American employees see less of a connection between their levels of performance and the pay they receive and are less likely to feel that they are paid well than their white counterparts.[38] Fortunately, the situation is improving and more and more organizations are taking concrete steps to reduce the negative effects of salience and stereotyping on minority employees. One such step that seems to be effective is linking managers' bonuses to diversity goals and initiatives. According to *Fortune* magazine, 38 of the 50 best companies for minorities to work for do this, and it is helping provide more opportunities and a fairer workplace for all employees.[39]

Another group of employees who have felt the negative effects of salience and stereotyping are people with disabilities. There are 15 million people with disabilities in the United States of working age and only one quarter of them are working. Of the 75 percent who are not employed, two-thirds wish they had a job.[40] The Americans with Disabilities Act (ADA), passed by Congress in 1990 and put into effect in 1992, requires that organizations make their buildings and workplaces accessible to the disabled and provide accommodations to enable disabled employees to do their jobs.[41]

Biases and Problems in Person Perception

We have been describing what perception is, how and why perceptions are formed, and the powerful effects they have on organizations and their members. Throughout this discussion, we emphasized the importance of accurate perceptions. Accurate perceptions enable managers to evaluate subordinates' performance correctly and make fair and ethical decisions about whom to hire and promote. They also enable members of an organization to understand and get along with each other and with clients, customers, and other people outside the organization.

You might think that once members of an organization are armed with this knowledge of perception (as you are now), their perceptions would be greatly improved, and they would do a better job of seeing other people (targets) as they really are. Unfortunately, biases and problems in person perception limit the accuracy of perception,[42] and dramatic improvement does not always come about.

A **bias** is a systematic tendency to use or interpret information about a target in a way that results in inaccurate perceptions. When bias and problems in person perception exist, perceivers form inaccurate perceptions of a target. In turn, when perceptions are inaccurate, decisions are likely to be inappropriate: An incompetent subordinate gets promoted, or a competent job candidate receives a negative rating from an interviewer. Managers, co-workers, and subordinates who are aware of biases and problems in person perception are in a good position to prevent them from affecting their subsequent behavior and decisions. We have already examined how stereotypes can bias perception. In this section, we look at primacy, contrast, and halo effects and other common biases (see Table 4.4).

Bias A systematic tendency to use or interpret information in a way that results in inaccurate perceptions.

TABLE 4.4

Biases and Problems in Person Perception

Source of Bias	Description	Example
Primacy effects	The initial pieces of information that a perceiver has about a target have an inordinately large effect on the perceiver's perception and evaluation of the target.	Interviewers decide in the first few minutes of an interview whether or not a job candidate is a good prospect.
Contrast effect	The perceiver's perceptions of others influence the perceiver's perception of a target.	A manager's perception of an average subordinate is likely to be lower if that subordinate is in a group with very high performers rather than in a group with very low performers.
Halo effect	The perceiver's general impression of a target influences his or her perception of the target on specific dimensions.	A subordinate who has made a good overall impression on a supervisor is rated as performing high-quality work and always meeting deadlines regardless of work that is full of mistakes and late.
Similar-to-me effect	People perceive others who are similiar to themselves more positively than they perceive those who are dissimilar.	Supervisors rate subordinates who are similar to them more positively than they deserve.
Harshness, leniency, and average tendency	Some perceivers tend to be overly harsh in their perceptions, some overly lenient. Others view most targets as being about average.	When rating subordinates' performances, some supervisors give almost everyone a poor rating, some give almost everyone a good rating, and others rate almost everyone as being about average.
Knowledge of predictor	Knowing how a target stands on a predictor of performance influences perceptions of the target.	A professor perceives a student more positively than she deserves because the professor knows the student had a high score on the SAT.

PRIMACY EFFECTS

Despite the old saying "You can't judge a book by its cover," you have probably heard or learned firsthand how important first impressions are. Scientific evidence, however, supports the folk wisdom of the adage. **Primacy effect** is the biased perception that results when the first pieces of information that people have about some target have an inordinately large influence on their perception of the target.

Primacy effects are common problems in interviews. Research has found that many interviewers decide in the first few minutes of an interview whether a job candidate is a good prospect and then spend the rest of the interview confirming their initial judgment by selectively paying attention to information that is consistent with that judgment and discounting or ignoring inconsistent information. An interviewer who falls victim to the primacy effect may turn down qualified interviewees who fail to perform well in the first minute or two of an interview because they are nervous.

Primacy effects can also be a problem in the perception and evaluation of longtime members of an organization. The manager of a subordinate who starts out on the fast track but then begins to slide downhill may fail to perceive the subordinate's performance problems because of the primacy effect. The manager's perception of the subordinate's current level of performance is biased by the subordinate's early success. As a result of this

Primacy effect The biased perception that results when the first information that a perceiver has about a target has an inordinately large influence on the perceiver's perception of the target.

faulty perception, the manager will fail to give the subordinate the feedback and coaching necessary to get the subordinate back on track. Organizational members who are aware of primacy effects can be on guard not to let their first impressions distort their perceptions. For example, if a new hire comes to work with visible tattoos or body piercings, this personal appearance choice should not influence perceptions of how capable or conscientious the new hire might be.

CONTRAST EFFECTS

A **contrast effect** is the biased perception that results when perceptions of a target person are distorted by the perceiver's perception of others in the situation. A manager's perception of a subordinate whose performance is average is likely to be less favorable if that subordinate is in a group of very high performers than it would be if that subordinate were in a group of average or low performers. An average job applicant will be perceived more favorably by an interviewer if he or she is preceded by two or three below-average applicants rather than by two or three above-average applicants. Both the manager and the interviewer in those examples are victims of the contrast effect. The subordinate's and the job applicant's performance and capabilities are not changed at all by the behavior of other employees and applicants.

Contrast effect The biased perception that results when perceptions of a target person are distorted by the perceiver's perception of others.

HALO EFFECTS

A **halo effect** occurs when the perceiver's general impression of a target distorts his or her perception of the target on specific dimensions.[43] A subordinate who has made a good overall impression on a supervisor, for example, may be rated as performing high-quality work and always meeting deadlines (specific dimensions of performance) even though the person's work is full of mistakes and is usually late. Because of the halo effect, the subordinate will not receive the feedback necessary to improve performance on the specific dimensions in question. Halos can be negative too: A supervisor who has a negative overall impression of a subordinate may mistakenly perceive that the subordinate is uncooperative and spends too much time on the telephone.

Halo effect The biased perception that results when the perceiver's general impression of a target distorts his or her perception of the target on specific dimensions.

SIMILAR-TO-ME EFFECTS

It is a fact of life that people tend to like others who are similar to themselves. In organizations, this "birds of a feather"/"like likes like" tendency can create problems because people tend (often unconsciously) to perceive those who are similar to themselves more positively than they perceive those who are dissimilar. During a performance appraisal, for example, supervisors may rate subordinates who are similar to them more positively than they deserve.[44] Likewise, interviewers may evaluate potential candidates who are similar to themselves more positively than they rate candidates who are dissimilar. Similar-to-me effects can be particularly problematic for women and minority group members trying to climb the corporate ladder. For example, similar-to-me effects may lead male CEOs to groom as their successors men who are like themselves and not perceive a woman as a viable successor.[45]

The similar-to-me bias is especially important to overcome today given the increasing diversity in organizational membership. In a workforce that includes many women, members of minority groups, and increasing numbers of people with disabilities, managers and subordinates have more frequent contact with people unlike themselves. When evaluating others who are different, people must try to be as objective as possible and avoid the similar-to-me trap.

Members of an organization also have to be on the lookout for the similar-to-me bias when interacting with people from other cultures. For example, when researchers from three global organizations—Siemens AG of Germany, Toshiba Corporation of Japan, and IBM—joined forces at IBM's East Fishkill, New York, facility to work together to develop a revolutionary computer chip, the similar-to-me bias struck. Some of the researchers tried to interact primarily with people from their own cultures. Some of the Japanese researchers, for instance, tried to work mainly with other Japanese researchers, rather than with the German or American researchers, whom they perceived as "so different."[46]

HARSHNESS, LENIENCY, AND AVERAGE TENDENCY BIASES

When rating a subordinate's performance, some supervisors tend to be overly harsh, whereas some are overly lenient. Others tend to rate everyone as being about average. Any of these tendencies is problematic for two reasons. First, the supervisor does not correctly perceive the variations in the performance of his or her subordinates. As a result, high performers do not receive appropriate recognition and rewards for their superior accomplishments, and low performers do not receive the constructive feedback they need to improve performance.

The second reason why these biases are problematic is that they make it difficult to evaluate and compare the performance of subordinates who have different supervisors. A subordinate who has received relatively poor ratings from a harsh supervisor may be just as accomplished as a subordinate who has received average or high ratings from a lenient one. Evaluations biased in this manner can result in faulty decision making about pay raises and promotions. These biases can also operate in classroom settings. One professor, for example, gives mostly A's in a course in which another professor maintains a C+ class average. Students in the first professor's class may be content, but those in the other professor's class are likely to feel that they are not being fairly treated.

KNOWLEDGE-OF-PREDICTOR BIAS

To decide whom to hire, how to assign jobs to newly hired and existing members of an organization, and whom to promote, organizations measure people's standing on different predictors of performance. Depending on the job in question, the indicators used to determine how well a person will be able to accomplish work activities in the future can range from educational background and prior work experiences, to standardized tests scores, and performance on certain critical job-related tasks.

If co-workers, managers, or others in the organization know what a person's standing on a predictor of performance is, the information may bias their perceptions of the person. This problem is known as **knowledge-of-predictor bias**. If a professor knows, for example, that a student has scored highly on some predictor of academic performance such as the Scholastic Aptitude Test (SAT) or the Graduate Management Admission Test (GMAT), this knowledge may lead the professor to perceive the student more positively than he or she deserves. This bias could also work to the disadvantage of a person who scored poorly on the predictor.

Sometimes, knowledge-of-predictor bias results in a **self-fulfilling prophecy**—a prediction that comes true because a perceiver expects it to come true.[47] The classic demonstration of this phenomenon took place in a classroom setting in the 1960s. At the beginning of the school year, teachers were told that a few of their students were potential "late bloomers" who, given the proper encouragement, should excel. In fact, these students had been randomly selected from the class rosters and were no different from their peers. Later on in the school year, however, the "late bloomers" were indeed doing better and had even improved their scores on standardized IQ tests compared to their earlier performance and the performance of the other children in the class.[48] What was responsible for the change? The teachers in the study probably gave the "late bloomers" more attention, encouragement, and feedback and had higher expectations of them, all of which resulted

Knowledge-of-predictor bias The biased perception that results when knowing a target's standing on a predictor of performance influences the perceiver's perception of the target.

Self-fulfilling prophecy A prediction that comes true because a perceiver expects it to come true.

in their improved performance. The teachers may have also looked more at these students and made encouraging body gestures toward them. In this way, knowledge of a predictor (in this case, a false predictor) resulted in behavior changes that caused that prediction to become true. Research has also shown that when an interviewer conveys negative expectations to a job applicant simply through nonverbal body language, the applicant performs poorly.[49] This situation hurts both the applicant and the organization; the applicant won't get the job, and the organization may lose a potentially capable member.

Sometimes, self-fulfilling prophecies can occur in an entire work group. A group of construction workers, for example, may be very responsible and perform highly when their supervisor has high expectations and treats them with respect. The same workers, however, may act lazy and perform at a low level when they have a supervisor who has low expectations and a derogatory attitude toward them.

Attribution Theory

Through the process of perception, people try to make sense of their environment and the people in it. Sometimes, however, just making sense of a target does not produce good understanding. To return to an earlier example, if you see your friend wearing a bathing suit at work, you perceive that he has a psychological problem. This perception may lead you to wonder why he has the problem. To answer the question of "why," you attribute your friend's behavior to a certain cause. Your explanation of his behavior is an **attribution**.

Attribution theory describes how people explain the causes of their own and other people's behavior. Attribution theory is interested in why people behave the way they do and what can be done to change their behavior. Consider the case of Martin Riley, a newly hired production worker at Rice Paper Products. Riley worked at a much slower pace than his co-workers; he always seemed to be lagging behind the other members of his production team. The big question in his supervisor's mind was why. Attribution theory focuses on how the supervisor and how Riley himself explain the cause of Riley's lackluster performance.

In organizations, the decisions that are made and the actions that are taken are based on attributions for behavior. Only when these attributions are accurate (that is, only when the real cause of a behavior has been determined) are good decisions likely to be made and appropriate actions taken. In a job interview, for example, whether a qualified applicant who is quiet and fails to ask questions receives an offer often depends on the interviewer's attributions for this behavior. Is the applicant a shy person who takes a while to warm up to new people? Was the applicant suffering from a bad case of nerves? Is the applicant not really interested in the job? If the interviewer makes the last attribution for the applicant's behavior, an offer will probably not be forthcoming. If that attribution is inaccurate, however, and the applicant was simply nervous, then the organization may be missing an opportunity to hire one of the best applicants for the job.

Similarly, supervisors' reactions to high or low performance by subordinates often depend on the attributions the supervisors make. A supervisor who attributes a subordinate's high performance to exceptional ability may give the subordinate increasingly challenging assignments and eventually recommend a promotion. If the subordinate's high performance is attributed to luck, however, no changes may be made in the subordinate's assignments. In either case, if the attributions are incorrect, problems are likely to result: The subordinate will be overwhelmed by challenging assignments or will not receive the challenges he or she thrives on. When subordinates perform poorly, supervisors are likely to provide additional on-the-job training if they attribute poor performance to a lack of knowledge rather than to laziness. If laziness is the real cause, however, training is not likely to improve performance.

Attribution An explanation of the cause of behavior.

Attribution theory A group of theories that describe how people explain the causes of behavior.

Smooth day-to-day interactions among members of an organization often hinge on the extent to which people's attributions are accurate.[50] If a co-worker snaps at you a couple of times one day, and you correctly attribute the co-worker's behavior to the personal problems he is having at home, these small incidents are not going to damage your relationship. If you incorrectly attribute this behavior to the co-worker's dislike for you, however, you may start avoiding him and treating him in a cold and distant manner, which will cause your relationship to deteriorate.

INTERNAL AND EXTERNAL ATTRIBUTIONS

Internal attribution An attribution that assigns the cause of behavior to some characteristic of the target.

People generally attribute someone's behavior to internal and external causes (see Figure 4.3). An **internal attribution** assigns the cause of behavior to some characteristic of the target and assigns credit or blame to the individual actor. Martin Riley's supervisor at Rice Paper Products might attribute Riley's poor performance to personal limitations: (1) Riley lacks the ability to perform at a higher level; (2) Riley is not making an effort to work faster; (3) Riley has a low need for achievement. Attributions to ability, effort, and personality are the most common internal attributions that people make.

External attribution An attribution that assigns the cause of behavior to outside forces.

However much people like to feel that they are in control of what happens in their lives, outside forces often play a decisive role in determining behavior. **External attributions** assign the cause of behavior to factors outside the individual. The most common external attributions relate to task difficulty and luck or chance. A salesperson who has just landed a major contract, for example, may have been successful because her company is the sole provider of a particular product in a certain geographic region or because the customer was in a particularly good mood at the time of negotiations. In the first case, the salesperson's success is attributed to the easiness of the task; in the second case, it is attributed to luck.

Whether attributions for a behavior are internal or external is an important determinant of how people respond to the behavior. If the supervisor of the salesperson mentioned previously correctly attributes the landing of the major contract to external causes such as an easy task or luck, getting this contract may have little impact on the supervisor's decisions about the salesperson's job assignments and suitability for promotion. But if the supervisor incorrectly attributes the behavior to an internal cause such as ability, the supervisor might promote this salesperson instead of another one who is more deserving but covers a more difficult territory.

The attributions people make for their own behavior also influence their own subsequent actions. An employee who fails on a task and attributes this failure to a lack of ability may be likely to avoid the task in the future or exert minimal effort

FIGURE 4.3
Types of Attributions

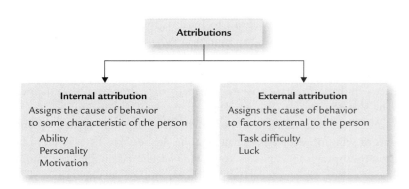

on it because he feels that his lack of ability will almost certainly guarantee a negative outcome. Conversely, attributing failure to a lack of effort may lead the employee to try harder in the future on the same task. As another example, an employee who succeeds on a task and attributes the outcome to luck is unlikely to be affected by her success, whereas attributing the success to her ability or effort will increase her confidence.

ATTRIBUTIONAL BIASES

The attributions people make to their own behaviors and those of others can have a profound impact on their subsequent actions. Like perceptions, however, attributions may sometimes be inaccurate because of certain biases. Here we consider three of these biases: the fundamental attribution error, actor–observer effect, and self-serving attributions (see Table 4.5).

The Fundamental Attribution Error. Behavior is often caused by a combination of internal and external factors, but situational factors are the sole determinants of behavior in certain circumstances. Regardless of how capable and motivated an employee might be, for example, if the employee does not have the proper resources to accomplish a task, she or he will not be able to perform at a high level. No matter how hard a waiter tries to have customers enjoy their meals, they are bound to be dissatisfied if the restaurant serves poorly prepared food. Despite the fact that external factors often determine behavior, people have a very strong tendency to attribute other people's behavior to internal factors. Because this tendency to overattribute other people's behavior to internal rather than to external causes is so basic to human nature, it has been called the **fundamental attribution error**.[51]

Why does the fundamental attribution error occur? Researchers have offered two explanations. According to the first, which concentrates on perception of the target's behavior, when we observe a person behaving, we focus on the person, and the situation is simply the background for the behavior. Because the person is the focus of our thinking and the situation receives little attention, we tend to think that something about the person prompted the behavior. According to the second reason for the occurrence of the fundamental attribution error, we often are simply unaware of all the situational factors that may be responsible for the behavior we observe.

Because of the tendency to overattribute other people's behavior to internal causes, managers are likely to think that a subordinate's behavior is due to some characteristic of the subordinate rather than to the situation. Similarly, subordinates are

Fundamental attribution error The tendency to overattribute behavior to internal rather than to external causes.

TABLE 4.5
Attributional Biases

Bias	Description
Fundamental attribution error	The tendency to overattribute behavior to internal rather than to external causes
Actor–observer effect	The tendency to attribute the behavior of others to internal causes and to attribute one's own behavior to external causes
Self-serving attribution	The tendency to take credit for successes and avoid blame for failures

likely to think that their supervisor's behavior is determined by internal rather than by external causes. Suppose a manager must lay off 30 percent of his or her staff because of a major decline in the organization's performance. Those who are laid off (and those who remain) may be likely to attribute this action to the manager's hard-heartedness and lack of concern for the well-being of others rather than to economic necessity.

People who manage diverse employees need to be especially aware of the fundamental attribution error and try to avoid it. Just as perceptions can be inaccurate as a result of stereotypes, so, too, can attributions. Inaccurate stereotypes about women, older workers, or African Americans, for example, may cause members of an organization to inappropriately attribute behavior to internal causes such as gender, age, or race when the behavior is actually caused by an external factor. If an older worker has difficulty getting new computer software to run, the worker's supervisor may fall victim to the stereotype that older workers have difficulty learning new things and inaccurately attribute this behavior to the worker's age, even though the real cause of the problem is that the computer has insufficient memory to handle the new software (an external cause).

The Actor–Observer Effect.   We make attributions not only for the behavior of other people but also for our own behavior. Researchers comparing these two types of attributions uncovered an interesting phenomenon: the **actor–observer effect**. The actor–observer effect is the tendency to attribute the behavior of others to internal causes (the fundamental attribution error) and to attribute one's own behavior to external causes.[52] We tend to think that other people's behavior is relatively stable from situation to situation because it is due to their very nature, but we think that our own behavior varies from situation to situation.

What causes this bias? According to one explanation, when we are behaving, we focus not on our behavior but rather on the situation we are in. Because we are totally aware of the external, situational pressures that we face, we see them as key. Because we are less aware of external pressures or factors that another person is dealing with, we are likely to see his or her behavior as internally driven.

Self-Serving Attribution.   Suppose you get promoted at work. Chances are you attribute this outcome to your superior abilities and the excellent job you have been doing. Now suppose that one of your co-workers gets the promotion that you have been expecting. You probably think that your supervisor has been unfair or that some political maneuvering has taken place. This example illustrates **self-serving attribution**, the tendency to take credit for successes and avoid blame for failures.[53] The considerable amount of research conducted on this phenomenon suggests that accepting the credit for success is more common than avoiding blame for failure.[54] Furthermore, people are most likely to accept the blame for failure when it is due to something they can control in the future, such as by working harder or planning their time better.[55]

Self-serving attribution can also bias one's perception of friends and spouses and even organizations.[56] People are more likely to attribute the good things that happen to their spouses to internal causes and the bad things that happen to their spouses to external causes.[57] When your organization makes a record contribution to the United Way, you are likely to attribute this generosity to the organization's being socially responsible (an internal cause). But when your organization is cited for polluting the environment, you may attribute its problems to external circumstances such as the unavailability or high cost of alternative ways to dispose of waste (an external cause).

Actor–observer effect The tendency to attribute the behavior of others to internal causes and to attribute one's own behavior to external causes.

Self-serving attribution The tendency to take credit for successes and avoid blame for failures.

you're the management expert

Helping a Co-Worker

Juan Coto works closely with one of his co-workers, Roger Brice. Coto and Brice work in the customer service department of Diamond Furniture and do everything from taking payments, approving credit, and arranging for furniture deliveries to responding to customer complaints and handling returns. Coto and Brice both work the same hours and often are the only full-time employees handling customer service at any one time. Periodically, the store manager will receive a complaint from a customer about Brice; the manager talks to Brice about it, Brice gets annoyed, and the matter is forgotten. Coto realizes that these incidents are probably not doing anyone any good, so he has decided to try to figure out why customers occasion- ally complain about Brice but very rarely about him, even though they both seem to be doing an equally good job. So, Coto has started watching Brice when he deals with customers who are having a problem and notices that Brice typically approaches these situations by essentially "blaming" the customer. For example, when a customer called to complain that her furniture had not been delivered on the day it was promised, Brice looked up her record and then told her that she must have made a mistake because the delivery had been scheduled for a different date than she thought. As an expert in OB, Coto has come to you for help. Why is Brice blaming customers for their problems, and how can he help Brice provide better customer service?

Effectively Managing a Diverse Workforce

Throughout this chapter, we have discussed how accurate perceptions and attributions are necessary to effectively manage a diverse workforce and the many issues involved with it. Effective management of a diverse workforce is necessary for an organization to make fair and ethical decisions, perform at a high level, and gain a competitive advantage. In this section, we explore four steps organizations can take to promote accurate perceptions and attributions and effectively manage diverse employees: securing the commitment of top management to diversity, diversity training, education, and mentoring. We also discuss the steps organizations can take to eliminate and prevent sexual harassment.

SECURING TOP-MANAGEMENT COMMITMENT TO DIVERSITY

Applied Materials, a $4 billion semiconductor equipment company in Silicon Valley, California, is a good example of an organization whose top management is committed to diversity. Applied Materials has made *Fortune* magazine's "America's 50 Best Companies for Minorities" list for five years in a row.[58] This commitment is shown in numerous ways, ranging from a financial commitment to promoting diversity and a commitment to hiring and giving diverse employees equal opportunities, to a commitment to helping minorities in the Silicon Valley area. Fifty-one percent of new hires at Applied Materials are minorities, as are 28.4 percent of the company's officials and managers and 26 percent of its highest-paid executives.[59]

Applied Materials has committed $1 million to help open up opportunities for minorities in Silicon Valley by, among other things, funding a center in East Palo Alto, California, devoted to teaching computer skills to community members and minority students. Another one of the company's program's links up employees with high school students in a nearby school district comprised largely of minority adolescents.[60] Applied Materials stands out among other Silicon Valley high-tech firms as one of a select few that demonstrated a commitment to diversity in multiple ways and are taking active steps both internally and externally to support it.[61]

Glen Toney, group vice president for corporate affairs, is an African American who has been with Applied Materials for more than 20 years. He is a mentor for several minority employees of various racial and ethnic backgrounds and provides career counseling, personal insights about how the company works, and positive feedback for a job well done. As Toney puts it, "People who come aboard here have to move faster than they ever have before, and the organization is complex and can be frustrating."[62] Toney and other top managers at Applied Materials really care that all employees are treated fairly and given the opportunities that they deserve. This benefits Applied Materials because it is able to capitalize on the many talents of its diverse workforce.

What is the likely outcome when top managers are committed to diversity? Their commitment helps ensure they will perceive and attribute the behavior of all of their employees in as accurate a light as possible and that they will understand and see them as they really are. Top-management commitment to diversity also helps to promote accurate perceptions and attributions of people throughout the organization. When supervisors support diversity, subordinates are more likely to be committed to it, too, and less likely to rely on stereotypes.

An important way to demonstrate and reinforce top-management commitment to diversity is the creation of an active and influential chief diversity officer, as indicated in the accompanying Global View.

global view

Use of Diversity Directors on the Rise

When an organization increases its global presence, one would think that effectively managing diversity would be a salient concern. Managing operations across country borders, by its very nature, increases the diversity of an organization. Ironically when accounting giants Price-Waterhouse and Coopers & Lybrand merged to form PricewaterhouseCoopers (PwC), diversity was temporarily put on the back burner. At that time, Toni Riccardi, who is currently a partner and chief diversity officer for PwC, was working in human resources and wanted to be involved in diversity initiatives for PwC.

As she puts it, "I wanted a role to lead diversity in the new firm, but our global head of human capital, who was from the United Kingdon said, 'No. That's an American problem. We're not going to do that.'"[63] As a result, Ricarrdi temporarily refocused her efforts on other special projects at PwC.

Management eventually realized the need to focus on effectively managing diversity at PwC, however. Riccardi has been leading this effort. In addition to being chief diversity officer, she sits on the U.S. Management Committee, a 12-person group that oversees global operations and includes PwC Chairman Samuel A. DiPiazza. Riccardi's responsibilities include managing the diversity and work-life initiatives for over 100,000 employees working in more than 140 countries. The U.S. Management

Companies frequently hire diversity directors like Toni Riccardi of Pricewaterhouse Coopers to implement programs promoting diversity, ensure the firm complies with equal opportunity laws, and investigate internal discrimination charges.

Committee must approve any task forces that are formed, and Riccardi makes sure that task forces reflect the diversity in PwC not only to increase their effectiveness but also to give the diverse members of the firm important leadership experience and visibility.[64]

Many other global organizations have diversity-designated director or officer positions to ensure diversity is effectively managed throughout the countries in which an organization operates. For example, Leslie Jones is the director of ethnicity and diversity at Ernst & Young. Jones strives to make the work environment at Ernst & Young attractive to minorities because they are key contributors to the success of the organization.[65] Sharon Hall, who focuses on senior executive placements at the Chicago search firm, Spencer Stuart, indicates that demand for chief diversity officers is strong and relatively recession-proof as more and more global organizations acknowledge how important it is to have a workforce that is as diverse and multicultural as their customers and consumers.[66] As Riccardi puts it, "The challenge is to make sure people view diversity and work-life as positive pieces of this new world rather than add-ons that you don't have time for."[67]

DIVERSITY TRAINING

Diversity training can facilitate the management of a diverse workforce. There are many diversity training programs that have a variety of objectives, including the following:

♦ Making explicit and breaking down organizational members' stereotypes that result in inaccurate perceptions and attributions

♦ Making members aware of different kinds of backgrounds, experiences, and values

♦ Showing members how to deal effectively with diversity-related conflicts and tensions

♦ Generally improving members' understanding of each other

Diversity training programs can last hours or days and can be run by consultants or existing members of an organization with diversity expertise. Small organizations are more likely to rely on consultants; larger organizations often have diversity managers. More than 50 percent of *Fortune* 500 organizations, for example, have diversity managers on staff.[68]

Diversity training can include but is not limited to:

1. Role-playing in which participants act out appropriate and inappropriate ways to deal with diverse employees

2. Self-awareness activities in which participants' own prejudices and stereotypes are revealed

3. Awareness activities in which participants learn about others who differ from them in lifestyle, culture, sexual orientation, gender, and so on

Cardiac Concepts Inc., a Texas medical laboratory that performs cardiovascular tests, helped to reduce conflict among employees with diverse ethnic backgrounds by using a training program in which pairs of participants from different ethnic backgrounds made lists of the stereotypes held about each other.[69] Prudential, the largest U.S. life insurance company, has its managers participate in other organizations in which they will be a minority so they can understand the challenges that minorities experience.[70] Simmons Associates, based in New Hope, Pennsylvania, provides diversity consulting services including a "Special Sensitivities" session. This session educates participants about words, phrases, situations, and scenarios that might be disturbing to certain groups due to their backgrounds and histories. For example, male African-American teens might take offense at being referred to as "boys." The goal of the sessions is to help avoid blunders whereby one person says something that is highly offensive to another, sometimes without realizing it.[71]

Many diversity programs are successful, but others do not change the ways that people perceive and treat each other in organizations. It appears that diversity training is most likely to be successful when it is ongoing or repeated (rather than a single session), when there are follow-up activities to see whether the training has accomplished its objectives, and when it is supplemented by other diversity-related activities in an organization, such as events focused on celebrating diversity. IBM's Systems Storage Division in San Jose, for example, sets aside one day a year as Diversity Day. On that day, employees dress in traditional ethnic clothing and share authentic dishes with their co-workers.[72]

EDUCATION

Sometimes effectively managing diversity requires that members of an organization receive additional education to make them better able to communicate and work with diverse employees and customers. The Kentucky state government, for example, realized that it was unable to provide employment opportunities for people with hearing impairments and could not provide high-quality service to hearing-impaired citizens wanting to use state-provided services and programs. The Americans with Disabilities Act requires organizations to be responsive to and accommodate people with disabilities (including deafness or hearing impairments).[73]

After considerable research, the Kentucky state government developed a three-stage program to improve its responsiveness to people (both customers and potential employees) who are hearing impaired or deaf. First, state employees chosen for the program participate in a one-day workshop that educates them about deaf culture and background. Second, employees attend a four-day workshop in which they learn some of the basics of American Sign Language (the most often used form of signing and a visual language that deaf people use to communicate). Finally, employees attend a week-long workshop on advanced American Sign Language.[74]

MENTORING PROGRAMS

Mentoring is a process through which an experienced member of an organization (the mentor) provides advice and guidance to a less experienced member (the protégé) and helps the less experienced person learn the ropes and do the right things to advance in the organization. Due to the similar-to-me effect and stereotyping, some young minority managers find that white senior colleagues aren't mentoring them. Ilene Wasserman, of the Cincinnati-based Kaleel Jamison Consulting Group, which specializes in helping organizations manage a diverse workforce, says that senior managers typically try to mentor someone who reminds them of themselves when they were younger—someone who, as she puts it, is a "clone."

Mentoring A process through which an experienced member of an organization (the mentor) provides advice and guidance to a less experienced member (the protégé) and helps the less experienced person learn the ropes and do the right things to advance in the organization.

Mentoring—both formal and informal—can help entry-level employees develop the skills they need to excel on the job. Seventy percent of minority executives, for example, say informal mentors helped them early their careers.

Mixed-race mentor–protégé relationships are rare. Benson Rosen, a management professor at the University of North Carolina at Chapel Hill, indicates that white managers sometimes feel uncomfortable dealing with minorities and may slight them (often unintentionally) in various ways such as failing to invite them to functions and giving them performance feedback that is less constructive than the feedback they give white subordinates. LaVon Stennis, a young African American lawyer who worked for a large corporation in Nebraska, found it difficult to relate to her white male superiors, so it was unlikely that any of them would serve as her mentor. These observations do not mean that white men cannot mentor minorities or that minorities do not want to receive help from white managers. Rather, they suggest that all members of an organization (regardless of race, gender, or other characteristics) need to be aware that the similar-to-me bias might predispose them to help members who are similar to them. In his study, Rosen found that white women were more likely than white men to mentor minorities of either gender.[75]

A recent study of minority executives found that more than 70 percent of the executives had informal mentors, and they generally believe that mentors helped them in their careers.[76] Lloyd David Ward, CEO of the Maytag Corporation and one of a handful of African-Americans to head a major U.S. corporation, was mentored by older African-American engineers when he was an employee at Procter & Gamble as well as by Dr. Price Cobbs, a psychiatrist and consultant who helped him deal with the anger he felt from being treated differently because of the color of his skin.[77] Former Coca-Cola president Donald R. Keough mentored Carl Ware, head of global public affairs and a senior African-American manager at Coca-Cola. Keough is currently chairman of Allen & Company (an investment bank).[78]

Mentors are not only important for managers and executives. The United Parcel Service relies on mentors to help entry-level employees develop basic skills and habits such as being punctual and dressing appropriately.[79] Mentors are also key for entrepreneurs trying to start their own businesses. African American Bernadette Williams, who founded i-strategy.com Inc., believes that mentors are particularly important for minority women trying to start a business, and her beliefs are confirmed by many surveys. Williams co-founded the Women's New Media Alliance to help young women interested in technology connect with a woman experienced in the area they wish to pursue.[80] Clearly, mentoring can be beneficial for all kinds of employees but it may be especially important for women and minorities trying to overcome the effects of the similar-to-me bias, stereotypes, and potential discrimination.[81]

Mentoring programs can be formal or informal. And protégés can benefit from mentors who are different from them as well as from mentors who are similar to them. What must exist for successful mentoring to take place is an atmosphere of mutual respect and understanding and for the mentor to have the protégé's best interests in mind. Maureen Giovanni, a multicultural consultant with J. Howard & Associates, suggests that when mentors and protégés are diverse or differ from each other on one or more salient dimensions, there can be enhanced opportunities for mutual learning. The mentor can learn about the background and experiences of the protégé, and the protégé can learn the ropes in the organization and how to be successful from the mentor.[82] Through this process, both the mentor and the protégé become more skilled in developing effective interpersonal relations with different kinds of people. At Prudential, managers are paired with mentors who are different from them to help them learn about differences between groups and the issues various groups face. Managers, in turn, are evaluated on their attention to diversity in multiple ways (on the amount of money they spend on ethnic marketing, for example, and how well they incorporate diversity issues into their meetings and speeches).[83]

Visible top-management commitment, training, education, and mentoring are just some of the ways in which organizations can effectively manage a diverse workforce. As we have discussed throughout this chapter, effectively managing diversity

In 1992, would-be military cadet Shannon Faulkner's sued South Carolina for admission to the Citadel, an all-male, military academy funded by the state. Faulkner fought for four years, ringing up a $6 million legal tab in the process. She was eventually admitted to the school but left just one week later because of the pressure.

begins by recognizing that the perceptions and attributions of the organization's members need to be as accurate as possible, regardless of the age, race, gender, ethnic background, religion, sexual orientation, or other characteristic of the target of perception.

SEXUAL HARASSMENT

After extensive study, the U.S. Army has indicated that sexual harassment exists throughout its ranks.[84] Unfortunately, sexual harassment is not just an Army problem but also a problem that many other organizations, such as Chevron Corporation and Ford Motor Company, have had to face.[85] There are two distinct types of sexual harassment: quid pro quo sexual harassment and hostile work environment sexual harassment. **Quid pro quo sexual harassment** is the most obvious type. It occurs when the harasser requests or forces an employee to perform sexual favors in order to receive some opportunity (such as a raise, a promotion, a bonus, or a special job assignment) or to avoid a negative consequence (such as a demotion, dismissal, a halt to career progress, or an undesired assignment or transfer).[86] **Hostile work environment sexual harassment** is more subtle and occurs when organizational members are faced with a work environment that is offensive, intimidating, or hostile because of their sex.[87] Pornographic pictures, sexual jokes, lewd comments, sexually oriented comments about a person's physical appearance, and displays of sexually oriented objects are all examples of hostile work environment sexual harassment. Hostile work environments interfere with organizational members' abilities to perform their jobs effectively and are illegal. Chevron settled a $2.2 million lawsuit with four employees who experienced a hostile work environment by, for example, receiving violent pornography through the company's mail system and being asked to deliver pornographic videos to Chevron employees in Alaska.[88] As another example, Ford settled a $17.5 million lawsuit involving employees at two factories in Illinois. The employees claimed they endured years of unwanted touching and massaging, being called sexually explicit names, having pornography and sexual graffiti displayed in the workplace, and other

Quid pro quo sexual harassment Requesting or forcing an employee to perform sexual favors in order to receive some opportunity (such as a raise, a promotion, a bonus, or a special job assignment) or avoid a negative consequence (such as demotion, dismissal, a halt to career progress, or an undesired assignment or transfer).

Hostile work environment sexual harassment Creating or maintaining a work environment that is offensive, intimidating, or hostile because of a person's sex.

forms of hostile work environment harassment.[89] Hostile work environment sexual harassment can also take place electronically when employees send or receive sexually oriented e-mails or pornography over the Internet. For example, Dow Chemical, Xerox, the *New York Times*, Edward Jones, and First Union Bank have all fired employees for using company e-mail systems to send sexually oriented messages.[90] According to a recent study, 70 percent of the employees surveyed indicated that they have viewed or sent e-mails at work that would be considered adult oriented. Moreover, over 60 percent admitted that they have sent e-mails that were either personally offensive or inappropriate.[91]

Research suggests that sexual harassment continues to occur in a wide variety of organizations[92] and has adverse effects on victims' job satisfaction, stress levels, life satisfaction, and psychological well-being. Victims of harassment may also be more likely to try to withdraw from the workplace, for example, by being late or absent, trying to avoid certain tasks or situations, or thinking about quitting and looking for another job.[93] They also tend to have negative attitudes about their supervisors and their co-workers.[94] Interestingly, a recent study found that regardless of whether employees experience sexual harassment themselves, being in a work group in which sexual harassment occurs results in employees being more dissatisfied with their work, their co-workers, and their supervisors and experiencing higher levels of stress.[95]

Organizations have a legal and ethical obligation to eliminate and prevent sexual harassment, which can occur at all levels in an organization. Many organizations, such as NBC, include segments on sexual harassment in their diversity training and education programs.[96] At a minimum, there are several key steps that organizations can take to combat the sexual harassment problem.[97]

♦ *Develop a sexual harassment policy supported by top management.* This policy should (1) describe and prohibit both quid pro quo and hostile work environment sexual harassment, (2) provide examples of types of behaviors that are prohibited, (3) outline a procedure employees can follow to report sexual harassment, (4) describe the disciplinary actions that will be taken in instances of sexual harassment, and (5) describe the organization's commitment to educating and training its members about sexual harassment.

♦ *Clearly communicate the organization's sexual harassment policy throughout the organization.* All members of an organization should be familiar with its sexual harassment policy.

♦ *Investigate charges of sexual harassment with a fair complaint procedure.* A fair complaint procedure should (1) be handled by a neutral third party, (2) be dealt with promptly and thoroughly, (3) protect victims and treat them fairly, and (4) treat alleged harassers fairly.

♦ *Take corrective action as soon as possible once it has been determined that sexual harassment has taken place.* The nature of these corrective actions will vary depending on the severity of the sexual harassment.

♦ *Provide sexual harassment training and education to all members of the organization.* Many organizations have such training programs in place, including Du Pont, NBC, Corning, Digital Equipment, and the U.S. Navy and Army.[98] A growing number of organizations are taking steps to ensure that new hires and interns are aware of their organization's sexual harassment policy. For example, the Katz Media Group, which helps to sell advertisements for television and radio stations, includes a 25-minute video on sexual harassment in its orientation program for new hires.[99] According to Christine Walters, sexual harassment prevention and resolution director at Johns Hopkins University, all new hires of that organization are educated about the behaviors that constitute sexual harassment.[100]

Summary

Perception and attribution are important topics because all decisions and behaviors in organizations are influenced by how people interpret and make sense of the world around them and each other. Perception is the process by which individuals select, organize, and interpret sensory input. Attribution is an explanation of the cause of behavior. Perception and attribution, thus, help to explain how and why people behave in organizations and how and why they react to the behavior of others. In this chapter, we made the following major points:

1. Perception is the process by which people interpret the input from their senses to give meaning and order to the world around them. The three components of perception are the perceiver, the target, and the situation. Accurate perceptions are necessary to make good decisions and to motivate employees to perform at a high level, to be fair and equitable, and to be ethical.

2. The perceiver's knowledge base is organized into schemas, abstract knowledge structures stored in memory that allow people to organize and interpret information about a given target of perception. Schemas tend to be resistant to change and can be functional or dysfunctional. A stereotype is a dysfunctional schema because stereotypes often lead perceivers to assume erroneously that targets have a whole range of characteristics simply because they possess one distinguishing characteristic (e.g., race, age, or gender). In addition to the perceiver's schemas, his or her motivational state and mood also influence perception.

3. Characteristics of the target also influence perception. Ambiguous targets are subject to a lot of interpretation by the perceiver; the more ambiguous the target, the more likely perceivers are to differ in their perceptions of it. The target's social status also affects how the target is perceived. Through impression management, targets can actively try to manage the perceptions that others have of them.

4. The situation affects perception by providing the perceiver with additional information. One

particularly important aspect of the situation is the target's salience—that is, the extent to which the target stands out in a group of people or things.

5. Biases and problems in person perception include primacy effects; contrast effects; halo effects; similar-to-me effects; harshness, leniency, and average tendencies; and knowledge-of-predictor bias. Inaccurate perceptions resulting from these biases can lead to faulty decision making.

6. Attributions are important determinants of behavior in organizations because how members of an organization react to other people's behavior depends on what they think caused the behavior. Attribution theory focuses on understanding how people explain the causes of their own and others' behavior. Common internal attributions for behavior include ability, effort, and personality. Common external attributions for behavior include task difficulty and luck or chance. Like perceptions, attributions can be inaccurate as a result of several biases, including the fundamental attribution error, the actor–observer effect, and self-serving attribution.

7. Three ways in which organizations can promote accurate perceptions and attributions and effectively manage diverse employees are securing top management's commitment to diversity, diversity training, education, and mentoring programs. Organizations also need to take steps to eliminate and prevent both quid pro quo and hostile work environment sexual harassment.

Exercises in Understanding and Managing Organizational Behavior

Questions for Discussion and Review

1. How do schemas help members of an organization make sense of each other and of what happens in the organization?
2. Are stereotypes ever functional for the perceiver? Why or why not?
3. Why might a supervisor be motivated to perceive a subordinate's performance as being poor when it really is not?
4. How might managers' moods affect organizational decision making?
5. In what ways might impression management be functional in organizations? In what ways might it be dysfunctional?
6. Can and should employees who are salient try to reduce their salience?
7. Why do perceptual biases exist?
8. Why might a supervisor make internal attributions for a subordinate's poor performance?
9. Why are attributions important determinants of behavior in organizations?
10. Why might members of an organization disagree about the nature of hostile work environment sexual harassment?

Building People Skills

Understanding Perceptions and Attributions in Group Meetings

Think about the last meeting or gathering that you attended. It could be a meeting that took place at the organization you are currently working for, a meeting of a club or student organization you are a member of, a meeting of a group you have been assigned to for a project in one of your classes, or any other recent gathering that involved more than two people.

1. Describe your perceptions of what took place during the meeting and explain why events unfolded as they did.
2. Describe the characteristics and behavior of the other people who were present at the meeting and explain why they acted the way they did.
3. Describe how you think you were perceived by other people during the meeting and explain why you behaved as you did.
4. After you have completed activities 1 through 3, pick another person who participated in the meeting and arrange to meet with her or him for around 15 minutes. Explain to the person that you want to ask a few questions about the meeting for one of your classes.
5. When you meet with the person, ask her or him to be as accurate and honest as possible. Remind the person that your get-together is part of an assignment for one of your classes and assure that person that answers to your questions are confidential. While the person is answering you, take careful notes and do not attempt to correct

anything that is said. Just listen and take notes. Ask the person to respond to each of these questions (one by one):

A. How would you describe what took place during the meeting, and why do you think it took place?

B. How would you describe the characteristics and behavior of the other people who were present at the meeting, and why do you think they behaved as they did?

C. How would you describe the reasons why I behaved as I did during the meeting?

6. Compare your own descriptions from activities 1 through 3 with the descriptions you obtained from activities 4 and 5. In what ways were your perceptions and attributions similar to those of the other person? In what ways were they different?

7. Use the knowledge you have gained from this chapter to explain why there were differences in your and the other person's perceptions and attributions and why there were similarities. Be specific.

A Question of Ethics

Given perceptual problems and biases, such as stereotyping and the similar-to-me effect, proponents of affirmative action argue that organizations need to take proactive steps to ensure that minorities and women are given the opportunities they deserve. Opponents, on the other hand, argue that these policies can inadvertently result in more discrimination rather than less.

Questions

1. Think about the ethical implications of affirmative action programs.
2. What obligation do organizations have to ensure that all members of the organization are treated fairly?

Small Group Break-Out Exercise

Dealing with Salience

Form groups of three or four people and appoint one member as the spokesperson who will communicate your conclusions to the rest of the class.

1. Take a few minutes to think about situations in which you were salient (i.e., you stood out in a group of people).
2. Take turns describing these situations and how you felt.
3. Then take turns describing what other people in these situations did to make the situation better or worse for you.
4. As a group, come up with ways that (a) individuals who are salient in a situation can effectively deal with their salience, and (b) those who are not salient in a situation can avoid paying undue attention to others who stand out and avoid forming extreme evaluations of them and stereotyping.

Topic for Debate

Perception and attribution have major effects on the decisions that are made in organizations and on how members of an organization respond to each other's behavior. Now that you have a good understanding of perception and attribution, debate the following issue.

Team A. There is not much that managers can do to reduce the negative effects of problems and biases in perception and attribution in organizations.

Team B. Managers can take active steps to reduce the negative effects of problems and biases in perception and attribution in organizations.

Experiential Exercise

Managing Diversity

Objective

Your objective is to gain firsthand experience in some of the issues involved in managing diversity.

Procedure

The class divides into groups of three to five people, and each group appoints one member as spokesperson to present the group's recommendations to the whole class. Each group plays the role of a team of diversity consultants who have been called in by a high-tech company in the computer industry to help effectively manage diverse employees. Here is the scenario.

Nick Hopkins is the team leader of a group of 10 programmers who are developing innovative software to be used in architectural design. The team is composed of seven men and three women. Hopkins thought that everything was going pretty smoothly in his team until the following two recent events. First, one of the women, Cara Lipkin, informed him that she would be resigning to work for a competing organization. Hopkins asked Lipkin why she decided to make this change, and she answered at length.

"I can't exactly explain it," she said, "but I never really felt that my contributions were valued by the team. I know you always appreciated the work I did and appraised my performance highly, but somehow I didn't really feel a part of things. In the long run, I was afraid that my prospects in the company might not be as good as other people's because I didn't seem to be included in certain activities and discussions. To give you what will probably sound like a real silly example, last month I overheard several of my team members planning a deep-sea fishing trip; I kept waiting to be included but never was. As another example, I sometimes feel like the last person people will come to for help with a programming problem."

The second event troubling Hopkins was as follows: Bob Risoto, another team member who at the time was unaware of Lipkin's resignation, complained that the women on the team always seemed to stick together.

"It's like they've got their own little clique going," Risoto said. "They go to lunch together. They talk to each other but not really to the rest of the team. When I have a programming problem that I think one of the women on the team would be able to help me with, for some reason I often feel hesitant to seek out her advice. Maybe it's just my fault. I don't know."

Hopkins has met with you (in your role as a team of diversity consultants) and asked you to help him effectively manage diversity as a team leader. He has indicated that he thought everything was going smoothly, but it evidently isn't and he wants to take some concrete steps to improve matters. Develop a plan of action to help Hopkins effectively manage diversity in his team.

Once your group has developed a plan, the spokesperson for the group will present the group's recommendations and the rationale behind them to the rest of the class.

Making the Connection

Find an example of an organization that has taken steps to improve the accuracy of its members' perceptions of diverse employees. What steps has this organization taken? How have organizational members responded to these diversity initiatives?

New York Times Cases in the News

The New York Times

Japan's Neglected Resource: Female Workers

BY HOWARD W. FRENCH

Tokyo, July 24—When Yuko Suzuki went into business for herself after the advertising company she worked for went bankrupt, no amount of talk she had heard about the hardships facing professional women here prepared her for the humiliations ahead.

As an independent saleswoman, she found that customers merely pretended to listen to her. Time and again when she finished a presentation, men would ask who her boss was. Eventually she hired a man to go along with her, because merely having a man by her side—even a virtual dummy—increased her sales significantly, if not her morale.

"If I brought a man along, the customers would only establish eye contact with him, even though I was the representative of the company, and doing the talking," she said. "It was very uncomfortable."

Japan has tried all sorts of remedies to pull itself out of a 13-year economic slump, from huge public works projects to bailouts of failing companies. Many experts have concluded that the expanding the role of women in professional life could provide a far bigger stimulus than any scheme tried so far.

But it often seems that the Japanese would rather let their economy stagnate than send their women up the corporate ladder. Resistance to expanding women's professional roles remains high in a country where the economic status of women trails far behind that of women in other advanced economies.

"Japan is still a developing country in terms of gender equality," Mariko Bando, an aide to Prime Minister Junichiro Koizumi, recently told reporters. This year the World Economic Forum ranked Japan 69th of 75 member nations in empowering its women.

While 40 percent of Japanese women work, a figure that reflects their rapid, recent entry into the job market, they hold only about 9 percent of managerial positions, compared with about 45 percent in the United States, according to the government and the International Labor Organization. Women's wages, meanwhile, are about 65 percent of those of their male counterparts, one of the largest gaps in the industrial world.

Japanese labor economists and others say it is no wonder, then, that Japan, which looked like a world beater 20 years ago, is struggling to compete economically today. With women sidelined from the career track, Japan is effectively fighting with one hand tied behind its back.

"Japan has gone as far as it can go with a social model that consists of men filling all of the economic, management and political roles," said Eiko Shinotsuka, assistant dean of Ochanomizu University and the first woman to serve on the board of the Bank of Japan.

"People have spoken of the dawn of a women's age here before," she said, "but that was always in relatively good times economically, and the country was able to avoid social change. We've never had such a long economic crisis as this one, though, and people are beginning to recognize that the place of women in our society is an important factor."

By tradition Japanese companies hire men almost exclusively to fill career positions, reserving shorter term work, mostly clerical tasks and tea serving, for women, who are widely known in such jobs here as office ladies, or simply O.L.'s.

Ms. Suzuki, who went into business for herself, is the exception. These days Ms. Suzuki, an impeccably groomed 32-year-old who dresses in crisp suits and speaks at a rapid, confident clip, is the proud owner of her own company, a short-term office suite rental business in one of Tokyo's smartest quarters. "I am the only professional out of all of my girlhood friends," she said. "The rest are housewives or regular office ladies, and they all say that what has happened to me is unbelievable."

Whatever a woman's qualifications, breaking into the career track requires overcoming entrenched biases, not least the feeling among managers that childbearing is an insupportable disruption.

That is so even though the country faces a steep population decline and keeping women sidelined has had economic costs. Women's relative lack of economic participation may be shaving 0.6 percent off annual growth, a study presented to the Labor Ministry estimated last year.

Meanwhile, at companies where women make up 40 to 50 percent of the staff average profits are double those where women account for 10 percent or less, the Economy Ministry reported last month.

A recent issue of Weekly Women magazine nonetheless recouned the stories of women who said they had been illegally dismissed because of pregnancy or had sought abortions for fear of being dismissed.

For the Record

How Women Fare

A comparison of professional women in Japan to those in other industrialized countries.

Women as a percentage of . . .

	All workers	Managerial workers	Civil workers service	General Managerial	National Parliament/ Congress
Japan	41.0%	8.9%	20.2%	1.4%	7.3%
United States	46.6	46.0	49.3	23.1	14.3
Sweden	48.0	30.5	43.0	51.0	45.3
Germany	44.0	26.9	39.0	9.5	32.2
Britain	44.9	30.0	49.1	17.2	17.9

Sources: The Cabinet Office of Japan: International Labor Organization. Inter-Parliamentary Union

"I reported to my boss that I was pregnant and would like to take off for a medical check," Masumi Honda, a 33-year-old mother was quoted as saying. "When I came home from the hospital, I was shocked that he had just left a message saying that I needn't bother coming to work any more."

Other women say the intense competitive pressure in the workplace can lead to resentment, even in progressive companies, against mothers who avail themselves of child care leave or flexible work hours.

One woman, who abandoned a career in marketing after similar experiences in two companies, recounted taking leave for three days to look after a sick child.

"After that I was not included in new projects," said the woman, who spoke on condition that she not be identified, "and after that I felt they saw me as an unreliable person. I finally decided that if I work in a company, I must understand the company's spirit, which means I couldn't feel comfortable taking maternal benefits."

The growing sense of urgency in official circles about these issues is driven largely by the projections of a population decline that could cause huge labor shortages over the next half-century and possibly even economic collapse. So far, though government efforts to expand women's place in the ecoomy have been modest and halting.

An advisory panel appointed by Prime Minister Koizumi recomended recently that the public and private sectors aim to have at least 30 percent of managerial positions filled by women by 2020. These days there is growing talk of affirmative action in Japan.

But changing mind-sets will be difficult. Earlier this year, former Prime Minister Yoshiro Mori, a member of a governement commission charged with finding solutions to the population crisis, was widely quoted as saying the main reason for Japan's falling birthrate was the overeducation of its women.

Mr. Koizumi's top aide, Yasuo Fukuda, was recently quoted as saying that often women who are raped deserve it, while a legislator from the governing party said, approvingly, that the men who carried out such acts were virile and "good specimens". The latter comment came last month at a seminar about the falling birthrate.

While senior politicians bemoan overeducation as the cause of Japan's population problems, women unsurprisingly cite other reasons that make it difficult for them to have children and also play a bigger role in the country's economic life.

Foremost is the lack of day care, which for many forces stark choices between motherhood and career. There are also the working hours of many offices, which extend deep into the evening and sometimes all but require social drinking afterward.

Haruko Takachi, 37, a postal manager, is luckier than most. Her child was accepted into a 20-student nursey school opened last year by the Ministry of Education.

It is the only public nursey school avaible for the 38,000 government employees who work in Kasumigaseki, central Tokyo's administrtive district. Unlike most private nurseries, which close earlier, the school remains open until 10 p.m.

"I work until 8 in the evening, but there are plenty of times when I work much later," she said. "That's just the social reality in Japan. There are some other women in my milieu, but most of them have just one child and don't plan for more."

Ms. Suzuki, who founded her own business, has been married for several years and has no children. She regards day care as just a small piece of what is needed in Japan. Men and women, she says, must rethink gender roles—an idea that she hesitantly concluded makes her a feminist.

"Men are really intimidated by professional women in Japan, "she said." But this is still a society where even when it looks like a woman has some authority, the men usually manage to stay on top."

SOURCE: "Japan's Neglected Resource: Female Workers" by H. W. French, *New York Times*, July 25, 2003, p. A3.

Questions for Discussion

1. Why are women treated so differently from men in the Japanese workplace?

2. What are the costs of this differential treatment?

3. What steps can be taken to ensure that women and men are on more of an equal footing in organizations in Japan?

The New York Times

Economic Scene

The Supreme Court finds the 'mushball middle' on affirmative action.

BY ALAN B. KRUEGER

"When we see a complicated, seemingly intractable problem," the comedian Al Franken once remarked about affirmative action, "we have the only really genuine, authentic human reaction you can have: we're confused."

Supreme Court justices do not have the same luxury.

The justices were forced to take sides last month in the landmark cases involving admissions practices at the University of Michigan. Their rulings will likely satisfy Mr. Franken's quest to find the "mushball middle" when it comes to affirmative action.

By a 5-4 margin, the court permitted the "narrowly tailored" use of race-conscious admissions policies used by the university's law school. The justices expressly prohibited the use of numerical quotas but ruled that race may be considered along with other factors on an individual basis if "serious, good faith consideration" was given to race-neutral alternatives to achieve diversity. Although the court ruled that achieving "student body diversity is a compelling state interest," its support is not indefinite.

"We expect that, 25 years from now," Justice Sandra Day O'Connor wrote in the majority opinion in the law-school case, "the use of racial preferences will no longer be necessary to further the interest approved today." That expectation led the majority to conclude, "We see no reason to exempt race-conscious admissions programs from the requirement that all governmental use of race must have a logical end point."

How likely is it that racial gaps will be substantially eroded in 25 years, so that the use of racial preferences is no longer desirable? Is the year 2028 a logical end-point for special efforts to ensure that underrepresented minority groups are given a fair chance in admissions or employment, or will the vestiges of past discrimination and unequal treatment still largely be with us then?

These are not the legal grounds on which the court ruled, but the question is not without interest, and it is undoubtedly tied to society's demand for diversity in institutions of higher education.

Although a definitive answer is impossible, estimates of the extent of income mobility from fathers to sons provide a rough forecast. Studies find that 40 to 60 percent of the gap in earnings between a particular individual and the average worker is closed from one generation to the next. Results specifically for blacks tend toward the lower end of this range but are not significantly different, according to research by Bhashkar Mazumder of the Federal Reserve Bank of Chicago.

In 1969, the average 30-to 39-year-old black male worker—who had attended separate and unequal schools and entered the labor force before the Civil Rights Act of 1964 barred discrimination—earned 37 percent less than the average white worker. This gap was mainly because of the legacy of discrimination.

If—and it is only a hypothetical if—the depressed income of black workers is not prevented from regressing to the mean because of subsequent discrimination,

then the gap would be expected to close to 15 to 22 percent for the next generation, and to 6 to 13 percent when members of the third generation reach their 30's, around a quarter century from now. The actual earnings gap for men in their 30's in 1999—roughly the second generation—was 19 percent, so the forecast appears on track.

Continuing discrimination or back-sliding on civil rights enforcement would slow this convergence, so Justice O'Connor's expectation is probably optimistic. Nevertheless, it is not unrealistic, at least when it comes to earnings, to think that the lingering effects of discrimination could be substantially reduced, though hardly eradicated, in the next quarter century or so.

For their part, many elite universities plan to continue using race-conscious admissions policies, according to the Chronicle of Higher Education.

In his bitter dissent in the law-school case, Justice Clarence Thomas made clear that he thought favorable treatment in admissions for minority students would prolong racial gaps in academic and economic achievement, not eradicate them: "These overmatched students take the bait, only to find that they cannot succeed in the cauldron of competition."

Beyond the alleged "harm" to students given favorable treatment in admissions, he went on to say that affirmative actions programs "stamp minorities with a badge of inferiority and may cause them to develop dependencies."

Instead of drawing on systematic evidence on the effect of affirmative action on students after they leave school, or on how the vast majority of minorities admitted to elite colleges actually viewed their college experience, Justice Thomas's opinion relied on introspection, selective anecdotes and the assertion that "no social science has disproved" his view that affirmative action is harmful.

"Somehow, someway, social scientists should say clearly to judges, even to

Clarence Thomas, that evidence matters," said William G. Bowen, president of the Andrew W. Mellon Foundation and co-author of "The Shape of the River" (Princeton University Press, 1998). In that book, Mr. Bowen and his co-author, Derek Curtis Bok, a former president of Harvard University, found that the more selective the college that black students attended, the more likely they were to graduate and earn an advanced degree, the more satisfied they were with their college experience, and the more successful they were later in life.

Moreover, these findings held for black students at the lower end of the College Boards distribution as well as those at the higher end, which is significant because those at the lower end were more likely to have been admitted to the elite schools because race was taken into account as background characteristic along with other factors.

Some people—including me—have questioned whether all the salutary out comes associated with attending an elite school are because of the school. (Staey Berg Dale, a researcher at Mathematical Police Research, and I have published a study that found the selectivity of the undergraduate college one attends does not materially affect one's earning power later in life.) But the evidence certainly does not suggest that attending top colleges harms minority students.

No one raises concerns that preference in admissions given to athletes, cheerleaders and children of wealthy alumni causes self-doubt or stigma. The fact that this concern only rises to prominence when it comes to considering race as one of many factors in admissions illustrates how difficult it will be to overcome the lingering discrimination in American society.

A quarter century from now, the Supreme Court will have a tougher call as to whether diversity is still a compelling state interest, but chances are it will wind up back in the mushball middle when it revisits the issue then.

SOURCE: "Economic Scene: The Supreme Court Finds the 'Mushball Middle' on Affirmative Action" by A. B. Krueger, *New York Times*, July 24, 2003, p. C2.

Questions for Discussion

1. What are the objectives of affirmative action programs?

2. What are the potential advantages of affirmative action programs?

3. What are the potential disadvantages of affirmative action programs?

Learning and Creativity

5

LEARNING OBJECTIVES

After studying this chapter, you should be able to:

■

Describe what learning is and why it is so important for all kinds of jobs and organizations.

■

Understand how to effectively use reinforcement to promote the learning of desired behaviors.

■

Describe the conditions necessary to determine if vicarious learning has taken place.

■

Appreciate the importance of self-control and self-efficacy for learning on your own.

■

Describe how learning takes place continuously through creativity, the nature of the creative process, and the determinants of creativity.

■

Understand what it means to be a learning organization.

OPENING CASE

Continuous Learning at Seagate Technologies

Why Is Continuous Learning a Necessity in Today's Business Environment?

Rapid changes in technology, multiple competitors, and a depressed economy—these conditions would seem to ring the death toll for an established disk drive maker in the 1980s. This was precisely the position of Seagate Technologies of Scotts Valley, California, in the late 1990s. Nonetheless, the disk maker has shown how continuous learning can put organizations and their members in charge of their own fate. Despite the business conditions surrounding it, Seagate Technologies has not only survived but also is thriving— thanks to ongoing learning throughout the organization. When Stephen J. Luczo became Seagate's new CEO in 1998, one of his top priorities was to instill a culture in Seagate that embraced and encouraged continuous learning.[1]

Luczo emphasized that Seagate needed to learn from multiple sources including its customers' customers. This was a departure from how Seagate had traditionally learned. As a major disk drive maker, Seagate used to rely on its large corporate customers that were market leaders in personal computer or server manufacturing to learn how to stay competitive. Luczo wanted employees to think beyond these large corporate customers and learn about the latest trends and what consumers might want in the years to come— despite the fact that consumers themselves were unlikely to know what that might be. As a result, Seagate is now a leading supplier of inexpensive, small disk drives used in video game consoles like X-Box. At Seagate, engineers and salespeople team up to learn what appeals to consumers and predict what will appeal to them five years down the road.[2]

Luczo also promoted learning on the part of suppliers. Rather than seeking the lowest prices from suppliers, Luczo thought of how suppliers could be most helpful to Seagate. Essentially, Seagate was dependent on suppliers to be able to get to market quickly with superior new disk drives. In order to promote learning on the part of suppliers, Seagate offered them financial rewards to the extent that they helped Seagate get to market more quickly with better disk drives than its competitors.[3]

Inside Seagate, Luczo emphasized that employees— engineers, salespeople, plant managers, R&D personnel, and so on—should learn from each other. Some of the learning is task based. But other kinds of learning are more interpersonal, for example, learning how to trust one another and work well together for the good of the whole company rather than one's own personal gain. This latter kind of learning takes place in different ways. For example, every year a group of senior managers from Seagate goes on a wilderness retreat where they work in teams climbing ropes, mountain biking, and navigating trails. These senior managers are typically accustomed to personal successes and pursuing their own agendas. In order to get them to learn how to work well in a team for the good of team, their performance on the retreat is determined by how well their five-person team does. Thus, rather than trying to shine themselves, the managers learn how important it is to help out team members who are having trouble.[4]

Additionally, Luczo emphasizes learning to behave differently in different markets. Some markets require high-end, technologically sophisticated drives, and customers are willing to pay for them. But other growing markets may be just the opposite. For example, consumers who buy game consoles are very sensitive to price. In order to compete with other disk drive makers, Seagate has learned that in these markets, inexpensive drives that do the job are key and expensive technological bells and whistles a detriment.[5]

Employees at Seagate realize that their learning is never over—they must engage in continuous learning to stay ahead of their competitors and carry on being a leading supplier of all kinds of disk drives. For example, Seagate is making inroads into supplying drives for video recorders, and it recently developed a new disk drive for notebook computers called the Momentus.[6] And all this learning is paying off. Annual revenues for Seagate's 2003 fiscal year were $6.5 billion compared to revenues of $6.1 billion in fiscal 2002.[7]

Overview

Learning is an ongoing process in everyone's life, both on and off of the job. In organizations, employees need to learn how to perform the tasks and duties that make up their jobs, how to effectively interact with others, and how things work in the wider organization. Although learning is particularly important to newcomers (discussed in more detail in Chapter 10), it is also important for experienced members at all levels in an organization because they are frequently called on to do things they haven't done before. Moreover, rapid rates of change in organizational environments require that employees continually learn on the job. Changes in knowledge, technology, markets, competition, and customer preferences are among the forces in the environment that necessitate ongoing learning. In the opening case, we described how employees at Seagate Technologies need to learn on an ongoing basis to remain competitive in the changing disk drive market.

In this chapter, we discuss the many ways in which learning takes place in organizations. We describe how to use reinforcement effectively to promote learning and how organizational members can "unlearn" undesired behaviors. Additionally, we explain how organizational members can learn from watching others, can learn on their own, and can learn by "by doing." Finally, we discuss how organizations can promote continuous learning through creativity. By the end of this chapter, you will have a good appreciation of why multiple kinds of learning are essential for an organization to be effective.

The Nature of Learning

Learning is a relatively permanent change in knowledge or behavior that results from practice or experience.[8] There are several key points in this definition. First, with learning comes *change*. For example, when you learn a second language, your knowledge about how to communicate evolves, and your behavior changes when communicating with native speakers of the language. Second, the change in knowledge or behavior has to be *relatively permanent* or long lasting. If you attempt to communicate with someone in another language by looking up words in a dictionary that you quickly forget once the interaction is complete, learning did not take place because there was no permanent change in your knowledge of the second language. The third key aspect of the definition is that learning takes place as a result of practice or through *experience*. Learning a second language requires much practice in pronunciation, word usage, and grammar. Similarly, through practice or experience, secretaries learn how to use new software packages, financial analysts learn the implications of new tax laws, engineers learn how to design more fuel-efficient automobiles, and flight attendants learn how to serve meals on airplanes. In this chapter, we discuss the multiples ways in which organizational members can and do learn.

> **Learning** A relatively permanent change in knowledge or behavior that results from practice or experience.

Learning Through Consequences

One of the most fundamental ways in which people learn throughout their lives is through the consequences they receive for their behaviors and actions. Psychologist B. F. Skinner was fascinated by the power of consequences to influence behavior, and his **operant conditioning** approach describes how learning takes place through consequences.[9] Operant conditioning is learning that takes place when the learner recognizes the connection between a behavior and its consequences (see Figure 5.1).[10] An individual learns to engage in specific behaviors (such as being responsive to customers' needs) in order to receive certain consequences (such as a bonus). This type of learning is called *operant* conditioning because individuals learn to operate in their environment in a certain way to achieve certain consequences.

> **Operant conditioning** Learning that takes place when the learner recognizes the connection between a behavior and its consequences.

You have probably learned that if you study hard, you will receive good grades, and if you keep up with your reading throughout the semester, you will not be overburdened during finals week. Thus, you have learned how to *operate* in your

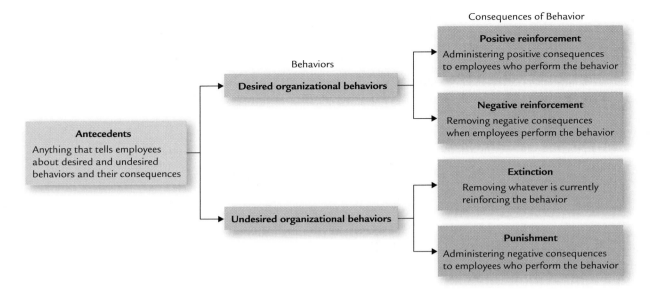

FIGURE 5.1
Operant Conditioning

environment to achieve your desired goals. In organizations, operant conditioning focuses on associating work behaviors (such as job performance, absenteeism, and lateness) with the consequences that will ensue in the employee's environment. These include *desired* consequences, such as pay and verbal praise, and *undesired* consequences, such as reprimands.

In addition to making the connection between a behavior and its consequences, antecedents play an important role in operant conditioning. Antecedents are instructions, rules, goals, advice from other members of an organization, and anything else that helps employees realize what behaviors they should and should not perform and what the consequences are for different behaviors. Antecedents play an educational role by letting employees know what the organizational consequences are (such as a pay raise or a promotion) for different behaviors (performing at a high level or impressing the division president during a presentation) and, thus, what behaviors they should perform.[11] For example, a rule (the antecedent) that three incidences of tardiness result in the loss of one vacation day (the consequence) lets employees know what will happen if they are continually late (the behavior).

Operant conditioning focuses on how organizations can use consequences to achieve two outcomes. One is increasing the probability that employees perform desired behaviors such as satisfying customers and coming to work on time. The other is decreasing the probability that employees perform undesired behaviors such as excessive Web surfing and making lengthy personal telephone calls at work. In the next section, we focus on the use of operant conditioning to promote desired behaviors in organizations; then we describe how operant conditioning can be used to discourage undesired behaviors.

ENCOURAGING DESIRED BEHAVIORS THROUGH POSITIVE AND NEGATIVE REINFORCEMENT

Reinforcement The process by which the probability that a desired behavior will occur is increased by applying consequences that depend on the behavior.

In operant conditioning, **reinforcement** is the process by which the probability that a desired behavior will occur is increased by applying consequences that depend on the behavior in question. One of a manager's major responsibilities is to ensure that subordinates learn and continue to perform desired behaviors consistently and dependably. In operant conditioning terms, managers need to increase the chances that this will occur. For example, they may want to encourage their subordinates to sell more products, assemble computer components faster, attend work more regularly, make more consistent use of safety equipment such as helmets, earplugs, and goggles, or provide higher-quality customer service.

Identifying Desired Behaviors.

The first step in the use of reinforcement is to identify desired behaviors that the organization wants to encourage or reinforce, such as using safety equipment or giving customers good service (see Figure 5.1). Surprisingly, correctly identifying these behaviors is not as easy as it might seem.

To an outside observer, for example, paying a commission on sales seems like a logical way to encourage salespeople to learn to satisfy customers. In this example, making sales is the behavior that is the focus of the reinforcement effort. However, this approach may result in short-run sales but not necessarily satisfied, loyal customers. It might lead to salespeople adopting a hard-sell approach, pushing customers to buy items that do not really meet their needs. Thus, the behaviors that result in satisfied long-term customers—behaviors such as building long-term relationships and making sure customers buy what is right for them—have not been identified correctly. What has been identified is the amount of actual sales.

Similarly, a professor who wants to encourage students to participate in class might reason that students have to regularly attend class in order to participate. The professor might, therefore, decide to reinforce attendance by making it worth 5 percent of a student's grade. Most students do come to class, but they do not actively participate because the behavior the professor has reinforced is attendance, not actual participation. The professor has not correctly identified the desired behavior. At Seagate Technologies in the opening case, CEO Stephen Luczo identified desired behaviors on the part of Seagate's suppliers—helping Seagate get to market quickly with superior new disk drives.

When desired behaviors are identified correctly, the second step in the reinforcement process is to decide how to reinforce the behavior. In operant conditioning, there are two types of reinforcement: positive and negative.[12]

Positive Reinforcement.

Positive reinforcement increases the probability that a behavior will occur by administering positive consequences to employees who perform the behavior. These positive consequences are known as *positive reinforcers*. To use positive reinforcement to facilitate the learning of desired behaviors, managers need

Positive reinforcement
Reinforcement that increases the probability of a desired behavior by administering positive consequences to employees who perform the behavior.

Companies frequently use award walls and plaques as positive reinforcers to motivate their employees. But reinforcers differ from person to person. A money-motivated employee, for example, may be less than pleased if presented with a plaque versus a bonus check.

to determine what consequences a given employee considers to be positive. Potential positive reinforcers include rewards such as higher pay, bonuses, promotions, job titles, interesting work, verbal praise, time off from work, and awards. Managers can determine whether these rewards are positively reinforcing for any given employee by seeing if that employee performs desired behaviors in order to obtain them.

It is important to keep in mind that individuals differ in what they consider to be a positive reinforcer. An employee who is independently wealthy, for example, may not view financial rewards as a positive reinforcer but may consider interesting work very reinforcing. In contrast, an employee with many financial needs and few financial resources may have exactly opposite preferences. Similarly, getting 5 percent credit for attending class regularly might be a powerful positive reinforcer for a student who is hoping to earn an A but not a positive reinforcer for a student who is content with a B or C in the course. Thus, managers need to take into account employees' individual preferences for different consequences.

With a little creative thinking, organizations can use reinforcement to promote the learning and performance of a wide variety of desirable behaviors. Many companies, for example, are trying to encourage their employees to give equal opportunities to an increasingly diverse workforce, yet are having a hard time getting a specific handle on the best ways to accomplish this objective. Positive reinforcement for diversity efforts may be one strategy that organizations can use. At Colgate-Palmolive, for example, a manager's pay is linked to diversity initiatives through the firm's Executive Incentive Compensation Plan. According to the plan, incentive compensation (such as a yearly bonus) depends on the extent to which a manager achieves certain predetermined objectives—one of which is supporting diversity. Colgate's diversity efforts in the United States have focused primarily on giving equal opportunities to women, African Americans, and Hispanics by having managers recruit and hire these employees, and once hired, giving them meaningful job assignments and opportunities for advancement and promotion.[13] At Seagate Technologies in the opening case, Luczo positively reinforced high quality and quick turnaround times on the part of suppliers through monetary incentives.

Negative Reinforcement. As in the case of positive reinforcement, subordinates experiencing negative reinforcement learn the connection between a desired organizational behavior and a consequence; however, the consequence is not a positive one that an employee wants to obtain but a negative one that the employee wishes to remove or avoid. **Negative reinforcement** increases the probability that a desired behavior will occur by removing, or rescinding, a negative consequence when an employee performs the behavior desired. The negative consequence that is removed is called a *negative reinforcer*. For example, if a manager complains every time an accountant turns in a report late, the complaints are a negative reinforcer if they result in the accountant learning to turn in the reports on time. By turning in reports when they are due, the accountant is able to "remove" the negative consequence of the complaints. Just as with positive reinforcement, managers need to take into account that individuals differ in what they consider to be a negative reinforcer.

When positive and negative reinforcement are used to promote learning, it is important for the consequences to be equivalent in magnitude to the desired behavior.[14] For example, even if pay is a positive reinforcer for an employee, a small increase in pay (a $5 weekly bonus) might not be significant enough to cause the employee to perform a desired behavior (say, make follow-up calls to all new customers). In the same way, 5 percent of the course grade might not be a big enough reinforcer to cause chronically absent students to come to class, and a professor's complaints in class might not be a big enough negative reinforcer to get some students to participate in class discussions (and by doing so, stop the professor from complaining).

Negative reinforcement
Reinforcement that increases the probability of a desired behavior by removing a negative consequence when an employee performs the behavior.

Using Reinforcement Appropriately. In general, positive reinforcement is better for employees, managers, and the organization as a whole than negative reinforcement. Negative reinforcement often has unintended side effects and makes for an unpleasant work environment. For example, a supervisor who continually complains may be resented and disliked. Even if positive reinforcement and negative reinforcement are equally successful in encouraging desired behaviors, the person or organization providing the reinforcement is likely to be viewed much more positively when positive reinforcement is consistently used.

When using reinforcement to promote the learning of desired behaviors in organizations, managers need to exercise some caution: When certain behaviors receive extensive reinforcement and others do not, employees may tend to focus on the former and ignore the latter. For example, if salespeople are paid solely on a commission basis, they may focus on making quick sales, and in doing so, may not perform the behaviors necessary for building long-term customer satisfaction (like making follow-up calls and sending service reminders, for example). Similarly, managers have to be careful to identify the right behaviors to reinforce.

Reinforcement Schedules. Managers using reinforcement to encourage the learning and performance of desired behaviors must choose whether to use continuous or partial reinforcement. When reinforcement is *continuous*, a behavior is reinforced every time it occurs. When reinforcement is *partial*, a behavior is reinforced intermittently. Continuous reinforcement can result in faster learning than can partial reinforcement. But if the reinforcement for some reason is curtailed, continuously reinforced behaviors will stop occurring more quickly than will partially reinforced behaviors.

Practical considerations often dictate whether reinforcement should be continuous or partial. A manager who is trying to encourage employees to use safety equipment, for example, may find continuous reinforcement infeasible. If she has to continually monitor her subordinates' use of safety equipment, she will never be able to get any work done herself.

Managers who decide to use partial reinforcement can choose from four schedules of partial reinforcement.[15] With a *fixed-interval schedule*, the period of time between the occurrence of each instance of reinforcement is fixed or set. An insurance agent whose supervisor takes him out to lunch at a fancy restaurant on the last Friday of the month if he has written a large number of policies during that month is being reinforced on a fixed-interval schedule. Once the supervisor has taken the agent out to lunch, a month will pass before the supervisor takes him out again for performing well. If in any given month the agent writes only a few policies, the supervisor does not treat him to lunch.

With a *variable-interval schedule*, the amount of time between reinforcements varies around a constant average. The owner of a car wash company who every so often watches each employee work on a car and praises those who do a good job is following a variable-interval schedule. The owner may watch and reinforce a given employee once a week, once every three weeks, or once a month, but over a six-month period the average amount of time between reinforcements is two weeks.

With a *fixed-ratio schedule*, a certain number of desired behaviors must occur before reinforcement is provided. Employees who are paid $5 for every three circuit boards they assemble are being reinforced on a fixed-ratio schedule. Many piece-rate pay plans currently in use at companies such as Lincoln Electric follow a fixed-ratio schedule.[16]

With a *variable-ratio schedule*, the number of desired behaviors that must occur before reinforcement varies around a constant average. A manager who allows an employee to leave early after she has stayed late for several evenings is following a variable-ratio schedule of reinforcement. Sometimes the manager allows the employee to leave early after working two late evenings, at other times after four late evenings, but over time the average is three evenings.

The choice of a schedule of partial reinforcement often depends on practical considerations: the particular behavior being encouraged, the type of reinforcer being used, or the nature of the employee's job. The specific type of schedule chosen is not as important as the fact that reinforcement is based on the performance of desired behaviors: Learning takes place only when the provision of a reinforcer depends on performance of a desired behavior.

SHAPING

Sometimes a desired behavior is unlikely to occur on its own or at any given point in time because an individual does not have the skills and knowledge necessary to perform the behavior or because the behavior can only evolve out of practice or experience. Consider, for example, a trainee who is learning to drive a bus in New York City. At the beginning of her training conducted by the firm's driving instructor, the trainee is unlikely to drive the bus properly and, thus, cannot be reinforced for this desired behavior. The instructor can use reinforcement to *stimulate* learning, however, by reinforcing successively closer approximations to the desired behavior (in this case, the proper handling of the bus in city traffic). Suppose the trainee initially jumps the curb when making left turns but after her sixth trip finally makes a turn that is still too wide but does not jump the curb. Even though the behavior was not at its ideal level, because the turn was a bit wider than it should have been, this behavior is positively reinforced by verbal praise from the instructor to increase the probability that it will occur again.

The reinforcement of successive and closer approximations to a desired behavior is known as **shaping**.[17] Shaping is particularly effective when employees need to learn complicated sequences of behavior. When it is unlikely that employees will be able to perform the desired behaviors all at once, managers reinforce closer and closer approximations to the desired behavior to encourage employees to gradually acquire the skills and expertise needed to perform at an adequate level.

DISCOURAGING UNDESIRED BEHAVIORS THROUGH EXTINCTION AND PUNISHMENT

Just as managers need to ensure that employees learn to perform desired behaviors dependably, they also need to ensure that employees learn *not* to perform undesired behaviors. Examples of undesired behaviors in organizations include (among hundreds of others) excessive absenteeism, excessive Web surfing on company time, operating heavy equipment such as bulldozers and cranes in a dangerous fashion, and sexually harassing other employees. Two main operant conditioning techniques reduce the probability of undesired behaviors: extinction and punishment (see Figure 5.1).

Extinction. According to the principles of operant conditioning, all behaviors—good and bad—are controlled by reinforcing consequences. Thus, any behavior that occurs is performed because the individual is receiving some form of reinforcement for it. If managers wish to lessen the probability that an undesired behavior will occur, they need to first determine what is currently reinforcing the behavior and then remove the source of reinforcement. Once the undesired behavior ceases to be reinforced, its frequency diminishes until it no longer occurs. This process is called **extinction**.

Suppose every time a manager has a meeting with one of her subordinates, Sam, he always tells jokes and fools around. At first, the manager thinks Sam's joking is harmless, but soon she realizes that the meetings are taking twice as long as they should, that certain items on the agenda are getting short shrift, and that Sam is having a hard time remembering the important points made during the meeting. After attending a man-

Stimulating learning involves reinforcing good performance bit-by-bit as employees learn the skills they need to do their jobs.

Shaping The reinforcement of successive and closer approximations to a desired behavior.

Extinction The lessening of undesired behavior by removing the source of reinforcement.

agement development seminar on operant conditioning, the manager realizes that she is actually positively reinforcing Sam's behavior by laughing at his jokes. At the next meeting, she treats Sam cordially but refrains from laughing at his jokes. Sam looks a little perplexed but soon stops joking and takes the meetings more seriously.

This example illustrates that extinction can be a relatively painless way to reduce the occurrence of undesired behaviors. The supervisor had considered talking directly to Sam or criticizing his behavior at their next meeting. Eliminating Sam's positive reinforcement for horsing around probably did less to hurt his feelings and disrupt their otherwise good relationship.

Punishment. Managers do not have the time to wait for extinction to lessen or eliminate some undesired behaviors. Certain behaviors are so detrimental or dangerous they need to stop their occurrence immediately. Just as a parent cannot rely on extinction to stop a child from touching a hot stove, a manager cannot rely on extinction to eliminate highly undesirable behaviors in the workplace such as sexual harassment or operating heavy equipment in a dangerous fashion. Under such circumstances, a manager can try to eliminate undesired behavior by using **punishment**—by administering a negative consequence when the undesired behavior occurs.

In operant conditioning, punishment and negative reinforcement are often confused. Students, employees, and managers alike think that these two techniques for managing behavior are similar or have the same result. However, they differ from each other in two important ways. First, punishment *reduces* the probability of an *undesired* behavior; negative reinforcement *increases* the probability of a *desired* behavior. Second, punishment involves administering a *negative* consequence when an *undesired* behavior occurs; negative reinforcement entails removing a *negative* consequence when a *desired* behavior occurs. Table 5.1 summarizes the effects of the different operant conditioning techniques that managers can use to encourage the performance of desired behaviors and eliminate undesired behaviors.

> **Punishment** The administration of a negative consequence when undesired behavior occurs.

TABLE 5.1

Operant Conditioning Techniques

Technique	How Consequence Is Administered	Effect on Behavior	Example
Positive reinforcement	Positive consequence is given when desired behavior is performed	Increases probability of desired behavior	Employee is praised for cleaning up work station
Negative reinforcement	Negative consequence is removed when desired behavior is performed	Increases probability of desired behavior	Supervisor complains about messy work station and stops only when worker cleans it up
Extinction	Positive consequence is removed when undesired behavior is performed	Decreases probability of undesired behavior	Manager refrains from laughing at a subordinate's disruptive jokes when the two have important matters to discuss
Punishment	Negative consequence is given when undesired behavior is performed	Decreases probability of undesired behavior	Manager criticizes subordinate for telling disruptive jokes when the two have important matters to discuss

Managers need to take into account the fact that people differ in what they consider to be punishment. If being scolded by a supervisor after coming to work late is a source of punishment for one employee, that employee will try as hard as possible not to be late after receiving a scolding. But an employee who hardly gives the scolding a second thought will come to work late again the next day. Some forms of punishment that organizations typically use are verbal reprimands, reductions in pay, elimination of privileges (such as personal days an employee can take off at his or her discretion), and temporary suspension. Organizations sometimes use a system of progressive punishment to try to curtail undesired behavior; the more an employee engages in the behavior, the stricter the punishment becomes.

Punishment can have some unexpected side effects and should be used only when necessary. It not only has the potential to threaten the employee's self-respect but can also create so much resentment and negative feelings toward the punisher and organization as a whole that the employee might want to retaliate. Thus, when punishment is used, managers need to be very careful that, while eliminating the undesired behavior, they do not create excessive hostility or negative feelings.

The following guidelines can help to ensure that punishment has its intended effect and does not generate negative side effects:

♦ Try to downplay the emotional element involved in punishment. Remember that you are punishing the person's undesirable behavior, not the person.

♦ Make sure the chosen negative consequence is indeed a punishment for the individual and punish the undesired behavior immediately.[18] Make sure employees know why they are being punished.

♦ Try to avoid punishing an employee in front of others. Although public punishment might seem like a good idea because it serves as a warning to others, it is likely to humiliate the individual being punished, reduce his or her esteem, and make co-workers uncomfortable. Remember: The key goal is to eliminate a person's undesirable behavior, not his or her self-respect.

♦ When possible, provide employees with a desired behavior in place of the undesired behavior.

When a manager does not follow those guidelines, not only is the individual who is being punished likely to suffer, but so too are his or her co-workers, the manager, and the whole organization.

ORGANIZATIONAL BEHAVIOR MODIFICATION

The systematic application of the principles of operant conditioning for learning desired behaviors is called **organizational behavior modification** (OB Mod). OB Mod has been successfully used to improve productivity, attendance, punctuality, safe work practices, customer service, and other important behaviors in a wide variety of organizations such as banks, department stores, factories, hospitals, and construction sites.[19] OB Mod can be used to encourage the learning of desired organizational behaviors as well as to discourage undesired behaviors.

Organizations that successfully use OB Mod follow a five-step process: identify, measure, analyze, intervene, and evaluate (see Figure 5.2).[20]

Identify the behavior to be learned. OB Mod should be used to encourage behaviors that can be observed by others (and can, therefore, be reinforced), are important for task performance, and can be measured. Examples include attendance, punctuality, the use of safety equipment, sales goals, customer service levels, productivity, and quality control.[21] The work behaviors also should be relevant to the job and to organizational perfor-

Organizational behavior modification The systematic application of the principles of operant conditioning for learning and managing important organizational behaviors.

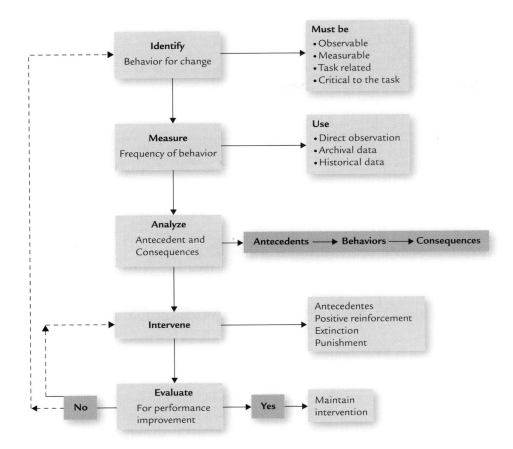

FIGURE 5.2

Steps in Organizational Behavior Modification

Source: Adapted from F. Luthans and A. D. Stajkovic, "Reinforce for Performance: The Need to Go Beyond Pay and Even Rewards," *Academy of Management Executive* 13(2) (1999): 49–57.

mance. For example, at the Treehouse Day Care Center in Chicago, the director of the center has identified punctuality as a critical behavior in need of improvement. OB Mod has been successfully used to promote desired behaviors ranging from safe driving by city bus drivers and timely and error-free registration and admittance procedures performed by hospital administrators to safe mining practices followed in open pit mines. It has also been used to encourage bank tellers to establish eye contact with their customers and greet them by name, improve the productivity of vineyard pruners, and the output of factory workers.[22]

Measure the frequency of the behavior. Before any actions are taken, it is important to get a baseline measure of how often the identified behavior occurs. For example, the director of Treehouse measured the punctuality of the center's staff over a two-week period and discovered that each staff member was late around three times per week.

Analyze the antecedents and consequences of the behavior. Once the frequency of the behavior has been determined, it is important to identify the current antecedents and consequences of the behavior. At Treehouse, the director realized that while it was assumed that staff would come to work on time for their shifts, there were no actual antecedents in place to cue punctuality. In terms of consequences, the director would occasionally reprimand workers who were excessively late for their shifts, and other staff members would occasionally complain when they had to remain on the job past their own quitting time because staff members on the next shift were late. However, the director realized there were no positive reinforcers in place to actually promote punctuality.

To improve punctuality, the Treehouse Day Care Center in Chicago first had to gauge how frequently its employees were tardy before it could correct the problem.

Intervene to change the frequency of the behavior. Interventions can include introducing antecedents and applying operant conditioning techniques including positive reinforcement, negative reinforcement, punishment, and extinction. Remember, whenever feasible, positive reinforcement is preferred to negative reinforcement and extinction is preferred to punishment. At Treehouse's next staff meeting, the director stressed how important punctuality was to the quality of child care, how important state-mandated children-to-caregiver ratios were, and the importance of being considerate to other staff members (who have to fill in for those who are late). The director also had a plaque made that summarized the reasons why "Punctuality Benefits Us All," which was hung next to the center's bulletin board. In addition to cuing punctuality with these antecedents, the director also positively reinforced punctuality in two ways. First, each week, staff members arriving on time were given verbal praise from the director. Second, staff with perfect punctuality records each month were allowed to take a half-day off the following month.

Evaluate whether the intervention was successful in changing behavior. At this last step, the frequency of the behavior is again measured to determine if the intervention was successful. If the behavior has been successfully modified, then all that needs to be done at this step is to maintain the intervention (for example, continue to use the antecedents and positive reinforcers from the prior step to encourage the behavior). If the behavior has not been successfully modified, then managers need to reconsider their intervention methods and modify them accordingly and/or reconsider the behavior they originally identified. At Treehouse, the director measured the punctuality of the staff over a two-week period following the intervention and was delighted to discover that no staff members were late for their shifts during the entire two weeks.

Research suggests that when OB Mod is appropriately used, it can be highly effective when it comes to promoting desirable organizational behavior.[23] For example, a recent review of research on OB Mod showed that it improved employee performance by 17 percent, on average. In a recent field experiment conducted by Alexander Stajkovic and Fred Luthans in a division of a large organization that processes credit card bills, it was found that OB Mod resulted in a 37 percent increase in performance when the reinforced behavior included financial incentives.[24] Interestingly, when performance was positively reinforced by simple supervisory feedback, the performance of employees increased by 20 percent. When social recognition and praise were used, performance increased by 24 percent.[25]

ETHICAL ISSUES IN OB MOD

There is some controversy surrounding the use of OB Mod in organizations. Proponents rightfully claim that OB Mod is a useful way to manage important organizational behaviors. Research indicating that OB Mod can be successfully used to increase productivity and cut down on accidents, waste, and absenteeism is certainly consistent with this view. Opponents of OB Mod complain that it is overly controlling, however. These critics believe that managers who explicitly manipulate consequences to control behavior strip employees of their dignity, freedom of choice, and individuality. They also believe that treating employees in such a cut-and-dried fashion may, over time, rob them of the initiative they might otherwise have had to respond appropriately to changing conditions.

Moreover, employees who are managed in such a fashion may refrain from performing important organizational behaviors that are not specifically part of their job duties, such as helping co-workers or coming up with new and good ideas, because these behaviors often cannot be assigned in advance and appropriately reinforced. These voluntary behaviors are essential for organizational survival and effectiveness but may not be covered by an organization's formal system of rewards because they are performed voluntarily. When employees are managed according to the principles of operant conditioning, they may become so reinforcement oriented that they refrain from doing anything that is *not* reinforced.

There is no clear-cut answer to the ethical dilemma posed by OB Mod, and there are counterarguments to each of the anti–OB Mod positions. In response to the criticism that OB Mod strips employees of their freedom of choice and individuality, for example, OB Mod proponents might assert that whether an employee performs a behavior or not is ultimately his or her own choice and that operant conditioning takes individuality into account when the individual preferences of different reinforcers are considered. Nonetheless, as a manager, it is important to be aware of the issues raised by this debate and think through their implications from one's own perspective. Additionally, any use of OB Mod must conform to employment laws. For example, in California and many other states, labor laws require that employers compensate employees for overtime work, even if they are paid on a piece-rate basis, to encourage them to work efficiently.[26]

Learning from Others

Although operant conditioning accurately describes some of the major factors that influence learning in organizations, certain aspects of learning are not covered in this theory. To get a more complete picture of how members of an organization learn, we now turn to **social cognitive theory** (also referred to as social learning theory). Albert Bandura, one of the principal contributors to social cognitive theory, suggests that any attempt to understand how people learn must also take into account a person's feelings and thoughts (cognitions) and their observations of the world around them (that is, their social environment) (see Figure 5.3). Social cognitive theory acknowledges the importance of the person in the learning process by taking cognitive processes into account.[27]

Cognitive processes are the various thought processes that people engage in. When people form attributions (see Chapter 4), for example, they are engaging in a cognitive process to determine why a person has performed a specific behavior. From

Social cognitive theory A learning theory that takes into account the fact that thoughts, feelings, and the social environment influence learning.

Cognitive processes Thought processes.

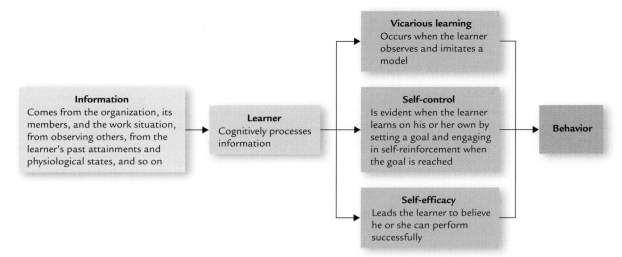

FIGURE 5.3
Social Cognitive Theory

the perspective of social cognitive theory, employees actively process information from the social environment and those around them when they learn.[28]

Suppose you study hard yet are doing poorly in one of your classes. A friend of yours doesn't seem to put in as much time as you do yet is maintaining a B+ average in the class. You think you are just as smart as your friend and notice how your friend studies for the class: He takes detailed notes in class, highlights the chapters and then summarizes the key points, and goes to see the professor whenever he is confused. You start doing this yourself, your grades improve, and you think you can salvage a B in the course after all. This example demonstrates how you have learned from observing another person. In learning how to do well in the class, your thoughts about your poor performance and about your friend's relatively good performance, your observations of how your friend studies for the class, your belief that you are just as smart as your friend, and your decision to copy your friend's approach to studying were the steps you took to learn how to perform well in the class.

In social cognitive theory, learning from observing others perform a behavior is called **vicarious learning**. When vicarious learning occurs, a person (the learner) observes another person (the model) perform a behavior. The learner observes the effect of the model's behavior on the environment (is it reinforced?), and when an appropriate situation arises, the learner imitates the model's behavior.

Several conditions must be met for vicarious learning to take place:[29]

Vicarious learning Learning that occurs when one person learns a behavior by watching another person perform the behavior.

◆ The learner must observe the model when he or she is performing the behavior.

◆ The learner must accurately perceive the model's behavior.

◆ The learner must remember the behavior.

◆ The learner must have the skills and abilities necessary to perform the behavior.

◆ The learner must see that the model receives reinforcement for the behavior in question. If the model is not reinforced (or is punished) for the behavior, there is obviously no incentive for the learner to imitate the behavior.

A substantial amount of the learning that takes place in organizations occurs vicariously. Training new recruits, for example, involves considerable amounts of vicarious learning. Formal training sessions often rely on demonstrations of appropriate behaviors by experienced employees and role-playing during which employees observe others performing appropriate and inappropriate behaviors. Retail organizations sometimes use films showing experienced salespeople giving customers good service in an effort to train new salespeople to do the same. For these films to be effective, it is essential for the model (the experienced salesperson) to be reinforced for the high-quality service behaviors. Often the reinforcement is the customer's decision to purchase something. Similarly, restaurants often have inexperienced waiters and waitresses follow and observe the behaviors of an experienced co-worker for a few days prior to serving their first customers. By watching others, new recruits learn appropriate on-the-job behaviors, such as those desired by the Ritz-Carlton, which is profiled in the accompanying Global View.

global view

Vicarious Learning at the Ritz-Carlton

The Ritz-Carlton luxury hotel chain is a global organization with 23,000 employees and 54 hotels scattered in more than 15 countries worldwide. Currently, new hotels are planned for Miami's South Beach area in Florida; Berlin, Germany; and Grand Cayman, Cayman Islands.[30] In order to appeal to its global customers around the world, the Ritz-Carlton recently partnered with NewspaperDirect, giving its guests access to over 150 daily newspapers from 40 countries.[31]

Providing high-quality customer service is the hallmark of the Ritz-Carlton, and it is embodied in the first sentence of its credo: "The Ritz-Carlton Hotel is a place where the genuine care and comfort of our guests is our highest mission."[32] In order to ensure that each new employee learns how to provide "the finest personal service" to Ritz-Carlton guests whether in Osaka, Japan, or Philadelphia, Pennsylvania, the Ritz-Carlton relies on vicarious learning.[33]

Take the case of a new employee who will be a room-service waiter at the Ritz-Carlton in Boston.[34] After a two-day orientation program, the new employee is teamed up with an experienced room-service waiter and literally follows the experienced waiter around for the next few days, observing what the waiter says and does and how customers react. The newcomer picks up certain tips along the way, such as the importance of trying to anticipate what customers might

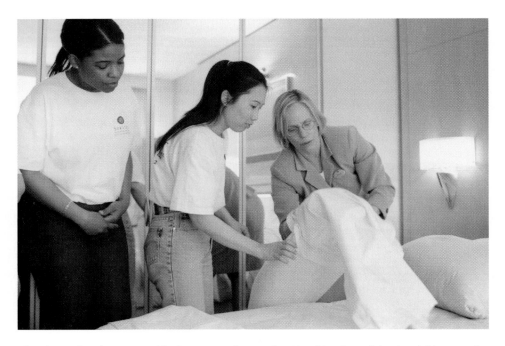

The Ritz-Carlton is renowned for its outstanding service. New hires learn "vicariously" how to give guests great service by accompanying experienced staff members and emulating their behavior.

want even if they don't ask for it. For example, a guest ordering one dinner and a bottle of wine might need two glasses. If he or she orders dinner along with ice cream, the dinner needs to stay hot while the ice cream needs to stay cold. After observing the experienced waiter model appropriate behavior, the newcomer starts playing a more active role by talking to customers or opening a bottle of wine, but the model waiter is never far from sight until the newcomer has learned all he needs to pass a test administered by the manager in charge of in-room dining services.[35] Clearly, vicarious learning has paid off handsomely for the Ritz-Carlton. It has won the prestigious Malcolm Baldrige National Quality Award and ranked first in *Business Travel News's* Top U.S. Hotel Chain survey for two years running.[36]

Vicarious learning also plays an important role in the day-to-day functioning of most organizations. Organizational members continually observe others and often try to remember behaviors that result in reinforcement. These behaviors can range from relatively routine matters, such as when to arrive at work and how long to take for lunch, to the best way to present a report to upper-level management and how to conduct oneself in a business meeting. Moreover, recent research suggests that employees can even learn how to be creative by observing the behavior of creative co-workers.[37]

Vicarious learning is also an important means of acquiring behaviors that are complicated and have a high cost of failure. Much of the learning that takes place through operant conditioning is the result of trial and error: The learner engages in a variety of behaviors and learns to repeat those that are reinforced and abandon those that are not. For some kinds of work, however, an organization simply cannot afford the costs of trial-and-error learning. No one would want to be at the mercy of a medical intern who is learning open-heart surgery by means of trial and error; the costs (a few dead patients) of learning in this manner are just too high. In such situations, vicarious learning is essential. A learner who has all the necessary knowledge, skills, and abilities can learn quite complicated sequences of behavior by carefully observing the behaviors and outcomes of others with more experience.

In organizations, there are many potential models available for members to imitate. However, only a few of these models will be used to acquire new behaviors vicariously. To take advantage of vicarious learning in organizations, managers should ensure that good performer models are available for newcomers and existing organizational members to learn from. Models that are most likely to be imitated by others tend to be provided by (1) members of the organization who are highly competent in the modeled behavior and may even have a reputation for being an expert, (2) individuals with high status in the organization, (3) employees who receive reinforcers that the learner desires, and (4) individuals who engage in desired behaviors in a friendly manner.[38]

Learning on Your Own

Self-control Self-discipline that allows a person to learn to perform a behavior even though there is no external pressure to do so.

Social cognitive theory acknowledges that people can learn on their own by using **self-control**—that is, by learning to perform a behavior even though there is no external pressure to do so. Several conditions indicate that a person is using self-control:[39]

1. An individual must engage in a low-probability behavior. A low-probability behavior is a behavior that a person would ordinarily not want to perform. This condition distinguishes individuals exhibiting self-control from those engaging in activities they enjoy. For example, Sylvia Crano, an administrative secretary, has had a new software package for graphics sitting on her desk for the past six months. She hates learning how to use new software and, fortunately, her boss hasn't put any pressure on her to learn the new software. Taking the initiative to learn how to use the new software is a

low-probability response for Crano. If she bites the bullet and comes in one Saturday to learn it, Crano will be exhibiting self-control.

2. Self-reinforcers must be available to the learner. **Self-reinforcers** are any consequences or rewards that individuals give to themselves. Potential self-reinforcers include buying oneself a present, eating a favorite food, going out to a movie, getting some extra sleep, and going out with friends. Sometimes self-reinforcement comes simply from a feeling of accomplishment or achievement. In the past, when Sylvia Crano has accomplished a particularly difficult task, she has rewarded or reinforced herself by buying a new CD or having lunch with a friend.

3. The learner must set goals that determine when self-reinforcement takes place. When self-control takes place, people do not indiscriminately reward themselves but set goals that determine when they will self-reinforce. How do people determine these goals or standards? Essentially, they rely on their own past performance, the performance of others on similar kinds of tasks, or some socially acquired performance standard. Crano's goal was to complete the software's tutorial and use the new program to reproduce some graphs she had done previously.

4. The learner must administer the reinforcer when the goal is achieved. Crano allowed herself to have lunch out with her friend only when she was able to use the new software to reproduce her existing graphs.

All people engage in self-control and self-reinforcement to learn behaviors on and off the job. These activities can range from the relatively mundane (such as cutting short a lunch hour to catch up on e-mails) to the more involved (learning how to appropriately give subordinates negative feedback). Managers need to be aware that self-control takes place at work, especially when individuals are interested in and care about their work. When opportunities for self-control are present and employees engage in it, managers do not need to take as active a role in controlling behavior and consequences because employees are taking responsibility for learning and performing desired behaviors themselves. In such cases, the managers' efforts at control may be not only redundant but also counterproductive because they may irritate and anger those who are self-controlled. Instead of trying to control individuals like this, managers would be wise to focus their efforts on those who need more guidance.

Self-reinforcers
Consequences or rewards that individuals can give to themselves.

Formal self-management training sessions teach employees to monitor themselves so managers don't have to.

Employees who manage their own behavior through self-control are often said to be self-managing. Sometimes, however, employees may need a bit of coaching and guidance to become truly self-managing. Managers can provide the training and support employees need to develop self-management skills and put them to use. Some organizations such as National Semiconductor explicitly recognize this need and have formal programs in place to teach self-management.[40]

BELIEFS ABOUT ONE'S ABILITY TO LEARN: THE ROLE OF SELF-EFFICACY

Self-efficacy A person's belief about his or her ability to perform a particular behavior successfully.

Social cognitive theory also emphasizes the importance of **self-efficacy**—a person's belief about his or her ability to perform a particular behavior successfully—in the learning process.[41] One secretary may believe that she can learn how to use a new software package on her own, and another may have strong doubts about his ability to learn new software without taking a formal training course. Self-efficacy has powerful effects on learning because people try to learn only those behaviors that they think they will be able to perform successfully.[42] Self-efficacy affects learning in three ways:[43]

1. *Self-efficacy influences the activities and goals that individuals choose for themselves:* Employees with a low level of self-efficacy may never try to learn how to perform challenging tasks because they think they will fail at them. Such employees tend to set relatively low goals for themselves. Conversely, an individual with high self-efficacy is likely to try to learn how to perform demanding tasks and set high personal goals. Consistent with this reasoning, research has found that individuals not only learn but also perform at levels consistent with their self-efficacy beliefs. Employees learn what they think they are able to learn.

2. *Self-efficacy affects learning by influencing the effort that individuals exert on the job:* Employees with high self-efficacy generally work hard to learn how to perform new behaviors because they are confident that their efforts will be successful. Employees with low self-efficacy may exert less effort when learning how to perform complicated or difficult behaviors, not because they are lazy but because they don't think the effort will pay off. Their lack of confidence in their ability to succeed causes them to think that exerting a lot of effort is futile because they are likely to fail anyway.

3. *Self-efficacy affects the persistence with which a person tries to master new and sometimes difficult tasks:* Because employees with high self-efficacy are confident that they can learn how to perform a given task, they are likely to persist in their efforts even in the face of temporary setbacks or problems. Conversely, employees with low self-efficacy who think they are unlikely to be able to learn a difficult task are likely to give up as soon as an obstacle appears or the going gets a little tough. Consistent with this reasoning, in a recent review of the extensive literature on self-efficacy, Albert Bandura and Ed Locke concluded that self-efficacy is a powerful determinant of job performance.[44]

SOURCES OF SELF-EFFICACY

Because self-efficacy can have such powerful effects on learning and performance in organizations, it is important to identify where it comes from. Bandura has identified four principal sources.[45]

Past performance is one of the most powerful sources of self-efficacy. Employees who have succeeded on job-related activities in the past are likely to have higher self-efficacy for such activities than employees who have failed. Managers can boost low levels of self-efficacy by ensuring that employees can and do succeed on certain tasks. "Small successes" boost self-efficacy and enable more substantial accomplishments in the future.

Vicarious experience or observation of others is another source of self-efficacy. Seeing co-workers succeed at a particular task may heighten the observer's self-efficacy. Conversely, seeing co-workers fail is likely to discourage the observer.

Verbal persuasion—that is, trying to convince people that they have the ability to learn and succeed at a particular task—can give rise to self-efficacy. Research has shown that when managers are confident that their subordinates can succeed at a particular task, the subordinates actually perform at a higher level.[46]

An individual's reading of his or her internal physiological states is the fourth source of self-efficacy that Bandura identified.[47] A person who expects to fail at some task or to find something too demanding is likely to experience certain physiological symptoms: a pounding or racing heart, feeling flushed, sweaty hands, headaches, and so on. The particular symptoms vary from individual to individual but over time become associated with doing poorly. If the symptoms start to occur in any given situation, self-efficacy for dealing with that situation may plummet.

Consider the case of Michael Pulinski, who was facing an important job interview. Pulinski really wanted to get this job and had spent a considerable amount of time preparing for the interview. He was familiar with the company and had prepared good questions to ask the interviewer about the job. He also had thoroughly rehearsed answers to typical interview questions (such as "Where do you see yourself in five years?") and had bought a new suit for the occasion. The day of the interview, Pulinski got up feeling quite good and was actually looking forward to the interview and to demonstrating that he was the right candidate for the job. He arrived to the interview a little early and paged through a recent copy of *Business Week* in the reception area. As he was thinking about how much this job meant to him, he started getting nervous. He could feel his face getting flushed, his hands were sweaty, and his heart started pounding in his chest. Pulinski's self-efficacy plummeted. Because of these physical symptoms, he decided that he was much too nervous to make a good impression in the interview. Unfortunately, his low self-efficacy resulted in his not doing well in the interview and failing to get a job offer.

Learning by Doing

Some learning takes place by actually engaging in a new or different activity. Often referred to as **experiential learning**, this learning occurs by the direct involvement of the learner in the subject matter being learned—learning by doing, in other words.[48] Consider, for example, how people learn to be air traffic controllers. They, of course, can read reference books on air traffic patterns, study Federal Aviation Administration rules and regulations, learn how to communicate with pilots who are flying planes, and study the configurations of different airports. However, if they only rely on these kinds of activities, they will never be an effective and safe air traffic controller. What's missing? Learning by doing. In order to master air traffic controlling, it is essential that prospective controllers learn their jobs by doing them. Clearly, it would be too dangerous for them to learn how to be an air traffic controller while directing real traffic in airspace. But they can and do learn by performing realistic simulations of actual air traffic controllers' jobs using the same equipment they will be using on the job.

Learning by doing is an important component of many kinds of jobs and occupations ranging from landscape architecture and nursing to sports, acting, and surgery. Moreover, learning by doing it not just important in order to be able to be

Experiential learning
Learning that occurs by the direct involvement of the learner in the subject matter being learned (that is, learning by doing).

Although it sounds counterintuitive, creativity on the job actually involves a number of methodical steps, including identifying the problem that needs to be solved, gathering information, and then generating ideas about how to do it.

able to execute technical, physical, or artistic tasks well—it is also important for interpersonal skills. In the opening case, senior managers at Seagate Technologies learn by doing on wilderness adventures.[49] What are they learning? The managers are learning valuable interpersonal skills that will enable them to work well in a team for the good of the team.

Continuous Learning Through Creativity

Creativity The generation of novel and useful ideas.

Creativity is the generation of novel and useful ideas.[50] By *novel* we mean ideas that represent new ways of thinking. By *useful* we mean ideas that have the potential to contribute to the performance and well-being of individuals, groups, and organizations. When people are being creative, they are engaged in continuous learning, whether it is to discover a vaccine for the HIV virus that causes AIDS, develop a new design for kitchen cabinets, or successfully revive a classic car model such as the Volkswagon Beetle. The idea of easy-to-use stick-on notes (Post-it Notes), the idea of offering healthy foods like salads in fast-food restaurants such as McDonald's, and the idea of flexible work schedules—all are examples of the results of creativity. Creative ideas such as these are novel and useful responses to problems and opportunities and result from continuous learning. From the opening case, it is clear that Seagate Technologies depends on continuous learning for its ongoing successes in the disk drive market.

Innovation The successful implementation of creative ideas.

Innovation is the successful implementation of creative ideas.[51] The 3M Corporation innovated when it successfully manufactured and marketed Post-it Notes; Apple Computer innovated when it designed and built the first personal computer, and it continues to innovate today with its new product offerings.

THE CREATIVE PROCESS

Each instance of creativity seems unique because an individual or group has come up with something that seems totally new or different. The creative process, however, usually entails a number of learning steps (see Figure 5.4).[52] The first two steps are recognizing a problem or opportunity and gathering information. Sometimes the first step

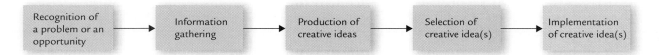

| Recognition of a problem or an opportunity | → | Information gathering | → | Production of creative ideas | → | Selection of creative idea(s) | → | Implementation of creative idea(s) |

FIGURE 5.4
The Creative Process

entails learning that something people think is a problem really isn't. Decades ago, some well-intentioned, but misinformed, educators thought it was a problem to be left-handed; so when left-handed children were learning how to write, they were urged to use their right hands no matter how awkward or difficult it was. Sometimes the problem needs redefining. Tooth decay in toddlers, for example, is not so much a function of what toddlers eat and drink but how and when they do it. (The real culprit is drinking from a bottle, especially right before bedtime.) Identifying a problem is also part of this first step—for example, recognizing that excessive exposure to the sun can lead to cancer—as is recognizing a potential opportunity—for example, that reality shows appeal greatly to today's TV viewers.[53]

An important part of learning about a problem or opportunity is involved in the second step—gathering information. Here, too, learning takes place as the learner figures out what kind of information to gather. In the process of gathering information, the learner might decide the problem or opportunity has been defined too broadly or too narrowly. He or she may then go back to step one and redefine the problem or opportunity before proceeding to learn about which information to gather and how to find it.

The third step in the creative process is the production of ideas. Once learners have gathered information, they need to come up with potential responses to problems or opportunities. During the production of ideas, it is important that learners feel free to come up with ideas that seem far-fetched or off the wall.

Once the ideas have been produced, learners are then ready for the fourth step of the creative process: selecting the idea or ideas they think will be useful. Sometimes learners assess each idea according to some criterion they may have previously determined to be important, such as the estimated annual sales of a new type of digital camera or the amount of computer memory needed to run a program. At this step, the information gathered during the second step can be helpful in evaluating the usefulness of each idea generated.

Once one or more ideas have been selected, it is time for implementation. At this stage in the creative process, innovation kicks in. Can the organization successfully implement the creative ideas it has developed and chosen to pursue?

Although the steps in the creative process are described previously and are shown in Figure 5.4 as if they always occur in a certain sequence, the order in which they occur is not fixed, nor does each step have to take place for creativity to occur. Let's see from the accompanying OB Today how the creative process unfolded at Hewlett-Packard (HP) and how it resulted in the company's successful Big Bang line of inexpensive printers.

Creativity and the creative process, by their nature, are hard to predict. It is difficult to tell in advance, for example, which decision makers will come up with creative ideas. Some people are naturally more creative than others, but, under the right circumstances, a person who is not very creative may come up with a creative solution. Evidence also shows that creativity is more likely to occur in some groups and organizations than in others. Researchers who have tried to identify some of the determinants of creativity have found that characteristics of individual decision makers and of the situations in which they make decisions contribute to creativity.

To create an entirely new line of printers, engineers at Hewlett-Packard, the industry's market leader, had to think outside the box. After some resistance, HP engineers altered the development process, producing a smaller, less-expensive line of printers.

ob today

HP's Big Bang

A few years ago, HP managers Tom Alexander and Vyomesh Joshi identified an unexpected problem and opportunity that led to an innovative line of inexpensive HP printers. In an early planning meeting with design engineers, Alexander and Joshi described how they wanted the engineers to develop an entirely new line of printers and related consumer products that were significantly less expensive than any of HP's existing offerings. And they didn't want the engineers to go about this task in their usual manner—trying to tinker with existing products to lower their costs. They wanted the engineers to develop the new line from scratch.[54]

The engineers were highly skeptical and resistant to the idea. So Alexander stood on an HP printer to drive home the message—HP was making printers that were strong enough to support the weight of a grown man. But that is not what customers wanted. Customers wanted inexpensive printers that will allow them to print from their digital cameras or make copies and send faxes. Joshi's vision was for HP to develop two totally new platforms that would be very inexpensive and the building blocks for over a dozen models of inkjet printers and combination models (printer/fax/scanner/copier).[55]

As the engineers gathered information, they realized that they needed to totally alter the way they were accustomed to developing new products. They needed to be incredibly cost-conscious. And they needed to develop ideas for platforms from the ground up—starting off with an empty box and then just adding features that were absolutely necessary at the lowest cost. Eventually, they settled on and developed two new platforms called the Malibu (for the higher end of the market) and the Crossbow (for the lower end of the market).[56]

HP successfully implemented these two new product lines, and the Big Bang (as this initiative was referred to) was a dramatic success. Not only did HP engineers develop products from these low-cost platforms that they thought impossible when they started out on the Big Bang, but also HP was able to increase its market share of all-in-one machines to close to 70 percent, and revenues and profit margins increased as a result. As manager John Solomon indicated, the new line is "much cheaper to make, much better in terms of image quality and speed, and it's half the size."[57] Clearly, continuous learning paid off handsomely for HP with its innovative line of new printers.[58]

CHARACTERISTICS OF EMPLOYEES THAT CONTRIBUTE TO CREATIVITY

Numerous characteristics of employees have been linked to creativity, but the ones that seem to be most relevant to understanding creativity in organizations are personal characteristics or individual differences, task-relevant knowledge, and intrinsic motivation (see Figure 5.5). These characteristics contribute to creativity whether employees work individually or in groups.

Although these factors contribute to creativity, they do not, of course, guarantee that any given employee or group of employees will be creative. And the lack, or low level, of any of these factors does not mean that a person or group will not or cannot be creative. Creativity is determined by the interaction or joint effects of a number of factors.

Individual Differences. In Chapter 2, we described a variety of ways in which people differ from each other and some of the personality traits and abilities especially relevant to understanding and managing organizational behavior. At least three of the personality traits we discussed earlier are likely to contribute to creativity.[59]

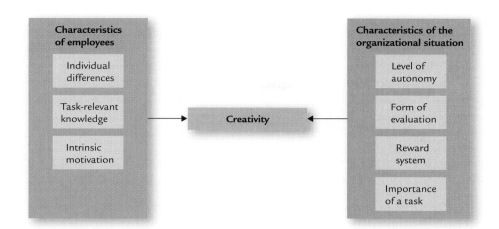

FIGURE 5.5
Determinants of Creativity

Recall that one of the Big Five general personality traits is *openness to experience*, which captures the extent to which an individual is original, is open to a wide variety of stimuli, has broad interests, and is willing to take risks. How does openness to experience contribute to creativity? It helps employees come up with new ideas and ways of doing things, and it helps to ensure that employees are willing to take the risks involved in proposing unusual ideas.

Two specific personality traits that are likely to contribute to creativity are *locus of control* and *self-esteem* (see Chapter 2). Locus of control captures the extent to which people think that their own actions and behaviors are important in determining what happens. *Internals* believe they have a lot of control over their environment and what happens to them. *Externals* believe that outside forces determine their fate. An *internal* locus of control contributes to creativity because it results in employees' feeling responsible for coming up with new ideas and being creative.[60] An *external* locus of control hinders creativity because employees believe that their own efforts are unimportant.[61]

Self-esteem is pride in oneself and in one's capabilities.[62] Self-esteem contributes to employees' confidence that they can come up with creative ideas, and it gives them the confidence to take risks and suggest ideas that may seem outlandish.

In addition to personality, it also is likely that ability contributes to creativity. At the broadest level, intelligence contributes to creativity because it helps employees come up with new ideas, see connections between things that other people do not see, view things from different perspectives, and synthesize a lot of information. Other cognitive abilities also contribute to creativity, especially when they are relevant to the kind of work an employee is engaged in. Numerical ability (the speed and accuracy with which a person can solve arithmetic problems), for example, is likely to contribute to creativity in a group of people who are looking at the overall cost implications of various changes to a manufacturing process.

Task–Relevant Knowledge. Task-relevant knowledge is all of the information, skills, and expertise that an individual or group has about the kind of work being performed.[63] Without task-relevant knowledge, it would be difficult for an architect to come up with a creative design for a new building, for a doctor to find a new way to treat arthritis, or for a secretary to discover a unique and useful filing system. To generate creative responses, the architect needs a good understanding of building design and architectural principles, the doctor needs knowledge pertaining to medicine in general and to arthritis in particular, and the secretary needs to be familiar with the kinds of information to be filed, the ways in which it needs to be accessed, and how frequently it's accessed.

Intrinsic Motivation. In Chapter 6, we distinguish between intrinsic and extrinsic motivation. For intrinsically motivated employees, the source of motivation is the work itself. These employees enjoy performing their jobs, often love their work, and get a sense of personal satisfaction when they do a good job or come up with a creative idea. Extrinsically motivated employees may perform at a high level, but the source of their motivation is external; they are motivated by, for example, the pay they receive and the chances of receiving a bonus, raise, or promotion—positive reinforcers provided by others, in other words.

In general, employees are more likely to be creative when they are intrinsically motivated.[64] The high level of involvement in the work that intrinsic motivation brings seems to spur creativity.

CHARACTERISTICS OF THE ORGANIZATIONAL SITUATION THAT CONTRIBUTE TO CREATIVITY

Although certain individuals may be more likely than others to be creative, creativity is also more likely to occur in certain situations than in others. Four situational characteristics are likely to affect creativity: level of autonomy, form of evaluation, reward system, and the importance of a task or problem (see Figure 5.5).

Level of Autonomy. More than 70 percent of the research and development (R&D) scientists who participated in a study of creativity indicated that autonomy was an important factor in instances of creativity that they were involved in or observed in their organizations.[65] Autonomy is the freedom and independence to make decisions and have personal control over one's work on a day-to-day basis. A high degree of autonomy is good for creativity. And when autonomy is low, creativity is unlikely.

Form of Evaluation. Imagine how William Shakespeare would have felt when he was writing some of his masterpieces if a supervisor had been standing over his shoulder critiquing scenes or bits of dialogue that didn't sound quite right ("A hero who believes in ghosts, talks to himself a lot, and kills his girlfriend's father? I don't think so, Will") and criticizing him when he took too long to complete a play. In all likelihood, these kinds of actions would have hampered some of Shakespeare's creativity.

Creative people and employees like to know how they are doing and to receive feedback and encouragement. But overly evaluative feedback and criticism can hamper creativity because it can make employees afraid to take risks.[66] If there is a strong likelihood that your boss will criticize the far-out idea you come up with, you may not risk expressing it. However, if your boss is interested in your ideas, provides constructive comments about how they may be improved, and points out some of their pros and cons, you may be encouraged to come up with an even better idea.

Reward System. People who come up with creative ideas like to be rewarded for them. But what happens if employees think that their salaries, bonuses, and chances for promotion hinge on their almost always being right, rarely or never making mistakes, and always being efficient in their use of time? Their creativity may be hampered, and they may be unlikely to take risks to come up with and choose creative responses to problems and opportunities.[67] By definition, creative responses are new, and there is always the potential that they may fail.

To help promote creativity, an organization's reward system should recognize and reward hard work and creativity. Creative employees and others in the organization need to see that hard work and creativity are recognized, appreciated, and rewarded— for example, through bonuses and raises. It is important, however, that these rewards not be seen as an attempt to control behavior and that employees do not feel they are being closely watched and rewarded based on what is observed.[68] It also is important that employees are *not* punished when some of their creative ideas do not pan out. Indeed, if employers want creativity, they need to encourage organizational members to take reasonable risks and be willing to accept failure.

By now it should be clear to you that OB Mod should *not* be used for behaviors that involve creativity or when creativity is desired. OB Mod assumes that desired behaviors can be objectively determined in advance; this is impossible for any kind of creative activity, which, by definition, is novel or new. Moreover, the relatively rigid matching of behavior and consequences in OB Mod ensures that any out-of-the-ordinary behavior (which could be creative) is discouraged. More generally, principles of operant conditioning, which are useful for learning desired behaviors that can be determined in advance, should not be used for creative kinds of work and tasks. However, even when creativity is desired, principles from operant conditioning can be used to promote the learning of certain kinds of behavior, such as using safety equipment, which can be objectively specified in advance. For example, suppose a welder is trying to come up with a way to join thin steel cylinders so that the place where they are joined together is invisible to the naked eye. In order to come up with the new procedure or process, the welder should have autonomy to experiment, and consequences such as rewards should not be directly linked to her current behaviors or her creativity will be hampered. However, a priori, her supervisor knows that she must wear safety goggles and follow certain safety procedures—for these kinds of behaviors, operant conditioning can be beneficial.

Importance of a Task. Being creative is intrinsically rewarding, but it also can be hard work. Creativity is enhanced when members of an organization feel that what they are working on is important.[69]

THE INTERACTION OF PERSONALITY AND SITUATIONAL FACTORS

Recall from Chapter 2 how behavior is often the result of the interaction of personality and the situation. Recent research suggests that this is the case for creativity. For example, a recent study found that whether or not openness to experience was related to creativity in jobs that do not necessarily entail creative work depended on the extent to which the employees' tasks provided them with the opportunity to be creative, or entailed some degree of flexibility and uncertainty, and the extent that the employees received positive feedback.[70] Results from this study and others are encouraging, as they suggest that all personality types have the potential to be creative if the situation they are in and those around them provide them with the right kinds of encouragement and support.[71]

you're the management expert

Encouraging Independent Thinking

Susan Armstrong, the owner and operator of a chain of nail salons in the southeastern United States, has recently hired a new store manager, Marcy Cook. Cook is not only very qualified for the job but also has many creative ideas that can increase the visibility of the salons and their sales. In fact, Cook runs circles around Armstrong's other store managers, who are good at keeping the stores running but do not seem that interested in doing much else. Since Cook took over as store manager, revenues at her salon have increased by 20 percent, and none of her staff members have quit. (The salons have generally been plagued by high turnover rates in the past.) After visiting the salons, Armstrong concluded that part of Cook's success as a store manager is due to her independent thinking—she takes the initiative to solve problems on her own, seeks and develops new opportunities, and creates a positive atmosphere in her salon both for clients and the staff. The other store managers are effective in terms of ensuring smooth operations, adequate staffing, and salon appearance, but they just don't take the initiative to go beyond the basics. Because you are an expert in OB, Armstrong has come to you for help. How can she foster the kind of independent thinking and creativity among her other store managers that Cook exhibits?

The Learning Organization

Organizational learning
The process through which managers instill in all members of an organization a desire to find new ways to improve organizational effectiveness.

Not only is it important that individuals learn to perform behaviors that contribute to organizational effectiveness but also that the organization as a whole adopts a learning mentality. **Organizational learning** involves instilling all members of the organization with a desire to find new ways to improve its effectiveness.[72] Moreover, learning organizations make sure their members actually have the knowledge and skills to learn continuously. They also take steps to ensure that new ideas are acted upon and knowledge is shared throughout the organization.[73]

Learning theorist Peter Senge has identified five key activities central to a learning organization.[74]

♦ *Encourage personal mastery or high self-efficacy.* In order for members of an organization to strive to find new ways of improving organizational effectiveness, they must have confidence in their ability to do so.

♦ *Develop complex schemas to understand work activities.* Recall from the Chapter 4 that schemas are abstract knowledge structures. In order for the members of an organization to learn new ways to cut costs or increase revenues, they must have an appreciation of not only their own jobs but also how the work they do affects the work of others and the organization as a whole.

♦ *Encourage learning in groups and teams.* New discoveries often take place in groups and teams.[75] Members of groups and teams need to strive to find new ways of doing things and manage the learning process by, for example, increasing the self-efficacy of group members who may question their own capabilities.

♦ *Communicate a shared vision for the organization as a whole.* Members of an organization need guidance in terms of what they should be striving for. For example, should they be striving to cut costs, or should they focus more on improving customer satisfaction even at the expense of higher costs? Recall how when Luczo took over as CEO of Seagate Technologies in the opening case, he instilled in Seagate's culture an emphasis on continuous learning from multiple sources.

♦ *Encourage system thinking.* Organizations are systems of interrelated parts. What one part of the organization does or learns affects other parts of the organization. Organizational members must be encouraged to think in these terms and address how their individual actions and their actions in groups and teams influence other parts of the organization.

Organizational learning is especially important for organizations in environments that are rapidly changing. As John Browne, CEO of British Petroleum, puts it, "Learning is at the heart of a company's ability to adapt to a rapidly changing environment. It is the key to being able both to identify opportunities that others might not see and to exploit those opportunities rapidly and fully."[76]

An important ingredient for a learning organization is *knowledge management*—being able to capitalize on the knowledge members of the organization have that might not be written down or codified in formal documents. As employees do their jobs, they gain knowledge about the tasks they perform and learn the best ways to get certain things done and solve specific problems. Through knowledge management, this information can be shared and used by others. This knowledge is not necessarily contained in job descriptions or written down in rules, standard operating procedures, or manuals. Rather, it is knowledge that has evolved from actually performing work tasks.[77] By disseminating and sharing this knowledge in an organization, other members will be able to take advantage of it.

A recent study of customer service representatives who repair Xerox machines confirms the importance of knowledge management. Repairing machines seems pretty straightforward—error codes on the machines indicate what the problems are, and written documents and manuals specify how to fix the problems. When anthropologist Julian Orr observed the representatives performing their jobs, however, their work didn't seem straightforward at all.[78] In a typical workday, the representatives came across many idiosyncratic breakdowns and problems and solutions that weren't predictable or detailed in the manuals. By actually performing their jobs, the representatives learned about the idiosyncrasies of the machines they repaired, how to solve a variety of problems not covered in the manuals, and how a variety of factors ranging from air temperature to the age of a certain part may affect their operation. Moreover, the representatives got together regularly over breakfast, coffee, lunch, or at the end of the workday and also at other times to share their knowledge while joking, playing games, or chatting. In these informal get-togethers, the representatives discussed problems they had encountered and how they were solved and shared their insights gleaned on the job.[79] Clearly, the people performing a certain job are likely to learn the most about it. Knowledge management seeks to share this learning and knowledge throughout an organization.

Summary

Organizational members can learn from multiple sources and in multiple ways. In this chapter, we made the following major points:

1. Learning is a relatively permanent change in knowledge or behavior that results from practice or experience.

2. In operant conditioning, the learner behaves in a certain way to achieve certain consequences. Antecedents let employees know which behaviors are desired, which should be avoided, and what the consequences are for performing different behaviors.

3. In operant conditioning, there are two ways to promote the learning of desired behaviors in organizations: positive reinforcement and negative reinforcement. Positive reinforcement increases the probability that a behavior will occur by administering positive consequences to employees who perform the behavior. Negative reinforcement increases the probability that a desired behavior will occur by removing a negative consequence if an employee performs the behavior. Positive reinforcement is generally preferred over negative reinforcement.

4. Reinforcement can be continuous or partial. Partial reinforcement can be administered according to one of four schedules: fixed interval, variable interval, fixed ratio, and variable ratio. The choice of reinforcement schedules in organizations is often influenced by practical considerations such as the nature of the behavior, job, and reinforcer in question. Shaping, or reinforcing progressively closer approximations to a desired behavior, can be used to encourage behaviors that are unlikely to occur on their own.

5. In operant conditioning, there are two ways to reduce the probability of undesired behaviors in organizations: extinction and punishment. Extinction, removing the source of reinforcement for an undesired behavior, can take time. Punishment, administering a negative consequence when an undesired behavior occurs, is sometimes needed to eliminate detrimental behaviors quickly. Punishment can have some unintended negative side effects (such as resentment) and should be used with caution.

6. The systematic application of the principles of operant conditioning to managing organizational behavior is known as organizational behavior modification (OB Mod). OB Mod works best for managing behaviors that are observable, important for task and organizational performance, and measurable.

7. In order for vicarious learning to take place, the learner must pay attention to the model, accurately perceive the model's behavior, remember the behavior, and have the skills and abilities necessary to perform the behavior; the model must also receive reinforcement for the behavior. Models who are most likely to be imitated by employees are competent or expert, have high status, receive positive reinforcers that the learner desires, and model behaviors in a friendly manner.

8. In order for self-control (taking the initiative to learn desired behaviors on one's own) to take place, the following conditions must be satisfied: An individual must engage in a low-probability behavior, self-reinforcers must be available, the learner must set performance standards or goals, and reinforcers must be self-administered when the goal is attained. Self-efficacy (beliefs about one's ability to perform particular behaviors successfully) influences the tasks employees choose to learn and the goals they set for themselves. Self-efficacy also affects employees' levels of effort and persistence when learning difficult tasks. Past

performance, observations of others, verbal persuasion, and physiological states are determinants of self-efficacy.

9. Continuous learning takes place through creativity. Creativity is the generation of novel and useful ideas and innovation is the successful implementation of creative ideas. The steps in the creative process are recognition of a problem or opportunity, information gathering, productions of ideas, selection of ideas, and implementation. Learners who are high on openness to experience, have an internal locus of control, have high self-esteem, have task-relevant knowledge, and are intrinsically motivated are especially likely to be creative. Situational characteristics that are likely to impact creativity are employees' levels of autonomy, the evaluation and reward system used in an organization, and the perceived importance of a decision.

10. Organizational learning is the process through which managers instill in all members of an organization a desire to find new ways to improve organizational effectiveness. Knowledge management is important for organizational learning.

Exercises in Understanding and Managing Organizational Behavior

Questions for Discussion and Review

1. Why might an organization prefer to use positive reinforcement rather than negative reinforcement?

2. How can a manager use the principles of operant conditioning to stop employees from bickering and fighting with each other?

3. Why do some organizations use punishment more often than others?

4. Is OB Mod ethical? Why or why not?

5. In what ways are the behaviors of taxi drivers controlled by the principles of operant conditioning?

6. On what kinds of jobs might vicarious learning be especially prevalent?

7. When might employees be especially likely to engage in self-control?

8. Why do some capable members of an organization have low levels of self-efficacy?

9. Why do organizations desiring creativity need to be willing to accept a certain level of failure?

10. What steps can organizations take to promote organizational learning and knowledge management?

Building People Skills

Learning Difficult Behaviors

Think about the last time you finally succeeded at something that had been giving you trouble. It could be a particularly troublesome class that you managed to pull through with a decent grade or a difficult project at work that you finally were able to finish satisfactorily.

1. Describe the specific behaviors that gave you trouble.

2. What antecedents prompted you to perform these behaviors?

3. What were the reinforcing consequences for performing these behaviors successfully?

4. Would you have been punished if you had not finally succeeded? If you had been punished, how would you have felt about being punished?

5. Did you use vicarious learning to try to solve your problem? If you did, who did you imitate and why? If you did not, why not?

6. Did you use self-control to try to solve your problem? If you did, what goal did you set for yourself, and what was your self-reinforcer? If you did not use self-control, why not?

7. Describe your level of self-efficacy when you first started out, when you were having a particularly troublesome time, and when you finally succeeded.

8. What do you think your level of self-efficacy will be for similar tasks in the future? Why do you think your self-efficacy will be at this level?

A Question of Ethics

Positive reinforcement can be used to promote the learning of desired behaviors in organizations. Commission pay plans, for example, reinforce salespeople for selling by paying them a percentage of their actual sales. However, sometimes these plans can be taken to extremes and may result in unethical behavior.

Questions

1. Think about the ethical implications of pay plans that link an employee's current pay to his or her current performance.
2. Under what conditions might linking pay to performance be questionable on ethical grounds?

Small Group Break-Out Exercise

Raising Self-Efficacy

Form groups of three or four people and appoint one member as the spokesperson who will communicate your conclusions to the rest of the class:

1. Take a few minutes to think about something that you are currently trying to learn and having trouble with—it could be a subject that you are having trouble with in school, learning a musical instrument, excelling in a sport, or learning a foreign language.
2. Take turns describing what you are trying to learn and how you have gone about it. After each person describes his or her "current learning challenge," as a team develop ways for this person to boost his or her self-efficacy for the challenge in question.
3. Each person then should take a few minutes to write down specific steps he or she can take based on the group's suggestions in Step 2.
4. Take turns describing the specific action steps generated in Step 3.

Topic for Debate

Creativity is the generation of new and useful ideas. Now that you have a good understanding of creativity, debate the following issue.

Team A. Creativity is only important in certain kinds of jobs and organizations.

Team B. Creativity is important in most jobs and organizations.

Experiential Exercise

Managing the Learning Process

Objective

Your objective is to gain experience in applying learning principles and theories and in understanding the challenges involved in managing the learning process.

Procedure

The class divides into groups of three to five people, and each group appoints one member as spokesperson to present the group's findings to the whole class. Here is the scenario:

You are a member of a group of supervisors that is responsible for teaching production workers how to operate a new, computerized production process. The new process requires employees to work in small teams, and each team member's performance influences the performance of the team as a whole. Prior to this major change, employees did not work in teams but performed simple, repetitive tasks that required few skills.

To operate the new production process, employees are required to learn new skills to perform their now more complicated jobs, and they are currently receiving formal training in a classroom setting and on-the-job instruction in their teams. Some employees are responding well to the changes, are doing well in training and instruction, and are performing up to expectations in their teams. Other employees are finding it difficult to adapt to their changed jobs and to teamwork and have been slow to acquire the necessary new skills. In addition, there have been reports of high levels of conflict among members of some teams. As a result, the overall performance of the teams is suffering and below expectations.

As the group of supervisors responsible for ensuring a smooth transition to the new production process and high performance in the production teams, do the following:

1. Develop a plan of action based on the principles of operant conditioning to facilitate learning and high team performance. Be specific about how operant conditioning techniques (positive reinforcement, negative reinforcement, punishment, and extinction) could be used to promote team members' learning of desired behaviors, working well together, and performing at a high level.

2. Develop a plan of action based on the principles of social cognitive theory (vicarious learning, self-control, and self-efficacy) to facilitate learning and high team performance. Be specific about how social cognitive theory could be used to promote team members' learning of desired behaviors, working well together, and performing at a high level.

3. Decide whether the two plans of action that you developed should be combined for the most effective learning to take place. Explain why or why not.

Making the Connection

Find an example of a company that recently used positive or negative reinforcement to try to change employees' behavior. What behaviors was the company trying to change? What reinforcers were used, and how were they administered? Was the company successful in changing behavior? Why or why not?

New York Times **Cases in the News**

The New York Times

Monitoring Calls in New World of Quality Assurance

BY CLAUDIA H. DEUTSCH

A few weeks ago, a customer called **Continental Airlines** to book tour tickets from San Antonio to London. An agent in Houston dutifully looked up routings and prices, and quoted a fare of $912 a person.

The agent was polite, the customer seemed happy and, until recently, any supervisor reviewing that call might have simply tagged it a job well done. But these days. Continental—along with a growing number of companies that interact with customers by phone—records not only voices but also every computer screen that agents view during calls and every mouse click they make along the way.

A supervisor, reviewing the booking session, noticed the agent had struggled with the routing screens. Retracing his steps, the supervisor found a $633 flight that left later in the day. He called the customer, who not only booked the lower-fare tickets but also parlayed part of the savings into a $375 membership in Continental's President Club.

"We spotted an agent who needed retraining, and we got a newly loyal customer, all because of one recording," said Martin Hand, Continental's managing director of reservations operations.

Continental and others that have adopted digital voice and data recording systems have moved beyond the mundane task of "monitoring this call for quality assurance purposes." In industries as diverse as financial services, health insurance and religious publishing, companies are using technology from Nice Systems, Witness Systems, Verint Systems or any of a handful of smaller players to mine customer interactions for insights into ways to improve their businesses.

"The need for customer retention is by far the biggest driver in our business," said David Gould, the chairman of Witness, which sold Continental its call recording system.

Sales of call recording software were $323 million last year, up from $278 million in 2001, according to Datamonitor, which predicts they will hit $538 million a year by 2007. In the last three years or so, "the whole market has moved from general recording to much higher value applications," said David Spindel, a managing analyst at Datamonitor.

In companies that have made the switch, computer hard drives have replaced the old storage rooms, with their stacks of tapes and cassettes. People with authorized passwords can replay the entire customer interaction on their desktop computers. They can e-mail copies to colleagues. Some can even use keyword searches to fast forward to parts of the voice-data sessions that most interest them.

Thus armed, a supervisor can reconstruct the incident if a customer complains. Agents can replay the phone call to recapture data lost if a computer system crashes. They can also forward copies of customer sessions that require action—say alerting the shipping department if an order has been lost.

Call center managers can spot examples of particularly smart techniques to share with other employees. Information technology executives can observe how well agents navigate the databases, then fine-tune cumbersome parts of programs. Marketing executives can search for nuggets about how customers use their products, and for features customers would like to see.

"Call centers used to be cost centers, but they are strategic centers now," said Shlomo Shamir, president of the American arm of Nice, an Israeli company that is the leader in this software field.

The new systems can also help hospitals and insurance companies ensure that their representatives understand what they can and cannot reveal by phone under new federal rules governing patient privacy. Do they realize, for example, that

while they cannot tell parents whether their child is pregnant, it is all right to say she has pneumonia? "We can spot and coach individuals who are erring on the side of caution," said Sharon Whitwam, vice president for member services at WPS Health Insurance, which installed a Nice system in January.

In contrast, financial services companies, under scrutiny in the wake of Wall Street scandals, want to make doubly sure their employees are going by the book. Last month, after an irate customer claimed that a broker at the CUNA Mutual Group had bought him stock without his approval, a call retrieved from CUNA Mutual's Nice system proved that he had requested the trade. The system "is an important safety net," said Barbara J. Ballweg, voice communication systems manager for CUNA Mutual.

The new Nice system at CCC Interactive, a telemarketer, flags calls in which an agent selling brokerage services records a customer's birth date or account number. "That means there was probably a sale, and we want to be sure we've validated all the data," explained CJ Johnson, CCC Interactive's senior vice president. He said that the automated system enabled him to reduce his quality assurance staff to 12 people from 15.

Software allows companies to turn their call centers into strategy centers.

Just as important for telemarketers, who face many new restrictions on whom they may call, the recording systems can help them make the most of the contacts they do make. Mariann McDonagh, vice president for global marketing at Verint, tells of a client who was hawking cellphone services. The client listened to every call that lasted more than five minutes without resulting in a sale, identified price as a sticking point, and reduced it by $10. Sales went up by 25 percent.

Businesses with widely dispersed call centers can also see whether customers get the same service from Bangkok and Bangor. And a new Nice system enabled Toyota Financial Services to spot that some new employees were having trouble explaining the value of a car after a lease expires. "We retrained them," Amy R. Olson, a team leader, said, "and rewrote that section of the manual."

Similarly, new Verint recording software spurred LifeWay Christian Resources, the events programming arm of the Southern Baptist Convention, to reword the voice menu that helps customers direct their calls. "Too many were inadvertently pushing the button that gave recorded instructions on using our Web site," said Nancy Marks, LifeWay's telecommunications manager.

The brisk sales of call recording software comes even as sales of other business software languish. According to the research firm Gartner Inc., sales of so-called customer relationship management software—which includes call recording software—were down nearly 25 percent in 2002. But Wendy S. Close, a Gartner research manager, noted that both Nice and Witness, the two biggest players in call recording, have had revenue growth.

Nice lost $34 million on revenues of $162.5 million last year, an improvement over 2001, when it lost $46.8 million on sales of $127 million. Witness essentially broke even last year, earning $48,000 on $68 million in sales. In 2001, it lost $5.2 million on $63 million in sales.

Sales are also improving for the Dictaphone Corporation, a pioneer in tape-based call recording systems that emerged from bankruptcy last year. Dictaphone, with only about 3 percent of the market for digital call center systems, receives 18 percent of its sales from the systems, and Robert G. Schwager, its chairman, said that number was growing.

Perhaps inevitably, the industry is consolidating. Last year Nice bought the smaller Thales Contact Solutions, while Witness Systems bought Eyretel.

"We spend $20 million a year on research," said Nice's president, Mr. Shamir. "Not many small players could do that."

Indeed, esoteric new features keep cropping up. Already, some recording systems can "hear" certain words or phrases—like a competitor's name or "cancel my account"—and automatically send that recording to someone who specializes in customer retention. Newer versions may soon automatically convert calls that mention key words to text, and send summaries to chosen executives. Several can even detect emotion in a voice, and flag those calls in which customers—or agents—became overly excited.

"It's a good way to spot if an agent is burning out," Mr. Shamir said.

SOURCE: "Monitoring Call in New World of Quality Assurance," by C. H. Deutch, *New York Times,* July 28, 2003, p. C3.

Questions for Discussion

1. How can monitoring calls help employees learn to perform desired behaviors?

2. What might be some unintended negative consequences of monitoring calls?

3. What ethical considerations should be taken into account when monitoring calls?

4. When might monitoring calls be inappropriate?

The New York Times

Working Mothers Swaying Senate Debate, as Senators

BY SHERYL GAY STOLBERG

Washington, June 6—Like working mothers everywhere, Blanche Lincoln spent her spring vacation tending to all the little things that fall by the wayside when she is busy on the job.

She went to Wal-Mart and Kmart to shop for blue jeans and sneakers for her twin sons, Reece and Bennett, who turn 7 later this month. She registered the boys for Little League and bought their uniforms. She sent checks to their school to cover two month's worth of cafeteria lunches and paid for their summer camp.

Then, Mrs. Lincoln returned to work—as a member of the United States Senate, where she promptly kicked up a fuss about an issue dear to millions of American families, the child tax credit.

This week, Mrs. Lincoln translated that fuss into public policy, using her spring break story as a way to persuade the Senate to increase the tax credit for minimum wage families. It was a defining moment for the 42-year-old Democrat from Arkansas, who briefly retired from politics when she became pregnant, deciding against running for reelection to the House of Representatives. And it underscored the emergence of a new and potentially powerful creature in the Capitol: the senator as working mother.

Until 1992, when Patty Murray, the self-described "mom in tennis shoes" was elected as a Democrat from Washington, no woman with children at home had become a senator. Today, Mrs. Murray is a grandmother and there are a record 14 female senators, four with children school age or younger.

As they juggle pediatricians' appointments and Cub Scout meetings with fundraisers and late-night roll call votes, these women—along with male senators who have young children—perform the same work-home tap dance as millions of American parents. But there are some notable differences: in the Senate, the dance plays out in public, voters get to rate the performance, and the outcome can affect public policy.

Senator Lisa Murkowski, Republican of Alaska, missed Thursday's child tax credit vote, a definite no-no for a freshman lawmaker who faces occusations of nepotism for having been appointed to her seat by her father. But Ms. Murkowski's oldest son, Nicolas Martell, 12, was graduating from sixth grade, and she was scheduled to speak at the ceremony. The plane ride to Anchorage would take 11 hours, so she left early.

Senator Kay Bailey Hutchison, Republican of Texas, was late to the Senate's prayer breakfast this week because her 2-year-old daughter, Bailey, slept late.

Senator Mary Landrieu, Democrat of Louisiana, brought her children, Connor Snellings, 11, and Mary Shanon Snellings, 5, to a fund-raiser on Wednesday night. Ms. Landrieu has given her staff strict instructions to limit her "work nights" to two a week. Weekends include time for soccer games and piano lessons.

"Just because I've chosen to be in the Senate," she said, "doesn't mean they deserve this kind of crazy life."

Though four working mothers are hardly enough to create a voting block in the Senate, they are making subtle changes in an institution that was long the exclusive province of men. Just as Senator Bill Frist, the majority leader who is a heart surgeon speaks with authority on matters of medicine, and Senator John McCain, a former prisoner of war, is a respected voice on the military, women like Mrs. Lincoln have a certain credibility, male senators say, on matters that affect women in the workplace.

"When a person in this body gets up and speaks from personal experience, it changes the whole nature of the debate," said Senator Christopher J. Dodd, Democrat of Connecticut himself the father of a 21-month-old daughter, Grace.

Mr. Dodd said that Mrs. Lincoln's presence was "important, in many ways, for her colleagues, because in some cases it's been decades since they were parents of young children."

This can make for some comic moments, as was the case several years ago when lawmakers considered a proposal to ban unapproved labels from being attached to prescription medicines.

"I said, 'If we do this, how is this going to affect Mr. Yuck?'" Mrs. Murray recalled. She was referring to the stickers with frowning faces used by parents, pediatricians and poison-control centers to warn children away from household hazards. But her colleagues were befuddled.

"Not one man in that room," said Mrs. Murray, "knew what Mr. Yuck was."

The Senate, of course, has long been home to fathers raising families, who also make difficult choices. Several years ago, Senator Evan Bayh, the Indiana Democrat and father of 7-year-old twins, declared that he would not run for president. "Political ambitions," Mr. Bayh said in a recent interview, "had to take a backseat to my responsibilities as a father."

Historically, women in the Senate were appointed as widows to fill vacancies created by their husband's death. As women have entered politics in their own right, they have done so later in life, said Ruth Mandel, an expert on women in politics at Rutgers University. So it is unusual, she said, for women to attain a high office like the Senate in their childbearing years.

Mrs. Lincoln, who began her career in Washington as a receptionist for a former member of the House, found that motherhood became an issue in her campaign. "There were some people that felt like I couldn't be a good mother and be a senator," Mrs. Lincoln said, "and they were not bashful about expressing that."

Yet the working mothers of the Senate say, it is extremely difficult to be both a good mother and a good senator. For one thing, the job is chaotic, with a schedule that changes at a moment's notice and votes that can occur in the middle of the night. For another, being a senator means working in two places, the Capitol and the home state.

Ms. Murkowski, who was appointed in December, decided to leave her two boys in Anchorage with her husband, Verne Martell, rather than uproot them in the middle of the school year. If she wins election next year, they will relocate.

Until then, Senator Murkowski jets back and forth each weekend, an exhausting trip. "I've often thought, what if something were to happen to one of the kids?" she said. "I'm a day away, and that's unsettling."

For all their efforts on behalf of other parents, the working mothers of the Senate agree that it is not a family-friendly place. Mrs. Lincoln, Ms. Landrieu and Mrs. Hutchison all said they had been pressing Dr. Frist, the majority leader, to refrain from scheduling votes during the dinner hour—a plea that they say has won them the quiet support of some men who would also like to have dinner with their children.

This was not a problem on Thursday, when the child credit vote—Senator Lincoln's shining moment—concluded at 6:20 p.m. When it was over, Mrs. Lincoln, glowing from her victory, dashed out of the Senate chamber. She said she felt good about the outcome and was looking forward to the weekend, when she was planning a quick trip to Arkansas for a fund-raiser, and hoped to take Reece and Bennett swimming.

SOURCE: "Working Mothers Swaying Senate Debate, as Senators," by S. G. Stolberg, *New York Times*, June 7, 2003, pp. A1, A11.

Questions for Discussion

1. What kinds of behaviors on the part of senators are encouraged in the U.S. Senate, and what kinds of behaviors are discouraged?

2. What role do consequences play in encouraging and discouraging these behaviors?

3. How is the U.S. Senate learning from experience?

4. To what extent is the U.S. Senate a learning organization?

The Nature of Work Motivation

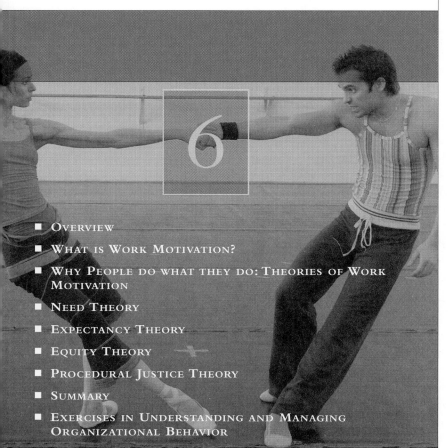

6

LEARNING OBJECTIVES

After studying this chapter, you should be able to:

■

Appreciate why motivation is of central importance in organizations and the difference between intrinsic and extrinsic motivation.

▧

Understand what we can learn about motivation from need theories.

▧

Describe why expectancy, valence, and instrumentality are of central importance for work motivation.

▧

Appreciate the importance of equity and the dangers of inequity.

▧

Understand why procedural justice is so important and how to promote it.

OPENING CASE

Motivating Employees at the SAS Institute: A Win-Win Situation

How Can Organizations Continue to Grow and Have Satisfied Employees in the Hard Times as Well as the Good Times?

With over 9,000 employees, the SAS Institute is the largest privately owned software company in the world.[1] Annual revenues at SAS have increased for 26 years in a row. In 2002, a tough year for many software companies, revenues at SAS increased by over 4 percent, and its spending on R&D continued to grow while many of its competitors' budgets shrank.[2] Moreover, SAS continues to win accolades for the way it treats its employees. For six years in a row, it was included in *Fortune* magazine's "100 Best Companies to Work for in America," and it has been cited 13 times as one of the "100 Best Companies for Working Mothers."[3] Moreover, SAS is well known for its ability to attract and retain top talent in the software industry.[4] How does SAS maintain this win–win situation of sustained growth and satisfied employees, even in an economic downturn? Essentially, by the way it goes about motivating its workforce.

SAS, founded in 1976, has always strived to ensure its employees enjoy their work and are motivated by the work they perform. Managers believe that employees should be interested and involved in the work they are doing and feel that they are making meaningful contributions. For example, whereas some software companies seeking to expand into new markets, such as video games or educational software, buy companies that have already developed these products, SAS does all its new product development internally. Although this approach might take longer, SAS believes it is beneficial because employees find that developing new products is interesting work. Moreover, SAS encourages its employees to change jobs within the company (getting additional training if needed)

so that they continue to be interested in their work and don't grow bored with what they're doing.[5]

The work itself is a major source of motivation for SAS employees, but managers at SAS are also concerned with fairly and equitably rewarding employees for a job well done. Pay and bonuses are linked to performance, and the company emphasizes fair treatment in numerous ways. For example, all employees have private offices. As another example, Jim Goodnight, one of SAS's co-founders and its current CEO and chairman, says that a founding and enduring principle of the company is that managers should treat employees the way the managers want to be treated themselves.[6]

The SAS Instiute also cares about its employees and their families' well-being both on and off the job. Some of the many other benefits employees receive, in addition to interesting work and equitable financial rewards, include an attractive work environment, with atriums overlooking rolling hills and artwork adorning the walls, access to the latest technology, 35-hour workweeks, two low-cost on-site child care facilities, a 77,000-square-foot fitness and recreation center,[7] on-site medical care, a putting green, and high chairs in the company cafeteria so employees can eat lunch with their children. The corporation's headquarters is located on 200 idyllic acres in Cary, North Carolina. Employees and their families can walk or jog around the campus's scenic trails or picnic on its grounds.[8]

Goodnight has been committed to motivating employees to develop creative and high-quality products that are responsive to customers' current and future needs since SAS's founding days; currently, 90 percent of *Fortune* 500 companies use SAS products for any number of purposes including risk management, monitoring and measuring performance, managing relationships with customers and suppliers, and detecting fraud.[9] At the SAS Institute, motivating employees really is a win–win situation.

As the SAS case suggests, motivating employees to make important contributions to their jobs can have a profound impact on organizational effectiveness. Motivation is central to understanding and managing organizational behavior because it explains why people behave as they do in organizations.[10] Just as your own motivation determines how many classes you take, how hard you study for exams, and the amount of time and effort you spend on research projects, similarly, motivation determines how hard members in an organization will work to help achieve its goals.

Motivation explains, for example, why one employee wants and tries to do a good job while another employee with the same abilities couldn't care less. Motivation also explains why some students strive for A's and study much harder than others, who are content with maintaining a solid B average.

In this chapter, we examine work motivation. We focus on the important distinctions between motivation and performance and between intrinsic and extrinsic motivation. We discuss several specific theories of work motivation—need theory, expectancy theory, equity theory, and procedural justice theory. Each theory seeks to explain why people behave as they do in organizations and suggests ways of increasing employee motivation and performance. An understanding of motivation is of utmost importance for organizational effectiveness. Managers need to ensure that employees choose to act in ways that help the organization achieve its goals and avoid behaving in ways that hinder the pursuit of organizational objectives.

What Is Work Motivation?

Motivation is a frequently used but poorly understood term. Over 140 definitions have been provided over the years,[11] and noted scholars of work motivation have said that trying to define *motivation* often gives them "a severe stomachache."[12] This remark may be a bit of an exaggeration, but it underscores the need to get a firm grasp on what motivation is before we try to understand its role in understanding and managing organizational behavior.

Motivation is important because it explains why employees behave as they do. **Work motivation** can be defined as the psychological forces within a person that determine the direction of a person's behavior in an organization, effort level, and persistence in the face of obstacles.[13] Because motivation involves psychological forces within a person, many of the topics that we cover in prior chapters are relevant to understanding motivation: personality and ability (see Chapter 2); values, attitudes, and moods (see Chapter 3); and perception and attribution (see Chapter 4).

The three key elements of work motivation are direction of behavior, level of effort, and level of persistence (see Table 6.1).

Work motivation The psychological forces that determine the direction of a person's behavior in an organization, a person's level of effort, and a person's level of persistence.

TABLE 6.1

Elements of Work Motivation

Element	Definition	Example
Direction of behavior	Which behaviors does a person choose to perform in an organization?	Does an engineer take the time and effort to convince skeptical superiors of the need to change the design specifications for a new product to lower production costs?
Level of effort	How hard does a person work to perform a chosen behavior?	Does an engineer prepare a report outlining problems with the original specifications, or does the engineer casually mention the issue when he or she bumps into a supervisor in the hall and hope that the supervisor will take the advice on faith?
Level of persistence	When faced with obstacles, roadblocks, and stone walls, how hard does a person keep trying to perform a chosen behavior successfully?	When the supervisor disagrees with the engineer and indicates that a change in specifications is a waste of time, does the engineer persist in trying to get the change implemented or give up despite his or her strong belief in the need for a change?

Direction of Behavior. Which behaviors does a person choose to perform? On any job, there are many behaviors (some appropriate, some inappropriate) that the jobholder can engage in. *Direction of behavior* refers to the behavior employees *choose* to perform from the many potential behaviors they *could* perform. If a stockbroker in an investment banking firm illegally manipulates stock prices, if managers advance their own careers at the expense of their subordinates, or if an engineer convinces skeptical superiors to change the design specifications of a new product in order to lower production costs—all of these actions reflect behaviors these employees chose to perform.

As the examples illustrate, employees can be motivated in *functional* ways that help an organization achieve its goals or in *dysfunctional* ways that hinder an organization from achieving its goals. In looking at motivation, managers want to ensure that the direction of their subordinates' behavior is functional for the organization. They want employees to be motivated to come to work on time, perform their assigned tasks dependably, come up with good ideas, and help others. They do not want employees to come to work late, ignore rules concerning health and safety, or pay lip service to quality.

Level of Effort. How hard does a person work to perform a chosen behavior? It is not enough for an organization to motivate employees to perform desired functional behaviors; the organization must also motivate them to work hard at these behaviors. If, for example, an engineer decides to try to convince skeptical superiors of the need for design changes, the engineer's level of motivation determines the lengths to which he or she will go to convince them. Does the engineer just mention the need for the change in casual conversation, or does he or she prepare a detailed report outlining the problems with the original specifications and describing the new, cost-saving specifications that are needed?

Level of Persistence. When faced with obstacles, roadblocks, and stone walls, how hard does a person keep trying to perform a chosen behavior successfully? Suppose the engineer's supervisor indicates that a change in specifications is a waste of time. Does the engineer persist in trying to get the change implemented or give up even though he or she strongly believes it's necessary? Likewise, if a factory employee's machine breaks down, does the employee simply stop working and wait for someone to come along to fix it, or does the employee try to fix the machine or at least alert others about the problem?

THE DISTINCTION BETWEEN MOTIVATION AND PERFORMANCE

Because motivation determines what employees do and how hard and diligently they do it, you might think that an employee's motivation to do a job is the same as the employee's job performance. In fact, motivation and performance, though often confused by employees and managers alike, are two distinct aspects of behavior in an organization. *Performance* is an evaluation of the results of a person's behavior: It involves determining how well or poorly a person has accomplished a task or done a job.[14] *Motivation* is only one factor among many that contributes to an employee's job performance. The performance of a screenwriter for a television series, for example, is the extent to which viewers find his scripts to be informative, entertaining, and engaging. Similarly, a research scientist's performance is the extent to which her research advances knowledge, and a physician's performance is the extent to which he provides high-quality care to patients.

What is the relationship between motivation and performance? All else being equal, one would expect a highly motivated screenwriter to write better scripts than those written by a poorly motivated screenwriter.[15] All else, however, is not always equal because so many other factors affect performance—factors such as personality and ability (see Chapter 2), the difficulty of the task, the availability of resources, working conditions, and

Starbucks is a model of employee learning, ownership, involvement, and motivation. Even part-time Starbucks employees, or "partners," as they are called, get stock options, full healthcare benefits, and extensive training.

chance or luck. A screenwriter who is highly creative, for example, may quickly turn out high-quality scripts, even though his or her motivation to do so is not high. And a physician in Somalia who is highly motivated to provide high-quality medical care may have difficultly providing it due to inadequate facilities or a lack of supplies.

In summary, because motivation is only one of several factors that can affect performance, a high level of motivation does not always result in a high level of performance. Conversely, high performance does not necessarily imply that motivation is high: Employees with low motivation may perform at a high level if they have a great deal of ability. Managers have to be careful not to automatically attribute the cause of low performance to a lack of motivation or the cause of high performance to high motivation (see Chapter 4). If they incorrectly assume that low performance stems from low motivation, managers may overlook the real cause of a performance problem (such as inadequate training or a lack of resources) and fail to take appropriate actions to rectify the situation. Similarly, if managers assume that employees who perform at a high level are highly motivated, they may inadvertently fail to take advantage of the talents of exceptionally capable employees: If employees perform at a high level when their motivation levels are low, they may be capable of making truly exceptional contributions to the organization if managers devote their efforts to boosting their motivation.

INTRINSIC AND EXTRINSIC MOTIVATION

Another distinction important to a discussion of motivation is the difference between the intrinsic and extrinsic sources of work motivation. **Intrinsically motivated work behavior** is behavior that is performed for its own sake; the source of motivation actually comes from performing the behavior itself, in other words.[16] A professional violinist who relishes playing in an orchestra regardless of relatively low pay and a millionaire CEO who repeatedly puts in 12-hour days because she enjoys her work are both intrinsically motivated. From the opening case, it is clear that employees at the SAS Institute are intrinsically motivated; they really enjoy their work. Employees who are intrinsically motivated often remark that their work gives them a sense of accomplishment and achievement or that they feel that they are doing something worthwhile. As indicated in the accompanying Managing Ethically feature, protecting the natural environment is a source of intrinsic motivation that benefits us all.

Intrinsically motivated work behavior Behavior that is performed for its own sake.

managing ethically

Saving the Planet

William McDonough is on a mission to save the planet, get rid of waste, and make large corporations believe it is worthwhile to take part in these efforts. And his mission is paying off. McDonough is an environmental designer who, along with partner Michael Braungart, are developing methods for organizations to make products in ways that do not result in waste and harm the natural environment. For example, McDonough and Braungart helped make a new material for the soles of Nike athletic shoes that biodegrades without toxic chemicals being released. They also helped Herman Miller design a factory that relies on solar heating and cooling, which reduced energy consumption at the facility by around 30 percent.[17]

McDonough is so intrinsically motivated to protect the environment that he believes even recycling does too much harm. Products that are made out of recycled substances still contain some of the toxic substances in the original products. For example, plastic bottles are often recycled, but the heavy metals and carcinogens in the bottles still make their way into the recycled products. And those products eventually make their way into landfills.[18]

Paul Tebo, vice president for safety, health, and environment at Du Pont, is also intrinsically motivated to protect the environment. Tebo is striving to develop a set of businesses that preserve natural resources.[19] Toward that end, Du Pont has been developing biodegradable material for plastic cutlery, extracting protein and milk from soy beans, developing a fabric for clothing made from corn, and inventing an automobile paint that doesn't emit toxic solvents when applied.[20] Fortunately, McDonough and Tebo are not alone in their efforts to save the planet and its inhabitants; organizations ranging from UPS and FedEx to McDonald's are focusing on social responsibility, sustainable growth, and protection and conservation of the natural environment. For example, McDonald's stopped buying chickens treated with certain antibiotics after it learned that the particular kind of antibiotics in question were no longer as effective when prescribed and taken by people who ate the chickens. As another example, UPS has 1,800 vehicles that run on alternative fuels, and plans are underway at FedEx to use more environmentally friendly trucks that run on a combination of electricity and diesel fuel.[21] Clearly, social responsibility and protecting and preserving the natural environment are ethical concerns that should be on many employees' minds.

Extrinsically motivated work behavior Behavior that is performed to acquire material or social rewards or to avoid punishment.

Extrinsically motivated work behavior is behavior that is performed to acquire material or social rewards or to avoid punishment.[22] The behavior is performed not for its own sake but rather for its consequences. The operant conditioning theory of learning discussed in Chapter 5 essentially deals with how consequences (positive and negative reinforcers and punishment) can be used to generate extrinsically motivated behavior. Examples of rewards that may be a source of extrinsic motivation include pay, praise, and status (discussed in detail in Chapter 8).

An employee can be extrinsically motivated, intrinsically motivated, or both.[23] When employees are primarily extrinsically motivated and doing the work itself is not a source of motivation, it is especially important for an organization and its managers to make a clear connection between the behaviors the organization wants employees to perform and the outcomes or rewards employees want.

You may be wondering whether there is any connection between intrinsic and extrinsic motivation and the intrinsic and extrinsic work values we describe in

Chapter 3. Employees who have intrinsic work values want challenging assignments, the opportunity to make important contributions to their jobs and organizations, and the opportunity to reach their full potential at work. Employees with extrinsic work values desire some of the consequences of working, such as earning money, having status in the community, social contacts, and time off from work for family and leisure. It stands to reason that employees with strong intrinsic work values are likely to want to be intrinsically motivated at work and those with strong extrinsic work values are likely to want to be extrinsically motivated at work.

Why People Do What They Do: Theories of Work Motivation

We have explored what motivation is, where it comes from, and how it is related to the performance of behaviors in an organizational setting. But we have not considered what motivates people, why they become motivated, and how they sustain their motivation.

Theories about work motivation provide answers to such questions by explaining why employees behave as they do in organizations. The key challenge facing managers in terms of motivation is how to encourage employees to contribute inputs to their jobs and to the organization. Managers want employees to be motivated to contribute inputs (effort, specific job behaviors, skills, knowledge, time, and experience) because inputs influence job performance and, ultimately, organizational performance. Employees are concerned with obtaining outcomes from the organization—both extrinsic outcomes (pay and job security) and intrinsic outcomes (a feeling of accomplishment from doing a good job or the pleasure of doing interesting work). These key concerns for managers and their employees lie at the heart of motivation. As indicated in Figure 6.1, we can graphically depict these concerns in an equation: Inputs→ Performance→ Outcomes.

The four theories that we describe in this chapter—need theory, expectancy theory, equity theory, and procedural justice theory—are *complementary* perspectives. Each theory addresses different questions about motivation in organizations and the relationships between inputs, performance, and outcomes, shown in Figure 6.1. Note that each of the four theories has its own merits. There is no "best" theory, in other words. To get a good understanding of motivation in organizations, we need to consider all four.

QUESTION ANSWERED BY NEED THEORY

Need theory focuses on the outcome side of the equation and on this question: *What outcome is an individual motivated to obtain from a job and an organization?* The principal message of need theory is that employees have needs that they are

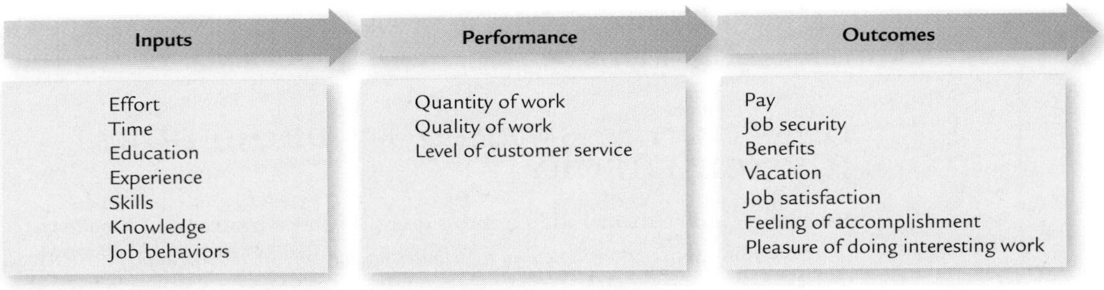

FIGURE 6.1

The Motivation Equation
Need theory, expectancy theory, equity theory, and procedural justice theory address different questions about the relationships shown in this equation.

Inputs →	Performance →	Outcomes
Effort	Quantity of work	Pay
Time	Quality of work	Job security
Education	Level of customer service	Benefits
Experience		Vacation
Skills		Job satisfaction
Knowledge		Feeling of accomplishment
Job behaviors		Pleasure of doing interesting work

motivated to satisfy in the workplace.[24] In order to determine which outcomes motivate employees the most, managers must first learn which needs employees are trying to satisfy.

After an employee's needs are determined the manager must make sure that she or he can control—either administer or withhold—the outcomes satisfying those needs. The manager should make it clear to the employee that receiving the outcomes depends on the desired behaviors being performed. Then the manager must administer the outcomes contingent upon that performance. In this way, the employee satisfies her or his needs while also contributing important inputs to the organization.

QUESTIONS ANSWERED BY EXPECTANCY THEORY

Expectancy theory addresses two questions about motivation. One question is: *Does the individual believe that his or her inputs (such as effort on the job) will result in a given level of performance?* Expectancy theory proposes that regardless of which outcomes are available, employees will not be motivated to contribute their inputs to the organization unless they believe it will result in achieving a given level of performance. Employees' beliefs about the relationship between their inputs (such as effort) and the performance level they reach are, thus, central to understanding motivation. Put simply, if employees do not think they are capable of performing at an adequate level even with maximum effort, their motivation to perform at that level will be zero.[25]

The other question that expectancy theory addresses is: *Does the individual believe that performing at this level will lead to obtaining the outcomes he or she wants (pay, job security, a feeling of accomplishment, and so forth)?* The second key part of expectancy theory indicates that employees will be motivated to perform at a given level only if that level leads to the desired outcomes.[26]

Only when the answer to both of these questions is "yes" will the individual be motivated to contribute effort and other inputs on the job. According to expectancy theory, a manager who wants to motivate an employee to perform at a certain level must first make sure the employee believes he or she can achieve the performance level. Then the manager must make sure the employee believes he or she will receive, and actually does receive, the desired outcomes after the performance level has been achieved.

QUESTION ANSWERED BY EQUITY THEORY

Equity theory focuses primarily on the relationship between inputs and outcomes and addresses this question: *Are the outcomes perceived as being at an appropriate level in comparison to the inputs?* The theory proposes that from past experience or the observation of others, employees will have a sense of the input levels that should result in certain outcomes.[27]

To motivate employees to contribute the inputs that the organization needs, managers need to administer outcomes based on those inputs. Moreover, managers need to ensure that different employees' outcome/input *ratios* are approximately equal so that employees who contribute more inputs receive more outcomes and vice versa.

QUESTION ANSWERED BY PROCEDURAL JUSTICE THEORY

Procedural justice theory addresses this question about motivation: *Are the procedures used to assess inputs and performance and distribute the outcomes perceived to be fair?* Procedural justice theory proposes that employees will not be motivated to contribute their inputs unless they perceive that fair procedures will be used to distribute outcomes in the

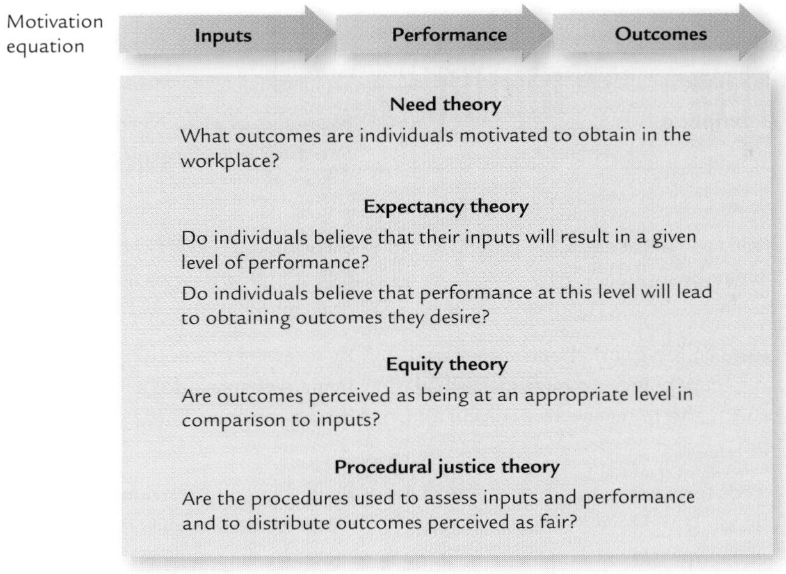

FIGURE 6.2
Questions Addressed by Four Theories of Motivation

Motivation equation

| Inputs | → | Performance | → | Outcomes |

Need theory
What outcomes are individuals motivated to obtain in the workplace?

Expectancy theory
Do individuals believe that their inputs will result in a given level of performance?
Do individuals believe that performance at this level will lead to obtaining outcomes they desire?

Equity theory
Are outcomes perceived as being at an appropriate level in comparison to inputs?

Procedural justice theory
Are the procedures used to assess inputs and performance and to distribute outcomes perceived as fair?

FIGURE 6.2
Questions Addressed by Four Theories of Motivation

organization. These procedures include those used to assess input levels, determine the level of performance achieved, and then actually distribute the outcomes.

When these procedures are perceived to be unfair, motivation suffers because *all* the relationships in the motivation equation (see Figure 6.1) are weakened: assessing the inputs, determining the performance, and ultimately distributing the outcomes.

Figure 6.2 summarizes the questions addressed by each of the four approaches. Each approach has different implications for what managers should do to motivate their subordinates to achieve high performance levels.

Need Theory

Although we just described need theory as if it is only one theory, **need theory** is actually a group of theories about work motivation. Collectively, these theories explain what motivates employees to behave in certain ways by focusing on employees' needs as the sources of motivation. Need theories propose that employees seek to satisfy many of their needs at work and that their behavior at work is, therefore, oriented toward need satisfaction.

A **need** is a requirement for survival and well-being. To determine what will motivate an employee, a manager first must determine what needs an employee is trying to satisfy on the job because needs will vary from person to person. The manager then must ensure the employee can satisfy his or her needs by engaging in behaviors that contribute to the organization's effectiveness. The two theories that we discuss next by Abraham Maslow and Clayton Alderfer describe several specific needs employees try to satisfy through their work behaviors and the order in which they try to satisfy them. In previous chapters, we discussed two other need-based approaches to understanding behavior in organizations: David McClelland's work on achievement, affiliation, and power needs (see Chapter 2) and Frederick Herzberg's motivator-hygiene theory (see Chapter 3).

MASLOW'S HIERARCHY OF NEEDS

Psychologist Abraham Maslow proposed that human beings have five universal needs they seek to satisfy: physiological needs, safety needs, belongingness needs, esteem needs, and self-actualization needs. These needs and examples of how they can be satisfied are described in Table 6.2. Maslow proposed that these needs can be arranged in a hierarchy of importance,

Need theory A group of content theories about work motivation that focuses on employees' needs as the sources of motivation.

Need A requirement for survival and well-being.

TABLE 6.2

Maslow's Hierarchy of Needs

Need Level	Description	Examples of How Needs are Met or Satisfied in an Organization
Highest-Level Needs		
Self-actualization needs	Needs to realize one's full potential as a human being	By using one's skills and abilities to the fullest and striving to achieve all that one can on a job
Esteem needs	Needs to feel good about oneself and one's capabilities, to be respected by others, and to receive recognition and appreciation	By receiving promotions at work and being recognized for accomplishments on the job
Belongingness needs	Needs for social interaction, friendship, affection, and love	By having good relations with co-workers and supervisors, being a member of a cohesive work group, and participating in social functions such as company picnics and holiday parties
Safety needs	Needs for security, stability, and a safe environment	By receiving job security, adequate medical benefits, and safe working conditions
Physiological needs	Basic needs for things such as food, water, and shelter that must be met in order for an individual to survive	By receiving a minimum level of pay that enables a worker to buy food and clothing and have adequate housing
Lowest-Level Needs (most basic or compelling)		

with the most basic or compelling needs—physiological and safety needs—at the base.[28] These basic needs must be satisfied before an individual seeks to satisfy needs higher up in the hierarchy. Maslow argued that after a need is satisfied, it is no longer a source of motivation.

There are many ways that organizations can help employees who are at different levels in Maslow's hierarchy satisfy their needs while at the same time also help the organization achieve its goals and a competitive advantage. Some organizations, for example, help satisfy employees' esteem needs by providing special recognition for their outstanding accomplishments. Managers at Los Angeles–based Unocal Corporation realized that research scientists need to feel good about their accomplishments and receive recognition and appreciation for them. One way Unocal has attempted to help satisfy these esteem needs is through the establishment of Creativity Week. Creativity Week was instituted by the Unocal Research Center, which employs scientists to do chemical research, create innovative ways to discover and develop energy resources, and transform those resources into usable products like fuel and electricity. Creativity is very important at the research center, and scientists and managers alike recognize the importance of acknowledging superior innovations benefiting the company.

During Creativity Week, scientists whose yearlong projects not only involved considerable creative effort but also benefited the company are singled out and called up onto a stage where their accomplishments are described. Colleagues applaud their achievements, and the researchers receive a cash award and plaque. A grand-prize winner is announced and receives a substantial bonus.

The Inventor's Wall of Fame provides another opportunity to recognize scientists for their accomplishments. Unocal has been very successful in obtaining patents and licenses for its inventions. Scientists who have obtained more than five patents for the company are honored during Creativity Week with plaques, statues, and other prizes. Those who have obtained more than 10 patents receive an additional acknowledgment: Their names are added to the Inventor's Wall of Fame. As Greg Wirzbicki, Unocal's head patent attorney, indicates, "The reaction of the inventors to being recognized was very positive. . . . It really meant a lot to them. One retiree listed on the Wall of Fame came in just to see his name, despite having to make a long journey with great difficulty."[29]

According to Maslow's theory, unsatisfied needs are the prime motivators of behavior, and needs at the lowest levels of the hierarchy take precedence over needs at higher levels.[30] At any particular time, however, only one set of needs motivates behavior, and it is not possible to skip levels. After an individual satisfies one set of needs, he or she tries to satisfy needs at the next level of the hierarchy, and this level becomes the focus of motivation.

By specifying the needs that contribute to motivation, Maslow's theory helps managers determine what will motivate any given employee. A simple but important lesson from Maslow's theory is that employees differ in the needs they try to satisfy at work and that what motivates one employee may not motivate another. What does this conclusion suggest? To have a motivated workforce, managers must identify which needs each employee is seeking to satisfy at work, and after these needs have been identified, managers must ensure that the employee's needs are satisfied if he or she performs the desired behaviors.

ALDERFER'S ERG THEORY

Clayton Alderfer's existence-relatedness-growth (ERG) theory is also a need theory of work motivation. Alderfer's theory builds on some of Maslow's thinking but reduces the number of universal needs from five to three and is more flexible in terms of movement between levels.[31] Like Maslow, Alderfer also proposes that needs can be arranged in a hierarchy. The three types of needs in Alderfer's theory are described in Table 6.3.

TABLE 6.3
Alderfer's ERG Theory

Need Level	Description	Examples of How Needs are Met or Satisfied in an Organization
Highest-Level Needs		
Growth needs	Needs for self-development and creative and productive work	By continually improving skills and abilities and engaging in meaningful work
Relatedness needs	Needs to have good interpersonal relations, to share thoughts and feelings, and to have open two-way communication	By having good relations with co-workers, superiors, and subordinates and by obtaining accurate feedback from others
Existence needs	Basic needs for human survival such as the need for food, water, clothing, shelter, and a secure and safe environment	By receiving enough pay to provide for the basic necessities of life and by having safe working conditions
Lowest-Level Needs		

Whereas Maslow assumes that lower-level needs must be satisfied before a higher-level need is a motivator, Alderfer lifts this restriction. According to ERG theory, a higher-level need can be a motivator even if a lower-level need is not fully satisfied, and needs at more than one level can be motivators at any time. Alderfer agrees with Maslow that as lower-level needs are satisfied, an employee becomes motivated to satisfy higher-level needs. But Alderfer breaks with Maslow on the consequences of need frustration. Maslow says that after a lower-level need is satisfied, it is no longer a source of motivation. Alderfer proposes that when an individual is motivated to satisfy a higher-level need but has difficulty doing so, the person's motivation to satisfy lower-level needs will increase.

To see how this process works, let's look at the case of a middle manager in a manufacturing firm whose existence and relatedness needs (lower-level needs) are pretty much satisfied. Currently, the manager is motivated to try to satisfy her growth needs but finds this hard to do because she has been in the same position for the past five years. She is very skilled and knowledgeable about all aspects of the job, and the wide variety and number of her current responsibilities leave her no time to pursue anything new or exciting. Essentially, the manager's motivation to satisfy her growth needs is being frustrated because of the nature of her job. According to Alderfer, this frustration will increase the manager's motivation to satisfy a lower-level need such as relatedness. As a result of this motivation, the manager becomes more concerned about interpersonal relations at work and continually seeks honest feedback from her colleagues.

THE RESEARCH EVIDENCE

Because Maslow's and Alderfer's theories were among some of the earliest approaches to work motivation, they have received a considerable amount of attention from researchers. Although they seem logical and intuitively appealing and many managers like them, by and large these theories have tended *not* to receive support from research.[32] There appear to be at least two major difficulties with the theories. First, it may be unreasonable to expect a relatively small set of needs ordered in a particular fashion to apply to all human beings. Second, it may be unrealistic to expect that all people become motivated by different types of needs in a set order (that is, that the satisfaction of higher needs is sought *only* when lower-level needs have been satisfied).

Studies of American employees generally do not support the main tenets of Maslow's and Alderfer's theories, and it is likely that international studies conducted in other cultures would yield even less support. Even though the conclusions of the theories have not been supported, we can still learn some important lessons about motivation from the work of Maslow and Alderfer.

Expectancy Theory

Expectancy theory
A process theory about work motivation that focuses on how employees make choices among alternative behaviors and levels of effort.

Need theories try to explain *what* motivates employees. Expectancy theory focuses on *how* employees decide which specific behaviors to perform and *how much* effort to exert. In other words, **expectancy theory** is concerned with how employees make choices among alternative behaviors and levels of effort.[33] With its emphasis on choices, expectancy theory focuses on employees' perceptions (see Chapter 4) and thoughts or cognitive processes (Chapter 5).

To understand the overall focus of expectancy theory, consider the *direction of behavior* of an experienced nurse who has just taken a job at a new hospital. Which behaviors could she choose to perform? Does she spend time casually chatting with patients, or does she limit her interactions to those directly pertaining to medical care? Does she discuss her patients' symptoms and complaints with their physicians in detail, or must doctors rely on her written records? Does she readily help other nurses when they seem to have a heavy load, or does she provide assistance only when asked?

After the nurse chooses what she will do, she also needs to decide how much *effort* to exert on the job. Should she push herself to do as much as she can, even if doing so means forgoing some of her authorized breaks? Should she do just enough to adequately perform her job requirements? Should she minimize her efforts by taking longer breaks, referring her most difficult patients to her supervisor, and avoiding conversations with patients and physicians?

Also, with what level of *persistence* should she report her fears that a junior doctor has made a misdiagnosis? Should she mention it to some of her more senior co-workers? Should she tell her supervisor? If her supervisor does nothing about it, should she raise the issue with the head nurse in charge of her unit? If the head nurse is unconcerned, should she discuss her fears with a more senior doctor?

Expectancy theory seeks to explain how employees go about making these various decisions. Because these choices determine what employees do on the job and how hard they work, they have profound effects on organizational effectiveness. By describing how employees make these choices, expectancy theory provides managers with valuable insights on how to get employees to perform organizationally functional behaviors and how to encourage employees to exert high levels of effort when performing these behaviors.

Because of its profound organizational implications, expectancy theory is among the most popular theories of work motivation. The theory, which was originally developed by Victor Vroom in the 1960s, assumes that employees are essentially pleasure seeking[34]—that is, they are motivated to receive positive outcomes (such as a weekly paycheck, a bonus, or an award) and to avoid negative outcomes (such as getting reprimanded, fired, or demoted). It also assumes that employees are rational, careful processors of information and use information about their jobs, abilities, and desires to decide what they will do on the job and how hard they will do it.

Expectancy theory identifies three major factors that determine an employee's motivation: valence, instrumentality, and expectancy.[35]

VALENCE: HOW DESIRABLE IS AN OUTCOME?

Employees can obtain a variety of outcomes from their jobs—pay, job security, benefits, feelings of accomplishment, the opportunity to do interesting work, good relationships with co-employees, and promotions. For any individual, the desirability of each outcome is likely to vary. The term **valence** refers to the desirability of an outcome to an individual employee. Valence can be positive or negative and can vary in size or magnitude. If an outcome has *positive valence*, an employee prefers having the outcome to not having it. If an outcome has *negative valence*, an employee prefers not having the outcome. For most employees, getting a raise is likely to have positive valence, and being fired is likely to have negative valence. The magnitude of valence is how desirable or undesirable an outcome is for an employee.[36] Maslow's and Alderfer's need theories suggest that employees will find outcomes that satisfy their needs to be especially attractive or valent. In the opening case, some highly valent outcomes for the SAS employees include the opportunity to do interesting and creative work, develop new products, and access the latest technology. Other valent outcomes at SAS include being fairly rewarded financially, working in a pleasant environment, and having access to a company-provided day care and gym.

Some motivation problems occur because highly valent outcomes are unavailable to employees. To determine what outcomes might motivate an employee, managers must determine what outcomes an employee desires or the valence of different outcomes for the employee.

Valence In expectancy theory, the desirability of an outcome to an individual.

INSTRUMENTALITY: WHAT IS THE CONNECTION BETWEEN JOB PERFORMANCE AND OUTCOMES?

Instrumentality In expectancy theory, a perception about the extent to which performance of one or more behaviors will lead to the attainment of a particular outcome.

In our discussion of learning and operant conditioning in Chapter 5, we emphasize how important it is for outcomes (or *consequences,* as they are called in operant conditioning) to be given to employees on the basis of their performance of desired behaviors. Like operant conditioning, expectancy theory proposes that outcomes should be directly linked to desired organizational behaviors or to overall levels of job performance.

Instrumentality, the second key determinant of motivation according to expectancy theory, is an employee's perception about the extent to which performing certain behaviors or performing at a certain level will lead to the attainment of a particular outcome. In organizations, employees are going to engage in desired behaviors and be motivated to perform them at a high level only if they perceive that high performance and desired behaviors will lead to positively valent outcomes such as a pay raise, a promotion, or sometimes even just a pat on the back.[37]

Just like valence, instrumentality can be positive or negative and varies in size or magnitude. Instrumentality, the *perceived* association between a certain level of job performance (or the performance of certain behaviors) and the receipt of a specific outcome, can be measured on a scale from −1 to +1. An instrumentality of −1 means that an employee perceives that performing a certain behavior, or performing it at a certain level, definitely *will not result* in obtaining the outcome. An instrumentality of +1 means that the employee perceives the performance *definitely will result* in obtaining the outcome.

An advertising executive, for example, perceives that if she obtains three new major corporate accounts this year (and holds on to all of her existing accounts), her performance definitely *will result* in her receiving a hefty year-end bonus (an instrumentality of +1) and definitely *will not result* in her being asked to relocate to one of the agency's less prestigious locations (an instrumentality of −1). The magnitude of instrumentalities between the extremes of −1 and +1 indicates the extent of the perceived association or relationship between the performance and the outcome. An instrumentality of zero means that an employee perceives *no* relationship between performance and outcome. Let's continue with the example of the advertising executive. She perceives that there is some possibility that if she performs at a high level she will be given a promotion (an instrumentality of .3) and a larger possibility that she will obtain a bigger office (an instrumentality of .5). She perceives that her medical and dental benefits will be unaffected by her level of performance (an instrumentality of zero).

In trying to decide which behaviors to engage in and how hard to work (the level of job performance to strive for), the advertising executive considers the *valences* of the outcomes that she perceives will result from different levels of performance (how attractive the outcomes are to her) and the *instrumentality* of performing at a certain level for attaining each outcome (how certain it is that performing at that level will result in that outcome). In this way, both instrumentality and valence influence motivation.

Instrumentalities that are, in fact, high and that employees believe are high are effective motivators. Managers need to make sure that employees who perform at a high level do in fact receive the outcomes that they desire—outcomes with high positive valence. In the opening case, the SAS Institute maintains high instrumentalities by linking employees' pay and bonuses to their performance. Managers also need to clearly communicate instrumentalities to employees by letting them know what outcomes will result from various levels of performance.

Sometimes employees are not motivated to perform at a high level because they do not perceive that high performance will lead to highly valent outcomes (such as pay raises, time off, and promotions). When employees think that good performance goes unrecognized, their motivation to perform at a high level tends to be low.

EXPECTANCY: WHAT IS THE CONNECTION BETWEEN EFFORT AND JOB PERFORMANCE?

Even though an employee perceives that a pay raise (a highly valent outcome) will result directly from high performance (high instrumentality), he or she still may not be motivated to perform at a high level. To understand why motivation is low even when instrumentalities and valences are high, we need to consider the third major factor in expectancy theory: expectancy.

Expectancy is an employee's perception about the extent to which his or her effort will result in a certain level of job performance. Expectancy varies from 0 to 1 and reflects the chances that putting forth a certain amount of effort will result in a certain level of performance. An expectancy of 0 means that an employee believes there is no chance that his or her effort will result in a certain level of performance. An expectancy of 1 signifies that an employee is absolutely certain that his or her effort will lead to a certain level of performance. Expectancies between 0 and 1 lie along the continuum between the two.

Employees are going to be motivated to perform desired behaviors at a high level only if they think they can do so.[38] If they think they actually *will perform* at a high level when they work hard, their expectancy is high. No matter how much the advertising executive in our earlier example wants the pay raise and promotion that she thinks will result from high performance, if she thinks she cannot possibly perform at the necessary level, she will not be motivated to do so. Similarly, no matter how much a student wants to pass a course, if she thinks she will flunk no matter how hard she studies, she will not be motivated to study. Expectancy is similar to the concept of self-efficacy, discussed in Chapter 5, which captures the idea that employees are not always certain that their efforts will be successful or result in a given level of performance.

If motivation levels are low because employees do not think their efforts will pay off with improved performance, managers need to reassure them they are capable of performing at a high level if they try hard. In addition, organizations can boost employees' expectancies by helping them improve their skills and abilities. Organizations ranging from the SAS Institute to the Container Store and Southwest Airlines are great believers in training to boost expectancies.[39]

Expectancy In expectancy theory, a perception about the extent to which effort will result in a certain level of performance.

THE COMBINED EFFECTS OF VALENCE, INSTRUMENTALITY, AND EXPECTANCY ON MOTIVATION

In order for an employee to be motivated to perform desired behaviors and to perform them at a high level, the following conditions are necessary (see Figure 6.3):

♦ *Valence* must be high: The employee wants outcomes the organization has to offer.

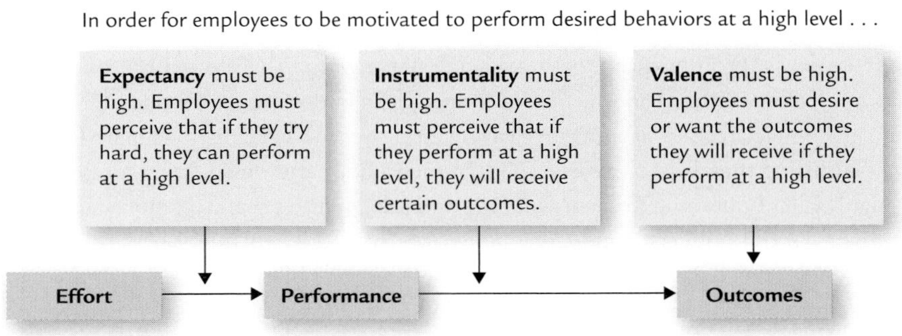

In order for employees to be motivated to perform desired behaviors at a high level . . .

Expectancy must be high. Employees must perceive that if they try hard, they can perform at a high level.

Instrumentality must be high. Employees must perceive that if they perform at a high level, they will receive certain outcomes.

Valence must be high. Employees must desire or want the outcomes they will receive if they perform at a high level.

Effort → Performance → Outcomes

FIGURE 6.3
Expectancy Theory

♦ *Instrumentality* must be high: The employee perceives that she or he must perform the desired behaviors at a high level to obtain these outcomes.

♦ *Expectancy* must be high: The employee thinks that trying hard will lead to performance at a high level.

If just one of these three factors—valence, instrumentality, or expectancy—is zero, motivation will be zero. Our advertising executive must perceive that (1) she is likely to receive desired (positively valent) outcomes if she performs at a high level and (2) she can perform at a high level if she tries (has a high expectancy).

High performance depends on what an employee does and how hard he or she does it. According to expectancy theory, in trying to decide what to do and how hard to do it, employees ask themselves questions such as these:

♦ Will I be able to obtain outcomes I want? (In expectancy theory terms: Is the valence of outcomes that the organization provides high?)

♦ Do I need to perform at a high level to obtain these outcomes? (In expectancy theory terms: Is high performance instrumental for obtaining these outcomes?)

♦ If I try hard, will I be able to perform at a high level? (In expectancy theory terms: Is expectancy high?)

Only when employees answer "yes" to each of these three questions are they motivated to perform as best they can. Expectancy theory suggests not only that rewards should be based on performance and that employees should have the abilities necessary to perform at a high level but also that managers must make sure that employees accurately perceive this to be the case.

Expectancy theory is a popular theory of motivation and has received extensive attention from researchers. Some studies support the theory and others do not,[40] but by and large, the theory has been supported.[41] The theory's lessons are heeded by a wide variety of organizations, including the U.S. steelmakers highlighted in the accompanying Global View.

global view

Motivating Steel Workers

LTV Corporation, a U.S. steelmaker failing for over a decade, finally went bankrupt in the early 2000s. LTV and its assets were subsequently purchased by businessman Wilbur Ross and his private equity firm. Thus, from LTV's idle mills, International Steel Group (ISG) was born.[42] ISG has gone on to acquire other defunct steelmakers, as have its competitors Nucor Corporation and U.S. Steel. Together these three companies are emerging as the "Big Three" in the troubled industry and are making major changes to regain their global competitiveness. Global competitiveness is essential, given the current worldwide excess of steelmaking capacity. And while consolidation in the industry (via mergers and acquistions) is argued by many to be necessary for global competitiveness, profound changes are taking place within these organizations that were once the crowning glory of the economy but have since been in decline for decades.[43]

Many of the changes revolve around motivating employees to take responsibility for enhancing efficiency, boosting their expectancies and instrumentalities and, in so doing, providing them with a very highly valent outcome (a secure income and job). In the past, steel mills had many layers of supervisors and managers and were rigidly constrained by rules.[44] Things are different today. Currently, ISG has fewer than 30 executives and responsibility for making improvements and efficiency gains is no longer the sole responsibility of managers.[45] Indeed, employees on the shop floor now believe they can and should take responsibility for improving efficiency. They know that if they do, their organizations will become more globally competitive, and they will benefit in terms of job security, pay incentives, and profit sharing.[46]

For example, at ISG, employees now believe there are things they can do on the job to improve efficiency. Rigid rules and layers of management no longer stand in their way. When these efficiency gains are realized, they also know they'll be rewarded. For example, mill workers at ISG recently suggested a change that resulted in an extra half-hour of productivity per day. Rather than waiting for a new slab of steel when a run was completed, as was customary, the employees suggested that the new slab be requested 10 minutes before the run was completed.[47] Although consolidations in the steel industry have resulted in painful layoffs, current efforts to motivate employees to increase efficiency may help the Big Three once again be globally competitive and, in the long run, perhaps save jobs in the industry.[48]

Once market leaders, American steelmakers like International Steel Group (ISG) today face stiff global competition from firms abroad. As a result, ISG employees have taken it upon themselves to make process improvements to improve the company's competitiveness.

Equity Theory

The equity theory of work motivation was developed in the 1960s by J. Stacy Adams (*equity* means "fairness"). Equity theory is based on the premise that an employee perceives the relationship between the *outcomes*—what the employee gets from a job and organization—and his or her *inputs*—what the employee contributes to the job and organization.[49] Outcomes include pay, fringe benefits, job satisfaction, status, opportunities for advancement, job security, and anything else the employees wants from the organization. Inputs include special skills, training, education, work experience, effort on the job, time, and anything else that employees believe they contribute. According to **equity theory**, however, it is *not* the objective level of outcomes and inputs that is important in determining work motivation. What is important to motivation is the way an employee perceives his or her outcome/input ratio compared to the **outcome/input ratio** of another person.[50]

Equity theory A process theory about work motivation that focuses on employees' perceptions of the fairness of their work outcomes and inputs.

Outcome/input ratio In equity theory, the relationship between what an employee gets from a job (outcomes) and what the employee contributes to the job (inputs).

This other person, called a *referent* by Adams, is simply another employee or group of employees perceived to be similar to oneself. The referent could also be oneself at a different place or time (for example, in a previous job), or it could be one's expectations (for example, one's beliefs about what the outputs and inputs of an entry-level accountant's job should be). Regardless of the referent an employee chooses, it is the *employee's perceptions* of the referent's outcomes and inputs that are compared—not any objective measure of actual outcomes or inputs.

EQUITY

Equity exists when an individual's outcome/input ratio equals the outcome/input ratio of the referent (see Table 6.4). Because the comparison of the ratios is what determines the presence or absence of equity (not the comparison of absolute levels of outcomes and inputs), equity can exist even if the referent receives more than the individual who is making the comparison.

Consider the case of two financial analysts who have been working at the same corporation for two years. At the end of the two years, analyst A gets promoted, but analyst B does not. Can both analysts consider this situation to be equitable? The answer is yes: Equity exists if analyst A and analyst B perceive that that their respective outcome/input ratios are equal or proportional and that analyst A generally worked more hours than analyst B. Perhaps, for example, added input, or overtime, accounts for analyst A's additional outcome (the promotion).

When an employee perceives that the employee's and the referent's outcome/input ratios are proportionally equal, the employee is motivated either to maintain the status quo or to increase his or her inputs to receive more outcomes.

INEQUITY

Inequity, or lack of fairness, exists when outcome/input ratios are not proportionally equal. Inequity creates tension and unpleasant feelings for an employee and motivates the individual to try to restore equity by bringing the two ratios back into balance.

TABLE 6.4
Conditions of Equity and Inequity

	Individual Referent	Example
Equity	$\dfrac{\text{Outcomes}}{\text{Inputs}} = \dfrac{\text{Outcomes}}{\text{Inputs}}$	A financial analyst contributes more inputs (time and effort) to her job and receives proportionally more outcomes (a promotion and a pay raise) than her referent receives.
Overpayment inequity	$\dfrac{\text{Outcomes}}{\text{Inputs}} > \dfrac{\text{Outcomes}}{\text{Inputs}}$ (greater than)	A financial analyst contributes the same level of inputs to her job as her referent but receives more outcomes than the referent receives.
Underpayment inequity	$\dfrac{\text{Outcomes}}{\text{Inputs}} < \dfrac{\text{Outcomes}}{\text{Inputs}}$ (less than)	A financial analyst contributes more inputs to her job than her referent but receives the same outcomes as her referent.

There are two basic types of inequity: overpayment inequity and underpayment inequity (see Table 6.4). **Overpayment inequity** exists when an individual perceives that his or her outcome/input ratio is greater than that of a referent. **Underpayment inequity** exists when a person perceives that his or her outcome/input ratio is less than that of a referent.

Consider the case of Steve and Mike, who are janitors in a large office building. Steve is a conscientious employee who always gets to work on time and keeps his areas of the building spotless. Mike is often late, takes long lunch hours, and often "forgets" to clean some of his areas. Steve and Mike receive the same level of pay, benefits, and other outcomes from their employer. According to equity theory, if both employees have accurate perceptions and choose each other as a referent, Mike should perceive *overpayment inequity*. This perception creates tension within Mike (perhaps it makes him feel guilty), and so he's motivated to restore equity. Steve, in contrast, perceives *underpayment inequity*. Because Steve is contributing more than Mike yet receiving the same level of outcomes, he, too, experiences tension (perhaps anger) and is motivated to restore equity.

WAYS TO RESTORE EQUITY

There are several ways by which equity can be restored in situations like the one involving Steve and Mike.[51]

1. *Employees can change their inputs or outcomes.* When employees perceive underpayment inequity, for example, they can restore equity by reducing their inputs. In the case of the two janitors, Steve could restore equity by cutting back on his inputs—by coming to work late, taking longer breaks, and working less conscientiously. An underpaid employee could also try to change his or her outcomes by asking for a raise.

2. *Employees try to change their referents' inputs or outcomes.* Steve might complain to his supervisor about Mike's coming to work late and not doing a very good job in the hope that the supervisor will alter Mike's inputs (perhaps by getting him to show up on time or do a better job) or his outcomes (cutting his pay or threatening his job security). On the other hand, Mike might encourage Steve to relax and take it easy on the job.

3. *Employees change their perceptions of inputs and outcomes (either their own or the referents').* Mike could restore equity by changing his perceptions about his inputs. He could start to think that his area is larger or harder to clean than Steve's or that he works faster, so his and Steve's ratios are really proportional after all. As this example illustrates, employees who perceive overpayment inequity are especially likely to change their perceptions (rather than their actual inputs or outcomes) to restore equity. This is why overpaid employees often do not feel guilty for very long.

4. *Employees can change the referent.*[52] An employee may decide that the original referent does not allow for an appropriate comparison and, thus, select another one. Steve might recall hearing that Mike is a relative of one of the managers in the company and conclude that he is not the most suitable basis for comparison. Conversely, Mike might decide that Steve is clearly an extraordinary, almost superhuman janitor and select someone else to compare himself to.

5. *Employees leave the job or organization or force the referent to leave.* The most common example of this approach is employee turnover and, not surprisingly, leaving the organization is most prevalent in situations of underpayment inequity. Thus, Steve might be motivated to look for a job elsewhere, or he might try to get Mike fired.

Overpayment inequity The inequity that exists when a person perceives that his or her outcome/input ratio is greater than the ratio of a referent.

Underpayment inequity The inequity that exists when a person perceives that his or her outcome/input ratio is less than the ratio of a referent.

THE EFFECTS OF INEQUITY AND THE RESEARCH EVIDENCE

Both underpayment inequity and overpayment inequity are dysfunctional for organizations, managers, and employees. In the case of overpayment, although employees are sometimes motivated to increase their inputs to restore equity (an effort that is functional for the organization), they are more likely to be motivated to change their perceptions of inputs or outcomes (an effort that is dysfunctional because there is no *actual* increase in the level of inputs contributed by the overpaid employees). In the case of underpayment, capable and deserving employees may be motivated to reduce their inputs or even leave the organization, both of which are dysfunctional for the organization. Moreover, sometimes when employees feel very unfairly treated, they engage in unethical behaviors such as stealing from the organization.[53]

All in all, motivation is highest when equity exists and outcomes are distributed to employees on the basis of their inputs to the organization. Employees who contribute a high level of inputs and receive, in turn, a high level of outcomes are motivated to continue to contribute inputs. Employees who contribute a low level of inputs and receive a low level of outcomes know that if they want to increase their outcomes, they must increase their inputs.

Like expectancy theory, equity theory is a popular theory of motivation and has received extensive research attention. Also, as in the case of expectancy theory, although there have been some nonsupportive results, by and large the research supports the main ideas of the theory.[54]

you're the management expert

When Equal Treatment Backfires

Tom Li manages the order processing department of a large catering company in New York City. Times have been tough, and he has been told that he will have very limited funds available for annual salary increases. In an effort to be fair, he has decided to take his entire pool of funds for raises and distribute a flat 3 percent salary increase equally to each of his subordinates. At the end of the last department meeting, he announced the 3 percent raise and noted that, given the decrease in the company's revenues over the past year, he was pleasantly surprised that any funds were available for raises. A few days after the meeting, one of Li's subordinates, Sebastian Saltado, came by his office and complained about his measly raise and asked why he was receiving the same percentage increase as everyone else in the department. Li told him that he knew that Saltado processed orders more quickly than others members in the department and was more responsive to customers, and he wished he could do something more to recognize his contributions. But, Li explained, because very limited funds were available for raises, he thought it only fair to share the raise pool equally. Two weeks later Saltado gave notice that he would be leaving the company because he found a better job working in a large department store. Li is concerned and confused—he thought Saltado really liked his work at the catering company and was satisfied with his job; in fact, Saltado had mentioned that a friend of his would be interested in a job in the same department if a position opened up. And Li is really going to miss having Saltado around; he could always count on Saltado to placate a disgruntled customer and somehow arrange for changes or replacements on an order to be processed and delivered in record time. As an expert in OB, Li has come to you for help. Why did Saltado quit, and was there anything that Li should have done differently?

Procedural Justice Theory

Because equity theory focuses on the fair distribution of outcomes across employees to encourage high levels of motivation, it is often called a theory of *distributive* justice.[55] Another dimension of fairness in organizations, *procedural* justice, is also important for understanding employee motivation.[56] **Procedural justice theory**, a relatively new approach to motivation, is concerned with the perceived fairness of the procedures used to make decisions about the distribution of outcomes. It is *not* concerned about the actual distribution of outcomes.[57] Procedural decisions pertain to how performance levels are evaluated, how grievances or disputes are handled (if, for example, an employee disagrees with a manager's evaluation of his or her performance), and how outcomes (like raises) are distributed. Like equity theory, employees' *perceptions* are key to procedural justice theory. That is, employees' reactions to procedures depend on how fair they *perceive* the procedures to be rather than how fair they actually are.[58]

Procedural justice theory holds that employees are going to be more motivated to perform at a high level when they perceive that the procedures used to make decisions about the distribution of outcomes are fair.[59] In other words, they'll be more motivated if they think their performance will be accurately assessed. Conversely, if employees think their performance will not be accurately assessed because the supervisor is not aware of their contributions to the organization or lets his or her personal feelings affect appraisals, employees will not be as strongly motivated to perform at a high level. Procedural justice theory seeks to explain what causes employees to perceive procedures as fair or unfair and the consequences of these perceptions.

Procedural justice theory A process theory about work motivation that focuses on employees' perceptions of the fairness of the procedures used to make decisions about the distribution of outcomes.

CAUSES OF PROCEDURAL JUSTICE

According to procedural justice theory, two factors are important in determining employees' perceptions of the fairness of procedures.[60] One factor is the interpersonal treatment of employees—that is, how employees are treated by the distributors of the outcomes (usually their managers). It is important for managers to be honest and courteous, to respect the rights and opinions of employees, and to provide employees with timely feedback about how they are doing.[61] It is also important for managers to allow their subordinates to contribute their own viewpoints, opinions, and perspectives to the decision-making process.[62]

The other factor that determines perceptions of procedural justice is the extent to which managers explain their decisions to employees.[63] For example, managers can explain to employees (1) how they assess inputs (including time, effort, education, and previous work experience), (2) how they appraise performance, and (3) how they decide to distribute outcomes. By treating employees with respect and courtesy, providing feedback, considering employees' viewpoints, and carefully explaining the manner in which decisions are made, managers can help ensure that perceptions of procedural justice are high.

Some companies hire firms to research compensation, employee satisfaction, and human resource practices to determine if employees perceive them to be fair. Perceptions of fairness on the part of employees is important for motivation.

CONSEQUENCES OF PROCEDURAL JUSTICE

Researchers have explored the specific consequences of procedural justice for work motivation. One can get a good handle on some of these consequences by considering the implications of procedural justice for the expectancy and equity theories of motivation.

Recall that expectancy theory asserts that individuals are motivated to work hard when they believe that (1) their effort will result in their achieving a satisfactory level of performance (expectancy is high) and (2) their performance will lead to desired outcomes such as pay raise or a promotion (instrumentality and valence of outcomes are high). Suppose, however, that an organization has a problem with procedural justice, and its employees do *not* perceive that the procedures used to distribute outcomes are fair. More specifically, suppose employees believe that the performance appraisal system is inaccurate and biased, so that performing at a high level does *not* ensure a good performance appraisal, and performing poorly has been known to result in an average performance rating. In this organization, employees may believe that they are capable of performing at a high level (their expectancy is high), but they cannot be sure that they will receive a high performance rating because the appraisal system is unfair (procedural justice is low). Employees will *not* be motivated to exert a lot of effort on the job if they think their performance will *not* be accurately and fairly assessed and they will *not* receive the outcomes they think they deserve.

From the perspective of equity theory, motivation will also suffer when perceptions of procedural justice are low. Employees may believe that their inputs to the organization are not going to be fairly assessed or that outcomes will not be distributed based on relative inputs. Under these circumstances, employees will not be motivated to contribute inputs, for there is no guarantee that they will result in the outcomes they think they deserve.

It appears that perceptions of procedural justice are especially important when the outcomes, like pay and benefits, are relatively low—that is, when there are few rewards to distribute to employees. Some research suggests that individuals who obtain medium or high outcome levels view them as fair *regardless* of whether the procedures in place to distribute them are really fair or not. However, they view low outcome levels—assuming they're the ones receiving them—as equitable only when the procedures used to distribute them really *are* fair.[64] In sum, although a lot of work still needs to be done in the area of procedural justice, it nevertheless appears to be an important factor to consider when it comes to understanding motivation in organizations.

Summary

Work motivation explains why employees behave as they do. Four prominent theories about work motivation—need theory, expectancy theory, equity theory, and procedural justice theory—provide complementary approaches to understanding and managing motivation in organizations. Each theory answers different questions about the motivational process. In this chapter, we made the following major points:

1. Work motivation is the psychological force within a person that determines the direction of the person's behavior in an organization, the person's level of effort, and the person's level of persistence in the face of obstacles. Motivation is distinct from performance; other factors besides motivation (for example, ability and task difficulty) influence performance.

2. Intrinsically motivated behavior is behavior performed for its own sake. Extrinsically motivated behavior is behavior performed to acquire material or social rewards or to avoid punishment.

3. Need theory, expectancy theory, equity theory, and procedural justice theory are comple-

mentary approaches to understanding motivation. Each answers different questions about the nature and management of motivation in organizations.

4. Need theories of motivation identify the needs that employees are motivated to satisfy on the job. Two major need theories of motivation are Maslow's hierarchy of needs and Alderfer's existence-relatedness-growth theory.

5. Expectancy theory focuses on how employees decide what behaviors to engage in on the job and how much effort to exert. The three major concepts in expectancy theory are valence (how desirable an outcome is to an employee), instru-

mentality (an employee's perception about the extent to which a certain level of performance will lead to the attainment of a particular outcome), and expectancy (an employee's perception about the extent to which effort will result in a certain level of performance). Valence, instrumentality, and expectancy combine to determine motivation.

6. Equity theory proposes that employees compare their own outcome/input ratio (the ratio of the outcomes they receive from their jobs and from the organization to the inputs they contribute) to the outcome/input ratio of a referent. Unequal ratios create tension inside the employee, and the employee is motivated to restore equity. When the

ratios are equal, employees are motivated to maintain their current ratio of outcomes and inputs or raise their inputs if they want their outcomes to increase.

7. Procedural justice theory is concerned with the perceived fairness of the procedures used to make decisions about inputs, performance, and the distribution of outcomes. How managers treat their subordinates and the extent to which they provide explanations for their decisions influence employees' perceptions of procedural justice. When procedural justice is perceived to be low, motivation suffers because employees are not sure that their inputs and performance levels will be accurately assessed or that outcomes will be distributed in a fair manner.

Exercises in Understanding and Managing Organizational Behavior

Questions for Discussion and Review

1. Why might a person with a very high level of motivation perform poorly?

2. Why might a person with a very low level of motivation be a top performer?

3. Why do people differ in the types of needs they are trying to satisfy at work?

4. Why might employees differ in their valences for the same outcomes?

5. Why might perceptions of instrumentality be relatively low in an organization?

6. Why might a very capable employee have low expectancy for performing at a high level?

7. How does the choice of a referent influence perceptions of equity and inequity?

8. Is inequity always dysfunctional for an organization? Why or why not?

9. Why might fair procedures be perceived as being unfair by some employees?

10. What steps can organizations take to encourage procedural justice?

Building People Skills

Peak Motivation Experiences

Think about the last time you felt really motivated to do well at some activity: in one of your classes, at work, or in some kind of hobby or leisure activity (such as playing golf, running, or singing).

1. Describe the activity and indicate how you felt while engaged in it.

2. Was your motivation extrinsic, intrinsic, or both?

3. What needs were you trying to satisfy by this activity?

4. What outcomes did you hope to obtain by performing this activity well?

5. Did you think it was likely that you would attain these outcomes if you were successful?

6. How would you characterize your expectancy for this activity? Why was your expectancy at this level?

7. Did you ever compare what you were putting into the activity and what you were getting out of it to the input and outcome of a referent? If not, why not? If so, how did you feel about this comparison, and how did it affect your behavior?

8. Did thoughts of procedural justice ever enter your mind and affect your motivation?

A Question of Ethics

Employees often differ in their needs for time off from work. Employees with small children, single parents, employees with health problems, and employees who are the primary caregiver for an elderly or infirm relative may need more time off, for example, than employees who are single with no dependents and in good health. And one could argue that organizations should be responsive to these differing needs on ethical grounds. However, some might feel that the same expectations should apply to all employees regardless of their needs.

Questions

1. Why should organizations take employees' personal needs into account in providing benefits such as time off from work?

2. How can organizations take employees' personal needs into account while at the same time ensuring that organizational members perceive that they are being fairly treated?

Small Group Break-Out Exercise

Promoting Procedural Justice

Form groups of three or four people and appoint one member as the spokesperson who will communicate your conclusions to the rest of the class:

1. Take a few minutes to think about a time in your life when you felt that you were really being treated unfairly and it was because of the procedures that were being used.

2. Take turns describing each of your experiences and the nature of the procedures that were unfair.

3. Then, as a group, come up with a list of the causes of a lack of procedural justice in the examples in your group.

4. Based on Step 3, develop specific recommendations for promoting procedural justice.

Topic for Debate

Motivation explains why members of an organization behave as they do and either help or hinder the organization from achieving its goals. Now that you have a good understanding of motivation, debate the following issue:

Team A. Equity and justice cannot be achieved in the workplace.

Team B. Equity and justice can be achieved in the workplace.

Experiential Exercise

Motivating in Lean Economic Times

Objective

Your objective is to gain experience in confronting the challenges of (1) maintaining high levels of motivation when resources are shrinking and (2) developing an effective motivation program.

Procedure

The class divides into groups of three to five people, and each group appoints one member as spokesperson to present the group's recommendations to the whole class. Here is the scenario.

Each group plays the role of a team of top managers in a magazine publishing company that has recently downsized and consolidated its businesses. Now that the layoff is complete, top management is trying to devise a program to motivate the remaining editorial and production employees, who range from rank-and-file employees who operate printing presses to upper-level employees such as magazine editors.

As a result of the downsizing, the workloads of most employees have been increased by about 30 percent. In addition, resources are tight. A very limited amount of money is available for things such as pay raises, bonuses, and benefits. Nevertheless, top management thinks the company has real potential and that its fortunes could turn around if employees could be motivated to perform at a high level, be innovative, and work together to regain the company's competitive advantage.

Your group, acting as the top-management team, answers the following questions:

1. What specific steps will you take to develop a motivation program based on the knowledge of motivation you have gained from this chapter?
2. What key features will your motivation program include?
3. What will you do if the program you develop and implement does not seem to be working—if motivation not only fails to increase, but also sinks to an all-time low?

When your group has completed those activities, the spokesperson will present the group's plans and proposed actions to the whole class.

Making the Connection

Find an example of an organization that uses outcomes such as pay and bonuses to motivate employees to perform at a high level. What behaviors is this organization trying to encourage? How does this organization use outcomes such as pay and bonuses to promote high motivation and performance?

New York Times Cases in the News

The New York Times

Top Users Of Sick Leave Face Transfer In Fire Dept.

BY MICHELLE O'DONNELL

Fire Commissioner Nicholas Scoppetta said yesterday that the Fire Department would transfer 20 firefighters with the most sick leave absences to other assignments in an effort to stem what he called abuses of its medical leave policy.

The measures may seem counter-intuitive: the firefighters will be moved from busy firehouses to less busy ones, which might seem an appealing fate to someone who is essentially being accused of not working hard enough. But within the ranks of the department, being reassigned to a quiet firehouse is akin to a direct attack on a firefighter's pride.

Working in a busy company—or, simply being able to say that one works in a busy company—provides certain status among firefighters. The companies in areas where fires are many, including the poorer neighborhoods of the Bronx, Brooklyn, Harlem and parts of Jamaica,

have long been relished assignments and, in some cases, have required some string-pulling to join.

The transfers, then, are meant to punish the 20 firefighters, each of whom averaged at least 40 days of sick time each year for the last three years for injuries like muscle strains and sprains. And while the union that represents firefighters cried foul—the 20 represent about one-fifth of 1 percent of the force, it said, hardly a representative body of the department's work ethic—some firefighters said the transfers were not entirely unwelcome.

"Most guys go to work to do it," said Lt. Greg Prial of Ladder Company 43 in East Harlem, which is considered a good or busy company—the two are synonymous in the department. "They don't want to hear about it from other firemen." Having a slacker in the ranks defeats company morale, Lieutenant Prial said, as company pride—and a chronic fear of losing face in front of other fire

companies—is critical to motivate the ranks at a fire. "That's the only thing that puts fires out."

In department parlance, slackers are called square roots. How the mathematical term came to represent those prone to call in sick around the holidays is not certain, but it might have something to do with how each tends to view his own interests at the heart of every matter.

In defense of its plan, the department yesterday trotted out some statistics—but not names—to show what it said were the egregious abuses of the 20.

Frequent absences can lead to quieter firehouses.

In one case, a Queens firefighter who has been with the department five years has been out on medical leave for a total of 521 days. One serious injury, a fractured vertebrae, kept him out of work for 142 days, but then a string of sprains and strains to his knee, back (twice) and shoulder (twice) kept him out the remainder of the 521 days.

Referring to the department's criticism of some firefighters, Stephen J. Cassidy, president of the Uniformed Firefighters Association, said, "There's a lemon or two in each company." Still, even singling out a select few sends the wrong message to the whole department, Mr. Cassidy maintained.

Part of the department's eagerness to nip any abuses in the bud is to protect itself from an extremely liberal medical leave policy. There is no limit to the medical leave a firefighter can take, and when he is out on a line-of-duty injury, he earns his income tax-free.

Despite the tough line, Commissioner Scoppetta hastened to point out that the department was not suspending these 20 firefighters from work, but merely placing them in companies where they would be less likely to see fire duty as often, and, as a result, be less likely to be injured.

So, just where do firefighters go to be exiled? For years, Staten Island served as the department's unofficial Isle of Elba, but the decreasing number of fires has left a sea of Elbas throughout the city. There is Riverdale in the Bronx; Bayside, Queens; Bay Ridge, Brooklyn; and even Lower Manhattan, which except for Sept. 11, was once considered an empty plain of false alarms in high-rises.

Reached yesterday by phone, a firefighter at Engine Company 151 in Tottenville, Staten Island, said they had not heard if the company would be receiving any new members, but that they would welcome whomever the department sent, even the square roots.

"Ten of those guys are already here," a firefighter in the background quipped.

SOURCE: "Top Users of Sick Leave Face Transfer in Fire Dept.," by M. O'Donnell, *New York Times,* August 28, 2003, p. A26.

Questions for Discussion

1. What outcomes are highly valent for firefighters?

2. From a motivation standpoint, what effect might the presence of top users of sick leave have on a fire company?

3. What are the implications of transferring top users of sick leave to less busy fire companies from an equity theory perspective?

4. What are the implications of transferring top users of sick leave to less busy fire companies from a procedural justice perspective?

The New York Times

Men in Teaching Fall to a 40-Year Low, Survey Finds

Washington, Aug. 27, (AP)—Two out of 10 teachers are men, the lowest figure in 40 years, a survey by the National Education Association has found. One in 10 teachers is a minority group member, another sign that teachers have far less diversity than their students.

About half of students are male, and almost 40 percent are from minorities, government figures show. The lopsided representation of whites and women in teaching is troubling, the president of the union, Reg Weaver, said, because it denies students a range of role models.

The union said the field was less attractive to men and minorities because it was easier to earn more with less stress in other fields.

"It takes so many years to finally get a salary that is high enough to support a family," said Edward Kelley, a teacher at A. B. Combs Elementary School in Raleigh, N.C.

A certified teacher with a master's, Mr. Kelley earns $65,000 in his 30th year.

In 2001, the average contract salary for teachers was $43,262.

Mr. Kelley, who spent years in Maine before starting to teach this year in North Carolina, finds himself in a category with one of the smallest shares of men. Nine percent of elementary school teachers are men, with the Southeast having the lowest share of men in all, 14 percent.

The N.E.A. report, "Status of the American Public School Teacher," is based on the 2000–2001 school year. The association is the largest union in the nation, with more than 2.7 million members. The union and others are pursuing diversity through programs to improve college access for minorities and encourage classroom aides to obtain teacher certifications.

The big teachers' union wants to match the diversity of students.

Men made up one-third of the teaching force in the 1960's, '70's and '80's. Their numbers slid through the 90's and hit 21 percent, a low point, in 2001. Whites have accounted for 90 percent of teachers for 30 years. Six percent of teachers are black, a declining number. Five percent of teachers said they are Hispanic.

Over all, students are most likely to be taught by a 15-year veteran with a growing workload and slightly eroding interest in staying in teaching, the study found. Teachers said they typically worked 50 hours a week and spent $443 of their own money to help students in the school year. Fifty-seven percent hold at least a master's, and 77 percent took courses through their districts during the year.

Six in 10 teachers said they would choose teaching again if they could go back to their college days and start over, but that number dipped in 2001 after having steadily increased since 1981.

Virginia Beauchamp, who returned to the classroom a few years ago after 25 years in teaching and 9 in private indus-try, said: "I love the art of convincing and explaining. That's a big part of teaching."

Ms. Beauchamp, a social studies teacher at Nicholas Orem Middle School in Hyattsville, Md., added, "I enjoy seeing kids accomplish."

Teachers face rising expectations. Federal law requires every teacher of a core academic subject to be highly qualified by the end of the 2005–2006 school year, including a provision to prove competence in every subject that the person teaches.

The survey, based on responses by 1,467 teachers, has a margin of error of plus or minus two percentage points.

These are among its findings:

The largest percentage of teachers, 43 percent, entered the field more than 20 years ago. The second biggest group, 23 percent, entered in the last five years.

Eighty-one percent said they spent no time teaching in subjects or grades outside their major fields of college preparation. Six percent worked all their time in those fields.

A large majority said they remained in the field for the same reason they entered it, a desire to work with young people.

Over all, 45 percent identified them-selves as Democrats and 28 percent as Republicans. The rest said they had no affiliation or belonged to another party.

SOURCE: "Men in Teaching Fall to a 40-Year Low, Survey Finds," Reprinted with permission of Associated Press.

Questions for Discussion

1. What needs do teachers seek to satisfy at work?

2. Why might men and minorities be underrepresented in the ranks of teachers?

3. How would you characterize expectancy, instrumentality, and valence levels for a typical teacher, based on the material in the article?

4. Are teachers being fairly treated?

Creating a Motivating Work Setting

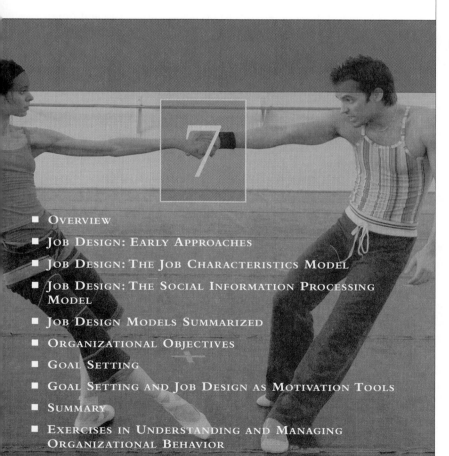

7

LEARNING OBJECTIVES

After studying this chapter, you should be able to:

■

Appreciate the advantages and disadvantages of the scientific management approach to job design.

■

Describe the job characteristics model and its implications for using job design to create a motivating work setting.

■

Understand the implications of the social information processing model.

■

Appreciate how and why organizational objectives can motivate employees.

■

Describe goal-setting theory and the kinds of goals that contribute to a motivating work setting.

OPENING CASE

Motivating Employees at Hydro

How Can Organizations Create a Motivating Work Setting?

Hydro, Norway's biggest industrial company, has operations in 40 countries and 35,000 employees globally.[1] The company operates in a variety of sectors, including oil, energy and aluminum, and agricultural industries.[2] A fundamental premise underlying Hydro's business model is social responsibility and corporate sustainability.[3] Corporate sustainability reflects a long-term commitment to protecting the environment and solving environmental problems and a commitment to social well-being.[4] Since 1998, Hydro has been listed on the prestigious Dow Jones Sustainability Index, a select list of companies that excel in sustainability in the industries in which they operate.[5] These companies are proactive in terms of integrating environmental and social concerns into their operations around the world.[6]

In Norway, Hydro is known for its many initiatives to promote the job satisfaction and well-being of its employees. Key to these initiatives is providing employees with interesting, meaningful, and intrinsically motivating work while allowing them to achieve a sense of balance between work and their personal lives.

Hydro has a holistic approach to job design and emphasizes the significance of the work employees perform for the company as a whole as well as for society in general. Employees are encouraged to develop and utilize multiple skills and bring their diverse talents to bear upon the tasks they perform. Managers acknowledge that each employee can contribute to the organization in multiple ways and strive to enable diverse and meaningful contributions from employees.

Employees at Hydro are also given considerable amounts of autonomy and feel personally responsible for the quality of their work. Whereas in the United States, employees are putting in ever longer hours, in Norway most people end the workday around 4:00 or 4:30 P.M., and women receive between seven and eight months of paid maternity leave (men can receive up to four weeks of paid paternity leave). Balance between work and personal life is a strong societal value in Norway and at Hydro.[7] Thus, not only are employees granted autonomy when it comes to the tasks they perform but also when and where they perform them.

Morten Lingelem owns a farm an hour and a half away from his job at Hydro in Oslo. Although he has demanding responsibilities as a manager and an engineer, he is still able to be back at his farm with his family by 6:00 P.M.; the commuter train he rides has an "office car" where he can work and use his laptop computer. Atle Taerum also lives on a farm an hour and a half away from his job; he comes to the office three days a week and stays home with his young daughter the remaining two days. When Unni Foss father was dying, she worked full-time from her parents' house so she could be there for both of them and help them out. Managers at Hydro gave Foss the autonomy to decide where she worked. They knew she was a responsible person and would ensure her work was coordinated with others. Allowing employees to have balance in their lives, according to Hydro, helps them perform better and contributes to their job satisfaction and organizational commitment.

Hydro also utilizes the latest developments in information technology to help employees do their jobs better, work from home, and still stay connected with their office colleagues. For example, Unni Foss works in the media group at Hydro, which produces internal communications documents and design work for other units in the company. Each of the 80 employees in her group has an office setup at home, including furniture and computer equipment provided by Hydro. From their home offices, these employees are able to manipulate data and graphics as easily as they can at the office.

Key to Hydro's approach is flexibility (known as the Hydroflex program)—flexibility in when and where one works, flexibility in the use of one's skills, and flexibility in the kinds of contributions one makes on the job. Even production workers are given autonomy in terms of how they perform their jobs. Some production workers have recently been reorganized into work teams to give them more responsibility and broaden their skills, which should contribute to their intrinsic motivation. As Hans Jørn Rønningen, vice president in human resources, puts it, "How do we keep the best people? We need to offer new challenges. We need to give people flexibility and options."[8]

Changes in the design of jobs and work processes, such as those being made at Hydro, are dramatically altering the nature of work. Employees are being required to develop and use more skills than ever before. They are also experiencing more autonomy because they are responsible for managing many aspects of the work process including, in the case of Hydro, when and where they work.

In Chapter 6, we examine the nature of work motivation and four approaches to understanding motivation in organizations. Building from this foundation, in this chapter we focus on how an organization can create a motivating work setting by the way it designs its jobs and the objectives and goals it sets for its employees.[9] Job design can have a profound effect on employee motivation. The specific goals employees strive for and the more general corporate objectives (such as Hydro's commitment to corporate sustainability) that an organization pursues over time are important sources of motivation for employees. In terms of the motivation equation, introduced in Chapter 6 (see Figure 6.2) and restated in Figure 7.1, job design and goal setting are key factors that motivate employees to contribute inputs to the organization.

Job Design: Early Approaches

Job design is the process of linking specific tasks to specific jobs and deciding what techniques, equipment, and procedures should be used to perform those tasks. The tasks that make up a secretary's job, for example, include answering the telephone, filing, typing letters and reports, and scheduling meetings and appointments. The techniques, equipment, and procedures the secretary uses to accomplish these tasks may include using a personal computer and one or more word-processing software packages to type documents and prepare graphs, using an answering machine to take calls, and keeping a weekly appointment book to schedule and keep track of meetings.

In general, managers try to design jobs to motivate employees to perform well, enjoy their work, and receive the outcomes they deserve. Job design also influences the motivation of employees and their input levels (see Figure 7.1). When employees are motivated to contribute inputs at a high level (to work harder, more efficiently, and more creatively) and perform their jobs more effectively, organizational effectiveness increases.

Job design The process of linking specific tasks to specific jobs and deciding what techniques, equipment, and procedures should be used to perform those tasks.

FIGURE 7.1
Motivation Tools

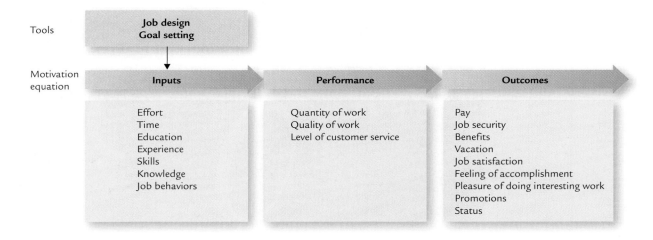

Tools	**Job design** **Goal setting**		
Motivation equation	**Inputs**	**Performance**	**Outcomes**
	Effort Time Education Experience Skills Knowledge Job behaviors	Quantity of work Quality of work Level of customer service	Pay Job security Benefits Vacation Job satisfaction Feeling of accomplishment Pleasure of doing interesting work Promotions Status

In the next sections, we examine scientific management, job enlargement, and job enrichment—three early approaches to job design. Each has implications not only for how *new* jobs should be designed but also for how *existing* jobs can be redesigned to improve motivation and performance. Some of the approaches can be used to design a job so the employee doing it gets more satisfaction from it (discussed in Chapter 3) along with the outcomes (pay, promotion, or other rewards) he or she desires.

SCIENTIFIC MANAGEMENT

Scientific management A set of principles and practices designed to increase the performance of individual employees by stressing job simplification and specialization.

Job simplification The breaking up of the work that needs to be performed in an organization into the smallest identifiable tasks.

Job specialization The assignment of employees to perform small, simple tasks.

In 1911, Frederick W. Taylor published one of the earliest approaches to job design, *The Principles of Scientific Management*.[10] Taylor was concerned that employees were slacking off and not performing as highly on the job as they should be. **Scientific management**, a set of principles and practices stressing job simplification and specialization, was developed by Taylor to increase the performance of individual employees. Taylor started with this premise: There is one best way to perform any job, and management's responsibility is to determine what that way is. He believed that following the principles of job simplification and specialization would help managers make this determination. **Job simplification** involves breaking up the work that needs to be done into the smallest identifiable tasks. Jobs are then designed around these narrow tasks. **Job specialization** results when employees are assigned to perform small, simple tasks and focus exclusively on them.

Many fast-food restaurants employ the principles of job simplification and specialization. The way food preparers at Subway (the sandwich shop chain) do their jobs illustrates the principles of simplification and specialization. One person puts the meat on a sandwich, another person puts on the trimmings (like lettuce, tomatoes, and condiments), and another person collects the money from customers. Because of simplification and specialization, Subway restaurants can make a large number of "custom" sandwiches in a short period of time. The effectiveness of this job design is easily illustrated by watching what happens when one or more employees are unavailable (because, for example, they are on the telephone or are replenishing supplies). When this occurs, the other Subway employees must do their own work plus the work of the tem-

Frederick W. Taylor, a pioneer in job design, envisioned the specialization of Henry Ford's first automobile assembly line. Taylor's time and motion studies led to dramatic productivity improvements, but they were criticized for dehumanizing employeess.

porarily absent employee(s). As a result, it generally takes much longer to serve a customer. A cashier who fills in for the "trimmings" employee, for example, must wash his or her hands after handling a customer's money before trimming another sandwich (in keeping with Subway's cleanliness policy).

Advocates of scientific management conduct time and motion studies to determine the one best way to perform each narrow task. **Time and motion studies** reveal exactly how long it takes to perform a task and the best way to perform it—for example, what body movements are most efficient for performing the task. Employees are then instructed in precisely how to perform their tasks.

Employees at Subway, for example, learn exactly how to slice the roll for a sandwich, how to place the meat on a sandwich, and how to add the trimmings. Because these tasks are simple, employees quickly learn to perform them correctly. Because managers know (from time and motion studies) exactly how long it should take to perform each task, they know how much output, on average, they can expect from an employee. Subway knows, for example, how many sandwiches can be made and how many customers can be served in each shop per hour. By clearly specifying exactly what an employee should do on the job, exactly how a task should be done, and exactly how long the task should take, scientific management ensures that employee inputs result in acceptable performance levels.

In the scientific management approach to job design, pay is the principal outcome used to motivate employees to contribute their inputs. Pay is often linked closely to performance by a piece-rate pay system in which employees are paid a set amount of money for performing a certain number of tasks. For example, an employee might be paid $5 for every eight sound mufflers that he or she attaches to computer printers.

Scientific management has been instrumental in helping organizations improve employee effectiveness and productivity. The early assembly lines that made the mass production of affordable automobiles possible reflected scientific management principles. These principles still guide some mass-production assembly lines in use today. Eventually, however, some disadvantages of designing jobs according to the principles of scientific management became apparent. Many problems stemmed from the fact that employees are intelligent human beings who have the capacity to be intrinsically as well as extrinsically motivated and who also like to have control over their work.

Recall from Chapter 6 that *extrinsically* motivated behavior is behavior performed to acquire rewards (such as pay) or to avoid punishment, and *intrinsically* motivated behavior is behavior performed for its own sake. Employees who are intrinsically motivated enjoy performing their jobs; the motivation comes from the work itself. However, scientific management focuses exclusively on extrinsic motivation and ignores the important role of intrinsic motivation. This narrow focus results in several disadvantages for employees and the organizations trying to motivate them.

First, employees may feel that they have lost control over their work behaviors. With its careful, exact specification of how a simple, repetitive, specialized task should be performed, and how long it should take, scientific management leaves no room for employees to feel that they have control over their actions. Second, employees tend to feel as if they are part of a machine and are being treated as such. Because they view their work as depersonalized, meaningless, and monotonous, their job satisfaction may decline. This decline, in turn, can lead to lower work life quality and potential increases in absenteeism and turnover. Finally, employees have no opportunity to develop and acquire new skills with job simplification and specification. These three drawbacks are part of the reason why Subway and other fast-food restaurants experience high turnover levels: Employees leave to find more interesting and demanding work.

Time and motion studies Studies that reveal exactly how long it takes to perform a task and the best way to perform it.

JOB ENLARGEMENT AND JOB ENRICHMENT

Job enlargement Increasing the number of tasks an employee performs but keeping all of the tasks at the same level of difficulty and responsibility; also called horizontal job loading.

The first widespread attempt to counteract some of the disadvantages related to the scientific management approach was job enlargement, a movement that started in the late 1940s and continued through the 1950s.[11] **Job enlargement** involves increasing the number of tasks an employee performs but keeping all of the tasks at the same level of difficulty and responsibility. Job enlargement is often referred to as *horizontal job loading* because the content of a job is expanded, but the difficulty remains constant. For example, one might enlarge the job of assembly-line workers who attach the paper tray to a computer printer by also requiring them to attach the sound muffler and the toner cartridge. The employees now do more tasks of equal difficulty with no increase in the level of responsibility.

Proponents of job enlargement thought that increasing the number of tasks performed on a job might increase intrinsic motivation. The job enlargement approach to job design was put into effect at a number of companies including IBM, Maytag, and AT&T.[12] Some companies reported increased employee productivity and satisfaction from job enlargement, but at other companies the effects were not clear-cut. This mixed success is not surprising because jobs that are "enlarged" may still be simple and limited with regard to how much control and variety employees have. Even though they no longer do one simple task, employees performing several simple tasks (each of which may quickly lose its appeal) may still be bored.

Job enrichment Increasing an employee's responsibility and control over his or her work; also called vertical job loading.

In response to the limited effects of job enlargement on work motivation, job enrichment emerged in the 1960s. **Job enrichment** involves designing jobs to provide opportunities for employee growth by giving employees more responsibility and control over their work. Job enrichment is often referred to as *vertical job loading* because employees are given some of the responsibilities that used to belong to their supervisors, such as planning for how to go about completing a project or checking the quality of one's work. Herzberg's motivator-hygiene theory (discussed in Chapter 3) was a driving force in the movement to enrich jobs. Recall that Herzberg's theory suggested that employees' motivator needs are satisfied by things such as having autonomy on the job and being responsible for one's work, and that employees are satisfied with their jobs only when these needs are met.

Managers can enrich jobs in a variety of ways. The following are some of the most common:[13]

- ◆ *Allow employees to plan their own work schedules.* For example, when possible, allow a secretary to determine when he or she does various tasks, such as typing, filing, and setting up meetings, and how much time to allow for each activity.

- ◆ *Allow employees to decide how the work should be performed.* If a manager wants a secretary to prepare a new company brochure or filing system, the manager may let the secretary decide how to design the brochure or filing system.

- ◆ *Allow employees to check their own work.* Instead of insisting that the secretary give a draft of the brochure to the manager to check for errors, the manager holds the secretary responsible for producing a top-quality, error-free brochure.

- ◆ *Allow employees to learn new skills.* A secretary may be given the opportunity to learn bookkeeping and some basic accounting procedures.

Like job enlargement, job enrichment is aimed at increasing intrinsic motivation so that employees enjoy their jobs more. When employees are given more responsibility, they are more likely to feel competent and like they have control over their own work behaviors. Job enrichment can also lead to efficiency gains, as indicated in the accompanying OB Today.

ob today

Cutting Costs and Increasing Efficiency at General Mills

When Randy G. Darcy, chief technical officer of General Mills, set out to dramatically reduce costs and improve efficiency at plants making Cheerios cereal, Betty Crocker cake mixes, and Hamburger Helper, he realized that much of his cost-cutting efforts would revolve around redesigning jobs.[14] As part of this effort, he enriched employees' jobs by making them responsible for thinking of ways to do their jobs more efficiently.

Darcy and other General Mills employees subsequently studied all kinds of different work groups ranging from U.S. SWAT teams and Air Force mechanics to mountain-climbing teams. By studying all kinds of high-performing, efficient groups and organizations, they hope to find new ways to lower costs at General Mills.[15] Being challenged to think about new and better ways to do their jobs has, in itself, been job enriching.

For example, by studying how racing car pit crews at NASCAR change tires in split seconds, General Mills employees figured out how to cut the amount of time it takes factories making Betty Crocker mixes to switch from one kind of mix to another. The employees managed to cut the process down from 4.5 hours to just 12 minutes, resulting in real cost savings and increases in efficiency. Essentially, they realized that by replacing traditional bolts with bolts that only need be turned one quarter and by equipping employees with tool boxes containing all the equipment they need to change over a production line, what was once a slow and tedious process could be accomplished in less than 15 minutes. Efficiency gains like these are essential if Darcy is to reach his goal of cutting costs by $1 billion at General Mills over the next 10 years.[16]

Studies of NASCAR teams helped food manufacturer General Mills speed up food manufacturing. General Mills employees used the NASCAR studies to figure out how to quickly change products on their assembly lines.

Not all employees, however, want the additional responsibility that job enrichment brings, and it can sometimes have disadvantages for the organization as a whole. Enriching some jobs can be expensive for an organization and may be impossible to do. Enriching other jobs may result in less efficiency. One of the reasons why Subway shops are able to make large numbers of customized sandwiches is because of job simplification and specialization. Enriching the jobs of Subway employees might increase the time it takes to serve customers, an outcome that would reduce organizational effectiveness.

Research evidence on the effects of job enrichment has been mixed. Although employees seem to be more satisfied with enriched jobs, it is not clear whether employees with enriched jobs are actually more motivated and perform at a higher level.

Job Design: The Job Characteristics Model

The job enlargement and job enrichment movements came about in part because of some of the negative effects observed when jobs were designed according to the principles of scientific management. Both movements attempted to increase employees' levels of intrinsic motivation to perform their jobs, in the hope that employees who found their jobs more interesting and meaningful would be more motivated to perform at higher levels and be more satisfied. Satisfied employees would mean less turnover and absenteeism. The **job characteristics model** proposed by Richard Hackman and Greg Oldham in the 1970s built on these early approaches but went further.[17] Based on the work of A. N. Turner and P. R. Lawrence, Hackman and Oldham attempted to identify exactly which job characteristics contribute to intrinsically motivating work and what the consequences of these characteristics are.[18]

The job characteristics model is one of the most popular approaches to job design. Hackman and Oldham sought to provide a detailed and accurate account of the effects of job design on motivation, performance, job satisfaction, and other important aspects of organizational behavior. Like the job enlargement and enrichment approaches, the job characteristics model focuses on what makes jobs intrinsically motivating. When employees are intrinsically motivated, Hackman and Oldham reasoned, good performance makes them feel good. This feeling motivates them to continue to perform at a high level, so good performance becomes self-reinforcing.[19]

CORE JOB DIMENSIONS

According to the job characteristics model, any job has five core dimensions that affect intrinsic motivation: skill variety, task identity, task significance, autonomy, and feedback. The higher a job scores on each dimension, the higher the level of intrinsic motivation.

1. **Skill variety** is the extent to which a job requires an employee to use a number of different skills, abilities, or talents. Employees are more intrinsically motivated by jobs that are high on skill variety.

   High variety: In the opening case, we described how employees at Hydro are required to use diverse skills to perform their jobs. Today, even factory jobs, which traditionally have had relatively low levels of variety, are increasing in skill variety due to the prevalence of sophisticated and computer-based technology. Factory employees now use a variety of skills, including computer skills, mathematics, statistical control, and quality control in addition to skills related to whatever they are producing such as metal products.

   Low variety: The jobs of employees in a Subway restaurant have a low level of skill variety. All the employees need to know is how to slice rolls and put meat and trimmings on them.

2. **Task identity** is the extent to which a job involves performing a whole piece of work from its beginning to its end. The higher the level of task identity, the more intrinsically motivated an employee is likely to be.

Job characteristics model An approach to job design that aims to identify characteristics that make jobs intrinsically motivating and the consequences of those characteristics.

Skill variety The extent to which a job requires an employee to use different skills, abilities, or talents.

Task identity The extent to which a job involves performing a whole piece of work from its beginning to its end.

High identity: A carpenter who makes custom wood cabinets and furniture has high task identity. The carpenter designs and makes cabinets and furniture from start to finish.

Low identity: For a factory worker assembling computer printers, task identity is low if the worker only attaches the paper tray.

3. **Task significance** is the extent to which a job has an impact on the lives or work of other people in or out of the organization. Employees are more likely to enjoy performing their jobs when they think their jobs are important in the wider scheme of things. Recall from the opening case how Hydro adopts a holistic approach to job design so employees see how their work benefits not only the organization but also society as a whole.

High significance: Medical researchers and doctors experience high levels of task significance because their work promotes the health and well-being of people.

Low significance: The job of an employee who dries cars off after the cars go through a car wash has low task significance because the employee doesn't think it has much impact on other people.

4. **Autonomy** is the degree to which a job allows an employee the freedom and independence to schedule work and decide how to carry it out. High autonomy generally contributes to high levels of intrinsic motivation.

High autonomy: From the opening case, it is clear that employees at Hydro have high autonomy concerning how, when, and where they perform their jobs.

Low autonomy: An employee at the Internal Revenue Service who opens tax returns and sorts them into different categories has a low level of autonomy because she or he must work at a steady, predetermined pace and follow strict guidelines for sorting the returns.

5. **Feedback** is the extent to which performing a job provides an employee with clear information about his or her effectiveness. Receiving feedback has a positive impact on intrinsic motivation.

High feedback: Computer-based technology in factories often gives factory workers immediate feedback on how well they are doing, and this information contributes to their intrinsic motivation.

Low feedback: An employee who reshelves books in the New York City Public Library rarely receives feedback as he or she performs the job and is often unaware of when he or she makes a mistake or does a particularly good job.

According to the job characteristics model, when managers consider the five core dimensions of a job, it is important for them to realize that *employees'* perceptions of the core dimensions (not the actual reality or a manager's perceptions) are the key determinants of intrinsic motivation. As we discussed in Chapter 4, two people can watch the same movie or take part in the same group meeting and have very different perceptions of what they have experienced. One person might hate a movie that another person loved, and one group member might perceive that a group meeting was a noisy, incomprehensible free-for-all while another perceives that a reasonable and lively discussion took place. In a like manner, two employees may have the same job yet perceive it differently. For example, one employee might perceive the job to be high on task significance while another perceives it to be low on this dimension.

THE MOTIVATING POTENTIAL SCORE

To measure employees' perceptions of their jobs on each of the core dimensions, Hackman and Oldham developed the *Job Diagnostic Survey*. The scales used to measure the five dimensions are shown in Figure 7.2. After an employee completes each of these scales for his or

Task significance The extent to which a job has an impact on the lives or work of other people in or out of the organization.

Autonomy The degree to which a job allows an employee the freedom and independence to schedule work and decide how to carry it out.

Feedback The extent to which performing a job provides an employee with clear information about his or her effectiveness.

Employees of the Federal Emergency Management Association (FEMA) help U.S. citizens recover from disasters. FEMA field workers, dispatched individually across the country to assist people, enjoy a great deal of autonomy, task significance, and skill variety on the job.

FIGURE 7.2

Measures of the Five Core Characteristics from Hackman and Oldham's *Job Diagnostic Survey*

Source: J. R. Hackman and G. R. Oldham, *Work Redesign*, copyright 1980 Addison-Wesley Publishing Co., Inc., Reading, Mass. Reprinted with permission.

Skill variety

1. How much *variety* is there in your job? That is, to what extent does the job require you to do many different things at work, using a variety of your skills and talents?

1	2	3	4	5	6	7
Very little; the job requires me to do the same routine things over and over again.			Moderate variety		Very much; the job requires me to do many different things, using a number of different skills and talents.	

2. The job requires me to use a number of complex or high-level skills.

How accurate is the statement in describing your job?

1	2	3	4	5	6	7
Very inaccurate	Mostly inaccurate	Slightly inaccurate	Uncertain	Slightly accurate	Mostly accurate	Very accurate

3. The job is quite simple and repetitive.*

How accurate is the statement in describing your job?

1	2	3	4	5	6	7
Very inaccurate	Mostly inaccurate	Slightly inaccurate	Uncertain	Slightly accurate	Mostly accurate	Very accurate

Task identity

1. To what extent does your job involve doing a *"whole" and identifiable piece of work*? That is, is the job a complete piece of work that has an obvious beginning and end? Or is it only a small *part* of the overall piece of work, which is finished by other people or by automatic machines?

1	2	3	4	5	6	7
My job is only a tiny part of the overall piece of work: the results of my activities cannot be seen in the final product or service.		My job is a moderate-sized "chunk" of the overall piece of work; my own contribution can be seen in the final outcome.			My job involves doing the whole piece of work, from start to finish; the results of my activities are easily seen in the final product or service.	

2. The job provides me the chance to completely finish the pieces of work I begin.

How accurate is the statement in describing your job?

1	2	3	4	5	6	7
Very inaccurate	Mostly inaccurate	Slightly inaccurate	Uncertain	Slightly accurate	Mostly accurate	Very accurate

3. The job is arranged so that I do *not* have the chance to do an entire piece of work from beginning to end.*

How accurate is the statement in describing your job?

1	2	3	4	5	6	7
Very inaccurate	Mostly inaccurate	Slightly inaccurate	Uncertain	Slightly accurate	Mostly accurate	Very accurate

Task significance

1. In general, how significant or important is your job? That is, are the results of your work likely to significantly affect the lives or well-being of other people?

1	2	3	4	5	6	7
Not very significant; the outcomes of my work are *not* likely to have important effects on other people.			Moderately significant		Highly significant; the outcomes of my work can affect other people in very important ways.	

2. This job is one where a lot of people can be affected by how well the work gets done.

How accurate is the statement in describing your job?

1	2	3	4	5	6	7
Very inaccurate	Mostly inaccurate	Slightly inaccurate	Uncertain	Slightly accurate	Mostly accurate	Very accurate

3. The job itself is *not* very significant or important in the broader scheme of things.[*]

How accurate is the statement in describing your job?

1	2	3	4	5	6	7
Very inaccurate	Mostly inaccurate	Slightly inaccurate	Uncertain	Slightly accurate	Mostly accurate	Very accurate

Autonomy

1. How much *autonomy* is there in your job? That is, to what extent does your job permit you to decide *on your own* how to go about doing your work?

1	2	3	4	5	6	7
Very little; the job gives me almost no personal "say" about how and when the work is done.		Moderate autonomy; many things are standardized and not under my control, but I can make some decisions about the work.			Very much; the job gives me almost complete responsability for deciding how and when the work is done.	

2. The job gives me considerable opportunity for independence and freedom in how I do the work.

How accurate is the statement in describing your job?

1	2	3	4	5	6	7
Very inaccurate	Mostly inaccurate	Slightly inaccurate	Uncertain	Slightly accurate	Mostly accurate	Very accurate

3. The job denies me any chance to use my personal initiative or judgment in carrying out the work.[*]

How accurate is the statement in describing your job?

1	2	3	4	5	6	7
Very inaccurate	Mostly inaccurate	Slightly inaccurate	Uncertain	Slightly accurate	Mostly accurate	Very accurate

Feedback

1. To what extent does *doing the job itself* provide you with information about your work performance? That is, does the actual *work itself* provide clues about how well you are doing—aside from any "feedback" coworkers or supervisors may provide?

1	2	3	4	5	6	7
Very little; the job itself is set up so I could work forever without finding out how well I am doing.		Moderately; sometimes doing the job provides "feedback" to me; sometimes it does not.			Very much; the job is set up so that I get almost constant "feedback" as I work about how well I am doing.	

2. Just doing the work required by the job provides many chances for me to figure out how well I am doing.

How accurate is the statement in describing your job?

1	2	3	4	5	6	7
Very inaccurate	Mostly inaccurate	Slightly inaccurate	Uncertain	Slightly accurate	Mostly accurate	Very accurate

3. The job itself provides very few clues about whether or not I am performing well.[*]

How accurate is the statement in describing your job?

1	2	3	4	5	6	7
Very inaccurate	Mostly inaccurate	Slightly inaccurate	Uncertain	Slightly accurate	Mostly accurate	Very accurate

Scoring: Responses to the three items for each core characteristic are averaged to yield an overall score for that characteristic. Items marked with a "*" should be scored as follows: 1 = 7; 2 = 6; 3 = 5; 5 = 3; 6 = 2; 7 = 1

$$\text{Motivating potential score} = \left(\frac{\text{Skill variety} + \text{Task identity} + \text{Task significance}}{3} \right) \times \text{Autonomy} \times \text{Feedback}$$

her job, it is possible to compute the job's motivating potential score. The **motivating potential score (MPS)** is a measure of the overall potential of a job to foster intrinsic motivation. MPS is equal to the average of the first three core characteristics (skill variety, task identity, and task significance) multiplied by autonomy and feedback, as indicated in Figure 7.2. Each of the three core dimensions is assigned a score ranging from a low of 1 to a high of 7. The lowest MPS possible for a job is 1 ($1 \times 1 \times 1$) and the highest MPS possible

Motivating potential score (MPS) A measure of the overall potential of a job to foster intrinsic motivation.

Before job redesign
Profile of a gardener
MPS + [(3.5 + 1 + 4)/3] × 1.2 × 6 = 20.4

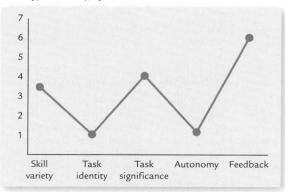

After job redesign
Profile of a gardener
MPS = [(3.5 + 5 + 4)/3] × 4 × 6 = 100

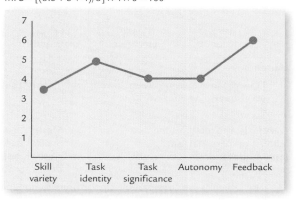

FIGURE 7.3

Sample *Job Diagnostic Survey* Profiles

is 343 (7 × 7 ×7). The lowest actual MPS score that Hackman and Oldham observed was 7 for a typist in an overflow typing pool; the typist waited at her typewriter all day for the occasional jobs she received when the regular pool got overloaded. The highest score was 300 for a management consultant. Hackman and Oldham suggest that an average motivating potential score for jobs in U.S. corporations is around 128.[20]

The *Job Diagnostic Survey* can be used to identify the core dimensions that are most in need of redesign in order to increase a job's motivating potential score and, thus, an employee's intrinsic motivation. Figure 7.3 shows a survey profile for a gardener who works for a landscape company. The gardener is a member of a three-person crew that provides landscape services to residential and commercial customers. The crew is headed by a landscape supervisor who assigns individual tasks (such as cutting grass, preparing flower beds, or planting trees) to crew members at each job site. As indicated in Figure 7.3, the gardener's levels of task identity and autonomy are especially low and should be the main focus of any redesign efforts. Currently, the supervisor assigns very specific and unrelated tasks to each crew member: At a particular site, the gardener might plant some flowers, cut some borders, and plant a tree. The supervisor also tells the crew members exactly how to do each task: Put the daisies here and the marigolds around the border.

To increase task identity and autonomy, the supervisor could change the way he assigns tasks to crew members: The supervisor could make each crew member responsible for a major aspect of a particular landscaping job and, after providing some basic guidelines, give the crew member the autonomy to decide how to accomplish this aspect of the job. On one job, for example, the gardener might be responsible for preparing and arranging all of the flower beds (resulting in high task identity). After the supervisor tells the gardener about the customer's likes and dislikes, the gardener would be free to design the beds as he sees fit and work on them in the order he wants (resulting in high autonomy). As a result of these changes, the MPS of the gardener's job would rise from 20.4 to 100 (see Figure 7.3).

Jobs can be redesigned in a variety of ways to increase levels of the five core dimensions and the MPS. Common ways to redesign jobs are described in Table 7.1.

CRITICAL PSYCHOLOGICAL STATES

Hackman and Oldham proposed that the five core job dimensions contribute to three critical psychological states that determine how employees react to the design of their jobs: experienced meaningfulness of the work, experienced responsibility for work outcomes, and knowledge of results.

First, employees who perceive that their jobs are high in skill variety, task identity, and task significance attain the psychological state of experienced meaningfulness of the work. **Experienced meaningfulness of the work** is the degree to which

Experienced meaningfulness of the work The degree to which employees feel their jobs are important, worthwhile, and meaningful.

TABLE 7.1

Ways to Redesign Jobs to Increase MPS

Change Made	Core Job Dimensions Increased	Example
Combine tasks so that an employee is responsible for doing a piece of work from start to finish.	Skill variety Task identity Task significance	A production worker is responsible for assembling a whole bicycle, not just attaching the handlebars.
Group tasks into natural work units so that employees are responsible for performing an entire set of important organizational activities rather than just part of them.	Task identity Task significance	A computer programmer handles all programming requests from one division instead of one type of request from several different divisions.
Allow employees to interact with customers or clients, and make employees responsible for managing these relationships and satisfying customers.	Skill variety Autonomy Feedback	A truck driver who delivers photocopiers not only sets them up but also trains customers in how to use them, handles customer billing, and responds to customer complaints.
Vertically load jobs so that employees have more control over their work activities and higher levels of responsibility.	Autonomy	A corporate marketing analyst not only prepares marketing plans and reports but also decides when to update and revise them, checks them for errors, and presents them to upper management.
Open feedback channels so that employees know how they are performing their jobs.	Feedback	In addition to knowing how many claims he handles per month, an insurance adjustor receives his clients' responses to follow-up questionnaires that his company uses to measure client satisfaction.

Source: Based on J. R. Hackman, "Work Redesign," in J. R. Hackman and J. L. Suttle, eds., *Improving Life at Work* (Santa Monica, CA: Goodyear, 1976).

employees feel their jobs are important, worthwhile, and meaningful as do many employees at Hydro in the opening case. The second critical psychological state, **experienced responsibility for work outcomes**, is the extent to which employees feel they are personally responsible or accountable for their job performance. This psychological state stems from the core dimension of autonomy. The third critical psychological state, **knowledge of results**, is the degree to which employees know how well they perform their jobs on a continuous basis; it stems from the core dimension of feedback. Figure 7.4 summarizes the relationships among the five core dimensions, the three critical psychological states, and work and personal outcomes (discussed next).

Experienced responsibility for work outcomes The extent to which employees feel personally responsible or accountable for their job performance.

Knowledge of results The degree to which employees know how well they perform their jobs on a continuous basis.

WORK AND PERSONAL OUTCOMES

Hackman and Oldham further proposed that the critical psychological states result in four key outcomes for employees and their organizations: high intrinsic motivation, high job performance, high job satisfaction, and low absenteeism and turnover (see Figure 7.4).

1. *High intrinsic motivation.* One of the major outcomes of job design is intrinsic motivation. When jobs are high on the five core dimensions, employees experience the three critical psychological states and are intrinsically motivated. When intrinsic motivation is high, employees enjoy performing a job for its own sake. Good

FIGURE 7.4

**The Job
Characteristics Model**

Source: Adapted from J. R.
Hackman and G. R. Oldham,
Work Redesign, copyright
1980 Addison-Wesley
Publishing Co., Inc.,
Reading, MA.

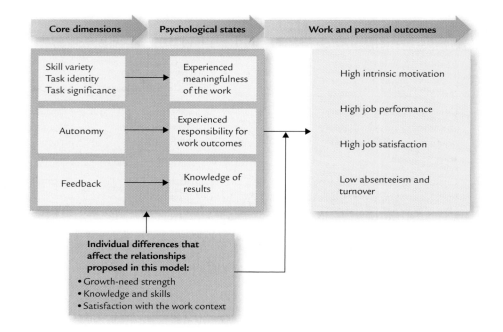

performance makes employees feel good, and this positive feeling further motivates them to continue to perform at a high level. Poor performance makes employees feel bad, but this feeling may motivate them to try to perform at a high level. In other words, because good performance is self-reinforcing (performance is its own reward), the motivation to perform well comes from inside the employee rather than from an external source like praise from a supervisor or the promise of pay.

2. *High job performance.* Jobs high in the five core dimensions, which lead to high levels of the three critical psychological states, motivate employees to perform at a high level.

3. *High job satisfaction.* Hackman and Oldham reasoned that employees are likely to be more satisfied with their jobs when the critical psychological states are high because they will have more opportunities for personal growth and development on the job.

4. *Low absenteeism and turnover.* When employees enjoy performing their jobs, Hackman and Oldham reasoned, they will be less likely to be absent or quit. (Also, recall from Chapter 3 that satisfied employees are less likely to be absent or quit.)

THE ROLE OF INDIVIDUAL DIFFERENCES IN EMPLOYEES' RESPONSES TO JOB DESIGN

The job characteristics model acknowledges the role that individual differences play in determining how employees respond to the design of their jobs. To see how individual differences interact with job design, let's look at the case of three sales managers, each of whom manages a different department in a department store. Mary Catalano, the manager of women's shoes, is a competent manager, eager to learn more about different aspects of retailing, and serious about her career. Ron Richards, the manager of men's shoes, is still mastering the responsibilities of his first supervisory position and is having a rough time. Roberta Doran, who has an M.B.A. in marketing, manages the china department. Doran is a competent manager but always complains about how low retailing salaries are compared to salaries she could be making in other organizations.

To increase the motivating potential score of each manager's job, the department store has recently redesigned each job. In the past, a manager's main responsibility was to supervise the sales teams in his or her respective departments. After the redesign, managers also became responsible for purchasing merchandise (an increase in skill variety and task significance), hiring and firing salespeople (also an increase in skill variety and task significance), and the profitability of their respective departments (an increase in task identity, autonomy, and feedback).

As you might expect, Catalano, Richards, and Doran have responded in different ways to their redesigned jobs. The job characteristics model helps explain why employees may respond somewhat differently to an increase in some of the core characteristics of their jobs. It identifies three types of individual differences that affect the relationships between the core dimensions and the psychological states and the relationships between the psychological states and the outcomes (see Figure 7.4). The nature of those relationships depends on the growth-need strength, knowledge and skills, and satisfaction with the work context of the individual employee.

1. *Growth-need strength* is the extent to which an individual wants his or her work to contribute to personal growth, learning, and development. When an individual wants his or her job to fuel personal growth, both relationships in the model (core dimensions–psychological states and psychological states–outcomes) are stronger. Such individuals are expected to be especially responsive both to increased levels in the core dimensions and to the critical psychological states. In our example, Mary Catalano is likely to have the most favorable response to the job redesign because she is most eager to learn what she can about her chosen career.

2. *Knowledge and skills* at an appropriate level enable employees to perform their jobs effectively. When employees do not have the necessary knowledge and skills, the relationships depicted in Figure 7.4 may be weak, nonexistent, or even negative. In our example, Ron Richards was barely keeping his head above water before the increases in the core dimensions of his job. After the job is redesigned, he may become frustrated because his lack of knowledge and skills prevent him from performing well. As a result, his intrinsic motivation and job satisfaction will probably suffer, and he will be unable to perform the more complicated job.

3. *Satisfaction with the work context* describes how satisfied employees are with extrinsic outcomes (such as pay, benefits, job security, and good relationships with co-workers) they receive from their jobs. Hackman and Oldham reasoned that when employees are dissatisfied with their work context, they spend much of their energy trying to deal with their dissatisfaction with the context and are not able to appreciate and respond to the potential for intrinsic motivation on their jobs.[21] When satisfaction with the work context is high, the relationships depicted in Figure 7.4 are expected to be strong; when context satisfaction is low, they are expected to be weak. In our example, Roberta Doran's dissatisfaction with her pay is intensified by the job redesign because she must now take on additional responsibilities but will receive no extra pay. (In terms of the equity theory that we discussed in Chapter 6, Doran sees her outcome/input ratio as being more unfavorable than it was before the job redesign because her inputs are going up but she is not receiving any additional outcomes.) Instead of increasing intrinsic motivation and job satisfaction, the changes in Doran's job make her even more dissatisfied with her pay, and she spends much of her time complaining, thinking about how to improve matters, and looking for another job.

Although the job characteristics model focuses on the relationships between the core job dimensions and psychological states and, in turn, psychological states and outcomes, cultural differences may also have an impact on these relationships. American employees are used to a certain amount of autonomy at work, but employees in other countries like China have traditionally had very little freedom and independence on the job.

Chinese employees, for example, may be motivated by core job dimensions such as autonomy, but it might take a little time and effort to convince them that they can really make decisions on their own. This proved to be the case at Minneapolis-based H. B. Fuller Company, which owns and runs a joint venture factory in China that makes adhesives used in products ranging from cardboard boxes to packages of cigarettes. The Chinese employees were originally reluctant to make decisions on their own but now find autonomy to be a source of motivation.[22]

THE RESEARCH EVIDENCE

Many research studies have tested different components of the job characteristics model since Richard Hackman and Greg Oldham originally proposed it. A recent review of this literature conducted by Fried and Ferris identified almost 200 studies. Fried and Ferris's overall conclusion from their review is that there is modest support for the model.[23] Some of their specific findings are as follows:

1. It is not clear that exactly five dimensions (the five core job dimensions outlined by Hackman and Oldham) best describe the job design of all jobs.

2. Research shows that job dimensions have the most significant effects on intrinsic motivation and on job satisfaction; the effects on actual work behaviors (such as job performance, absenteeism, and turnover) are not as strong.

3. Simply adding the scores for the job characteristics might be a better way of calculating the motivating potential score than using the multiplicative formula proposed by Hackman and Oldham.

The results of this review of the job characteristics model as well as other reviews and studies[24] lead to these overall conclusions: Employees tend to prefer jobs that are high in the five core dimensions in the model, they tend to be more satisfied with these types of jobs, and they have higher levels of intrinsic motivation. Thus, job design can

you're the management expert

Redesigning Jobs

Marcia Long has recently been hired as the manager of a group of five employees who process mortgage applications for a bank in West Hempstead, New York. When Long was interviewing for the position, her boss told her there were certain morale problems in the group. This was confirmed during Long's first week on the job when her boss shared the results of an employee attitude survey with her. The employees in her group were very dissatisfied with the work they did—they found it monotonous and boring. They were actually satisfied with extrinsic factors such as pay, benefits, and their co-workers. But the nature of their actual jobs was a real problem. In Long's group there are basically three different kinds of jobs. Two employees focus on the beginning of the process of granting a mortgage; they interact with home buyers, provide them with applications, and make sure their applications are complete with all supporting documents attached. They also run credit and background checks. Two employees focus on the next stage of the process—getting surveys and appraisals conducted, interacting with builders in the case of new homes, and arranging for title searches and a title policy. The remaining employee focuses on arranging closings, making sure everything is complete and in good order beforehand, and interacting with customers once they have been approved for a mortgage. Much to Long's surprise, the employees were about equally dissatisfied with their jobs, regardless of which of the three positions they had. Because you are an expert in OB, Long has come to you for help. She wants to redesign her employees' jobs so that they are more motivated and satisfied, but she has no idea where to start and what to focus on. What should she do?

contribute to the quality of work life and may also have some indirect effects on absenteeism and turnover rates. In addition, when the intrinsic motivation of employees is high, they are internally motivated to perform well. As a result, managers do not need to supervise them as closely as they do when their intrinsic motivation is low. The need for less supervision may free up some management time for other activities. Nevertheless, it is not clear that job performance will actually be higher when core dimensions are high.

Job Design: The Social Information Processing Model

The job characteristics model is complemented by another approach to job design, the social information processing model developed in 1978 by Gerald Salancik and Jeffrey Pfeffer.[25] According to the **social information processing model**, factors other than the core dimensions specified by Hackman and Oldham influence how employees respond to the design of their jobs. Salancik and Pfeffer propose that how employees perceive and respond to the design of their jobs is influenced by *social information* (information from other people) and by employees' own past behaviors. The following example highlights the social information processing model.

Joseph Doherty and Robert Cantu have recently received their law degrees from Columbia University and accepted associate positions with the same prestigious Wall Street law firm. They work in different sections of the corporate law department and report to different partners in the firm, for whom they do a lot of research and grunt work. The design of their jobs and the extrinsic outcomes (pay and perks) that they receive are similar. About half of their work is interesting and challenging, and the other half is tedious. They are expected to put in between 60 and 70 hours each week and are well paid, receiving $100,000 a year.

Despite these and other similarities, Doherty's and Cantu's reactions to their jobs are different. Doherty still can't believe his luck at landing a job that is so interesting and challenging. He enjoys his work and thinks nothing of the long hours; his high salary is the icing on the cake. Cantu complains that he didn't spend four years in college and three years in law school (never mind the year spent studying to pass the bar exam) to spend half of his time at work running errands for the partners of a law firm. He resents the fact that he is not able to deal directly with corporate clients (this job is reserved for the partners) even though he is the one who does most of the work on their cases. In his view, his high salary barely makes up for the long working hours.

Doherty is both intrinsically motivated by and very satisfied with his job. The opposite is true for Cantu, whose motivation (both intrinsic and extrinsic) is low and dissatisfaction is high. Why do they have such different reactions to jobs that are similar on most dimensions?

THE ROLE OF THE SOCIAL ENVIRONMENT

Salancik and Pfeffer's social information processing model suggests several reasons why Doherty's and Cantu's reactions are so different. First, the model proposes that the social environment provides employees with information about which aspects of their job design and work outcomes they should pay attention to and which they should ignore. Here, *social environment* means the other individuals with whom employees come into contact at work. An employee's social environment, thus, includes his or her co-workers, supervisors, and other work group members. Second, the model suggests that the social environment provides employees with information about how they should evaluate their jobs and work outcomes.

Doherty and Cantu belong to two different work groups, each of which has three other associates in it. In Doherty's work group, there is one other new associate and two

Social information processing model An approach to job design based on the idea that information from other people and employees' own past behaviors influence employees' perceptions of and responses to the design of their jobs.

Contingent workers, like those hired by temporary employment agencies, are motivated by different factors than full-time employees with more job security.

Contingent workers
Employees whom organizations hire or contract with on a temporary basis to fill needs for labor that change over time.

experienced associates who have been with the firm for several years. Rumor has it that the experienced associates are soon to be promoted to the position of managing attorney. From day one, these two associates impressed on Doherty and the other newcomer to the group the valuable experience they would obtain if they did their jobs well. They acknowledged the dullness of the grunt work but made light of it and instead stressed the considerable autonomy the new associates had in conducting their research. These two associates are very satisfied with their jobs and are intrinsically motivated. Interestingly enough, the long hours expected of all the associates never became a topic of conversation in this group. Doherty's social environment emphasizes the importance of the valuable experience he is obtaining from his job, points out the considerable autonomy he has, and suggests that this job provides high levels of intrinsic motivation and satisfaction.

Cantu's work group is also composed of one other newcomer and two experienced associates who have been with the firm for several years. These two associates, however, do not expect to be promoted, and both are on the job market. They are bitter about their experiences in the law firm and warn Cantu and the other newcomer that they can look forward to being "the personal slaves" of the partners for the next several years. They also complain that most of the work they had to do when they first joined the firm didn't require someone with a law degree and that the long hours were simply inhumane. Given the type of social environment Cantu encountered, his dissatisfaction with his new job and his lack of intrinsic and extrinsic motivation are hardly surprising. If two seasoned veterans evaluate the job so negatively, why should he think any differently?

The different social environments that Doherty and Cantu encounter cause them to focus on different aspects and outcomes of their jobs and how they should evaluate these factors.

The increasing reliance of organizations on contingent employees has some interesting implications for social environments at work. **Contingent workers** are employees organizations hire or contract with on a temporary basis to fill needs for labor that change over time.[26] Contingent workers have little job security and loyalty toward their organizations because they know their employment is on a temporary, as-needed basis.[27] Contingent workers often face a different social environment on the job than do regular employees.

THE ROLE OF PAST BEHAVIORS

The social information processing model proposes another reason why Doherty and Cantu view their similar jobs so differently: Employees' past behaviors have implications for how they view their current jobs and work outcomes. Doherty made considerable sacrifices to get through law school. He worked at night as a waiter to supplement the $60,000 worth of student loans he took out to pay his tuition and living expenses over the three-year period. His hectic schedule made his social life practically nonexistent. Cantu, in contrast, did not have to take out any loans or work to pay for law school. His father, an attorney, always assumed that Cantu would follow in his footsteps. In fact, Cantu was not overjoyed by the prospect of going to law school but couldn't find a decent job with his B.A. in anthropology. His parents were pleased that he decided to attend the Columbia law school and thought nothing of paying the high tuition and living expenses involved.

Because Doherty freely chose to become a lawyer, made a lot of sacrifices to attend law school, and will be paying off his debts from law school for the next several years, his intrinsic motivation is high, and his attitude toward his job is extremely positive. Having such a good job justifies all the sacrifices he has made. Cantu, who didn't have many options after graduating from college, was pressured by his parents to become a lawyer and didn't have to sacrifice much at all to attend law school. In terms of his past behaviors, Cantu has much less to justify because he didn't have much choice, nor was he required to make many sacrifices.

The social information processing model, thus, identifies a second factor that affects employees' reactions to the design of their jobs: Employees' past behaviors have implications for their evaluations of their current jobs, their levels of intrinsic motivation, and their levels of job satisfaction, especially when these behaviors are freely chosen and involve certain personal sacrifices.

To sum up, the social information processing model points to the importance of the social environment and past behaviors for an understanding of how employees react to the design of their jobs.[28] It helps explain why two employees with the same job and outcomes may have very different levels of motivation and satisfaction. As you might expect, research has found that both the objective features of a job (its actual design in terms of the five core dimensions of the job characteristics model) and an employee's social environment and past behavior all interact to affect motivation levels and satisfaction.[29] Research has found that the social environment is an especially potent source of information when employees with limited information and experience are new to a job or to an organization. After employees have gained firsthand experience with their jobs, the social environment may play less of a decisive role in molding reactions, and the actual design of the job itself may become more important.

Job Design Models Summarized

Scientific management, job enlargement, job enrichment, the job characteristics model, and the social information processing model—each theory highlights different aspects of job design that are important to consider when it comes to understanding work motivation. The main features and motivational focus of each approach are recapped in Table 7.2.

Scientific management advocates job simplification and job specialization, and its key goal is maximizing performance. Scientific management implicitly assumes that extrinsic motivation is the primary determinant of performance and provides no opportunity for intrinsic motivation. Proponents believe employees can be motivated to contribute inputs to their jobs and organizations if pay is closely linked to performance by means of piece-rate pay systems. Jobs designed according to the principles of scientific management tend to be boring, monotonous, and dissatisfying.

Job enlargement and *job enrichment* focus on expanding the simple jobs created by scientific management (enlargement through horizontal loading; enrichment through vertical loading) to promote intrinsic motivation.

In response to some of the problems related to designing jobs according to the principles of scientific management, Hackman and Oldham proposed the *job characteristics model*. The job characteristics model outlines the job dimensions that lead to high levels of intrinsic motivation. When employees are intrinsically motivated, they contribute inputs to their jobs because they enjoy the work itself. According to this model, how jobs are designed along five core dimensions can affect intrinsic motivation, job performance, job satisfaction, and absenteeism and turnover rates.

The *social information processing model* makes the important point that how employees view their jobs and their levels of intrinsic and extrinsic motivation are affected not just by the objective nature of the job but also by the social environment at work and the employees' own past behaviors.

As we mentioned at the beginning of this chapter, the primary aim of the different approaches to job design is to try to ensure employees are motivated to contribute their inputs (time, effort, knowledge, and skills) to their jobs and organizations. Approaches such as scientific management, which stress extrinsic motivation, advocate designing jobs from an efficiency standpoint and closely linking pay and performance to them. Approaches such as the job characteristic model, which stress intrinsic motivation, suggest designing

TABLE 7.2

Approaches to Job Design

Approach	Main Features	Motivational Focus
Scientific management	Work simplification Specialization Time and motion studies Piece-rate pay	Extrinsic
Job enlargement	Horizontal job loading (increase number of tasks with no increase in difficulty and responsibility)	Intrinsic
Job enrichment	Vertical job loading (increase responsibility and provide employee with opportunities for growth)	Intrinsic

Job characteristics model	Core job dimensions
	  Skill variety
	  Task identity
	  Task significance
	  Autonomy
	  Feedback
	Motivating potential score
	Critical psychological states
	  Experienced meaningfulness of the work
	  Experienced responsibility for work outcomes
	  Knowledge of results
	Work and personal outcomes
	  Intrinsic motivation
	  Job performance
	  Job satisfaction
	  Absenteeism and turnover
		Intrinsic

Social information processing model	Emphasis on social environment (what aspects to consider and how to evaluate a job) Emphasis on implications of past behaviors (on how jobs and outcomes are perceived)	Extrinsic and intrinsic

jobs to make them interesting and enjoyable. Regardless of whether the motivational focus is intrinsic, extrinsic, or both, job design affects motivation levels primarily by influencing the level and amount of inputs employees contribute to their jobs and organizations.

Organizational Objectives

Organizational objectives
The overarching purpose of an organization, what it stands for, and what it seeks to accomplish.

Organizational objectives describe the overarching purpose of an organization—what it stands for and what it seeks to accomplish. From the opening case, it is clear that a key objective of Hydro is corporate sustainability and integrating environmental and social concerns with business concerns. Organizational objectives contribute to creating a motivating work setting because they can provide employees with a sense of meaning and purpose. Just as a hospital's objective of providing high-quality patient care can be motivating, so, too, can Hydro's objective of protecting the environment and playing a positive role in the communities in which it operates. Take the case of a janitor in a not-for-profit teaching hospital known for its superior patient care and the fact that needy patients are never turned away. A key source of motivation for the janitor might be knowing he is contributing to an organization that really helps people regardless of their financial means.

Organizational objectives also can help employees determine what they should be striving for on the job. This is true at Google, profiled in the accompanying OB Today.

ob today

Google's Quest to Be the Best

Google is the most popular search engine on the Internet today.[30] Its popularity is due, in no small part, to Google, Inc.'s steadfast objective to provide the best search results possible to its users. One thousand people work at Google, many of them top-notch engineers.[31] Creating algorithms that make searches on Goggle the most efficient in the industry is a consuming passion for these engineers.[32]

In order to provide users with the ultimate search, employees at Google concentrate on giving them exactly what they want at breakneck speed. Searches on Google currently take, on average, about 0.2 seconds; four years ago, they took about 3 seconds. In order to achieve results like these, employees at Google are given the flexibility to experiment, take risks, and sometimes fail. They are encouraged to learn from their failures, however, and apply what they've learned to subsequent projects.[33]

Google's organizational objective dictates that users' experiences are paramount. Consequently, employees are continually collecting data on what users like and don't like and what will improve that experience. Given that more than 50 percent of Internet searches are conducted on Google and some estimate that the actual figure is closer to 75 percent, they must be doing a pretty good job at it.[34]

Some companies' organizational objectives can be fuzzy. Not Google's. The no. 1 Internet search company's objective is crystal clear: Make Google users' searches faster and better than any other they can experience.

Social identity theory A theory that describes how individuals use the groups and organizations they are members of to define themselves.

Social identity theory explains how and why an organization's objectives can serve to motivate its employees. **Social identity theory** postulates that people tend to classify themselves and others into social categories, such as being members of a certain group or team, religion, political party, or organization. When people identify with an organization, they define themselves in terms of being a member and see their destiny as being connected to it.[35]

Identification helps people answer the "who am I?" question.[36] People also prefer positive identifications to negative ones. Thus, for example, most employees would prefer to work for and identify with an organization that makes safe, life-improving products for consumers rather than for an organization whose products have a questionable safety record. When individuals identify with an organization, they are motivated to make positive contributions to it because their organizational membership is one way in which they see themselves.[37] At Google, as engineering director Peter Norvig puts it, "There are people who think they are creating something that's the best in the world. . . . And that product is changing people's lives."[38]

Identifying with an organization can also help employees keep things in perspective when doing tedious or unpleasant tasks or when they're frustrated by a persistent work-related problem. Knowing they are adding real value to society can help them get through tough times and prop up their motivation. Although individual employees typically focus on achieving the goals tied to their own jobs, they are more likely to realize that by meeting their individual or group goals, they are helping the organization to reach its objectives, when they identify with their organization. In addition to general organizational objectives, the individual goals employees work toward play an important role in creating a motivating work setting. Goal-setting theory (discussed next) describes when, how, and why goals contribute to creating a motivating work setting.[39]

Goal Setting

Goal What an individual is trying to accomplish through his or her behavior and actions.

A **goal** is what an individual is trying to accomplish through his or her behavior and actions.[40] Goal-setting theory, like the different approaches to job design, focuses on how to motivate employees to contribute inputs to their jobs[41] (see Figure 7.1). The theory also stresses the importance of ensuring their inputs result in acceptable job performance levels.

Edwin Locke and Gary Latham, leaders in goal-setting theory and research, suggest that the goals employees try to attain at work have a major impact on their levels of motivation and performance. Just as you might have a goal to get an A in this course or to find a good job or nice apartment upon graduation, employees likewise have goals that direct their behaviors in organizations. Salespeople at Dillard's department stores, for example, have weekly and monthly sales goals they are expected to reach, and telephone operators have goals for the number of customers they should assist each day. CEOs of organizations such as IBM, Chrysler, and Acme Metal strive to meet growth, profitability, and quality goals.

Goal-setting theory A theory that focuses on identifying the types of goals that are most effective in producing high levels of motivation and performance and why goals have these effects.

Goal setting is used in organizations not just to influence input levels employees are motivated to contribute but also to ensure the inputs are directed toward furthering organizational goals.[42] **Goal-setting theory** explains what types of goals are most effective in producing high levels of motivation and performance and why goals have these effects.

WHAT KINDS OF GOALS LEAD TO HIGH MOTIVATION AND PERFORMANCE?

According to goal-setting theory, there are two major characteristics of goals that, together, lead to high levels of motivation and performance. One is specificity; the other is difficulty.

Specific goals lead to higher performance than do vague goals or no goals. Specific goals are often quantitative, such as a salesperson's goal of selling $600 worth of merchandise in a week, a telephone operator's goal of assisting 20 callers per hour, or a CEO's goal of increasing monthly and annual revenues by 10 percent. Vague goals are

Goals that are difficult but attainable, like building Hoover Dam, for example, are generally more motivating than easier goals. Thousands of men worked to tame the Colorado River during the Great Depression, creating what's been called the Eighth Wonder of the World. Some lost their lives.

much less precise than specific goals. A vague goal for a salesperson might be to "sell as much as you can." A vague goal for a CEO might be to "increase revenues and quality."

Difficult goals lead to higher motivation and performance than do easy or moderate goals. Difficult goals are goals that are hard (but not impossible) for most employees to reach. Practically all employees can achieve easy goals. Moderate goals can be achieved, on average, by about half of the people working toward the goal.

The theory states that specific and difficult goals lead to higher motivation and performance than do easy, moderate, or vague goals or no goals at all. Goal-setting theory is supported by research studies conducted in a wide variety of organizations.[43] Although most of the studies have been conducted in the United States, research conducted in Canada, the Caribbean, England, Israel, and Japan suggests that specific, difficult goals lead to high levels of motivation and performance in different cultures as well.[44]

Specific, difficult goals lead to high motivation and performance whether the goals are set by managers for their subordinates, by employees themselves,[45] or by managers and employees together. When managers set goals for subordinates, it is important that the subordinates accept the goals—that is, agree to try to meet them.[46] It is also important that employees are committed to attaining goals—that is, they want to attain them. Sometimes managers and employees may set goals together (a process often referred to as allowing subordinates to *participate* in goal setting) to boost subordinates' acceptance of and commitment to the goals. High self-efficacy also helps ensure employees will be motivated to try to reach difficult goals. Recall from Chapter 5 that self-efficacy is a person's belief that she or he can successfully perform a behavior. Employees with high self-efficacy believe that they can attain difficult goals, and this belief contributes to their acceptance, commitment, and motivation to achieve them. Sometimes providing employees with flexibility to achieve their difficult goals can increase their self-efficacy and performance. For example, at TechTarget, an interactive media company in Needham, Massachusetts, employees are given specific, difficult goals on a quarterly basis, but they are then given the flexibility to set their own hours and schedules to meet them.[47] Finally, goal setting seems to work best when employees are given feedback about how they are doing.[48]

WHY DO GOALS AFFECT MOTIVATION AND PERFORMANCE?

Why do specific, difficult goals lead to consistently higher levels of motivation and performance than easy or moderate goals or vague goals such as "do your best"? There are several reasons, and they are illustrated in the case of Mary Peterson and Allison Rios, who are the division managers of the frozen desserts and frozen vegetables divisions, respectively, of a food-processing company. Both divisions overran their operating budgets the previous year. One of the priorities for the current period is to cut operating expenses. When Peterson and her supervisor, the vice president who oversees the dessert division, met to decide Peterson's goals for the year, they agreed that she should aim to cut operating expenses by 10 percent. Rios met with the vice president of the vegetables division on the same issue, and they decided on a goal of reducing operating expenses by 25 percent. At year-end, even though Peterson met her goal of reducing expenses by 10 percent and Rios failed to meet her goal, Rios's performance was still much higher than Peterson's because she had reduced expenses by 23 percent.

Why did Rios's more difficult goal motivate her to perform at a level higher than Peterson? First, Rios's difficult goal prompted her to direct more attention toward reducing expenses than Peterson felt she needed to expend. Second, it motivated her to put forth more effort than Peterson felt she had to put forth. Consequently, Rios spent a lot of time and effort working out ways to reduce expenses; she developed more efficient inventory and product distribution systems and upgraded some of her division's production facilities. Peterson, on the other hand, devoted much less attention to reducing expenses and focused exclusively on cutting back inventories. Third, Rios's difficult goal motivated her to create a plan for achieving her goal. The plan outlined the cost savings from each change she was proposing. By contrast, Peterson, confident that she could reach her goal through improved inventory management, didn't do much planning at all. Fourth, Rios's difficult goal made her more persistent than Peterson. Both Rios and Peterson changed their inventory-handling procedures to try to cut costs, and they originally decided to focus on reducing their inventories of both raw materials and finished products. The former, however, was much easier than the latter to cut back. Peterson, confident that she could attain her easy goal, decided to maintain her finished-product inventories as they were and focus solely on reducing the raw-materials inventories. Rios also encountered problems in reducing her finished-product inventory but persisted until she was able to come up with a viable plan to do so.

To sum up, specific, difficult goals affect motivation and performance by

♦ Directing employees' attention and action toward goal-relevant activities
♦ Causing employees to exert higher levels of effort
♦ Causing employees to develop action plans to achieve their goals
♦ Causing employees to persist in the face of obstacles or difficulties[49]

It is important to note that research shows that goal setting affects motivation and performance even when employees are *not* given any extra extrinsic rewards for achieving their goals. Not surprisingly, however, specific, difficult goals tend to have more powerful effects on performance when some financial reward *is* given for goal attainment. Goal setting can operate to enhance both intrinsic motivation (in the absence of any extrinsic rewards) and extrinsic motivation (when employees are given extrinsic rewards for achieving their goals).

Because goals work so well, setting them may lead employees to *not* perform activities *not* related to the specific goals they're supposed to attain (recall the discussion of organizational citizenship behavior in Chapter 3). Research has found, for example, that employees with specific, difficult goals may be less likely to help a co-worker who is having a problem because it might interfere with the achievement of their goals.[50] A telephone operator who spends time explaining how to use a new electronic directory to a co-worker, for example, might fail to meet her own goal of assisting 20 callers per hour because of the 15 minutes she spent helping her co-worker. Some of these unassigned goals, however, may be paramount to the organization's overall effectiveness.

Moreover, it's important that employees do not so single-mindedly pursue their goals that they behave in questionable or unethical ways. Clearly, no goal is so important that a person or organization's ethics should be compromised. As indicated in the accompanying Managing Ethically feature, questionable behavior took place at Coca-Cola when a few managers became too eager to get good results from a market test of a new product.

managing ethically

There's No Such Thing as a Free Burger

Coca-Cola Co. made news after auditors discovered some irregular actions two managers took in pursuit of their goals. Evidently the managers very much wanted a test market of a promotion to deliver positive results.[51]

Coca-Cola wanted Burger King to do a national promotion with Frozen Coke, a slushy-type drink Coca-Cola hoped would yield millions in additional revenues. Before doing a national promotion, however, Burger King wanted to test market the promotion in Richmond, Virginia.[52] The deal was this: When customers purchased a Value Meal during a certain two-week period, they were given a coupon for a free Frozen Coke. Whether or not Burger King would go ahead with the national promotion hinged on how many Value Meals were sold and how many Frozen Coke coupons were redeemed.[53]

After the first week, things did not look good for Frozen Coke. Despite all of Coca-Cola's effort to push the promotion, the numbers were bad, and Burger King managers were disappointed. In an effort to save the promotion, two midlevel managers at Coke then crossed the line into ethically questionable territory. Evidently, they paid a consultant $9,000 to distribute cash to Boys and Girls Clubs and other not-for-profit organizations in Richmond to be used to purchase Value Meals at Richmond Burger Kings. The administrators of the organizations were not aware of the motivation underlying the "free" Value Meals, and it is not clear that the consultant knew all that was going on either.[54] However, what is clear is that any efforts to attain goals must be, first and foremost, defensible on ethical grounds.[55]

LIMITS TO GOAL-SETTING THEORY

Although goal-setting theory has received extensive research support for a variety of jobs and organizations, some recent research suggests that there may be certain limits on the theory's applicability. Research suggests that there are three circumstances under which setting specific, difficult goals will not lead to high motivation and performance:

1. *When employees lack the skills and abilities needed to perform at a high level.* Giving an employee the goal of writing a computer program to calculate production costs will not result in high levels of motivation and performance if the employee does not know how to write computer programs.

2. *When employees are given complicated and difficult tasks that require all of their attention and require a considerable amount of learning.* Good performance on complicated tasks depends on employees being able to direct *all* of their attention to learning the task at hand. When employees are given difficult goals for such tasks, some of their attention will be directed toward trying to attain the goal and not toward actually learning about the task. Under these circumstances, assigning a specific, difficult goal actually *reduces* performance.[56] After the task has been mastered, goal setting will then have its customary effects.

   Ruth Kanfer and Philip Ackerman of the University of Minnesota explored the effects of goal setting on the performance of Air Force personnel who were learning the complicated, difficult tasks involved to become air traffic controllers.[57] During the early stages of learning, assigning goals to the recruits resulted in lower levels of performance because it distracted some of their attention away from learning how to direct air traffic and toward trying to achieve the goal. After the recruits had developed a certain level of mastery over the task, setting specific, difficult goals did enhance performance.

3. *When employees need to be creative.* As we discussed in Chapter 5, creativity is the generation of new and useful ideas whether they be products, services, or processes.[58] Given that creativity involves coming up with something that is novel and has not been thought of before, it is often not appropriate to provide employees with specific, difficult goals if the outcome of their creative efforts is unknown. If they are coming up with something that is really new, a specific, difficult goal cannot be set as a priority because managers do not yet know what it is that they will create. Additionally, if creativity is desired and employees are given specific, difficult goals, it is likely they will focus on achieving the goals rather than being creative. However, this does not mean that more general kinds of goals cannot help motivate creativity. Indeed, research has found that giving employees the general goal to be creative can help encourage creativity. And, clearly, creative pursuits are driven by organizational objectives and group goals such as providing new services that will meet clients' needs.

MANAGEMENT BY OBJECTIVES

Management by objectives (MBO) A goal-setting process in which a manager meets with his or her supervisor to set goals and evaluate the extent to which previously set goals have been achieved.

Some organizations adopt formal systems to ensure that goal setting actually takes place on a periodic basis.[59] **Management by objectives (MBO)** is a goal-setting process in which a manager meets periodically with his or her supervisor to set goals and evaluate how well previously set goals have been met.[60] The objective of MBO is to make sure that all goal setting contributes to the organization's effectiveness. Most MBO programs are usually reserved for managers, but the programs can also be used as a motivational tool for nonmanagers. Although the form and content of MBO programs vary from organization to organization, most programs have three basic steps: goal setting, implementation, and evaluation (see Figure 7.5).[61]

1. *Goal setting.* The manager and the supervisor meet and jointly determine the goals the manager will try to achieve during a specific time period, say, 6 or 12 months. In our earlier example, Allison Rios, the division manager for frozen vegetables, met with the vice president to whom she reports, and together they decided that she should work throughout the coming year toward the goal of reducing operating expenses by 25 percent.

2. *Implementation.* The manager is given the autonomy to decide how to meet the goals in the specified time period. Progress toward goal attainment is periodically assessed and discussed by the manager and her or his supervisor. In our example, Rios came up with several ways to cut expenses, including the development of more efficient inventory and product distribution systems and upgrading the production facilities. Rios made and implemented these decisions on her own and periodically met with her supervisor to review how her plans were working.

3. *Evaluation.* At the end of the specified time period, the manager and supervisor again meet to assess the extent of goal attainment, discuss why some goals may not have been attained, and set goals for the next period.

FIGURE 7.5

Basic Steps in Management by Objectives

Goal setting	**Implementation**	**Evaluation**
The manager and the supervisor meet and jointly determine goals the manager will try to achieve during a specified period.	The manager is given the autonomy to decide how to meet the goals, but progress toward goal attainment is periodically assessed and discussed by the manager and the supervisor.	The manager and the supervisor meet to assess the extent of goal attainment, discuss why some goals have not been attained, and set goals for the next period.

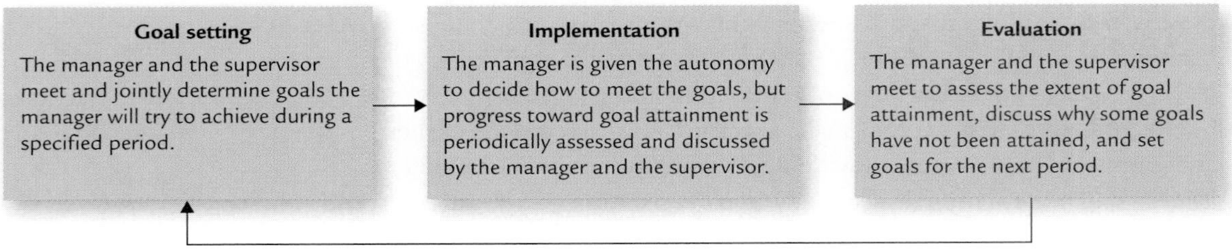

The success of an MBO program depends on the appropriateness and difficulty of the goals that are set. Clearly, the goals should focus on key dimensions of a manager's performance such as cutting operating expenses, expanding sales, or increasing the profitability of a division's product line that are under the manager's control. And, as we've seen, goals should be specific and difficult. Finally, for MBO to work, a certain amount of rapport and trust must exist between managers and their supervisors. A manager who doesn't trust her supervisor, for example, might fear that if some unforeseen, uncontrollable event prohibits her from attaining a difficult goal, the supervisor will penalize her (for example, by not giving a raise). To avoid this situation, the manager may try to set easy MBO goals. Managers and supervisors must be committed to MBO and be willing to take the time and effort needed to make it work. Moreover, when conditions change, a willingness to change objectives in midstream can be important; if an objective is no longer appropriate, there is no point in continuing to work toward it.

Goal Setting and Job Design as Motivation Tools

Recall from Chapter 6 that motivating employees to contribute their inputs (which include their time, effort, and skills) to their jobs is a key challenge in an organization. Goal-setting theory suggests that one way to meet this challenge is to set specific, difficult goals. Employees exert more effort for such goals than they do for easy or vague goals, and they are more likely to persist in the face of obstacles. In addition to motivating employees, goals focus employee inputs in the right direction so that the inputs result not only in acceptable levels of job performance but also in the achievement of organizational goals.

Together, job design and goal setting address some of the many questions managers face in the realm of motivation: How can I make my subordinates more interested in doing a good job? What is the best way to assign specific tasks to each of my subordinates? How can I get my subordinates to care about their work? How can I achieve increases in performance and quality necessary for the organization to achieve its goals? In terms of the motivation equation (Inputs$\rightarrow$ Performance$\rightarrow$ Outcomes), job design and goal setting focus primarily on how to motivate employees to contribute their inputs to their jobs and organizations (see Figure 7.1).

Summary

Job design and goal setting are the foundations of a motivating work setting. The ways in which jobs are designed and the types of goals that are set can have profound effects on employee motivation and performance and the extent to which an organization is able to achieve its goals. In this chapter, we made the following major points:

1. One of the earliest systematic approaches to job design was scientific management, which stresses job simplification and job specialization. Scientific management focuses on extrinsic motivation and can result in an efficient production process. It also may result in high levels of job dissatisfaction.

2. Job enlargement and job enrichment focus, respectively, on the horizontal and the vertical loading of jobs. Each attempts, by raising levels of intrinsic

motivation, to overcome some of the problems that arise when jobs are designed according to the principles of scientific management.

3. The job characteristics model also focuses on intrinsic motivation. The model proposes that five core dimensions (skill variety, task identity, task significance, autonomy, and feedback) lead to three critical psychological states (experienced meaningfulness of the work, experienced responsibility for

work outcomes, and knowledge of results) that in turn lead to several outcomes (intrinsic motivation, job performance, job satisfaction, and low absenteeism and turnover). Individual differences (growth-need strength, knowledge and skills, and satisfaction with the work context) affect the key relationships in the model. Research suggests that intrinsic motivation and job satisfaction do tend to result from the core characteristics and psychological states as proposed by the model; however, job performance is not necessarily affected.

4. The social information processing model suggests that the social environment provides employees with information about which aspects of their job design and work outcomes they should pay attention to and how they should evaluate them. This information influences motivation. In addition, employees' past behaviors have implications for how they view their current jobs and current levels of motivation, particularly when these past behaviors were freely chosen or entailed personal sacrifices.

5. Goal-setting theory and research suggest that specific, difficult goals lead to higher motivation and performance than do easy goals, moderate goals, vague goals, or no goals. Specific, difficult goals influence motivation and performance by directing employees' attention toward goal-relevant activities, influencing effort expenditure, influencing levels of persistence, and causing employees to develop action plans. When employees are performing very complicated and difficult tasks that require all of their attention and a considerable amount of learning, specific, difficult goals should not be set until the employees have mastered the tasks.

Exercises in Understanding and Managing Organizational Behavior

Questions for Discussion and Review

1. Why might an organization want to design jobs according to the principles of scientific management?

2. Why might some employees not want their jobs enriched?

3. How might a manager redesign the job of a person who delivers newspapers to raise levels of the core job dimensions identified by the job characteristics model?

4. Can principles of scientific management and the job characteristics model both be used to design a job? Explain.

5. Why do individual differences affect the relationships in the job characteristics model?

6. Why does the social environment influence employees' responses to the design of their jobs?

7. Why should organizations clearly communicate organizational objectives to their employees?

8. What kinds of goals should be set for a supermarket cashier?

9. Why do people try to attain difficult goals?

10. When might specific, difficult goals result in low levels of performance?

Building People Skills

Extrinsic and Intrinsic Motivation

Pick two people you know pretty well who are working (such as friends or relatives). Try to pick one person who is primarily extrinsically motivated by his or her job and another person who is primarily intrinsically motivated (or both intrinsically and extrinsically motivated). Informally meet with each of these people and ask them about their jobs (especially what their jobs entail, the social environment at work, and their work goals, if any). Then do the following:

1. Describe each person's job.

2. Is either job designed according to the principles of scientific management? If so, how?

3. Describe each job in terms of the five core dimensions of the job characteristics model.

4. Describe each person in terms of the individual differences in the job characteristics model.

5. How are the people's social environments at work similar? How are they different?

6. Is either person assigned goals? If so, what kinds of goals?

7. What do you think accounts for the extrinsic motivation and the intrinsic motivation of the people you have chosen?

A Question of Ethics

Some employees are given specific, difficult goals and their very livelihood depends on how well they perform. For example, salespeople who are paid strictly on a commission basis have all their earnings hinging on the extent to which they are successful in selling to customers. This can sometimes cause salespeople considerable stress, especially when they are very dependent on their earnings to support themselves and/or loved ones.

Questions

1. Think about the ethical implications of assigning specific, difficult goals to employees.
2. Is it ethical to have employees' earnings based entirely on the extent to which they attain their goals?

Small Group Break-Out Exercise

The Power of Social Influence

Form groups of three or four people and appoint one member as the spokesperson who will communicate your conclusions to the rest of the class.

1. Take a few minutes to think about a situation in which your opinion differed from the general consensus of the group of people you were with.
2. Write down a brief description of the situation, how you felt, whether or not you expressed your opinion, and whether or not you or anyone in the group changed their opinions.
3. Take turns describing these situations and the information you wrote down for Step 2.
4. As a group, try to come up with explanations for why sometimes people who disagree with a majority fail to express their opinions and/or end up changing them.

Topic for Debate

Job design and goal setting are two major motivational tools that managers can use to increase motivation and performance. Now that you have a good understanding of job design and goal setting, debate the following issue.

Team A. Managers should try to avoid designing jobs according to the principles of scientific management whenever possible.

Team B. Designing jobs according to the principles of scientific management can help an organization achieve its goals and should be used whenever appropriate.

Experiential Exercise

Increasing Autonomy

Objective

Your objective is to gain experience in redesigning a job to increase employee autonomy.

Procedure

Assume the role of a manager in charge of a group of artists who draw pictures for greeting cards. You currently assign the artists their individual tasks. Each artist is given a particular kind of card to work on (one works on birthday cards for female relatives, one on birthday cards for children, and so on). You inform each artist of the market research that has been done on his or her particular category of cards. You also communicate to each artist your ideas about what you would like to see in the cards he or she creates. The artists then produce sketches based on this information. You review the sketches, make changes, sometimes make the decision to abandon an idea or suggest a new one, and eventually give the artists the go-ahead to proceed with the drawing.

You thought everything was working pretty smoothly until you accidentally overheard one of your subordinates complaining to another that you are stifling his creativity. This exchange brought to mind another troubling incident. One of your artists who had drawn some of the company's best-selling cards quit a few months ago to work for a competitor. You began to wonder whether you have designed the artists' jobs in the best way possible.

You decide to administer the *Job Diagnostic Survey* to your subordinates. They complete it anonymously, and you are truly shocked by the results. Most of your subordinates indicate that their jobs are low on autonomy. Being an artist yourself, you are disturbed by this outcome because you see autonomy as being a necessary ingredient for creativity.

1. Develop an action plan to increase levels of autonomy in the artists' jobs. Although you want to increase autonomy, you also want to make sure that your group creates cards that are responsive to market demands and customer taste.
2. The class divides into groups of three to five people, and each group appoints one member as spokesperson to present the group's recommendations to the whole class.
3. Group members take turns describing their own specific action plans for increasing autonomy in the artists' jobs while making sure the cards are responsive to market demands and customer taste.
4. Discuss the pros and cons of the different alternative action plans and create an action plan that group members think will best increase autonomy while at the same time meet the organizational goal of creating best-selling cards.

When your group has completed those activities, the spokesperson will present the group's action plan to the whole class.

Making the Connection

Find an example of a company that uses goals to motivate its employees. What kinds of jobs do the employees in this company have? What kinds of goals does the company use?

New York Times Cases in the News

The New York Times

After Many Generations, Floating Hospital Is Still Going, Just Not Floating

BY DIANE CARDWELL

The Floating Hospital was not a true hospital, and that was precisely its charm. For more than a century it floated up and down New York City's waterways, making a clinical checkup feel like a day at the beach.

In the summer, the familiar barge would ply the harbor as its staff offered primary health care, nutrition counseling and entertainment for children and for the needy who might shy away from other clinics. In the colder months of recent decades, it offered its services while tethered to a Manhattan pier. Generations of patients climbed aboard to have their teeth examined, watch a magic show or just take a refreshing cruise and see the Statue of Liberty.

"We've had patients come and say, 'Oh, my grandmother was on this ship, and so I wanted to come,'" said Angela Amendola, a physician assistant.

But the ship has run aground. Though it still calls itself the Floating Hospital, the clinic has moved off the barge and is looking for a permanent home on land.

While the hospital's basic mission has not changed in its 130-odd years on the water, the waterfront has. In the past, there were few objections to a barge that tended to the sick and indigent near working or derelict piers, far from the homes of the elite. But now, as city residents and officials are rediscovering the potential for commercial development, housing and recreational oases along the waterways, the Floating Hospital has found itself largely unwelcome.

The barge, the Lila Acheson Wallace, has sat idle in Brooklyn since December, and the agency has set up shop on East Broadway, near Clinton Street, in Manhattan, in a non-descript clinic where it began seeing patients last week. The hospital plans to settle in Long Island City. Queens, as soon as it can find an available building or lot. Hospital officials say the area has been designated by the federal government as an underserved community.

"Our mission doesn't say we will be a ship," said Ken Berger, president and chief executive officer of the agency, who described the decision to abandon ship as painful. "Our mission says that we will provide health care and social services to underserved people."

The boat—where many patients were treated at no charge—was the flagship and headquarters of a much larger enterprise with 66 satellite clinics throughout the city (except Staten Island), in Westchester and on Long Island. In addition to medical care, the organization provides rehabilitation and social services to homeless and immigrant families, the retarded, victims of domestic violence and people with H.I.V.

But it was the ship, a barge powered by a tugboat, that gave the agency its identity over the years, as more than five million patients went aboard the Lila Acheson Wallace and her many predecessors.

The concept evolved from cruises begun in 1866 by *The New York Times* for newsboys toiling in the smoggy, sweltering city. It became a summer institution, touring the East and Hudson Rivers with children, the elderly and the disabled. Later, it was not only a mobile clinic whose many distractions offset the fear and pain of a trip to the doctor, but also a summer retreat for those without a cottage or beach.

At the same time, the ship was an extreme example of the beliefs about disease in the late 19th century, said David Rosner, a director of the Center for the History and Ethics of Public Health at Columbia University. In that period, before the role of bacteria was fully understood, disease was seen as being rooted in personal behavior, he said.

By removing patients, some of them tubercular, from congested areas of the city, the Floating Hospital was trying both "to cure them and to isolate them from the evil influences that had gotten them sick in the first place," he said, including "immorality, bad habits and lousy decisions" on the part of the patients, who were, for the most part, poor residents of the city's slums.

By the 1870's the hospital was shuttling poor children around the city's waterways so they could breathe the sea breezes, take a salt bath and see a doctor while their mothers relaxed on the boat. Throughout the years, the hospital, operated until 1980 by St. John's Guild, a private philanthropic group, also staged festive events. In 1949, sanitation workers dressed up as cowboys to entertain 1,200 children who had participated in city cleanup drives.

Over the decades, the barge has come to rest at several spots, including piers on the Lower East Side, in West Midtown and in Harlem, said Ellie Tinto-Poitier, the hospital's chief operating officer, adding that its last regular home was at Pier 11, near Wall Street. After the terror attack, the city moved the barge temporarily to Pier 17, at the South Street Seaport, to make way for ferries in Lower Manhattan.

The barge was displaced again by plans for emergency ferry service in December as a threatened transit strike loomed. The strike never materialized, but officials of the company that manages the seaport would not let the barge return, saying it was inappropriate in an area full of stores, restaurants and tourists.

City and hospital officials considered many other piers, they say, but none worked out. Finally, Floating Hospital officials decided earlier this year that it was time to come ashore.

Mr. Berger said the new headquarters in Long Island City would be a boon. Its central location will make it easier for clients to be brought there from shelters and schools around the city. The neighborhood also has a large public housing project in need of health care services, he said.

"In years to come, people will ask, 'Why is it called the Floating Hospital?' because it's anchored in Queens," said Councilman Eric Gioia, who represents the area. "This will dramatically improve people's access to health care."

So the blue and white boat now sits like a ghost at a pier in Sunset Park, Brooklyn, its dental chairs and theater and exam rooms empty. Mr. Berger said he held out hope that the hospital would float once again, or that at least a new use would be found for the ship.

In Boston, the Floating Hospital for Children also began in the late 19th century as a ship, inspired by the New York vessel. The boat was destroyed by fire in the late 1920's, but the institution survives on land as a full-fledged children's hospital.

"There's a lot more you can do for children than provide them fresh air and sunlight, so we've changed to be a modern children's hospital," said Dr. Ivan Frantz, the chief pediatrician at the Boston hospital.

New York's ship may have been historically and emotionally important, he added, but it is no longer necessary in providing care. "The original concept is now something that just doesn't exist."

SOURCE: "After Many Generations, Floating Hospital Is Still Going, Just Not Floating" by D. Cardwell, *New York Times*, September 1, 2003, p. W1.

Questions for Discussion

1. What are the organizational objectives of the Floating Hospital?

2. To what extent have the organizational objectives changed over time?

3. How might these organizational objectives motivate employees and be translated into more specific operational goals?

The New York Times

Korean Steel Maker Finds Strength in Flexibility

Posco Faces Challenge in a Changing Market

BY JAMES BROOKE

POHANG, South Korea—With a metallic roar, a new strip of orange steel heated to 1,200 degrees shot angrily through a hot rolling mill, a cavernous shed that stretched farther than the eye could see.

"Every 110 seconds, we can produce a 25-ton coil of steel," Min Kyung Zoon, the superintendent of the mill, shouted during a recent tour. As a wall of heat rose to hit visitors on a catwalk, he added: "We can produce 640 tons of stainless steel an hour—that's better than Europe, better than Japan."

Down below, the heavily automated line ran around the clock in an inferno of gyrating temperatures, but only a handful of workers tended the building, a hall the size of several football fields.

While American steel producers struggle to cut losses, Posco, one of the world's most profitable steel makers, is a model of efficiency. Ships carrying iron ore from Australia dock at one end of the horseshoe-shaped mill. At the other end, different ships, often built with Posco steel, load finished steel. China, the world's biggest consumer and biggest importer of steel, is one day away by ship from these docks.

It is this kind of efficiency that has made South Korea, sandwiched between the industrial giants of China and Japan, the world's biggest per capita steel producer—almost one ton for each of South Korea's 48 million people. About 60 percent of that steel comes from Posco, as the **Pohang Iron and Steel** Company is known, the world's third-largest steel maker, after Europe's Arcelor and Japan's Nippon Steel Company.

Elsewhere, in Europe and the United States, steel production is often synonymous with expensive union labor, looming pension costs, government subsidies and tariff barriers.

In contrast, Posco, a nonunion company that has not had a strike in its 30 years of steel production, saw its net profits hit $850 million in the first half of this year, nearly triple the level of the same period last year. Less than three years after Posco's privatization was completed, it is the darling of private investors, with foreigners owning 64 percent of shares in a company with a market capitalization of $10.7 billion.

This year, World Steel Dynamics, a steel information service, studied the world's 17 largest steel makers. It ranked Posco as the most competitive.

"No one doubts the competitiveness of Posco," Hwang Tae Hyun, Posco's vice president for finance, said in an interview at the company's steel-trimmed headquarters in Seoul. "Even two years ago, when steel prices were at 25-year lows, and investors elsewhere got burned, Posco had double-digit profits. Posco is one of the most transparent companies in Korea today."

Posco has to be agile because it operates in a virtually wide open market, one with essentially no import barriers. In contrast, the United States imposed steel tariffs of up to 30 percent in March 2002.

Operating in a market with few import barriers requires creativity.

With a far more open market, South Korea was a net importer of steel products this year, importing a net $83 million. South Korea's net exports of $1 billion in steel to China were canceled out by its net imports of $1.5 billion in steel from Japan.

In June, Prime Minister Junichiro Koizumi of Japan promised to start talks at an early date with South Korea on a free-trade pact, a move that could increase Korean steel exports to Japan. But Posco is not holding its breath. Instead, this steel mastodon has learned to dance.

After investing heavily in computerization and better customer service, Posco has over the last two years cut average inventories of finished steel by two-thirds, to 360,000 tons; has cut in half delivery lead time to 14 days; and has sharpene on-time deliveries to 97 percent.

The big jump in profits comes largely from China's rapid growth, which this nation generally embraces as a challenge, rather than a threat.

Posco's average sales price is up 18.7 percent from a year earlier, while sales volume is up only 3.7 percent, to 13.8 million tons.

China is the world's largest steel producer making 100 million tons last year. But a shortfall between supply and demand has nearly double prices in two years, pushing them to levels not seen in nearly a decade.

Steel prices have been maintained by the huge growth in China's demand for steel, said Mr. Hwang, predicting that Posco's strong numbers would be maintained through this year.

Rolled steel from plants like these is used to make cars in China, which is expanding car production by 60 percent a year.

By crossing the Yellow Sea, Posco is joining a flotilla that has made South Korea the sixth largest foreign investor in China.

"At present, we have 14 strategic joint ventures in China and $780 million invested in China," Cho Soung Sik, Posco's vice president for strategic planning, said in Seoul. "A decade ago our investment in China was zero."

Despite the importance of China as a market, about three quarters of Posco's steel is sold domestically. In the first half of this year, South Korea suffered its first recession in five years, with the economy contracting slightly.

But industrial output in June was up 7.8 percent over the same period a year ago, and economists are forecasting that a rebound will bring growth to 3 percent for the year, about half of last year's rate.

During the first six months, South Korean shipyards received orders for 233 ships, or $10.6 billion worth, slightly more than the 230 orders recorded all of last year.

The South Korean economy, however, is sluggish, Andy Xie, Morgan Stanley's Asia economist, wrote recently. Noting that South Korea's exports to China jumped by nearly a quarter in the first six months, he added: "The only growth engine is exports to China."

Despite this sunny season for steel, three clouds float on the horizon, and are problems that may also apply to South Korea's economy as a whole: the possibility of conflict with North Korea; the rise of China as a low-cost labor competitor; and the migration of steel-intensive industries out of South Korea because of rising wages.

Few South Koreans seem to think there will be an armed conflict with the North.

Indeed, if North Korea's Communist government collapses one day, there will be a massive demand for steel for railroads, construction and vehicles to make up for half a century of foregone development.

But if China, with its lower wages, sharply expands its steel production, South Korea will have to fight harder for export markets.

"There is a high possibility that the home appliance factories will move, in which case we have to increase steel exports to those countries," said Ryoo Kyeong Ryul, Posco's executive vice president for process innovation.

"Last year, I visited South Korean factories in Vietnam," he said. "I saw young people working very hard."

Another possibility would be for South Korea's steel-consuming industries to migrate to North Korea, which has low wages. Ground was broken six weeks ago on South Korean-run industrial park just north of the demilitarized zone.

SOURCE: "Korean Steel Maker Finds Strength in Flexibility" by J. Brooke, *New York Times*, August 5, 2003, pp. W1, W7.

Questions for Discussion

1. What are the organizational objectives of Posco?

2. What kinds of goals motivate Posco's employees?

3. How has Posco been able to succeed in the challenging environment it faces?

Pay, Careers, and Changing Employment Relationships

8

LEARNING OBJECTIVES

After studying this chapter, you should be able to:

■

Describe the determinants and types of psychological contracts and what happens when they are broken.

■

Appreciate the two major roles of performance appraisal.

■

Understand the different kinds and methods of performance appraisal.

■

Appreciate the importance of merit pay and the choices organizations face in using pay to motivate employees.

■

Understand the importance of careers, different kinds of careers, and effective career management.

OPENING CASE

Changing with the Times at Briggs & Stratton

How Can Organizations in Traditional Industries Remain Competitive?

Briggs & Stratton Corp. is one of the largest manufacturers of engines that run on gasoline, are cooled by air, and are used in lawn mowers, tractors, pressure washers, and other kinds of lawn and garden equipment.[1] In the mid-1990s, Briggs & Stratton was at a crossroads. Its huge factory outside Milwaukee was so unwieldy it was difficult to even determine the profitability of its different product lines. Costs were rising just as competitors and customers were seeking to lower their costs by outsourcing and purchasing overseas. Although Briggs & Stratton was still earning a profit, managers realized that times were changing, and the company had to change, too, to remain competitive. As Chairman and CEO John S. Shiely put it, "We had become a battleship."[2]

Briggs & Stratton proceeded to make major changes, which have paid off handsomely. In fiscal year 2003, net sales were $1.66 billion, and net income was $80.6 million—52 percent higher than in 2002.[3] In an effort to change with the times, Briggs & Stratton relocated some of its manufac-

turing work to smaller-sized plants in southern states that have lower cost structures and are easier to manage because they specialize in just one or two product lines.

Moreover, all Briggs & Stratton employees now work toward the goal of increasing productivity and efficiency and reducing costs. Importantly, a portion of employees' pay is linked to their productivity, which, according to Senior Vice President Paul Neylon, causes them to "go to extremes to take even a half a cent of cost out of each engine."[4] Productivity and profitability can now be measured precisely and engines are assembled in about half of the time it took 10 years ago.[5]

Briggs & Stratton also recognizes the importance of career development and guidance for its employees. Its Career Development Program helps employees explore their career options within the company by providing them with career counseling and holding career-planning workshops.[6] Via an internal job posting system, employees are continually informed about open positions they might pursue to enhance their careers. Recognizing the value of ongoing learning, Briggs & Stratton also fully reimburses tuition and book costs for employees who want to continue their education on a part-time basis.[7] Changing with the times has helped Briggs & Stratton remain competitive by motivating its employees and bucking the trend to outsource jobs to low-cost markets overseas.

Overview

Building off of Chapters 6 and 7, in this chapter we focus on the broader context in which employee motivation takes place. Although it is important to understand what motivates people, how they are motivated, and why, it is also important to understand how key aspects of the employment relationship can serve to encourage and maintain high levels of motivation. If mismanaged, these factors can lower motivation. In the opening case, it is clear that employees at Briggs & Stratton are responding well to the initiatives the organization has undertaken to promote employee motivation, including giving employees incentive pay and career development opportunities.

The nature of the relationship between employees and organizations is changing. Organizations in the United States are increasingly outsourcing not only manufacturing jobs but also white-collar jobs, such as computer programming, engineering, and consulting, to countries with lower labor costs.[8] Recent waves of layoffs have changed U.S. workers' expectations about their careers and how they might unfold. In this chapter, we discuss these changes in depth. We describe the nature of the psychological contract an individual has with an organization and factors that cause psychological contracts to change over time. Psychological contracts and the motivation equation, explained in Chapter 6, all underscore the fact that the relationship between an organization and its employees is an exchange relationship: Employees make certain contributions to the organization and, in exchange, expect to receive certain outcomes.[9] We then discuss three factors that play a central role in this exchange relationship: performance appraisal, pay, and careers. In order to have a meaningful, reciprocal exchange, organizations need to be able to accurately assess the nature of the contributions employees make through performance appraisals. Given that pay is one of the most important outcomes for employees, regardless of the kinds of jobs they hold and organizations they belong to, we focus on pay and how it can be used to enhance motivation. Lastly, we take a longer-term perspective on the employment relationship and address the careers of an organization's employees.

Psychological Contracts

A good way to think about the exchange relationship between an employee and an organization is in terms of a psychological contract.[10] A **psychological contract** is an employee's perception of his or her exchange relationship with an organization: outcomes the organization has promised to provide and contributions the employee is obligated to make.[11] There are a few key points worth emphasizing in this definition. First, psychological contracts are perceptual in nature[12] (see Chapter 4). Hence, they can be subject to errors and biases and also can be somewhat idiosyncratic. Having said this, though, does little to diminish the impact psychological contracts have on employee motivation. Second, psychological contracts refer to the perceived exchange relationship between an employee and an organization in terms of reciprocal promises or obligations.[13] Given the prevalence of reciprocity norms in the United States and other countries such as China, Singapore, and Belgium,[14] organizations and the people within them generally seek to abide by psychological contracts. (The belief that making a contribution should lead to a commensurate outcome is an example of one such norm.)

> **Psychological contract** An employee's perception of his or her exchange relationship with an organization, outcomes the organization has promised to provide to the employee, and contributions the employee is obligated to make to the organization.

DETERMINANTS OF PSYCHOLOGICAL CONTRACTS

How do individuals form their psychological contracts? Essentially, by piecing together information from a variety of sources to determine what is expected of them and what they can expect from the organization in return. Three sources of information are particularly influential in helping individuals form their psychological contracts—direct

Not only are manufacturing jobs outsourced today, so are many white collar jobs. India, for example, has carved out a niche for itself handling computer programming work for other countries.

FIGURE **8.1**
Determinants of
Psychological
Contracts

communication from co-workers and supervisors, observations of what actually tran-spires in the organization, including how similar employees behave and are treated, and written documents (see Figure 8.1).[15]

Direct Communication. Psychological contracts can begin to form before a prospective employee even joins an organization. For example, when managers try to recruit new employees, they often focus on the advantages of joining the organization and accepting a particular job. Take the case of Maria Gomez who was recruited to be a marketing assistant for a large consumer products firm. Gomez has a B.A. in marketing and was attracted to the position because she hoped it would put her on track for eventually assuming the position of brand manager. When she was recruited, she was told that upward mobility at the firm was encouraged, and if she performed well and proactively sought to advance, she would have opportunities. This promise was one of the reasons she accepted the position.

After employees are on the job, they continue to receive direct communication from organizational members that form the basis of their psychological contracts.[16] In Gomez's case, however, two co-workers who held similar positions to hers complained they were stuck in dead-end, glorified clerical positions. This upset Gomez because of her own aspirations and what she was told when she was recruited. She began to won-der to what extent she might have been misled by the recruiter. Gomez's experience is, unfortunately, not uncommon. Organizations often seek to hire the best applicants by making lofty promises. However, this strategy often backfires after employees are on the job and realize how things really are. Thus, research suggests that to promote motivation, satisfaction, and retention of employees—as well as create more accurate psychological contracts—organizations should provide prospective employees with realistic job pre-views. A **realistic job preview (RJP)** is an honest assessment of the advantages and disadvantages of a particular job and working in a particular organization.[17] RJPs enable employees to make informed decisions and form realistic expectations and more accu-rate psychological contracts.

Realistic job preview (RJP)
An honest assessment of the
advantages and
disadvantages of a particular
job and working in a
particular organization.

Observation. Although the adage, "actions speak louder than words," is somewhat of a cliché, it certainly rings true when it comes to psychological contracts. Essentially, employees observe how they are treated, how their co-workers are treated, what kinds of decisions are made and in what manner, how their managers behave, and how outcomes are distributed in an organization to form their psychological contracts.[18] In Gomez's case, she observed that two of the current brand managers in her division had started out as marketing assistants and also that her boss made the effort to explain the kinds of things she (the boss) did and how it fit in with the plan for the brand.

Written Documents. Written documents are also used in forming psychological contracts. For example, documents describing compensation and benefit policies, performance appraisal processes, and career development become the basis for forming psychological contracts.[19] During her first few weeks on the job, Gomez periodically would consult her company's Web site and online human resources and career development programs to get a better understanding of what to expect and see if the promises made to her were likely to be fulfilled. Fortunately for her, all signs pointed to a good potential for advancement to the brand manager position—except for the complaints of two of her co-workers. The pair had been passed over for a promotion a few months earlier, but because of the information Gomez had garnered, she was able to dismiss those complaints as "sour grapes."

TYPES OF PSYCHOLOGICAL CONTRACTS

There are two major types of psychological contracts: transactional and relational (see Figure 8.2).[20]

Transactional Contracts. Transactional contracts tend to be short term and very specific.[21] They are narrow in focus and relatively flexible given their short-term nature. If either party terminates the relationship, a replacement can be found.[22] In transactional contracts, individuals focus primarily on extrinsic outcomes such as pay. Recall the discussion of contingent workers. Contingent workers have transactional kinds of psychological contracts—they transact with an organization to provide some good or service (for example, extra help during a busy time of year or clerical services to fill in for an employee on medical leave) for a set economic return (say, hourly pay). The employing organization expects adequate performance on the part of the contingent worker but not much else, and the contingent worker expects pay for the hours worked but little more of the organization. Of course, sometimes organizations decide that they want a longer-term relationship with a valued contingent worker and may seek to employ that individual on a more permanent basis. Another example of a transactional contract is an employment situation in which there is an initial probationary period during which either party can terminate the relationship.

Relational Contracts. Relational contracts are longer term, more general, and evolve more gradually over time. They imply a mutual commitment on the part of both parties.[23] Employees are affectively committed to their organizations (see Chapter 3), and the organization is committed to promoting the well-being of the employees.[24] Relational contracts cover much more ground than transactional contracts and are also more subjective because they entail more intangible kinds of factors, such as, for example, opportunities for career development. Although extrinsic outcomes like pay are still important to relational contracts, so too are intrinsic factors such as making an important contribution to the organization and a sense of achievement. University professors who are tenured have relational kinds of psychological contracts.

FIGURE 8.2

Types of Psychological Contracts

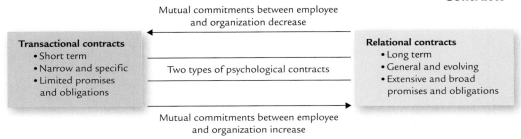

The previous scenarios involving contingent workers and tenured professors are relatively clear-cut examples of transactional and relational contracts. For other jobs, however, the distinction becomes a bit murkier. One way to think about the distinction is in terms of the extent to which the employment relationship is more transactional (short term) or more relational (long term) (see Figure 8.2). Indeed, theories and research suggest it is useful to think of psychological contracts as varying along a continuum, with transactional contracts falling at one end of the continuum and relational contracts falling at the other. Of course, the nature of the psychological contract is essentially determined by an employee's perceptions of it.

A number of recent developments have caused researchers to question to what extent psychological contracts are undergoing some sweeping changes. Massive layoffs by both major corporations and smaller start-ups and high-tech companies have caused employees to question how committed their organizations are to them. Today, it is probably more the exception than the rule to expect to spend one's entire career in a single organization. As indicated in the accompanying Global View, outsourcing work to countries with lower-cost labor such as China and India is becoming pervasive in more and more industries.[25] Increased reliance on outsourcing might also lead to fundamental changes in psychological contracts over time.

global view

Outsourcing White-Collar Jobs

Outsourcing is not a new phenomenon. From 2000 to 2003, approximately 2.6 million U.S. manufacturing jobs where outsourced to China.[26] However, what *is* new is a dramatic increase in the outsourcing of white-collar jobs. Jobs for financial analysts, telemarketers, accountants, engineers, computer programmers, claims adjusters, loan processors, and architectural drafters are among those being outsourced to China, India, and other countries with low labor costs. Even mainstay American organizations such as IBM, Microsoft, and Procter & Gamble are outsourcing their white-collar jobs.[27]

In India, for example, the software industry is booming. Salaries are approximately one-tenth what they are in the United States, and there is an abundant supply of workers skilled in engineering, computer science, and other white-collar fields.[28] Tata Consultancy Services, one of India's largest companies providing software services to multinationals, recently received outsourcing contracts—each worth over $50 million—from GE Medical Systems, Verizon, and United Utilities.[29] Due to the international time differences, workers in India are leaving for home when their U.S. counterparts are arriving at work. This makes it possible for organizations to operate around the clock and turn time-sensitive projects around, in some instances, in just a day.[30]

Multinational organizations are also setting up their own offices in countries such as India to take advantage of lower costs. For example, Oracle has recently opened two large centers in India that employ approximately 4,000 people.[31] IBM has offices in India that employ engineers, and Hewlett-Packard has approximately 5,000 employees working in centers in India on software development and research, and manning call centers.[32] Although outsourcing has resulted in less job security for U.S. workers, many multinational organizations believe they must outsource at least some white-collar work to reap the benefits of low labor costs and remain competitive. Given the economic benefits of outsourcing, it appears to be here to stay.[33]

WHEN PSYCHOLOGICAL CONTRACTS ARE BROKEN

When employees perceive that their psychological contracts have been breached or broken due to the failure of the organization to live up to its promises, their motivation and performance can suffer. Breached contracts can also result in employees experiencing more negative moods and emotions, being more dissatisfied with their jobs, and looking for employment elsewhere. The larger the perceived violation, the more intense the potential negative reaction. When contracts are intentionally breached by an organization in significant ways, employees' levels of trust in the organization plummet.[34] In our prior example, had Maria Gomez found out that there was no chance of ever being promoted to the position of brand manager (even though she was promised this when she was recruited), in all likelihood, her commitment to the company would plummet, and she would have started looking for another job.

Sometimes observing other employees having their psychological contracts breached can cause people to be concerned about their own future in an organization.[35] For example, if an organization is outsourcing more and more jobs, a computer programmer who is still employed might fear that his job, too, will eventually be outsourced and might act on this fear by finding another job. However, if the programmer was a valued member of the organization, and his job was not actually in jeopardy, both parties stand to lose. The organization has lost a valued member and the programmer has lost a good job. Thus, whenever organizations take actions that have the potential to affect their members' psychological contracts, care must be taken to accurately and honestly communicate what the action was, why it was taken, and what the future is likely to hold. Moreover, how an organization treats workers whose contracts have been broken is important.[36] For example, during a layoff, whether workers are given adequate advance notice, given help in finding other positions, provided with additional training to make them more employable, and whether the organization is doing all it can to help them through a tough time and transition out of it can have profound effects on how survivors of the layoff view their own psychological contracts.

Performance Appraisal

Psychological contracts and almost all of the theories and approaches to motivation we have covered so far assume that managers can accurately *appraise*—that is, evaluate—their subordinates' performance and contributions to their jobs and to the organization. In expectancy theory (see Chapter 6), two of the main determinants of motivation are *expectancy* (the perceived connection between effort and performance) and *instrumentality* (the perceived connection between performance and outcomes such as pay, praise, and career opportunities). Employees are likely to have high levels of expectancy, instrumentality, and, thus, motivation only if their managers can accurately appraise their performance.

According to equity theory, employees will be motivated to perform at a high level only if they perceive that they are receiving outcomes in proportion to their inputs or contributions. Accurately appraising performance is necessary for determining employees' contributions. From the perspective of equity theory, then, employees will be motivated to perform at a high level only if their performance can be and is accurately appraised.

Procedural justice theory suggests that the procedures that are used to appraise performance must be perceived as fair in order for motivation to be high. If employees think managers' appraisals are biased or that irrelevant information is used to evaluate performance, their motivation is likely to suffer. No matter which approach managers use to motivate employees, employees will be motivated to contribute their inputs to the organization and perform at a high level only if they think that their managers can and do appraise their performance accurately.

Because motivation and performance have so great an impact on organizational effectiveness, many researchers have focused on how to appraise performance in organizations. **Performance appraisal** has two overarching goals:

Performance appraisal
Evaluating performance to encourage employee motivation and performance and to provide information to be used in managerial decision making.

◆ To encourage high levels of employee motivation and performance
◆ To provide accurate information to be used in managerial decision making[37]

ENCOURAGING HIGH LEVELS OF MOTIVATION AND PERFORMANCE

As we mentioned earlier, all the approaches to motivation we discussed in Chapter 6 depend on the accurate assessment of an employee's performance. An accurate appraisal gives employees two important pieces of information: (1) the extent to which they are contributing the appropriate level of inputs to their jobs and the organization and (2) the extent to which they are focusing their inputs in the right direction on the right set of tasks. Essentially, performance appraisal gives employees *feedback* that contributes to intrinsic motivation.

A positive performance appraisal lets employees know that their current levels of motivation and performance are both adequate and appreciated. In turn, this knowledge makes employees feel valued and competent and motivates them to sustain their current levels of inputs and performance. Many employees consider a good performance appraisal an important outcome or reward in itself.

An inadequate performance appraisal tells employees that their performance is unacceptable and may signal that (1) they are not motivated to contribute sufficient inputs to the job, (2) they cannot contribute certain inputs that are required (perhaps because they lack certain key abilities), or (3) they are misdirecting their inputs, which in and of themselves are at an adequate level.

The case of Susan England, Ramona Michaels, and Marie Nouri, salespeople in the women's clothing department of a large department store, illustrates the important role of performance appraisals in encouraging high levels of motivation and performance. England, Michaels, and Nouri have just met individually with the department supervisor, Ann Rickels, to discuss their latest performance appraisals. The performances of all three sales clerks were assessed along four dimensions: quality of customer service, dollar amount of sales, efficient handling of transactions (for example, processing sales and returns quickly to avoid long lines), and housekeeping (returning clothing from dressing rooms to display racks and shelves and keeping the shelves and racks neat).

England received a very positive evaluation on all four dimensions. This positive feedback on her performance helps sustain England's motivation because it lets her know that her efforts are appropriate and appreciated.

Michaels received a positive evaluation on the customer service dimension but a negative evaluation on sales, efficiency, and housekeeping. Michaels tried very hard to be a good performer and provided exceptionally high levels of service to the customers she served. Rickels noted, however, that even though her shifts tended to be on the slow side in terms of customer traffic, there was often a long line of customers waiting to be served and a backlog of clothes in the dressing room to be restocked. Rickels judged Michaels's sales performance to be lackluster. She thought the problem might be that Michaels' attempts to help individual customers arrive at purchase decisions were consuming most of her time. Discussions with Michaels confirmed that this was the case. Michaels indicated that she was working as hard as she could, yet she knew that her performance was lacking on three of the four dimensions. She confessed to feeling frustrated that she couldn't get everything done even though she always seemed to be busy. Michaels's negative performance evaluation let her know that she was misdirecting her inputs. The time and effort she was spending to help customers were preventing her from performing her other job duties. Even though Michaels's performance evaluation was negative, it helped sustain her level of motivation (which had always been high) because it showed her how she could become a good performer.

Nouri received a negative evaluation on all four dimensions. Because Nouri was an experienced salesperson who had the necessary skills and abilities, the negative evaluation signaled Nouri and her manager that Nouri's level of motivation was unacceptable and in need of improvement.

PROVIDING INFORMATION FOR DECISION MAKING

As mentioned earlier, the second goal of performance appraisal is to provide information for managerial decision making. Part of Rickels's job as supervisor of the women's clothing department, for example, is training the salespeople in her area and making decisions about pay raises and promotions.

On the basis of the performance appraisals, Rickels decides that England should receive a pay raise and is most deserving of a promotion to the position of senior sales associate. The performance appraisals let Rickels know that Michaels needs some additional training in how to provide an "appropriate" level of customer service. Finally, Rickels decides to give some counseling to Nouri because of the negative evaluation of her performance. Rickels knows that Nouri is looking for another job and doesn't expect to remain with the department store for long. Rickels lets Nouri know that as long as she remains in the department, she must perform at an acceptable level to receive the outcomes she desires—pay, not having to work in the evenings, and good working relationships with the other members of the department.

In this example, performance appraisal is used to decide how to distribute outcomes such as pay and promotions equitably and how to improve the performance of employees who are not performing as well as they should be. Performance appraisal can also be useful for other aspects of decision making. For example, information from performance appraisals may allow managers to more effectively use the talents of employees, assign them specific tasks, and group them into high-performing work teams. Performance appraisals also can alert managers to problems in job design or shortcomings in an organization's approach to motivating employees and distributing outcomes.

Finally, performance appraisals provide employees and supervisors with career planning information. By helping managers identify an employee's strengths and weaknesses,[38] the performance appraisal sets the scene for meaningful discussions about the employee's career aspirations and how he or she can best progress toward those goals. The performance appraisal can also signal areas of improvement for the employee and the skills he or she needs to develop.

DEVELOPING A PERFORMANCE APPRAISAL SYSTEM

Managers can use the information gained from performance appraisal for two main purposes:

♦ *Developmental purposes* such as determining how to motivate an employee to perform at a high level, evaluating which of an employee's weaknesses can be corrected by additional training, and helping an employee formulate appropriate career goals

♦ *Evaluative, decision-making purposes* such as deciding whom to promote, how to set pay levels, and how to assign tasks to individual employees

Regardless of which purpose is most important to a manager, there are a number of choices he or she needs to make when it comes to developing an effective performance appraisal system. In this section, we discuss four of these choices: the extent to which formal and informal appraisals are to be used, what factors are to be evaluated, what methods of appraisal are to be used, and who is to appraise performance (see Figure 8.3).

Choice 1: The Mix of Formal and Informal Appraisals. When a performance appraisal is formal, the performance dimensions and the way employees are evaluated on them are determined in advance. IBM, GE, ExxonMobil, and most other large organizations use formal appraisals, which are usually conducted on a fixed schedule (such as every six months or once a year).[39] In a meeting between the employee whose performance is being appraised and the person doing the evaluating, the employee is given feedback on his or her performance. Feedback contributes to intrinsic motivation.

Sometimes employees want feedback on a more frequent basis than that provided by the formal system. Similarly, managers often want to use performance feedback to motivate subordinates on a day-to-day basis. If an employee is performing poorly, for example, a manager might not want to wait until the next 6- or 12-month performance review to try to rectify the problem. In these situations, an informal performance appraisal, in which managers and subordinates meet informally to discuss ongoing progress, can meet the needs of both employees and managers. Informal appraisals vary in form and content and range from a supervisor commending an employee for doing an outstanding job on a project to criticizing an employee for slacking off and missing a deadline.

Informal performance appraisals are beneficial. Because they often take place right after desired or undesired behavior occurs, employees immediately have a good idea of what they are doing right or wrong. As you learned in Chapter 5, employees will learn to perform desired behaviors and learn not to perform undesired behaviors only when it is clear to them that consequences such as praise (for a desired behavior) or a reprimand (for an undesired behavior) result from performing the behavior in question. The smaller an organization is, the more likely it is to rely exclusively on informal performance appraisals.

Ideally, an organization should rely on both formal and informal performance appraisals to motivate its members to perform at a high level and to make good decisions. The formal appraisal ensures that performance gets assessed periodically along the dimensions important to the organization. Because many managers and employees

Top Nordstrom salespeople, or "Nordies," as they're called, can earn as much as $80,000 annually. Nordstrom's doesn't have to persuade Nordies to sell hard. Instead, the company's computer systems offer up-to-the minute data on each person's sales, giving everyone instant feedback.

FIGURE 8.3

Choices in Developing an Effective Performance Appraisal System

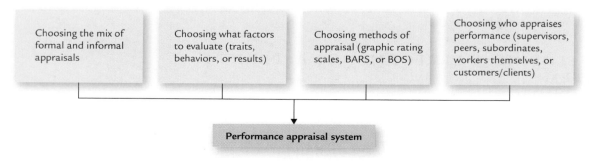

| Choosing the mix of formal and informal appraisals | Choosing what factors to evaluate (traits, behaviors, or results) | Choosing methods of appraisal (graphic rating scales, BARS, or BOS) | Choosing who appraises performance (supervisors, peers, subordinates, workers themselves, or customers/clients) |

Performance appraisal system

believe that formal performance appraisals should not yield any "surprises," however, ongoing informal appraisals should be part of an organization's performance appraisal system. An employee who is performing poorly should not have to wait six months or a year to find out about it; likewise, good performers should frequently be told that they are on the right track. Informal performance appraisals are important for motivation and performance on a day-to-day basis because they identify and rectify problems as they arise. Although managers in small organizations may not want to spend time and money on the development of a formal system, and managers of large organizations may spend less time than they should appraising performance informally, in most cases the motivational benefits of using formal and informal appraisals outweigh the costs.

Choice 2: What Factors to Evaluate. In addition to varying in degree of formality, performance appraisals can also vary in content. Traits, behaviors, and results are the three basic types of information that can be assessed.[40]

When traits are used to assess performance, personal characteristics (such as personality, skills, or abilities) that are deemed relevant to job performance are evaluated. A division manager of a large corporation may be evaluated on personal initiative, forecasting skills, and the ability to identify and promote managerial talent. A hotel reservations clerk may be evaluated on patience, politeness, and the ability to remain calm under pressure.

Using traits to assess performance has several disadvantages. First, recall from Chapter 2 that the *interaction* of individual differences such as personality traits or abilities and situational influences usually determines behavior. For this reason, traits or individual differences *alone* are often poor predictors of performance because the possible effects of the situation are not taken into account. Traits may be good indicators of what an employee is like but not very good indicators of what the employee actually does on the job.

Second, because traits do not necessarily have clear-cut relationships with actual behaviors performed on the job, employees and law courts involved in cases of potential employment discrimination are likely to view trait-based performance appraisals as unfair. To avoid the negative effects of perceived unfairness on employee motivation, as well as costly litigation, organizations should use trait-based approaches only when they can clearly demonstrate that the traits are *accurate* indicators of job performance.

Finally, the use of traits to assess performance does little to help motivate employees because it focuses on relatively enduring characteristics that cannot be changed in the short term, if at all. For example, telling a division manager that she lacks

Managers need to be able to accurately appraise the performance of their employees. Otherwise, worker motivation will suffer, no matter what incentives managers try to utilize.

initiative or a hotel reservations clerk that he is impatient does not give either employee much of a clue about how to do the job differently.

When *behaviors* are used to appraise performance, the focus is on the actual behaviors or actions an employee displays on the job: What an employee *does* is appraised, not what the employee is *like*. A division manager's behavior might be appraised in terms of the extent to which she has launched successful new products and scrapped unprofitable existing products. A hotel reservations clerk might be assessed on his ability to make accurate reservations accommodating guests' requests and the extent to which he satisfactorily explains unmet requests to guests.

Relying on behaviors to assess performance is especially useful because it lets employees know what they should do differently on the job. For example, telling a hotel reservations clerk that he should explain why a certain request can't be met and should answer guests' questions calmly and clearly regardless of how many people are in line waiting to check in gives the clerk a lot more direction than simply telling him he needs to be more patient, polite, and calm.

One potential problem with relying on behaviors to assess performance is that sometimes the *same* level of performance can be achieved through *different* behaviors. For example, two managers may be equally effective at launching new products and scrapping unprofitable ones, even though one reaches decisions through careful, long-term research and deliberation while the other relies more on gut instincts. To overcome this problem, performance appraisals sometimes focus on the results of behaviors rather than on the behaviors themselves.

When *results* are used to appraise performance, the focus is not on what employees *do* on the job but on the *effects* of their behaviors, or their actual output. The performance of a hotel clerk might be assessed in terms of the number of reservations handled per day and on guests' satisfaction ratings with their check-in experience. When there are many ways to achieve the same result, and the avenue the employee chooses is inconsequential, the result itself can be a useful way of assessing performance.

Just like the other two approaches, however, using results alone to assess performance has its disadvantages. Sometimes results are not under an employee's control: A division's profitability might suffer because sales were lost when foreign trade regulations changed unexpectedly. A day's worth of reservations might be lost because of a computer malfunction. Employees may also become so results oriented that they engage in unethical practices such as overcharging customers or failing to perform important organizational citizenship behaviors such as helping their co-workers.

Sometimes organizations can use both behaviors and results to appraise employee performance, as is the case at USAA, an insurance and investment management firm.[41] It is a good idea to appraise both behavior and results when both dimensions of performance are important for organizational effectiveness. In most sales jobs, for example, the results of a salesperson's behavior (number of items sold) are crucial, but the kinds of behaviors employed (treating customers courteously and politely and processing transactions efficiently) are often equally important. Because traits generally bear less directly on many kinds of jobs, they are not as useful in performance appraisals.

Choice 3: Methods of Appraisal. Regardless of the approach to performance appraisal (formal or informal) and the types of information assessed (traits, behaviors, or results), the measures managers use to appraise performance can be of two types: objective or subjective. **Objective measures** such as numerical counts are based on facts. They are used primarily when results are the focus of performance appraisal. The number of televisions a factory worker assembles in a day, the dollar value of the sales a salesperson makes in a week, the number of patients a physician treats in a day, and the return on capital, profit margin, and growth in income of a business are all objective measures of performance.

Objective measures
Measures that are based on facts.

you're the management expert

Promoting High-Quality Customer Service

Mark Milstein is the manager of an upscale sporting goods store. There are 15 full-time sales associates in the store who are paid, in part, based on commissions. The store is more expensive than its competitors in the local market it serves, but it also stocks higher-quality items that are difficult to find for the sports enthusiast. The store also prides itself on outstanding customer service. When customers enter the store, they are approached by a sales associate who helps them find what they are looking for and actually stays with them until they are ready to check out. The sales associates then escort their customers to the checkout counter where they pay for their purchases, and the cashier enters the ID numbers of the sales associates who helped them. Although sales associates are paid the minimum wage per hour, the commissions on their sales can double or triple their actual earnings. Milstein uses weekly sales per associate to appraise their performance and works with new sales associates and those with relatively low sales to improve their performance. Lately, however, Milstein has noticed a troubling trend. Fall sales are up compared to fall sales a year ago, but so are returns. In fact, taking returns into account, sales are actually down from a year ago. Milstein is concerned that perhaps the sales associates are encouraging customers to buy items they may not need or want; thus, the relatively high volume of returns. Given that high-quality, individualized customer service is the distinguishing competitive advantage of the store, Milstein is worried that his sales associates are perhaps too overzealous in their attempts to "perform" at a high level. And he wonders if the way he appraises their performance and compensates them might have something to do with it. Because you are an expert in OB, Milstein has come to you for help. Does he need to change the way he appraises the sales associates' performance to promote high-quality customer service?

Subjective measures are based on individuals' perceptions and can be used for appraisals based on traits, behaviors, and results. Because subjective measures are based on perceptions, they are vulnerable to many of the biases and problems that can distort person perception (discussed in Chapter 4). Because for many jobs there is no alternative to subjective appraisal measures, researchers and managers have focused considerable attention on the best way to define these measures.

Typically, when subjective measures are used, managers identify specific dimensions of performance (traits, behaviors, or results) that are important in a job. Then they develop some kind of rating scale or measure to assess an individual's standing on each dimension. Various rating scales can be used. Three of the most popular types are graphic rating scales, behaviorally anchored rating scales, and behavioral observation scales (see Figure 8.4). Graphic rating scales can be used to assess traits, behaviors, or results. Behaviorally anchored rating scales and behavioral observation scales focus exclusively on behaviors.

When a **graphic rating scale** is used, the rater—the person responsible for the performance appraisal—assesses the performance of an employee along one or more continua with clearly specified intervals. As indicated in Figure 8.4(a), for example, level of customer service may be assessed by rating a salesperson in terms of how courteous she or he is to customers on a five-point scale ranging from "very discourteous" to "very courteous." Graphic rating scales are popular in organizations because they are relatively easy to construct and use.[42] One potential disadvantage of these scales is that different raters may disagree about the meaning of the scale points. For example, what is "very discourteous" behavior to one rater may be only "discourteous" to another.

A **behaviorally anchored rating scale (BARS)** attempts to overcome that problem by carefully defining what each scale point means. Examples of specific work-related behaviors correspond to each scale point.[43] Figure 8.4(b) is an example of a

Subjective measures
Measures that are based on individual perceptions.

Graphic rating scale
A subjective measure on which performance is evaluated along a continuum.

Behaviorally anchored rating scale (BARS)
A subjective measure on which specific work-related behaviors are evaluated.

a. Graphic rating scale

How courteous is this salesperson toward customers?

Very discourteous	Discourteous	Neither discourteous nor courteous	Courteous	Very courteous

b. Behaviorally anchored rating scale

1	2	3	4	5	6	7
Ignores customers who need help	Keeps customers waiting unnecessarily	Fails to thank customers for purchases	Answers customers' questions promptly	Completes transactions in a timely manner	Greets customers pleasantly and offers assistance	Always tries sincerely to help customers locate items to suit their needs

c. Behavioral observation scale

	Almost never				Almost always
Sincerely thanks customers for purchases	1	2	3	4	5
Pleasantly greets customers	1	2	3	4	5
Answers customers' questions promptly	1	2	3	4	5

FIGURE 8.4

Examples of Subjective Measures of Performance

Behavioral observation scale (BOS) A subjective measure on which the frequency with which an employee performs a behavior is indicated.

BARS rating for a salesperson on the courtesy dimension. One potential problem with behaviorally anchored rating scales is that sometimes employees exhibit behaviors corresponding to more than one point on the scale. For example, a salesperson may thank customers for their purchases but otherwise tend to ignore them. BARS can also take a considerable amount of time and effort to develop and use.

A **behavioral observation scale (BOS)** overcomes the BARS problem of employees exhibiting behaviors corresponding to more than one scale point by not only describing specific behaviors (as does BARS) but also asking raters to indicate the frequency with which an employee performs the behaviors, as shown in Figure 8.4(c).[44] BOS, however, tends to be even more time consuming than BARS for raters to complete.

These are just a few of the types of scales that are available for subjective appraisals of performance. As we indicated, each scale has its advantages and disadvantages, and it is not clear at this point that any one type is better to use than another. BARS and BOS can be a lot more time consuming to develop and use than graphic rating scales, but they can be more beneficial for giving feedback to employees because they appraise more precise behaviors.

Choice 4: Who Appraises Performance? We have been assuming that supervisors are the people who appraise their subordinates' performance. This is usually a fair assumption. In most organizational settings, supervisors are responsible for performance appraisals because they are generally the most familiar with their subordinates' behavior and are responsible for motivating them to perform at acceptable levels. Sometimes, however, self-appraisals, peer appraisals, subordinate appraisals, customer/client appraisals, and multiple raters are also used to appraise performance.[45]

Self-appraisal may offer some advantages because an employee is likely to be familiar with his or her own level of performance. But most people consider themselves to be above average, and no one likes to think of him or herself as a poor performer, so a self-appraisal is likely to be inflated.

Peer appraisals are appraisals given by an employee's co-workers. Peers are often very familiar with performance levels, yet they may be reluctant to provide accurate appraisals. An employee may not want to give his friend a poor rating. An employee may not want to give her co-worker a high rating if she thinks it will make her look bad in comparison. Nevertheless, peer evaluations can be useful, especially when employees are members of a team, and the team's performance depends on each member being motivated to perform at a high level. Under these circumstances, team members are motivated to provide accurate peer ratings because the whole team suffers if one member performs poorly. By accurately appraising one another's performance, members can motivate each other to perform well and ensure everyone does their share of the work. It is for this reason that many professors who assign group projects have the members appraise each other's performance. Peer ratings help to ensure that no group member gets a "free ride" or takes advantage of the other hardworking students in the group.

Subordinate appraisals are appraisals given to a manager by the people he or she supervises. Subordinates rate the manager on, for example, his or her leadership behaviors. In order for subordinates to feel free to give an accurate appraisal (especially a negative one), it is often desirable for the appraisals to be anonymous so they need not fear retaliation from their supervisors. Many universities use anonymous student evaluations to appraise the quality of their teachers.

Customer/client appraisals are another source of performance information. Recall from Chapter 5 that some health maintenance organizations, such as U.S. Healthcare and AvMed–Sante Fe, evaluate their physicians' performance, in part, on the basis of scores they receive on patient surveys. These surveys measure whether the doctors are available for emergencies, provide clear explanations of treatments, and show concern for patients' needs.

The advantage of using other sources of information, such as customers, subordinates, or peers, is that each of these sources is likely to be familiar with a different dimension of an employee's performance. But because each source has considerable disadvantages if used exclusively, some organizations rely on 360-degree appraisals. In a **360-degree appraisal**, an employee's performance is evaluated by a variety of people who are in a position to evaluate the employee's performance. A 360-degree appraisal of a manager, for example, may include evaluations made by peers, subordinates, superiors, and clients or customers who are familiar with the manager's performance. The manager would then receive feedback based on evaluations from each of these sources. When 360-degree appraisals are used, managers have to be careful that each evaluator is familiar with the performance of the individual he or she is evaluating. Although 360-degree appraisals can be used for many different kinds of employees, they are most commonly used for managers.

The growing popularity of 360-degree appraisals attests to the need for more feedback in organizations. And who is in a better position to give employees feedback than all the different individuals they come into contact with on the job? An employee's peers, for example, may have a different perspective on his or her performance than the boss. A manager who lacks assertiveness when dealing with superiors may be too assertive and dictatorial when dealing with subordinates. Receiving feedback based on evaluations from these multiple sources has the potential to provide employees with a richer picture of their strengths, weaknesses, and areas for improvement.

The lending cooperative, Farm Credit Service Southwest, relies on 360-degree appraisals for about 50 percent of its annual performance appraisal process. Although the company's chief financial officer, John Barkell, found the process a bit intimidating, he did receive useful feedback that he has subsequently acted upon, including the need to communicate more with his subordinates. Barkell subsequently instituted weekly meetings with his staff to open lines of communication and answer questions.[46]

360-degree appraisal A performance appraisal in which an employee's performance is evaluated by a number of people who are in a position to evaluate the employee's performance such as peers, superiors, subordinates, and customers or clients.

At Public Service Electric & Gas in Newark, New Jersey, manager Gordon Smouther's 360-degree appraisal indicated he was too controlling and defensive, which resulted in him dismissing other people's ideas without giving them a chance. As a result of the appraisal, Smouther and his boss put together a plan that included his taking a course at a center specializing in creative leadership and giving him private lessons with an executive coach. Smouther's ratings improved dramatically.[47]

Experiences such as these point to the advantages of 360-degree appraisals—they can provide managers and other employees with valuable feedback that they can use to improve their performance. However, there are also certain potential problems with 360-degree appraisals. Some managers fear that 360-degree appraisals might turn into popularity contests, with managers who are well liked being rated more highly than those who may be less popular but produce better results. Others fear that managers will be reluctant to make unpopular decisions or difficult choices because they may have a negative effect on how their subordinates evaluate them. On the one hand, if appraisals are anonymous, disgruntled subordinates may seek revenge by giving their bosses negative evaluations. On the other hand, some bosses coach their subordinates and sometimes even threaten them to get positive ratings.[48]

A manager at Citibank indicated that he received a very negative appraisal from a subordinate that was almost like a personal attack; he was pretty sure it came from a poor performer.[49] At Baxter International, although employees in the information technology unit were very familiar with each other's performance, they were reluctant to provide any negative evaluations and gave each other positive ratings because they knew the ratings were being used for pay raise decisions and the evaluations were not anonymous. Baxter decided to continue using the peer evaluations but more for developmental purposes rather than decision making.[50]

Clearly, 360-degree appraisals have both advantages and disadvantages. In order to reap the benefits of 360-degree appraisals, research suggests the appraisals should focus on behaviors rather than traits or results and that much care be taken to ensure appropriate raters are chosen. The research also suggests that appraisals are more likely to be honest when they are anonymous, and raters should receive training in how to use the rating form.[51]

Regardless of whether a formal 360-degree appraisal system is in place, organizations need to be careful that managers and all employees are accurately appraised by individuals who are knowledgeable about their behavior. Subordinates can be particularly knowledgeable about their supervisor's behaviors but sometimes lack the means to communicate this knowledge in ways that can motivate their supervisors to improve. The Web site ImproveNow.com provides a potential solution to this problem.[52] The site contains a 60-item questionnaire subordinates can complete to appraise the performance of their supervisors. After multiple subordinates complete the form independently online, the results are tabulated, and the supervisor receives specific feedback about how he or she is doing in different areas. Those areas might include standing up for their subordinates and being supportive, rewarding them, or having a good sense of what the organization or work group should strive for in the future.[53]

Lee Burnley and eight of her co-workers at Alliance Funding, a mortgage lending unit of Superior Bank FSB located in Orangeburg, New Jersey, completed the appraisals online for their supervisor Sonia Russomanno. Russomanno received an overall score of B on the appraisal, based on specific dimensions in the rating form. Her reaction? At first, she was grateful that her rating wasn't worse but then let down that it wasn't better. More importantly, she realized the value of getting honest feedback from her subordinates to help her improve her performance. For example, as a result of the feedback she received, Russomanno realized that she needs to work on using rewards to motivate her subordinates. She plans to have her subordinates evaluate her again at the ImproveNow.com Web site in the future to see how she is doing.[54]

TABLE 8 1

Problems and Biases in Person Perception That May Result in Inaccurate Performance Appraisals

Problem or Bias	Description	Example of Problem or Bias Leading to an Inaccurate Performance Appraisal
Stereotypes	A type of schema (abstract knowledge structure stored in memory) built around some distinguishing, often highly visible characteristic such as race, gender, or age.	A 35-year-old supervisor gives a 60-year-old engineer a negative performance appraisal that indicates that the engineer is slow and unwilling to learn new techniques although this is not true.
Primacy effect	The initial pieces of information that people have about a person have an inordinately large effect on how that person is perceived.	A subordinate who made a good first impression on his supervisor receives a better performance appraisal than he deserves.
Contrast effect	People's perceptions of a person are influenced by their perception of others in an organization.	A subordinate's average level of performance is appraised more harshly than it should be by her supervisor because all the subordinate's co-workers are top performers.
Halo effect	People's general impressions of a person influence their perceptions on specific dimensions.	A subordinate who has made a good overall impression on a supervisor is appraised as performing high-quality work and always meeting deadlines although this is not true.
Similar-to-me effect	People perceive others who are similar to themselves more positively than they perceive those who are dissimilar.	A supervisor gives a subordinate who is similar to her a more positive performance appraisal than the subordinate deserves.
Harshness, leniency, and average tendency biases	When rating their subordinates' performance, some supervisors tend to be overly harsh, some overly lenient. Others tend to rate everyone as about average.	An exceptionally high-performing secretary receives a mediocre performance appraisal because his supervisor is overly harsh in rating everyone.
Knowledge-of-predictor bias	Perceptions of a person are influenced by knowing the person's standing on a predictor of performance.	A computer programmer who scored highly on cognitive and numerical ability tests used to hire programmers in an organization receives a more positive performance appraisal than she deserves.

POTENTIAL PROBLEMS IN SUBJECTIVE PERFORMANCE APPRAISAL

Recall from Chapter 4 that a number of problems and biases can result in inaccurate perceptions of other people in an organization. These problems and biases (recapped in Table 8.1) can be particularly troublesome for subjective performance appraisals. Awareness of these perception problems can help prevent these problems and biases from leading to an inaccurate appraisal.

Pay and the Employment Relation

The accurate assessment of performance is central to the goals of motivating employees to perform at acceptable levels and improving the effectiveness of managerial decision making. One area of decision making that often has profound effects on the motivation of all members of an organization—managers and employees alike—is the distribution of outcomes, such as pay, benefits, vacations, perks, promotions and other career opportunities, job titles, offices, and privileges. In this section, we focus on the outcome that is one of the most powerful of all motivation tools: pay. Pay can be used not only to motivate people to perform highly but also to motivate them to join and remain with an organization. Thus, pay is a central aspect of psychological contracts and a key component of the exchange relationship between employees and an organization.

The principles of operant conditioning discussed in Chapter 5 and all of the approaches to motivation covered in Chapter 6 suggest that outcomes should be distributed to employees *contingent* on their performing desired organizational behaviors:

♦ Operant conditioning theory suggests that to encourage the learning of desired organizational behaviors, positive reinforcers or rewards should be distributed to employees contingent on performance.

♦ Need theory suggests that when pay is contingent on performance, employees are motivated to perform because doing so will help satisfy their needs.

♦ Expectancy theory takes into account the fact that pay is an outcome with high valence (highly desirable) for most employees and that instrumentality (the association between performance and outcomes) must be high for motivation to be high.

♦ Equity theory indicates that outcomes (pay) should be distributed in proportion to inputs (performance).

♦ Procedural justice theory suggests that the methods used to evaluate performance and distribute pay need to be fair.

From a learning and motivational perspective, the message is clear: Whenever possible, pay should be based on performance.[55]

MERIT PAY PLANS

Merit pay plan A plan that bases pay on performance.

A plan that bases pay on performance is often called a **merit pay plan**.[56] When pay is not based on merit, it might be based on the particular job an employee has in an organization or on an employee's tenure in the organization. Merit pay, however, is likely to be much more motivational than pay that is not based on performance.

Merit pay plans tend to be used most heavily at the upper levels in organizations,[57] but basing pay on performance has been shown to be effective for employees at lower levels in an organization's hierarchy as well. Many organizations are increasingly using merit pay to attract, motivate, and retain employees. Manufacturing companies, accounting firms, law offices, and investment banks have all stepped up their use of merit pay to motivate employees at all levels.[58]

Merit pay is an important motivation tool not only in the United States but in many other countries as well. In 1979, only 8 percent of companies in Great Britain used some form of merit pay, but in 1994, 75 percent of British companies used merit pay to motivate their members. On average, 40 percent of an upper manager's pay in Britain is based on performance. Merit pay is also increasing in popularity in Japan. Honda, for example, based 40 percent of its managers' pay on performance in 1992, and in 1994 their pay totally depended on their performance levels. Similarly, at Nissan, 85 percent of managers' salaries are based on their performance levels. Merit pay also is increasing in popularity in Germany, and even the pay of some European government employees or civil servants (such as those in Britain) is based in part on their performance levels.[59]

SHOULD MERIT PAY BE BASED ON INDIVIDUAL, GROUP, OR ORGANIZATIONAL PERFORMANCE?

One of the most important choices managers face in designing an effective merit pay plan is whether to base merit pay on individual, group, or organizational performance. The following guidelines, based on the theories of learning and motivation discussed in previous chapters, can be used to make this choice:

1. When individual performance can be accurately assessed (for example, the number of cars a salesperson sells, the number of insurance policies an insurance agent writes, a lawyer's billable hours), the maximum motivational impact is obtained from basing pay on individual performance.[60]

2. When employees are highly interdependent—when what one employee does affects the work of others—and individual performance levels cannot be accurately assessed, an individual-based pay-for-performance plan is not a viable option. In this case, managers can implement a group or organization-level pay-for-performance plan. Under such a system, employees' pay levels depend on how well their group or the organization as a whole performs. It is impossible, for example, to accurately assess the performance of individual members of a group of carpenters who jointly design and construct large, elaborate pieces of custom furniture. Together they produce pieces of furniture that none of them could construct alone.

3. When organizational effectiveness depends on individuals working together, cooperating with each other, and helping each other out, group- or organization-based pay-for-performance plans may be more appropriate than individual-based plans.[61] When a team of research scientists works together in a laboratory to try to come up with a cure for a disease such as AIDS, for example, it is essential for group members to share their insights and findings with each other and build upon each other's findings.

Sometimes it is possible to combine elements of an individual and group or companywide plan to get the benefits of both. Lincoln Electric, for example, uses a combination of individual- and organization-based plans.[62] Each year, Lincoln Electric establishes a bonus fund, the size of which depends on the whole organization's performance that year. Money from the bonus fund is then distributed to employees on the basis of their individual levels of performance. Lincoln Electric employees are motivated to cooperate and help each other because when the firm as a whole performs well, everybody benefits by receiving a larger bonus at year-end. Employees are also motivated to perform at a high level individually not only because their individual performance determines their share of the fund but also because they are paid on piece-rate basis, which is discussed next.

SHOULD MERIT PAY BE IN THE FORM OF A SALARY INCREASE OR A BONUS?

There are two major ways to distribute merit pay: salary increases and bonuses. When salary increases are used, individual salaries are increased by a certain amount based on performance. When bonuses are used, individuals receive a lump-sum amount (in addition to their regular salary) based on performance. Bonus plans such as the one used by Lincoln Electric tend to have a greater impact on motivation than do salary increase plans, for three reasons.

First, an individual's current salary level is based on performance levels, cost-of-living increases, and so on, from the day the person started working in the organization; thus, the absolute level of one's salary is based largely on factors not related to current performance. Increases in salary levels based on current performance tend to be small (for example, 6 percent) in comparison to total salary amounts. Second, current salary increases may be only partially based on performance. This occurs when, for example, across-the-board, cost-of-living raises are given to all employees. Third, organizations rarely cut salaries, so salary levels across employees tend to vary less than performance levels. Bonus plans overcome some of the limitations of salary increases because a bonus can be tied directly and exclusively to performance and because the motivational effect of a bonus is not mitigated by the other factors mentioned previously. Bonuses can vary considerably from time period to time period and from employee to employee, depending on performance levels.[63] When organizations want all employees to cooperate and work together for an organizational objective, bonuses can be based on organizational performance, as indicated in the accompanying Managing Ethically feature.

managing ethically

Rewarding Employees and Protecting the Environment: A Winning Combination at Dofasco

Dofasco, Inc., is a steel company based in Hamilton, Ontario, that seems to have a magic formula. Its employees are satisfied, it has outperformed many of its competitors, and it is also socially responsibile and strives to protect the environment.[64] As former CEO John Mayberry puts it, "How do you get happy shareholders? Start with satisfied customers. How do you get satisfied customers? Start with happy employees. How do you please employees? Try not to wreck the community they live in."[65] Dofasco cares about the effects its operations have on society and the environment, and it has been on the Dow Jones Sustainability Index for five years in a row. Firms on this index are leaders in their industries in terms of three key areas: protecting the environment, protecting the well-being of people, and profitability.[66]

Each of DoFasco, Inc.'s 7,400 skilled employees is part of a proactive team, responsible for suggesting better ways of working. Turnover at the Canadian steelmaking company is less than one percent, and productivity has increased 50 per cent since 1990. That's about twice the rate of the Canadian manufacturing sector as a whole.

Although protecting the environment is an ethical imperative for Dofasco, it has also contributed to its profitability and ability to provide its employees with hefty bonuses. Over the past 10 years, Dofasco has reduced the amount of energy it consumes to make a ton of steel by over 20 percent.[67] Moreover, the company has been able to improve quality as well save energy by finding new ways to use its electric furnaces.

Dofasco's efforts to promote sustainability not only benefit the environment but also its customers and employees. In terms of the latter, employees receive an annual bonus of 14 percent of Dofasco's pretax income. The bonus pool is divided equally among its 8,500 employees to motivate them to work together for the good of the company, its customers, the environment, and society.[68]

Employees are proud of Dofasco's organizational objectives, and organizational identification (see Chapter 7) among its employees runs high.[69] One indication of this is the fact that Dofasco has an exceptionally low turnover rate of 7 percent. The company relies on its employees to achieve its objectives. Mayberry sums it up this way: "People can make a phenomenal difference if you can tap into them, if you stop telling them to come to work, put their brains in a box, and do whatever the supervisor says."[70] Clearly, Dofasco does seem to have a winning combination.[71]

EXAMPLES OF MERIT PAY PLANS

Two clear examples of individual-based merit pay plans are piece-rate pay and commission pay. In a *piece-rate pay plan*, an employee is paid for each unit he or she produces, as in the case of a tailor who is paid for each piece of clothing he sews or alters, or a factory worker who is paid for each television she assembles. With commission pay, often used in sales positions, salaries are a percentage of sales. Salary levels in *full commission plans* fluctuate directly in proportion to sales that are made. Salary levels in a *partial commission plan* consist of fixed salaries plus an amount that varies with sales levels. The maximum motivational impact is obtained when pay is based solely on performance, as in a full commission plan. Employees operating under such a plan, however, are not likely to develop any kind of team spirit.

When pay is based solely on individual performance, employees are motivated to perform at a high level, and organizations may be able to attract and retain top performers because they will receive maximum levels of pay. But such plans can also cause employees to adopt a highly individualized approach to their jobs and not work together as a team.

Pay plans that are linked strictly to organizational performance are often called *gain-sharing plans*. Employees in organizations that have these kinds of plans are given a certain share of the profits that the organization makes or a certain share of the expenses that are saved during a specified time period. Gain sharing is likely to encourage camaraderie and a team spirit among employees because all of the organization's members stand to benefit if it does well. But, because pay is based on organizational rather than on individual performance, each individual may not be so motivated to perform at the high level he or she would have achieved under a pay plan based on individual merit.

One kind of gain-sharing plan is the *Scanlon plan*, developed by Joseph Scanlon, a union leader at a steel and tin plant in the 1920s.[72] The Scanlon plan focuses on reducing costs. Departmental and organizationwide committees are established to evaluate and implement cost-saving suggestions provided by employees. Employees are motivated to make suggestions, participate on the committees, and help implement the suggestions because they get a portion of the cost savings realized.

Another kind of gain-sharing pay plan is *profit sharing*. Employees participating in profit-sharing plans receive a certain share of an organization's profits. Approximately 16 percent of employees in medium and large companies and 25 percent of employees in small firms receive some form of profit sharing. Rutgers University economist Douglas

Kruse estimates that productivity tends to increase from 3 to 5 percent when companies institute profit sharing. Profit-sharing plans that give employees their share of profits in cash tend to be more successful than programs that use some sort of deferred payment (such as contributing employees' shares of profits to their retirement funds).[73] If an organization has a bad year, then no money may be available for profit sharing regardless of individual or group performance levels.

THE ETHICS OF PAY DIFFERENTIALS AND COMPARABLE WORTH

It is well established that women earn less money than men. Women earn approximately 74 cents for every dollar earned by men.[74] Some of the gender gap in rates of pay may be due to overt discrimination or to the fact that some men have more experience or better qualifications.[75] But there is another reason for these discrepancies in pay. This subtle form of discrimination works as follows: Jobs that women have traditionally held (as nurses, teachers, secretaries, librarians, and so forth) have lower pay rates than jobs that men have traditionally held (as carpenters, managers, doctors, and construction workers, for example), even though the jobs require similar skill levels, and the organization values them equally.

Pay differentials between men and women have the potential to adversely affect the motivation of high-performing women who perceive they are not receiving as much pay as the job is worth. From the perspective of equity theory, women who perceive themselves as contributing levels of inputs equivalent to those of their male counterparts but receiving lower levels of outcomes (in particular, pay) may be motivated to reduce their inputs (perhaps by exerting less effort) to restore equity. More critical than their effects on motivation, pay differentials based on gender, age, race, ethnic background, or any other nonperformance characteristic are unethical.

Comparable worth The idea that jobs of equivalent value to an organization should carry the same pay rates regardless of differences in the work and the personal characteristics of the employee.

The principle of **comparable worth** suggests that jobs of equivalent value to an organization should carry the same pay rates regardless of differences in the nature of the work itself and the personal characteristics of the people performing the work.[76] Pay rates should be determined by factors such as effort, skill, and job responsibility— not by the type of person who usually performs the job. The gender, race, or ethnic background of jobholders is an irrelevant input that managers should not consider when they establish pay rates for different positions. When pay rates are determined by comparable worth, it is more likely that all members of an organization will be motivated to perform at a high level because they are more likely to perceive that they are being paid on an equitable basis.

Although comparable worth makes a lot of sense in principle, it has been hard to put into practice. Organizations have resisted basing salaries on comparable worth because pay levels for some jobs would have to be raised (organizations rarely lower pay rates). On a more fundamental level, however, determining what the value or worth of a job is to an organization and comparing this value to that of other very different types of jobs is difficult. Such comparisons are often value laden and the source of considerable disagreement. Even so, comparable worth is an ethical issue that managers need to be aware of and a goal worth striving for.

Another pay differential that has been receiving increasing attention is the difference between the pay received by those at the very top of an organization and the many employees under them. Today, the average CEO earns 400 times what the average hourly worker earns.[77] While some employees are actually seeing their pay being cut and raises eliminated, CEOs, on the other hand, seem to be earning ever more money.[78] For example, the median compensation of CEOs of large public companies increased by 32 percent from 2000 to 2002.[79] During 2002, a year in which many companies' stock prices plummeted, CEOs continued to earn mammoth salaries that could have been used to pay hundreds of employees lower down in the corporate hierarchy.[80] At companies such as Apple Computer, Honeywell, Cisco Systems, Lucent Technologies, and Sun Microsystems, CEO total compensation ranged from over $30 million to over $75 million.[81] By contrast, the average raises received by employees in large public companies were the smallest in 25 years, according to a study by Hewitt Associates. Deloitte Consulting, for example, recently cuts its employees' pay by 8 percent.[82] Huge pay differentials between those at the top of the corporate hierarchy and those lower down raise concerns about distributive justice, especially when layoffs take place, salaries are cut, or raises are minimal.

Careers

There are outcomes in addition to pay that are part of many employees' psychological contracts and central to their exchange relationship with their employers. One of these outcomes, career opportunities, is related not just to the specific job a person holds today but also to the jobs a person expects to perform or advance to over the course of his or her entire career.

Career opportunities often include things such as being in a fast-track management program or getting a promotion, but they can include other specific career-related outcomes such as having the opportunity to do the kind of work you really want to do, receiving career-relevant experiences and training, and having exposure to people who can help you advance your own career. Many of these career opportunities affect intrinsic motivation levels because they help people pursue the kind of work they enjoy.

Sometimes it is possible to give employees the chance to do what they love, even when they are performing a job that is not directly related to their career aspirations. At a restaurant called Applause in New York City, many aspiring singers and actors take what they hope are temporary jobs waiting tables to support themselves because Applause allows waiters and waitresses to sing and entertain customers while serving meals. The restaurant, thus, gives aspiring singers and actors the chance to do what they love, to gain experience performing in front of a live audience, and meet customers who might be talent scouts, directors, and producers who, of course, can further their careers.

Both organizations and individual employees should engage in career management. When careers are effectively managed, organizations make the best use of their members' skills and abilities, and employees are motivated to perform at a high level and tend to be satisfied with their jobs, all of which help the organization achieve its goals. To use career opportunities as a motivational tool, managers must understand what careers are, how people progress through them, and how they can be managed by both employees and organizations.

THE NATURE OF CAREERS

A **career** can be defined as the sum of work-related experiences throughout one's lifetime.[83] A career includes the number and types of jobs a person has had as well as the different organizations a person has worked for.

Career The sum of work-related experiences throughout a person's lifetime.

Why are individuals concerned about their careers? A career can have major effects on a person's economic and psychological well-being. At a basic economic level, work provides most people in modern society with the income they need to support themselves and their loved ones and pursue their personal interests such as their hobbies and leisure activities. From this economic perspective, career opportunities are an important source of *extrinsic motivation* for employees.[84] As a source of psychological well-being, work can provide personal fulfillment and give a sense of meaning and purpose to people's lives. From this psychological perspective, career opportunities are an important source of *intrinsic motivation*.

Why are organizations concerned with the careers of their members? Effectively managing careers helps an organization motivate its members to achieve individual and organizational goals and perform at a high level. Effective career management in an organization means that there will be well-qualified employees at all levels who can assume more responsible positions as needed to help the organization achieve its goals. Organizations can help motivate their members through career management by helping them develop the knowledge, skills, abilities, and other inputs needed for high levels of performance[85] and by rewarding high performers with career opportunities such as valuable experience and training, choice job assignments, and promotions.

TYPES OF CAREERS

Although every individual's career is unique, careers fall into four general categories: steady-state careers, linear careers, spiral careers, and transitory careers.[86]

Steady-State Careers. A steady-state career reflects a one-time commitment to a certain kind of job that is maintained throughout one's working life.[87] Employees with steady-state careers can become very skilled at, and intrinsically motivated by, the work they do and often see themselves as experts. A family doctor who sets up a medical practice in her hometown when she finishes her medical training and keeps the same practice throughout her career until she retires at age 70 has a steady-state career.

Linear Careers. In a linear career, a person progresses through a sequence of jobs, and each job entails progress over the prior one in terms of responsibility, skills needed, level in the hierarchy of an organization, and so on.[88] Employees can stay with the same organization or move from company to company as they pursue linear careers. Edwin L. Artzt, former chairman of Procter & Gamble, started working for Procter & Gamble over 40 years ago in a low-level job and worked his way up the corporate ladder through each of the corporate divisions to assume the top position.[89]

Spiral Careers. In a spiral career, a person holds different types of jobs that build on each other but tend to be fundamentally different.[90] An associate professor of management with a spiral career leaves university teaching and research to head up the human resources department at a large company, then, after working at that job for 10 years, leaves to start a consulting company.

Transitory Careers. A person with a transitory career changes jobs frequently, and each job is different from the one before it.[91] After graduating from college, Paul Jones worked as the manager of a hardware store for two years, then worked in a bank for a year, and is currently training to become a police officer.

CAREER STAGES

Although each person's career is unique, there are certain career stages that at least some people seem to progress through. And even if a person does not progress through each stage, he or she experiences some subset of the stages. Each stage is associated with challenges to be met and tasks to be tackled. Researchers disagree about the exact number of career stages; here, we discuss five stages that are useful to understand a person's career, even if each of these stages is not experienced to the same extent (see Figure 8.5).[92]

More often than not, these career stages are experienced in different organizations. As we have said, given the high levels of uncertainty in the environment, layoffs, outsourcing, and increased global competition, many people's psychological contracts do not include expectations of a lifelong career with a single organization or even a relatively long-term relationship. The **boundaryless career** captures the idea that careers

Dr. Novella Clevenger has taught accounting to students at Washburn University in Topeka, Kan., for 16 years. Clevenger, who has no plans to retire, is an example of someone whose career is in a steady-state.

Boundaryless career A career that is not tied to a single organization and in which a person has a variety of kinds of work experiences in different organizations.

FIGURE 8.5
Career Stages

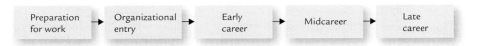

are not tied to (or bound to) a single organization and that people will have a variety of work experiences in different organizations over the course of their careers.[93] Boundaryless careers are becoming increasingly prevalent in the United States.[94]

Preparation for Work. During the first stage, individuals must decide what kind of career they want and learn what qualifications and experiences they need to obtain a good career-starting job.[95] Critical tasks faced in the preparation stage involve acquiring the necessary knowledge, skills, education, and training either from formal classroom education or from on-the-job apprenticeships or other programs.

Personality, ability, attitudes, and values are among the factors that affect initial career choice.[96] Individuals who are high on the Big Five dimension of extroversion (see Chapter 2), for example, may tend to gravitate toward careers such as sales that require a lot of social interaction with others. Individuals with exceptional numerical abilities may lean toward a career in engineering. A person who has extrinsic work values (Chapter 3) and values work for its consequences may choose a law career earning him or her a high income. By contrast a person who has intrinsic work values and values work for its own sake may choose a nursing career leading to feelings of personal accomplishment and fulfillment.

A recent study by researchers Jacquelynne Eccles and Mina Vida sought to understand why young men and women who desired science careers tended to concentrate on different subjects, with women being more likely to focus on the biological sciences (including social science, environmental science, and medicine) rather than mathematically based sciences such as physics, engineering, astronomy, and information technology.[97] Evidently, it seems that the young women in the study were more people oriented and saw areas such as medicine as more social and important for society. Young men who were more people oriented also were more likely to go into the biological sciences but, on the whole, young men were more interested in the mathematical sciences than young women.[98] Eccles suggests that educators need to focus more on communicating to young people how different kinds of careers contribute to society. For example, engineers design many things that help people ranging from safe, functional buildings, to wheelchairs and other medical equipment that improve the quality of life for the disabled.[99] By having more information about how different jobs and careers contribute to society and help people, young women and men will be able to make more informed career choices.

Organizational Entry. During the second stage, people try to find a job that will be a good start to their chosen career. People in the entry stage find out as much as they can about potential jobs and organizations from various sources, including business newspapers and magazines, college placement offices and career/job fairs, company-sponsored information and seminars, and personal contacts.

After job seekers have gathered this information, they want to become jobholders. Getting an interview with an organization you're interested in is sometimes as simple as signing up with a company representative visiting on campus or getting "the friend of a friend" to put in a good word for you with his wife, who is a manager at the company.

After an interview is scheduled, it is crucial to make the most of it. Finding out as much as possible about the company, doing practice interviews, and thinking of interesting questions to ask the interviewer and good answers to frequently asked questions (for example, "Where do you see yourself in five years?" or "Why do you want to be an accountant?") are things job applicants can do to increase their prospects. In Chapter 4, we discussed many of the factors that affect perception and, thus, both how interviewers perceive job applicants and how job applicants can actively influence the perception process through impression management. We also explained how perception is distorted by biases such as the primacy effect, which leads interviewers to make an initial decision about someone in the first few minutes of the interview and then spend the rest of the interview selectively hearing and seeing things that confirm that initial impression. In an interview, then, job applicants must make a good impression from the minute they walk in the door.

In addition to selling themselves to an organization, applicants also need to find out as much information as they can about the job they are seeking, their career prospects with the organization, and the organization as a whole to make a good choice. Sometimes what people think a job or an organization will be like is very different from what they actually experience on the job. A new assistant to the division president might find, to her dismay, that her job is really a secretarial position and not the start to the management career she envisions.

Organizations should provide applicants with accurate information about the jobs they apply for, their career prospects, and the organization as a whole. Sometimes, in an effort to attract outstanding applicants who might have several job offers, members of an organization might be tempted to paint a rosy picture of what their organization has to offer. This practice can lead new hires to experience disappointment and negative attitudes, both of which might prompt them to quit. Research has found that organizations that disseminate realistic job information can reduce turnover.[100]

Early Career. The early career stage starts once a person has obtained a job in a chosen career. There are two distinct steps in this stage. The first step is *establishment*, during which newcomers are motivated to learn how to perform their jobs, what is expected of them, and more generally how to fit in (see Chapter 10).[101] The second step is *achievement*.[102] After newcomers have mastered their jobs and "know" the organization, they are motivated to accomplish something worthwhile and make a significant contribution to the organization. Achievement can mean different things to different people. For some, achievement is synonymous with moving up the corporate ladder; for others, it can mean becoming an expert in a certain area or devising creative solutions to difficult problems.

Organizations can do several things to help ensure members are motivated to achieve individual, group, and organizational goals. In Chapters 6 and 7, we discussed how organizations motivate members to perform at a high level and how jobs should ideally be designed. In addition, managers need to convince employees that they are able to achieve difficult goals (have high expectancy) and will receive the outcomes they desire when they do (have high instrumentality).

According to equity theory, managers must also distribute outcomes (pay, status, choice job assignments, promotions, and other career opportunities) to employees based on their inputs to the organization (ability, education, experience, time, and effort). Earlier in this chapter, we saw the important role that performance appraisals can play by providing employees with feedback to motivate them. Accurate performance appraisals help employees assess their own levels of achievement, determine how to improve in the future, and more generally assess their career progress.

In addition to identifying where and how they can make the most valuable contributions to an organization, individuals can advance their careers during the achievement step by seeking out a mentor (see Chapter 4) and setting their own career goals. Getting help from a mentor has been found to increase levels of pay and pay satisfaction and the rate of promotion for protégés.[103] Although it has commonly been assumed that mentors seek out protégés, protégés can and do seek out mentors. One recent study found that employees who had an internal locus of control, were high on self-monitoring, and were low on negative affectivity (see Chapter 2) were most likely to seek out and obtain help from a mentor. Moreover, the mentoring clearly benefited the employees in terms of salary levels and the extent to which the protégés felt good about their accomplishments and the progress they were making.[104]

Some organizations have formal mentoring programs that assign experienced members to newcomers. Often, however, mentoring is an informal process in which mentors and protégés seek each other out because of some common interest or bond. One researcher who interviewed successful working women found that 77 percent of them had received help from a mentor. Jennie Coakley received extensive help from her mentor, Ronnie Andros, when she began teaching the fifth grade at Columbia Elementary School in Fairfax County, Virginia. Andros helped Coakley cope with many of the challenges new teachers face. For example, Andros clarified official rules and procedures, introduced Coakley to important school administrators, and gave Andros tips about how to obtain textbooks.

Mentors are often in the same organizations as their protégés, but sometimes protégés can obtain help from mentors outside their organizations. For example, Lee Cooke was the office manager of the American Automobile Association in Washington, DC, when he met his mentor at a local Rotary Club meeting. Lee's mentor was an orchid breeder, and their relationship eventually led Lee to land a position with the American Orchid Society in West Palm Beach, Florida.[105]

In addition to seeking out the help of a mentor, employees can also advance their careers by formulating career goals. In Chapter 7, we said that goals are useful motivational tools because they help to focus employees' attention and effort in the right direction. Career goals are the experiences, positions, or jobs that employees would like to have in the course of their careers.[106] **Career goals** are good guides for achievement because they help employees decide what activities to concentrate on to advance their careers.

Career goals The experiences, positions, or jobs that employees would like to have in the course of their careers.

Midcareer. Employees in the midcareer stage have generally been in the workforce between 20 and 35 years and face the challenge of remaining productive. Many employees achieve the height of career success during the midcareer stage, as exemplified by current or one-time CEOs Scott McNealy of Sun Microsystems, Steve Jobs of Apple Computer; John Chambers of Cisco Systems, Carly Fiorina of Hewlett Packard, and Pat Russo of Lucent Technologies. Many other midcareer employees, however, need to come to terms with career plateaus, obsolescence, and major career changes.

A person is said to have reached a **career plateau** when the chances of being promoted within his or her own organization or another organization are slim.[107] There are several reasons why employees reach a career plateau. First, because of the hierarchical nature of most organizations, there are fewer and fewer positions to be promoted into as employees advance. Second, competition for upper-level positions in organizations is intense, and the number of these positions has been reduced because of downsizing.[108] Third, if some employees delay retirement past the traditional age of 65, their positions do not open up for midcareer employees to assume.[109] Finally, changes in technology or the lack of important new skills and abilities may limit the extent to which employees can advance in organizations.[110]

Career plateau A position from which the chances of obtaining a promotion or a job with more responsibility become very small.

How can organizations help "plateaued" employees remain satisfied, motivated, and productive? Encouraging lateral moves and job rotation is often an effective means of keeping plateaued employees motivated when they no longer have the prospect of a major promotion to work toward. Chevron is one of many organizations using this strategy.[111] At the SAS Institute (see the opening case for Chapter 6), all employees are encouraged and have the opportunity to make lateral moves and learn new skills.[112]

What steps can plateaued employees take to remain valuable, motivated members of the organization who are satisfied with their jobs? They might take on the role of mentor. They might become "good citizens" of their organizations by suggesting changes, improvements, and generally engaging in the various forms of organizational citizenship behavior discussed in Chapter 3. Employees in early career stages often concentrate on activities that advance their careers and do not take the time to do things that help the organization as a whole. Plateaued employees, who often have a good understanding of their organization, are sometimes in an especially good position to help start a major companywide recycling program, establish an outreach program to encourage members of an organization to volunteer time to community causes, or organize social activities such as company picnics, for example.

Employees face obsolescence when their knowledge and skills become outmoded and prevent them from effectively performing their organizational roles. Obsolescence is caused by changes in technology or in an organization's competitive environment that alter how jobs are performed. Organizations can help prevent obsolescence by providing their members with additional training whenever possible and allowing employees time off from work to take courses in their fields to keep them up-to-date. Whenever possible, employees should seek out additional training to keep their skills current.

Late Career. The late career stage extends as long as an individual's career is active. Obsolescence and other potential midcareer problems also carry over into the late career stage, and it is important for employees and organizations to take some of the steps discussed earlier to overcome these problems and help older employees remain motivated, productive, and satisfied. Unfortunately, age-related stereotypes sometimes cause members of an organization to perceive older employees as slower, resistant to change, or less productive than younger employees, although this characterization is simply not true. Organizations need to dispel these myths by educating their members about the capabilities and contributions of their most senior members. Some older employees choose to continue working at their current occupations, others switch occupations, and still others choose to volunteer in nonprofit organizations.

All in all, organizations and individual employees can do many things to manage careers. When careers are effectively managed, employees are satisfied with their jobs and careers and are motivated to perform at a high level and thereby help organizations achieve their goals.

CONTEMPORARY CAREER CHALLENGES

In Chapter 1, we discuss contemporary challenges for organizational behavior and management. Some of these challenges are very relevant to the motivation of organizational members as they pursue their careers. When career management is effective, employees are given a series of motivating job assignments that they value and that contribute to their own development. In this case, the organization makes good use of its human resources to accomplish its goals. In this section, we discuss three career challenges that organizations face: ethical career management, career management that supports diversity, and career management in an era of dual-career couples. In Chapter 9, we discuss in more detail some of the specific steps organizations can take to meet these challenges as well as the challenges that arise when organizations downsize and lay off some of their members.

Ethical Career Management. In Chapter 1, we define *ethics* as rules, beliefs, and values that outline the ways that managers and employees should behave when confronted with a situation in which their actions may help or harm other people inside or outside an organization. A key challenge for organizations and their managers is to ensure that career practices are ethical and that members of the organization pursue their own careers in an ethical manner.

Ethical career practices are practices built on honesty, trust, and open communication. Honesty means that managers are frank with employees concerning their career prospects, their strengths and weaknesses, and their progress to date. As we saw earlier, honesty begins before an employee actually joins an organization, when an organization informs job applicants about the good and not-so-good things in various positions and in the organization itself. Honesty continues when managers appraise performance and give employees clear and accurate feedback, which contributes to employees' being motivated to perform at a high level. To motivate subordinates, managers should also provide honest feedback concerning how subordinates' careers are progressing and information about future career opportunities and prospects. Honesty continues into the later career stages when organizations follow through on their commitments regarding provisions for retirement.

Trust is also built on organization members following through on their commitments to each other. If a manager or an organization motivates an employee by promising a certain type of career progression given adequate job performance, the opportunities should be forthcoming whenever possible. Likewise, if an employee promises his or her supervisor to remain on the job and vows that the organization will benefit by, say, enrolling him or her in an expensive course to learn a new technology, trust results when the employee follows through on this commitment.

Ethical career management cannot take place without open communication between managers and subordinates. Open communication leads to a clear and shared understanding of the development of careers, career prospects, and mutual expectations.

When careers are managed in an ethical fashion, promotions are based on performance. When employees understand the link between performance and promotion and other career opportunities (such as receiving challenging assignments and special training), they are more likely to be motivated to perform at a high level. Moreover, ethical career management means that supervisors do not abuse their power to make career decisions and provide career opportunities to their subordinates. An extreme case of a supervisor abusing his or her power happens, for example, when sexual harassment occurs, and a subordinate is led to believe he or she can't advance without tolerating inappropriate behavior or language. To advance their careers, employees should not be coerced to do things compromising their own ethical standards or those of the organization. Figure 8.6 contains a short ethics quiz that provides some examples of behaviors that supervisors may request subordinates to perform that may be unethical.[113]

Career Management That Supports Diversity. The increasing diversity of the workforce means that managers have to make sure the organization's diverse members are given the career opportunities they deserve. Although progress has certainly been made with regard to diversity and hiring, somewhat less progress has been made when it comes to motivating diverse employees and making sure they're given equal career opportunities.

FIGURE 8.6
Ethics Quiz

Source: Adapted from G. Graham, "Would You Lie for Your Boss or Would You Just Rather Not," *Bryan-College Station Eagle*, October 24, 1994, p. C3. Reprinted with permission.

Supervisors sometimes ask subordinates to do things that may be questionable on ethical grounds. Ethical career management means that subordinates do not have to engage in unethical behaviors to advance their own careers. Which of the following behaviors would you feel comfortable performing, and which do you think are basically unethical?

1. Your supervisor asks you to sign her name on some letters.
2. Your supervisor asks you to respond to a request and send it under her name.
3. Your supervisor asks you to tell callers that she is with a customer when you know that this is not true.
4. Your supervisor asks you to delay recording expenses until the next quarter.
5. Your supervisor asks you to tell others that she hasn't made a decision yet even though you know she has.
6. Your supervisor tells you to record the purchase of office equipment as an advertising expense.
7. Your supervisor asks you to backdate invoices to last quarter.
8. Your supervisor requests that you tell people you don't know certain things that you do know.
9. Your supervisor tells you to tell top management that she is working on a project that she hasn't begun yet (if top management happens to ask you).
10. Your supervisor tells you not to report sexist language you overheard if anyone asks about it.

According to Gerald Graham, Dean of the W. Frank Barton School of Business at Wichita State University, most people would consider items 3, 4, 5, 6, 7, 8, 9, and 10 to be deceptive or unethical and probably should not be agreed to.

In Chapter 4, we discuss several reasons why people have a tendency to perceive others who are similar to themselves in gender, race, age, or cultural background more favorably than they perceive those who are different, and we described ways to overcome these biases. Problems such as the similar-to-me bias can result in certain members of an organization not receiving the career opportunities they deserve because they are dissimilar to managers making the career-related decisions. This inequity can result in a lack of motivation among employees who think they won't receive their "due." Managers who are aware of these biases and problems and ways to overcome them are in a good position to motivate their employees and promote career management diversity.

Organizations, too, can take specific steps to ensure equal career opportunities to their diverse members. Pacific Bell, for example, has undertaken a number of initiatives to promote the careers of minorities—in particular, Hispanics. Summer internships and scholarships are offered to minorities even before they join Pacific Bell, to help seek out minority applicants with the college degrees necessary for management positions. Minorities without college degrees are hired into nonmanagement positions, but these employees nonetheless can eventually advance into management. One of the ways Pacific Bell does this is by holding efficacy seminars, which prepare minority employees for future promotions. The company has also instituted a special two-year development track for minority managers to support their career development, help them develop their knowledge and skills, and provide them with access to mentors.[114]

Xerox Corporation is another organization that supports diversity via career management. Xerox is careful to place women and minorities in positions that will give them the experiences they need for future promotions. Minority and female caucus groups at Xerox provide guidance to diverse employees on how to manage their careers. Because managers often make important decisions that affect the careers of women and minorities, Xerox's Balanced Work Force process links the performance appraisals and compensation managers receive to their efforts to provide women and minorities with career opportunities.[115] The Balanced Work Force process thereby motivates managers to support diversity at Xerox and use career opportunities to motivate their diverse subordinates.

Career Management in an Era of Dual-Career Couples. In managing careers, organizations have to take into account the fact that the dual-career couple is now the norm rather than the exception. Individual employees cannot make career decisions such as relocating, accepting a promotion, and transferring to another state without considering the preferences and careers of their spouses. When dual-career couples have children, the needs of the entire family have to be taken into account as the couple's careers unfold. To help dual-career couples, employees who are single parents, and those caring for elderly parents effectively manage their careers, organizations can take several steps:

1. *Organizations can limit unnecessary moves and travel as much as possible.* When employees do need to relocate in the course of their careers, relocation programs can be used to help their partners find new jobs and the families adjust to their new surroundings.

2. *Organizations can use flexible working arrangements to allow their members time off when needed.* Sometimes these arrangements may entail simply changing the hours worked (for example, from 6 A.M. to 2 P.M. instead of from 9 A.M. to 5 P.M.) like Xerox does. Sometimes that may mean that employees perform some of their assigned tasks at home. At other times, that may mean managers accommodate employees who need to take time off to, for example, take care of sick children or parents.

3. *Organizations can have on-site day care centers.* One of the most pressing concerns for dual-career couples with small children and for single parents is finding quality day care for their children. On-site day care centers are growing in popularity and give working parents the peace of mind that comes from knowing that their children are in good hands.

These are just a few of the steps that organizations can take to help members manage their careers in light of the many other demands and constraints that employees face from their personal lives. Rather than ignoring these demands and constraints, as some organizations have tried to do in the past, organizations should take steps to help employees effectively meet them.

Summary

The relation between employees and an organization is an exchange relationship that is embodied in the employees' psychological contracts. Accurate performance appraisals are essential for the fulfillment of psychological contracts and a motivated workforce. Pay and career opportunities are two of the most important outcomes in the exchange relationship between employees and an organization and have important implications for motivation. In this chapter, we made the following major points:

1. A psychological contract is an employee's perception of his or her exchange relationship with an organization, outcomes the organization has promised to provide to the employee, and contributions the employee is obligated to make to the organization. The determinants of psychological contracts include direct communication, observation, and written documents. The two major types of psychological contracts are transactional contracts and relational contracts.

2. The goals of performance appraisal are to encourage high levels of employee motivation and performance and to provide accurate information to be used in managerial decision making. Performance appraisal can focus on the assessment of traits, behaviors, or results, be formal or informal, and rely on objective or subjective measures. Supervisors most often appraise the performance of their subordinates.

3. Pay is an important outcome for most employees. Motivation and learning theories suggest that pay should be based on performance. When individual performance can be accurately assessed, the maximum motivational impact is obtained from basing pay on individual performance. When employees are highly interdependent, individual levels of performance cannot be accurately appraised, or high levels of cooperation across employees are desired, it can be advantageous to base pay on group or organizational performance.

4. Merit pay in the form of bonuses generally is preferable to salary increases because salary levels have multiple determinants in addition to current performance. The ethics of pay differentials and comparable worth are important issues that managers face in using pay as a motivational tool and

striving for the equitable distribution of pay in organizations.

5. A career can be defined as the sum of work-related experiences throughout a person's lifetime. Effective career management helps to ensure that members of an organization are motivated to perform at a high level and receive the career opportunities they should while also ensuring that the organization is making the best use of its human resources.

6. Four general types of careers are steady-state careers, linear careers, spiral careers, and transitory careers. Increasingly, careers are boundaryless meaning that people have a variety of kinds of work experiences in different organizations during their careers. Careers can be thought of as progressing through stages, although each individual's career is somewhat unique and these stages are not necessarily experienced by all people. At each stage, organizations and individuals can take steps to ensure high levels of employee motivation and effective career management. The five stages are (1) preparation for work, (2) organizational entry, (3) early career, (4) midcareer, and (5) late career. The early career stage is made up of two steps: establishment and achievement. Mentors and career goals can be especially helpful to employees during the achievement step.

7. Contemporary career challenges include ethical career management (built on honesty, trust, and open communication), career management that supports diversity (ensures that diverse members of an organization are given the career opportunities they deserve), and career management in an era of dual-career couples (acknowledges the many demands on employees arising from their jobs and personal lives).

Exercises in Understanding and Managing Organizational Behavior

Questions for Discussion and Review

1. Under what conditions will an employee be likely to perceive that his or her psychological contract has been broken?

2. Why are accurate performance appraisals a key ingredient in having a motivated workforce?

3. How can performance appraisals be used to form high-performing work teams?

4. Why might employees perceive appraisals based on traits as unfair?

5. Despite the positive effects of merit pay on motivation, when might an organization not want to use it?

6. Do all employees want their pay to be based on their performance? Why or why not?

7. Why do bonuses tend to be more effective motivational tools than salary increases?

8. Why are corporations reluctant to put comparable worth into practice in establishing levels of pay?

9. Is motivation likely to be higher at some career stages than at others? Why or why not?

10. Are career plateaus inevitable for most employees? Why or why not?

Building People Skills

Determining Career Aspirations and Goals

Think about the kind of career you would like to have and are trying to pursue.

1. Describe your desired career. Why do you want to have this career?

2. Describe three specific jobs that you think would be excellent for your desired career.

3. Which career stage is each of these jobs relevant to?

4. What would you find especially motivating in each of these jobs?

5. How do you think your performance should be appraised on each of these jobs to result in high levels of motivation?

6. How should pay be determined on each of these jobs to result in high levels of motivation?

A Question of Ethics

Given that employees depend on their pay for many things, including taking care of themselves and their loved ones, some would argue that basing pay on team or organizational performance might be questionable on ethical grounds because the performance of other team or organizational members is not under an individual employee's control. Others might argue that merit pay based on team or organizational performance is a powerful motivational tool to encourage organizational members to work together, cooperate, and perform at a high level.

Questions

1. Think about the ethical implications of merit-based pay.
2. Under what conditions is the use of merit-based pay to motivate employees questionable on ethical grounds?

Small Group Break-Out Exercise

When Performance Appraisals Seem Unfair

Form groups of three or four people and appoint one member as the spokesperson who will communicate your conclusions to the rest of the class.

1. Take a few minutes to think about situations in which you believe your performance was judged in an unfair manner. These situations could be related to work, school, a sport, or a hobby.
2. Take turns describing these situations and how you felt.
3. Then take turns describing why you felt that you were not being judged in a fair manner.
4. As a group, come up with a list of the determinants of perceived unfairness in performance appraisals.
5. As a group, come up with a list of recommendations to help ensure that performance appraisals are perceived to be fair.

Topic for Debate

The exchange relationship employees have with their organization is embodied in their psychological contracts. Performance appraisal, pay, and careers are important aspects of the exchange relationship between an employee and an organization and also have important implications for motivation. Now that you have a good understanding of these important elements of psychological contracts, debate the following issues.

Team A. Given that psychological contracts are perceptual in nature, they are highly idiosyncratic and there is not much that organizations can do to influence them.

Team B. Organizations play an active and important role in shaping their members' psychological contracts.

Experiential Exercise

Designing Effective Performance Appraisal and Pay Systems

Objective

Your objective is to gain experience in designing a performance appraisal and pay system to motivate employees.

Procedure

The class divides into groups of three to five people, and each group appoints one member as spokesperson to present the group's recommendations to the whole class. Here is the scenario.

Assume the role of a gourmet cook who has just started a catering business. You are located in a college town with approximately 150,000 residents. Sixty thousand students attend the large state university located in this town. Your customers include professors who host parties and receptions in their homes, student groups who hold parties at various locations, and local professionals such as doctors and lawyers who hold parties both in their homes and at their offices.

Your staff includes two cooks who help you prepare the food and four servers who help you set up and serve the food on location. Often one or both cooks go to the location of a catering job to help the servers prepare food that needs some cooking on site, such as a soufflé with hot raspberry sauce.

Your business is getting off to a good start, and you want to make sure that you have an effective performance appraisal and pay system in place to motivate your cooks and servers. It is important that your cooks are motivated to prepare high-quality and imaginative dishes, are flexible and willing to help out as needed (you often get last-minute jobs), work well with each other and with you, and are polite to customers on location. It is crucial that your servers follow your specific instructions for each job, attractively set up the food on location, provide excellent service, and are also polite and pleasant to customers.

1. Using the concepts and ideas in this chapter, design an effective performance appraisal system for the cooks.
2. Using the concepts and ideas in this chapter, design an effective performance appraisal system for the servers.
3. How should you pay the cooks to ensure that they are motivated to prepare high-quality and imaginative dishes, are flexible and willing to help out as needed, work well with each other and with you, and are polite to customers on location?
4. How should you pay the servers to ensure that they are motivated to do a good job and provide high-quality service to your customers?

When your group has completed those activities, the spokesperson will present the group's recommendations to the whole class.

Making the Connection

Find an example of a company that tries to manage the careers of its members effectively. What steps has this company taken to try to ensure effective career management?

New York Times Cases in the News

The New York Times

Chairman Quits Stock Exchange In Furor Over Pay

Grasso Resigns Under Pressure—Ally May Be Interim Chief

BY GRETCHEN MORGENSON AND LANDON THOMAS JR.

Richard A. Grasso resigned yesterday as chairman and chief executive of the New York Stock Exchange after three weeks of blistering criticism of his pay package.

Mr. Grasso had a remarkable rise at the exchange, from a clerk earning $82.50 a week in 1968 to its top executive in 1995. When it was announced last month that he was taking out $140 million in deferred pay and retirement benefits, a furor erupted as critics noted that he was not just a market leader but a regulator whose pay was set by some of the people he oversaw. The outrage over his pay threatened to engulf the exchange itself.

Under pressure from the board and after several public pension funds Tuesday called for him to leave, Mr. Grasso offered his resignation yesterday in a hastily arranged telephone meeting with directors that began after the markets closed and lasted for two hours. A heated discussion among the directors ensued,

with 13 of the 20 participants ultimately voting to accept Mr. Grasso's resignation. The seven other directors on the call opposed the resignation of Mr. Grasso.

During the meeting, the directors proposed that one of their own become the interim chairman. He is Lawrence W. Sonsini, chairman and chief executive of Wilson Sonsini Goodrich & Rosati, a law firm based in Palo Alto, Calif., and one of Mr. Grasso's few public supporters in recent days.

"I believe this course is in the best interest of both the exchange and myself," Mr. Grasso said in a statement, adding that he was leaving "with the deepest reluctance."

While Mr. Grasso's exit from the exchange will help it quiet the compensation controversy and get back to the business of trading stocks, his departure will by no means put an end to investor scrutiny of the Big Board and its practices. Indeed, his resignation may bring significant change to the Big Board, under pressure from critics who may seize on weakness at the institution. For years, they have complained about what they call the exchange's obsolete trading platforms, secrecy in its operations and potential conflicts of interest in its dual role of regulator and protector of member firms. [Page C1.]

The board of the exchange is already considering additional changes in the composition and selection of its members to achieve more independence and represent investors. After Mr. Grasso's resignation was announced, Laura Cox, managing executive for external affairs at the Securities and Exchange Commission, said: "The S.E.C. will continue its review of governance standards and will work closely with the new leadership at the exchange to put an appropriate structure in place that will ensure the credibility and integrity of the governance of the exchange."

The seeds of Mr. Grasso's downfall were sown with the disclosure of an employment contract struck in August that provided payments totaling $139.5 million in deferred compensation, savings and pension benefits. Exchange officials said that Mr. Grasso accumulated the sum by deferring significant components of his pay during his 20 years as an executive at the exchange.

Less than a week after the pay package was disclosed, William H. Donaldson, chairman of the Securities and Exchange Commission, wrote a letter to the Big Board demanding details of Mr. Grasso's compensation. "In my view, the approval of Mr. Grasso's pay package raises serious questions regarding the effectiveness of the N.Y.S.E.'s current governance structure," Mr. Donaldson wrote to H. Carl McCall, the new chairman of the Big Board's compensation committee.

The firestorm over Mr. Grasso only escalated as politicians and pension fund managers said he had lost credibility. To demonstrate his desire to change the exchange's governance practices, Mr. Grasso had called a meeting of all 26 members of the board for next Wednesday to discuss a set of proposals.

But as the clamor grew, the directors of the Big Board agreed to a telephone meeting yesterday.

Mr. Grasso began his final day at the stock exchange by calling a handful of directors who had supported him or who were undecided about his future to gauge their opinions, said a director who requested anonymity. Several of the directors said they advised him gently to resign. The final straw seemed to come at around 1 p.m. in a telephone conversation with a director who suggested that Mr. Grasso put the interest of the exchange before his own.

On the conference call with directors yesterday, Mr. Grasso said that he would be prepared to resign if asked by the board, saying that he had always put the exchange's interest ahead of his own. The board then went into executive session, with him absent, and voted to accept Mr. Grasso's resignation.

Those favoring his departure were a group of Wall Street chief executives who have been critical of Mr. Grasso's pay package since it was disclosed. They included Henry M. Paulson Jr. of Goldman Sachs, William B. Harrison Jr. of J. P. Morgan Chase and Philip J. Purcell of Morgan Stanley. H. Carl McCall, the co-chair of the corporate governance committee and the former comptroller of New York, also voted with this group, according to several directors.

These directors also said that Mr. Grasso's exit was opposed by Kenneth G. Langone, a longtime friend of Mr. Grasso's and a member of the compensation committee when his biggest contract was approved; William B. Summers Jr., the chairman of McDonald Investments, and James E. Cayne, the chief executive of Bear Stearns.

After the vote, with Mr. Grasso back on the phone, Mr. McCall told Mr. Grasso that the board would accept his resignation.

Unlike many executives whose pay has drawn fire in recent years, Mr. Grasso has been applauded for his management of the exchange, including his strong leadership and ability to reopen the markets after Sept. 11.

"This will be the first time in American history where someone who is said to have done a good job is being fired because the board is paying him too much," said Jeffrey A. Sonnenfeld, associate dean of the Yale School of Management. "The board's accountability is the second issue to be dealt with."

The board held a follow-up meeting late last night to vote formally on the matter and to form a search committee to find a permanent replacement for Mr. Grasso. For the time being, directors said yesterday, Robert G. Britz and Catherine R.

Kinney would continue in their posts as co-presidents of the exchange.

Even as Mr. Grasso was phoning directors yesterday morning to get a sense of their thinking, lawmakers in Washington were questioning the management of the exchange. At a congressional hearing, Mr. Donaldson was pressed for his views on Mr. Grasso's tenure. Mr. Donaldson declined to say whether Mr. Grasso should step down or whether any broader structural changes should be imposed on the exchange but said that the commission would soon be sending additional questions to the exchange about Mr. Grasso's compensation.

"I was upset by the disclosure as were my fellow commissioners, but we need to look at this in the context not of personalities, but procedures," Mr. Donaldson told the House Financial Services Committee.

While the House committee discussed Mr. Grasso, Senator Joseph Lieberman became the first lawmaker and presidential candidate to call on Mr. Grasso to step down. "Instead of setting an example of ethical leadership for the market he oversees, Mr. Grasso's behavior has shaken the faith of investors and the foundation of the stock exchange," Mr. Lieberman said in a statement. "For the sake of confidence in the market, it is time for Mr. Grasso to resign."

Another Democratic presidential candidate, Senator John Edwards of North Carolina, issued a similar statement later in the day.

Officials at the S.E.C. said Mr. Grasso's departure would have no impact on its review of the exchange. The commission is considering whether to force the exchange to change its structure and separate the regulatory unit from the trading floor.

Lawmakers continue to question board's management.

During his years at the exchange, Mr. Grasso worked hard to burnish its image as an icon of United States capitalism and as a place where even the smallest investor can buy his share of the American dream and be treated fairly.

During the bull market in stocks that swept the nation during the late 1990's, Mr. Grasso became the public face of the exchange. By inviting celebrities such as Muhammad Ali, Walter Cronkite and Hank Aaron to ring the opening bell that starts each day's trading activity, Mr.

Grasso brought glamor to the relatively arcane operations of the 211-year-old institution.

Raised in Jackson Heights, Queens, by a single mother and two maiden aunts, Mr. Grasso rose to the heights of American capitalism without a college degree. His story is one of grit and an uncanny ability to ingratiate himself with some of the country's most powerful corporate executives.

Mr. Grasso was the first president in the exchange's history who worked his way up through its ranks. When he became an officer, he called his mother to give her the good news, said a friend of his. She replied that if he had listened to her and joined the police department, he would be a sergeant by now. He never worked anywhere else.

In a remarkable transformation over 36 years, Mr. Grasso evolved from a low-level technician to an elder statesman of the financial world. Under his leadership, the Big Board's power and prestige grew even though its old-fashioned trading practices were under threat from technologically advanced platforms. His behind-the-scenes work to open the exchange for trading six days after the terrorist attacks of Sept. 11 made him a national figure. And his role last year brokering the peace between warring regulators investigating Wall Street conflicts of interest earned him additional respect.

But even as his stature rose, Mr. Grasso failed to realize that his statesman role required him to be beyond reproach in his activities and in those of the institution. Nevertheless, he joined boards of companies whose shares were traded on the exchange, setting up a potential for conflicts of interest. For example, he was a director of Computer Associates, whose accounting was the subject of an S.E.C. investigation and whose executive compensation was criticized by shareholder advocates as outsized.

Another misstep came last March when the exchange board nominated Sanford I. Weill, the chairman of Citigroup, to join as a public representative. Mr. Weill withdrew after Eliot Spitzer, the attorney general of New York, vowed to oppose the nomination because Citigroup had just agreed to pay $400 million in penalties as part of a broad settlement between regulators and major brokerage firms.

And while the Big Board instituted new and tougher governance standards for the companies whose shares it trades, the exchange did not hold itself to such standards. It has since said that it would do so.

"Grasso's resigning goes a long way to resolving corporate governance issues at the exchange, but it takes two to tango," said Charles M. Elson, the director of the Weinberg Center for Corporate Governance at the University of Delaware. "The board has a lot of soul searching to do. It is clear that the reputation of the exchange has been damaged."

SOURCE: "Chairman Quits Stock Exchange in Furor Over Pay," by G. Morgenson and L. Thomas, Jr., *New York Times*, September 18, 2003, pp. A1, C4.

Questions for Discussion

1. Why was there so much concern over Richard Grasso's pay as chairman of the New York Stock Exchange?

2. Why was Grasso pressured into resigning his position and why did the board accept his resignation?

3. What ethical obligations do CEOs and other top leaders of organizations such as Grasso have to organizational members and the public at large regarding their own pay and how their pay is determined?

The New York Times

Older Workers Are Thriving Despite Recent Hard Times

BY LOUIS UCHITELLE

Without fanfare, older workers—the ones seemingly left behind by the dot.com boom—are turning out to be the only group thriving in the jobless recovery.

Even as younger workers have lost ground, a higher percentage of those aged 55 to 64 hold jobs today than when the economy plunged into hard times in early 2001. Their success has shifted the composition of the work force: older people now make up 12 percent of the nation's workers, up from 10.2 percent in 2000. That was the year the dot-com boom, so favorable to the young, began to collapse.

As if to rub in the point, the raises given in America today go disproportionately to workers in their last decade before retirement.

These older workers, particularly women, are enjoying an unusual late-in-life success—as survivors of the disintegrating job security that began to spread through the work force early in their careers, undermining pensions and lifetime employment. Layoffs and retirement reduced their ranks in the recession in the early 1990's and its aftermath, but not this time.

"I am surprised by their resilience," said Robert M. Hutchens, an economist at Cornell University's School of Industrial and Labor Relations. So were a dozen other experts interviewed. Like the wider public, most had the impression that older workers were suffering. The data compiled by the Labor Department's Bureau of Labor Statistics now tells an unmistakably different story.

The reasons vary. Men who got new jobs after layoffs are trying to recoup lost pay in their final preretirement years. Or they never lost a job, but with pensions shrinking, they cannot afford to retire, even taking Social Security into account. Women play a big role. Many entered the work force in their 40's and still consider themselves in midcareer, or they have not saved enough to retire.

Many employers are holding onto older staff members until the economy strengthens and they hire again, among younger people.

Since March 2001, when the last recession began, the percentage of working people in the population of 55- to 64-year-olds has steadily risen, reaching a peak of 60 percent in the spring, or 16.4 million men and women, up from 58.1 percent and 14.5 million workers. While that gain appears to have tapered off this summer, the older workers were still the only age group to improve their lot in the recession and jobless recovery.

Demographics play a role in these numbers. The oldest baby boomers are 57 and as they have entered the ranks of the nation's older workers over the last three years, the job holders among them have increased both the number and the percentage of those employed in the group as a whole. But even without counting the baby boomers—counting only the 60- to 64-year-olds, for example—the percentage at work has still held up better since March 2001 than for any other age group, the Bureau of Labor Statistics reports.

Reflecting this success, the average weekly wage of the 55- to 64-year-olds, adjusted for inflation, reached $673 by the end of last year, up 4.5 percent from the $644 in 2000. That is a faster pace than the wage gains of any other age group, according to the Economic Policy Institute, which analyzed the bureau's wage data. Only the 25- to 34-year-olds, earning $590 in 2002, came close, increasing their average wage by 2.7 percent over the same period.

Union membership, more concentrated among older workers, may have played a role in lifting their wages. And good fortune helped. Wages and employment have risen in health care, for example, and this is a sector where 55- to 64-year-olds are disproportionately represented.

"The pure economist in me says that if the wage numbers are going in the same direction as the employment, then that is demand driven," said Harry Holzer, a labor economist at Georgetown University.

The demand among employers for older workers does seem to have risen,

but other experts argue that supply also plays a role. More than in the past, older people seem determined to stay in the work force at least until retirement age.

And as the baby boomers age, employers have less of an alternative. That is because the youngest baby boomers are now 38 and behind them is the baby-bust generation. Those employers who are hiring have fewer choices among younger workers. And those who have stopped hiring until the economy improves "hope the older workers will hold on until the hiring resumes," said Mark Zandi, chief economist at Economy.com.

Some of the 55- to 64-year-olds postponed retirement when their nest eggs were depleted in the stock market decline. Or they simply do not have enough savings to retire. In 2001, 53.4 percent of the men and women 55 to 64 who headed families had only their 401(k) savings and similar "defined contribution" plans to finance their retirement, according to the Employee Benefit Research Institute.

That was up from 33.4 percent in 1992, when many more older workers— 43.8 percent of all heads of families— looked forward to company-financed defined-benefit pensions featuring guaranteed monthly amounts. A proliferation of early-retirement packages helped thin the ranks of workers before they entered the 55-to-64 age group. Rather than resort to layoffs, many companies sweetened their defined-benefit plans in the 1990's to get workers to retire early on full pensions.

Nynex, now part of Verizon, persuaded thousands of employees to retire early, including Kingsley H. Nelson of Briarcliff Manor, N.Y. He is 60 now and back in the work force.

Like many others in his age group, Mr. Nelson, an industrial engineer, joined Nynex in the 1960's, right out of Clarkson University, expecting to remain with the company until he retired. He left instead in 1997, at 54, for a combination of reasons. The full pension was a lure. His operation at Nynex, an interactive information system, was being phased out, and he faced transfer to a job in another department.

The early-retirement package gave him an out, and in the weeks before his departure, he searched for another job. In the booming late 1990's, he soon found one. The Volt Telecom Group, a construction and engineering company, offered to make him vice president for marketing and sales at a six-figure salary that was double his pay at Nynex.

"I am not the kind of person to sit home and do nothing," Mr. Nelson said. "I passionately love what I am doing, but make no mistake, I am doing it because I have to." The salary plus the pension allow Mr. Nelson and his wife, Lynn, to maintain their lifestyle and to whittle away at $250,000 in debt.

While Mr. Nelson chose re-employment, some others who left with early-retirement packages were brought back on consulting contracts by the companies that had pushed them out. "Older workers are disproportionately represented in the data on independent contractors," said Sara Rix, a senior policy adviser for AARP.

In manufacturing, seniority and union membership helped older blue-collar workers escape the relentless layoffs in that sector, which have accounted for most of the nation's job losses over the last 30 months. Older workers, as a result, now represent 12.2 percent of those employed in manufacturing, up from 11 percent, on average, in 2000.

"These older survivors have managed to close the gap in technology skill with younger workers," said Phyllis Eisen, a vice president of the National Association of Manufacturers.

Laws against age discrimination have protected older workers. So has government employment, where layoffs have been far fewer than in the private sector. As in manufacturing, the percentage of older workers in public employment has risen in recent years.

But women have been the heavy lifters, taking jobs or staying in the labor force as they have grown older. Without them, the rate of job growth as a percentage of the 27.5 million people in this country who are 55 to 64 would have been roughly zero since 2001. Men of similar age lost a little ground, although not as much as younger men.

More people aged 55 to 64 hold jobs today than when hard times hit in 2001.

The women were in their 20's in the late 1960's, when the women's movement came to life. They started to move into the work force 20 years later, after raising children or getting a divorce or both. As they turned 55 and as older women turned 65, leaving the 55-to-64 age group, the share holding jobs rose, by a percentage point or more almost every year since 1996.

"The recession, if anything, is motivating them to recoup the time lost when they were out of the labor market earlier in their lives," said Heidi Hartmann, director of the Institute for Women's Policy Research.

Judith Bourgeois, who is 64, certainly needs the money. While her children were young, she earned a degree in American studies at Mount Holyoke College, not far from her home in Wilbraham, Mass. After completing college, she held sales jobs, got into career counseling; divorced her husband, a policeman, in 1993; and in 1998 she set up JCS Consulting, hiring herself out to run training classes and workshops for the employees of corporate clients.

The recession crimped that business and Ms. Bourgeois moved into the counseling of laid-off workers, contracting with three outplacement companies, which specialize in helping the former employees of corporate clients search for new jobs.

"I either go in and conduct workshops," Ms. Bourgeois said, "or I do one-on-one counseling."

With less than $100,000 in savings, $50,000 a year in income and a meager Social Security pension just ahead, she does not even think of retirement. Nor does she want to stop working.

"I have a lot of energy and a lot of ambition," she said, "and I almost think in terms of I have not done my best work yet."

SOURCE: "Older Workers Are Thriving Despite Recent Hard Times" by L. Uchitelle, *New York Times*, September 8, 2003, pp. A1, A15.

Questions for Discussion

1. How have changes in the economy affected the careers and career stages of older workers?

2. What effect do you think changes in the economy and laws against age discrimination have had on the psychological contracts of older workers?

3. What are the implications of your conclusions in 1 and 2 (above) for younger workers?

Managing Stress and Work–Life Balance

9

- OVERVIEW
- THE NATURE OF STRESS
- SOURCES OF STRESS
- COPING WITH STRESS
- SUMMARY
- EXERCISES IN UNDERSTANDING AND MANAGING ORGANIZATIONAL BEHAVIOR

LEARNING OBJECTIVES

After studying this chapter, you should be able to:

■

Describe how the experience of stress is based on employees' perceptions and influenced by individual differences.

■

Appreciate the fact that stress can have both positive and negative consequences for employees and their organizations.

■

Be aware of stressors that can arise from employees' personal lives, their jobs, their work groups and organizations, the pursuit of work–life balance, and uncertainty in the wider environment.

■

Describe problem-focused and emotion-focused coping strategies for individuals.

■

Described problem-focused and emotion-focused coping strategies for organizations.

OPENING CASE

Doing More With Less

Is Work Stress Out of Control?

Uncertainty in the world today is creating heightened levels of anxiety for more and more people. The sources of this anxiety are varied. They include a challenging global economy, layoffs, and fear in the aftermath of September 11, as well as a series of high-profile scandals at corporations such as Enron, WorldCom, and Tyco.[1]

Work stress, moreover, is at an all-time high. Employees at all levels of organizations are being asked to accomplish more with less.[2] Our ability (and sometimes our need) to stay electronically connected to the job 24 hours a day, 7 days a week has also contributed to mounting levels of stress. Increasingly, employees with laptops and company-provided cell phones are taking work home at night and on their vacations.

The fact is employees are trying to juggle a myriad of responsibilities, including responsibilities related to their jobs, raising their children, and caring for their elderly parents. Maintaining a balance between work and the rest of one's life is becoming a huge challenge. Is it any surprise the stress management industry is booming as organizations and individuals seek relief from the never-ending pressures they face?

A key challenge for organizations is to ensure that efficiency, quality, and innovation do not suffer and that their members retain their sanity and well-being. In terms of the former, some organizations have been able to do more with less by examining work processes and making creative changes to improve effectiveness.[3] For example, Debbie DeGabrielle, vice president of corporate marketing at WRQ, a software integration company based in Seattle, Washington, recently had her staff of 50 reduced to 22 while she was aiming to increase sales. DeGabrielle took a proactive approach to her dilemma, and with the help of her staff, came up with creative ways to do more with less by developing things such as an online "toolbox" to help staff members during sales calls and presentations. However, she also recognizes the need to make sure that she doesn't push her staff too hard, so after strenuous periods of nonstop work, she encourages them to take a day off. As she puts it, "You have to make sure that you don't push so hard that you burn out."[4]

John Seiple, president for North American operations at ProLogis, a distribution facilities company based in Denver, Colorado, was similarly challenged when the volume of his operations increased 40 percent while his work-force was reduced by 5 percent. Seiple met this challenge by eliminating unnecessary activities and paperwork. Rather than worrying about getting their paperwork done, employees are urged to remain focused on customers and give customers their undivided attention.[5]

For some employees, stress can be so intense that their bodies literally shut down. This is precisely what happened to Naomi Henderson, the CEO of a market-research firm in Bethesda, Maryland.[6] Henderson was accustomed to working very long hours on little sleep, and vacations were out of the question. One night, Henderson tried to get out of bed but couldn't move her legs. Fearing the worst, such as some incurable disease, her husband rushed her to the hospital. It turns out Henderson's temporary paralysis was due to intense stress. Her doctor recommended that she rest in bed for six weeks. She got better and started back into her intense routine of never-ending work. During a particularly trying time, she experienced the temporary paralysis and again was put on bed rest. However, this time she realized her need to change and worked with Dr. Pamela Peeke to alter her approach to work, learn to take time out for breaks, get enough sleep, and say "no" when demands become too intense. Dr. Peeke also insisted that Henderson take a 10-day vacation three times each year. After seeing Dr. Peeke once a week for two years to learn how to manage her stress and achieve a sense of balance in her life, Henderson now checks in quarterly with her to help keep her stress levels under control.[7]

Stress is not just rampant among the managerial ranks. It also appears to be afflicting all kinds of employees. A recent study by the National Institute for Occupational Health and Safety Administration (OSHA) found that over 50 percent of the employees surveyed considered job stress to be a big problem for them personally, and over 40 percent of the employees believed that their co-workers required some kind of assistance to manage their job stress.[8] A study by Marlin Company, a research firm specializing in the workplace, found that 29 percent of the employees surveyed categorized their stress levels as being high.[9] According to research conducted by the American Institute of Stress, job stress and its consequences, such as absenteeism and mental health deterioration, carry a heavy price tag for corporate America—estimated at over $300 billion annually, in fact.[10] Moreover, job stress appears to be a global problem. The European Community proclaimed job stress to be among the top work-related health problems in Europe. Unfortunately, stress is not going to go away, so what is important, stress management experts say, is helping employees change how they respond to and cope with stress.[11]

n previous chapters, you learned about many of the ways in which working in an organization affects individuals. In Chapter 3, you learned how people's experiences in organizations shape important attitudes they have, such as their job satisfaction and organizational commitment. In Chapters 5, 6, 7, and 8, you learned how and why different aspects of an organization—the way it designs jobs, sets goals, appraises performance, and administers rewards such as pay and praise—affect motivation and performance. In this chapter, we continue to explore how working in an organization affects individuals by focusing on stress and work–life balance (the relationships between people's work and their lives as a whole).

Stress affects how people feel and behave both on and off the job. Stress is a national and global concern and unfortunately an all-too-familiar problem.[12] Most of us at one time or another have experienced some of the consequences of too much stress: sleepless nights, anxiety, nervousness, and headaches or stomachaches. A recent study found that around 40 million Americans experienced stress during a two-week period.[13] And, as indicated in the opening case, stress costs organizations billions of dollars a year in lost productivity, absenteeism, turnover, and health care costs for stress-related illnesses. Understanding and managing stress is important not only for the well-being of the members of an organization but also for the effectiveness of the organization itself.

In this chapter, we describe the nature of stress and the consequences it has for individuals and organizations. We discuss the sources of stress and the steps that employees and their organizations can take to help employees cope effectively with stress. By the end of this chapter, you will have a good understanding of how stress affects people and how employees and organizations can manage stress effectively.

The Nature of Stress

When was the last time you felt particularly stressed? Maybe you had a paper due in a couple of days, but you hadn't even started it. Perhaps you had three big exams on the same day, and you weren't getting along with your roommate, or you were worried about not being able to find a good job when you graduate. You might have had a sense of being overwhelmed, of facing a problem that seemed insurmountable, or of being expected to do too many things at once. Or you may have felt uncertain about how to respond to an opportunity that had the potential to benefit you but also was very challenging.

Stress is the experience of opportunities or threats that people perceive as important and also perceive they might not be able to handle or deal with effectively.[14] Several significant aspects of stress are highlighted in this definition. First, stress can be experienced because of both opportunities and threats. An *opportunity* is something that has the potential to benefit a person. A *threat* is something that has the potential to harm a person.[15] Opportunities such as learning new skills or getting a new job can be stressful if employees lack self-efficacy (see Chapter 5) and fear that they will not be able to perform at an acceptable level. When an organization reduces the size of its workforce, employees experience stress because their financial security, psychological well-being, and career development are threatened. From the opening case, it is clear that having to work long hours causes employees to experience stress because it threatens their family lives.

A second aspect of stress is that the threat or opportunity experienced is important to a person. By *important* we mean that it has the potential to affect a person's well-being or the extent to which someone is happy, healthy, or prosperous. Many of the things that people encounter in their daily lives could be classified as opportunities or threats, but usually only the important ones result in stress. Driving through traffic on the way to work is a threat, for example, but for many people it is not significant enough to result in stress. The threat of heavy traffic may become important enough to cause stress, however, if you are caught in a traffic jam at 7:50 A.M. and are scheduled to make a crucial presentation to upper management at 8:00 A.M.. In this situation, heavy traffic

Stress The experience of opportunities or threats that people perceive as important and also perceive they might not be able to handle or deal with effectively.

has the potential to affect your well-being negatively—being late for your own presentation will not make you look good in the eyes of your superiors.

Clearly, workplace violence is one of the most life-threatening sources of stress. How real is the threat, and what can be done to overcome it? Managing Ethically discusses this.

managing ethically

Violence in the Workplace

A Xerox employee in Honolulu shoots and kills seven co-workers; two employees of a Seattle boat repair business are shot and killed by a man dressed in camouflage clothing; a troubled employee of a Lockheed Martin aircraft plant in Meridian, Mississippi, shoots and kills five of his co-workers and then kills himself.[16] Unfortunately, these examples of workplace violence underscore a national problem.

In the 1990s, widely publicized tragedies involving violence by postal workers[17] led people to believe that violence in the U.S. Postal Service was more prevalent than elsewhere. The truth is postal employees are only about one-third as likely as employees in general in the United States to be killed on the job.[18] That said, approximately 2 million employees in the United States are victims of workplace violence (ranging from threats and verbal abuse to physical attacks and homicide). Workplace violence, believe it or not, is one of the major causes of work-related deaths.[19]

The threat of violence on the job is highest for employees in service jobs whose work hours or places of employment put them particularly at risk, and for employees whose interactions with the public entail the exchange of money.[20] Overall, employees in retail settings are more than five times more likely to be victims of homicides at work than post office workers. Taxicab drivers and chauffeurs tend to be at most risk for homicide while on the job, followed by sheriffs and police officers; gas station, convenience store, and garage workers; and security guards. More often

Despite heightened publicity about violence in the 1990s, U.S. Postal Service employees are only about one-third as likely to be killed on the job as other employees in United States. Nonetheless, the postal service has instituted a workplace violence awareness program along with a hotline employees can call to report hostile situations.

than not, the perpetrators of these crimes are not current or former co-workers and do not know their victims. Sometimes domestic violence spills over into the workplace such as when an abusive partner attacks his or her estranged spouse in the spouse's place of employment.[21]

It is an ethical imperative that managers and organizations take whatever steps they can to minimize the threat of workplace violence. When a former employee of Intel Corporation made violent threats, managers decided to take swift action to ensure that the work environment was safe. They instituted a multipronged program that includes guidelines, training, and awareness programs for employees. At each Intel location in the United States, a workplace violence team composed of members from security, human resources, and nursing helps employees deal with threats and responds to any incidents that might occur.[22]

According to the Occupational Health and Safety Administration (OSHA), all organizations should have a "zero-tolerance policy" toward violence in the workplace.[23] Organizations should also take specific steps to ensure that employees are aware of the policy and what it covers. Additionally, pragmatic steps should be taken to make the workplace as safe as possible so that employees are not put in risky situations. These steps can range from installing security systems, surveillance cameras, and locked drop safes to limiting the amount of available cash in stores and providing employees with safety equipment such as handheld alarms and cell phones. It might also include security officers escorting employees to their cars at night.[24]

A third key aspect of stress is *uncertainty*: The person who is experiencing an important opportunity or threat is not sure that he or she can effectively deal with it. When people are confident that they can effectively handle an opportunity or threat, they usually do not experience stress. An orthopedic surgeon performing a routine knee operation is not likely to experience stress if he or she has performed similar operations in the past and feels confident about doing a good job. Performing a complicated hip replacement on an elderly patient in poor health, however, might be stressful for the surgeon if he or she is uncertain about the outcome. Similarly, employees experience stress from the uncertainty of being able to have a good family life while still advancing their careers.

The last aspect of stress emphasized in our definition is that stress is rooted in perception. Whether people experience stress depends on how they *perceive* potential opportunities and threats and how they *perceive* their capabilities to deal with them. One person might perceive a job change or a promotion as an opportunity for learning and career advancement, and another person might perceive the same job change or promotion as a threat because of the potential for failure. Similarly, a person with high self-efficacy might feel well equipped to take on additional responsibility. However, an equally capable employee with low self-efficacy might perceive that he or she can't handle any more responsibility.

INDIVIDUAL DIFFERENCES AND STRESS

Our definition emphasizes that an individual's experience of stress depends on a number of factors such as how important a person thinks a given opportunity or threat is and the extent to which a person thinks he or she can deal effectively with the opportunity or threat. Above all else, stress is a very personal experience. Although it may be terrifying for some students to make a presentation in front of class, others enjoy being in the spotlight and having a chance to display their knowledge and wit. Similarly, some nurses who care for AIDS patients find this duty highly stressful because of the threat of accidental infection or the emotional pain caused by the death of their patients. But other nurses consider caring for AIDS patients a professional opportunity that they have the skills and knowledge to deal with. Members of an organization must realize that individuals may respond differently to the same potential source of stress and that what might seem trivial to one employee might be a real source of stress for another.

In Chapter 2, we discuss the two major ways in which people differ from each other, in personality and ability, and their implications for understanding and managing organizational behavior. Individual differences also play a significant role in determining how members of an organization perceive and think about potential sources of stress, their ability to deal with stress effectively, and ultimately the extent to which they experience stress.

Personality.   Several of the personality traits we discuss in Chapter 2 are important for understanding why employees exposed to the same potential source of stress may differ in the extent to which they actually experience stress. Employees who are high on the Big Five personality dimension of *neuroticism*, or *negative affectivity*, for example, have a general tendency to view themselves, their organizations, their jobs, and the people they work with in a negative manner. These employees are likely to view ambiguous conditions and changes at work as potential threats and feel ill-equipped to deal with both threats and opportunities. Consistent with this reasoning, employees high on negative affectivity tend to experience more stress than those low on negative affectivity.[25]

As another example, employees who are high on the Big Five dimension of *extraversion*, or *positive affectivity*, tend to be outgoing and enjoy interacting and socializing with other people. In the classroom, extraverts are less likely than introverts to experience stress when making presentations. Similarly, extraverts are less likely to experience stress in jobs requiring frequent presentations or meeting with new people on a day-to-day basis. Sales and service jobs are examples.

Openness to experience, which captures the extent to which employees are daring and open to a wide range of experiences, is a final example of a personality trait from the Big Five model that is likely to affect the extent to which employees experience stress. For most people, taking risks and making frequent changes can be stressful. Even entrepreneurs are stressed by the risks of starting their own companies and the frequent changes needed to be innovative. Nevertheless, it is likely that employees who are high on openness to experience may find risk taking and frequent change less stressful than those who are low on openness to experience.

In Chapter 2, we also discuss some other, more specific personality traits that are relevant to understanding and managing organizational behavior, and it is likely that these traits also affect stress. Employees who are high on *self-esteem*, for example, are less likely to experience stress from challenging work assignments and are also more likely to think they can deal effectively with sources of stress. As another example, *Type A employees* have stress experiences different from those of *Type B employees*. Type A's, as you recall, have a strong desire to achieve, are competitive, have a sense of time urgency, are impatient, and can be hostile. They have a strong desire to get a lot done in a short period of time. The more relaxed Type B's are not so driven. Initially, researchers thought that Type A's would experience more stress than Type B's; however, recent research suggests that only Type A's who are very hostile experience high levels of stress. A final example of a personality trait that is likely to play a role in the extent to which employees experience stress is *locus of control*. Employees with an internal locus of control may experience less stress than those with an external locus of control because they feel that they can influence what happens to them. However, when events are largely beyond an employee's control (for example, when his or her company goes bankrupt), internals may experience stress because they are not in control of the situation.

Ability.   In addition to having different personalities, employees also differ in their abilities, which can affect stress levels. Stress can be experienced when employees lack the abilities necessary to perform their jobs. Employees at the Collins & Aikman carpet factory in Dalton, Georgia, for example, experienced stress when the factory was computerized. Some of the employees were not able to read or perform the calculations necessary to work with the new computers and felt that their jobs were threatened.

Collins & Aikman helped employees deal with this source of stress by providing extensive additional training. The training itself was a source of stress for some employees who were afraid that they would not be able to improve their skills because of other time demands at work and at home.[26]

Somewhat related to ability is another factor that affects whether employees feel stressed or not: experience. People are more likely to feel stressed when they lack experience at doing something, and they are less likely to feel stressed as they gain experience. This explains why employees starting new jobs often feel stressed and nervous—their lack of on-the-job experience breeds uncertainty. A new supervisor in a bank, for example, is uncertain about how to settle work-scheduling conflicts among his subordinates, how to run a group meeting most effectively, how to get help from his boss without seeming incompetent, and how to motivate a capable but poorly performing subordinate. These sources of uncertainty create stress for the supervisor, but the stress diminishes over time as he gains experience.

CONSEQUENCES OF STRESS

Because what an employee considers stress is highly personal, employees differ in the extent to which they experience the consequences of stress, even when they are exposed to the same sources of stress (such as making a presentation or getting laid off). At some point in their lives, however, all employees experience some of the consequences of stress. These consequences are of three main types: physiological, psychological, and behavioral. Each consequence has the potential to affect well-being, performance, and effectiveness at the individual, group, and organizational levels.

Physiological Consequences. Were you ever unable to fall asleep or stay asleep at night when you were experiencing particularly high levels of stress during the day? Such sleep disturbances are just one of the potential physiological consequences of stress. Other potential physiological consequences range from sweaty palms, feeling flushed, trembling, a pounding heart, elevated blood pressure, headaches, dizziness, nausea, stomachaches, backaches, and hives to heart attacks and impaired immune system functioning. Rock singer Stevie Nicks, for example, says that when she experiences stress before a live performance, her stomach gets upset, she breaks out in a sweat, and her asthma bothers her.[27]

The relationship between stress and physiological consequences is complicated, and researchers are still struggling to understand the dynamics involved.[28] Two individuals experiencing the same high levels of stress may have different physiological reactions. Moreover, some people seem to experience more physiological consequences than others do. People also differ in the extent to which they complain about physical symptoms of stress such as headaches and stomachaches.[29] The most serious physiological consequences of stress are likely to occur only after considerably high levels of stress are experienced for a prolonged period of time. High blood pressure, cardiovascular disease, and heart attacks, for example, may result from excessive levels of prolonged stress.

Psychological Consequences. One of the major psychological consequences of stress is the experience of stressful feelings and emotions. Stressful feelings and emotions can range from being in a bad mood, feeling anxious, worried, and upset to feeling angry, scornful, bitter, or hostile. Any or all of these feelings will detract from employees' well-being.[30]

Another psychological consequence of stress is that people tend to have more negative attitudes when they experience stress. Employees who are highly stressed tend to have a more negative outlook on various aspects of their jobs and organizations and are more likely to have low levels of job satisfaction and organizational commitment.

FIGURE 9.1

A Stress Quiz

This quiz was adapted from a stress scale developed by Marlin Company and the American Institute of Stress. Employees respond to each of the items based on the following scale:

1	2	3	4	5
Never	Rarely	Sometimes	Often	Very Often

1. Conditions at work are unpleasant or sometimes even unsafe.   _____
2. I feel that my job is making me physically or emotionally sick.   _____
3. I have too much work or too many unreasonable deadlines.   _____
4. I can't express my opinions or feelings about my job to my boss.   _____
5. My work interferes with my family or personal life.   _____
6. I have no control over my life at work.   _____
7. My good performance goes unrecognized and unrewarded.   _____
8. My talents are underutilized at work.   _____

                              TOTAL   _____

Responses to each item are summed to yield an overall stress score. Scores at or below 15 are indicative of low stress whereas those above 25 are indicative of high stress. The higher the score, the higher the level of stress.

Burnout Psychological, emotional, or physical exhaustion.

Stressed employees may feel underappreciated, feel a lack of control, and also feel that their work is interfering with their personal lives. Marlin Company and the American Institute of Stress developed a short quiz that measures the extent of stress based on the severity of its psychological consequences (see Figure 9.1).

Burnout—psychological, emotional, or physical exhaustion—is a special kind of psychological consequence of stress that afflicts some employees who experience high levels of work stress day in and day out for an extended period of time. Burnout is especially likely to occur when employees are responsible for helping, protecting, or taking care of other people.[31] Nurses, doctors, social workers, teachers, lawyers, and police officers, for example, can be at risk for developing burnout due to the nature of their jobs.

Three key signs of burnout are feelings of low personal accomplishment, emotional exhaustion, and depersonalization.[32] Burned-out employees often feel that they are not helping others or accomplishing as much as they should be. Emotionally, they are worn out from the constant stress of dealing with people who are sometimes in desperate need of assistance. Burned-out employees sometimes depersonalize the people they need to help, thinking about them as objects or things rather than as feeling human beings. A burned-out social worker, for example, may think about a foster child in need of new home as a case number rather than as a very scared 12-year-old. This psychological consequence may lead to a behavioral consequence when the burned-out social worker treats the child in a cold and distant manner.

Behavioral Consequences. The potential consequence of stress on job performance is perhaps of most interest to managers. One way to summarize the relationship between stress and performance is in terms of an inverted U (see Figure 9.2). Up to a certain point (point A in the figure), increases in stress enhance performance. Beyond that point, further increases in stress impair performance. Stress up to point A is *positive stress* because it propels employees to perform at a high level. Stress beyond point A is *negative stress* because it impairs performance. Dr. Allen Elkin, who works at the Stress Management Counseling Center in New York City, suggests that each person has to find the right level of stress for himself or herself—enough to feel productive and fulfilled but not too much to be overwhelming. Dr. Elkin likens finding the optimal level of stress to tuning the strings on a violin or guitar. If the strings are too

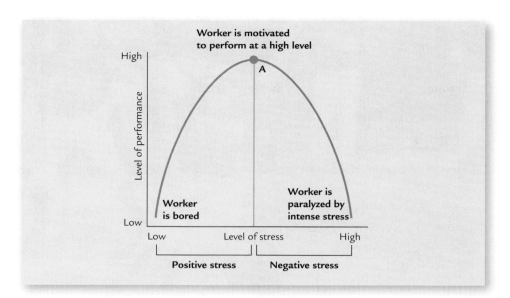

FIGURE 9.2

An Inverted U Relationship Between Stress and Performance
Stress up to point A is positive because it prompts a worker to perform at a high level. Stress beyond point A is negative because it impairs performance.

loose, there is no sound; if they are too tight, they break; when they are tuned correctly, they can make beautiful music.

The fact that stress can be positive is illustrated by considering the motivational theories and tools we discuss in Chapters 6, 7, and 8. These theories and tools can be used to raise levels of motivation and job performance, but they also have the potential to increase levels of stress. For example, giving an employee a difficult goal to reach and then telling the employee that he or she will receive a hefty bonus only if the goal is attained is likely to result in a certain level of stress. In this case, however, the stress is positive because it energizes the employee to try to reach the goal. Similarly, the stress that most students experience as exams approach is positive because it propels them to study. As a final example, many performers and athletes find that a certain amount of stress (or stage fright) gets their adrenaline pumping and helps them do their best. As singer Stevie Nicks indicates, "If I wasn't really nervous before walking on stage, I'd be really worried."[33] The expression "I work best under pressure" captures the feeling that positive stress can propel people to reach their goals and perform at a high level.

Stress levels that are too high, however, can impair performance and, thus, are negative. Students who suffer from serious test anxiety cannot remember material they may have known quite well the day before the test. Their stress and anxiety interfere with their ability to take the test, and thoughts of how poorly they are going to do prevent them from concentrating on the questions being asked. Similarly, excessively high levels of stress may prevent employees from effectively performing their jobs. Entertainers who experience excessive levels of negative stress may avoid live performances altogether, as Barbra Streisand did for 27 years.[34] In 1994, world-renowned speed skater Dan Jansen was able to win the gold medal that had eluded him for three previous Olympic Games only when he was able to relax and control his dysfunctional level of stress with the help of sports psychologist James E. Loehr.[35]

Individual differences also affect the relationship between stress and performance. Some employees, because of their personalities and abilities, are able to withstand high levels of stress that seem to propel them on to even higher levels of performance; for such employees, high levels of stress are positive. The performance levels of other employees suffer when stress becomes too high. For each employee, the point at which increases in levels of stress result in decreases in performance depends on the employee's personality traits and abilities.

On-the-job stress can be good, if it's kept at an optimal level. Sports teams like the New York Yankees and the Florida Marlins can actually use stress to enhance their performance in high stakes games like the World Series.

Besides enhanced or diminished job performance, other potential behavioral consequences of stress include strained interpersonal relations, absenteeism,[36] and turnover. When employees are experiencing excessively high levels of stress (negative stress), it is often hard for them to be as caring and understanding with others (co-workers, subordinates, superiors, customers) as they normally would be. A normally agreeable employee who suddenly flies off the handle may be experiencing a very high level of stress. Joseph Strickland, a vice president in charge of Amoco's Dallas plant, realized that stress levels were getting out of hand when one of the managers at the plant started giving everyone a hard time. "He was yelling at the secretaries, he was screaming at the human resources people," Strickland recalled. "It was very unlike him."[37] Employees experiencing high levels of stress may also have strained relationships with their spouses and families. This was found to be the case with some employees who were laid off at Phillips Petroleum Company.[38]

Excessively high levels of stress may also lead to absenteeism and turnover, especially when employees have other employment options. A recent study found that many nurses experience so much stress and burnout that they are planning to quit their jobs or leave nursing altogether.[39]

In Japan, where work overload is a significant source of stress for many employees, an extreme behavioral consequence of negative stress is what the Japanese call *karoshi*, death from overwork.[40] A study conducted by the Japanese government found that in 1993 about one out of six men worked a minimum of 3,100 hours a year (60 hours a week, 52 weeks a year), a schedule that physicians suggest can lead to karoshi. Karoshi is not limited to Japan; the British Medical Association has investigated claims that karoshi took the life of a young doctor who worked 86 continuous hours in England.[41] Unfortunately, if anything, it appears that work overload is on the rise, in Japan and around the globe. According to Japan's Health, Labor, and Welfare Ministry, 317 deaths in Japan in 2002 could directly be associated with excessive working hours.[42] However, experts believe the actual figure is many times higher than this, especially among professional workers.[43] A recent study conducted by the Japanese Trade Union Confederation estimates that around 33 percent of male employees in Japan in their early thirties work approximately 58 hours per week.[44] England, Australia, and the United States also appear to be trending toward increasingly long working hours.[45] And, as illustrated in the opening case, excessive working hours can be not only a significant cause of stress but can also lead to health problems.

Sources of Stress

What causes stress? Five major potential **stressors**, or sources of stress, are one's personal life, one's job responsibilities, membership in work groups and organizations, work–life balance, and environmental uncertainty. Whether potential stressors become actual stressors and produce stress and whether the stress an employee experiences is positive or negative depend on individual differences and how the individual perceives and interprets the stressors. Between the five categories of potential stressors (discussed next) a nearly infinite combination of them can lead to the physiological, psychological, and behavioral consequences of stress (see Figure 9.3). The effects of these stressors combine to determine the overall level of stress a person experiences. Each stressor contributes to or influences how stressed a person generally feels.

Stressor A source of stress.

PERSONAL STRESSORS

Why are we bothering to discuss stressors from one's personal life in a book on organizational behavior? What happens to employees off the job can affect their attitudes, behaviors, and performance on the job as well as their own well-being. A normally polite and helpful salesperson may lose his temper with a disgruntled customer because he is preoccupied by the fight he had with his wife that same morning. Similarly, a marketing manager who normally has an open-door policy may avoid interacting with her colleagues because she can't get her mind off her teenage son's drug problem. Marriott International found that personal and family problems are a significant cause of the high turnover rates of employees in some of its restaurants and hotels.[46] From the opening case, it is clear that family responsibilities and home life are an important concern for employees both on and off the job.

One way of viewing these and other personal sources of stress is in terms of major and minor life events.[47] *Major life events* can have serious implications for stress and well-being and include the death of a loved one, divorce, serious illness of oneself or a loved one, and getting arrested. These are all sources of stress involving emotional or physical "threats" and are negative. Other major life events are positive "opportunities" that can be stressful, such as getting married, buying a house, having or adopting a baby, and moving to another state. Relatively *minor life events* also can be sources of stress, such as getting a speeding ticket, having trouble with your in-laws or child care provider, and even going on vacation.

How stressed a person generally feels appears to depend not only on the extent to which the stressors occur and how significant they are for the person but also on how many of them occur simultaneously during any given period.[48] New college graduates, for example, sometimes experience high levels of stress because many potentially stressful life events (both positive and negative) occur in a short period of time—moving, losing old friends, making new friends, getting married, and becoming financially independent while at the same time starting or looking for a job. Although each event might be only mildly stressful by itself, the fact that they are all happening together results in a high level of stress.

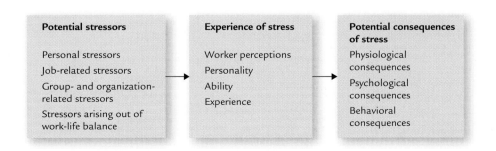

FIGURE 9.3

Sources and Consequences of Stress

Researchers have developed questionnaires that contain checklists of stressful life events and their perceived impact. Overall stress levels are determined by the number of events that have occurred during a certain period (such as the past three years) and their significance to a person. Overall stress levels, in turn, have been shown to be related to the extent to which some of the negative consequences of stress we discussed earlier occur.[49] Items from one of these questionnaires are listed in Table 9.1.

TABLE 9.1

Sample Items from a Life Event Checklist to Determine Overall Stress Levels

	Happened in Last Three Years?		Current Impact on You?				
	No	Yes	Negative		None	Positive	
1. Started school or a training program after not going to school for a long time	No	Yes	−3 −2 −1		0	+1 +2 +3	
2. Started work for the first time	No	Yes	−3 −2 −1		0	+1 +2 +3	
3. Changed jobs for a better one	No	Yes	−3 −2 −1		0	+1 +2 +3	
4. Changed jobs for a worse one	No	Yes	−3 −2 −1		0	+1 +2 +3	
5. Changed jobs for one that was no better or no worse than the last one	No	Yes	−3 −2 −1		0	+1 +2 +3	
6. Had trouble with boss	No	Yes	−3 −2 −1		0	+1 +2 +3	
7. Demoted at work	No	Yes	−3 −2 −1		0	+1 +2 +3	
8. Found out was *not* going to be promoted at work	No	Yes	−3 −2 −1		0	+1 +2 +3	
9. Conditions at work got worse, other than demotion or trouble with boss	No	Yes	−3 −2 −1		0	+1 +2 +3	
10. Had significant success at work	No	Yes	−3 −2 −1		0	+1 +2 +3	
11. Fired from previous job	No	Yes	−3 −2 −1		0	+1 +2 +3	
12. Promoted on present job	No	Yes	−3 −2 −1		0	+1 +2 +3	
13. Started a business or profession	No	Yes	−3 −2 −1		0	+1 +2 +3	
14. Suffered a business loss or failure	No	Yes	−3 −2 −1		0	+1 +2 +3	
15. Sharply increased workload	No	Yes	−3 −2 −1		0	+1 +2 +3	
16. Sharply reduced workload	No	Yes	−3 −2 −1		0	+1 +2 +3	
17. Had trouble with a co-worker or peer	No	Yes	−3 −2 −1		0	+1 +2 +3	
18. Had trouble with a subordinate	No	Yes	−3 −2 −1		0	+1 +2 +3	
19. Had trouble with a customer or client	No	Yes	−3 −2 −1		0	+1 +2 +3	
20. Spouse started work for the first time	No	Yes	−3 −2 −1		0	+1 +2 +3	
21. Spouse changed jobs for a worse one	No	Yes	−3 −2 −1		0	+1 +2 +3	
22. Spouse promoted	No	Yes	−3 −2 −1		0	+1 +2 +3	
23. Spouse demoted at work	No	Yes	−3 −2 −1		0	+1 +2 +3	
24. Spouse fired	No	Yes	−3 −2 −1		0	+1 +2 +3	
25. Took out a mortgage	No	Yes	−3 −2 −1		0	+1 +2 +3	
26. Started buying a car, furniture, or other large purchase on an installment plan	No	Yes	−3 −2 −1		0	+1 +2 +3	

27.	Foreclosure of a mortgage or loan	No	Yes	−3	−2	−1	0	+1	+2	+3
28.	Did not get an expected wage or salary increase	No	Yes	−3	−2	−1	0	+1	+2	+3
29.	Took a cut in wage or salary without a demotion	No	Yes	−3	−2	−1	0	+1	+2	+3
30.	Spouse did not get an expected wage or salary increase	No	Yes	−3	−2	−1	0	+1	+2	+3
31.	Robbed	No	Yes	−3	−2	−1	0	+1	+2	+3
32.	Got involved in a court case	No	Yes	−3	−2	−1	0	+1	+2	+3
33.	Acquired a pet	No	Yes	−3	−2	−1	0	+1	+2	+3
34.	Pet died	No	Yes	−3	−2	−1	0	+1	+2	+3
35.	Was not able to take a planned vacation	No	Yes	−3	−2	−1	0	+1	+2	+3
36.	Remodeled a home	No	Yes	−3	−2	−1	0	+1	+2	+3
37.	Became engaged	No	Yes	−3	−2	−1	0	+1	+2	+3
38.	Engagement was broken	No	Yes	−3	−2	−1	0	+1	+2	+3
39.	Spouse was physically ill	No	Yes	−3	−2	−1	0	+1	+2	+3
40.	Expecting a baby	No	Yes	−3	−2	−1	0	+1	+2	+3
41.	Child started college	No	Yes	−3	−2	−1	0	+1	+2	+3
42.	Serious family argument other than with spouse	No	Yes	−3	−2	−1	0	+1	+2	+3

Source: Adapted from R. S. Bhagat, S. J. McQuaid, H. Lindholm, and J. Segouis. "Total Life Stress: A Multimethod Validation of the Construct and Its Effects on Organizationally Valued Outcomes and Withdrawal Behaviors," *Journal of Applied Psychology* 70 (1985): 202–14; A. P. Brief, M. J. Burke, J. M. George, B. S. Robinson, and J. Webster, "Should Negative Affectivity Remain an Unmeasured Variable in the Study of Job Stress?" *Journal of Applied Psychology* 73 (1988): 193–98: B. S. Dohrenwend, L. Krasnoff, A. R. Askenasy, and B. P. Dohrenwend, "Exemplification of a Method for Scaling Life Events: The PERI Life Events Scale," *Journal of Health and Social Behavior* 19 (1978): 205–29; J. H. Johnson and I. G. Sarason, "Recent Developments in Research on Life Stress." In V. Hamilton and D. M. Warburton (eds.), *Human Stress and Cognition: An Information Processing Approach* (New York: Wiley, 1979), 205–36.

JOB–RELATED STRESSORS

Just as a wide variety of life events can be potentially stressful, a wide variety of potential stressors arise from a person's job. Here, we consider six job-related stressors: role conflict, role ambiguity, overload, underload, challenging assignments, promotions, and conditions that affect employees' economic well-being.

In Chapter 1, we defined a *role* as a set of behaviors or tasks a person is expected to perform because of the position he or she holds in a group or organization. **Role conflict** occurs when expected behaviors or tasks are at odds with each other.[50] A social worker experiences role conflict when he is told to (1) spend more time and effort to determine whether children in foster care should be returned to their parents and (2) double the number of cases he handles each month. A middle manager experiences role conflict when her supervisor expects her to increase production levels, and her subordinates complain they are being overworked.

Role ambiguity is the uncertainty that occurs when employees are not sure about what is expected of them and how they should perform their jobs.[51] Role ambiguity can be an especially potent source of stress for newcomers to an organization, work group, or job. Newcomers are often unclear about what they are supposed to do and how they should do it. Most employees, however, experience some degree of role ambiguity at one time or another because organizations frequently change job responsibilities to adapt to changing conditions in the competitive environment. Ford Motor Company, for example, realized it needed to adapt to increased customer demands for high-quality

Role conflict The struggle that occurs when the behaviors or tasks that a person is expected to perform are at odds with each other.

Role ambiguity The uncertainty that occurs when employees are not sure what is expected of them and how they should perform their jobs.

Truck drivers working for Kellogg Brown & Root faced considerable role ambiguity during the U.S.-Iraq war. The pay was high, but so were the risks. Many of them quit and returned to the United States.

automobiles and workers' demands for more autonomy. To address the need for change, Ford reorganized some of its factories so that employees performed their jobs in teams rather than individually. Some team members experienced role ambiguity because they were unsure about their new responsibilities in the teams.

Sometimes employees experience job-related stress not because of conflicting demands (role conflict) or uncertain expectations (role ambiguity) but because of **overload**—the condition of having too many tasks to perform.[52] Robert Kakiuchi, vice president of human resources at the U.S. Bank of Washington, often works nights, weekends, and holidays to accomplish all of the tasks he is assigned. Layoffs reduced Kakiuchi's department from 70 employees to six, but the number of human resource services that he is expected to provide to other departments in the bank has not been reduced at all.[53] Kakiuchi is experiencing overload because his organization expects the remaining human resource workers to perform the tasks that used to be performed by laid-off workers.[54] Nadine Billard, a manager of export sales for the book publisher HarperCollins, experiences so much overload that she typically works 15-hour days and takes work home on weekends.[55] According to a recent study conducted by the Families and Work Institute, dual-career couples worked, on average, 91 hours per week in 2003, compared to an average of 81 hours per week in 1977.[56] Whether the high level of stress an overloaded employee experiences is negative and impairs performance depends on the employee's personality traits and abilities.

Overload is particularly prevalent among middle and top managers,[57] as was illustrated in the opening case. A recent study conducted by the American Management Association found that 41 percent of the middle managers surveyed had more work to do than time in which to do it. Another study conducted by the Seattle consulting firm Priority Management found that many middle managers are working much longer hours because of the extent of their overload.[58] Earlier we discussed how overload is a significant problem in Japan and sometimes leads to karoshi (death by overwork).

Underload, not having enough work to do, can also be a source of stress for employees. When was the last time you were really bored? Maybe it was a slow day at work, or you were doing research for a paper at the library. Perhaps you were bored while studying for an exam or watching a bad movie. Now imagine that you were truly bored for eight hours a day, five days a week. You would probably experience stress just because you were bored. As we know from the job characteristics model (see

Overload The condition of having too many tasks to perform.

Underload The condition of having too few tasks to perform.

Chapter 7), most employees like to use different skills on the job and feel like they're doing something worthwhile. More generally, a certain level of stress is positive and leads to high levels of motivation and performance, as indicated in Figure 9.1.

Promotions and challenging assignments can be a source of stress for employees who are not sure that they can perform effectively or have low self-efficacy. An employee promoted to a supervisory position who has never before had subordinates reporting to him may experience stress because he is not sure that he will be able to be assertive enough. Barbra Streisand was so negatively stressed by the challenge of performing in front of 125,000 people in New York's Central Park in 1967 that she forgot the lyrics to three of her songs and avoided live performances for the next 27 years. Madonna found the opportunity of singing at the 1991 Oscar presentation (which is broadcast to billions of television viewers) so stressful that her hand shook.[59]

Stressors that affect employees' *economic well-being and job security* are also powerful sources of stress.[60] When job-related income is very low or threatened by layoffs and downsizing, a lack of job security, or pay cuts, the well-being of employees and their families is put in jeopardy.

Numerous studies have shown that when organizations lay off employees, unemployment stress can be very damaging to employees and their families and may result in physical and mental illness, including depression, suicide, family violence, and even a family's breakup.[61] Layoffs can also be stressful for members of an organization who do not lose their jobs or are survivors of the layoff.[62] Layoff survivors can feel guilty, angry, unhappy, lonely, or fearful that they will be the next to lose their jobs. Sometimes they become physically ill from their high levels of stress. A 46-year-old geologist who has worked for a Houston oil company for the past 11 years survived a layoff and was promoted to be the leader of a group of 12 of her close colleagues. One of her first assignments in her new supervisory role was to lay off half of the geologists in the group. Her stress levels were so high that she started to go to bed earlier and earlier at night so that she would not have to think about work.[63] As indicated in the accompanying Managing Ethically, extensive layoffs and resultant financial difficulties are significant sources of stress for increasing numbers of employees in the United States.

managing ethically

Laid Off and On Your Own

Increasing numbers of employees in the United States are being laid off[64] and given little assistance to deal with the sudden loss of income and challenges of finding another job. According to a recent study conducted by the John J. Heldrich Center for Workforce Development at Rutgers University, one out of five employees randomly interviewed was laid off in the period from 2000 to 2003.[65] Less than half of those laid off received unemployment insurance, less than one-third had their health insurance coverage extended by their employer during their unemployment period, and less than one-fifth received any help from their former employer when it came to retraining or finding another job. Furthermore, approximately one-third of those laid off received no advance warning that their jobs were being terminated, and another third received only one or two weeks' notice.[66]

Unfortunately, for those laid off, finding another job is often a real challenge. Many workers are being forced to take part-time work or jobs for which they are overeducated and overskilled just to try to make ends meet. For example, John Wilkins was a software specialist with many years of work experience who was laid off from his job. After his search for another job in the computer industry was unsuccessful, he now works two part-time jobs (unloading packages for UPS in Palatine, Illinois, and counseling teenagers in a family service agency). And he is only

A job loss is one of life's most traumatic experiences. Sometimes the effects of a job loss on a person's emotional outlook can be so severe it interferes with his or her finding another job.

making 25 percent of what his salary used to be.[67] Greg Fuller is in a similar bind. He used to be the director of program management for Motorola's cell phone division prior to being laid off. Now he sells cell phones at Best Buy, earns 15 percent of what he used to at Motorola, and is thinking about selling his house and finding less expensive housing.[68]

Unemployment and underemployment are growing problems in the United States. An estimated 4.8 million Americans are working at part-time jobs because they have been unable to find full-time work.[69] Organizations such as Home Depot are receiving record numbers of applications for jobs from people like Scott Zucker, a former software engineer, who now is a salesperson in the home and garden department of a Home Depot for $10 an hour.[70] While CEOs and top managers continue to take home record salaries, many laid-off, lower-level employees are struggling to find other jobs or make ends meet on a fraction of the pay they used to earn. This is a troubling ethical concern for corporate America that does not appear to be resolving itself.

Given how important job income is to employees and their families, opportunities for increasing pay levels also can be stressful to employees who are not sure that they can meet the requirements for pay increases.[71] A car salesman working strictly on a commission basis experiences considerable stress every day because his ability to support his family and buy them the things they need depends on how many cars he sells. He likes his job because he has a lot of autonomy and is given the opportunity to earn high commissions by his hard work. But the job is stressful because so much is riding not only on what he does but also on things that are beyond his control, such as the economy, company-sponsored discounts, and advertising.

The previous examples constitute just a few of the potential stressors people face. But there are still many others, some of which we discussed in previous chapters. For example, being a victim of discrimination or sexual harassment (see Chapter 4) is typically very stressful for employees.[72]

Although we discuss how employees and organizations can cope with stressors in general later in the chapter, at this point it is useful to list some of the steps managers can take to make sure that job-related stressors do not cause employees to experience stress levels so high that their well-being and performance are impaired:

◆ To make sure that role conflict does not get out of hand, managers should be sure not to give employees conflicting expectations. They should try to ensure that what they expect of subordinates does not conflict with what others (customers, co-workers, and other managers) expect from them.

♦ Role ambiguity can be kept to a manageable level by telling employees clearly what is expected of them, how they should do their jobs, and what changes are being made.

♦ Managers should try to avoid overloading their subordinates and redesign jobs with too many tasks and responsibilities.

♦ When underload is a problem, managers should consider redesigning jobs so they score higher on the five core dimensions in the job characteristics model (skill variety, task identity, task significance, autonomy, and feedback).

♦ When employees experience stress from promotions or challenging job assignments, managers should take steps to raise their self-efficacy—their belief that they can be successful. We discuss several ways to boost self-efficacy in Chapter 5, such as encouraging small successes, letting subordinates know that others like themselves have succeeded in similar kinds of situations, having high expectations, and expressing confidence in subordinates' abilities.

♦ Organizations should do whatever they can to minimize the negative effects of layoffs and downsizing on their employees' economic well-being by giving employees advance notice of layoffs, fair and equitable severance pay, and providing them with counseling services. Similar steps can also be taken to reduce the stress of layoff survivors.

♦ When employees are experiencing stress due to, for example, a pay-for-performance plan, managers should actively work on boosting employees' self-efficacy.

GROUP- AND ORGANIZATION-RELATED STRESSORS

Potential stressors that can cause too high a level of stress also can arise at the work group and organizational levels. At the work group level, for example, misunderstandings, conflicts, and interpersonal disagreements can be sources of negative stress for group members. In Chapters 10 and 11, we discuss the benefits of using groups in organizations, some of the specific problems they face, and ways to alleviate them.

Given increasing globalization, more and more organizations are assembling cross-cultural teams whose members come from different countries. Misunderstandings and conflicts due to cultural differences sometimes are sources of stress in these teams. For example, in an impressive cross-cultural business venture, researchers from three competing companies—Siemens AG of Germany, Toshiba Corporation of Japan, and IBM worked together at IBM's East Fishkill, New York, facility to build a new computer memory chip. The more than 100 scientists from the three different cultures working on the project called themselves the Triad. The managers (from all three companies) who organized the effort were initially concerned the scientists might encounter problems working together because of their different cultural backgrounds. Their concerns were borne out: Misunderstandings and conflicts became a significant source of stress for many of the scientists. For instance, the German scientists from Siemens were aghast when their Japanese counterparts from Toshiba closed their eyes during meetings and appeared to be sleeping. (Apparently, overworked scientists and managers frequently do this in Japan during parts of meetings that don't relate to them.) As another example, the American scientists from IBM experienced stress because they thought that the Germans spent too much time on planning, the Japanese spent too much time reviewing ideas, and neither spent enough time actually getting the project done.

Working through potential misunderstandings such as these in cross-cultural teams is important because international joint ventures have many advantages: Participants get different perspectives on a project or problem, a wide variety of skills and expertise is represented, and participants are able to benefit from their exposure to new ways of doing things. To take advantage of the benefits of diversity without experiencing too much stress from "culture shock," individuals and groups need to be sensitive to the role that national culture plays when it comes to behavior in groups and organizations.

Uncomfortable working conditions are another source of stress for groups and entire organizations. Excessive noise, temperature extremes, and poorly designed office equipment and machinery can be very stressful when employees are exposed to them day in and day out. In recent years, more than 2,000 lawsuits have been filed by employees who claim that poorly designed computer keyboards—some made by well-known companies such as Eastman Kodak, IBM, and AT&T—have resulted in high levels of stress and painful, sometimes crippling, injuries to the employees' hands and wrists.[73]

Uncomfortable working conditions took on new meaning at Jim Beam's Clermont, Kentucky, bourbon distillery when a new policy prevented workers from using the rest room whenever they needed to. Bottling line employees at the plant complained to the United Food and Commercial Workers Union when they were restricted to four breaks to use the restroom during their 8 1/2-hour shifts with only one of the breaks being unscheduled.[74] Employees found enforcement of this policy highly stressful, uncomfortable, and for some, a medical challenge. Employees who received notes from their doctors did not have to follow the policy and were able to use the restroom whenever nature called.[75]

Potentially *unsafe* or dangerous jobs that involve, say, working in nuclear power plants, with toxic chemicals or dangerous machinery, or with people who have communicable diseases such as AIDS, can cause stress and injuries.[76] A recent study by Circadian Technologies Inc. found that pilots who fly for United Parcel Service face dangerous working conditions between 15 percent and 31 percent of the time. The pilots' union attributes these dangerous working conditions to flights that cross several time zones, and flight schedules that cause pilots to alternate between flying at night and flying during the day.[77] Dangerous working conditions can also lead to on-the-job injuries. A recent study conducted by the University of Michigan School of Public Health found that employees in Michigan missed 8.9 million days of work in a year for injuries they received while performing their jobs.[78]

Mergers and acquisitions are often an organizational source of stress, particularly for employees in the acquired firm. Employees in the acquired firm often feel like second-class citizens and fear being laid off. Such fears are often justified because after an acquisition is completed, the acquiring firm or parent company typically restructures the organization it has acquired to capitalize on synergies across the two companies and eliminate duplication of effort.[79] Some employees in the acquired firm may be likely to lose their jobs. Others will be required to do more with less. This is what happened at Kentucky Fried Chicken when PepsiCo acquired the franchise.[80] Employees in the newly merged firm might experience stress from heightened uncertainty about the future and potential culture clashes between the two organizations.

We discuss what individuals and organizations can do to cope with stressors in general later in the chapter, but at this point it is useful to consider what managers and organizations can do to try to make sure that group- and organizational-level stressors do not get out of hand. First, members of work groups can be trained to work together as a team and communicate effectively with each other. (In Chapter 19, we discuss some team-building strategies.) Second, organizations should make sure that employees have comfortable working conditions whenever possible. Third, organizations should ensure that employees are not exposed to any unnecessary risks on the job and that all safety precautions are in place to limit the risk of injury on the job. Fourth, when organizations are undergoing major changes such as mergers and acquisitions,[81] they should provide employees with accurate and timely information about how the change will proceed and how it may affect them. This is just a sampling of the steps managers and organizations can take to try to limit the extent to which these potential stressors have negative effects on the employees exposed to them.

STRESSORS ARISING OUT OF WORK–LIFE BALANCE

People employed as factory workers, receptionists, managers, nurses, and truck drivers are also often parents, spouses, children of elderly parents, volunteers in community organizations, and hobbyists. A recent study conducted by the nonprofit Families and Work Institute based in New York found that 85 percent of U.S. employees are responsible for family members living at home.[82] In light of the fact that employees are working longer hours than they did 20 years ago, this suggests that achieving a balance between work and life outside of work can be a real challenge.[83] When work roles conflict with one's personal life, stress is often the result, as we saw in the opening case. New accountants and attorneys working in major accounting and law firms, for example, are expected to put in very long hours. Although working long hours can be stressful in its own right, it can be even more stressful when it conflicts with demands from one's personal life. Many employees have young children at home and a spouse who is putting in equally long hours. Add in the responsibility of taking care of an ill parent or being president of a local charity and the stress can be overwhelming. Single parents often feel even more burdened because they do not have a spouse to help them deal with family problems and responsibilities.[84]

Even when employees do not have children, family responsibilities often cause stress when they conflict with work demands. Faith Merrens, a manager of software designers at U. S. West Communications Inc., indicates that "elder care is the biggest personal issue we face in maintaining productivity from day to day."[85] Most of her subordinates have been forced to take time off from work to care for elderly relatives. Even Merrens and her boss had to take time off when their parents were hospitalized.

In 2005, an estimated 37 percent of the workforce will be between ages 40 and 54, and their elderly parents will often need their assistance at this point.[86] Around 22 percent of the workforce expects to be caring for elderly relatives in the next three or four years. Later in the chapter, we discuss some of the steps organizations can take to help prevent these kinds of conflicts from overwhelming their employees.

Another form of conflict between work and personal life occurs when employees are asked to do things that conflict with their personal values or when they work in organizations with ethics different from their own. It is very stressful, for example, for some emergency room personnel at private hospitals to turn away potential patients because they lack medical insurance. Likewise, it is sometimes stressful for loan officers at banks to foreclose on a family's mortgage because the family can't keep up the payments. Similarly, it may be difficult for insurance agents to cancel medical insurance or deny coverage to patients for certain kinds of ailments. An environmentalist may feel stressed out working for an organization that fails to recycle; salespeople may experience stress selling products they know are low quality.

ENVIRONMENTAL UNCERTAINTY

Just as employees can experience stress from their personal lives, so too can they experience stress from uncertainty and crises in the wider environment in which organizations operate. The tragic and devastating terrorist attacks on the United States on September 11, 2001, shocked the nation and the world. Research suggests the attacks were a significant source of stress for the employees directly affected by the attacks and those people in the vicinity of the attacks. The attacks were also stressful for people living and working hundreds of miles away who didn't know anyone personally affected. This is a stressor that unfortunately continues to be present and heightened security at airports and public venues reminds us all of potential risks. Governmental warnings and security lapses contribute to a sense of threat and vulnerability over which many people feel they have little control. Although the threat of terrorism continues to be a potential source of stress around the world, research suggests that it does not appear to have changed employees' attitudes about their jobs and organizations.[87]

Other examples of contemporary stressors stemming from the wider environment include global instability and wars in Afghanistan, Iraq, and elsewhere; The outbreak of a deadly disease in Asia (SARS); a growing number of corporate scandals in which top managers engaged in deception and fraud;[88] tragic accidents such as the crash of a Staten Island, New York, ferry in October 2003 that killed 10 people and injured many more;[89] and pollution of the natural environment and exposure to toxins are just a few examples. Stressors like these that stem from uncertainty in the wider environment can affect the well-being and stress levels of employees in organizations—whether or not they have a close connection to the stressor. Such stressors can be particularly troubling because many individuals feel they have little personal control over the stressors.

Although people may have little control over terrorism, war, or contagious diseases, there are steps they can take to manage how they feel, think about, and deal with environmental stressors. The accompanying Global View explains how.

global view

Keeping Stress and Fear from Getting Out of Hand

Psychologists Dr. James Gordon, director of the Center for Mind–Body Medicine in New York, and Dr. Barrie Cassileth, a medical social worker and director of Integrative Medicine at Memorial Sloan-Kettering Cancer Center, both have helped people manage stress resulting from traumatic events.[90] Dr. Cassileth helps patients and their families deal with life-threatening diseases. Dr. Gordon helps people in countries such as Bosnia, Macedonia, and Kosovo return to a sense of normalcy in the aftermath of war. He also helped New York City firefighters in the wake of September 11, 2001. *New York Times* reporter Jane E. Brody recently spoke with these caregivers about the steps people can take to deal with the stress caused by traumatic environmental events. Here are some of their recommendations.[91]

Gordon and Cassileth say that, first of all, a person needs to try to maintain a healthy balance between knowing what is going on in the world and avoiding overexposure to it. Thus, it might be beneficial for you to be cognizant of the events that are occurring around you and how you might deal with them—perhaps by volunteering or expressing your feelings to others—but it is not a good idea to spend excessive amounts of time dwelling on trauma (say, watching endless news reports and films, reading articles, listening to reports on the radio, and so forth). Second, if you feel overwhelmed, try to take things one day at a time and focus on your key priorities. Gordon and Cassileth suggest you also maintain some kind of routine on a daily or weekly basis. Last, but not least, try to take care of yourself physically and emotionally. Exercise, relaxation techniques, meditation, and seeking help and support from others are all beneficial ways to try to maintain your physical and emotional balance.[92]

Research done a few months after September 11, 2001, suggests that sometimes people respond to traumatic environmental events by altering their values and priorities. A significant number of employees who participated in one survey indicated they had changed their values and priorities.[93] Some employees were struck by how very important their families had become to them and the fact they shouldn't take them for granted. Others decided to spend more time with their families and resolved to tell them how important they are.[94]

Sometimes traumatic events can set the stage for personal improvement. Lauren Howard, a psychotherapist in New York City, had this to say following September 11: "There is . . . a greater sense of community in New York. We care more about other people," Howard explained.[95]

Indeed, the city mourned the deaths of the 2,792 people who died at the World Trade Center, and 265 others who perished just two months later in a plane crash in Queens.[96] Such caring on the part of New Yorkers was also evident following a Staten Island Ferry crash in 2003.[97, 98] The tragic events caused the citizens to pull together like never before.

The accompanying Global View clearly suggests that how people deal or cope with stressors can have important effects on how they react to them. While we have discussed coping in reaction to certain specific stressors, we now turn to a more general discussion of ways of coping with stress.

Coping With Stress

Ultimately, the extent to which stress is experienced and whether it is positive or negative depends on how people *cope*—that is, manage or deal with stressors. There are two basic types of coping: problem-focused coping and emotion-focused coping. **Problem-focused coping** relates to the steps people take to deal directly with and act on the source of stress.[99] For example, employees facing the threat of a layoff may cope in a problem-focused manner by looking for other jobs in organizations that are not downsizing. When problem-focused coping is successful, it helps employees deal with opportunities and threats that are causing stress.

Emotion-focused coping relates to the steps people take to deal with and control their stressful feelings and emotions.[100] For example, some employees facing the threat of a layoff may try to alleviate some of their stressful feelings and emotions by exercising regularly or meditating. When emotion-focused coping is successful, stressful feelings and emotions generated by threats and opportunities do not get out of hand.

Research suggests that most of the time people engage in both kinds of coping when dealing with a stressor.[101] Individuals cope with stressors in a variety of problem- and emotion-focused ways, and there are steps organizations can take to help employees cope with the many stressors they face.

PROBLEM-FOCUSED COPING STRATEGIES FOR INDIVIDUALS

Problem-focused coping is coping directly tailored to the stressor being experienced. A college senior experiencing stress due to an upcoming job interview copes in a problem-focused way by finding out as much information as possible about the company and doing some practice interviews with a friend. When Dale Morley moved his family from London to New York so that he could assume the position of vice president of sales and marketing for Avis International, he and his family coped with the stress of being away from relatives by periodically making audiocassettes and sending them back home.[102] In addition to problem-focused coping strategies devised to manage a very specific source of stress, such as preparing for a job interview or relocating, more general strategies can be used to deal with several kinds of stressors. Here we consider three: time management, getting help from a mentor, and role negotiation.

Time Management. One strategy for coping with overload is **time management**, a series of techniques that can help people accomplish more with the amount of time they do have. Time management usually entails these steps:

- Employees make lists of all the tasks they need to accomplish during the day.
- The tasks are then prioritized in terms of those that are most important and must be done and those that are less important and can be put off, if need be.

Problem-focused coping
The steps people take to deal directly with and act on the source of stress.

Emotion-focused coping
The steps people take to deal with and control their stressful feelings and emotions.

Time management
Prioritizing and estimating techniques that allow employees to identify the most important tasks and fit them into their daily schedule.

♦ Employees estimate how long it will take to accomplish these tasks and plan their workday accordingly.[103]

Time management is a coping strategy for individuals, but organizations can help their members learn effective time management techniques. Valerie Nossal is employed as a time management expert at MeadWestvaco Consumer and Office Products in Stamford, Connecticut, to help employees better manage their time.[104] She suggests that employees need to be proactive and also set priorities and limits. Given the high volumes of work many employees are faced with, they could work around the clock and not get everything done. Thus, employees need to set priorities not only in terms of what is more and less important to get done at work but also in terms of making sure they have a balance between work and the rest of their lives. Nossal advises employees to schedule time to exercise and be with their families because these are important activities that should not be neglected due to work pressures.[105] Moreover, not paying attention to one's priorities and achieving a work–life balance may actually make employees less efficient.

Given pressures to get more done in less time, some employees engage in multitasking—doing two or more things at once—such as writing a report during a meeting, answering e-mails while talking on the telephone, or opening mail while listening to a co-worker. Does multitasking save time? Preliminary research suggests that rather than saving time, multitasking might actually make people become less, rather than more, efficient, especially when they are working on complex tasks or activities.[106] Multitasking that relies on the same parts of the brain makes a person especially vulnerable to efficiency losses.[107] For example, if you are trying to compose an e-mail while carrying on a conversation with your boss over your speaker phone, both of these tasks require you to use and process language. One will likely interfere with the other, resulting in lower efficiency. However, photocopying documents while talking with a co-worker might be more feasible, though the co-worker is probably receiving a bit less of your attention than she would have received if you weren't multitasking.[108]

Getting Help from a Mentor. Recall from Chapter 4 that more experienced members of an organization (mentors) can offer advice and guidance to less experienced members (protégés). Getting help from a mentor can be an effective problem-focused coping strategy for dealing with stressors such as role conflict, role ambiguity, overload, and challenging assignments and promotions. A mentor can advise an overloaded protégé, for example, about how to prioritize tasks so the important ones get accomplished, how to determine what tasks can be put aside, and when to say "no" to additional assignments or requests.

Like time management, getting help from a mentor is an individual-based, problem-focused coping strategy, but organizations can take steps to help ensure that mentors are available to protégés. For example, some organizations have formal mentoring programs to help new employees get the guidance and advice they need to achieve their goals.

Role negotiation The process through which employees actively try to change their roles in order to reduce role conflict, role ambiguity, overload, or underload.

Role Negotiation. **Role negotiation** is the process through which employees actively try to change their roles in order to reduce role conflict, role ambiguity, overload, or underload.[109] Sometimes simply saying "no" to additional assignments can be an effective means of role negotiation for overloaded employees.

Role negotiation can also be an effective problem-focused coping mechanism for employees experiencing stress due to work–life linkages. Blake Ashdown, a consultant based in East Lansing, Michigan, helps resorts develop and manage exercise programs and facilities. He has engaged in role negotiation by being more selective about the assignments he takes and by turning down some resorts. Ashdown has found this strategy to be an effective means of coping with the conflict between his demanding work schedule and his responsibilities at home. By negotiating his role, Ashdown is able to spend more time with his wife and five children and avoid high levels of stress from his work.[110]

EMOTION-FOCUSED COPING STRATEGIES FOR INDIVIDUALS

In addition to trying to manage problems and opportunities that are stressful, employees also have to learn to manage the feelings and emotions they give rise to. Here we consider four emotion-focused coping strategies for individuals: exercise, meditation, social support, and clinical counseling.

Exercise. One of the reasons why exercise is so popular today is that it is an effective means of emotion-focused coping. Jogging, aerobics, swimming, tennis, and walking are just a few of the types of exercise that employees ranging from entry-level employees to CEOs and even American presidents use to cope with stressors in an emotion-focused way. Regular exercise can reduce stress, improve cardiovascular functioning, and enhance well-being.

Yoga is growing in popularity as a means to alleviate stress and can also increase people's ability to concentrate. According to the magazine *Yoga Journal*, 15 million adults in the United States engage in yoga, and over 35 million say they want to try it in the next 12 months.[111] Yoga involves practicing certain postures and poses, controlling breathing, and achieving a sense of calm and alleviating stress. Some organizations are actually providing optional yoga classes to help their employees combat stress. For example, Katz Media Company in New York and Lomangino Studio, a Washington, D.C., graphic design company, both offer on-site yoga classes for their employees.[112] And some counselors in the New York City fire department who worked 80-hour weeks after September 11 found yoga helped them cope with the stress of helping firefighters and their families deal with the deaths of 343 fellow firefighters. Bill Crawford, who has over 30 years experience with the department and heads its counseling group, is a yoga devotee himself. As he puts it, yoga "makes me focus and put aside all the stray thoughts of the day that overwhelm us and cause us stress."[113]

Meditation. Some employees deal with stressful emotions through meditation. There are various forms of meditation, and some of them require professional training to learn. Generally, however, meditation entails being in a quiet environment, sitting in a comfortable position, and tuning out everyday cares and worries by focusing mentally on some visual image or verbal phrase.[114]

Buddhist monks are masters of the practice of meditation and excel at the kind of trained introspection that meditation involves. In fact, neuroscientists at MIT have met with the Dalai Lama to understand how meditation works and what it can reveal about the workings and power of the brain.[115] The French monk Matthieu Ricard met with neuroscientists at the University of Wisconsin for similar reasons. Not only do the scientists hope to learn from the Buddhists but the Buddhists hope to learn from the scientists as well.[116]

Social Support. People naturally seek help from others—social support—when they are having problems or feeling stressed. The social support of friends, relatives, co-workers, or other people who care about you and are available to discuss problems, give advice, or just be with you can be an effective means of emotion-focused coping.[117] Both the number of people you can turn to and the quality of the relationships you have with those people are important in helping to alleviate stress. A sample measure that is used to determine the extent to which a person is satisfied with the social support available to him or her is provided in Figure 9.4.

Clinical Counseling. Sometimes employees have difficulty coping on their own and seek professional help or clinical counseling. Trained psychologists and psychiatrists can help employees learn how to cope with stressors that may seem overwhelming and at times unbearable.

Instructions: The following questions ask about people in your environment who provide you with help or support. Each question has two parts. For the first part, list all the people you know, excluding yourself, whom you can count on for help or support in the manner described. Give the persons' initials, their relationship to you (see example). *Do not list more than one person next to each of the numbers beneath the question.*

For the second part, circle how *satisfied* you are with the overall support you have.

If you have had no support for a question, check the words "No one," but still rate your level of satisfaction. Do not list more than nine persons per question.

Please answer all the questions as best you can. All your responses will be kept confidential.

Example

Who do you know whom you can trust with information that could get you in trouble?

_____ No one	**1** T.N. (brother)	**4** T.N. (father)	7
	2 L.M. (friend)	**5** L.M. (employer)	8
	3 R.S. (friend)	6	9

How satisfied?

6	(5)	4	3	2	1
very satisfied	fairly satisfied	a little satisfied	a little dissatisfied	fairly dissatisfied	very dissatisfied

1. Whom can you really count on to be dependable when you need help?

_____ No one	1	4	7
	2	5	8
	3	6	9

2. How satisfied?

6	5	4	3	2	1
very satisfied	fairly satisfied	a little satisfied	a little dissatisfied	fairly dissatisfied	very dissatisfied

3. Whom can you really count on to help you feel more relaxed when you are under pressure or tense?

_____ No one	1	4	7
	2	5	8
	3	6	9

4. How satisfied?

6	5	4	3	2	1
very satisfied	fairly satisfied	a little satisfied	a little dissatisfied	fairly dissatisfied	very dissatisfied

5. Who accepts you totally, including both your worst and best points?

_____ No one	1	4	7
	2	5	8
	3	6	9

6. How satisfied?

6	5	4	3	2	1
very satisfied	fairly satisfied	a little satisfied	a little dissatisfied	fairly dissatisfied	very dissatisfied

7. Whom can you really count on to care about you, regardless of what is happening to you?

_____ No one	1	4	7
	2	5	8
	3	6	9

8. How satisfied?

6	5	4	3	2	1
very satisfied	fairly satisfied	a little satisfied	a little dissatisfied	fairly dissatisfied	very dissatisfied

9. Whom can you really count on to help you feel better when you are feeling generally down in the dumps?

_____ No one	1	4	7
	2	5	8
	3	6	9

10. How satisfied?

6	5	4	3	2	1
very satisfied	fairly satisfied	a little satisfied	a little dissatisfied	fairly dissatisfied	very dissatisfied

(Continued)

FIGURE 9.4

A Measure of Satisfaction with Social Support

Source: Scale obtained from I. G. Sarason, Psychology Department NI-25, University of Washington, Seattle, WA 98195. Reprinted with permission. Scale described in I. G. Sarason, B. R. Sarason, E. N. Shearin, and G. R. Pierce, "A Brief Measure of Social Support: Practical and Theoretical Implications," *Journal of Social and Personal Relationships* 4 (1987): 497–510.

11. Whom can you count on to console you when you are very upset?

_____ No one	1	4	7
	2	5	8
	3	6	9

12. How satisfied?

6	5	4	3	2	1
very satisfied	fairly satisfied	a little satisfied	a little dissatisfied	fairly dissatisfied	very dissatisfied

Scoring: Satisfaction with social support is measured by averaging responses to the even-numbered questions (2, 4, 6, 8, 10, and 12).

FIGURE 9.4
(continued)

Nonfunctional Strategies. The four emotion-focused coping strategies that we have discussed are functional for individuals because they generally help alleviate stressful feelings and emotions without creating new problems or sources of stress. Unfortunately, however, there are other emotion-focused ways of coping that are less functional for employees. Some people react to high levels of stress by eating too much, drinking too much, or taking drugs. Some employees employed by Phillips Petroleum Company, for example, started having problems with alcohol when they experienced high levels of stress from a big layoff.[118] These ways of coping are never effective in alleviating stressful feelings and emotions in the long run, and they create more problems, such as being overweight, being addicted to alcohol or drugs, and being unable to function to one's fullest capacity.

PROBLEM–FOCUSED COPING STRATEGIES FOR ORGANIZATIONS

Managers and organizations can do several things to deal with problems and opportunities that are sources of stress for employees. Some problem–focused coping strategies for organizations are job redesign and rotation, reduction of uncertainty, job security, company day care, flexible work schedules, job sharing, and telecommuting.

you're the management expert

Coping With the Stress of a Challenging New Job

Pamela Perkins recently took a new job as the managing director of a chain of day care centers in the northeastern United States. After three weeks on the job, she already feels burned out. She has been putting in 15-hour days, five days a week and spending her weekends catching up on paperwork and visiting individual centers. Perkins feels pressure from all sides: The relatively low-paid teachers and aides who staff the centers have a high absenteeism and turnover rate that creates logistical nightmares. Each day, there is at least one parent who calls on Perkins with a concern at one of the centers. Her own staff members lack initiative, and she does not feel comfortable delegating tasks to them. And as a single parent of a toddler who is enrolled in one of the centers, she feels guilty she's not spending more time with her son in the evenings and on weekends. The owner of the centers recently complimented Perkins on her swift adjustment to the new job and the seamless way in which she seems to have gotten up to speed. He remarked that Perkins has actually become much more adept at managing the centers than her predecessor, who never seemed quite on top of things and took too long to address problems and make changes. Perkins was pleased that her boss recognized the fruits of her labor, but it was a bittersweet kind of feeling because she was feeling so stressed out at the time. Perkins has come to the realization that something must change if she is to keep this job. Because you are an expert in OB, Perkins has come to you for help. How can she effectively cope with the excessive levels of stress she is experiencing?

Job Redesign and Rotation. Sometimes it is possible to redesign jobs to reduce negative stress caused by high levels of role conflict, role ambiguity, overload, or underload, or to improve working conditions. The job characteristics model (see Chapter 7) outlined the aspects of the job especially important to consider—namely, skill variety, task identity, task significance, autonomy, and feedback. Increasing autonomy can be useful to combat role conflict, and providing feedback can help cut down on role ambiguity. When overload is a problem, reducing the number of tasks a jobholder must perform is a viable option. Underload can be remedied by raising the skill levels, variety, task identity, and task significance related to the job. Uncomfortable and dangerous working conditions should be remedied whenever possible. Redesigning jobs to reduce unnecessary travel and job relocations can also help reduce levels of stress, particularly for dual-career couples and single parents.

Job rotation Assigning employees to different jobs on a regular basis.

When job redesign is not a viable option, **job rotation**, assigning employees to different jobs (which themselves do not change) on a regular basis, can sometimes alleviate stress. Physicians, for example, often rotate on-call duty for hospital emergency rooms and thereby reduce the level of stress that any one physician experiences from this job assignment.

Reduction of Uncertainty. Often employees experience stress because they are uncertain about how to perform their assigned tasks, how to deal with conflicting goals or expectations, or how to prioritize assignments. Uncertainty also can cause stress when employees are unsure about how an organization expects or wants them to deal with competing demands at work and home. Whatever gives rise to it, uncertainty often results in stress.

One way to reduce uncertainty in organizations is by allowing employees to participate in making decisions that affect them and their jobs. When employees participate in decision making, they often have a lot more information about changes an organization can make and how to adjust to them. We discuss participation in decision making in more detail in Chapters 12 and 14. As we discuss in Chapter 14, participation can be taken one step further by empowering employees—giving them the authority to make decisions and be responsible for the outcomes of those decisions.

Another way to reduce uncertainty is to improve communication throughout an organization. Employees need clear, accurate information on a timely basis, and steps should be taken to ensure that employees understand what this information essentially means for them as well as the organization as a whole. Good communication is so important in understanding and managing organizational behavior that it is the focus of Chapter 14.

Job Security. Whenever possible, providing employees with job security so that they know they will be able to support themselves and their loved ones helps to eliminate stressors related to the economic functions of work. Employees in Japan and Europe typically have higher levels of job security than do employees in the United States.

In lean economic times, it may be hard for organizations to guarantee job security. IBM and other companies that in the past prided themselves on high levels of security have been forced to lay off employees. Nevertheless, organizations can take steps to reduce the impact a layoff has on employees and their families. If a layoff is a real possibility, managers should provide employees with clear, honest information about their prospects in the organization. When laying off employees is necessary, it is best to give them as much advance notice as possible so they can prepare themselves and explore their options. Whenever possible, outplacement counseling should be made available to help employees find other positions or obtain additional training to increase their employment options. Employees should also receive fair severance packages.

Company Day Care. The problem of finding good, safe, affordable day care for young children is well known to many working parents. So is the problem of knowing what to do with their children when they get sick. Many organizations are coming up with innovative ways to help employees cope with stressors arising out of this work–life linkage. For example, Tallahassee Memorial Hospital in Florida spends around $300,000 a year to run a child care center for its employees. The facility is open from 7 A.M. to midnight.[119] As another example, when four staff members, three of whom were supervisors, at the San Jose National Bank became pregnant, bank president James Kenny and human resources director Laura Graves gave the women the option of taking the standard 12-week maternity leave allowed by San Jose National Bank or coming back to work after 8 weeks with their babies in tow. Bank employees are allowed to bring their babies to work until they are six months old or are crawling.[120]

Organizations can also help employees cope with the problem of what to do when children become ill. Such assistance not only helps reduce employees' stress but also can reduce absenteeism. Schering-Plough, a pharmaceutical company in Memphis, Tennessee, has a special sick room in its child care center (run by a pediatrician), so employees' children receive proper care when they are ill. In its first six months of operation, the sick room reduced employee absenteeism by 133 days. The money the company saves in six months from lower absenteeism covers the cost of operating the sick room for a whole year.[121] Time Warner has an emergency child care service for its employees. Babysitters take care of employees' sick children in their homes. They also step in to care for children should an employee's regular babysitter miss work.[122]

Flexible Work Schedules and Job Sharing. Many organizations use flexible work schedules to help their employees cope with conflicts between work and personal life. Stride Rite, a shoemaker, and eight other organizations have joined together to find ways to promote flexibility in the workplace. Companies such as Du Pont and Corning train their supervisors to manage employees on flexible schedules.[123] Flexible schedules allow employees to take time off when they need to take care of a sick child or an elderly parent. Employees at Xerox have this option and keep records of how they make up for their absences.[124] (For more information on flexible work schedules, see the closing case for this chapter.)

When job sharing is used, two or more employees are responsible for a single job and agree on how to divide job tasks and working hours. One employee might perform the job in the mornings and another in the afternoons; employees might alternate days; one might work on Mondays, Wednesdays, and Fridays and the other on Tuesdays and Thursdays; or each employee might be accountable for particular tasks and assignments. Job sharing helps employees cope with the competing demands they face at work and home. In order for job sharing to be effective, however, good communication and understanding between the organization and its employees are necessities.

The prospect of increased flexibility leads some people to become contingent workers, hired on a temporary basis by organizations. If a contingent worker is finished with an assignment at one company and wants to take some time off before the next job, he or she is free to do so. However, this increased flexibility comes at the expense of job security, and a lack of job security can be a source of stress in and of itself. Art director David Debowski works on a freelance basis out of San Francisco, choosing the projects he wants to work on from ad agencies. Although he enjoys the flexibility of freelance work, he initially found it stressful to not know if he would have a new project to work on when he finished his current project. He coped with this source of stress by listing himself with a temporary employment agency that specializes in his kind of work.[125]

Telecommuting. When **telecommuting** is used, employees are employed by an organization and have an agreement that enables them to work out of their homes regularly but not necessarily all the time.[126] Some employees' telecommuting

Telecommuting is growing at a brisk pace in the United States. Today, about 20 percent of U.S. employees telecommute from home, satellite office, or on the road.

Telecommuting A work arrangement whereby employees are employed by an organization and have an agreement that enables them to work out of their homes regularly but not necessarily all the time.

Employers know exercise improves employee morale and productivity and cuts health care costs. Steelcase Corporation, a Michigan-based office equipment manufacturer, was able to cut its health care claims by 50 percent by taking a proactive approach to its employees' health.

arrangements may entail working three days at home and two days in the office. Other employees may work primarily at home but come to the office for meetings on an as-needed basis. Still others have the option of working from home as the need arises. New advances in information technology offer telecommuters multiple ways to communicate and stay in constant contact with their co-workers, bosses, customers, and clients.

Telecommuting can help employees cope with stress by providing them with more flexibility, freeing up time that would ordinarily be spent commuting, and giving them more autonomy. However, some telecommuters feel isolated, and others think that they end up working longer hours than they would have because their work is always "there"—at home, that is. Telecommuting also has potential advantages and disadvantages for the employing organization. On the plus side, telecommuting can help organizations attract and retain valuable employees. It can also lead to higher productivity and less time lost due to absences. On the downside, telecommuting can result in coordination problems and tensions between employees who telecommute and those who don't.[127]

Research suggests that employees tend to appreciate the opportunity to telecommute. For example, one recent study found that telecommuters were generally satisfied with telecommuting.[128] Another study found that telecommuters perceived lower levels of role conflict and ambiguity, had higher levels of organizational commitment, and were more satisfied with their supervisors than employees who did not telecommute. However, the telecommuters were less satisfied with their co-employees and opportunities for promotions.[129] Research also suggests that telecommuting may be more likely to reduce stress levels when telecommuters perceive that their organizations are supportive and really care about their well-being.[130]

Clearly, more organizations are making telecommuting an option for employees, and more employees are choosing to telecommute. Estimates of the number of telecommuters in the United States tend to range from around 3 to 9 million employees.[131] A recent study found that 41 percent of the organizations surveyed provided some kind of telecommuting options for their employees.

EMOTION-FOCUSED COPING STRATEGIES FOR ORGANIZATIONS

Organizations can help employees cope effectively with stressful feelings and emotions through such things as on-site exercise facilities, organizational support, employee assistance programs, and personal days and sabbaticals.

On-Site Exercise Facilities. Realizing the benefits of exercise, many organizations such as General Foods Corporation and the SAS Institute have exercise facilities and classes that employees can use before and after work and during their lunch hours.

Organizational Support. **Organizational support** is the extent to which an organization cares about the well-being of its members, listens to their complaints, tries to help them when they have a problem, and treats them fairly.[132] Feeling and knowing that an organization cares about, and is committed to, its members is likely to help reduce employees' stressful feelings and emotions.[133] Research has found, for example, that nurses who perceive high levels of organizational support are less likely to experience negative feelings and emotions when they take care of AIDS patients.[134] Organizational support is also likely to help mitigate some of the negative feelings and emotions generated by downsizing and layoffs. An example of a measure of employees' perceptions of how supportive their organizations are is provided in Figure 9.5.

Organizational support The extent to which an organization cares about the well-being of its members, tries to help them when they have a problem, and treats them fairly.

Workers indicate the extent to which they agree or disagree with each of the following statements about their organizations using the following scale:

1	2	3	4	5	6	7
Strongly disagree	Disagree	Slightly disagree	Neither agree nor disagree	Slightly agree	Agree	Strongly agree

1. The organization values my contribution to its well-being.	1	2	3	4	5	6	7
2. If the organization could hire someone to replace me at a lower salary, it would do so.*	1	2	3	4	5	6	7
3. The organization fails to appreciate any extra effort from me.*	1	2	3	4	5	6	7
4. The organization strongly considers my goals and values.	1	2	3	4	5	6	7
5. The organization would ignore any complaint from me.*	1	2	3	4	5	6	7
6. The organization disregards my best interests when it makes decisions that affect me.*	1	2	3	4	5	6	7
7. Help is available from the organization when I have a problem.	1	2	3	4	5	6	7
8. The organization really cares about my well-being.	1	2	3	4	5	6	7
9. Even if I did the best job possible, the organization would fail to notice.*	1	2	3	4	5	6	7
10. The organization is willing to help me when I need a special favor.	1	2	3	4	5	6	7
11. The organization cares about my general satisfaction at work.	1	2	3	4	5	6	7
12. If given the opportunity, the organization would take advantage of me.*	1	2	3	4	5	6	7
13. The organization shows very little concern for me.*	1	2	3	4	5	6	7
14. The organization cares about my opinions.	1	2	3	4	5	6	7
15. The organization takes pride in my accomplishments at work.	1	2	3	4	5	6	7
16. The organization tries to make my job as interesting as possible.	1	2	3	4	5	6	7

Scoring: Responses to items are averaged for an overall score.
Items marked with a "*" should be scored as follows: 1 = 7, 2 = 6, 3 = 5, 5 = 3, 6 = 2, 7 = 1.

FIGURE 9.5

A Measure of Perceived Organizational Support

Source: Copyright © 1977 by the American Psychological Association. Reprinted with permission.

Employee Assistance Programs. Many organizations realize that employees sometimes face stressors that they simply cannot handle on their own. IBM, General Motors, Caterpillar, and many other organizations use **employee assistance programs (EAPs)** to provide their members with professional help to deal with stressors. Some EAPs simply provide employees with free professional counseling by trained psychologists. Others are structured to deal with particular types of stressors and problems, such as alcohol or drug abuse by employees or members of their families or problems with troubled teens. Champion International Corporation, for example, offers workshops to its employees on how to deal with potential drug abuse in their families.[135]

> **Employee assistance programs (EAPs)** Company-sponsored programs that provide employees with counseling and other kinds of professional help to deal with stressors such as alcohol and drug abuse and family problems.

In order for EAPs to be effective, however, employees must be guaranteed confidentiality so they're not afraid their jobs and careers will be jeopardized by seeking help.

Employee health management programs (EHMPs) are a special kind of EAP designed to promote the well-being of members of an organization and encourage healthy lifestyles. These programs focus on helping employees improve their well-being and ability to cope with stressors by, for example, controlling their weight, quitting smoking, improving their eating habits and nutrition, and detecting potential health problems such as high blood pressure early.[136] Eighty-one percent of large organizations have at least one kind of EHMP in place.[137] Du Pont, for example, offers classes ranging from 4 to 10 weeks long that are held during lunch and before and after work. How to stop smoking, control one's weight and eat a healthy diet, and deal with back-related problems are among the topics discussed.[138]

FIGURE 9.6
Coping Strategies

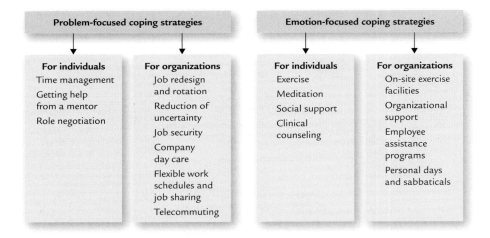

Personal Days and Sabbaticals. Providing personal days and sabbaticals can help reduce stressful feelings and emotions by allowing employees to put their work-related stress aside for a day or two (in the case of personal days) or for a more extended period (in the case of sabbaticals). Personal days are common at many large and small organizations and are available to all employees.

People usually cope with stressors in both problem-focused and emotion-focused ways. When coping is successful, it helps employees effectively deal with stressful opportunities and threats without experiencing too many stressful feelings and emotions. Figure 9.6 summarizes the various coping strategies available to individuals and organizations.

Summary

Stress affects individual well-being and has the potential to affect the extent to which individuals and organizations achieve their goals and perform at a high level. Stress is bound up with employees' personal lives; thus, the study of stress also entails exploring the nature of work–life balance. In this chapter, we made the following major points:

1. People experience stress when they face opportunities or threats that they perceive as important and also perceive they might not be able to handle or deal with effectively. An opportunity is something that has the potential to benefit a person. A threat is something that has the potential to harm a person. Stress is a highly personal experience influenced by an individual's personality, abilities, and perceptions; what is stressful for one person might not be stressful for another.

2. Stress can have physiological, psychological, and behavioral consequences. The relationship between stress and physiological consequences is complicated, and the most serious physiological consequences (for example, cardiovascular disease and heart attack) result only after considerably high levels of stress have been experienced for a

prolonged period of time. Psychological consequences of stress include negative feelings, moods, and emotions; negative attitudes; and burnout. Potential behavioral consequences of stress include poor job performance, strained interpersonal relations, absenteeism, and turnover.

3. Employees who are responsible for helping others sometimes experience burnout. The three key signs of burnout are feelings of low personal accomplishment, emotional exhaustion, and depersonalization.

4. A certain level of stress is positive in that it can result in high levels of job performance. When stress levels are excessively high, negative stress is experienced, and performance suffers. Other potential behavioral consequences of high stress include strained interpersonal relations, absenteeism, and turnover.

5. Potential stressors can arise from employees' personal lives, job responsibilities, membership in work groups and organizations, work–life balance, and environmental uncertainty. Stressors from employees' personal lives include major and minor life events. Job-related stressors include role conflict, role ambiguity, overload, underload, challenging assignments and promotions, and conditions that affect employees' economic well-being. Group- and organization-related stressors include misunderstandings, conflicts, and interpersonal disagreements; uncomfortable working conditions; and dangerous or unsafe working conditions. Stressors arising out of work–life balance result when work roles conflict with people's personal lives. Stressors arising out of environmental uncertainty result from events and conditions in the wider environment in which organizations function such as the threat of terrorism, pollution of the natural environment, and infectious diseases.

6. Coping methods are the steps people take to deal with stressors. Problem-focused coping involves steps people take to deal directly with the source of stress. Emotion-focused coping involves steps people take to deal with their stressful feelings and emotions. Most of the time, people engage in both types of coping when dealing with a stressor.

7. Some problem-focused coping strategies that individuals can use are time management, getting help from a mentor, and role negotiation. Some emotion-focused coping strategies for individuals are exercise, meditation, social support, and clinical counseling. Some problem-focused coping strategies that organizations can use are job redesign and rotation, reduction of uncertainty, job security, company day care, flexible work schedules and job sharing, and telecommuting. Some emotion-focused coping strategies for organizations are on-site exercise facilities, personal days and sabbaticals, organizational support, and employee assistance programs.

Exercises in Understanding and Managing Organizational Behavior

Questions for Discussion and Review

1. Why are opportunities such as a job promotion stressful for some people?

2. Why might excessively high levels of stress lead to turnover?

3. Should managers try to eliminate all or most role conflict and ambiguity? Why or why not?

4. Is underload as stressful as overload? Why or why not?

5. Do organizations have an ethical obligation to guarantee their members job security? Why or why not?

6. How can managers help their subordinates learn how to cope with stressors in a problem-focused way?

7. What should a manager do if he or she thinks a subordinate is using a dysfunctional form of emotion-focused coping (such as abusing drugs)?

8. Is a certain level of stress necessary to motivate employees to perform at a high level? Why or why not?

9. Why might some employees be reluctant to use an employee assistance program?

10. Why should an organization care whether its members eat well or exercise regularly?

Building People Skills

The Nature of Stressful Experiences

Think about the last significant stressful experience that you had on the job or at school. For the experience you have chosen, do the following:

1. Describe the experience and the surrounding circumstances.

2. Explain whether the experience was stressful because it entailed an opportunity or a threat. What was the opportunity or threat?

3. Describe your feelings when you first encountered the source of stress.

4. Describe the (a) physiological, (b) psychological, and (c) behavioral consequences of the stress.

5. Describe how you actually coped with the stressor in a problem-focused manner.

6. Describe how you actually coped with the stressor in an emotion-focused manner.

7. Describe how your employing organization or university helped you cope with the stressor. If your employing organization or university did not help you cope with the stressor, do you think it should have? How?

8. Describe the extent to which your coping efforts were successful in helping you deal with the source of stress and with your stressful feelings and emotions.

A Question of Ethics

As many organizations continue to lay off employees, CEOs and top managers are taking home record salaries. In the United States, the differences between what employees at the very top of an organization make and those at the very bottom tend to be much greater than they are in other countries. When layoffs take place, CEOs and top managers typically indicate that they are an economic necessity. Yet these very same people might be earning millions of dollars a year. There are many cases of a major layoff taking place in the same year that a CEO of the company laying off employees earned a record salary.

Questions

1. Think about the ethical implications of organizations laying off hundreds of employees in the same year that the CEO earns a record salary.
2. What ethical obligations do organizations have when they are considering laying off employees?

Small Group Break-Out Exercise

Emotion-Focused Ways of Coping

Form groups of three or four people, and appoint one member as the spokesperson who will communicate your conclusions to the rest of the class.

1. Take a few minutes to think about the emotion-focused ways of coping that you personally rely on to cope with stressful feelings and emotions.
2. Take turns describing your emotion-focused ways of coping and have the spokesperson list them on a piece of paper.
3. Now go through the list and determine as a group to what extent each way of coping is likely to be effective/functional or ineffective/dysfunctional.
4. As a group, come up with a list of effective emotion-focused coping strategies. (This list may include but is not limited to the list that was generated previously in Step 2.)

Topic for Debate

Stress can have major impacts on people and their organizations. Now that you understand how stress affects individual employees as well as organizations, debate the following issue:

Team A: The primary responsibility for managing work-related stress lies with the employing organization.

Team B: The primary responsibility for managing work-related stress lies with the individual employee.

Experiential Exercise

Developing Effective Coping Strategies

Objective

Your objective is to gain experience in developing effective strategies for helping members of an organization cope with stress.

Procedure

Assume the role of a supervisor of a group of 12 financial analysts for a petroleum company. Your subordinates tend to be in their late twenties and early thirties. Although some of them are single, others are married and have young children, and one is a single parent. Because of their job demands, they often work late and take work home on weekends.

Your company has fallen on hard times and has recently downsized. You were forced to lay off three subordinates. The layoff has really shaken up the survivors, who fear that they may be next to get a "pink slip." Workloads have increased, and lately your subordinates always seem to be on edge.

Recently, four of the financial analysts got into a serious and loud argument over a project they were working on. One of the participants in this fight came to you practically in tears. She said that things had gotten so bad that members of the group always seemed to be at each other's throats, whereas in the past they had helped each other. This incident, along with your recent observations, suggested the need to take steps to help your subordinates cope effectively with the stress they seem to be experiencing.

1. Describe the steps you, as the supervisor, should take to determine which problem-focused and emotion-focused coping strategies might be effective in helping the financial analysts deal with the stress they are experiencing.
2. The class divides into groups of three to five people, and each group appoints one member as spokesperson to present the group's recommendations to the whole class.
3. Group members in the role of supervisor take turns describing the steps each would take to determine effective problem-focused and emotion-focused coping strategies to help subordinates deal with the stress they are experiencing.
4. Group members develop an action plan that the group as a whole thinks would best lead to the development of effective problem-focused and emotion-focused coping strategies.

When your group has completed those activities, the spokesperson will present the group's action plan to the whole class.

Making the Connection

Find an example of an organization that has recently taken steps to help employees cope with stressors. At which potential stressors are the organization's coping strategies directed? Are these strategies related to problem-focused coping or to emotion-focused coping?

New York Times Cases in the News

The New York Times

Employers Take a United Stand in Insisting on Labor Concessions

BY STEVEN GREENHOUSE

Jefferson, Wis., July 7—For the 470 workers on strike at the Tyson Foods sausage and pepperoni plant here, the big question is why the company is so eager to cut starting salaries, freeze pensions and adopt a health plan with less coverage when the plant is so profitable.

In the first strike in the plant's 128-year history, the workers have been picketing since Feb. 28, carrying signs accusing Tyson of greed and hoping to persuade it to withdraw its demands for a string of concessions.

"They figure that this is the time to take money out of our pockets and put it back in theirs," said Chuck Moehling, who made $13.10 an hour in the sausage-stuffing operation before the strike. "The fact that they're making record profits doesn't seem to matter."

Healthy profits or not, Tyson has joined hundreds of companies nationwide demanding concessions from organized labor. As corporations grapple with a weak economy, fierce overseas competition and soaring health costs, they have made concessions a focus of labor negotiations, often demanding wage freezes, lower starting pay, stingier pensions and higher health insurance premiums and co-payments.

This push comes not only from businesses, but also the public sector—states, cities and school boards that face their biggest budget deficits in decades.

The examples extend far beyond this southern Wisconsin town, where Tyson officials say concessions are needed to keep costs in line with those of its other plants. Verizon, the telephone company, wants concessions from 75,000 workers in 12 northeastern states. New York City has demanded wage freezes from nearly 300,000 municipal workers. In Pennsylvania, 48,000 state employees have had to accept a two-year pay freeze.

Demanding concessions is common in teetering industries, most notably airlines and steel, but now it has spread to thriving industries as well. Even General Electric, one of the nation's most profitable companies, with more than $45,000 in profits per worker, demanded health-care concessions in recent negotiations. The Big Three automakers also insist that their workers contribute more toward health coverage.

"We're seeing a return to the bargaining climate of the 1980's as a lot of negotiations appear to focus on concessions, givebacks and reductions," said Paul Clark, a labor relations professor at Pennsylvania State University who edited a recent book on collective bargaining.

With unemployment rising and unions on the defensive, Professor Clark said: "There's no question that employers recognize that they have the upper hand in these relationships, and it's not surprising that they're trying to take advantage of it."

Manufacturers are making the biggest demands because they feel intense pressures from low-wage countries like China and from fast-rising health and natural gas costs. Citing the loss of 2.3 million factory jobs in 30 months, many manufacturers warn their workers that their jobs might disappear unless they accept cost-cutting measures.

Such a battle is taking place 30 miles east of Jefferson, where 460 workers have been on strike since May 2 at Waukesha Engine, which makes power-generating equipment. The company seeks a two-tier pay system, far higher health payments from retirees and the right to lay off workers regardless of seniority.

"Now more than ever we compete in a global economy," said Stewart Yee, a spokesman for Dresser Inc., Waukesha Engine's parent corporation. "When you're talking about competition from low-cost countries, you have to get your work force to help position your company to compete effectively. We tell our workers we have to set ourselves up going forward to keep these jobs in our country."

Patrick Cleary, senior vice president for human resources policy at the National Association of Manufacturers, said, "The pressures out there on manufacturers are enormous. It's the worst pricing pressures we've ever experienced. Our guys can't push these costs along. That's why they're seeking to reduce labor costs."

Most unions try to resist concessions, as is clear in Jefferson, a usually quiet, two-stoplight town of 7,500, surrounded by rolling farmland. Local supermarkets, restaurants and bakeries are donating food to sustain the strikers, while scores of homes have signs out front saying, "No Greed," and "We Need More Than Chicken Feed."

Some unions have successfully rebuffed concessions—G.E.'s two main unions beat back the company's demand that they pay 30 percent of health-care costs, up from the current 18 percent. But many other unions have reluctantly accepted them, fearful that a prolonged strike could mean months without paychecks and perhaps the loss of jobs to permanent replacement workers.

Some labor experts say the current era, like the 1980s, could portend another ratcheting down in labor's strength. The nation's unions have seen their power slip steadily as unionized workers have dropped to 13 percent of the work force, from 35 percent in the 1950s.

"Until unions turn things around, these pressures will continue," said Richard Hurd, a labor relations professor at Cornell University.

Labor leaders boast of examples where unions have obtained impressive contracts, notably in cities where unions have organized the vast majority of the workers in a nonmanufacturing industry. In Chicago, the Hotel Employees and Restaurant Employees International Union mobilized 7,300 workers at 27 hotels, threatened a strike and obtained a 54 percent increase in wages and benefits over four years, including a two-thirds reduction in worker-paid premiums for family health coverage. In recent talks involving janitors in Boston, Denver and Washington, the Service Employees International Union won raises of 25 percent over five years and health insurance for many part-time workers.

The economy spurs a return to the 1980s' era of tough bargaining.

"In 1985, we took concessions in 23 out of 25 agreements," said Stephen Lerner, director of the union's Justice for Janitors campaign. "Nowasdays we represent 70 to 90 percent of building service workers in these cities. That means a lot in terms of bargaining power."

Even many employers with solid profits are demanding concessions. For example, the Tribune Company, facing a weak and disorganized bargaining unit, demanded substantial concessions from the Newspaper Guild at The Baltimore Sun. In contract talks last month, the company obtained a one-year wage freeze and more flexibility to transfer workers.

"There's an old theory in industrial relations that two main factors determine who has the upper hand," Professor Clark said. "These factors are the economy and the degree to which the government in power supports workers' interests. In the early 1980's, management had the upper hand because the economy was in bad shape, unemployment was rising and the Reagan administration was very unfriendly toward unions. We haven't had the stars aligned that way since the 1980's until now."

Ken Kimbro, Tyson's senior vice president for human resources, said the company, which acquired the Jefferson plant two years ago, merely wanted to get the plant's costs in line with other Tyson plants.

That, he explained, is why Tyson has demanded a four-year wage freeze in Jefferson and wants to cut starting pay to $9 an hour from $11.10, and ultimately to cut the maximum base pay to $11 an hour, from $13. For new workers, the company would reduce maximum vacation to four weeks compared with six weeks for current workers. Tyson also wants workers to contribute, more toward their health coverage and accept a less comprehensive plan and to freeze pensions so that workers would not get larger pensions the longer they work. Instead, Tyson wants to institute a 401 (k) program, which is less costly to the company.

"Jefferson was in a luxurious position from our perspective," Mr. Kimbro said, "It's just a case of being an outlier."

Mr. Moehling, who has worked at the plant for 22 years, said: "The company asked, 'Why should we be sitting on this pedestal in Wisconsin?' Well, we're just scraping by. We're making $27,000 a year. That's not a lot of money. It's just enough to survive in this state. We have high heating bills and some of the highest tax rates in the nation."

If the union accepted Tyson's demands, he said, the lower pension and higher health premiums would force him to take a second job. "We can't afford to live on the concessions they're demanding," he said.

"If you take a second job, you end up with less time for your family," Mr. Moehling continued. "You hear that the reason kids end up the way they do today is because parents don't spend enough time with them. I have an 11-year-old girl and 9-year-old twin boys, and I do a lot of coaching, but if I have to take a second job, you can forget about the coaching."

Mr. Kimbro said Tyson was mindful of such considerations. "We're not pleading poverty," he said. "We're not saying the Jefferson facility is losing money. We're saying the cost in Jefferson is out of line and we have to make adjustments."

SOURCE: "Employers Take a United Stand in Insisting on Labor Concessions," by S. Greenhouse, *New York Times,* July 11, 2003, pp. A1, A12.

Questions for Discussion

1. Why are employees resisting the concessions that their organizations are asking them to make?

2. Why are the organizations seeking these concessions?

3. Considering the point of view of the employees and the organizations, what do you think is an appropriate resolution of the conflicts described in the article? Why?

The New York Times

Workplace Deaths Rise in China Despite New Safety Legislation

BY JOSEPH KAHN

Beijing, Oct. 23—New work safety rules and beefed-up enforcement have failed to reduce the death toll in China's mines and factories so far this year, and a government official acknowledged that the problem "has not been completely addressed."

Accidents took the lives of 11,449 workers through September, an increase of 9 percent over the corresponding period a year earlier, according to national data released Thursday. The official tally shows the number of deaths dropping slightly in notorious coal mines, but rising in other mines and jumping by 19 percent at factories and construction sites.

The undiminished carnage reflects the relatively low priority that China's government puts on safety. There is heavy emphasis on raising production, and workers are forbidden to form independent unions.

Although China's new leaders have promised to overhaul the way they manage the economy to better reflect the needs of workers and peasants, top lead-

ers rarely speak about the enormous numbers of casualties in a wide variety of industries. They have continued to repress workers who voice concerns about poor labor conditions as potential threats to the Communist Party's hold on power.

Since a new work safety law was enacted last year, the State Administration on Work Safety has begun regularly releasing statistics about accident rates. The authorities have also increased penalties for mine or factory owners who allow hazardous conditions to persist.

Huang Yi, the chief legal officer of the work safety administration, told a news conference on Thursday that the State Council, China's cabinet, had ordered the agency to improve its procedures and given it fresh powers of enforcement, but did not provide details.

"We have to make sure that the work of the new administration is not just a resumption of our earlier work," Mr. Huang said. Overall, though, the agency's power appears to be limited.

Coal mines continued to be the most dangerous place to work. Officials said 4,620 miners lost their lives in accidents so far this year, a reduction of just under 1

percent from the corresponding period in 2002. The modest improvement came despite an intense effort to shut illegal mines and crack down on managers who run substandard operations.

Liang Jiakun, deputy director of the work safety administration, said the death toll was down from earlier in the decade, when as many as 10,000 miners were killed annually, but acknowledged that the numbers remained too high. Mr. Liang said his agency had set a seemingly modest goal of capping annual coal mining fatalities at 5,000 by 2007.

Foreign labor activists say the official statistics reflect only part of the problem because many smaller mining accidents are covered up by local officials who do not want to disrupt production.

Han Dongfang, a labor activist based in Hong Kong, says his research indicates that more than 10,000 people die in mines each year, almost double the official count.

Other industries that contributed to the spike in workplace deaths this year are fireworks and construction, both of which rely heavily on migrant workers who receive little or no training.

SOURCE: "Workplace Deaths Rise in China Despite New Safety Legislation," by J. Kahn, *New York Times*, October 24, 2003, p. A12.

Questions for Discussion

1. Why is there such a high rate of workplace deaths in China?

2. How can this problem be rectified?

3. What are the implications of this problem on a global scale?

The Nature of Work Groups and Teams

IO

LEARNING OBJECTIVES

After studying this chapter, you should be able to:

■

Describe the different types of work groups and the difference between a group and a team.

■

Appreciate the characteristics of work groups and their effects on the behavior of group members.

■

Describe how groups control their members through roles, rules, and norms.

■

Appreciate the need for conformity and deviance in groups and why and how group goals need to be aligned with organizational goals.

■

Understand the socialization process and how socialization tactics can result in an institutionalized or an individualized role orientation.

OPENING CASE

Hummer's Winning Team

How Can a Team Achieve Fantastic Results With Very Limited Resources?

In 1999, mass marketing the Hummer—a 3.2-ton truck used by the U.S. military during the Gulf War—was just a crazy idea buzzing around in the head of Mike DiGiovanni, General Motors' director of market intelligence. In fact, the Hummer had actually been just one of three ideas pitched by DiGiovanni to GM's strategy board. So how did the company's Hummer H2 evolve so quickly from the idea stage in 1999 to a pricey, top-seller in 2003?[1] And how was it launched on an unusually modest budget and with a minimal amount of resources committed to it? Essentially, the H2 success story can be credited to the team GM formed to pull the feat off.[2]

Despite the fact that DiGiovanni lacked the depth of general management experience typical for someone heading up a new division, GM's strategy board nonetheless decided to let him run with the idea and head up the H2 team. What DiGiovanni *did* have was the enthusiasm and drive to turn his wild idea into a reality. He realized that whether the H2 succeeded or failed would depend as much on the other members of his team as himself. As he puts it, "I knew Hummer would never get out of the box without a good team . . . But I needed some cockiness, irreverence, and a belief that you could change the rules. I needed people who would constantly push each other out of the comfort zone."[3] These people included Ken Lindensmith, an employee with 30 years of GM experience who negotiated the contract with AM General (the manufacturer of the original Hummer) to market GM's H2. Also on the team were Marc Hernandez, an employee with 18 years of GM experience in sales, service, and marketing; Liz Vanzura, a former marketing executive at Volkswagen; and Paul Beckett, an executive in GM's Pontiac Division. Each of the team members had a wealth

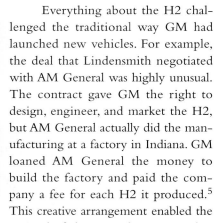

of experience to draw upon, knew the ins and outs of GM and the car industry, and was fully committed to the H2.[4] Moreover, these veterans were not afraid to take risks, were committed to their own ideas, and were unafraid to speak their minds. Ultimately, the composition of the H2 team ended up being a key contributor to the vehicle's success.

Everything about the H2 challenged the traditional way GM had launched new vehicles. For example, the deal that Lindensmith negotiated with AM General was highly unusual. The contract gave GM the right to design, engineer, and market the H2, but AM General actually did the manufacturing at a factory in Indiana. GM loaned AM General the money to build the factory and paid the company a fee for each H2 it produced.[5] This creative arrangement enabled the H2 to come out in a timely fashion on the very modest budget allocated to it. The H2 team thrived on finding creative solutions to problems like these. It was almost as if an informal rule existed among the members to challenge the status quo.

Mutual respect and commitment enabled the team to make the most of each of its members' talents and skills, trusting one another to follow through with their ideas. This was exemplified, for example, by the decision to include Paul Beckett on the team. Beckett was receiving chemotherapy treatments for colon cancer at the time but was committed to the H2 and eager to work on the team. DiGiovanni's decision to hire Beckett, despite the draining treatments he would be receiving, was based on Beckett's passion for the project and his willingness to be creative and challenge the status quo. For example, it was Beckett's idea to have H2 "personal consultants" take preorders for the H2 and keep in contact with potential customers.[6] The personal consultants shared the team's enthusiasm for the new vehicle and conveyed this excitement to prospective buyers. This creative sales tool was so effective that now GM's Cadillac division is also using personal consultants.[7] All in all, the H2 went from a tentative idea to a top-selling vehicle.[8] And DiGiovanni's team made it happen.

Overview

n previous chapters, we focused on how various traits, thoughts, and feelings an individual has (his or her personality, ability, values, attitudes, moods, perceptions, and attributions) and organizational characteristics and practices (its rewards, punishments, promotion practices, goals, and so on) determine how employees feel, think, and behave and ultimately how well the organization achieves its goals. Of course, organizations don't consist of individuals working alone. Employees are usually assembled or clustered into groups or teams. Organizations use groups or teams because they can sometimes accomplish things that no one individual could accomplish working alone, such as designing, manufacturing, and marketing a new vehicle like the H2. For example, in a group, individuals can focus on particular tasks and become better at performing them. Performance gains that result from the use of groups have led to the popular saying, "A group is more than the sum of its parts."

Groups are the basic building blocks of an organization. Just as the effective functioning of a university depends on the performance of the various groups in the university (departments such as management and psychology; student groups and athletic teams; and governing bodies such as the university's student council and the faculty senate), so, too, does the effectiveness of GM, Yahoo!, and other organizations depend on the performance of groups.

Using groups in organizations, however, can sometimes be very challenging for organizations.[9] People behave differently when they work in groups than when they work alone.[10] And although groups can sometimes work wonders for an organization, they can also wreak havoc if they function improperly. Digital Equipment Corporation, prior to its acquisition by Compaq Computer Corporation in 1998, disbanded a good number of its cross-functional teams (groups of people from different departments such as engineering, marketing, and finance) because the teams spent so much time in meetings trying to reach agreement that they weren't getting much work done.[11]

Given the important role groups play in all organizations, in this and the next chapter, we concentrate on the nature and functioning of work groups and teams. We start by describing what a group is, how work groups develop, key characteristics of work groups, and how being a member of a group affects individual behavior. We describe how groups control their members' behavior and turn newcomers into effective group members through the socialization process. Essentially, in this chapter, we explain what work groups are like and why they are this way. In the next chapter, we build on this foundation and explore what causes some groups to perform at a high level and help an organization achieve its goals.

Introduction to Groups

Is any gathering of individuals a group? If not, what distinguishes a group from a mere collection of individuals? Two basic attributes define a group:

1. Members of a group interact with each other: What one person does affects everyone else and vice versa.[12]

2. Members of a group believe there is the potential for mutual goal accomplishment—that is, group members perceive that by belonging to the group they will be able to accomplish certain goals or meet certain needs.[13]

A **group**, then, is a set of two or more people who interact with each other to achieve certain goals or meet certain needs.

It is important to note at the outset that although group members may have one or more goals in common, this does not mean that all their goals are identical. For example, when a person from each of four different departments in an organization (research and development, sales, manufacturing, and engineering) is assigned to a group to work on a new product, all members of the group may share the common goal of developing the best product they can. But the person from research and development might define the *best product* as the one that has the most innovative features; the person from sales might define it as the one that most appeals to price-conscious customers; the

Group A set of two or more people who interact with each other to achieve certain goals or to meet certain needs.

representative from manufacturing might define it as one that can be produced the most inexpensively; and the person from engineering might define it as one that will be the most reliable. Although they agree on the common goal—giving the customer the best product they can devise—deciding what *best product* means can be a difficult task. A **group goal** is one that all or most members of a group can agree on.

TYPES OF WORK GROUPS

There are many types of groups in organizations, and each type plays an important role in determining organizational effectiveness. One way to classify groups is by whether they are formal or informal. Managers establish **formal work groups** to help the organization achieve its goals. The goals of a formal work group are determined by the needs of the organization. Examples of formal work groups include a product quality committee in a consumer products firm, the pediatrics department in a health maintenance organization (HMO), and a task force created to end sex discrimination in a law firm. Managers establish each of these groups to accomplish certain organizational goals—increasing product quality in the case of the product quality committee, providing health care to children who belong to the HMO in the case of the pediatrics department, and ending discrimination at the law firm in the case of the task force.

Informal work groups emerge naturally in organizations because members believe that working together in a group will help them achieve their goals or meet their needs. A group of five factory workers who go bowling every Thursday night to satisfy their common need for affiliation and friendship is an example of an informal group.

Types of Formal Work Groups. Four important kinds of formal work groups are command groups, task forces, teams, and self-managed work teams (see Figure 10.1). A **command group** is a collection of subordinates who report to the same supervisor. Command groups are based on the basic reporting relationships in organizations and are frequently represented on organizational charts as departments (marketing, sales, accounting, and so on). The pediatrics department in an HMO, the research and development department in a pharmaceutical company, and the financial aid department in a university are all examples of command groups. Command groups are the vehicle through which much of the work in an organization gets accomplished. Thus, they have a huge impact on the extent to which an organization is able to achieve its goals. The supervisors or leaders of command groups play such an important role in determining the effectiveness of these groups that we devote Chapter 12 to the topic of leadership.

A **task force** is a collection of people who come together to accomplish a specific goal. After the goal has been accomplished, the task force is usually disbanded. The group established to end sex discrimination in a law firm and the product quality committee in

Group goal A goal that all or most members of a group can agree on as a common goal.

Formal work group A group established by management to help the organization achieve its goals.

Informal work group A group that emerges naturally when individuals perceive that membership in a group will help them achieve their goals or meet their needs.

Command group A formal work group consisting of subordinates who report to the same supervisor.

Task force A formal work group consisting of people who come together to accomplish a specific goal.

FIGURE 10.1
Types of Work Groups

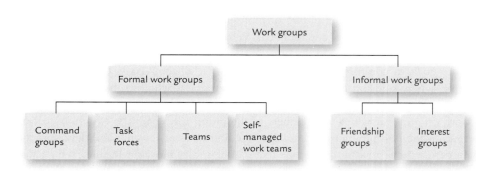

a consumer products firm are examples of task forces. Sometimes, when task forces address a goal or problem of long-term concern to an organization, they are never disbanded, but their membership periodically changes to offer new insights about the goal or problem as well as to relieve existing task force members of their duties so they can focus on their regular jobs. These kinds of tasks forces are sometimes referred to as *standing committees* or *task groups.* The consumer products firm, for example, may always have a standing committee assigned to product quality to ensure that feature is a foremost consideration as new products are developed and existing ones modified.

A **team** is a formal group of members who interact at a high level and work together intensely to achieve a common group goal. When teams are effective, they draw on the abilities and experience of their members to accomplish things that could not be achieved by individuals working separately or by other kinds of work groups. Boeing, for example, uses *cross-functional teams* (described earlier) to design and build new kinds of airplanes. Some organizations run into trouble effectively managing teams because their members spend too much time trying to come to an agreement on important issues. This, as we explained, is precisely what happened at Digital Equipment. Just because people work in a group does not mean they work as a *team,* which is further characterized by *intense* interaction and a strong commitment to its goals.

A team with no manager or a team member assigned to lead the team is called a **self-managed work team**. Members of a self-managed work team are responsible for ensuring the team accomplishes its goals and for performing leadership tasks such as determining how the group should go about achieving its goals, assigning tasks to individual group members, disciplining group members who are not performing at an adequate level, coordinating efforts across group members, and hiring and firing.[14] Self-managed work teams are becoming increasingly popular because they can have a dramatic impact on organizations and their members. We discuss them in detail in the next chapter.

Types of Informal Work Groups. Two important types of informal work groups are friendship groups and interest groups. A **friendship group** is a collection of organizational members who enjoy each other's company and socialize with each other (often both on and off the job). A group of factory workers who go bowling or a group

Team A formal work group consisting of people who work intensely together to achieve a common group goal.

Self-managed work team A formal work group consisting of people who are jointly responsible for ensuring that the team accomplishes its goals and who lead themselves.

Friendship group An informal work group consisting of people who enjoy each other's company and socialize with each other on and off the job.

Starbucks' coffee bean roasting plants are managed by work teams of employees. Although Starbucks' managers at the plants are responsible for initially organizing the teams, employees, or "partners," as Starbucks calls them, assume day-to-day operation and decision-making responsibility.

of accountants at a Big Four firm who frequently have lunch together can be described as friendship groups. Friendship groups help meet employees' needs for social interaction, are an important source of social support (see Chapter 9), and can contribute to job satisfaction and employees' experiencing positive moods.

Interest group An informal work group consisting of people who come together because they have a common goal or objective related to their organizational membership.

Members of an organization form **interest groups** when they have a common goal or objective (related to their organizational membership) that they are trying to achieve by uniting their efforts. Interest groups are often formed in response to pressing concerns that certain members of an organization have. Those concerns might include lobbying the company to sponsor a day care or elder care center, extend the amount of time allowed for maternity leave, actively protect the environment, or improve conditions in the community at large. Interest groups help members of an organization voice their concerns and can be an important impetus for needed organizational changes.

Although many of the concepts we discuss in the rest of this chapter and in the next apply to both formal and informal work groups, we focus mainly on the formal side of the organization because this is where managers can have the most impact.

GROUP DEVELOPMENT OVER TIME: THE FIVE-STAGE MODEL

All groups change over time as group members come and go (because of turnover, hiring, and promotions, among other things); group tasks and goals change, and group members gain experience as they interact with one another. Some researchers have tried to determine the stages groups normally go through over time. Understanding how groups change is important because, as we discuss later in the chapter, groups and their members face different challenges at different stages of development. In order for groups to be effective and perform at a high level, it is important for these challenges to be effectively managed. Think back to the last group project you worked on for one of your classes. It is likely that your first group meeting was dramatically different from your last group meeting or from the meetings that took place in between. At each point, the group faced different challenges. Likewise, as work groups evolve from their initial inception, they too undergo important changes.

One well-known model of group development is Bruce W. Tuckman's five-stage model, outlined in Figure 10.2.[15] During stage 1, which Tuckman called *forming,* group members try to get to know each other and establish a common understanding as they struggle to clarify group goals and determine appropriate behavior within the group. Once individuals truly feel they are members of the group, the forming stage is completed.

Stage 2, called *storming,* is characterized by considerable conflict, as its name implies. In the storming stage, members resist being controlled by the group and might disagree about who should lead the group or how much power the leader should have. This stage is completed when members no longer resist the group's control, and there is mutual agreement about who will lead the group. Members usually complete this stage because they see it is in their best interests to work together to achieve their goals.

FIGURE 10.2
Tuckman's Five-Stage Model of Group Development

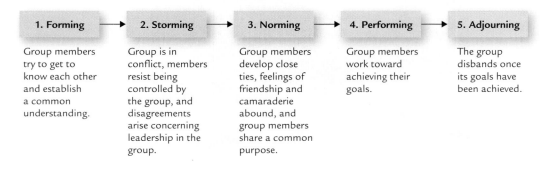

1. Forming	2. Storming	3. Norming	4. Performing	5. Adjourning
Group members try to get to know each other and establish a common understanding.	Group is in conflict, members resist being controlled by the group, and disagreements arise concerning leadership in the group.	Group members develop close ties, feelings of friendship and camaraderie abound, and group members share a common purpose.	Group members work toward achieving their goals.	The group disbands once its goals have been achieved.

In stage 3, *norming*, members really start to feel like they belong to the group, and they develop close ties with one another. Feelings of friendship and camaraderie abound, and a well-developed sense of common purpose emerges in the group. By the end of this stage, group members agree on standards to guide behavior in the group.

By the time stage 4, *performing*, is reached, the group is ready to tackle tasks and work toward achieving its goals. This is the stage at which the real work is done, so ideally, it shouldn't take long to reach it. Sometimes, however, it can take as long as two or three years to get to the performing stage, especially when the groups are self-managed work teams. Saturn Corporation, for example, experienced a slowdown when it started using self-managed work teams.[16]

In the last stage of group development—*adjourning*—identified by Tuckman as stage 5, the group disbands after having accomplished its goals. Ongoing work groups in organizations do not go through this stage and often remain at the performing stage. In contrast, a task force is likely to be adjourned after it has achieved its goals.

The five-stage "forming-norming-storming-performing-adjourning" model is intuitively appealing, but research indicates that not all groups go through each of the stages. Nor do they go through them one at a time or in the order specified by Tuckman. Some groups are characterized by considerable levels of conflict throughout their existence, in fact,[17] and always experience elements of the storming stage. Organizational researcher Connie Gersick's studies of task forces found that groups with deadlines for goal accomplishment did not go through a series of stages. Rather, they alternated between periods of inertia in which little was accomplished and periods of frenzied activity in which the group rapidly progressed toward its goals.[18] Interestingly enough, these studies found that the timing of these stages depended on how long the group was given to achieve its goals. All of the groups studied experienced inertia for approximately the first half of their duration. For example, a group given six months to accomplish its goal might experience an initial stage of inertia for its first three months, and a group given three months to accomplish its goals may be in an initial stage of inertia for its first month and a half.

As research into group development continues, it is probably safest to conclude that although all groups change over time, there doesn't seem to be a single set of stages all groups go through in a predetermined sequence.

Characteristics of Work Groups

Work groups vary in many other respects in addition to type. Here we examine five characteristics of groups that profoundly affect the way members behave and the group's overall performance. Those characteristics are the group's size, composition, function, status, and efficacy. We also discuss a characteristic that groups have on their members: social facilitation.

GROUP SIZE

The size of a group is measured by the number of full-time members who work together to achieve the group's goals. Groups may be composed of just three people or more than 20.[19] Group size is an important determinant of the way group members behave. When groups are small, members are likely to know one another and interact regularly with each other on a day-to-day basis. When groups are small, it is relatively easy for members to share information, recognize individual contributions to the group, and identify with the group's goals. Strong identification with the group and its goals may lead to increased motivation and commitment to group goals and higher levels of satisfaction.

In large groups, members are less likely to know one another and may have little personal contact with each other on a day-to-day basis. The lower level of interaction between members of large groups makes sharing information difficult. In addition, because of the many members, individuals may consider their own contributions to the group unimportant, and this can reduce their motivation and commitment to the group. For all these reasons, people generally tend to be less satisfied in large groups than in smaller ones.[20]

The disadvantages of large groups have to be weighed against their advantages, however. On the advantage side, larger groups have a greater number of resources at their disposal to accomplish their goals. These resources include the skills, abilities, and accumulated work experience and knowledge of their members. A second advantage of larger groups are the benefits that come from the **division of labor**—dividing up work assignments to individual group members. When individual members focus on particular tasks, they generally become skilled at performing these tasks at a high level. In fact, one of the primary reasons why groups (as well as whole organizations) exist is to make the division of labor possible.

When making a decision about group size, an organization needs to balance the skill and resource advantages that large groups offer against certain disadvantages. Chief among these disadvantages are the communication and coordination problems that occur as the number of members increases. For example, as a group gets bigger, it is much more difficult to let group members know about a change in procedures. Imagine communicating complex procedural changes to each member of a 40-member group versus each member of a group of four. It is also gets more difficult to coordinate members as the size of the group increases. If, for example, a group of 20 students (versus, say, five) is doing a joint research project, it is much more likely that two students will inadvertently cover the same material, that the project report the group is submitting will be disjointed, and that some students will not do their share of the work. In general, the larger a group is, the greater is the potential for conflict, duplication of effort, and low motivation. Some of these problems are discussed in detail in the next chapter. Table 10.1 summarizes some of the potential advantages of small and large group size.

Division of labor Dividing up work and assigning particular tasks to specific workers.

GROUP COMPOSITION

Group composition refers to the characteristics of members of a group.[21] In the opening case, recall how members of the H2 team were GM veterans unafraid to challenge the status quo.[22] One way to think about group composition is in terms of how similar or different the members are from each other. In the H2 team, members were similar in that they all had many years of experience working at GM, but they were different in terms of the kinds of experiences they had and their areas of expertise.

TABLE 10.1

Group Size Advantages

Potential Advantages of Smaller Groups	Potential Advantages of Larger Groups
Interactions among group members are more frequent.	Group has many resources at its disposal to accomplish its goals, including members' skills, abilities, knowledge, and experience.
Information is more easily shared among group members.	
Group members recognize their contributions to the group.	Group can have a greater division of labor, so group members focus on particular tasks. When group members focus on particular tasks, they generally become skilled at performing them.
Group members are motivated and committed to the group's goals.	
Group members are satisfied.	

Members of a **homogeneous group** have many characteristics in common. These characteristics can be demographic characteristics (such as gender, race, socioeconomic background, cultural origin, age, educational background, or tenure with an organization), personality traits, skills, abilities, beliefs, attitudes, values, or types of work experience. A group of white men from the northeastern United States who all attended Ivy League colleges, place a great deal of importance on their careers, and work for the same New York law firm is a homogeneous group. In contrast, a group of men and women of diverse races and cultural origins who possess degrees from both large and small state and private universities, have differing beliefs about the centrality of work in their lives, and work for the same New York law firm constitutes a heterogeneous group. Members of a **heterogeneous group** do not have many characteristics in common. Heterogeneous groups are characterized by diversity, homogeneous groups by similarity.

The relationships between group composition, members' behaviors, and the group's performance are complex. On the one hand, people tend to like and get along well with others who are similar to themselves. Thus, members of homogeneous groups may find it easier to share information, have lower levels of conflict, and fewer communication and coordination problems than members of heterogeneous groups. On these grounds you might expect the performance and goal attainment of homogeneous groups to be higher than that of heterogeneous groups. Because group members are more likely to get along with each other in homogeneous groups, you might also expect their motivation and satisfaction to be high as well.

On the other hand, a group that is composed of people with different backgrounds, experiences, personalities, abilities, and "views of the world" may be better able than a homogeneous group to make good decisions because more points of view are represented in the group. A heterogeneous group may also be able to perform at a high level because the group has a variety of resources at its disposal. Because of their differences, group members may be more likely to challenge each other and existing ways of doing things, and the outcome may be valuable and needed changes. The homogeneous group of lawyers, for example, might have few disagreements and little trouble communicating with one another but have difficulty dealing with female clients or clients from different ethnic or racial backgrounds. The more heterogeneous group of lawyers might have more disagreements and communication problems but fewer problems interacting with clients from different races and cultural backgrounds.

To reap the advantages of heterogeneity, it is important for group members to understand each others' differences and points of view and use these diverse perspectives to enable the group to perform at a high level and achieve its goals.[23] Table 10.2 summarizes some of the potential advantages of homogeneous and heterogeneous groups.

Toyota used heterogeneous groups, called *oobeyas*, to facilitate the design, manufacturing, marketing, and sales of its new Corolla and Corolla Matrix, as profiled in the accompanying Global View.

Homogeneous group A group in which members have many characteristics in common.

Heterogeneous group A group in which members have few characteristics in common.

TABLE 10. 2

Group Composition Advantages

Potential Advantages of Homogeneous Groups	Potential Advantages of Heterogeneous Groups
Group members like and get along well with each other.	Group makes good decisions because diverse points of view are represented.
Group members share information, have low levels of conflict, and have few coordination problems.	Group performs at a high level because the group has a variety of resources at its disposal.

global view

Oobeyas Design the Matrix

In Japanese, *oobeya* means "big, open office." However, the term pertains more to what goes on in the big, open space rather than the actual physical environment. An *oobeya* is a meeting of a heterogeneous group (that can be large) including people from all parts of an organization to work on a project in new and different ways. Takeshi Yoshida, Toyota's chief engineer for the 2003 Corolla and the five-door Corolla Matrix, utilized *oobeyas* around the globe to design and bring the new Corolla and Matrix to market. Yoshida's goals were to keep the sales price of the new Corolla under $15,000 while improving the car's design to appeal to drivers under 30 and incorporating the latest technology.[24]

Yoshida responded to this challenge by using an *oobeya* from day one. The initial *oobeya* brought people together from all parts of Toyota, including design, engineering, manufacturing, marketing, logistics, and sales to meet once a month for the two year period prior to the actual production of the new models. In an *oobeya*, there are no givens and everything is up for discussion. All participants are treated as equals and respected for their expertise. Sharing knowledge and information and improving communication across employees from heterogeneous units and divisions are emphasized.[25]

A key focus for the *oobeyas* was cutting costs both to keep the price of the Matrix under $15,000 and to enable important design changes and upgrades to be made.[26] By having employees involved in the design process who ordinarily would not be involved or involved only at a later point, Yoshida was able to cut costs in ways that a traditional design group would never have thought of. For example, an employee from logistics pointed out that Corollas with sunroofs were produced in a plant in Canada (where demand for sunroofs is low) and then shipped to states such as Florida, Texas, Louisiana, and California at a cost of $300 per vehicle shipped. Toyota has a plant in California, but that plant was not configured to produce vehicles with sunroofs. During a discussion between manufacturing and logistics in an *oobeya*, the decision was made to spend the money to modify the California plant to produce vehicles with sunroofs. Although the plant modification cost $600,000, the result was millions of dollars in reduced costs. Other *oobeya* meetings held in various locations resulted in more unique ways to cut costs that would probably have never occurred to employees if they hadn't met on a regular basis to share ideas. Still other *oobeya* meetings led to improvements in the design and standard features of the Matrix prior to production (at a lower cost than if they had been tacked on later in the process). The improvements included wheel covers, a 60–40 split back seat, and a CD player.[27] *Oobeyas* were critical to the successful design and production of both product lines,[28] and it was their use early on and throughout the process that was key.

GROUP FUNCTION

Group function *The work that a group performs as its contribution to the accomplishment of organizational goals.*

Group function is the work that a group contributes to the accomplishment of organizational goals. A manufacturing department, for example, is a command group that has the responsibility for producing the goods (automobiles, televisions, etc.) that an organization sells. The manufacturing department's function is to produce these goods in a cost-effective manner and maintain appropriate levels of quality.

Within the manufacturing department are small groups of employees responsible for performing a specific aspect of the manufacturing process. In an automobile-manufacturing plant, for example, one group's function might be to make the automobile bodies, another's to attach the transmission to the body, and another's to paint the body. In fact, we can think of an entire organization as a series of groups linked together according to the functions they perform.

The function of a group affects the behavior of its members by letting them know how their work contributes to the organization achieving its goals. A group's function gives its members a sense of meaning and purpose.[29] When members see how the work of their group influences the work of other groups, they may become motivated to perform at a high level. Just as task significance—the extent to which a job affects the lives and work of other people (see Chapter 7)—affects the intrinsic motivation of individuals, so, too, does a group's function. To motivate members, managers should remind them that their activities, behaviors, and the group's function all are important contributions to the organization.

GROUP STATUS

The work that some groups in an organization do is often seen as being more important to the organization's success than the work of other groups. **Group status** is the implicitly agreed upon, perceived importance of what a group does in an organization. The status of a top management team is likely to be very high because it sets the organization's goals and determines how it will achieve them. The work performed by a group of accountants who prepare quarterly profit-and-loss statements and balance sheets is certainly important. However, it is often seen as less central to the organization's performance as a whole than the work performed by the top management team. Thus, the status of the group of accountants is lower than that of the top management team. The more important the task performed by a work group or a group's function is, the higher is the group's status in the organization. Members of groups with high status are likely to be motivated to perform at a high level because they see their work as especially important for the success of the organization as a whole.

Group status The implicitly agreed upon, perceived importance for the organization as a whole of what a group does.

GROUP EFFICACY

Recall from Chapter 5 how self-efficacy is a powerful determinant of employees' behavior in an organization. Groups and teams have a sense of collective efficacy.[30] **Group efficacy** is the shared belief group members have about the ability of the group to achieve its goals and objectives.[31] How do members come to share a belief about the group's ability to coordinate and mobilize its members to perform effectively? By taking into account many of the factors that contribute to the group's effectiveness, such as its composition (including the ability, knowledge, and skills of its members), members' willingness to work together and share information, the resources the group has to work with, and the extent to which the group is able to develop effective strategies to achieve its goals.[32]

Group efficacy The shared belief group members have about the ability of the group to achieve its goals and objectives.

Thus, group efficacy develops over time as members come to understand each other, how the group functions, the tasks it needs to accomplish, and the group's capabilities.[33] We know from the stages of group development discussed earlier that it takes time for groups to perform up to their capabilities. Efficacy is not something that exists when a group is initially formed, but rather it is a shared belief that emerges over time as members work together. Just as a newly formed soccer league comprised of members who have never played together before will not have a sense of group efficacy until the league practices and competes with other leagues, so too will a newly formed group of computer programmers developing a novel software package lack a sense of what the group will be able to accomplish when it is first formed. However, as the soccer league practices and wins and loses games and as the group of programmers share their ideas, develop a strategy, and start writing code, both groups' collective sense of efficacy begins to emerge.

Once members come to share a sense of group efficacy, this will also play an important role in the future of the group.[34] For example, group efficacy can influence the aspirations members have for the group, their effort levels, how they approach tasks, and their persistence when the going gets tough.[35] A group of computer programmers with high group efficacy are likely to put forth more effort, be more persistent when problems arise, and have higher aspirations for what the group can achieve than a group of programmers with low efficacy.

When a group has low efficacy, there are a number of things that can be done to improve it. For example, if certain skills or capabilities are lacking in the group, there is a variety of ways to get them. That might mean adding new members with the requisite skills to the group, training existing members, or seeking outside help. If members are not able to effectively work together, group training and development might be in order (see Chapters 11 and 18). If the group is having trouble developing appropriate task strategies, members can reexamine the strategies they do rely on, reevaluate what seems to work and what doesn't, explicitly consider their strategies before they begin their tasks, and evaluate how effective the new strategies they utilized were upon completing their tasks. If communication problems exist, group members can take steps to become better communicators (see Chapter 14). Just as self-efficacy is an important determinant of individual accomplishments, group efficacy is an important determinant of group accomplishments.[36]

SOCIAL FACILITATION

Does a secretary type more or fewer letters when placed in a room with three other secretaries or in a private office? Does a computer programmer take more or less time to find an error in a complex program when working on the program in the presence of other computer programmers or when working alone? Research on social facilitation provides answers to questions such as these.

Social facilitation is the effect the physical presence of others has on an individual's performance. The presence of other group members tends to arouse or stimulate individuals, often because the individuals feel that others will evaluate their performance and give them positive or negative outcomes dependent on how well or poorly they do.

Two types of social facilitation effects have been studied. *Audience effects* are the effects of passive spectators on individual performance. In this case, other group members are not engaged in the task itself but are present as an audience. *Co-action effects* are the effects of the presence of other group members on the performance of an individual when the other group members are performing the same task as the individual.

Research on both types of social facilitation has produced some contradictory results, summarized in Figure 10.3. A typist might type more letters in the presence of other group members than when typing alone. But a computer programmer might take more time to find an error in a complex program when working in a group. Why?

> **Social facilitation** The effects that the presence of others has on performance, enhancing the performance of easy tasks and impairing the performance of difficult tasks.

FIGURE 10.3
Social Facilitation

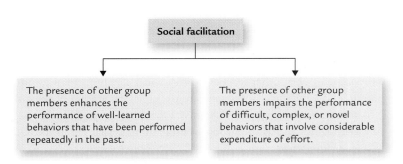

When individuals are stimulated by the presence of other group members, their performance of well-learned tasks and behaviors they have performed repeatedly in the past is enhanced.[37] Typing letters is a well-learned behavior for a secretary. She or he knows exactly how to do it—it doesn't require much thought. The presence of other group members enhances the secretary's performance, and she or he types more letters. More generally, when individuals are stimulated or aroused, their performance of well-learned tasks tends to be enhanced.

However, when individuals are stimulated by the presence of other group members, their performance of difficult, complex, or novel tasks and behaviors is impaired.[38] Finding an error in a complex computer program is a difficult task. The programmer will need to spend a considerable amount of attention, time, and effort to detect the error. It will probably take longer to locate it working in the presence of others, who might create distractions. More generally, when individuals are stimulated or aroused, their performance of difficult tasks tends to be impaired.

When people realize the presence of others is distracting them or interfering with their performance, they often try to isolate themselves by closing office doors, letting the answering machines take their calls, or finding quiet places to work alone.

Organizations can actually buy special furniture to maximize the benefits of social facilitation and minimize the drawbacks. Furniture and the arrangement of it can provide members with the space they need to work alone yet still provide the opportunity they need to meet together as a group. For example, Aetna Life & Casualty's employees in its home office are organized into self-managed work teams. Team members need to be able to meet with one another and coordinate their efforts. At the same time, they need to be alone to concentrate on complicated tasks, such as calculating the projected risks and returns for different types of insurance policies. Aetna's solution to the problem was to purchase some new "team" furniture manufactured by Steelcase.[39] The furniture divides the total work space into areas called "neighborhoods." In each neighborhood, a central work space is created with a table where members can meet. Individual work areas that are clustered around the central work space give employees the privacy they need to perform their tasks.[40]

How Groups Control Their Members: Roles and Rules

In order for any group (formal or informal, command group or self-managed work team, large or small, homogeneous or heterogeneous) to accomplish its goals, the group must *control*—that is, influence and regulate—its members' behavior. Controlling members' behavior is crucial whether a group is charged with writing superior computer programs, providing excellent customer service, raising quality levels, or cutting costs. Effective groups are groups that control their members' behavior and channel it in the right direction. A group of waiters and waitresses in a restaurant, for example, needs to ensure customers are promptly and courteously waited on, that staff members do not wait on each other's tables or grab each others' food orders, and that customers are given their checks in a timely fashion. Three mechanisms through which groups control their members' behavior are roles, rules, and norms. We discuss each next.

ROLES

The division of labor that occurs in groups and organizations necessitates the development of roles. Recall from Chapter 9 that a *role* is a set of behaviors or tasks a person is expected to perform by virtue of holding a position in a group or organization. When a group divides up its work and assigns particular tasks to individual members, different roles are established within the group. For example, there are four roles in a group of employees responsible for the evening news program at a small television station. The local news reporter's role is to compile local stories of interest and provide on-the-scene reports as needed. The state and national news reporter's role is to cover statewide news stories and help the news anchor cover important national stories. The anchor's role is to select the stories to be covered each night (based on the input of the local reporter and the state and national reporter) and prepare and deliver the news. The editor's role is to oversee this entire process and make sure that the time allotted for the news is efficiently and effectively used, that important stories are covered in a meaningful order, and that there is the right amount of on-the-scene reporting.

As we mentioned earlier, sometimes organizations form cross-functional teams. In a cross-functional team, a member's role is likely to be representing his or her function's perspective on the group's project.

Associated with each role in a group are certain responsibilities and rights. All of the behaviors expected of a role occupant (the individual assigned to a role) are the role occupant's *responsibilities.* On a news team, for example, the anchor's responsibility is to prepare and deliver the news. Each role occupant also has *rights or privileges*, such as the right to use resources assigned to the role. Resources can include people, money, specialized equipment, or machinery. The local news reporter on a news team has the right to use the local camera crew and its equipment and has a monthly budget at his or her disposal for tracking down stories.

Roles facilitate the control of group members' behaviors for several reasons. First, roles tell members what they should be doing. Second, roles not only enable a group to hold its members accountable for their behavior but also provide the group with a standard by which to evaluate the behavior. Finally, roles help managers determine how to reward members who perform the behaviors that make up their various roles.

Role relationships The ways in which group and organizational members interact with one another to perform their specific roles.

Members or managers also define the **role relationships** within the group. Role relationships dictate the way members should interact with one another to perform their specific roles. Role relationships may be formally specified in a written job description or emerge informally over time (for example, at the storming or norming stage of group development) as members work out methods for getting the job done.

On a news team, the anchor's role relationships with the local reporter and state and national reporter are formally specified in all three group members' job descriptions: The two reporters and the anchor are to work together to decide what stories will be covered each night, but the final decision is ultimately up to the anchor. The anchor has also developed an informal role relationship with the local reporter, who is given considerable autonomy to determine what local news gets covered. This informal role relationship developed when the anchor realized how skilled and motivated the local news reporter was.

A large part of a person's role in a group may not be specified but emerge over time as members interact with one another. For example, one member of a group may assume a significant number of responsibilities for the group and emerge as an informal leader when she handles those responsibilities well. Sometimes a manager notices that an informal leader performs certain tasks effectively and then promotes the informal leader to become the new formal leader, should the formal leader of the group leave, be promoted, or replaced. The process of taking the initiative to create a role by assuming certain responsibilities that are not part of one's assigned role is called **role making**. In contrast, **role taking** is the process of performing one's responsibilities associated with an assigned role. Role taking is the common process of assuming a formal organizational role.

Role making Taking the initiative to create a role by assuming responsibilities that are not part of an assigned role.

Role taking Performing the responsibilities that are required as part of an assigned role.

On the news team, for example, the local news reporter did such a good job covering the local scene for the evening news that the anchor always followed her suggestions for stories. Station managers recognized her initiative and high performance, and when the anchor left for a better position in a larger city, the local reporter was promoted to become the new anchor. Role making can be an important process in self-managed work teams where members are jointly trying to find innovative ways to accomplish the group's goals.

WRITTEN RULES

Effective groups sometimes use written rules to control their members' behavior. Written rules specify behaviors that are required and those that are forbidden. The news team, for example, developed a rule that requires members to determine at the beginning of each year when they will take their allotted three weeks of vacation. Other rules require them to arrange their schedules so that only one person is on vacation on any given day, and no one can take more than one week off at a time. The rules help the group cover and present each day's news thoroughly and maintain the continuity of the news from the viewer's perspective. Over time, groups should experiment with their rules and try to find better ones to replace those that currently exist.

Some rules groups develop, often called *standard operating procedures*, specify in writing the best way to perform a particular task. Standard operating procedures help ensure the group's tasks will be performed correctly and efficiently. For example, a rule specifies exactly when and in what form the news anchor should communicate his or her plans for the evening news each night to the editor so that the editor has enough time to review the format and make any needed changes before the program airs. Zingerman's Community of Businesses (ZCoB) has developed its own unique standard operating procedures. ZCoB's procedures have been so effective that other companies send their employees to its training center to learn them, as profiled in the accompanying OB Today.

ob today

Zingerman's "Steps" to Success

Zingerman's Delicatessen was founded in 1982 by Ari Weinzweig and Paul Saginaw in Ann Arbor, Michigan.[41] Weinzweig and Saginaw are food aficionados. From the start, they have prided themselves on making wonderful sandwiches and tracking down unique, traditional foods. Finding tasty treasures from around the world and endless selections of the best condiments, including exotic oils, vinegars, and olives has been a labor of love for the two.[42] In order to expand their business yet maintain high quality service and an intimate atmosphere, Weinzweig and Saginaw expanded their deli concept to encompass a community of related businesses that they call ZCoB. ZCoB now includes the original deli, a mail-order unit, a bakery, a caterer, and a creamery.[43] The founders' persistent emphasis on great food, high-quality service, and commitment to people and community are part and parcel to their savvy business expertise.[44]

A primary tool that ZCoB uses to manage its businesses and train employees is its unique brand of standard operating procedures. These procedures encapsulate the key steps necessary to accomplish important objectives at ZCoB. During training, new employees learn the "Four Steps to Selling Great Food." Step 1 is "know the food"—whether it's how a certain artisan bread rises or olives are cured.[45] There are also distinct steps for particular food groups. For example, "Six Steps to Selecting Superior Cheese" include a primary emphasis on taste, choosing handmade cheeses, and getting your cheese cut to order.[46] Having trouble with a co-worker? "Four Steps to Productive Resolution of Your Differences" suggests you speak directly to the co-worker about your concerns.[47] And not forgetting the need to make a profit, ZCoB's "Three Steps to Great Finance" suggests you should understand how finance works, measure your financial performance on a weekly basis, and make sure all employees benefit from good financial performance.[48]

As word of ZCoB's success spread, other organizations sought to emulate it. Enter Zing Train, ZCoB's training, development, and consulting business. Hospitals, restaurants, banks, and grocery store chains have all sent employees to Zing Train in Ann Arbor to learn ZCoB's steps to success in different business areas.[49] The steps not only seem to work, but they also lead to satisfied employees who love what they do.

Rules have several advantages that help groups control and manage behavior and performance:

◆ Rules help groups ensure members will engage in behaviors that contribute to the effectiveness of the group and the organization and avoid behaviors that hinder performance and goal attainment.

◆ Rules facilitate the control of behavior because members and managers know how and when role occupants are expected to perform their assigned tasks.

◆ Rules facilitate the evaluation of individual group members' performance levels because their behavior can be compared to the behavior specified by the rules.

◆ When the membership in a group changes, rules help newcomers learn the right way to perform their roles.

A group can develop rules at any stage of its development. Rules developed at early stages are often changed or abandoned as the nature of the group's work, group goals, or organizational goals change. A healthy group recognizes the need for change and is willing to alter its rules and roles when warranted.

How Groups Control Their Members: Group Norms

Roles and rules help group members and managers control the behavior in groups because they specify the behaviors members should engage in. Norms serve the same purpose.[50] Norms signal members about the behavior expected of them. Unlike written rules, however, which are *formal* descriptions of actions and behaviors required by a group or organization, **group norms** are *informal* rules of conduct. Often they are not put in writing. Recall from the opening case how the H2 team norms included speaking out and challenging the status quo.

Group norms Informal rules of conduct for behaviors considered important by most group members.

When members share a common idea of acceptable behavior, they can monitor each other's behavior to make sure everyone is following the group's norms. This is key to controlling the group. Groups enforce their norms by rewarding members who conform to the norms by behaving in the specified manner and punishing members who deviate from the norms.[51] Rewards for conforming to group norms can include being treated in a friendly manner by other group members, verbal praise, receiving help from others when needed, and tangible rewards, such as bonuses or perks. Punishments for deviations can include being ignored by other members, criticized or reprimanded, stripped of certain privileges, or expelled from the group.

A group of waiters and waitresses in a busy restaurant may develop informal norms to the effect that members should not steal each other's tables or orders in the kitchen and should always inform others when they observe that customers at another member's table are ready for their check. These norms help the group effectively accomplish its goal of providing good service to customers and earning the best tips possible. A group member who does not follow the norm (a waiter, for example, who steals an order in the kitchen on a particularly busy day) might be reprimanded. If deviation from the norm continues, the individual might even be expelled from the group. A waitress who continually steals tables to earn more tips, for example, might be brought to the attention of the restaurant manager and eventually fired. Waiters and waitresses who conform to the group's norms are rewarded with continued membership in the group and other perks. Those perks might include verbal praise from the restaurant manager and other members and bigger tips from customers.

Like formal roles and rules, norms develop to channel the behavior of members in a direction that leads to the achievement of group and organizational goals.[52] When norms exist, members do not have to waste time thinking about what to do in a particular situation; norms guide their actions and specify how they should behave. Furthermore, when people share common norms, they can predict how others will behave in certain situations and thus anticipate one another's actions. This improves the interaction among members and results in fewer misunderstandings between them.

WHY DO GROUP MEMBERS CONFORM TO NORMS?

Individuals conform to group norms for three main reasons. The first and most widespread basis for conformity to group norms is **compliance**—assenting to a norm in order to attain rewards or avoid punishment.[53] When individuals comply with norms, they do not necessarily believe the behavior specified by the norm is important for its own sake. However, they know that abiding by the norm will result in certain benefits and ignoring it will result in certain costs. Consider how norms operate in the following example. The internal auditing department of a chemical company annually solicits contributions for the United Way, a charitable organization. Mary Kelly is a group member who doesn't really like the United Way because she has read some articles questioning the way the charitable organization uses its funds. Nevertheless, Kelly always contributes to the United Way because she is afraid her co-workers will think less of her and perhaps avoid her if she does not.

     The second reason for conformity is **identification**—associating oneself with supporters of a norm and conforming to the norm because those individuals do. John Bickers, one of the newest members of the auditing department, really looks up to Ralph Diaz and Steve Cashion, who have been in the department for several years and are ripe for promotion. Around the time of the United Way campaign, Bickers casually asks Diaz and Cashion over lunch how they feel about the United Way. Both Diaz and Cashion indicate they think it's a worthy cause, and both tell Bickers they contributed to it during the annual fund drive. This information causes Bickers to decide to contribute as well.

     The third and potentially most powerful basis for conformity to group norms is **internalization**—believing that the behavior dictated by the norm is truly the right way to behave. Diaz and Cashion's basis for conformity is internalization: They wholeheartedly believe in the United Way's cause. Norms have the most influence on group members when the basis for conformity is internalization. Similarly, members of the H2 team profiled in the opening case internalized their norms, believing they were in the best interest of GM and its customers.

IDIOSYNCRASY CREDIT

Although most group members are expected to conform to group norms, one or a few group members sometimes are allowed to deviate from the norms without being punished. These privileged individuals are generally group members who have contributed a lot to the group in the past. Their above-average contributions to the group give them what has been termed **idiosyncrasy credit**—the freedom to violate group norms without being punished.[54]

     In the restaurant described earlier, John Peters, the waiter who has been with the restaurant for the longest period of time, generally takes on the responsibility of training new waiters and waitresses and settling conflicts that arise in the group. On very busy days, Peters sometimes "mistakes" other group members' orders in the kitchen for his own. However, he is never reprimanded for stealing orders. His beyond-the-call-of-duty contributions to the group give him idiosyncrasy credit, which allows him to deviate

Compliance Assenting to a norm in order to attain rewards or avoid punishment.

Identification Associating oneself with supporters of a norm and conforming to the norm because those individuals do.

Internalization Believing that the behavior dictated by a norm is truly the right and proper way to behave.

Idiosyncrasy credit The freedom to violate group norms without being punished that is accorded to group members who have contributed a lot to the group in the past.

from the group's norms. Similarly, a highly skilled developer in a group of computer programmers might frequently fight with other group members and with the supervisor yet never be reprimanded. Although her behavior violates the group's norm of members being polite and considerate to one another, the behavior is tolerated because this programmer is the one who always finds the bug in a program.

THE PROS AND CONS OF CONFORMITY AND DEVIANCE

From our discussion of group norms, you probably get the impression that conformity is good in all situations. Conformity *is* good when norms help a group control and influence its members' behavior so that the group can accomplish its goals. But what if a group's norms are inappropriate or unethical? Or what if a norm that was once appropriate is no longer appropriate because the situation has changed? Many norms, such as always behaving courteously to customers or always leaving a work area clean, promote organizational effectiveness, but some group norms do not.

Studies have shown that groups of employees can develop norms that actually hurt the group's performance. A group of employees on an assembly line might develop norms to control the speed at which the work is performed. An employee who works very quickly (and, thus, produces "too much") may be called a "rate buster." An employee who works very slowly (or below the group norm) may be called a "gold-bricker," a "slacker," or a "chiseler."[55] Other members of the group may reprimand slackers and rate busters alike. In the case of a rate buster, the reprimand may hinder group performance, because rate busters generally tend to lower their levels of performance to fall more in line with the group norm.

This same kind of process can occur at all levels in an organization. A group of middle managers may adopt a don't-rock-the-boat norm that signals managers to agree with whatever top management proposes, regardless of whether they think the ideas are right or wrong. A new middle manager soon learns that it doesn't pay to rock the boat because this behavior will incur the wrath of not only the top manager but his or her co-managers, too. When such a norm exists, all middle managers might be reluctant to speak up even when they all realize that a change is sorely needed for the organization's success. In cases like this, conformity maintains dysfunctional group behaviors, and deviance from the norm is appropriate.

Deviance Deviation from a norm.

Deviance—deviation from a norm—occurs when a member of a group violates a norm. Groups usually respond to deviance in one of three ways.[56] First, the group might try to get the deviant to change by, for example, explaining to the deviant why the norm is so important, pointing out that he or she is the only member of the group violating the norm, or reprimanding and punishing the deviant for violating the norm. Second, the group might reject[57] or try to expel the deviant, as the group of restaurant employees did when a waitress violated the norm of not stealing tables. Third, the group might actually change the norm in question to be more in line with the deviant's behavior. When group norms are inappropriate, deviance can spark a needed change within the group.

BALANCING CONFORMITY AND DEVIANCE

As illogical as it might sound, groups need both conformity and deviance to accomplish their goals and perform at a high level. In our restaurant example, conformity to the group norms of not stealing tables or food orders and of informing members when customers are ready for their checks helps the group meet its goals. A group norm for handling customer complaints, however, has recently changed.

In the past, whenever customers complained about a meal, the norm was to refer the complaint to the restaurant manager. The manager would talk to the customer and invariably offer him or her an alternative selection. Then, on a particularly busy day, one of Sally Schumaker's customers had a complaint. Rather than seek out the manager, Schumaker decided to handle the problem herself. She offered the customer another meal because that was how the manager always solved such a problem. After that, Schumaker continued to take matters into her own hands whenever one of her customers had a complaint. Over time, other members of the group noticed Schumaker's behavior and asked her why she was circumventing the restaurant manager. She explained her reasons for violating the group norm, and they made sense to the other members: Handling problems themselves would enable them to please dissatisfied customers more quickly and avoid bothering the manager with every problem.

John Peters, the senior waiter, decided to check with the manager to make sure it was all right with him if the waitstaff offered a new meal for a customer who had a complaint about the food. The manager thought this was a great idea and was surprised he hadn't thought of it himself. He informed the waitstaff that from then on they should handle complaints themselves (as Schumaker was already doing), but that they should be sure to let the cook know about the nature of the complaints.

The norm of referring all complaints to the restaurant manager was dysfunctional for the group of waiters and waitresses for two reasons: (1) It meant keeping dissatisfied customers waiting (which prevented the group from achieving its good-service goal), and (2) it meant seeking out the manager, which took time that could have been used to serve other customers (preventing members from earning the maximum amount of tips they could). Deviance from this norm was functional for the group because it stimulated the group to reexamine the norm and change it.

As this story shows, *conformity* ensures that a group can control members' behaviors to get tasks accomplished, and *deviance* forces group members to reexamine the appropriateness of norms. Figure 10.4 depicts the relationship between levels of conformity and deviance in a group and the group's goal accomplishment. The group at point A has a low level of conformity and a high level of deviance. This group has difficulty controlling members' behaviors and fails to attain its goals. The group at point B has achieved just the right balance: Conformity helps the group direct members' behaviors toward its goals, and deviance forces it to periodically reexamine the appropriateness of it norms. In the group at point C, conformity is so high that it is stressed at the expense of the group achieving its goals. Because group members are extremely reluctant to deviate from its norms, this group retains dysfunctional norms and resists any sort of change.

Because deviance can be an impetus for change and improvement, how groups respond to deviance can be an important determinant of group effectiveness. For example, research has found that groups can benefit by allowing members who deviate from the norms or hold a position at odds with the majority to air their views.[58] Sometimes the deviant or dissenter is justified, and the norm or majority position is ineffective or unwarranted. In this case, by listening to the deviant and thinking through his or her arguments, the group might improve how it functions. Even if the deviant's position is not justified, listening to him or her and discussing his or her perspective is likely to lead the group to a better understanding of the issues at hand, including the deviant.[59] Additionally, when the group's tasks require creativity[60] (see Chapter 5), it is especially important that all views are expressed and heard, regardless of how outlandish or deviant they might seem.

Some national cultures promote high levels of conformity. In cultures such as these group members are likely to abide by the norms at all cost and fear change. This phenomenon is prevalent in Japan. In Japan, young children are taught the importance of conforming to group norms at an early age because the Japanese tend to see conformity as desirable and change as threatening. For example, JAL Coordination Service

FIGURE 10.4

The Relationship Between Levels of Conformity and Deviance in a Group and Group Goal Accomplishment

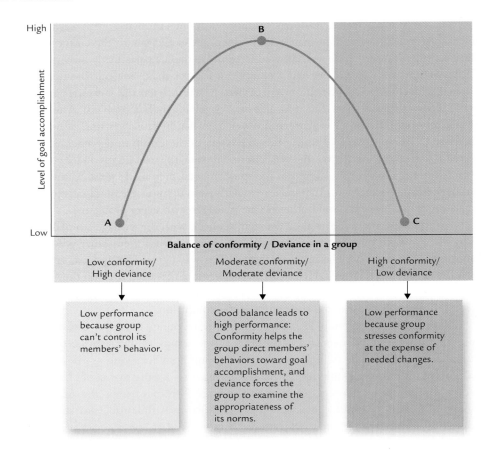

Company, a Japanese company, teaches its female office employees the proper ways to bow and smile, per the norm. Proper bowing and smiling are deemed to be so important, in fact, other companies send hundreds of their members to JAL each year for a two-day, bowing-and-smiling training seminar. The cost is about $240 per employee. The Japanese stress conformity to group norms to such a great extent that harmony is sometimes valued over needed change. Sociologist Akira Fujitake suggests that change in Japan may be slow because of "a barrier called 'the group.'"[61] The use of *oobeyas*, profiled earlier in a Global View, can be an effective way of alleviating the pressures related to conformity. In an *oobeya*, everyone is on equal footing, has a voice, and is listened to, and all issues are open for discussion and potential disagreement.

ENSURING THAT GROUP NORMS ARE FUNCTIONAL FOR THE ORGANIZATION

In our restaurant example, because the group's goals are aligned with the restaurant's goals, the norms that are functional for the group are also functional for the organization. Similarly, the norms that are dysfunctional for the group (such as referring all customer complaints to the manager) are dysfunctional for the organization. When group and organizational goals are closely aligned, groups are inclined to develop norms that help the groups achieve its goals and are also functional for the organization. Likewise, they are inclined to discard norms that are dysfunctional for the group and the organization.

Group goals, however, are not always congruent with organizational goals. The goal of a group of employees who assemble radios, for example, might be to *minimize* the amount of effort each member exerts on the job. To achieve this goal, the employees develop the norm of assembling no more than 50 radios a day. The group could easily assemble 75 radios each day, but this performance level would entail additional effort on the part of members.

In this case, the group norm is clearly dysfunctional for the organization because group goals are inconsistent with organizational goals. The norm, however, is functional for the group because it helps members achieve their goal of not having to work too hard.

How can managers ensure that group norms are functional and aligned with those of the organization? One way is by making sure members are rewarded when the organization achieves its goals. In our restaurant example, members benefited from the restaurant achieving its goal of providing good service because good service leads to bigger tips. Another way is by rewarding group members on the basis of individual or group performance.

The group of employees assembling radios, on the other hand, receives no tangible benefits when the organization reaches its performance goal. Members are paid on an hourly basis and receive the same amount of money regardless of how many radios they assemble. Their group goal (minimizing effort expenditure) is not aligned with their organization's goal (performance) because they do not benefit if the organizational goal is met. The norms the group has developed (restricting production) are functional for its members but dysfunctional for the organization.

The need to align group and organizational goals has a very clear implication for how outcomes (such as pay) should be distributed to members of the group when their individual contributions or performance levels cannot be readily identified or evaluated. Essentially, the outcomes members receive should be based on the group's levels of performance. In other words, members should be rewarded when the group is effective and contributes to the attainment of the organization's overall goals. When members are rewarded for their high performance, this then becomes a group goal, and norms develop toward that end. If our radio employees were able to increase their earnings by assembling more radios, it is likely the group's goal would be to increase production rather than to limit it, and new norms would probably develop toward this end.

you're the management expert

Aligning Goals

Marcy Long heads a diagnostic laboratory that performs a wide variety of blood tests in a large city. When physicians give their patients medical orders to have certain blood tests performed, Long's lab is one of many in the city patients have the option to use. The laboratory accepts most major insurance plans in the area and has a close relationship with many of the nearby medical practices. Some of these practices direct their patients exclusively to Long's lab. Patients, of course, can choose to go elsewhere, but often they do not. Although Long is generally satisfied with the performance of her employees, several physicians recently complained to her that the staff are inflexible in terms of making exceptions and being responsive to special requests. For example, if a certain blood test typically takes three days but can be performed in one or two days if needed, staff members are unwilling to do the test sooner, even when the reasons for doing so are compelling. As another example, when a patient has multiple tests performed and some take longer

than others, the lab typically waits until all or most of the test results are in before faxing them over to the physicians. In some cases, physicians and/or patients are anxious to get the results as they become available, and the lab's policy is to accommodate these requests. However, some physicians have told Long they've repeatedly had to request partial results before receiving them. Long has always told her staff members that they the need to be sensitive to the needs of patients and their doctors and as responsive as possible while maintaining the highest standards in the field. While her staff excels at the latter, she has come to realize they are not as responsive as they could be. Although she has emphasized this point repeatedly in staff meetings, the complaints from physicians and their patients have not stopped. In one instance, Long herself had to intervene to satisfy a special request.

Because you are an expert in OB, Long has come to you for help. How can she get her staff to be flexible and responsive to the special requests and needs of physicians and their patients?

Socialization: How Group Members Learn Roles, Rules, And Norms

Socialization The process by which newcomers learn the roles, rules, and norms of a group.

The ability of a group to control its members' behaviors depends on the extent to which newcomers learn the group's roles, rules, and norms. Newcomers do not initially know what is expected of them and what they can and cannot do.[62] A newcomer to a group of secretaries, for example, does not know whether it is all right to take a long lunch one day and make up the time the next day or whether it is acceptable to work from 8:30 to 4:30 instead of from 9:00 to 5:00. Newcomers are outsiders, and only when they have learned the group's roles, rules, and norms do existing group members accept them as insiders. The process by which newcomers learn the roles, rules, and norms of a group is **socialization**.

A newcomer can learn how the group controls members' behavior by simply observing how existing members behave and inferring from this behavior what is appropriate and what is inappropriate. This might be perfectly acceptable to the newcomer, but from the group's point of view, it could be risky because the newcomer might observe and learn bad habits that are unacceptable to the group. In one of our earlier examples, a computer programmer gets away with argumentative behavior that violates the group norm of being cooperative because of her idiosyncrasy credit. A newcomer to the group observing her combative behavior, however, might mistakenly assume this behavior is acceptable—that it is in conformity with a group norm.

SOCIALIZATION AND ROLE ORIENTATION

Role orientation The characteristic way in which members of a group respond to various situations.

John Van Mannen and Edgar Schein developed a model of socialization describing the different ways in which groups socialize their members. How groups socialize newcomers, in turn, influences the role orientation that newcomers adopt.[63] **Role orientation** is the characteristic way in which members of a group respond to various situations. For example, do members react passively and obediently to commands and orders? Are they creative and innovative when it comes to finding solutions to problems?

Van Mannen and Schein identified six pairs of contrasting socialization tactics that influence a newcomer's learning and role orientation. The use of different combinations of these tactics leads to two different role orientations: institutionalized and individualized. In an **institutionalized role orientation**, newcomers are taught to respond to situations in the same way that existing group members respond to similar situations. An institutional orientation encourages obedience and conformity to existing roles, rules, and norms. Newcomers who have an institutionalized orientation are more likely to engage in role taking rather than in role making because this orientation emphasizes the importance of following existing ways of doing things.

Institutionalized role orientation A role orientation in which newcomers are taught to respond to situations in the same way that existing group members respond to similar situations.

Individualized role orientation A role orientation in which newcomers are taught that it is acceptable and desirable to be creative and to experiment with changing how the group does things.

In an **individualized role orientation**, individuals are taught that it is acceptable and desirable to be creative and to experiment with changing how the group does things.[64] Although group members with an individualized orientation still need to learn and follow existing roles, rules, and norms, they realize that these ways of controlling behavior are not cast in stone and that the group will consider changing them if a more effective way of behaving is identified. Members with an individualized orientation tend to engage more in role making rather than in role taking.

SOCIALIZATION TACTICS

The socialization tactics identified by Van Mannen and Schein are discussed next and summarized in Table 10.3. Groups or organizations can use all six tactics or a subset of the six tactics, depending on their needs and goals. Each of the six tactics actually represents a pair of contrasting tactics from which a choice can be made.

Tactics That Lead to an Institutionalized Orientation	Tactics That Lead to an Individualized Orientation
Collective tactics	Individual tactics
Formal tactics	Informal tactics
Sequential tactics	Random tactics
Fixed tactics	Variable tactics
Serial tactics	Disjunctive tactics
Divestiture tactics	Investiture tactics

Collective Versus Individual Tactics. When *collective* tactics are used, newcomers go through a common learning experience designed to produce standardized or highly similar responses to different situations. For example, all of the new sales associates hired by a department store receive collective socialization by participating in the same two-week training program. They watch videotapes showing the proper way to greet customers, process a sale or returned item, and deal with customer complaints.

When *individualized* tactics are used, newcomers are taught individually how to behave. Because learning takes place on an individual basis, each newcomer's learning experiences are somewhat different, and newcomers are encouraged to behave differently in the various situations they may encounter on the job. For example, newcomers to a group of cosmetics salespeople, each of whom is responsible for a different line (Estée Lauder, Lancôme, and so one), are socialized individually by company representatives to ensure they develop the appropriate knowledge about the line and the type of customers it appeals to.

Collective tactics tend to lead to an *institutionalized* orientation; *individual* tactics tend to lead to an *individualized* orientation.

Formal Versus Informal Tactics. When tactics are *formal*, newcomers are segregated from existing group members during the learning process. For example, new sales associates receive their two-week training in the department store's training room. During this period, they never interact with members of the groups they are to join after their training is complete.

When tactics are *informal*, newcomers learn on the job. For example, many restaurants socialize new waiters and waitresses by having them work alongside experienced waiters and waitresses.

Formal tactics tend to lead to an *institutionalized* orientation; *informal* tactics tend to lead to an *individualized* orientation.

Sequential Versus Random Tactics. When *sequential* tactics are used, newcomers are provided with explicit information about the sequence in which they will perform new behaviors. For example, a new assistant in a veterinarians' office is told that during her first two weeks she will assist the vets with routine checkups. After that, she will also weigh the animals and administer injections. After one month on the job, she will also assist the vets in surgery.

When *random* tactics are used, the order in which socialization proceeds is based on the interests and needs of the individual newcomer, and no set sequence is followed. For example, an apprentice woodworker who has just joined a group of custom furniture makers might be told that the order in which he learns to make the different types of furniture is up to him.

Sequential tactics tend to lead to an *institutionalized* orientation; *random* tactics tend to lead to an *individualized* orientation.

Fixed Versus Variable Tactics.

Fixed tactics give newcomers precise knowledge about the timetable for completing each stage in the learning process. The socialization of the assistant in the veterinarians' office relies on fixed tactics. The assistant knew that two weeks would have to elapse before she moved on to the next stage in her training.

Variable tactics provide no information about when newcomers will reach a certain stage in the learning process; the speed of socialization depends on the individual newcomer. The woodworker was socialized with variable tactics; he was never told how long it should take him to learn how to make different types of furniture.

Fixed tactics tend to lead to an *institutionalized* orientation; *random* tactics tend to lead to an *individualized* orientation.

Serial Versus Disjunctive Tactics.

When *serial* tactics are used, existing group members socialize newcomers. (Waiters and waitresses training newcomers is one example.)

When *disjunctive* tactics are used, newcomers must figure out and develop their own way of behaving. They are not told what to do by experienced group members. For example, many new professors learn how to teach and do research through disjunctive socialization. Experienced professors in the groups or department they join often do not give them training or guidance in how to teach and do research.

Serial tactics tend to lead to an *institutionalized* orientation; *disjunctive* tactics tend to lead to an *individualized* orientation.

Divestiture Versus Investiture Tactics.

With *divestiture* tactics, newcomers receive negative interpersonal treatment from other members of the group. For example, they are ignored or taunted. Existing group members refrain from treating newcomers kindly and with respect until they learn existing roles, rules, and norms. The classic example of divestiture is in military boot camp, where new recruits are insulted and subject to a wide variety of abuse until they learn the ropes.

With *investiture* tactics, newcomers immediately receive positive social support from other group members. For example, a group of nurses might go out of its way to teach a new member how things are done in the group and make the member feel welcome.

Divestiture tactics tend to lead to an *institutionalized* orientation; *investiture* tactics tend to lead to an *individualized* orientation.

To summarize, collective, formal, sequential, fixed, serial, and divestiture tactics tend to lead newcomers to develop an institutionalized orientation. Individual, informal, random, variable, disjunctive, and investiture tactics tend to lead newcomers to develop an individualized orientation.[65] What is the significance of this model for socialization in organizations?

Consider the use of socialization tactics by the military. New recruits are placed in platoons with other new recruits (*collective*), are segregated from existing group members (*formal*), go through preestablished drills and learning experiences (*sequential*), know exactly how long basic training will take and what they have to do (*fixed*), have superior officers such as platoon sergeants who socialize them (*serial*), and are treated with little respect and tolerance until they have learned their duties and "gotten with the program" (*divestiture*). As a result of their socialization experiences, new recruits develop an institutionalized role orientation in which obedience and conformity to group roles, rules, and norms are signs of success. New members who cannot, or will not, perform according to these standards either leave the military or are asked to leave.

Few groups exert the same amount of control over its members as the military, but other groups do use similar tactics to socialize their members. For example, Disneyland prides itself on visitors having a fun-filled experience in a wholesome, clean, cheerful, and friendly theme park. How does an organization that employs over 30,000 people ensure its employees will behave in accordance these standards? A careful socialization process geared toward developing an institutionalized role orientation is one important means for Disney.

Disney wants all its employees to carefully follow its roles (such as their individual job duties), rules (such as refraining from growing mustaches or wearing dangling earrings), and norms (such as always going the extra mile to help guests have a good time). The institutionalized orientation helps employees do their jobs the Disney way and helps the company succeed in its quest to maintain its competitive advantage.

New recruits, or "cast members" as they are called at Disney, receive formal training at Disney University in groups of around 45. Their collective socialization follows a set sequence of activities. During the Traditions I program, which lasts for a day and a half, newcomers learn the Disney language and the four Disney guiding principles: safety, courtesy, show or entertainment, and efficiency. They also receive training in how to answer guests' questions no matter how difficult the questions may be.

Once cast members complete Traditions I, they move on to further socialization in the attraction areas (Adventureland, Fantasyland, and so on) that they will be joining. This session, which can last as long as a day and a half, covers the rules for each specific area. Last, but not least, is on-the-job training the newcomers will be given by the experienced cast members in the groups they're joining (a serial tactic). This part of the socialization process can take up to two and a half weeks to complete and includes new cast members' learning their roles and their accompanying responsibilities, privileges, and role relationships. All in all, careful socialization ensures new cast members learn how to do things the Disney way.[66]

Should a group encourage an institutional role orientation in which newcomers accept the status quo? Or should it encourage an individual role orientation whereby newcomers are allowed to develop creative and innovative responses to the tasks required of them? The answer to this question depends on the goals of the group and organization.

The main benefit of an institutionalized orientation is also its main danger: the homogeneity it produces among group members. If all members of a group have been socialized to share the same way of looking at the world and have the same strong allegiance to existing roles, rules, and norms, the group may become resistant to change and lack the wherewithal to come up with creative solutions to problems. As we discuss in Chapter 18, however, the very survival of groups and organizations

Disney socializes its thousands of employees, or "cast numbers," by sending them to Disney University. Careful socialization and training ensures new cast members learn how to act the Disney way.

depends on their willingness and ability to change as needed in response to changes in the environments in which they exist. Such changes include changes in customer demands, in the nature and diversity of the workforce, and changes in economic conditions or technology. Groups such as marketing departments, self-managed work teams, and research and development teams, and organizations such as consumer products firms, auto companies, and computer manufacturers are likely to have to respond to frequent changes in the business climate. These groups and organizations can benefit from an individualized orientation and should try to use individual, informal, random, variable, disjunctive, and investiture tactics whenever feasible. Microsoft, for example, tends to rely on many of these tactics to promote individualized role orientations. Microsoft takes this approach because the effectiveness of the various groups in the organization depends not on standardized individual behavior (like at Disneyland) but on encouraging members to come up with new and improved solutions to software problems.

Socialization helps groups achieve whatever goals they have established—to provide consistently high-quality audits, to assemble 75 radios a day, and to develop new software—by helping them control their members' behaviors. Whether a group wants its members to closely follow established ways of doing things or offer suggestions for ways to do things differently, it needs to exert control over its members' behaviors and actions in order to make this happen.

Summary

Work groups are the basic building blocks of an organization. Work groups use roles, rules, and norms to control their members' behavior, and they use several socialization tactics to turn newcomers into effective group members. Groups contribute to organizational effectiveness when group goals are aligned with organizational goals. In this chapter, we made the following major points:

1. Two attributes separate work groups from random collections of individuals in an organization. Members of a work group (a) interact with each other and (b) perceive the potential for mutual goal accomplishment. Work groups vary in whether they are formal or informal. Formal work groups include command groups, task forces, teams, and self-managed work teams. Informal work groups include friendship groups and interest groups. Teams are characterized by intense interactions between team members to achieve team goals.

2. Groups develop and change over time. The five-stage model of group development proposes that groups develop in five sequential stages: forming, storming, norming, performing, and adjourning. Research, however, has not indicated that there is a universal set of stages that all groups experience in the same order.

3. Five important characteristics of groups are size, composition, function, status, and group efficacy. Each has the potential to affect the extent to which a group achieves its goals, performs at a high level, and ultimately is effective in helping an organization attain its goals. Social facilitation is a characteristic effect that the presence of other group members has on individual performance such that having others present enhances performance of well-learned tasks and impairs performance of difficult tasks.

4. All groups, regardless of their type or characteristics, need to control their members' behaviors to be effective and attain their goals. Roles and rules can be used to control behavior in groups.

5. A role is a set of behaviors or tasks that a person is expected to perform by virtue of holding a position in a group or organization. Roles have rights

and responsibilities attached to them. Role relationships are the ways in which group and organizational members interact with each other to perform their specific roles. Group members acquire roles through role making and through role taking.

6. Written rules specify behaviors that are required of group members or are forbidden. They also specify how particular tasks should be performed.

7. Groups also control their members' behavior by developing and enforcing group norms. Group norms are shared expectations for behavior within a group. There are three bases for conformity to group norms: compliance, identification, and internalization.

8. To accomplish goals and perform at a high level, groups need both conformity to and deviance from norms. Whether group norms result in high levels of group performance depends on the extent to which group goals are consistent with organizational goals. To facilitate goal alignment, group members should benefit or be rewarded when the group performs at a high level and contributes to the achievement of organizational goals.

9. Group members learn roles, rules, and norms through the process of socialization. Collective, formal, sequential, fixed, serial, and divestiture socialization tactics tend to lead to an institutionalized role orientation. Individual, informal, random, variable, disjunctive, and investiture socialization tactics tend to lead to an individualized role orientation.

Exercises in Understanding and Managing Organizational Behavior

Questions for Discussion and Review

1. At what stage in the five-stage model of group development might groups exert the most control over their members' behavior?

2. Do most members of an organization want to work in teams? Why or why not?

3. In what situations might the advantages of large group size outweigh the disadvantages?

4. In what kinds of situations might it be especially important to have heterogeneous groups?

5. Why are roles an important means of controlling group members' behaviors in self-managed work teams?

6. Why do groups need rules?

7. How are rules that specify how to perform a particular task developed?

8. Why might a group keep following a dysfunctional norm or a norm that prevents the group from achieving its goals?

9. Do all groups socialize their members? Do all groups need to socialize their members? Why or why not?

10. Is socialization ever completely finished, or is it an ongoing process?

Building People Skills

Analyzing a "Real" Group

Choose a work group featured in a television series (e.g., *Karen Cisco, The Practice, CSI Miami, Will & Grace*). For the group you have chosen, answer these questions:

1. Is this a formal or an informal group? What kind of formal or informal group is it?

2. What stage of development is this group at according to the five-stage model of group development?

3. What can you say about the size, composition, function, and status of this group?

4. What are the roles and role relationships in this group?

5. What rights and responsibilities are attached to each role in the group?

6. What rules does this group use to control its members' behavior?

7. What norms does this group use to control its members' behavior?

8. How does the group react to deviance from its norms?

9. Do any members of this group have idiosyncrasy credit?

A Question of Ethics

In many organizations, some groups of employees typically have higher status than others. And sometimes the groups with the lower status feel that they are not appreciated and are "second-class citizens." For example, in hospitals, physicians generally have higher status than nurses; in universities, faculty typically have higher status than staff; and in law firms, partners have higher status than attorneys who are not partners and paralegals.

Questions

1. Think about the ethical implications of these kinds of status differences in organizations.
2. To what extent should groups with different status in an organization be treated differently and to what extent should they receive equal treatment? Why?

Small Group Break-Out Exercise

Encouraging Dissenting Views

Form groups of three or four people, and appoint one member as the spokesperson who will communicate your conclusions to the rest of the class.

1. Take a few minutes to think about groups that you were a member of in which there was a high level of conformity to group norms.
2. Think about how someone who openly disagreed with the majority would feel and be treated in these groups.
3. Take turns describing these groups and the bases for conformity in them. And then discuss how deviants would likely be treated in these groups.
4. As a group, come up with ways that groups in which conformity is emphasized at the expense of deviance can encourage group members to express dissenting views.

Topic for Debate

Groups are the basic building blocks of organizations. Now that you have a good understanding of the nature and types of groups and how groups control and socialize their members, debate the following issue.

Team A. In most organizations, an institutionalized role orientation is more desirable than an individualized role orientation.

Team B. In most organizations, an individualized role orientation is more desirable than an institutionalized role orientation.

Experiential Exercise

Developing Roles, Rules, and Norms

Objective

Your objective is to gain experience in developing roles, rules, and norms that contribute to group effectiveness.

Procedure

The class divides into groups of three to five people, and each group appoints one member as spokesperson, to present the group's findings to the whole class. Here is the scenario.

Assume the role of a group of jazz musicians who recently started performing together. Each member of the group has had some individual success as a musician and hopes that the group will become a top-performing jazz ensemble. The immediate goals of the group are to develop a repertoire of pieces that showcase each member's individual strengths and display the energy, vitality, and creativity of the group as a whole; to play as many gigs as possible at bars and clubs within a 500-mile radius of home; and to start making contacts with recording companies. The group's long-range goal is to be a nationally visible and successful jazz group with a major-label recording contract.

The group has gotten together and played several times both with and without an audience present and thinks it has what it takes to "make it big." The group realizes, however, that it needs to get its act together to meet both its short- and long-range goals.

1. What roles should the musicians develop to help achieve group goals?
2. What rules should the musicians develop to help achieve group goals?
3. What norms should the musicians develop to help achieve group goals?
4. What steps should the musicians take to help ensure that the group has the right balance of conformity and deviance?

When your group has answered those questions, the spokesperson will describe to the rest of the class the roles, rules, and norms that your group thinks will help the jazz group achieve its goals. The spokesperson also will discuss the steps group members think should be taken to help ensure that the jazz group has the right balance of conformity and deviance.

Making the Connection

Find an example of a company that recently increased its use of groups or teams. Why did this company start to use groups or teams more heavily? What kinds of groups or teams is the organization using? How do the groups or teams control their members' behaviors? What effect has the increase in the use of groups or teams had on organizational performance? How do employees feel about working in the groups or teams?

New York Times Cases in the News

The New York Times

Japanese Workers Told From on High: Drop the Formality

BY NORIMITSU ONISHI

HIROSHIMA, Japan—The change in policy came directly from the Tokyo headquarters of Elpida Memory, a semiconductor maker, but it had nothing to do with computer chips.

The 1,366 workers at Elpida's factory here were told to stop addressing each other by their titles and simply to add the suffix -san to their names.

Yukio Sakamoto, the president and chief executive in Tokyo, believes that using titles like "department chief" impedes decision-making and innovation.

"To call someone 'president' is to deify him," said Mr. Sakamoto, who was influenced by the 28 years he worked at Texas Instruments. "It's part of Japan's hierarchical society. Now that has no meaning. If you have ability, you can rise to the top and show your ability."

Many Japanese companies, traditionally divided rigidly by age and seniority, have dropped the use of titles to create a more open—and, they hope, competitive—culture.

The long economic slump has forced companies to abandon seniority in favor of performance, upsetting the traditional order. This has led to confusion in the use of titles as well as honorific language, experts say.

The shift also mirrors profound changes in Japanese society, experts say. Equality-minded parents no longer emphasize honorific language to their children, and most schools no longer expect children to use honorific language to their teachers. As a result, young Japanese entering the work force have a poor command of honorific language and do not feel compelled to use it.

"There's confusion and embarrassment," said Rika Oshima, the 43-year-old president of Speaking Essay, a school that instructs new employees on the use of honorific language. "Junior staffers aren't strict about using respectful forms to their bosses, whereas bosses want their staffers to use respectful forms to them, but bosses cannot say that."

What is clear is that the use of honorific language, called keigo, to elevate a person or humble oneself, has especially fallen out of use among young Japanese.

Japanese, perhaps more than any other language, has long taken account of social standing. While French speakers must decide between the familiar "tu" and the formal "vous" in addressing someone in the second person, in Japanese, there are many ways to say I or you, calibrated by age, circumstance, gender, social position and other factors. Verb endings, adjectives and entire words also shift according to the situation.

Mistakes have been deadly. In 1975, two workers, Kunihiro Fukuda, 30, and Tomohiko Okabe, 27, were having a drink in a Tokyo bar, according to magazine reports at the time. Although Mr. Okabe was younger, he had entered the company first and had taken to addressing his colleague in a manner usually reserved for someone younger, calling him Fukuda instead of Fukuda-san. Mr. Fukuda protested. But Mr. Okabe said, "What's wrong if a senior guy calls his junior in this way?" Enraged, Mr. Fukuda grabbed his colleague by the neck and pummeled his face, killing him, the magazines reported.

These days, companies hope the use of -san—less cumbersome than the longer titles traditionally used—will allow workers to exchange ideas more freely and make decisions more quickly. In 2001, 59 percent of companies with more than 3,000 employees had adopted such a policy, compared with 34 percent in 1995, according to the Institute of Labor Administration of Japan.

Mr. Sakamoto, 56, made the change last December, immediately after becoming the chief executive of Elpida, a company owned by NEC and Hitachi.

"It's easier to talk now," said Kazuyoshi Iizuka, a 32-year-old employee at the Tokyo headquarters.

Mr. Sakamoto said he also discouraged the use of honorific language that Japanese have traditionally used toward an older person, a boss, a customer, a stranger.

Mr. Sakamoto decided that the factory here would adopt the new policy on Sept. 1. The factory's president, Takehiko Kubota, 59, who describes himself as "old-fashioned," sent an e-mail message on Sept. 5 explaining the policy to his staff.

"I think a free and frank atmosphere existed already here, so I don't know if this policy will be significant," he said. "But by adopting this policy, it might give birth to something new. If we don't try, we won't find out."

A few weeks later, workers still found it awkward. "It will change little by little," said Hiromichi Iwabuchi, 48, a manager. "Even I sometimes say, 'President Kubota-san.' I think people will become more frank and free to talk thanks to this change. And it will show in our new ideas and products."

Naoko Okamoto, Mr. Kubota's 26-year-old secretary, said that now "there is less distance and human relations have improved."

At companies emphasizing performance, it is not unusual for younger bosses to supervise older workers. That has created uncomfortable moments. Kazuo Aizawa, a 39-year-old division chief, added the suffix -kun, usually used to address someone younger, to his workers' names. But he could not bring himself to do so with a worker who was a year older.

"For two or three months, our conversations were awkward," Mr. Aizawa said. But one day, he did it. The worker, Yoshitaka Ishihara, 40, shifted uncomfortably in front of his boss when he was asked about his reaction. "I'm starting to sweat here," Mr. Ishihara said, pulling back his shirt collar during an interview. Being addressed as Ishihara-kun by someone younger gave him "a strange feeling," he said.

A move to enhance creativity unsettles a traditional culture.

Fumio Inoue, a professor of linguistics at Tokyo University of Foreign Studies, said honorifics began with the nobility a millennium ago. At first, they were strictly based on social hierarchy, but after World War II and the democratisation of Japanese society, they began to be used according to the level of intimacy between speakers.

For many older Japanese, the decline of the honorific form amounted to losing the deep beauty of their language and the coarsening of the social culture.

"In the past, Japanese children were taught well at home to elevate men and their elders," said Mr. Kubota, the factory manager. "Here in Hiroshima, because we are in the country, some of the old ways remain. But in Tokyo, it's chaos."

In Tokyo, at Talyo General, a futures trading company, Hideki Matama, the 51-year-old deputy general manager of personnel, said training for new employees included honorific language.

To him, the decline of honorific language symbolized Japan's shift away from an older generation concerned with its place in companies or society, to a younger one focused on personal satisfaction.

"At company seminars, I often get questions whether weekends are off, or whether women have maternity leave," he said.

"One time, when I asked one boy about his dreams, he said, 'Good marriage, good home and children.' Can you believe that?"

SOURCE: "Japanese Workers Told From on High: Drop the Formality," by N. Onishi. *New York Times*, October 30, 2003, pp. A1, A6.

Questions for Discussion

1. What norms are changing in Japan?

2. Why are these norms changing?

3. How might changing norms influence the behavior and effectiveness of work groups?

The New York Times

Ex-Executive Admits Inflating Company Profit

BY BLOOMBERG NEWS

The former chief accounting officer of **Symbol Technologies** Inc. pleaded guilty yesterday to criminal fraud and conspiracy charges for overstating earnings to meet the targets of senior executives, the Securities and Exchange Commission said.

The S.E.C. said the former executive, Robert Korkuc, adjusted Symbol's preliminary financial reports to make them match analysts' and executives' numbers. He also knowingly played a role in a sales practice known as channel stuffing, in which the company recognized revenue from distributors and resellers who were not obligated to pay for products, the commission said.

Symbol "was a numbers-driven company obsessed with meeting financial projections," the S.E.C. said in a civil complaint it also filed against Mr. Korkuc, 40.

The S.E.C. is continuing to investigate accounting practices at Symbol, which makes bar-code scanners, said John J. O'Donnell, a lawyer at the S.E.C. Symbol, based in Holtsville, N.Y., has said it expects to complete a restatement of its earnings from 1998 through the first quarter of 2003 by June 30.

The company's chief executive, Richard Bravman, said in a statement, "We anticipate the financial impact of this restatement to be consistent with the company's previous disclosures."

In investigations of accounting fraud suspected at Enron, WorldCom and other companies, securities regulators and prosecutors have focused on whether executives manipulated earnings to meet analysts' quarterly expectations and drive share prices higher. At Symbol, "there was often a mad scramble at the end of financial reporting periods to hit the number," the S.E.C. said in its complaint, which repeats language used in cases involving companies like Global Crossing Ltd. and WorldCom.

Symbol's former president, Tomo Razmilovic, set "ambitious financial performance targets that either drove or mirrored Wall Street expectations, and he aggressively enforced the targets," the agency's complaint said. "Management's primary function was to make sure that the company's reported results matched those figures."

Mr. Razmilovic, who took early retirement from the company in 2002, could not be reached for comment. He is not charged in the complaint, nor is the company, which announced Mr. Korkuc's resignation in March.

Questions for Discussion

1. Why is it inappropriate for a top management team to have norms that indicate that earnings expectations should be met?

2. Why would they develop these norms?

3. Why didn't Robert Korkuc deviate from these norms? How can organizations promote deviance in response to norms that might lead to unethical behavior?

Effective Work Groups and Teams

H

LEARNING OBJECTIVES

After studying this chapter, you should be able to:

■

Describe the sources of process losses and gains and understand how they affect group or team potential performance.

■

Understand how social loafing can occur in groups and the steps that can be taken to prevent it.

■

Differentiate between three forms of task interdependence and discuss the team performance implications associated with them.

■

Understand the ways in which a group's cohesiveness affects its performance and explain which level of cohesiveness results in the highest team performance.

■

Describe the nature of four important kinds of groups in organizations and how and why they help an organization achieve its goals.

OPENING CASE

Creating High-Performing Teams Is a Difficult Thing to Do

How Should Teams Be Organized?

Thousands of companies now organize their employees into groups and teams to make and sell their goods and services because teamwork can significantly improve employee productivity and efficiency. Whether or not a company succeeds in creating high-performing teams depends crucially on the way managers and supervisors structure and control team members' behaviors, however. The different experience of two companies when they began to use teams illustrates many of the issues associated with creating effective groups and teams.

Mantua Manufacturing Co. is a leading supplier of mattress components, such as bedsprings, foam pads, wire, and fabrics, to mattress makers.[1] Competition among suppliers for mattress makers' business is fierce, and suppliers have been unable to raise their prices for several years for fear of losing business. As a consequence, Mantua Manufacturing was forced to take a close look at the way it makes its products. Edward Weintraub, its owner and president, has led the search to find ways to reduce costs and increase productivity in its factories. One of Mantua's major innovations was to change how its employees worked together.

Making a bed frame involves taking angle iron, cutting it to size, punching holes, inserting rivets, painting the bed frame, and then putting the frame and casters into a cardboard box for shipping. Mantua employees used to work separately and in sequence to perform the different activities necessary to make and pack each bed frame. Often bottlenecks arose during production because employees at one stage of the process could perform their jobs faster than those at other stages. To encourage employees to help each other out when this occurred, Weintraub decided to organize them into work groups.

Employees were grouped into teams that are responsible for all the activities necessary to make and pack bed frames. In the new group work system, in addition to the $12 an hour each employee receives for performing his or her own specific task, he or she also receives a $3 or 25 percent bonus if the group as a whole hits its assigned production target. To obtain the bonus, employees must not only achieve the performance target associated with their own jobs, but they must also cooperate and help other employees who are falling behind for whatever reason. So, for example, if riveters or packers are falling behind, those employees responsible for punching holes quickly move to help their team members out to achieve the group bonus.

Team members have learned to think for themselves in the new group system and self-manage their teams to control their own activities. This change has freed up supervisors to think about new ways to increase productivity, such as improving the design of the machines used to make the frames and finding better ways to physically organize the production process to save time and effort.[2] Mantua's use of self-managed teams has resulted in substantial and continuing gains in productivity, enabling the company to prosper despite its inability to increase prices.

Levi-Strauss was much less successful in its attempt to use self-managed teams to increase productivity in its jeans factories. In the 1990s, Levi-Strauss's competitors outsourced their manufacturing activities to low-cost Asian companies; Levi-Strauss, being more committed to its employees, decided it would instead try to increase the productivity of its U.S. factory employees with work groups. The company abandoned its piece-rate plan whereby each employee worked separately on a specific task and was paid according to how many tasks, or pieces, he or she completed. Instead, employees were assigned to work groups of up to 35 people who were now jointly responsible for all the jean-making tasks, such as sewing on pockets, zippers, and belt loops. They were paid according to the number of pairs of jeans the whole team made.

But after the new team system was implemented, productivity plunged. In part, this was because employees weren't used to the new issues and problems the groups created. Levi's most skilled employees, for example, found that they could only work as fast as the slowest members of their teams and that their paychecks were falling. On the other hand, the paychecks of less skilled employees were increasing because they were benefiting by being teamed up with the faster, more highly skilled workers. Soon the fastest employees began to feel that some team members were not pulling their weight, in-fighting between team members increased, and employee morale fell.[3]

To improve the situation Levi's began to group employees according to their skill level, and they reduced the size of the teams so employees had more control over each other. Supervisors also gave more training to slower employees and helped group members develop new team skills to improve their group performance. Even after it made these changes, however, Levi's found that team production had not increased productivity; in fact, productivity was just 93 percent of what it was when employees worked separately. With its attempts to increase productivity failing, Levi's was forced to close down more of its U.S. manufacturing plants. Its final plant was closed in 2004.[4]

In Chapter 10, we discuss the nature of work groups, how they control their members' behavior, and how they socialize newcomers to contribute to the attainment of group and organizational goals. In this chapter, we continue our study of work groups and focus on what makes groups like the teams used at Mantua and Levi's work effectively. Recall from the last chapter that effective work groups perform at a high level and help an organization achieve its goals.

Numerous factors determine how effective a work group is and how well its members work together. In fact, the group characteristics we discuss in Chapter 10, the ways that groups control their members, and the socialization process all have the potential to influence how effective a work group is. In this chapter, we build on this foundation and examine why and under what conditions groups can be more than the sum of their parts and thereby help an organization perform at a high level. We also examine the factors that can lead to problems in groups and can contribute to poor group and organizational performance, such as the problems Levi-Strauss experienced. Finally, we examine four important types of work groups in detail: top management teams, self-managed work teams, research and development teams, and virtual teams. By the end of this chapter, you will have a good understanding of what makes work groups effective in organizations.

Process Losses, Process Gains, and Group Effectiveness

Effective work groups contribute to the attainment of organizational goals by providing the organization with important outputs. The outputs might be finished products, such as correctly typed reports and high-quality automobiles, or less tangible but no less important outputs, such as satisfied customers and patients. Desired outputs also include behaviors not related to a group's specific tasks. These behaviors include promptly reporting broken-down machinery, suggesting ways of improving work processes, going out of one's way to help customers, helping group members when they are under pressure, and other forms of organizational citizenship behavior (see Chapter 3). As you will learn in this chapter, effective work groups perform at the highest level possible by minimizing performance difficulties or process losses. Moreover, effective work groups increase their potential performance over time by achieving process gains or finding better ways to work.

POTENTIAL PERFORMANCE

Managers strive to have groups perform at the highest level possible, which is called a group's **potential performance**.[5] Although potential performance is important because it reflects a work group's capabilities, it is often difficult to know in advance and can change as conditions change. When Japanese car companies such as Toyota were experimenting with ways to improve the productivity of groups of assembly-line employees, one innovative approach they took was to continually increase groups'

Potential performance The highest level of performance that a group is capable of achieving at a given point in time.

343

expected or potential performance levels. Realizing that the capabilities of groups are often underestimated, Japanese managers strove to push groups to produce up to their true potential.

In order for an organization to achieve its goals, managers and work groups need to strive to ensure that a group's *actual* performance comes as close as possible to its *potential* performance. In many situations, however, a group's actual performance falls short of its potential performance, even though the group is capable of achieving its potential. To see what this can mean for an organization, consider the following situation. A group of six salesmen staff the men's clothing department in a small, exclusive department store. This group is fully capable of providing excellent customer service, keeping the department clean and neat, and stocking and restocking merchandise in a timely fashion. Recently, however, the group's actual performance has fallen below its potential performance. Customers wishing to return merchandise are often kept waiting unnecessarily, and counters and dressing rooms are often cluttered with clothes. Why is the actual performance of this group below its potential performance, and what can the store's management do to remedy it?

PROCESS LOSSES AND PERFORMANCE

Process losses Performance difficulties that a group experiences because of coordination and motivation problems.

Research has shown that **process losses**—performance difficulties that a group experiences because of coordination and motivation problems—are an important factor when a group's actual performance falls short of its potential performance.[6] Coordination problems arise when group activities are divided among the group's members (because of the division of labor that occurs in groups) and then group members' contributions are merged or combined into some group product or output. At Levi-Strauss, for example, the move to make groups of workers jointly responsible for assembling complete pairs of jeans resulted in major problems of cooperation between group members. Figure 11.1 depicts the relationship between actual and potential performance and process losses (the figure also includes process gains, which we discuss in the next section).

The group of six salesmen described earlier experienced a coordination problem when they tried to keep the counters and dressing rooms clean and tidy. Often, when a salesman knew that one of his customers was coming to the store, he selected some clothes he thought the customer would like and displayed them on a counter or hung them in a dressing room. At the same time, clothing remained on the counters and in the dressing rooms from customers who had already been served and left the store. Even though keeping counters neat and restocking shelves were among their job responsibil-

FIGURE 11.1
The Relationship between Actual and Potential Performance, Process Losses and Process Gains

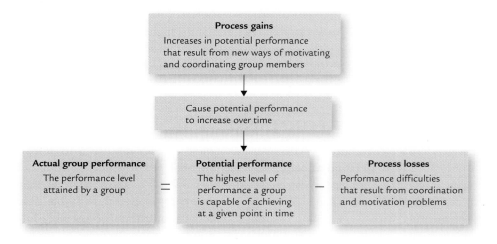

Process gains
Increases in potential performance that result from new ways of motivating and coordinating group members

↓

Cause potential performance to increase over time

↓

Actual group performance		**Potential performance**		**Process losses**
The performance level attained by a group	=	The highest level of performance a group is capable of achieving at a given point in time	−	Performance difficulties that result from coordination and motivation problems

ities, the salesmen tended to avoid these tasks because they did not want to make the mistake of restocking clothes that one of their co-employees had just picked out for a customer. As a result of this coordination problem, counters and dressing rooms were usually cluttered.

The group's motivation problem revolved around processing returned clothing. All of the group's members were equally responsible for processing returned clothing, yet customers wishing to return an item were often kept waiting even though several of the salesmen appeared to be available to wait on them. Because the salesmen received no commission for processing returns and disliked all the paperwork involved, each one of them would wait a minute or two before volunteering to help a customer with a return in the hope that one of his colleagues would handle the transaction.

To meet the challenge of ensuring that a group's actual performance equals its potential performance, managers must try to eliminate as many process losses as possible. The manager of the men's clothing department eliminated the coordination problem by designating one counter and one dressing room to be used for displaying clothes for particular customers and by instructing all salesmen to restock the clothes they had selected once they were finished helping their customers. In addition, all salesmen were explicitly instructed to restock clothes on the remaining counters and in the other dressing rooms whenever they saw them. The manager solved the motivation problem by keeping track of the returns that each salesman processed. After the salesmen knew that their returns were being tracked, customers were never again kept waiting. Sometimes process losses can also arise from interpersonal difficulties among group members, like those that ensued in the Levi's factory when employees started to blame one another for their pay falling.

PROCESS GAINS AND PERFORMANCE

In addition to eliminating process losses that prevent a group from performing up to its potential, managers also need to increase a group's potential performance. To increase the effectiveness of a work group, managers need to identify ways to improve the group's motivation and coordination to achieve **process gains**—increases in potential performance that result from new ways of motivating and coordinating group members.[7] (See Figure 11.1.) The Japanese managers experimenting with ways to continuously improve group performance in automobile assembly-line settings were searching for process gains: new and better ways to coordinate and motivate employees to raise levels of potential performance. Process gains can lead to groups being more creative and coming up with innovative solutions to problems.[8]

The manager of the men's clothing department successfully eliminated process losses, for example, so that the department no longer was sloppy and returns were handled efficiently. But the manager believed the salesmen's potential performance could still be higher. He thought that if group members pooled their skills and abilities they could create new kinds of attractive merchandise displays that would boost sales. To achieve this process gain (and raise the group's potential level of performance), the manager needed to raise the group's motivation.

Together, the store manager and all of the department managers devised a strategy to achieve process gains by increasing the motivation of the groups throughout the store: The store manager announced a quarterly competition among the groups of salespeople from the different departments for the most innovative and attractive merchandise display. Winning groups would have their pictures displayed in the employee lunchroom, and each member of the winning group would receive a $75 gift certificate for store merchandise. This strategy worked: The quality of merchandise displays increased dramatically in many of the departments, and the salespeople enjoyed their new challenge.

Process gains Increases in potential performance that result from new ways of motivating and coordinating group members.

Sometimes process gains can be achieved by encouraging group members to be more creative and willing to take risks.[9] Corporate finance departments, for example, are not usually known for their willingness to take risks, but many companies are trying to change that. One company, Nortel Networks, spent over $15,000 on improvisational comedy training for its finance staff members to encourage them to be creative and think and act like a team.[10] Nortel hired comedian Rob Nickerson, an independent contractor with the renowned Second City comedy group,[11] whose roster of alumni includes Bill Murray and John Belushi. During the training, staff members were encouraged to work as a team to develop creative stories or monologues, perform in front of each other, take risks, and think quickly on their feet. As financial analyst Lori Ozaki puts it, "You can't help but be nervous . . . But you get through it; you have to, because your team is depending on you. You realize that if you act a fool and I act a fool, we are all foolish together and you are not alone. If we can support each other onstage like that, doing it in the office should be easy."[12] Second City provides over 500 training workshops a year to companies such as AT&T, Motorola, Kraft Foods, and Accenture to help them promote teamwork throughout their organizations.[13]

In the next sections, we examine various aspects of groups that can influence group performance by increasing or decreasing process gains and losses. A manager's key objectives in creating and sustaining highly effective work groups are to (1) eliminate process losses by ensuring that the actual performance of a group is as close as possible to potential performance and (2) create process gains by continually raising the level of potential performance.[14]

Social loafing The tendency of individuals to exert less effort when they work in a group than when they work alone.

Social Loafing: A Problem in Group Motivation and Performance

In some groups, any given individual's contribution to group performance cannot be easily recognized or identified by other group members or by outsiders such as supervisors. Consider a group of custodians who are jointly responsible for keeping the food court in a busy shopping mall clean. The custodians are not assigned to particular areas but work together to patrol the whole food court, picking up trash and cleaning dirty tables. Because the custodians work together, it is difficult to identify the performance of any individual custodian. When individuals work in groups in which individual performances are not readily observable, there exists the potential for **social loafing**—that is, the tendency for people to exert less effort when they work in a group than when they work alone.[15]

Social loafing can seriously impact work group effectiveness and lead to process losses; it occurs for two main reasons. First, recall from our discussions of learning and motivation in earlier chapters that motivation, effort, and performance tend to be highest when outcomes such as praise and pay are administered to employees contingent on their level of individual performance. Because the custodians are working in a group and their individual levels of performance cannot easily be identified and evaluated by a supervisor, the custodians realize that they will not receive positive outcomes (such as praise) for performing at a high level or negative outcomes (such as a reprimand) for performing at a low level.[16] As a result of this lack of a connection between inputs and outcomes, the custodians' motivation is lower than it would be if they were working separately, so they do not exert as much effort.

A second reason why social loafing occurs is that employees who are performing in a group sometimes think that their own efforts are unimportant or not really needed. This belief lowers their level of motivation.[17] For example, a custodian might not clean off many tables when he works in a group because he thinks that his input is not really necessary and that some other member of the group will clean the tables he misses. This problem also arose in Levi's factory discussed earlier, as less skilled workers came to rely on the efforts of the highest performers. Have you observed social loafing when you

Sam Solovey, a contestant on Donald Trump's hit reality TV show, "The Apprentice," took social loafing to new lows. While the group he was assigned to was working, Solovey curled up on the floor and napped. "They're all going to be working for me when this is over," predicted Solovey about his fellow contestants.

were working on a group project for one of your classes? Sometimes one or two students in a group do not do their share of the work. They think they will receive the same grade as everyone else in the group regardless of how much or little effort they exert, or they may think their contributions aren't really needed for the group to do a good job.

Social loafing is a serious problem for groups and teams because it results in process losses that lower group performance. When social loafing occurs, actual group performance is lower than potential performance because some members of the group are not motivated to work as hard as they would if they were working on their own. Furthermore, social loafing by one or a few members of a group sometimes induces other members of the group to cut back on their efforts as well—as happened at Levi's factory. This type of process loss is a result of the **sucker effect**. The sucker effect occurs when group members who were not originally inclined to engage in social loafing lower their efforts when they observe other group members loafing.[18] Because they do not want to be taken advantage of, or considered "suckers," their motivation suffers when they see others in the group slack off.[19] The sucker effect is consistent with the equity theory of motivation, which suggests that employees who perceive inequity are motivated to try to restore equity by bringing their outcome/input ratios back into balance with the ratios of their referents—other group members (see Chapter 6).

Sucker effect A condition in which some group members, not wishing to be considered suckers, reduce their own efforts when they see social loafing by other group members.

GROUP SIZE AND SOCIAL LOAFING

Several studies have found that the tendency for group members to put forth less effort increases as the size of the group increases.[20] This increase in social loafing occurs because larger numbers of people in a group increase the problems associated with identifying and evaluating each person's individual performance. The more custodians a supervisor has to monitor, for example, the less time the supervisor can devote to evaluating each custodian. As group size increases, members may also be more likely to think that their own efforts are not an important part of the group's performance, something that also occurred in the Levi's factory.

Other kinds of process losses also occur as group size increases.[21] As you learned in Chapter 10, in a large group, there is much potential for conflict and coordination problems. Both widen the gap between potential and actual performance due to process losses.[22]

WAYS TO REDUCE SOCIAL LOAFING

Managers can try to reduce or eliminate social loafing by making each employee's individual contribution to group performance identifiable, by making each employee feel he or she is making a valuable contribution to the group, and by keeping the group as small as possible.

Making Individual Contributions Identifiable. One way to eliminate social loafing is to make individual contributions to group performance identifiable.[23] For example, the contributions of individual custodians could be made identifiable by dividing the food court into separate zones and giving each custodian a separate area to keep clean. The contributions of each employee could then be evaluated on the basis of how clean each zone is. Sometimes, when it is difficult for supervisors to identify individual contributions, other group members can do so by using a peer evaluation or performance appraisal system (see Chapter 8). Some professors, for example, try to eliminate social loafing on group projects by having students evaluate each others' contributions to a group project and assigning grades to individual students based, in part, on these evaluations.

Making Individuals Feel That They Are Making Valuable Contributions to a Group. In some kinds of groups, it is impossible for supervisors or group members to monitor individual behavior or make individual

One way managers can prevent social loafing is by keeping group sizes small. Social loafing tends to increase as groups get larger.

contributions identifiable. In a professional singing group that provides background music for commercials and movies, for example, it is very difficult to assess the effort of any individual singer. Indeed, each singer's contribution (the quality of a person's singing) cannot be distinguished from the performance of the group as a whole.

In situations in which each employee's contribution cannot be separated from the performance of the group as a whole, managers can reduce social loafing by making each individual feel that he or she makes an important and worthwhile contribution to the group.[24] Making individuals feel valued is the second way to reduce social loafing and increase work group effectiveness. This goal could be accomplished in the group of singers by periodically reminding each singer of his or her special talents and the contribution he or she makes to the group. A singer with a very deep and resonant voice, for example, could be reminded that his singing adds unique richness to the group's overall sound. Another way to stress the importance of each member's value and contributions is to let individual members know that the success or failure of the group sometimes hinges on his or her efforts.

Bill Walsh, celebrated former coach of the San Francisco 49ers and the Stanford University football team, tried to make each football player feel that he made an important contribution to team performance in order to motivate him to do his best and eliminate any potential for social loafing. As Coach Walsh put it, "You develop within the organization and the players an appreciation for the role each athlete plays on the team. You talk to each player and let each one know that, at some point, he will be in a position to win or lose a game. It may be one play in an entire career for a certain player or many plays each game for a Joe Montana. But the point is that everyone's job is essential. Everyone has a specific role and specific responsibilities. . . . You talk to each player and indicate the importance of everyone's participation in the process—that it is important for everyone to express himself, to offer ideas, explanations, solutions, formulas."[25] Walsh's ability to make each member feel like his or her unique contributions are important to the team's success comes from his years of experience as a football coach. Still, that ability is important for managers of teams in small and large companies alike to have.

Another way to reduce social loafing is by reminding each employee why their individual talents led them to be chosen as a member of the group. In forming task forces, for example, managers typically select individuals with different kinds of expertise and experience to get the full range of perspectives a heterogeneous group provides (see Chapter 10). By reminding members that they were selected for the task force because of the unique contributions they can make, managers can drive home the message that members can (and are expected to) make an important and worthwhile contribution to the group.

Keeping the Group as Small as Possible. The third way to reduce social loafing is to keep the group as small as possible.[26] Social loafing is more likely as groups get bigger because individuals perceive that their own effort and performance levels are unidentifiable, unnecessary, or likely to be duplicated by others in the group. In Levi-Strauss's factories, work groups were originally as large as 35 members. This resulted in the motivation and coordination problems discussed in the opening case. To prevent problems like these, managers should try to identify the optimal size of a group, given the tasks members are performing. If managers sense that process losses are increasing as a group gets larger, they should take steps to reduce the group's size.

One way to do this is to divide the work so that two smaller groups perform it. In the men's wear department, for example, rather than have six different salespeople interacting to manage the whole department, two people could be given the responsibility to manage men's designer clothes, such as Polo and Tommy Hilfiger, and the other four could manage the lower-priced clothing section. Indeed, one reason why organizations consist of so many different groups is to eliminate the process losses that occur because of social loafing inherent in larger-sized groups. The accompanying OB Today illustrates an example of this.

ob today

How GlaxoSmithKline Used Groups to Boost Productivity

The need to develop new kinds of prescription drugs is a continual battle for pharmaceutical companies. In the last few years, many of these companies have been merging to try to increase their research productivity. In 2001, GlaxoSmithKline was created when Glaxo Wellcome and SmithKline Beechum merged. Prior to the merger, both companies had seen steep declines in the number of new prescription drugs their scientists had been able to deliver. How could the newly formed company combine the talents of its scientists and researchers to quickly create exciting new drugs?

GlaxoSmithKline's top managers realized that after the merger there would be enormous problems associated with coordinating the activities of the thousands of research scientists who were working on hundreds of different kinds of drug programs. Understanding the problems associated with large size, top managers decided to group researchers into eight smaller groups so they could focus on particular clusters of diseases such as heart disease or viral infections. Each of the groups was instructed to behave like a company in its own right, and they were told that they would be rewarded based on the number of new prescription drugs they were able to invent and the speed with which they could bring them to market.

To date, GlaxoSmithKlein's new group approach to research seems to have worked. The company claims that research productivity has more than doubled since it reorganized its scientists into teams: The number of new drugs moving into clinical trials doubled from 10 to 20, and the company has 148 new drugs currently being tested. Moreover, the company claims that the morale of its researchers has increased, and turnover is down because the disease-focused groups enjoy working and collaborating together. The company expects to have the best new drug "pipeline" in its industry in the next three to four years.

How Group Tasks Affect Group Performance

Process losses, particularly those that result from social loafing, are most prevalent when group members feel their individual contributions are not identifiable or important. In some groups, however, process losses occur because of the types of tasks that members perform. Process losses are especially likely to occur when the nature of the task itself makes it difficult to identify individual performance levels and reward employees on that basis.

To determine how to assign outcomes to the individual members in the group, the kinds of tasks it performs must be taken into account. James D. Thompson's model of group tasks helps managers identify (1) task characteristics that can lead to process losses and (2) the most effective ways to distribute outcomes or rewards to group members to generate high motivation. Thompson's model is based on the concept of **task interdependence**—the extent to which the work performed by one member affects what other group members do.[27] As task interdependence within a group increases, the degree and intensity of the interactions among group members who are required to perform the tasks also increase.[28] Thompson identifies three types of task interdependence: pooled, sequential, and reciprocal.[29]

Task interdependence The extent to which the work performed by one member of a group affects what other members do.

Pooled task interdependence The task interdependence that results when each member of a group makes a separate and independent contribution to group performance.

POOLED INTERDEPENDENCE

If a group task involves **pooled task interdependence**, each member of the group makes a separate and independent contribution to group performance. Because each member's contribution is separate, it can be readily identified and evaluated.

On group tasks that involve pooled interdependence, group performance is determined by summing up the contributions or performances of the individual members.[30] Pooled interdependence is depicted in Figure 11.2A. Members A, B, and C make independent contributions to group performance, and their contributions are added together to measure the group's performance.

Examples of tasks with pooled interdependence include the work performed by the members of a typing pool, by the waiters and waitresses in a restaurant, by a group of physicians in a health maintenance organization, and by a group of sales representatives for a book publisher. In each of these examples, group performance is the result of adding up the performances of individual group members: the amount of correspondence typed, the number of customers served, the number of patients treated, or the number of books sold.

One common source of process losses on tasks with pooled interdependence is duplication of effort, such as when two waiters inadvertently take orders from the same table or two typists mistakenly type the same report. This coordination problem can usually be solved by carefully and clearly assigning tasks to group members.

Motivation problems can easily be avoided on tasks with pooled interdependence by evaluating the performance levels of the individuals in the group and rewarding them on that basis. Distributing rewards based on individual performance is likely to result in high levels of motivation, as theories of learning and motivation suggest. In fact, because pooled interdependence allows each member's contribution to be measured and rewarded, the potential for process losses due to a lack of motivation is relatively low. When Levi's used a piece-rate system to reward employees, it was using pooled task interdependence.

SEQUENTIAL INTERDEPENDENCE

Sequential task interdependence The task interdependence that results when group members must perform specific behaviors in a predetermined order.

A group task based on **sequential task interdependence** requires specific behaviors to be performed by the group's members in a predetermined order. The level of each member's performance, therefore, affects the performance of other members down the line. The output of one employee depends on another employee, in other words. In Figure 11.2B, for example, the performance of member A affects the ability of member B to perform her task; in turn, the activities of member B affect the ability of member C to perform his task. Examples of sequential interdependence include all types of assembly-line work—from the production of cars, to televisions, or Subway sandwiches—where the finished product is the result of the sequential inputs of group members. When Levi's decided to group its employees into teams, it switched from using pooled to sequential task interdependence.

As Levi's found out, sequential interdependence makes identifying the individual performances of group members difficult because each member contributes to the same final product. (In contrast, when task interdependence is pooled, each member contributes his or her own final product, and group performance depends on the sum of

FIGURE 11.2
Three Types of Task Interdependence

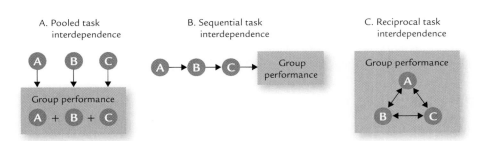

A. Pooled task interdependence

B. Sequential task interdependence

C. Reciprocal task interdependence

these contributions.) Identification of individual performance is also difficult because an error made by a group member at the beginning of a work sequence can affect how well members later in the sequence perform their tasks. If an employee on a car assembly line fails to align the axle correctly, for example, employees farther down the line will have a hard time aligning the wheels and making the brakes work properly. Similarly, if an employee sews the waist of the jeans improperly, a second employee will have difficulty attaching belt loops.

When the activities of group members are sequentially interdependent, the performance level of the least capable or poorest-performing member of the group determines group performance. In a plant that produces televisions on an assembly line, for example, televisions move along the line at a set speed, and employees stationed along the line complete their required tasks on each television that passes by. The assembly line can move only at the speed of the slowest employee along the line; thus, the number of televisions produced by the group of assembly-line employees is limited by the performance capabilities of the group's poorest performer.

For these reasons, the potential for process losses is higher with sequential interdependence than with pooled interdependence. Motivation and social loafing problems are also encountered more often because all of the group's members work on the same product, and so it's hard to discern what individual performance levels are. This was the problem Levi's encountered; its most skilled workers could only work as fast as its less skilled workers.

How can organizations try to overcome the motivation and social loafing problems associated with sequential interdependence? One way is by closely monitoring on-the-job behaviors of group members. Assembly lines, for example, usually employ a relatively large number of supervisors to do this. A second way to counteract the negative effects of sequential task interdependence is to form work groups consisting of individuals with similar levels of ability, as Levi-Strauss subsequently did. When that is done, the talents and motivation of high performers will not be hampered by the presence of a low performer in the group.

In some situations, a third way to overcome motivation problems in sequentially interdependent groups is to reward group members on the basis of the group level of performance. Because social loafing by one member impairs group performance and reduces the rewards received by all members of the group, this leads members to monitor and control each other's behavior. The more skilled employees are also likely to help the less skilled learn how to perform at a high level, too, so that over time the group's performance as a whole increases. Because rewards based on group performance can lead to hostility among team members, however, supervisors must be willing to help train the team's members, and the most skilled workers should be guaranteed their old rates of pay until the group's performance is brought up to speed. Levi-Strauss failed to anticipate the problems the move from using pooled to sequential task interdependence would cause. Japanese companies have long recognized how to take advantage of sequential interdependence to continuously improve group performance over time, a process called *kaizen* that we discuss in Chapter 18.

Process losses arising from coordination problems also occur when tasks are sequentially interdependent. If an employee at the start of an assembly line comes to work late or needs to stop working during the day, for example, the whole line must be shut down until a replacement can be found. How can managers try to overcome coordination difficulties? They can reward employees for good attendance and punctuality, and they can have a pool of multiskilled employees on hand who can step in at different points in production for those who are absent.

RECIPROCAL INTERDEPENDENCE

Reciprocal task interdependence The task interdependence that results when the activities of all work group members are fully dependent on one another.

Group tasks are characterized by **reciprocal task interdependence** when the activities of all work group members are fully dependent on one another so that each member's performance influences the performance of every other member of the group. Figure 11.2C shows that not only do member A's actions affect B's, and member B's actions affect C's (as would be the case with sequential interdependence), but also member C's actions affect A's and B's, member A's actions affect C's, and member B's actions affect A's. Examples of work groups whose tasks are reciprocally interdependent include high-tech research and development teams, top management teams, emergency room personnel, and an operating room team in a hospital. In all these cases, team members work very closely together, communicate frequently, and each member of the team depends on the others for decision-making input.

The potential for process losses is highest when tasks are reciprocally interdependent because motivation and coordination problems can be particularly troublesome. Motivation problems such as social loafing ensue because it is difficult, if not impossible, to identify an individual's level of performance when the final product is the result of the complex interplay of the contributions made by everyone.

How can managers try to minimize process losses when a group's activities are reciprocally interdependent? They should keep groups relatively small, emphasize that each member can make an important and distinct contribution to the group, and encourage members to feel personally responsible for meeting the group's goals.[31] To reduce the tendency for social loafing, managers should reward the members for the group's performance and encourage them to continuously improve their own performance over time by offering them increased pay and incentives for doing so.

An example of a group characterized by reciprocal interdependence is the top management team of a small company that manufactures toys. On the team are the vice presidents in charge of marketing and sales, production, research and development, and finance. Leading the team is the president of the company. How well the company as a whole does depends on the complex interplay between those various functions, but at any point in time it is difficult to evaluate the performance of any one of the top managers. Under these circumstances, there is a high potential for social loafing, but it does not often occur because (1) the group is relatively small, (2) each vice president thinks that his or her contributions are indispensable to the success of the company because each is an expert in a particular function, and (3) group members' salaries depend on how well the firm does.

Work groups performing tasks characterized by reciprocal interdependence experience considerable coordination problems because of the inherent unpredictability of group relations and interactions. There is no set ordering of the group's activities when its tasks are organized reciprocally, unlike when its tasks are organized in a sequential fashion. The top management team described previously experiences coordination problems on a day-to-day basis. When sales of a new dinosaur board game greatly exceeded expectations, for example, the managers in charge of marketing, production, and finance had to work out a plan to increase production runs for the game while keeping costs down and not interfering with the production of other products. But the production manager was on a monthlong trip to Taiwan, China, and Singapore to evaluate the feasibility of moving some of the firm's manufacturing facilities overseas. Because the group had difficulties coming up with a viable plan, sales were lost.

How can managers alleviate coordination problems when it comes to complex tasks? Again, one way is to keep group sizes relatively small to limit the number of individuals who must coordinate their efforts. Another way is to locate group members close to one another so that whenever one member needs input from another, the input is readily available. With the electronic forms of communication available today, team members in different locations can now keep in constant communication with one another. If the production manager scouting out factory sites in East Asia had been electronically in touch with other members of the group, for example, the manufacturing problem at the plant might have been averted. Finally, coordination difficulties can be reduced if groups develop norms encouraging members to help one an other when needed.

As task interdependence moves from pooled to sequential to reciprocal interdependence, the potential for *process losses* increases because identifying individual performances becomes increasingly harder and because coordination becomes more difficult. The potential for *process gains* also increases as task interdependence becomes more complex. As the level and intensity of group members' interactions increase and the expertise and skills of group members are brought to bear on the group's tasks, the potential for synergy increases. **Synergy** (a type of process gain) occurs when members of a group acting together are able to produce more or better output than would have been produced by the combined efforts of each person acting alone.

For example, the top management team of the toy company recently developed a new line of compact travel toys that was an instant success with children and very profitable for the company. The managers in charge of marketing, production, research and development, and finance worked closely throughout the development and launch of the new line. As a result, their reciprocally interdependent interactions enabled them to come up with a winner in record time. If each of the managers had worked independently, the new line would never have been developed successfully or launched so quickly. Employees at Mantua Manufacturing in the opening case were able to achieve much more by working as a team than they did when each employee worked alone.

In sum, the potential for process gains often increases as the level of task interdependence increases but so too does the potential for process losses. Thus, the actual performance gains an organization achieves depends on its managers' abilities to choose the form of task interdependence that best matches the products being produced and then create a work setting minimizing motivation and coordination problems related to them.

> **Synergy** A process gain that occurs when members of a group acting together are able to produce more or better output than would have been produced by the combined efforts of each person acting alone.

you're the management expert

What Kinds of Groups and Tasks?

You have just completed your degree in computer science. You have decided to refurbish and upgrade used PCs and then rent them to college students for a low monthly fee. As a part of this service you will also repair them as the need arises.

To get your business off the ground, you'll need to hire about 20 college students on a part-time basis to buy used PCs, bring them to the workshop for servicing, deliver them to customers, and make on-site repairs as necessary. You know that your ability to provide good customer service is vital in the rental business and your problem is how to group employees to get the best out of them—to get them to increase and realize their performance potential.

Using the material provided in the chapter and given the tasks that your business requires, what kind of task interdependence do you think is most appropriate for your business? Also, do you think you should organize employees into just one large group, or would you divide them into several smaller groups? If so, how many? What kinds of motivation and coordination problems are you trying to prevent with your decisions?

Group Cohesiveness and Performance

Regardless of the kinds of tasks performed, work groups also differ in another important respect—how *attractive* they are to their members. When a group is very attractive to its members, the individuals within it value their membership and strongly want to remain in it. The attractiveness of a group to its members is called **group cohesiveness**.[32] Groups high in cohesiveness are very appealing to their members; those low in cohesiveness are not appealing to their members and may even repulse them to the point at which they try to leave the team. An important property of work groups, group cohesiveness affects group performance and effectiveness.

Group cohesiveness
The attractiveness of a group to its members.

FACTORS THAT CONTRIBUTE TO GROUP COHESIVENESS

A variety of factors influences a group's level of cohesiveness.[33] Here we examine five: group size, similarity of group members, competition between groups, success, and the exclusiveness of the group (see Figure 11.3).

Group Size. As you learned in Chapter 10, as groups get bigger, their members tend to be less satisfied. For this reason, large groups do not tend to be cohesive. In large groups, a few members of the group tend to dominate group discussions, and the opportunities for participation by other group members are limited. Large groups have the greatest potential for conflict, and members find it difficult to form close ties with one other. A small or medium group size (between 3 and 15 people), on the other hand, tends to promote cohesiveness.

Similarity/Diversity of Group Members. People generally like, get along with, and most easily communicate with others who are similar to themselves. Moreover, people tend to perceive others who are similar to themselves more positively than they perceive those who are different (due to the similar-to-me bias discussed in Chapter 4). Groups tend to be most cohesive when group members are homogeneous or share certain attitudes, values, experiences, and so on. For example, a task force composed of individuals (such as engineers) with the same educational background and

Diversity in a group gives it a wider range of skills, abilities, and experiences to draw upon.

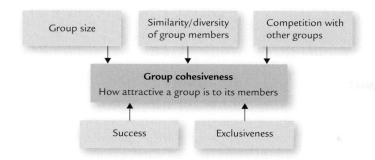

FIGURE 11.3

Determinants of Group Cohesiveness

work experiences will tend to be more cohesive than a task force whose members (an engineer, an accountant, a financial analyst, and a biochemist) have dissimilar backgrounds. One caveat, however, needs to be made about the similarity or homogeneity of group members. As you saw in Chapter 10, diversity (or heterogeneity) can be beneficial because it offers the group varied resources and perspectives (a wider range of skills, abilities, experiences, and so forth) on which to draw.[34] If the diversity of the group's members helps it achieve its goals, then *diversity*, rather than similarity, is likely to facilitate group cohesiveness.[35]

Competition Between Groups. Competition between groups in an organization increases group cohesiveness when it motivates members of each group to band together to achieve its goals.[36] For this reason, organizations often promote group cohesiveness by having work groups compete against each other.[37] Groups of salespersons compete to see which can sell the most each month, groups of production employees compete to see which can maintain the highest quality standards, and groups of maintenance employees compete to achieve the best attendance record. Healthy competition is also encouraged by naming groups and recognizing the ones doing especially well. Sometimes groups compete not so much with groups inside their organization as much as with groups from other organizations.

   Although a certain level of competition across groups can help each group be cohesive, too much competition can be dysfunctional and impair effectiveness. When competition is too intense, groups sometimes try to sabotage each other. They become more concerned with "winning the battle" than achieving the organization's goals, in other words. If an organization is to achieve its goals, the different groups within it must be willing and able to work together and cooperate, even when they are competing with one another.[38]

Success. "Nothing breeds success like success," according to an old adage. When groups are successful, they become especially attractive to their members and others, and the cohesiveness of the group increases.

Exclusiveness. A group's exclusiveness is indicated by how difficult it is to become a member of the group, the extent to which outsiders look up to the group's members, the group's status within the organization (see Chapter 10), and the special rights and privileges accorded its members. When group members must undergo a very tough initiation process or are required to undertake extensive training to join the group, being a member becomes more highly prized.[39] For example, individuals who want to become firefighters must meet stringent physical criteria and engage in extensive training exercises. Groups of firefighters tend to be highly cohesive, in part because of how difficult it is to become a member of the group. Fraternities, sororities, football teams, and cheerleading squads at universities also tend to be high on cohesiveness. It is often difficult to become a member of these groups. These groups tend to have high status as a result, and outsiders look up to the members, who often have special rights and privileges.

CONSEQUENCES OF GROUP COHESIVENESS

Is cohesiveness a group property that managers should encourage? Is there such a thing as too much cohesiveness? As we saw when discussing group norms in Chapter 10, the consequences of group cohesiveness for an organization depend on the extent to which group goals are aligned with organizational goals. Recall from the restaurant example in Chapter 10 how the goals of the group of waiters and waitresses (providing good service and getting good tips) were aligned with the restaurant's goal of having satisfied customers. In examining the consequences of group cohesiveness, we first focus on the case in which group and organizational goals are aligned, and then we look at the case in which they are not.

Consequences When Group Goals Are Aligned With Organizational Goals. The first major consequence of group cohesiveness when group and organizational goals are aligned is *the level of participation and communication within the group.*[40] As cohesiveness increases, members become more active participants in the group, and the level of communication within it increases. This outcome can be beneficial for the organization. Members will be more likely to perform behaviors necessary for the group and organization to achieve its goals, and information will be readily shared among members. (As we discuss in Chapter 15, an exception to this consequence occurs in cohesive decision-making groups that fall victim to groupthink.)

The group of waiters and waitresses, for example, was moderately cohesive. As a result, its members performed a variety of behaviors to ensure that customers received good service. They kept the salt and pepper shakers and sugar bowls on the tables filled, helped each other with especially large tables, and kept the restaurant clean and tidy. Moreover, information flowed through the group very quickly. When the group changed its norm of always referring complaints to the manager, for instance, the change was communicated to all group members on the very same day that it was discussed with the manager.

Although good communication within groups is important, too much communication can be dysfunctional if members waste a lot of time talking to each other, especially about nonwork matters such as the Monday night football game or last night's episode of *CSI.* Thus, a moderate amount of group cohesiveness is functional for the group and the organization when it encourages members to participate in the group and share information. Too much cohesiveness, however, can be dysfunctional if members waste time chitchatting.

The World Team consists of hundreds of skydivers representing over 40 countries. The skydivers come together every few years to set world records freefalling into various countries around the world.

The second major consequence of cohesiveness when group and organizational goals are aligned is *the level of conformity to group norms.*[41] As group cohesiveness increases, conformity to the group's norms tends to increase as well. Increased conformity can be functional for groups and the organization because it enables the groups to control and direct their members' behaviors toward achieving those goals. Too much conformity, however, can be dysfunctional if a group eliminates all deviance. As we discussed in Chapter 10, deviance can benefit a group by helping it recognize and discard dysfunctional norms, but excessive conformity can make a group resistant to change.

A moderate amount of cohesiveness gives groups the level of conformity they need to achieve their goals but still allows for some deviance. Too much cohesiveness can stifle opportunities for change and growth. There was enough conformity within the restaurant group that it was able to control its members' behavior, but there wasn't so much conformity that members were afraid to deviate from a dysfunctional norm (for example, referring all food complaints to the manager when they were able to handle some of the complaints themselves).

The third major consequence of cohesiveness when group and organizational goals are aligned is *group goal accomplishment.*[42] Cohesive groups tend to be very effective at achieving their goals. Group members who value their membership are motivated to help the group achieve its goals. Such members generally work well together, help each other when needed, and perform the behaviors necessary for the group to be effective. This consequence certainly seems to be effective for the organization, and for the most part it is. If groups become too cohesive, however, the members may be so driven toward group goal accomplishment that they lose sight of the fact that the group is part of a larger organization. When this happens one group may fail to cooperate with another because the members are solely loyal to their own groups. Once again, a moderate amount of group cohesiveness is functional for groups and organizations because it facilitates goal accomplishment. Too much cohesiveness is dysfunctional because it can lead members to fail to cooperate with people outside the group.

By now it should be clear that a certain level of cohesiveness contributes to group effectiveness. When that level is insufficient (1) group members are not motivated to participate in the group, (2) group members do not effectively communicate with each other, (3) the group has difficulty influencing its members' behavior, and (4) the group often fails to achieve its goals. When that level is excessive—when groups are *too* cohesive (1) time is wasted by members socializing on the job, (2) conformity is stressed at the expense of needed change, and (3) group goal accomplishment becomes more important than cooperation with other groups to achieve the organization's goals.

A *moderate* amount of group cohesiveness results in the most favorable group and organizational outcome. A moderately cohesive group has (1) the appropriate level of communication and participation between members, (2) the ability to influence members' behavior to ensure conformity while still allowing for some deviation, and (3) the capacity to stress the importance of the group's accomplishments but not at the expense of other groups and the organization. Indicators or signs of the level of cohesiveness in a work group are as follows:

♦ *Signs that a group has a moderate level of cohesiveness.* Members work well together, there is a good level of communication and participation in the group, the group is able to influence its members' behavior, and it tends to achieve its goals.

♦ *Signs that a group has a low level of cohesiveness.* Information flows slowly within the group, the group has little influence over its members' behavior, and it tends not to achieve its goals.

♦ *Signs that a group has a very high level of cohesiveness.* Group members socialize excessively on the job, there is a very high level of conformity in the group and intolerance of deviance, and the group achieves its goals at the expense of other groups or the organization as a whole.

TABLE 11.1

Consequences of High Cohesiveness When Group Goals Are Aligned With Organizational Goals

Consequences of High Cohesiveness	Advantages	Potential Disadvantages
A high level of participation and communication within the group	Group members are more likely to perform behaviors necessary for the group and organization to achieve their goals, information flows quickly in the group, and turnover may be relatively low.	Group members may waste time socializing on the job and chatting about nonwork matters.
A high level of conformity to group norms	The group is able to control its members' behavior to achieve group goals.	Excessive conformity within the group may result in resistance to change and failure to discard dysfunctional norms.
Group goal accomplishment	The group achieves its goals and is effective.	Group members may not cooperate with other groups as much as they should.

Table 11.1 summarizes some of the advantages and potential disadvantages of a *high level* of cohesiveness when group goals are aligned with organizational goals. The way in which Nokia has achieved this balancing act is profiled in the accompanying Global View.

global view

Teams, Teams, and More Teams at Nokia

Nokia Corporation, headquartered in Espoo, Finland, employs 60,000 people around the world and is the market leader in the global wireless communications industry.[43] Nokia has research and development (R&D) units in 14 countries, to which it dedicates one-third of its workforce.[44] The company's success and competitive advantage are the result of its use of teams throughout the organization. In fact, it has been said that any task or project that is of any significance in the company is assigned to a team. This commitment to teams starts at the top of the organization, where managers work together as a team to make all of Nokia's important business decisions.[45] The number of teams cascades on down through the organization, with almost all its employees mirroring the model set by the company's top managers.

Why does Nokia get good results from its teams? Teams are given high levels of autonomy and encouraged to be creative. High emphasis is placed on letting those people who are most knowledgeable about a problem or opportunity make decisions concerning it regardless of their position in the hierarchy (which by nature is very flat at Nokia).[46] Teams and their members take personal responsibility for decisions and believe that their efforts and contributions are important for Nokia's continued success. Good communication, mutual respect, and a high regard for the members of one's team are its central values and norms. Annual meetings, referred to as the Nokia Way, also help keep teams on track as well provide a vehicle for teams throughout the organization to help actualize Nokia's vision for the future.[47] Through these means, Nokia ensures that team goals are aligned with organizational goals and that its cohesive groups work to benefit the organization as a whole.

Consequences When Group Goals Are Not Aligned With Organizational Goals. Our conclusions about the consequences of cohesiveness apply only when the group's goals are aligned with the organization's goals. What are the consequences when group goals are *not* aligned with organizational goals?

When group goals are not aligned with organizational goals (recall from Chapter 10 the radio assemblers whose goal was to minimize effort expenditure), the consequences for the organization are almost always negative. In this case, group cohesiveness is dysfunctional for the organization because it helps the group achieve its goals at the expense of organizational goals.

Like the group of restaurant employees, the group of radio assemblers was moderately cohesive. However, the radio assemblers' group goal to minimize the expenditure of effort was inconsistent with the organization's performance goal. Consequently, the moderate level of cohesiveness within the group was dysfunctional for the organization. There was a high level of communication within the group, but it usually revolved around nonwork concerns like football and baseball scores. There also was a sufficient amount of conformity to group norms, which resulted in members restricting their output so that the group never produced more than 50 radios a day, even though it could have produced 75. Finally, the group was very effective at achieving its goal of producing no more than 50 radios.

Table 11.2 summarizes the consequences of a *high level* of cohesiveness when group goals are not aligned with organizational goals.

Important Organizational Groups

Now that you understand some of the problems and challenges that groups face in organizations and the factors that influence work group effectiveness, we turn to a discussion of four types of work groups: top management teams, self-managed work teams, research and development teams, and virtual teams. Although we could discuss other important types of groups in organizations (such as whole departments, assembly-line groups, or task forces), we concentrate on these four because they have the potential to dramatically affect an organization's performance.

THE TOP MANAGEMENT TEAM

An organization's **top management team** is the team of managers who report to the chief executive officer (CEO). Top management teams (chosen by an organization's CEO and its board of directors) profoundly affect organizational performance because they decide which overall goals should be pursued, and they establish the plan of action

Top management team
The team of managers who report to the chief executive officer (CEO) and determine what an organization is trying to accomplish and develop plans for goal attainment.

TABLE 11.2

Disadvantages of High Cohesiveness When Group Goals Are Not Aligned With Organizational Goals

Consequences of High Cohesiveness	Disadvantages
A high level of participation and communication within the group	Group members waste time socializing on the job and chatting about nonwork matters.
A high level of conformity to group norms	Group members behave in ways that are dysfunctional for the organization.
Group goal accomplishment	The group achieves its goals at the expense of organizational goals.

or means to achieve these goals. Because the complex nature of top management activities requires intensive interaction among team members, top management teams are characterized by reciprocal task interdependence.

What steps can a CEO take to reduce process losses associated with reciprocal task interdependence? First, team size should be kept relatively small (most top management teams average between five and seven members). Second, members of the team need to be assured that their individual input to the group is important for the team's and the organization's success. Third, group members need to be persuaded to be honest and open in their communication with one another. Finally, a CEO should make sure that members are readily available and accessible whenever other group members need their input and expertise.

The quality of decision making in the top management team is a function of the personal characteristics and backgrounds of team members.[48] It has been found, for example, that the best decisions are made by top management teams that are diverse or heterogeneous, consisting of managers from different functions (such as marketing, finance, and production). Diversity in team membership ensures that the team will have the adequate complement of skills, knowledge, expertise, and experience to guide the activities of the organization as a whole. Also, when managers bring different points of view and information to the table, an organization can avoid the dangerous problem of *groupthink*, a pattern of faulty decision making that occurs when like-minded people reinforce one another's tendencies to interpret events and information in similar ways (see Chapter 15).[49] Finally, the top management team affects its company's performance by the way the team uses human resource practices such as performance appraisal and rewards to encourage performance.[50]

SELF–MANAGED WORK TEAMS

In a self-managed work team, team members have the autonomy to lead and manage themselves and determine how the team will perform its tasks (see Chapter 10). Self-managed teams can be found at all levels in an organization.

Some organizations use self-managed work teams, rather than more traditional types of groups or individuals working separately. The idea is to enhance job satisfaction and motivate members to perform at higher levels.[51] In a self-managed work team, separate tasks normally performed by individual employees and managed by a supervisor fall under the responsibility of a group of employees empowered to ensure they get done and get done well.[52]

As an example of how a self-managed work team operates, consider the following situation. Requests for credit from AT&T Credit Corporation used to be processed by individuals. Extending or denying credit to customers involved a number of steps: reviewing the application, verifying the customer's credit rating, notifying the customer of whether his or her request for credit had been accepted or rejected, preparing a written contract, and collecting payments from the customer. Individuals were assigned to one of these steps. Some employees focused exclusively on reviewing applications, others on checking credit ratings, others on collecting payments, and so on. As a result, with this grouping of tasks, employees had little sense of how their individual jobs contributed to AT&T's organizational goal of first-class customer service. To remedy this situation, AT&T decided to combine these individual tasks and give teams of employees the responsibility for all activities, ranging from the initial review of an application to collecting payments from approved customers. The switch to the use of self-managed work teams resulted in customers being notified of the acceptance or rejection of their applications several days sooner than under the old system and the daily processing of twice as many applications.[53]

The job characteristics model of job design (see Chapter 7) provides a good framework for understanding why the use of self-managed work teams can lead to higher levels of motivation, performance, and satisfaction. Recall that this model suggests that jobs will be motivating and result in high levels of performance and satisfaction when they are high in skill variety, task identity, task significance, autonomy, and feedback.[54] Often it is difficult to design individual jobs that are high on each of these dimensions. The job of reviewing applications at AT&T Credit Corporation, for example, required a limited number of skills, was low on task identity because the employee often did not know whether the application was eventually accepted or rejected, low on task significance because the employee did not have a sense of how the job affected the customer, and low on autonomy. Combining the tasks of this job with the tasks of other jobs involved in the process, and then giving a group of employees responsibility for performing all of these tasks, heightens the job characteristic levels for *each group member*. Skill variety increases because members use a full array of skills to perform all of the various activities. Task identity and task significance are heightened because the groups perform all the activities necessary to provide credit to customers and have a real sense of how their activities impact customer satisfaction.

A number of conditions must be present for self-managed work teams to be effective.[55]

1. The group must be truly self-managing. The group itself must have the autonomy and authority to do many of the things traditionally reserved for managers, such as setting the group's goals, determining how the group should go about reaching them, and assigning individual tasks to members. Some managers are reluctant to give up these responsibilities. One of the advantages of using self-managed teams is that the number of middle managers needed in an organization may decrease.

2. Self-managed work teams appear to be most effective when the work performed by group members is sufficiently complex and results in some sort of finished end product. By "complex," we mean that a number of different steps and procedures must be performed to accomplish the group's goals. By "finished end product," we mean some identifiable group output such as extending or rejecting credit to customers and collecting payments.

3. Managers in the organization must support and be committed to utilizing self-managed work teams. Sometimes self-managed teams fail because managers are reluctant to relinquish their authority to the teams, or they don't support the teams by giving them the guidance and coaching they need. Managers need to be available to the groups in an advisory capacity and provide coaching when needed as well as help groups that veer off course to get back on track. When members of a self-managed work team have serious disagreements, for example, managers should be available to help team members settle their differences fairly.[56]

4. Members of successful self-managed work teams must be carefully selected to ensure that the team has the right complement of skills and expertise to get the job done.[57]

5. Team members need to be able to work with one another and want to be part of the team. Not all employees want to work closely with others on a team or want the responsibility that goes along with being a member of a self-managed team.[58]

Self-managed work teams have been used successfully by a number of organizations, such as General Mills, Federal Express, Chaparral Steel, 3M, Aetna Life &

Casualty, and Johnsonville Foods.[59] However, more research is needed to understand why they have been successful as well as why they are sometimes not so successful. One study suggests that members of self-managed work teams may be somewhat reluctant to discipline each other (for example, withhold rewards or punish a member who is not performing acceptably).[60] This can result in some members performing at a lower level in self-managed teams. Other studies suggest that the success of a self-managed team depends on the extent to which its members value being part of the team and the status the group has within the organization.[61] In any case, additional research is needed to explain why some self-managed teams succeed and others fail.

RESEARCH AND DEVELOPMENT TEAMS

Research and development (R&D) team A team that is formed to develop new products, may be cross-functional, and is often used in high-tech industries.

Organizations often use **research and development (R&D) teams** to develop new products, especially in high-tech industries such as electronics, pharmaceuticals, and computers.[62] Some R&D teams are cross-functional; team members represent each of the different functions or departments necessary to develop and launch a new product. An R&D team trying to develop a sophisticated electronic notepad, for example, might include members from research and development, engineering, manufacturing, finance, marketing, and sales (see Figure 11.4). A team with each of these capabilities represented is in a good position to develop a successful new product.

Skunk works An R&D team that is created to expedite new product design and promote innovation in an organization.

An R&D team that is created to expedite new product designs and promote innovation in an organization is known as a **skunk works**. The group consists of members of the engineering and research departments and other support functions such as finance and marketing. Skunk works often meet and work in facilities that are separated from the rest of the organization. Having their own facilities gives group members the opportunity for the intensive interactions necessary for innovation (or other process gains) and ensures the group will not be interrupted or distracted by the day-to-day problems of the organization. Members of skunk works often become very possessive of the products they are developing and feel completely responsible for the success or failure of them.

Ford Motor Company established a skunk works to develop a new Mustang coupe and convertible. Interestingly enough, when Ford managers projected that

FIGURE 11.4
A Cross-Functional Research and Development Team

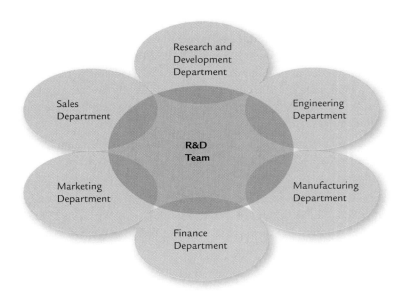

Ford created an "extreme" team to develop a new version of its classic Mustang coupe and convertible. Members of the group—also known as the "skunk works"—literally barricaded themselves in an empty furniture warehouse until they got the job done.

developing the new Mustang would cost approximately $1 billion, top executives almost abandoned the project. However, the project was ultimately spared and turned over to a skunk works. When all was said and done, developing the new Mustang cost Ford only about $700 million and was accomplished in 25 percent less time than Ford usually takes to develop a new model. This helped Ford in its quest to regain its competitive advantage.

John Coletti, one of the champions of the Mustang and founders of the skunk works, along with other team members, realized that to develop the new Mustang in a timely fashion while at the same time lowering costs, the team would need the freedom to make its own decisions and not follow Ford's usual development process. Will Boddie, the engineer who led the team, recognized the need to have everyone working on the project in close proximity to one another but distanced from Ford itself so that they would not be encumbered by the company's prevailing procedures and norms. A furniture warehouse in Allen Park, Michigan, was converted to become the home of the skunk works, and team members—everyone from drafters to engineers and stylists to "bean counters"—moved into cramped offices to work on the Mustang.

A turning point in the team's development occurred when an unexpected problem arose during the testing of the prototype for the Mustang convertible. When chief engineer Michael Zevalkink test-drove the prototype, the car shimmied and shook. Engineers worked for a year to resolve the problem, but when Zevalkink test-drove the "corrected" model, the car still shook. Senior executives at Ford were aware of the problem but did not renege on their promise to preserve the independence and autonomy of the skunk works.

During an eight-week period, the convertible was furiously reengineered (the engineers working on it even slept on the floor of the warehouse at night), and the problem was solved by installing braces in the car and redesigning its mirrors. Will Boddie, however, wasn't satisfied with these changes. When he saw a new Mercedes convertible in a parking lot, he thought, "Why shouldn't the Mustang convertible have as smooth a ride as a Mercedes convertible?" He told the skunk works engineers to purchase a Mercedes convertible and take it apart to learn the key to its smooth ride. The consequence of this research was the attachment of a 25-pound cylinder behind the front fender of the Mustang (a similar attachment on the Mercedes contributes to its smooth ride).[63]

The skunk works was successful in developing the new Mustang in record time and at a lower-than-usual cost because the team members closest to the issues involved not only had the autonomy to make decisions and changes as circumstances warranted but also a high level of commitment to the team's goal of keeping the Mustang alive. The skunk works' autonomy and relative isolation enabled it to respond to problems and make needed changes quickly and efficiently.

A skunk works approach to R&D can be very successfully used to to develop new and innovative products. Even when new product development requires the involvement of many different people in an organization, skunk works can still be effective. The skunk works that developed the Mustang, for example, included about 400 people grouped into what were called "chunk teams," each of which worked on developing a particular aspect, or "chunk," of the car.[64]

VIRTUAL TEAMS

Virtual team A team in which a significant amount of communication and interaction occurs electronically rather than face-to-face.

Virtual teams are teams in which a significant amount of communication and interaction among members occurs electronically, using computer hardware and software.[65] Organizations use virtual teams to help people in different places and/or time zones work together.[66]

Members of virtual teams use a variety of new information technologies to share information, interact with one another, and achieve their goals. More specifically, there are two types of information technologies that virtual teams use. Synchronous technologies enable team members to communicate with each other in real time and simultaneously. These technologies include videoconferencing, teleconferencing, instant messaging, and electronic meetings.[67] When asynchronous technologies are used, communication among team members is delayed rather than instantaneous. For example, using e-mail, electronic bulletin boards, and Web sites often results in some communication delays.[68] Many virtual teams rely on both kinds of technologies, depending on the tasks they are performing. The kind of technologies teams use also hinges on levels of task interdependence in a virtual team. For example, teams whose members are reciprocally interdependent have greater need for synchronous technologies than teams characterized by pooled interdependence.

Globalization has increased the need for and use of virtual teams linked together by fax, phone, e-mail, and videoconferencing. Technologies allowing instant communication and the growing complexity of multinational organizations are likely to lead to more virtual teams in the future.

According to researcher Lee Sproull, who studies virtual teams, organizations will increase their reliance on virtual teams because of increasing levels of globalization. When team members live and work in different countries, virtual teams are often a necessity.[69] Virtual teams allow organizations to keep their members apprised of the knowledge, expertise, and experience they need to accomplish the task at hand, regardless of where they are located.

Virtual teams face all the challenges that members of ordinary teams face, such as curbing social loafing and maintaining a good balance between conformity and deviance. They also face the additional challenge of building trust and cohesiveness among people who rarely interact with one another in person.[70] To meet this additional challenge, some virtual teams make it a point to schedule group recreational activities such as skiing trips so that their members can get to know, understand, and trust each other.[71] Many virtual teams also schedule periodic face-to-face meetings to supplement electronic forms of communication, which can be especially important for newly formed virtual teams.[72]

Research on virtual teams is at an early stage, but preliminary studies suggest that while some virtual teams can perform as well as teams whose members meet face-to-face, team members may be less satisfied with the experience, and cohesiveness may be lower in virtual teams.[73] Periodic face-to-face meetings and scheduled recreational and social activities can improve the cohesiveness of virtual teams, however.

In some virtual teams, some members are located in the same physical location and often interact in person, whereas other members of the same team work in a different location and interact with the rest of the team primarily through electronic forms of communication.[74] Although this kind of arrangement has the benefits of increased flexibility, it also presents some special challenges as indicated in the accompanying OB Today.

ob today

The Challenges of Being a Virtual Team Member

Hewlett-Packard, the electronics and computer technology giant, prides itself on taking advantage of the latest developments in information technology to support flexibility and diversity.[75] Thus, telecommuting, using new information technology to facilitate working from home, and virtual teams are all realities at Hewlett-Packard. Take the case of Barbara Recchia, who is a member of a team in the company's human resources department. The other members of Recchia's team work at corporate headquarters in Palo Alto, California, while Recchia works from her home in Santa Rosa, California (which is north of San Francisco) and communicates with the team by phone and e-mail.[76]

Although Recchia likes her virtual arrangement, she also sometimes gets lonely and feels isolated from the other members of her team. She recalls when she first started working from her home, she used to come to the office in Palo Alto around once a month. She soon realized, however, that she was feeling very disconnected from her team and the organization as a whole. Now she comes to headquarters about once a week, and she tries to attend important meetings on site. She also finds that it is important to sometimes meet face-to-face with her supervisor to get some sense of how her supervisor really feels about key issues and decisions.[77]

Equally important is making time to socialize with members of her team when she comes to Palo Alto. Getting together for lunch after a morning meeting helps to build a sense of camaraderie and enables Recchia to feel connected with her team and the company. These occasions also help satisfy her need for social interaction.[78]

Summary

Group and organizational effectiveness hinge on minimizing process losses, achieving process gains, aligning group goals with organizational goals, and having the appropriate level of group cohesiveness. Four types of groups that are especially important in many organizations include the top management team, self-managed work teams, research and development teams, and virtual teams. In this chapter, we make the following major points:

1. Actual group performance often falls short of potential performance because of process losses due to coordination and motivation problems in groups. Process gains cause the potential performance of a group to rise, and they enhance group effectiveness.

2. Social loafing, a motivation problem that leads to process losses, is the tendency of individuals to exert less effort when they work in a group than when they work alone. Social loafing occurs for two reasons: (a) Individuals in a group think that they will not receive positive outcomes for performing at a high level or negative outcomes for substandard performance because individual levels of performance cannot easily be identified and evaluated. (b) Individuals think that their own efforts are unimportant or not really needed. Social loafing can be eliminated or reduced by making individual performance levels identifiable, making each individual feel that he or she can make an important and worthwhile contribution to the group, and by keeping group size small.

3. Group tasks can be characterized in terms of the nature of interdependence between group members. Thompson describes three types of task interdependence: pooled, sequential, and reciprocal. The nature and causes of process losses and process gains depend on the type of task involved and the degree of interdependence among group members.

4. Group cohesiveness is the attractiveness of a group to its members. Group size, the similarity/diversity of group members, competition with other groups, success, and the exclusiveness of the group help to determine the level of group cohesiveness. Consequences of group cohesiveness are the level of participation and communication within a group, the level of conformity to group norms, and group goal accomplishment. When group goals are aligned with organizational goals, there is an optimal level of group cohesiveness that results in high levels of performance. When group goals are not aligned with organizational goals, group cohesiveness is dysfunctional for an organization.

5. Four kinds of work groups that have the potential to affect organizational performance dramatically are top management teams, self-managed work teams, research and development teams, and virtual teams.

Exercises in Understanding and Managing Organizational Behavior

Questions for Discussion and Review

1. Give an example of (a) a process gain in a research and development team and (b) a process loss in a research and development team.

2. Give an example of (a) a process gain in a self-managed work team and (b) a process loss in a self-managed work team.

3. Why do some individuals engage in social loafing while others do not?

4. Can managers change the type of task interdependence in a work group, or is task interdependence a relatively fixed characteristic? If managers can change it, how might they do so?

5. Why is it sometimes hard to manage groups that are reciprocally interdependent?

6. Is social loafing a problem in top management teams? Why or why not?

7. What kinds of employees would probably prefer to work in a virtual team rather than in a team that meets face-to-face?

8. How can excessive group cohesiveness result in low levels of performance?

9. How can too little group cohesiveness result in low levels of performance?

10. In what kinds of organizations might it be especially important for work groups to be cohesive?

Building People Skills

Group Effectiveness

Think of a group that you are currently a member of—a work group, a club, or any other group that you belong to and actively participate in. Briefly describe the group. Then answer each of these questions:

1. What process losses are experienced in this group? Why?

2. What process gains are experienced in this group? Why?

3. Does the actual performance of this group equal its potential performance? Why or why not?

4. How might this group raise its potential performance?

5. Is social loafing a problem in this group? Why or why not?

6. How would you characterize the major tasks performed by this group in terms of Thompson's model of task interdependence?

7. Is this a cohesive group? Why or why not?

8. Does cohesiveness help or hinder the group's performance?

9. Are group goals aligned with any larger organizational goals?

A Question of Ethics

Group Processes and Ethics

As the chapter notes, sometimes when groups or teams become too large the problem of social loafing arises as some employees withhold their own effort and let other members of the team bear the work burden. If this happens, the members of a group are likely to come into conflict because they do not think this is fair and because some people are putting their own self-interest above that of other group members. With this in mind, think about the following issues.

Questions

1. To what extent should the members of a group attempt to correct and change the behavior of a group member whom they feel is shirking?
2. At what point is it appropriate to inform their supervisor about this member's behavior?
3. At what point does conflict among group members become unethical?

Small Group Break-Out Exercise

When and How to Use Groups

After reading the following scenario, break up into groups of three or four people and discuss the issues involved. Be prepared to share your thinking with the rest of the class.

You are the managers who are in charge of the operations of a large building products supply company. In the past you were each responsible for a different department and each of you were responsible for managing 10 employees who worked separately to stock the shelves, answer customer questions, and check out customers. You have decided that you can operate more efficiently if you organize these employees into work teams. You believe that the old system did not encourage your employees to behave proactively. Indeed, you think that the way the work situation was designed prevented them from finding ways to improve operating procedures, and this is why you have chosen to use work teams.

Teams will change how employees perform their tasks in many ways. You are meeting to decide how to change the way you motivate employees to encourage employees in the new work groups to perform at a higher level. Using the chapter material:

1. Identify the kinds of process gains and losses associated with this change to work groups and discuss ways to solve potential motivational and coordination problems.
2. Discuss how to change the incentive system to encourage employees to cooperate and work together in their new teams to improve performance.
3. Discuss some steps you can take to smooth the transition to teams and help employees become used to working in their new groups.

Topic for Debate

Organizational effectiveness hinges on the effectiveness of the groups that make up an organization. Now that you have a good understanding of what makes for effective work groups, debate the following issue.

Team A. Process losses in work groups are more common than process gains.

Team B. Process gains in work groups are more common than process losses.

Experiential Exercise

Curtailing Social Loafing

Objective

Your objective is to gain experience in developing a strategy to reduce social loafing in an ongoing group.

Procedure

Assume the role of a manager of a home improvements/building supply store that sells a wide range of products, including lumber, plumbing fixtures, windows, and paint, to both commercial accounts and individual customers. The store is staffed by three types of employees who work in three different groups: (1) a group of six cashiers who check out purchases made by individuals on site, (2) a group of five floor employees who help customers locate items they need, stock merchandise, and reshelve returns; and (3) a group of four employees who handle commercial accounts. All the employees are paid on an hourly basis. The cashiers and floor employees earn the minimum wage; the commercial account employees earn one and a half times the minimum wage.

You are pleased with the performance of the cashiers and the commercial account employees. The floor employees, however, seem to be putting forth less effort than they should. On several occasions, customers have complained about not being able to find items, and you personally have located the items for them even though there were ample floor employees on duty. The floor employees do not seem busy, and their workloads have not increased recently, yet they have a backlog of work to be done, including stocking of new merchandise and reshelving. Despite their backlog, you often see members of this group chatting with each other, taking cigarette breaks outside the back of the store, and making personal telephone calls, all outside their regularly scheduled breaks.

1. Develop a plan of action to reduce social loafing in the group of floor employees.
2. The class divides into groups of three to five people, and each group appoints one member as spokesperson to present the group's action plans to the whole class.
3. Group members take turns describing their action plans for reducing social loafing among the floor employees.
4. After discussing the pros and cons of each different approach, the group develops a plan of action to reduce social loafing among the floor employees.

When your group has completed these activities, the spokesperson will present the group's action plan to the whole class.

Making the Connection

Find an example of a company that groups many of its employees into self-managed work teams. Why does this company use self-managed work teams? What process gains (if any) occur in these teams? What process losses (if any) occur in these teams? Do the employees like working in self-managed work teams? What contributes to the level of cohesiveness in the teams?

New York Times Cases in the News

The New York Times

For Group Doctors, a Winning Model

BY CHRISTOPHER WEST DAVIS

While the business problems of hospitals like Westchester Medical Center are acute and well known, some private practice doctor groups are doing just fine.

Take the Mount Kisco Medical Group, for example. It started with five doctors in 1942, and now has 87 doctors, double the number it had six years ago, in offices here and in Yorktown Heights and Carmel. Offering virtually every specialty in modern medicine, from rheumatology and neurology to sports medicine and plastic surgery, the group is the dominant provider in the northern part of the county, with all-in-one convenience for what group officials say is a roster of 200,000 patients, pulled from 60 miles in every direction.

The problems of the health-care industry are well known: reimbursement rates for virtually every service are fixed, managed care and health insurance are complicated, and government reimbursements for the poor and the elderly under Medicaid and Medicare are slim. As a result, it seems, doctors are forced to take more and more of a business role, at which Mount Kisco Medical Group has apparently excelled.

"Medicine has changed, unfortunately, for everyone in the country," said Dr. Scott D. Hayworth, chief executive officer of the Mount Kisco Medical Group, "a medical group is really a business."

The equation seems to be pretty clear. The group has expanded and taken over or merged with doctors in other practices, or has recruited specialists one by one. Almost all specialties are represented, so patients feel they can do one-stop shopping. The group has developed especially lucrative procedures like outpatient ambulatory surgery, taking a substantial chunk of that business away from local hospitals.

Most of Westchester's 2,500 private practice doctors work in groups of one to five, according to Stuart A. Hayman, executive director of the Westchester County Medical Society. Because of its affluence, "Westchester is really a bastion for small groups, reminiscent of the old days," he said. Success with "the big model," like Mount Kisco's, he said, is "unusual for this county."

Acknowledged as pioneers by the medical community, the group has still come in for criticism. Doctors outside the group worry, in general, that large group practices risk becoming businesses that feed on themselves, supplying incentives for in-house referrals and de-emphasizing outside second opinions and spending time with patients.

Dr. Daniel F. Peters, a solo-practice surgeon in the area, said there were too many trade-offs to joining a large group. "Every decision is my own," he said. "Nobody's over my shoulder saying, 'Come on, there are patients waiting out there.'" An independent affiliate of Mount Sinai Hospital, the Mount Kisco Medical Group, according to Dr. Hayworth, is "the oldest multispecialty group in New York State." Last spring the group moved into all 60,000 square feet of T.W.A.'s old corporate headquarters on Bedford Road, in a purchase and remodeling aided by Mount Sinai. Patients are pulled from "Manhattan, New Jersey, tip of Long Island and up north," he said. The group is held privately, and Dr. Hayworth declined to make the group's revenue or cost figures public. He said that of the 87 doctors, 63 were shareholders and that new doctors had to practice two years before being voted a piece of the pie.

One of the things Mount Kisco offered is convenience: with a range of specialists, lab and imaging equipment and so on under the same roof, with the patient's records accessible instantaneously through a PC network and no need to go through the trouble of registering all over again, it is convenient for the patient. It also makes sense for a primary care physician or pediatrician to refer in-house. There is a financial incentive for the doctor to refer to a partner. At the end of the day, there will be more revenues in the common till.

SOURCE: Christopher Davis, "For Group Doctors, a Winning Model," *New York Times*, February 1, 2004, p. 14WC.4.

Questions for Discussion

1. What are some advantages and disadvantages of physicians working in large groups as opposed to small groups?

2. What form of task interdependence would you expect to find in a large group of physicians? How would this likely affect the level of group cohesiveness?

𝕿𝖍𝖊 𝕹𝖊𝖜 𝖄𝖔𝖗𝖐 𝕿𝖎𝖒𝖊𝖘

A Firehouse Culture Where Taunts and Teasing Flourish

MICHELLE O'DONNELL, JANON FISHER AND JASON GEORGE CONTRIBUTED REPORTING FOR THIS ARTICLE.

First came the teasing: one man made a crack about another's sexual orientation. Others may have laughed. The target of the teasing responded with a taunt, a firefighter familiar with the case said, and then, in a flash, a metal chair sailed through the air, shattering bones in the teased man's face and partly severing his nose.

In that horrifying instant last Wednesday, a verbal fight swiftly escalated into violence in a Staten Island firehouse, officials say, leaving one firefighter on a respirator in a hospital and another under arrest, his career in peril. While the details are still under investigation and more charges against firefighters accused of covering up the incident are possible, the fight has opened a window of sorts on New York City's firehouse culture, including certain aspects that may have combined to disastrous effect.

Fire Commissioner Nicholas Scoppetta said last week that the fight at least partially stemmed from the close confines of firehouse living, where shared meals and sleeping quarters can lead to a boiling over of sibling-like relationships fueled by constant ribbing and full of all the tensions, personal feuds and intense competition of any family ties. To be sure, razzing is as much a part of firehouse life as communal meals and the shattering peal of alarm bells. But what set the Staten Island incident apart, surprising even longtime firefighters, was that it culminated in violence.

Part of the mystique of firefighters is their seeming ability to remain forever young and daring. But as admirable as those traits can be, this youthfulness can at times translate into what the outside world might consider adolescent behavior. The endless flow of taunts can seem vicious and cruel. Those who have lived in and studied the world of firefighters–which remains overwhelmingly male–say there are good reasons why such an atmosphere is cultivated. After all, who but someone with a teenage boy's daring sense of immortality would willingly run into a burning building to save someone's life?

"Everybody verbally abuses young firefighters," said Vincent Dunn, a retired deputy chief, who added that even longtime firefighters do not outgrow the sport of razzing. "Nobody wants physical violence–that's a no-no. But there's a lot of verbal abuse. It's like society."

In firehouses across the city, firefighters say they use taunts to build camaraderie. The idea, firefighters say, is to find a colleague's greatest weakness and taunt him–or her–about it over and again until it no longer wounds the person's pride. That colleague will be a stronger individual at a moment of crisis, firefighters say.

There is, for example, the firefighter who once worked as a manager at Bloomingdale's before joining the department. His colleagues learned of his former job and, for more than a decade, the only personal pronouns they have used to refer to him have been "she" and "her."

Another firefighter, teased by his colleagues about having a small skull, once found a photo of his head nestled in a pea pod on the label of a can of peas. And a short firefighter was given a child's oxford shirt when he passed the lieutenant's test.

"One thing in the firehouse is that they love anyone who has the ability to make them laugh," said Mr. Dunn. That person is held in high esteem in the firehouse, he said.

A firefighter at a firehouse in Astoria, Queens, yesterday explained it this way: "To be picked on is to be liked. It's like being out with friends. You have to be a sport about it. If you can't take it, don't give the heat."

A firefighter familiar with the Staten Island fight said that Firefighter Silvestri was known to call Firefighter Walsh by homosexual slurs, as he allegedly did last Wednesday evening. Using taunts to emphasize seniority could have been a factor, the firefighter said. Firefighter Silvestri, 41, had 15 years with the department, while Firefighter Walsh, 40, had just 8.

"It's just a way of ranking each other," the firefighter said, speaking on the condition of anonymity because of the investigation. "It's just one more way to get at one another."

To defend himself, the firefighter said, Firefighter Walsh mentioned that Firefighter Silvestri had arranged for a junior firefighter to work his regular shift on Thanksgiving Day, then came in to work on overtime pay. According to the firefighter, Firefighter Walsh had mentioned that subject more than a few times since Thanksgiving. Alleging that a firefighter is taking advantage of his colleagues in making the system work to his own benefit is a sore subject in any firehouse, and the firefighter said that Firefighter Walsh's references to this galled Firefighter Silvestri.

In firehouse culture, people who work the system to their advantage are all too familiar, just as any family knows who it is that never washes the dishes or carries out the trash. (Firefighters even have a name for these types: "squarerooters.")

Usually, these disputes are resolved without violence. "If a guy comes in and he doesn't do the right thing, that's where some of the needling comes in," said a firefighter in Jackson Heights, Queens. "Hopefully, he'll get the idea and set things right."

"If you got a problem, all you need to do is mention it at the dinner table," the Jackson Heights firefighter said, a reference to the large kitchen table where anywhere from 6 to 20 firefighters take their three meals a day. "You get all the advice you need. It's firehouse therapy."

SOURCE: Michelle O'Donnell, Janon Fisher, and Jason George, "A Firehouse Culture Where Taunts and Teasing Flourish." *New York Times*, January 5, 2004, p. B.1.

Questions for Discussion

1. What effect do taunts and teasing have on group relationships in a firehouse?

2. What might be some positive and negative effects of taunts and teasing?

Leaders and Leadership

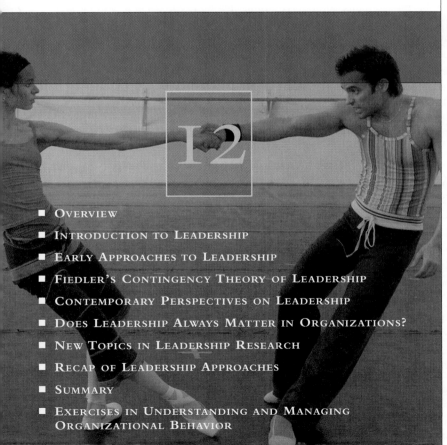

I2

LEARNING OBJECTIVES

After studying this chapter, you should be able to:

■

Describe what leadership is, when leaders are effective and ineffective, and the difference between formal and informal leaders.

▨

Identify the traits that show the strongest relationship to leadership, the behaviors leaders engage in, and the limitations of the trait and behavior models of leadership.

■

Explain how contingency models of leadership and differentiate between four different contingency approaches.

▨

Describe why leadership is not always a vital process in some work situations because substitutes for leadership exist.

▨

Discuss transformational leadership and how it is achieved, explain how a leader's moods affects followers, and appreciate how gender may affect leadership style.

OPENING CASE

No "One Size Fits All" Approach to Leadership

Is There an "Ideal" Leadership Style?

Many companies whose performance is falling significantly often search for a new leader or chief executive officer (CEO) who they believe will be able to solve its problems and turn around its performance. What is interesting about these CEOS is that they often have very different approaches to leadership—and not all of them are successful. There is no "one size fits all" approach when it comes to understanding what leaders do and what leadership is; neither is there just one way of solving a company's problems.

Take the example of Jacques Nasser, an experienced global executive who was appointed as CEO of Ford Motors to turn around its performance. Nasser was a brilliant, creative thinker who involved Ford in many different global projects to compete against efficient Japanese car companies. Nasser was a micromanager who sought to manage all major operating decisions and was reluctant to delegate authority to his top executives.[1] He had an achievement-oriented leadership approach based on setting his subordinates challenging and difficult goals and then driving them to succeed. He created a tough performance appraisal system to evaluate Ford's middle managers, one that sought to identify and weed out those he felt were poor performers.

By contrast, when struggling General Motors (GM) searched for a new leader, its selection was Rick Waggoner, a top executive known for being a team player and a Type B leader compared to hard-driving Nasser who was seen as a typical Type A leader. As a Type B leader with a participative leadership style, Waggoner recognizes the competence of his top executives and he delegates to them the authority they need to make the decisions in the areas and functions that they are in charge of. He lets people get on with their jobs, and believes that "you've got to work well with people . . . you've got to be a good judge of talent."[2]

As it turned out, whereas Rick Waggoner is still the CEO of GM and his company's performance is improving, Jacques Nasser's approach didn't work for Ford. Its performance continued to slip and William Clay Ford, who has a consensus-building leadership style similar to Waggoner's, replaced him as CEO. He has delegated authority to his top managers to try to jump-start Ford's turnaround; he has also abandoned Nasser's tough performance appraisal system that discouraged managers from taking risks for fear of being fired for making mistakes.[3]

An example of a CEO who has adopted a leadership style that includes elements of both Nasser's and Waggoner's approach is Ellen Hancock, CEO of Exodus Communications, Inc., a prominent Web site hosting company. Like Waggoner, Hancock is a strong believer in participation in decision making and gives the managers who report to her the authority to make important decisions in their areas of expertise. At the same, however, like Nasser, Hancock is very goal oriented and excels at creating a work situation that provides managers with guidance so important things get done and nothing slips through the cracks. In addition, Hancock also is supportive of her subordinates and has mentored many women who want to succeed in the male-dominated world of high technology.[4]

A final example of the effect of different leadership approaches comes from Time Warner, the giant entertainment company.[5] In 2003, to turn around its performance it replaced its visionary, achievement-oriented CEO, Gerald Levin, with another Time Warner executive, Richard Parsons.[6] Although both these CEOs believe in delegating authority to their managers, Parsons, unlike Levin, has a participative approach to leadership. When he became CEO, the diplomatic Parsons worked in a methodical way to encourage Time Warner's managers to cooperate with each other across the organization.[7] Levin's hard-driving approach had led these managers to compete with one another, and turf battles between different business units were common. As a result, Time Warner's performance had fallen. Currently, Parsons's approach is working well for Time Warner and its performance has improved.

Overview

When things go wrong in an organization, blame is most often laid at the leader's feet. Similarly, when organizations are doing particularly well, people tend to think that their leaders are doing an especially good job. The common belief that leaders "make a difference" and can have a major impact on people, groups, and whole organizations has prompted OB researchers to exert considerable effort to try to explain the nature of leadership. Researchers have focused primarily on two leadership issues: (1) Why do some members of an organization become leaders while others do not? and (2) Why are some leaders more successful or effective than others? As the opening case suggests, answering these questions is not easy because there are many different kinds of leaders and leadership approaches. Although some approaches work in a particular situation, others do not.

This chapter addresses these two important issues and explores the nature of leadership in organizations. First, we define leadership and discuss the different types of leaders found in organizations. Second, we explore several different approaches to leadership that provide answers to the questions of why some people become leaders and what makes some people able to perform at a higher level than others. We then consider the issue of substitutes and neutralizers for leadership, that is, factors that also help to motivate and coordinate employee behavior, and factors that can reduce leader effectiveness. Finally, we examine some new topics in leadership theory and research: transformational and charismatic leadership, the effect of a leader's mood on his or her subordinates, and gender and leadership. By the end of this chapter, you will understand how and why leaders so profoundly affect organizational behavior at all levels.

Introduction to Leadership

Although you can often recognize a leader when you see one in action, coming up with a precise definition of leadership is difficult. Even researchers often disagree about which characteristics best describe leadership but, in general, two are regarded as being the most important.[8] First, leadership involves *exerting influence* over other members of a group or organization. Second, leadership involves *helping a group or organization achieve its goals*. Combining these two key characteristics, we can define **leadership** as the exercise of influence by one member of a group or organization over other members to help the group or organization achieve its goals.[9] The **leaders** of a group or organization are the individuals who exert such influence. *Leader effectiveness* is the extent to which a leader actually does help a group or organization to achieve its goals.[10] An *effective* leader helps achieve goals; an *ineffective* leader does not.[11] Rick Waggoner has proved to be an effective leader at GM because he helped improve the company's performance; Jacques Nasser was an ineffective leader at Ford because he did not.

Leaders influence and shape many aspects of organizational behavior that we have discussed in previous chapters: attitudes (see Chapter 3), learning (see Chapter 5), motivation (see Chapters 6, 7, and 8), stress (see Chapter 9), and work group effectiveness (see Chapters 10 and 11). Research has shown, for example, that leaders influence their subordinates' or followers' levels of motivation, performance, absenteeism, and turnover, and the quality of their decision making. (We use *followers* and *subordinates* interchangeably to refer to the members of a group or organization who are influenced by a leader).[12]

All leaders exert influence over members of a group or organization. Some leaders, however, have formal authority to do so while others do not. **Formal leaders** are those managers who are given the authority to influence other members in the organization to achieve its goals.[13] With this authority comes the responsibility to make the best use of an organization's resources, including its money and capital and the abilities and skills of its employees. Note that not all managers are leaders; some managers do not have subordinates who report to them.[14] For example, the accounting manager of a restaurant who is responsible for keeping the books is a manager but not a formal leader—this person could be an informal leader, however.

Informal leaders have no formal job authority to influence others but sometimes exert just as much influence in an organization as formal leaders—and sometimes even more. The ability of informal leaders to influence others often stems from special

Leadership The exercise of influence by one member of a group or organization over other members to help the group or organization achieve its goals.

Leader An individual who is able to influence group or organizational members to help the group or organization achieve its goals.

Formal leader A member of an organization who is given authority by the organization to influence other organizational members to achieve organizational goals.

Informal leader An organizational member with no formal authority to influence others who nevertheless is able to exert considerable influence because of special skills or talents.

skills or talents they possess—skills the organization's members realize will help it achieve its goals. Eight waiters employed in a restaurant all have the same job of serving customers, for example, but the waiter who was the most experienced and had the best interpersonal skills became the informal leader of the group. He made sure that the other waiters provided good service, and he always stepped in to help settle arguments before they got out of hand. The other waiters listened to him because his advice about customer service helped them earn large tips and because his social skills made the restaurant a nice place to work.

In general, both formal leaders and informal leaders influence others in groups and organizations. The various approaches to leadership that we describe in this chapter seek to explain why some people become leaders and others do not and why some leaders are more effective than others.

Early Approaches to Leadership

Each of the various approaches to leadership we discuss in the next sections of this chapter complements the other approaches—no one theory describes the "right" or "only" way to become a leader or be a good leader. Each of the theories focuses on a different set of issues, but taken together they provide a better understanding of how to become an effective leader. Two of the earliest perspectives on leadership were offered by the trait approach and the behavior approach.

THE LEADER TRAIT APPROACH

Early studies of leadership sought to identify *enduring personal traits* that distinguish leaders from followers and effective from ineffective leaders. Recall from Chapter 2 that traits are a person's particular tendencies to feel, think, and act in certain ways. The search for leadership traits began in the 1930s, and after nearly 300 studies, the list was narrowed to several traits that showed the strongest relationship to effective leadership:[15]

Tommye Jo Daves (right), a 60-year-old grandmother, was promoted and became the plant manager of Levi's factory in Murphy, North Carolina. She began as a seamstress at the plant in 1959 and rose to the top because her job knowledge and personal qualities earned her the trust and respect of the workforce.

- *Intelligence* helps a leader solve complex problems.

- *Task-relevant knowledge* ensures that a leader knows what has to be done, how it should be done, and what resources are required for a group and organization to achieve its goals.

- *Dominance*, an individual's need to exert influence and control over others, helps a leader channel followers' efforts and abilities toward achieving group and organizational goals.

- *Self-confidence* helps a leader influence followers and motivates them to persevere in the face of obstacles or difficulties.

- *Energy/activity levels*, when high, help a leader deal with the many demands he or she faces on a day-to-day basis.

- *Tolerance for stress* helps a leader deal with the uncertainty inherent in any leadership role.

- *Integrity* and *honesty* ensure that a leader behaves ethically and is worthy of his or her followers' trust and confidence.

- *Emotional maturity* ensures that a leader is not overly self-centered, can control his or her feelings, and can accept criticism.[16]

There is an important point to understand when viewing leadership using the trait approach. For some traits, it is not clear what comes first: *being in a leadership position or possessing the trait in question.* In other words, is it possession of the appropriate trait that leads a person to become a leader? Or, as we learned in Chapter 2, given that personality traits *can* change over the long term (several years), does being put in a leadership position result in a person developing leadership traits? The answer to this question is not clear or unambiguous. Individuals who possess the traits associated with effective leadership may be more likely to become effective leaders than those who do not. But many individuals who possess the appropriate traits may never become leaders, and many leaders who possess them are not effective. The difficulty of this question prompted researchers to look for other ways to understand effective leadership and search for other factors that contribute to it.

THE LEADER BEHAVIOR APPROACH

Rather than looking at the personal traits of leaders, in later years, researchers focused on what leaders actually do—that is, on the *specific behaviors* performed by effective leaders. Researchers at Ohio State University in the 1940s and 1950s were at the forefront of the leader behavior approach.[17] The Ohio State researchers realized one of the key ways in which leaders influence followers is through their concrete behaviors. The behavior approach seeks to identify leader behaviors that help individuals, groups, and organizations achieve their multiple goals.

The Ohio State researchers developed a list of over 1,800 specific, concrete behaviors they thought leaders might engage in, such as setting goals for followers, telling followers what to do, being friendly, and making sure that followers are happy.[18] The researchers then developed scales to measure these behaviors and administered the scales to thousands of employees. Employees were asked to indicate the extent to which their leaders performed the various leader behaviors. After analyzing their responses, the researchers found that most leader behaviors involved either *consideration* or *initiating structure.* The Ohio State results have been replicated in many studies and in other countries such as Germany.[19]

Consideration. Behaviors indicating that a leader trusts, respects, and values good relationships with his or her followers is known as **consideration**. Stanley Gault, a former CEO of Goodyear Tire and Rubber, demonstrated consideration on

Consideration Behavior indicating that a leader trusts, respects, and values good relationships with his or her followers.

his very first day as CEO. He showed his followers that he trusted them. While moving into his luxurious office, he was offered a set of keys for the locked cabinets lining the office walls. Gault indicated that he didn't want the keys because he liked to keep things unlocked. The employee who offered Gault the keys urged him to reconsider because many people would be going in and out of his office every day and the cleaning staff would come in at night. Gault's response was that he didn't need the keys because, as he put it, "This company should be run on the basis of trust."[20] Other examples of consideration include a leader's being friendly, treating group members as his or her equals, and explaining to them why he or she has done certain things.

A leader who engages in consideration also shows followers that he or she cares about their well-being and is concerned about how they feel and what they think. David Pottruck, co-CEO of the brokerage firm Charles Schwab & Company, learned the importance of consideration by observing how subordinates react when their boss does *not* engage in consideration.[21] Early in his career, Pottruck adopted a very directed, competitive approach to leading and rarely engaged in consideration behaviors. Charles Schwab himself delivered a wake-up call to Pottruck when he let Pottruck know that people didn't like working with him and didn't trust him because he was forcing his initiatives on others and not soliciting their involvement.[22]

With the help of an executive coach, Pottruck began to alter his leadership style to incorporate consideration behaviors. Now, rather than forcing initiatives on others, Pottruck shows he respects his subordinates by explaining problems to them and soliciting their input. For example, when he came to the realization that Schwab might need to keep its branch offices open on Saturdays, he explained the need for this unpopular move to branch managers and also acknowledged the big imposition this might have on their lives and lives of their subordinates. Rather than encountering resistance, the consideration behaviors Pottruck engaged in garnered enthusiasm and support for the initiative.[23] Pottruck now believes that consideration is a key contributor to a competitive advantage in the new Internet economy because it breeds collaboration and encourages teamwork.

Initiating Structure. Behaviors that a leader engages in to make sure the work gets done and subordinates perform their jobs acceptably is known as **initiating structure**. Assigning individual tasks to followers, planning ahead, setting goals, deciding how the work should be performed, and pushing followers to get their tasks accomplished are all initiating-structure behaviors.[24] In the opening case, both Rick Waggoner and Richard Parsons's delegate authority to their subordinates. But, at the same time, from regular, structured meetings they can assess these managers' progress toward meeting current goals, and they can intervene and provide guidance and advice as needed.

Leaders at lower levels also engage in initiating structure. The informal leader of the group of waiters in the restaurant described earlier, for example, engaged in initiating structure by developing a system in which waiters serving very large tables would receive help from other waiters whose stations were not full. This leader also engaged in consideration by taking an interest in the personal lives of the other waiters and by having a cake made and throwing a small party to celebrate each of their birthdays.

Note that consideration and initiating structure are complementary but independent leader behaviors. They are *complementary* because leaders can engage in both types of behaviors. They are *independent* because knowing the extent to which a leader engages in consideration says nothing about the extent to which he or she engages in initiating structure and vice versa.

Initiating structure
Behavior that a leader engages in to make sure that work gets done and subordinates perform their jobs acceptably.

With the help of an executive coach, David Pottuck learned how to incorporate consideration behaviors into his management style in order to overcome his unpopular "directive approach," wich was antagonizing both managers and employees alike.

THE BEHAVIOR APPROACH: LEADER REWARD AND PUNISHING BEHAVIOR

In addition to engaging in consideration and initiating structure, leaders behave in other ways that have important effects on their followers. Recall from Chapter 5 that *reinforcement* can increase the probability of desirable behaviors and *punishment* can decrease the probability of undesirable behaviors occurring. In organizations, managers who are leaders administer reinforcements and punishments.

Leader reward behavior occurs when a leader positively reinforces subordinates' desirable behavior.[25] Leaders who notice when their followers do a good job and acknowledge it with compliments, praise, or more tangible benefits such as a pay raise or promotion are engaging in reward behavior. Leader reward behavior helps to ensure that employees perform at a high level. Gurcharan Das, while CEO of Vicks Vaporub's Indian subsidiary, recalls engaging in leader reward behavior when he gave annual raises to all employees who met at least 20 customers and 20 retailers or wholesalers during the year. Why did Das reward this behavior? It helped the employees keep in touch with the marketplace and come up with ways to improve the company's products and services.[26]

Leader reward behavior A leader's positive reinforcement of subordinates' desirable behavior.

Leader punishing behavior occurs when a leader reprimands or otherwise responds negatively to subordinates who perform undesired behavior.[27] A factory foreman who docks the pay of any subordinate who fails to wear safety glasses on the job is engaging in leader punishing behavior.

Leader punishing behavior A leader's negative response to subordinates' undesired behavior.

Although punishing behavior can be an effective means of curtailing undesirable or potentially dangerous behavior in organizations (see Chapter 5), it is generally more effective to use reinforcement to encourage desired behavior than to use punishment to stop undesired behavior. Punishment can have unintended side effects such as resentment. The foreman mentioned previously would obtain more desirable organizational results by engaging in leader reward behavior, such as giving a bonus of some sort to subordinates who wear their safety glasses every day for a three-month period. Despite the research evidence, however, leaders often engage in punishing behavior.

MEASURING LEADER BEHAVIORS

Considerable research has been done to develop scales to measure the leader behaviors described previously. The *Leadership Behavior Description Questionnaire* asks a leader's subordinates to indicate the extent to which their leader or supervisor engages in a number of different consideration and initiating-structure behaviors. The *Leadership Opinion Questionnaire*, completed by the leaders themselves, asks leaders to indicate which of a variety of consideration and initiating-structure behaviors they think result in good leadership.[28] Researchers have also developed measures of leader reward behavior and leader punishing behavior. Figure 12.1 is an example of one of these measures, which is completed by a leader's subordinates.

Some of the leadership models that management consultants use to help managers learn how to be effective also employ scales to measure consideration and initiating structure. As we discuss in Chapter 18, an approach to organizational change designed to make managers more effective as leaders (Robert Blake and Jane Mouton's Managerial Grid) focuses on identifying the extent to which a company's leaders are concerned about people (consideration) and production (initiating structure).[29] Paul Hersey and Kenneth Blanchard's model, which is quite popular with consultants, also focuses on consideration and initiating structure behaviors.[30]

The subordinates of a leader are asked to indicate the extent to which they agree or disagree with each of the following statements on the following scale:

1 = Strongly disagree	**5** = Slightly agree
2 = Disagree	**6** = Agree
3 = Slightly disagree	**7** = Strongly agree
4 = Neither agree nor disagree	

1. My supervisor always gives me positive feedback when I perform well.
2. My supervisor gives me special recognition when my work performance is especially good.
3. My supervisor would quickly acknowledge an improvement in the quality of my work.
4. My supervisor commends me when I do a better than average job.
5. My supervisor personally pays me a compliment when I do outstanding work.
6. My supervisor informs his or her boss and/or others in the organization when I do outstanding work.
7. If I do well, I know my supervisor will reward me.
8. My supervisor would do all that she/he could to help me go as far as I would like to go in this organization if my work was consistently above average.
9. My good performance often goes unacknowledged by my supervisor.*
10. I often perform well in my job and still receive no praise from my supervisor.*
11. If I performed at a level below that which I was capable of, my supervisor would indicate his/her disapproval.
12. My supervisor shows his/her displeasure when my work is below acceptable standards.
13. My supervisor lets me know about it when I perform poorly.
14. My supervisor would reprimand me if my work was below standard.
15. When my work is not up to par, my supervisor points it out to me.

    * For these items, scoring is reversed such that 1 = 7, 2 = 6, 3 = 5, 5 = 3, 6 = 2, 7 = 1.
    Leader reward behavior = the sum of items 1–10
    Leader punishment behavior = the sum of the items 11–15

FIGURE 12.1

A Measure of Leader Reward and Punishing Behavior

Source: P. M. Podsakoff, W. D. Todor, R. A. Grover, and V. L. Huber, "Situational Moderators of Leader Reward and Punishment Behaviors. Fact or Fiction?" *Organizational Behavior and Human Decision Processes*, 1984, 34, pp. 21-63. Reprinted with permission of Academic Press, Inc.

WHAT IS MISSING IN THE TRAIT AND BEHAVIOR APPROACHES?

Although the trait and behavior approaches to leadership are different from each other—one focuses on what effective leaders are *like*, and the other on what they *do*—they do have something in common: Each approach essentially ignores the situation in which leadership takes place. Recall from Chapter 2 that the *interaction* of personal characteristics (such as traits and behaviors) with the organizational situation (including the amount of formal authority that leaders have and the nature of their subordinates) determines a person's behavior (for example, leadership and performance) in an organization.

The trait approach takes into account leaders' personal characteristics but ignores the situations in which they try to lead. However, certain leadership traits might result in effective leadership in some situations but ineffective leadership in others. Dominance, for example, may make a football coach a good leader for a football team. But the same trait in the head research scientist at a medical laboratory might not be effective because his or her subordinates are likely to be highly educated people who think independently and work best when left alone.

In a similar way, the behavior approach seeks to identify the behaviors responsible for effective leadership without considering how the situation affects behavior. The behavior approach implicitly assumes that regardless of the situation (such as a group's characteristics and composition or the type of task being done), certain leadership behaviors will result in high subordinate levels of satisfaction and performance. However, just as the situation can change how a leader's personal traits affect subordinates' responses, so, too, can it influence how subordinates respond to a leader's specific behaviors. Consider the performance of a group of carpenters who are building a complicated custom-built house. Their performance may increase if their leader engages in initiating structure by scheduling the work so the house is completely framed before the roof is put on and by pushing employees to perform their tasks as quickly as possible. By contrast, the performance of a group of furniture assembly-line workers who have been performing the same tasks day in and day out for several years know exactly how to do their jobs. Not only is their leader's initiating structure behavior unnecessary, but it also might actually lower their job satisfaction if they become annoyed by their leader constantly telling them what to do.

In sum, the trait and behavior approaches contribute to our understanding of effective leadership by indicating what effective leaders tend to be like and what they do (see Table 12.1). A fuller understanding of leadership, however, can be gained only by also considering how the situation affects leadership.

Fiedler's Contingency Theory of Leadership

The trait and behavior approaches ignore how the situation at hand influences a leader's effectiveness. Recognizing that effectiveness is determined by both (1) the characteristic of individuals and (2) the situations in which they find themselves, Fred Fiedler developed the **contingency theory of leadership**.[31] One of the most popular approaches to understanding leadership, Fiedler's theory sheds light on two important leadership issues: (1) why, in a particular situation, some leaders will be more effective than other leaders even though they have equally good credentials, and (2) why a particular leader may be effective in one situation but not in another.

Contingency theory of leadership The theory that leader effectiveness is determined by both the personal characteristics of leaders and by the situations in which leaders find themselves.

LEADER STYLE

Like the trait approach, Fiedler's theory acknowledges that personal characteristics influence the effectiveness of leaders. Fiedler was particularly interested in styles of leadership—how a person approaches being a leader. He identified two distinct leader styles—relationship-oriented and task-oriented styles—and proposed that all leaders are characterized by one style or the other.

Leaders who are *relationship oriented* want to be liked by and get along well with their subordinates. Although they want their subordinates to perform at a high level, relationship-oriented leaders' first priority is developing good relationships with their followers. Their second priority is making sure that the job gets done (task accomplishment). Ken Franklin, who manages American-owned factories (*maquiladoras*) in Mexico's Bermúdez Industrial Park in Ciudad Juárez, has learned that a relationship-oriented style is particularly important when leading Mexican subordinates. Every morning at 6 o'clock he greets factory employees personally when they begin work.[32]

Leaders who are *task oriented* want their subordinates to perform at a high level and accomplish all of their assigned tasks. Their first priority is task accomplishment, and they push subordinates to make sure that the job gets done. Having good relationships with their subordinates is their second priority.

According to Fiedler, a leader's style, whether relationship oriented or task oriented, is an enduring personal characteristic. Leader style cannot easily be changed. A relationship-oriented leader cannot be trained to be task oriented and vice versa. A leader's style also cannot easily change with the situation. In other words, a leader will not be relationship oriented in one situation and task oriented in another; he or she will use the same style in all leadership situations.

Which style of leadership is most effective depends on the kind of situation the leader is dealing with. Because leaders cannot change their style, an organization must do one of two things to ensure that its leaders are able to help their subordinates and the

TABLE 12.1

The Nature of Leadership: The Role of Traits and Behaviors

Approach	Premise	Drawbacks
Trait approach	Effective leaders possess certain qualities or traits that help a group or an organization achieve its goals.	Some effective leaders do not possess all of these traits, and some leaders who possess these traits are not effective. The approach ignores the situation in which leadership takes place.
Behavior approach	Effective leaders perform certain behaviors, which may include consideration, initiating structure, reward behavior, and punishing behavior.	The relationship between these behaviors and subordinate performance and satisfaction is not necessarily clear-cut. The behavior approach ignores the situation in which leadership takes place.

Least preferred co-employee scale A questionnaire that measures leader style by scoring leaders' responses to questions about the co-employee with whom they have the most difficulty working.

organization as a whole attain important goals. *An organization must either assign leaders to situations in which they will be effective or change the situation to fit the leader.*

Fiedler devised and used a unique scale to measure leader style: the **least preferred co-employee scale.** He asked leaders to think about their least preferred co-employee (LPC), or the co-employee with whom they have the most difficulty working. The leader was then asked to rate the LPC on a number of dimensions such as the extent to which the LPC was friendly, enthusiastic, and pleasant. Relationship-oriented leaders (also called *high LPC leaders*) described their least preferred co-employee in relatively positive terms. They were able to say some good things about the co-employee with whom they had the most difficulty working. They were able to set aside the work-related problems they had with the LPC and see that this person had merit as another human being. In contrast, task-oriented leaders (also called *low LPC leaders*) described their least preferred co-employee negatively. They believed their LPC had few redeeming qualities. Because they had difficulty working with the LPC, their overall impression of this person was very negative.

Fiedler theorized that the way in which leaders described their least preferred co-employee provided insight into their approach to leading. Specifically, relationship-oriented leaders would try to think positively about others—even the LPC—because a positive outlook fosters good relationships. Task-oriented leaders, on the other hand, would think negatively about others who were difficult to work with because their undesired behavior might hinder task accomplishment.

SITUATIONAL CHARACTERISTICS

Fiedler proposed that situations vary in their *favorability* for leading—that is, the extent to which the situation allows the leader to easily guide and channel subordinate behavior in the direction of high performance and goal attainment. When a situation is favorable for leading, it is easier for a leader to exert influence than it is when a situation is unfavorable. According to Fiedler, three characteristics determine how favorable situations are for leading: leader–member relations, task structure, and position power.

Leader–member relations The relationship between a leader and his or her followers.

Leader–Member Relations. When **leader–member relations**—the relationship between the leader and his or her followers—are good, followers appreciate, trust, and feel a certain degree of loyalty toward their leader, and the situation is favorable for leading. When leader–member relations are poor, followers dislike or distrust their leader, and the situation is unfavorable for leading. Consider the following situations: Robert Holkan, as head mechanic, leads a group of mechanics in a garage. He gets along well with the mechanics, and they often go out to lunch together. In Holkan's leadership situation, leader–member relations are good. Mary Lester is head of the English department of a small liberal arts college. The other professors in the department think Lester is a snob and a bit pretentious. Leader–member relations are poor in Lester's leadership situation.

Task Structure. **Task structure** is the extent to which the work to be performed by a group is clearly defined. When a group has specific goals that need to be accomplished and every group member knows how to go about achieving the goals, task structure is high. When group goals are vague or uncertain and members are not sure how to go about performing their jobs, task structure is low. Situations are more favorable for leading when task structure is high.

Task structure is high for head mechanic Robert Holkan because the garage has the clear goal of repairing customers' cars in a timely fashion and because the highly skilled mechanics generally know exactly what needs to be done on each car. Task structure is low for Mary Lester. Within the English department there is considerable turmoil about the relative emphasis on teaching and research. The English professors are split about which is more important, and there is considerable disagreement about how to evaluate professors' research and teaching performance. A result of the uncertainty about what the "work" of the department should be (teaching or research) is low task structure.

Position Power. **Position power** is the amount of formal authority that a leader has. If a leader has the power to reward and punish subordinates by, for example, granting them pay raises and bonuses or docking their pay, position power is high. If a leader can do little to reward or punish subordinates, position power is low. A situation is more favorable for leading when position power is high.

At the garage, Robert Holkan has low position power because he has little control over rewards and punishments for the mechanics. The owner of the garage determines pay rates, benefits, and other rewards, and Holkan has little input into the process. Conversely, Lester has high position power as head of the English department. Each year, the department has a set amount of money for faculty raises, and Lester determines how to distribute the money among the faculty. She also determines who teaches which courses and the times at which all courses are taught. Members of the department are reluctant to disagree with her because they are afraid that she may assign them undesirable teaching times (a class, say, from 3 to 5 P.M. on Fridays).

THE CONTINGENCY MODEL

All possible combinations of good and poor leader–member relations, high and low task structure, and high and low position power yield eight leadership situations. Fiedler applied the word *octant* to each type of situation (see Figure 12.2). According to Fiedler's theory, octant I, II, and III situations are very favorable for leading; octant IV, V, VI, and VII situations are moderately favorable for leading; and an octant VIII situation is very unfavorable for leading.

Head mechanic Robert Holkan has good leader–member relations, high task structure, and low position power (octant II in Figure 12.2), a very favorable situation for leading. Professor Mary Lester, in contrast, has poor leader–member relations, low task structure, and high position power (octant VII in Figure 12.2), a moderately favorable situation for leading.

Task structure The extent to which the work to be performed by a group is clearly defined.

Position power The amount of formal authority a leader has.

FIGURE 12.2

Favorability of Situations for Leading

Source: Adapted from F. E. Fiedler, *A Theory of Leadership Effectiveness* (New York: McGraw-Hill, 1967). Reprinted with permission.

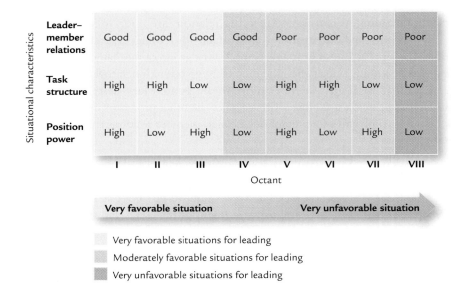

Situational characteristics								
Leader–member relations	Good	Good	Good	Good	Poor	Poor	Poor	Poor
Task structure	High	High	Low	Low	High	High	Low	Low
Position power	High	Low	High	Low	High	Low	High	Low
Octant	I	II	III	IV	V	VI	VII	VIII

Very favorable situation ⟶ Very unfavorable situation

Very favorable situations for leading
Moderately favorable situations for leading
Very unfavorable situations for leading

To determine whether Robert Holkan or Mary Lester will be the more effective leader, we need to look at Holkan and Lester's leadership styles and the favorability of their situations. The impact of each of these factors on leader effectiveness depends or is contingent on the other. To identify their leadership style, we ask both of them to describe their least preferred co-employee. Holkan describes his least preferred co-employee very negatively; he thinks this mechanic is basically stupid and difficult to get along with. This description indicates that Holkan is a task-oriented or low LPC leader. Lester describes her least preferred co-employee in positive terms. Even though she has trouble working with this professor, she thinks that he is intelligent and pleasant. This description indicates that Lester is a relationship-oriented or high LPC leader.

According to Fiedler's theory, task-oriented leaders are most effective in situations that are very favorable or very unfavorable, and relationship-oriented leaders are most effective in moderately favorable situations (see Table 12.2). Thus, even though Holkan's and Lester's leadership situations are different as are their styles, they are actually equally effective leaders. Holkan is a task-oriented leader in a very favorable situation, and Lester is a relationship-oriented leader in a moderately favorable situation.

TABLE 12.2

Fiedler's Contingency Theory of Leadership

Leader Style	Nature of Leader	Situations in Which Style is more Effective
Relationship oriented	Wants to be liked by and to get along well with subordinates *First priority*: Developing good relationships with subordinates *Second priority*: Getting the job done	Moderately favorable for leading (octants IV, V, VI, and VII in Figure 12.2)
Task oriented	Wants subordinates to perform at a high level and accomplish all assigned tasks. *First priority*: Getting the job done *Second priority*: Developing good relationships with subordinates	Very favorable or very unfavorable for leading (octants I, II, III, and VIII in Figure 12.2)

Why are task-oriented leaders more effective in very favorable and in unfavorable situations? And why are relationship-oriented leaders more effective in moderately favorable situations? Recall that the first priority of task-oriented leaders is task accomplishment and their second priority is good interpersonal relations. Fiedler suggests that when leaders and people in general are under stress, they concentrate on their first priorities. A very unfavorable situation for leading is stressful for most leaders, and task-oriented leaders will focus on getting the job done because that is their first priority. This focus is likely to be effective in such situations because it increases the chances that a group will at least accomplish its tasks. In very favorable situations, task-oriented leaders, realizing that the group will achieve its goals because the situation is so good, can focus on their second priority—good interpersonal relations—because they know the job will get done. In moderately favorable situations, relationship-oriented leaders can focus on both interpersonal relations and task accomplishment.[33] Some leadership experts have questioned these explanations and Fiedler's model. Research studies provide some support for the model but also suggest that it (like most theories) needs modifying.[34]

In summary, Fiedler considers leadership styles to be relatively fixed or enduring. Leaders cannot be "taught" to be relationship oriented or task oriented, nor can a leader alter his or her style according to the situation. Instead, contingency theory holds that leaders must be assigned to situations in which they will be effective. If that won't work, the situation must be changed to fit the leader. In the first case, task-oriented leaders should be assigned to very unfavorable or to very favorable situations, whereas relationship-oriented leaders should be assigned to moderately favorable situations. In the second case, to improve the favorability of a situation for leading, it may be possible to increase the levels of task structure by giving a leader specific goals to be accomplished and guidelines for how to channel subordinates' behavior to reach those goals. Another alternative would be for the organization to improve the favorability of the situation by giving the leader the formal authority to make decisions about pay raises, bonuses, and promotions for subordinates, there by increasing the leader's power position.

Contemporary Perspectives on Leadership

Several newer theories or approaches to leadership—each dealing with a different aspect of leadership—have been proposed in recent years. Like Fiedler's model, they are based on a contingency approach that takes into account both the characteristics of leaders and the situations in which they're trying to lead.

Path-goal theory describes how leaders can *motivate* their followers to perform at a high level and can keep them satisfied. The Vroom and Yetton model deals with a specific aspect of leadership: the extent to which leaders should *involve their subordinates in decision making*. Leader–member exchange theory takes into account the fact that leaders often do not treat each of their subordinates equally but instead develop *different kinds of relationships* with different subordinates. Each of these perspectives adds to an understanding of what makes leadership effective in organizations.

PATH–GOAL THEORY: HOW LEADERS MOTIVATE FOLLOWERS

Robert House, a widely respected leadership researcher, realized that much of what leaders try to do in organizations involves motivating their followers. House's **path-goal theory** describes how leaders can motivate their followers to achieve group and organizational goals and the kinds of behaviors they can engage in to accomplish that (see Table 12.3).

Path-goal theory A theory that describes how leaders can motivate their followers to achieve group and organizational goals and the kinds of behaviors leaders can engage in to motivate followers.

TABLE 12.3

Path-Goal Theory

> Effective leaders motivate their followers to achieve group and organizational goals.
>
> Effective leaders make sure that they have control over outcomes their subordinates desire.
>
> Effective leaders reward subordinates for performing at a high level or achieving their work goals by giving them desired outcomes.
>
> Effective leaders raise their subordinates' beliefs about their ability to achieve their work goals and perform at a high level.
>
> In determining how to treat their subordinates and what behaviors to engage in, effective leaders take into account their subordinates' characteristics and the type of work they do.

Path-goal theory suggests that effective leaders follow three guidelines to motivate their followers. The guidelines are based on the expectancy theory of motivation (see Chapter 6). Effective leaders who follow these guidelines have highly motivated subordinates who are likely to meet their work goals and perform at a high level:

1. *Determine what outcomes subordinates are trying to obtain in the workplace.* For example, what needs are they trying to satisfy, or what goals are they trying to meet? After gaining this information, the leader must have control over those outcomes or over the ability to give or withhold the outcomes to subordinates.[35] The new manager of a group of five attorneys in a large law firm determined that salary raises and the opportunity to work on interesting cases with big corporate clients were the outcomes that her subordinates most desired. She already controlled the assignment of cases and clients, but her own boss determined salary raises. After realizing the importance of salary raises for the motivation of her subordinates, the manager discussed with her boss the importance of being able to determine her own subordinates' raises. The boss gave her sole authority to determine their raises as long as she kept within the budget. In this way, the manager made sure she had control over outcomes that her subordinates desired.

2. *Reward subordinates for performing at a high level or achieving their work goals by giving them desired outcomes.* The manager in the law firm had two important goals for her subordinates: completing all assignments within the budgeted hours and winning cases. When subordinates met these goals, they were performing at a high level. To motivate her subordinates to attain these goals, the manager made sure that her distribution of interesting monthly case assignments and semiannual raises reflected the extent to which her subordinates met these two goals. The subordinate who always stayed within the budgeted hours and won all of his cases in the last six months received not only the biggest raise but also the choicest assignments.

3. *Make sure the subordinates believe that they can obtain their work goals and perform at a high level.* Leaders can do this by showing subordinates the paths to goal attainment (hence, the name *path-goal theory*), by removing any obstacles that might come up along the way, and by expressing confidence in their subordinates' capabilities. The manager in the law firm realized that one of her subordinates had low expectations. He had little confidence in his ability to stay within budget and to win cases no matter how hard he worked. The manager was able to raise this subordinate's expectations by showing him how to allocate his billable hours among the various cases he was working on and explain-

ing to him the key ingredients to winning a case. She also told him to ask her for help whenever he came across a problem he thought might jeopardize his chances of winning a case. The subordinate followed her advice, and together they worked out ways to get around problems that came up on the subordinate's various cases. By clarifying the paths to goal attainment and helping to remove obstacles, the supervisor helped raise this subordinate's expectations and motivation, and he actually started to win more cases and complete them within the budgeted hours.

House identified four types of behavior that leaders can engage in to motivate subordinates:

♦ *Directive behavior* (similar to initiating structure) lets subordinates know what tasks need to be performed and how they should be performed.

♦ *Supportive behavior* (similar to consideration) lets subordinates know that their leader cares about their well-being and is looking out for them.

♦ *Participative behavior* enables subordinates to be involved in making decisions that affect them.

♦ *Achievement-oriented behavior* pushes subordinates to do their best. Such behavior includes setting difficult goals for followers, expecting high performance, and expressing confidence in their capabilities.

In determining how to motivate subordinates or which of these behaviors to engage in, a leader has to take into account the nature of his or her subordinates and the work they do. If a subordinate is under a lot of stress, a leader who engages in supportive behavior might be especially effective. Directive behaviors are likely to be beneficial when subordinates work on complex and difficult projects, such as the lawyer who was having trouble winning cases. As discussed earlier, when subordinates are performing easy tasks at which they are already proficient, initiating-structure or directive behaviors are not necessary and are likely to be resented; people don't like to be told how to do something they already do quite well. When it is important for subordinates to accept a decision that a leader needs to make, participative leadership behavior is likely to be effective, as the accompanying OB Today suggests.

Microsoft manager Tammy Savage relied on a participative leadership model to motivate her team members because she knew they were highly competent and driven. Savage convinced them that by working as a team, they could quickly develop software to capture the NetGen market segment.

ob today

Tammy Savage and the NetGen

Tammy Savage joined Microsoft's New York City sales office straight out of Cal State, Fresno, in 1993 when she was 22. A marketing whiz, Savage soon gained a reputation as an expert in understanding the needs of under-30 Internet users—the "Net Generation" or "NetGen." She became a central figure in the New York sales office's dealings with programmers back at Microsoft's Redmond, Washington, headquarters, and her knowledge of the NetGen led to her promotion. She became a manager in Microsoft's business development group, and she moved to Redmond.

Business development keeps a company's products alive and up-to-date with changing customer needs. Savage used her new more senior position to reevaluate the whole of Microsoft's business development efforts for the NetGen. Her conclusion was that Microsoft was missing the boat and risked losing the NetGen to rival companies such as AOL and Yahoo! whose instant messenger services were already very popular. Savage's goal was to earn back the loyalty of the NetGen and thereby increase the popularity of Microsoft's own Internet service and instant messaging system. The goal was to come up with a product that the NetGen would just "have to have." Savage used her new power and position to begin a major research program to find out what needs members of the NetGen were trying to satisfy and develop software to meet those needs.

In 2000, Savage presented her new ideas to Microsoft's top managers including Bill Gates. She explained that the kinds of products NetGen customers wanted were not being made by Microsoft and that it risked losing an entire generation of Internet users if it could not provide a product that inspired them and met the principal needs they were trying to satisfy—the need for online companionship and socialization. Microsoft's top brass heard her out. Although they knew she had a track record of success, they were not persuaded by her arguments. They could not understand why it was so important to the NetGen that they have a product they could use to share their experiences and foster friendships on the Web. Luckily for her, though, Microsoft Group Vice President Jim Allchin did understand what Savage was driving at. He was persuaded by her vision to develop a new generation of Microsoft Internet software that would attract young people.

Savage was made the manager and leader of a project team put together to develop the ideal NetGen Web software. In early 2001, she began recruiting new college software graduates and "NetGeners" to join her team. From the beginning, she adopted the approach to leadership that Microsoft is well known for—a participative and achievement-oriented approach. Because she was recruiting people who were highly competent, showed a drive for achievement, and would have to work in teams where cooperation is vital, Savage knew she had to adopt its participative and achievement-oriented approach. Savage made it clear to team members that if they worked together to push the development of the product quickly along, they would see the results of their efforts right away. In other words, it was up to them to work together to find new ways to develop superior software quickly and take back the NetGen.

The result of Savage's team's efforts was the 3-degrees Windows peer-to-peer networking application that allows users to listen to a shared play list, send digital photos, and initiate group chats with MSN messenger. The goal of this new kind of relationship software is to further the development of online relationships. Its users can build a "club," so to speak, of up to 10 friends. The software allows them to create a unique identity for the club through shared images, sounds, and animations called "winks." Whenever a club member has something interesting to say, he or she can share it with the others and instant message everyone simultaneously. Members can build online "togetherness" by sharing their music, feelings, and experiences with one another using the software.

When the 3-degrees team debuted the new software on Microsoft's internal Web site in 2002, its popularity soared. Even thousands of Microsoft employees got into the game, forming online clubs to get to know each other better. The true test now will be to see if it succeeds with the NetGen.[36]

Although each relationship between a leader and a subordinate is unique, employees nevertheless can be part of the "in-group" or "out-group," and this affects the way they perceive their relationship with their supervisor.

In sum, path–goal theory enhances our understanding of effective leadership in organizations by specifying how leaders should motivate their followers. As we discuss in previous chapters, motivation is one of the key determinants of performance in organizations, and the ability to motivate followers is a crucial aspect of a leader's effectiveness.[37]

THE VROOM AND YETTON MODEL: PARTICIPATION IN DECISION MAKING

One of the most important things that leaders do in organizations is make decisions. Good decisions help the organization achieve its goals; bad decisions hinder goal attainment. The **Vroom and Yetton model**, developed in the 1970s by Victor Vroom and Philip Yetton, describes the different ways in which leaders can make decisions, and it offers guidelines regarding the extent to which subordinates should participate in decision making.[38]

As many leaders have learned, allowing subordinates to participate in decision making and problem solving can enhance leadership.[39] Participation helps to ensure that subordinates will accept a decision that affects them or requires their support. Participation may result in better decisions if, for example, subordinates have information pertaining to the decision that the leader does not have. Additionally, participation can help foster subordinates' growth and development and may result in higher performance levels and job satisfaction.[40]

There are, however, certain disadvantages to employee participation. The biggest disadvantage is time. Not only does decision making take longer when subordinates participate, but also both the subordinates and the leader now spend time making the decision. Another disadvantage of participation is that subordinates may disagree among themselves about the appropriate course of action or even begin to question the way others are doing their jobs. In team situations, this can lead to conflict and lower performance.

Given the advantages and disadvantages of subordinates' participation in decision making, the Vroom and Yetton model seeks to specify when and to what extent leaders should allow their subordinates to participate. To identify the optimal amount

Vroom and Yetton model
A model that describes the different ways in which leaders can make decisions and guides leaders in determining the extent to which subordinates should participate in decision making.

of participation, the Vroom and Yetton model first requires leaders to determine whether an individual or a group decision needs to be made. Individual decisions pertain to a single subordinate. An example is the decision the law firm manager had to make about how to motivate a subordinate with low confidence in his ability. Group decisions pertain to a group of subordinates. An example is the decision the law firm manager had to make about how to distribute raises.

Leaders making either individual or group decisions can choose from four different decision-making styles, which vary in the extent to which subordinates participate in making the decision.

♦ *Autocratic:* The leader makes the decision without input from subordinates.

♦ *Consultative:* Subordinates have some input, but the leader makes the decision.

♦ *Group:* The group makes the decision; the leader is just another group member.

♦ *Delegated:* The leader gives exclusive responsibility to subordinates.

The Vroom and Yetton model then instructs leaders to choose among these alternative decision-making styles on the basis of their answers to a series of questions about the nature of the situation and the subordinates involved. The following criteria must be considered: The nature of the tasks being performed by employees, the level of task interdependence, the output being produced, and the characteristics of the employees involved, such as their skill level. As such, the model adopts the same kind of contingency approach as the models of Fiedler and House, but it focuses on choosing the right leader *decision-making* style. Today, allowing subordinates to participate in decision making is a very important issue because so many companies have organized their employees into self-managed work teams (discussed in Chapter 10) with decision-making authority.[41]

LEADER–MEMBER EXCHANGE THEORY: RELATIONSHIPS BETWEEN LEADERS AND FOLLOWERS

Leader–member exchange theory A theory that describes the different kinds of relationships that may develop between a leader and a follower and what the leader and the follower give to and receive back from the relationship.

Leaders do not treat all of their subordinates in exactly the same way and may develop different types of relationships with different subordinates. **Leader–member exchange theory** describes the different kinds of relationships that may develop between a leader and a follower and describes what the leader and the follower bring to and get back from the relationship. The theory focuses on the *leader–follower dyad*—that is, the relationship between the leader and the follower (a *dyad* is two individuals regarded as a pair).[42] Leader–member exchange theory proposes that each leader–follower dyad develops a unique relationship that stems from the unfolding interactions between the leader and the follower.

Although each relationship is unique, the theory suggests that two general kinds of relationships develop in leader–follower dyads (see Figure 12.3). In some dyads, the

FIGURE 12.3

Leader-Member Exchange Theory
The relationship between in group followers and the leader is characterized by trust commitment, and involvement. The relationship between out-group followers and the leader is based on the formal authority of the leader and obedience to rules.

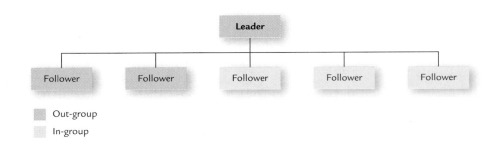

Out-group

In-group

leader develops a special relationship with the subordinate, characterized by mutual trust, commitment, and involvement. In these dyads, the subordinate helps the leader, the leader helps the subordinate, and each has substantial influence over the other. The leader spends a lot of time with the subordinate, who is given latitude or freedom to use his or her own judgment on the job. In turn, the subordinate tends to be satisfied and to perform at a high level. Subordinates who develop this special kind of relationship with their leader are said to be in the *in-group*.[43]

Other subordinates develop a more traditional relationship with their leader. In these dyads, the leader relies on his or her formal authority and position in the organization to influence the subordinate, and the subordinate is expected to perform his or her job in an acceptable manner and to follow rules and the directives of the leader.[44] The subordinate has considerably less influence over the leader, and the leader gives the subordinate less freedom to use his or her own judgment. These dyads are characterized by an impersonal, distant, or cold relationship between the leader and the subordinate. Subordinates who develop this kind of relationship with their leaders are said to be in the *out-group*. They tend to be less satisfied and perform at a lower level than in-group subordinates.

The relationship between a leader and his or her own supervisor is also a dyad that can be classified as an in-group or out-group relationship. Leaders who have high-quality relationships with their own supervisors are more likely to develop high-quality relationships with their subordinates. Furthermore, research conducted in Japan suggests that leaders who have high-quality relationships with their supervisors are more likely to advance quickly in an organization.[45]

Research suggests that it is desirable for leaders to develop special relationships with as many of their subordinates as they can because those who are in the in-group are more likely to perform at a higher level and exhibit loyalty than those in the out-group.[46] Research further suggests that a sharp distinction between the in-group and the out-group may not be desirable because subordinates in the out-group might resent their relatively inferior status and differential treatment.[47]

In summary, path-goal theory suggests that leaders need to focus on what outcomes motivate their followers and then to distribute those outcomes to subordinates when they attain their work goals and perform at a high level. It also suggests the need to tailor leadership styles to the characteristics of subordinates and the situation. The Vroom and Yetton model focuses on how much to allow subordinates to participate in decision making, which depends on the decision-making situation and the subordinates involved. Finally, leader–member exchange theory suggests that leaders should develop high-quality relationships with as many subordinates as possible. They should have as big an in-group and as small and out-group as possible.

Does Leadership Always Matter in Organizations?

By and large, research suggests that leaders *can* make a difference. Some researchers, however, have questioned whether leadership *always* makes a difference. Does it always help individuals, groups, and organizations perform at high levels, achieve their goals, and increase the organization's market share and profits? These researchers argue that although it might make people within the organization feel secure to think there is "someone" in charge, leadership may be more a figment of the imagination than a fact of organizational life.[48] These researchers suggest that leaders sometimes have little effect on the attitudes and behaviors of their followers. Sometimes, no matter what a leader does, employees are dissatisfied with their jobs or fail to perform highly. At other times, subordinates are satisfied with their jobs, attain or exceed their work goals, and perform at a high level without a leader's exerting much influence at all.

As an example of an employee of the latter type, consider Jason Jackson, a scriptwriter for a hit situation comedy on a major television network. Jackson prefers to work at home, where he has few interruptions. He stops by his office only a couple of times a week to pick up his mail. Jackson rarely sees his supervisor outside the quarterly planning and scheduling meetings that they both attend. Nevertheless, Jackson is very satisfied with his job and by all counts is a top performer. The show is in the top 10 and Jackson has received numerous industry awards for his scripts.

Jackson's case may be a bit extreme, but it does suggest in some situations leadership might not be very important. Two organizational behavior researchers, Steven Kerr and John Jermier, realized that leadership "substitutes" and "neutralizers" sometimes act to limit the influence that leaders have in organizations.[49]

LEADERSHIP SUBSTITUTES

Leadership substitute
Something that acts in place of a formal leader and makes leadership unnecessary.

A **leadership substitute** is something that acts in place of a formal leader and makes leadership unnecessary. Characteristics of the subordinate, the work, the group, and the organization all have the potential to act as substitutes for leadership. In Jackson's case, for example, both his personal characteristics and the nature of his work serve as leadership substitutes. Jackson is intelligent and skilled and has a high level of intrinsic motivation. (Recall from Chapter 6 that an employee who is intrinsically motivated enjoys his or her job and performs it well for its own sake.) Jackson loves writing and happens to be very creative. Because he is the way he is, Jackson does not need a supervisor to push him to write good scripts; his intrinsic motivation and capabilities ensure that he performs at a high level.

That Jackson's work tends to be interesting is an additional substitute for leadership: It contributes to his high performance and job satisfaction. It is not necessary for Jackson's supervisor to push him to perform, try to keep him happy, or even see him on a regular basis because of these powerful leadership substitutes. Fortunately, Jackson's supervisor realizes this and basically leaves Jackson alone, thereby freeing up some time to concentrate on his many other subordinates who *do* require leadership.

LEADERSHIP NEUTRALIZERS

Sidney Harman, CEO of Harman International Industries, realized that not seeing his subordinates on a day-to-day basis was leading them and his whole organization to imminent ruin. Harman International, located in California, manufactures audio equipment such as speakers for stereo systems. Although the company is located on the West Coast, Sidney Harman tried to lead the company from his office in Washington, DC. How successful was he as a long-distance CEO? Not very. Harman International began to lose million of dollars. Fortunately, Harman acted quickly to turn around his company's performance. He moved to California, and by the next year, the company was making millions of dollars.[50]

Why did Harman's move to California coincide with the dramatic change in his company's fortunes? Harman suggests that when he was 3,000 miles away he was unable to have as much influence on his subordinates as he needed. Not having their leader around on a day-to-day basis caused managers to tolerate and accept mediocre performance.[51] Essentially, the physical distance separating Harman from his subordinates neutralized his leadership efforts.

Leadership neutralizer
Something that prevents a leader from having any influence and negates a leader's efforts.

A **leadership neutralizer** is something that prevents a leader from having any influence and negates the leader's efforts. When neutralizers are present, there is a leadership void. The leader has little or no effect, and there is nothing to take the leader's place (there are no substitutes). Characteristics of the subordinate, the work, the group, and the organization can all serve as potential neutralizers of leadership. When subordinates lack *intrinsic* motivation and are performing boring tasks, for example, it is often necessary to use *extrinsic* rewards such as pay to motivate them to perform at a high level. Sometimes, however, the leaders of these subordinates do not have control over rewards such as pay.

Elizabeth Williams, the leader of a group of ticket takers on a commuter railroad, had little at her disposal to motivate her subordinates' performance. The ticket takers' pay and benefits were based on seniority, and their employment contract specified they could be disciplined and dismissed only for a major infraction, such as coming to work intoxicated. Like Sidney Harman when he lived on the East Coast, Williams often did not see her subordinates. The ticket takers worked on the trains but she did not. Because of those powerful neutralizers, Williams had little influence over her ticket takers, who often failed to collect tickets during rush hour because they didn't want to force their way through crowded passenger cars. Leadership neutralizers contributed to the railroad's losing money from lost ticket sales just as the transcontinental distance between Harman and his managers contributed to Harman International's losses in the early 1990s.

As these examples indicate, *substitutes* for leadership are actually *functional* for organizations because they free up some of a leader's time for other activities. But *neutralizers* are *dysfunctional* because a leader's influence is lacking. The fact that substitutes and neutralizers exist probably contributes to the perception that leadership is unimportant. Despite their existence, however, research suggests that leaders do in fact make a difference and can have positive effects on the attitudes and behaviors of their followers.[52]

THE ROMANCE OF LEADERSHIP

Finally, it is worth noting that some researchers believe that the kinds of attribution errors and stereotypes discussed in Chapter 4 may sometimes lead people to perceive leaders in too positive or "romantic" a way. For example, perceptual biases can lead followers to attribute too much importance to a leader's personal style and too little importance to situational characteristics, such as substitutes and neutralizers. In other words, followers may sometimes want to believe leaders have the ability to make a difference, and so they attribute qualities or powers to them they really don't possess. This is referred to as the *romance of leadership*.[53] Even if these beliefs aren't "real," they influence the way followers perceive a leader.[54] So, leaders may be wise to conform to popular beliefs about what a successful leader should be "like"—for example, what they should wear, how they should behave toward subordinates, and how they should appear to the public.

you're the management expert

How to Lead *Me*

Each person has his or her own personality, values, beliefs, attitudes, and way of viewing the world. To help you gain insight into how different kinds of leadership approaches are likely to affect your *own* future work behaviors and attitudes, use the chapter material to think about the following issues:

1. What kind of personal characteristics should a leader possess to influence *you* to perform at the highest level you are capable of?

2. Which of the approaches to leadership described in the chapter would be (1) most likely or (2) least likely to influence and persuade *you* to perform at a high level? Why?

3. Which approach would *you* be most likely to adopt as a leader?

New Topics in Leadership Research

Given the prominence of the subject of leadership in scholarly literature and the popular press, it is not surprising there are always new developments, theories, and research on leadership. In this section, we explore some new topics of research: transformational and charismatic leadership, the effects of a leader's moods on his or her followers, and gender and leadership.

TRANSFORMATIONAL AND CHARISMATIC LEADERSHIP

Leadership researcher Bernard Bass has proposed a theory that looks at how leaders can sometimes dramatically affect their followers and organizations and literally transform them. Although several other theories focus on transformational and charismatic leadership, Bass's theory is highly thought of by other researchers, is relatively comprehensive, and incorporates ideas from some other well-known leadership approaches.[55]

According to Bass, **transformational leadership** occurs when a leader transforms, or changes, his or her followers in three important ways that together result in followers' trusting the leader, performing behaviors that contribute to the achievement of organizational goals, and being motivated to perform at high levels (see Figure 12.4):

> **Transformational leadership** Leadership that inspires followers to trust the leader, perform behaviors that contribute to the achievement of organizational goals, and perform at a high level.

1. Transformational leaders increase subordinates' awareness of the importance of their tasks and the importance of performing them well.

2. Transformational leaders make subordinates aware of their needs for personal growth, development, and accomplishment.

3. Transformational leaders motivate their subordinates to work for the good of the organization rather than exclusively for their own personal gain or benefit.[56]

How do transformational leaders influence their followers and bring these changes about? Transformational leaders are **charismatic leaders**—leaders who have a vision of how good things *could be* in an organization in contrast to how things currently are.[57] Charismatic leaders clearly communicate this vision to their followers, and their excitement and enthusiasm induce their followers to enthusiastically support this vision.[58] To convey the excitement of their vision, charismatic leaders tend to have high levels of self-confidence and self-esteem, which further encourage their followers to respect and admire them.[59]

> **Charismatic leader** A self-confident, enthusiastic leader able to win followers' respect and support for his or her vision of how good things could be.

FIGURE 12.4
Transformational Leadership

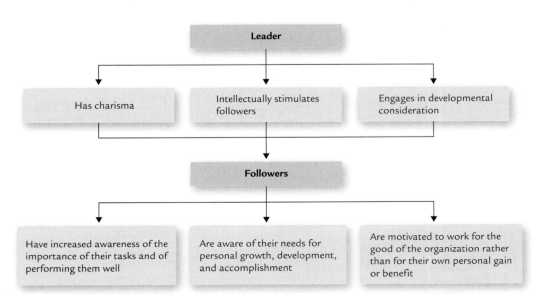

Transformational leaders influence their followers by **intellectually stimulating** them to become aware of problems in their groups and organization and view these problems from a new perspective—one consistent with the leader's vision.[60] Before the leader makes his or her influence felt, followers may not realize a problem exists, and if they do, they probably do not see the problem as something that directly concerns them. A transformational leader causes followers to view problems differently and feel some degree of responsibility for helping to solve them.[61]

Transformational leaders also influence their followers through developmental consideration.[62] **Developmental consideration** includes not only the consideration behavior discussed earlier in the chapter (which indicates a leader's concern for the well-being of his or her followers) but also behavior that supports and encourages followers and gives them opportunities to develop and grow on the job by acquiring new skills and capabilities.[63] Building trust is also an important aspect of transformational leadership.[64] Andrea Jung, CEO of Avon, is a transformational leader who has moved the company into the Internet age, as illustrated in the accompanying Global View.

Intellectual Stimulation Behavior that a leader engages in to make followers aware of problems in their groups and organization and to view these problems from a new perspective consistent with the leader's vision.

Developmental consideration Behavior that a leader engages in to provide support and encouragement to followers and give them opportunities to develop and grow on the job.

global view

Avon Is Calling Everywhere

If any company was ever in need of transformation it was Avon, the well-known, door-to-door selling cosmetics giant founded in 1886. Avon had over 3 million sales reps around the globe in 2000, but does door-to-door selling make sense in the Internet era when 75 percent of women in America work 9 to 5? After several years of declining sales, Avon recognized the need for change and appointed Andrea Jung as its CEO in 2000—its first woman CEO ever. Transforming the tradition-laden company would be a tough task for Jung.[65] She began by searching for a new vision for Avon.

In 2001, Jung began to enthusiastically communicate her vision to 13,000 sales representatives who gathered in Las Vegas to preview Avon's new product lines, take in some shows, and listen to the new CEO. Jung let the sales representatives know that Avon's future success depended on their efforts and that they were at the heart of Avon.

Jung preached about the importance of Internet sales and sought to help reps do more business online.[66] This was important because Avon's reps initially saw the Internet as a way of bypassing them and costing them their commissions. However, Jung worked hard to prove to them that the company cared about them and that customers who purchased products online would likely end up being good prospects for personal selling in the future, once they had tried Avon's products. Jung's predictions proved to be correct. Internet sales actually increased—not decreased—the reps' commissions, and they now actively embrace the opportunities it has opened up for personal selling.

Moreover, Jung realized that a serious problem facing Avon was reaching beyond the typical 30- to 55-year-old woman who had always been its main customer. She decided to target the important 16- to 24-year-old segment and attract and build brand loyalty among young customers who will one day comprise its customer base. The potential of this market segment is enormous. The 17 million women in this segment have a total purchasing power of almost $100 billion a year and spend 20 percent of their income on beauty products.

In the summer of 2003, a new Avon division called Mark began to distribute a new line of hip cosmetics designed specifically to meet the needs of this younger market segment. To meet the sales challenge of direct distribution to customers through a personal selling approach, Jung also decided to recruit a new generation of sales reps from the same demographic groups as younger customers. She hoped that being served by peers would enable Avon to gear up to the needs of this younger age group, and the company's sales reps would be trained to respond to them.

Today, Avon has 3.9 million reps located around the world, and it plans to increase the number of its U.S. sales reps from 500,000 to 750,000 in the next few years.[67] In 2004 it reported record global profits on booming worldwide sales of its growing range of makeup, soaps, hair care, jewelry, and other products. Jung continues to emphasize that the possibilities are endless if its sales reps continue to work toward achieving her vision of making it the number-one cosmetics shopping place for women around the globe.

Andrea Jung, CEO of Avon Cosmetics, is a transformational leader. She inspires the company's salespeople, who are the backbone of the company, to new heights by the enthusiastic way she conveys her message of what she wants Avon to become: a provider of everything women want to purchase.

Transactional leadership
Leadership that motivates followers by exchanging rewards for high performance and noticing and reprimanding subordinates for mistakes and substandard performance.

Transformational leadership is often distinguished from transactional leadership. **Transactional leadership** occurs when a leader motivates followers purely by exchanging rewards for good performance and noticing and reprimanding subordinates for mistakes and substandard performance.[68] Transformational leaders, however, also may engage in transactional leadership. But they go one step further by actually *inducing* followers to support their vision and put aside their personal interests for the sake of the organization and take responsibility for solving its problems. Subordinates thereby grow and develop more than they would under exclusively incentive-based transactional leadership styles.

Research on transformational leadership suggests that it is positively related to subordinate job satisfaction and job performance.[69] Moreover, transformational leaders may be more likely to instill trust in their subordinates. This can elevate members' perceptions of procedural justice (see Chapter 6), which in turn can lead to the performance of organizational citizenship behaviors (see Chapter 3).[70]

THE EFFECT OF LEADER MOOD

Megan Kelly and Rachel Feinstein are two bank tellers working for a medium-sized bank in New York City. They work different hours and have different supervisors but are close friends and frequently compare notes about their jobs and supervisors. Kelly recently complained to Feinstein that her boss, Bob Griffith, always seems so down. Even when everything is going smoothly on his shift, he rarely smiles and often looks as though the world is coming to an end. Although Griffith treats all the tellers on his shift fairly and is a capable supervisor, Kelly decided to try to switch to Feinstein's shift.

Part of the reason why Kelly requested a transfer to Feinstein's shift was some of the things that Feinstein told her about her boss, Santiago Ramirez. He almost always is in a good mood, and it is nice to be around him. He frequently jokes with the tellers, and smiles and laughs are as common on his shift as they are rare on Griffith's.

Kelly's experience (and probably your own) suggests that subordinates prefer to work for upbeat leaders than for those who are downbeat. Likewise, you might expect subordinates to work even harder when their leaders are happy and enthusiastic. Surprisingly, little research has been conducted on the effects that leader mood has on subordinates. Some preliminary research, however, suggests that leader mood may be an important factor when it comes to understanding why some leaders are more effective than others.

One recent study explored the effects of positive leader mood in a retail setting. The leaders were branch managers in a national chain. The researchers found that the managers who were in positive moods at work had stores that provided better customer service and had lower turnover rates than stores whose managers were not in positive moods. Although more research is needed, this initial study suggests that leader mood may be an important determinant of leader effectiveness.[71]

In addition to the moods a leader experiences, a leader's level of *emotional intelligence* (see Chapter 2) may also contribute to leader effectiveness. Emotional intelligence may help leaders develop a vision that is collective and shared throughout the organization and energize subordinates to enthusiastically work toward achieving it. It can also help leaders develop a meaningful identity for their organizations and instill an atmosphere of trust and cooperation. Finally, emotional intelligence can help leaders remain flexibile in rapidly changing environments.[72]

GENDER AND LEADERSHIP

One common stereotype in organizations is that women are supportive, nurturing, and generally good at managing interpersonal relations. The male counterpart to the stereotype of the relationship-oriented woman is the notion that men are directive and focus on getting the job done—in other words, that men tend to be task oriented. Judging from these stereotypes, you might expect that gender would have an effect on leadership. For example, you might expect female leaders to engage in more consideration behaviors than men and male leaders to engage in more initiating-structure behaviors than women.

Indeed, researchers have investigated this question. One recent review of the literature conducted by well-respected researcher Alice Eagly and a colleague found quite the opposite. It suggested that when men and women have leadership positions in organizations, they tend to behave in a similar manner. Men do not engage in more initiating structure just as women do not engage in more consideration.[73]

One difference did emerge, however. Women tended to lead in a more democratic style, and men tended to lead in a more autocratic style.[74] When leaders are democratic, they tend to involve their subordinates in decision making and seek their subordinates' input on a variety of matters. Autocratic leaders tend to discourage subordinate participation in decision making and like to do things their own way.

Why are women more democratic than men when they occupy leadership positions in organizations? Researchers have offered two potential explanations.[75] One is that women's interpersonal skills (they way they interact with other people) tend to be better than men's. To be democratic or participative, a leader needs to have good interpersonal skills. To encourage subordinates to express their opinions, for example, it is important for a leader to understand how subordinates feel. To reject subordinates' ideas or proposed solutions to problems and still maintain a good relationship with them requires a certain amount of sensitivity. Women may be more democratic as leaders than men simply because they are more skilled interpersonally.

The other potential explanation for the finding that women leaders tend to be more democratic than men is that women in leadership positions encounter more resistance from subordinates than do men in leadership positions. (Consistent with this reasoning is the tendency that people have to evaluate female leaders a bit more harshly than they evaluate male leaders.[76]) Gender stereotypes (see Chapter 4) may lead members of an organization to readily accept men in leadership positions but to resist women taking on these same roles. For example, a 55-year-old male executive in an engineering firm who has always had a male supervisor throughout his professional career may resist having to report to a woman. His female supervisor, recognizing his resistance and resentment, might try to overcome it by involving the subordinate in decision making and seeking his input on a variety of matters. Given that women are assuming more leadership positions in organizations, it is important to understand whether and why they might be different from men when it comes to leading.

Interestingly enough, some recent research suggests that women may actually have better leadership skills in some respects. Some recent studies suggest that women leaders, when evaluated by co-employees, supervisors, and subordinates, receive somewhat higher ratings on skills such as good communication and listening, work quality, and being able to motivate others.[77] Thus, to the extent that women are better listeners, less autocratic and more participative, more flexible, and more willing to admit they are wrong, watching and learning from women leaders may actually help men lacking one

TABLE 12.4

Approaches to Understanding Effective Leadership

Approach	Focus
Trait approach	Specific traits that contribute to effective leadership
Behavior approach	Specific behaviors that effective leaders engage in
Fiedler's contingency model	Characteristics of situations in which different kinds of leaders (relationship oriented and task oriented) are most effective
Path-goal theory	How effective leaders motivate their followers
Vroom and Yetton model	When leaders should involve their subordinates in decision making
Leader–member exchange theory	The kinds of personal relationships that leaders develop with followers
Substitutes and neutralizers	When leadership is unnecessary and when a leader is prevented from having influence
Transformational and charismatic leadership	How leaders make profound changes in their followers and organizations
Leader mood	How leaders' feelings influence their effectiveness
Gender and leadership	Similarities and differences in men and women as leaders

or more of these skills.[78] By the same token, watching how men network and seize opportunities to become leaders may help women advance further up the organizational hierarchy, where they are still significantly underrepresented.

Recap of Leadership Approaches

In this chapter, we have described several approaches to understanding effective leadership in organizations. These leadership approaches are complementary: Each sheds light on a different aspect of, or set of issues pertaining to, effective leadership. The approaches are recapped in Table 12.4.

Summary

Leaders at all levels in an organization help individuals, groups, and the organization as a whole achieve their goals and can, thus, have profound effects in organizations. The approaches to leadership covered in this chapter help explain how leaders influence their followers and why leaders are sometimes effective and sometimes ineffective. In this chapter, we made the following major points:

1. Leadership is the exercise of influence by one member of a group or organization over other members to help the group or organization achieve its goals. Formal leaders have formal authority to influence others by virtue of their job responsibilities. Informal leaders lack formal authority but influence others by virtue of their special skills or talents.

2. The trait approach to leadership has found that good leaders tend to be intelligent, dominant, self-confident, energetic, honest, mature, and knowledgeable and are able to withstand stress. Possessing these traits, however, does not guarantee that a leader will be effective, nor does the failure to have one or more of these traits mean that a leader will be ineffective.

3. A lot of the behaviors that leaders engage in fall into two main categories: consideration and initiating structure. Consideration includes all leadership behaviors that indicate that leaders trust, respect, and value a good relationship with their followers. Initiating structure includes all the behaviors that leaders engage in to help subordinates achieve their goals and perform at a high level. Leaders also engage in reward and punishing behaviors.

4. Fiedler's contingency theory proposes that leader effectiveness depends on both leader style and situational characteristics. Leaders have either a relationship-oriented style or a task-oriented style. Situational characteristics, including leader–member relations, task structure, and position power, determine how favorable a situation is for leading. Relationship-oriented leaders are most effective in moderately favorable situations. Task-oriented leaders are most effective in extremely favorable or unfavorable situations. Leaders cannot easily change their style, so Fiedler recommends changing situations to fit the leader or assigning leaders to situations in which they will be most effective.

5. Path-goal theory suggests that effective leaders motivate their followers by giving them outcomes they desire when they perform at a high level or achieve their work goals. Effective leaders also make sure their subordinates believe that they can obtain their work goals and perform at a high level, show subordinates the paths to goal attainment, remove obstacles that might come up along the way, and express confidence in their subordinates' capabilities. Leaders need to adjust the type of behavior they engage in (directive, supportive, participative, or achievement oriented) to correspond to the nature of the subordinates they are dealing with and the type of work they are doing.

6. The Vroom and Yetton model specifies the extent to which leaders should have their subordinates participate in decision making. How much subordinates should participate depends on aspects of the decision that needs to be made, the subordinates involved, and the information needed to make a good decision.

7. Leader–member exchange theory focuses on the leader–follower dyad and suggests that leaders do not treat each of their followers the same but rather develop different kinds of relationships with different subordinates. Some leader–follower dyads have high-quality relationships. Subordinates in these dyads are members of the in-group. Other leader–follower dyads have low-quality relationships. Subordinates in these dyads form the out-group.

8. Sometimes leadership does not seem to have much of an effect in organizations because of the existence of substitutes and neutralizers. A leadership substitute is something that acts in place of a formal leader. Substitutes make leadership unnecessary because they take the place of the influence of a leader. A leadership neutralizer is something that prevents a leader from having influence and negates a leader's efforts. When neutralizers are present, there is a leadership void—the leader is having little or no effect, and nothing else is taking the leader's place.

9. Transformational leaders increase their followers' awareness of the importance of their jobs and the followers' own needs for personal growth and accomplishment and motivate followers to work for the good of the organization. Leaders transform their followers by being charismatic, intellectually stimulating their followers, and engaging in developmental consideration. Transactional leadership occurs when leaders motivate their subordinates by exchanging rewards for high performance and reprimanding instances of low performance.

10. Leader mood at work and levels of emotional intelligence have the potential to influence leader effectiveness. Preliminary research suggests that when leaders tend to be in a good mood at work, their subordinates may perform at a higher level and be less likely to resign.

11. Women and men do not appear to differ in the leadership behaviors (consideration and initiating structure) that they perform in organizations. Women, however, appear to be more democratic or participative than men as leaders.

Exercises in Understanding and Managing Organizational Behavior

Questions for Discussion and Review

1. In what ways are the trait and behavior approaches to leadership similar?

2. Under what circumstances might leader punishing behavior be appropriate?

3. Are Fiedler's contingency model and the trait approach consistent with one another or inconsistent? Explain.

4. How might a relationship-oriented leader who manages a restaurant and is in a very unfavorable situation for leading improve the favorability of the situation so that it becomes moderately favorable?

5. In what kinds of situations might it be especially important for a leader to focus on moti-

vating subordinates (as outlined in path-goal theory)?

6. What might be some of the consequences of a leader having a relatively small in-group and a large out-group of subordinates?

7. Can organizations create substitutes for leadership to cut down on the number of managers they need to employ? Why or why not?

8. When might having a charismatic leader be dysfunctional for an organization?

9. Do organizations always need transformational leaders, or are they needed only some of the time? Explain.

Building People Skills

Contemporary Leaders

Choose a public figure you are familiar with (you know the individual, you have read about the person in magazines and newspapers, or you have seen him or her on TV) who is in a leadership position. Pick someone other people in your class are likely to know. The person could be a leader in politics or government (at the national, state, or local level), a leader in your community, or a leader at the college or university you attend. For the leader you have selected, answer the following questions:

1. What traits does this leader appear to possess?

2. What behaviors does this leader engage in?

3. Is this leader relationship oriented or task oriented? How favorable is the leadership situation according to Fiedler's contingency model?

4. How does this leader try to motivate his or her followers?

5. To what extent does this leader allow his or her followers to participate in decision making?

6. Do any substitutes or neutralizers exist with regard to this leader? What are they?

7. Is this a transformational leader? Why or why not?

8. Does this leader engage in transactional leadership?

A Question of Ethics

Influence at Work

Influence and persuasion are a central part of a leader's job; leaders routinely attempt to influence employees to work hard and perform at a high level. Leadership can have a dark side if managers influence employees to behave in unethical ways, however. Think about the ethical issues involved in leadership and address the following questions:

1. What kinds of leader actions would you regard as being clearly unethical in attempts to influence and persuade employees?
2. Do you think some kinds of leadership approaches are more ethical than others?
3. At what point does transformational leadership become unethical in an organizational setting?

Small Group Break-Out Exercise

A Leadership Problem at HighandTall

After forming groups of three to five people, discuss the following scenario. Discuss the questions and be prepared to share your discussions with your class.

You are the founding entrepreneurs of HighandTall Company, a fast-growing digital software company that specializes in home consumer electronics. Customer demand to license your software has boomed so much that in just two years you have added over 50 new software programmers to help develop a new range of software products. These people are young and inexperienced but are highly skilled and used to putting in long hours to see their ideas succeed. The growth of the company has been so swift that you still operate informally. As top managers, you have been so absorbed in your own work that you have paid little attention to the issue of leading your growing company. You have allowed your programmers to find solutions to problems as they go along. They have also been allowed to form their own work groups, but there are signs that problems are arising.

There have been increasing complaints from employees that as managers you do not recognize or reward good performance and that they do not feel equitably treated. Moreover, there have been growing concerns that top managers are either too busy or not willing to listen to their new ideas and act on them. A bad atmosphere seems to be developing in the company and recently several talented employees have left.

As top managers, you realize in hindsight that you have done a poor job of leading your employees and that you need to develop a common leadership approach to encourage employees to perform well and stay with your company.

1. Analyze this leadership situation to uncover the contingency factors that will be important in choosing a leadership approach. Examine the four approaches to leadership against these factors.
2. Which is the most effective leadership approach to adopt?
3. In what other ways could you influence and persuade your employees to perform well and stay with your company?

Topic for Debate

Leaders can have powerful effects on their subordinates and their organizations as a whole. Now that you have a good understanding of leadership, debate the following issue:

Team A. Managers can be trained to be effective leaders.

Team B. Managers either have what it takes to be effective leaders or they don't. If they don't, they cannot be trained to be effective leaders.

Experiential Exercise

Effectively Leading a Work Group

Objective

Your objective is to gain experience in effectively leading a group of employees who have varying levels of ability and motivation.

Procedure

Assume the role of Maria Cuellar, who has just been promoted to the position of supervisor of a group of four employees who create designs for wallpaper. The group's goal is to create imaginative and best-selling wallpaper designs. Cuellar is excited but apprehensive about assuming her first real leadership position. As a former member of this group, she has had ample opportunity to observe some of her new subordinates' (and former group members') on-the-job behaviors.

Each person brings different strengths and weaknesses to his or her job. Ralph Katten can turn out highly creative (and occasionally) best-selling designs if he tries. But often he does not try; he seems to daydream a lot and not take his work seriously. Elisa Martinez is a hard-working employee who does an acceptable job; her designs are not particularly noteworthy but are not bad either. Karen Parker is new to the group and is still learning the ins and outs of wallpaper design. Tracy McGuire is an above-average performer; her designs are good, and she turns out a fair number of them.

1. Using the knowledge you have gained from this chapter (e.g., about the behavior approach, path-goal theory, and leader–member exchange theory), describe the steps Maria Cuellar should take to effectively lead this group of wallpaper designers. Should she use the same approach with each of her subordinates, or should her leadership approach differ depending on the subordinate involved?
2. The class divides into groups of three to five people, and each group appoints one member as spokesperson to present the group's recommendations to the whole class.
3. Group members take turns describing the steps Cuellar should take to be an effective leader.
4. Group members compare and contrast the different leadership approaches that Cuellar might take and assess their advantages and disadvantages.
5. Group members decide what advice to give Maria Cuellar to help her be an effective leader of the four designers.

When the group has completed those activities, the spokesperson will present the group's recommendations to the whole class.

Making the Connection

Find an example of a leader who has recently had dramatic effects on the performance of his or her work group or organization. Describe the leader and his or her behavior. Is this leader transformational? Why or why not?

New York Times Cases in the News

The New York Times

An Apparent Heir at Xerox

BY CLAUDIA H. DEUTSCH

Ursula M. Burns doesn't play golf. She doesn't belong to the local country club. Small talk is not her strong suit. And she insists on being home on weekends.

She sounds like an unlikely climber on the Xerox corporate ladder. But up she is going, rung by rung. Since she joined the company two decades ago, Ms. Burns has moved through engineering, manufacturing, various product divisions and a senior vice presidency.

Now she is close to the top. In December, Ms. Burns, 44, was named president of Xerox Business Group Operations. Under her umbrella—or, more appropriately now, circus tent—are the businesses that provide more than 80 percent of Xerox's sales, as well as the engineering, manufacturing and other logistical functions that keep Xerox humming.

Even though Anne M. Mulcahy, Xerox's first female chief executive, is only 50, many people have already pegged Ms. Burns as her successor.

"When you think about who will follow Anne Mulcahy, you can't not consider Ursula Burns," said David A. Nadler, chairman of Mercer Delta Consulting and a longtime consultant to Xerox.

One can almost hear Xerox outsiders asking, Ursula who?

Xerox's crises of the last few years, which included a near bankruptcy (as well as accounting problems that resulted in a $10 million fine), made Ms. Mulcahy a familiar figure as she traveled, trying to reassure employees, customers, shareholders and reporters that Xerox, while ailing, was not dead. In the meantime, Ms. Burns was streamlining things back home.

She wrenched $250 million from Xerox's manufacturing operations by hiring an outside contractor, Flextronics International, in 2001, to make many Xerox products. She masterminded last year's often-contentious union negotiations. She coordinated security procedures before the war in Iraq.

All told, she washed away the red ink and prepared Xerox to go from defense to offense. A month ago, Xerox effectively declared war on Canon and Ricoh, its archrivals in the lucrative market for midspeed digital copiers and printers, by introducing 21 new products and cutting prices on many older ones.

"Ten percent of that was Anne, 90 percent was me," Ms. Burns said during a recent two-hour phone conversation. "Essentially, I'm the Ms. Inside for the operational side of the business."

Hmm. For a self-described Ms. Inside, Ms. Burns has been fielding media calls, talking at investor meetings, visiting customers and otherwise building up a lot of outside credibility. "Ursula is articulate, she has deep knowledge, she's credible—and, yes, we are developing her externally," Ms. Mulcahy said.

Ms. Mulcahy says she has not anointed a successor—yet. For Ms. Burns, that may be just as well; even her fans point to parts of her executive persona that need work.

"It's hard sometimes to persuade her that the right thing to do is not always apparent from the financials," said Gary Bonadonna, director of the Rochester unit of the Union of Needletrades, Industrial and Textile Employees, which represents Xerox's manufacturing workers.

Others say she has yet to strike a perfect balance of over- and under-managing. "She's quick to help when I ask, and rarely butts in when I don't," said James J. Miller, president of the Xerox Office Group, who has reported to Ms. Burns since January. "But, yes, she sometimes asks for signature authority over things I think should be my decision."

Even Ms. Mulcahy suggests that Ms. Burns "focus more on listening skills, and on not acting too quickly." But, she added, "every area of weakness is one that she can easily fix."

Ms. Burns has burnished rough edges before. After all, she is not to the executive manner born.

Ursula Burns grew up in "the Projects," a large low-income housing community on Delancey Street in Manhattan. "There were lots of Jewish immigrants, fewer Hispanics and African-Americans, but the common denominator and great equalizer was poverty," she recalled.

Ms. Burns was the middle child of three born to two different fathers. Neither man participated much in the family's life, she said, and her mother took in ironing and ran a day care center from home. Somehow, she was able to send all her children to Catholic schools. "She felt it was the only way to get us good educations, and keep us safe," Ms. Burns said.

She excelled at math and received an engineering degree from the Polytechnic Institute of New York. Xerox, through the graduate engineering program for minorities, paid for part of her graduate work at Columbia. That program included a sum-

mer internship at Xerox, and when she graduated in 1981, she joined Xerox full time.

African-Americans from New York ghettos were not common at Xerox, but Ms. Burns never saw her "otherness" as a liability. "My perspective comes in part from being a New York black lady, in part from being an engineer," she said. "I know that I'm smart and have opinions that are worth being heard."

Others recall that she was never intimidated by superiors. "Even in her 30's, she was a smart, unconventional thinker who'd embrace new ideas even while older executives at the table were rejecting them," said Mr. Nadler, the consultant. Her youthful fearlessness was particularly attractive to Lloyd F. Bean, a Xerox scientist 20 years her senior whom she began dating in 1981. They were married in 1988. They live in Rochester with Malcolm, Mr. Bean's 14-year-old son, and Melissa, their 10-year-old daughter.

Mr. Bean retired two years ago, and Ms. Burns could theoretically spend more time at work. She does not. She is adamant about spending weekends with the family and about working at home only after the children are asleep. She tries to run 35 minutes a day and works out with a personal trainer twice a week—but those activities, too, are done either in the early morning or late at night.

She also fits community service into the schedule, never missing a board meeting of the Rochester Business Alliance. "She always makes it, even if she has to come straight here from the plane," said Sandra A. Parker, the alliance president.

There are a lot of reasons for that. Yes, she feels a sense of duty to the group. And yes, she likes kibitzing with Ms. Parker, a personal friend. But she is also able to talk up Xerox to other executives on the alliance board. "It's a good place to hone my selling skills," Ms. Burns said.

Honing Ms. Outside skills, eh? So she really is preparing to assume the chairman's mantle?

"Come on, it's too soon to think of that," she said. But, she could not resist adding, "I guess I'm a darned good option for a candidate."

SOURCE: "An Apparent Heir at Xerox," by C. H. Deutsch, *New York Times*, June 1, 2003, p. 3.2.

Questions for Discussion

1. Using the chapter material, describe Ursula Burns's approach to leadership.

2. Will her approach help her to become Xerox's next CEO? What other skills might she need to learn or develop to become CEO?

The New York Times

Chief Seeks to Revive J. Crew's Preppy Heyday

BY TRACIE ROZHON

Millard S. Drexler, known as the Merchant Prince before his fall from grace at the Gap, has made his mark quickly and aggressively at the ailing J. Crew, with a rackful of big changes planned for early August.

In just 15 weeks as J. Crew's chief executive, Mr. Drexler has partly redesigned the stores (visible) and has ordered new, more colorful and supposedly better-fitting merchandise (not yet visible). He has begun consulting with the company's co-founder, Emily Woods, who had fallen out of favor with previous chief executives, and he has tried to repair employee relationships that had worn as thin as some of the flimsy fabric used by the company in the recent past.

Employees say that Mr. Drexler has repeatedly told them, "Everything and anything is under attack."

Including J. Crew's prices. In a retail atmosphere redolent of falling prices, Mr. Drexler is trying another tack: he plans to raise some, if not most, prices, people at the company say. But he also plans to offer a decidedly different product, made of much more expensive materials: tight, military-style suede jackets, Shetland sweaters and sleek coats, designed in a range of colors—from pimento red to green the shade of a new-mown lawn.

Analysts call the pricing strategy a daring move, and wonder aloud if Mr. Drexler can turn the company around; the Texas Pacific Group bought the controlling interest in J. Crew when Ms. Woods's father, Arthur Cinader, retired in 1997.

"He's got the brand name," said Richard Jaffe, a retail analyst with UBS Warburg. "But can Mickey Drexler, with the right product and the brand name,

inspire the consumer, get us excited? I'm going to wait and see."

Mr. Drexler has said little about his strategy; he refuses to speak publicly about his plans, saying "less is more."

But from interviews with people in both management and design at the company, it seems clear that he means to regain his previous prominence in the apparel industry, a reputation tarnished by more than 29 straight months of declining same-store sales at the Gap. Before that, he had led the Gap through 17 years of rising revenues and rapidly advancing stock valuations.

By most accounts, J. Crew, once a stylish powerhouse of preppy catalog retailing, had been floundering, running through four chief executives in five years. Sales per square foot, once surpassing $500, have fallen to $350, analysts say. Mr. Drexler, who had been looking for the right company to run since he was ousted from the Gap last year, has told friends he decided on J. Crew because he felt the company was ripe for a turnaround—and he invested $10 million of his own money in it.

On his first day, Mr. Drexler held the first of what would become weekly meetings of everyone who works at company headquarters in downtown Manhattan, sessions that have come to be called town hall meetings. By his second week, a handful of top executives, including the executive vice president/creative director and several merchant managers, were gone. (Of J. Crew's recent chief executives, Mark Sarvary was dismissed last year and Ken Pilot left in late January to make room for Mr. Drexler.)

"He has flattened the pyramid—there were too many bosses," said an executive in the financial end of the business. Since

Mr. Drexler arrived, about 30 people at headquarters—nonexecutive employees involved in merchandising, planning and catalog production, among others—were let go or quit. Most will not be replaced, the executive said.

Mr. Drexler brought in Jeff Pfeifle, who had been running the Old Navy division of the Gap (and had met Mr. Drexler 16 years before, when Mr. Pfeifle was working for Polo Ralph Lauren), as the new president.

Working with Mr. Pfeifle, Mr. Drexler has switched manufacturing plants in Asia, and added factories in Italy to make the new suits and jackets.

"We're not going to be Armani, exactly," one design executive at the company said, "but we're upgrading." Mr. Drexler has also raised the target age of the J. Crew customer; from teenagers back to 25- to 45-year-olds. "But it's still very much a work in progress," one company executive explained.

Mr. Drexler is also bringing back some of the old crowd; not only his closest allies at the Gap (like Mr. Pfeifle), but former J. Crew employees, some of whom were fired under previous chief executives.

At a session with store managers and buyers last week, Mr. Drexler appeared ready to ditch anything that did not represent the new J. Crew image, which he has defined as a return to the preppy clothes of the company's heyday in the early to mid-1990s. According to one store manager who was at the meeting, Mr. Drexler even junked one printed backless top that is selling snappily.

Some analysts remain pessimistic about J. Crew's chances for a turnaround in a saturated market—even with Mr. Drexler at the helm.

SOURCE: "Chief Seeks to Revive J. Crew's Preppy Heyday," by T. Rozhon, *New York Times*, May 6, 2003, p. C.1.

Questions for Discussion

1. What steps did Mickey Drexler take to improve J. Crew's performance after he was appointed CEO?

2. Given his actions and the chapter material, how would you describe his approach to leadership? How well is J. Crew doing now?

Power, Politics, Conflict, and Negotiation

13

LEARNING OBJECTIVES

After studying this chapter,
you should be able to:

■

Understand the nature of power and explain
why organizational politics exists and how it
can help or harm an organization and its
members.

▪

Differentiate between the main sources
of formal and informal power people can
use to engage in organizational politics as
well as the sources of functional and
divisional power.

▪

Discuss the nature of organizational conflict
and the main sources of conflict in an
organizational setting.

▪

Describe a model of the conflict process that
illustrates how the conflict process works.

▪

Explain how negotiation can be used to
manage the conflict process and resolve
disputes between people and groups.

OPENING CASE

A Power Struggle at Gucci

Why Do Disputes between People and Groups at Work Occur?

Gucci, the Italian luxury fashion house, is one of the best-known companies in the world; its clothes, shoes, and accessories are bought and worn by the rich and famous everywhere.[1] The success of a luxury fashion house rests on its claim to offer customers products that are unique and different, and people who pay the incredibly high prices Gucci charges must feel they are part of the select crowd who can afford to wear its stylish creations.

Gucci's fortunes were saved in 1990, when its CEO Domenico De Sole invited the brilliant, Texas-born gay clothes designer Tom Ford to become its principal clothes designer. With De Sole's backing, Ford designed new clothes collections that led to record sales, and Gucci once again became the fashion leader of the world. Together, the two men, known as "Tom and Dom" within Gucci and the fashion world, were admired and respected for their creative endeavors and design expertise.[2]

In 2004, however, the peace at Gucci was shattered when a huge conflict broke out at the top about who should lead the company into the future. Gucci is a part of the huge French luxury goods company Pinault-Printemps-Redoute (PPR). The biggest shareholder of PPR is Francois-Henri Pinault, who appointed a top executive named Serge Weinberg to head the PPR empire. In 2004, Tom and Dom's contracts were due to expire, and Weinberg assumed responsibility for negotiating the conditions under which Ford and De Sole would run Gucci over the next decade.

Prior to 2004, De Sole and Ford had been given total control over Gucci and made all the important design and business decisions. Weinberg had no experience in high fashion and freely admitted that, until recently, his main contact with high fashion had been through his wife, who was a fashion model. Nevertheless, Weinberg was determined to exert his authority as the top executive of the whole PPR empire over Gucci's top executives. He wanted the right to sign off on Tom and Dom's major business decisions; essentially, he wanted them to recognize his greater power and authority. They, on the other hand, wanted to protect their autonomy and feared Weinberg's interference would harm Gucci's performance. Thus, the stage was set for a major power struggle between Tom and Dom, who felt Gucci's current success owed everything to their design talents, and Weinberg, who felt he had the right to decide under what conditions they should lead Gucci because he represented the interests of its owner.

For several months, Weinberg negotiated with Tom and Dom over who should have control of Gucci. Over time, the struggle escalated, and conflict arose because neither Weinberg nor Ford and De Sole would give in on the ultimate question of who should have the power to determine Gucci's future. Things came to a head in January 2004 when Ford and De Sole announced they would leave Gucci when their contracts expired in March of that year.[3] The fashion world was stunned. Would they join a competitor like Dior or Yves St. Laurent or to start their own company? Weinberg was faced with the major problem of whom to replace them with. Very often, when power struggles between managers escalate into conflict, it ultimately does no one any good. If the parties could only have found a way to negotiate and resolve their differences, perhaps by bringing in a neutral third party or mediator, the breakup might not have occurred. Possible replacements for Tom and Dom include Alexander McQueen, a British designer, and Narciso Rodriguez, an American designer, who are both reported to be feisty and self-determined. Because creative people are often those with great self-confidence who frequently start their own companies, it's possible the House of Gucci will experience new competition in the future from the "House of Tom and Dom." Will Gucci's principal owner, Pinault, be happy that Weinberg allowed Gucci's top manager and designer to leave? On the other hand, will Tom and Dom be happy with their choice to leave what many believe to be the best fashion house in the world?

Overview

At Gucci, top managers fought over who would control the future of the company. Weinberg used the power derived from his position as CEO of the PPR empire, and De Sole and Ford used the power they had gained from their design expertise and success at running the fashion house to battle for ultimate control of

Gucci. Essentially, these managers were locked in a power struggle. In this chapter, we explore power, politics, conflict, and negotiation and their effect on organizations.

We discuss the nature of power and politics, how they can help and harm an organization, and where the power of individuals, functions, and divisions comes from. We survey the political tactics that managers can use to gain control of organizational resources. We then turn our attention to organizational conflict, examining its sources, the way a typical conflict plays out, and the strategies that can be used to manage it so that it helps rather than harms the organization. Finally, we discuss the role of negotiation as a means to resolve political struggles and conflict. By the end of this chapter you will understand why power, politics, and conflict play central roles in organizational life and how the ability of managers to learn to negotiate and manage these processes can improve the organization's effectiveness.

The Nature of Power and Politics

Whenever people come together in an organization, their activities must be directed and controlled so that they can work together to achieve their common purpose and goals. **Power**, the ability of one person or group to cause another person or group to do something they otherwise might not have done, is the principal means of directing and controlling organizational goals and activities.[4]

Managers often disagree about what an organization's goals should be and what the best ways of achieving them are. One way in which managers can attempt to control the decision-making process to support their interests is to use their power to engage in politics.[5] **Organizational politics** are activities in which managers engage to increase their power and pursue goals that favor their individual and group interests.[6] Managers at all levels may engage in political behavior to gain promotion or to influence organizational decision making in their favor.

Is the use of power and politics to promote personal or group interests over organizational interests necessarily a bad thing? There are various answers to this question.

On the one hand, the terms *power* and *politics* often have negative connotations because people associate them with attempts to use organizational resources for one's personal advantage and goals at the expense of the goals of others. When Jacques Attali took over as head of the European Bank for Reconstruction and Development, for example, he took advantage of his power as head of the bank to make personal use of its resources. Attali spent over $1.5 million to change the marble in the bank's new London offices to suit his taste, and he spent almost the same amount to hire private planes for his personal use. During his reign at the bank, the organization spent $310 million on itself—twice the amount it invested or lent to countries in Eastern Europe and the former Soviet Union.[7] Similarly, in 2004, Dennis Kozlowski, ex-CEO of Tyco, was accused of behaving illegally by diverting millions of dollars of Tyco's money for his personal use. His expenses included millions spent on a birthday party for his wife where Jimmy Buffet serenaded partygoers. Additional millions were spent to refurbish his New York apartment—reportedly, Kozlowsi spent a whopping *$6,000* on a new shower curtain alone.

Managers who use (or, more correctly, abuse) power and politics to promote their own interests are likely to harm the interests of others—in these cases, countries that were to receive aid from the bank Attali was overseeing and Tyco's stockholders.

On the other hand, there are ways in which power and politics can help organizations. First, when different managers or groups champion different solutions to a problem and use their power to promote these solutions, the ensuing debates over the appropriate course of action can help improve the quality of organizational decision making.[8] In other words, **political decision making**—decision making characterized by active disagreement over which organizational goals to pursue and how to pursue them—can lead to a more efficient use of organizational resources. Second, different

Power The ability of one person or group to cause another person or group to do something that they otherwise might not have done.

Organizational politics Activities in which managers engage to increase their power and to pursue goals that favor their individual and group interests.

Political decision making Decision making characterized by active disagreement over which organizational goals to pursue and how to pursue them.

"Organizational politics" takes on nasty connotations when employees like former Tyco CEO Dennis Kozlowski, use their influence for personal gain. Kozlowski went on trial in 2004, accused of bilking millions from Tyco, which he allegedly spent lavishly.

Coalition A group of managers who have similar interests and join forces to achieve their goals.

managerial perspectives can promote the change that allows an organization to adapt to its changing environment. When **coalitions**, groups of managers who have similar interests, lobby for an organization to pursue new strategies or change its structure, the use of power can move the organization in new directions.[9]

We have more to say about organizational politics later in the chapter. For now, the main point is that power and politics can help an organization in two main ways: (1) Managers can use power to control people and other resources so that they cooperate to achieve an organization's current goals. (2) Managers can also use power to engage in politics and influence the decision-making process to help promote new, more appropriate organizational goals. An organization has to guard continually and vigilantly against managers who might use power to harm the organization. Power-hungry managers are people to be feared and avoided. Nevertheless, power is necessary for the efficient functioning of organizations, and in any group of people, the question of how to distribute power and establish a power structure is an important one.[10]

An organization's power structure—partially revealed by its organizational chart—is the manifestation of the formal and informal sources of the power that managers, functions, and divisions possess. The chart shows how the organization makes decisions and whose interests those decisions favor.[11]

To see how power can be acquired formally and informally, it is necessary to examine where organizational power comes from. When managers at the top of an organization understand the sources of power, it is easy for them to manage power and politics to gain the benefits while minimizing the negative effects. Indeed, a prerequisite of managerial success is the ability to analyze and chart an organization's power structure accurately. Such an analysis enables managers to develop coalitions and build a power base from which they can influence organizational decision making.

Sources of Individual Power

Most individuals in an organization have some ability to control the behavior of other individuals or groups, but some have more power than others. Where do individuals in an organization get their power from, and how do they get it? Researchers distinguish between the formal and informal power that individuals possess (see Figure 13.1).[12]

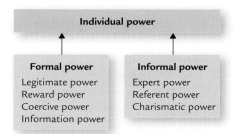

FIGURE 13.1
Sources of Individual Power

SOURCES OF FORMAL INDIVIDUAL POWER

Formal individual power is the power that stems from a person's position in an organization's hierarchy. When individuals accept a position in an organization, they accept the formal responsibility to carry out agreed-upon tasks and duties. In return, the organization gives them formal authority to use its people and other resources to accomplish job-related tasks and duties. Serge Weinberg in the opening case possessed the most formal power as the top executive of the PPR empire, which gave him authority over Domenico De Sole, its Gucci division's CEO. Formal power is a reflection of an individual's *legitimate*, *reward*, *coercive*, and *information* power.

Formal individual power
Power that originates from a person's position in an organization.

Legitimate Power. **Legitimate power** confers on an individual the legitimate authority to control and use organizational resources to accomplish organizational goals.[13] The legitimate power of a CEO, for example, is granted by an organization's board of directors, which, representing its owners' interests, gives the CEO authority over all organizational resources. The CEO, in turn, has the right to confer legitimate power upon managers further down in the organization's hierarchy. Continuing down through the hierarchy, upper-level managers give lower-level managers the authority to hire, fire, monitor, and oversee the behavior of subordinates. The CEO and lower-level managers also possess the power to withdraw authority from their subordinates by firing, demoting, or otherwise stripping away a subordinate's authority to control organizational resources.

Legitimate power
The power to control and use organizational resources to accomplish organizational goals.

Legitimate power is the ultimate source of an individual's power in an organization. One day, a CEO such as Jeff Immelt of GE or Carly Fiorino of HP may have a personal staff of five hundred people, a private jet, a chauffeur-driven limousine, and the

Elected in 1978, Pope John Paul II, is the recognized authority in one of the world's largest organizations, the Roman Catholic Church. As such, he has legitimate organizational power until the time of his death.

right to use the company's New York penthouse. But if a CEO is removed from office by the board of directors, the next day all of his or her authority and privileges are gone. The greater a manager's legitimate power is, the greater is the manager's authority and the more accountable and responsible is the person for his or her performance and use of organizational resources. This is why CEOs who perform poorly are often quickly replaced, as the former CEOs of Ford, Motorola, Lucent, McDonald's, and many other poorly performing companies have recently discovered.

Reward power The power to give pay raises, promotions, praise, interesting projects, and other rewards to subordinates.

Reward Power. **Reward power** is the power to give pay raises, promotions, praise, interesting projects, and other rewards to subordinates. As long as subordinates value the rewards, a manager can use reward power to influence and control their behavior. In Chapter 5 on learning, we discussed how important positive reinforcement could be in influencing behavior. In Chapters 6 and 7, we discussed how rewards can influence motivation.

The amount of rewards that an organization can give is limited. When extrinsic rewards such as raises and promotions are scarce, intrinsic rewards such as praise and interesting job assignments can become more important. One challenge that managers face is motivating their subordinates when their ability to confer tangible rewards is limited.

Coercive power The power to give or withhold punishment.

Coercive Power. **Coercive power** is the power to give or withhold punishment. Punishments range from suspension to demotion, termination, unpleasant job assignments, or even the withholding of praise and goodwill.

The ability to reward or punish subordinates gives supervisors great power, which is sometimes abused. As we discussed in Chapter 5, punishment has negative side effects and should be used with caution. It is for this reason that most organizations have clearly defined rules concerning when and how employees are to be rewarded or punished. Clearly specified rules and procedures that govern how coercive power and reward power are used prevent superiors from arbitrarily using their legitimate power to benefit their supporters and hurt opponents or people they simply dislike or disagree with.[14] The function of review boards and promotion committees in organizations, for example, is to ensure that people are promoted on the basis of merit and *what* they know, not *whom* they know.

In Chapter 6, we discussed the importance of perceptions of equity in determining motivation in organizations. No matter what rewards or punishments people actually receive, they compare their rewards or punishments to those received by others. If they feel inequitably treated, they may perform poorly, be dissatisfied with their jobs, or quit. The ability to confer rewards and punishments fairly and equitably is a crucial managerial skill, and organizations usually provide managers with written guidelines to help them perform this function.

Information power The power that stems from access to and control over information.

Information Power. **Information power** is power stemming from access to and control over information.[15] The greater a manager's access to and control over information, the greater is his or her information power. The more information a manager possesses, the better able he or she is to solve problems facing subordinates. As a result, the greater is subordinates' dependence on the manager. Some managers are reluctant to share information with subordinates. They fear that if their subordinates know as much as they do, the power to control and shape their behavior will be lost.

Although individual managers sometimes benefit from keeping information to themselves, the most effective organizations are those in which organizational members share, not hoard, information. Indeed, in organizations that recognize the value of empowering employees, managers deliberately decentralize authority and make information easily accessible to everyone. This allows subordinates to assume more responsibility for the organization's performance and feel more motivated.[16]

SOURCES OF INFORMAL INDIVIDUAL POWER

Several managers in a group or department may be at the same level in the organizational hierarchy or hold the same position, but some will have more power than others. Similarly, some lower-level managers may seem to have as much power and authority as higher-level managers—or even more. What accounts for this paradox? Power comes not only from an individual's formal position in an organization but also from a person's personality, skills, and capabilities. Power stemming from personal characteristics is **informal individual power**.[17] Researchers have identified several sources of it: *expert*, *referent*, and *charismatic* power.

Informal individual power Power that stems from personal characteristics such as personality, skills, and capabilities.

Expert Power.
In any group, some individuals have skills or talents that allow them to perform at a higher level than others. In a group of engineers, there may be one or two individuals who always seem to find a simple or inexpensive design solution to a problem. In a group of salespeople, there may be a few individuals who always seem to land large new accounts. Group members often look to these individuals for advice, and in doing so, come to depend on them. This dependence gives these individuals expert power.

Expert power is informal power that stems from superior ability or expertise in performing a task. Generally, people who possess expert power are promoted up the hierarchy of authority so that their informal power eventually becomes formal. Sometimes, however, individuals with expert power are mavericks: They have little ability or desire to assume formal authority over others. When that is the case, managers with formal power must take pains to develop good working relationships with subordinates who have expert power; otherwise, conflict may arise as formal leaders and informal leaders with expert power battle for control over people and resources. At Gucci, for example, Ford and De Sole used their expert power in their battle with Weinberg for control of decision making.

Expert power Informal power that stems from superior ability or expertise.

Referent Power.
People who gain power and influence in a group because they are liked, admired, and respected are said to possess **referent power**. Individuals who are high on the personality traits of agreeableness, extroversion, or even conscientiousness are often liked or admired (see Chapter 2). Willingness to help others may also lead to someone's being liked or admired. Fame is one sign that a person has acquired referent power. Why are famous film stars and athletes paid to endorse goods and services? Advertisers expect their referent power to attract their admirers to buy the companies' products. People with referent power are liked because of who they are, not just because of their expertise or their ability to influence people, obtain resources, or achieve their own ends. Tennis star Serena Williams is one of these people. In 2004, William negotiated a contract with Nike paying her over $60 million for eight years of tennis product endorsements.

Referent power Informal power that stems from being liked, admired, and respected.

Charismatic Power.
Charismatic power is an intense form of referent power stemming from an individual's personality, physical, or other abilities that induces others to believe in and follow that person.[18] Domenico De Sole and Tom Ford not only possess expert power, but they also gained charismatic power because of their ability to turn Gucci around and restore its position as a leading fashion house. In Chapter 12, we discussed how transformational leaders—leaders who possess charismatic power—often inspire awe and loyalty in their followers. These followers buy into the leader's vision and work with excitement and enthusiasm toward goals set by the leader.[19] When charismatic power exists, legitimate power, reward power, and coercive power lose their significance because followers give the charismatic leader the right to hold the reins of power and make the decisions that define the vision and goals of an organization and its members.

Charismatic power An intense form of referent power that stems from an individual's personality or physical or other abilities, which induce others to believe in and follow that person.

Unlike Microsoft CEO Bill Gates, some people with expert power never rise up through the corporate ranks. Many of these people with expert power, however, nonetheless wield considerable influence in their organizations.

Many charismatic leaders can excite a whole organization and propel it to new heights, as have Tom Ford at Gucci, Bill Gates at Microsoft, and Steve Jobs at Apple. But charismatic power can have a dark side, evident when followers of the charismatic leader blindly follow the leader and fail to take personal responsibility for their actions because they think the leader knows what is best for the organization. When charismatic power is abused by a leader who has a mistaken or evil vision, no checks or balances exist to resist the leader's directives, no matter how outrageous they may be. This appears to have happened at Enron. Enron dramatically became one of the largest and seemingly most successful U.S. companies in the last decade of the twentieth century. The company's success was attributed largely to the brilliance of its CEO Kenneth Lay and its CFO Andrew Fastow. Fastow and Lay's followers blindly obeyed the orders of their charismatic leaders. When fraud, rather than expertise or charisma, was shown to be the source of Enron's profits, the company imploded. Most of these employees lost their jobs.

Some researchers have argued that charismatic leadership is an advantage only when a formal hierarchy of authority places some checks on the power of this person.[20] Thus, only when the power of a charismatic CEO is balanced by the power of the board of directors or a strong top management team is the CEO a force for good and someone who can stir people to work together to pursue common goals. Michael Eisner, CEO of Walt Disney, is one manager who is currently under scrutiny. Critics claim Eisner can control Disney's board of directors and make decisions that are often not in the company's best interests. The battle is described in a *New York Times* case at the end of this chapter.

SOURCES OF FUNCTIONAL AND DIVISIONAL POWER

Although formal individual power, particularly legitimate power, is the primary source of power in organizations, managers in particular functions or divisions can take advantage of other sources of power to enhance their individual power. A division or function becomes powerful when the tasks that it performs give it the ability to control the behavior of other divisions or functions, to make them dependent on it, and thereby increase its share of organizational resources (see Figure 13.2).[21]

ABILITY TO CONTROL UNCERTAIN CONTINGENCIES

A contingency is an event or problem that could occur and must be planned for, by having people and resources in place to deal with it. A function or division has power over others if it can reduce the uncertainty they experience or manage the contingency or problem that is troubling them.[22] The marketing function, for example,

you're the management expert

Identifying Who Has Power

Think about one of the organizations that you have worked for in the past or that you are currently employed by. Create a chart of the managers you come most in contact with and the employees who seem to have the most influence in your department or organization. List the formal and informal sources of power of these people. Show on your chart how these people form a network that influences decision making. Which employees have the most influence? Which employees do you expect to be promoted the soonest? Why?

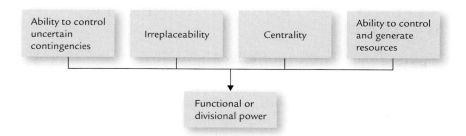

FIGURE 13.2
Sources of Functional and Divisional Power

often has power over the manufacturing function because it can forecast potential demand for a product (a contingency facing manufacturing). This ability to forecast demand reduces the uncertainty manufacturing faces by enabling it to plan production runs so as to minimize costs. Similarly, the public relations department and legal function are able to manage problems for other functions after those problems have occurred, and in doing so they reduce uncertainty for those functions and gain power over them. In general, functions or divisions that can solve the organization's problems and reduce the uncertainty it experiences are the ones that have the most power in the organization.[23] Today the ability to control information technology is one way to gain such power.[24]

IRREPLACEABILITY

A function or division gains power when it is irreplaceable—that is, when no other function or division can perform its activities.[25] In one study of a French tobacco plant, for example, Michael Crozier found that the relatively low-status repair engineers had great power in the plant. The plant managers were very respectful toward them.[26] The source of the engineers' power, Crozier discovered, was their irreplaceability. Although the engineering function was low in the formal hierarchy, the engineers as a group were the only employees who knew how to fix the plant's machines when they broke down. If they chose to, the engineers could cause problems for the manufacturing function. To maintain their status as irreplaceable employees, the engineers jealously hoarded their knowledge and refused to write it down.

All functions and divisions are irreplaceable to a certain degree. How irreplaceable they are depends on how easy it is to find a replacement for them.[27] For example, many organizations can assemble their products in low-cost foreign locations and thereby reduce the power of their domestic manufacturing functions relatively easily. Because it is difficult for an organization to gain access to high-quality research and development information, the R&D function in many companies is more irreplaceable than is manufacturing.

CENTRALITY

The power of a function or division also stems from its importance, or centrality, to the organization—that is, how central it is to the organization's operations and the degree to which it lies at the center of information flows.[28] Central functions, whose activities are needed by many other functions, have access to a lot of information, which gives them power in their dealings with others.[29] The product development department, for example, has a high degree of centrality because R&D, engineering, marketing, and manufacturing all need product specifications in order to plan their activities. In the course of its dealings with other functions, product development acquires a lot of valuable information about many aspects of organizational activities—information that it can use to make other functions dependent on it.

ABILITY TO CONTROL AND GENERATE RESOURCES

The ability to control and generate resources for an organization is another source of functional and divisional power. The ability to control resources is, for example, a principal source of power for top managers such as Serge Weinberg.[30] These managers control the purse strings of the organization and have the ability to give or withhold rewards—money and funding—to functions and divisions. This ability is important because the more money a division is given, the more people it can hire and the more advanced facilities it can build so that it increases its chance of success. In contrast, when divisions are starved for funds, they cannot hire new skilled employees or buy new technology to increase their efficiency and this lack reduces their efficiency in the long run.

Although controlling resources is important, the ability to *generate* them is also important. The division whose goods and services provide the organization with the most profits will be the most important division in the organization. Very often, new CEOs and corporate headquarters staff are promoted from the divisions that have been most successful in generating resources. In the past, IBM's top managers came from its mainframe division, which generated most of the company's revenues and profits. Today, most of IBM's profits are being generated from computer services, so more top managers from this division are being promoted. Similarly, most of General Motors' top managers come from its most profitable car divisions.

To fully understand the power structure of an organization, a manager needs to analyze all sources of power. The sources of individual power, such as position in the hierarchy, are the most important determinants of power. But a manager must also take into consideration the sources of functional and divisional power when determining the relative power of functional and divisional managers in the organization.[31]

Organizational Politics: The Use of Power

Organizational politics are activities that managers engage in to increase their power. After they acquire it, they can use power to influence decision making so that the organization pursues goals that favor their individual, functional, and divisional interests.[32]

One reason why many people engage in organizational politics is that jobs are a scarce resource.[33] The higher a manager rises in a hierarchy, the more difficult it is to continue to rise because fewer and fewer jobs are available at the upper levels. To compete for these scarce jobs and to increase their chances of promotion and share of organizational resources, employees try to increase their power and influence.[34] Without constant vigilance, organizational politics can get out of hand and prevent the organization from achieving its goals.[35] For this reason, it must try to manage the politics to promote positive effects and prevent negative ones.[36]

To understand how organizations can manage politics, we need to look at the tactics that managers use to increase their individual power and the power of their functions and divisions.[37]

TACTICS FOR INCREASING INDIVIDUAL POWER

Managers can use many kinds of political tactics to increase their power, become experts at political decision making, and increase their chances of obtaining their goals.[38] In the following pages we describe some commonly used tactics (see Figure 13.3).

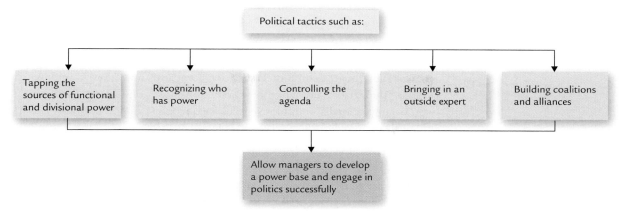

FIGURE 13.3
Political Tactics for Increasing Individual Power

Tapping the Sources of Functional and Divisional Power. The way in which functions and divisions gain informal power suggests several tactics that managers can use to increase their individual power. First, managers can try to make themselves irreplaceable.[39] For example, they may develop specialized skills such as knowledge of computers or special relationships with key customers that allow them to solve problems or limit uncertainty for other managers in the organization. Second, managers may specialize in an area of increasing concern to the organization so that they eventually control a crucial contingency facing the organization.[40] Third, managers can try to make themselves more central in an organization by deliberately accepting responsibilities that bring them into contact with many functions or managers. Politically astute managers cultivate both people and information, and they are able to build up a personal network of contacts in the organization—contacts that they can use to pursue personal goals such as promotion.[41]

Recognizing Who Has Power. Another way to increase individual power is to develop the ability to recognize who has power in the organization. With this knowledge, a person knows whom to try to influence and impress. By supporting a powerful manager and being indispensable to him or her, it is possible to rise with that person up the organizational ladder. There are five factors to assess in order to determine the relative power of different managers in an organization.[42]

1. *Sources of power:* Power has many sources in an organization. The power of a manager or subunit may come from legitimate authority, from the possession of scarce resources, or from expertise. A manager who assesses the source of various managers' power will learn whom to influence to obtain his or her objectives.

2. *Consequences of power:* The people who have the most power can be identified by an assessment of who benefits the most from the decisions made in an organization. For example, managers compete for resources through the budgeting process, and obtaining access to scarce resources is a measure of how much power a manager has.

3. *Symbols of power:* Many symbols of prestige and status are generally associated with power in an organization. Job titles, for example, are a prized possession; and titles such as "chief executive officer" and "president" confer great prestige on the officeholder. The use of a corporate jet or a chauffeured car, occupying a corner office with a wonderful view, and having a reserved parking place are other signs of power.

4. *Personal Reputations:* A person's reputation within an organization is likely to indicate the person's power to influence decision making.

5. *Representational Indicators:* The organizational roles persons or subunits play and the responsibilities they possess are indications of power. A manager's membership on an influential committee, such as a company's operations committee, is a sign of the person's influence in organizational decision making. Managers who occupy central administrative roles have access to important information and derive power from this access. It strengthens their ability to make sound decisions and to alter the bargaining process in their favor.

By focusing on those five factors, a person new to an organization can assess which people or groups have the most power. Armed with this knowledge, the newcomer can make certain predictions about which groups will be favored by the decision-making process to receive a large share of organizational resources or be protected from cutbacks if resources are scarce.

After managers have accurately assessed the power structure of an organization and have obtained some individual power, they can use several other tactics to enhance their power.

Controlling the Agenda. An important tactic for influencing decision making is to control the agenda—that is, to determine what issues and problems decision makers will consider. The ability to control the agenda is one reason why managers like to be members of or in charge of committees. By controlling the agenda, managers can limit the consideration of alternatives in the course of decision making. Powerful managers, for example, can prevent formal discussion of any issue they do not support by not putting the issue on the agenda.

Bringing in an Outside Expert. When a major disagreement over goals emerges, as it often does when an organization is undergoing change or restructuring, managers know that every subunit is fighting to safeguard its own interests. Managers in charge of different functions want the ax to fall on functions other than theirs and want to benefit from whatever change takes place. Knowing that one function or one person's preferred alternative will be perceived by others as politically motivated and self-interested, a manager may bring in an outside expert who is considered to be a neutral observer. The manager then uses the "objective" views of this expert to support his or her position.

Building Coalitions and Alliances. Managers may form a coalition with other managers to obtain the power they need to influence the decision-making process in their favor. Many coalitions result from agreements to trade support: Function A agrees to support function B on an issue of interest to function B, and in return function B supports function A on an issue of interest to function A. Skills in coalition building are important in organizational politics because functional interests frequently change as the organizational environment changes. Because of such changes, coalitions must be actively managed by their members.

The ability to forge coalitions and alliances with the managers of the most important divisions provides aspiring top managers with a power base from which they can promote their personal agenda. Having many supporters enhances a manager's claims to power in the organization, but there is a downside to alliances: the possibility that individual members will request alliance support for their losing propositions. It is particularly important for top-level managers to build personal relationships with members of the board of directors. CEOs need the support of the board in any contest between top managers; without it CEOs might lose their job to another top-level manager. The way in which politics and power struggles have influenced Kodak is discussed in the accompanying OB Today.

ob today

Politics at Kodak

Eastman Kodak, whose little yellow film boxes have long been a part of the global photo scene, has experienced declining performance for years. Kodak was slow to react to the threat of global competition in its central film-making business, and a successive series of political contests between its managers has stifled its attempts to restructure its activities. The problems have been going on for at least a decade.

In the early 1990s, Kay Whitmore, a Kodak veteran, was appointed as CEO. He gained the top job as the leader of a coalition of Kodak's most senior managers. Because any attempt of his to raise Kodak's performance would require massive cuts in some of Kodak's businesses, Whitmore was reluctant to make the drastic changes that Kodak needed to regain its competitiveness.

So, in 1993, investors were delighted to hear about the appointment of Christopher Steffen as Kodak's new chief operating officer.

Steffen has a reputation as a "turnaround artist" who performed miracles at Chrysler and Honeywell. Investors thought that an outsider would finally bring fresh ideas to Kodak's inbred top management team. Investors were, therefore, shocked when Steffen announced his resignation from the company less than a week after his appointment, citing "differences with the company's approach to problem solving." Apparently he and the coalition of Kodak's top managers headed by CEO Whitmore had very different ideas about how to restructure the company and the speed at which restructuring should be done. Steffen wanted to massively reduce operating costs by closing several business units and laying off large numbers of employees. Whitmore's coalition resisted this and, as in the past, Kodak's entrenched management had the power to carry the day by firing Steffen.

After this event Kodak's stock plunged, and within months Whitmore was ousted by a concerned board of directors. He was replaced by George Fisher in 1994, the first outsider ever to lead Kodak. The hope was that Fisher would be able to change the way organizational politics worked at Kodak and that this would enhance the company's performance. Fisher made many changes, but he, too, had to fight against the no-change tactics used by Kodak's top brass to protect their interests. He never gained their support.[43]

Behind the scenes, another Kodak veteran, Dan Karp, was waiting to become its CEO. In 2000, supported by a coalition of Kodak's top managers, Karp became Kodak's new CEO, and Fisher was out. Karp has been able to do little to turn the company around; every year Kodak's performance has continued to decline. Finally, in January 2004, Karp announced that Kodak was going to make the radical changes needed to reduce its high costs.[44] It would lay off 20 percent of its workforce, shut down many plants that made film, and focus its resources on digital technology. If the company's top managers had made these hard choices two decades earlier, far fewer employees would have lost their jobs. Given its position in the industry at the time, Kodak's early entry into digital imaging would have likely made it a leader in the field.

Building alliances and coalitions is a crucial task for CEOs. Daniel Karp, a Kodak veteran, was appointed to the head of Kodak in 2000 after previous CEOs failed to win the support of the company's entrenched management.

MANAGING ORGANIZATIONAL POLITICS

The exercise of power is an essential ingredient of organizational life, so it is important for an organization to manage organizational politics and harness it to support organizational interests. The management of organizational politics falls primarily to the CEO because only the CEO possesses legitimate power over all other managers. This power allows the CEO to control political contests so that they help rather than harm the organization. If the CEO is perceived as being weak, however, other top managers (who may possess their own stock of expert, referent, or charismatic power) will lobby for their own interests and compete among themselves for control of resources.

Power struggles, as at Gucci in the opening case, sap the strength of an organization, waste resources, and distract the organization from achieving its goals. To avoid power struggles, an organization must have a strong CEO who can balance and manipulate the power structure so that no manager or coalition of managers becomes strong enough to threaten organizational interests. At the same time, a strong CEO should not fear to delegate significant responsibilities to managers below when they have demonstrated their personal success. When there is a balance of power, the decisions that result from the political process are more likely to favor the long-term interests of the organization.[45]

In summary, because power and politics influence many kinds of decision making in organizations, members need to be able to tell what's going on around them. They can do this by analyzing the sources of power at the functional, divisional, and organizational levels, and by identifying powerful people and observing their approach to leadership. To increase their chances of promotion most managers try to develop a personal power base to heighten their visibility and individual power.

What Is Organizational Conflict?

Organizational conflict The struggle that arises when the goal-directed behavior of one person or group blocks the goal-directed behavior of another person or group.

Organizational politics gives rise to conflict as one person or group attempts to influence the goals and decision making of an organization to advance its own interests—usually at the expense of some other person or group. **Organizational conflict** is the self-interested struggle that arises when the goal-directed behavior of one person or group blocks the goal-directed behavior of another person or group.[46]

The effect of conflict on organizational performance has received considerable attention. In the past, researchers viewed conflict as always bad or dysfunctional for an organization because it leads to lower organizational performance.[47] According to this view, conflict occurs because managers have not designed an organizational structure that allows people, functions, or divisions to cooperate to achieve corporate objectives. The current view of conflict, however, is that, although it is unavoidable, it can often increase organizational performance if it is carefully managed and negotiated.[48]

Figure 13.4 illustrates the effect of conflict on organizational performance. At first, conflict can increase organizational performance because it exposes weaknesses in organizational decision making and design and prompts the organization to make changes. Managers realign the organization's power structure and shift the balance of power in favor of the group that can best meet the organization's current needs. At some point—after point A in Figure 13.4—an increase in conflict leads to a decline in performance because conflict between managers gets out of control, and the organization fragments into competing interest groups.[49]

The job of top managers is to prevent conflict from going beyond point A and to channel conflict in directions that increase organizational performance. Thus, managing conflict, like managing politics, is a way to improve organizational decision making and resource allocation, making the organization more effective.[50]

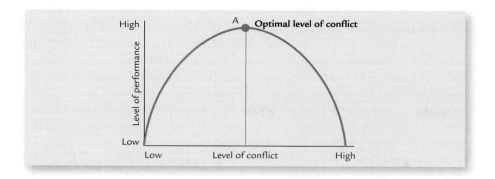

FIGURE **13.4**
The Effect of Conflict on Organizational Performance

SOURCES OF ORGANIZATIONAL CONFLICT

Conflict, both between individuals and between groups, has many sources, and managers need to be aware of them so that when conflict occurs they can either control or resolve it. Three major sources of interpersonal and intergroup conflict are differentiation, task relationships, and scarcity of resources.[51]

DIFFERENTIATION

Differentiation in an organization occurs when people and tasks are grouped or split up into functions and divisions to produce goods and services. The splitting of the organization into functions or divisions produces conflict because it makes the differences in functional orientations and status inconsistencies apparent.

Differences in Functional Orientations. Different functions commonly develop different orientations toward the organization's major priorities.[52] Their views of what needs to be done to increase organizational performance differ because their tasks, jobs, and goals differ. Manufacturing generally has a short-term, cost-directed efficiency orientation. Research and development is oriented toward long-term, technical goals, and sales is oriented toward satisfying customer needs. Thus, manufacturing may see the solution to a problem as one of reducing costs, research and development as one of promoting product innovation, and sales as one of increasing demand.

Because of differences in their functional orientation, functional groups can have differing views of the organization's priorities. These differences can lead to conflict that can do considerable harm, undermining the organization's cohesiveness and functional integration and reducing its performance.

Status Inconsistencies. Over time, some functions or divisions come to see themselves as more vital than others to an organization's operations and believe that they have higher status or greater prestige in the organization.[53] In this situation, high-status functions make little attempt to adapt their behaviors to the needs of other functions, thus blocking the goals of other functions.[54] Similarly, functions that are most central and essential to a company's operations may come to see themselves as more important than other functions and attempt to achieve their goals at the expense of the less central functions.

TASK RELATIONSHIPS

Task relationships generate conflict between people and groups because organizational tasks are interrelated and affect one another. Overlapping authority, task interdependence, and incompatible evaluation systems may stimulate conflict among functions and divisions.[55]

Overlapping Authority. If two different functions or divisions claim authority for the same task, conflict may develop. Such confusion often arises when a growing organization has not yet fully worked out relationships between different groups.[56] As a result, functions or divisions fight for control of a resource and, thus, spawn conflict. At the individual level, too, managers can come into conflict over the boundaries of their authority, especially when one manager attempts to seize another's authority and resources. If a young manager starts to upstage his or her boss, for example, the boss may react by assigning the subordinate to relatively unimportant projects or by deliberately withholding the resources the person needs to do a good job.

Task Interdependencies. The development or production of goods and services depends on the flow of work from one function to another; each function builds on the contributions of other functions.[57] If one function does not do its job well, the ability of the function next in line to perform is compromised, and the outcome is likely to be conflict.[58] For example, the ability of manufacturing to reduce costs on the production line depends on how well research and development has designed the product for cheap manufacture and how well sales has attracted large, stable customer accounts. When one function fails to perform well, all functions suffer.

The potential for conflict increases as the interdependence of functions or divisions increases. Thus, as task interdependence increases from pooled, to sequential, to reciprocal interdependence (see Chapter 11), the potential for conflict among functions or divisions is greater.[59]

Incompatible Evaluation Systems. Inequitable performance evaluation systems that reward some functions but not others sometimes create conflict.[60] Typical problems include finding ways to jointly reward sales and production to avoid scheduling conflicts that lead to higher costs or dissatisfied customers. Also, the more complex the task relationships between functions are, the harder it is to evaluate each function's individual contribution to performance and reward it appropriately, which also increases the likelihood of conflict.

SCARCITY OF RESOURCES

Competition for scarce resources produces conflict.[61] Conflict over the allocation of capital occurs among divisions and between divisions and corporate headquarters. Budget fights can be fierce when resources are scarce. Other organizational groups also have an interest in the way a company allocates scarce resources. Shareholders care about the size of the dividends. Employees want to maximize their salaries and benefits. Managers in competition for scarce resources may fight over whom should get the biggest pay raise.

Pondy's Model of Organizational Conflict

Because conflict of one kind or another is inevitable in organizations, it is an important influence on behavior. Louis Pondy developed one of the most widely accepted models of organizational conflict.[62] Pondy views conflict as a dynamic process that consists of five sequential stages (see Figure 13.5). No matter how or why conflict arises in an organization, managers can use Pondy's model to analyze a conflict and guide their attempts to manage it.

LATENT CONFLICT

In the first stage of Pondy's model there is no actual conflict. The potential for conflict to arise is present, though latent, because of the sources of conflict that we just examined.

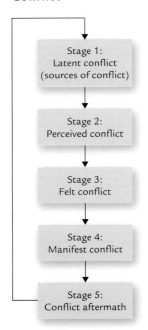

FIGURE 13.5

Pondy's Model of Organizational Conflict

PERCEIVED CONFLICT

The stage of perceived conflict begins when one party—individual or group—becomes aware that its goals are being thwarted by the actions of another party. Each party searches for the origins of the conflict, defines why the conflict is emerging, analyzes the events that led to its occurrence, and constructs a scenario that accounts for the problems it is experiencing with other parties. For example, the manufacturing function of a company may trace its production problems to defective inputs used in the assembly process. Manufacturing managers wonder why the inputs are substandard and, after an investigation, discover that the materials management function chose to buy inputs from the lowest-cost supplier instead of paying for high-quality inputs. This decision reduces input costs and improves materials management's performance but raises production costs and worsens manufacturing's performance. Manufacturing comes to see materials management as thwarting its goals and interests.

What usually happens at the stage of perceived conflict is that the conflict escalates as functions start to battle over the cause of the problem. In an attempt to get materials management to change its purchasing practices, manufacturing complains about materials management to the CEO or to anyone else who will listen. Materials management argues that low-cost inputs do not reduce quality and claims that manufacturing does not properly train its employees. Each party perceives the conflict and its causes differently.[63] Thus, although both functions share the same goal of superior product quality, they attribute the cause of poor quality very differently.

FELT CONFLICT

During the stage of felt conflict, the parties in conflict develop negative feelings about each other. Typically, each group closes ranks, develops an us-versus-them attitude, and blames the other group for the problem. As conflict escalates, cooperation between groups declines, as does organizational effectiveness.[64] For example, it is almost impossible to speed new product development if materials management and manufacturing are fighting over the quality of inputs and final products.

As the parties in conflict battle and argue for their points of view, the significance of the disputed issue is likely to be blown out of proportion. Consider, for example, a relatively simple kind of conflict: conflict between roommates. Roommate A consistently neglects to put his dirty dishes in the dishwasher and clean the kitchen counters. To get the sloppy roommate to clean up, roommate B first makes a joke about the messy kitchen. If no change occurs in roommate A's behavior, roommate B starts to complain. If there is still no improvement, the roommates begin fighting and become so antagonistic toward one another that they not only cease to be friends but also begin looking for other living arrangements. The original problem was relatively minor, but when roommate A did nothing to solve it, the problem escalated into something that became increasingly difficult to manage. This may well have been the situation that developed at Gucci as both sides grew more and more antagonistic to the other as time went on.

MANIFEST CONFLICT

In the stage of manifest conflict, one party decides how to react to or deal with the party that it sees as the source of the conflict, and both parties try to hurt each other and thwart each other's goals.

Manifest conflict can take many forms. Open aggression or even violence between people and groups may occur. There are many stories and myths in organizations about boardroom fights in which managers actually came to blows as they sought to promote their interests. Infighting in the top management team is a more indirect form of aggression

Arguing managers is one of the many forms that manifest conflict takes. On some occasion managers have been known to resort to loud shouting matches as they seek to exert control and win the decision-making battle.

that occurs as managers seek to promote their own careers at the expense of others in the organization. When Lee Iacocca was at Ford, for example, Henry Ford II decided to bring in the head of General Motors as the new Ford CEO. Within one year, Iacocca engineered the new CEO's downfall to clear his own path to the top. Eventually, he lost the battle when Henry Ford forced him out because he feared that Iacocca would take his power.

Manifest conflict between groups such as teachers and parents, prisoners and guards, and unions and managers is also common. In the past in industrial disputes, for example, managers often obtained their goals by using tactics such as sabotage, strikebreaking, hiring new workers as permanent replacements for striking workers, and physical intimidation.

Manifest conflict also takes the form of a lack of cooperation between people or functions, a result that can seriously hurt an organization. If an organization's members do not cooperate, integration declines, and the organization is less likely to come together to achieve its goals. One particularly dysfunctional kind of manifest conflict occurs when parties accommodate or avoid managing a conflict. In this situation, one party might try to frustrate the goals of its opponent by passivity—that is, by doing nothing. Suppose there is a history of conflict between sales and production, but sales desperately needs a rush on an order for an important client. What might manufacturing do? One strategy is to agree informally to sales' requests and then do nothing. When sales comes banging on the door looking for its products, manufacturing says: "Oh, you meant *last* Friday? I thought you meant *this* Friday." In general, the stronger manifest conflict is, the more organizational effectiveness suffers because coordination and integration between managers and subunits decline. A particularly strong form of manifest conflict is illustrated in the accompanying OB today.

Managers need to do all they can to prevent manifest conflict from becoming dysfunctional and to intervene as early as possible in this stage. If they cannot prevent the breakdown in communication and coordination that usually occurs in this stage, the conflict advances to the last stage: the conflict aftermath.

CONFLICT AFTERMATH

Sooner or later conflict in an organization is resolved in one way or another—someone gets fired, a CEO tells a division to shape up, the organization gets reorganized, or the conflict becomes so destructive that the organization fails. Regardless of the outcome, it

ob today

When Partners Battle for Control of Their Company

CIC Inc. was founded by two partners, David Hickson and Glenn S. Collins III, in College Station, Texas, in 1985. Each founder took a 50-50 stake in the small business. CIC's strategy was to maintain and service high-tech equipment, such as CT scanners, X rays, and lasers, in hospitals and universities across the United States.[65] Hickson and Collins's new venture proved very successful, business increased very rapidly, and by 2000, the company had over 200 employees. In the 1990s, CIC upgraded its service program so that all maintenance transactions could be handled electronically over the Internet using the company's in-house software programs. Because CIC's new Internet service could save hospitals up to 20 percent of their maintenance costs, savings would amount to millions of dollars a year. Hospitals flocked to join the program, and CIC's future looked bright indeed.

Imagine then the impact of the bombshell that occurred when Hickson, on vacation with his family, returned to College Station to find that in his absence Collins had staged a coup. He found that he had been replaced as president by a CIC manager who was one of Collins's closest friends, that CIC managers and workers who had been loyal to Hickson had been fired, and that all the keys and security codes to CIC buildings had been changed. Hickson immediately sought and obtained a legal restraining order from a judge that allowed him back into the company and reinstated fired employees. The judge also issued an order preventing the two men from taking any actions that were not part of their normal job duties.

Apparently this extraordinary situation had occurred because the two owners had not been able to agree on the company's future direction—a problem that had resulted in a deteriorating personal relationship between them. Because they were equal partners, neither had power over the other to resolve the conflict. As a result, the conflict had become worse over time. Different camps had formed in the organization with different CIC managers being a member of one camp or the other, loyal either to Collins or Hickson.

In the months following this episode, it became clear that the two men would be unable to resolve the conflicts and problems between them. The only solution to the conflict seemed to be for one person to buy out the other, and they each searched for bank financing to do so. Finally, it was announced that Hickson had purchased Collins's share of the business. However, the problems between the two men were apparently not to be resolved by the buyout.[66] Collins immediately announced that he would use the money from his share of CIC to start another company that would essentially provide the same kind of service as CIC!

is almost certain that the causes of the conflict will occur again in another context. Suppose that sales, still angry over the earlier "mix-up" with manufacturing, approaches manufacturing with a new request. How will these functions behave? Probably, their wariness and lack of trust will make it hard for them to agree on anything.

Now suppose that after the earlier encounter sales and manufacturing were able to solve their dispute amicably through compromise and collaboration. In that case, when sales next has a special request for manufacturing, the two departments will be able to sit down together and work out a joint plan that suits the needs of both functions.

Every conflict episode leaves a conflict "aftermath" that affects the way both parties perceive and respond to future episodes. If conflict can be resolved by compromise or collaboration before it progresses to the manifest stage, the conflict aftermath will promote good future working relationships. But if conflict is not resolved until late in the process, the competition that takes place will result in a conflict aftermath that sours future working relationships and leads to an organizational culture poisoned by the presence of permanently uncooperative relationships like that at CIC.

Negotiation: Resolving Conflict

One of management's major responsibilities is to help parties in conflict—subordinates, functions, or divisions—cooperate in resolving their disputes. Indeed, much of a manager's time can be spent in managing conflict. If a company is to achieve its goals, managers must be able to resolve conflicts between employees and groups, and it is always best that conflict is settled by compromise between the parties involved.[67] Compromise is possible when each party is willing to engage in a give-and-take exchange and to make concessions until a reasonable resolution of the conflict is reached. When the parties to a conflict are willing to cooperate with each other to find an acceptable solution to the conflict, a company is more likely to achieve its goals.

Negotiation Negotiation is a process in which groups with conflicting interests meet together to make offers, counteroffers, and concessions to each other in an effort to resolve their differences.[68] Negotiation is an important technique that managers can use to increase the chances of reaching compromise between individuals and groups in conflict.[69] Through negotiating and bargaining, the parties to a conflict try to come up with an acceptable solution by considering various ways to allocate resources. Sometimes the parties believe that the more one party gains, the more the other loses. This makes them competitive and adversarial in the bargaining and negotiation process.[70] They "take a hard line," make unrealistic demands, and use all of their power to get what they want. Managers need to help the parties avoid viewing the conflict competitively—as a win-or-lose situation. Instead, they need to frame the situation so it can be viewed by both parties as a win-win situation. Negotiation is an important tool that managers can use to handle conflict in ways that lead to cooperative, functional outcomes rather than competitive, dysfunctional outcomes.

Negotiation A process in which groups with conflicting interests meet together to make offers, counteroffers, and concessions to each other in an effort to resolve their differences.

INDIVIDUAL-LEVEL CONFLICT MANAGEMENT

The management of conflict between individuals is directed at changing the attitudes or behavior of those involved in the conflict.[71] If the conflict is due to a clash of personalities and the parties in conflict simply do not understand one another's point of view, the organization can help the people involved by bringing in outside help to give advice and counsel. Education and sensitivity and awareness training help people learn to understand and to deal with those who are not like themselves. If the conflict is due to workforce diversity, such as when a young person supervises older, more experienced

When conflicts arise, managers can help employees by framing a settlement both parties perceive to be a "win-win" situation.

workers or a female manager supervises an all-male work group, the organization can use education and training to help employees appreciate the differences in their attitudes and avoid or successfully resolve conflict.

If the conflict is due to a basic disagreement about how the work should be performed or about the performance of the other party, managers can use a step-by-step negotiation approach to help resolve a dispute between employees. This is especially useful when the conflict has reached the felt and manifest conflict stage and the dispute is poisoning not just personal but also work group relationships. The steps in the process are as follows:[72]

1. A manager meets with both the employees in conflict and forcefully outlines how their behavior is affecting the way they perform their jobs and other members of the department. Each employee then is asked to express his or her thoughts and feelings about the conflict to open up the conflict so that the manager, and the employees, understand the facts of the conflict and each other's positions.

2. The manager summarizes the dispute between the employees in written form, creating a report that carefully matches both sides of the case to identify the main factors that are in dispute. For example, if the dispute is about one employee not pulling his or her weight or performing substandard work, each employee's interpretation of the facts is balanced against the other.

3. The manager discusses the facts in the report with each employee separately acting as a neutral third party; the manager uses the fact-finding report to work out a solution each employee can accept, going back and forth between the employees until they can accept a common solution.

4. The manager meets with both employees to discuss the agreement and get their commitment to resolving the dispute. Each employee also agrees to meet with the manager should subsequent problems arise.

If the conflict cannot be negotiated successfully, another solution is to move people around. Managers can transfer employees to new positions where they will not have contact with each other or where they can come to better appreciate the other's point of view. Job rotation and assignments to new teams or departments or even to new countries help people to develop fresh perspectives on issues in dispute. Promotion can also be used to change attitudes. Managers might deal with troublesome union shop stewards by making them supervisors. They might deal with troublesome manufacturing managers by promoting them sideways into a position in training, plant security, or elsewhere. In this way parties to the conflict are permanently removed from the conflict situation.[73] As a last resort, an organization can fire the people involved and replace them with others who have no history of dysfunctional conflict. Replacing managers from the CEO down to first-level supervisors is also a common method of eliminating conflict.

GROUP–LEVEL CONFLICT MANAGEMENT

Group-level conflict management is aimed at changing the attitudes and behaviors of groups and departments in conflict.[74] Managers can physically separate work groups and deny them the opportunity to interact face-to-face, thus eliminating the potential for direct conflict. Coordination between separate groups is then made possible by using integrating roles (see Chapter 16) and giving some people the full-time responsibility to coordinate the groups' activities while keeping them physically separate. Sometimes managers can develop rules and standard operating procedures to coordinate the groups' activities or give them common goals, allowing them to achieve their goals simultaneously.

Often, however, these solutions provide only a temporary solution to the problem. If the underlying causes are not addressed, the conflict is never truly resolved, and the organization's performance may continue to suffer. Because few organizations can afford this outcome, most usually try to resolve the conflict at its source by negotiating at the group level.

Third-party negotiator An outsider skilled in handling bargaining and negotiation.

Mediator A neutral third party who tries to help parties in conflict reconcile their differences.

Arbiter A third party who has the authority to impose a solution to a dispute.

Direct negotiations between groups are held either with or without a **third-party negotiator**—an outsider who is skilled in handling bargaining[75] and negotiation. The third party facilitates the bargaining process and helps the parties in dispute find a solution to their problem.[76] Sometimes the common superior of the parties in conflict acts as the third party. If the third party plays the role of **mediator**, he or she takes a neutral stance and helps the parties to reconcile their differences. If the parties cannot find an equitable solution, the third party may act as **arbiter**, or judge, and impose a solution.

There are five basic forms that negotiation may take as groups handle conflict with others: compromise, collaboration, accommodation, avoidance, and competition (see Figure 13.6).[77] The horizontal axis of Figure 13.6 measures the degree to which a person or group is concerned with obtaining its own goals. The vertical axis measures the extent to which the person or group is concerned with helping some other person or group to achieve its goals. Using this model, it is possible to compare the different ways of handling conflict during the felt stage.

At the middle of the figure is *compromise*. Compromise usually involves bargaining and negotiation to reach a solution that is acceptable to both parties. Sometimes the parties in dispute use *collaboration* to find a solution: Each side tries to satisfy not only its own goals but also the goals of the other side. Collaboration can benefit an organization because the parties work together to find a solution that leaves them both better off. Compromise and collaboration enable the parties in dispute to solve their differences.[78]

Accommodation is a style of handling conflict in which one party simply allows the other to achieve its goals. With *avoidance*, both parties refuse to recognize the real source of the problem and act as if there were no problem. Both of these conflict solutions are unsatisfactory from the organization's perspective and from the perspective of one or both of the parties in conflict. Accommodation means that one group uses its power to force the other to submit—to accommodate its demands, in other words. This solution is unlikely to lead to cooperation; furthermore, the weaker party is likely to become resentful and be on the lookout for any opportunity to get back at the stronger party. Similarly, avoidance means that the conflict will smolder, and the parties will remain uncooperative or uncommunicative.

Competition leads to the greatest and most visible conflict. Each party is looking out for its own interests and has little interest in understanding the other's position or taking the other's needs into account. When a conflict is handled competitively, or when accommodation or avoidance are typical styles of handling conflict, the conflict escalates to the next stage in Pondy's model.

Promoting Compromise. There are five specific tactics that managers can use to structure the negotiation and bargaining process to make compromise and collaboration more likely: Emphasize common goals; focus on the problem, not the people; focus on interests, not demands; create opportunities for joint gain; and focus on what is fair.

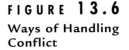

FIGURE 13.6
Ways of Handling Conflict

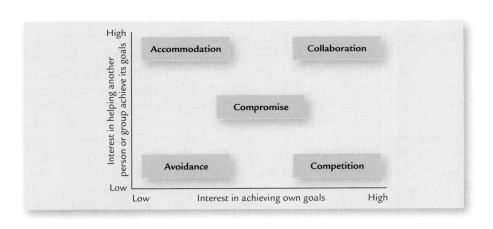

Emphasize Common Goals. Common goals are goals that all parties agree on regardless of the source of their conflict. Increasing organizational effectiveness, increasing responsiveness to customers, and gaining a competitive advantage are just a few of the many common goals that members of a company can emphasize during bargaining. Emphasizing common goals helps parties in conflict to keep in mind the big picture and the fact that they are working together to help the company succeed despite their disagreements.

Focus on the Problem, Not the People. People who are in conflict may not be able to resist the temptation to focus on the shortcomings and weaknesses of the other person or group. Now instead of attacking the problem itself, people start to attack one another. For example, they talk about the mistakes the other group has made in the past, and they criticize the personality of the other person or their personal habits. This approach is inconsistent with reaching a compromise through bargaining. All parties to a conflict need to remain focused on the problem or the source of the conflict and avoid the temptation to discredit each other personally.

Focus on Interests, Not Demands. Demands are what a person wants; interests are why the person wants them. When two people are in conflict, it is unlikely that the demands of both can be met. Their underlying interests, however, can be met, and meeting them is what bargaining and negotiation is all about.

Create Opportunities for Joint Gain. Once the parties to a conflict focus on their interests, they are on the road to achieving creative solutions that will benefit them both. This win-win scenario means that, rather than having a fixed set of alternatives from which to choose, the parties can come up with new alternatives that might even expand the resource "pie."

Focus on What Is Fair. Focusing on what is fair is consistent with the principles of equity theory. Equity theory emphasizes the fair distribution of outcomes based on the inputs or contributions that people make to companies. It is likely that parties in conflict will prefer different alternatives; each party wants the solution that best serves his or her interests. Emphasizing fairness and equity will help the parties come to a mutual agreement about what the best solution is to the problem.

When managers pursue those five strategies and encourage other members of the company to do so, they are more likely to resolve their conflicts effectively through negotiation and bargaining. Then managers can use conflict to help increase a company's performance and avoid destructive fights that harm the people involved in conflict as well as the organization.

Union–Management Negotiations. One of the most common types of negotiation and bargaining takes place between unions and management during contract talks. Suppose this year, management is in a strong position because the economy is in recession. When management and the union sit down to negotiate, management crushes the union, which goes back to its members empty-handed. Next year, the economy has recovered, and the negotiations begin again. What will be the attitude of the union this time? Management probably will confront a no-holds-barred attempt to beat management and get everything the union thought it should have gotten last year.

When two parties are in continual negotiation with one another, they realize that, for the survival of the organization, they need to adopt a long-term perspective that emphasizes their joint objectives and minimizes differences. In a negotiation situation, such as management–union bargaining, it is important to note that two different processes go on simultaneously. First, in *distributive bargaining* the parties bargain over how to divide resources, deciding who gets what and how much.[79] Second, in *attitudinal structuring* the parties try to influence their opponent's attitudes. For example, either managment or union negotiators might decide to act in an aggressive manner to increase their share of the resources, or perhaps act in a conciliatory manner to preserve long-term working relationships, save face, or demonstrate how much power they have should they choose to use it.[80]

Union and management negotiators often develop long-term relationships with one another and try to cooperate because they know that stalemate and attempts to destroy one another result in an antagonistic, destructive conflict aftermath in which everyone loses. Negotiation and bargaining is a difficult and delicate process in which the art of give-and-take and posturing for position is finely developed. Negotiations typically take place over a period of months as the parties discover what they can and cannot get. This is true of negotiations not only between management and unions but also between corporate headquarters managers and divisional managers and between managers and subordinates as they discuss pay and promotions.

In summary, negotiation and bargaining is an important means to resolve and manage conflict in work and organizational settings. Conflict can never be eliminated because differences in interests and in attitudes, as well as competition over resources, are integral to the way organizations operate. For the outcome of conflict to be beneficial, an organization's members have to learn how to deal with conflict when it occurs and to adopt the appropriate way of resolving it. Managing conflict through negotiation is an important part of a manager's job and an important aspect of organizational behavior at all levels.

Summary

Understanding and managing power, politics, conflict, and negotiation is an integral part of a manager's job. Organizations are composed of people who come together to achieve their common goals. When resources are scarce, people and groups have to compete for them, and some achieve their goals while others do not. In an organization managers have the primary responsibility to ensure that competition for resources is free and fair and that people who obtain power over resources do so because they possess skills and abilities that will, in the long run, benefit all members of the organization. Managers also have the responsibility to manage conflicts as they arise to ensure the long-term success of the organization and to maintain a balance of power to ensure that politics and conflict benefit rather than harm the organization. In this chapter, we made the following major points:

1. Power is the ability of one person or group to cause another person or group to do something they otherwise might not have done. Managers engage in political activities to increase their power and to pursue goals that favor their individual and group interests. Power and politics can benefit or harm an organization.

2. Sources of formal individual power include legitimate power, reward power, coercive power, and information power. Sources of informal individual power include expert power, referent power, and charismatic power.

3. Sources of functional and divisional power include the ability to control uncertain contingencies, irreplaceability, centrality, and the ability to control and generate resources.

4. Managers can use many kinds of political tactics to increase their individual power. These tactics include making oneself irreplaceable and central, controlling contingencies and resources, recognizing who has power, controlling the agenda, bringing in an outside expert, and building coalitions and alliances. Managing politics to obtain positive effects requires a balance of power in an organization and a strong CEO who has the ability to keep powerful people and groups in check.

5. Conflict is the struggle that arises when the goal-directed behavior of one person or group blocks the goal-directed behavior of another person or group. Whether conflict benefits or harms an organization depends on how it is managed.

6. The three main sources of conflict are differentiation, task relationships, and the scarcity of resources. When conflict occurs, it typically moves through a series of stages. In Pondy's model of conflict, these stages are latent conflict, perceived conflict, felt conflict, manifest conflict, and the conflict aftermath.

7. Negotiation and bargaining is an important means of managing and resolving conflict at both the individual and group level. The ability to negotiate an agreement is an important skill a manager needs to cultivate.

Exercises in Understanding and Managing Organizational Behavior

Questions for Discussion and Review

1. In what ways can the use of power and politics help or harm an organization?

2. What are the principal sources of a manager's formal power and informal power? How does the way a manager exercises power affect subordinates?

3. Think of a manager you have worked under or a leader you have been in close contact with. What were the main sources of this person's individual power? What was your reaction to the way this person exercised power?

4. What are the main sources of functional and divisional power?

5. Why is it important to have a power balance in an organization?

6. In what ways can the manager of a function deliberately set out to gain power inside an organization?

7. Why may conflict be good or bad for an organization?

8. What are the main sources of conflict between functions?

9. Why is it important for managers to try to reduce manifest conflict and create a good conflict aftermath?

10. What are the main conflict resolution strategies?

Building People Skills

Understanding Conflict and Politics

Think of the last time you came into conflict with another person or group, such as a manager you worked for or even a friend or family member. Then answer these questions:

1. Was this the first time you came into conflict with this party, or was the conflict one in a series of conflicts?

2. What was the source of the conflict? Did you and the other party see the source of the conflict differently? If so, why?

3. How would you describe the way you both reacted to the conflict?

4. Did the conflict reach the stage of manifest conflict? If it did not, how did you manage to avoid coming into manifest conflict? If it did, what form did the manifest conflict take?

5. How was the conflict resolved?

6. What kind of conflict aftermath resulted from the way you or the other party managed the conflict?

7. How well do you think you managed the conflict with the other party?

8. Given what you know now, how could you have handled the conflict more effectively?

A Question of Ethics

Power, Politics, and Negotiation

Managers routinely use organizational politics and negotiation to try to convince other managers to agree with their goals and follow the course of action they are championing. They may also seek ways to increase their personal power in an organization to further their own interests. Think about the ethical issues involved in politics, power, and negotiation and address the following issues:

1. At what point does it become unethical to use organizational politics to promote either personal interests or the interests of a function or division?
2. What is the role played by ethical values in the negotiation and bargaining process to ensure that outcomes are fair and equitable?

Small Group Break-Out Exercise

What Are the Sources of Conflict?

Form groups of three or four people and appoint one member as the spokesperson who will communicate your conclusions to the rest of the class.

Think of an organization you are all familiar with, such as a local restaurant or supermarket, and discuss the way it operates. Using the material in the chapter:

1. Identify how *differentiation* might potentially give rise to conflict between different employees or groups in this organization (e.g., because of status inconsistencies).
2. Identify how *task relationships* might potentially result in conflict between different employees or groups in this organization (e.g., because of task interdependencies).
3. How does the way the organization operates, such as its hierarchy of authority and the way it groups activities into departments, help to prevent such conflict from arising?

Topic for Debate

Organizational politics and conflict are part of the fabric of behavior in organizations. Now that you understand how these processes work in organizations, debate the following issue.

Team A. The use of power by self-interested managers and groups has the potential to do an organization more good than harm.

Team B. The use of power by self-interested managers and groups has the potential to do an organization more harm than good.

Experiential Exercise

Managing Conflict Successfully

Objective

Your objective is to gain an appreciation of the conflict process and to understand the difficulties involved in managing conflict successfully.

Procedure

The class divides into groups of from three to five people, and each group appoints one member as spokesperson to report on the group's findings to the whole class. Here is the scenario.

You are a group of top managers who have been charged with resolving an escalating conflict between manufacturing and sales managers in a large company that manufactures office furniture. The company's furniture can be customized to the needs of individual customers, and it is crucial that sales provides manufacturing with accurate information about each customer's specific requirements. Over the last few months, however, manufacturing has been complaining that sales provides this information too late for it to make the most efficient use of its resources, that sales is increasingly making errors in describing each customer's special needs, and that sales demands unreasonably quick turnaround for its customers. For its part, sales is complaining about sloppy workmanship in the final product, which has led to an increased level of customer complaints, about increasing delays in delivery of the furniture, and about manufacturing's unwillingness to respond flexibly to unexpected last-minute customer requests. Problems are increasing, and in the last meeting between senior manufacturing and sales managers harsh words were spoken during a bitter exchange of charges and countercharges.

1. As a group, use the concepts discussed in this chapter (particularly Pondy's model) to analyze the nature of the conflict between manufacturing and sales. Try to identify the sources of the conflict and ascertain how far the conflict has gone.
2. Devise a detailed action plan for resolving the conflict. Pay particular attention to the need to create a good conflict aftermath. In devising your plan, be sure to analyze (a) the obstacles to resolving the conflict, (b) the appropriate conflict management techniques to use, and (c) ways to design a new control and reward system to help eliminate such conflict in the future.

When asked by your instructor, the spokesperson will describe your group's analysis of this conflict between functions and the action plan for resolving it.

Making the Connection

Find an example of an organization in which two or more managers, functions, or divisions have been coming into conflict or have been engaged in a power struggle for control of organizational resources. What was the source of the problem, how are they behaving toward one another, and how is the problem being managed?

New York Times Cases in the News

The New York Times

Criticism of Disney Chief Grows Bolder

BY LAURA M. HOLSON AND SHARON WAXMAN

Michael D. Eisner faces a paradox these days. His position as the chief executive of the Walt Disney Company appears secure, as Mr. Eisner has skillfully beaten back a revolt among his board and steered the company's performance upward, nearly doubling the stock price in the last year.

Yet former board executives, crucial employees and other people in Hollywood now feel emboldened to criticize Mr. Eisner in a manner more vociferous than at any other time in his nearly 20 years as chief executive.

Mr. Eisner's antagonists—including Roy E. Disney, the nephew of the company's founder, whose resignation last Sunday set off some of the public discontent—have their individual reasons for speaking out now. But one common strand is their growing dismay over Mr. Eisner's management style, which has left in its wake a large number of alienated former executives and colleagues.

Despite a charm offensive by Mr. Eisner in response to the board uprising last year—wooing anxious or skeptical directors, institutional investors, partners and members of the news media over cocktails and in interviews—many say he

has just papered over a lack of substantive change at the company.

In this view, Mr. Eisner, 61, feinted in the direction of more transparent corporate governance, a plan for succession, and an easing of his micromanaging ways. But all the while, he was apparently consolidating power and becoming less inclined than ever to brook dissent from his board, his staff or his partners.

"Michael wants to be the Walt Disney Company," said Andrea Van de Kamp, a Los Angeles civic leader and head of Sotheby's West coast operations, who was forced off the board early in the year. "But he can't do that." Although an earlier leaked memorandum had expressed some of Ms. Van de Kamp's concerns, she had not spoken in detail with a reporter until last week.

And Mr. Disney, who recruited Mr. Eisner to the company in 1984, said: "Certainly in the last couple of years, it has become very personal. It seems to be a pattern: 'My ego vs. yours' has become the issue, not what's best for the company."

Mr. Eisner declined to comment for this article. A spokeswoman for the Walt Disney Company said if you had placed a $10,000 bet on Disney shares in 1984, today you'd have about $220,000, which she said was double the return of the Standard & Poor's 500-stock index.

As recently as two and half weeks ago, when Disney announced its fourth-quarter results, the worst of Mr. Eisner's troubles and a four-year earnings slump appeared to be behind him. Helped by movies like *Pirates of the Caribbean: Curse of the Black Pearl* and *Freaky Friday*, and cable television networks like ESPN, the company's net profit more than doubled and operating income rose 54 percent from the period a year earlier.

Beginning last Sunday, though, Disney executives found themselves on the defensive.

Roy Disney, 73, resigned from his posts as board vice chairman and chairman of the feature animation division after discovering that he would be asked to step down for retirement-age reasons. To show his displeasure, Mr. Disney's resignation letter was delivered to the news media before it reached Mr. Eisner, who was watching a football game in New York when it was slipped under his door. And the letter, which lauded Mr. Eisner's first 10 years on the job before listing a seven-point bill of complaint, included criticisms of Mr. Eisner for failing to restore the glory and profits of ABC's prime-time line-up, to build good relationships with creative partners like Pixar Animation Studios, and to feed sufficient capital to the company's theme parks.

Stanley P. Gold, Mr. Disney's investment adviser and close ally, quit the board

the next day, pledging to join him in his efforts to rally institutional investors and oust Mr. Eisner.

A week before the resignations of Mr. Disney and Mr. Gold, in an interview with a reporter for *The New York Times* for a book about Hollywood in the 1990's, Harvey Weinstein, the co-chairman of Miramax, criticized Mr. Eisner in a public way unlike any in their often-fractious relationship as business partners since 1993.

"All the great executives have been driven from the company," he said in the interview. "I think there is no camaraderie anymore, no great esprit de corps that I found earlier."

Mr. Weinstein, with his brother Bob, the other Miramax co-chairman, has been in a dispute with Mr. Eisner over several financial matters. He said on National Public Radio late last month, when asked about possibly breaching a ban on sending movie tapes to Academy Award voters, "There's always the case of Michael Eisner firing us, but that might be a cause for celebration in all quarters—ours included."

Complaints about Mr. Eisner's ways are nothing new, particularly since the death in 1994 of Frank G. Wells, his former No. 2 and a moderating influence on his boss's more confrontational style. Over the last decade, there have been a dizzying series of changes in the executive suites of Disney's various divisions—from the acrimonious departure of a former studio chief, Jeffrey Katzenberg, in 1994, to the expensive leave-taking of the former superagent Michael Ovitz from the president's position after just 18 months. And whispers that Mr. Eisner is reluctant to groom a powerful No. 2 as a replacement have continued to grow louder.

But scathing on-the-record comments—at least those not part of legal proceedings, like Mr. Katzenberg's against Disney—are a rarity in a business where the knives truly come out when someone is considered finished.

"Michael Eisner's agenda most of the time is to make everyone feel replaceable," said Rob Moore, who left Disney in

2000 after 13 years, to join Revolution Studios and his old boss, Joe Roth, who himself clashed with Mr. Eisner before departing from the company.

Mr. Moore added: "If you draw a line at Frank Wells's death, and what's happened since, the company used to attract the best and brightest minds in entertainment. Nearly all those people work somewhere else."

Ms. Van de Kamp expressed concern last week over what she said was Mr. Eisner's growing tendency to personalize any disagreement over corporate matters. She recalled a meeting with him in the midst of the board turmoil more than a year ago, nominally over new ideas, when she said he recited every instance in her four years as a board member where she disagreed with him.

"It appeared that Michael was focusing more on staying in power instead of focusing on the best interests of the company," she said.

Much of the animosity toward Mr. Eisner, some Disney and Hollywood executives suggest, is purely a result of his long tenure.

"If there's animosity, it's that he's been in the job longer than anyone in Hollywood for quite some time," said Bill Mechanic, a producer who has worked as an executive for Mr. Eisner both at Paramount and Walt Disney. "It's very hard to survive in all this stuff and not pick up enemies or backbiting or whatever."

Few dispute Mr. Eisner's talents, particularly his creative zeal. "He always micromanaged, mainly in the creative areas, not in the business arenas," Mr. Mechanic said. "I thought he was the best creative executive I've ever dealt with, even though I didn't like it."

Mr. Eisner, who colleagues say seemed vulnerable last year for the first time in his career, has since tried to soften his image. His get-togethers with institutional investors appear to have quieted most of their qualms. But the results of his wooing have not been entirely encouraging.

SOURCE: "Criticism of Disney Chief Grows Bolder," by Laura M. Olson and Sharon Waxman, *New York Times*, Dec. 8, 2003, p. C1.

Questions for Discussion

1. What are the origins of the conflict between Michael Eisner, his top managers, and Disney's board of directors?

2. What sources of power is Eisner using to manage the political process and retain control of Disney?

The New York Times

Viacom's Top 2 Remain Icy as Deadline Looms

BY GERALDINE FABRIKANT WITH
BILL CARTER

The executives who run the media giant Viacom, Mel Karmazin and Sumner Redstone, are barely speaking, and their relationship has become so poisonous that even if they resolve their current contract dispute, their dealings are not likely to improve, people who know them said late last week.

The drama of their bitter alliance will undoubtedly receive some attention when Viacom directors hold their regularly scheduled meeting on Wednesday. On the agenda will probably be the future of Mr. Karmazin, the company's president, whose contract is coming up for renewal. With only two months left before the new proxy statement is mailed to investors, board members are eager for a peace treaty.

For good reason. To be sure, despite the internal conflicts, Viacom's stock has performed well, compared with that of its competitors. Still, Wall Street has become so skittish about the future of Mr. Karmazin, who is given sizable credit for the success of the company, that Viacom's stock jumped 5 percent, to $39.88 a share, on Thursday as rumors swept the investment community that his contract had been extended for one year. A company spokesman denied the rumors, and the stock closed the week at $38.78 a share.

The two men do discuss business matters, the spokesman said. But the situation appears to have little to do with strategic business issues. And the blame cannot be placed entirely on either executive, people who know them say.

The two got off to a bad start shortly after Viacom and CBS merged in 2000, these people said. At the heart of the rift, they said, is the belief of the chairman, Mr. Redstone, that he gave away too much power when Mr. Karmazin, the CBS executive, became president of Viacom.

Their personal styles clashed, too. Mr. Redstone is a gregarious figure. But Mr. Karmazin resisted his social overtures and did not go out of his way to consult Mr. Redstone on business matters. Mr. Redstone is reported to have felt snubbed, and jealous of the attention given to Mr. Karmazin.

Mr. Redstone has been telling associates that he wants to keep Mr. Karmazin but that he wants some of his power back.

"Sumner did give up a lot of power to get the deal done, but in the back of his mind there was always a clock ticking as to how long it would last," said one of the people who know both Mr. Redstone and Mr. Karmazin well. "When the contract was up, he thought he would get that power back."

Meanwhile, Mr. Karmazin has become so angry about Mr. Redstone's comments that he recently complained to one board member in exasperation that it was not possible to negotiate a new contract with Mr. Redstone, according to one of these people.

Despite the battle over a new contract, one executive close to Mr. Karmazin said that he was happy in his job, wanted to stay at the company and expected to work out a deal with Mr. Redstone, even though it could be a short-term contract, for a year or two. Mr. Karmazin's initial contract was for three years.

This executive said he was confident that the board would address the issue of Mr. Karmazin's level of control. "The board is going to put strong pressure on the two men to make a deal that keeps the status quo in the company," this person said, adding, "The board will act because it has a fiduciary responsibility to maintain a management team that has been so successful."

Both executives are trying to manage the public perception of the negotiations, as well as the talks themselves, in the opinion of one person who knows both of them. This person pointed out that when Mr. Redstone says he wants to keep Mr. Karmazin, in part he is attempting to convince the public that he did not try to get rid of him. That way, if the talks fail, it will look as if Mr. Karmazin was to blame.

People who know both men well say both can be difficult. In part, they say, the strains developed because Mr. Karmazin had run Infinity Broadcasting and then CBS and was not willing to consult Mr. Redstone about management issues immediately after the merger.

"Mel miscalculated when he first came in," one person said. "His attitude was that he had operating control, and he decided he would simply use it and not consult Sumner.

"He really didn't understand the nature of the beast," the person continued. "Mel never invited Sumner to dinner to keep him

abreast of issues at the company. Sumner's daughter Shari and his son Brent, who are both on the board, had attended divisional management meetings, and Mel told them they could no longer participate." Mr. Redstone, who has always seen his business life as part of his social life, was angered by what he saw as Mr. Karmazin's dismissive attitude.

Mr. Karmazin's style was in stark contrast to Mr. Redstone's. He had long had close relationships with top executives at his company. He dines with Viacom Entertainment's chairman, Jonathan Dolgen, and Paramount Pictures' chairwoman, Sherry Lansing. He attended the wedding of Mr. Dolgen's daughter in Mexico and grew close to Ms. Lansing's husband, the director William Friedkin. He has long had a warm relationship with MTV Networks' chairman, Tom Freston, and grew friendly with the CBS president, Leslie Moonves, after the merger.

Nevertheless, Mr. Redstone, who is 79, could also be faulted for letting the relationship with Mr. Karmazin, 59, deteriorate. "He has a huge ego," said one of the executives who know the pair.

Mr. Redstone had had great success in running his movie theater business. He was prescient in deciding to buy land at important intersections of major highways so he could construct large, well-appointed theaters. Their high-quality sound and picture equipment helped differentiate the movie theater experience from television.

But by the 1980s, Mr. Redstone had become convinced that outlets for entertainment—whether movie theaters or television stations—would always be eroded by new technologies. The best strategy, he believed, would be to buy the companies that made the programming. His 1994 purchase of Paramount Communications, after a lengthy battle with QVC Inc., proved to be a smart financial bet. It also put him among a handful of the more visible and glamorous executives in American media.

And Mr. Redstone loved the attention. He enjoyed speaking to investors and seeing himself on the cover of magazines. Some people who know him say he always resented sharing the stage with his lieutenants and would inevitably find an excuse to oust a No. 2, as he did with the former Viacom chief executive, Frank Biondi, in 1996. It is a criticism Mr. Redstone has hotly disputed, arguing to associates that Mr. Biondi simply did not work hard enough.

Indeed, Mr. Redstone may be willing to withstand investor ire if Mr. Karmazin leaves because he was vindicated in both the dismissal of Mr. Biondi and the costly purchase of Paramount Communications. After both incidents, Viacom stock rose over the long term.

One of the people who know both Mr. Redstone and Mr. Karmazin said that in recent months it had particularly galled Mr. Redstone to read that Wall Street analysts and large investors believed that the company would suffer without Mr. Karmazin. In Mr. Redstone's view, Viacom's stock would suffer only a temporary setback if

Mr. Karmazin left because underlying management is so strong, the person said.

Mr. Karmazin has a preference for businesses like radio and cable programming, which have steady earnings and are not capital-intensive. When he recently attended the MTV Networks' annual retreat in Puerto Rico, several people who also attended said he appeared to be enjoying himself.

Mr. Karmazin is said to have far less interest in the movie business, which requires large amounts of capital and where earnings, which depend on hit films, are erratic. Several people close to the company say that Mr. Karmazin has a respectful relationship with Mr. Dolgen and Ms. Lansing but has never, for example, had social dinners with either of them. But Mr. Dolgen has had some lunches with Mr. Karmazin, and they talk several times a week.

In contrast, Mr. Redstone enjoys Hollywood; the film business is in his blood. He appeared at a recent New York opening of *The Hours*, a Paramount movie.

Whatever the relationship between Mr. Dolgen and Mr. Karmazin, several people familiar with the situation said, Mr. Dolgen might well prefer the status quo to having Mr. Karmazin leave, a move that could destabilize the current management. If Mr. Moonves gained more power, these people say, he might have an interest in running the film studio. Mr. Dolgen declined to comment.

For now, many people at Viacom are simply throwing up their hands in despair at the endless publicity. "They just want it to be over," one of the people close to the company said.

SOURCE: "Viacom's Top 2 Remain Icy as Deadline Looms," by Geraldine Fabrikant and Bill Carter, *New York Times*, January 27, 2003, p. C.1.

Questions for Discussion

1. Why are Sumner Redstone and Mel Karmazin involved in a continuing conflict situation?

2. What would be the best way of resolving this conflict between them?

Communication

in

Organizations

14

LEARNING OBJECTIVES

After studying this chapter, you should be able to:

■

Describe the four main functions of communication and differentiate between different kinds of communications networks.

■

Discuss the steps in the communications process and the requirements for successful communication to take place.

■

Differentiate between the main kinds of barriers to communication and explain how they can reduce the effectiveness of communication.

■

Identify the main kinds of communication media and explain how they vary along the dimension of information richness.

■

Appreciate the importance of persuasive communication and describe how to create persuasive messages to influence others.

OPENING CASE

Combining Face-to-Face and Intranet Communication Pays Off

How Did Effective Communication Promote Alteon's Performance?

Founded in 1996, Alteon Websystems quickly became a leading maker of the advanced hardware and software necessary to manage Web sites and e-businesses. It achieved its dominant position because of the way its managers developed one of the most effective systems of communication to speed new product innovation in the Internet industry.[1]

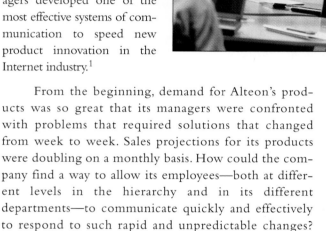

From the beginning, demand for Alteon's products was so great that its managers were confronted with problems that required solutions that changed from week to week. Sales projections for its products were doubling on a monthly basis. How could the company find a way to allow its employees—both at different levels in the hierarchy and in its different departments—to communicate quickly and effectively to respond to such rapid and unpredictable changes? How could the communication process be changed so that Alteon's software engineers could communicate with manufacturing managers to develop and produce new products quickly and reliably?

Alteon's answer was to develop an in-house, Web-based software platform, or intranet, making it possible for its work groups, teams, and subunits such as production, engineering, and sales to communicate quickly and effectively. For companies that rely mainly on written communication, it can take considerable time and many phone calls and e-mails before managers can agree on what to do. Using its new intranet, however, all Alteon's salespeople can now communicate with each other electronically and work together in real time on an ongoing basis to discuss the changing nature of customer needs.

When salespeople have decided what those needs are, they then use the intranet to communicate them to the company's engineers, who then work together in real time online to work out how to change the design of the company's hardware to meet those needs. Not only does this speed new product design but also, because manufacturing managers are connected to the Web-based intranet, they are fully aware of all the information and knowledge being developed in other parts of the organization. Using the company's intranet they can also offer their own inputs into the product development process. The combined result of its improved communication has been rapid, high-quality decision making that has made Alteon a market leader.[2]

Interestingly enough, however, Alteon still recognizes the need for face-to-face, oral communication. Every Friday afternoon, its 240 employees meet together for informal give-and-take sessions in which employees ask managers tough questions and then break into groups to confront specific problems.[3] Any decisions made in these groups are then inputted into the company's Web-based intranet. This information is then communicated to all the company's employees everywhere.

Alteon, in fact, has been so successful that the Canadian communication giant Nortel Networks announced it would purchase the company. Nortel will use its huge global sales force and manufacturing facilities to help make Alteon's products more quickly and hasten their distribution and sale around the world. Nortel also decided to make Alteon's managers responsible for replicating the company's communication system in the merged organization. The goal is to speed the flow of information across operations and improve communication between employees around the world.[4]

O v e r v i e w

As the story of Alteon suggests, communication is one of the most important processes that takes place in organizations; it has a major impact on individual, group, and organizational performance.[5] High-performing organizations such as Alteon have mastered the communication process; their members have the information they need when they need it to achieve the organization's goals. In contrast, the poor performance of many organizations is often the result of communication problems within the organization.

Given the sheer impact that communication has on individual, group, and organizational effectiveness, this chapter appropriately focuses on its nature.[6] First, we define communication, outline its implications for organizational behavior, and describe the functions that communication serves in organizations. Second, we examine common patterns of communication in organizations. Third, we describe a model of the communication process and discuss common communication problems and ways to avoid them. We then explore one of the key components of the communication process—the communication medium or method—in depth. Finally, we discuss the steps involved in persuasive communication. By the end of this chapter, you will understand why effective communication is so important in organizations.

What Is Communication?

One of the defining features of communication is the *sharing of information with other people*.[7] An accountant for Ernst & Young communicates with his boss when he informs him how well a large auditing project is going, when he asks to take his vacation at the beginning of June, and when he requests that his boss purchase a new software package to help in the preparation of complicated income tax forms.

The simple sharing of information is not enough for communication to take place, however. The second defining feature of communication is the *reaching of a common understanding*.[8] The sharing of information does not accomplish much in organizations unless people concur on what this information means. For example, suppose the accountant at Ernst & Young informs his supervisor that he has run into some problems on the auditing project and it will take longer to complete than was originally thought. The supervisor might assume that the audit is simply more complicated and time consuming than most others. The accountant, however, might suspect that the top management team at the company it is auditing is trying to hide questionable, and perhaps illegal, accounting practices. In this situation, effective communication has not taken place. The supervisor does not understand the source and magnitude of the problems the auditor has encountered. In other words, a common understanding has *not* been reached. This reduces the effectiveness of both the auditor and the supervisor. The auditor doesn't get the supervisor's advice and help in handling the tricky situation, and the supervisor isn't living up to an important responsibility—namely, working closely with his employees on an unusual or especially difficult auditing project.

In this case, **communication**—sharing information between two or more individuals or groups to reach a common understanding—hasn't occurred. Reaching a common understanding does *not* mean that people have to agree with each other. What it does mean is that people must have a relatively accurate idea of what a person or group is trying to tell them.[9] Communication is good or effective when members of an organization share information with each other and all parties involved are relatively clear about what this information means. Communication is ineffective when people either do not receive the information they need or are not quite sure what the information they do receive means.[10]

Communication The sharing of information between two or more individuals or groups to reach a common understanding.

THE FUNCTIONS OF COMMUNICATION

Effective communication is important in organizations because it affects practically every aspect of organizational behavior.[11] For example, members of an organization are likely to come to understand each other's personalities, attitudes, and values only when they communicate effectively with one another. Likewise, employees are motivated to perform at a high level when someone communicates clearly what is expected of them and expresses confidence in their ability to perform. Finally, leaders can influence and persuade their followers only when effective communication takes place.

When organizations experience problems such as unmotivated employees or excessively high turnover, poor communication is often partially to blame. A secretary may have low motivation to develop new bookkeeping skills or to take on the additional responsibility of planning conferences because he thinks he is in a dead-end job. In reality, no one has bothered to communicate to him that secretaries do have opportunities to advance in the company. Similarly, a software company that announces that a larger rival has purchased it may see its turnover rate triple, even though no layoffs and few internal changes will result from the change in ownership. The reason for the exodus is that its top managers have not clearly communicated to employees that their jobs are not at risk. Expecting the worst, the best performers (who have the most opportunities available to them elsewhere) will find another job.

Good communication prevents many problems like these from occurring and serves several important functions in organizations: providing knowledge, motivating the organization's members, controlling and coordinating group activities, and expressing feelings and emotions (see Figure 14.1).

Providing Knowledge.   A basic function of communication is to give members of the organization the information they need to do their jobs effectively.[12] By providing knowledge about, for example, ways to perform tasks and the decisions that have been made, an organization makes sure its members have the information they need to perform at a high level.

The importance of communication is most apparent when an employee has just started a new job. As you learned in Chapter 10, individuals starting a new job face considerable uncertainty about what they are supposed to do, how they should go about doing it, and what standards are acceptable. Communication from co-workers,

FIGURE 14.1

Functions of Communication

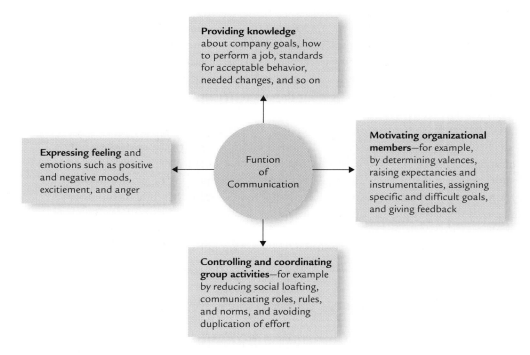

supervisors, customers, clients, and others helps reduce this uncertainty and provides newcomers with the knowledge they need to perform their jobs effectively.

Communication is essential for the socialization of newcomers at all levels in an organization. When Mickey Drexler became CEO of J. Crew in 2003, he spent the first couple of weeks on the job communicating with as many employees as he could to learn about the troubled company he was hired to help turn around. Drexler instituted a series of "town hall" meetings and talked to employees at all levels about J. Crew's problems.

The knowledge function also is important for even the most experienced members of an organization because things change. Just as the products or services an organization provides change in response to customers' desires, so does the nature of an employee's job responsibilities. Clearly communicating the new tasks, responsibilities, and policies required helps ensure that the members of the organization will continue to understand what needs to be done so it will achieve its goals.

The vast amount of information and knowledge available on the World Wide Web (WWW) today allows employees to access all kinds of data to help them perform their jobs and solve problems. On the other hand, employees can also plan vacations, shop for clothes, sell antiques, and make stock trades through the Internet on company time, which has raised ethical dilemmas for many organizations as the accompanying Managing Ethically suggests.

Employers know their workers need access to the Internet to do their jobs and that they expect a measure of privacy. Still, three-quarters of firms say they monitor their employees' communications and activities online.

managing ethically

What's the Right Way to Use the WWW?

A growing problem for more and more organizations is employee Web surfing at work.[13] According to Dr. David Greenfield, who runs the Center for Internet Addiction based in West Hartford, Connecticut, pornographic Web sites are among the most common non-work-related sites employees visit while they are supposed to be working.[14] The majority of the visits to pornographic Web sites occur during the normal workday. Similarly, the majority of stock trades made using online broker Charles Schwab & Company are made from the workplace. It has been estimated that Web surfing results in significant losses in productivity, with total costs tallying in the billions of dollars.[15]

This trend creates a number of ethical dilemmas for organizations. On the one hand, employees value their privacy, and access to the Internet is considered a perk on some jobs. On the other hand, when employees surf the WWW on company time, their job performance might suffer. Moreover, companies expose themselves to potential legal conundrums ranging from copyright infringement to hostile work environment charges and sexual harassment allegations.[16] The combined productivity losses and and legal risks have led more organizations to actively monitoring their employees' Internet activities and e-mail messages.[17] According to an American Management Association survey of medium to large organizations in the United States, almost 75 percent of the companies surveyed indicated that they engage in some monitoring of employees' activities and communications.[18] Some organizations also install firewalls that prevent employees from accessing particular Web sites on the job. And when employees violate their organization's Internet use policies, negative consequences often ensue. Many companies, including Xerox and IBM, have fired employees for visiting pornographic Web sites on the job.[19] Hence, employees may want to think twice before they surf the WWW on company time.

Motivating Organizational Members. As you learned in Chapters 6 and 7, motivation is a key determinant of performance in organizations, and communication plays a central role in motivating members of an organization to achieve their goals. Expectancy theory (see Chapter 6) proposes, for example, that managers do the following:

♦ Determine what outcomes subordinates are trying to obtain from their jobs—that is, the valences of various outcomes.

♦ Make sure that employees perceive that obtaining these outcomes is contingent on performing at a high level—that is, make sure that instrumentalities are high.

♦ Make sure that employees believe that they can perform at a high level—that is, make sure that expectancies are high.

The only way that a manager can determine the valences of different outcomes for any given employee is by talking *and* listening to the employee to find out what the employee wants. Likewise, managers need to communicate with employees to assure them they are capable of performing at high levels and will be rewarded for doing so.

As another example of the role of communication in motivating employees, consider goal-setting theory (examined in Chapter 7). It suggests that employees will perform at a high level when they have specific and difficult goals and are given feedback concerning how they are doing. Managers use communication to let employees know what goals they should be striving for and how they are progressing in their efforts to achieve those goals.

Controlling and Coordinating Group Activities. As you learned in Chapters 10 and 11, it is essential for groups to control their members' behaviors so that they perform their jobs in an acceptable fashion. Recall, for example, that a key challenge for self-managed work teams is to reduce social loafing—the tendency of people to exert less effort when working in groups than when working on their own. When a member of a group engages in social loafing, one of the primary ways that other members of the group can reduce it is by communicating to the loafer that his or her behavior has been observed and is not going to be tolerated. Groups and organizations exert control over their members by regularly communicating information about roles, rules, and norms to them. Similarly, as the interdependence between group members increases, the need for communication to coordinate their efforts in order to achieve group goals also increases.[20] For example, communication can help to eliminate duplication of effort in a team and to prevent one poorly performing member from keeping the other members from achieving the group's goals.

Expressing Feelings and Emotions. One of the most important functions of communication is to allow people to express their feelings and emotions.[21] These feelings and emotions can be general or specific and can originate from inside or outside the workplace.

Recall from Chapter 3 that *work moods* are the feelings people experience on a day-to-day basis as they perform their jobs. Often individuals and groups can better achieve their goals if they can communicate their moods to others. The moods employees experience on the job influence their perceptions and evaluations of people and situations as well as their behavior.[22]

For example, when the manager of an electronics store snapped at a subordinate who was proposing an innovative way to increase customer traffic through the store and, thus, increase sales, the hurt look on the subordinate's face made the manager realize that such impatience was out of line. The manager decided to communicate his feelings to the subordinate, and he frankly told him that he was in a lousy mood and that they should wait until the next day to discuss what sounded like a promising proposal.

This simple communication of feelings helped to prevent a minor incident from turning into a major problem.

Emotions such as excitement or anger are often stirred by specific events at work or at home, so it is often useful for individuals to communicate their emotions to others in the organization. A employee who has just learned she has received a promotion may be so elated she can't think straight enough to have an in-depth discussion with her supervisor about finding and training her successor. Simply communicating this fact to the supervisor and postponing the conversation for a while is the sensible thing to do. Similarly, as you learned in Chapter 9, a employee who is upset and angry about his spouse's terminal illness may feel a little bit better when he communicates his emotions to others and receives their social support.[23] Moreover, supervisors, co-employees, and subordinates will be more understanding of the employee's lack of enthusiasm or recent tendency to be overly critical when they realize the tremendous strain he is under. Communication of moods and emotions helps organizational members understand each other, and when people understand each other, they are better able to work together to perform well and achieve their goals.

In summary, communication is vital to ensure subordinates have all the information they need to perform their jobs and achieve their goals. Effective communication also lets subordinates know a leader is confident they can perform at a high level and that they will benefit from performing well. Communication is also vital to help subordinates understand the goals they should strive for and give them clear feedback about how they are performing. Employees can also be encouraged to communicate effectively with each other to coordinate their activities, avoid duplication of effort, and limit social loafing. Finally, to avoid misunderstandings, managers use communication to express their own feelings and emotions to others and should encourage their subordinates to do the same.

COMMUNICATION NETWORKS IN ORGANIZATIONS

Communication in an organization, both between employees at different levels in the hierarchy and between employees in different functions and departments, tends to occur in certain recurring patterns. The set of pathways through which information flows within a group or organization is called a **communication network**. Communication networks are found at both group and organizational levels.

Communication network
The set of pathways through which information flows within a group or organization.

Group Communication Networks. As we discussed in Chapters 10 and 11, self-managed work teams, top management teams, and other work groups play an important role in most organizations. Among the communication networks that can develop in such groups are the wheel, the chain, the circle, and the all-channel network (see Figure 14.2).

In a wheel network, most information travels through one central member of the group. This central member receives information from all other group members and is the sole sender of information to them; the other members of the group do not communicate directly with each other. Wheel networks are most common when there is *pooled task interdependence,* that is, when group members work independently and group performance is determined by summing up the performances of the members of the group. Examples of such groups are typing pools and groups of sales reps covering different geographic regions in which members have little need to communicate directly with each other. Most communication flows to and from either the formal or the informal leader of the group. For these kinds of group tasks, the wheel is an effective communication pathway because it is fast and efficient.

In a chain network, communication flows in a predetermined sequence from one group member to the next. Chain networks are common when there is *sequential*

FIGURE **14.2**
Group Communication
Networks

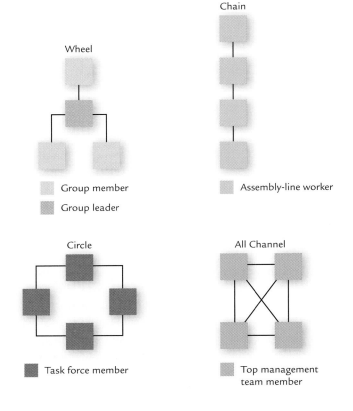

task interdependence, and members are required to perform specific behaviors in a predetermined order. Examples of such groups include all types of assembly-line work, where the finished product is the result of the sequential inputs of the group's members. While working on an assembly line, individuals are able to communicate only with others who are adjacent to them on the line. Chain networks also characterize communication up and down the hierarchy.

The circle network occurs in groups whose members communicate with others who are similar to them on some dimension ranging from experience, interests, or area of expertise to the location of their offices or even whom they sit next to when the group meets. Employees tend to communicate with group members whose offices are located next to theirs, for example. Similarly, when groups sit at a round table, members tend to talk to those on either side of them.

In an all-channel network, every group member communicates with every other group member. All-channel networks are prevalent when there is *reciprocal task interdependence*, that is, when the activities of work group members depend on one another. Each group member's behavior influences the behavior of every other member of the group. Examples of groups that use an all-channel communication network because of the complex nature of the work they perform include high-tech research and development teams, top management teams, emergency room personnel, and surgical teams.

Organizational Communication Networks. Organization charts that summarize the formal reporting relationships in an organization reflect one type of organizational communication network. Formal reporting relationships emerge from the chain of command established by an organization's hierarchy. The hierarchy determines which subordinates report to a given supervisor, to whom that supervisor reports, and so on, up and down the chain of command. A simple organization chart is provided in Figure 14.3. When an organizational communication network is accurately

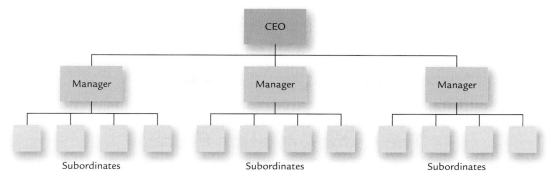

FIGURE 14.3
A Simple Organization Chart

described by an organization chart, communication flows up and down the hierarchy of the organization from superiors to subordinates and vice versa.

Newcomers to an organization may not see an organization chart until they have been on the job for several months. But when they see the chart, they are often surprised because the communication patterns that they have been observing bear little resemblance to the communication patterns specified by the chart. Lack of congruence between actual communication patterns and those specified in an organization chart is common. Communication in organizations often flows around issues, goals, projects, and problems rather than upward and downward from one formal reporting relationship to another. The roundabout flow ensures that members of the organization have access to the information they need to perform their jobs.

Actual communication patterns in an organization may look more like the informal network shown in Figure 14.3 than like the formal organization chart in Figure 14.4. Although the relationships shown on an organization chart are somewhat stable, actual communication patterns, such as in the network shown in Figure 14.4, are likely to change as conditions in the organization change. Members of an organization develop new patterns of communication as the type of information they need changes.[24]

Communication experts David Krackhardt and Jeffrey Hanson suggest that there are at least three informal communication networks in organizations: the advice network, the trust network, and the communication network. The *advice network* provides paths of communication for obtaining technical information. Examples might include determining the countries abroad that offer the lowest manufacturing costs and solving problems

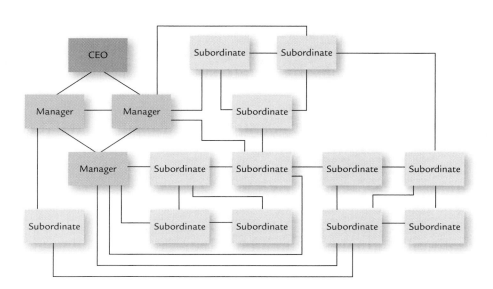

FIGURE 14.4

An Example of Actual Communication Patterns in an Organization

such as how to fix a complicated machine when it breaks down. The *trust network* provides paths of communication for delicate information such as information pertaining to conflicts, disagreements, and power struggles, as well as the handling of potential and actual crisis situations such as a product recall. The *communication network* provides paths of communication that are used on a day-to-day basis for ordinary work-related matters such as a change in accounting procedures or the upcoming company picnic.[25]

The Communication Process

Regardless of the nature of the communication network, effective communication involves a series of distinct steps shown in the model of the communication process presented in Figure 14.5 and described here.[26] The model is cyclical because effective communication is a continually repeated process. However, the sender initiates the communication process, so we start by discussing the sender and the message.

THE SENDER AND THE MESSAGE

Sender The individual, group, or organization that needs or wants to share information with some other individual, group, or organization.

Receiver The individual, group, or organization for which information is intended.

Message The information that a sender needs or wants to share with other people.

The **sender** is the individual, group, or organization that wants or needs to share information with some other individual, group, or organization to accomplish one or more of the four functions of communication described earlier. The **receiver** is the individual, group, or organization for which the information is intended. For example, a supervisor may wish to send information to a subordinate about his or her performance, a task force on diversity may need to communicate to top management its assessment of the promotion barriers facing minorities, or the organization may need to communicate to the Environmental Protection Agency about what it's doing to comply with new waste disposal regulations.

The **message** is the information that the sender needs or wants to share with other people. Effective communication depends on messages that are as clear and complete as possible. Clarity is important regardless of the content of the message, whether it relates to performance feedback, task force findings and conclusions, or an organization's response to new government regulations. A message is *clear* when it contains information that is easily interpreted or understood. A message is *complete* when it contains all the information necessary to achieve a common understanding between the sender and the receiver. Sometimes problems in the communication process crop up because the sender is vague or unsure about what the message should be. A supervisor, for example, might give vague feedback to a subordinate about performance on a recent assignment because the supervisor gave too little thought to how the subordinate actually performed or how his or her performance could improve in the future.

FIGURE 14.5
The Communication Process

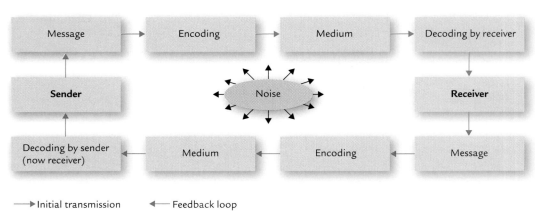

→ Initial transmission   ← Feedback loop

ENCODING

Once the sender has decided what the message is, the next step in the process is **encoding**, or translating the message into symbols or language the receiver can understand. A supervisor who puts ideas about how a subordinate is performing and ways that performance can be improved into words, a task force that summarizes the results of its investigations and weekly meetings into words and statistics such as the number of African Americans and women in top management positions, and a member of an organization who shows a government inspector the organization's waste disposal operations—all of these are examples of the encoding of messages.

Although encoding ideas by putting them into words seems simple enough, some organizations are finding that their employees lack the basic writing and oral communication skills needed to do this and are taking action to improve encoding. First Bank Systems Inc., in Minneapolis, Minnesota, for example, helps employees ranging from clerks to managers improve their grammar through skills-upgrading classes. Smith Corona Corporation, located in New Canaan, Connecticut, teaches employees how to answer telephone calls.[27]

For communication to be effective, the sender must translate the message into a form that the receiver can understand. When ideas are translated into words, for example, the sender must take care to use words the receiver understands. Have you ever listened to a computer expert explain the workings of a new software package using terminology that meant nothing to you? His or her failure to communicate probably added to your confusion instead of providing you with the knowledge you needed. A visit to a doctor can also be an exercise in frustration if the doctor describes your problem and its treatment in words you can't understand.

Jargon. In both of those examples, a breakdown in communication occurs because of the use of **jargon**, specialized terminology or language that members of a profession, occupation, or other group develop to improve communication among themselves. Computer experts have their own jargon, as do physicians, lawyers, and people pursuing most occupations or professions. Jargon facilitates communication within an occupation because it simplifies encoding. Rather than having to describe a complex array of symptoms and their likely causes, when a nurse uses a single medical term such as *gastroenteritis*, other health care providers will know immediately the ailment the nurse is referring to.

Messages encoded with jargon can lead to *effective* communication when senders and receivers are members of the same occupation or profession. Jargon becomes a problem only when the receiver of a jargon-laden message is outside the sender's profession or occupational group. In this case, the use of jargon leads to *ineffective* communication.

Sometimes even individual companies have their own jargon. For example, at the Coors brewery, newly developed beers are called "the liquid." At Microsoft, an employee's knowledge and ability are referred to as his or her "bandwidth." At Wal-Mart, training new employees to smile and offer a high level of customer service is known as being "Wal-Martized." And Intel executives "Intellize" new businesses they are trying to enter and compete in, such as telecommunications.[28]

THE MEDIUM

Once a message is encoded, it is transmitted to the receiver through some medium. The **medium** is the pathway through which an encoded message is transmitted to a receiver. (*Media* is the plural form.)

Encoding Translating a message into symbols or language that a receiver can understand.

Jargon Specialized terminology or language that members of a group develop to aid communication among themselves.

Medium The pathway through which an encoded message is transmitted to a receiver.

Verbal communication The sharing of information by means of words, either spoken or written.

Verbal Communication. **Verbal communication** is the sharing of information by means of words, either spoken or written. For messages that are encoded into words, the media can include face-to-face oral communication, oral communication over the telephone, and written communication through the use of memos, letters, and reports that may be electronically transmitted via e-mail or fax machines.

Each medium of verbal communication has advantages and disadvantages. Although there are no clear-cut rules about when to use one rather than another, there are two guidelines for selecting a medium.

One guideline is to select a medium that the receiver monitors—a medium that the receiver pays attention to, in other words. People differ in their preferences for communication media. Mickey Drexler, CEO of J. Crew, prefers to use oral face-to-face communication. Ron Shaich, president of the Boston-based, fast-food chain Au Bon Pain, likes to see things in writing. The most effective forms of communication for people like Shaich are written memos, reports, and letters.[29] A sender who ignores receivers' individual preferences for media is asking for trouble. A receiver may not realize the importance of a message delivered in casual conversation over lunch if he or she expects the message to be delivered via a formal report. A receiver who is inundated with memos and letters and more accustomed to having important messages delivered orally might toss a letter containing an important message into the trash without ever reading it.

The second guideline to follow in selecting a medium is to try to select one that is appropriate to the message you are trying to convey and to use multiple media when necessary. Common sense suggests that if you are communicating a personal and important message to an individual (such as information about being fired, being promoted, receiving a raise, or being transferred to another unit), oral communication is called for, preferably face-to-face. Alternatively, if the message you are trying to communicate is involved and complex, such as a proposal to open a new factory in Singapore, written communication is appropriate. If the message is important, you might want to back up the written communication with oral communication as well.

Nonverbal Communication. Words are not the only way people communicate. **Nonverbal communication** is the sharing of information by means of facial expressions (smiles and grimaces), body language (posture and gestures), and even mode of dress (elegant business attire versus jeans and a T-shirt).[30] The boss's look of disgust when you tell him the recent sales promotion you designed was a flop, your co-employee slamming his door in your face after a recent argument, and the uniform worn by a police officer standing next to your illegally parked car all transmit encoded messages to you. Many organizations have informal dress days to communicate that employees and managers are partners who should trust one another.

Nonverbal communication The sharing of information by means of facial expressions, body language, and mode of dress.

Often, when people do not feel comfortable about expressing part of a message verbally, they express it nonverbally. In general, because people tend to have less control over their nonverbal than over their verbal communication, their facial expressions or body language give them away when they wish to withhold some information. A sender who compliments someone he dislikes but fails to look the receiver in the eye, for example, is not concealing his insincerity.

Nonverbal communication also can be useful for communicating support, acceptance, and a sense of camaraderie. Researchers have long noted the value of hugs as a form of communication. Hugs help reduce stress, raise self-confidence, and make people feel connected with those around them. Studies of newborns, the elderly, and children in orphanages have shown that touch is necessary for psychological well-being. Sometimes a good hug at the right time can express powerful feelings and emotions. This was the case when retiring Supreme Court Justice William Brennan greeted his successor David Souter after Souter's confirmation hearings. According to

Souter, "He hugged me and he hugged me, and he went on hugging me for a very, very long time."[31]

We have covered just some of the issues involved in selecting a communication medium. Given the importance of choosing the right medium and the difficulty of making the right choice, we focus on additional aspects of this step in the communication process later in this chapter, in the sections on information richness and the impact of technological advances on organizational communication.

THE RECEIVER: DECODING AND THE FEEDBACK LOOP

Just as senders have to translate their ideas or messages into a form that can be sent to the receiver, receivers have to make sense of the messages they receive. **Decoding** is interpreting or trying to make sense of a sender's message. For messages that are relatively clear-cut, such as information about a raise or about a specific goal, decoding can be straightforward. Some messages, however, are ambiguous. For example, what caused your boss's look of disgust when you told him your sales promotion was a flop? Was the look due to his displeasure with your performance or his concern over the dwindling sales of the product involved? Or was it just the result of one more piece of bad news that day? During decoding, the receiver tries to determine which interpretation of the message, of all the possible interpretations, is accurate.

When messages are ambiguous, the receiver may have difficulty with decoding or may think that the message means something other than what the sender intended. When messages are ambiguous, the likelihood increases that the receivers' own beliefs, attitudes, values, moods, perceptual biases, and so on will influence decoding.

You may be tempted to think that communication is largely complete after decoding has taken place. As indicated in Figure 14.5, however, only about half of the communication process has occurred up to this point—the initial-transmission half. Recall that communication is the sharing of information to reach a common understanding. Up until and including the point at which the receiver decodes the message, the communication process has largely been one of sharing information. Members of an organization know they have reached a common understanding and have communicated effectively by completing the feedback loop, the second half of the process illustrated in Figure 14.5.

After decoding the message, the receiver has to respond to it and start the feedback loop. The receiver must first decide what message to pass on to the original sender. Sometimes the receiver's message is as simple as "I got your memo and agree that we need to meet to discuss this issue." At other times, the receiver may provide, in a long and detailed message, the information that the sender requested. Or the receiver's response might be that he or she did not understand the message.

After the receiver decides on a response, he or she *encodes* the message and transmits it, using a *medium* that the original sender monitors. The original sender *decodes* the response. If the original sender is confident that the receiver properly interpreted the initial message and a common understanding has been reached, the communication process is complete. However, if during decoding the original sender realizes that the receiver did not properly interpret or decode the message, the whole communication process needs to continue until both parties are confident that they have reached a common understanding.

The feedback loop in the communication process can be just as important as the initial transmission of the message because it confirms that the message has been received and properly understood. Thus, effective communicators do whatever they can to make sure they receive feedback. For example, an advertising executive hoping to convince a car company to use her firm to promote a new model may send a detailed

Decoding Interpreting or trying to make sense of a sender's message.

proposal to the manager at the car company who will make the decision. In the letter accompanying the proposal, the advertising executive makes sure she will receive feedback by telling the manager that she will be calling him in two or three weeks to answer any questions he might have. During the phone conversation, the advertising executive makes sure that the manager has understood the key components of the proposal.

Barriers to Effective Communication

Noise Anything that interferes with the communication process.

Noise is anything that interferes with the communication process. Noise can include the use of jargon, poor handwriting, a broken answering machine, a heavy workload that prevents a receiver from reading a written report, a receiver's bad mood resulting in the misinterpretation of a message, or the operation of perceptual biases (see Chapter 4). One of the key challenges for managers is to eliminate as much noise as possible.

Noise is a general term, but there are specific communication problems that result in ineffective communication. Here we examine six important potential communication problems in organizations and ways to overcome them so that individuals, groups, and organizations can communicate effectively and, thus, better achieve their goals: filtering and information distortion, poor listening, lack of or inappropriate feedback, rumors, workforce diversity, and differences in cross-cultural linguistic styles. (See Figure 14.6.)

FILTERING AND INFORMATION DISTORTION

Filtering A sender's withholding part of a message because the sender thinks the receiver does not need or will not want to receive the information.

Filtering occurs when senders withhold part of a message because they think the receiver does not need the information or will not want to receive it. Nobody wants to be the bearer of bad news, and subordinates are particularly loath to pass negative information on to their bosses. However, if subordinates withhold negative information or filter it out of their messages, a supervisor may not even be aware of a problem until it's almost too late to resolve it. What was once a minor problem that could have been easily fixed now becomes a potential disaster. Supervisors also sometimes filter information in their communications with subordinates. As a result, subordinates may have more negative attitudes, be less effective, or experience more stress. Sometimes when an organization is making major changes, such as downsizing, supervisors fail to give their subordinates information about the changes, and the result is high levels of stress as subordinates become uncertain about their future with the organization.

The magnitude of the filtering problem is underscored by the fact that subordinates are sometimes reluctant to convey negative information to their superiors even in crisis situations. A tragic example of this problem was the Air Florida plane that crashed

FIGURE 14.6
Barriers to Effective Communication

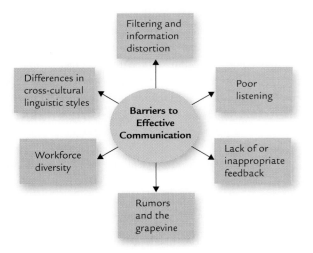

into a bridge over the Potomac River after taking off from National Airport in Washington, DC. Federal Aviation Administration (FAA) investigators determined that the crash resulted in part from the copilot's failure to tell the pilot about problems with engine power readings that were caused by ice on the engine sensors. Because of this and other instances of poor communication and filtering, the FAA now has mandatory assertiveness and sensitivity training for airline crew members to make sure that they communicate effectively and do not engage in filtering.[32]

Related to the problem of filtering is **information distortion**, the change in meaning that occurs when a message travels through a series of different senders to a receiver. Experiments (and the children's game "Telephone") have shown, for example, that a message that starts at one end of a chain of people is likely to become something quite different by the time it reaches the last receiver at the other end of the chain. In addition, senders may deliberately alter or distort a message to serve their own interests—to make themselves look good or to advance their own individual or group goals at the expense of organizational goals.

Filtering and information distortion can be avoided by establishing *trust* in an organization, as discussed earlier. One aspect of trust is the policy of *not* blaming the sender for bad news. When subordinates trust their supervisors, supervisors trust their subordinates, and co-workers trust each other, and when all members of an organization are confident that they will not be blamed for problems out of their control, filtering and distortion are much less likely to occur.

Information distortion The change in meaning that occurs when a message travels through a series of different senders to a receiver.

POOR LISTENING

Many people enjoy talking more than they enjoy listening to others. So, not surprisingly, poor listening is responsible for many communication problems in organizations. Consistent with this observation are findings from a recent study that suggests that managers think the voice mail they send is more important than the voice mail they receive and that senders generally think their messages are more important, urgent, and helpful than do the receivers.[33] In addition, people sometimes listen only to the part of a message they want to hear.

Members of an organization can do several things to become better listeners or receivers of messages. Being a good listener entails giving a sender your undivided attention, looking him or her in the eye, and not interrupting. Rather than thinking about what they are going to say next, good listeners focus on trying to understand what they are hearing and how the sender feels about it. Being a good listener also means asking questions and rephrasing key points to make sure you understand their meaning, avoiding distracting the sender (by glancing at the clock or tapping a pencil, for example), and accepting what the sender is telling you, even if it is not what you want to hear. It is especially important for supervisors to be good listeners when their subordinates are trying to communicating with them and avoid the natural tendency to pay more attention to the information coming from their superiors. The FAA's mandatory sensitivity training for airline crews, for example, may help pilots become better listeners. An interesting example of a manager who learned the importance of being a good listener is profiled in the accompanying OB Today.

LACK OF OR INAPPROPRIATE FEEDBACK

Sometimes communication breaks down because receivers either fail to provide feedback or provide feedback in an inappropriate manner. This barrier to effective communication is especially likely to occur when feedback is negative because negative feedback makes people feel uncomfortable. A manager at a bank, for example, may be reluctant to let one of her subordinates know that a loan application the subordinate worked closely on with a customer is going to be turned down. He or she may avoid

ob today

Consequences of Poor Listening Skills

I n 1997, Marc Brownstein decided to return to his native city, Philadelphia, and assume the position of president of the small ad agency his father Bernie had founded, the Brownstein Group.[34] Months later, Marc Brownstein was confident that he had made the right decision and was leading the agency effectively because the Brownstein Group's revenues were up and it was gaining clients and garnering more industry recognition.[35] Seeking to further enhance his leadership skills, Brownstein decide to enroll in a short executive development course. One of his assignments for the course was to have his managers complete an anonymous questionnaire rating his job performance as president of the agency.[36]

Brownstein was shocked to learn that his managers did not think that he was an effective leader. Although they thought that he meant well, managers complained about a breakdown in communication at the agency. They claimed that Brownstein failed to keep them informed about important matters such as how the agency was doing and who its new clients were, and that he also often failed to give them feedback about how they were performing. Moreover, they claimed that Brownstein didn't seem to consider his subordinates' preferences when handing out assignments and that he was generally a poor listener. For example, when a manager would meet with him in his office, Brownstein would often interrupt him or her several times to take phone calls.[37]

Brownstein realized that he had to make some major changes quickly or he would lose talented employees. Turnover at the agency was already surprisingly high, and now he knew why. So, he decided to change his communication style and schedule regular meetings with everyone on staff to open up the lines of communication. Any topic was fair game at these meetings, and Brownstein made a point of really listening to his managers. He focused his attention solely on what the person he was talking to was saying and put his phone calls on hold. His employees immediately sensed the change in his leadership style. Believing their contributions were now being appreciated, they more actively suggested ways to improve the agency's operations, including how it managed its clients.[38] With the lines of communication opening up, Brownstein also began to understand what was really going on his employees' minds. Above all, he learned that leaders need to pay attention to and listen to what their subordinates have to say—that the feedback they provide is just as important as the feedback their superiors give to them![39]

When his subordinates told him the wasn't communicating well, Marc Brownstein, the head of a Philadelphia advertising agency, took steps to become a better listener and give staff members more feedback.

broaching the issue, putting the subordinate in an embarrassing position if the bad news is divulged by the customer whose loan has been rejected. By developing good feedback skills, managers and employees at all levels in an organization will be more likely to respond in an appropriate manner to messages they receive, whether they're positive or negative.

Good feedback concentrates on the message being responded to, not on the sender's personality, attitudes, capabilities, or more general performance levels. Good feedback is specific and focuses on things the sender controls. When giving feedback, the receiver should try to put himself or herself in the original sender's shoes, understand how the sender feels, and relay the feedback in a manner that conveys the right message without unnecessarily hurting the sender's feelings.

RUMORS AND THE GRAPEVINE

A **rumor** is unofficial information on topics that are important or interesting to an organization's members. Rumors usually spread quickly and uncontrollably around communication networks and, once started, are often hard to stop. They are especially likely to spread when members of the organization are not informed about matters that have the potential to affect them personally, such as a takeover attempt by another company, impending layoffs, or a scandal involving a top manager. Sensational rumors sometimes help relieve the everyday boredom of organizational life. These rumors often entail gossip about the personal lives and habits of the organization's various members.

How can companies halt the spread of inaccurate and sometimes damaging rumors and also provide employees with up-to-date, accurate information on issues that are important to them? One way is with an IT network consisting of computer monitors and/or television screens linked to the Internet or via a company-owned satellite system that can beam information to employees working in many places. Wal-Mart, for example, has a state-of-the-art IT system that allows for the rapid communication of information to its thousands of stores.[40]

According to the Atlanta consulting firm KJH Communications, companies can use these systems to control the spread of rumors, communicate accurate information to large numbers of employees, and coordinate emergency efforts.[41] For example, when Jeff Imelt took over as CEO of GE, he appeared on GE's company-wide Intranet

Rumor Unofficial information on topics that are important or interesting to an organization's members.

Managers can't discount the power of the "grapevine" to spread rumors. Sometimes the rumors aren't accurate. In other cases, however, they provide legitimate information to employees that managers could have provided.

several times during his first months on the job to communicate to employees that they had no need to worry about the future of their jobs and organization. And when heavy fog in Memphis, Tennessee, halted delivery of thousands of Federal Express's overnight packages and letters, the company used its intranet to keep employees informed and instruct them on what to do. Federal Express also uses its intranet to communicate accurate information and halt the spread of unfounded rumors, such as those that sprang up when the company stopped making deliveries between European countries and laid off 4,000 European employees. American employees learned of these changes on Federal Express's computer monitors and were reassured that their own jobs were secure. The European employees who were actually let go were informed of the layoff face-to-face.

Grapevine A set of informal communication pathways through which unofficial information flows.

Rumors are often spread through the **grapevine**, a set of informal communication pathways through which unofficial information flows in an organization.[42] In any group, department, or division of an organization, some individuals seem to know everything about everyone and everything and pass along large quantities of unofficial information to others. Rumors that spread through the grapevine can be about the private or work lives of key members in the organization, the organization itself, or the future of the organization and its members. Although rumors that are spread through the grapevine are often inaccurate, sometimes information transmitted through the grapevine *is* accurate. For example, Mike O'Connell, a marketing manager in an airline company, told one of his co-employees over lunch that he was quitting his job, had given his supervisor two weeks' advance notice, and would be joining British Airways in London. By the end of the same workday, everyone in O'Connell's department knew of his plans even though he hadn't mentioned them to anyone else (nor had his supervisor).

WORKFORCE DIVERSITY

Diversity lends strength to groups, but it can also cause communication problems between the people in them. Managers can help facilitate group cooperation by encouraging members to think about their joint goals instead of focusing on their individual differences.

Increasing diversity might also become a barrier to effective communication when the members of a group or organization don't see eye to eye or fail to respect and appreciate each other's points of view. To counter this effect, many organizations are instituting diversity training programs so their employees can learn to communicate and work well together. For example, Federal Express has a voluntary four-and-a-half-day diversity training program available to its 5,500 managers to help them learn to understand and appreciate each other's points of view. Similarly, Pacific Gas & Electric has a mandatory four-hour diversity training for its 12,000 employees. Employees must find the training valuable because the classes often run long, sometimes up to six or eight hours.[43]

What goes on in a diversity training program? The training can be approached several different ways. One approach involves having a panel of minority members in the organization describe and share with their co-workers their own experiences and difficulties.

Another approach involves having members of an organization work for a period of time with people who are different from themselves. New recruits to the San Diego Police Department, for example, are assigned a one-week tour of duty working with citizens who are very different from them. A white woman might be sent to work with an all-male Hispanic teenage gang to gain some understanding of how these youths view society and learn how to communicate with them and people who are very different from her. Regardless of how it is done, helping diverse groups and members in an organization get along so that they communicate effectively and work together to achieve their goals is imperative—especially as diversity within the workforce (and the world) continues to increase.

DIFFERENCES IN CROSS-CULTURAL LINGUISTIC STYLES

When people from different cultures interact, communication difficulties sometime arise because of differences in linguistic styles. **Linguistic style** is a person's characteristic way of speaking including tone of voice, volume, speed, use of pauses, directness or indirectness, choice of words, use of questions and jokes, and willingness to take credit for ideas.[44] Within a culture, linguistic styles can vary between, for example, different regions of a country or between men and women. Across cultures, however, linguistic style differences are typically much greater, and this can lead to many misunderstandings.

Linguistic style A person's characteristic way of speaking.

In Japan, for example, employees tend to communicate more formally and be more deferential toward their bosses than employees are in the United States. On the one hand, Japanese employees don't mind lengthy pauses in a conversation while they are thinking about something under discussion. On the other hand, American employees often find lengthy pauses in conversations uncomfortable and feel the need to fill the void by talking. Americans are also more likely to take individual credit for ideas and accomplishments in conversations whereas Japan's more group-oriented culture makes individual credit taking less likely.[45]

These cross-cultural differences can result in many communication difficulties. For instance, U.S. employees' tendencies to take credit for their ideas and accomplishments may cause Japanese employees to think they are being boastful when this is not the case. Lengthy pauses on the part of Japanese communicators may cause U.S. employees to feel that the Japanese aren't interested in the discussion. On the other hand, U.S. employees' tendency to fill these pauses may cause the Japanese to think they are being pushy and not giving them a chance to think. Neither of these scenarios may be correct.

Cultures also differ in terms of the physical distance between speakers and listeners deemed appropriate for conversations at work.[46] For example, people in Brazil and Saudi Arabia favor closer physical distances than do people in the United States. Americans may feel uncomfortable when Brazilians stand "too" close to them during a conversation, whereas Brazilians may be wondering why Americans keep backing up and seem so standoffish.

Cross-cultural communication difficulties such as these can be overcome by understanding cross-cultural differences in linguistic styles. Before interacting with people from a different culture, members of an organization should try to learn as much as possible about the linguistic style of that culture. Expatriate managers who have lived in the country in question can often be a good source of information about its linguistic style because they have firsthand experience interacting with the culture's members. Learning about more general, cross-cultural differences is also often helpful because these differences are often linked to differences in linguistic styles.

Selecting an Appropriate Communication Medium

The communication difficulties that many companies experience demonstrate that sharing information to reach a common understanding is often more difficult than it appears. Choosing the right communication medium for any given message can help ensure that a message is received and properly understood, but selecting a medium involves trade-offs for both the sender and the receiver. One way to examine these trade-offs is by exploring the information richness of various media, their demands on the receiver's and the sender's time, and the paper trail they leave. In this section, we explore these issues and the implications of advances in information technology for communication in organizations.

INFORMATION RICHNESS

Information richness The amount of information a medium of communication can carry and the extent to which it enables senders and receivers to reach a common understanding.

Communication media differ in their **information richness**—that is, the amount of information they can carry and the extent to which they enable senders and receivers to reach a common understanding.[47] Media that are high in information richness are capable of transmitting more information and are more likely to generate a common understanding than are media that are low in richness. The various media available to organizational members can be categorized into four general groups based on their information richness (see Figure 14.7).[48]

Face-to-Face Communication. Face-to-face communication is the medium highest in information richness for at least two reasons. The first is that it provides the receiver not only with a verbal message but also with a nonverbal message conveyed by the sender's body language and facial expressions.[49] The nonverbal part of the communication gives receivers additional information they can use to decode the messages. When Joan Schmitt, an engineer for a construction firm, met with her supervisor Fred Johnston to discuss the plans for a Brazilian project the company was bidding on, Johnston got up from behind his desk to sit in a chair next to Schmitt as she described her proposal. His action provided Schmitt with information: He respected her and wanted her to feel that they were on equal footing in their discussion of the bidding. Similarly, when Johnston mentioned that the newly hired and inexperienced son of the owner of the firm was to be a member of the team preparing the bid, his failure to look her in the eye and his pursed lips conveyed that he was not pleased with this situation.

The second reason why face-to-face communication is highest in information richness is that it allows receivers to give senders instant feedback. Senders can clarify ambiguous information immediately, and the communication process can be cycled through as many times as needed until a common understanding is reached.[50] At the engineering firm, Fred Johnston was quite familiar with the Brazilian clients for whom the bid was being prepared and thought it best they be more involved in the bidding process than was normally the case. He suggested, for example, that the clients have more input into materials specifications and quality parameters than was usual. Joan Schmitt was taken aback by Johnston's suggestion. She wasn't sure why it was important and how to carry it out. After a 20-minute discussion, however, Schmitt realized that what Johnston was suggesting was not unreasonable or difficult and that it made sense given the clients' desire to have more input into the details of the building's construction than was customary.

Verbal Communication Electronically Transmitted. Verbal communication that is electronically transmitted over telephone lines is the communication medium next

FIGURE 14.7
The Information Richness of Communication Media

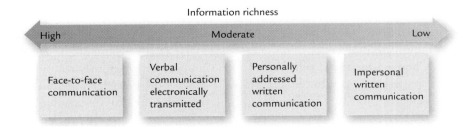

Information richness

High — Moderate — Low

| Face-to-face communication | Verbal communication electronically transmitted | Personally addressed written communication | Impersonal written communication |

highest in information richness. Telephone conversations do not provide the receiver with nonverbal information from body language and facial expressions, but they still are a rich source of information. The receiver can hear the message, interpret the tone of voice in which it is delivered, hear clearly which parts of the message the sender emphasizes, and get a sense of the sender's general demeanor while communicating. Because this type of verbal communication is personally addressed to the receiver, the receiver is likely to pay attention to it. When Johnston was talking on the telephone with the Brazilian clients about the building they wanted, for example, he could sense their enthusiasm and was pleased that they sounded comfortable talking with him.

Telephone conversations also allow for instant feedback so misunderstandings can be cleared up quickly. Although not commonly used, video telephones allow callers to see the person they are talking to. As the use of broadband increases, computers are likely to serve as video telephones in the future.[51] Visual images add to the information richness of this medium.

Also in this category of electronic verbal media is communication using voice mail and answering machines, which both allow receivers to gather information from the sender's tone of voice and inflections in the sender's verbal communication, but they do not permit immediate feedback. When using this medium to communicate with a receiver, the sender needs to make sure that the receiver monitors this medium by calling in frequently to receive messages.

Personally Addressed Written Communication. Written communications (such as letters and memos) addressed personally to the receiver are next in information richness. Personally addressing the communication helps to ensure the receiver will pay attention to it, and writing for one person allows the sender to tailor the message in such a way that the receiver is most likely to understand it. Feedback is not instantaneous, but this may not always be a disadvantage. In some situations, it is important for receivers to have time to reflect on a message and then formulate a response. E-mail is also included in this category of media. However, for communication to be effective receivers have to check periodically to see whether they have any electronic messages.

Impersonal Written Communication. Lowest in information richness is written communication that is not addressed to a particular receiver. This form of communication is used when a sender needs to communicate with a large number of receivers simultaneously, such as when a company president wants to dispel rumors of an impending layoff. Because this type of medium is impersonal, receiving feedback is unlikely. For this reason, it is especially important for the sender to use language that all receivers will be able to interpret correctly, so a common understanding will be reached.

This kind of medium is also useful when a large amount of information needs to be communicated, such as the monthly sales of a company's products by state, enrollment in a large state university by college and major, or the instructions for running a complicated printing press. When information is complicated (such as the printing press instructions), some form of written communication is a necessity so that receivers can go back and review the information as needed.

TRADE-OFFS IN THE CHOICE OF MEDIA

In choosing a medium, one of the most significant trade-offs is between *information richness* and the *amount of time* it takes to communicate the message by using the medium. Oral, face-to-face communication, for example, has high information richness but can be very time consuming. When messages are important, and the sender is not certain that a written message will be understood, then taking the time to communicate orally is usually worthwhile. However, when a message is clear-cut and easy to understand, such as an announcement that a company will close at noon on the Friday before Memorial Day weekend, a written memo or letter may be most expedient.

Another trade-off that needs to be taken into account is the trade-off between *information richness* and the *need for a paper or electronic trail*—written documentation of a message, in other words. When messages are complicated and need to be referred to later, such as those containing operating instructions or elaborate procedures, a paper or electronic trail is a clear advantage. Similarly, written communication is advantageous when a sender requires proof that a message was sent. A patient who is denied medical insurance coverage for a particular procedure and appeals the insurance company's decision wants to be able to prove that the insurance company was notified about the procedure and approved it.

USING NEW INFORMATION TECHNOLOGY

Recent advances in information technology (IT) not only have given members of organizations new ways to communicate with each other but also timely access to more information than ever before.[52] An organization must be careful not to overwhelm its employees with so much information that they spend more time reading e-mail and bulletin boards than doing their jobs.[53] Most employees in corporate America who use e-mail receive around 30 messages per day and spend about two hours a day responding and completing tasks related to the messages, according to Ferris Research based in San Francisco, and these figures are expected to increase significantly over the next few years.[54] Joseph Galli, who used to receive around 150 e-mails a day when he was president of Amazon.com, suggests that e-mail should be used only for those tasks it is most suited for, such as sending data, memos, summaries, or relevant information. Other kinds of messages are more efficiently and effectively handled on the phone or in person. Also Galli suggests that when it is important to express feelings such as congratulations for a job well done or motivate employees to excel, voice mail is superior to e-mail because feelings as well as words can be communicated.[55]

Despite these problems, IT has the potential to significantly reduce the costs of communicating information.[56] For example, at Aetna Life & Casualty Company, most

A state-of-the-art satellite system helps "Wal-Martize" the employees of the world's largest retailer by broadcasting information to them at stores worlwide.

training manuals, rate books, and other insurance documents (which used to be on paper) are now on computer. Aetna estimates that this change from paper to electronic communication saves about $6 million annually due to, for example, the elimination of costly storage fees for extra manuals and binders (around $2,000 a month) and the 4.5 cents-per-page cost of updating and changing employees' manuals when procedures are altered (often involving millions of pages).

Intranets. Communication information technology advances such as the Internet have also dramatically altered the nature of communication in almost all organizations.[57] The United States has the most Internet users, but other countries in Europe and Asia also have high numbers of Internet users.[58] Many organizations, using the same technology that the Internet is based on, have created their own company-wide computer networks, called **intranets**, which use software to facilitate real-time online communication within an organization. Intranets contain a wide variety of information ranging from directories, manuals, and product specifications to delivery schedules, minutes of meetings, and current financial performance. They can be accessed by all members of the organization. Organizations use intranets to efficiently communicate information to their members as well as give them easy access to the information they need to do their jobs, when they need it.[59]

> **Intranet** A company-wide computer network.

As we discussed in the opening case, intranets also enable employees to work together electronically to facilitate joint problem solving.[60] In real time, all of the members of one group, and even those of others, can see the messages being relayed back and forth via the intranet and technology like instant messaging (IM). The use of teleconferencing, which is relatively high in information richness because group members can see as well as talk to each other face-to-face in real time, is also growing in popularity.[61] The Japanese company Hitachi Limited, for example, uses teleconferencing to facilitate communication between its 29 research laboratories in Japan. Scientists and engineers in the different laboratories use teleconferencing to share knowledge and cooperate on joint research projects. Teleconferencing is also a good choice of medium when members of a group or organization are located in different countries.[62] Hewlett-Packard and IBM are among the many companies that use teleconferencing to facilitate communication between managers in its foreign and domestic divisions. Nevertheless, when it comes to solving thorny problems, face-to-face communication is still often necessary because it is information rich. Recall from the opening case how Alteon combined both methods.

In summary, research suggests that face-to-face communication works best when a message is important and there is a good chance that the receiver will have difficulty understanding it. Moreover, when messages are important and complex it is best to use multiple communication media such as face-to-face communication and written reports. On the other hand, written communication is appropriate when it is necessary to document that a message has been transmitted and when the message needs to be referred to more than once. Finally, in some situations, electronically transmitted oral or written communication is just as effective as face-to-face communication and can save time.

Persuasive Communication

In organizations one person's ability to understand another is not the only objective of communication. Often a person wants to persuade and influence other people. **Persuasive communication** is an attempt by one person or group to transmit and share information with another person or group in order to get the other to accept, agree with, follow, or otherwise achieve the objectives the communicator desires. When it comes to persuasive communication, not only is the accurate transfer of information necessary but also important is how the message is "framed" or "packaged" so as to influence other people.

> **Persuasive communication** The attempt by one person or group to transmit and share information with another person or group to get the other to accept, agree with, follow, and seek to achieve the former's goals and objectives.

you're the management expert

How to Speed Product Development

You have been called in by the top managers of a small, high-tech start-up company to advise them how to solve a major communication problem. The company makes flat-panel LCD displays that function both as computer monitors and as TV screens. The market is growing rapidly and there is increasing demand for a wider variety of sizes of screens and for screens with brighter displays that also offer a clearer picture when viewed at an angle. You have different teams of engineers working on the design of the different-sized screens, and even more teams are working to design brighter displays that can be viewed from wider angles.

Recently, members of many of these teams have been complaining that they are not learning quickly enough about the technical advances being made by other teams. This is slowing down their progress and many teams are falling behind the schedule you have set for launching your new displays in the marketplace. Currently, top managers are responsible for monitoring the progress of the various teams and disseminating new information to them. The managers hold regular meetings with the team leaders, and together they summarize any new information into technical e-mails that are sent to all team members. However, these methods of communication are obviously not sufficient.

Using the material in the chapter, design a new communications system for this company that will allow the teams to better share information and coordinate their actions to speed the product development process.

Persuasive communication is important in many different kinds of situations. We discussed in Chapter 12 how leaders attempt to influence and persuade their employees, but employees also attempt to influence their leaders. Some of the most important situations in which there is a need to communicate persuasively occur when one party lacks the power to direct the other party as he or she wishes. In this case, persuasion must be used. For example, managers in one functional department or group are often in a situation in which they need to influence managers from other functional departments or groups. Because these managers have no power over one another, they have to influence and persuade their counterparts to follow or adopt their goals or objectives. Also, employees who work in a group often wish to influence their co-workers to follow their ideas. Because they have no legitimate power over their co-workers, they'll need to persuade them. Even employees who *do* have expert or referent power need to know how to persuade their co-workers to successfully influence them.

In each of the instances, communication becomes the vehicle through which attempts to influence and persuade others are made. Some studies have found that managers spend most of their time in meetings and committees in which their primary goal is to provide accurate information about their plans and goals to elicit support for them. Small wonder then that people in organizations need to develop a competence in persuasive communication.

A MODEL OF PERSUASIVE COMMUNICATION

To examine how persuasive communication competence is developed, we follow the steps in the communications model outlined previously but focus on how persuasive communication works. Recall that the two main parties involved in communication are known as the sender and the receiver. The sender's task is to influence the receiver's response to the message—that is, to persuade the receiver to agree with and act on the message. Five factors determine how persuasive a message will be: the characteristics of the sender, active listening, the content of the message, the medium or channel through which the message is sent, and finally the characteristics of the receiver.

Characteristics of the Sender. As you might expect, messages are always more persuasive when they are sent from those people who are *credible*, meaning that the receiver believes that the sender is in a position to know what the appropriate objective is. Leaders, of course, are credible because they have legitimate power they can use to gain the compliance of their employees. In addition, leaders who have expert and referent power are also credible and can use these qualities to secure the commitment of employees. Other factors that promote credibility are moral integrity and emotional intelligence. If the receiver believes the sender is an honest, trustworthy person, then the receiver is more likely to believe that the information he or she is receiving is true and should, therefore, be acted upon. People who have empathy—those who can understand and appeal to the feelings and emotions of others—can use empathy to gain credibility and influence others. Emotional intelligence can be used to good effect, but it can also be harmful, say, when a con artist takes advantage of his or her personal appeal to deliberately trick or deceive others.

People who are able to persuade others also often possess good speaking and listening skills. As speakers, they know how to use every word to effect. They don't speak too quickly, they marshal their arguments logically, and subtly come back to the same point again and again to make sure the key facts are not only being communicated but also emphasized. Good speakers invite listeners to ask questions to clarify issues and generate feedback, interest, and support for their ideas. They use personal qualities such as their referent power or emotional intelligence to "emotionally charge" their words to convince others they *know* what they are doing, that their approach is the *right* one, and that it will *succeed*.

Active Listening. Active listening is an important ingredient of persuasive communication. Recall from Chapter 3 that we discussed how job applicants, even though they are receivers, should ask questions of company interviewers to demonstrate their interest and enthusiasm. The same is true of persuasive senders. They need to actively listen to see how their arguments are being received, and then they can clarify issues and add information to get their points across.

People who are active listeners pay attention not only to the words that are being said but also to the many unsaid things that are also going on in the communication process. Both the sender's and receiver's voice tones and the nonverbal cues they exhibit, such as hesitation or laughter, also shed light on what is being said or heard by the other party. Active listeners also avoid interrupting and maintain their interest in what the other party is saying. They give the other party time to frame his or her thoughts and get to the punch line. People who interrupt and finish another person's sentences for them often miss the real intention behind the words and message being conveyed because they put their own views first.

Active listeners also try to show interest and ask questions to solicit more information from the sender than perhaps he or she ever wanted to reveal. As the saying goes, "If you give people enough rope (time to talk about themselves), they will hang themselves." By rephrasing questions and picking up on throwaway statements, it is usually possible to learn much more about the other party's intentions than he or she was planning to reveal.

For the receiver, active listening is a way of finding out how important the message he or she is receiving is to the sender. For the sender, actively listening to the receiver's response provides the sender with the same clues about the other's intentions. Often, for example, a busy employee might say, "Sure, boss—I'll get right on that," then does nothing because it would just slow their other tasks down. A boss who picks up on this by listening actively can take pains to reemphasize the point and ask probing questions to discover just how likely the employee is to act upon the boss's wishes.

Content of the Message. The content of the message, that is, the information and arguments it contains, is also a crucial ingredient in the communication process. The receiver of the message, especially if he or she is an active listener, is always evaluating the meaning and implications of the information being given, looking for the theme behind it and ambiguities or inconsistencies in the arguments.

A competent sender knows this and is careful not to offer the receiver a one-sided or incomplete account of why some issue is important. To gain credibility, the sender knows he or she needs to present all sides of an argument—even those contrary to his or her position. The sender can always later shift back to the major theme being communicated, using a few strong arguments to persuade and win over the receiver.

As you might expect, the content of a message can be greatly augmented by framing the argument with an emotional appeal that "it's in the best interests of every-one in our department and vital to the future of our company." In other words, the content of a message can be made much more persuasive when it appeals to the receiver's feelings and emotions as well as to his or her intellect.

Method of Communication. In general, face-to-face communication and telephone conversations offer the greatest facility for persuasive communication, whereas formal written letters and memos and e-mail are most suited for conveying factual, detailed information, which requires time and effort to digest and act upon. In practice, these electronic methods of communication might be used at the beginning of an "influence attempt" when managers and employees are collecting information to work out how to respond to some new development, such as a change in the work setting. The sender and receiver share such information and try to persuade the other as to the best course of action to pursue. In the hours or days before the final decision is made, the sender and receiver are likely to resort to a more persuasive approach. The exchange of e-mails declines and they start to use the telephone. Depending on the level of disagreement or complexity of the issue they are dealing with, face-to-face meetings then become the communication method of choice. These face-to-face meetings allow them to process the most information, both logically and emotionally, and to arrive at the best decision.

People who are competent persuasive communicators have a good understanding of how these different methods of communication should be used. They know when and when not to send an e-mail, when it is time to make a phone call, and when it is vital to knock on the other person's door. Former President Lyndon Johnson was a master at this approach. To persuade senators to vote for his bills he would first send his aides to talk to them and give them written information. Later he would call them on the telephone to discuss the issues and further his case. Then, in the days and hours before the final vote on a bill, he would charge down to Congress, locate the "swing-vote" senators and literally push them against the wall and into a corner. There he would put his hands on their shoulders, squeeze their arms, put his face close to theirs, and either cajole or threaten them until they agreed to do what he wanted. This physical approach is very common among powerful people or people who know how to get their way. Failing to communicate persuasively can sometimes prove catastrophic, as accompanying OB Today on the space shuttle *Columbia* illustrates.

Characteristics of the Receiver. What about the receiver? Because in any influence attempt a receiver upon replying becomes a sender, much of the preceding information applies to receivers, too. Receivers, for example, can learn to enhance their credibility, use their emotional intelligence, and select the best method to transmit a message back to the sender. However, there are certain characteristics of the receiver that come into play when persuasive communication takes place.

First, receivers who are themselves highly competent and have high self-esteem are less likely to be "taken in," or swayed, by logical or emotional arguments they believe are flawed. They are more likely to be able to "cut through the chaff" to determine if the sender is acting out of personal interest or in a way that will benefit others. Then they can decide how to react to what the sender has said.

ob today

A Failure in Communication

One day before the breakup and crash of the space shuttle *Columbia* in the spring of 2003, senior NASA engineers worried that the shuttle's left wing might burn off and cause the deaths of its crew. But they never sent their warnings to NASA's top managers. After intense debate via phone and e-mail, the engineers, supervisors, and the head of the space agency's Langley research facility in Hampton, Virginia, decided against taking the matter to top NASA managers.[63]

The engineers suggested they should ask the U.S. Strategic Command to use its sophisticated ground-based imaging equipment to inspect the shuttle for damage that might have been caused by debris striking the left wing during launch. However, after asking for such help, a senior space agency official later withdrew the request before the NASA engineers had completed their analysis of how serious the tile damage problems might be. Once again, all this communication was handled by phone calls and e-mail.

Later NASA top administrator Sean O'Keefe commented that he probably should have taken part in the decision to cancel the survey, but he had not been asked directly, face-to-face, to participate, so he had just followed the debate through e-mail. Moreover, he said he had not known for most of the mission about the shuttle's problems.[64]

All these events point to the choice of the wrong method of persuasive communication. All the people involved in the investigation were communicating by e-mail and phone calls. NASA engineers knew all about the problems and risks involved and had reported them through e-mails. However, at no point had they asked for a face-to-face meeting with top managers where all the issues could be laid out on the table. Thus, even though a few NASA engineers knew there was the possibility of a potential disaster and had communicated this to middle managers electronically, this method did not persuade others, and the survey of the craft was not conducted.[65] Managers at all levels failed to request face-to-face meetings in which the engineers with firsthand knowledge could have been present to communicate their fears. The tragic event demonstrates the importance of managers knowing how to engage in and choose the right methods to communicate persuasively.

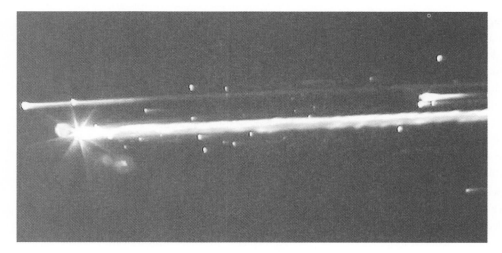

Choosing the best method of communication can be a matter of life and death, as the demise of the space shuttle Columbia in 2003 sadly illustrated. NASA engineers and mid-level managers were aware of a problem that could potentially destroy the shuttle. Because the problem was communicated only through e-mails and phone calls, however, it never made its way the organization's top decision makers.

Devil's advocate A person willing to stand up and question the beliefs of more powerful people that a planned course of action is flawed.

People with high self-esteem are very useful to have around because they are frequently the ones who will challenge the ideas or suggestions of a leader, or more senior manager, when they sense they are flawed. They act as what is known as the **devil's advocate**—a person willing to stand up and question the beliefs of more powerful people, resist influence attempts, and convince others that the planned actions are flawed. At this level, the issue of self-interest and the intent to persuade to personally benefit does come into play. Now persuasive communication extends into the realm of organizational politics, a topic we discussed in the last chapter.

In summary, the goal of persuasive communication is to sway and influence others by the kind of messages that are sent. Effective leaders, either managers, supervisors, or informal group leaders, understand the issues involved in persuasive communication and use them to promote individual, group, and organization goals.

Summary

Communication is one of the most important processes that takes place in organizations. Effective communication allows individuals, groups, and organizations to achieve their goals and perform at a high level, and it affects virtually every aspect of organizational behavior. In this chapter, we made the following major points:

1. Communication is the sharing of information between two or more individuals or groups in an organization to reach a common understanding. Communication serves four major functions in organizations: providing knowledge, motivating organizational members, controlling and coordinating individual efforts, and expressing feelings and emotions.

2. Four types of work group communication networks are the wheel, the chain, the circle, and the all-channel network. As the level of task interdependence increases in a group, so too does the need for communication between group members. When a group's task is characterized by pooled interdependence, the wheel network is likely to be used. When a group's task is characterized by sequential interdependence, a chain network is likely to be used. When a group's task is characterized by reciprocal interdependence, an all-channel network is likely to be used. An organization's actual communication network is seldom accurately depicted in its formal organization chart. Networks change as communication needs change within the organization or group.

3. The communication process entails a number of steps including the sender's encoding of the message, selection of a medium, decoding of the message by the receiver, and completing the feedback loop. Jargon (specialized language used by members of a group) facilitates communication within the group and hinders communication outside the group.

4. Filtering and information distortion, poor listening, lack of or inappropriate feedback, rumors, and cross-cultural differences in linguistic styles can all lead to ineffective communication in organizations. Communication can be improved by establishing trust and encouraging open communication, improving listening skills, developing good feedback skills, using company TVs to spread accurate information, and understanding cross-cultural differences in linguistic styles.

5. Communication media vary in information richness (the amount of information they can carry and the potential they have for enabling senders and receivers to reach a common understanding). Face-to-face communication is the medium highest in information richness. It is followed by verbal communication electronically transmitted, personally addressed written communication, and impersonal written communication. Other factors that affect the selection of a medium include how much of the sender's and receiver's time it takes and whether it leaves a paper or electronic trail.

6. Advances in information technology such as global computer networks such as the Internet generally tend to contribute most to the knowledge function of communication. Given the vast array of information currently available to organizational members, organizations have to be careful that their members are not overloaded with information. Using electronic communication to replace face-to-face communication in work groups has certain disadvantages that tend to increase as the level of task interdependence between group members increases.

7. Persuasive communication is the use of information and messages to influence others to act in the way desired by the sender.

Exercises in Understanding and Managing Organizational Behavior

Questions for Discussion and Review

1. Why is reaching a common understanding a necessary condition for communication to have taken place?

2. Why are members of an organization sometimes reluctant to express their feelings and emotions?

3. Why is feedback a necessary component of the communication process?

4. What jargon have you encountered? How did it hamper or help your understanding of messages being communicated to you?

5. Is filtering always dysfunctional? Why or why not?

6. Why do almost all organizations have grapevines?

7. Why are some people annoyed by the increasing use of voice mail in many organizations (instead of having secretaries and assistants take messages for people who are away from their desks)?

8. Is using a medium high in information richness always desirable? Why or why not?

9. How have advances in technology changed the ways that you communicate with other people on a day-to-day basis?

10. Should organizations have organization charts? If not, why not? If so, what should they be used for?

Building People Skills

Effective and Ineffective Communication

Think of two communication experiences you had in the last six months—one in which you felt that you communicated especially effectively with another individual or group (call it Communication Experience 1, or CE1) and one in which you felt that you had particularly poor communication with another individual or group (call it Communication Experience 2, or CE2). If you are working, try to pick experiences that occurred at work. Describe both experiences and then answer these questions:

1. Which of the functions of communication were served in CE1 and CE2? Which of the functions of communication should have been served in CE2 but were not?

2. Which parts of the communication process worked especially well in CE1? Which parts of the communication process failed in CE2?

3. Was any jargon used in either CE1 or CE2? If not, why not? If so, did the use of jargon lead to effective or ineffective communication?

4. Did any filtering take place in CE1 or CE2? Why or why not?

5. Were rumors or the grapevine involved in CE1 or CE2?

6. Describe the information richness of the communication media that were involved in CE1 and CE2.

7. Did either CE1 or CE2 involve the use of any advances in information technology? If so, how did these advances aid or hinder good communication?

A Question of Ethics

Communication is often used to influence other people and to persuade them to behave in ways that help an organization achieve its goals. Sometimes, however, influence and persuasion can be used for unethical purposes. Managers, for example, might persuade employees to overcharge customers for products such as legal or accounting services or encourage employees to sell expensive products to customers who obviously cannot afford to buy them. On the other hand, employees might try to persuade their managers they are doing a good job by only communicating information that makes them looks good and "hiding" the rest.

1. How can managers decide if their attempts to influence employees are ethical or unethical?
2. How can employees decide if their attempts to influence their managers or co-workers are ethical or unethical?
3. What kind of rules could be created in an organization to ensure attempts to influence and persuade others never become unethical?

Small Group Break-Out Exercise

Implementing IT in a Medical Clinic

After reading the following scenario, break up into groups of three or four people and discuss the issues involved. Be prepared to discuss your thinking with the rest of the class.

You have been called in by the doctors in a large medical clinic to advise them how to take advantage of their new information technology to improve organizational communication. Although the clinic does have an e-mail system and doctors are connected into a local area network (LAN) that allows them to post information on bulletin boards and access shared patient records, in practice they rarely use these means to communicate. Most communication takes place face-to-face when they meet each other in the coffee rooms or by playing telephone tag as they meet their busy schedules. As a communications expert, your job is to get the doctors to appreciate the potential of their new information technology.

1. What kinds of advantages can you tell the doctors they will obtain when they use the new IT?
2. How could you use persuasive communication to convince the doctors to use the new IT? Create an action plan to help the doctors learn how to use and appreciate the new IT.

Topic for Debate

Good communication is central to the functioning and effectiveness of all organizations. Now that you have a good understanding of communication in organizations, debate the following issue.

Team A. Advances in IT can make it easier for members of an organization to communicate with each other.

Team B. Advances in IT can make it more difficult for members of an organization to communicate with each other.

Experiential Exercise

Troubling Communication

Objective

Your objective is to gain experience in communicating effectively in a troublesome situation.

Procedure

The class divides into groups of three to five people, and each group appoints one member as spokesperson to present the group's conclusions to the whole class. Here is the scenario.

One group member assumes the role of David Gimenez, the supervisor of a group of chemical engineers. Another group member assumes the role of Stuart Kippling, one of the chemical engineers. The remaining members of the group are observers. Once Gimenez and Kippling assume their roles, the observers take notes on the verbal and nonverbal communication they observe as well as instances of effective and ineffective communication between the two.

For the past several months, Kippling has been designing a prototype of a new waste control processing device. He has just discovered that his device does not conform to a new Environmental Protection Agency (EPA) regulation that will go into effect in one year. This is a major setback. Although some of the design work can be salvaged, at least several weeks of work will be lost. Gimenez and Kippling are meeting in Gimenez's office to discuss the problem, why it occurred, and how it can be avoided in the future. Gimenez's position is that extrapolating from recent EPA regulations, requirements, and deliberations, Kippling should have been able to anticipate EPA's most recent ruling and take it into account in his design work, or at least he should have drawn up a contingency plan in case such a ruling was put into effect. Kippling's position is that there is no way he could have known what EPA was going to do.

1. Gimenez and Kippling assume their roles. They are meeting to discuss the problem, why it occurred, and how it can be avoided in the future. Gimenez is to meet with his boss in 15 minutes to discuss the problem, so he and Kippling have only 15 minutes to come to some kind of resolution of this matter.

2. When Gimenez and Kippling's meeting is finished, the observers should discuss the verbal and nonverbal communication they observed as well as what was particularly effective and ineffective.

3. The entire group determines which instances of communication between Gimenez and Kippling were especially effective and why and which instances of communication were especially ineffective and why.

When the group has finished those activities, the spokesperson will present the group's conclusions to the whole class.

Making the Connection

Find an example of a company that has experienced communication problems. What communication problems has this company experienced? Why did these problems occur? What steps, if any, has the company taken to solve these problems?

New York Times Cases in the News

The New York Times

Learning to Wow 'Em With Stage Presence

BY MELINDA LIGOS

Jennifer Newsom's face is bright red. Ms. Newsom, a vice president at Chubb & Son, part of the Chubb Group of Insurance Companies, is ranting to a group of colleagues about her husband, Jack. "I can't believe that Jack won't wipe the toast crumbs off the toaster!" she yells, fists clenched. With a stomp of her foot, she rattles off a list of her husband's minor imperfections, appearing to become more enraged by the moment.

But, suddenly, her face softens and her voice becomes tender. "Jack really loves our dachshund, Henry," she says, holding her hands to her heart. "He is a very sweet man."

Then she takes a bow, and her colleagues are on their feet, applauding wildly. Ms. Newsom has just finished her first exercise in a two-day workshop intended to give her more presence as a leader.

The workshop, held last month for eight Chubb vice presidents, was led by the Ariel Group, a company founded by two performers who use theatrical techniques to help business leaders improve communication skills. During the sessions—in a hotel ballroom about 45 miles west of New York City—the executives were required to scream, gesticulate wildly, jog in place, pretend to ice skate and tell tear-inducing stories about lost pets and bitter divorces. All that effort is meant to help the attendees become more effective managers and leaders.

Bringing actors into management training classes may still be unusual, but the idea could soon gain favor in business, said Deborah Brown-Volkman, a career

coach based in Long Beach, N.Y. As the economy picks up, she said, more companies may want to train their managers in how to rev up their teams.

"We're emerging from a time where workers are fatigued, and they don't necessarily believe in their companies anymore," she said. "Leaders are going to have to work to be more galvanizing."

During the first exercise in which Ms. Newsom participated, she was instructed to talk about her husband while a colleague whispered every 30 seconds into her ear, telling her a new emotion to project. The exercise was intended to teach an executive to think on the run, and to adopt different tones of voice and emotions, said Kathy Lubar, an actress and a founder of Ariel.

Ms. Lubar and Belle Halpern, a cabaret singer who is the other founder, have run similar seminars for executives from companies including Deloitte & Touche, ExxonMobil and General Electric.

The Chubb executives were all identified by their bosses as having high potential, but as needing certain advanced leadership qualities, said Bettina Kelly, worldwide manager of Chubb's training department. Some are quiet leaders, she said, who "need to step out of their shells a bit."

In the insurance industry in particular, said Sharon Emek, director of the New York City office of the CBS Coverage Group, "Most managers are not animated enough."

"Most leaders in our industry could use a little more passion," she added, "as long as it's real, instead of some sort of charade." Ms. Emek is also a board member of the Independent Insurance Agents and Brokers Association in New York.

Ms. Lubar tells her students that by using acting techniques to be more expressive and spontaneous, they will be able to connect more effectively with others. That was the goal of Ms. Newsom, 33, who said she sometimes had trouble coming across as serious in the workplace. Recently, she had to discuss the poor performance of a subordinate and did not feel that she was able to convey to that employee the seriousness of the matter. "I'm naturally upbeat and positive, which doesn't always play well when

you're in a management situation," she said.

For Kirk Voisin, a soft-spoken vice president of Chubb who moved to the United States from Trinidad 10 years ago, the workshop was a chance to become more comfortable at social events for work. In October, Mr. Voisin recalled, he was entertaining clients on a boat in Savannah, Ga., and became so weary of small talk that he retreated onto the deck. He said he was also concerned about the tone of his voice. "When I'm speaking in front of a large room of people, my voice tends to fade," he said.

Luckily for Mr. Voisin, the first afternoon of the workshop focused on voice projection. He and his colleagues were required to belt out lines spoken by Ariel in "The Tempest," using different emotions for each line. "All hail, great master! Grave sir, hail!" the executives shouted, as Ms. Halpern urged them to use the most commanding voices they could muster.

Then she instructed them to recite another line, using exaggerated hand gestures and elevated vocal tones. "Be't to fly, to swim, to dive into the fire, to ride on the curl'd clouds," they recited. Doug Vahey, a Chubb manager based in Chicago, became so involved in the activity that he nearly fell over while pretending to dive into a fire.

Next, the managers were asked to share a personal story about one of their colleagues in the room.

When Mr. Voisin rose to tell his story, Ms. Halpern made him repeat it, this time standing on a chair.

On Day 2, participants were required to act out longer stories. Judith Heim, a senior litigation counsel for Chubb, told of going with her father when she was a small child to put her dog, Rusty, to sleep. The story brought tears to the eyes of some audience members.

The final activity of the day required participants to incorporate storytelling into everyday work situations. With the help of a partner, Ms. Newsom practiced having a difficult conversation with a colleague. She used new breathing techniques to make her voice resonate more.

Mr. Voisin was the first of his peers to try his new skills back in the real world. The evening the workshop ended, he took three clients to Jean Georges, the Manhattan restaurant. "I was more emotional and projected my voice much more," said Mr. Voisin, clearly proud of his efforts. He said that he felt comfortable all evening, and that he had been able to sustain his energy through dessert. Was it the workshop that helped? "Certainly," he said. "That, and a couple of glasses of wine."

SOURCE: "Learning to Wow 'Em With Stage Presence," by Melinda Ligos, *New York Times*, December 21, 2003, p. 3.11.

Questions for Discussion

1. In what ways can developing a "stage presence" make communication more effective?

2. Take turns standing in front of a group and practice telling a story using the kinds of voice intonations and hand gestures mentioned in the story. What did you learn about communicating to a group?

The New York Times

Big Blue's Big Bet: Less Tech, More Touch

BY STEVE LOHR

People tend to underestimate Samuel J. Palmisano, the chairman and chief executive of IBM. It's not just that he is an IBM lifer, who joined Big Blue more than 30 years ago and rose through the ranks, while the famous names of the computer industry are mostly entrepreneurial founders—Bill Gates, Steve Jobs, Andy Grove, Larry Ellison, Scott McNealy.

There is also the understandable comparison with Mr. Palmisano's predecessor, Louis V. Gerstner Jr. A respected outsider, whose resume included RJR Nabisco, American Express and McKinsey & Company, Mr. Gerstner was recruited in 1993 to resurrect a fallen corporate icon. He saved the day, became a celebrity chief executive and wrote a best-selling book about the turnaround. Mr. Gerstner's manner was formal, sometimes curt; his brilliance was obvious, his comments concise, and he led from the front.

Mr. Palmisano, who is 52, is very different, from his body language to his conversation. Where Mr. Gerstner marched down a hall, Mr. Palmisano ambles. Ask him a question, and the reply often includes an informal digression or two. Tall, beefy and relaxed, he looks every inch the former college football lineman he is.

His sense of humor is reflexively self-deprecating. Earlier this month, at an IBM meeting in Las Vegas, he observed, as an aside: "I'd be a lousy politician. I don't have much curb appeal."

But if the style is understated, the moves Mr. Palmisano has made since he became chief executive less than two years ago have been bold, even risky. And if successful, his strategy promises to redefine not only IBM, but also what it means to be a computer company—making it far more a side-by-side partner with businesses, helping them improve their marketing, planning, procurement and customer service, rather than merely a supplier of hardware and software.

"The aim is to create a very deep connection between IBM and its customers, and at that level it is a very powerful strategy," said David B. Yoffie, a professor at the Harvard Business School. "But it's making IBM more like a service business with technology thrown in than a technology business."

To pursue his strategy, Mr. Palmisano needed to add expertise in business consulting and software. The largest purchases came in 2002, when he acquired PricewaterhouseCoopers Consulting for $3.5 billion and Rational Software for $2.1 billion.

More fundamental changes have come in the last year, and some are just now falling into place. In particular, IBM has shaken up its software, services and research divisions. With the addition of PwC Consulting, the big IBM services unit is more focused on executive-level business consulting instead of traditional technology services, like managing data centers for corporate customers.

This year, the 38,000 people in IBM's software group are being reorganized and retrained to focus on making and selling products tailored to the most common business problems of 12 major industries, including banking, insurance, automobiles, utilities, consumer packaged goods, telecommunications and life sciences.

Likewise, the 3,000 researchers in IBM's labs are moving well beyond the hard science of making computers and programs run faster and more efficiently. They are also focusing on solving business problems and modeling patterns of human behavior, giving their work more of the flavor of social science. "I think it's a huge opportunity, but it is also a huge cultural change in research," said Paul M. Horn, the director of IBM labs.

In an e-mail message to his senior management team on Oct. 29, 2002, Mr. Palmisano wrote. "While they share many attributes, there is one thing that sets all great companies apart—they define and lead the agendas for their industries. This has been a hallmark of IBM throughout its history."

"We now see an opportunity to set the agenda again," he added. He concluded: "I am confident that we are on the verge of the next great opportunity for our company, and for the entire information technology industry."

A day later, Mr. Palmisano announced the on-demand campaign to an audience of corporate customers, industry analysts and journalists, at the American Museum of Natural History in Manhattan. Next, IBM's huge advertising budget—$500 million a year—began promoting "e-business on demand."

Initially, rivals heaped derision on the marketing campaign. Then most of them mimicked it. These days, Hewlett-Packard speaks of its corporate offerings as its "adaptive enterprise initiative"; Microsoft says its offerings will make companies "agile" businesses; and Computer Associates simply copied the "on demand" phrase.

In late January 2003, IBM held its annual worldwide management committee meeting at a company conference center in upstate New York. At the two-day session, there was a lengthy discussion of how to harness the company's resources around the on-demand vision—until Mr. Palmisano cut it short. "I was listening very patiently, and they were very sincere," he recalled. "These are some very good people." But all the discussion was about internal moves.

So he told everyone to go out and talk to customers about their most nettlesome business problems, and to try to figure out how IBM might be able to help solve them. "If they got out there and actually solved the problem with the client," he said, "they would understand what we needed to do."

They found that a team approach was required, typically involving the sales executive in charge of a corporate account, a representative from the services division, a person in the software unit and, increasingly, someone from the research labs. At IBM, this team approach is called "four in a box." Previously, the common pattern had been "two in a box": a sales manager and a services person.

The reorganization of the company's software around 12 industry groups grew out of those meetings with clients. The hardware systems business is following suit, tailoring its server computers with specialized features for specific industries like telecommunications and banking.

"So once they all got into the marketplace, they all saw it and it just took off," Mr. Palmisano said. When the management committee holds its yearly meeting this week, internal organization, he noted, will not be on the agenda. "For us to deliver the value of on demand, we had to reintegrate IBM," he said. "That's really what we've been doing for the last 15 months."

SOURCE: "Big Blue's Big Bet: Less Tech, More Touch," by Steve Lohr, *New York Times*, January 25, 2003, p. 3.1.

Questions for Discussion

1. What kind of people, groups, and organizations is Sam Palmisano trying to persuade and influence?

2. What kinds of communications media does he makes use of?

3. Why is communication with customers so important to IBM?

Decision Making and Organizational Learning

LEARNING OBJECTIVES

After reading this chapter, you should be able to:

■

Differentiate between nonprogrammed and programmed decisions and explain why nonprogrammed decision making is a complex, uncertain process.

■

Explain the difference between the two main models of decision making and describe which is the more realistic.

■

Discuss the main sources of error in decision making.

■

Describe the advantages and disadvantages of group decision making and explain the techniques that can be used to improve it.

■

Understand how organizational learning can improve decision making and explain the steps involved in creating a learning organization.

OPENING CASE

A Big Turnaround in Nike's Decision Making

In What Ways Has Decision Making at Nike Changed?

Nike, headquartered in Beaverton, Oregon, is the biggest sports shoemaker in the world. In the 1990s, it seemed that its founder and CEO Phil Knight and his team of shoe designers could put no foot wrong, and all their design decisions led to global acceptance of Nike's shoes and record sales and profits for the company. At the heart of Nike's business plan was its decision to design very expensive high-performance shoes that often sold for more than $100. Frequently, the shoes were touted by celebrities like Michael Jordan and Tiger Woods.[1]

As time went on, however, and Nike's fortunes soared, some strange dynamics took place. The company's managers and designers became convinced they "knew best" what customers needed and that their choices and decisions about future shoe lines would unquestionably be well received by customers who would continue to flock to buy their new creations.

But things were changing in the sports shoe environment. Many new competitors had entered the market, and they began to offer alternative kinds of sports shoes targeted at specific market segments such as skateboarders, soccer players, and power walkers. Nike had no shoes in these market segments. Moreover, Nike also failed to notice that sports shoes were evolving into performance shoes for more everyday uses such as walking and backpacking. It also failed to take note of consumers' increasing preferences for dark blue and black shoes that wore well in cities and that could double as work and walking shoes.

By the end of the 1990s, Nike's sales and profits started to fall sharply. Many of its new lines of sports shoes were not well received by customers, and CEO Phil Knight knew he had to find a way to turn around his company's performance. Realizing that his designers were starting to make poor decisions, he decided to bring in people from outside the company to try to change the way decisions were made. One of these was an executive named Gordon O. McFadden, who was brought in to lead the outdoor products division. He advised Knight to take over and purchase some of these small companies, such as North Face, to quickly widen Nike's product line. But Nike's managers and designers resisted this idea believing that they could still make the best decisions and that Nike should continue to grow its product lines from within. So McFadden quit.[2]

By 2000, with sales still slumping, it became obvious Nike would have to take over some competing shoe companies to grow successfully. One of the first of its acquisitions was ColeHann, the luxury shoemaker, and Nike's designers proceeded to revitalize its line of shoes by using their skills to make them more comfortable. Then, realizing it had to get into small markets, in 2002, Nike bought other small companies such as Hurley, the skate and surfboard apparel maker.

To try to overcome its past errors in decision making, however, Knight decided on a new way to design shoes for specialized niche markets, such as the skateboarding, golf, and soccer markets. Henceforth, rather than having Nike's designers all grouped together in one large design department, they would be split up into different teams. Each team would focus on developing unique products to match the needs of customers in its assigned market segment. The skate team, for example, was set up as a separate and independent unit, and its 11 designers and marketing experts were charged with coming up with a unique line of shoes for the sport. Similarly, because of poor sales, Nike separated golf products from the rest of the company and created an independent unit to develop new golf shoes, clubs, and other golfing products.[3]

What Nike was trying to accomplish with the change was to obliterate the company-wide, decision-making mind-set that had resulted in past decision-making errors. With many different teams, each working on different lines of shoes and other products, Nike was hoping to build diversity into its decision making and create teams of experts who were attuned to changing customer needs in their segments of the sports product market.

So far, it seems that Nike's new approach to decision making is working better. Many of its new products lines have been well received, and its sales and profits have started to rebound. Nike has apparently learned from its mistakes. Indeed, Knight is trying to promote organizational learning—the process of helping the members of an organization to "think outside the box" and be willing to experiment, take risks, and be different. Knight's current willingness to delegate authority and empower the different units to take responsibility for their own product lines is one example of this.

Making decisions is an essential part of behavior in organizations. Good decisions help individuals, groups, and organizations achieve their goals and perform well. Bad decisions hinder goal attainment and lower performance. Nike's experience illustrates the way in which the quality of decision making can change quickly over time in a company. It suggests how complex the process of making good decisions can be and how factors at the individual and group levels (such as people's personalities and the company's rules, values, and norms) can affect it. Decision making is one more important organizational behavior we need to understand.

In this chapter, we discuss how members of organizations make decisions. We examine the types of decisions that need to be made in organizations and the decision-making process. We explore some biases and problems in decision making. We look at the pros and cons of using groups instead of individuals to make decisions and some of the issues involved in group decision making. Finally, we discuss how a company can encourage organizational learning to both maintain and improve the quality of its decision making over time. By the end of the chapter, you will understand how decision making is a crucial determinant of whether or not individuals, groups, and organizations perform at a high level and achieve their goals.

Types of Decisions

In previous chapters, we discussed some of the choices that organizational members make every day—decisions ranging from how managers should motivate and reward subordinates to what is the best way for subordinates to communicate important information to their supervisors and to how group members should respond to a deviant co-worker. Making such choices is the essence of decision making. In fact, **decision making** can be defined as the process by which members of an organization choose a specific course of action to respond to the opportunities and problems that confront them. Good decisions help an individual, group, or organization be effective. Bad decisions hinder effectiveness and result in poor performance and negative attitudes at all organizational levels.

Decision making The process by which members of an organization choose a specific course of action to respond to both opportunities and problems.

Decision making in response to *opportunities* occurs when members of an organization make choices or act in ways that result in benefits or gains. Such decisions range from those made by an upper-level manager in a successful electronics company trying to decide whether to market the firm's products in Europe to a telephone operator at the same company deciding whether to take an online business course to expand his or her skills and opportunities. Individuals, groups, and entire organizations reach their full potential only when they take advantage of opportunities to increase their efficiency and effectiveness. Many famous managers such as Andrew Grove, former CEO of Intel, and Steve Jobs, who was fired as CEO of Apple but is now its current CEO, suggest that successful companies often fail because they get complacent, fail to take advantage of opportunities, or misread the way the future of their industry is changing. Thus, managers at Intel and Apple are constantly on the lookout for new opportunities and spend a lot of time figuring out how to respond to them.[4]

Decision making in response to *problems* occurs when individual, group, or organizational goal attainment and performance are threatened. A doctor's goal to provide good medical care in a rural community is threatened when the doctor lacks the financial resources to purchase medical equipment. A production group's goal of winning the monthly quality contest is threatened when two of its members engage in social loafing. And an organization's goal of being profitable is threatened when the top management team experiences communication problems. Through the decision-making process, organizational members choose how to respond to these and other kinds of problems.

Whether they are responding to a potential opportunity or deciding how to solve a problem, two basic types of decisions are made in organizations: nonprogrammed decisions and programmed decisions.

NONPROGRAMMED DECISIONS

Nonprogrammed decision making Decision making in response to novel opportunities and problems.

When members of an organization choose how to respond to new or novel opportunities and problems, they engage in **nonprogrammed decision making**.[5] Nonprogrammed decision making involves searching for the extra information that is needed to make the right choice.[6] Because the problem or opportunity has not been experienced before, members of the organization are uncertain about how they should respond and, thus, they search for any information they can find to help them make their decision.

Mike Castiglioni, the manager of a successful Italian restaurant called Ciao! in a small Texas town, for example, was confronted with a novel problem when a nationwide Italian restaurant chain, The Olive Garden, opened a new restaurant a few blocks away. The arrival of a strong competitor posed a novel problem for Mike; previously, Ciao! had been the only Italian restaurant in town. Similarly, staff members at Ciao! faced new potential employment opportunities when The Olive Garden advertised for waiters and waitresses.

As soon as he learned The Olive Garden was planning to open a restaurant, Mike tried to find out as much as he could about his new competitor—its lunch and dinner menus and prices, the kinds of customers it appeals to, the quality of its food, and so on. Mike also traveled to the nearby cities of Houston and Dallas and ate in several Olive Garden restaurants to sample the food and ambience and record customer traffic.

As a result of these search activities, Mike decided that the quality of the food he served at Ciao! was better and that the prices the two restaurants charged were similar. The Olive Garden, however, had a wider selection of menu items and offered a soup or salad with every entrée. Mike decided to expand his menu by adding three new items to the lunch menu and four to the dinner menu. He also decided to serve a house salad with all entrées, which would appeal to his health-conscious customers. As a result of his search for information, Mike Castiglioni was able to decide how to respond to the problem of competition in a successful way, and Ciao! continues to thrive despite its new competition.

PROGRAMMED DECISIONS

Programmed decision making Decision making in response to recurring opportunities and problems.

Performance program A standard sequence of behaviors that organizational members follow routinely whenever they encounter a particular type of problem or opportunity.

Although members of an organization frequently make unprogrammed decisions, they also need to engage in **programmed decision making**—that is, making decisions in response to recurring opportunities and problems.[7] To make a programmed decision, the decision maker uses a **performance program**, a standard sequence of behaviors that organizational members follow routinely whenever they encounter a particular type of problem or opportunity.[8] Department stores develop performance programs that specify how salespeople should respond to customers who return items that have been worn and are defective. Grocery stores develop performance programs that indicate how clerks should respond when sale items are out of stock. Universities develop performance programs dictating how to deal with students who cannot complete their courses.

Organizations develop performance programs whenever the same kinds of opportunities or problems keep cropping up. After a performance program is developed, members of the organization initiate the performance program almost automatically as soon as the opportunity or problem is encountered. They do not have to search for information or think about what they should do in response. Organizational rules (see Chapter 10) are types of performance programs developed to help members make programmed decisions.

FIGURE 15.1
Nonprogrammed and Programmed Decision Making

Because of improvements in the local economy, Mike Castiglioni was faced with the recurring problem of Ciao!'s experienced waiters and waitresses being offered jobs at The Olive Garden and other new restaurants opening up in town. Although the waiters and waitresses at Ciao! were generally satisfied with their jobs, they interviewed at some of the new restaurants to see whether they could earn more money and get better benefits or working hours. Periodically, waiters or waitresses came to Mike and told him that they had been offered better benefits or working hours by one of his competitors. The first couple of times this happened, Mike needed to make a *nonprogrammed* decision because the problem was relatively novel. Accordingly, he searched for information to help him with his decision: How costly would it be to hire and train a new waiter or waitress? How important was it to have experienced waiters and waitresses who knew many of Ciao!'s regular customers? As a result of his search for information, Mike concluded that, whenever possible, he should try to retain as many of Ciao!'s waiters and waitresses as he could by matching the hourly rates, benefits, and working hours they were offered at other restaurants.

After Mike made this decision, whenever waiters or waitresses came to him and told him of better job offers they received, he matched the offers whenever he could. Mike Castiglioni essentially decided on a standard response to a recurring problem—the essence of *programmed* decision making and the use of performance programs.

As this example illustrates, performance programs often evolve from nonprogrammed decisions. Essentially, if what was once a novel problem or opportunity keeps recurring, it calls for a programmed decision, and the organization comes up with a standard response or performance program (see Figure 15.1).

Performance programs save time because they make it unnecessary for organizational members to search for information to make a decision; instead, all they need to do is follow the performance program. Managers, however, must be able to realize when performance programs need to be changed and take the steps necessary to alter them. Organizations tend to be slow to change performance programs because doing things the way they have always been done in the past is often easier than devising and implementing new procedures.

The Decision-Making Process

When people think of decision making in organizations, the kinds of decisions they usually have in mind are nonprogrammed decisions involving a search for new and necessary information. Thus, in the remainder of this chapter, we focus on nonprogrammed decisions. Whenever we use the term *decision,* we are referring to a *nonprogrammed* decision. Two widely studied models of the decision-making process are the classical decision-making model and James March and Herbert Simon's administrative decision-making model.

THE CLASSICAL MODEL OF DECISION MAKING

The **classical decision-making model** is a *prescriptive model;* it describes how people *should* make decisions.[9] This model rests on two assumptions: (1) People have access to all the information they need to make a decision, and (2) people make decisions by choosing the best possible solution to a problem or response to an opportunity.[10] According to the classical model, a decision maker should choose how to respond to opportunities and problems by engaging in these four steps:[11]

1. Listing all alternatives from which a choice will be selected: These alternatives represent different responses to the problem or the opportunity.

2. Listing the consequences of each alternative: The consequences are what would occur if a given alternative were selected.

3. Considering his or her own preferences for each alternative or set of consequences and then ranking the sets from most preferred to least preferred.

4. Selecting the alternative that will result in the most preferred set of consequences.

According to the classical model, if members of an organization follow those four steps, they will make optimal decisions, given the decision maker's preferences.[12] Do members of an organization actually make decisions according to the classical model? If they do not, could they make better decisions if they did? The answer to both questions is "no" because of several basic problems with the classical model.

The classical model is unrealistic.[13] Its assumption that decision makers have all the information needed to make optimal decisions bears little resemblance to the conditions facing most organizations. Even if the decision makers did have all necessary information, they probably would not be able to use it all. This is because the cognitive abilities of decision makers are limited; often they cannot take into account the large quantities of information available to them.

One way to consider the difficulties of the classical model is to compare the four steps described previously to actual decision making in organizations. With regard to the first step, decision makers often *do not know all the alternatives* they can choose from.[14] One of the defining features of nonprogrammed decisions is that they involve an extensive search for information. Even after this search is complete, however, it is likely that decision makers are aware of only some of the possible alternatives.

For example, the challenge facing Sarah Hunter, a marketing manager at a Fortune 500 food products company, was to solve the problem of lackluster sales of a line of frozen desserts. Hunter's search for alternatives yielded three potential solutions to the problem: (1) The company could launch a series of newspaper and magazine advertisements with coupons; (2) the company could negotiate with major grocery store chains to give the desserts a more visible location (at eye level) in the frozen foods sections; or (3) the company could develop a series of expensive television ads airing during prime time. Hunter's information search failed to uncover other alternatives: (1) rename the products, (2) change the products' packaging, (3) reorient the packaging and marketing of some of the products to appeal to certain segments of the market (for example, pitch angel food cake to health-conscious adults and frozen yogurt bars to young children), and (4) dropping the line altogether.

In the second step of the classical model, decision makers list the consequences of each alternative. As in the first step, however, decision makers often *do not know all of the consequences* that will ensue if they choose a given alternative.[15] One reason it's hard to make decisions is that the decision maker often does not know what will happen if a given course of action is chosen. Sarah Hunter did not know whether coupons in newspapers and magazines would significantly boost sales because her company had experienced mixed success with this approach in the past. She knew that television ads were likely to increase sales, but it was not clear whether the increase in sales would be temporary or long lasting or be large enough to offset the high costs of purchasing airtime in prime viewing hours.

As the third step in the classical model, decision makers must consider their own preferences for sets of consequences. Once again, the classical model assumes that decision makers are able to rank sets of consequences and know their own preferences.[16] However, decision makers *don't always know for sure what they want.* Stop and think about some of the important and difficult decisions you have had to make. Sometimes these decisions were difficult to make precisely because *you weren't sure what you wanted.* A graduating senior with an accounting degree from the University of Wisconsin, for example, finds it hard to choose between a job offer from a Wisconsin bank and one from a major accounting firm in New York City because he doesn't know whether he prefers the security of staying in Wisconsin, where most of his family and friends are, to the excitement of living in a big city and the opportunity to work for a major firm. Similarly, Sarah Hunter did not know whether she preferred to dramatically improve frozen dessert sales or improve them just enough to maintain profitability and then move on to another product line.

Because of these problems with the first three steps in the classical model, (1) *it is often impossible for an organization's members to make the best possible decisions,* and (2) *even if they make a good decision, the time, effort, and cost that were spent making it might not be worthwhile.*[17] Realizing these problems with the classical model, James March and Herbert Simon developed a more realistic account of decision making: the administrative decision-making model.[18]

MARCH AND SIMON'S ADMINISTRATIVE MODEL OF DECISION MAKING

The classical model is prescriptive; it indicates how decisions *should* be made. In contrast, March and Simon's **administrative decision-making model** is *descriptive;* it explains how people *actually make* decisions in organizations.[19] March and Simon stress that incomplete information and the decision maker's cognitive abilities and psychological makeup affect decision making. Consequently decision makers often choose *satisfactory,* not optimal, solutions.[20]

According to the administrative decision-making model, decision makers choose how to respond to opportunities and problems on the basis of a simplified and approximate account of the situation—the decision maker's definition of it, in other words. Decision makers do not take into account all information relevant to a problem or opportunity, nor do they consider all possible alternatives and their consequences.

Sarah Hunter did not consider renaming or changing the packaging of the frozen desserts, or reorienting them to appeal to certain segments of the market, or even recommending that the company drop the products altogether. She did not define the situation in those terms. She defined the situation in terms of increasing sales of existing products, not changing the products to make them more attractive to customers. In addition, the thought of dropping the line never entered her mind, although that is what the company ended up doing two years later.

Decision makers may follow some of the steps in the classical model, such as generating alternatives and considering the consequences of the alternatives and their own preferences. But the information they consider is based on their definition of the situation, which is the result of psychological and sociological factors. Psychological factors include the decision maker's personality, ability, perceptions, experiences, and knowledge. Sociological factors include the groups, organization, and organizational and national culture of which the decision maker is a member.

The alternatives Sarah Hunter considered and, more generally, her definition of the situation were based in part on two factors. One was her past marketing

Administrative decision-making model A descriptive approach stressing that incomplete information, psychological and sociological processes, and the decision maker's cognitive abilities affect decision making and that decision makers often choose satisfactory, not optimal, solutions.

experiences: She had always worked on improving and maintaining sales of "successful" products. The other was the marketing department in which she worked. It was quite conservative. For example, it rarely made changes to product names and packaging, it had introduced few new products in the past 10 years, and it had not dropped an existing product in 12 years' time.

Satisficing Searching for and choosing an acceptable response or solution, not necessarily the best possible one.

Satisficing. Rather than making optimal decisions, organizational members often engage in **satisficing**—that is, they search for and choose *acceptable* responses to opportunities and problems, not necessarily the *best* possible responses.[21] One way that decision makers can satisfice is by listing criteria that would lead to an acceptable choice and picking an alternative that meets the criteria. When deciding among many job applicants to hire, for example, organizations often satisfice by listing criteria that an acceptable candidate should meet (such as having an appropriate degree from a college or university, job-related experience, and good interpersonal skills) and then choosing a candidate who meets the criteria. If organizations were to make the optimal hiring decision rather than a satisfactory one, they would have to pick the best candidate—the person with the best educational background, prior experience, and interpersonal skills. Often it would be very difficult and time-consuming (if not impossible) to do this.

Ethical Decision Making. One criterion of a satisfactory decision in any organization is that it be *ethical*. Ethical decisions promote well-being and do not cause harm to members of an organization or to other people affected by an organization's activities. Although it is easy to describe what an ethical decision is, sometimes it is difficult to determine the boundary between ethical and unethical decisions in an organization. Is it ethical, for example, for a pharmaceutical company to decide to charge a high price for a lifesaving drug, thus making it unaffordable to some people? On the one hand, it can be argued that the drug is costly to produce and the company needs the revenues to continue producing the drug as well as to research ways to improve its effectiveness. On the other hand, it can be argued that the company has a moral or ethical obligation to make the drug available to as many people as possible. In 2004, for example, Sheering Plough raised the price of its best-selling AIDS prevention drug by 500 percent, causing an uproar among doctors and patients who claimed that this would lead to great hardship for patients, many of whom would no longer be able to afford it. Sheering Plough simply said that it had been charging too low a price for its valuable drug and that it had the right to increase its price.

Some people deliberately make unethical decisions to benefit themselves or their organizations, but even decision makers who strive to be ethical are sometimes faced with difficult choices or ethical dilemmas. Under these circumstances, satisficing, or making acceptable decisions that are ethical, can be difficult. One example of blatantly unethical decision making by pharmaceutical companies occurred in 1999 when six of them admitted they had conspired to artificially raise the price of vitamins, such as vitamins A, B^2, C, E, and beta carotene. Swiss giant Hoffman-La Roche agreed to pay $500 million in criminal fines, and German Company BASF paid a $225 million fine; the others were also fined large amounts.[22] How could this happen?

Senior managers from each of these companies' vitamin divisions jointly made the decision to inflate their division's profits and to act unethically at the expense of consumers. In several meetings around the world, they worked out the details of the plot, which went undiscovered for several years. Many of the top managers involved have been prosecuted in their home countries, and all have been fired. BASF, for example, completely replaced its worldwide management team.[23]

What has been the end result of this fiasco for these companies? All have agreed to create a special "ethics officer" position within their organizations. The ethics officer is responsible for developing new ethical standards with regard to how decisions are made. The ethics officer is also responsible for listening to employees' complaints about unethical behavior, training employees to make ethical decisions, and counseling top managers to prevent further wrongdoing.

Bounded Rationality. Unlike the classical model, which disregards the cognitive limitations of the decision maker, March and Simon acknowledge that decision makers are constrained by **bounded rationality**—an ability to reason that is restricted by the limitations of the human mind itself. March and Simon's model assumes that bounded rationality is a fact of organizational life. Members of an organization try to act rationally and make good decisions that benefit the organization, but their rationality is limited by their own cognitive abilities.[24] It is often impossible for decision makers to simultaneously consider all the information relevant to a decision (even if it were available) and use all this information to make an optimal choice. Even though the information provided by advances in IT can help members of an organization make better decisions, rationality is always limited, or bounded, by the capabilities of the human mind. Thus, decision makers approach decisions on the basis of their own subjective definitions of the situation, and they usually satisfice rather than optimize.[25]

When members of an organization realize that decision making proceeds more often as described by March and Simon than as outlined in the classical model, they are better able to understand why both good and bad decisions are made in organizations and how decision making can be improved. Good decisions are often made when decision makers are able to identify and focus on the key aspects of the situation. Bad decisions may result from defining a situation improperly.

How did Sarah Hunter, in our earlier example, define the situation she was in? She believed that her challenge was to improve sales of an existing product rather than to change the product or evaluate whether it should be dropped. Her definition of the situation limited the potential solutions she considered. Only after trying two of those solutions and failing did she and her company realize the need to redefine the situation and recognize that the product line needed to be either dramatically changed or dropped.

In summary, it is important to realize that different members of an organization are going to define the same problem or opportunity in different ways, depending on their personalities, abilities, knowledge, expertise, and the groups they belong to. As a result, decision makers need to carefully examine how they define opportunities and problems and the implications these definitions have. To help improve decision making, it is important to focus on the information most relevant to the decision at hand and be cognizant of the sources of decision-making errors. We discuss these sources of errors next.

Bounded rationality
An ability to reason that is constrained by the limitations of the human mind itself.

Sources of Error in Decision Making

Given that decision makers often do not have all the information they need to make a good decision and are boundedly rational, it is not surprising that a variety of sources of error in decision making exists.[26] Some of these sources of error are pervasive and recurring.[27] Many decision makers succumb to these errors and make less than satisfactory decisions because of them.[28] Two major sources of error arise from (1) the shortcuts, or rules of thumb, people use to make decisions, which can lead to both good and bad decisions, and (2) the human tendency to throw good money after bad and continue involvement in unfruitful activities.

HEURISTICS AND THE BIASES THEY MAY LEAD TO

Given the number and complexity of the many decisions that people have to make at work and in their personal lives, it is not surprising that they often try to simplify things or use certain rules of thumb to help them make decisions. The rules of thumb that help

Heuristics Rules of thumb that simplify decision making.

people simplify decision making are called **heuristics**.[29] Heuristics are involved in much of the decision making that takes place in organizations; people tend to use them without even knowing they are doing so. Because they simplify matters, heuristics can aid in the decision-making process, but they can also lead to *biases*—systematic errors in decision making.[30] Three common rules of thumb are availability heuristics, representativeness heuristics, and anchoring and adjustment heuristics (see Figure 15.2). We discuss each of these next.

Availability Heuristic. When making decisions, organizational members often have to judge the frequency with which different events will occur and their likely causes. The **availability heuristic** reflects the tendency to determine the frequency of an event and its causes by how easy these events and causes are to remember (that is, how *available* they are from memory).[31] People tend to judge an event that is easy to remember as occurring more frequently than an event that is difficult to remember. Likewise, if a potential cause of an event comes to mind quickly, people are likely to think that it is an important causal factor.

Availability heuristic The rule of thumb that says an event that is easy to remember is likely to have occurred more frequently than an event that is difficult to remember.

The availability heuristic can aid decision making because events and causes that actually do occur frequently come easily to mind. However, factors other than frequency of occurrence also determine the availability of information that can be recalled. As a result, the availability heuristic can cause certain biases to enter into decision making. One such bias is the overestimation of the frequency of *vivid* or *extreme* events and their causes because they are easy to remember.[32] Another is the overestimation of the frequency of *recent* events and their causes because they also tend to be easy to remember.[33]

When Sarah Hunter was trying to decide how to increase sales of frozen desserts, for example, she remembered that one of her co-employees recently experienced dramatic success boosting fruit drink sales with a series of advertisements and coupons placed in magazines and Sunday newspaper supplements. The fact that the success was *recent* and *extreme* led Hunter to *overestimate* the extent to which this approach would increase the sales of her product line. This same bias led her to ignore instances in which the same kinds of advertisements and coupons failed to improve the sales of other products. As a result of the biases emanating from the availability heuristic, Hunter decided to place advertisements and coupons in magazines and Sunday supplements in the hope of increasing frozen dessert sales—a strategy that ultimately proved to be unsuccessful.

Representativeness heuristic The rule of thumb that says similar kinds of events that happened in the past are a good predictor of the likelihood of an upcoming event.

Representativeness Heuristic. The **representativeness heuristic** reflects the tendency to predict the likelihood of an event occurring from the extent to which the event is typical (or *representative*) of similar kinds of events that have happened in the past.[34] A manager in the United States trying to determine whether a domestically popular hand cream will sell in Spain, for example, compares the extent to which Spain

FIGURE 15.2
Heuristics and the Biases They May Lead To

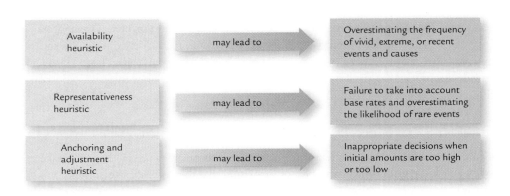

Availability heuristic	may lead to	Overestimating the frequency of vivid, extreme, or recent events and causes
Representativeness heuristic	may lead to	Failure to take into account base rates and overestimating the likelihood of rare events
Anchoring and adjustment heuristic	may lead to	Inappropriate decisions when initial amounts are too high or too low

is similar to foreign countries in which the cream has sold especially well or to countries in which the cream has not sold well. The manager decides not to export the hand cream to Spain because Spain is typical of the countries in which the product had bombed (the cream had bombed in other Spanish-speaking countries, for example).

The representativeness heuristic can sometimes be a good shortcut used to estimate the likelihood of an upcoming event because the fact that similar kinds of events happened in the past may be a good predictor of the upcoming event.[35] Sometimes, however, this heuristic can cause decision makers to disregard important information about the frequency of events. In such cases, the representativeness heuristic leads to biased decision making.

One source of bias emanating from the representativeness heuristic is the failure to take into account the **base rate**, or the actual frequency with which events occur.[36] The manager in the hand cream example should have considered the number of times the hand cream did not sell well in foreign countries. If he had, he would have found that the product sold well in *most* countries to which it was exported and that its failure in foreign markets was rare. Using this information in the decision-making process would have told the manager that chances that the cream would sell well in Spain were pretty high. However, the manager did not take this base-rate information into account. He decided not to export the hand cream to Spain and missed out on a good opportunity. To avoid the pitfalls of the representativeness heuristic, it is important to take base rates into account because it is likely that common events (the hand cream's high sales in foreign countries) will occur again and that rare events (the product's failure in a few countries, some of which were Spanish speaking) will not occur again.

Base rate The actual frequency with which an event occurs.

Anchoring and Adjustment Heuristic.

The **anchoring and adjustment heuristic** reflects the tendency to make decisions based on adjustments from some initial amount (or *anchor*).[37] Decisions about salary increases are often made by choosing a percentage increase from an employee's current salary. Budget decisions are often made by deciding whether the current budget should be increased or decreased. Decisions about the degree to which costs must be cut are often based on the current level of costs. In situations such as these, if the initial amounts are reasonable, then the anchoring and adjustment heuristic might be a good shortcut for decision making.

By using this heuristic, decision makers need to consider only the degree to which the current level needs to be changed. They do not, for example, need to determine a person's salary from scratch or build a budget from ground zero. But if the original amount from which a decision or adjustment is made is *not* reasonable, the anchoring and adjustment heuristic will lead to biased decision making. If employees' current salary levels are low in comparison to what they could be earning in similar kinds of jobs and companies, even a relatively large percentage increase (such as 15 percent) may still leave them underpaid. Likewise, if a department's budget is much too high, a 10 percent decrease will lead to the department's still being allocated more money than it really needs.

Anchoring and adjustment heuristic The rule of thumb that says that decisions about how big or small an amount (such as a salary, budget, or level of costs) should be can be made by making adjustments from some initial amount.

ESCALATION OF COMMITMENT

A second source of error in decision making (in addition to biases) is **escalation of commitment**, the tendency of decision makers to invest additional time, money, or effort into what are essentially bad decisions or unproductive courses of action that are already draining the organization's resources.[38] Here is a typical escalation-of-commitment scenario: (1) A decision maker initially makes a decision that results in some kind of loss or negative outcome. (2) Rather than change the course of action contained in the initial decision, the decision maker commits more time, money, or

Escalation of commitment The tendency to invest additional time, money, or effort into what are essentially bad decisions or unproductive courses of action.

Escalation of commitment proved to be undoing of President Lyndon Johnson in the 1960s. Johnson believed that pulling out of Vietnam would be seen as a sign of weakness by the world. Instead, he continued to send troops and equipment to Vietnam to fight a war the United States ultimately lost.

effort to the course of action. (3) Further losses are experienced because of this escalation of commitment to a failing course of action. Escalation of commitment is graphically illustrated in Figure 15.3.

Sarah Hunter experienced escalation of commitment in her quest to improve sales of frozen desserts. First, she embarked on a series of magazine and newspaper ads. When this approach failed to boost sales and the money was spent, she decided to negotiate with grocery store chains to make the products more visible in their frozen foods sections. This was difficult to do, but she nonetheless persevered and was successful at getting it done. This strategy, however, also failed to boost sales. Instead of reassessing her original decision to try to boost frozen dessert sales, Hunter gave her boss a proposal for a series of expensive television advertisements. Luckily for the organization, the boss denied her request and halted her escalation of commitment.

FIGURE 15.3

Escalation of Commitment

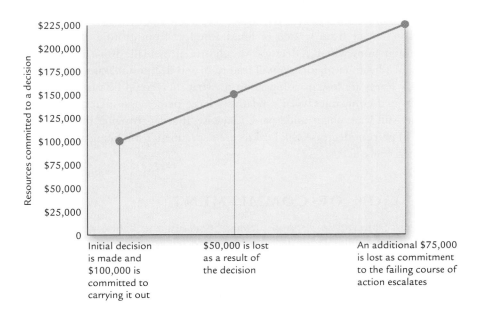

Escalation of commitment is common in organizations (even at top management levels) and in people's personal lives. Investors in stocks and real estate, for example, often continue to invest in losing ventures, pouring good money after bad. Why does escalation of commitment occur, even among presumably knowledgeable decision makers? There appear to be at least three causes of this type of faulty decision making:

1. *Decision makers often do not want to admit to themselves or to others that they have made a mistake.*[39] Rather than reassess the wisdom of their original decision in light of the negative consequences they have experienced, decision makers commit more resources to the course of action in order to reconfirm the "correctness" of the original decision.

2. *Given the amount of money or resources that has been lost, decision makers erroneously believe that an additional commitment of resources is justified to recoup some of those losses.*[40] When the newspaper and magazine ads and the increased visibility in the grocery stores failed to boost sales, what did Sarah Hunter do? She decided that after investing so much time, effort, and money into boosting sales, she had no alternative but to push ahead with the TV ads. The costs that she has already incurred, however, were **sunk costs**—costs that could not be recovered or affected by subsequent decision making. The sunk costs should not have entered into Hunter's decision making.

3. *Decision makers tend to take more risks when they frame or view decisions in negative terms (for example, as a way to recover money that has been lost) rather than in positive terms (for example, as a way to generate more money).*[41] When Sarah Hunter originally thought about TV ads, she decided against them because they were too risky; they would cost too much money given the uncertainty about whether or not they would boost sales. At that point, Hunter had spent no resources on boosting sales; the TV ads were framed (in her mind) in positive terms: as a way to boost sales. But after her first two strategies failed, the TV ads were framed in negative terms: as a way to recover some of the time, effort, and money she had already spent unsuccessfully trying to boost sales. Once the decision was framed negatively, Hunter was willing to risk the high cost of the ads.[42]

Biases resulting from escalation of commitment and the use of heuristics can result in poor decision making at all levels in an organization. This problem is compounded by the fact that decision makers often use heuristics without being aware that they are doing so. Escalation of commitment also occurs without decision makers realizing that they are throwing good money after bad. No matter how knowledgeable a decision maker is, the potential for poor decision making as a result of biases and the escalation of commitment is always present.

THE ROLE OF INFORMATION TECHNOLOGY (IT)

The use of IT can often help to reduce the effect of these biases and heuristics on decision making.[43] IT systems can generate much more information on which managers can base their decisions. Likewise, new software programs can generate improved tables and charts making the data more meaningful to managers. This in, turn, can reduce the effects of the availability and representativeness biases.[44]

Additionally, because IT can be used to link managers at different levels and in different parts of the organization, there is less likelihood of their making errors. For example, the escalation-of-commitment bias is likely to become far less of a problem when more objective information is available that a serious problem does exist in the organization. Managers with different perspectives can simultaneously examine that

Sunk costs Costs that cannot be reversed and will not be affected by subsequent decision making.

information before deciding what to do. IT can also turn many nonprogrammed decisions into programmed ones. For example, when salespeople can turn to online databases and software programs to access instant solutions for their customers, this frees up their time to make more sales calls or provide better-quality customer service. At all levels in the organization, the application of IT allows managers to spend more time making nonprogrammed decisions that can enhance organizational performance. The accompanying Global View profiles how the enterprise resource planning system designed and sold by the German IT company SAP can improve the quality of organizational decision making. An *enterprise resource planning (ERP) system* is a company-wide intranet based on multimodule software that allows an organization to link and coordinate its functional activities and operations.

global view

SAP's ERP System

SAP is the world's leading supplier of ERP software; it introduced the world's first ERP system in 1973. So great was the demand for its software that it had to train thousands of consultants from companies such as IBM, HP, Accenture, and Cap Gemini to install and customize its software to meet the needs of companies in different industries around the world.[45]

The popularity the ERP system is that it manages and connects all of a company's different functions. SAP's software has modules specifically devoted to each of a company's core functional activities, such as marketing and manufacturing. Each module contains a set of functional "best practices," or rules, SAP has found work best to improve the function's efficiency and effectiveness.[46] SAP claims that when a company reconfigures its IT system to make the software work, it can achieve productivity gains of 30 to 50 percent, which for large companies can amount to billions of dollars in savings.

For each function, SAP has a software module that it installs on the function's intranet. The function inputs its data into that module in the way specified by SAP. For example, the sales function inputs all the information about customer needs into SAP's sales module, and the materials management function inputs information about the product specifications it requires from suppliers into the materials management module. These modules give functional managers real-time feedback on the status of their particular functional activities. Essentially, each SAP module functions as an expert decision-making system that can reason through the information functional managers input into it. It then provides managers with recommendations for improvement. The magic of ERP does not stop there, however.[47]

SAP's ERP software also connects people across functions. Managers in all functions have access to the other functions' decision-making systems, and SAP's software is designed to alert them when their functional activities will be affected by decisions being made by managers in another function. Thus, the ERP system allows managers across the organization to better coordinate their decision making. This can be a big competitive advantage. Moreover, the software installed on the corporation's mainframe takes the information from all of the different functional expert systems and creates a company-wide overview of its operations. In essence, SAP's ERP software creates a sophisticated top-level decision-making system that can reason through the huge volume of information being provided by the organization's functions.[48] It can then diagnose common problems and issues and recommend organization-wide solutions. Top managers armed with this information can then use these recommendations to improve the decisions they make in the changing environment the organization faces.

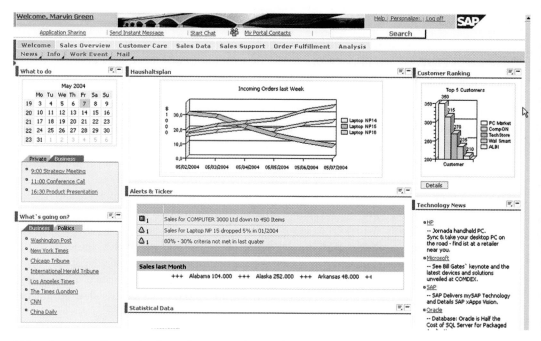

SAP, a German software developer, began producing planning programs over 30 years ago to help firms operate more efficiently. The software integrates their functional groups, taking some of the guesswork out of decision making.

Group Decision Making

Frequently groups rather than individuals make decisions in organizations. These groups might have a formal leader or functional manager who oversees the decision-making process. Self-managed work teams also need to make decisions, however. In this section, we consider some of the potential advantages, disadvantages, and consequences of group decision making. (See Figure 15.4.)

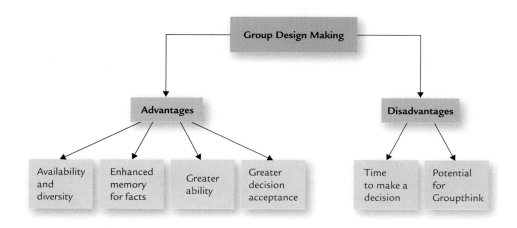

FIGURE 15.4

Advantages and Disadvantages of Group Decision Making

ADVANTAGES OF GROUP DECISION MAKING

Advantages of using groups to make decisions include the availability and diversity of members' skills, knowledge, and expertise; enhanced memory for facts; greater ability to correct errors; and greater decision acceptance.

Availability and Diversity of Members' Skills, Knowledge, and Expertise. When groups make decisions, each group member's skills, knowledge, and expertise can be brought into play. For certain kinds of decisions, an individual decision maker is very unlikely to have all the different capabilities needed to make a good decision. For example, when Jack Welch, General Electric's (GE) former CEO, needed to decide whether to invest $70 million to modernize GE's washing machine manufacturing facilities near Louisville, Kentucky, or buy washing machines from another company and sell them under the GE brand name, he clearly did not have all the skills, knowledge, and expertise needed to make the decision by himself. He needed input from various managers about manufacturing costs, product development costs, and quality considerations. He also needed input from union representatives about whether GE's unionized employees would agree to needed changes in their jobs to cut costs if the company decided to go ahead with the modernization program. Relying on group decision making, Welch undertook the modernization program, which proved to be a wise choice.[49] Whenever a decision requires skills, knowledge, and expertise in several areas (such as marketing, finance, engineering, production, and research and development), group decision making has clear advantages over individual decision making.

This advantage of group decision making suggests that there should be *diversity* among group members (see Chapter 10). In addition to diversity in knowledge and expertise, it is often desirable to have diversity in age, gender, race, and ethnic backgrounds. Diversity gives a group the opportunity to consider different points of view. Traditionally, for example, groups that design new automobiles for major car companies have been all male. But some companies are now realizing it's important to have women and foreign designers on the team. They bring new, different, and important insights to the process that result in features appealing to women and car buyers in other countries.[50]

NutraSweet Corporation is another company that values diversity. NutraSweet is attempting to improve its product's foreign sales and sales to African Americans and

The members of a work group learn to appreciate each other's point of view at a diversity-training workshop. Such workshops are now routine for employees at many firms.

Hispanics, who have relatively high incidences of diabetes. Given this aim, NutraSweet CEO Robert E. Flynn views a diverse workforce as a practical business necessity.[51]

Although diverse work groups can improve decision making, they can give rise to a problem: Group members who have different points of view because of their varied backgrounds sometimes find it hard to get along with each other. Many organizations are trying to respond to this challenge through diversity training programs, which aim to help members of an organization understand each other so they can work together effectively and make good decisions.

Enhanced Memory for Facts.

When a decision requires the consideration of a substantial amount of information, groups have an advantage over individuals because of their memory for facts.[52] Most people engaged in the process of making a decision have experienced the frustrating problem of forgetting an important piece of information. Because a group can rely on the memory of each of its members, the problem of forgetfulness is minimized. Information that one member of the group forgets is likely to be remembered by another. For example, even if Jack Welch had all the information he needed to decide whether General Electric should make or buy washing machines, it is highly unlikely he would be able to remember all of it when the time came to make the final decision. Having a group of GE managers and employees available to participate in the decision making helped to ensure that important information was not forgotten or overlooked.

Capability of Error Detection.

No matter how experienced decision makers are, they all make mistakes. Some errors occur in the information-gathering stage or in the evaluation of alternatives. Other errors occur when the final decision is made. When a group makes a decision, errors made by some group members might be detected and corrected by others.[53] If, for example, a manager at GE made a mistake in calculating production costs at the new manufacturing facility that was being contemplated, there was always the chance that another manager would detect the error.

Greater Decision Acceptance.

For a decision to be implemented, it is often necessary for several members of an organization to accept the decision. Suppose, for example, a grocery store manager decides to extend the store's operating hours from 18 to 24 hours a day by scheduling employees to work for longer periods of time (and not hiring any new employees). The employees must accept this decision for it to work. If none of the employees is willing to work the new 10 P.M. to 6 A.M. shift, the decision cannot be implemented.

The likelihood that employees will accept a decision increases when they take part in the decision-making process. The successful implementation of GE's decision to invest $70 million to modernize its washing machine manufacturing facilities, for example, depended on union leaders agreeing to changes in the employees' jobs.[54] By involving the union in the decision making, Jack Welch helped ensure these employees would accept and support the decision to go ahead with the modernization plan.

DISADVANTAGES OF GROUP DECISION MAKING

Group decision making has certain advantages over individual decision making (particularly when the decisions are complex, require the gathering and processing of a variety or large amount of information, and require acceptance by others for successful implementation). But there are also disadvantages to group decision making. Two of them are time and the potential for groupthink.

Time to Make a Decision.

Have you been in the annoying situation of being in a group that seemed to take forever to make a decision that you could have made yourself in half the time? One of the disadvantages of group decision making is the amount of time it consumes. Groups seldom make decisions as quickly as individuals can. Moreover, if you multiply the amount of time a group takes to make a group decision by the number of people in the group, you can see the extent to which group decision making consumes the time and effort of organizational members.

For decisions that meet certain criteria, individual decision making takes less time than group decision making and is likely to result in a decision that's just as good. Organizations should use individual and not group decision making when (1) an individual is likely to have all the capabilities needed to make a good decision, (2) an individual is likely to be able to gather and accurately take into account all the necessary information, and (3) the acceptance of the decision by the organization's other members is either unnecessary or is likely to occur, regardless of their involvement in decision making.

Groupthink A pattern of faulty decision making that occurs in cohesive groups whose members strive for agreement at the expense of accurately assessing information relevant to the decision.

The Potential for Groupthink.

Groupthink is a pattern of faulty decision making that occurs in cohesive groups whose members strive for agreement at the expense of accurately assessing information relevant to the decision.[55] Irving Janis coined the term *groupthink* in 1972 to describe a paradox that he observed in group decision making: Sometimes groups of highly qualified and experienced individuals make very poor decisions.[56] The decision made by President John F. Kennedy and his advisers to carry out the ill-fated Bay of Pigs invasion of Cuba in 1962, the decisions made by President Lyndon B. Johnson and his advisers between 1964 and 1967 to escalate the war in Vietnam, the decision made by President Richard M. Nixon and his advisers to cover up the Watergate break-in in 1972, and the decision made by NASA and Morton Thiokol in 1986 to launch the *Challenger* space shuttle, which exploded after takeoff, killing all crew members—all these decisions were influenced by groupthink. After the fact, the decision makers involved in these and other fiascoes are often shocked that they and their colleagues were involved in such poor decision making. Janis's investigations of groupthink primarily focused on government decisions, but the potential for groupthink in business organizations is just as likely.

Recall from Chapter 11 that cohesive groups are very attractive to their members. The individuals in the group value their membership and strongly want to remain part of it. When groupthink occurs, members of a cohesive group unanimously support a decision favored by the group leader without carefully assessing its pros and cons.

This unanimous support is often based on members' exaggerated beliefs about the group's capabilities and moral standing. They think the group is more powerful than it is and could never make a decision that might be morally or ethically questioned. As a result, the group becomes closed-minded and fails to pay attention to information that suggests that the decision might not be a good one. Moreover, when members of the group do have doubts about the decision being made, they are likely to discount those doubts and not mention them to other group members. As a result, the group as a whole perceives that there is unanimous support for the decision, and group members actively try to prevent any negative information pertaining to the decision from being brought up for discussion.[57] Figure 15.5 summarizes Janis's basic model of the groupthink phenomenon. It is important to note that although groupthink occurs only in cohesive groups, many cohesive groups never succumb to this faulty mode of decision making.

A group leader can take the following steps specifically to prevent the occurrence of groupthink; these steps also contribute to good decision making in groups in general:[58]

◆ The group leader encourages all group members to be critical of proposed alternatives, to raise any doubts they may have, and to accept criticism of their own ideas. It is especially important for a group leader to subject his or her own viewpoint to criticism by other group members.

F I G U R E **15.5**
Groupthink
Source: Adapted from *Irvin L. Janis, Groupthink Psychological Studies of Policy Decisions and Fiascoes* 2nd ed. Copyright ©1982 by Houghton Mifflin Company. Reprinted with permission.

Symptoms of groupthink

1. **Illusion of invulnerability**
   Group members are very optimistic and take excessive risks.
2. **Belief in inherent morality of the group**
   Group members fail to consider the ethical consequences of decisions.
3. **Collective rationalizations**
   Group members ignore information that suggests they might need to rethink the wisdom of the decision.
4. **Stereotypes of other groups**
   Other groups with opposing views are viewed as being incompetent.
5. **Self-censorship**
   Group members fail to mention any doubts they have to the group.
6. **Illusions of unanimity**
   Group members mistakenly believe they are all in total agreement.
7. **Direct pressure on dissenters**
   Members who disagree with the group's decision are urged to change their views.
8. **Emergence of self-appointed mind guards**
   Some group members try to shield the group from any information that suggests that they need to reconsider the wisdom of the decision.

↓

Defective decision-making process

↓

Bad decisions

♦ The group leader refrains from expressing his or her own opinion and views until the group has had a chance to consider all alternatives. A leader's opinion given too early is likely to stifle the generation of alternatives and productive debate.

♦ The group leader encourages group members to gather information pertaining to a decision from people outside the group and to seek outsiders' perspectives on the group's ideas.

♦ Whenever a group meets, the group leader assigns one or two members to play the role of **devil's advocate**—that is, to criticize, raise objections, and identify potential problems with any decisions the group reaches. The devil's advocate should raise these problems even if he or she does not believe the points are valid.

Devil's advocate Someone who argues against a cause or position in order to determine its validity.

♦ If an important decision is being made and time allows, after a group has made a decision, the group leader holds a second meeting. During the second meeting, members can raise any doubts or misgivings they might have about the course of action the group has chosen.

OTHER CONSEQUENCES OF GROUP DECISION MAKING

Three other consequences of group decision making are not easily classified as advantages or disadvantages: diffusion of responsibility, group polarization, and the potential for conflict.

Diffusion of Responsibility. Group decisions are characterized by a diffusion of responsibility.[59] That is, the group as a whole rather than any one individual is accountable for the decision. If the decision was a good one, the group gets the credit; if the decision was a poor one, a single individual is not blamed.

Sometimes, when important decisions are made that entail considerable uncertainty, it can be very stressful for one individual to assume sole responsibility for the decision. Moreover, under these conditions, some people are inclined to make a decision they know will not come back to haunt them rather than the decision they think is best for the organization. When this is the case, diffusion of responsibility can be an advantage of group decision making.

Diffusion of responsibility can also be a disadvantage if group members do not take the time and effort needed to make a good decision because they are not held individually accountable. This consequence is related to the concept of social loafing (see Chapter 11), the tendency for individuals to exert less effort when they work in a group.

Group Polarization. Another consequence of group decision making is that groups tend to make more extreme decisions than do individuals. This tendency is called group polarization.[60] By *extreme decisions* we mean making more risky or conservative decisions rather than taking a middle-of-the-road approach. For example, on the one hand, the group might commit a vast amount of resources to develop a new product that may or may not be successful. On the other hand, it might decide not to introduce any new products because of the uncertainty involved.

Why are decisions made by groups more extreme than decisions made by individuals? The diffusion of responsibility is one reason.[61] But there are at least two more explanations for group polarization. First, knowing that other group members have the same views or support the same decision can cause group members to become more confident of their positions.[62] Group members who initially supported committing a moderate amount of resources to the development of a new product may become more confident in the product's potential success after learning that other members of the group also feel good about the product. As a result of this increased confidence, the group makes the more extreme decision to commit a large amount of resources. Second, as a group discusses alternatives, members of the group often come up with persuasive arguments to support their favored alternative (say, for example, why the new product is "bound to be" a success).[63] As a result of these persuasive arguments, the group's confidence in the chosen alternative increases, and the decision becomes more extreme.

Potential for Conflict. There is always the potential for conflict in decision-making groups. Group members differ in their knowledge, skills, and expertise as well as in their past experiences. These differences cause them to view opportunities and problems and responses to them in different ways. Moreover, certain group members may stand to benefit from one alternative being chosen over another, and self-interest may cause them to push for that alternative. Other group members may resent this pressure and disagree or push for an alternative that benefits them. Such conflict can be functional for groups and organizations when it forces them to evaluate the alternatives carefully. However, it can be dysfunctional when individual members become more concerned about winning the battle than making a good decision.

In summary, groups are used to make decisions when the decision requires a wide range of skills, knowledge, and expertise, or more information than a single individual could be expected to possess. Group decision making is time consuming, however, although IT can help reduce this problem. In addition, it is important to encourage group members to be critical of each other's ideas, to evaluate the different alternatives, and to follow the five steps that help prevent groupthink.

you're the management expert

Group Decision-Making Techniques

Several techniques have been developed to help groups make good decisions that promote high levels of performance and positive attitudes and avoid some of the potential disadvantages of group decision making. In this section, we describe three of those techniques: brainstorming, the nominal group technique, and the Delphi technique. We also discuss some of the group decision-making techniques used in total quality management programs.

BRAINSTORMING

Sometimes groups do not consider as wide a range of alternative responses to opportunities and problems as they should. At other times, group members prematurely make a decision without adequately considering other alternatives. **Brainstorming** is a spontaneous, participative, decision-making technique that groups use to generate a wide range of alternatives from which to make a decision.[64] A typical brainstorming session proceeds like this:

> **Brainstorming**
> A spontaneous, participative decision-making technique that groups use to generate a wide range of alternatives from which to make a decision.

1. Group members sit around a table, and one member of the group describes the problem or opportunity in need of a response.

2. Group members are encouraged to share their own ideas with the rest of the group in a free and open manner without any critical evaluation of the ideas.

3. Group members are urged to share their ideas no matter how far-fetched they may seem, to come up with as many ideas as they can, and to build on each others' suggestions.

4. One member of the group records the ideas on a chalkboard or flip chart as they are presented.

Although it seems that brainstorming groups would come up with a wide range of alternatives, research suggests that individuals working separately tend to generate more ideas than do brainstorming groups.[65] A group of marketing managers who brainstorm to come up with a catchy name for a new convertible sports car, for example, will in all likelihood come up with fewer ideas than will individual managers who dream up ideas on their own and then pool them. Why does this outcome occur? There are at least two reasons. First, even though members of brainstorming groups are encouraged to share even the wildest or strangest idea, and even though criticism is suppressed, group

Production blocking Loss of productivity in brainstorming groups due to various distractions and limitations inherent to brainstorming.

members tend to be inhibited from sharing all their ideas with others. Second, **production blocking** takes place. This loss of productivity has several causes.[66] Group members cannot give their full attention to generating alternatives because they are listening to other people's ideas. They forget some of their ideas while they are waiting for their turn to share them with the rest of the group. And only one person can speak at a time, so the number of ideas that can be presented is limited.

Electronic brainstorming can overcome some of these problems.[67] Group members can use personal computers to record their ideas while at the same time have access to alternatives generated by other group members on their computer screens. Electronic brainstorming is an effective means of preventing some of the production blocking that occurs when brainstorming groups meet face-to-face.[68]

THE NOMINAL GROUP TECHNIQUE

Nominal group technique (NGT) A decision-making technique that includes the following steps: Group members generate ideas on their own and write them down, group members communicate their ideas to the rest of the group, and each idea is then discussed and critically evaluated by the group.

The **nominal group technique (NGT)** also can be used to overcome production blocking and is a way for groups that need to make a decision quickly to select an alternative.[69] Group members sit around a table, and one member of the group describes the problem or opportunity. Members are then given a certain amount of time (perhaps 20 or 30 minutes) to come up with ideas or alternative ways to respond to the problem or opportunity and write them down on a piece of paper. Because each member comes up with alternatives while brainstorming privately, the NGT avoids production blocking. Moreover, when the NGT is used, group members are encouraged to write down all their ideas no matter how bizarre they may seem. Doing this individually may help to overcome the inhibition that limits some brainstorming groups.

After writing down all of their ideas, members present them in a round-robin fashion: Each person seated at the table presents one idea at a time. One member records the ideas on a chalkboard or flip chart, and no discussion of the ideas takes place at this point. After all the ideas are listed, the group discusses them one by one. Members are allowed to raise questions and objections and critically evaluate each idea. After each alternative has been discussed, each member privately ranks all of the alternatives from most preferred to least preferred. The alternative that receives the highest ranking in the group is chosen, and the decision-making process is complete.

The NGT helps a group reach a decision quickly (sometimes in just a couple of hours), and it allows all of the ideas generated by the members to be considered. NGT is not feasible for complex decisions requiring the processing of large amounts of information and repeated group meetings. It is also not appropriate when it is important that all, or most, group members agree on the alternative chosen (a decision by a jury would be such an example).

THE DELPHI TECHNIQUE

Delphi technique A decision-making technique in which a series of questionnaires is sent to experts on the issue at hand, who never actually meet face-to-face.

When the **Delphi technique** is used, group members never meet face-to-face.[70] When a leader is faced with a problem or opportunity that needs a response, the advice of experts in the area is sought through written communication. The leader describes the problem or opportunity and solicits their help by asking them to complete and return a questionnaire. After all the questionnaires have been returned, the leader compiles the responses and sends a summary of them to all group members, along with additional questions that need to be answered for a decision to be made. This process is repeated as many times as needed to reach a consensus or a decision that most of the experts think is a good one.

The Delphi technique has the advantage of not requiring group members who may be scattered around the country or the globe to meet face-to-face. Its principal disadvantages are that it can be time consuming and it does not allow for group interaction.

It also depends on the cooperation of the experts to respond promptly to the questionnaires and take the time needed to complete them carefully. These disadvantages can be overcome, to some extent, by using some of the new computer software being developed for work groups by companies such as Microsoft.

GROUP DECISION-MAKING TECHNIQUES USED IN TOTAL QUALITY MANAGEMENT

Total quality management (TQM)[71] is a philosophy and set of practices that have been developed to improve the quality of an organization's goods and services and the efficiency with which they are produced. Total quality management (which we discuss in detail in Chapter 18) includes two group decision-making techniques, benchmarking and empowerment, which can be used to improve group decision making in general. The objective of these techniques is to encourage group members to make suggestions and use their knowledge to come up with ways to reduce costs and waste and increase quality with the ultimate goal of pleasing the final customer. Benchmarking and empowerment can be used, for example, in manufacturing settings to reduce defects and recalls of new cars, in customer service departments to shorten the time it takes to respond to a customer complaint, and in accounting departments to make bills easier for customers to read.

Benchmarking. When groups make decisions, it is often difficult for group members to grasp exactly what they should be striving for or trying to achieve when they evaluate alternatives. A group's overall goal, for example, may be to increase performance and quality, but the level of performance or quality that the group should aim for may not be clear to group members. Benchmarking helps groups figure out what they should be trying to accomplish when making a decision. A benchmark is a standard against which something can be measured or judged.

Benchmarking involves selecting a high-performing group or organization that is currently providing high-quality goods or services to its customers and using this group or organization as a model. When a low-performing group needs to make a decision, members compare where their group is with where the benchmark group or organization is on some criterion of quality. They then try to determine how to reach the standard set by the group or organization being benchmarked. For example, when groups in express delivery organizations such as DHL and UPS need to decide how to improve the quality of their services to customers, they sometimes use Federal Express's guarantee of next-day delivery and continuous tracking of letters and packages as benchmarks of what they should be striving for.

> **Benchmarking** Selecting a high-performing group and using this group as a model.

Empowerment. A guiding principle of total quality management is that performance and quality improvements are the responsibility of all organizational members. Employees are often in the best position to come up with ways to improve performance and quality. **Empowerment** is the process of giving these employees the authority to make decisions and be responsible for their outcomes. Empowerment often requires managers and other employees to change the way they think about decision making. Rather than managers making the decisions and the rest of an organization's employees carrying them out, empowerment requires that the responsibility for decision making be shared throughout an organization.

> **Empowerment** The process of giving employees throughout an organization the authority to make decisions and be responsible for their outcomes.

Getting employees and managers to change the way they think about decision making in an organization can be difficult but also worth the effort. McDonald's, Federal Express, Citibank, and Xerox are among the growing list of companies using empowerment to improve group decision making.[72] Xerox has gone so far as to push its suppliers to use empowerment (and other TQM practices) to improve the quality of the parts Xerox buys from them.[73] For example, Trident Tools, located in Rochester, New

York, supplies Xerox with electromagnetic components. Xerox helped train Trident employees to use TQM techniques such as empowerment to improve the quality of Trident's parts. As a result of the training, groups of employees at Trident cut the number of steps in the company's materials-ordering process from 26 to 12, reducing the lead time needed to fill customer orders from 16 to 7 weeks. The employees also reduced the amount of time needed to design new components from 5 years to 16 months. The story of how managers at Plexus empowered the company's employees and created a learning organization is discussed in the accompanying OB Today.

ob today

How Plexus Decided It Could Make Flexible Manufacturing Pay Off

In the United States, over 2.3 million manufacturing jobs were lost to factories in low-cost countries abroad in 2003. Although many large U.S. manufacturing companies have given up the battle, some companies such as Plexus Corporation, based in Neenah, Wisconsin, have been able to craft the decisions that have allowed them to survive and prosper in a low-cost manufacturing world.

Plexus started out making electronic circuit boards in the 1980s for IBM. In the 1990s, however, it saw the writing on the wall as more and more of its customers began to turn to manufacturers abroad to produce the components that go into their products or even the whole product itself. The problem facing managers at Plexus was how to design a production system that could compete in a low-cost manufacturing world. U.S. companies cannot match the efficiency of foreign manufacturers in producing high volumes of a single product, such as millions of a particular circuit board used in a laptop computer. So Plexus's managers decided to focus their efforts on developing a manufacturing technology, called "low-high," that could efficiently produce low volumes of many different kinds of products.

Other companies outsourced jobs to low-cost countries, but Plexus, a Wisconsin-based circuit board maker, focused on teamwork, adaptation, and flexibility instead. Today, the company produces 2.5 times the number of circuit boards it did ten years ago when it had twice as many employees.

Plexus's engineers worked as a team to design a manufacturing facility in which products would be manufactured in four separate "focused factories." The production line in each factory is designed to allow the operations involved in making each product to be performed separately, although operations still take place in sequence. Workers are cross-trained so they can perform any of the operations in each factory. So, when work slows down at any point in the production of a particular product, a worker further along the line can step back to help solve the problem that occurred at the earlier stage on the line.

These workers are organized into self-managed teams empowered to make all of the decisions necessary to make a particular product in one of the four factories. Because each product is different, these teams have to quickly make the decisions necessary to assemble them if they are to do so cost-effectively. The ability of these teams to make rapid decisions is vital on a production line because time is money. Every minute a production line is idle adds hundreds or thousands of dollars to the cost of production. To keep costs down, employees have to be able to react to unexpected contingencies and make nonprogrammed decisions, unlike workers on a conventional production line who simply follow a set performance program.

Team decision making also comes into play when the line is changed over to make a different product. Because nothing is being produced while this occurs, it is vital the changeover time be kept to a minimum. At Plexus, engineers and teams working together have reduced this time to as little as 30 minutes. Eighty percent of the time the line is running and making products; only 20 percent of the time is it idle.[74] This incredible flexibility, developed by the members of the company working for years to improve the decisions involved in the changeover process, is the reason why Plexus is so efficient and can compete against low-cost manufacturers abroad. In fact, today, Plexus has about 400 workers, who can produce 2.5 times the product value that 800 workers could just a decade ago.

Quality is also one of the goals of the self-managed work teams. Employees know nothing is more important in the production of complex, low-volume products than a reputation for products that are reliable and have very low defect rates. By all accounts, both managers and workers are very proud of the way they have developed such an efficient operation. The emphasis at Plexus is on continuous learning to improve the decisions that go into the design of the production process.[75]

Organizational Learning

Because decision making takes place under uncertainty, and because of the errors that can affect decision making, it is not surprising that many of the decisions that managers and organizations make are mistakes and end in failure. Others, of course, allow an organization to succeed beyond managers' wildest dreams. Organizations survive and prosper when their members make the right decisions—sometimes through skill and sound judgment, sometimes through chance and good luck. For decision making to be successful over time, however, organizations must improve their ability to make better decisions and reduce decision-making errors.

One of the most important processes that can help managers make better decisions is organizational learning.[76] **Organizational learning** is a process managers seek out to improve the decision-making ability of employees and enhance organizational efficiency and effectiveness.[77] Because of the rapid pace of change in today's business environment, organizational learning is a vital activity that must be managed. This requires an understanding of how organizational learning occurs and the factors that can promote or impede it.

TYPES OF ORGANIZATIONAL LEARNING

James March, whose work on decision making was discussed earlier, proposed that two principal types of organizational learning strategies can be pursued to improve decision making: exploration and exploitation.[78] **Exploration** involves organizational members searching for and experimenting with new kinds or forms of behaviors and procedures to increase effectiveness. Learning that involves exploration might involve finding new ways to make and sell goods and services or inventing new ways to organize employees, such as developing cross-functional or virtual teams.

Exploitation involves organizational members learning ways to refine and improve existing organizational behaviors and procedures to increase effectiveness. This might involve implementing a TQM program to promote the continuous refinement of existing operating procedures or developing an improved set of rules to enable a work group to more effectively perform its specific tasks.[79] Exploration is, therefore, a more radical learning process than exploitation although both are important for improved decision making that enhances the organization's effectiveness.[80]

Organizational learning The process through which managers seek to increase organization members' desire and ability to make decisions that continuously raise organizational efficiency and effectiveness.

Exploration Learning that involves organizational members searching for and experimenting with new kinds or forms of organizational behaviors and procedures to increase effectiveness.

Exploitation Learning that involves organizational members finding ways to refine and improve existing organizational behaviors and procedures to increase effectiveness.

A **learning organization** is an organization that purposefully takes steps to enhance and maximize the potential for explorative and exploitative organizational learning to take place.[81] How do managers create a learning organization, one capable of allowing its members to appreciate and respond quickly to changes taking place around it? By increasing the ability of employees at every level in the organization to question and analyze the way the organization performs its activities and to experiment with new ways to change it to increase effectiveness.

PRINCIPLES OF ORGANIZATIONAL LEARNING

In order to create a learning organization, managers need to promote learning at the individual and group levels.[82] Some principles for creating a learning organization have been developed by Peter Senge and are discussed next.[83] (See Figure 15.6.)

Personal Mastery. At the individual level, managers need to do all they can to facilitate the learning of new skills, norms, and values so that individuals can increase their own personal ability to help build the organization's core competencies. Senge has argued that for organizational learning to occur, each person needs to develop a sense of *personal mastery*. Essentially, that means the organization should empower individuals to experiment and create and explore what they want. The goal is to give employees the opportunity to develop an intense appreciation for their work that translates into a distinctive competence for the organization.[84]

Complex Mental Models. As part of attaining personal mastery, and to give employees a deeper understanding of what is involved in a particular activity, organizations need to encourage employees to develop and use *complex mental models* that challenge them to find new or better ways to perform a task. As an analogy, a person might mow the lawn once a week and treat this as a chore that has to be done. However, suppose the person decides to study how the grass grows and to experiment with cutting the grass to different heights and using different fertilizers and watering patterns. Through this study, he or she notices that cutting the grass to a certain height and using specific combinations of fertilizer and water promote thicker growth and fewer weeds, resulting in a better-looking lawn that needs less mowing. What had been a chore may become a hobby, and personal mastery is achieved. Looking at the task in a new way has become a source of deep personal

FIGURE 15.6
Principles of Organizational Learning

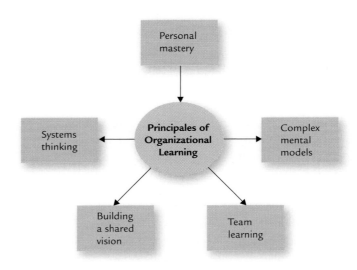

satisfaction. This is the message behind Senge's principles for developing a learning organization. Namely, organizations must encourage each of their individual members to develop a taste for experimenting.[85]

A learning organization can encourage employees to form complex mental models and develop a sense of personal mastery by providing them with the opportunity to assume more responsibility for their decisions. This can be done in a variety of ways. Employees might be cross-trained so that they can perform many different tasks, and the knowledge they gain may give them new insight into how to improve work procedures. On the other hand, perhaps a specific task that was performed by several different employees can be redesigned or reengineered so that one employee, aided by an advanced information system, can perform the complete task. Again, the result may be an increase in the level of organizational learning as the employee finds new ways to get the job done.

Team Learning. At the group level, managers need to encourage learning by promoting the use of various kinds of groups—such as self-managed groups or cross-functional teams—so that individuals can share or pool their skills and abilities to solve problems. Groups allow for the creation of *synergy*—the idea that the whole is much more than the sum of its parts—which can enhance performance. In terms of Thompson's model of task interdependence discussed in Chapter 11, for example, the move from a pooled, to sequential, to reciprocal task interdependence will increase the potential for group-level learning because the group's members have more opportunity to interact and learn from one another over time. "Group routines" that enhance group effectiveness may develop from such interactions.[86] Senge refers to this kind of learning as *team learning,* and he argues that team learning is as important, or even more important, than individual-level learning in promoting organizational learning. This is due to the fact that most important decisions are made in groups, such as departmental and functional groups.

The ability of teams to bring about organizational learning was unmistakable when Toyota revolutionized the work process in a former GM factory in California. Large performance gains were achieved in the factory when Toyota's managers created work teams and empowered team members to take over the responsibility for measuring, monitoring, and controlling their own behavior to find ways to continuously increase performance.

Building a Shared Vision. Another one of Senge's principles for designing a learning organization emphasizes the importance of *building a shared vision*. Building a shared vision involves creating an ongoing frame of reference or mental model that all of the organization's members use to frame problems or opportunities and that binds them to an organization. At the heart of this vision is likely to be the set of work values and norms that guides behavior in a particular setting.

Systems Thinking. Senge's last principle of organizational learning, *systems thinking,* emphasizes that in order to create a learning organization, managers must recognize how learning at the individual and group levels affects each other. For example, there is little point in creating teams to facilitate team learning if an organization does not also take steps to give its employees the freedom to develop a sense of personal mastery. By encouraging and promoting organizational learning at each of these levels—that is, by looking at organizational learning as a system—managers can create a learning organization that facilitates an organization's ability to make high-quality decisions rapidly to respond to the changes that are constantly taking place around it.

Summary

The decisions made by employees at all levels in organizations can have a major impact on levels of performance and well-being and on the extent to which individuals, groups, and whole organizations achieve their goals. In this chapter, we made the following major points:

1. Decision making is the process by which members of an organization choose how to respond to opportunities and problems. Nonprogrammed decision making occurs when members of an organization choose how to respond to novel opportunities and problems. Nonprogrammed decision making involves a search for information. Programmed decision making occurs when members of an organization respond to recurring opportunities and problems by using standard responses (performance programs). This chapter focuses on nonprogrammed decision making.

2. The classical model of decision making is a prescriptive model that assumes that decision makers have access to all the information they need and will make the best decision possible. A decision maker using the classical model takes these four steps: (a) listing all alternatives, (b) listing the consequences of each alternative, (c) considering his or her preferences for each alternative or set of consequences, and (d) selecting the alternative that will result in the most preferred set of consequences. Decisions made according to the classical model are optimal decisions.

3. There are problems with the classical model because it is not realistic. Decision makers often do not know all the alternatives they can choose from, often do not know the consequences of each alternative, may not be clear about their own preferences, and in many cases lack the mental ability to take into account all the information required by the classical model. Moreover, the classical model can be very time consuming.

4. March and Simon's administrative decision-making model is descriptive; it explains how decisions are actually made in organizations. March and Simon propose that decision makers choose how to respond to opportunities and problems on the basis of a simplified and approximate account of the situation called the decision maker's definition of the situation. This definition is the result of both psychological and sociological processes. Rather than making optimal decisions, decision

makers often satisfice, or make an acceptable decision, not necessarily an optimal decision. Satisficing occurs because of bounded rationality.

5. Heuristics are rules of thumb that simplify decision making but can lead to errors or biases. The availability heuristic reflects the tendency to determine the frequency of an event and its causes by how easy they are to remember (how available they are from memory). The availability heuristic can lead to biased decision making when the frequency of events and causes is overestimated because they are vivid, extreme, or recent. The representativeness heuristic reflects the tendency to predict the likelihood of an event from the extent to which the event is typical (or representative) of similar kinds of events that have happened in the past. Representativeness can lead to biased decision making when decision makers fail to take into account base rates. The anchoring and adjustment heuristic reflects the tendency to make decisions based on adjustments from some initial amount (or anchor). The anchoring and adjustment heuristic can lead to biased decision making when the initial amounts were too high or too low.

6. Escalation of commitment is the tendency of decision makers to invest additional time, money, or effort into losing courses of action. Escalation of commitment occurs because decision makers do not want to admit that they have made a mistake, view further commitment of resources as a way to recoup sunk costs, and are more likely to take risks when decisions are framed in negative rather than in positive terms.

7. The advantages of using groups instead of individuals to make decisions include the availability and diversity of members' skills, knowledge, and expertise; enhanced memory for facts; capability of error detection; and greater decision acceptance. The disadvantages of group decision making include the time it takes to make a decision and the potential for group-

think. Other consequences include diffusion of responsibility, group polarization, and the potential for conflict.

8. Group decision-making techniques used in organizations include brainstorming, the nominal group technique, and the Delphi technique. Two group decision-making techniques used in total quality management are benchmarking and empowerment.

9. Two main types of organizational learning that can lead to improved decision making are explorative and exploitative learning. Organizations can improve their members' ability to make high-quality decisions by encouraging them to develop personal mastery and complex mental models through team learning, by building a shared vision, and through systems thinking.

Exercises in Understanding and Managing Organizational Behavior

Questions for Discussion and Review

1. Do programmed decisions and the use of performance programs always evolve from what were originally nonprogrammed decisions? Why or why not?

2. For what kinds of decisions might the classical model be more appropriate than March and Simon's model?

3. How might the anchoring and adjustment heuristic affect goal setting?

4. Can the availability and the representativeness heuristics operate simultaneously? Why or why not?

5. How might decision-making groups fall into the escalation-of-commitment trap?

6. Why do members of diverse groups sometimes find it hard to make a decision?

7. In what ways can conflict in a decision-making group be both an advantage and a disadvantage?

8. Do all employees want to be empowered and make the decisions that their bosses used to make? Why or why not?

9. What is the relationship between the anchoring and adjustment heuristic and benchmarking?

Building People Skills

Analyzing Individual and Group Decisions

Think of two important decisions that you have recently made—one that you made individually and one that you made as a member of a group. Describe each decision. For each decision, answer these questions:

1. Was the process by which you made the decision more accurately described by the classical model or by March and Simon's model? Why?

2. In what ways were heuristics involved in making the decision?

3. Was escalation of commitment involved in making the decision?

4. Why did you make the individual decision on your own rather than in a group? Do you think a better decision would have been made if the decision had been made in a group? Why or why not?

5. Why did you make the other decision as a member of a group rather than on your own? Do you think that you could have made a better decision on your own? Why or why not?

A Question of Ethics

As the chapter discusses, the question of whether a decision is ethical or not is an important aspect of the decision-making process. In group decision making, sometimes the diffusion of responsibility can lead a group to make an extreme and unethical decision because the responsibility for it is spread over all group members. With this in mind think about the following issues:

- To what extent to you believe each member of the group is aware that *collectively* they might be making an unethical decision?
- What steps could be taken to make individual group members be more outspoken in suggesting a possible course of action is unethical?

Small Group Break-Out Exercise

Brainstorming

After reading the following scenario break up into groups of three or four people and discuss the issues involved. Be prepared to discuss your thinking with the rest of the class.

You and your partners are trying to decide which kind of restaurant to open in a new shopping center in your city. The problem confronting you is that the city already has many restaurants that provide different kinds of food in all price ranges. Your challenge is to decide which type of restaurant is most likely to succeed. Using the brainstorming technique, follow these steps to make your decision:

1. As a group spend 5 or 10 minutes generating ideas about the alternative kinds of restaurants you think will be most likely to succeed. Write down the alternatives.
2. Spend 5 to 10 minutes debating the pros and cons of the alternatives and try to reach a group consensus.

Topic for Debate

Decision making is one of the most important processes in all organizations. Now that you have a good understanding of decision making, debate the following issue.

Team A. Individuals generally make better decisions than groups.

Team B. Groups generally make better decisions than individuals.

Experiential Exercise

Using the Nominal Group Technique

Objective

Your objective is to gain experience in using the nominal group technique.

Procedure

The class divides into groups of three to five people, and each group appoints one member as spokesperson to report the group's experiences to the whole class. Here is the scenario.

Assume the role of a self-managed work team. The team is one of the best-performing teams in the company, and the members like and get along well with each other. Currently, team members are paid an hourly wage based on seniority. The company has decided to change the way in which members of all self-managed teams are paid and has asked each team to propose a new pay plan. One plan will be chosen from those proposed and instituted for all teams.

Use the nominal group technique to decide on a pay plan by following these steps:

1. Each team member comes up with ideas for alternative pay plans on his or her own and writes them down on a piece of paper.
2. Team members present their ideas one by one while one member records them on a piece of paper. There is no discussion of the merits of the different alternatives at this point.
3. Team members discuss the ideas one by one and raise any questions or objections. Critical evaluation takes place at this step.
4. Each team member privately ranks all the alternatives from most preferred to least preferred.
5. The team chooses the alternative that receives the highest ranking.

After the decision has been made, team members discuss the pros and cons of using the nominal group technique to make a decision such as this one.

When your group has completed the exercise, the spokesperson will report back to the whole class on the decision the group reached as well as the group's assessment of the pros and cons of the nominal group technique.

Making the Connection

Find an example of a company that has recently made and successfully implemented one or more important decisions that have had a major effect on its performance. What was the nature of the decision? Do decisions in this organization tend to be made by individuals or by groups?

New York Times Cases in the News

The New York Times

Sweet Taste of Start-Up Success

BY PATRICIA R. OLSEN

Even for entrepreneurs who seem to do everything right, old-fashioned luck sometimes makes all the difference between scraping by and enjoying rapid growth. Just ask David A. Hammond.

Mr. Hammond, 55, was no neophyte when he founded DLH Inc., a maker of specialized first-aid kits, six years ago. As a Navy medic in Vietnam in the 1970s, he knew how to treat severe wounds and injuries. After he left active duty, he served as director of instructional programs for the Navy's medical department, and he later advised the Transportation Department about the creation of the 911 national emergency medical response service.

Besides his technical expertise, Mr. Hammond had honed his business skills. In 1982, he started a company called Itest in Newport News, Va., that made first-aid stations—steel cabinets packed with supplies and video instructions—for oil rigs and construction sites. The company had annual sales of about $500,000 and was profitable, he said.

But to Mr. Hammond, two much larger markets—the home, and workplaces like office buildings and schools—were ripe for kits that could enable untrained people to cope with a wide range of emergencies. So he tinkered with scaled-down versions of his products. After ending Itest's operations, he began DLH in the bedroom of his home in Tinton Falls, N.J., with his wife,

Linda, in 1997. Formerly a regional manager of custom decorating for J. C. Penney, Linda Hammond designed the kits' packaging and the company logo and was in charge of product development.

DLH's patented kits contain supplies and instruction cards in plastic envelopes labeled and color-coded for specific injuries.

The home kit, costing $30.95, has a packet for bleeding, another for sprains or broken bones, a third for bites and stings and one that contains extras, like latex-free gloves and plastic bandages. The kit for vehicles and outdoor enthusiasts, also $30.95, contains packs for aiding breathing, stanching bleeding and treating shock. The industrial kit, which comes in two sizes, priced at $99.95 and $49.95, contains additional packs for burns, head and spine injuries, eye injuries and other medical emergencies.

Like many other start-ups, DLH went on a marketing blitz. It persuaded organizations like the Newport News, Va., school system and businesses like the Chesapeake Corporation, a paper company, to try the industrial kits. It signed up the National Safety Council as a distributor and landed contracts with Hertz and the Federal Bureau of Investigation.

It wasn't a bad beginning, but even so, revenues averaged only $250,000 in the first five years, Mr. Hammond said; the profit last year was $100,000.

Then came the big break that every entrepreneur dreams of.

In 1999, Mr. Hammond demonstrated his kits at the National Safety Council's annual conference. A few occupational nurses for the United States Postal Service saw them and suggested that he get in contact with their medical office.

It turned out that the Occupational Safety and Health Administration had just mandated that Postal Service employees be supplied with first-aid training and kits. So DLH designed customized kits for the agency, one for its buildings and another for its trucks, and sold 180 of the larger industrial ones for testing.

Last May, Mr. Hammond got the good news: a Postal Service contract that he estimates will bring in $10 million over the next four years.

"My heart was in my throat waiting for the final decision," he said.

Now comes the hard part. Suddenly, DLH must start producing more than 100,000 kits a year, quintuple the roughly 20,000 kits it has been turning out until now. To handle the surge, Mr. Hammond says, he plans to hire several staff members, including three national sales representatives, directors of public relations and information management, and a chief operating officer over the next few months and to lease 6,000 square feet of office and warehouse space.

He is negotiating with two New Jersey organizations that hire disabled workers to supplement assembly work now being done by a Missouri company that also hires the disabled.

"We have to go from a two-person operation to about five times that number without breaking stride," he said.

DLH continues to search for new customers. It has given test kits to the Drug Enforcement Administration, the John Jay College of Criminal Justice in New York and U.S. Cavalry, a company that sells military and adventure gear; it is also hoping to do business with the Department of Homeland Security. The consumer kit was named a "best buy" last year by the Good Housekeeping Institute. And the National Safety Council has asked the company to develop a first-aid kit for farms that will contain supplies for amputations, for handling farmers' injuries around heavy equipment.

Mr. Hammond plans to add audio instructions, available at the press of a button, to the kits, and to branch out into foreign languages. He expects huge growth in the home market and says his research shows that even people with emergency training like the detailed instruction sheets in his kits.

"We think we've found the weak points in the chain," he said.

Still, it won't be easy sailing. Amit Bohora, a health care analyst at Frost & Sullivan in San Jose, Calif., gave DLH high marks for "making information-rich 'smart' kits in an industry which has traditionally been fairly stagnant." But he noted that it was up against several established players like Zee Medical, a subsidiary of the McKesson Corporation, a health care services company; Johnson & Johnson; and many independent online suppliers.

Patrick Dunkerley, a portfolio manager at Victory Capital Management in Cleveland, said: "Given their innovation and success so far, they may have a decent chance of being a long-term survivor, but customers vote with their money every day. Numerous competitors would like to eat their lunch."

But Mr. Hammond has a good shot at getting more good breaks, experts say, because such luck doesn't just materialize out of nowhere.

"People talk about overnight successes," said Julian E. Lange, an associate professor of entrepreneurial studies at Babson College in Wellesley, Mass. "But they are rare. A big break, like landing a major customer, is usually the result of a lot of preparation, with lots of successes and setbacks along the way. You may have to try 100 leads before you get a live one."

SOURCE: Patricia R. Olsen, "Sweet Taste of Start-Up Success," *New York Times*, September 21, 2003, p. 3.2.

Questions for Discussion

1. What kind of organizational learning is going on at DLH?

2. How would you describe David Hammond's approach to decision making?

3. What new kinds of decisions will face his company as it grows rapidly?

The New York Times

After a Fast Start, Growing Pains

BY EVE TAHMINCIOGLU

Raising millions of dollars in venture capital, landing big-name customers and measuring sales growth in percentages of four digits may seem to be every entrepreneur's dream. But there can be a nasty side to breakneck growth, and Kevin Laracey can tell you all about it.

Revenue at edocs Inc., the company Mr. Laracey founded in 1997, has surged by more than 7,000 percent in the past four years. But Mr. Laracey quickly found that coping with such growth can be tricky. Other parts of the business, like staff and space, have to grow, too.

Edocs provides software that helps corporations put customer bills online. After it raised $4 million in June 1998 in its first round of venture-capital financing, it moved its three executives and two other employees into a 1,000-square-foot office in Westborough, Mass.

Just a few months later, in early 1999, the staff had grown to 17 employees and the company moved again, to Wayland, Mass., to a building that under the state code was supposed to hold a maximum of 45 office workers. But it was soon busting at the seams with 77 employees, who occasionally used picnic tables near the parking lot for meetings.

So in the fall of 1999, with 160 employees, edocs began negotiating to lease 25,000 square feet in an office park in Natick, Mass., with a guarantee that 17,000 square feet across the street would also be available as it grew. With eight other companies vying for that same space in a hot real-estate market, Mr. Laracey persuaded business colleagues and even investment bankers to talk up his company to the landlord.

"I remember putting on my suit and getting my PowerPoint slides ready to do a presentation on how fast we were growing, how well we were raising money and how good our prospects were," he recalled.

He got the deal. And now he wishes he hadn't. Soon after he signed a lease for the additional 17,000 square feet in December 2000, the stock market tumbled, and so did the office-rental market. No longer needing the extra room, edocs subleased some of it at a loss. To date, it estimates that it has paid $1.6 million for essentially idle space.

In March 2000, edocs filed to go public, in part to secure "additional financing to fuel our growth," Mr. Laracey said. But the plan was shelved in February 2001 because technology shares tumbled.

It wasn't just Mr. Laracey's aggressive moves into real estate that ultimately backfired. With sales growing so rapidly, he said, he became caught up in the euphoria and sometimes spent money unwisely. Edocs shelled out $1 million in 2000 on a product that made it easy for customers to download and manage bills on their personal computers rather than do everything on the Internet. But the Internet won out, and the product flopped.

Furthermore, in his rush to build staff, he said, he sometimes hired candidates he instinctively felt weren't right for the job. In one case in particular, he recalled, "although I had my reservations on how he fit into the culture, we went ahead and hired this person," he said.

"He created some real problems and impacted morale at the company," Mr. Laracey added. "He wouldn't interact with people. Other employees would come to me and say, 'Why won't he talk to me?'"

Expanding overseas likewise led to hiccups. Decisions to open offices in countries like Australia and Britain often came on a moment's notice, Ms. Smith [chief financial officer] said, forcing her to scramble to figure out the logistics. "I'd find out in a sales meeting that in two to three weeks we're deciding to go to another country," she said.

Business functions that were simple in the United States seemed daunting elsewhere, she said. "In order to accomplish the practical matter of getting our international folks a paycheck," she said, "we needed referrals to local bookkeepers in Melbourne and in London to help us reg- ister the company to withhold employer taxes and establish local-country benefit and pension schemes, which vary by country and are often very different from what is offered to U.S. employees."

Despite all the bumps, edocs kept roaring ahead. While the wobbly econ- omy of the last couple of years has slowed its growth pace, Deloitte & Touche ranked it as the 16th-fastest- growing technology company in North America last year, and *Inc.* magazine has just rated it the 13th-fastest-growing pri- vately held company in the United States. Today, the company has 202 employees, 80 major corporate customers and offices in Australia, Europe and Asia. Revenue in 2002 was $34.5 million, the company said; Mr. Laracey would not project the total for this year.

Not all fledgling businesses are so lucky, or so well run, or both. "The most prominent cause of death in a start-up is growth," said Mark Lipton, author of *Guiding Growth: How Vision Keeps Companies on Course* (Harvard Business School Press) and chairman of the organizational change management program at the New School for Social Research in New York. "Growth is what kills them, especially the inability to manage growth."

One particularly severe self-inflicted wound is the refusal by many entrepre- neurs to delegate authority. "The biggest issue I see is whether the founder or owners are willing to let go," said Lynn Daniel of the Daniel Group, a strategic planning and market research firm in Charlotte, N.C. "Letting go means hav- ing the discipline to say: 'I have some- one here that's responsible for that. Let them do it.'"

Mr. Laracey acknowledged that it had taken awhile for him to hand over the reins. Even so, his tenacity and attention to detail apparently rubbed off on his staff. Rob Orgel, vice president for busi- ness development at edocs, said he often got after-hours e-mail from his boss. "Kevin is notorious for his midnight Google searches," he said. "He'll say, 'Go read this,' if we're trying to get a new cus- tomer or we're looking at a new product. He feels if you have those three or four extra nuggets of information, you will look better prepared."

Ms. Smith, the chief financial officer, ruefully recalled a conference call that her boss organized last year when she and her husband were out Christmas shopping on a Sunday. "Here I am on the cellphone, walking around the mall," she said. "There's a frenzy around getting every deal."

Avivah Litan, a research analyst who focuses on financial services at Gartner Inc., a consulting group, can attest to that. "They really do their homework, getting to know each industry and coming up with more cost-saving-tailored products," she said. "Edocs salespeople and account managers are like dogs on your heels that don't let go."

SOURCE: Eve Tahmincioglu, "After a Fast Start, Growing Pains," *New York Times*, October 5, 2003, p. 3.2.

Questions for Discussion

1. How did bounded rationality impact decision making at edocs Inc. over time?

2. What kinds of decision-making errors did Kevin Laracey make as his company grew quickly over time?

3. How could he have taken advantage of group decision making to avoid some of these errors and improve the quality of decision making?

Organizational Design and Structure

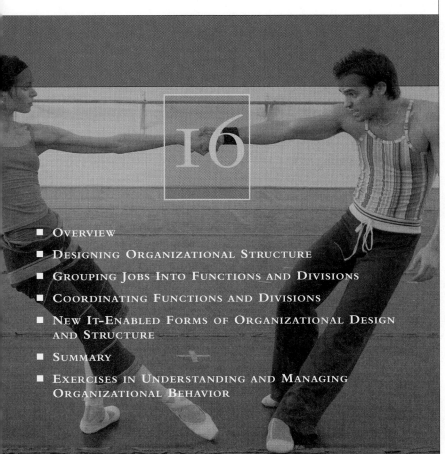

16

- OVERVIEW
- DESIGNING ORGANIZATIONAL STRUCTURE
- GROUPING JOBS INTO FUNCTIONS AND DIVISIONS
- COORDINATING FUNCTIONS AND DIVISIONS
- NEW IT-ENABLED FORMS OF ORGANIZATIONAL DESIGN AND STRUCTURE
- SUMMARY
- EXERCISES IN UNDERSTANDING AND MANAGING ORGANIZATIONAL BEHAVIOR

LEARNING OBJECTIVES

After reading this chapter, you should be able to:

■

Understand the relationship between organizational design and an organization's structure.

■

Explain the main contingencies affecting the process of organizational design and differentiate between a mechanistic and an organic structure.

■

Cite the advantages of grouping people into functions and divisions and distinguish among the main forms of organizational structure from which an organization can choose.

■

Explain why coordination becomes a problem with the growth of an organization and differentiate among the three main methods it can use to overcome this problem and link its functions and divisions.

■

Gain an understanding of the enormous impact modern information technology has had on the process of organizational design and structure both inside organizations and among them.

OPENING CASE

A New Approach to Organizing at Sun Life Financial

Why Did Sun Life Financial Change Its Structure?

Sun Life Financial, which is based in Toronto, Canada, is one of the largest financial and insurance companies in North America.[1] Like most other life insurance companies in the 1990s, Sun Life Financial had an organizational structure that was very rigid and bureaucratic. Over the years it had developed a tall, centralized structure. Information was sent via the hierarchy to upper-level managers, who made the final decisions about whether or not to offer prospective customers insurance and how much their policies should cost.

Sun Life Financial also operated with a functional structure, however. When a potential customer requested information about insurance coverage, a member of the company's customer service department took the application and handed it over to the company's order fulfillment department for processing. The order fulfillment department then sent the application to the actuarial department, which calculated the insurance premium. Only after several more steps were completed could the company inform a would-be customer about the outcome of his or her request.

The process of channeling the request through many different levels in the hierarchy and across so many different functions took considerable time. Frequently, because most potential customers obtained multiple quotes from several insurance companies, the long time lag often resulted in lost business. Customers simply "satisficed" and chose an insurance policy from one of the first two or three companies that promptly gave them an insurance quote.

Sun Life Financial realized it had to find a way to respond more quickly to its customers. It was also aware of the fact that the insurance business was changing in many ways. New aggressive competitors were entering the market, including large established banks such as Citicorp, which were acquiring insurance companies and expanding their operations. Also, a number of dot-com companies had begun selling policies on the Internet; this left insurance companies operating in a traditional manner scrambling to develop technologies to do business online, too. Other advances in information technology were affecting the company's internal operations as well.

Sun Life Financial decided that it had to change the way it operated and do so fast. It needed a structure that would allow it to respond quickly and flexibly to the needs of its current and prospective customers. It knew it must empower its frontline employees to quote and issue policies.

Toward that end, Sun Life Financial decided on the following course of action: First, it discarded its functional structure and reorganized its 13 different functional groups into a series of cross-functional product teams. Employees from sales, customer service, order fulfillment, and other departments of the company became members of "service teams." Each team was also equipped with an IT system, which gave it access to all the information it needed to respond to a customer's request.[2] For example, each team was empowered to perform all the steps necessary to process a customer's request for insurance. No longer was it necessary for subordinates to go to their managers for approval on policies; the team could make its own decisions.

When all the requests and exchanges between departments were eliminated, Sun Life Financial was astonished at the impact the new structure had on the company's activities. Its new teams operated so quickly and with such flexibility that the time needed to process a request fell by 75 percent. With such rapid service, the company found it much easier to attract new customers, and its business started growing rapidly as a result.

Sun Life Financial soon realized that it could use IT in other ways to improve the way it coordinated its activities. As the company grew, for example, it began to offer a wider range of financial services such as pension management and investment and estate planning. In addition to realizing it could use its cross-functional teams to offer a wider range of new services, it decided to bring its customers "inside" the organization.

For example, via the Internet, today the company's customers can self-manage their accounts. When they want to change their insurance policies or add additional services, they can easily do so online. If they should need additional help, however, they can interact electronically with company's teams, make online inquiries, and normally receive a response within 24 hours. In fact, in 2003 Sun Life Financial won a national award for the way it had transformed its organizational design to improve customer service. Moreover, its new organizational structure and processes have resulted in record revenues and profits.[3]

S un Life Financial's experience suggests that an organizational design can have a major effect on the way a company's employees behave and how well it operates. Moreover, with the marketplace changing at every turn, it is imperative that organizations continue to find new ways to operate efficiently and flexibly. In this chapter, we first examine the nature of organizational design and structure, and then we examine the main contingencies or changing conditions that affect the way an organization is designed. Second, we look at the different ways in which people and groups can be arranged to create an organizational structure that allows employees to achieve the organization's goals. Third, we examine the methods organizations use to coordinate and integrate people and groups to ensure that they work together well. Finally, we focus on the way new forms of information technology are changing the way organizations manage their activities.

Designing Organizational Structure

Organizing is the process of establishing the structure of working relationships among employees to allow them to achieve organizational goals effectively. **Organizational structure** is the formal system of task and job reporting relationships that determines how employees use resources to achieve the organization's goals.[4] **Organizational design** is the process of making the specific choices about how to arrange the tasks and job relationships that comprise the organizational structure.[5]

According to **contingency theory**, an organization's structure needs to be designed to fit or match the set of contingencies—factors or conditions that affect it the most and cause it the most uncertainty.[6] Because each organization faces a different set of contingencies, there is no "one best way" to design an organization: The best design is one that fits the organization's specific situation. Three important contingencies that factor into the design of organizational structure are (1) the nature of the organization's environment, (2) advances in technology (increasingly, information technology), and (3) the characteristics of an organization's human resources.[7] (See Figure 16.1.) Each of these is discussed in detail next, followed by the way they affect an organization's structure.

THE ORGANIZATIONAL ENVIRONMENT

We examined several forces in the environment that affect organizational behavior, such as changes in the social, cultural, and global environment, in Chapter 1. In general, the more quickly forces in the environment are changing, the greater the uncertainty within it and the greater are the problems of quickly accessing resources the organization needs

Organizational structure
The formal system of task and reporting relationships that controls, coordinates, and motivates employees so that they cooperate and work together to achieve an organization's goals.

Organizational design The process by which managers select and manage various dimensions and components of organizational structure and culture so that an organization can achieve its goals.

Contingency theory Organizational structure should be designed to match the set of contingencies— factors or conditions—that cause an organization the most uncertainty.

FIGURE 16.1
Three Contingencies Affecting Organizational Design

The Organization's Environment → Organizational Design ← The Organization's Technology

Human Resources and the Employment Relationship → Organizational Design

to perform well, such as additional capital, plants, and equipment. In order to speed up the decision-making and communication processes related to obtaining resources, the most likely choice of design will be one that brings flexibility to the organization.[8] In this case, an organization is more likely to decentralize authority and empower its employees to make important operating decisions.[9] Because change is occurring everywhere in today's global environment, finding ways to structure organizations to empower self-managed teams and employees is imperative.[10]

In contrast, if the environment is stable, resources are readily available, and uncertainty is low, then less coordination and communication among people and functions are needed to obtain resources. Organizational design choices can be made that bring more stability or formality to the structure. A more clearly defined hierarchy of authority and an extensive body of rules and regulations are likely to be appropriate in this case.

TECHNOLOGY

Technology The combination of skills, knowledge, tools, machines, computers, and equipment used in the design, production, and distribution of goods and services.

Technology is the combination of skills, knowledge, tools, machines, computers, and equipment used in the design, production, and distribution of goods and services. As a rule, the more complicated the technology that an organization uses, the more difficult it is to regulate and control it. Thus, in contingency theory, the more complicated the technology, the greater is the need for a flexible structure to allow an organization to respond to unexpected situations and provide its employees with the freedom to work out new solutions to the problems they encounter using it.[11] In contrast, the more routine the technology, the more appropriate is a formal structure because tasks are simple and the steps needed to produce goods and services have been worked out in advance.

What makes a technology routine or complicated? One researcher who investigated this issue, Charles Perrow, argued that two factors determine how complicated or nonroutine technology is: task variety and task analyzability.[12] *Task variety* is the number of new or unexpected problems or situations that a person or functional group encounters while performing tasks or jobs. *Task analyzability* is the degree to which programmed solutions are available to people or functional groups to solve the problems they encounter. Nonroutine or complicated technologies are characterized by high task variety and low task analyzability; this means that many varied problems occur and that solving these problems requires significant nonprogrammed decision making. In contrast, routine technologies are characterized by low task variety and high task analyzability; this means that the problems encountered do not vary much and are easily resolved through programmed decision making.

Examples of nonroutine technology are found in the way scientists in a research and development laboratory develop new products or discover new drugs or in the way emergency or operating room personnel cooperate to quickly respond to each patient's particular medical needs. Examples of routine technology include typical mass-production or assembly operations in which employees perform the same task repeatedly and the programmed solutions necessary to perform a task efficiently have already been identified and refined. Similarly, in service organizations, such as fast-food restaurants, the tasks that crew members perform in making and serving the food are very routine.

The extent to which the process of actually producing or creating goods and services depends on people or machines is another factor that determines how nonroutine a technology is. The more the technology used to produce goods and services is based on the skills, knowledge, and abilities of people working together on an ongoing basis and not on automated machines that can be programmed in advance, the more complex the technology is. Joan Woodward, a professor who investigated the relationship between technology and organizational structure, differentiated among three kinds of technology on the basis of the relative contributions made by people or machines.[13]

Skilled workers at Steinway and Sons wrap a 22-foot-long maple rim around the press that will shape it into the case for a Model D grand piano, an example of small-batch production in action. Roughly 200 people are involved in making and assembling the piano, which has 12,000 parts and costs about $ 60,000 to buy.

Small-batch technology is used to produce small quantities of customized, one-of-a-kind products and is based on the skills of people who work together in small groups. Examples of goods and services produced by small-batch technology include custom-built cars, such as Ferraris and Rolls Royces, highly specialized metals and chemicals that are produced by the pound rather than by the ton, and the evaluation services performed by a small team of auditors hired to evaluate the accuracy of a firm's financial statements. Because small-batch goods or services are customized and unique, employees need to respond to each situation in a more unique fashion; a decentralized structure of authority allows them to respond flexibly. Such a structure is, therefore, appropriate with small-batch technology.

Woodward's second kind of technology, **mass-production technology**, is based primarily on the use of automated machines that are programmed to perform the same operations time and time again. Mass production works most efficiently when each person performs a repetitive task. There is less need for flexibility; in this case, a formal organizational structure is preferred because it gives managers the most control over the production process. Mass production results in an output of large quantities of standardized products such as tin cans, Ford Tauruses, washing machines, and lightbulbs, and services such as a car wash or dry cleaner.

The third kind of technology that Woodward identified, **continuous-process technology**, is almost totally mechanized. Products are produced by automated machines working in sequence and controlled through computers from a central monitoring station. Examples of continuous-process technology include large steel mills, oil refineries, nuclear power stations, and large-scale brewing operations. The role of employees in continuous-process technology is not to produce individual products but instead to watch for problems that may occur unexpectedly and adversely affect the overall process. The possibility of a machinery or computer breakdown, for example, is a major hazard associated with continuous-process technology. If an unexpected situation does occur (such as an explosion in a chemical complex), employees must be able to respond quickly and appropriately to prevent a disaster. In this case, the flexible response required will necessitate a flexible organizational structure.

As we discussed in previous chapters, new information technology is profoundly affecting how organizations operate. An IT-enabled organizational structure allows for new kinds of tasks and job reporting relationships among electronically connected people that promotes superior communication and coordination. For

Small-batch technology A method used to produce small quantities of customized, one-of-a-kind products based on the skills of people who work together in small groups.

Mass-production technology A method of production using automated machines that are programmed to perform the same operations time and time again.

Continuous-process technology A method of production involving the use of automated machines working in sequence and controlled through computers from a central monitoring station.

example, one type of IT-enabled organizational relationship discussed in Chapter 15 is *knowledge management,* the sharing and integrating of expertise within and between functional groups and divisions in real time.[14] Unlike more rigid or bureaucratic organizing methods, new IT-enabled organizations can respond more quickly to changing conditions in the competitive environment.

HUMAN RESOURCES AND THE EMPLOYMENT RELATIONSHIP

A third important contingency affecting an organization's choice of structure is the characteristics of its human resources and the nature of the employment relationship. In general, the more highly skilled an organization's workforce, the more people are required to work together in groups or teams to perform their tasks. In this case, an organization is more likely to use a flexible, decentralized structure. Also, the longer and better the employment relationship a company has with its employees, the more likely it is to choose a design structure giving them the freedom to make important decisions.[15] Highly skilled employees usually desire freedom and autonomy and dislike close supervision.[16] For example, no one needs to tell a scientist to report his or results accurately and impartially or doctors and nurses to give patients the best care possible.

Moreover, when people work in teams like doctors and nurses and groups of research scientists do, they must be able to interact freely. A more flexible organizational structure makes this possible. When it comes to designing an organizational structure, both the work and the people who do it are important.

ORGANIC AND MECHANISTIC STRUCTURES

As the previous discussion suggests, an organization's environment, technology, and human resources are three main factors that influence the design of its structure. The greater the level of uncertainty in the environment of the organization, the complexity of its technology, and the skill of its workforce, the more likely managers are to design a flexible structure.

Organic structure
An organizational structure designed to promote flexibility so that employees can initiate change and adapt quickly to changing conditions.

In contingency theory, the term **organic structure** is used to describe an organizational structure that is designed to promote flexibility so that employees can initiate change and adapt quickly to changing conditions. In an organic structure, employees working in empowered teams assume the responsibility to make decisions as organizational needs dictate. Employees also are expected to continually develop skills in new kinds of tasks and to work together to find the best ways to perform a task. Shared work norms and values become the main means through which employees coordinate their activities to achieve organizational goals.

Mechanistic structure
An organizational structure designed to induce employees to behave in predictable, accountable ways.

In contrast, the more stable the organization's environment, the less complex and more well understood its technology, and the less skilled its workforce, the more likely are managers to design an organizational structure that is formal and controlling. In contingency theory, the term **mechanistic structure** is used to describe an organizational structure that is designed to induce employees to behave in predictable, accountable ways. In a mechanistic structure decision-making authority is retained at the top of the organization, and each employee performs a clearly defined task and knows exactly what his or her area of responsibility is. The work process is coordinated by an extensive system of rules and regulations that links employee activities and makes them ordered and predictable. How do you design an organization structure to be either flexible or formal? The way an organization's structure works depends on the organizing choices managers make about two principal issues:

- ♦ How to group jobs into functions and divisions
- ♦ How to coordinate or integrate jobs, functional groups, and divisions

you're the management expert

Which Work System Is Better?

You're an expert on organizational design who has been called in to advise a new Web development company about how to organize its work activities. The company's goal is to design Web sites to suit the needs of specific clients, usually small- to medium-sized companies. This will require that the Web site developers work closely with each client. After the site is built to the satisfaction of the client, it will have to be constantly updated to incorporate new software technology and to reflect changes in the client's business needs. The managers of the new company want to know if they should (1) design the work processes so that, using a sophisticated IT system, each employee working alone can make all the necessary decisions to satisfy a particular customer's request, or (2) use small-batch production and group employees into teams to develop several different Web sites at once. Which system do you think is likely to be more effective? Why?

Grouping Jobs Into Functions and Divisions

As we note in Chapter 1, organizations are groups of people working together to achieve a wide variety of goals. One of the main reasons people work together is so that the organization can experience gains in productivity that result from the division of labor and specialization.[17]

The first issue in organizational design is to choose a division of labor or way to group different jobs together to best meet the needs of the organization's environment, technology, and human resources. Most organizations group jobs together according to their function and thereby develop a functional structure. A **function** is a group of people working together who possess similar skills or use the same kind of knowledge, tools, or techniques to perform their jobs. A **functional structure** is an organizational structure composed of all the job specializations that an organization requires to produce its goods or services. For example, the salespeople in a car dealership belong to the sales function. Together, car sales, car repair, car parts, and accounting are the set of functions that allow an automotive dealership to sell and maintain cars. Consider how Michael Dell developed a functional structure for Dell Computer. To effectively control the activities of his employees as his company grew, Dell created the functional structure illustrated in Figure 16.2.

Dell groups all employees who perform tasks related to assembling personal computers into the manufacturing function and all employees who handle Dell's telephone sales into the sales function. Engineers responsible for designing Dell's computers are grouped into the product development function, and employees responsible for obtaining supplies of hard discs, chips, and other inputs are grouped into the materials management function. The functional structure suited the needs of Dell's growing company, especially as it battled with Compaq, now a part of HP, and Gateway for control of the personal computer market—a battle in which it is currently winning hands down.[18]

Function A set of people who perform the same types of tasks or hold similar positions in an organization.

Functional structure An organizational structure that groups together people who hold similar positions, perform a similar set of tasks, or use the same kinds of skills.

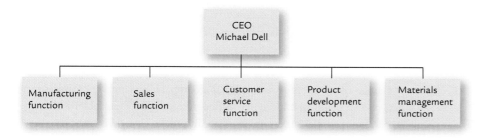

FIGURE 16.2
Dell's Functional Structure

Division A group of functions created to allow an organization to produce and dispose of its goods and services to customers.

If an organization subsequently grows and prospers, it often employs a second grouping by division and adopts a more complex form of divisional structure. A **division** is a group of functions created to specialize in making and selling a particular kind of good or service.[19]

Choosing a structure and then designing it so that it works as intended is a significant challenge. The ability to make the right kinds of organizing choices is often what differentiates effective from ineffective organizations. Organizational design is such an important decision because it affects the behavior of people in so many different ways. First, it affects employees' motivation to work hard and to develop supportive work attitudes. Second, it affects the likelihood that different groups, functions, or divisions will want to cooperate with one another, share resources, and work together effectively.[20] To be effective, an organization must decide how it wants its members to behave, what attitudes it wants to encourage, and what it wants its members to accomplish. Then it can make design choices based on these goals.

ADVANTAGES OF A FUNCTIONAL STRUCTURE

A functional structure offers several advantages when it comes to managing an organization's activities. All organizations (even relatively small ones) group their activities by function, at least to some extent, to capture the benefits that result from the division of labor and specialization.

Coordination Advantages. People grouped together according to similarities in their positions can easily communicate and share information with each other. As we saw in Chapter 14 on communication and Chapter 15 on decision making, people who approach problems from the same perspective can often make decisions more quickly and effectively than can people whose perspectives differ. A functional grouping also makes it easier for people to learn from one another's experiences. In this way, a functional structure helps employees improve their skills and thereby enhances individual and organizational performance.

Motivational Advantages. Grouping by function improves an organization's ability to motivate employees. When employees are grouped together by function, supervisors are in a good position to monitor individual performance, reward high performance, and discourage social loafing. Functional supervisors find monitoring easy because they usually possess high levels of skill in the particular function. Grouping by function also allows group members to monitor and control one another's behavior and performance levels. Functional grouping can also lead to the development of norms, values, and group cohesiveness that promote high performance (see Chapter 11). Finally, grouping by function creates a career ladder to motivate employees: Functional managers and supervisors are typically employees who have been promoted because of their superior performance.

DISADVANTAGES OF A FUNCTIONAL STRUCTURE

To manage the division of labor, most organizations develop a functional structure because of the coordination and motivation advantages associated with it. But as an organization continues to grow and its activities become more diverse and complex, a functional structure may no longer allow it to coordinate its activities effectively. It may even hinder the organization for any one of the following three reasons:

1. When the range of products or services that a company produces increases, its various functions can begin to experience difficulties. Imagine the problems that would occur, for example, if a company started to make cars, then went into

computers, followed by clothing, but used the same sales force to sell all three products. Most salespeople would not be able to learn enough about all three products quickly enough for the company to provide its customers good service.

2. Coordination problems may arise. As organizations attract customers with different needs, it may find it hard to service these different needs by using a single set of functions. The needs of individual customers, for example, are often very different from the needs of large corporate customers, although each still requires a high level of personalized service.

3. As companies grow, they often expand their operations nationally. Servicing the needs of different regional customers with a single set of manufacturing, sales, or purchasing functions becomes very difficult.

To cope with coordination problems such as these, organizations typically overlay their functional structures with divisional structures.

DIVISIONAL STRUCTURES: PRODUCT, MARKET, AND GEOGRAPHIC

When a divisional structure overlays its functional groups, an organization can coordinate its activities more effectively. Organizations can choose from three kinds of divisional structure: product, market, and geographic structures (see Figure 16.3). Each is suited to a particular kind of coordination problem facing an organization.[21]

U.S. computer maker Dell is organized, in part, by function. Dell employees are grouped according to what they do: manufacturing, engineering, product development, sales, and so forth.

Product Structure. When an organization chooses to group people and functions so that it can produce a wide variety of different products, it moves to a **product structure**. Each product division contains the functions necessary to service the specific goods or products. Figure 16.3A shows the product structure used by a company such as General Electric, which has many separate product-oriented divisions—for example, divisions responsible for producing lightbulbs, aerospace products, and appliances. Each of these divisions has its own set of functions (such as accounting, marketing, and research and development).

What are the advantages of a product structure? It allows a company to increase its division of labor so that it can make and sell a wider range of products. Dell, for example, created product divisions when it began to sell new electronic goods such as workstations, minicomputers, printers, and personal data assistants (PDAs) in the 2000s. Each product division is responsible for the success of its new products, so the members of each division focus their energies on making those products a success.

Market Structure. Sometimes the most pressing problem facing an organization is to deliver products to customers in a way that best meets customer needs. To accomplish this goal, an organization is likely to choose a **market structure** and group functions into divisions to respond to the needs of particular types of customers. (See Figure 16.3B.) For example, companies such as Staples and OfficeMax serve individual customers, but they also have large accounts with small companies and accounts with large companies and government agencies. Customers who buy large quantities of office supplies require special service and often demand special payment or delivery terms. To suit the specific needs of each group of customers, firms group their functions according to the type of customer needs. That way, each market division can specialize in and become more effective at meeting them.

Geographic Structure. When organizations expand rapidly both at home and abroad, functional structures can become problematic because managers in one central location may find it increasingly difficult to deal with the different issues

Product structure A divisional organizational structure that groups functions by types of product so that each division contains the functions it needs to service the products it produces.

Market structure A divisional organizational structure that groups functions by types of customers so that each division contains the functions it needs to service a specific segment of the market.

FIGURE 16.3

Three Types of Divisional Structure

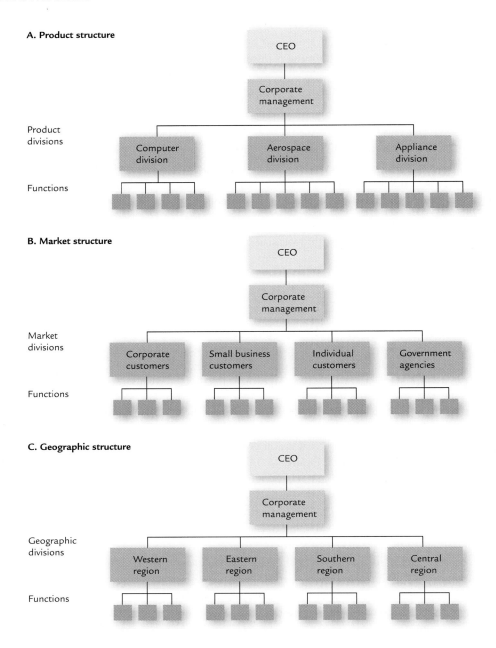

A. Product structure

B. Market structure

C. Geographic structure

Geographic structure
A division organizational structure that groups functions by region so that each division contains the functions it needs to service customers in a specific geographic area.

facing different regions. In these cases, a **geographic structure**, in which divisions are broken down by location, is often chosen (see Figure 16.3C). To achieve Federal Express's corporate mission of providing next-day mail service, CEO Fred Smith chose a geographic structure with regional divisions. Large retailers such as Macy's, Neiman Marcus, and Brooks Brothers also use a geographic structure. Because retail customers' purchases can vary dramatically by region (more down parkas are likely to be sold in the Midwest than in California, for example), a geographic structure gives regional managers the flexibility they need to choose the range of products best suited to their customers.

If it adopts a *global geographic structure,* then an organization locates different divisions in each of the world regions in which it operates. Often, for example, products that appeal to U.S. customers do not appeal to customers in Europe, the Pacific Rim, or South America. The goal is to customize products to meet the needs of customers in those different world regions, and a global geographic structure allows an organization to do this.

ADVANTAGES OF A DIVISIONAL STRUCTURE

A divisional structure—whether it's based on products, markets, or geography—has coordination and motivational advantages that overcome many of the problems associated with a functional structure as the size and complexity of an organization increase.

Coordination Advantages. Because each division contains its own set of functions, functional groups are able to focus their activities on a specific kind of good, service, or customer. This narrow focus helps a division create high-quality products and provide high-quality customer service. Each product division, for example, has its own sales force that specializes in selling its particular product. This specialization enables salespeople to perform more effectively.

A divisional structure also facilitates communication between functions and can improve decision making, thereby increasing performance. Burlington Northern Santa Fe Railway began dividing up its shipping operations into product divisions by the commodities customers ship—cars, chemicals, food products, and so on. The change from a functional to a product structure allowed the company to reduce costs and make better use of its resources.[22]

Similar kinds of advantages can result from using a market structure. Grouping different functions together in a market division to serve one type of customer enables the functions to coordinate their activities and better serve their customers. For example, KPMG, the third-largest accounting company in the United States, reorganized from a functional structure (in which people were organized into traditional functions such as accounting, auditing, taxes, and consulting) to a market structure. Employees in each of these functional areas were grouped together to serve customers in different industries, such as manufacturing, financial, and retail sectors, for example.[23] KPMG moved to a market structure to make better use of its human and other resources.

A geographic structure puts managers closer to the scene of operations than managers at central headquarters. Regional managers are well positioned to respond to the regional needs of customers and fluctuations in resources in those areas. Often they are able to find solutions to specific problems in those areas and use available resources more effectively than managers at headquarters can.

Finally, on an individual level, people who are grouped together into divisions are sometimes able to pool their skills and knowledge and brainstorm new ideas for products or improved customer service. As divisions develop a common identity and approach to solving problems, their cohesiveness increases, and the result is improved decision making.

Motivational Advantages. Grouping into divisions offers organizations a wide range of motivational advantages as well. First, a divisional structure gives rise to a new level of management: **corporate management** (see Figure 16.3). The responsibility of corporate managers is to supervise and oversee the managers of the various divisions. Corporate managers coordinate and motivate divisional managers and reward them on the basis of the performance of their individual divisions. A divisional structure makes it easier for organizations to evaluate the performance of individual divisions and their managers and reward them in a way that is closely linked to their performance.[24] Recall from Chapter 8 that a clear connection between performance and reward increases motivation. Corporate managers can also evaluate one regional operation against another and share ideas developed by one region with the others to improve performance.

A second motivational advantage is that divisional managers enjoy a large measure of autonomy because they—not corporate managers—are responsible for operations. Their autonomy tends to promote positive work attitudes and boost performance.

Corporate management
The set of managers whose responsibility is to supervise and oversee the divisional managers.

Another motivational advantage of a divisional structure is that regional managers and employees are close to their customers and more likely to develop personal relationships with them as a result. These relationships give the managers and employees an extra incentive to perform well. Finally, on an individual level, employees' close identification with their division can increase their commitment, loyalty, and job satisfaction.

DISADVANTAGES OF A DIVISIONAL STRUCTURE

Although divisional structures offer large, complex organizations a number of coordination and motivational advantages over functional structures, they have certain disadvantages as well. The disadvantages can be overcome with good management, but some of them are simply the result of the way a divisional structure works.

First, because each division has its own set of functions, the costs of operating and managing an organization increase. The number of managers in an organization, for example, increases because each division has its own set of sales managers, manufacturing managers, accountants, and so on. It also creates a completely new level of management that must be paid for—the corporate level of management.

Second, as we discuss later, communication may suffer when a divisional structure is implemented. Because divisional structures normally have more managers and more levels of management than functional structures, communication can become more complex as managers at various levels in different divisions attempt to exchange information with one another and coordinate their activities.

Third, divisions may start to compete for organizational resources and pursue their own goals at the expense of organizational goals. These conflicts reduce cooperation and can sometimes result in friction between divisions.

In summary, an organization must compare the benefits and costs of using a functional or a divisional structure. When the benefits exceed the costs, it should move to a divisional structure. Even with a divisional structure, however, an organization must manage the structure to overcome some of the disadvantages inherent to it and keep divisions and functions coordinated and motivated.

MATRIX STRUCTURE

Moving to a product, market, or geographic divisional structure allows managers to respond more quickly and flexibly to the particular set of contingencies they confront. However, when the environment is dynamic and changing rapidly and uncertainty is high, even a divisional structure may not provide managers with enough flexibility to respond quickly enough.[25] This can occur, for example, when information technology or the needs of customers are evolving rapidly. In this case managers must design the most flexible kind of structure available to their organization. This is called the *matrix structure*.

Matrix structure An organizational structure that simultaneously groups people by function and by product team.

In a **matrix structure**, managers group people and resources in two ways simultaneously: by function and by product.[26] Employees are grouped by *functions* to allow them to learn from one another and become more skilled and productive. In addition, employees are grouped into *product teams* in which members of different functions work together to develop a specific product. The result is a complex network of reporting relationships among product teams and functions that makes the matrix structure very flexible. Each person in a product team reports to two bosses: (1) a functional boss, who assigns individuals to a team and evaluates their performance from a functional perspective, and (2) the boss of their product team, who evaluates his or her performance on the team. Thus, team members are known as *two-boss employees*.

Figure 16.4 illustrates a matrix structure. The vertical lines show the functions of an organization, and the horizontal lines show the product teams responsible for devel-

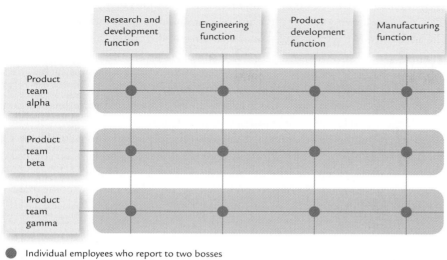

FIGURE 16.4
A Matrix Structure

● Individual employees who report to two bosses

▭ Product team composed of employees with two bosses

oping or manufacturing the organization's products. At the intersection of the lines are employees who report to both a functional boss and a product boss. The members of the teams are each developing a specific product. One team in Figure 16.4 is working on the Alpha computer workstation for small businesses; another team is working on the Beta workstation designed for large corporate customers.

Coordination Advantages. Typically, a company uses a matrix structure (rather than an ordinary divisional structure) for three reasons:

1. It needs to develop new products very rapidly.
2. It needs to maximize communication and cooperation between team members.
3. Innovation and creativity are the key to the organization's continuing success.[27]

Product teams permit face-to-face problem solving and create a work setting in which managers with different functional expertise can cooperate to solve nonprogrammed decision-making problems. Product team membership in a matrix structure is not fixed. Two-boss employees are transferred from team to team when their functional expertise is needed. For example, three electrical engineers work in the Alpha team to design the most efficient system to link electronic components. When they solve the Alpha design problem, they may then move to the Beta team if it requires their expertise. The flexibility of a matrix structure allows an organization to make the best use of its human resources.

Motivational Advantages. To understand how the matrix structure influences motivation, it is important to understand that the members of the product teams are generally highly qualified and skilled employees with advanced degrees and expertise in their fields. The matrix structure provides a work setting giving employees freedom and autonomy over their work activities. As we saw in Chapter 7, job design is important in determining work attitudes and behaviors, and many people enjoy jobs with a high motivating potential score. Matrix structures allow for such motivation and encourage work behaviors that enhance quality and innovation.

Disadvantages of a Matrix Structure. As you might expect, matrix structures have some disadvantages as well. Inherent to them are several properties that can cause job dissatisfaction. Matrix structures can increase role conflict and ambiguity (see Chapter 9), and high levels stress within them can sometimes ensue. Two bosses making conflicting demands on an employee can cause him or her to feel some role conflict; the very loose system of reporting relationships can make employees vulnerable to role ambiguity. The result is stress. Another source of discomfort for employees is that they might have trouble demonstrating their personal contributions to team performance because they move so often from team to team. For reasons such as these, some people dislike working within a matrix structure.[28]

As this discussion suggests, the matrix structure is associated with the most complex coordination and motivational issues. On the one hand, it has enormous coordination advantages, but on the other hand, it can cause complex motivational problems. The extent of these problems explains why only companies that depend for their survival on rapid product development designed to meet very specific customer needs use matrix structures. They are especially common in high-tech and biotechnology companies.

SUMMARY

Large organizations are more complex than small organizations. They have a greater number and variety of functions and divisions because they produce a greater number and variety of goods and services. As organizations grow, they can implement one or more different organizational structures. Each structure offers coordination and motivational advantages and disadvantages, and each is suited to addressing a particular contingency or problem facing the organization. Most companies use a functional design to group organizational activities and then overlay it with a product, market, geographic, or matrix structure to manage the specific contingencies they face.

Coordinating Functions and Divisions

The first organizational design task is to group functions and divisions and create the organizational structure best suited to the contingencies an organization faces. The second organizational design task is to ensure that there is sufficient coordination or integration among functions and divisions so that the organization's resources are used effectively. Having discussed the way in which organizational activities are divided up into functions and divisions, we now look at how the parts are put back together. We look first at the way in which the hierarchy of authority is used to coordinate functions and divisions so that they work together well. Then we focus on integration and examine the many different integrating mechanisms that can be used to coordinate functions and divisions.

ALLOCATING AUTHORITY

Authority The power that enables one person to hold another person accountable for his or her actions.

Hierarchy of authority An organization's chain of command that defines the relative authority of each level of management.

Span of control The number of employees who report to a manager.

As organizations grow and produce a wider range of goods and services, the size and number of their functions and divisions increase. To coordinate the activities of people, functions, and divisions, managers must develop a clear hierarchy of authority.[29] **Authority** is the power vested in a manager to make decisions and use resources to achieve organizational goals by virtue of his or her position in an organization. The **hierarchy of authority** is an organization's chain of command—the relative authority that each manager has—extending from the CEO at the top down through the middle managers and first-line managers to the nonmanagerial employees who actually make the goods or provide the services. In a hierarchy, each lower position is under the supervision of a higher one; as a result, authority links and integrates the activities of managers and employees across hierarchical levels. The term **span of control** refers to the number of subordinates who report directly to a manager.

Recall from the last section, for example, how the position of divisional manager emerges when an organization splits apart into divisions and how a corporate-level manager emerges to integrate the activities of divisional managers. Similarly, a hierarchy emerges inside each function to integrate the activities of employees within each function. As an organization grows and the problem of integrating activities within and between functions and divisions increases, the organization typically increases the number of levels in its hierarchy. As it does so, the span of control narrows.[30]

Compare the hierarchies shown in Figures 16.5A and 16.5B. The CEO in Figure 16.5A supervises six different functions, so the CEO's span of control is six subordinates. There are three levels in the hierarchy—the CEO, the managers in charge of each function, and the employees who report to each functional manager. Suppose the CEO decides that he can no longer effectively monitor the activities of the six functions because they are growing so rapidly. One way of solving this problem is to create a new level in the hierarchy. To do this, the CEO adds a level to the hierarchy by creating the positions of operations manager and product development manager, as shown in Figure 16.5B. Each of the new managers supervises three functions. These two managers and the CEO then work together as a team to integrate the activities of all six functions. The organization now has four levels in the hierarchy, the CEO's span of control narrows from six to two, and the span of control of the two new managers is three. Increasing the number of levels in an organization's hierarchy increases the coordination between the activities of different functions. Also, as the number of levels in the organizational hierarchy increases, the span of control narrows, so managers are better able to coordinate and motivate their subordinates.

FIGURE 16.5

Using the Hierarchy to Manage Intergroup Relations

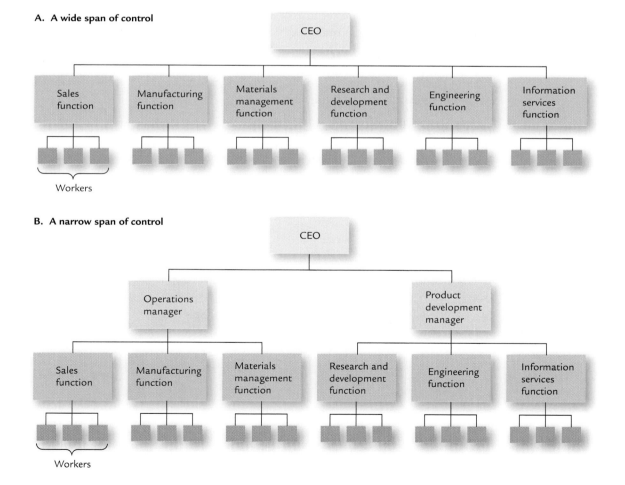

A. A wide span of control

B. A narrow span of control

Tall and Flat Hierarchies. The number of levels in a hierarchy varies from organization to organization. In general, the larger and more complex an organization is, the taller is its hierarchy. Tall organizations have many hierarchical levels relative to their size; flat organizations have few (see Figure 16.6).

Just as it becomes more difficult to coordinate the activities of different functions as their number increases, it becomes more difficult to achieve coordination between hierarchical levels when an organization's hierarchy becomes too tall. Communication and decision-making problems start to occur. As the number of managerial levels increases, the time it takes to send messages up and down the chain increases. The result is slower decision making. In addition, information passed from person to person is more likely to get distorted or filtered as messages become garbled and managers interpret them according to their own interests. These problems detract from the quality of decision making. In fact, all the communications problems discussed in Chapter 14 increase as an organization's hierarchy becomes taller and taller.

The Minimum Chain of Command. An important organizational design principle is the *principle of the minimum chain of command*. A minimum chain of command principle can help mitigate problems that ensue when the hierarchical structure becomes too tall. The principle states that an organization should operate with the fewest levels possible. Effective organizations should scrutinize their hierarchies to see whether the number of levels can be reduced—for example, whether one level can be eliminated and its responsibilities assigned to managers or employees above or below it.

This practice has become increasingly common in the United States as companies battling low-cost global competitors search for ways to cut costs. One manager who is constantly trying to empower employees and keep the hierarchy flat is Colleen C. Barrett, the number-two executive of Southwest Airlines.[31] At Southwest, she is well known for continually reaffirming the company's message that employees should feel free to go above and beyond their prescribed roles to provide customers better service. Southwest employees are encouraged not to look to their superiors for guidance but rather to themselves to find ways to do their jobs better. As a result, Southwest keeps the number of its middle managers to a minimum.

Centralization Versus Decentralization. Another way to keep the organizational hierarchy flat is to decentralize authority to lower-level managers and nonmanagerial employees.[32] When lower-level managers and nonmanagerial employees

FIGURE 16.6

Examples of Flat and Tall Hierarchies

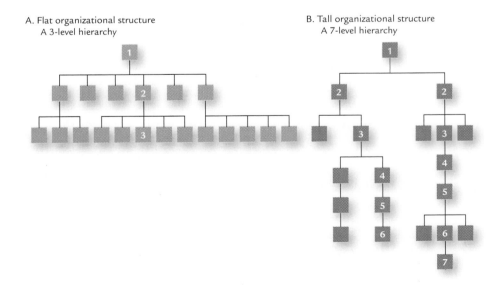

A. Flat organizational structure
A 3-level hierarchy

B. Tall organizational structure
A 7-level hierarchy

have the responsibility to make important decisions, the problems of slow and distorted communication noted previously are kept to a minimum. This can increase motivation by making lower-level jobs more interesting and rewarding. Moreover, fewer managers are needed because their role is not to make decisions but to act as coach and facilitator and to help other employees make the best decisions.

Decentralizing authority allows an organization and its employees to behave in a flexible way even as the organization grows and becomes taller. This is why managers are so interested in empowering employees, creating self-managed work teams, establishing cross-functional teams, and even moving to a product team structure.

Although more and more organizations are taking steps to decentralize authority, too much decentralization has certain disadvantages. If divisions, functions, or teams are given too much decision-making authority, they may begin to pursue their own goals at the expense of the organization's goals. Managers in engineering design or R&D, for example, may become so focused on making the best possible product that they fail to realize that the best product may be so expensive that few people will be willing or able to buy it! Also, with too much decentralization, a lack of communication among functions or divisions may prevent synergies among them from materializing and organizational performance may suffer.

An organization must seek the balance between centralization and decentralization of authority that best meets the major contingencies it faces. If an organization operates in a stable environment using well-understood technology, for example, then there is no pressing need to decentralize authority, and top-level managers can make most of the decisions.[33] However, in uncertain, changing environments like those in surrounding high-tech industries, companies are speeding new products to market. Employees and teams must be empowered to make important decisions so that the organization can keep pace with the changes taking place. These companies are more likely to prefer a higher degree of decentralization.

In summary, the design of the organizational hierarchy is one of the most important decisions an organization makes as it attempts to coordinate its functions and divisions and achieve its goals. Managers need to continually scrutinize the hierarchy to make sure it meets the organization's needs, and they must be prepared to change it if it does not. We discuss issues and problems in changing organizational structure in detail in Chapter 18.

MUTUAL ADJUSTMENT AND INTEGRATING MECHANISMS

The organizational hierarchy is an important method of coordination because it links and allows the activities performed by employees at all levels of the organization to be controlled. If necessary, for example, the operations manager in Figure 16.5B can tell the sales, manufacturing, and materials management managers what to do and how to coordinate their activities. However, the operations manager cannot tell the product development manager what to do because the two managers are at the *same level in the hierarchy*. Furthermore, the operations manager cannot tell anyone in R&D, engineering, or information systems what to do even though they are at a lower hierarchical level because they do not report to the operations manager. These functions report to the product development manager, who is responsible only to the CEO. Ultimately, only the CEO, the person at the top of the hierarchy, has the authority to tell everyone in the organization what to do, and that is why an organization's top manager is so powerful.

Because managers at the same level or in different functions have no power over each other, organizations need to use tools other than the organizational hierarchy to coordinate their activities. One important form of coordination takes place through mutual adjustment and the use of integrating mechanisms. **Mutual adjustment** is the ongoing communication among different people and functions that is necessary for an

Mutual adjustment The ongoing informal communication among different people and functions that is necessary for an organization to achieve its goals.

organization to achieve its goals. Mutual adjustment makes an organization's structure work smoothly because it facilitates communication and the free flow of information between functions. Mutual adjustment, for example, prevents the emergence of different orientations that can cause significant communication and decision-making problems between functions and divisions.

To facilitate mutual adjustment, organizations use various kinds of integrating mechanisms. **Integrating mechanisms** are organizing tools used to increase communication and coordination among functions and divisions. Here we discuss several kinds of integrating mechanism that facilitate mutual adjustment in the order of their importance.[34]

Integrating mechanisms
Organizing tools used to increase communication and coordination among functions and divisions.

Direct Contact. With direct contact, managers from different functions establish face-to-face working relationships that allow them to solve common problems informally without having to go through the formal channels of authority in the hierarchy. In a functional structure, for example, managers in sales try to develop good, informal working relationships with managers in manufacturing so that both can simultaneously make decisions to achieve their goals. Reaching agreement may not be easy because the goals of the two groups are not always identical. Manufacturing's goal is to keep costs at a minimum; to do this it is often necessary to maintain production according to a particular schedule to smoothly manufacture goods in large batches. The goal of the sales function is to respond to the needs of customers; it often needs to ask manufacturing to change production schedules on short notice to accommodate unexpected customer requests. Because such sales-dictated changes raise manufacturing's costs, the potential for conflict arises. A high level of direct contact between sales and manufacturing managers, however, can lead to a give-and-take relationship that fosters cooperation between functions.

Liaison Roles. Because organizations recognize that direct contact is important, they often establish liaison roles giving specific functional managers the *formal* responsibility of communicating with managers in another function to solve common problems. To facilitate communication, managers in liaison roles meet regularly to exchange information, and members of one function transmit requests to other functions through these liaison personnel. Over time, the personal working relationships that develop between the managers performing these roles enhance coordination throughout the organization.

Teams and Task Forces. Organizations often create teams and task forces composed of employees from different functions to facilitate communication and cooperation. Whereas a team is a permanent group made up of representatives from two or more functions that meets regularly, a task force is a temporary, or ad hoc, group set up to solve a specific problem. An organization might set up a task force to study problems it expects to encounter as it expands its operations into another country, for example. After the task force comes up with a solution to the problem to which it is assigned, it disbands.

In contrast, an organization may use a team to increase coordination between functions such as the product development team shown in Figure 16.7. Because product development is an ongoing activity, an organization is likely to create a permanent team composed of members from several functions whose job it is to constantly scrutinize new product ideas and make recommendations about the ones that should be funded.

The important role teams and task forces play to promote mutual adjustment cannot be overemphasized. It has been estimated that managers spend over 70 percent of their time in face-to-face meetings with other managers making decisions and solving problems that cannot be dealt with through the formal hierarchy or in any other way.[35]

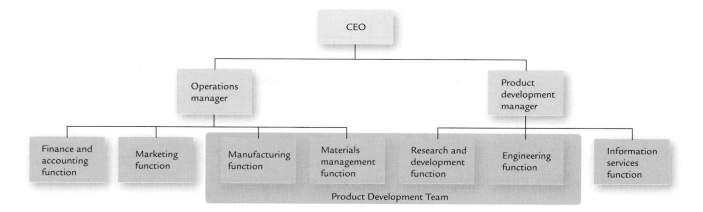

Cross-Functional Teams. Recently, many organizations have implemented cross-functional teams to facilitate mutual adjustment. *Cross-functional teams* consist of people from different functions who are permanently assigned to work full-time on a team to bring a new good or service to the market.[36] Cross-functional teams are different from ordinary teams in several ways. Members of an ordinary team are full-time members of the same function or division; members of cross-functional teams are full-time members of different functions or divisions and report to the leader of the team. Figure 16.8 shows an example of a cross-functional team structure formed to facilitate mutual adjustment.

Hallmark Cards moved to a cross-functional team structure when it decided to organize its tasks according to specific types of cards—birthday cards, Christmas cards, Mother's Day cards, and so on. Rather than having card designers, artists, rhyme writers, and other specialists work in separate functions, Hallmark assigned them to cross-functional teams to reduce the need to coordinate among functions. The new structure greatly speeded product development. A new card used to take a year to get to the market; now it takes only a few months. Chrysler Corporation was a pioneer in the use of cross-functional teams, which have greatly contributed to its current strong performance in the car market as the accompanying OB Today discusses.

FIGURE 16.7

Using a Team to Increase Coordination Between Functions

FIGURE 16.8

A Cross-Functional Team Structure
Cross-functional teams are composed of functional personnel who are assigned full-time to work in the team.

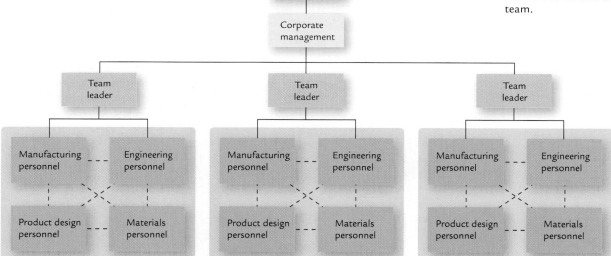

ob today

DaimlerChrysler's Cross-Functional Product Team Structure

After almost going bankrupt in the early 1990s, Chrysler earned record profits in the 1990s and merged with Daimler Benz to form DaimlerChrysler in 1998.[37] Daimler's desire to merge with Chrysler came about because Chrysler had pioneered the use of cross-functional teams and new information technology to lower manufacturing costs and speed the introduction of new products. Daimler needed this expertise.[38]

Chrysler's decision to use cross-functional teams linked to a sophisticated computer network came about in the following way. In 1988, Chrysler acquired American Motors (AMC) and its 700 design engineers. Rather than distributing these engineers among Chrysler's different engineering functions—transmissions, brakes, engines, and so on—Chrysler made a radical decision. It chose to keep the engineers together and have all 700 of them work together in a cross-functional team devoted to redesigning the Jeep Grand Cherokee, infamous among consumers for its poor reliability.

The 700 engineers from all areas of design engineering worked together on a single huge work floor. They were joined by marketing, finance, purchasing, and other functional experts who gave them information about customers' needs, input costs, and so on. All of the information communicated between functional specialists was recorded and exchanged electronically through sophisticated computer systems so that each member of the team knew what the others were doing. Top management then gave the team a target price for the car and told the team to design it to fit within that price range. The result was astounding. The new design was finished in just two years, and the Jeep Cherokee was an instant success when it was introduced in 1992. Chrysler was so pleased with the results the cross-functional team achieved that it decided to change the entire structure of the company from one that revolved around functions to one that utilized cross-functional teams.

In the new structure, functional personnel are assigned to one of four major teams—the small car, large car, minivan, or Jeep/truck team—and each team has its own vice president. Chrysler also built a $1 billion technology center with separate floors to house each team. Its cross-functional team structure allows Chrysler's functional experts to meet and share ideas to speed the development process. It also allows for the intense interaction among people that is necessary for successful innovation and product development.

The biggest challenge Chrysler faced after its merger with Daimler was not just transferring new product information from one team to another but also transferring information to its far-flung German and U.S. operations so that all design teams could quickly capitalize on the advances made by the other teams. For example, Mercedes-Benz, Daimler's car division, is renowned for the high quality and safety of its cars; Chrysler's managers wanted to disseminate that expertise to the personnel making its brands.[39] The result was an outpouring of new, innovative vehicles in the 2000s such as the Chrysler Crossfire, Pacifica, and PT cruiser convertible.[40]

DaimlerChrysler employees assemble one of the company's best-selling lines—the PT Cruiser cars.

STANDARDIZATION

The third principal tool that organizations can use to coordinate their activities and integrate functions and divisions is **standardization**—the development of programmed responses, performance standards, written rules, and standard operating procedures (SOPs) that specify how employees and functions should respond to recurring problems or opportunities. An organization can standardize activities at the input, conversion, and output stages.[41]

Standardizing Inputs. Organizational inputs include the skills and capabilities of managers and employees, the quality of the raw materials and component parts used to make products, and the machinery and computers used in the production process. Organizations develop performance standards, such as quality or reliability specifications, used to evaluate and assess inputs before they are put into production. Japanese car companies, for example, are renowned for the stringent quality specifications that they require suppliers of car components such as engine blocks to meet. Increasingly, more global companies are recognizing that high input standards result in a higher-quality products.

Organizations can standardize the skills of their managers and employees by requiring them to have certain qualifications and experiences. An assembly-line employee might be required to have a high school diploma, an R&D scientist might be required to have a Ph.D. from a prestigious research university, and a CEO might be required to show that he or she has successfully managed similar kinds of businesses in the past. Organizations that recruit and select employees who meet stringent criteria can be relatively confident that their employees will respond in appropriate ways to uncertain events. This is why organizations spend so much time recruiting and selecting employees.

Standardizing Conversion Processes. To standardize the conversion processes an organization uses to make the final product, organizations specify the kinds of behavior they expect from their employees. When these behaviors are specified, both individuals and groups are more likely to act consistently in ways that allow an organization to achieve its goals. The principal way in which organizations standardize behaviors is through the use of rules and standard operating procedures (SOPs). (See Chapter 10.)[42] Because rules and SOPs specify the series of actions or decisions that employees are expected to perform in a given situation, they standardize employee responses to the situation.

Formalization is the use of rules and standard operating procedures to control an organization's activities. The more an organization can rely on formalization to specify required behaviors, the less it needs to use either direct supervision from the hierarchy or mutual adjustment. Formalization results in lower operating costs, once rules have been developed. They are also inexpensive to implement and cost the organization little to maintain. All that is required is that new employees be taught the appropriate rules to follow in certain situations. (Recall from Chapter 10 that socialization is the process by which employees learn organizational rules and SOPs.)

Although some rules are necessary to the smooth running of an organization, too many rules can give rise to a number of problems:

♦ Excessive formalization can "straitjacket" employees and prevent them from responding creatively and flexibly to new situations.

♦ Employees' inclination to obey rules without thinking about their consequences can reduce the quality of organizational decision making.

♦ Too much emphasis on the use of existing rules and procedures can make it especially difficult for an organization to make changes and develop new rules.

Despite these drawbacks, formalization is a powerful tool as the accompanying OB Today suggests.

Standardization The development of routine responses to recurring problems or opportunities.

Formalization The use of rules and standard operating procedures to control an organization's activities.

ob today

This Dot-Com Thrives on Rules

Most people don't associate high-tech, dot-com companies with elaborate rule systems and SOPs. Normally, we would think that the need to adjust to rapid technological change would dictate a decentralized structure. There are exceptions, however. One exception was a company called siteROCK based in Emeryville, California.

Before later being acquired by Avasta, a San Francisco firm, siteROCK hosted and managed other companies' Web sites, and was known for its ability to keep them up and running and error free. When a site went down at siteROCK, it was enemy number one.

The company was run by Dave Lilly, who was once nuclear submarine commander. To maximize the performance of his employees and increase their ability to respond to unexpected online events, Lilly decided the siteROCK needed a comprehensive set of rules and SOPs to cover all the major known problems that could crash a site.[43] He insisted that every problem-solving procedure be written down. siteROCK had over 30 thick binders listing all the processes and checklists that employees needed to follow when an unexpected event happened.

At siteROCK, these written rules and SOPs were used to control employee behavior to achieve high levels of customer service. Because the goal of the company was 100 percent reliability, detailed blueprints guided planning and decision making—not seat-of-the-pants solutions that might have worked 80 percent of the time but resulted in disaster the other 20 percent of the time. Before siteROCK employees were allowed in the control room each day, they had to read over the most important rules and SOPs. At the end of a shift, they spent 90 minutes doing paperwork logging what they had done and detailing any new or improved rules that they came up with.

Moreover, Lilly instituted a "two-person rule." Whenever the unexpected happened, each employee had to immediately tell a co-employee and the two together would then attempt to solve the problem. The goal was simple: Use the rules to achieve a quick resolution to a complex issue. If the existing rules didn't work, then employees were told to experiment. When they found a solution, it went into the rule book to aid the future decision making of all employees in the organization.

Formals sets of rules undoubtedly helped siteROCK achieve a great deal of operational control—for a time. Lilly tried to control the things he could at siteROCK, but there were other things he couldn't. Amid a wave of consolidation in the IT industry beginning in 2002, siteROCK was acquired by Avasta, which provided outsource services to companies running large-scale applications like Oracle and PeopleSoft. Six months later, Avasta was acquired by NaviSite, a Massachusetts IT company.

Standardizing Outputs. Finally, output standards are also an effective way to standardize behavior. Instead of specifying the behaviors the organization expects from its employees with rules and SOPs, the organization specifies what the final output of its employees must be for the organization to achieve its goals.[44]

Imagine, for example, how difficult it is for a manager to monitor the behavior of employees such as salespeople or R&D scientists. It is impossible to watch a scientist to see how well he or she "does research." Likewise, the cost involved to have managers shadow salespeople and give them instructions would be exorbitant. So, organizations specify the level of performance they require from their employees and set standards—or performance goals—by which to measure actual employee outputs. In the case of salespeople, for example, an organization might set a sales target for how much each salesperson should sell each month or how many customers they should visit each day. Specifying the goals for researchers is more difficult because their work is so long term and complex, but an R&D function can be measured by the number of new products it develops or the number of new patents that it files. As we saw in Chapter 7, setting specific, challenging goals can be an effective way to motivate employees.

By using specific goals and targets to measure the performance of individuals and groups, an organization increases the control it has over their activities. The more ways an organization can devise to measure its performance, the more effective it becomes.

New IT-Enabled Forms of Organizational Design and Structure

The increasing use of new information technology is changing the nature of organizational design and structure.[45] The principal reason is because IT changes companies and allows them to behave in more flexible, organic ways. The effects of IT on organizational design can be seen both inside and between organizations.[46]

THE EFFECTS OF IT INSIDE ORGANIZATIONS

In the last decade, information technology has had a dramatic effect on the way in which organizations group and coordinate their activities.[47] First, IT increases communication and coordination and promotes mutual adjustment among teams, functions, and divisions.[48] Second, IT permits the greater decentralization of decision making because employees have instant access to the information they need to make a decision.[49] The opening case showed how Sun Life Financial used IT to reorganize from a functional structure to one based on cross-functional product teams. Company's new IT system gave teams the information they needed to handle each customer's specific request. As a result of using IT, organizations no longer need tall management hierarchies. They can operate with flatter structures that speed decision making and enable the organization to act in a more flexible and organic way.

Some organizations, especially those that provide complex services and employ highly trained workers, have gone one step further and created what has been called a virtual organization. A **virtual organization** is one in which employees are linked to an organization's centralized databases by computers, faxes, and videoconferencing and rarely see one another face-to-face, if ever.[50] These employees might only infrequently visit the physical premises of their companies; they receive their assignments electronically, report back to their superiors electronically, and operate autonomously.[51] Almost all their employees are out in the field, working anywhere around the globe working with clients to solve their problems. Large consultancy companies like EDS and Accenture operate in this fashion as the following OB Today illustrates. It provides an interesting example of how IT, by decentralizing authority to employees, can promote flexibility and allow a company to behave organically.

THE EFFECTS OF IT BETWEEN ORGANIZATIONS

Another innovation in organizational design—the use of outsourcing and networking structures between organizations—has largely been the result of information technology. Recall from Chapter 1 that *outsourcing* involves moving a functional activity that was done *inside* an organization to the *outside,* where another company

Virtual organization
A company that operates largely using new information technology in which people and functions are linked through company intranets and databases.

ob today

Accenture's "Virtual" Organization

Accenture, a global management consulting company, has been one of the pioneers in using IT to revolutionize its organizational structure. Its managing partners realized that because only its consultants in the field could diagnose and solve clients' problems, the company should design a structure that facilitated creative, on-the-spot decision making. To accomplish this, Accenture decided to replace its tall hierarchy of authority with a sophisticated IT system to create a virtual organization.[52]

First, it flattened the organizational hierarchy, eliminating many managerial levels. Then it went about setting up a shared organization-wide IT system that provides each of Accenture's consultants with the information and knowledge they need to make their own decisions. If the consultant still lacks specific knowledge to solve a client's problem, the system is designed to provide data from Accenture's thousands of consultants located around the globe who can provide each other with expert backup help.[53]

To implement the change, Accenture first equipped every one of its consultants with a wireless laptop computer, and each consultant was linked to the others via a sophisticated corporate intranet, depending on the particular kind of client he or she served. For example, consultants who work with consumer product firms are linked together in one group, and those that work with brokerage companies are linked together in another. Often the members of these groups e-mail their counterparts working at different client sites to see if any of them have encountered a client problem similar to one they are presently facing and what they did to solve it. If members of the consultant's core group can't solve the problem, he or she can then communicate with members of other groups by tapping into Accenture's large information databases containing volumes of potentially relevant information. The consultant can also communicate directly with other company employees through a combination of phone, voice mail, e-mail, and teleconferencing in an attempt to gain access to more current information presently being gathered and applied at other client sites.[54]

Often employees uncover useful information that can pertain to other employees in very different areas of the firm. For example, if the project involves installing an enterprise-wide computer system, the consultant has quick access to the information of hundreds of others consultants who have dealt with the software in question but applied it in different contexts. By utilizing these resources consultants stay abreast of the innovative practices being implemented within their own firm and within client firms.

Accenture found that the effects its virtual organization had on flattening the structure, decentralizing authority, and enlarging and enriching roles increased the creativity of its consultants and enhanced their performance. By providing employees with more information and enabling them to easily confer with other people, Accenture gave its consultants much more freedom to make decisions. Moreover, because they often work far away from Accenture's headquarters, the electronic connections have made consultants much more independent. They are able to make their own decisions, which has been a source of motivation. The end result for Accenture is that it is now one of the best-known global consulting companies.[55]

Because its employees are scattered at client sites worldwide, Accenture, a global management consultant company, linked them together electronically, transforming itself into a virtual organization. Being able to access one another and problem-solution databases electronically has helped consultants working solo solve more problems.

performs it. Many companies have found that the use of the Internet and software platforms linking organizations together in real time makes it easier and cheaper for them to send a specific kind of functional activity, such as making component parts, manufacturing the final product, or even managing the IT function itself, to other companies to perform. For example, the U.S. military signed a 10-year, $15 billion contract to let EDS, the computer services company, manage its vast array of computer networks and information systems. The move to outsource manufacturing to low-cost countries such as China and Malaysia has been accelerating. Companies such as Black and Decker, Sony, and Levi-Strauss now contract with manufacturers abroad to produce most, if not all, of their products, which are then shipped to the markets in which they will be sold.

Some companies radically alter their organizational structures by focusing only on that one specific functional activity such as product design or research and development at which they excel and then outsource the rest of their functional activities to other companies. In doing so, they operate within what is called a **network structure**.[56] Nike, for example, the largest and most profitable sports shoe manufacturer in the world, uses a network structure to make, distribute, and sell its shoes.[57] At the center of the network is Nike's product design and research function located in Beaverton, Oregon, where Nike's designers are constantly developing new, innovative sports shoe designs. However, that is almost all that Nike does in Beaverton, besides the corporation's administrative activities. All the other functional work that Nike needs to make and sell its shoes has been outsourced to companies around the world. Nike manages its relationships with the companies in its network through advanced IT. Its designers use sophisticated computer software systems to design its shoes, and all of the new product information, including its technical and manufacturing instructions and specifications, is stored electronically. When the designers have completed their work, they then relay the blueprints for the new products electronically to Nike's network of suppliers and manufacturers in Southeast Asia.[58] For example, instructions for the design of a new sole may be sent to a supplier in Taiwan and instructions for the leather uppers to a supplier in Malaysia. These suppliers then produce the shoe parts, which are subsequently sent for final assembly to a manufacturer in China with whom Nike has established an alliance. From China, the shoes are shipped to distributors throughout the world and are marketed in each country by organizations having contracts with Nike.

The advantage of this network structure is that Nike can respond quickly and flexibly to changes in customer needs and tastes. If demand for a particular kind of shoe drops and demand for another soars, Nike can rapidly transmit new instructions to its network of manufacturers abroad to change their production plans. Moreover, because it does not have to coordinate many different functional activities, Nike can preserve its flat hierarchy and stay small and nimble. In essence, a network structure allows Nike and many other companies to act in an organic way.

Companies are increasingly recognizing the many opportunities outsourcing and networking afford when it comes to reducing costs and increasing flexibility. Clearly, managers have to carefully assess the relative benefits of having their own organization perform a functional activity or make a particular product versus forming an alliance with another organization to do it. As you can see, designing an organizational structure is becoming increasingly complex in today's rapidly changing global world.

Network structure A structural arrangement whereby companies outsource one or more of their functional activities to other specialist companies.

Summary

Organizational structure affects how people and groups behave in an organization by providing a framework that shapes employee attitudes and behavior. Organizations need to create a structure that allows them to coordinate and motivate people, functions, and divisions effectively. This chapter makes the following major points:

1. Organizational structure is the formal system of task and job reporting relationships that determines how employees use resources to achieve organizational goals. Organizational design is the process of making the specific choices about tasks and job relationships that result in the construction of a particular organizational structure.

2. Contingency theory argues that an organization's structure needs to be designed to fit or match the set of contingencies—factors or conditions—that affect it the most and cause it the most uncertainty. Three important contingency factors are the organizational environment, advances in technology (especially information technology), and an organization's human resources.

3. The greater the level of uncertainty in the environment, the more complex its technology, and the more highly skilled its workforce, the more likely are managers to design an organic structure, one that is flexible and that can change quickly. The more stable the environment, the less complex its technology, and the less skilled its workforce, the more likely an organization is to have a mechanistic structure, one that is formal, controlling, and designed to induce employees to behave in predictable, accountable ways.

4. The main structures that organizations use to differentiate their activities and to group people into functions or divisions are functional, product, market, geographic, and matrix structures. Each of these is suited to a particular purpose and has specific coordination and motivation advantages and disadvantages associated with it.

5. As organizations grow, problems of coordinating activities between functions and divisions arise. Three methods organizations can use to solve coordination problems are to use the hierarchy of authority, mutual adjustment, and standardization.

6. To coordinate their activities, organizations develop a hierarchy of authority and decide how to allocate decision-making responsibility. Two important choices that they must make are how many levels to have in the hierarchy and how much authority to decentralize to managers throughout the hierarchy and how much to retain at the top.

7. To coordinate their activities, organizations develop mechanisms for promoting mutual adjustment (the ongoing informal communication and interaction among people and functions). Mechanisms that facilitate mutual adjustment include direct contact, liaison roles, teams and task forces, and cross-functional teams.

8. Organizations that use standardization to coordinate their activities develop programmed responses and written rules that specify how people and functions are to coordinate their actions to accomplish organizational objectives. Organizations can standardize their input, throughput, and output activities.

Exercises in Understanding and Managing Organizational Behavior

Questions for Discussion and Review

1. What is the relationship between organizational design and structure?

2. What contingencies would cause an organization to choose an organic rather than a mechanistic structure?

3. Why do organizations group activities by function?

4. Why do organizations move to some kind of divisional structure?

5. What kind of organizational structure would you expect to find in (a) a fast-food restaurant, (b) a company such as General Electric or General Motors, and (c) a biotechnology company?

6. What kind of structure does your college or business use?

7. Why is coordinating functions and divisions a problem for an organization?

8. What are the main issues in deciding on the design of an organization's hierarchy of authority?

9. Why is mutual adjustment an important means of integration in most organizations?

10. What kinds of organizational activities are easiest to standardize? What kinds are most difficult?

Building People Skills

Understanding Organizational Structure

Think of an organization that you are familiar with—a university, restaurant, church, department store, or an organization that you have worked for—and answer these questions:

1. What form of structure does the organization use to group people and resources? Draw a diagram showing the major functions. Why do you think the organization uses this form of structure? Would another form of structure (for example, divisional) be more appropriate?

2. How many levels are there in the organization's hierarchy? Draw a diagram showing the levels in the hierarchy and the job titles of the people at each level. Do you think this organization has

the right number of levels in its hierarchy? How centralized or decentralized is authority in the organization?

3. To what degree does the organization use mutual adjustment and standardization to coordinate its activities? What mechanisms does it use to increase mutual adjustment? Does it use teams or cross-functional teams? What kinds of rules and standard operating procedures does it use?

A Question of Ethics

How to Lay Off Employees?

You are the manager(s) charged with reducing high operating costs. You have been instructed by the CEO to eliminate 25 percent of the company's workforce, both managers and employees. You also must manage the layoff process and then find a new way to allocate authority in the company to increase efficiency.

Some managers charged with deciding which employees should be laid off might decide to keep the employees whom they like, and who are obedient to them, rather than the ones who are difficult or the best performers. They might decide to lay off the most highly paid employees. When redesigning the hierarchy, they might try to keep most of the power and authority in their hands. Think of the ethical issues involved in layoffs and organizational design and answer the following questions:

1. What ethical rules should managers use when deciding which employees to terminate?
2. What ethical rules can help managers to best allocate authority and design their hierarchies?
3. Why can the use of ethical principles help managers make the layoff process less painful for employees?
4. What effects do you think the way the layoff is carried out will have on the employees who remain?

Small Group Break-Out Exercise

Speeding Up Web Site Design

You have been called in as consultants by the top functional managers of a Web site design, production, and hosting company whose new animated Web site designs are attracting a lot of attention and a lot of customers. Currently, employees are organized into different functions such as hardware, software design, graphic art, Web site hosting as well as functions such as marketing and human resources. Each function takes its turn to work on a new project from initial customer request to final online Web site hosting.

The problem this company is experiencing is that it typically takes one year from the initial idea stage to the time that the Web site is up and running. The company wants to shorten this time by half to protect and expand its market niche. The managers believe their current functional structure is the source of the problem because it is not allowing employees to develop Web sites fast enough to satisfy customers' demands. They want you to suggest a better organizational structure.

1. Discuss ways in which you can improve the way the current functional structure operates to speed Web site development.
2. Discuss the pros and cons of changing to a matrix structure to reduce Web site development time. Then discuss the pros and cons of using cross-functional teams to coordinate activities between functions.
3. Which of these structures do you think is most appropriate and why?

Topic for Debate

Different kinds of organizational structures lead people to behave in different ways. Now that you understand the kinds of choices that organizations face when they create their organizational structures, debate the following issues.

Team A. Today the hierarchy of authority is more important than mutual adjustment in coordinating and motivating people and functions to achieve an organization's goals.

Team B. Today mutual adjustment is more important than the hierarchy of authority in coordinating and motivating individuals and functions to achieve an organization's goals.

Experiential Exercise

Analyzing Organizational Structure

For this chapter you will analyze the structure of a real organization such as a department store, restaurant, hospital, fire station, or police department. In the next chapter, you will identify the contingencies that have influenced the development of the organization's culture.

Objective

Your objective is to gain experience in analyzing and diagnosing an organization.

Procedure

The class divides into groups of three to five people. Group members discuss the kind of organization the group will analyze and then explore the possibility of gaining access to the organization by using a personal contact or by calling and going to see the manager in charge of the organization. After the group gains access to the organization, each member of the group interviews one or more members of the organization. Use the questions that follow to develop an interview schedule to guide your interview of the organization's employees, but be sure to ask additional questions to probe more deeply into issues that you think are interesting and reveal how the organization's structure works.

After all of the groups complete the assignment, the instructor either will allocate class time for each group to make a presentation of its findings to the whole class or will request a written report.

1. Draw an organizational chart showing the major roles and functions in your organization.
2. What kind of structure does your organization use? Why does it use this structure? What are the advantages and disadvantages of this structure?
3. How does your organization integrate and coordinate its activities?
   A. Describe the organization's hierarchy of authority. Is it tall or flat? Is it centralized or decentralized? How wide a span of control does the top manager have?
   B. What integrating mechanisms does the organization use to coordinate its activities?
   C. To what degree does the organization standardize its activities, and how does it do this?
4. Summarizing this information, would you say the organization operates with a mechanistic or organic structure? Are there elements of both?

Making the Connection

Find an example of an organization that has been changing its structure recently. What changes did the organization make, why did it make them, and what does it hope to achieve from them?

New York Times Cases in the News

The New York Times

Sony Music to Cut 1,000 Jobs in a Broad Restructuring Plan

BY LYNETTE HOLLOWAY

Sony Music Entertainment is making sweeping layoffs in the first reorganizational move by its new chairman and chief executive, Andrew Lack.

Mr. Lack, who succeeded Thomas D. Mottola about three months ago, plans to eliminate 1,000 jobs in the United States and abroad as part of a broad cost-reduction plan that would try to cut expenses by more than $100 million a year, people close to the company said yesterday.

They said that the plan was scheduled to take effect yesterday and today in New York. The company hopes to complete its restructuring before the fiscal year of its parent company, the Sony Corporation, concludes at the end of the month.

The cuts include about 300 positions in the United States. The layoffs will affect people who work in distribution, manufacturing, administrative support and corporate offices, and at Sony's two major record labels, Columbia Records and Epic Records.

The layoffs come as Mr. Lack seeks to restructure, streamline and leave an imprint on a company that was run for 14 years by Mr. Mottola, an industry giant. Mr. Mottola left under a pall after the music division experienced huge financial losses as its market share continued to shrink, at a time when CD sales in general had fallen. Mr. Lack, formerly the president and chief operating officer of NBC, was hired by Sir Howard Stringer, chief of the Sony Corporation of America, in the hopes that he could help improve the division's finances.

"We are also combining some functions, most notably in sales and distribution, in order to minimize duplication of efforts and more efficiently serve the needs of our artists, employees and customers," Mr. Lack said in an undated memorandum to employees.

It is expected that Mr. Lack, in about two weeks, will announce management changes that will dismantle the structure of Mr. Mottola's longtime administration, but keep many of its players.

Donnie Ienner, chairman of Columbia Records, is expected to oversee the Sony Music America division and both Columbia and Epic. Michele Anthony, executive vice president for Sony Music, who works closely with the labels, is expected to continue in her role. Will Botwin, president of Columbia Records, will continue to oversee the label and will report to Mr. Ienner. Polly Anthony, president of Epic Records, will continue to oversee Epic Records and will report to Mr. Ienner.

Sony is the third-largest music company in the nation, after BMG, which is owned by Bertelsmann, and Universal Music Group, which is owned by Vivendi Universal.

SOURCE: Lynette Holloway, "Sony Music to Cut 1,000 Jobs in a Broad Restructuring Plan," *New York Times*, March 28, 2003, p. C3.

Questions for Discussion

1. In what ways is Sony changing its structure?
2. How will these changes help to improve its effectiveness?

The New York Times

3M, Textron, and Lockheed Reorganize Their Structures

The 3M Company, the maker of products ranging from Post-it notes to medical inhalers, reorganized into seven businesses from six to give more focus to faster-growing markets. Three of the business divisions will be new: safety, security and protection services; display and graphics; and transportation. The health care; industrial, consumer and office; and electro and communications divisions will remain. E. James McNerney Jr., the chief executive, is managing 2,500 cost-cutting projects, borrowing from methods he learned during his 18 years at General Electric.

Textron Inc., a maker of airplanes, helicopters and other products, said yesterday that it would combine industrial components and industrial products areas to cut employment costs and speed decisions. Textron has been battling a downturn in its Cessna Aircraft business and said in April that is was stepping up plans to cut jobs and other costs to meet reduced profit forecasts. Combining the two segments to create a single industrial segment will eliminate two division president positions and lead to staff cuts of 40 to 50 people, a Textron spokeswoman, Susan Bishop, said. The chief operating officer, Steve Loranger, will become head of the combined unit and keep his other duties, Textron said. Textron is based in Providence, R.I.

The military contractor Lockheed Martin Corporation said yesterday that it would form a new business unit to focus on technology integration. Lockheed said the unit, called Integrated Systems and Solutions, would bring together specialists from its space, air and ground businesses to help design systems compatible with one another. Albert Smith, currently executive vice president at Lockheed's space systems business, will head the unit, which will employ about 11,000 and be based in Gaithersburg, Md. Lockheed, based in Bethesda, Md., said formation of the division, its fifth business unit, would not affect its previous forecasts.

SOURCE: "3M, Textron, and Lockheed Reorganize Their Structures," *New York Times*, September 28, 2002; June 7, 2003, p. C.4; June 28, 2003, p. C4.

Questions for Discussion

1. In what ways are these companies changing the design of their organizations?
2. What benefits do they hope to obtain from their reorganization?

Organizational Culture and Ethical Behavior

17

LEARNING OBJECTIVES

After reading this chapter, you should be able to:

■

Distinguish between values and norms and discuss how they are the building blocks of organizational culture.

▪

Appreciate how a company's culture is transmitted to employees through its formal socialization practices and through informal on-the-job learning.

▪

Discuss five main factors that shape organizational culture and explain why different organizations have different cultures.

▪

Appreciate how differences in national culture affect the culture of organizations within a particular society.

▪

Understand the importance of building and maintaining an ethical organizational culture.

OPENING CASE

How 3M Built a Culture for Innovation

How Does 3M's Culture Affect Creativity?

3M is a company known worldwide for its organizational skills that promote creativity and new product innovation. To promote the creativity of its employees, 3M has developed cultural values and norms that strongly emphasize the need for employees to feel empowered, to experiment, and to take risks to come up with new product ideas. The company has many famous stories about employees who charged ahead and pursued their own product ideas—even when their managers doubted the success of their efforts. Take the case of masking tape.[1]

The story of masking tape began when Dick Drew, a 3M abrasives lab technician, visited an auto body shop in St. Paul, Minnesota to test some new sandpaper samples.[2] Two-tone cars were popular then, and Drew watched as paint shop employees improvised a method to keep one color of paint from being over sprayed onto the other using a paint shield made up of a combination of glue and butcher paper. As they pulled their shield off when the paint was dry, however, it often took the other color paint with it. Employees joked with Drew that since 3M knew something about glue (since it was used to hold the abrasive grain and the paper backing), it would be a good idea if 3M could develop a product to make their painting task easier as well.

Drew went back to his boss and explained his idea for a new product—a roll of paper with glue already applied that would not pull the paint off. But his boss was not convinced this was a viable project, and he told Drew to go back to work on developing improved abrasive products as he had been. Drew went back to his lab but decided that while he pursued his assigned work, he would also pursue his new idea. Over time, he began to divert more and more resources to his project and made repeated attempts to invent a weaker glue and find a suitable paper backing. Word of his efforts spread throughout, but his boss decided to turn a blind eye to his efforts. Within two years Drew perfected his glue and found just the right "crepe" paper. It was an instant success with paint shop employees.

His boss realized they had a potential winner. Once it hit the market it soon became clear that masking tape had potentially thousands of other applications. Drew was now an organizational hero. He was given control of a major lab and the resources he needed to develop new kinds of tape for these varied uses. In 1930, for example, he invented clear cellophane tape; "Scotch" cellophane tape became one of 3M's most successful products.[3]

The fact that employees spend their time on projects of their own choosing is the source of many of 3M's cultural values and its success. 3M, for example, developed an informal norm that its researchers can spend 15 percent of their time to develop projects of their own choosing. It was this norm that brought about the development of other new products such as Post-it® Notes. To encourage more innovation and risk taking, 3M is careful to recognize its heroes—the people invent its new products and improve business processes. 3M established its "Golden Step Program," which rewards successful businesses. Also, to recognize career-long efforts, researchers may become members of its "Carlton Society," which gives them recognition throughout the company and access to a career ladder that can take them to the top. All of these and numerous other practices gain the loyalty and support of 3M's scientists and helped create a culture of innovation.

To speed innovation 3M also realizes the importance of creating organization-wide values to encourage employees to cooperate and share their ideas with one another. To avoid the problem of people in different functions focusing solely on their own tasks, 3M established a system of cross-functional teams made up of members from product development, process development, marketing, manufacturing, packaging, and other functions. So that all the groups have a common focus, the teams work closely with customers. Customer needs, in other words, are the common denominator linking all the teams. For example, one of 3M's cross-functional teams worked closely with disposable diaper manufacturers to develop the right kind of sticky tape for their needs. Clearly, all this attention to creating a culture of innovation that conveys to its employees the values of excellence and innovation has paid off for 3M.

3M attributes a large part of its success to a culture that encourages employees like Dick Drew to take risks in order to pursue their own ideas. In this chapter, we first define organizational culture and discuss the way it influences employees' work attitudes and behaviors. Then we discuss how employees learn about an organization's culture from the company's formal socialization practices and informal processes, such as watching how things "get done." Five major building blocks of organizational culture discussed are (1) the characteristics of people within the organization, (2) organizational ethics, (3) the employment relationship, (4) organizational structure, and (5) national culture. Finally, we explore an issue that is especially important in the 2000s—how and why it is necessary for organizations to build and maintain an ethical culture.

What Is Organizational Culture?

Organizational culture is the set of shared values, beliefs, and norms that influence the way employees think, feel, and behave toward each other and toward people outside the organization. In Schein's view, culture is "a pattern of shared basic assumptions a group learns as it solves its problems of external adaptation and internal integration, that is considered valid, is taught to new members as the correct way you perceive, think and feel in relation to those problems."[4] Just as an organization's structure can increase employee cooperation and motivation, so the values and assumptions in an organization's culture also can promote work attitudes and behaviors that increase organizational effectiveness.[5] This is because the organization's culture controls the way employees perceive and respond to their environment, what they do with information, and how they make decisions.[6]

What are organizational values, and how do they affect work attitudes and behavior? **Values** are general criteria, standards, or guiding principles that people use to determine which types of behaviors, events, situations, and outcomes are desirable or undesirable.[7] There are two kinds of values: terminal and instrumental values (see Figure 17.1).[8] A **terminal value** is a desired end, state, or outcome that people seek to achieve. Organizations might adopt any of the following as terminal values or guiding principles: quality, responsibility, innovativeness, excellence, economy, morality, or profitability. Large insurance companies, for example, may value profitability, but their terminal values are often stability and predictability because the company cannot afford to take risks. It must be there to pay off policyholders' claims.

Organizational culture The set of shared values, beliefs, and norms that influences the way employees think, feel, and behave toward each other and toward people outside the organization.

Values General criteria, standards, or guiding principles that people use to determine which types of behaviors, events, situations, and outcomes are desirable or undesirable.

Terminal value A desired end, state, or outcome that people seek to achieve.

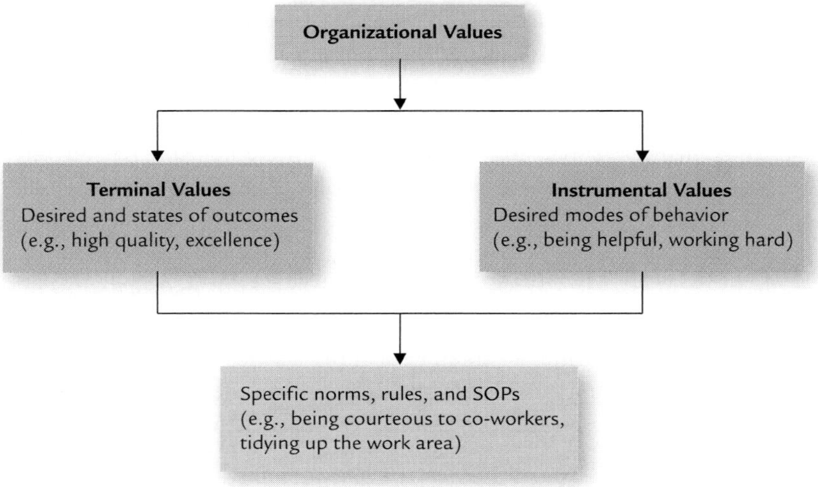

FIGURE 17.1
Terminal and Instrumental Values in an Organization's Culture

Organizational Values

Terminal Values
Desired and states of outcomes
(e.g., high quality, excellence)

Instrumental Values
Desired modes of behavior
(e.g., being helpful, working hard)

Specific norms, rules, and SOPs
(e.g., being courteous to co-workers, tidying up the work area)

Instrumental value A desired mode or type of behavior that people seek to follow.

An **instrumental value** is a desired mode or type of behavior. Modes of behavior that organizations advocate include working hard, respecting traditions and authority, being conservative and cautious, being frugal, being creative and courageous, being honest, taking risks, and maintaining high standards.

An organization's culture, thus, consists of the end states that the organization seeks to achieve (its *terminal values*) and the modes of behavior the organization encourages (its *instrumental values*). Ideally, instrumental values help the organization achieve its terminal values. For example, computer companies such as HP and Microsoft whose cultures emphasize the terminal value of innovativeness might attain this outcome by encouraging instrumental values such as working hard, being creative, and taking risks. That combination of terminal and instrumental values leads to an entrepreneurial culture—one in which employees are challenged to take risks or go out on a limb to test their ideas.[9] On the other hand, insurance companies or accounting firms generally emphasize the terminal value of stability and predictability and try to attain this outcome by encouraging instrumental values that emphasize behaving cautiously, following the appropriate rules, and obeying instructions. The result will be a conservative culture.

To encourage members to adopt certain terminal and instrumental values and behave in certain ways as they pursue their goals, the organization develops specific norms. In Chapter 10 we defined a *norm* as a shared expectation for behavior. Norms are standards or styles of behavior that are considered acceptable or typical for a group of people. In essence, norms are informal rules of conduct that emerge over time to encourage employees to cultivate work attitudes and behaviors that are considered important to an organization. So, for example, the specific norms of being courteous, keeping one's work area clean, or being a team player will develop in an organization whose more general terminal or instrumental values include being helpful and hardworking or cooperative.[10]

Norms are largely informal, so many of the most crucial values an organization has are also not written down. They exist only in the shared norms, beliefs, assumptions, and ways of thinking and behaving that people within an organization use to relate to each other and analyze and deal with problems.[11] For example, from one another, members learn how to perceive and respond to various situations in ways that are consistent with the organization's accepted values. Eventually, members choose and follow appropriate values without even realizing they are doing so.[12] Over time, they *internalize* the organization's values and the specific rules, norms, and standard operating procedures that govern behavior; that is, organizational values become part of members' mind-set and affect the way they perceive and respond to a situation.[13]

Southwest Airlines' organizational culture is the envy of its industry and possibly all of corporate America. Four times a year, Southwest managers work as baggage handlers, ticket agents, and flight attendants so they get a feel for the problems facing the company's other employees.

Values and norms work in a subtle, indirect fashion yet have a powerful effect on behavior.[14] To get a feel for the effect of organizational values, consider how differences in behavior at Southwest Airlines and Value Line reflect differences in values. When Southwest Airlines was formed to compete against giant airlines such as American and United, its CEO Herbert Kelleher and his second in command, Colleen Barrett, knew they had their work cut out for them. To compete they had to provide low-cost, high-quality airline service to customers. Kelleher and Barrett set out to develop terminal and instrumental values that would create a culture accomplishing this goal—and they succeeded. Today, Southwest's organizational culture is the envy of its competitors.

Southwest managers and employees are committed to the success of the organization. They do everything they can to help one another and provide customers with excellent service (a terminal value). Four times a year, Southwest managers work as baggage handlers, ticket agents, and flight attendants so they get a feel for the problems facing other employees. An informal norm makes it possible for employees to meet with Barrett (and Kelleher sometimes although he has retired as CEO) every Friday at noon in the company's Dallas parking lot for a company cookout. Both managers have encouraged employees to be creative and to develop rules and norms to solve their own problems. To please customers, for example, employees dress up on special days such as Halloween and Valentine's Day and wear "fun uniforms" every Friday. In addition, they try to develop innovative ways to improve customer service and satisfaction.

All employees participate in a bonus system based on the company's performance, and employees own over 20 percent of the airline's stock, which, not surprisingly, has consistently performed well. The entrance hall at Southwest Airline's headquarters at Love Field in Dallas is full of plaques earned by employees for their outstanding performance. Everybody in the organization cooperates to achieve Southwest's goal of providing low-cost, high-quality service, and Southwest's culture seems to be working to its advantage.

Contrast Southwest's culture with that of Value Line, Inc. Jean Buttner, publisher of the Value Line Investment Survey, fashioned an organizational culture that employees hate and no one envies. In her attempt to reduce costs and improve efficiency, Buttner created instrumental values of frugality and economy that soured employees' attitudes toward the organization. Among the other strict rules she created, employees were told to sign in by 9:00 A.M. every day and sign out when leaving. If they faked their arrival or departure time, they faced dismissal. Because at Value Line messy desks are considered signs of unproductivity, Buttner required department managers to file a "clean surfaces report" every day, certifying that employees have tidied their desks.[15] Buttner keeps salary increases as small as possible, and she has kept the company's bonus plan and health plan under tight rein.

Did promoting these terminal and instrumental values pay off? Many highly trained, professional workers left Value Line because of the hostile atmosphere produced by these "economical" values and work rules that debase employees. This turnover generated discontent among the company's customers. The relationship between employees and Buttner become so poor that employees reportedly put up a notice on their bulletin board criticizing Buttner's management style and suggesting that the company could use some new leadership. Buttner's response to this message was to remove the bulletin board. Clearly, Buttner did not create a culture of cooperation at Value Line.

The terminal and instrumental values that Kelleher and Buttner developed to manage their organizations elicited very different responses from their employees. The cultural values at Southwest led employees to perceive that they were appreciated by the organization and that the organization wanted to reward behavior that supported its goals. The cultural values at Value Line, on the other hand, alienated employees, reduced commitment and loyalty, and increased employee turnover.[16] Clearly, an organization's cultural values are important shapers of members' behaviors.[17] Shared cultural values provide a common reference point and smooth interactions among organizational members. People who share an organization's values may come to identify strongly with the organization, and feelings of self-worth may flow from their membership in it.[18] Employees of Southwest Airlines, for example, seem to value greatly their membership in the organization and are committed to it.

How Is an Organization's Culture Transmitted to Its Members?

The ability of an organization's culture to motivate employees and increase its effectiveness is directly related to the way in which members learn the organization's values. They learn the pivotal values and norms from an organization's formal socialization practices and from the signs, symbols, stories, rites, ceremonies, and organizational language that develop informally as an organization's culture matures (see Figure 17.2).

FIGURE 17.2
Ways of Transmitting Organizational Culture

SOCIALIZATION AND SOCIALIZATION TACTICS

As we discuss in Chapter 10, newcomers to an organization must learn the values and norms that guide existing members' behavior and decision making.[19] Newcomers are outsiders, and only when they have learned an organization's values and act in accordance with its values and norms will longtime members accept them as insiders. To learn an organization's culture, newcomers must obtain information about cultural values, and they do so formally by participating in an organization's socialization program. They do so informally by observing and working with other employees.

We discussed socialization in detail in Chapter 10. Recall Van Mannen and Schein's model for structuring the organization's socialization experience so newcomers learn its values. In turn, these values influence the way in which newcomers respond to a situation: Do they react passively and obediently to commands and orders? Are they creative and innovative in searching for solutions to problems? When organizations combine these tactics as suggested in Table 10.1, there is some evidence that they can influence an individual's role orientation. Military-style socialization discussed in Chapter 11 is one such example. Dell has built a culture using socialization practices that are very instructive in this respect. The Texas-based computer maker has developed a lean organizational culture focused on cutting costs and providing excellent customer service to help sell its products. How does Dell socialize its new employees so they learn the vales ands norms of its culture? In a very specific way: Just like the army, Dell has a "boot camp" to which it sends its employees for training.[20] For four weeks employees go to a Dell training center outside Austin, Texas, where they are educated about the basic software that operates Dell's products: MS office, WindowsNT, and Visual basic, the main programming language installed on the machines, are among the programs they study. At the end of the boot camp there is a miniproject in which six to nine people are given a real business problem facing Dell. They must arrive at a solution to the problem and then present their findings to a panel of instructors. During this training process, new employees also learn the basic values and norms that guide Dell employees; they are also taught how to provide excellent customer service. Employees form many common bonds because they are all socialized together and trained in such a focused, concentrated way.[21]

After "boot camp" a week of shadowing is required, the new hire observes an experienced Dell employee performing the tasks that comprise his or her organizational role. The new hire is able to ask questions and absorb information quickly and effectively. In this way Dell's lean cost-cutting organizational values are transmitted quickly to employees. The careful socialization process has become increasingly important at Dell because its rapid growth has required the company to recruit many new employees who must be brought quickly up to speed.[22]

STORIES, CEREMONIES, AND ORGANIZATIONAL LANGUAGE

The cultural values of an organization are often evident in the stories, ceremonies, and language found in the organization.[23] At Southwest Airlines, for example, employees wearing costumes on Halloween, the Friday cookouts with top managers, and employees pitching in to help to speed aircraft turnaround as needed all reinforce and communicate the company's culture.

Organizations use several types of ceremonial rites to communicate cultural norms and values.[24] *Rites of passage* mark an individual's entry to, promotion in, and departure from the organization. The socialization programs used by the army and by Dell are rites of passage; so, too, are the ways in which an organization grooms people for promotion or retirement. *Rites of integration*, such as shared announcements of organizational success, office parties, and company cookouts, build and reinforce common bonds between members. *Rites of enhancement*, such as awards dinners, newspaper releases, and employee promotions, give an organization the opportunity to publicly acknowledge and reward employees' contributions and thereby enhance their commitment to its values.

The stories and language of an organization are also important media for communicating culture. Stories (be they fact or fiction) about organizational heroes provide important clues about cultural values and norms. Such stories can reveal the kinds of behaviors that the organization values and the kinds of practices it frowns on. Studying the stories and language can reveal the values that guide behavior.[25] At 3M, for example, to build cooperative team values and norms each team is headed by a "product champion," who takes the responsibility for building cohesive team relationships. Each team is also given a "management sponsor," one of 3M's top managers, whose job it is to help the team get resources and provide support when the going gets tough. After all, product development is a very risky undertaking, and many projects do not succeed. Clearly, a team with a champion and a sponsor is more likely to experience success!

This is not a boot camp for the U.S. army; it is a boot camp for new Pizza Hut managers, where as a group they learn about the company's norms and values. Attending boot camp is a rite of passage at Pizza Hut.

Because language is the principal medium of communication in organizations, the characteristic names or phrases a company uses to frame and describe events provide important clues about norms and values. Many organizations use technical languages to facilitate cooperation between their employees.[26] For example, because many 3M products are flat such as Scotch tape, Post-it notes, floppy disks, sandpaper, and transparencies, the quality of "flatness" has come to be closely associated with 3M's terminal values. Flatness is often a winning theme in 3M's corporate language. At Microsoft, employees have developed a shorthand language of software-type phrases to describe communication problems. Technical languages are used by the military and sports teams and in hospitals and many other specialized work contexts.

The concept of organizational language encompasses not only spoken language but also how people dress, the offices they occupy, the company cars they drive, and how they formally address one another. In Microsoft and some other organizations casual dress is the norm. Indeed, in the last decade many large companies that used to emphasize conservative business-type clothing such as Ford and IBM now encourage "business casual" clothing and "dress-down" days when employees can wear whatever they feel most comfortable in.

Like socialization practices, organizational language, ceremonies, and stories help people "learn the ropes" and the organization's cultural values. As the accompanying OB Today shows, Wal-Mart uses many of these means to socialize its employees and enhance its organizational culture.

ob today

Sam Walton and Wal-Mart's Culture

Wal-Mart, headquartered in Bentonville, Arkansas, is the largest retailer in the world. In 2003, it sold over $250 billion worth of products.[27] A large part of Wal-Mart's success is due to the nature of the culture that its founder, the late Sam Walton, established for the company. Walton wanted all his managers and workers to take a hands-on approach to their jobs and be totally committed to Wal-Mart's main goal, which he defined as total customer satisfaction. To motivate his employees, Walton created a culture that gave employees at all levels, who are called associates, continuous feedback about their performance and the company's performance.

To involve his associates in the business and encourage them to develop work behaviors focused on providing quality customer service, Walton established strong cultural values and norms for his company. Some of the norms associates are expected to follow include the "ten-foot attitude." The ten-foot attitude encourages associates, in Walton's words, to "promise that whenever you come within 10 feet of a customer, you will look him in the eye, greet him, and ask him if you can help him." The "sundown rule" states that employees should strive to answer customer requests by sundown of the day they are made. The Wal-Mart cheer ("Give me a W, give me an A," and so on) is used in all its stores.[28]

The strong customer-oriented values that Walton created are exemplified in the stories its members tell one another about Wal-Mart's concern for its customers. They include stories such as the one about Sheila, who risked her own safety when she jumped in front of a car to prevent a little boy from being struck; about Phyllis, who administered CPR to a customer who had suffered a heart attack in her store; and about Annette, who gave up the Power Ranger she had on layaway for her own son to fulfill the birthday wish of a customer's son.[29] The strong Wal-Mart culture helps to control and motivate employees to achieve the stringent output and financial targets the company has set for itself.[30]

A notable way Wal-Mart builds its culture is at its annual stockholders' meeting, an extravagant ceremony celebrating the company's success.[31] Every year Wal-Mart flies thousands of its highest performers to its annual meeting at corporate headquarters in Arkansas for a show featuring performers such as exercise guru Richard Simmons and singers Reba McIntyre and Andy Williams. Wal-Mart feels that expensive entertainment is a reward its employees deserve and that it reinforces the company's high-performance values and culture. The proceedings are even broadcast live to all of Wal-Mart's stores so employees can celebrate the company's achievements together.[32] This is just one way Wal-Mart uses information technology to bolster its culture.[33] Online training programs and company announcements are electronically sent to all its stores on a regular basis so managers and employees know exactly what is happening at the company's many stores around the world.

Finally, organizational symbols often convey an organization's cultural values to its members and to others outside the organization.[34] In some organizations, for example, the size of peoples' offices, their location on the third floor or the thirty-third floor, the luxury of the furniture in them, and so on symbolize the cultural values an organization holds. Is the organization hierarchical and status-conscious, for example, or are informal, participative work relationships encouraged? At General Motors, the executive suite on the top floor of the Detroit headquarters is isolated from the rest of the building and open only to top GM executives. A private corridor and stairway link top managers' offices, and a private elevator connects them to a heated parking garage.

Sometimes the very design of the building itself is a symbol of an organization's values. For example, the Walt Disney Company hired famed Japanese architect Arata Isozaki to design the Team Disney Building, which houses Disney's "imagineering unit" in Orlando, Florida. This building's contemporary and unusual design featuring unusual shapes and bright colors conveys the importance of imagination and creativity to the Walt Disney Company and to the people who work in it. When Louis Gerstner took control of IBM in the early 1990s when its sales were collapsing, one of his first actions was to build a brand-new, campus-style headquarters building similar to Disney's. He moved all IBM's managers to open-plan offices and suites in the new building. IBM's old high-rise skyscraper building, which Gerstner believed reduced teamwork and innovation and encouraged conservative thinking, was sold.

you're the management expert

A Culture of Cleanliness

You're the training expert for a fast-food restaurant chain that is opening up a location in a new city. One of your company's major priorities is food safety and cleanliness. The chain has never in its history had a case of food poisoning, and preserving this record is central to its culture. In fact, the chain insists its employees exhibit high personal hygiene and that they thoroughly clean and disinfect the restaurants each night upon closing. Your job is to instill these core values in the new hires quickly. How will you design your socialization program?

FIGURE 17.3

Where an Organization's Culture Comes From

The goal of the late Mary Kay Ash, founder of Mary Kay Cosmetic (famous for the pink Cadillacs its sales representatives drive) was to empower women to succeed financially and personally. Still, Ash encouraged her employees to put God first, family second, and career third. It's a motto still embraced by Mary Kay employees.

Factors Shaping Organizational Culture

Now that you have seen what organizational culture is and how members learn and become part of it some difficult questions can be addressed: Where does organizational culture come from? Why do different companies have different cultures? Why might a culture that for many years helps an organization achieve its goals suddenly harm the organization?

Organizational culture is shaped by the interaction of four main factors: the personal and professional characteristics of people within the organization, organizational ethics, the nature of the employment relationship, and the design of its organizational structure (see Figure 17.3). These factors work together to produce different cultures in different organizations and cause changes in culture over time.

CHARACTERISTICS OF PEOPLE WITHIN THE ORGANIZATION

The ultimate source of organizational culture is the people who make up the organization. If you want to know why cultures differ, look at their members. Organizations A, B, and C develop distinctly different cultures because they attract, select, and retain people who have different values, personalities, and ethics.[35] Recall the attraction-selection-attrition model from Chapter 2. People may be attracted to an organization whose values match theirs; similarly, an organization selects people who share its values. Over time, people who do not fit in leave. The result is that people inside the organization become more and more similar, the values of the organization become more and more pronounced and clear-cut, and the culture becomes more and more distinct from that of similar organizations.[36]

The founder of an organization has a substantial influence on the organization's initial culture because of his or her personal values and beliefs.[37] Founders set the scene for the later development of culture because they not only establish the new organization's values but also hire its first members. Presumably, the people selected by the founder have values and interests similar to the founder's.[38] Over time, members buy into the founder's vision and perpetuate the founder's values in the organization.[39] This has certainly been the case at Microsoft and Dell, whose founders championed innovative and frugal values, respectively.

An important implication of this is that an organization's members become similar over time and come to share the same values. This, in fact, may actually hinder their ability to adapt and respond to changes in the environment.[40] This happens when the organization's values and norms become so strong and promote so much group cohesiveness that members misperceive the environment.[41] Also, groupthink might appear as members reinforce one another's misperceptions and respond inappropriately to them. Groupthink has been a problem at many companies. Even though Microsoft has strong, cohesive values that bond its members, Bill Gates has worked hard to make it clear that employees should express their own personal views, even though they might differ from his and everyone else's in the organization. One example of how Gates's policy has worked to Microsoft's advantage occurred when the company started its Internet service, MSN. The company believed the popularity of its Windows platform would allow it to control the future development of the Internet, even though Netscape had introduced a popular browser. Two concerned Microsoft programmers working in its Internet division wrote a memo to top managers arguing that Microsoft would end up with *no* control over the Internet, given the pace at which it was developing. They also argued that Netscape's browser would become the dominant way people would access the Internet. The programmers argued that to compete with Netscape, Microsoft should rush to develop its own Web browser.

After reading their memo, Gates convened a major organization-wide meeting. Top managers listened while all of the issues were aired and admitted they were wrong. The company then diverted most of its human talent to develop its own browser as quickly as possible. Within one year, the first version of Internet Explorer was ready, and Microsoft even went so far as to give it away free to users. This posed a major challenge for Netscape, which had been charging users for Netscape Navigator.

Successful companies such as Microsoft certainly need a strong set of terminal values emphasizing innovation and hard work. However, they need to be careful their very success doesn't lead members to believe their company will always be the "best" in the business or "invincible." Some companies have made this mistake. The old IBM of the 1980s believed its control of the mainframe market made it invincible; IBM employees laughed off the potential threat personal computers posed. The CEO of another dominant computer maker at that time, Digital Equipment, reportedly commented that "personal computers are just toys." Within a few years, Digital Equipment was experiencing huge losses.

The "people make the place" view of organizational culture explains how an organization develops the shared cultural values that can have such a powerful effect on work attitudes and behaviors. The "people make the place" view also implies the culture of an organization must be managed by the people who control it to ensure it does not lead to problems.[42] For this reason, some experts advocate that a company should have a board of independent-minded directors who aren't afraid to challenge top management and that CEOs and top managers should be changed regularly. We look at this issue later in the chapter when we discuss ethics.

ORGANIZATIONAL ETHICS

An organization can purposefully develop some kinds of cultural values to control the way its members behave. One important class of values that falls into this category stems from **organizational ethics**, the moral values, beliefs, and rules that establish the appropriate way for an organization and its members to deal with each other and people outside the organization. Ethical values rest on principles stressing the importance of treating everyone fairly and equally.

Organizations are constantly making choices about the right, or ethical, thing to do. A company such as IBM, Target, or Sears might wonder whether it should have procedures in place giving advance notice to its employees about impending layoffs or plant closings. Traditionally, companies have been reluctant to do so because they fear

Organizational ethics The moral values, beliefs, and rules that establish the appropriate way for an organization and its members to deal with each other and with people outside the organization.

employees will become hostile or apathetic and perform poorly. Similarly, a company has to decide whether to allow its managers to pay bribes to government officials in foreign countries where such payoffs are an accepted way of doing business, even though they may actually be illegal.[43]

To make these decisions, an organization purposefully implants ethical instrumental values in its culture.[44] Such ethics outline the right and wrong ways to behave when the action taken may help one person or group but hurt another.[45] Ethical values, and the rules and norms that reflect them, are an integral part of an organization's culture because they help to determine how its members will manage situations and make decisions.

The question is how are organizational ethics formed? Ethical values are a product of societal, professional, and individual ethics.[46] (See Figure 17.4.) We discuss each of the aspects next.

Societal Ethics. The ethics of the country or society in which the organization exists are important determinants of its ethical values. Societal ethics are the moral values formalized in a society's legal system, in its customs and practices, and in the unwritten norms and values that its people follow in their daily lives. Most people automatically follow the ethical norms and values of the society in which they live because they have internalized them and made them their own.[47] When societal ethics are codified into law (rules), an organization is legally required to follow these laws in its dealings with people inside and outside of the organization.

One of top management's main responsibilities is to ensure that the organization's members obey the law. Indeed, in certain situations top managers can be held accountable for the conduct of their subordinates. One of the main ways top managers ensure ethical behavior on the part of their organizations is by instilling good values in their members. However, although some companies (such as Johnson & Johnson and Merck) are well known for their ethical cultures, many organizations nonetheless act illegally, immorally, and unethically. These organizations frequently do little to develop ethical values for their employees to follow.

Professional Ethics. Professional ethics are the moral values that a group of similarly trained people develop to control their performance of a task or use their resources.[48] People internalize the values and norms of their professions just as they do the values and norms of their societies. Generally, they follow these norms when deciding how to behave.[49] Some organizations have many types of professionals

FIGURE 17.4
Sources of Organizational Ethics

working for them—nurses, lawyers, researchers, doctors, and accountants—whose behavior is governed by professional ethics. These ethics help shape the organization's culture and determine how members deal with other people and groups. Medical ethics, for example, control how doctors and nurses do their jobs and help establish the culture of the organizations they work for. Professional ethics, for example, encourage doctors to act in the best interests of their patients; performing unnecessary medical procedures for one's own financial benefit, for example, is considered unethical. Similarly, at companies such as Merck and Johnson & Johnson, professional ethics induce scientists and technicians to behave ethically when preparing and presenting the results of their research.

Most professional groups have the authority to enforce the ethical standards of their profession. Doctors and lawyers, for example, can be barred from practicing their profession if they violate professional rules.

Individual Ethics. Individual ethics are the personal moral values that people use to structure their interactions with other people. In many instances, personal ethics mirror societal ethics and originate in the law. But personal ethics are also the result of an individual's upbringing. They may stem from his or her family, friends, or membership in a church or other social organization. Because personal ethics influence how a person will act in an organization, an organization's culture is strongly affected by the people who are in a position to establish its ethical values. As we saw earlier, the founder of an organization plays a particularly important role when it comes to establishing the ethical norms and values of the organization.

THE EMPLOYMENT RELATIONSHIP

A third factor shaping organizational culture is the nature of the employment relationship a company establishes with its employees via its human resource policies and practices. Recall from Chapter 8 our discussion of the changing employment relationships between organizations and their employees: Human resource policies, such as a company's hiring, promotion, and layoff policies along with pay and benefits, can influence how hard employees will work to achieve the organization's goals, how attached they will be to the organization, and whether or not they will buy into its values and norms.[50]

Whenever people must work together to accomplish a common goal, the potential for miscommunication, competition, and conflict is always present. Well-designed human resource policies function as the "oil" preventing "people problems" from occurring and can align an employee's goals with the goals of the company's. They are also a good indicator of how the organization values its employees. Consider the effects of a company's promotion policy, for example. If a company pursues a policy of promoting "from within," employees who already work for the organization are recruited to fill higher-level positions. On the other hand, a company with a policy of promotion "from without" will fill its open positions with qualified outsiders. What impact will this have?

Promoting from within will bolster strong values and norms, build loyalty, and encourage employees to work hard to advance within the organization. Upward mobility is a major motivating factor for many people. Promoting from within also helps a company retain its highest-performing employees. If employees see no prospect of being promoted from within, they are likely to begin looking for opportunities elsewhere. As a result, values and norms emerge that lend themselves to employee turnover and a temporary relationship between companies and employees. This is what has happened at many companies in the high-tech sector, which has gone through great turmoil in recent years. An estimated 1 million U.S. tech employees lost their jobs following the burst of the dot-com bubble at the turn of the century. Companies such as Apple Computer, Hewlett-Packard, and IBM—all well known for their strong corporate values, long-term employment, risk-taking initiatives, and employee commitment—were some of the corporations forced to lay off the greatest number of employees.

Another important human resource policy relates to the company's pay level and incentive systems. A company can choose to pay its employees above, below, or at the industry-average pay level. Some companies, Microsoft, Merck, and IBM among them, choose to pay their employee above the average-industry pay level. Above-average pay attracts the best-qualified employees. On the other hand, some companies pay below-average wages and accept a high level of employee turnover as normal. Similarly, there are many different kinds of incentive pay linked to individual, group, and company performance that affect employee work attitudes and behaviors. To retain their employees, many companies give them bonuses and company stock linked to their contributions or years of service. This tends to make employees feel like "owners" of the company. Companies such as IBM, Microsoft, and Accenture believe these types of incentives encourage the development of values and norms that improve organizational effectiveness.[51] We saw how Jean Buttner's attempt to limit Value Line employees' benefits resulted in hostility and high turnover. We also saw how Herbert Kelleher, by establishing a company-wide stock option system and encouraging employees to find better ways to make customers happy, fostered commitment and loyalty at Southwest Airlines. Indeed, evidence suggests that linking pay to performance creates a culture of committed and motivated employees who perform at high levels. The accompanying OB Today shows how one company did just this.

ob today

Bimba Changes Its Approach

The Bimba Manufacturing Company, based in Monee, Illinois, manufactures aluminum cylinders. Its owner, Charles Bimba, decided to sell the company to its employees by establishing an employee stock ownership plan (ESOP). He kept 10 percent of the shares; the other 90 percent was sold to employees. Some of the employees' money came from an already existing profit-sharing plan; the rest was borrowed from a bank.[52]

Changes in the company since the ESOP was introduced have been dramatic, and the orientation of the workforce to the organization has totally changed. Previously, the company had two groups of employees: managers who made the

Before Bimba, Inc., employees purchased shares in their company, they merely followed managers' orders. Now these same employees think like owners. Teamwork and innovation have dramatically improved the aluminum cylinder maker's operations.

rules and workers who carried them out. Workers rarely made suggestions and generally just obeyed orders. Now, cross-functional teams composed of managers and workers meet regularly to discuss problems and find new ways to improve quality. These teams also meet regularly with customers to better understand their needs.

Because of the incentives provided by the new ESOP, management and workers have developed new working relationships based on teamwork to achieve excellence and high quality. Each team hires its own members and spends considerable time socializing new employees in the culture of the organization. The new cooperative spirit in the plant has forced managers to relearn their roles. They now listen to workers and act as advisers rather than superiors.

So far, changing the company's property rights system has paid off. Both its sales and employment have doubled. Bimba has expanded to a new, larger facility, and it has opened facilities in both Europe and Asia. Furthermore, workers have repaid the entire loan they took out to finance the employee stock purchase.[53] In the words of one worker, the ESOP has led to "an intense change in the way we look at our jobs."[54] It has totally changed Bimba's corporate culture and the commitment of its workforce.

ORGANIZATIONAL STRUCTURE

As the Bimba story illustrates, redesigning human resource policies and introducing new training, promotion, and incentive systems can alter an organization's culture by changing its instrumental values and norms. Bimba's culture changed because it altered its organizational structure and empowered self-managed teams. At Bimba, this change eliminated the need for close supervision. Coordination is achieved by teams of employees who value cooperation and are motivated by the prospect of sharing in the wealth the organization generates.

We have seen how the values and norms that shape employee work attitudes and behaviors are derived from the organization's people, ethics, and human resources management policies. A fourth source of cultural values comes from the organization's structure. Recall from Chapter 16 that *organizational structure* is the formal system of task and reporting relationships that an organization establishes to coordinate and motivate its employees. Because different structures give rise to different cultures, managers need to design a certain kind of organizational structure in order to create a certain kind of culture. Mechanistic structures, for example, give rise to totally different sets of norms, rules, and cultural values than do organic structures.

Recall from Chapter 16 that *mechanistic structures* are tall, highly centralized, and standardized, and *organic structures* are flat and decentralized and rely on mutual adjustment. In a tall, centralized organization, people have relatively little personal autonomy, and desirable behaviors include being cautious, obeying authority, and respecting traditions. Thus, a mechanistic structure is likely to give rise to a culture in which predictability and stability are desired end states. In a flat, decentralized structure, people have more freedom to choose and control their own activities, and desirable instrumental values include being creative or courageous and taking risks. Thus, an organic structure is likely to give rise to a culture in which innovation and flexibility are desired terminal values.

An organization's structure can promote cultural values that foster integration and coordination. Out of stable task and role relationships, for example, emerge shared norms and rules that help reduce communications problems, prevent the distortion of information, and speed the flow of information. Moreover, norms, values, and a common organizational language can improve the performance of teams and task forces. It is easier for different functions to share information and trust one another when they share similar cultural values. One reason why product development time is short and the organization is flexible in product team structures and matrix structures is that the reliance on face-to-face contact between functional specialists in teams forces those teams to quickly develop shared values and common responses to problems.

Whether a company is centralized or decentralized also leads to the development of different kinds of cultural values. By decentralizing authority, an organization can establish values that encourage and reward creativity or innovation. As mentioned earlier, at 3M employees are encouraged to spend 15 percent of their time working on personal projects. By decentralizing authority and empowering its members, an organization signals them that it's "okay" to be innovative and do things their own way—as long as their actions are consistent with the good of the organization.

Conversely, in some organizations, it is important that employees do not make decisions on their own and that their actions be open to the scrutiny of superiors. In cases such as this, centralization can be used to create cultural values that reinforce obedience and accountability. For example, in nuclear power plants, values that promote stability, predictability, and obedience to authority are deliberately fostered to prevent disasters.[55] Through norms and rules, employees are taught the importance of behaving consistently and honestly, and they learn that sharing information with supervisors, especially information about mistakes or errors, is the only acceptable form of behavior.[56]

ADAPTIVE CULTURES VERSUS INERT CULTURES

Adaptive cultures are those whose values and norms help an organization build momentum, grow, and change as needed to achieve its goals and be effective. Inert cultures are those that lead to values and norms that fail to motivate or inspire employees; they lead to stagnation and often failure over time. What leads to an adaptive or inert culture? Researchers have found that organizations with strong adaptive cultures such as 3M, Microsoft, and IBM invest in their employees. They adopt human resource practices that demonstrate their commitment to their members by, for example, emphasizing the long-term nature of the employment relationship and trying to avoid layoffs. These companies develop long-term career paths for their employees and invest heavily in training and development to make them more valuable to the organization. In these ways, terminal and instrumental values pertaining to the worth of the people working within the organization encourage the development of supportive work attitudes and behaviors.

In adaptive cultures employees often receive rewards linked directly to their performance and to the performance of the company as a whole. Sometimes employee stock ownership plans (ESOPs) are developed. In an ESOP, workers as a group are allowed to buy a significant percentage of their company's stock. Workers who are owners of the company have an incentive to develop skills improving their performance levels. These employees are also more likely to search actively for ways to improve quality, efficiency, and performance. At Dell, for example, employees are able to buy Dell stock at a steep (15 percent) discount and build a sizable stake in the company over time.

However, some organizations develop cultures with values that do not include protecting and increasing the worth of their people as a major goal. Their employment practices are based on short-term employment needs and minimal investment in employees, who perform simple, routine tasks. Moreover, employees are not often rewarded based on their performance and, therefore, have little incentive to improve their skills to help the organization meet its goals. In a company with an inert culture and poor relationships with its employees, the instrumental values of noncooperation, laziness, and output restriction norms are common. Employees are content to be told what to do because they have little motivation to perform beyond the minimum requirements. Unfortunately, such a hierarchical structure and emphasis on close super-vision produce a culture that doesn't readily adapt to a change. By contrast, an adaptive culture emphasizes entrepreneurship and respect for employees. Innovative organizational structures such as cross-functional teams that empower and motivate employees are likely to develop in such a culture. This puts the organization in a better position to adapt to the changing business climate.

An organization that seeks to manage and change its culture must take a hard look at all four factors that shape culture: the characteristics of its members (particularly the founder), its ethical values, human resource policies, and organizational structure. Changing a culture can be difficult, however, because of the way these factors interact and affect one another.[57] Often a major reorganization is necessary for a cultural change to occur, as we discuss in Chapter 18. Next, we discuss how the values of a national culture shape a company's ability to adapt.

Values From the National Culture

The values and norms of a nation have a profound impact on the culture of each and every organization operating or headquartered within it. Culture, whether organizational or national, is a product of the values and norms that people use to guide and control their behavior. On a national level, a country's values and norms determine what kinds of attitudes and behaviors are acceptable or appropriate. Members of a particular national culture are instilled with these values as they grow up. Norms and social guidelines dictate the way they should behave toward one another and, often, toward people of different cultures.

Recall from Chapter 1 that national culture is the particular set of economic, political, and social values that exists in a particular country. U.S. national culture, for example, is based on capitalistic economic values, democratic political values, and individualistic, competitive social values—all characteristic of the way people in the United States live and work. The culture of a U.S. company is distinct from the cultures of Japanese, French, and German companies, for example, because the values of these countries differ in significant ways.

HOFSTEDE'S MODEL OF NATIONAL CULTURE

Researchers have spent considerable time and effort identifying similarities and differences between the cultural values and norms of different countries. A model of national culture developed by Geert Hofstede argues that differences in the values and norms of different countries are captured by five dimensions of culture.[58]

Individualism Versus Collectivism. The dimension that Hofstede called individualism versus collectivism focuses on the values that govern the relationship between individuals and groups. In countries where individualism prevails, values of individual achievement, freedom, and competition are stressed. In countries where collectivism prevails, values of group harmony, cohesiveness, and consensus are very strong, and the importance of cooperation and agreement between individuals is stressed. In collectivist cultures, the group is more important than the individual, and group members follow norms that stress group rather than personal interests. Japan epitomizes a country where collectivist values dominate, and the United States epitomizes a country where individualist values prevail.[59]

Power Distance. Hofstede used power distance to refer to the degree to which a country accepts the fact that differences in its citizens' physical and intellectual capabilities give rise to inequalities in their well-being. This concept also measures the degree to which countries accept economic and social differences in wealth, status, and well-being as natural. Countries that allow inequalities to persist or increase are said to have high power distance. Professionally successful workers in high-power-distance countries amass wealth and pass it on to their children. In these countries, inequalities increase over time; the gap between rich and poor, with all the attendant political and social consequences, grows very large. In contrast, countries that dislike the development of large inequality gaps between their citizens are said to have low power distance. These countries use taxation or social welfare programs to reduce inequality and improve the lot of the least fortunate members of society. Low-power-distance countries are more interested in preventing a wide gap between rich and poor and discord between classes.

Advanced Western countries such as the United States, Germany, the Netherlands, and the United Kingdom score relatively low on power distance and are high on individualism. Poor Latin American countries such as Guatemala, Panama, and Asian countries such as Malaysia and the Philippines score high on power distance and low on individualism.[60] These findings suggest that the cultural values of richer countries emphasize protecting the rights of individuals and, at the same time, provide a fair chance of success to every member of society. But even among Western countries there are differences. Both the Dutch and the British see their countries as more protective of the poor and disadvantaged than Americans, who believe that people have the right to be rich as well as the right to be poor.

Achievement Versus Nurturing Orientation. Countries that are achievement oriented value assertiveness, performance, success, and competition and are results oriented. Countries that are nurturing oriented value the quality of life, warm personal relationships, and service and care for the weak. Japan and the United States tend to be achievement oriented. The Netherlands, Sweden, and Denmark tend to be nurturing oriented.

Uncertainty Avoidance. Just as people differ in their tolerance for uncertainty and willingness to take risks, so do countries. Countries low on uncertainty avoidance (such as the United States and Hong Kong) are easygoing, value diversity, and are tolerant of differences in what people believe and do. Countries high on uncertainty avoidance (such as Japan and France) tend to be rigid and intolerant. In high-uncertainty-avoidance cultures, conformity to the values of the social and work groups to which a person belongs is the norm, and structured situations are preferred because they provide a sense of security.

Differences in national culture help explain why the cultures of companies in one country tend to be different from those of companies in another. French and German organizations, for example, admire the entrepreneurial drive of U.S. managers and the American work ethic but treat their managers and workers in different ways than do U.S. organizations. French and German organizations are far less concerned with issues of equity and opportunity in their human resource policies. In France, for example, social class still determines the gender, ethnicity, and background of employees who will successfully climb the organizational ladder. Moreover, German and French companies employ far fewer foreign nationals in their management ranks than do U.S. companies. In the Unites States, the most talented employees are likely to be promoted regardless of their national origin.[61]

Long-Term Versus Short-Term Orientation. The last dimension that Hofstede identified concerns whether citizens of a country have a long- or a short-term orientation toward life and work.[62] A long-term orientation is likely to be the result of values that include thrift and persistence. A short-term orientation is likely to be the result of values that express a concern for maintaining personal stability or happiness and for living in the present. Countries with long-term orientations include Japan and

Hong Kong, well known for their high rate of per capita savings. The United States and France, which tend to spend more and save less, have a short-term orientation.

Table 17.1 lists the ways people in 10 countries score on Hofstede's five dimensions of national culture.

National cultures vary widely, as do the values and norms that guide the way people think and act. When an organization expands into foreign countries, it employs citizens whose values reflect those of the national culture. The fact that national culture is a determinant of organizational culture poses some interesting problems for an organization seeking to manage its global operations.[63]

If differences in values between countries cause differences in attitudes and behaviors between workers in different subsidiaries, an organization will find it difficult to obtain the benefits of global learning. Different parts of the company located in different countries may develop different orientations toward the problems facing the company and their own subcultures. They will become concerned more with their own local problems than with the global problems facing the company as a whole, and this will hinder organizational effectiveness.

Another major problem can occur when a company in one country seeks to cooperate with a company in a different country, perhaps via a joint venture. Differences in national values and norms can make such cooperation difficult for many reasons. The accompanying Global View illustrates the problems that emerged when Corning and Vitro formed a joint venture in Mexico.

To prevent the emergence of different national subcultures within a global organization, an organization must take steps to create a global culture and organization-wide values and norms that foster cohesiveness among divisions. But what does that entail?

TABLE 17.1

Culture Dimension Scores for 10 Countries

	Power Distance	Individualism	Achievement Orientation	Uncertainty Avoidance	Long-Term Orientation
United States	L	H	H	L	L
Germany	L	H	H	M	M
Japan	M	M	H	H	H
France	H	H	M	H	L
Netherlands	L	H	L	M	M
Hong Kong	H	L	H	L	H
Indonesia	H	L	M	L	L
West Africa	H	L	M	M	L
Russia	H	M	L	H	L
China	H	L	M	M	H

Note: H = top third
M = medium third } among 53 countries and regions for the first four dimensions; among 23 countries for the fifth
L = bottom third

Source: Adapted from G. Hofstede, "Cultural Constraints in Management Theories." *Academy of Management Executive,* 7 (1993):91.

global view

Different Cultures Make Cooperation Difficult

Pittsburgh-based Corning Glass Works and Vitro, a Mexican glass-making company, formed a joint venture to share technology and market one another's glass products throughout the United States and Mexico. They formed their alliance to take advantage of the opportunities presented by the North American Free Trade Agreement (NAFTA), which opened up the markets of both countries to one another's products. At the signing of the joint venture, both companies were enthusiastic about the prospects for their alliance. Managers in both companies claimed they had similar organizational cultures. Both companies had top management teams dominated by the family members of the founders; both were global companies with broad product lines; both had been successful managing alliances with other companies in the past.[64] Nevertheless, within two years, Corning Glass terminated the joint venture, returning the $150 million Vitro had given it for access to its technology. Why had the venture failed? The cultures and values of the two companies were so different that Corning managers and Vitro managers could not work together.

Vitro, the Mexican company, did business the Mexican way, in accordance with values prevailing in Mexican culture. In Mexico, business is conducted at a slower pace than in the United States. Used to a protected market, Mexican companies are inclined to sit back and make their decisions in a "very genteel," consensual way.[65] Managers typically come to work at 9 A.M., spend two or more hours at lunch, often at home with their families, and then work late, often until 9 P.M.. Mexican managers and their subordinates are intensely loyal and respectful to their superiors. The corporate culture is based on paternalistic, hierarchical values, and most important decisions are made by small teams of top managers. This centralization slows down decision making because middle managers may come up with a solution to a problem but will not take action without top management's approval. In Mexico, building relationships with new companies takes time and effort because trust develops slowly. Personal contacts that develop only slowly between managers in different companies are important for doing business in Mexico.

Corning, the American company, did business the American way, in accordance with values prevailing in American culture. Managers in the United States take short lunch breaks or work through lunch so they can leave early in the evening. In many American companies, decision-making authority is decentralized to lower-level managers, who make important decisions and commit their organization to certain courses of action. U.S. managers like to make decisions quickly and worry about the consequences later.

Aware of the differences in their approaches to doing business, managers from Corning and Vitro tried to compromise and find a mutually acceptable working style. Managers from both companies agreed to take long working lunches together. Vitro's managers agreed to forgo going home at lunchtime, and Corning's managers agreed to work a bit later at night so they could talk to each other and speed up the decision-making process. Over time, however, the differences in management styles and approaches to work became a source of frustration for both sets of managers. The slow pace of decision making was frustrating for Corning's managers. The pressure from Corning's managers to get everything done quickly was frustrating for Vitro's managers. In the end, the Americans withdrew from what had seemed to be a promising venture.[66] Corning's managers working in Mexico discovered that the organizational cultures of Vitro and Corning were not so similar after all, and they decided to go home. Vitro's managers also realized that it was pointless to prolong the venture when the differences were so great.

Corning and many other U.S. companies that have entered into global agreements have found that doing business in Mexico or in any other country is different from doing business at home. American managers living abroad should not expect to do business the American way. Because values, norms, customs, and etiquette differ from one country to another, expatriate managers must learn to understand the differences between their national culture and the culture of the host country, if they are to manage global organizational behavior successfully.

Global information technology, networks, and teams can be used to transmit values to the organization's worldwide divisions. Via global networks, expatriate managers can move from one country to another, spreading the company's values and norms throughout its divisions. Indeed, the transfer of employees from one division to another helps them understand they are members of a global organization. Global teams—both real and virtual—formed of managers from different countries can also facilitate the development of shared values.

Many large companies attempt to develop a cohesive set of values and norms throughout their organization by transferring their top managers to their global divisions. When Nissan, Honda, and Sony, for example, expand abroad, the entire top management team of the new global division consists of Japanese managers whose job it is to disseminate the companies' values. The Japanese have been very successful at maintaining control of the organizational culture of their plants in the United States and England. Quality levels at Japanese auto plants in the United States are close to levels in Japan, in fact.

Creating an Ethical Culture

We mentioned earlier that ethics—the moral values, beliefs, and rules that govern the way organizations and their members should act toward one another and people outside the organization—form an important part of an organization's cultural values. In an era when most companies' actions are being more intensively scrutinized by customers, investors, and government agencies, organizations and their employees cannot afford to engage in actions that will harm the company's reputation. Creating an ethical organizational culture has now become a major priority for many companies because failing to do so can be catastrophic.

One of the most important effects of ethical rules is to regulate and control the pursuit of unbridled self-interest. To understand why self-interest needs to be regulated, consider the "tragedy of the commons." The tragedy of the commons holds that it is rational for people to maximize their use of "common" land or resources (parks and open range are examples) because it's free. For example, cattle owners will all want to graze their herds on the open range to promote their individual interests. As a result, the land will almost certainly be overgrazed, and erosion will render it unusable. The rational pursuit of individual self-interests, in other words, will result in a collective disaster.

The same thing can happen in organizations: Left to their own devices, people will pursue their own goals at the expense of collective goals. Top managers, for example, may run the organization to their own advantage and to the detriment of shareholders, employees, and customers. Similarly, powerful unions may negotiate wages so high that in the long run a company becomes uncompetitive.

Ethical values and rules control self-interested behavior that might threaten the collective interests of an organization and society in general. Ethical values establish desired end states—for example, equitable or "good" business practices—and the modes of behavior needed to achieve those end states, such as being honest or being fair. Ethical values in an organization's culture also reduce the need for people to always evaluate what is right or wrong. By automatically following an ethical rule, people are also more productive because they spend less time and effort trying to decide what course of action to take.[67]

Another important reason to act ethically is that when an organization follows accepted ethical rules, it gains a good reputation.[68] This is a valuable asset that entices people to do business with it, including customers, suppliers, and the best job applicants. On the other hand, organizations with unethical reputations breed hostility and mistrust. Although unethical organizations might reap short-term benefits, they are penalized in the long run because eventually people will refuse to deal with them. This happened in the 2000s. People dumped companies such as WorldCom/MCI and Qwest in droves because they "cooked their books" to inflate their profits. Unfortunately, even unethical behavior on the part of just a few individuals can harm the organization as a whole. Ethical rules, laws, and social customs were designed precisely because of this. Without them, organizations and societies would suffer.

WHY DOES UNETHICAL BEHAVIOR OCCUR?

If there are good reasons for individuals and organizations to behave ethically, why do we see so many instances of unethical behavior?

Lapses in Individual Ethics. In theory, individuals learn how to behave ethically as they mature. People learn right from wrong from family members, friends, religious institutions, schools, professional associations, and other organizations. However, imagine that your father is a mobster, that your mother is a political terrorist, or your family belongs to a warring ethnic or religious group. Brought up in such an environment, you might be led believe that any act—including murder—is acceptable if it benefits you, your family, or your friends. In a similar way, individuals within an organization may come to believe that any action that promotes or protects the organization is acceptable, even if it does harm to others.

This apparently happened at now defunct accounting company Arthur Andersen, when its unscrupulous partners ordered middle managers to shred records of its dealings with Enron to hide evidence of its illegal accounting practices. Although middle managers knew this was wrong, they followed orders because of the power the firm's partners had over them. They were afraid they would lose their jobs if they did not behave unethically and shred the documents—and they were used to obeying orders. Nonetheless, in the end, their actions still cost them their jobs.

Ruthless Pursuit of Self-Interest. We normally confront ethical issues when we weigh our personal interests against the effects our actions will have on others. Suppose you will be promoted to vice president of your company if you can secure a $100 million contract, but that to get the contract, you must bribe the contractor with $1 million. Your career and future will probably be assured if you perform this act. "What harm will it do?" you ask yourself. Bribery is common; if you don't pay the million dollars, you are certain that someone else will. So what do you do? Research suggests that people who believe they have the most at stake are the ones most likely to act unethically. Similarly, it has been shown that organizations that are doing badly economically and are struggling to survive are the ones most likely to commit unethical and illegal acts such as bribery, although many other organizations will do so if they are given the opportunity.[69]

A woman carrying her boxed-up work belongings wipes away a tear as she leaves the Enron building, following the company's implosion. Lacking ethical boundaries, a few, self-interested employees can threaten an organization's very existence.

Outside Pressure. Many studies have found that the likelihood of unethical or criminal behavior increases when people feel outside pressure to perform. If company performance is deteriorating, for example, top managers may be pressured by shareholders to boost the corporation's performance. Fearful of losing their jobs, they may engage in unethical behavior to increase the value of the company's stock. If all outside pressures work in the same direction, it is easy to understand why unethical organizational cultures develop. Managers at all levels buy into unethical acts, and the view that the end justifies the means filters through the organization. If the organization's members pull together to disguise their unethical actions and protect one another from prosecution, the organization becomes increasingly defensive.

The social costs of unethical behavior are hard to measure but can be easily seen in the long run. They take the form of mismanaged organizations that become less innovative. Such organizations spend less and less money developing new and improved products and more and more money on advertising or managerial salaries. When new competitors arrive who refuse to play the same game, the mismanaged organization begins to crumble.

Organizations that lack ways for employees to air their ethical concerns or don't take them seriously risk being exposed by whistleblowers like Sherron Watkins, formerly of Enron.

WAYS TO CREATE AN ETHICAL CULTURE

There are several ways to create an ethical organizational culture to help members resist the temptation to engage in illegal acts for personal gain. First, an organization can encourage people to act ethically by putting in place incentives for ethical behavior and disincentives to punish those who behave unethically. A company's top managers—the people who have the ultimate responsibility for ensuring an organization behaves ethically—must be proactive in establishing the company's ethical position. Managers create an ethical culture by making a personal commitment to uphold ethical values and transmit them to subordinates.

As a leader, a manager can promote the moral values that determine how employees will make decisions by establishing appropriate rules and norms of behavior that outline the organization's ethical position. It is also important for managers to demonstrate their commitment to following the rules via their own behavior. That includes being honest and acknowledging errors or omissions quickly and disclosing the facts accurately.

Second, organizations can design an organizational structure that reduces the incentives for people to behave unethically. The creation of authority relationships and rules that promote ethical behavior and punish unethical acts, for example, will encourage members to behave in a socially responsible way. The federal government, for example, has a set of uniform standards of conduct for executive branch employees to follow. These standards cover ethical issues such as giving and receiving gifts, impartially assigning work to government contractors, and avoiding conflicts of interest when it comes to one's financial matters and outside work activities. These regulations cover 5 million federal workers.

Third, an organization can develop fair and equitable human resource procedures toward the management of its diverse employees. This signals workers that they can expect to be treated in an ethical way, that they are working for an ethical organization, and that they should behave in a like manner.

Fourth, organizations can put procedures into place giving subordinates access to upper-level managers to voice their concerns about unethical organizational behaviors they might observe. Ten percent of Fortune 500 companies now have ethics officers in their employ. An ethics officer is a manager responsible for training employees about ethical conduct and investigating claims of unethical behavior. Ethics committees within the organization can then make formal judgments depending on the officer's findings. Ethical values, of course, flow down from the top of the organization but are strengthened or weakened by the design of the organizational structure and programs such as these.

Michael Eisner, CEO of Disney, pocketed hundreds of millions of dollars in corporate bonuses in recent years, despite Disney's lackluster performance. In addition to his bonuses, critics say Eisner has Disney's board members in his back pocket too.

Whistle-blowing When an employee decides to inform an outside person or agency about illegal or unethical managerial behavior.

Organizations that lack avenues for employees to air their ethical concerns or fail to follow up on those concerns risk being exposed by whistle-blowers. **Whistle-blowing** occurs when an employee informs an outside person or organization, such as a government agency or newspaper or television reporter, about an organization's illegal or unethical behaviors (frequently on the part of its top managers). Employees typically become whistle-blowers when they feel powerless to prevent an organization from committing an unethical act or when they fear retribution from the company if they voice their concerns.[70]

Fifth, an organization can create a strong board of directors, from outside the company with no ties to top management. The directors should oversee the actions of top managers and, if they see any sign of wrongdoing or mismanagement, "nip it in the bud." In the 2000s, there have been many calls to strengthen the power of boards to scrutinize the decisions made by managers. One company forced to respond to this call is the Walt Disney Company, profiled in the accompanying Managing Ethically.

managing ethically

A Change in Disney's Board of Directors

In the last few years, the performance of Walt Disney Company has fallen precipitously. Many analysts are wondering if Michael Eisner, who has been its CEO for the last 18 years, is still the right person to run the company. For example, Eisner pushed through the merger of Disney with Capital/ABC. Since then, the ABC television network has been a poor performer, and this has caused Disney's stock price to plunge. Despite that poor performance, Eisner has received over $800 million in stock options from the company over the years. Some critics argue this is hardly ethical when the company's shareholders are losing money.

One of the things Eisner has been criticized for is creating a weak, or captive, board of directors unable or unwilling to scrutinize his decisions. Of the 16 members on the board, at least eight have personal ties to him. There are few outspoken outsiders on the board willing to rein Eisner in.

To counter such criticism, in 2003 Disney announced a reorganization of its board of directors. Two new special outside directors were appointed; one of them will chair two board meetings a year that Eisner—who normally chairs the meetings—will not be permitted to attend. The board will now have more freedom to assess Eisner's performance. Some analysts say the changes are not enough, though. Eisner still has the backing of the majority of the members, who are beholden to him, and he is still in control of all of Disney's important committees. What Disney's board of directors will do if Eisner's performance continues to deteriorate is anyone's guess.

Finally, just as pressures from those at the top of the organization can help prevent unethical behavior, so can pressures from people and groups outside the company.[71] Government agencies, industry councils, regulatory bodies, and consumer watchdog groups all play a role when it comes to making sure corporations follow the rules. In the last few years in particular, government regulators have very actively prosecuted managers at companies such as WorldCom and Enron. WorldCom (now renamed MCI) later brought in new top managers who took many of the steps just discussed to rebuild that organization's ethical culture. The steps are summarized in Table 17.2.[72]

In sum, there are many steps that can be taken to help strengthen managers' and employees' commitment to behave ethically. When ethical values are instilled, a strong adaptive culture develops, which, in turn, helps organizations achieve their goals.

TABLE 17.2

Creating an Ethical Culture at MCI/WorldCom

In order to create an ethical culture at the old WorldCom, MCI's new managers took the following steps:

♦ Recruited a new CEO who was not at the company during the events at issue, and who brought a reputation for integrity and forthrightness in his leadership skills

♦ Recruited a new president and chief operating officer from outside the company who has more than 25 years of telecom experience

♦ Recruited a new chief financial officer, general counsel, and director of internal controls, all of whom came from outside the company

♦ Replaced its entire board of directors who were present at the time the fraud was discovered, thereby removing 100 percent of the directors who were participants in governance under the regime of the prior CEO Bernard J. Ebbers

♦ Recruited new and highly qualified independent directors

♦ Consented to the establishment (and continuation) of the Corporate Monitor program, which represents an unprecedented level of independent oversight of management activity

♦ Closed the finance and accounting department located in the company's former Clinton, Mississippi, headquarters where most of the fraudulent activities were conducted

♦ Hired more than 400 new finance and accounting personnel

♦ Retained a new outside auditor and commissioned a complete reaudit of the years 1999–2002 to document the company's actual performance as best as it can be reconstructed from available records and personnel

♦ Evaluated all corporate assets for value impairment, wrote off all goodwill, and wrote down asset-carrying values for property, plant, and equipment to achieve a realistic balance sheet

♦ Initiated a widespread and intensive review led by three new directors to identify wrongdoing that occurred and those who participated. Also funded a separate thorough investigation by the bankruptcy examiner and responded to his findings concerning wrongful activities of different types

♦ Terminated dozens of employees, including a number of senior officers, who either participated in inappropriate activities, who appeared to look the other way in the face of indications of suspicious activity, or who otherwise acted in a manner inconsistent with necessary standards of conduct

♦ Agreed to abolish use of stock options in favor of restricted stock with full expensing of the value of equity grants on the company's profit and loss statement

♦ Initiated a thorough review of internal controls to strengthen the company's systems and procedures for capturing and reporting financial data and a widespread program to create a much stronger system

♦ Put in place a new Ethics Pledge program pursuant to which senior officers including the CEO pledge to pursue ethics and integrity, compliance programs, and transparency and candor in financial reporting well beyond SEC requirements

♦ Established a new Ethics Office

♦ Commenced a training program for employees on their responsibilities under the federal securities laws, accounting issues that may signal inappropriate behavior or fraud, and ethical issues

♦ Consented to the Permanent Injunction

♦ Consented to a financial settlement with the SEC under which $500 million in cash and $250 million in stock will be paid into a trust for victims

Summary

Organizational culture is an important means through which organizations coordinate and motivate the behavior of their members. An organization can shape work attitudes and behaviors by the way it invests in and rewards its employees over time and by its attempts to encourage values of excellence. The chapter has made the following main points:

1. Organizational culture is the set of shared values, beliefs, and norms that influences the way employees think, feel, and behave toward each other and toward people outside the organization.

2. There are two kinds of organizational values: terminal (a desired outcome) and instrumental (a desired mode of behavior). Ideally, instrumental values help the organization to achieve its terminal values.

3. Culture is transmitted to an organization's members by means of (a) socialization and training programs and (b) stories, ceremonies, and language used by members of the organization.

4. Organizational culture develops from the interaction of four factors: the personal and professional characteristics of people within the organization, organizational ethics, the nature of the employment relationship between a company and its employees, and the design of its organizational structure. These factors work together to produce different cultures in different organizations and cause changes in culture over time.

5. Different organizations have different kinds of cultures because they attract, select, and retain different kinds of people. Because an organization's founder is instrumental in initially determining what kind of people get selected, a founder can have a long-lasting effect on an organization's culture.

6. Ethics are the moral values, beliefs, and rules that establish the right or appropriate ways in which one person or group should interact and deal with another person or group. Organizational ethics are a product of societal, professional, and individual ethics.

7. The nature of the employment relationship between a company and its employees causes the development of particular norms, values, and attitudes toward the organization.

8. Different organizational structures give rise to different patterns of interaction among people. These different patterns lead to the formation of different organizational cultures.

9. Adaptive cultures are those whose values and norms help an organization to build momentum and to grow and change as needed to achieve its goals and be effective. Inert cultures are those that lead to values and norms that fail to motivate or inspire employees; they lead to stagnation and often failure over time.

10. Another important determinant of organizational culture is the values of the nation in which a company is founded and has its home operations.

11. A company can help to build and sustain an ethical culture by establishing the right kinds of incentives and rules for rewarding ethical behavior, by establishing a strong board of directors, and by making sure employees follow the legal rules and guidelines established by government agencies and watched by consumer groups.

Exercises in Understanding and Managing Organizational Behavior

Questions for Discussion and Review

1. What are the building blocks of organizational culture?

2. How do newcomers learn the culture of an organization?

3. Find a manager or person in charge of helping new employees "learn the ropes" and question this person about how the organization socializes its new members.

4. What four factors affect the kind of culture that develops in an organization?

5. In what ways can organizational culture increase organizational effectiveness?

6. If you were starting a new restaurant, what kind of culture would help promote organizational effectiveness? How would you try to build such a culture?

7. How does national culture affect organizational culture?

8. Why is it important that an organization's members behave ethically? Why does unethical behavior occur?

9. How can you build and maintain an ethical culture?

Building People Skills

Understanding Culture

Pick an organization you are very familiar with such as a local school, church, or one in which you have worked for a long period of time. Use the chapter material to think about its culture and answer the following questions:

1. What are the terminal and instrumental values of the organization? How do they affect its members' attitudes and behaviors?

2. Identify the main beliefs and norms of organizational members. How do these norms relate to the organization's values? Is there a fit between them? Identify areas for improvement.

3. How does the organization socialize new members? Could the ways it helps newcomers learn the organization's culture be improved?

4. What kinds of organizational ceremonies does the organization have to help reinforce its values and norms?

5. Try to identify the source of the values and norms of your organization's culture. For example, do you think the people or the organization's rules and procedures have the most effect on organizational culture?

A Question of Ethics

When Is Culture Too Strong?

An organization's managers may attempt to influence their employees' attitudes and behaviors by building a particular kind of culture. The process of building a strong culture can have a dark side if managers create values and norms that ultimately cause employees to behave in unethical ways. In other words, sometimes a culture can become too strong and its members may all begin to act unethically and without regard to the effects of their actions on others. Think about the ethical issues involved in building organizational culture and address the following issues:

1. When and under what conditions can values and norms become so strong that they cause employees to act in unethical ways?

2. Think about the four main factors influencing organizational culture. How could they be used to create a culture that causes employees to act in unethical ways?

3. Why might differences in national culture lead to unethical behavior in a global organization?

Small Group Break-Out Exercise

Developing a Service Culture

Form groups of three to five people and discuss the following scenario:

You are the owner/managers of a new five-star resort hotel opening up on the white sand beaches of the west coast of Florida. For your venture to succeed you need to make sure that hotel employees focus on providing customers with the highest-quality customer service possible. You are meeting to discuss how to create a culture that will promote such high-quality service, that will encourage employees to be committed to the hotel, and that will reduce the level of employee turnover and absenteeism, which are typically high in the hotel business.

1. What kinds of organizational values and norms encourage employees to behave in ways that lead to high-quality customer service?

2. Using the concepts discussed in this chapter (for example, people, employment relationship, socialization), discuss how you will create a culture that promotes the learning of these customer service values and norms.

3. Which factor is the most important determinant of the kind of culture you expect to find in a five-star hotel?

Topics for Debate

Different contingencies—the environment, technology, and strategy—cause organizations to design their structures and cultures in different ways. Now that you understand the contingencies facing an organization, debate the following issues.

Debate One

Team A. An organization can never be too organic because the environment constantly changes and an organization has to be able to respond to change quickly.

Team B. A structure that is too organic can be a problem because ill-defined task and authority relationships can slow decision making and responses to change.

Debate Two

Team A. Efficiency and quality are the most important sources of competitive advantage.

Team B. Innovation and responsiveness to customers are the keys to competitive success.

Experiential Exercise

A Culture Problem at HighandTall

Form groups of three to five people to discuss the following scenario and the questions. Be prepared to share your discussions with your class.

You are the founding entrepreneurs of HighandTall Company, a fast-growing digital software company that specializes in home consumer electronics. Customer demand to license your software has boomed so much that in just two years you have added over 50 new software programmers to help develop a new range of software products. These people are young and inexperienced but are highly skilled and used to putting in long hours to see their ideas succeed. The growth of your company has been so swift that you still operate informally. You have been so absorbed in your own work that you have paid little attention to the issue of developing a culture for your growing company. Your programmers have been learning how your company works by observing you and by seeing what goes on in their own work groups. There are increasing signs that all is not well, however.

There have been increasing complaints from employees that as managers you do not recognize or reward good performance and that they do not feel equitably treated. Moreover, there has been growing concern that you are either too busy or not willing to listen to new ideas and act on them. A bad atmosphere seems to be developing in the company and recently several talented employees have left.

You realize in hindsight that you have done a poor job of creating a culture that encourages employees to perform well and stay with your company.

1. What kinds of values and norms do you want to make the heart of your organization's culture?
2. Think about this work situation, how could you try to build an adaptive culture, based on the desired values and norms, for your organization? (Hint: Focus on the four sources of culture.)
3. In what other ways could you influence and persuade your employees to perform well and stay with your company?

Making the Connection

Identify an organization that has been trying to change its culture. Describe the culture that it is trying to alter. Why is this culture no longer effective? How has the organization tried to bring about change? How successful has it been?

New York Times Cases in the News

The New York Times

Many Find an Office's Culture Is More Than Dress-Shirt Deep

BY DAVID KOEPPEL

At first, Joyce Hansen wondered if leaving journalism for the more conservative world of banking was a career mistake. When she was a reporter and editor, dressing for work had meant pulling on jeans and a Gap T-shirt. At her jobs in New York City and Harrisburg, Pa., from 1990 to 1999, Ms. Hansen, 44, had loved the sometimes raucous and chaotic atmosphere of a newsroom, and had relished the freedom to speak her mind.

But in time, she tired of the hectic pace, fierce competition and relatively low pay. In February 2001, after taking some time off to write a book, she accepted a job as a technical writer with the Bank One Corporation of Chicago. She got a taste of what was to come from the hiring process, when she was fingerprinted, tested for drugs and given a criminal background check. But it was still a shock to have to show up for work at 9 a.m. sharp every day, wearing subdued colors and Calvin Klein skirts. The calm, polite tenor of the frequent meetings she was required to attend also took some getting used to.

Not only that, but for almost a year, her supervisor kept her on a tight leash, criticizing her choice of clothing and her way of speaking and writing whenever they were deemed to have fallen short of company standards. "She was studying me on an almost daily basis, to make sure I was conservative enough," Ms. Hansen recalled about her supervisor. "She wanted to make sure that I looked and acted like a banker."

So did Ms. Hansen begin to yearn for the old days as a reporter? Not a bit. Instead, she learned an important lesson about the workplace: surface manifestations of a company's culture don't matter; what counts are its core values.

Ms. Hansen came to view the formality and strict rules at Bank One as little more than a mild annoyance—and to appreciate what she saw as its principles of shared purpose, open communication and mutual respect among employees.

The money helped, too. "The new job required me to adapt my personality to the new circumstances," she said. "But I knew that in making these changes there would be a payoff. I've been able to achieve my personal goals. There's better money, excellent benefits. I'm saving to make a down payment on a mortgage and for the first time I'm debt free."

In March, Ms. Hansen began working at Banc One Capital Markets, a subsidiary of Bank One, as a research editor, a job that she called "a perfect fit."

There is a lesson in her experience for people looking for a job, or thinking of switching careers. It has always been accepted wisdom among workplace experts that employees thrive best in a company whose culture matches their personality. But as Ms. Hansen's shaky but ultimately successful transition shows, it is important for job candidates to peer below the surface to figure out what really matters to them.

Similarly, if you love what you are doing, maybe you should stay put, even if more lucrative offers beckon. Christine Bracco, 31, an executive assistant for the Anschutz Entertainment Group, a sports and entertainment company in Los Angeles, says she never felt more professionally fulfilled than when she worked from 1997 to 2000 as an executive assistant at Scholastic, the Manhattan publisher that specializes in children's books.

Ms. Bracco, a certified teacher, strongly identified with its mission to educate children and improve literacy. And she said she felt that management cared about employees, treating them to lectures and workshops by authors and educators, giving them perks like a rooftop restaurant and an on-site library. The management kept employees informed through the company's newsletter and Intranet site.

Though she left Scholastic to move to California in 2000, she is hoping a return is not out of the question, especially if the company opens an office there, as she has heard it plans to do.

Of course, in this sagging economy, people desperate for work can be forgiven for ignoring potential employers' culture altogether. "You don't think about it if you're just concerned about survival," said Randall S. Hansen, the publisher of Quintessential Careers, an online job site.

"Any offer is a good one if it allows you to pay the bills or ensure you won't be homeless," said Dr. Hansen, who is no relation to Joyce Hansen.

But the economy is starting to show signs of life. Last week, surveys from May showed that factory activity exceeded expectations and job cuts by employers declined sharply. If the economy rebounds this summer, as some expect, people looking for work might find they have more flexibility to take a close look at the companies that want to hire them.

Sometimes, of course, it is obvious where you belong and where you don't. An environmental activist would not have to scratch much below the surface to realize she would not enjoy working for an oil company with a spotty record on pollution.

Job seekers should think hard about what, exactly, in a company's culture is important to them and what is not, experts say. For some, a rooftop restaurant or large office with a north-south exposure might matter a lot. Others might prefer a laid-back environment, and some value opportunities for advancement and to make more money.

Dr. Hansen offered a basic test: "You want to be happy going to work. You don't want to be one of these people who spend Sundays thinking, 'Oh my God, I can't face my job tomorrow.'"

There are many ways to learn about a company's culture, from doing online research to chatting with employees off the premises.

Benjamin Dattner, president of Dattner Consulting and an adjunct assistant professor of organizational psychology at New York University, says you can pick up clues by making a casual visit. "Does the receptionist smile?" he asked. "Are people sitting in the reception area responded to? Ask people to flat-out describe what it's like to work there and what types of people are happiest."

Job hunters should be aware that employers, too, are intent on finding the right match. In fact, because they are hiring fewer people than they were a few years ago, they are paying closer attention to the personalities of applicants to make sure they share the company's values and goals, according to Herbert Greenberg, chief executive of Caliper Human Strategies, a job-aptitude assessment company in Princeton, N.J.

Caliper charges $265 for its personality and job-aptitude test, a two-hour exam used by companies like FedEx and Avis, and it says that business has increased 20 percent over the last year.

Another method that has been gaining favor recently for scrutinizing job candidates, Dr. Hansen says, is something called the situational interview, which uses role-playing techniques to gauge applicants' responses to situations they might encounter on the job.

For all the emphasis on finding the right fit, employers should not lose sight of the value of a diversity of viewpoints, workplace experts say. Sometimes, new hires with contrarian ideas can shake things up in a positive way.

"They're coming from a fresh perspective," Dr. Dattner said. "They can ask, 'Why do we do it this way? Let's try it that way.'"

SOURCE: "Many Find an Office's Culture Is More Than Dress-Shirt Deep," *New York Times*, June 8, 2003, p. 10.1.

Questions for Discussion

1. What kinds of ways of learning about an organization's culture are suggested in the case?

2. What are some things prospective employees should learn about an organization's culture before they join it?

The New York Times

Excerpts From Report of the Columbia Accident Investigation Board

Following are excerpts from the report of the Columbia Accident Investigation Board, which was released yesterday. The full text is online at nytimes.com/columbia.

The Board Statement

For all those who are inspired by flight, and for the nation where powered flight was first achieved, the year 2003 had long been anticipated as one of celebration—Dec. 17 would mark the centennial of the day the Wright Flyer first took to the air. But 2003 began instead on a note of sudden and profound loss. On Feb. 1, Space Shuttle Columbia was destroyed in a disaster that claimed the lives of all seven of its crew. . . .

It is our view that complex systems almost always fail in complex ways, and we believe it would be wrong to reduce the complexities and weaknesses associated with these systems to some simple explanation.

Too often, accident investigations blame a failure only on the last step in a complex process, when a more comprehensive understanding of that process could reveal that earlier steps might be equally or even more culpable. In this board's opinion, unless the technical, organizational and cultural recommendations made in this report are implemented, little will have been accomplished to lessen the chance that another accident will follow. . . .

Organizational Causes

. . . The organizational causes of this accident are rooted in the space shuttle program's history and culture, including the original compromises that were required to gain approval for the shuttle program, subsequent years of resource constraints, fluctuating priorities, schedule pressures, mischaracterizations of the shuttle as operational rather than developmental and lack of an agreed national vision.

Cultural traits and organizational practices detrimental to safety and reliability were allowed to develop, including reliance on past success as a substitute for sound engineering practices (such as testing to understand why systems were not performing in accordance with requirements/specifications); organizational barriers which prevented effective communication of critical safety information and stifled professional differences of opinion; lack of integrated management across program elements; and the evolution of an informal chain of command and decision making processes that operated outside the organization's rules.

In the board's view, NASA's organizational culture and structure had as much to do with this accident as the external tank foam. Organizational culture refers to the values, norms, beliefs and practices that govern how an institution functions. At the most basic level, organizational culture defines the assumptions that employees make as they carry out their work. It is a powerful force that can persist through reorganizations and the reassignment of key personnel. Given that today's risks in human space flight are as high and the safety margins as razor thin as they have ever been, there is little room for overconfidence. Yet the attitudes and decision making of shuttle program managers and engineers during the events leading up to this accident were clearly overconfident and often bureaucratic in nature. They deferred to layered and cumbersome regulations rather than the fundamentals of safety.

The shuttle program's safety culture is straining to hold together the vestiges of a once-robust systems safety program. As the board investigated the Columbia accident, it expected to find a vigorous safety organization, process and culture at NASA bearing little resemblance to what the Rogers Commission identified as the ineffective "silent safety" system in which budget cuts resulted in a lack of resources, personnel, independence and authority.

NASA's initial briefings to the board on its safety programs espoused a risk-averse philosophy that empowered any employee to stop an operation at the mere glimmer of a problem. Unfortunately, NASA's views of its safety culture in those briefings did not reflect reality. Shuttle program safety personnel failed to adequately assess anomalies and frequently accepted critical risks without qualitative or quantitative support, even when the tools to provide more comprehensive assessments were available.

Similarly, the board expected to find NASA's Safety and Mission Assurance organization deeply engaged at every level of shuttle management: the Flight Readiness Review, the Mission Management Team, the Debris Assessment Team, the Mission Evaluation Room and so forth. This was not the case. In briefing after briefing, interview after interview, NASA remained in denial. In the agency's eyes, "there were no safety-of-flight issues," and no safety compromises in the long history of debris strikes on the thermal protection system.

The silence of program-level safety processes undermined oversight; when they did not speak up, safety personnel could not fulfill their stated mission to provide "checks and balances." A pattern of acceptance prevailed throughout the organization that tolerated foam problems without sufficient engineering justification for doing so.

Connecting the parts of NASA's organizational system and drawing the parallels with Challenger demonstrate three things. First, despite all the post-Challenger changes at NASA and the agency's notable achievements since, the causes of the institutional failure responsible for Challenger have not been fixed. Second, the board strongly believes that if these persistent, systemic flaws are not resolved, the scene is set for another accident.

Therefore, the recommendations for change are not only for fixing the shuttle's technical system, but also for fixing each part of the organizational system that produced Columbia's failure. Third, the board's focus on the context in which decision making occurred does not mean that individuals are not responsible and accountable. To the contrary, individuals always must assume responsibility for their actions. What it does mean is that NASA's problems cannot be solved simply by retirements, resignations or transferring personnel.

The constraints under which the agency has operated throughout the shuttle program have contributed to both shuttle accidents. Although NASA leaders have played an important role, these constraints were not entirely of NASA's own making. The White House and Congress must recognize the role of their decisions in this accident and take responsibility for safety in the future.

Through its recommendations in Part 2, the board has urged that NASA's human spaceflight program adopt the characteristics observed in high-reliability organizations. One is separating technical authority from the functions of managing schedules and cost. Another is an independent safety and mission assurance organization. The third is the capability for effective systems integration.

Perhaps even more challenging than these organizational changes are the cultural changes required. Within NASA, the cultural impediments to safe and effective shut-tle operations are real and substantial, as documented extensively in this report. The board's view is that cultural problems are unlikely to be corrected without top-level leadership. Such leadership will have to rid the system of practices and patterns that have been validated simply because they have been around so long. Examples include the tendency to keep knowledge of problems contained within a center or program, making technical decisions without in-depth peer-reviewed technical analysis, and an unofficial hierarchy or caste system created by placing excessive power in one office. Such factors interfere with open communication, impede the sharing of lessons learned, cause duplication and unnecessary expenditure of resources, prompt resistance to external advice and create a burden for managers, among other undesirable outcomes. Collectively, these undesirable characteristics threaten safety. . . .

SOURCE: "Excerpts From Report of the Columbia Accident Investigation Board," *New York Times*, August 27, 2003, p. A18.

Questions for Discussion

1. In what ways does the accident board attribute the *Columbia* disaster to NASA's culture?

2. How could NASA's culture *and* structure be changed to ensure such a tragedy never happens again?

Organizational Change and Development

- OVERVIEW
- FORCES FOR AND RESISTANCE TO ORGANIZATIONAL CHANGE
- EVOLUTIONARY AND REVOLUTIONARY CHANGE IN ORGANIZATIONS
- MANAGING CHANGE: ACTION RESEARCH
- ORGANIZATIONAL DEVELOPMENT
- SUMMARY
- EXERCISES IN UNDERSTANDING AND MANAGING ORGANIZATIONAL BEHAVIOR

LEARNING OBJECTIVES

After reading this chapter, you should be able to:

■

Appreciate the forces that lead to organizational change and the various impediments to change that arise during the change process.

■

Distinguish between evolutionary and revolutionary change and identify the main types of each of these kinds of change process.

■

Discuss the main steps involved in action research and identify the main issues that must be addressed to manage the change process effectively.

■

Understand the process of organizational development and how to use various change techniques to facilitate the change process.

OPENING CASE

Toyota Is a Master at Managing Change

Why Is Change Important at Toyota?

Toyota has long been known as a company that has constantly strived to change its production systems to enhance efficiency, quality, and customer responsiveness. It pioneered the system of "lean production," a form of reengineering the work process that resulted in dramatic improvements in the quality of its vehicles. And Toyota has always pursued total quality management or *kaizen*, a change strategy that involves a continuous incremental improvement of work procedures. Using *kaizen*, production-line employees are made responsible for finding ways to improve work procedures to drive down costs and drive up quality. Individually, and in quality groups or circles, employees suggest ways to improve how a particular Toyota car model is made. Over time, from their thousands of suggestions, incremental innovations made to the car assembly process result in major improvements to the final product. Employees receive cash bonuses and rewards for finding ways to improve work procedures, and the result has been a continuous increase in car quality and reduced manufacturing costs.

In the 2000s, however, under the leadership of Toyota's new president, Jujio Cho, the company sought to increase the speed of change to further improve its efficiency and quality to gain an edge over its major competitors such as GM, Ford, and DaimlerChrysler. It has begun a series of new kinds of change programs, each directed at improving some aspect of its operations, which Toyota hopes will bring both incremental and radical changes to the way it operates.

Some incremental change programs involve strengthening its *kaizen* program, such as "pokayoke," or mistake-proofing. This initiative concentrates on the stages of the assembly process that have led to most previous quality problems; employees are required to double- and triple-check a particular stage to discover defective parts or to fix improper assembly operations that lead to subsequent customer complaints. Another program is "CCC21," which involves working with the company's suppliers to find ways to reduce the costs of Toyota's car components

by 30 percent—something that will result in billions of dollars in savings. Toyota has also introduced a new manufacturing process called "GBL," which uses a sophisticated new assembly process to hold a car body firmly in place during production. This allows welding and assembly operations to be performed more accurately, resulting in better-quality cars. GBL has also enabled Toyota to build factories that can assemble several different kinds of models on the same production line with no loss in efficiency or quality. This is a major competitive advantage. The company's global network of plants can now quickly change the kinds of cars they are making depending on buyers' demands for various models at different points in time.

Other radical change efforts have focused on revamping Toyota's development and design process to keep up with changing customer needs and demographics. In the 1990s, for example, the age of the average Toyota car buyer steadily rose. Despite Toyota's climbing global sales (which exceeded $146 billion in 2003), the company was criticized for failing to understand how the market was changing. Analysts blamed the problem on centralized decision making at the company and a culture that had long been dominated by Toyota's cautious and frugal Japanese designers. Rather than designing innovative, flexible vehicles customers were increasingly demanding, Toyota continued to focus on cutting costs and increasing the quality of its vehicles. When the company's U.S. designers, for example, argued with designers in Tokyo that an eight-cylinder pickup truck was what Toyota needed to keep pace with GM and Ford, they were ignored. Headquarters also turned a deaf ear to the call to manufacture other new kinds of vehicles appealing to younger customers. Slow sales of small pickups and compact cars soon showed that both these design changes were necessary, however.

To quickly get an improved design process into gear, President Cho championed two new change techniques to radically alter the design process: PDCA and *obeya*. *Obeya* is based on frequent brainstorming sessions among engineers, designers, production managers, and marketers designed to speed new model cars to the market. PDCA ("plan," "do," "check," "action") is a program designed to empower the company's designers outside of Japan to intervene in the car development process and champion designs that meet the needs of local customers. The results of promoting a flexible, decentralized car design process were the speedy introduction of the rugged eight-cylinder Tundra pickup truck and the angular, ScionxB compact in the United States, as well as the Yaris, Toyota's best–selling European car. The Yaris was designed in Europe, and its success there led to its subsequent introduction in Japan where it also sold well.

Toyota's mastery of the need to manage change has made it by far the most profitable of the major carmakers. With all its new change processes operating at full speed, Toyota replaced Ford as the world's second largest carmaker in 2004 and Cho has set his sights on Toyota replacing GM as the world's biggest carmaker by 2010.

Toyota and all carmakers have been under increasing pressure to change in order to survive and prosper in today's competitive car market. In an era when technology is advancing rapidly, most organizations are confronting the need to learn new ways to reduce costs and offer better goods and services to customers. The need to change is a fact of life for most organizations. Indeed in today's environment, organizations cannot afford to change only when their performance is deteriorating; like Toyota, they need continuously to predict and anticipate the need for change.

There are many reasons why organizations change and many types of change they can pursue, such as restructuring, reengineering, e-engineering, innovation, and total quality management. In this chapter, we complete our analysis of organizational behavior by examining the nature and process of organization change. We look at forces for and resistance to change, and we examine different types of changes that occur in organizations. We also look at action research, a method organizations can use to plan, implement, and ease the change process. We examine various techniques that managers can use to overcome resistance to change and facilitate the process.[1] By the end of this chapter you will understand why managing change successfully is a vital part of organizational behavior.

Forces for and Resistance to Organizational Change

Organizational change is the movement of an organization away from its present state and toward some desired future state to increase its effectiveness. Why does an organization need to change the way it performs its activities? The business environment is constantly changing, and the organization must adapt to these forces in order to survive.[2] Table 18.1 lists the most important forces for and impediments to change that confront an organization and its managers.

Organizational change
The movement of an organization away from its present state and toward some desired future state to increase its effectiveness.

FORCES FOR CHANGE

Recall from Chapter 16 that many environmental forces have an impact on the organization and that recognizing the nature of these forces is one of a manager's most important tasks.[3] If managers are slow to respond to competitive, economic, political, global, and other forces, the organization will lag behind its competitors and its effectiveness will be compromised.

Competitive Forces. Organizations are constantly striving to achieve a competitive advantage.[4] Competition is a force for change because unless an organization matches or surpasses its competitors in at least one competitive area (either in terms of efficiency, quality, innovation, or responsiveness), it will not survive.[5]

To excel in the area of *efficiency* or *quality*, an organization must constantly adopt the latest technology as it becomes available. The adoption of new technology usually

TABLE 18.1

Forces for and Impediments to Change

Forces for Change	Impediments To Change
Competitive forces	*Organizational impediments*
	Power and conflict
Economic and political forces	Differences in functional orientation
	Mechanistic structure
Global forces	Organizational culture
Demographic and social forces	*Group impediments*
	Group norms
	Group cohesiveness
Ethical forces	Groupthink and escalation of commitment
	Individual impediments
	Uncertainty and insecurity
	Selective perception and retention
	Habit

brings a change to task relationships as employees learn new skills or techniques to operate the new technology.[6] Later in this chapter we discuss total quality management and reengineering, two change strategies that organizations can use to achieve superior efficiency or quality.

To excel in the area of *innovation* and obtain a technological advantage, a company must skillfully manage the process of innovation, another source of change. (We discuss innovation later in the chapter.) Central to the ability to capture and sustain a competitive advantage is the ability to excel in the most important area of all: *responsiveness to customers.*

Economic, Political, and Global Forces. As we saw in Chapter 1, economic and political forces continually affect organizations and compel them to change how and where they produce goods and services. Economic and political unions between countries are becoming an increasingly important force for change.[7] The North American Free Trade Agreement (NAFTA) paved the way for cooperation among Canada, the United States, and Mexico. Many organizations in these countries have taken advantage of NAFTA to find new markets for their products and new sources of inexpensive labor and inputs.

The European Union (EU), an alliance of European countries that traces its origin to the end of World War II, includes over 20 members eager to exploit the advantages of a large protected market. Poland and many other formerly communist countries of Eastern Europe, and Georgia and other former republics of the Soviet Union, have now joined the European Union to foster their own economic and political development. Many more countries such as Turkey are seeking entry as well.

Japan and other fast-growing Asian countries such as Malaysia, Thailand, and China, recognizing that economic unions protect member nations and create barriers against foreign competitors, have moved to increase their presence in countries abroad. Numerous Japanese companies, for example, have opened manufacturing plants in the United States, Mexico, and in European countries such as Spain, Poland, and the United Kingdom to capitalize on the advantages the European Union and trade agreements such as NAFTA offer. Toyota, Honda, and Nissan have all opened large car plants in England to supply cars to EU member countries, for example. These firms are also taking advantage of the low labor costs in England (compared to those in France, Germany, or Japan), and the products made in England are not subject to EU import tariffs. Similarly, in the Far East, Pacific Rim countries such as Japan, Thailand, Taiwan, Malaysia, and Singapore all face the problem of how to develop an economic union of their own as the world divides into three distinct economic spheres: North America, Europe, and Asia.

No organization can afford to ignore the effects of global economic and political forces on its activities. The rise of low-cost foreign competitors, the development of new technology that can erode a company's competitive advantage, and the failure to exploit low-cost inputs abroad all spell doom for an organization competing in the global marketplace.[8]

Other global challenges organizations face include the need to help their managers who work abroad adjust to a variety of national cultures and understand the economic, political, and cultural values of the countries in which they are located.[9] Toyota, for example, has realized the importance of sending its Japanese car designers and engineers to work with their counterparts in other countries. This helps the company meet the needs of customers in overseas markets as well as spread its *kaizen* manufacturing methods to its other divisions.

Demographic and Social Forces. Managing a diverse workforce is one of the biggest challenges confronting organizations in the 2000s.[10] We discussed in previous chapters how changes in the composition of the workforce and the increasing diversity of employees have presented organizations with many challenges and opportunities. Increasingly, changes in the demographic characteristics of the workforce have led managers to alter their styles of managing employees in an effort to learn how to best understand, supervise, and motivate minority and female members. This includes abandoning the stereotypes they unwittingly held in the past when making promotion decisions. It also means understanding the importance of equity in the recruitment process and acknowledging that employees today are looking for a better balance between work and leisure. As more and more women have entered the workforce, companies have had to accommodate the needs of dual-career and single-parent families. This might include providing employees with child and elder care and allowing them to keep flexible work schedules to better manage their busy lives.[11]

Many companies have helped their employees keep up with changing technology by supporting advanced education and training for them. Increasingly, organizations are coming to realize that the ultimate source of competitive advantage and organizational effectiveness lies in fully utilizing the skills of their members by, for example, empowering their employees to make important decisions.[12] As we discuss later in this chapter, reengineering and total quality management are change strategies that aim to alter how an organization views its activities and the employees who perform them.

Ethical Forces. While it's important for an organization to change in response to demographic and social forces, it also is important for them to do so in an ethical way—especially in the face of increasing government, political, and social scrutiny.[13] Many companies have created the role of ethics officer, a person to whom employees can report ethical lapses on the part of the organization's managers or turn to for advice when faced with ethical business dilemmas. Organizations are also trying to promote ethical behavior by giving employees direct access to important decision makers and by protecting whistle-blowers who expose ethical problems.

Many organizations need to make changes to allow managers and employees at all levels to report unethical behavior so that the organization can move quickly to eliminate this behavior and thereby protect the organization, its members, and customers from reputational harm.[14] Similarly, if organizations operate in countries that pay little attention to human rights or the well-being of employees, they have to learn how to change these standards—at least within their own organization—to protect their foreign employees. The story of how U.S. sporting goods makers have battled accusations about their products being produced in third-world sweatshops illustrates this issue.

managing ethically

Nike, Reebok, Adidas, and the Sweatshops

More products are increasingly being manufactured in poor, third-world countries today, but the behavior of the companies that outsource their production to subcontractors in these countries has increasingly been called into question. Nike, a giant in the sportswear industry, was one of the first companies to experience this when it came to light how employees working abroad for Nike's subcontractors were being treated. Indonesian employees were stitching together shoes in hot, noisy factories for only 80 cents a day, or about $18 a month.[15] Employees in Vietnam and China fared better; they could earn about $1.60 a day. Critics charged that at least a $3-a-day wage was needed for these workers to make a living.

These facts surrounding Nike's subcontracting practices abroad generated an outcry in the United States. Nike was roundly attacked for its practices, which resulted in a sales backlash for the company. Phil Knight, Nike's billionaire owner, was asked how, when his own net worth was over $3 billion, he could defend paying a worker 80 cents a day. As criticism mounted, Knight was forced to reevaluate Nike's labor practices. The company subsequently announced that henceforth all of the factories producing its shoes and clothes would be independently monitored and inspected. Then, after Reebok, a competitor criticized for similar labor practices, announced it was raising wages in Indonesia by 20 percent, Nike raised its wages by 25 percent, to about $23 a month.[16] Small though this may seem it was a boon to employees in these countries.

In Europe, Adidas, another sportswear company, had largely escaped such criticism. But in 1999, it was reported that a Taiwan-based Adidas subcontractor in El Salvador was employing girls as young as 14 in its factories and making them work for over 70 hours a week. They were only allowed to go to the rest room twice a day, and if they stayed in the rest room longer than three minutes, they were penalized a day's wages.[17] Adidas moved swiftly to avoid the public relations nightmare that Nike had experienced. It announced that, henceforth, its subcontractors would also be required to abide by more strict labor standards. Thus, throughout the industry companies were forced to reevaluate the ethics of their labor practices and promise to keep a vigilant watch on their subcontractors in the future.

The changes these companies have made have had a major impact. As working conditions have improved abroad, the number of complaints has fallen.[18] Moreover, the movement to protect the rights of employees manufacturing clothing abroad has spread to include all types of other products and other retailers and wholesalers. A particularly good example of a company's description of its ethical position on the treatment of overseas employees can be found at Gap's Web site (**www.gapinc.com/social_resp/ifpr.htm**).

IMPEDIMENTS TO CHANGE

From customer design preferences to the issue of where clothes should be produced and whether economic or political unrest will affect the availability of raw materials, the forces of change bombard organizations from all sides. Effective organizations are agile enough to adjust to these forces. But many internal forces make the organization resistant to change.[19]

In the last decade, many of America's best-known (and formerly strongest and most successful) companies—General Motors, Ford, Xerox, Kodak, TWA, and Macy's among them—have seen their fortunes decline. Some, such as Macy's and TWA, have gone bankrupt; others such as Xerox and Kodak are still in deep financial trouble. But some companies, such as General Motors and Ford, seem to have reversed the decline and embarked on a recovery. How did such former powerhouses lose their effectiveness? The main explanation for such decline is almost always an organization's inability to change in response to changing environmental conditions such as increased competition. Research suggests that one of the main reasons for some organizations' inability to change is **organizational inertia**, or the tendency to maintain the status quo.[20] Impediments to change that cause inertia are found at the organization, group, and individual levels.[21] (See Table 18.1)

Organizational inertia The tendency of an organization to maintain the status quo.

ORGANIZATION-LEVEL RESISTANCE TO CHANGE

Many forces inside an organization make it difficult for the organization to change in response to changing conditions in its environment.[22] The most powerful organization-level impediments to change include power and conflict, differences in functional orientation, mechanistic structure, and organizational culture.

Power and Conflict. Change usually benefits some people, functions, or divisions at the expense of others. When change causes power struggles and organizational conflict, an organization is likely to resist it.[23] Suppose that a change in purchasing practices will help the materials management group in an organization achieve its goal of reducing input costs but that it will harm manufacturing's ability to reduce manufacturing costs. Materials management will push for the change, but manufacturing will resist it. The conflict between the two functions will slow down the process of change and perhaps prevent it from occurring at all.

Many large companies have experienced resistance to change on the part of their functional groups. In the 1990s, for example, managers in IBM's mainframe computer division were the most powerful in the corporation. To preserve their established position, prestige, and power in the organization, these managers fought off attempts to redirect IBM's resources to produce workstations and network computers that customers desperately wanted. This failure to change in response to customer demands severely hampered IBM's speed of response to its competitors. As a result, the company lost billions of dollars. It was not until a new CEO took over operations and ruthlessly laid off thousands of mainframe managers and diverted resources toward making and servicing network computers that the company's fortunes began to change.

Differences in Functional Orientation. Differences in functional orientation are another major impediment to change and a source of organizational inertia. Different functions and divisions often see the source of a problem or issue differently as a result of their own viewpoints. This "tunnel vision" increases organizational inertia because the organization must spend time and effort to secure agreement about the source of a problem before it can even consider how the organization needs to respond to the problem.

Mechanistic Structure. Recall from Chapter 16 that tall hierarchies, centralized decision making, and the standardization of behavior through rules and procedures characterize mechanistic structures. In contrast, organic structures are flat and decentralized and rely on mutual adjustment between people to get the job done.[24] Which structure is likely to be more resistant to change?

Mechanistic structures are more resistant to change. People who work within a mechanistic structure are expected to act in certain ways and do not develop the initiative to adjust their behavior to changing conditions. The extensive use of mutual adjustment and decentralized authority in an organic structure, on the other hand, foster the development of skills that enable employees to be creative, responsive, and find solutions to new problems. A mechanistic structure typically develops as an organization grows and is a principal source of inertia, especially in large organizations.

Organizational Culture. The values and norms in an organization's culture can be another source of resistance to change. Just as role relationships result in a series of stable expectations between people, so values and norms cause people to behave in predictable ways. If organizational change disrupts taken-for-granted values and norms and forces people to change what they do and how they do it, resistance is likely to ensue. Many organizations develop conservative values that support the status quo and make managers reluctant to search for new ways to compete. As a result, if the environment changes and a company's products become obsolete, the company has nothing to fall back on; failure is, therefore, likely.[25] Sometimes values and norms are so strong that even when the environment is changing and it is clear that a new strategy needs to be adopted, managers cannot do so because they are wed to the way they presently do business.

GROUP-LEVEL RESISTANCE TO CHANGE

As we discuss in Chapters 10 and 11, groups perform much of an organization's work, and several group characteristics can produce resistance to change. Here we consider four: group norms, group cohesiveness, groupthink, and escalation of commitment.

Group Norms. Many groups develop strong informal norms that specify appropriate and inappropriate behaviors and govern the interactions between group members (see Chapter 10). Often change alters task and role relationships in a group and, when it does, it disrupts group norms and the informal expectations that members have of one another. As a result, members of a group may resist change because a whole new set of norms may have to be developed to meet the needs of the new situation.

Group Cohesiveness. Group cohesiveness, or the attractiveness of a group to its members, affects group performance (see Chapter 11). Although some level of cohesiveness promotes group performance, too much cohesiveness can actually reduce performance because it stifles opportunities for the group to change and adapt. A highly cohesive group may resist attempts by management to change what it does or even who its members are. Group members may unite to preserve the status quo and to protect their interests at the expense of other groups.

Groupthink and Escalation of Commitment. Groupthink is a pattern of faulty decision making that occurs in cohesive groups when members discount negative information in order to agree. Escalation of commitment worsens this situation. Escalation occurs when members realize their course of action is wrong but continue to pursue it. Groupthink and escalation can make changing a group's behavior very difficult.

INDIVIDUAL–LEVEL RESISTANCE TO CHANGE

Individuals within an organization may be inclined to resist change because of uncertainty, selective perception, and force of habit.[26]

Uncertainty and Insecurity. People tend to resist change because they feel uncertain and insecure about what its outcome will be.[27] Employees might be given new tasks; role relationships may change; some employees might lose their jobs while others might be promoted. Employees' resistance to the uncertainty and insecurity surrounding change can cause organizational inertia. Absenteeism and turnover may increase as change takes place, and employees may become uncooperative, attempt to delay or slow down the change process, or passively resist it.

Selective Perception and Retention. Perception and attribution play a major role in determining work attitudes and behaviors (see Chapter 4). There is a general tendency for people to selectively perceive information that is consistent with their existing views (or schemas) of their organizations. Thus, when change takes place, employees tend to focus only on how it will personally affect them or their function or division. If they perceive few benefits, they may reject the change. Not surprisingly, it can be difficult for an organization to develop a common platform to promote change across an organization and get people to see the need for it.

Habit. Habit, people's preference for familiar actions and events, is another impediment to change. The difficulty of breaking bad habits and adopting new styles of behavior indicates how hard it is for people to change their habits. Why are habits hard to break? Some researchers have suggested that people have a built-in tendency to return to their original behaviors, a tendency that stymies change.

LEWIN'S FORCE-FIELD THEORY OF CHANGE

As you have seen, a wide variety of forces make organizations resistant to change, and a wide variety of forces push organizations toward change. Researcher Kurt Lewin developed a theory about organizational change. According to his **force-field theory**, these two sets of forces are always in opposition in an organization.[28] When the forces are evenly balanced, the organization is in a state of inertia and does not change. To get an organization to change, managers must find a way to increase the forces for change and reduce resistance to change, or do both simultaneously. Any of these strategies will overcome inertia and cause an organization to change.

Figure 18.1 illustrates Lewin's theory. An organization at performance level P1 is in balance: Forces for change and resistance to change are equal. Management, however, decides that the organization should strive to achieve performance level P2. To get to

> **Force-field theory** The theory that organizational change occurs when forces for change strengthen, resistance to change lessens, or both occur simultaneously.

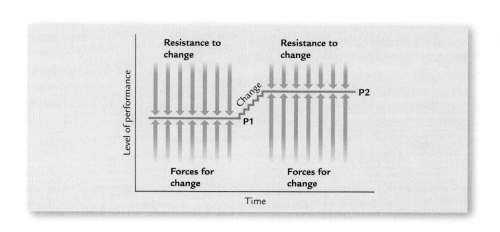

FIGURE 18.1
Lewin's Force-Field Theory of Change

level P2, managers must *increase* the forces for change (the increase is represented by the lengthening of the up-arrows), *reduce* resistance to change (the reduction is represented by the shortening of the down-arrows), or both. If managers pursue any of the three strategies successfully, the organization will change and reach performance level P2.

Before we look in more detail at the techniques that managers can use to overcome resistance and facilitate change, we need to look at the types of change they can implement to increase organizational effectiveness.

Evolutionary and Revolutionary Change in Organizations

Managers continually face choices about how best to respond to the forces for change. There are several types of change that managers can adopt to help their organizations achieve desired future states.[29] In general, types of change fall into two broad categories: evolutionary change and revolutionary change.[30]

Evolutionary change is gradual, incremental, and narrowly focused. Evolutionary change is not drastic or sudden but a constant attempt to improve, adapt, and adjust strategy and structure incrementally to accommodate to changes taking place in the environment.[31] Sociotechnical systems theory and total quality management, or *kaizen*, are two instruments of evolutionary change. Such improvements might entail utilizing technology in a better way or reorganizing the work process.

Some organizations, however, need to make major changes quickly. Faced with drastic, unexpected changes in the environment (for example, a new technological breakthrough) or with an impending disaster resulting from mismanagement, an organization might need to act quickly and decisively. In this case, revolutionary change is called for.

Revolutionary change is rapid, dramatic, and broadly focused. Revolutionary change involves a bold attempt to quickly find new ways to be effective. It is likely to result in a radical shift in ways of doing things, new goals, and a new structure for the organization. The process has repercussions at all levels in the organization—corporate, divisional, functional, group, and individual. Reengineering, restructuring, and innovation are three important instruments of revolutionary change.

EVOLUTIONARY CHANGE I: SOCIOTECHNICAL SYSTEMS THEORY

Sociotechnical systems theory was one of the first theories that proposed the importance of changing role and task or technical relationships to increase organizational effectiveness.[32] The theory emerged from a study of changing work practices in the British coal-mining industry.[33]

After World War II, new technology that changed work relationships between miners was introduced into the British mining industry. Before the war, coal mining was a small-batch, or craft, process. Teams of skilled miners dug coal from the coalface underground and performed all the other activities necessary to transport the coal to the surface. Work took place in a confined space where productivity depended on close cooperation between team members. Employees developed their own routines and norms to get the job done and provided one another with social support to help combat the stress of their dangerous and confining working conditions.

This method of coal mining, called the "hand got method," approximated small-batch technology (see Chapter 16). To increase efficiency, managers decided to replace it with the "long wall method." This method utilized a mechanized, mass-production technology. Miners used powered drills to cut the coal, and it was then transported to

Evolutionary change Change that is gradual, incremental, and narrowly focused.

Revolutionary change Change that is rapid, dramatic, and broadly focused.

Sociotechnical systems theory Ideas about how organizations should choose specific kinds of control systems that match the technical nature of the work process.

the surface on conveyor belts. Tasks became more routine as the work process became programmed and standardized. On paper, the new technology promised impressive increases in efficiency. But after its introduction, mine efficiency rose only slowly and absenteeism among miners, which had always been high, increased dramatically. Consultants were called to the mines to figure out why the expected gains in efficiency had not occurred.

The researchers pointed out that to operate the new technology efficiently, management had changed the task and role relationships among the miners. The new task and role relationships had destroyed informal norms and social support, disrupted long-established informal working relationships, and reduced group cohesiveness. To solve the problem, the researchers recommended linking the new technology with the old social system by recreating the old system of tasks and roles and decentralizing authority to work groups. When managers redesigned the production process, productivity improved and absenteeism fell.

This study illustrates the need to fit, or "jointly optimize," the workings of an organization's technical and social systems. The lesson learned from sociotechnical systems theory is that when managers change task and role relationships, they must gradually adjust the technical and social systems so that group norms and cohesiveness are not disrupted. By taking a gradual approach, an organization can avoid group-level resistance to change.

EVOLUTIONARY CHANGE II: TOTAL QUALITY MANAGEMENT

Total quality management (TQM) or *kaizen* is an ongoing and constant effort by all of an organization's functions to find new ways to improve the quality of the organization's goods and services.[34] In many companies, the initial decision to adopt a TQM approach signals a radical change in the way they organize their activities. Once TQM is adopted by an organization, it generally leads to continuous, incremental change, and all functions are expected to cooperate with each other to improve quality.

First developed by a number of American business consultants such as W. Edwards Deming and Joseph Juran, total quality management was eagerly embraced by Japanese companies after World War II. For Japanese companies, with their tradition of long-term working relationships and cooperation between functions, the implementation of the new TQM system was an incremental step. Shop-floor employees in Japan, for example, had long been organized into **quality circles**—groups of employees who met regularly to discuss the way work was performed in order to find new ways to improve performance.[35]

Changes frequently inspired by TQM include altering the design or type of machines used to assemble products and reorganizing the sequence of an organization's activities to provide better service to customers. As in sociotechnical systems theory, the emphasis in TQM is on the fit between technical and social systems. Changing cross-functional relationships to help improve quality is very important in TQM. Poor quality often originates at crossover points or after handoffs—that is, when people turn over the work they are doing to people in different functions. The job of intermediate manufacturing, for example, is to assemble inputs to make the final product. Coordinating the design of the various inputs so that they fit together smoothly and operate effectively together is one area of focus in TQM. Members of the different functions work together to find new ways to reduce the number of inputs needed or to suggest design improvements to help the inputs to be assembled more easily and reliably.

TQM and *kaizen* can help increase product quality and lower costs, as we saw earlier with Toyota. The results of TQM activities can also dramatically affect an organization's responsiveness to its customers as Citibank found out. Citibank is one of the

Total quality management (TQM) An ongoing and constant effort by all of an organization's functions to find new ways to improve the quality of the organization's goods and services.

Quality circles Groups of employees who meet regularly to discuss the way work is performed in order to find new ways to increase performance.

leading global financial institutions and has established the goal to become *the* premier institution in the twenty-first century. To achieve this lofty goal the company started to use TQM to increase its responsiveness to customers. It recognized that, ultimately, its customer base and loyalty determine a bank's future success. As the first step in its TQM effort, Citibank focused on identifying the factors that dissatisfy its customers. When it analyzed the complaints, it found that most of them centered around the time it took to complete a customer's request, such as responding to an account problem or getting a loan. So Citibank's managers began to examine how they handled each kind of customer request.

For each distinct kind of request, they formed a cross-functional team of people whose job was to break down a specific request into the steps between people and departments needed to fulfill the request. These teams found that often many steps in the process were unnecessary and could be eliminated if the right information systems tools were used. They also found that very often delays occurred because employees simply were not being given the right kind of training and did not know how to handle the request. As a result, Citibank decided to implement an organization-wide TQM program.

Managers and supervisors at the company were charged with reducing the complexity of the work process and finding the most effective way to process requests. They were also charged with teaching employees how to answer each specific request. The results were remarkable. For example, in the loan department, the TQM program reduced the number of handoffs necessary to process a request by 75 percent; average time taken to respond to a customer dropped from several hours to 30 minutes. By 2000, over 100,000 employees had been trained worldwide in the new TQM processes and Citibank could easily measure TQM's effectiveness by the increased speed with which it was handling an increased volume of custom requests. By 2003, it had over 120 million customers in over 100 countries.[36]

More and more companies are embracing the continuous, incremental type of change that results from the implementation of TQM, or *kaizen* programs. Many companies have found, however, that implementing a TQM program is not always easy because it requires employees and managers to adopt new ways of looking at their roles in the organization. Managers must be willing to decentralize decision making, empower employees, and become facilitators rather than supervisors. The "command and control" model gives way to an "advise and support" model. It is also important that employees, as well as managers, share in the increased profits that successful TQM programs can provide. In Japan, for example, performance bonuses frequently account for 30 percent or more of employees' and managers' salaries, and salaries can fluctuate widely from year to year because organizational performance changes.

Resistance to the changes a TQM program requires can be serious unless management explicitly recognizes the many ways that TQM affects relationships between functions and even divisions. We discuss ways to deal with resistance to change at length later in this chapter.

Despite the success that organizations such as Toyota, Citibank, Harley-Davidson, and Ford have had with TQM, many other organizations do not achieve the increases in quality and cost reductions associated with TQM and abandon their programs. One reason TQM can fail is because top managers underestimate the degree of commitment from people at all levels in an organization necessary to implement the program. A second reason is the long time frame necessary for TQM efforts to yield results. Unfortunately, TQM is not a quick fix that can turn an organization around overnight.[37] It is an evolutionary process that bears fruit only when it becomes a way of life in an organization as it has become at Toyota, which is perhaps the world's leader in championing the *kaizen* process.

REVOLUTIONARY CHANGE I: REENGINEERING

Reengineering involves the "fundamental rethinking and radical redesign of business processes to achieve dramatic improvements in critical, contemporary measures of performance such as cost, quality, service, and speed."[38] Change resulting from reengineering requires managers to go back to the basics and dissect each step in the work process. Instead of focusing on an organization's *functions*, the managers of a reengineered organization focus on business processes, just as Toyota did when reengineering its car development and design process.

A **business process** is any activity (such as order processing, inventory control, or product design) vital to the quick delivery of goods and services to customers or a process that promotes high quality or low costs. Business processes are not the responsibility of any one function; they involve activities across functions. Because reengineering focuses on business processes and not functions, a reengineered organization always adopts a new approach to organizing its activities.

Organizations that take up reengineering ignore the existing arrangement of tasks, roles, and work activities. Management starts the reengineering process with the customer (not with the product or service) and asks the question "How can we reorganize the way we do our work, our business processes, to provide the best-quality, lowest-cost goods and services to the customer?" Frequently, when companies ponder this question, they discover better ways to organize their activities. For example, a business process that currently involves members of 10 different functions working sequentially to provide goods and services might be performed by one person or a few people at a fraction of the cost after reengineering. Because reengineering often results in such changes, job enlargement and enrichment (discussed in Chapter 7) are common results of reengineering. Individual jobs become increasingly complex, and people are grouped into cross-functional teams as business processes are reengineered to reduce costs and increase quality.

Reengineering and TQM are highly interrelated and complementary. After revolutionary reengineering has taken place and the question "What is the best way to provide customers with the goods or service they require?" has been answered, evolutionary TQM takes over. The focus for the organization then becomes: "How can we now continue to improve and refine the new process and find better ways of managing task and role relationships?" Successful organizations examine both questions simultaneously, and they continuously attempt to identify new and better processes for meeting the goals of increased efficiency, quality, and responsiveness to customers.[39] An example of a reengineering change at Hallmark Cards is described in the accompanying OB Today insight box.

E-Engineering. In fact, the term e-engineering has been coined to refer to companies' attempts to use all kinds of information systems to improve their performance. In previous chapters, there have been many examples of how the use of Internet-based software systems can change the way a company's strategy and structure operate. New information systems can be employed in all aspects of an organization's business and for all kinds of reasons.[41] For example, Cypress Semiconductor's CEO, T. J. Rodgers, uses the company's online management information system to continually monitor his managers' activities and help him keep the organizational hierarchy flat. Rodgers claims that he can review the goals of all his 1,500 managers in about four hours, and he does so each week.[42] In earlier chapters we discussed how Oracle and Citibank are using Internet-based systems to streamline their operations and to better link their operations to their customers. The importance of e-engineering is only likely to increase in the future as it changes the way a company organizes people and tasks and links them together to improve its performance.

Business process Any activity that is vital to the quick delivery of goods and services to customers or that promotes high quality or low costs.

ob today

Reengineering at Hallmark Cards

Hallmark Cards, based in Kansas City, Missouri, sells 55 percent of the 8 billion birthday, Christmas, and other kinds of cards sold each year in the United States.[40] However, in the 1990s, Hallmark fell prey to smaller and more agile competitors that pioneered new kinds of specialty greeting cards and sold them—often at discount prices—in supermarkets and discount stores. To keep Hallmark on top of its market the company decided to examine how things were currently being done and determine what changes were needed.

Top management began this evaluation by organizing a hundred managers into teams to analyze Hallmark's competitors, the changing nature of customer needs, the organizational structure the company was using to coordinate its activities, and the way it was developing, distributing, and marketing its cards—its basic business processes, in other words. What the teams found startled managers from the top down and showed there was a desperate need for change.

Managers discovered that although Hallmark had the world's largest creative staff—over 700 artists and writers who design over 24,000 new cards each year—it was taking over three years to get a new card to market. After an artist designed a new card and a writer came up with an appropriate rhyme or message, it took an average of three years for the card to be produced, packaged, and shipped to retailers. Information on changing customer needs, a vital input into decisions about what cards should be designed, took many months to reach artists. That delay made it difficult for Hallmark to respond quickly to its competitors.

Armed with this information, the hundred team managers presented top management with a hundred recommendations for changes that would allow the company to do its work more quickly and effectively. The recommendations called for a complete change in the way the company organized its basic business processes. Hallmark began by completely restructuring its activities. Previously the company had relied on a functional structure. Artists worked separately from writers, and both artists and writers worked separately from materials management, printing, and manufacturing personnel. Twenty-five handoffs between employees were needed to produce the final product, and 90 percent of the time, work was simply sitting in somebody's in- or out-basket. Taking the advice of the teams, Hallmark changed to a cross-functional team structure. People from different functions—artists, writers, editors, and so on—were grouped into teams responsible for producing a specific kind of card, such as Christmas cards, get-well cards, or new lines of specialty cards.

To eliminate the need for handoffs between departments, each team is now responsible for all aspects of the design process. To reduce the need for handoffs within a team, all team members work together from a card's inception to plan the steps in the design process, and all are responsible for reviewing the success of their efforts. To help each team evaluate its efforts and give it the information it needs about what customers want, Hallmark introduced a computerized point-of-sales merchandising system in each of its Hallmark Cards stores. This gives each team instant feedback on what and how many kinds of cards are selling at any given point in time. Each team can now continuously experiment with new card designs to attract more customers.

The effects of these changes have been dramatic. Not only are cards introduced in less than one year, but some reach the market in a matter of months. Quality has increased as each team focuses on improving its cards, and costs have fallen because the new work system is so efficient. However, increased competition from free online greeting card sites is putting pressure on Hallmark again. Its managers are currently seeking to increase its online presence in order to fight back and are once again reengineering its processes to make the company a leader in the e-card business, too.

REVOLUTIONARY CHANGE II: RESTRUCTURING

Organizations experiencing a rapid deterioration in performance may try to turn things around by restructuring. An organization that resorts to restructuring usually attempt to simplify its organizational structure by eliminating divisions, departments, or levels in the hierarchy and downsizing employees to lower operating costs. It also contracts with other companies to perform manufacturing, customer service, and other functional activities.

When William F. Malec, for example, took over as the head of the federally administered Tennessee Valley Authority (TVA), the organization had over 14 levels in its hierarchy of 37,000 employees, and its customers had experienced an average increase in their utility rates of over 10 percent per year. Describing TVA as a top-heavy bureaucracy, Malec quickly moved to slash costs and restructure the organization; he reduced the levels in the hierarchy to nine and the employees to 18,500, and he froze utility rates for 10 years. Another example of restructuring that illustrates the important role played by outsourcing is discussed in the accompanying Global View insight.

global view

eMachines Joins With Gateway

In 2001, eMachines, a low-price computer maker whose machines sold for less than $800, was going bankrupt. The main problem? Low product quality because of eMachines' inefficient manufacturing operations and poor service from its customer service reps who seemed unable to help customers fix problems with their new computers. Wayne Inouye, a Japanese American who has been in charge of Best Buy's computer retailing division, was put in charge of turning around the company or shutting it down if he could not.

To turn around the company, Inouye adopted a radical approach to change. He decided to outsource both the company's manufacturing, sales, and customer service operations. Henceforth, eMachines computers would be assembled at low-cost global locations in countries such as China or Malaysia, and software specialists in Bangalore, India, would handle its customer service operations. Furthermore, although eMachines used to sell most of its computers online or by advertising, in the future Inouye decided to sell the computers through retail partners such as Best Buy.

After outsourcing all these activities, Inouye now focuses his company's efforts on marketing. He and his employees are constantly monitoring what kinds of new features customers want from their computers and how much they are willing to pay for them. eMachines is electronically linked to its retailers and its managers have real-time information on what kinds of computers are selling and why. Using this information, they can then redesign computers and electronically ship new computer specifications to their overseas manufacturers. In this way, the computers coming off the assembly line match customers' current needs, thereby increasing eMachines' sales. The results of all these changes were astounding. In 2003, the company's sales exceeded $1 billion, and it replaced Gateway to become the number-three leading computer maker.

By outsourcing his company's functional operations and changing its distribution strategy, Wayne Inouye turned eMachines into a leading computer maker.

Inouye's success in leading eMachines' business turnaround led Gateway's board of directors to decide to buy eMachines in 2004 and make Inouye the CEO of the combined company. As the CEO of Gateway, Inouye's job now is to find ways to create advanced PCs that can compete with those of Dell, the low-cost leader. Inouye plans to introduce new kinds of laptops and notebook PCs and compete in this fast-growing market segment.

Why does restructuring become necessary, and why may an organization need to downsize or outsource its operations? Sometimes an unforeseen change in the environment occurs: Perhaps a shift in technology makes the company's products obsolete, or a worldwide recession reduces demand for its products. Sometimes an organization has excess capacity because customers no longer want the goods and services it provides because they are outdated, low quality, offer little value, or the customer service related to them is poor, as at eMachines. Sometimes organizations downsize because they have grown too tall and bureaucratic and their operating costs have become much too high. Organizations even restructure, at times, when they are in a strong position simply to stay on top in the face of competition. Microsoft, for example, is constantly changing its structure to realign its resources with the changing computing environment. In 2003, for example, the company broke its MSN division into two distinct units, one to handle its Internet customers, and one to handle its growing Internet activities such as X-Box gaming.[43]

All too often, companies are forced to downsize and lay off employees because they do *not* continually monitor the way they operate and do not make the incremental adjustments to their strategies and structures allowing them to contain costs and adapt.[44] Paradoxically, because they have not paid attention to the need to reengineer themselves, they are forced into a position in which restructuring becomes the only way they can survive to compete in an increasingly cutthroat environment.

Restructuring, like reengineering, TQM, and other change strategies, generates resistance to change. Often the decision to downsize will require the establishment of new task and role relationships. Because this change may threaten the jobs of some employees, they resist the changes taking place. Many plans to introduce change, including restructuring, take a long time to implement and fail because of the high level of resistance encountered at all levels of the organization.

REVOLUTIONARY CHANGE III: INNOVATION

Restructuring is often necessary because advancing technology makes the technology an organization is currently using to produce goods and services (or the goods and services themselves) obsolete. For example, advancing technology has made computers much more powerful and cheaper to manufacture. This in itself has changed the type of computers customers want. Laptops are rapidly becoming more popular than home PCs, for example. If organizations are to avoid falling behind in the competitive race to produce new goods and services, they must take steps to introduce new products or develop new technologies to produce them reliably and at a low cost. Innovation, as we discuss in Chapter 15, is the successful use of skills and resources to create new technologies or new goods and services so that an organization can change and better respond to the needs of customers.[45] Innovation can result in spectacular success. Apple Computer changed the face of the computer industry when it introduced its personal computer. Honda changed the face of the small motorbike market when it introduced small 50cc motorcycles. Mary Kay changed the way cosmetics are sold to customers when it introduced at-home cosmetics parties and personalized selling.

Although innovation does bring about change, it is also associated with a high level of risk because the outcomes of research and development activities are often uncertain.[46] It has been estimated that only from 12 to 20 percent of R&D projects result in products that make it to the market.[47] Thus, innovation can lead not only to change organizations want—the introduction of profitable new technologies and products—but also to the kinds of change they want to avoid—technologies that are inefficient or products that customers *don't* want. In the 2000s, for example, cell phone users have increasingly demanded new features such as calendars, color screens, word processing, games, and even digital cameras built into their phones. Companies such as Motorola and Nokia that were slow to build in these new features have seen their sales fall, and companies such as Sanyo and Sony that moved quickly to introduce these features have prospered.

Innovation is one of the most difficult instruments of change to manage, in fact.[48] Recall from Chapter 16 that when organizations rely on innovation as the source of their competitive advantage, they need to adopt organic, flexible structures such as matrix or cross-functional team structures, giving employees the freedom to experiment and be creative.[49] As with reengineering, the need for functions to coordinate their activities and to work together is important for successful innovation, and companies that rely on innovation have to facilitate the change effort and support the efforts of their members to be creative. For example, the term *skunk works* was coined at Lockheed Corporation when that company set up a specialized unit, separate from its regular functional organization, to pioneer the development of the U-2 spy plane. Ford copied the skunk works model to develop a new version of the Mustang and other cars. To try to increase the success rate of innovation and new product development, many high-tech organizations have developed the role of **product champion**, an expert manager appointed to head a new product team and see a new product from its inception to sale.[50] Many of the techniques for managing change that we discuss in the next section were developed to help facilitate innovation. Of all the instruments of revolutionary change, innovation offers the best prospect for long-term success but also poses the most risk.

Product champion An expert manager appointed to head a new product team and lead a new product from its beginning to commercialization.

Managing Change: Action Research

No matter what type of evolutionary or revolutionary change an organization adopts, managers face the problem of getting the organization to change. Kurt Lewin, whose force-field theory argues that organizations are balanced between forces for change and resistance to change, has a related perspective on how managers can bring change to their organizations (see Figure 18.2).

In Lewin's view, implementing change is a three-step process: (1) unfreezing the organization from its present state, (2) making the change, and (3) "refreezing" the organization in the new desired state so that its members do not revert to their previous work attitudes and role behaviors.[51] Lewin warns that resistance to change will quickly cause an organization and its members to revert to their old ways of doing things unless the organization actively takes steps to refreeze the organization with the changes in place. It is not enough to make some changes in task and role relationships and expect the changes to be successful and endure. To get an organization to remain in its new state, managers must actively manage the change process.[52]

Action research is a strategy for generating and acquiring knowledge that managers can use to define an organization's desired future state and to plan a change program enabling

Action research A strategy for generating and acquiring knowledge that managers can use to define an organization's desired future state and to plan a change program that allows the organization to reach that state.

| 1. Unfreeze the organization from its present state | → | 2. Make the desired type of change | → | 3. Refreeze the organization in a new desired state |

FIGURE 18.2
Lewin's Three-Step Change Process

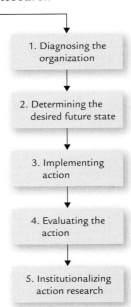

1. Diagnosing the organization

2. Determining the desired future state

3. Implementing action

4. Evaluating the action

5. Institutionalizing action research

it to reach that state.[53] The techniques and practices of action research help managers unfreeze an organization, move it to its new desired position, and refreeze it again so that the benefits of the change are retained. Figure 18.3 identifies the main steps in action research.

DIAGNOSIS OF THE ORGANIZATION

The first step in action research requires managers to recognize the existence of a problem that needs to be solved and acknowledge that some type of change is needed. In general, recognition of the need for change arises because someone in the organization thinks there is a gap between desired performance and actual performance. Perhaps customer complaints about the quality of goods or services have increased. Perhaps profits have recently fallen or operating costs have escalated. Or perhaps turnover among managers or employees has been excessive. In the first stage, managers need to analyze what is going on and why problems are occurring. Recall that slow sales of its small pickup trucks and the aging of its typical car buyer caused managers at Toyota to reevaluate the organization's present state.

Diagnosing the organization can be a complex process. Like a doctor, managers have to distinguish between symptoms and causes. For example, there is little point in introducing new technology to reduce production costs if the problem is that demand is falling because customers do not like the design of the product. Toyota needed to introduce new change programs to address just this problem. Managers have to carefully collect information about the organization to diagnose the problem correctly and get employees committed to the change process. At this early stage it is important for managers to collect information from people at all levels in the organization and from outsiders such as customers and suppliers. Questionnaire surveys given to employees, customers, and suppliers and interviews with employees and managers can provide information essential to a correct diagnosis.

DETERMINING THE DESIRED FUTURE STATE

After identification of the present state, the next step is to identify where the organization needs to be—its desired future state. This step also involves a difficult planning process as managers work out various alternative courses of action that could move the organization to where they would like it to be. Identifying the desired future state involves deciding what the organization's strategy and structure should be. For example, should the organization focus on reducing costs and increasing efficiency? Or are improving quality and responsiveness to customers the key to future success? What is the best kind of structure for the organization to adopt to realize organizational goals—a product structure or perhaps a cross-functional team structure?

IMPLEMENTING ACTION

Implementing action is the third step of action research.[54] It is a three-step process. First, managers need to identify possible impediments to change that they will encounter as they go about making changes. These include impediments at the organization, group, and individual levels.[55] Suppose managers choose to reengineer the company from a functional to a cross-functional team structure to speed product development and reduce costs. They must anticipate the obstacles they will encounter when they "unfreeze" the organization and make the changes. Functional managers, for example, might strongly resist efforts to change the company because their power and prestige in the organization might suffer. Similarly, members of each function who have grown accustomed to working with the same people and to stable task and role relationships will resist being assigned to a new team where tasks and roles have to be worked out again and new interpersonal relationships have to be forged.

The more revolutionary the change that is adopted, the greater will be the problem of implementing it. Managers need to find ways to minimize, control, and co-opt resistance to change. They also need to devise strategies to bring the organization's members on board and foster their commitment to the change process. Moreover, they must look to the future and seek ways to refreeze the changes they have made.

The second step in implementing action research is deciding who will be responsible for actually making the changes and controlling the change process. The choices are to employ **external change agents**, outside consultants who are experts in managing change, or **internal change agents**, managers from within the organization who are knowledgeable about the situation, or some combination of both.[56]

The principal problem with using internal change agents is that other members of the organization may perceive them as being politically involved in the changes and biased toward certain groups. External change agents, in contrast, are likely to be perceived as being less influenced by internal politics (although recall from Chapter 13 that one political tactic is to bring in an outside expert to provide support for one's own view of what needs to be changed). Another reason for employing external change agents is that, as outsiders, they have a detached view of the organization's problems and can distinguish between the "forest and the trees." Insiders can be so involved in what is going on within the organization that they cannot see the true source of the problems. Management consultants, such as those from McKinsey & Co. and Accenture, are frequently brought in by large organizations to help the top management team diagnose the organization's problems and suggest solutions. Many consultants specialize in certain types of organizational change, such as restructuring, reengineering, or implementing total quality management.

The third step in implementing action research is deciding which specific change strategy will most effectively unfreeze, change, and refreeze the organization. Specific techniques for implementing change are discussed later in this chapter. The types of change that these techniques give rise to fall into two categories: top-down and bottom-up changes.[57]

Top-down change is change that is implemented by managers at a high level in the organization. The result of radical organizational restructuring and reengineering is top-down change. Managers high up in the organization decide to make a change, realizing full well that it will reverberate at all organizational levels. The managers choose to manage and solve problems as they arise at the divisional, functional, and individual levels during the process.

Bottom-up change is change that is implemented by employees at low levels in the organization and gradually rises until it is felt throughout the organization. When an organization wants to engage in bottom-up change, the first step in the action research process—diagnosing the organization—becomes pivotal in determining the success of the change. Managers involve employees at all levels in the change process to get their input and lessen their resistance. By reducing the uncertainty employee's experience, bottom-up change facilitates unfreezing and increases the likelihood that employees will retain the new behaviors they learn during the change process. In contrast, top-down change proceeds rapidly, forcing employees to keep up with the pace of change and troubleshoot problems as they arise.

In general, bottom-up change is easier to implement than top-down change because it provokes less resistance. Organizations that have the time to engage in bottom-up change are generally well-run organizations that pay attention to change, are used to change, and change often. Poorly run organizations, those that rarely change or postpone change until it is too late, are frequently forced to engage in top-down restructuring simply to survive. For example, Lucent did not have the luxury of being able to use bottom-up change when its performance declined precipitously in the early 2000s. Lucent's new CEO, Patricia Russo, had to take immediate action to reduce costs and develop new products that would turn around the company when she took over in 2003.[58] Russo slashed the number of Lucent's product development teams from 14 to 5, closing 9 of Lucent's operating divisions in the process. She also focused its resources on developing fewer, but more advanced, products. In contrast, even though Microsoft dominates its competitors, Bill Gates constantly seeks change to improve his organization's performance. Even though Microsoft was earning record profits in 2003, Gates announced programs to develop new Windows software for all kinds of digital devices

External change agent
An outside consultant who is an expert in managing change.

Internal change agent
A manager from within an organization who is knowledgeable about the situation to be changed.

Top-down change Change that is implemented by managers at a high level in the organization.

Bottom-up change Change that is implemented by employees at low levels in the organization and gradually rises until it is felt throughout the organization.

Bill Gates tries to promote creativity and innovation at Microsoft by allowing employees to dress and to decorate their office space as they like. Shown here is software designer Sean Selitrennikoff, clearly pleased with his personal workspace at Microsoft.

including cell phones and MP3 players. He also established new operating divisions to develop these products to stay on top of the industry.[59]

Organizations that change the most are able to exploit the advantages of evolutionary bottom-up change because their managers are always open to the need for change and constantly use action research to find new and better ways to operate and increase effectiveness. Organizations in which change happens rarely are likely candidates for revolutionary top-down change. Because their managers do not use action research on a continuing basis, they attempt change so late that their only option is some massive restructuring or downsizing to turn their organization around.

EVALUATING THE ACTION

The fourth step in action research is evaluating the action that has been taken and assessing the degree to which the changes have accomplished the desired objectives. Armed with this evaluation, management decides whether more change is needed to reach the organization's desired future state or whether more effort is needed to refreeze the organization in its new state.[60]

The best way to evaluate the change process is to develop measures or criteria to help managers assess whether the organization has reached its desired objectives. When criteria developed at the beginning of action research are used consistently over time to evaluate the effects of the change process, managers have ample information to assess the impact of the changes they have made. They can compare costs before and after the change to see whether efficiency has increased. For example, they can survey employees to see whether they are more satisfied with their jobs. They can survey customers to see whether they are more satisfied with the quality of the organization's products. As part of its *kaizen* effort, managers at Toyota carefully survey their customers to make sure that the quality and features of the company's new car models meet their expectations. That information helped them to evaluate the success of their change effort.

Assessing the impact of change is especially difficult because the effects may emerge slowly. The action research process that we have been describing may take several years to complete. Typically, reengineering and restructuring take months or years, and total quality management, once under way, never stops. Consequently, managers need valid and reliable measures that they can use to evaluate performance. All too often poorly performing organizations fail to develop and consistently apply criteria to evaluate their performance. For those organizations, the pressure for change often comes from the outside when shareholders complain about poor profits, customers complain about their products, or regulatory bodies investigate their practices.

you're the management expert

Bringing Change to a Restaurant

You're the change agent called in to help a local restaurant find out why its sales are not increasing. The restaurant's major problem is a low level of repeat business—customers just don't seem to return often. After visiting the restaurant several times posing as a customer, you discover that there seems to be a high level of conflict between the chefs in the kitchen and the waiters and a high level of conflict between the waiters themselves. The chefs are also playing favorites with the waiters to get a share of their tips; waiters who give the chefs a cut of their tips get better food for their customers than those who do not, and their customers are served more quickly. Unfortunately, customers notice the strife between employees and react to it negatively. That means smaller tips for both waiters and chefs and fewer repeat customers for the restaurant. Draw up a plan for changing this situation and develop some before-and-after measures to evaluate how well your plan is succeeding.

INSTITUTIONALIZING ACTION RESEARCH

The need to manage change is so vital in today's quickly changing environment that organizations must institutionalize action research, that is, make it a required habit or a norm adopted by every member of the organization. The institutionalization of action research is as necessary at the top of the organization (where the top management team plans the organization's future strategy) as it is on the shop floor (where employees meet in quality circles to find new ways to increase efficiency and quality). Because change is so difficult and requires so much thought and effort to implement, members at all levels of the organization must be rewarded for being part of successful change efforts. Top managers can be rewarded with stock options and bonus plans linked to organizational performance. Lower-level members can be rewarded through an employee stock ownership plan and by performance bonuses and pay linked to individual or group performance. Indeed, tangible rewards are one way of helping to refreeze the organization in its new state because, as we discuss in Chapter 8, pay is an important motivational tool for helping people learn and sustain desired organizational behaviors.

Organizational Development

Organizational development (OD) is a series of techniques and methods that managers can use in their action research program to increase the adaptability of their organization.[61] In the words of organizational theorist Warren Bennis, OD refers to a "complex educational strategy intended to change beliefs, attitudes, values, and structure of organizations so that they can better adapt to new technologies, markets, and challenges and the dizzying rate of change itself."[62] The goal of OD is to improve organizational effectiveness and help people reach their potential and realize their goals. As action research proceeds, managers need to continually unfreeze, change, and refreeze managers' and employees' attitudes and behaviors. Many OD techniques have been developed to help managers do this. We first look at OD techniques to help managers unfreeze an organization and overcome resistances to change. We then look at OD techniques to help managers change and refreeze an organization in its new desired state.

> **Organizational development (OD)** A series of techniques and methods that managers can use in their action research program to increase the adaptability of their organization.

OD TECHNIQUES TO DEAL WITH RESISTANCE TO CHANGE

Resistance to change occurs at all levels of an organization. It manifests itself as organizational politics and power struggles between individuals and groups, differing perceptions of the need for change, and so on. Tactics that managers can use to reduce resistance to change include education and communication, participation and empowerment, facilitation, bargaining and negotiation, manipulation, and coercion.[63]

Education and Communication. One of the most important impediments to change is uncertainty about what is going to happen. Through education and communication, internal and external agents of change can inform members of the organization about the change and how it will affect them.[64] Change agents can communicate this information in formal group meetings, by memo, in one-on-one meetings, and, increasingly, through electronic means such as e-mail and videoconferencing. Wal-Mart, for example, has a state-of-the-art videoconferencing system. Managers at corporate headquarters put on presentations that are beamed to all Wal-Mart stores so that both managers and employees are aware of the changes taking place.

Even when plant closures or massive layoffs are planned, it is still best—from both an ethical and a change standpoint—to inform employees about what will happen to them as downsizing occurs. Many organizations fear that disgruntled employees may try to hurt the organization as it closes or sabotage the closing process. More often, however, employees are cooperative until the end. As organizations become more and more aware of the benefits offered by incremental change, they are increasing communication with the workforce to gain employees' cooperation and to overcome their resistance to change.

Participation and Empowerment. Inviting employees to participate in the change process is becoming a popular method of reducing resistance to change. Participation complements empowerment by increasing employees' involvement in decision making and giving them greater autonomy to change their work procedures. In addition, to encourage employees to share their skills and talents, organizations are opening up their books to inform employees about the organization's financial condition. Some organizations use employee stock ownership plans (ESOPs) to motivate and reward employees and to harness their commitment to change. Wal-Mart, for example, has an ESOP for all of its store employees and encourages their continual input regarding decision making. Participation and empowerment are two key elements of most TQM programs.

Facilitation. Both managers and employees find change stressful because established task and role relationships alter as it takes place. As we discuss in Chapter 9, there are several things organizations can do to help their members manage stress: Provide employees with training to help them learn their how to perform new tasks, and allow them time off from work to recuperate from the stressful effects of change. Companies such as Microsoft and Apple Computer, for example, give their most talented programmers time off from ordinary job assignments to think about ways to create new kinds of products. Other companies offer senior managers sabbaticals to "recharge their batteries" following stressful events.

Many companies employ psychologists and consultants to help employees handle the stress associated with change. During organizational restructuring, especially when large layoffs are common, many organizations employ consultants to help employees deal with the stress and uncertainty of being laid off and having to find new jobs. Some companies pay consultants to help their CEOs manage the stress associated with being forced to reduce their number of employees.

Bargaining and Negotiation. Bargaining and negotiation are important tools that help managers manage conflict (see Chapter 13). Because change causes conflict, bargaining can counter resistance to change. By using action research, managers can anticipate the effects of change on interpersonal and intergroup relationships. Managers can use this knowledge to help different people and groups negotiate their future tasks and roles and reach compromises that will lead them to accept change. Negotiation also helps individuals and groups understand how change will affect others so that the organization as a whole can develop a common perspective on why change is taking place and why it is important.

Manipulation. When it is clear that change will help some individuals and groups at the expense of others, senior managers need to intervene in the bargaining process and manipulate the situation to secure the agreement, or at least the acceptance, of various people or groups to the results of the change process.[65] As we discuss in Chapter 13, powerful managers have considerable ability to resist change, and in large organizations infighting among divisions can slow or halt the change process unless it is carefully managed. Politics and political tactics such as co-optation and building alliances become important as ways of overcoming the opposition of powerful functions and divisions that feel threatened by the changes taking place.

Coercion. The ultimate way to eliminate resistance to change is to coerce the key players into accepting change and threaten dire consequences if they choose to resist. Employees and managers at all levels can be threatened with reassignment, demotion, or even termination if they resist or threaten the change process. Top managers attempt to use the legitimate power at their disposal to quash resistance to change and to eliminate it. The advantage of coercion can be the speed at which change takes place. The disadvantage is that it can leave people angry and disenchanted and can make the refreezing process difficult.

Managers should not underestimate the level of resistance to change. Organizations work because they reduce uncertainty by means of predictable rules and routines that people can use to accomplish their tasks. Change wipes out the predictability of rules and routines and perhaps spells the end of the status and prestige that accompany some positions. It is not surprising that people resist change and that organizations themselves, because they are made up of people, are so difficult to change.

OD TECHNIQUES TO PROMOTE CHANGE

Many OD techniques are designed to make changes and to refreeze the organization in its new state. These techniques can be used at the individual, group, and organization levels. The choice of techniques is determined by the type of change. In general, the more revolutionary a change is, the more likely is an organization to use OD techniques at all three levels. Counseling, sensitivity training, and process consultation are OD techniques directed at changing the attitudes and behavior of individuals. Different techniques are effective at the group and organization levels.

Counseling, Sensitivity Training, and Process Consultation. Recall from Chapter 2 that the personalities of individuals differ and that the differences lead individuals to interpret and react to other people and events in a variety of ways. Even though personality cannot be changed significantly in the short run, people can be helped to understand that their own perceptions of a situation are not necessarily the correct or the only possible ones. People can also be helped to understand that they should learn to tolerate differences in perception and to embrace and accept human diversity. Counseling and sensitivity training are techniques that organizations can use to help individuals to understand the nature of their own and other people's personalities and to use that knowledge to improve their interactions with others.[66] The highly motivated, driven boss, for example, must learn that his or her subordinates are not disloyal, lazy, or afflicted with personality problems because they are content to go home at five o'clock and want unchallenging job assignments. Instead, they have their own set of work values, and they value their leisure time. Traditionally, one of OD's main efforts has been to improve the quality of the work life of organizational members and increase their well-being and satisfaction with the organization.

Trained professionals such as psychologists counsel organizational members who are perceived by their superiors or peers to have certain problems in appreciating the viewpoints of others or in dealing with certain types of organizational members. Through counseling they learn how to more effectively manage their interactions with other people in the organization. Recall from Chapter 1, for example, that one challenge facing growing numbers of white male managers is learning how to manage female and minority employees effectively. Similarly, a female manager might receive counseling because her peers find her too aggressive or ambitious and her drive to succeed is poisoning work relationships in a group.

Sensitivity training is an intense type of counseling.[67] Members who have problems dealing with others meet in a group with a trained facilitator to learn more about how they and other group members view the world. Group members are

> **Sensitivity training** An OD technique that consists of intense counseling in which group members, aided by a facilitator, learn how others perceive them and may learn how to deal more sensitively with others.

encouraged to be forthright about how they view themselves and others, and through discussion they learn the degree to which others perceive them as similar or different from themselves. By examining the source of differences in perception, members can reach a better understanding of the way others perceive them and become more sensitive when dealing with others.

Participation in sensitivity training is a very intense experience because a person's innermost thoughts and feelings are brought to light and dissected in public. This process makes many people very uncomfortable, so certain ethical issues may be raised by an organization's decision to send "difficult" members for sensitivity training in the hope that they will learn more about themselves.

Is a manager too directive, too demanding, or too suspicious of subordinates? Does a manager deliberately deprive subordinates of information in order to keep them dependent? **Process consultation** provides answers to such questions. Process consultation bears a resemblance to both counseling and sensitivity training.[68] A trained process consultant, or facilitator, works closely with a manager on the job, to help the manager improve his or her interaction with other group members. The outside consultant acts as a sounding board so that the manager can gain a better idea about what is going on in the group setting and can discover the interpersonal dynamics that are affecting the quality of the relationships within the group.

Process consultation, sensitivity training, and counseling are just three of the many OD techniques that have been developed to help individuals learn to change their attitudes and behavior in order to function more effectively. It is common for many large organizations to provide their higher-level managers with a yearly budget to be spent on individual development efforts such as these or on more conventional executive education programs.

Team Building and Intergroup Training.   To manage change within a group or between groups, change agents can employ three different kinds of OD techniques. **Team building**, a common method of improving relationships within a group, is similar to process consultation except that all the members of a group participate together to try to improve their work interactions.[69] For example, group members discuss with a change agent (who is a trained group facilitator) the quality of the interpersonal relationships between team members and between the members and their supervisor. The goal of team building is to improve the way group members work together—to improve the interaction in the group to achieve process gains and reduce process losses. Team building does *not* focus on what the group is trying to achieve but, rather, on the members' relationships.

Team building is important when reengineering reorganizes the way people from different functions work together. When new groups are formed, team building can help group members quickly establish task and role relationships so that they can work effectively together. Team building facilitates the development of functional group norms and values and helps members develop a common approach to solving problems.

The change agent begins the team-building process by watching group members interact and identifying the way the group currently works. Then the change agent talks with some or all of the group members one on one to get a sense of the problems that the group is experiencing or just to identify where the group process could be improved. In a subsequent team-building session that normally takes place at a location away from the normal workplace, the change agent discusses with members the observations he or she has made and asks for their views on the issues brought to their attention. Ideally, through this discussion team members develop a new appreciation about the group dynamics that affect their behavior. Group members may form small task forces to suggest ways of improving the group process or to discuss specific ways of handling problems that have been arising. The goal is to establish a platform from which group members themselves, with no input from the change agent, can make continuous improvements in the way the group functions.

Process consultation An OD technique in which a facilitator works closely with a manager on the job to help the manager improve his or her interaction with other group members.

Team building An OD technique in which a facilitator first observes the interactions of group members and then helps them become aware of ways to improve their work interactions.

A training workshop was held in Poughkeepsie, New York, to improve understanding of how people interpret what takes place in a mediation or bargaining situation.

Intergroup training takes team building one step further and uses it to improve the ways different functions or divisions work together. Its goal is to improve organizational performance by focusing on a function or division's joint activities and output. Given that cross-functional coordination is especially important in reengineering and total quality management, intergroup training is an important OD technique that organizations can exploit to implement change.

A popular form of intergroup training is called **organizational mirroring**, an OD technique designed to improve the effectiveness of interdependent groups.[70] Suppose that two groups are in conflict or simply need to learn more about each other, and one of the groups calls in a consultant to improve cooperation between the two. The consultant begins by interviewing members of both groups to understand how each group views the other and uncover possible problems the groups are having with each other. The groups are then brought together in a training session, and the consultant tells them that the goal of the session is to explore perceptions and relations in order to improve their work relationships. Then, with the consultant leading the discussion, one group describes its perceptions of what is happening and its problems with the other group, while the other group sits and listens. Then the consultant reverses the situation—hence, the term *organizational mirroring*—and the group that was listening takes its turn discussing its perceptions of what is happening and its problems, while the other group listens.

As a result of this initial discussion, each group appreciates the other's perspective. The next step is for members of both groups to form task forces to discuss ways to deal with the issues or problems raised. The goal is to develop action plans that can be used to guide future intergroup relations and provide a basis for follow-up. The change agent guiding this training session needs to be skilled in intergroup relations because both groups are discussing sensitive issues. If the process is not managed well, intergroup relations can be further weakened by this OD technique.

Total Organizational Interventions. A variety of OD techniques can be used at the organization level to promote organization-wide change. One is the **organizational confrontation meeting**.[71] At this meeting, all of the managers of an organization meet to confront the issue of whether the organization is effectively meeting its goals. At the first stage of the process, again with facilitation by a change agent, top management invites free and open discussion of the organization's situation. Then the consultant divides the managers

Intergroup training An OD technique that uses team building to improve the work interactions of different functions or divisions.

Organizational mirroring An OD technique in which a facilitator helps two interdependent groups explore their perceptions and relations in order to improve their work interactions.

Organizational confrontation meeting An OD technique that brings together all of the managers of an organization to confront the issue of whether the organization is effectively meeting its goals.

into groups of seven or eight, ensuring that the groups are as heterogeneous as possible and that no bosses and subordinates are members of the same group (so as to encourage free and frank discussion). The small groups report their findings to the total group, and the sorts of problems confronting the organization are categorized. Top management uses this statement of the issues to set organizational priorities and plan group action. Task forces are formed from the small groups to take responsibility for working on the problems identified, and each group reports back to top management on the progress that has been made. The result of this process is likely to be changes in the organization's structure and operating procedures. Restructuring, reengineering, and total quality management often originate in organization-wide OD interventions that reveal the kinds of problems that an organization needs to solve.

Summary

Organizational change is an ongoing process that has important implications for organizational performance and for the well-being of an organization's members. An organization and its members must be constantly on the alert for changes from within the organization and from the outside environment, and they must learn how to adjust to change quickly and effectively. Often the revolutionary types of change that result from restructuring and reengineering are necessary only because an organization and its managers ignored or were unaware of changes in the environment and did not make incremental changes as needed. The more an organization changes, the easier and more effective the change process becomes. Developing and managing a plan for change are vital to an organization's success. In this chapter, we made the following major points:

1. Organizational change is the movement of an organization away from its present state and toward some future state to increase its effectiveness. Forces for organizational change include competitive forces, economic, political, and global forces, demographic and social forces, and ethical forces. Organizations are often reluctant to change because resistance to change at the organization, group, and individual levels has given rise to organizational inertia.

2. Sources of organization-level resistance to change include power and conflict, differences in functional orientation, mechanistic structure, and organizational culture. Sources of group-level resistance to change include group norms, group cohesiveness, and groupthink and escalation of commitment. Sources of individual-level resistance to change include uncertainty and insecurity, selective perception and retention, and habit.

3. According to Lewin's force-field theory of change, organizations are balanced between forces pushing for change and forces resistant to change. To get an organization to change, managers must find a way to increase the forces for change, reduce resistance to change, or do both simultaneously.

4. Types of changes fall into two broad categories: evolutionary and revolutionary. The main instruments of evolutionary change are sociotechnical systems theory and total quality management. The main instruments of revolutionary change are reengineering, restructuring, and innovation.

5. Action research is a strategy that managers can use to plan the change process. The main steps in action research are (1) diagnosis and analysis of the organization, (2) determining the desired future state, (3) implementing action, (4) evaluating the action, and (5) institutionalizing action research.

6. Organizational development (OD) is a series of techniques and methods to increase the adaptability of organizations. OD techniques can be used to overcome resistance to change and to help the organization to change itself.

7. OD techniques for dealing with resistance to change include education and communication, participation and empowerment, facilitation, bargaining and negotiation, manipulation, and coercion.

8. OD techniques for promoting change include, at the individual level, counseling, sensitivity training, and process consultation; at the group level, team building and intergroup training; and at the organization level, organizational confrontation meetings.

Exercises in Understanding and Managing Organizational Behavior

Questions for Discussion and Review

1. What are the main forces for and impediments to change?
2. How do evolutionary change and revolutionary change differ?
3. What is the main purpose of total quality management?
4. What is a business process, and why is reengineering a popular instrument of change today?
5. Why is restructuring sometimes necessary for reengineering to take place?
6. Which type of change is likely to encounter the greatest resistance?
7. What are the main steps in action research?
8. What is organizational development and what is its goal?
9. In what ways can team building and intergroup training promote organizational effectiveness?

Building People Skills

Coping with Change

Imagine that you are the manager of a design group that is soon to be reengineered into a cross-functional team composed of people from several different functions who have had little contact with each another.

1. Discuss the resistance to change at the organization and individual levels that you will likely encounter.
2. Using action research, chart the steps that you will use to manage the change process.
   A. How will you diagnose the work group's present state?
   B. How will you determine the cross-functional team's desired future state?
   C. What will be the most important implementation choices you will face? For example, how will you manage resistance to change?
   D. What criteria will you use to evaluate the change process?
3. How might you use team building and other organizational development techniques to implement the change?

A Question of Ethics

Managing the Change Process

Some people find change a very difficult thing for reasons described in the chapter. Managers often find it difficult also to change an organization's culture because they cannot get people to develop new kinds of work attitudes or to adopt new kinds of values and norms, such as those involved in implementing *kaizen*.

Sometimes *kaizen* requires both people and groups to change their work attitudes and behaviors in important ways, often in ways they do not wish, and they resist the changes being made. Also, there have been cases in which organizations actively involve employees in the change process by, for example, suggesting ways to change their jobs and perform them more effectively. Then, after the change process has taken place, they proceed to lay off employees. Think about the ethical issues involved in this situation and address the following questions:

1. What kinds of techniques should managers be allowed to use to change employee attitudes and behavior before their actions would be considered unethical?

2. Under what conditions it is ethical to terminate employees as a result of implementing an organizational change program?

3. What kind of guarantees should managers offer employees to enlist their support if they suspect layoffs may be necessary?

Small Group Break-Out Exercise

Practicing *Kaizen*

Form groups of three to five people and discuss the following scenario:

You are a group of software engineers meeting to discuss how to implement a *kaizen* program to reduce the number of mistakes made in developing and writing computer code. Presently, your employees are each responsible for a different section of the code and they typically just hand off their work to the person next in line, which is the point at which errors often creep in. You are contemplating introducing a computer-aided design process that will make each employee's code-writing activities visible to everyone else *and* that will alert employees when changes they make impact other employees' code-writing activities. This will likely cause considerable conflict among employees because it will complicate their work activities.

1. How can you manage the change process to reduce employees' likely resistance to the changes that will take place in the work process?

2. What kind of reward system could you devise to motivate employees to contribute and make suggestions for improving the new system?

Topic for Debate

Organizational change alters role and task relationships at all levels of an organization. Now that you understand the nature and process of organizational change, debate the following issue:

Team A. Changing people's attitudes and behavior is easier than changing organizational structure and culture.

Team B. Changing organizational structure and culture is easier than changing people's attitudes and behavior.

Experiential Exercise

Analyzing Forces for and Impediments to Change

Objective

Your objective is to understand the complex problems surrounding organizational change.

Procedure

The class divides into groups of from three to five people. Each member of the group assumes the role of supervisor of a group of manufacturing employees who assemble mainframe computers. Here is the scenario.

The employees' jobs are changing because of the introduction of a new, computer-controlled manufacturing technology. Using the old technology, employees stationed along a moving conveyor belt performed a clearly defined set of operations to assemble the computers. The new, computerized technology makes it possible to produce many different models of computers simultaneously.

To operate the technology effectively, employees have to learn new, more complex skills, and they also have to learn how to work in teams because the new technology is based on the use of flexible work teams. In the new work teams, the employees themselves, not a supervisor, will be responsible for product quality and for organizing work activities. The new role of the supervisor will be to facilitate, not direct, the work process. Indeed, a major part of the change to flexible work teams involves introducing a total quality management program to improve quality and reduce costs.

1. Chart the main impediments to change at the organization, group, and individual levels that you, as internal change agents, are likely to encounter as you assign employees to flexible work teams.
2. Discuss some ways to overcome resistance to change in order to help the organization move to its future desired state.
3. Discuss the pros and cons of top-down change and bottom-up change, and decide which method should be used to implement the change in the work system.
4. Which specific organizational development techniques might be most useful in helping to implement the change smoothly?

Making the Connection

Find an example of a company that has recently gone through a major change. What type of change was it? Why did the organization make the change, and what does it hope to achieve from it?

New York Times Cases in the News

The New York Times

IBM Explores Shift of Some Jobs Overseas

BY STEVEN GREENHOUSE

With American corporations under increasing pressure to cut costs and build global supply networks, two senior IBM officials told their corporate colleagues around the world in a recorded conference call that IBM needed to accelerate its efforts to move white-collar, often high-paying, jobs overseas even though that might create a backlash among politicians and its own employees.

During the call, IBM's top employee relations executives said that three million service jobs were expected to shift to foreign workers by 2015 and that IBM should move some of its jobs now done in the United States, including software design jobs, to India and other countries.

"Our competitors are doing it and we have to do it," Tom Lynch, IBM's director for global employee relations, said in the call. A recording was provided to The New York Times recently by the Washington Alliance of Technology Workers, a Seattle-based group seeking to unionize high-technology workers. The group said it had received the recording—which was made by IBM and later placed in digital form on an internal company Web site—from an IBM employee upset about the plans.

IBM's internal discussion about moving jobs overseas provides a revealing look at how companies are grappling with a growing trend that many economists call off-shoring. In decades past, millions of American manufacturing jobs moved overseas, but in recent years the movement has also shifted to the service sector, with everything from low-end call center jobs to high-paying computer chip design jobs migrating to China, India, the Philippines, Russia and other countries.

Executives at IBM and many other companies argue that creating more jobs in lower cost locations overseas keeps their industries competitive, holds costs down for American consumers, helps to develop poorer nations while supporting overall employment in the United States by improving productivity and the nation's global reach.

"It's not about one shore or another shore," an IBM spokeswoman, Kendra R. Collins, said. "It's about investing around the world, including the United States, to build capability and deliver value as defined by our customers."

But in recent weeks many politicians in Washington, including some in the Bush administration, have begun voicing concerns about the issue during a period when the economy is still weak and the information-technology, or I.T., sector remains mired in a long slump.

At a Congressional hearing on June 18, Bruce P. Mehlman, the Commerce Department's assistant secretary for technology policy, said, "Many observers are pessimistic about the impact of offshore I.T. service work at a time when American I.T. workers are having more difficulty finding employment, creating personal hardships and increasing demands on our safety nets."

Forrester Research, a high-technology consulting group, estimates that the number of service sector jobs newly located overseas, many of them tied to the information technology industry, will climb to 3.3 million in 2015 from about 400,000 this year. This shift of 3 million jobs represents about 2 percent of all American jobs.

"It's a very important, fundamental transition in the I.T. service industry that's taking place today," said Debashish Sinha, principal analyst for information technology services and sourcing at Gartner Inc., a consulting firm. "It is a megatrend in the I.T. services industry."

Forrester also estimated that 450,000 computer industry jobs could be transferred abroad in the next 12 years, representing 8 percent of the nation's computer jobs.

For example, Oracle, a big maker of specialized business software, plans to increase its jobs in India to 6,000 from 3,200, while Microsoft plans to double the size of its software development operation in India to 500 by late this year. Accenture, a leading consulting firm, has 4,400 workers in India, China, Russia and the Philippines.

Critics worry that such moves will end up doing more harm to the American economy than good.

"Once those jobs leave the country, they will never come back," said Phil Friedman, chief executive of Computer Generated Solutions, a 1,200-employee computer software company. "If we continue losing these jobs, our schools will stop producing the computer engineers and programmers we need for the future."

In the hourlong IBM conference call, which took place in March, the company's executives were particularly worried that the trend could spur unionization efforts.

"Governments are going to find that they're fairly limited as to what they can do, so unionizing becomes an attractive option," Mr. Lynch said on the recording. "You can see some of the fairly appealing arguments they're making as to why employees need to do some things like organizing to help fight this."

The IBM executives also warned that when workers from China come to the United States to learn to do technology jobs now being done here, some American employees might grow enraged about being forced to train the foreign workers who might ultimately take away their jobs.

"One of our challenges that we deal with every day is trying to balance what the business needs to do versus impact on people," Mr. Lynch said. "This is one of these areas where this challenge hits us squarely between the eyes."

Mr. Lynch warned that with the American economy in an "anemic" state, the difficulties and backlash from relocating jobs could be greater than in the past.

"The economy is certainly less robust than it was a decade ago," Mr. Lynch said, "and to move jobs in that environment is going to create more challenges for the reabsorption of the people who are displaced."

The IBM executives said openly that they expected government officials to be angry about this trend.

"It's hard for me to imagine any country just sitting back and letting jobs go offshore without raising some level of concern and investigation," Mr. Lynch said.

Those concerns were pointedly raised on June 18, when the House Small Business Committee held a hearing on "The Globalization of White-Collar Jobs: Can America Lose These Jobs and Still Prosper?"

"Increased global trade was supposed to lead to better jobs and higher standards of living," said Donald A. Manzullo, an Illinois Republican who is the committee chairman. "The assumption was that while lower-skilled jobs would be done elsewhere, it would allow Americans to focus on higher-skilled, higher-paying opportunities. But what do you tell the Ph.D., or professional engineer, or architect, or accountant, or computer scientist to do next? Where do you tell them to go?"

The technology workers' alliance is highlighting IBM's outsourcing plans to help rally IBM workers to the union banner.

"It's a bad thing because high-tech companies like IBM, Microsoft, Oracle and Sun, are making the decision to create jobs overseas strictly based on labor costs and cutting positions," said Marcus Courtney, president of the group, an affiliate of the Communications Workers of America. "It can create huge downward wage pressures on the American work force."

Mr. Mehlman, the Commerce Department official, said companies were moving more service jobs overseas because trade barriers were falling, because India, Russia and many other countries have technology expertise, and because high-speed digital connections and other new technologies made it far easier to communicate from afar.

Another important reason for moving jobs abroad is lower wages.

"You can get crackerjack Java programmers in India right out of college for $5,000 a year versus $60,000 here," said Stephanie Moore, vice president for outsourcing at Forrester Research. "The technology is such, why be in New York City when you can be 9,000 miles away with far less expense?"

Company executives say this strategy is a vital way to build a global company and to serve customers around the world.

General Electric has thousands of workers in India in call center, research and development efforts and in information technology. Peter Stack, a G.E. spokesman, said, "The outsourcing presence in India definitely gives us a competitive advantage in the businesses that use it. Those businesses are some of our growth businesses, and I would say that they're businesses where our overall employment is increasing and our jobs in the United States."

David Samson, an Oracle spokesman said the expansion of operations in India was "additive" and was not resulting in any jobs losses in the United States.

"Our aim here is not cost-driven," he said. "It's to build a 24/7 follow-the-sun model for development and support. When a software engineer goes to bed at night in the U.S., his or her colleague in India picks up development when they get into work. They're able to continually develop products."

SOURCE: Steven Greenhouse, "IBM Explores Shift of Some Jobs Overseas," *New York Times*, July 22, 2003, p. C1.

Questions for Discussion

1. What kind of forces in the environment are pushing IBM and other high-tech companies to change the way they operate and build global supply networks?

2. If this shift to move high-tech jobs abroad continues, how would you expect U.S. organizations to restructure and reengineer their operations in the future?

The New York Times

Schering-Plough Details Its Steps for a Turnaround

BY GARDINER HARRIS

On his 100th day as chief executive of the ailing Schering-Plough Corporation, Fred Hassan took drastic steps toward a turnaround yesterday by announcing job cuts, a steep reduction in the company's dividend, a prediction of lower profit this year and next year, and even the sale of a corporate jet.

But Mr. Hassan skipped an evening conference call with analysts to discuss the moves, infuriating some analysts. "The question really is, 'Where's Fred?'" asked Tony Butler, an analyst for Lehman Brothers. "Here, when a bad piece of news needs to be released, quite frankly he goes and hides."

Mr. Butler's comments were echoed by Barbara Ryan, an analyst for Deutsche Bank. "We all recognize these things didn't happen on Fred's watch; this is Fred's watch," she said. "I think it damages his credibility" to be absent from the conference call.

Staff members were left to answer analysts' questions, and they said Mr. Hassan had a previous commitment. "You all have got to remember that he has barely been at this company," a spokeswoman, Geraldine Foster, said. "This is his first full quarter. And I know you all

want things done immediately, but this is not a quick fix."

In a press release, Mr. Hassan said he hoped his actions would stabilize Schering-Plough, which has been spiraling downward each quarter for nearly two years. The biggest blow came last year with the expiration of its patent on Claritin, a huge-selling allergy drug. Claritin's sales in the second quarter dropped 98 percent in the United States.

In a letter to shareholders released yesterday, Mr. Hassan wrote, "In hindsight, it is clear that by depending on just one large product, a company in our industry runs a high risk of problems and unanticipated challenges, and that is what we have seen."

But a series of other problems have enveloped the company. The company's second-biggest seller, the Intron A franchise of hepatitis C drugs, is also experiencing a decline in sales in the face of competition from Roche Holding Ltd. Sales of another big seller, the allergy drug Nasonex, are also being affected by competition. What is needed to address the problems, Mr. Hassan said, is aggressive cost-cutting "in order to stabilize the company and to create a realistic base on which to build a turnaround."

Mr. Hassan also plans to invest in a few projects that are needed to pull the company out of its tailspin, including the marketing of the company's cholesterol drug, Zetia, and selective research projects. Mr. Hassan had warned for months that he would be willing to spend money on selective programs because, he said, he has no interest in presiding over a sale or dismantling of Schering-Plough.

Among Mr. Hassan's moves announced yesterday:

- The quarterly dividend will drop to 5.5 cents a share in the fourth quarter from 17 cents in the third. The company had recently announced that it did not have enough cash on hand to pay the dividend and also finance its operations. Most drug companies are awash in cash, highlighting Schering-Plough's distress.

- Costs will be cut even further beyond the $200 million in annual savings already announced.

- Executive bonuses and employee profit-sharing and merit raises will be eliminated, and a program is being created to cut staff by 1,000 by encouraging early retirements.

- Some executive perks, including a separate dining room and health plan, are being eliminated.

Mr. Hassan succeeded Richard Kogan, Schering-Plough's longtime chairman and chief executive. Mr. Kogan is being investigated by the Securities and Exchange Commission for comments he made to an investment group that may have led to a steep drop in the company's shares.

Mr. Kogan was in charge when Schering-Plough was buffeted by a series of preventable crises, including manufacturing problems that may have endangered some users of its allergy medicines and led federal regulators to freeze the approval of its new allergy drug, Clarinex. The freeze led to a long delay in Clarinex's introduction and crippled the company's plans to switch sales from Claritin to Clarinex.

The difficulties led Schering-Plough to add hundreds of employees to its manufacturing operation just as the volume of products coming out of the plants was plummeting. As revenue dropped, expenses rose. The company seemed to have little choice, however. Schering-Plough paid a $500 million fine to the Food and Drug Administration and agreed to a series of steps to improve manufacturing processes.

"These manufacturing problems will be with us until 2005," Ms. Foster said. "Are these tough decisions? Sure they're tough decisions. And Fred Hassan has been willing to do that, and we're all pretty pleased about that. It's not easy."

SOURCE: Gardiner Harris, "Schering-Plough Details Its Steps for a Turnaround," *New York Times*, August 22, 2003, p. C1.

Questions for Discussion

1. What kinds of steps is Fred Hassan taking to turn around Schering-Plough?

2. What kinds of resistances to change might he encounter, and how should he implement the change process?

APPENDIX

Research Methods in Organizational Behavior

OVERVIEW

Research methods is a broad term that refers to the set of techniques used to acquire knowledge or learn about something of interest. In organizational behavior, research methods are the techniques used to learn about how individuals and groups respond to and act in organizations and how organizations respond to their environments.

An understanding of research methods is important for several reasons:

1. It allows researchers, managers, and other members of organizations to learn about why people feel and behave as they do in organizations.

2. It helps people to solve problems in organizations and, more generally, come up with ways to increase performance and well-being.

3. It can help managers and other members of an organization use findings from research done by others to improve conditions in their organizations.

4. It can help members of an organization properly evaluate advice and recommendations provided by others such as consultants.

5. It allows people to evaluate the various theories of organizational behavior.[1]

Our discussion of research methods proceeds as follows. We present a general model of the scientific process used to learn about organizational behavior. We discuss how researchers develop theories to explain some aspect of organizational behavior and how theories can be evaluated. We move on to the actual testing of theories. We discuss the different types of research designs that are used throughout the scientific process. We conclude with a discussion of ethical considerations.

THE SCIENTIFIC PROCESS

A basic model of the scientific process is provided in Fig. A.1.[2] Because the model is cyclical, we could start describing the process at any point. For convenience, we start at point A, the observation of organizational behavior. At point A, a researcher notices something about organizational behavior that she or he wishes to learn more about. The researcher may observe, for example, that levels of absenteeism are higher in some groups than in others, that

employees performing some jobs experience much higher levels of stress than do those performing other jobs, or that some employees put forth much more effort than others.

After making observations like these, the researcher tries through induction to come up with a general explanation for what she or he has observed (point B in Fig. A.1). *Induction* is the process that researchers use to come up with general ways to account for or explain specific observations or instances of organizational behavior. Researchers who observed that individuals varied in the amounts of effort they exerted on the job, for example, tried to come up with some general explanations for what they observed. The outcome was theories of work motivation.

Once a researcher has a general explanation to account for a phenomenon, then, through deduction, she or he makes specific predictions that seem likely to be true if the general explanation was a good one. *Deduction* is the process of making specific predictions (point C in Fig. A.1) from general explanations. A general explanation for absenteeism (arrived at through induction), for example, might be that employees are most likely to be absent from their jobs when they are dissatisfied and have a lot of personal responsibilities in addition to their work responsibilities. Having made this general explanation from induction, the researcher might use deduction to predict that nurses who

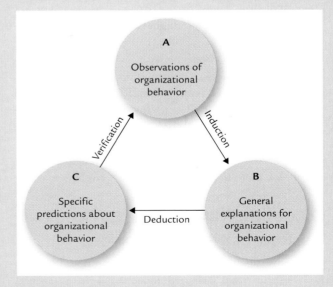

FIGURE A.1
The Scientific Process

are dissatisfied with their jobs and have children will have higher levels of absence from work during a year than will nurses who are satisfied and do not have children.

Once a researcher has made a prediction, the next step in the scientific process is to test this prediction and determine the extent to which it is true. *Verification* is the process by which researchers determine whether their predictions are accurate by making specific observations about organizational behavior. The researcher might ask 150 nurses employed by a large hospital to complete a questionnaire that includes measures of job satisfaction and also asks them how many children they have. The researcher might also ask the hospital to supply the number of days each nurse is absent for one year. These observations allow the researcher to verify whether her predictions are accurate. Verification completes the cycle of the scientific process and the researcher is back at point A in Fig. A.1.

Because human behavior in organizations is complex and determined by many factors, it is often the case that at least part of the predictions researchers make are not verified or found to be accurate by observations of actual organizational behavior. When this occurs, a new cycle of induction and deduction begins. Researchers cycle through the process again and try to come up with another general explanation for what they observed, make predictions from this explanation, and then test these predictions through verification.

Research in organizational behavior, as in all fields of study is a cooperative undertaking. Several different researchers might all be studying the same phenomenon and learning from each other's research. One researcher who studies absenteeism, for example, might come up with a new explanation for absenteeism. Based on this explanation, another researcher might make certain predictions and test them in several organizations. Some of these predictions might be verified, and others might not be. A third researcher then might seek to modify the original explanation to account for these new observations.

Researchers cooperate with each other or learn and build from each other's research in several ways. Researchers who already know each other often share ideas and research findings informally as well as ask for each other's advice. At professional meetings and conferences researchers present their work to other researchers who are interested in the same topic. And researchers write up their ideas and findings and publish them in journals and books for others to read.

COMING UP WITH GENERAL EXPLANATIONS: THE ROLE OF THEORY BUILDING

A *theory* is a general explanation of some phenomenon. Theories are arrived at through induction. When researchers build theories, they are moving from point A to point B in the scientific process shown in Fig. A.1. Theories summarize and organize what researchers have already learned about some phenomenon as well as provide direction for future research. Theories can never be proved to "be correct" because there is always the possibility that a future study will not support the theory. When research findings are consistent with or support a theory, confidence in the theory increases. Above all else, theories should be useful. Theories should help us understand organizational behavior as well as provide direction for future research in organizational behavior.

Four basic criteria that researchers can use to determine how useful a theory are correspondence, coherence, parsimony, and pragmatism.[3] *Correspondence* is the extent to which a theory is congruent with what is actually observed in organizations. One way to determine correspondence is to see whether predictions derived from the theory are verified or found to be accurate. *Coherence* is the extent to which the logic in the theory is straightforward and the theory is free of any logical contradictions. *Parsimony* is the extent to which a theory is free of concepts or relationships than are not necessary to provide a good explanation. Suppose there are two theories of absenteeism, one includes five concepts and the other ten, and each does an equally good job of explaining absenteeism. The simpler theory is preferred because of its greater parsimony. *Pragmatism* is the extent to which a theory stimulates further research. A minimal condition for pragmatism is that the theory is able to be tested. No matter how eloquent a theory is, if no one is able to test it, the theory is not very useful at all.

DEVELOPING SPECIFIC PREDICTIONS: FORMULATING HYPOTHESES

Once a theory is in place, researchers need to make specific predictions based on the theory; in other words, through deduction, move from point B to point C in Fig. A.1. Specific predictions in organizational behavior are often stated in the form of hypotheses. A *hypothesis* is a statement about the relationship between two or more variables.[4] A *variable* is a dimension along which some aspect of individuals, groups, or organizations differs or varies. Variables pertaining to individuals include age, gender, job satisfaction, organizational commitment, motivation, and job performance. Variables pertaining to groups include group size, group norms, and group cohesiveness. Variables pertaining to organizations include organizational structure, technology, and culture.

Some hypotheses simply state that two or more variables are related to each other. Other hypotheses state how variables affect each other—that is, they describe a causal relationship between variables. Ultimately, researchers always prefer to be able to state their hypotheses in causal terms; causal relationships provide explanations for *why* things happen. When hypotheses are not stated in causal

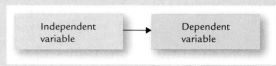

FIGURE A.2 A Casual Relationship

terms, the reason often is that the researcher is very uncertain about what causal relationship to expect or knows that she or he will not be able to conduct research to test a causal relationship.

When hypotheses do describe a causal relationship between variables, the variables can be categorized into four types: independent variables, dependent variables, mediator variables, and moderator variables. An *independent variable* is a variable that causes another variable to change when it varies or changes. The variable that changes in response to the independent variable is called the *dependent variable* (see Fig. A.2). A hypothesis might state, for example, that when the payment of production workers changes from an hourly basis to a piece-rate basis, levels of performance or production increase. In this example, the method of pay is the independent variable, and performance is the dependent variable.

Sometimes independent variables do not directly affect dependent variables but rather operate through a third variable. A *mediator variable* is a mechanism through which an independent variable has an effect on a dependent variable (see Fig. A.3). In organizational behavior, mediator variables often refer to something that is hard to observe directly, such as motivation. In our previous example, a mediator of the relationship between method of pay and performance may be motivation. Method of pay impacts motivation such that employees are more motivated to perform at a high level when their pay is based on their performance rather than on an hourly rate. When motivation increases, performance increases (assuming all else is equal).

A *moderator variable* is a variable that when it changes, changes the nature of the relationship between the independent and the dependent variables (see Fig. A.3). When the moderator variable changes, for example, it can turn strong positive relationships into weaker

positive relationships, into negative relationships, or into no relationships at all. Positive, negative, and no relationships are depicted graphically in Fig. A.4. An example of a moderator of the relationship between method of pay and performance is financial need. A hypothesis might state that there is a strong, positive relationship between method of pay and performance for employees who have high financial needs and a weak positive relationship for employees who have low financial needs.

TESTING HYPOTHESES: OPERATIONALIZING VARIABLES

Once researchers have specific predictions or hypotheses, they then have to test them through the process of verification—that is, they must move from point C to point A in the scientific process illustrated) in Fig. A.1. In order to test hypotheses, researchers need to find ways to measure the variables in the hypotheses. Many of the variables of interest in organizational behavior are abstract. Job satisfaction, motivation, stress, culture, and organizational structure, for example, are abstract terms that are sometimes hard to define, let alone measure. Nevertheless, finding measures for these variables is necessary in order to test hypotheses.

As a first step, researchers need to have clear conceptual definitions of the variables or be certain about what exactly they are trying to measure. Then they need to find ways of *operationalizing*, or measuring, these variables. A specific measure of a variable is sometimes called an *operational definition* of the variable.

There are two important criteria by which to judge whether a good operational definition or measure of a variable is being used in a research study: reliability and validity. *Reliability* is the extent to which a measure of a variable is free of error. Suppose you are weighing people but the scale you are using is not reliable. Each time you weigh them their weight varies by three or four pounds even though their actual weight has not changed. Your measure of weight lacks reliability because it contains a significant amount of error.

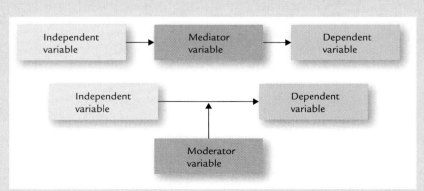

FIGURE A.3
Mediator and Moderator Variables

FIGURE A.4

Relationships Between Independent Variables (IV) and Dependent Variables (DV)

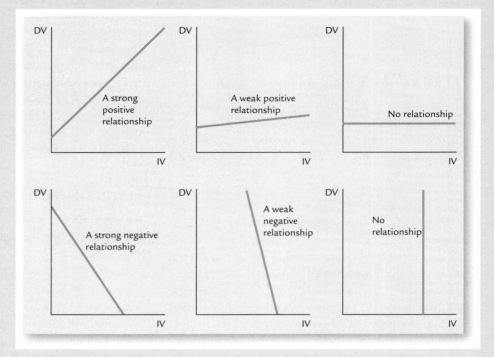

Measures of job satisfaction, performance and other organizational behavior variables need to be reliable in order for researchers to be able to have good tests of their hypotheses. For some organizational behavior variables, such as job satisfaction, reliable measures have already been created in the past and used in many research studies. These measures typically ask employees to answer a number of questions about their current jobs. Sample items from two of these measures are provided in Fig. 3.7 in Chapter 3. When using an existing measure of a variable, researchers should always determine how reliable or free of error the measure is in their own particular study.

There are several ways to assess the reliability of a measure. For example, if a questionnaire measure of job satisfaction asks employees to answer ten questions about their current job, each of the questions should be assessing job satisfaction. One way to determine whether the measure is reliable is to assess the extent to which each person's answers to the questions are consistent with each other. If each question taps job satisfaction, but on some questions people indicate that they are very satisfied and on others that they are very dissatisfied, then there is a lot of error in the measure and it is not reliable. This technique assesses *internal consistency reliability.*

Another way of determining reliability is assessing the extent to which repeated measures of a variable agree with each other (assuming that the variable itself has not changed). This technique assesses *test-retest reliability.* For example, the height of adults should not change from day to day, and a way to assess the reliability of a measure of height is to use the measure to determine people's height

on several different days and assess the extent to which the measures of height are the same from day to day.

The second criterion by which to judge an operational definition or measure is validity. *Validity* is the extent to which an operational definition of a variable is actually measuring the variable in question. Given that many of the variables in organizational behavior research are abstract, it is essential that measures of variables are valid or that the measures are actually measuring what the researcher wants to measure. A measure of job satisfaction, for example, is not valid if it is simply measuring the extent to which people tend to have a positive outlook on life in general and not how they feel about their current jobs. Reliability is a necessary but not sufficient condition for validity. In order for a measure to be valid, at a minimum the measure has to be free of error. However, the measure also has to be tapping into the right variable.

Determining the validity of measures in organizational behavior is an ongoing and complicated process. Researchers cannot be sure from one research study that their measures are valid. Only through repeated use of measures can researchers be confident in the validity of their measures. Moreover, there are multiple indicators of validity. One indicator is the extent to which experts in an area think that the measure is adequately gauging the variable in question. Another indicator is the extent to which the measure is related to measures of other variables in expected ways and is different from other measures of different variables. Only through using a measure many times and relying on multiple indicators of validity can researchers be confident in the validity of their measures.

RESEARCH DESIGNS

The design of a specific research study is geared toward what the researcher wishes to accomplish from the study. Different research designs or ways of conducting research are well suited to different stages in the research process. Here, we discuss three types of research designs: qualitative research, cross-sectional research, and experimental research.[5] Qualitative research can help researchers move from point A to B and from point B to C in the scientific process (see Fig. A.1). Cross-sectional and experimental research can help researchers move from point B to C and from point C to A. Each research design can be helpful in other ways as well. Cross-sectional research, for example, sometimes helps researchers move from point A to point B.

Qualitative Research

One hallmark of qualitative research is the careful *observation* of actual behavior in organizations. Researchers watch what members of an organization do and listen to what they say in the hopes of getting an accurate picture of what naturally occurs in an organization. Researchers keep careful records of what they have observed. Qualitative research can provide researchers with a rich description of organizational life and the many factors that affect it.

There are two basic ways of doing qualitative research: participant observation and direct observation. In *participant observation,* the researcher actually becomes a member of the organization that he or she is observing, and often other members of the organization do not realize that the newest member of the department or team is conducting research. Participant observation gives the researcher the opportunity to experience firsthand what it is like to be a member of the organization, and it helps the researcher gain the confidence and trust of other members of the organization. In *direct observation,* the researcher enters an organization as an observer and records what he or she sees (often as it occurs). Direct observation can be less time-consuming than participant observation.

Because qualitative research entails detailed observations, it is often conducted in one or a few organizations. A key question that arises from this kind of research design pertains to the *generalizability* of the findings—the extent to which what researchers discover in one organization is true of other organizations.

Cross-sectional Research

When using a cross-sectional design, researchers develop and test specific hypotheses about relationships between variables. To do so, they must develop or use existing measures of variables that are both reliable and valid. Questionnaires and interviews are often used to gather measures of variables. Although qualitative designs are well suited for making observations and coming up with general explanations for them, cross-sectional designs are well-suited for testing specific hypotheses because the researcher is actually collecting measures of variables. However, researchers cannot test hypotheses that state causal relationships between variables by using cross-sectional designs because they have no control over the many other factors that might impact a dependent variable in addition to the independent variable. Hence, with cross-sectional designs, researchers can test only hypotheses that state that certain variables are related to each other.

Experimental Research

The hallmark of experimental research designs is the controlled *manipulation,* or changing, of an independent variable to determine what effect it has on a dependent variable. There are two types of experimental research designs: true experiments and quasi-experiments.

True experiments are the only kind of research design that allows researchers to test causal hypotheses and draw conclusions about causal relationships. True experiments allow researchers to do this by controlling for everything else that might affect a dependent variable besides changes in the independent variable. Two features of true experiments provide this control: a control group and random assignment of participants to the experimental and the control groups.

Suppose a researcher is interested in the relationship between method of pay and performance and decides to do an experiment. The researcher hypothesizes that switching from an hourly pay plan to a piece-rate pay plan results in an increase in performance. He or she takes a group of employees who are currently being paid on an hourly rate and switches them to a piece-rate plan and measures their performance before and after the change. Performance does increase after the change. Can the researcher conclude that the change in pay plan caused the change in performance? No, and the reason is that the researcher did not control for other things—in addition to the change in pay plan—that might have been responsible for a change in performance, such as the fact that the employees have gained more job experience and thus their performance would have increased regardless of the change in pay plan.

By having a *control group*—a group of participants for whom the researcher does not change the independent variable (in this case, the pay plan)—the researcher is able to control for, or take into account, other things besides the pay plan that might affect performance because the control group also will be exposed to these things. By randomly assigning participants to the experimental and control groups, the researcher guarantees that these groups start out at an equivalent position. Because the experimental and control groups start out in equivalent positions (because of random assignment), the *only* difference between the groups is the change in pay plan.

Thus, if the performance level of the control group stays the same but rises for the experimental group, the researcher can confidently conclude that the change in pay plan caused the change in performance. Conversely, if the performance levels of both groups stay the same or increase, then the change in pay plan is not having the hypothesized effect.

For practical reasons it is very difficult to conduct true experiments in real organizations. Manipulating variables like pay and randomly assigning employees to experimental and control groups is often very disruptive to the ongoing activities of an organization, and few managers are willing to tolerate these disruptions. Partially for this reason, true experiments are often conducted in laboratory settings at universities using college students as participants rather than employees. The logic behind this practice is that if a researcher is studying some fundamental aspect of human functioning like motivation, she or he should be able to observe its operation in a laboratory with students or in an organization with employees. Although this assumption makes sense, it might also be the case that conditions in organizations are so different from conditions in the lab (or that some differences between employees and college students are so fundamental) that results from the lab do not generalize to the field or to real organizations. In other words, what might occur in the laboratory might not occur in an organization and vice versa. To be on the safe side, researchers need to supplement laboratory research with field research whenever possible.

Similar to a true experiment, *quasi-experiments* also involve the manipulation of an independent variable. The major difference is that in a quasi-experiment a researcher does not have a control group or does not randomly assign participants to experimental and control groups. Quasi-experiments are often a practical necessity when researchers want to conduct experiments in real organizations. For example, a researcher might find an organization that currently operates six factories that employ a hundred employees each. The organization wants to experiment with changing from an hourly pay plan to a piece-rate pay plan. Management decides to make the change in three of the factories and leave the other three (to be used as a control group) on the existing hourly plan. In this quasi-experiment, there is a control group but no random assignment because of the practical problem that all employees in a single factory need to be working under the same pay system.

Because of the lack of a control group or random assignment, researchers cannot test causal hypotheses or arrive at causal conclusions from quasi-experiments. Nevertheless, quasi-experiments can provide valuable insights into organizational behavior.

Tradeoffs in the Choice of Research Designs

By this time, it should be clear to you that multiple tradeoffs affect the choice of a research design. Qualitative designs have the advantage of providing researchers with a rich account of the many factors that influence organizational behavior. True experiments have the advantage of allowing researchers to test causal relationships. Researchers cannot come to causal conclusions from qualitative designs, and they might be neglecting important organizational behavior variables in true experiments. No one design is preferable over another, and each one is well suited to different stages in the scientific process. Moreover, research on any topic in organizational behavior benefits from research using all three types of designs.

ETHICAL CONSIDERATIONS IN ORGANIZATIONAL BEHAVIOR RESEARCH

Researchers have ethical obligations to research participants. There is disagreement about the exact nature of these obligations, but here are some guidelines that many researchers would agree with:[6]

1. The researcher should obtain the informed consent of research participants. When consent is *informed,* participants know that they are taking part in a research study and do so voluntarily. Obtaining informed consent becomes troublesome in a participant observation design because an integral feature of this design is that members of an organization do not realize that research is actually being conducted.

2. Participants should not be harmed in any way by the research being conducted.

3. Participants' rights to privacy should be respected.

4. Participants in a control group should not be denied treatment that the researcher knows would benefit them. This guideline is most clearly relevant to medical research. However, there are instances when it might be relevant to organizational behavior research, such as the case when a researcher knows that a certain type of training benefits employees yet gives only some of the employees the training (that is, those in the experimental group).

5. Participants should be debriefed. Once researchers have completed a study, they should let participants know what the study was about, and they should be available to answer questions.

6. Data should be treated confidentially.

Summary

Only through conducting research on organizational behavior can progress be made in understanding how individuals and groups respond to and act in organizations and how organizations respond to their environments.

references

Chapter 1

1. www.ikea.com, 2003.
2. www.ikea.com, 2003; K. Kling and I. Goteman, "IKEA CEO Anders Dahlvig on International Growth and IKEA's Unique Corporate Culture and Brand Identity," *Academy of Management Executive* 17 (2003): 38–46.
3. www.forbes.com, 2003.
4. H. Fayol, *Industrial and General Administration* (London: Pitman, 1949); P. F. Drucker, *Management Tasks, Responsibilities, Practices* (New York: Harper and Row, 1974).
5. www.flysouthwest.com, 2000.
6. www.ddir.com, 2003.
7. http://seattletimes.nwsource.com/html/obituaries/2001211576_dicks23m.html.
8. H. Mintzberg, *The Nature of Managerial Work* (New York: Harper and Row, 1963).
9. R. L. Katz, "Skills of an Effective Administrator," *Harvard Business Review* (September–October 1974): 90–102.
10. T. Donaldson, "Taking Ethics Seriously—A Mission Now More Possible," *Academy of Management Review* 28 (2003): 363–67.
11. E. Soule, "Managerial Moral Strategies—In Search of a Few Good Principles," *Academy of Management Review* 27 (2002): 114–25.
12. R. C. Soloman, *Ethics and Excellence* (New York: Oxford University Press, 1992).
13. D. L. Swanson, "Towards an Integrative Theory of Business and Society: A Research Strategy for Corporate Social Performance," *Academy of Management Review* 24 (1999): 506–22.
14. L. K. Trevino, "Ethical Decision Making in Organizations: A Person–Situation Interactionist Model," *Academy of Management Review* 11 (1986): 601–17.
15. T. M. Jones, "Convergent Stakeholder Theory," *Academy of Management Review* 24 (1999): 206–22.
16. www.consumerreports.com, 2003.
17. www.yahoo.com, 2003.
18. H. Mintzberg, "The Case for Corporate Social Responsibility," *Journal of Business Strategy* (December 1983): 3–15; J. J. Chrisman and A. B. Carroll, "Corporate Responsibility—Reconciling Economic and Social Goals," *Sloan Management Review* 25 (1984): 59–65.
19. G. R. Weaver, L. Trevino, and P. L. Cochran, "Corporate Ethics Programs as Control Systems: Influences of Executive Commitment and Environmental Factors," *Academy of Management Journal* 42 (1999): 41–58.
20. H. Mintzberg, "The Case for Corporate Social Responsibility," *Journal of Business Strategy* (Winter 1973): 3–15.
21. B. R. Agle and R. K. Mitchell, "Who Matters to CEOs? An Investigation of Stakeholder Attributes and Salience," *Academy of Management Journal* 42 (1999): 507–26.
22. T. M. Jones, "Ethical Decision Making by Individuals in Organizations: An Issue Contingent Model," *Academy of Management Review* 16 (1991): 366–95; G. R. Shea, *Practical Ethics* (New York: American Management Association, 1988).
23. L. I. Kessler, *Managing Diversity in an Equal Employment Opportunity Workplace* (Washington, DC: National Foundation for the Study of Employment Policy, 1990).
24. W. B. Johnson and A. H. Packer, *Workforce 2000: Work and Employees in the 21st Century* (Indianapolis: Hudson Institute, 1987); M. Galen and A. T. Palmer, "White, Male and Worried," *Newsweek* (January 31, 1994): 50–55.
25. Ibid.
26. M. Fine, F. Johnson, and M. S. Ryan, "Cultural Diversity in the Workforce," *Public Personnel Management* 19 (1990): 305–19.
27. W. E. Hopkins and S. A. Hopkins, "Effects of Cultural Recomposition on Group Interaction Processes," *Academy of Management Journal* 45 (2002): 1029–46.
28. P. M. Elsass and L. M. Graves, "Demographic Diversity in Decision Making Groups," *Academy of Management Review* 22 (1997): 946–72.
29. T. Cox, Jr., *Cultural Diversity in Organizations* (San Francisco: Berrett Koehler, 1994).
30. D. Jamieson and J. O'Mara, *Managing Workforce 2000: Gaining the Diversity Advantage* (San Francisco: Jossey-Bass, 1991).
31. C. Muir, "Can We All Get Along? The Interpersonal Challenge at Work," *Academy of Management Executive* 14 (2000): 143–45.
32. R. C. Orlando, "Racial Diversity, Business Strategy, and Firm Performance: A Resource-Based View," *Academy of Management Journal* 43 (2000): 164–78.
33. www.uboc.com, 2003.
34. G. Colvin, "The 50 Best Companies for Asians, Blacks, and Hispanics," *Fortune* (July 19, 1999): 53–57.
35. "Union Bank of California Honored by U.S. Labor Department for Employment Practices," Press Release, September 11, 2000.
36. G. A. Gilbert and J. M. Ivancevich, "Valuing Diversity: A Tale of Two Organizations," *Academy of Management Executive* 25 (2000): 93–106.
37. M. C. Higgins, "Reconceptualizing Mentoring at Work: A Developmental Network Perspective," *Academy of Management Review* 26 (2001): 264–89.

38. P. Dass and B. Parker, "Strategies for Managing Human Resource Diversity: From Resistance to Learning," *Academy of Management Executive* 13 (1999): 68–81.

39. C. K. Prahalad and Y. L. Doz, *The Multinational Mission: Balancing Local Demands and Global Vision* (New York: Free Press, 1987); C. A. Bartlett and S. Ghoshal, *Transnational Management* (Homewood, IL.: Irwin, 1992).

40. A. K. Gupta and V. Govindarajan, "Cultivating a Global Mindset," *Academy of Management Executive* 16 (2002): 116–27.

41. S. A. Zahra, "The Changing Rules of Global Competitiveness in the 21st Century," *Academy of Management Executive* 13 (1999): 36–43.

42. P. J. Dowling and R. S. Schuler, *International Dimensions of Human Resource Management* (Boston: PWS-Kent, 1990).

43. N. Adler, *International Dimensions of Organizational Behavior* (Boston: Kent, 1991).

44. L. Van Dyne and A. Soon, "Organizational Citizenship Behavior of Contingent Workers in Singapore," *Academy of Management Journal* 41 (1998): 692–704.

45. T. W. Malnight, "Emerging Structural Patterns Within Multinational Corporations: Towards Process Based Structures," *Academy of Management Journal* 44 (2001): 1187–1211.

46. G. Hofstede, "The Cultural Relativity of Organizational Practices and Theories," *Journal of International Business Studies* (Fall 1983): 75–89.

47. C. A. Bartlett and S. Ghoshal, *Managing Across Borders* (Boston: Harvard Business School Press, 1989).

48. Ibid.

49. E. Kelley, "Keys to Effective Virtual Global Teams," *Academy of Management Executive* 15 (2001): 132–34.

50. T. W. Malone and J. F. Rockart, "Computers, Networks, and the Corporation," *Scientific American* 263 (1991): 128–37.

51. R. Forrester and A. B. Drexler, "A Model for Team-Based Organizational Performance," *Academy of Management Executive* (August, 1999): 36–49.

52. T. H. Davenport, and L. Prusak, *Information Ecology* (Oxford: Oxford University Press, 1997).

53. C. K. Prahalad and V. Ramaswamy, "Co-opting Customer Competence," *Harvard Business Review* (January–February 2000): 79–90.

54. D. M. Rousseau and Z. Shperling, "Pieces of the Action: Ownership and the Changing Employment Relationship," *Academy of Management Review* 28 (2003): 553–71.

55. D. P. Lepak, "The Human Resource Architecture: Toward a Theory of Human Capital Allocation and Development," *Academy of Management Review* 24 (1999): 31–49.

56. R. J. Trent and R. M. Monczka, "Pursuing Competitive Advantage Through Integrated Global Sourcing," *Academy of Management Executive* 16 (2002): 66–81; S. J. Freeman and K. S. Cameron, "Organizational Downsizing: A Convergence and Reorientation Framework," *Organizational Science* 4 (1993): 10–29.

57. S. L. Robinson and M. S. Kraatz, "Changing Obligations and the Psychological Contract: A Longitudinal Study," *Academy of Management Journal* 37 (1994): 137–53.

58. E. W. Morrison and S. L. Robinson, "When Employees Feel Betrayed: A Model of How Psychological Contract Violation Develops," *Academy of Management Review* 22 (1997): 226–57.

59. A. Yuan, Z. Guorong, and D. T. Hall, "International Assignments for Career Building: A Model of Agency Relationships and Psychological Contracts," *Academy of Management Review* 27 (2002): 373–92.

60. W. A. Randolph and M. Sashkin, "Can Organizational Empowerment Work in Multinational Settings?" *Academy of Management Executive* 16 (2002): 102–16.

61. F. W. Taylor, *Shop Management* (New York: Harper, 1903); F. W. Taylor, *The Principles of Scientific Management* (New York: Harper, 1911).

62. L. W. Fry, "The Maligned F. W. Taylor: A Reply to His Many Critics," *Academy of Management Review* 1 (1976): 124–29.

63. J. A. Litterer, *The Emergence of Systematic Management as Shown by the Literature from 1870–1900* (New York: Garland, 1986).

64. D. Wren, *The Evolution of Management Thought* (New York: Wiley, 1994), 134.

65. L. D. Parker, "Control in Organizational Life: The Contribution of Mary Parker Follett," *Academy of Management Review* 9 (1984): 736–45.

66. P. Graham, *M. P. Follett–Prophet of Management: A Celebration of Writings from the 1920s* (Boston: Harvard Business School Press, 1995).

67. M. P. Follett, *Creative Experience* (London: Longmans, 1924).

68. E. Mayo, *The Human Problems of Industrial Civilization* (New York: Macmillan, 1933); F. J. Roethlisberger and W. J. Dickson, *Management and the Employee* (Cambridge: Harvard University Press, 1947).

69. D. W. Organ, "Review of Management and the Employee, by F. J. Roethlisberger and W. J. Dickson," *Academy of Management Review* 13 (1986): 460–64.

70. D. Roy, "Banana Time: Job Satisfaction and Informal Interaction," *Human Organization* 18 (1960): 158–61.

71. For an analysis of the problems in determining cause from effect in the Hawthorne studies and in social settings in general, see A. Carey, "The Hawthorne Studies: A Radical Criticism," *American Sociological Review* 33 (1967): 403–16.

72. D. McGregor, *The Human Side of Enterprise* (New York: McGraw-Hill, 1960).

73. Ibid., 48.

Chapter 2

1. A. Barrett, "Staying on Top: Can He Keep Up the Growth?" *Business Week* 5 (May 2003): 60–68.

2. L. Nathans Spiro, "In Search of Leaders," *Chief Executive* Issue 192 (October 2003); R. Pierson, "Johnson & Johnson, 116 and Growing Like a Teenager," *Reuters* (2003).

3. R. Alsop, "Scandal-Filled Year Takes Toll on Firms' Good Names," *The Wall Street Journal Online* (February 12, 2003), www.wsj.com; "Johnson & Johnson Ranks #1 in National Corporate Reputation Suvey for the Fourth Consecutive Year," *HarrisInteractive* (February 12, 2003), www.harrisinteractive.com.

4. Barrett, "Staying on Top: Can He Keep Up the Growth?"

5. Ibid.

6. F. Arner and A. Weintraub, "J&J: Toughing Out the Drought," *Business Week* (January 26, 2004): 84–85.

7. Barrett, "Staying on Top: Can He Keep Up the Growth?"

8. Arner and Weintraub, "J&J: Toughing Out the Drought."

9. Ibid.

10. P. T. van den Berg and J. A. Feij, "Complex Relationships Among Personality Traits, Job Characteristics, and Work Behaviors," *International Journal of Selection and Assessment* 11(4), (December 2003): 326–49.

11. R. Ilies and T. A. Judge, "On the Heritability of Job Satisfaction: The Mediating Role of Personality," *Journal of Applied Psychology* 88(4), (2003): 750–59.

12. A. Tellegen, D. T. Lykken, T. J. Bouchard et al., "Personality Similarity in Twins Reared Apart and Together," *Journal of Personality and Social Psychology* 54 (1988): 1031–39.

13. Ibid.

14. J. M. George, "The Role of Personality in Organizational Life: Issues and Evidence," *Journal of Management* 18 (1992): 185–213.

15. R. D. Arvey, T. J. Bouchard, N. L. Segal, and L. M. Abraham, "Job Satisfaction: Environmental and Genetic Components," *Journal of Applied Psychology* 74 (1989): 187–92; A. P. Brief, M. J. Burke, J. M. George, B. Robinson, and J. Webster, "Should Negative Affectivity Remain an Unmeasured Variable in the Study of Job Stress?" *Journal of Applied Psychology* 73 (1988): 193–98; J. L. Holland, *Making Vocational Choices: A Theory of Careers* (Upper Saddle River, NJ: Prentice Hall, 1973); R. J. House, W. D. Spangler, and J. Woycke, "Personality and Charisma in the U.S. Presidency: A Psychological Theory of Leader Effectiveness," *Administrative Science Quarterly* 36 (1991): 364–96.

16. M. R. Barrick, M. K. Mount, and J. P. Strauss, "Conscientiousness and Performance of Sales Representatives: Test of the Mediating Effects of Goal Setting," *Journal of Applied Psychology* 78 (1993): 715–22.

17. A. Davis-Blake and J. Pfeffer, "Just a Mirage: The Search for Dispositional Effects in Organizational Research," *Academy of Management Review* 14 (1989): 385–400.

18. R. C. Carson, "Personality," *Annual Review of Psychology* 40 (1989): 227–48; D. T. Kenrick and D. C. Funder, "Profiting from Controversy: Lessons from the Person–Situation Debate," *American Psychologist* 43 (1988): 23–34; D. C. Rowe, "Resolving the Person–Situation Debate: Invitation to an Interdisciplinary Dialogue," *American Psychologist* 42 (1987): 218–27.

19. B. Schneider, "The People Make the Place," *Personnel Psychology* 40 (1987): 437–53.

20. J. Schaubroeck, D. C. Ganster, and J. R. Jones, "Organization and Occupation Influences in the Attraction-Selection-Attrition Process," *Journal of Applied Psychology* 83 (1998): 869–91.

21. "Who Hires at Small Concerns? Often, It Is the Head Honcho," *Wall Street Journal*, November 17, 1992, p. A1.

22. J. M. Digman, "Personality Structure: Emergence of the Five-Factor Model," *Annual Review of Psychology* 41 (1990): 417–40.

23. Ibid.; R. R. McCrae and P. T. Costa, "Validation of the Five-Factor Model of Personality Across Instruments and Observers," *Journal of Personality and Social Psychology* 52 (1987): 81–90; R. R. McCrae and P. T. Costa, "Discriminant Validity of NEO-PIR Facet Scales," *Educational and Psychological Measurement* 52 (1992): 229–37.

24. J. Sandberg, "Case Study," *Newsweek* (January 24, 2000): pp. 31–36.

25. J. M. George and A. P. Brief, "Personality and Work-Related Distress," in B. Schneider and B. Smith (Eds.), *Personality and Organization* (Mahwah, NJ: Erlbaum, 2004).

26. M. J. Simmering, J. A. Colquitt, R. A. Noe, and C. O. L. H. Porter, "Conscientiousness, Autonomy Fit, and Development: A Longitudinal Study," *Journal of Applied Psychology* 88(5), (2003): 954–63.

27. M. R. Barrick and M. K. Mount, "The Big Five Personality Dimensions and Job Performance: A Meta-Analysis," *Personnel Psychology* 44 (1991): 1–26; Barrick, Mount, and Strauss, "Conscientiousness and Performance of Sales Representatives."

28. J. O'C. Hamilton, "Roger Salquist," *Business Week, Reinventing America*, 1992, p. 186.

29. L. A. Witt and G. R. Ferris, "Social Skills as Moderator of the Conscientiousness–Performance Relationship: Convergent Results Across Four Studies," *Journal of Applied Psychology* 88(5), (2003): 809–20.

30. J. M. George and J. Zhou, "When Openness to Experience and Conscientiousness Are Related to Creative Behavior: An Interactional Approach," *Journal of Applied Psychology*, forthcoming.

31. "A Gallery of Risk Takers," *Business Week, Reinventing America* (1992): p. 183.

32. I. M. Kunii, "Making Canon Click," *Business Week* 16, (September 2002): 40–42.

33. Ibid.

34. S. Ballmer, "Repeat Performers," *Business Week Online* (January 13, 2003), www.buinessweek.com/@@X9eC1IQQvgmr3QcA/magazine/content/03_0; F. Mitarai, "Market-Leading Value Creation through Strength in Innovative Technologies," (January 24, 2004), www.canon.com/about/greeting/index.html; "Corporate Philosophy—Kyosei," (January 24, 2003), www.canon.com/about/philosophy/index.html.

35. Kunii, "Making Canon Click."

36. Ibid.

37. M. A. Burke, A. P. Brief, and J. M. George, "The Role of Negative Affectivity in Understanding Relationships Between Self-Reports of Stressors and Strains: A Comment on the Applied Psychology Literature," *Journal of Applied Psychology* 78 (1993): 402–12.

38. Barrick and Mount, "The Big Five Personality Dimensions and Job Performance"; J. M. George, "Mood and Absence," *Journal of Applied Psychology* 74 (1989): 317–24; J. M. George, "Time Structure and Purpose as a Mediator of Work-Life Linkages," *Journal of Applied Social Psychology* 21 (1991): 296–314.

39. J. B. Rotter, "Generalized Expectancies for Internal vs. External Control of Reinforcement," *Psychological Monographs* 80 (1966): 1–28; P. Spector, "Behavior in Organizations as a Function of Employees' Locus of Control," *Psychological Bulletin* 91 (1982): 482–97.

40. M. Snyder, "Self-Monitoring of Expressive Behavior," *Journal of Personality and Social Psychology* 30 (1974): 526–37; M. Snyder, "Self-Monitoring Processes." In L. Berkowitz (Ed.), *Advances in Experimental Social Psychology* 12 (1979): 85–128.

41. T. A. Judge, A. Erez, J. E. Bono, and C. J. Thoresen, "The Core Self-Evaluations Scale: Development of a Measure," *Personnel Psychology* 56 (2003): 303–31.

42. J. Brockner, *Self-Esteem at Work* (Lexington, MA: Lexington Books, 1988).

43. D. C. Ganster, J. Schaubroeck, W. E. Sime, and B. T. Mayes, "The Nomological Validity of the Type A Personality Among Employed Adults," *Journal of Applied Psychology* 76 (1991): 143–68; R. H. Rosenman, "Current and Past History of Type A Behavior Pattern." In T. Schmidt, J. M. Dembrowski, and G. Blumchen (Eds.), *Biological and Psychological Factors in Cardiovascular Disease* (New York: Springer-Verlag, 1986).

44. R. A. Baron, "Personality and Organizational Conflict: Effects of the Type A Behavior Pattern and Self-Monitoring," *Organizational Behavior and Human Decision Processes* 44 (1989): 281–97.

45. D. C. McClelland, *Human Motivation* (Glenview, IL: Scott, Foresman, 1985); D. C. McClelland, "How Motives, Skills, and Values Determine What People Do," *American Psychologist* 40 (1985): 812–25; D. C. McClelland, "Managing Motivation to Expand Human Freedom," *American Psychologist* 33 (1978): 201–10.

46. D. C. McClelland, "Achievement and Entrepreneurship: A Longitudinal Study," *Journal of Personality and Organizational Behavior* 1 (1965): 389–92.

47. L. Goldberg, "Continental Executive Is Still a Pilot," *Houston Chronicle* (February 26, 2000): pp. 1C, 3C; Continental Airlines News Release, September 20, 1999; www.continental.com/corporate.

48. L. Goldberg, "Continental Executive Is Still a Pilot."

49. D. G. Winter, *The Power Motive* (New York: Free Press, 1973).

50. R. J. House, W. D. Spangler, and J. Woycke, "Personality and Charisma in the U.S. Presidency: A Psychological Theory of Leader Effectiveness," *Administrative Science Quarterly* 36 (1991): 364–96.

51. M. J. Stahl, "Achievement, Power, and Managerial Motivation: Selecting Managerial Talent with the Job Choice Exercise," *Personnel Psychology* 36 (1983): 775–89.

52. Ibid.

53. D. C. McClelland and D. H. Burnham, "Power Is the Great Motivator," *Harvard Business Review* 54 (1976): 100–10.

54. D. S. Ones and C. Viswesvaran, "Job-Specific Applicant Pools and National Norms for Personality Scales: Implications for Range-Restriction Corrections in Validation Research," *Journal of Applied Psychology* 88(3), (2003): 570–577.

55. L. M. Hough, N. K. Eaton, M. D. Dunnette, J. D. Kamp, and R. A. McCloy, "Criterion-Related Validities of Personality Constructs and the Effect of Response Distortion on Those Validities," *Journal of Applied Psychology* 75 (1990): 581–95.

56. D. Lubinski and R. V. Dawis, "Aptitudes, Skills, and Proficiencies." In M. D. Dunnette and L. M. Hough (Eds.), *Handbook of Industrial and Organizational Psychology*, 2nd ed., vol. 3. (Palo Alto, CA: Consulting Psychologists Press, 1992), pp. 1–59.

57. Ibid.

58. J. C. Nunnally, *Psychometric Theory*, 2nd ed. (New York: McGraw-Hill, 1978); T. G. Thurstone, "Primary Mental Abilities and Children," *Educational and Psychological Measurement* 1 (1941): 105–16.

59. K. R. Murphy, B. E. Cronin, and A. P. Tam, "Controversy and Consensus Regarding the Use of Cognitive Ability Testing in Organizations," *Journal of Applied Psychology* 88(4), (2003): 660–71.

60. Ibid.

61. J. F. Salgado, N. Anderson, S. Moscoso, C. Bertua, F. de Fruyt, and J. P. Rolland, "A Meta-Analytic Study of General Mental Ability Validity for Different Occupations in the European Community," *Journal of Applied Psychology* 88(5), (2003): 1068–81; J. F. Salgado, N. Anderson, S. Moscoso, C. Bertua, and F. de Fruyt, "International Validity Generalization of GMA and Cognitive Abilities: A European Community Meta-Analysis," *Personnel Psychology* 56 (2003): 573–605.

62. J. A. LePine, "Team Adaptation and Postchange Performance: Effects of Team Composition in Terms of Members' Cognitive Ability and Personality," *Journal of Applied Psychology* 88(1), (2003): 27–39.

63. M. D. Dunnette, "Aptitudes, Abilities, and Skills." In M. D. Dunnette (Ed.), *Handbook of Industrial and Organizational Psychology* (Chicago: Rand McNally, 1976), pp. 473–520.

64. E. A. Fleishman, "The Description and Prediction of Perceptual-Motor Skill Learning." In R. Glaser (Ed.), *Training Research and Education* (Pittsburgh: University of Pittsburgh Press, 1962); E. A. Fleishman, "On the Relation Between Abilities, Learning, and Human Performance," *American Psychologist* 27 (1972): 1017–32.

65. H. M. Chipuer, M. Rovine, and R. Plomin, "LISREL Modeling: Genetic and Environmental Influences on IQ Revisited," *Intelligence* 14 (1990): 11–29; N. L. Pedersen, R. Plomin, J. R. Nesselroade, and G. E. McClearn, "A Quantitative Genetic Analysis of Cognitive Abilities During the Second Half of the Life Span," *Psychological Science* 3 (1992): 346–53.

66. "Think About It: Your Brainpower May Be Vastly Underused on the Job," *Wall Street Journal*, May 11, 1997, p. A1.

67. R. Merle, "Technology Workers See No Sizzle in What They Do," *Wall Street Journal*, April 26, 2000, p. T2.

68. "Drug Tests Keep Paying Off, But Continued Gains Are Tougher," *Wall Street Journal*, April 5, 1998, p. A1.

69. L. McGinley, " 'Fitness' Exams Help to Measure Worker Acuity," *Wall Street Journal*, April 21, 1992, pp. B1, B6.

70. D. Goleman, *Emotional Intelligence* (New York: Bantam Books, 1994); J. D. Mayer and P. Salovey, "The Intelligence of Emotional Intelligence," *Intelligence* 17 (1993): 433–42; J. D. Mayer and P. Salovey, "What Is Emotional Intelligence?" In P. Salovey and D. Sluyter (Eds.), *Emotional Development and Emotional Intelligence: Implications for Education* (New York: Basic Books, 1997); P. Salovey and J. D. Mayer, "Emotional Intelligence," *Imagination, Cognition, and Personality* 9 (1989–1990): 185–211.

71. Ibid.

72. A. Farnham, "Are You Smart Enough to Keep Your Job?," *Fortune*, January 15, 1996 pp. 34–48; M. E. P. Seligman, *Learned Optimism* (New York: A. A. Knopf, 1990).

73. K. Law, C. Wong, and L. Song, "The Construct and Criterion Validity of Emotional Intelligence and Its Potential Utility for Management Studies," *Journal of Applied Psychology* (in press).

74. "Leading by Feel," *Inside the Mind of the Leader* (January 2004): 27–37.

75. J. M. George, "Emotions and Leadership: The Role of Emotional Intelligence," *Human Relations*, 2000.

76. J. Zhou and J. M George, "Awakening Employee Creativity: The Role of Leader Emotional Intelligence," *The Leadership Quarterly* 14 (2003): 545–68.

77. A. Farnham, "Are You Smart Enough to Keep Your Job?"

78. Ibid. p. 35.

79. Ibid.

80. A. Jung, "Leading by Feel: Seek Frank Feedback," *Inside the Mind of the Leader* (January 2004): 31.

81. Barrett, "Staying on Top: Can He Keep Up the Growth?"

82. M. Austria Farmer, "Christine Poon: The Powerhouse Who Leads a Billion-Dollar Drug Business," *Diversity Inc.* (September 2003): 52–56.

83. M. Austria Farmer, "The Power Who Leads a Billion-Dollar Business," *Diversity Inc. Magazine Cover Story, July 2003* www.diversityinc.com.

84. Farmer, "Christine Poon: The Powerhouse Who Leads a Billion-Dollar Drug Business."

85. Farmer, "Christine Poon: The Powerhouse Who Leads a Billion-Dollar Drug Business."

86. Farmer, "The Power Who Leads a Billion-Dollar Business."

87. Farmer, "Christine Poon: The Powerhouse Who Leads a Billion-Dollar Drug Business."

88. W. Arthur, Jr., W. Bennett, Jr., P. S. Edens, and S. T. Bell, "Effectiveness of Training in Organizations: A Meta-Analysis of Design and Evaluation Features," *Journal of Applied Psychology* 88(2), (2003): 234–45.

89. H. Cooper, "Carpet Firm Sets Up an In-House School to Stay Competitive," *Wall Street Journal*, October 5, 1992, pp. A1, A5.

90. Ibid.

91. "Collins & Aikman Recognized as One of Metro Detroit's " 'Best and Brightest,' " October 22, 2003. C&A Media Center-Press Release, www.collinsaikman.com/profile/news.asp?newsid =483, January 28, 2004.

Chapter 3

1. B. Morris, "What a Life," *Fortune* (October 6, 2003): 50–62.

2. Ibid.

3. Ibid.

4. W. Zellner, "Is JetBlue's Flight Plan Flawed?" *Business Week Online* (February 16, 2003), www.businessweek.com/ @@/98GiyGUQXRKr3QcA/premium/content/04_07.

5. Morris, "What a Life."

6. G. Khermouch and C. Yang, "Richard Branson: Winning Virgin Territory," *Business Week Online* (December 22, 2003), www.businessweek.com/@@/u8MUxoUQXRKrQcA/ magazine/content/03_5.

7. Morris, "What a Life."

8. Ibid.

9. W. R. Nord, A. P. Brief, J. M. Atieh, and E. M. Doherty, "Work Values and the Conduct of Organizational Behavior." In B. M. Staw and L. L. Cummings (Eds.), *Research in Organizational Behavior*, vol. 10 (Greenwich, CT: JAI Press, 1988), 1–42.

10. M. Rokeach, *The Nature of Human Values* (New York: Free Press, 1973).

11. Ibid.

12. Nord, Brief, Atieh, and Doherty, "Work Values and the Conduct of Organizational Behavior"; A. Malka and J. A. Chatman, "Intrinsic and Extrinsic Work Orientations as Moderators of the Effect of Annual Income on Subjective Well-Being: A Longitudinal Study," *Society for Personality and Social Psychology, Inc.* 29 (6) (June 2003): 737–46.

13. T. L. Beauchamp and N. E. Bowie (Eds.), *Ethical Theory and Business* (Englewood Cliffs, NJ: Prentice-Hall, 1979).

14. Rokeach, *The Nature of Human Values*.

15. R. E. Goodin, "How to Determine Who Should Get What," *Ethics* (July 1975): 310–21.

16. M. York, "With More Layoffs at Kodak, Rochester's Corporate Identity Erodes," *New York Times*, January 25, 2004.

17. D. C. Johnston, "Kodak to Reduce Its Work Force by Up to 15,000," *New York Times* (January 23, 2004): C5.

18. T. M. Jones, "Ethical Decision Making by Individuals in Organizations: An Issue Contingent Model," *Academy of Management Journal* 16 (1991): 366–95; G. F. Cavanaugh, D. J. Moberg, and M. Velasquez, "The Ethics of Organizational Politics," *Academy of Management Journal* 6 (1981): 363–74.

19. Ibid.

20. L. K. Trevino, "Ethical Decision Making in Organizations: A Person–Situation Interactionist Model," *Academy of Management*
Review 11 (1986): 601–17; W. H. Shaw and V. Barry, *Moral Issues in Business*, 6th ed. (Belmont, CA: Wadsworth, 1995).

21. Jones, "Ethical Decision Making by Individuals in Organizations."

22. M. S. Frankel, "Professional Codes: Why, How, and with What Impact?" *Ethics* 8 (1999): 109–15; J. Van Maanen and S. R. Barley, "Occupational Communities: Culture and Control in Organizations" In B. Staw and L. Cummings (Eds.), *Research in Organizational Behavior*, vol. 6 (Greenwich, CT: JAI Press, 1984): 287–365; D. Denby, "The Lies of the Party," *Fortune* (January 26, 2004): 99–108; M. France, "White-Collar Crime: Heiress in Handcuffs," *Business Week* (November 24, 2003): 32–40; R. Lowenstein, "The Rigases Tried Desperately to Maintain Control of Their Cable Company Adelphia," *The New York Times Magazine* (February 1, 2004): 27–42, 62.

23. A. S. Watermann, "On the Uses of Psychological Theory and Research in the Process of Ethical Inquiry," *Psychological Bulletin* 103 (3), (1988): 283–98; R. B. Schmitt, "Companies Add Ethics Training: Will It Work?" *Wall Street Journal*, November 4, 2002, pp. B1–B3.

24. Frankel, "Professional Codes"; Van Maanen and Barley, "Occupational Communities"; Denby, "The Lies of the Party"; France, "White-Collar Crime"; Lowenstein, "The Rigases Tried Desperately to Maintain Control of Their Cable Company Adelphia"; G. Colvin, "Get Ready: It's Going to Be a Trying Year," *Fortune* (February 10, 2004), www.furtune.com/fortune/subs/columnist/ 0,15704,575738,00.html.

25. Watermann, "On the Uses of Psychological Theory and Research in the Process of Ethical Inquiry"; Schmitt, "Companies Add Ethics Training."

26. S. N. Mehta, "ENRON 'Employees Are the Best Line of Defense,' " *Fortune* (October 14, 2003), www.fortune.com/fortune/subs/ print/0,15935,518339,00.html.

27. "2 Entries for Whistleblower" (February 9, 2004), http://dictionary.reference.com; M. P. Miceli and J. P. Near, "Whistleblowing: Reaping the Benefits," *Academy of Management Review* 8 (3), (1994): 65–72.

28. Watermann, "On the Uses of Psychological Theory and Research in the Process of Ethical Inquiry"; Schmitt, "Companies Add Ethics Training."

29. Ibid.

30. Ibid.

31. "Sarbanes-Oxley Act of 2002," *CPE Online* (February 7, 2004), www.cpeonline.com/cpenew/sarox.asp.

32. Ibid.

33. Ibid.

34. Watermann, "On the Uses of Psychological Theory and Research in the Process of Ethical Inquiry"; Schmitt, "Companies Add Ethics Training."

35. "National Whistleblower Center: About the Center" (February 9, 2004), www.whistleblowers.org/html/ about_the_whistle-blow.htm; S. M. Kohn, "National Whistleblower Center: Corporate Whistleblowers" (February 9, 2004), www.whistleblowers.org/html/corporate_whistleb lowers.htm.

36. M. Fishbein and I. Ajzen, "Attitudes and Opinions," *Annual Review of Psychology* 23 (1972): 487–544.

37. D. Watson and A. Tellegen, "Toward a Consensual Structure of Mood," *Psychological Bulletin* 98 (1985): 219–35.

38. D. Watson, *Mood and Temperament* (New York: Guilford Press, 2000).

39. Ibid.

40. J. M. George and A. P. Brief, "Feeling Good–Doing Good: A Conceptual Analysis of the Mood at Work–Organizational Spontaneity Relationship," *Psychological Bulletin* 112 (1992): 310–29.

41. J. M. George, "Trait and State Affect." In K. R. Murphy (Ed.), *Individual Differences and Behavior in Organizations* (San Francisco: Jossey-Bass, 1996), 145–74; J. Zhow and J. M. George, "Awakening Employee Creativity: The Role of Leader Emotional Intelligence," *The Leadership Quarterly* 14 (2003): 545–68.

42. J. M. George, "Mood and Absence," *Journal of Applied Psychology* 74 (1987): 317–24; J. M. George, "State or Trait: Effects of Positive Mood on Prosocial Behaviors at Work," *Journal of Applied Psychology* 76 (1991): 299–307.

43. George, "State or Trait."

44. J. M. George and K. Bettenhausen, "Understanding Prosocial Behavior, Sales Performance, and Turnover: A Group Level Analysis in a Service Context," *Journal of Applied Psychology* 75 (1990): 698–709.

45. A. M. Isen and R. A. Baron, "Positive Affect as a Factor in Organizational Behavior." In B. M. Staw and L. L. Cummings (Eds.), *Research in Organizational Behavior*, vol. 13 (Greenwich, CT: JAI Press, 1991), 1–53; J. P. Forgas (Ed.), *Feeling and Thinking: The Role of Affect in Social Cognition* (Cambridge, UK: Cambridge University Press, 2000); J. P. Forgas, "Mood and Judgment: The Affect Infusion Model," *Psychological Bulletin* 117 (1995): 39–66; A. M. Isen, "Positive Affect and Decision Making." In M. Lewis and J. M. Haviland-Jones (Eds.), *Handbook of Emotions*, 2nd ed. (New York: Guilford Press, 2000), 417–35; R. C. Sinclair, "Mood, Categorization Breadth, and Performance Appraisal: The Effects of Order of Information Acquisition and Affective State on Halo, Accuracy, Informational Retrieval, and Evaluations," *Organizational Behavior and Human Decision Processes* 42 (1988): 22–46.

46. L. L. Martin and A. Tesser (Eds.), *Striving and Feeling: Interactions Among Goals, Affect, and Self-Regulation* (Mahwah, NJ: Erlbaum, 1996).

47. A. M. Isen, K. A. Daubman, and G. P. Nowicki, "Positive Affect Facilitates Creative Problem Solving," *Journal of Personality and Social Psychology* 52 (1987): 1122–31; A. M. Isen, M. M. S. Johnson, E. Mertz, and G. R. Robinson, "The Influence of Positive Affect on the Unusualness of Word Associations," *Journal of Personality and Social Psychology* 48 (1985): 1413–26.

48. J. M. George and J. Zhou, "Understanding When Bad Moods Foster Creativity and Good Ones Don't: The Role of Context and Clarity of Feelings," Manuscript submitted for publication; G. Kaufmann and S. K. Vosburg, "Paradoxical' Mood Effects on Creative Problem-Solving," *Cognition and Emotion* 11 (1997): 151–70; L. L. Martin and P. Stoner, "Mood as Input: What We Think About How We Feel Determines How We Think." In L. L. Martin and A. Tesser (Eds.), *Striving and Feeling: Interactions Among Goals, Affects and Self-Regulation* (Mahwah, NJ: Erlbaum), 279–302.

49. Martin and Stoner, "Mood as Input."

50. J. P. Forgas, "Affect in Social Judgements and Decisions: A Multi-Process Model." In M. Lanna (Ed.), *Advances in Experimental and Social Psychology* vol. 25, (San Diego, CA: Academic Press, 1992): 227–75; J. P. Forgas and J. M. George, "Affective Influences on Judgements and Behavior in Organizations" "An Information Processing Perspective,"

Organizational Behavior and Human Decision Processes 86 (2001): 3–34; J. M. George, "Leadership and Emotions: The Role of Emotional Intelligence," *Human Relations* 52 (2000): 1027–55; W. N. Norris, *Mood: The Frame of Mind* (New York: Springer-Verlag, 1989).

51. J. M. George, "Affect Regulation in Groups and Teams." In R. G. Lord, R. J. Klimoski, and R. Kanfer, (Eds.), *Emotions in the Workplace: Understanding the Structure and Role of Emotions in Organizational Behavior* (San Francisco, CA: Jossey-Bass, 2002); A. R. Hochschild, "Ideology and Emotion Management: A Perspective and Path for Future Research." In T. D. Kemper, (Ed.), *Research Agendas in the Sociology of Emotions* (Albany: University of New York Press, 1990): 117–42; J. M. Diefendorff and R. H. Gosserand, "Understanding the Emotional Labor Process: A Control Theory Perspective," *Journal of Organizational Behavior* 24 (2003): 945–59.

52. J. M. Diefendorff and E. M. Richard, "Antecedents and Consequences of Emotional Display Rule Perceptions," *Journal of Applied Psychology* 88 (2), (2003): 284–94.

53. T. D. Kemper, "Social Models in the Explanation of Emotions." In M. Lewis and J. M. Haviland-Jones, (Eds.), *Handbook of Emotions*, 2nd ed. (New York: Guilford Press, 2000): 45–58.

54. Ibid.

55. D. R. Middleton, "Emotional Style: The Cultural Ordering of Emotions," *Ethos* 17 (2), (1989): 187–201; A. R. Hochschild, "Ideology and Emotion Management."

56. J. A. Morris and D. C. Feldman, "The Dimensions, Antecedents, and Consequences of Emotional Labor," *Academy of Management Review* 21 (4), (1996): 986–1010.

57. T. Matthews, "The Inn at Little Washington," *Wine Spectator Online* (September 30, 2001), www.winespectator.com/Wine/Archives/Show_Article/0,1275,3363,00.html; J. Lustig, "Virginia: A Dream Dinner at the Inn at Little Washington," *NewYorkmetro.com* (March 26, 2001), www.newyorkmetro.com/travel/guides/52weekends/locations/Virginia.htm.

58. T. Raz, "A Recipe for Perfection," *Inc.* (July, 2003): 36–38.

59. Ibid.

60. Ibid.

61. Ibid.

62. J. A. Fuller, J. M. Stanton, G. G. Fisher, C. Spitzmüller, S. S Russell, and P. C. Smith, "A Lengthy Look at the Daily Grind: Time Series Analysis of Events, Mood, Stress, and Satisfaction," *Journal of Applied Psychology* 88 (6), (2003): 1019–33; C. J. Thoresen, S. A. Kaplan, A. P. Barsky, C. R. Warren, and K. de Chermont, "The Affective Underpinnings of Job Perceptions and Attitudes: A Meta-Analytic Review and Integration," *Psychological Bulletin* 129 (6), (2003): 914–25.

63. G. R. Jones and J. M. George, "The Experience and Evolution of Trust: Implications for Cooperation and Teamwork," *Academy of Management Review* 23 (1998): 531–46.

64. R. Axelrod, *The Evolution of Cooperation* (New York: Basic Books, 1984); P. Bateson, "The Biological Evolution of Cooperation and Trust." In D. Gambetta (Ed.), *Trust: Making and Breaking Cooperative Relations* (New York: Basil Blackwell, 1988), 14–30; L. G. Zucker, "Institutional Theories of Organization," *Annual Review of Sociology* 13 (1997): 443–64.

65. R. Galfor and A. S. Drapeau, "The Enemies of Trust," *Harvard Business Review* (February 2003): 89–95.

66. G. Korentz, "Hate Your Job? Join the Club," *Business Week* (October 6, 2003): 40.

67. Ibid.

68. Ibid.

69. J. M. George, "The Role of Personality in Organizational Life: Issues and Evidence," *Journal of Management* 18 (1992): 185–213; P. T. van den Berg and J. A. Feij, "Complex Relationships Among Personality Traits, Job Characteristics, and Work Behavior," *International Journal of Selection and Assessment*, 11 (4), (December 2003): 326–40; R. Ilies and T. A. Judge, "On the Heritability of Job Satisfaction: The Mediating Role of Personality," *Journal of Applied Psychology* 88 (4), (2003): 750–59; T. A. Judge, A. Erez, J. E. Bono, and C. J. Thoresen, "The Core Self-Evaluation Scale: Development of a Measure," *Personnel Psychology* 56 (2003): 303–31.

70. J. M. George, "Time Structure and Purpose as Mediator of Work-Life Linkages," *Journal of Applied Social Psychology* 21 (1991): 296–314.

71. R. D. Arvey, T. J. Bouchard, N. L. Segal, and L. M. Abraham, "Job Satisfaction: Environmental and Genetic Components," *Journal of Applied Psychology* 74 (1989): 187–92.

72. A. P. Brief, *Attitudes In and Around Organizations* (Thousand Oaks, CA: Sage, 1998).

73. "Mothers Want Flexibility Most," *Houston Chronicle* (September 23, 2003): 3B.

74. Ibid.

75. Ibid.

76. T. DeAngelis, "The 'Who Am I' Question Wears a Cloak of Culture," *APA Monitor* (October 1992): 22–23.

77. Ibid.

78. S. Shellenberger, "More Job Seekers Put Family Needs First," *Wall Street Journal*, November 15, 1991, pp. B1, B6.

79. "100 Best Companies to Work for 2004," *Fortune* (February 10, 2004), www.fortune.com/fortune/bestcompanies.

80. "Biotech Firm Offers Remedy for Parents," *Houston Chronicle*, June 13, 2000, p. 10C.

81. R. W. Rice, K. Markus, R. P. Moyer, and D. B. McFarlin, "Facet Importance and Job Satisfaction: Two Experimental Tests of Locke's Range of Affect Hypothesis," *Journal of Applied Social Psychology* 21 (1991): 1977–87.

82. D. Milbank, "More Business Graduates Snap Up Jobs in Rust Belt That Promise Them Clout," *Wall Street Journal*, July 21, 1992, pp. B1, B6.

83. Ibid.

84. F. Herzberg, *Work and the Nature of Man* (Cleveland: World, 1966).

85. N. King, "Clarification and Evaluation of the Two-Factor Theory of Job Satisfaction," *Psychological Bulletin* 74 (1970): 18–31; E. A. Locke, "The Nature and Causes of Job Satisfaction." In M. Dunnette (Ed.), *Handbook of Industrial and Organizational Psychology* (Chicago: Rand McNally, 1976), 1297–349.

86. D. B. McFarlin and R. W. Rice, "The Role of Facet Importance as a Moderator in Job Satisfaction Processes," *Journal of Organizational Behavior* 13 (1992): 41–54; R. A. Katzell, "Personal Values, Job Satisfaction, and Job Behavior." In H. Borow (Ed.), *Man in a World of Work* (Boston: Houghton Mifflin, 1964).

87. T. Lee, "What Kind of Job Are You Likely to Find?" *National Business Employment Weekly* (Spring 1992): 5–6.

88. McFarlin and Rice, "The Role of Facet Importance as a Moderator in Job Satisfaction Processes."

89. F. J. Landy, "An Opponent Process Theory of Job Satisfaction," *Journal of Applied Psychology* 63 (1978): 533–47.

90. B. M. Staw and J. Ross, "Stability in the Midst of Change: A Dispositional Approach to Job Satisfaction," *Journal of Applied Psychology* 71 (1985): 469–80.

91. R. W. Griffin, "Effects of Work Redesign on Employee Perceptions, Attitudes, and Behaviors: A Long-Term Investigation," *Academy of Management Journal* 34 (1991): 425–35.

92. D. J. Weiss, R. V. Dawis, G. W. England, and L. H. Lofquist, *Manual for the Minnesota Satisfaction Questionnaire, Minnesota Studies in Vocational Rehabilitation*, vol. 22, Industrial Relations Center, University of Minnesota, 1967.

93. R. B. Dunham and J. B. Herman, "Development of a Female Faces Scale for Measuring Job Satisfaction," *Journal of Applied Psychology* 60 (1975): 629–31; T. Kunin, "The Construction of a New Type of Attitude Measure," *Personnel Psychology* 8 (1955): 65–78.

94. P. C. Smith, L. M. Kendall, and C. L. Hulin, *The Measurement of Satisfaction in Work and Retirement* (Chicago: Rand McNally, 1969).

95. M. T. Iaffaldano and P. M. Muchinsky, "Job Satisfaction and Performance: A Meta-Analysis," *Psychological Bulletin* 97 (1985): 251–73.

96. T. A. Judge, C. J. Thoresen, J. E. Bono, and G. K. Patton, "The Job Satisfaction–Job Performance Relationship: A Qualitative and Quantitative Review," 127 (2001): *Psychological Bulletin* 376–407.

97. D. R. Dalton and D. J. Mesch, "On the Extent and Reduction of Avoidable Absenteeism: An Assessment of Absence Policy Provisions," *Journal of Applied Psychology* 76 (1991): 810–17; D. R. Dalton and C. A. Enz, "Absenteeism in Remission: Planning, Policy, and Culture," *Human Resource Planning* 10 (1987): 81–91; D. R. Dalton and C. A. Enz, "New Directions in the Management of Employee Absenteeism: Attention to Policy and Culture." In R. S. Schuler and S. A. Youngblood (Eds.), *Readings in Personnel and Human Resource Management* (St. Paul: West, 1988), 356–66; "Expensive Absenteeism," *Wall Street Journal*, July 7, 1986, p. 1.

98. G. E. Hardy, D. Woods, and T. D. Wall, "The Impact of Psychological Distress on Absence from Work," *Journal of Applied Psychology* 88 (2), (2003): 306–14.

99. R. M. Steers and S. R. Rhodes, "Major Influences of Employee Attendance: A Process Model," *Journal of Applied Psychology* 63 (1978): 391–407.

100. George, "Mood and Absence."

101. W. H. Mobley, "Intermediate Linkages in the Relationship Between Job Satisfaction and Employee Turnover," *Journal of Applied Psychology* 62 (1977): 237–40.

102. George and Brief, "Feeling Good–Doing Good"; D. W. Organ, *Organizational Citizenship Behavior: The Good Soldier Syndrome* (Lexington, MA: Lexington Books, 1988).

103. George and Brief, "Feeling Good–Doing Good."

104. Organ, *Organizational Citizenship Behavior*.

105. "Finding Motivation in the Little Things," *Wall Street Journal*, November 2, 1992, p. B1.

106. "We Caught You Doing Something Right," *Texas A&M University Human Resources Newsletter*, October 1992, p. 6.

107. N. Schmitt and A. G. Bedeian, "A Comparison of LISREL and Two–Stage Least Squares Analysis of a Hypothesized Job Satisfaction–Life Satisfaction Reciprocal Relationship," *Journal of Applied Psychology* 67 (1982): 806–17.

108. A. Cortese, "Bored to Death at Work—Literally," *Business Week* (July 1, 2002): 16.

109. N. J. Allen and J. P. Meyer, "Affective, Continuance, and Normative Commitment to the Organization: An Examination of Construct Validity," *Journal of Vocational Behavior* 49 (1996): 252–76.

110. Ibid.

111. S. Alexander, "Life's Just a Bowl of Cherry Garcia for Ben & Jerry's," *Wall Street Journal*, July 15, 1992, p. B3.

112. Allen and Meyer, "Affective, Continuance, and Normative Commitment to the Organization"; J. E. Mathieu and D. M. Zajac, "A Review and Meta–Analysis of the Antecedents, Correlates, and Consequences of Organizational Commitment," *Psychological Bulletin* 108 (1990): 171–94.

113. R. Cropanzano, D. E. Rupp, and Z. S. Byrne, "The Relationship of Emotional Exhaustion to Work Attitudes, Job Performance, and Organizational Citizenship Behaviors," *Journal of Applied Psychology* 88 (1), (2003): 160–69.

114. Allen and Meyer, "Affective, Continuance, and Normative Commitment to the Organization"; Mathieu Zajac, "A Review and Meta–Analysis of the Antecedents, Correlates, and Consequences of Organizational Commitment."

115. Ibid.

Chapter 4

1. "Hotel to Pay $8 Million in Settlement," March 22, 2000, *Houston Chronicle*, March 22, 2000, p. 3A.

2. M. France and T. Smart, "The Ugly Talk on the Texaco Tape," *Business Week* (November 18, 1996): 58; J. S. Lublin, "Texaco Case Causes a Stir in Boardrooms," *Wall Street Journal*, November 22, 1996, pp. B1, B6; T. Smart, "Texaco: Lessons from a Crisis-In-Progress," *Business Week* (December 2, 1996): 44.

3. "Ford, Settling Bias Case, Will Hire More Women, Minorities," *Houston Chronicle*, February 19, 2000, p. 8C.

4. C. Salter, "A Reformer Who Means Business," *Fast Company* (April 2003): 102–11.

5. Ibid.

6. C. Daniels, "GM Tried: How to Love a Bad Report Card," *Fortune* (July 10, 2000): 189.

7. Salter, "A Reformer Who Means Business."

8. Ibid.

9. H. R. Schiffmann, *Sensation and Perception: An Integrated Approach* (New York: Wiley, 1990).

10. W. B. Swann, Jr., J. T. Polzer, D. C. Seyle, and S. J. Ko, "Finding Value in Diversity: Verification of Personal and Social Self-Views in Diverse Groups," *Academy of Management Review* 29 (1), (2004): 9–27.

11. S. T. Fiske and S. E. Taylor, *Social Cognition* (Reading, MA: Addison-Wesley, 1984).

12. J. S. Bruner, "Going Beyond the Information Given." In H. Gruber, G. Terrell, and M. Wertheimer (Eds.), *Contemporary Approaches to Cognition* (Cambridge, MA: Harvard University Press, 1957); Fiske and Taylor, *Social Cognition*; G. R. Jones, R. Kosnik, and J. M. George, "Internalization and the Firm's Growth Path: On the Psychology of Organizational Contracting." In R. W. Woodman and W. A. Pasmore (Eds.), *Research in Organizational Change and Development* (Greenwich, CT: JAI Press, 1993): 105–35.

13. Fiske and Taylor, *Social Cognition*.

14. A. B. Fisher, "When Will Women Get to the Top?" *Fortune* (September 21, 1992): 44–56; S. Hamm, "Why Women Are So Invisible," *Business Week* (August 25, 1997): 136.

15. D. J. Schneider, "Social Cognition," *Annual Review of Psychology* 42 (1991): 527–61.

16. Fiske and Taylor, *Social Cognition*.

17. K. D. Elsbach, "How to Pitch a Brilliant Idea," *Harvard Business Review* (September 2003): 117–123.

18. R. King, "If Looks Could Kill," *Business* 2.0 (December 2001): 24–26.

19. J. Simons, "Living in America," *Fortune* 7 (January 2002): 92–94.

20. M. Conlin, "Taking Precautions—Or Harassing Workers?" *Business Week* 3 (December 2001): 84.

21. A. Salkever, "The INS Hurts Uncle Sam Most of All: By Detaining Hundreds of the Foreign Muslims It Lured into West Coast Offices, the Agency Succeeded Only Harming U.S. Security," *Business Week Online* (January 23, 2003).

22. D. C. McClelland and J. W. Atkinson, "The Projective Expression of Needs: The Effect of Different Intensities of the Hunger Drive on Perception," *Journal of Psychology* 25 (1948): 205–22.

23. C. J. Thoresen, S. A. Kaplan, A. P. Barsky, and K. de Chermont, "The Affective Underpinnings of Job Perception and Attitudes: A Meta-Analytic Review and Integration," *Psychological Bulletin* 129 (6): 914–45.

24. J. M. George and A. P. Brief, "Feeling Good–Doing Good: A Conceptual Analysis of the Mood at Work–Organizational Spontaneity Relationship," *Psychological Bulletin* 112 (1992): 310–29; A. M. Isen and R. A. Baron, "Positive Affect as a Factor in Organizational Behavior." In B. M. Staw and L. L. Cummings (Eds.), *Research in Organizational Behavior* 13 (Greenwich, CT: JAI Press, 1991), 1–54.

25. J. Merritt, "Wanted: A Campus That Looks Like America," *Business Week* 11 (March 2002): 56–58.

26. M. R. Leery and R. M. Kowalski, "Impression Management: A Literature Review and Two-Component Model," *Psychological Bulletin* 107 (1990): 34–47.

27. Ibid.

28. C. N. Alexander Jr. and G. W. Knight, "Situated Identities and Social Psychological Experimentation," *Sociometry* 34 (1971): 65–82; Fiske and Taylor, *Social Cognition*; K. J. Gergen and M. G. Taylor, "Social Expectancy and Self-Presentation in a Status Hierarchy," *Journal of Experimental Social Psychology* 5 (1969): 79–92.

29. C. Stephenson, "Business Etiquette's More Than Minding Peas, Queues," *The Bryan-College Station Eagle*, February 8, 1993, pp. A1, A3.

30. Leery and Kowalski, "Impression Management."

31. Fiske and Taylor, *Social Cognition*.

32. Fiske and Taylor, *Social Cognition*; R. M. Kanter, *Men and Women of the Corporation* (New York: Basic Books, 1977).

33. P. R. Sackett, C. M. Hardison, and M. J. Cullen, "On Interpreting Stereotype Threat as Accounting for African American–White Differences on Cognitive Tests," *American Psychologist* 59 (1), (January 2004): 7–13; P. R. Sackett, C. M. Hardison, and M. J. Cullen, "On the Value of Correcting Mischaracterizations of Stereotype Threat Research," *American Psychologist* 59 (1), (1995): 47–48.

34. C. M. Steele and J. A. Aronson, "Stereotype Threat Does Not Live by Steele and Aronson (1995) Alone," *American Psychologist* 59 (1), (January 2004): 47–48; J. Aronson, M. Lustina, C. Good, K. Keough, C. M. Steele, and J. Brown, "When White Men Can't Do Math: Necessary and Sufficient Factors in Stereotype Threat," *Journal of Experimental Social*

Psychology 35 (1999): 29–46; Sackett, Hardison, and Cullen, "On Interpreting Stereotype Threat as Accounting for African American–White Differences on Cognitive Tests"; C.M. Steele and J. Aronson, "Stereotype Threat and the Intellectual Test Performance of African Americans," *Journal of Personality and Social Psychology* 69 (1995): 797–811.

35. Sackett, Hardison, and Cullen, "On Interpreting Stereotype Threat as Accounting for African American–White Differences on Cognitive Tests"; Sackett, Hardison, and Cullen, "On the Value of Correcting Mischaracterizations of Stereotype Threat Research."

36. Steele and Aronson, "Stereotype Threat Does Not Live by Steele and Aronson (1995) Alone"; Aronson, Lustina, Good, Keough, Steele, and Brown, "When White Men Can't Do Math"; Sackett, Hardison, and Cullen, "On Interpreting Stereotype Threat as Accounting for African American–White Differences on Cognitive Tests"; Steele and Aronson, "Stereotype Threat and the Intellectual Test Performance of African Americans."

37. S. H. Mehta, "America's 50 Best Companies for Minorities: What Minority Employees Really Want," *Fortune* (July 10, 2000): 181–86.

38. Ibid.

39. Ibid.

40. M. Conlin, "The New Workforce," *Business Week* (March 20, 2000): 64–68.

41. J. Williams, "A Kind Act Indeed," *Business Week* (March 20, 2000): 74.

42. E. Bonabeau, "Don't Trust Your Gut," *Harvard Business Review* (May 2003): 116–23.

43. S. A. Fisicaro, "A Reexamination of the Relation Between Halo Errors and Accuracy," *Journal of Applied Psychology* 73 (1988): 239–44.

44. E. D. Pulakos and K. N. Wexley, "The Relationship Among Perceptual Similarity, Sex, and Performance Ratings in manager–Subordinate Dyads," *Academy of Management Journal* 26 (1983): 129–39.

45. A. B. Fisher, "When Will Women Get to the Top?"; L. Himelstein and S.A. Forest, "Breaking Through," *Business Week* (February 17, 1997): 4–70; S. Hamm, "Why Women Are So Invisible."

46. E. S. Browning, "Computer Chip Project Brings Rivals Together, but Cultures Clash," *Wall Street Journal*, May 3, 1994, pp. A1, A8.

47. R. K. Merton, *Social Theory and Social Structure* (New York: Free Press, 1957).

48. R. Rosenthal and L. F. Jacobson, *Pygmalion in the Classroom* (New York: Holt, Rinehart and Winston, 1968).

49. C. O. Wood, M. P. Zanna, and J. Cooper, "The Nonverbal Mediation of Self-Fulfilling Prophecies in Interracial Interaction," *Journal of Experimental Social Psychology* 10 (1974): 109–20.

50. R. Galford and A. Seibold Drapeau, "The Enemies of Trust," *Harvard Business Review* (February 2003): 889–95.

51. F. Heider, *The Psychology of Interpersonal Relations* (New York: Wiley, 1958); L. Ross, "The Intuitive Psychologist and His Shortcomings: Distortions in the Attribution Process." In L. Berkowitz (Ed.), *Advances in Experimental Social Psychology* 10 (New York: Academic Press, 1977).

52. E. E. Jones and R. E. Nisbett, "The Actor and the Observer: Divergent Perceptions of the Causes of Behavior." In E. E. Jones, D. E. Kanouse, H. H. Kelley et al. (Eds.), *Attribution:*

Perceiving the Causes of Behavior (Morristown, NJ: General Learning Press, 1972).

53. J.A. Knight and R. R.Vallacher, "Interpersonal Engagement in Social Perception: The Consequence of Getting into the Action," *Journal of Personality and Social Psychology* 40 (1981): 990–99; M. Zuckerman, "Attribution of Success and Failure Revisited, or: The Motivational Bias Is Alive and Well in Attribution Theory," *Journal of Personality* 47 (1979): 245–87.

54. D.T. Miller and M. Ross, "Self-Serving Biases in Attribution of Causality: Fact or Fiction?" *Psychological Bulletin* 82 (1975): 213–25.

55. Fiske and Taylor, *Social Cognition.*

56. J. M. Burger, "Motivational Biases in the Attribution of Responsibility for an Accident: A Meta-Analysis of the Defensive-Attribution Hypothesis," *Psychological Bulletin* 90 (1981): 496–512; Fiske and Taylor, *Social Cognition.*

57. J.A. Hall and S. E. Taylor, "When Love Is Blind: Maintaining Idealized Images of One's Spouse," *Human Relations* 29 (1976): 751–61.

58. E. R. Robinson and J. Hickman, "The Diversity Elite," *Fortune* (July 19, 1999): 62–70; C.Y. Chen and J. Hickman, "America's 50 Best Companies for Minorities," *Fortune* (July 10, 2000): 190–200; J. Hickman, "America's 50 Best Companies for Minorites," *Fortune* (July 8, 2002): 110–20.

59. Hickman, "America's 50 Best Companies for Minorites."

60. Robinson and Hickman, "The Diversity Elite"; Chen and Hickman, "America's 50 Best Companies for Minorities."

61. J. Dreyfuss, "Valley of Denial," *Fortune* (July 19, 1999): 60–61.

62. E. Robinson, "Father Figure at the Front Door," *Fortune* (July 19, 1999): 66.

63. K. Hynes, "PwC's Toni Riccardi: Her Seat at the Table Makes Others Accountable," *DiveristyInc* (March/April 2003) 65–70.

64. Ibid.

65. Y. Cole, "Corporate Recruitment Matters: How to Attract Top Candidates of Color," *DiversityInc* (November/December 2002): 53–56.

66. Y. Cole, "The Diversity Director: An Evolving Position with a Hand in All Business Aspects," *DiversityInc* (March/April 2003): 72.

67. Hynes, "PwC's Toni Riccardi."

68. S. Gelston, "The '90s Work Force Faces Diverse Challenges," *Boston Herald*, January 25, 1994, p. N18.

69. M. Lee, "Diversity Training Brings Unity to Small Companies," *Wall Street Journal*, September 2, 1993, p. B2.

70. Y. Cole, "Learning from the Winners," *DiversityInc* (November/December 2002): 12–27.

71. E. L. Hinton, "When Words Go Too Far: How to Handle Offensive Talk at the Office," *DiversityInc* (November/December 2002): 58–59.

72. Hinton, "When Words Go Too Far."

73. Rutkowski and Associates, *Employment Law Update* (September 1991): 1–12.

74. E. Klee, L. Hayes, and G. W. Childress, "A Kentucky Response to the ADA," *Training & Development* (April 1994): 48–49.

75. "Racial Differences Discourage Mentors," *Wall Street Journal*, October 29, 1991, p. B1.

76. C. Comeau-Kirschner, "Navigating the Roadblocks," *Management Review* 88 (5) (May 1999): 8.

77. D. Leonhardt, "The Saga of Maytag's Lloyd Ward," *Business Week* (August 9, 1999): Business Week Archives.

78. D. Foust, "Will Coke Go Better with Carl Ware?" *Business Week* (January 24, 2000): Business Week Archives.

79. A. T. Palmer, M. McBride, D. Rocks, and L. Woellert, "Poverty in America: Finally There's Some Good News," *Business Week* (October 18, 1999): Business Week Archives.

80. "A Mentor for the Asking: Bernadette Williams Wants to Provide Minority Women with Experienced Guides to the Tech Biz," *Business Week* (December 6, 1999): Business Week Archives.

81. S. Wellington, M. Brumit Kropf, and P. R. Gerkovich, "What's Holding Women Back?" *Harvard Business Review* (June 2003): 18–19.

82. Y. Cole, "The Truth About Mentoring, Especially Between Races: Supportive Relationships Add Real Value," *DiversityInc* (November/December 2002): 44–46.

83. Y. Cole, "Learning from the Winners," *DiversityInc* (November/December 2002): 12–27.

84. S. M. Shafer, "Sexual Harassment Exists at All Levels, Army Says," *The Bryan-College Station Eagle*, September 12, 1997, p. A4.

85. "Chevron Settles Claims of 4 Women at Unit as Part of Sex Bias Suit," *Wall Street Journal*, January 22, 1995, p. B12; J. Muller, "Ford: The High Cost of Harassment," *Business Week* (November 15, 1999): 94–96.

86. R. L. Paetzold and A. M. O'Leary-Kelly, "Organizational Communication and the Legal Dimensions of Hostile Work Environment Sexual Harassment." In G. L. Kreps (Ed.), *Sexual Harassment: Communication Implications* (Cresskill, NJ: Hampton Press, 1993).

87. A. M. O'Leary-Kelly, R. L. Paetzold, and R. W. Griffin, "Sexual Harassment as Aggressive Action: A Framework for Understanding Sexual Harassment," paper presented at the annual meeting of the Academy of Management, Vancouver, August 1995.

88. "Chevron Settles Claims of 4 Women at Unit as Part of Sex Bias Suit."

89. J. Muller, "Ford: The High Cost of Harassment," *Business Week* (November 15, 1999): 94–96.

90. S. Olafson, "Dow Fires Workers for E-Mail Abuse," *Houston Chronicle*, August 22, 2000, p. 13A; A. Carrns, "Bawdy E-Mails Were Funny Till Times' Parent Fired 22," *Houston Chronicle*, February 6, 2000, p. 3D.; M. Conlin, "Workers, Surf at Your Own Risk," *Business Week* (June 12, 2000): 105–6.

91. "What Productivity Revolution?" *Business Week* (June 12, 2000): 106.

92. R. Ilies, N. Hauserman, S. Schwochau, and J. Stibal, "Reported Incidence Rates of Work-Related Sexual Harassment in the United States: Using Meta-Analysis to Explain Reported Rate Disparities," *Personnel Psychology* 56 (2003): 607–31.

93. T. M. Glomb, L. J. Munson, C. L. Hulin, M. E. Bergman, and F. Drasgow, "Structural Equation Models of Sexual Harassment: Longitudinal Explorations and Cross-Sectional Generalizations," *Journal of Applied Psychology* 84 (1999): 14–28.

94. K. T. Schneider, S. Swan, and L. F. Fitzgerald, "Job-Related and Psychological Effects of Sexual Harassment in the Workplace: Empirical Evidence from Two Organizations," *Journal of Applied Psychology* 82 (1997): 401–15.

95. T. M. Glomb, W. L. Richman, C. L. Hulin et al. "Ambient Sexual Harassment: An Integrated Model of Antecedents and Consequences," *Organizational Behavior and Human Decision Processes* 71 (September 1997): 309–28.

96. E. Jensen and J. Lippman, "NBC's Problem: Gifted Executive Who Drank," *Wall Street Journal*, December 13, 1996, pp. B1, B19.

97. S. J. Bresler and R. Thacker, "Four-Point Plan Helps Solve Harassment Problems," *HR Magazine* (May 1993): 117–24.

98. "Du Pont's Solution," *Training* (March 1992): 29; Jensen and Lippman, "NBC's Problem"; J. S. Lublin, "Sexual Harassment Moves up Agenda in Many Executive Education Programs," *Wall Street Journal*, December 2, 1991, pp. B1, B4; "Navy Is Teaching Sailors What Proper Conduct Is," *The Bryan-College Station Eagle*, April 19, 1993, p. A2.

99. "Training New Workers to Avoid Sexual Harassment Is a Summer Priority," *Wall Street Journal*, June 29, 1999, p. A1.

100. Ibid.

Chapter 5

1. G. Anders, "The Innovator's Solution," *Fast Company* (June 2002): 132–38; R. Barker, "Seagate: Is the Tide Still Rising?" *Business Week Online* (July 28, 2003); S. Hamm, "Reversals of Fortune: How Dozens of Companies Managed to Pull Off Impressive Recoveries in the Midst of Tech's Deepest, Longest Slump." *Business Week Online* (June 23, 2003).

2. Anders, "The Innovator's Solution."

3. Ibid.

4. Ibid.

5. Ibid.

6. Barker, "Seagate."

7. Ibid.

8. W. C. Hamner, "Reinforcement Theory and Contingency Management in Organizational Settings." In H. Tosi and W. C. Hamner (Eds.), *Organizational Behavior and Management: A Contingency Approach* (Chicago: St. Clair Press, 1974).

9. B. F. Skinner, *Contingencies of Reinforcement* (New York: Appleton-Century-Crofts, 1969).

10. F. Luthans and R. Kreitner, *Organizational Behavior Modification and Beyond* (Glenview, IL: Scott, Foresman, 1985).

11. J. L. Komaki, "Applied Behavior Analysis and Organizational Behavior: Reciprocal Influence of the Two Fields." In B. M. Staw and L. L. Cummings (Eds.), *Research in Organizational Behavior*, vol. 8 (Greenwich, CT: JAI Press, 1986), 297–334.

12. H. M. Weiss, "Learning Theory and Industrial and Organizational Psychology." In M. D. Dunnette and L. M. Hough (Eds.), *Handbook of Industrial and Organizational Psychology,* 2nd ed., vol. 1 (Palo Alto, CA: Consulting Psychologists Press, 1990), 171–221.

13. S. Overman, "When It Comes to Managing Diversity, a Few Companies Are Linking Pay to Performance," *HRMagazine* (December 1992): 38–40.

14. J. D. Shaw, M. K. Duffy, A. Mitra, D. E. Lockhart, and M. Bowler, "Reactions to Merit Pay Increases: A Longitudinal Test of Signal Sensitivity Perspective," *Journal of Applied Psychology* 88(3), (2003): 538–44.

15. Weiss, "Learning Theory and Industrial and Organizational Psychology."

16. "Working at Lincoln," (December 15, 2003), www.lincolnelectric.com/corporate/career/default.asp; "About Lincoln," (December 15, 2003), www.lincolnelectric.com/corporate/about/about.asp; "Our History—A Century of Excellence, A Future of Innovation," (December 15, 2003), www.lincolnelectric.com/corporate/about/history.asp; "Lincoln Electric Vision and Missions," (December 15, 2003), www.lincolnelectric.com/corporate/about/visions.asp.

17. J. P. Houston, *Fundamentals of Learning and Memory*, 3rd ed. (New York: Harcourt Brace Jovanovich, 1986); Weiss,

"Learning Theory and Industrial and Organizational Psychology."

18. R. D. Arvey and J. M. Ivancevich, "Punishment in Organizations: A Review, Propositions, and Research Suggestions," *Academy of Management Review* 5 (1980): 123–32.

19. A. D. Stajkovic and F. Luthans, "Behavioral Management and Task Performance in Organizations: Conceptual Background, Meta-Analysis, and Test of Alternative Models," *Personnel Psychology* 56 (2003): 155–94.

20. Luthans and Kreitner, *Organizational Behavior Modification and Beyond*; F. Luthans and A. D. Stajkovic, "Reinforce for Performance: The Need to Go Beyond Pay and Even Rewards," *Academy of Management Executive* 13(2), (1999): 49–56.

21. Luthans and Stajkovic, "Reinforce for Performance."

22. Stajkovic and Luthans, "Behavioral Management and Task Performance in Organizations"; Luthans and Stajkovic, "Reinforce for Performance"; G. Billikopf Encina and M. V. Norton, "Pay Method Affects Vineyard Pruner Performance"; www.cnr.berkeley.edu/ucce50/ag-labor/7research/7calag05.htm.

23. A. D. Stajkovic and F. Luthans, "A Meta-Analysis of the Effects of Organizational Behavior Modification on Task Performance, 1975–95," *Academy of Management Journal* 40(5), (1997): 1122–49.

24. A. D. Stajkovic and F. Luthans, "Differential Effects of Incentive Motivators on Work Performance," *Academy of Management Journal* 4(3), (2001): 580–90.

25. Ibid.

26. "In California Garment: Workers Have Rights," (October 2002), www.dir.ca.gov, www.workitout.ca.gov.

27. A. Bandura, *Social Learning Theory* (Upper Saddle River, NJ: Prentice Hall, 1977); A. Bandura, *Self-Efficacy: The Exercise of Control* (New York: W. H. Freeman and Co., 1997).

28. Ibid.

29. Bandura, *Social Learning Theory*; T. R. V. Davis and F. Luthans, "A Social Learning Approach to Organizational Behavior." In Luthans and Kreitner, *Organizational Behavior Modification and Beyond*.

30. "Fact Sheet," The Ritz-Carlton (July 28, 2003) www.ritzcarlton.com/corporate/about_us/fact_sheet.asp.

31. In T. Gutner, "Dividends," *Business Week Online* (July 28, 2003).

32. "Gold Standards," The Ritz-Carlton (July 28, 2003) www.ritz-arlton.com/corporate/about_us/fact_sheet.asp.

33. Ibid.

34. P. Hemp, "My Week as a Room-Service Waiter at the Ritz," *Harvard Business Review* (June 2002): 50–62.

35. Ibid.

36. "Fact Sheet."

37. J. Zhou, "When the Presence of Creative Coworkers Is Related to Creativity: Role of Supervisor Close Monitoring, Developmental Feedback, and Creative Personality," *Journal of Applied Psychology* 88(3), (2003): 413–22.

38. A. P. Goldstein and M. Sorcher, *Changing Supervisor Behavior* (New York: Pergamon Press, 1974); Luthans and Kreitner, *Organizational Behavior Modification and Beyond*.

39. A. Bandura, "Self-Reinforcement: Theoretical and Methodological Considerations," *Behaviorism* 4 (1976): 135–55.

40. M. Moravec, K. Wheeler, and B. Hall, "Getting College Hires on Track Fast," *Personnel* (May 1989): 56–59.

41. T. J. Maurer, E. M. Weiss, and F. G Barbeite, "A Model of Involvement in Work-Related Learning and Development Activity: The Effects of Individual, Situational, Motivational and Age Variables," *Journal of Applied Psychology* 88(4), (2003): 707–24.

42. M. E. Gist and T. R. Mitchell, "Self-Efficacy: A Theoretical Analysis of Its Determinants and Malleability," *Academy of Management Review* 17 (1992): 183–211.

43. A. Bandura, "Self-Efficacy Mechanism in Human Agency," *American Psychologist* 37 (1982): 122–47.

44. A. Bandura and E. A. Locke, "Negative Self-Efficacy and Goal Effects Revisited," *Journal of Applied Psychology* 88(1), (2003): 87–89.

45. Bandura, "Self-Efficacy Mechanism in Human Agency."

46. D. Eden and A. B. Shani, "Pygmalion Goes to Boot Camp: Expectancy, Leadership, and Trainee Performance," *Journal of Applied Psychology* 67 (1982): 194–99.

47. Bandura, "Self-Efficacy Mechanism in Human Agency."

48. C. Rogers, "Experimental Learning," http://tip.psychology.org/rovers.html (June 26, 2003); M. K. Smith, "David A. Kolb on Experiential Learning," www.infed.org/biblio/b-explrn.htm (June 26, 2003).

49. Anders, "The Innovator's Solution."

50. T. M. Amabile, "A Model of Creativity and Innovation in Organizations." In B. M. Staw and L. L. Cummings, *Research in Organizational Behavior*, vol. 10 (Greenwich, CT: JAI Press, 1988), 123–67.

51. Ibid.

52. Ibid.

53. J. L. Adams, *Conceptual Blockbusting: A Guide to Better Ideas*, 4th ed. (Cambridge, MA: Perseus Publishing, 2001).

54. N. Watson, "What's Wrong with This Printer?" *Fortune* (February 17 2003): 120C–120H.

55. Ibid.

56. Ibid.

57. Ibid.

58. Ibid.; L. Armstrong, "Printers You Can Tote," *Business Week Online* (July 30, 2003); T. J. Mullaney, "Commentary: Why the Tech Rally Is No Freak Performance," *Business Week Online* (July 30, 2003); B. Elgin, "Can HP's Printer Biz Keep Printing Money?" *Business Week Online* (July 30, 2003).

59. F. B. Barron and D. M. Harrington, "Creativity, Intelligence, and Personality," *Annual Review of Psychology* 32 (1981): 439–76; R. W. Woodman, J. E. Sawyer, and R. W. Griffin, "Toward a Theory of Organizational Creativity," *Academy of Management Review* 18 (1993): 293–321.

60. R. W. Woodman and L. F. Schoenfeldt, "Individual Differences in Creativity: An Interactionist Perspective." In J. A. Glover, R. R. Ronning, and C. R. Reynolds (Eds.), *Handbook of Creativity* (New York: Plenum Press, 1989), 77–92.

61. Ibid.

62. Barron and Harrington, "Creativity, Intelligence, and Personality."

63. Amabile, "A Model of Creativity and Innovation in Organizations."

64. Ibid.; Woodman, Sawyer, and Griffin, "Toward a Theory of Organizational Creativity."

65. Amabile, "A Model of Creativity and Innovation in Organizations."

66. Ibid.

67. Ibid.

68. Ibid.

69. Ibid.

70. J. M. George and J. Zhou, "When Openness to Experience and Conscientiousness Are Related to Creative Behavior: An Interactional Approach," *Journal of Applied Psychology* 86(3), (2001): 513–24.

71. J. Zhou and J. M. George, "Awakening Employee Creativity: The Role of Leader Emotional Intelligence," *The Leadership Quarterly* (July 24, 2003).

72. P. Senge, *The Fifth Discipline: The Art and Practice of the Learning Organization* (New York: Doubleday, 1990).

73. J. Goldenberg, R. Horowitz, A. Levav, and D. Mazursky, "Finding Your Innovation Sweet Spot," *Harvard Business Review* (March 2003): 120–29.

74. Senge, *The Fifth Discipline: The Art and Practice of the Learning Organization*.

75. M. J. Grawitch, D. C. Munz, E. K. Elliott, and A. Mathis, "Promoting Creativity in Temporary Problem-Solving Groups: The Effects of Positive Mood and Autonomy in Problem Definition on Idea-Generating Performance," *Group Dynamics: Theory, Research, and Practice* 7(3), (2003): 200–13; M. J. Grawitch, D. C. Munz, and T. J. Kramer, "Effects of Member Mood States on Creative Performance in Temporary Workgroups," *Group Dynamics: Theory, Research, and Practice* 7(1), (2003): 41–54.

76. S. E. Prokesch, "Unleashing the Power of Learning: An Interview with British Petroleum's John Browne," *Harvard Business Review* (September–October 1997): 148.

77. J. S. Brown and P. Duguid, "Balancing Act: How to Capture Knowledge Without Killing It," *Harvard Business Review* (May–June 2000): 73–80.

78. Ibid.

79. Ibid.

Chapter 6

1. J. Goodnight, "Welcome to SAS" (August 26, 2003): www.sas.com/corporate/index.html.

2. "SAS Continues Annual Revenue Growth Streak" (August 28, 2003): www.sas.com/news/prelease/031003/news1.html.

3. "Worklife" (August 26, 2003): www.sas.com/corporate/worklife/index.html.

4. "Saluting the Global Awards Recipients of Arthur Andersen's Best Practices Awards 2000" (September 6, 2000): www.fortune.com.

5. J. Pfeffer, "SAS Institute: A Different Approach to Incentives and People Management Practices in the Software Industry" (January 1998): Harvard Business School Case HR-6.

6. Ibid.

7. "Worklife" (August 26, 2003): www.sas.com/corporate/worklife/index.html.

8. Pfeffer, "SAS Institute"; N. Stein, "Winning the War to Keep Top Talent" (September 6, 2000): www.fortune.com.

9. Goodnight, "Welcome to SAS"; "By Solution" (August 26, 2003): www.sas.com/success/solution.html.

10. G. P. Latham, and M. H. Budworth, "The Study of Work Motivation in the 20th Century." In L. Koppes (Eds.), *The History of Industrial and Organizational Psychology* (Hillsdale, NJ: Laurence Erlbaum Associates Inc., in press).

11. F. J. Landy and W. S. Becker, "Motivation Theory Reconsidered." In B. M. Staw and L. L. Cummings (Eds.), *Research in Organizational Behavior*, vol. 9 (Greenwich, CT: JAI Press, 1987), 1–38.

12. J. P. Campbell and R. D. Pritchard, "Motivation Theory in Industrial and Organizational Psychology." In M. D. Dunnette (Ed.), *Handbook of Industrial and Organizational Psychology* (Chicago: Rand McNally, 1976), 63–130.

13. R. Kanfer, "Motivation Theory and Industrial and Organizational Psychology." In M. D. Dunnette and L. M. Hough (Eds.), *Handbook of Industrial and Organizational Psychology*, vol. 1 (Palo Alto, CA: Consulting Psychologists Press, 1990), 75–170.

14. Kanfer, "Motivation Theory and Industrial and Organizational Psychology."

15. A. K. Kirk and D. F. Brown, "Latent Constructs of Proximal and Distal Motivation Predicting Performance Under Maximum Test Conditions," *Journal of Applied Psychology* 88 (1), (2003): 40–49.

16. A. P. Brief and R. J. Aldag, "The Intrinsic-Extrinsic Dichotomy: Toward Conceptual Clarity," *Academy of Management Review* 2 (1977): 496–99.

17. M. Conlin and P. Raeburn, "Industrial Evolution," *Business Week* (April 8, 2002): 70–2.

18. Ibid.

19. "DuPont Donates 16,000 Acres to the Conservation Fund, Georgia Tract Borders Okefenokee National Wildlife Refuge" (August 30, 2003): www1.dupont.com/NASApp/dupont-global/corp/index.jsp?page=/c. . ./nr8_27_03a.htm.

20. M. Gunther, "Tree Huggers, Soy Lovers, and Profits," *Fortune* (June 23, 2003): 98–104.

21. Ibid.

22. Brief and Aldag, "The Intrinsic-Extrinsic Dichotomy."

23. N. Nicholson, "How to Motivate Your Problem People," *Harvard Business Review* (January 2003): 57–65.

24. A. H. Maslow, *Motivation and Personality* (New York: Harper & Row, 1954); C. P. Alderfer, *Existence, Relatedness, and Growth: Human Needs in Organizational Settings* (New York: Free Press, 1972).

25. V. H. Vroom, *Work and Motivation* (New York: Wiley, 1964).

26. Ibid.

27. J. S. Adams, "Toward an Understanding of Inequity," *Journal of Abnormal and Social Psychology*, 67: 422–436.

28. Maslow, *Motivation and Personality*; Campbell and Pritchard, "Motivation Theory in Industrial and Organizational Psychology,"

29. V. Anderson, "Kudos for Creativity," *Personnel Journal* (September 1991): 90–93.

30. Maslow, *Motivation and Personality*; Campbell and Pritchard, "Motivation Theory in Industrial and Organizational Psychology."

31. C. P. Alderfer, "An Empirical Test of a New Theory of Human Needs," *Organizational Behavior and Human Performance* 4 (1969): 142–75; Alderfer, *Existence, Relatedness, and Growth*; Campbell and Pritchard, "Motivation Theory and Industrial and Organizational Psychology."

32. Kanfer, "Motivation Theory and Industrial and Organizational Psychology."

33. Vroom, *Work and Motivation*.

34. Ibid.

35. Ibid.

36. Campbell and Pritchard, "Motivation Theory in Industrial and Organizational Psychology"; T. R. Mitchell, "Expectancy-Value Models in Organizational Psychology." In N. T. Feather (Ed.), *Expectations and Actions: Expectancy-Value Models in Psychology* (Hillsdale, NJ: Erlbaum, 1982), 293–312.

37. T. J. Maurer, E. M. Weiss, and F. B. Barbeite, "A Model of Involvement in Work-Related Learning and Development Activity: The Effects of Individual, Situational, Motivational, and Age Variables," *Journal of Applied Psychology* 88 (4), (2003): 707–24.

38. N. Shope Griffin, "Personalize Your Management Development," *Harvard Business Review* (March 2003): 113–19.

39. P. A. Galagan, "Training Keeps the Cutting Edge Sharp for the Andersen Companies," *Training & Development* (January 1993): 30–35.

40. M. J. Stahl and A. M. Harrell, "Modeling Effort Decisions with Behavioral Decision Theory: Toward an Individual Differences Model of Expectancy Theory," *Organizational Behavior and Human Performance* 27 (1981): 303–25.

41. Campbell and Pritchard, "Motivation Theory in Industrial and Organizational Psychology"; Kanfer, "Motivational Theory and Industrial and Organizational Psychology."

42. M. Arndt, "Wilbur Ross: Pulling LTV Out of the Scrap Heap," *Business Week Online* (February 3, 2003): www.businessweek.com.

43. M. Arndt, "Up from the Scrap Heap," *Business Week Online* (July 21, 2003): www.businessweek.com.

44. N. D. Schwartz, "Bent but Unbowed," *Fortune* (July 22, 2002): 118–26.

45. Arndt, "Wilbur Ross."

46. Schwartz, "Bent but Unbowed."

47. Arndt, "Wilbur Ross."

48. Arndt, "Up from the Scrap Heap."

49. Adams, "Toward an Understanding of Inequity."

50. Ibid.

51. Ibid.

52. Ibid.

53. R. Cropanzano, B. Goldman, and R. Folger, "Deontic Justice: The Role of Moral Principles in Workplace Fairness," *Journal of Organizational Behavior* 24 (2003): 1019–24.

54. J. Greenberg, "Approaching Equity and Avoiding Inequity in Groups and Organizations." In J. Greenberg and R. L. Cohen (Eds.), *Equity and Justice in Social Behavior* (New York: Academic Press, 1982), 389–435; J. Greenberg, "Equity and Workplace Status: A Field Experiment," *Journal of Applied Psychology* 73 (1988): 606–13; R. T. Mowday, "Equity Theory Predictions of Behavior in Organizations." In R. M. Steers and L. W. Porter (Eds.), *Motivation and Work Behavior* (New York: McGraw-Hill, 1987), 89–110.

55. L. J. Skitka and F. J. Crosby, "Trends in the Social Psychological Study of Justice," *Personality and Social Psychology Review* 7 (4), (2003): 282–85.

56. Y. R. Chen, J. Brockner, and J. Greenberg, "When Is It "A Pleasure to Do Business with You?" The Effects of Relative Status, Outcome Favorability, and Procedural Fairness," *Organizational Behavior and Human Decision Processes* 92 (2003): 1–21.

57. R. Folger and M. A. Konovsky, "Effects of Procedural and Distributive Justice on Reactions to Pay Raise Decisions," *Academy of Management Journal* 32 (1989): 115–30; J. Greenberg, "Organizational Justice: Yesterday, Today, and Tomorrow," *Journal of Management* 16 (1990): 399–432.

58. E. E. Umphress, G. Labianca, D. J. Brass, E. Kass, and L. Scholten, "The Role of Instrumental and Expressive Social Ties in Employees' Perceptions of Organizational Justice," *Organization Science* 14 (6), (November–December 2003): 738–53.

59. M. L. Ambrose and M. Schminke, "Organization Structure as a Moderator of the Relationship Between Procedural Justice, Interactional Justice, Perceived Organizational Support, and Supervisory Trust," *Journal of Applied Psychology* 88 (2), (2003): 295–305.

60. Greenberg, "Organizational Justice: Yesterday, Today, and Tomorrow."

61. Ibid.; T. R. Tyler, "What Is Procedural Justice?" *Law and Society Review* 22 (1988): 301–35; J. M. Jackman and M. H. Strober, "Fear of Feedback," *Harvard Business Review* (April 2003): 101–06.

62. Greenberg, "Organizational Justice: Yesterday, Today, and Tomorrow"; E. A. Lind and T. Tyler, *The Social Psychology of Procedural Justice* (New York: Plenum, 1988).

63. R. J. Bies, "The Predicament of Injustice: The Management of Moral Outrage." In L. L. Cummings and B. M. Staw (Eds.), *Research in Organizational Behavior*, vol. 9 (Greenwich, CT: JAI Press, 1987), 289–319; R. J. Bies and D. L. Shapiro, "Interactional Fairness Judgments: The Influence of Causal Accounts," *Social Justice Research* 1 (1987): 199–218; J. Greenberg, "Looking Fair vs. Being Fair: Managing Impressions of Organizational Justice." In B. M. Staw and L. L. Cummings (Eds.), *Research in Organizational Behavior*, vol. 12 (Greenwich, CT: JAI Press, 1990), 111–57; T. R. Tyler and R. J. Bies, "Beyond Formal Procedures: The Interpersonal Context of Procedural Justice. " In J. Carroll (Ed.), *Advances in Applied Social Psychology: Business Settings* (Hillsdale, NJ: Erlbaum, 1989), 77–98.

64. J. Greenberg, "Reactions to Procedural Injustice in Payment Distributions: Do the Means Justify the Ends?" *Journal of Applied Psychology* 72 (1987): 55–61.

Chapter 7

1. "About Hydro" (September 5, 2003): www.hydro.com.

2. C. Fishman, "The Way to Enough: Norsk Hydro's Work-Life Experiments Test a Radical Idea: A Company Can Compete on the Basis of Balance," *Fast Company* (July/August 1999): 160–74; A. Sains, "Is Norway's Oil Patch at Last Open to Outsiders?" *Business Week (Online)*, June 14, 1999; A. Sains, "What Happened to Norway's Gusher," *Business Week (Online)*, November 16, 1998; www.hydro.com/en/about/index.html.

3. "Social Responsibility" (September 5, 2003): www.hydro.no/en/about/global_commitment/social_resp/index.html; E. Reiten, "Dear Shareholder" (September 5, 2003): www.hydro.no/en/investor_relations/financial_rep/2002_annual_report/share_letter.html.

4. "Sustainable Development Good for Environment—and Bottom Line" (September 5, 2003): www.americas.hydro.com; "Talking Environment with Suppliers" (September 5, 2003): www.hydro.no/en/about/ global_commitment/environment.

5. E. Bull-Hansen and T. Aasland, "Hydro on Dow Jones Sustainability Index for Fifth Year" (September 5, 2003): www.hydro.com/en/press_room/news/archive/2003_09/dowjones_sustainindex_en.html.

6. "Welcome to the Dow Jones Sustainability Indexes," *Dow Jones Sustainability Indexes* (September 5, 2003): www.sustainability-indexes.com; "Frequently Asked Questions," *Dow Jones Sustainability Indexes* (September 5, 2003):

www.sustainability-indexes.com; "Corporate Sustainability," *Dow Jones Sustainability Indexes* (September 5, 2003): www.sustainability-indexes.com.

7. Fishman, "The Way to Enough."

8. Ibid.

9. G. P. Latham and M. H. Budworth, "The Study of Work Motivation in the 20th Century." In L. Koppes (Eds.), *The History of Industrial and Organizational Psychology* (Hillsdale, NJ: Laurence Erlbaum Associates Inc., in press).

10. F. W. Taylor, *The Principles of Scientific Management* (New York: Harper and Brothers, 1911).

11. R. W. Griffin, *Task Design: An Integrative Approach* (Glenview, IL: Scott, Foresman, 1982).

12. A. C. Filley, R. J. House, and S. Kerr, *Managerial Process and Organizational Behavior* (Glenview, IL: Scott, Foresman, 1976); C. R. Walker, "The Problem of the Repetitive Job," *Harvard Business Review* 28 (1950): 54–58.

13. Griffin, *Task Design*.

14. P. Gogoi, "Thinking Outside the Cereal Box," *Business Week* (July 28, 2003): 74–75; "Hamburger Helper Announces 'Better Tasting' Product Line," *General Mills* (June 17, 2003): www.generalmills.com; "NASCAR Driver Bill Lester Featured on Honey Nut Cheerios Package," *General Mills* (July 16, 2003): www.generalmills.com.

15. Ibid.

16. Ibid.

17. Latham and Budworth, "The Study of Work Motivation in the 20th Century."

18. J. R. Hackman and G. R. Oldham, "Motivation Through the Design of Work: Test of a Theory," *Organizational Behavior and Human Performance* 16 (1976): 250–79; J. R. Hackman and G. R. Oldham, *Work Redesign* (Reading, MA: Addison-Wesley, 1980); A. N. Turner and P. R. Lawrence, *Industrial Jobs and the Worker* (Boston: Harvard School of Business, 1965).

19. Hackman and Oldham, "Motivation Through the Design of Work"; Hackman and Oldham, *Work Redesign*.

20. Hackman and Oldham, *Work Redesign*.

21. Ibid.

22. M. W. Brauchli, "When in Huangpu . . .," *Wall Street Journal*, December 10, 1993, p. R3.

23. Y. Fried and G. R. Ferris, "The Validity of the Job Characteristics Model: A Review and Meta-Analysis," *Personnel Psychology* 40 (1987): 287–322.

24. B. T. Loher, R. A. Noe, N. L. Moeller, and M. P. Fitzgerald, "A Meta-Analysis of the Relation of Job Characteristics to Job Satisfaction," *Journal of Applied Psychology* 70 (1985): 280–89.

25. G. R. Salancik and J. Pfeffer, "A Social Information Processing Approach to Job Attitudes and Task Design," *Administrative Science Quarterly* 23 (1978): 224–53.

26. S. Nolen, "Contingent Employment." In L. H. Peters, C. R. Greer, and S. A. Youngblood (Eds.), *The Blackwell Encyclopedic Dictionary of Human Resource Management* (Oxford: Blackwell Publishers, 1997): 59–60.

27. Ibid.

28. Ibid.

29. R. W. Griffin, "Objective and Social Sources of Information in Task Redesign: A Field Experiment," *Administrative Science Quarterly* 28 (1983): 184–200; J. Thomas and R. Griffin, "The Social Information Processing Model of Task Design: A Review of the Literature," *Academy of Management Review* 8 (1983): 672–82.

30. R. D. Hof, "Why Tech Will Bloom Again," *Business Week Online* (August 25, 2003): www.businessweek.com.

31. J. Kerstetter, "Still the Center of This World," *Business Week Online* (August 25, 2003): www.businessweek.com.

32. K. H. Hammonds, "Growth Search," *Fast Company* (April 2003): 74–81.

33. Ibid.

34. Ibid.

35. H. Tajfel and J. C. Turner, "The Social Identity Theory of Intergroup Behavior." In S. Worchel and W. G. Austin (Eds.), *Psychology of Intergroup Relations* (2nd ed.). (Chicago: Nelson-Hall, 1985), pp. 7–24.

36. B. E. Ashforth and F. Mael, "Social Identity Theory and the Organization," *Academy of Management Review* 14(20–39): 1989; Tajfel Turner, "The social Identity Theory of Intergroup Behavior."

37. M. E. Brown, "Identification and Some Conditions of Organizational Involvement," *Administrative Science Quarterly* 14 (1969): 346–55; Tajfel and Turner, "The Social Identity Theory of Intergroup Behavior"; Ashforth and Mael, "Social Identity Theory and the Organization."

38. K. H. Hammonds, "Growth Search," p. 76.

39. Latham and Budworth, "The Study of Work Motivation in the 20th Century."

40. E. A. Locke and G. P. Latham, *A Theory of Goal Setting and Task Performance* (Upper Saddle River, NJ: Prentice Hall, 1990).

41. J. J. Donovan and K. J. Williams, "Missing the Mark: Effects of Time and Causal Attributions on Goal Revision in Response to Goal-Performance Discrepancies," *Journal of Applied Psychology* 88 (3), (2003): 379–90.

42. N. Nicholson, "How to Motivate Your Problem People," *Harvard Business Review* 81 (1), (January 2003): 57–65.

43. Locke and Latham, *A Theory of Goal Setting and Task Performance*; M. E. Tubbs, "Goal Setting: A Meta-Analytic Examination of the Empirical Evidence," *Journal of Applied Psychology* 71 (1986): 474–83.

44. P. C. Earley, "Supervisors and Shop Stewards as Sources of Contextual Information in Goal Setting: A Comparison of the U.S. with England," *Journal of Applied Psychology* 71 (1986): 111–17; M. Erez and I. Zidon, "Effect of Goal Acceptance on the Relationship of Goal Difficulty to Performance," *Journal of Applied Psychology* 69 (1984): 69–78; G. P. Latham and H. A. Marshall, "The Effects of Self-Set, Participatively Set and Assigned Goals on the Performance of Government Employees," *Personnel Psychology* 35 (1982): 399–404; T. Matsui, T. Kakkuyama, and M. L. Onglatco, "Effects of Goals and Feedback on Performance in Groups," *Journal of Applied Psychology* 72 (1987): 407–15; B. J. Punnett, "Goal Setting: An Extension of the Research," *Journal of Applied Psychology* 71 (1986): 171–72.

45. A. Bandura and E. A. Locke, "Negative Self-Efficacy and Goal Effects Revisited," *Journal of Applied Psychology* 88 (1), (2003): 87–99.

46. F. K. Lee, K. M. Sheldon, and D. B. Turban, "Personality and the Goal-Striving Process: The Influence of Achievement Goal Patterns, Goal Level, and Mental Focus on Performance and Enjoyment," *Journal of Applied Psychology* 88 (2), (2003): 256–65.

47. P. J. Sauer, "Open-Door Management," *Inc.* (June, 2003): 44.

48. J. M. Jackman and M. H. Strober, "Fear of Feedback," *Harvard Business Review* (April 2003): 101–06.

49. E. A. Locke, K. N. Shaw, L. M. Saari, and G. P. Latham, "Goal Setting and Task Performance: 1969–1980," *Psychological Bulletin* 90 (1981): 125–52.

50. P. M. Wright, J. M. George, S. R. Farnsworth, and G. C. McMahan, "Productivity and Extra-Role Behavior: The Effects of Goals and Incentives on Spontaneous Helping," *Journal of Applied Psychology* 78 (1993): 374–81.

51. C. Terhune, "How Coke Officials Beefed Up Results of Marketing Test," *Wall Street Journal*, August 20, 2003, p. A1, A6.

52. S. Day, "Coke Executive to Leave His Job After Rigged Test at Burger King," *New York Times* (August 26, 2003), p. C1, C2.

53. C. Terhune, "How Coke Officials Beefed Up Results Of Marketing Test."

54. Ibid.

55. S. Day, "Coke Moves with Caution to Remain in Schools," *New York Times*, September 3, 2003, p. C1, C5.

56. P. C. Earley, T. Connolly, and G. Ekegren, "Goals, Strategy Development, and Task Performance: Some Limits on the Efficacy of Goal Setting," *Journal of Applied Psychology* 74 (1989): 24–33; R. Kanfer and P. L. Ackerman, "Motivation and Cognitive Abilities: An Integrative/Aptitude-Treatment Interaction Approach to Skill Acquisition," *Journal of Applied Psychology* 74 (1989): 657–90.

57. Kanfer and Ackerman, "Motivation and Cognitive Abilities."

58. J. Zhou, "When the Presence of Creative Coworkers Is Related to Creativity: Role of Supervisor Close Monitoring, Developmental Feedback, and Creative Personality," *Journal of Applied Psychology* 88 (3), (2003): 413–22.

59. H. Levinson, "Management by Whose Objectives?" *Harvard Business Review* (January 2003): 107–16.

60. S. J. Carroll and H. L. Tosi, *Management by Objectives: Applications and Research* (New York: Macmillan, 1973); P. F. Drucker, *The Practice of Management* (New York: Harper & Row, 1954); C. D. Fisher, L. F. Schoenfeldt, and J. B. Shaw, *Human Resource Management* (Boston: Houghton Mifflin, 1990); R. Rodgers and J. E. Hunter, "Impact of Management by Objectives on Organizational Productivity," *Journal of Applied Psychology* 76 (1991): 322–36.

61. Fisher, Schoenfeldt, and Shaw, *Human Resource Management*.

Chapter 8

1. "Overview," Briggs & Stratton, **www.briggsandstratton.com**.

2. M. Arndt, "How Briggs Is Revving the Engines," *Business Week* (May 5, 2003): 92.

3. "Briggs & Stratton Corporation Reports Improved Results for the Fourth Quarter and Twelve Months of Fiscal 2003," *Company News On Call* (September 9, 2003), **www.prnewswire.com**.

4. Arndt, "How Briggs Is Revving the Engines."

5. Ibid.

6. "Work @ Briggs & Stratton," **www.briggsandstratton.com**, (September 9, 2003).

7. "Frequently Asked Questions," **www.briggsandstratton.com**, (September 9, 2003).

8. B. Einhorn, "Move Over, India," *Business Week* (August 11, 2003): 42–43.

9. L. M. Shore and J. A-M. Coyle-Shapiro, "Editorial: New Developments in the Employee–Organization Relationship," *Journal of Organizational Behavior* 24 (John Wiley & Sons, Ltd. 2003): 443–50.

10. Ibid.

11. D. M. Rousseau and J. McLean Parks, "The Contracts of Individuals and Organizations," *Research in Organizational Behavior* 15 (JAI Press, Inc. 1993): 1–43; S. L. Robinson, "Trust and Breach of the Psychological Contract," *Administrative Science Quarterly* 41 (Cornell University, 1996): 547–99; S. L. Robinson et al., "Changing Obligations and the Psychological Contract: A Longitudinal Study," *Academy of Management Journal* 37 (1994): 137–152; I. R. MacNeil, "Relational Contract: What We Do and Do Not Know," *Wisconsin Law Review* (1985): 483–525.

12. L. Schurer Lambert, J. R. Edwards, and D. M. Cable, "Breach and Fulfillment of the Psychological Contract: A Comparison of Traditional and Expanded Views," *Personnel Psychology* 56 (2003): 895–934.

13. Rousseau and Parks, "The Contracts of Individuals and Organizations"; Robinson, "Trust and Breach of the Psychological Contract"; Robinson et al., "Changing Obligations and the Psychological Contract"; MacNeil, "Relational Contract."

14. Shore and Coyle-Shapiro, "Editorial."

15. J. Aselage and R. Eisenberger, "Perceived Organizational Support and Psychological Contracts: A Theoretical Integration," *Journal of Organizational Behavior* 24 (2003): 491–509; D. M. Rousseau, *Psychological Contracts in Organizations* (Thousand Oaks CA: Sage, 1995).

16. Ibid.

17. S. L. Premack and J. P. Wanous, "A Meta-Analysis of Realistic Job Preview Experiments," *Journal of Applied Psychology* 70 (1985): 706–19; J. P. Wanous, "Realistic Job Previews: Can a Procedure to Reduce Turnover Also Influence the Relationship Between Abilities and Performance?" *Personnel Psychology* 31 (1978): 249–58; J. P. Wanous, *Organizational Entry: Recruitment, Selection, and Socialization of Newcomers* (Reading, MA: Addison-Wesley, 1980).

18. Aselage and Eisenberger, "Perceived Organizational Support and Psychological Contracts"; Rousseau, *Psychological Contracts in Organizations.*

19. Ibid.

20. Rousseau and Parks, "The Contracts of Individuals and Organizations"; Robinson, "Trust and Breach of the Psychological Contract"; Robinson et al., "Changing Obligations and the Psychological Contract"; MacNeil, "Relational Contract."

21. R. Cropanzano, D. E. Rupp, and Z. S. Byrne, "The Relationship of Emotional Exhaustion to Work Attitudes, Job Performance, and Organizational Citizenship Behaviors," *Journal of Applied Psychology* 88 (1), (2003): 160–69.

22. Rousseau and Parks, "The Contracts of Individuals and Organizations"; Robinson, "Trust and Breach of the Psychological Contract"; Robinson et al., "Changing Obligations and the Psychological Contract"; MacNeil, "Relational Contract."

23. D. N. Sull, "Managing By Commitments," *Harvard Business Review* (June 2003): 82–91.

24. Rousseau and Parks, "The Contracts of Individuals and Organizations"; Robinson, "Trust and Breach of the Psychological Contract"; Robinson et al., "Changing Obligations and the Psychological Contract"; MacNeil, "Relational Contract."

25. M. Kripalani, "Calling Bangalore: Multinations Are Making It a Hub for High-Tech Research," *Business Week* (November 25, 2002): 52–53.

26. B. Stone, "Men at Overwork: The Good News Is We're More Productive. The Bad News? They Don't Need as Many of Us," *Newsweek* (August 11, 2003): 38–39.

27. S. Armour and M. Kessler, "USA's New Money-Saving Export: White-Collar Jobs," *USA Today* (August 5, 2003): 1B–2B.

28. Armour and Kessler, "USA's New Money-Saving Export."

29. "America's pain, India's gain," *The Economist* (January 11, 2003): 57.

30. M. Kripalani, "Calling Bangalore."

31. Armour and Kessler, "USA's New Money-Saving Export."

32. Ibid.

33. "Outsourcing Jobs: Is it Bad?" *Business Week* (August 25, 2003): 36–38; K. Madigan, "Yes . . ." *Business Week* (August 25, 2003): 36–38; M. J. Mandel, " . . . No" *Business Week* (August 25, 2003): 36–38.

34. Rousseau and Parks, "The Contracts of Individuals and Organizations"; Robinson, "Trust and Breach of the Psychological Contract"; Robinson et al., "Changing Obligations and the Psychological Contract"; MacNeil, "Relational Contract."

35. Ibid.

36. Ibid.

37. C. D. Fisher, L. F. Schoenfeldt, and J. B. Shaw, *Human Resource Management* (Boston: Houghton Mifflin, 1990).

38. J. M. Jackman and M. H. Strober, "Fear of Feedback," *Harvard Business Review* (April 2003): 101–06.

39. Fisher, Schoenfeldt, and Shaw, *Human Resource Management.*

40. Ibid.; G. P. Latham and K. N. Wexley, *Increasing Productivity Through Performance Appraisal* (Reading, MA: Addison-Wesley, 1982).

41. R. Henkoff, "Make Your Office More Productive," *Fortune* (February 25, 1991): 72–84.

42. R. S. Schuler, *Managing Human Resources* (New York: West, 1992).

43. T. A. DeCotiis, "An Analysis of the External Validity and Applied Relevance of Three Rating Formats," *Organizational Behavior and Human Performance* 19 (1977): 247–66; Fisher, Schoenfeldt, and Shaw, *Human Resource Management.*

44. Schuler, *Managing Human Resources.*

45. N. Nicholson, "How to Motivate Your Problem People," *Harvard Business Review* (January 2003): 56–65.

46. H. Lancaster, "Performance Reviews Are More Valuable When More Join In," *Wall Street Journal*, July 9, 1996, p. B1.

47. Ibid.

48. Ibid.; J. S. Lublin, "Turning the Tables: Underlings Evaluate Bosses," *Wall Street Journal*, October 4, 1994, p. B1; J. S. Lublin, "It's Shape-Up Time for Performance Reviews," *Wall Street Journal*, October 3, 1994, p. B1; S. Shellenbarger, "Reviews from Peers Instruct—and Sting," *Wall Street Journal*, October 4, 1994, pp. B1, B4.

49. Lublin, "Turning the Tables."

50. Shellenbarger, "Reviews From Peers Instruct—and Sting."

51. W. C. Borman and D. W. Bracken, "360 Degree Appraisals." In C. L. Cooper and C. Argyris (Eds.), *The Concise Blackwell Encyclopedia of Management* (Oxford, UK: Blackwell Publishers, 1998), 17; D. W. Bracken, "Straight Talk About Multi-Rater Feedback," *Training and Development* 48 (1994): 44–51; M. R. Edwards, W. C. Borman, and J. R. Sproul, "Solving the Double-Bind in Performance Appraisal: A Saga of Solves, Sloths, and Eagles," *Business Horizons* 85 (1985): 59–68.

52. "Problems With Your Boss?" ImproveNow.com (September 23, 2003), **www.improvenow.com.**

53. A. Harrington, "Workers of the World, Rate Your Boss!" *Fortune* (September 18, 2000): 340, 342.

54. Ibid.; J. Montgomery, "They Mean It When They Ask, 'Is Everything All Right Here?' " *Wall Street Journal*, February 6, 2000, p. 6D.

55. E. E. Lawler III, *Pay and Organization Development* (Reading, MA: Addison-Wesley, 1981).

56. J. D. Shaw, M. K. Duffy, A. Mitra, D. E. Lockhard, and M. Bowler, "Reactions to Merit Pay Increases: A Longtitudinal Test of a Signal Sensitivity Perspective," *Journal of Applied Psychology* 88 (3), (2003): 538–44.

57. A. Bennett, "Paying Workers to Meet Goals Spreads, but Gauging Performance Proves Tough," *Wall Street Journal* (September 10, 1991, pp. B1, B8.

58. M. Conlin, "Give Me That Old-Time Economy," *Business Week* (April 24, 2000): BusinessWeek.Online; G. Hardesty, "-Dot-compensation Makes Some Green," *Houston Chronicle*, May 21, 2000.

59. "Just Deserts," *The Economist* (January 29, 1994): 71.

60. Lawler, *Pay and Organization Development.*

61. Ibid.

62. J. F. Lincoln, *Incentive Management* (Cleveland: Lincoln Electric Company, 1951); R. Zager, "Managing Guaranteed Employment," *Harvard Business Review* 56 (1978): 103–15.

63. Lawler, *Pay and Organization Development.*

64. "Dofasco Reports $38.8 Million Second Quarter Net Income," Dofasco Inc. (September 9, 2003) **www.dofasco.ca/NEWS/ press_releases/Q2-03results.htm.**

65. C. Dahle, "A Steelmaker's Heart of Gold," *Fast Company* (June 2003): 46–48.

66. "Fifth Consecutive Year on Sustainability Index Only Canadian Market Sector Leader," Dofasco, Inc. (September 9, 2003) **www.dofasco.ca/NEWS/press_releases/sustainability2-003.htm.**

67. Dahle, "A Steelmaker's Heart of Gold."

68. Ibid.

69. "Media Information Kit," Dofasco, Inc. (September 9, 2003), **www.dofasco.ca.**

70. Dahle, "A Steelmaker's Heart of Gold."

71. P. Coy, "The Power of Smart Pricing," *Business Week Online* (September 9, 2003) **www.businessweek.com/ @@JrYQloQQdk@r3QcA/archives/2000/ b3676133.arc.htm.**

72. Fisher, Schoenfeldt, and Shaw, *Human Resource Management;* B. E. Graham-Moore and T. L. Ross, *Productivity Gainsharing* (Upper Saddle River, NJ: Prentice Hall, 1983); A. J. Geare, "Productivity from Scanlon Type Plans," *Academy of Management Review* 1 (1976): 99–108.

73. J. Labate, "Deal Those Workers In," *Fortune* (April 19, 1993): 26.

74. D. Duston, "Women Tend to Pay More in Marketplace, Author Claims," *Bryan–College Station Eagle*, May 18, 1993, p. A1; F. C. Whittelsey, *Why Women Pay More* (Washington, DC: Center for Responsive Law, 1993).

75. Fisher, Schoenfeldt, and Shaw, *Human Resource Management.*

76. D. J. Treiman and H. I. Hartmann, *Women, Work, and Wages: Equal Pay for Jobs of Equal Value* (Washington, DC: National Academy Press, 1981).

77. A. Borrus, "A Battle Royal Against Regal Paychecks," *Business Week* (February 24, 2003): 127.

78. M. Conlin, "Going Sideways on the Corporate Ladder," *Business Week* (September 30, 2002): 39.

79. J. Useem and E. Florian, "Have They No Shame?" *Fortune* (April 23, 2003): 57–64.

80. Borrus, "A Battle Royal Against Regal Paychecks."

81. Useem and Florian, "Have They No Shame?"

82. Conlin, "Going Sideways on the Corporate Ladder"; K. J. Dunham, and K. Maher, "Companies Cut Costs Where It Hurts: Employee Pay," *Wall Street Journal*, October 15, 2002, pp. B1, B8.

83. J. H. Greenhaus, *Career Management* (New York: Dryden Press, 1987).

84. A. Malka and J. A. Chatman, "Intrinsic and Extrinsic Work Orientations as Moderators of the Effect of Annual Income on Subjective Well-Being: A Longtiduinal Study," *Society for Personality and Social Psychology, Inc.* 29 (6), (June 2003): 737–46.

85. N. Shope Griffin, "Personalize Your Management Development," *Harvard Business Review* (March 2003): 113–19.

86. M. J. Driver, "Careers: A Review of Personal and Organizational Research." In C. L. Cooper and I. Robertson (eds.), *International Review of Industrial and Organizational Psychology* (New York: Wiley, 1988).

87. Ibid.

88. Ibid.

89. C. Hymowitz and G. Stern, "At Procter & Gamble, Brands Face Pressure and So Do Executives," *Wall Street Journal*, May 10, 1993, pp. A1, A8.

90. Driver, "Careers: A Review of Personal and Organizational Research."

91. Ibid.

92. Greenhaus, *Career Management.*

93. M. B. Arthur, "The Boundaryless Career: A New Perspective for Organizational Inquiry," *Journal of Organizational Behavior*, 15 (1994): 295–306; M. B. Arthur and D. M. Rousseau, *The Boundaryless Career: A New Employment Principle for a New Organizational Era* (New York: Oxford University Press, 1996a), 237–55; "Introduction: The Boundaryless Career as a New Employment Principle." In M. B. Arthur and D. M. Rousseau (Eds.) *The Boundaryless Career: A New Employment Principle for a New Organizational Era.* (New York: Oxford University Press, 1996b): 3–20; L. T. Eby et al., "Predictors of Success in the Era of the Boundaryless Career," *Journal of Organizational Behavior* 24 (2003): 689–708.

94. S. C. de Janasz, S. E. Sullivan, and V. Whiting, "Mentor Networks and Career Success: Lessons for Turbulent Times," *Academy of Management Executive* 17 (4), (2003): 78–91.

95. Greenhaus, *Career Management.*

96. J. L. Holland, *Making Vocational Choices: A Theory of Careers* (Upper Saddle River, NJ: Prentice Hall, 1973); M. B. Barrick, M. K. Mount, and R. Gupta, "Meta-Analysis of the Relationship Between the Five-Factor Model of Personality and Holland's Occupational Types," *Personnel Psychology* 56 (2003): 45–74.

97. J. Chamberlin, "Study Offers Clues on Why Women Choose Medicine over Engineering," *Monitor on Psychology* (September, 2003): 13.

98. Ibid.

99. Ibid.

100. J. P. Wanous, "Realistic Job Previews: Can a Procedure to Reduce Turnover Also Influence the Relationship Between Abilities and Performance?" *Personnel Psychology* (1978): 249–58; J. P. Wanous, *Organizational Entry: Recruitment, Selection and Socialization of Newcomers* (Reading, MA: Addison-Wesley, 1980).

101. Greenhaus, *Career Management.*

102. Ibid.

103. G. Dreher and R. Ash, "A Comparative Study of Mentoring Among Men and Women in Managerial, Professional, and Technical Positions," *Journal of Applied Psychology* 75 (1990): 525–35; T. A. Scandura, "Mentorship and Career Mobility: An Empirical Investigation," *Journal of Organizational Behavior* 13 (1992): 169–74; W. Whitely, T. W. Dougherty, and G. F. Dreher, "Relationship of Career Mentoring and Socioeconomic Origin to Managers' and Professionals' Early Career Success," *Academy of Management Journal* 34 (1991): 331–51.

104. D. B. Turban and T. W. Dougherty, "The Role of Protégé Personality in Receipt of Mentoring and Career Success," *Academy of Management Journal* 37 (1994): 688–702.

105. L. Clyde Jr., "Would You Make a Good Protégé?", *National Business Employment Weekly: Managing Your Career* (Spring–Summer 1993): 15–17.

106. Greenhaus, *Career Management.*

107. T. P. Ference, J. A. F. Stoner, and E. K. Warren, "Managing the Career Plateau," *Academy of Management Review* 2 (1977): 602–12.

108. B. T. Abdelnor and D. T. Hall, *Career Development of Established Employees* (New York: Center for Research in Career Development, Columbia University, 1981); J. M. Bardwick, "Plateauing and Productivity," *Sloan Management Review* 24 (1983): 67–73.

109. Abdelnor and Hall, *Career Development of Established Employees;* J. Sonnenfeld, "Dealing with the Aging Workforce," *Harvard Business Review* 56 (1978): 81–92.

110. Ference, Stoner, and Warren, "Managing the Career Plateau."

111. J. Fierman, "Beating the Midlife Career Crisis," *Fortune* (September 6, 1993): 52–62.

112. J. Pfeffer, "SAS Institute: A Different Approach to Incentives and People Management Practices in the Software Industry," *Harvard Business School Case* HR-6 (January 1998).

113. G. Graham, "Would You Lie for Your Boss or Would You Just Rather Not?" *Bryan–College Station Eagle*, October 24, 1993, p. C3.

114. L. S. Gottfredson, "Dilemmas in Developing Diversity Programs." In S. E. Jackson and Associates (Eds.), *Diversity in the Workplace: Human Resources Initiatives* (New York: Guilford Press, 1992).

115. Ibid.

Chapter 9

1. C. Daniels, "The Last Taboo," *Fortune*, October 28, 2002, pp. 135–44.

2. In E. LaFreniere (Ed.), "Attitudes in the American Workplace VII, The Seventh Annual Labor Day Survey," The Marlin Company by Harris Interactive, pp. 1–11.

3. C. Hymowitz, "Doing More with Less, Avoiding Shoddy Work and Burned-Out Staff," *In the Lead*, February 25, 2003, p. B1.

4. Ibid.

5. Ibid.

6. In E. LaFreniere (Ed.), "Attitudes in the American Workplace VII, The Seventh Annual Labor Day Survey."

7. Ibid.

8. Ibid.

9. Ibid.

10. Ibid.

11. "Bad Jobs Are a Problem Europe-wide," *hazards magazine*, October 22, 2003, **www.hazards.ord/workedtodeath/wordedtodeath3.htm**.

12. J. A. Fuller, J. M. Stanton, G. G. Fisher, C. Spitzmiller, and S. S. Russell, "A Lengthy Look at the Daily Grind: Time Series Analysis of Events, Mood, Stress, and Satisfaction," *Journal of Applied Psychology* 88 (6), (2003): 1019–33.

13. "Negative Feelings Afflict 40 Million Adults in U.S.," *Wall Street Journal*, November 26, 1993, p. B1.

14. R. S. Lazarus, *Psychological Stress and Coping Processes* (New York: McGraw-Hill, 1966); R. S. Lazarus and S. Folkman, *Stress, Appraisal, and Coping* (New York: Springer, 1984); R. S. Lazarus, "Psychological Stress in the Workplace," *Journal of Social Behavior and Personality* 6 (7) (1991): 1–13.

15. Lazarus and Folkman, *Stress, Appraisal, and Coping.*

16. J. Cole, "Fight Workplace Violence: Safeguard Yourself and Your Employees," *Fortune Small Business*, October 21, 2003, **www.fortune.com/fortune/print/0,15935,360655,00.html**; S. Gold and L. Hart, "Factory Worker Kills 5, Self in Plant Shooting," *Miami Herald*, July 9, 2003, p. 3A; D. M. Halbfinger, "Factory Killer Had a Known History of Anger and Racial Taunts," *New York Times*, July 10, 2003, NYTimes.com.

17. T. DeAngelis, "Psychologists Aid Victims of Violence in Post Office," *APA Monitor* (October 1993): 1, 44–45.

18. R. C. Clay, "Securing the Workplace: Are Our Fears Misplaced?" *Monitor on Psychology* (October 2000): 46–49; Washington Post, "Mail Workers Not More Inclined to 'Go Postal,' Workplace Report Says," *Houston Chronicle*, September, 1, 2000, p. 8A; T. DeAngelis, "Psychologists Aid Victims of Violence in Post Office."

19. "Workplace Violence: OSHA Fact Sheet," U. S. Department of Labor: Occupational Safety and Health Administration, 2002, **www.osha.gov**.

20. Ibid.

21. Clay, "Securing the Workplace: Are Our Fears Misplaced?"; Washington Post, "Mail Workers Not More Inclined to 'Go Postal,' Workplace Report Says."

22. Clay, "Securing the Workplace: Are Our Fears Misplaced?"

23. "Workplace Violence: OSHA Fact Sheet."

24. Ibid.

25. M. J. Burke, A. P. Brief, and J. M. George, "The Role of Negative Affectivity in Understanding Relations Between Self-Reports of Stressors and Strains: A Comment on the Applied Psychology Literature," *Journal of Applied Psychology* 78 (1993): 402–12; D. Watson and L. A. Clark, "Negative Affectivity: The Disposition to Experience Aversive Emotional States," *Psychological Bulletin* 96 (1984): 465–90.

26. H. Cooper, "Carpet Firm Sets Up an In-House School to Stay Competitive," *Wall Street Journal*, October 5, 1992, pp. A1, A5.

27. J. Seligmann, T. Namuth, and M. Miller, "Drowning on Dry Land," *Newsweek*, May 23, 1994, pp. 64–66.

28. D. Watson and J. W. Pennebaker, "Health Complaints, Stress, and Distress: Exploring the Central Role of Negative Affectivity," *Psychological Review* 96 (1989): 234–54.

29. Ibid.

30. D. Watson and A. Tellegen, "Toward a Consensual Structure of Mood," *Psychological Bulletin* 98 (1985): 219–35.

31. C. Maslach, *Burnout: The Cost of Caring* (Upper Saddle River, NJ: Prentice Hall, 1982).

32. R. T. Lee and B. E. Ashforth, "On the Meaning of Maslach's Three Dimensions of Burnout," *Journal of Applied Psychology* 75 (1990): 743–47.

33. Seligmann, Namuth, and Miller, "Drowning on Dry Land."

34. Ibid.

35. D. Jansen, "Winning: How the Olympian Quit Trying Too Hard—and Finally Won," *USA Weekend*, July 15–17, 1994, pp. - 4–5.

36. G. E. Hardy, D. Woods, and T. D. Wall, "The Impact of Psychological Distress on Absence from Work," *Journal of Applied Psychology* 88 (2), (2003): 306–14.

37. A. B. Fisher, "Welcome to the Age of Overwork," *Fortune*, November 30, 1992, pp. 64–71.

38. "Stress Busters: Employers Fight Anxiety as Staffs Shrink and Work Increases," *Wall Street Journal*, December 1, 1992, p. A1.

39. "A Nurse Shortage May Be Easing, but Stress Persists," *Wall Street Journal*, January 5, 1993, p. A1.

40. Y. Wijers-Hasegawa, "JPN Rise in Work-Related Suicides," IWW-news, May 10, 2003, **www.japantimes.co.jp/cgi-bin/getarticle.p15?nn20030510b3.htm**, B. Lafayette De Mente, "Asian Business Codewords," May 2002, **www.apmforum.com/columns/boye51.htm**.

41. A. Stevens, "Suit over Suicide Raises Issue: Do Associates Work Too Hard?" *Wall Street Journal*, April 15, 1994, pp. B1, B7.

42. "Japan Wakes Up to Fatal Work Ethic," *Japan Forum*, June 15, 2003, **http://forum.japanreference.com/showthread.php?s=&threadid=2886**.

43. Ibid.

44. J. Ryall, "Japan Wakes Up to Fatal Work Ethic," *Scotland on Sunday*, June 15, 2003, **www.scotlandonsunday.com/international.cfm?id=660412003**.

45. "Bad Jobs Are a Problem Europe-wide."

46. S. Shellenbarger, "Keeping Workers by Reaching Out to Them," *Wall Street Journal*, June 1, 1994, p. B1.

47. J. M. George and A. P. Brief, "Feeling Good—Doing Good: A Conceptual Analysis of the Mood at Work–Organizational Spontaneity Relationship," *Psychological Bulletin* 112 (1992): 310–29.

48. T. H. Holmes and M. Masuda, "Life Change and Illness Susceptibility." In B. S. Dohrenwend and B. P. Dohrenwend (Eds.), *Stressful Life Events: Their Nature and Effects* (New York: Wiley, 1974), 45–72; T. H. Holmes and R. H. Rahe, "Social Readjustment Rating Scale," *Journal of Psychosomatic Research* 11 (1967): 213–18.

49. R. S. Bhagat, S. J. McQuaid, H. Lindholm, and J. Segovis, "Total Life Stress: A Multimethod Validation of the Construct and Its Effect on Organizationally Valued Outcomes and Withdrawal Behaviors," *Journal of Applied Psychology* 70 (1985): 202–14; A. P. Brief, M. J. Burke, J. M. George, B. Robinson, and J. Webster, "Should Negative Affectivity Remain an Unmeasured Variable in the Study of Job Stress?", *Journal of Applied Psychology* 73 (1988): 193–98; B. S. Dohrenwend, L. Krasnoff, A. R. Askenasy, and B. P Dohrenwend, "Exemplification of a Method for Scaling Life Events: The PERI Life Events Scale," *Journal of Health and Social Behavior* 19 (1978): 205–29; J. H. Johnson and I. G. Sarason, "Recent Developments in Research on Life Stress." In V. Hamilton and D. M. Warburton (Eds.), *Human Stress and Cognition: An Information Processing Approach* (New York: Wiley, 1979), 205–36.

50. R. L. Kahn and P. Byosiere, "Stress in Organizations." In M. D. Dunnette and L. M. Hough (Eds.), *Handbook of Industrial and Organizational Psychology*, 2nd ed., vol. 3 (Palo Alto, CA: Consulting Psychologists Press, 1992), 571–650; S. Jackson and R. Schuler, "A Meta-Analysis and Conceptual Critique of Research on Role Ambiguity and Role Conflict in Work Settings," *Organizational Behavior and Human Decision Processes* 36 (1985): 16–78.

51. R. L. Kahn and P. Byosiere, "Stress in Organizations." In M. D. Dunnette and L. M. Hough (Eds.), *Handbook of Industrial and Organizational Psychology*, 2nd ed., vol. 3 (Palo Alto, CA: Consulting Psychologists Press, 1992), 571–650; S. Jackson and R. Schuler, "A Meta-Analysis and Conceptual Critique of Research on Role Ambiguity and Role Conflict in Work Settings," *Organizational Behavior and Human Decision Processes* 36 (1985): 16–78.

52. Kahn and Byosiere, "Stress in Organizations."

53. Fisher, "Welcome to the Age of Overwork."

54. J. A. Byrne, "The Pain of Downsizing," *Fortune*, May 9, 1994, pp. 60–68.

55. Fisher, "Welcome to the Age of Overwork."

56. L. W. Winik, "What You May Not Know About Workers in America Today," *Parade Magazine*, October 26, 2003, p. 10.

57. J. M. Brett and L. K. Stroh, "Working 61 Plus Hours a Week: Why Do Managers Do It?" *Journal of Applied Psychology* 88 (1), (2003): 67–78.

58. Fisher, "Welcome to the Age of Overwork."

59. Seligmann, Namuth, and Miller, "Drowning on Dry Land."

60. A. P. Brief and J. M. Atieh, "Studying Job Stress: Are We Making Mountains Out of Molehills?" *Journal of Occupational Behaviour* 8 (1987): 115–26.

61. Brief and Atieh, "Studying Job Stress"; R. L. Kahn, *Work and Health* (New York: Wiley, 1981); S. V. Kasl and S. Cobb, "Blood Pressure Changes in Men Undergoing Job Loss: A Preliminary Report," *Psychosomatic Medicine* 32 (1970): 19–38.

62. J. Brockner, "The Effects of Work Layoffs on Survivors: Research, Theory, and Practice." In B. M. Staw and L. L. Cummings (Eds.), *Research in Organizational Behavior* (Greenwich, CT: JAI Press, 1988).

63. J. Fierman, "Beating the Midlife Career Crisis," *Fortune*, September 6, 1993, pp. 52–62.

64. M. Davis, "Anadarko to Jettison 400 Jobs: Senior Managers Depart in Wave," *Houston Chronicle*, August 1, 2003, p. 1C.

65. L. A. Johnson, "Study: 1 in 5 Laid Off in Recent Recession," *Houston Chronicle*, July 28, 2003, p. 9A.

66. Ibid.

67. B. Rose, "Part-Time Work, Full-Time Worries," *Houston Chronicle*, April 7, 2003, p. 10D.

68. Ibid.

69. Ibid.

70. Ibid.

71. Brief and Atieh, "Studying Job Stress"; L. Levi, "Psychological and Physiological Reaction to and Psychomotor Performance During Prolonged and Complex Stressor Exposure," *Acta Medica Scandinavica*, 191 Supplement no. 528, (1972): 119; M. Timio and S. Gentili, "Adrenosympathetic Overactivity Under Conditions of Work Stress," *British Journal of Preventive and Social Medicine* 30 (1976): 262–65.

72. R. Ilies, N. Hauserman, S. Schwochau, and J. Stibal, "Reported Incidence Rates of Work-Related Sexual Harassment in the United States: Using Meta-Analysis to Explain Reported Rate Disparities," *Personnel Psychology* 56 (2003): 607–31.

73. K. Pope, "Keyboard Users Say Makers Knew of Problems," *Wall Street Journal*, May 4, 1994, pp. B1, B5.

74. B. Schreiner, "Hot Water over Bathroom Breaks," *Houston Chronicle*, August 28, 2002, p. 21A.

75. Ibid.

76. J. M. George, T. F. Reed, K. A. Ballard, J. Colin, and J. Fielding, "Contact with AIDS Patients as a Source of Work-Related Distress: Effects of Organizational and Social Support," *Academy of Management Journal* 36 (1993): 157–71; J. Barling, E. K. Kelloway, and R. D. Iverson, "High-Quality Work, Job Satisfaction, and Occupational Injuries," *Journal of Applied Psychology* 88 (2), (2003): 276–83.

77. "Cargo Pilots Say They Are Flying Tired, and Seek Tougher Schedule Rules," *Wall Street Journal*, April 5, 1994, p. A1.

78. "Workplace Injuries May Be Far Worse Than Government Data Suggest," *Wall Street Journal*, February 2, 1993, p. A1.

79. J. A. Krug, "Why Do They Keep Leaving?" *Harvard Business Review* (February 2003): 14–15.

80. Ibid.

81. Ibid.

82. Y. Cole, "Work-Life in a Down Economy: Morale Boost or Revenue Flush?" *DiversityInc* (March/April 2003): 96–101.

83. Ibid.

84. S. Shellenbarger, "Single Parenting Boosts Career Stress," *Wall Street Journal*, June 1, 1994, p. B1.

85. S. Shellenbarger, "The Aging of America Is Making 'Elder Care' a Big Workplace Issue," *Wall Street Journal*, February 16, 1994, pp. A1, A8.

86. Ibid.

87. A. M. Ryan, B. J. West, and J. Z. Carr, "Effects of the Terrorist Attacks of 9/11/01 on Employee Attitudes," *Journal of Applied Psychology* 88 (4): 647–59.

88. "Credibility of Witness Is Attacked at Tyco Trial," *New York Times*, October 21, 2003, p. C5; "First Trails Monday in Series of Corporate Scandals," CNN.com./LAW CENTER, September 28, 2003, www.cnn.com/2003/LAW/09/28/white.collar.tirals.ap/; "Enron 'Bribed Tax Officals'," BBC NEWS, February 17, 2003, www.bbc.co.uk/1/hi/in_depth/business/2002/scandals.

89. "Tragedy Strikes at Staten Island Ferry Pier," LowerManhatten.info, October 16, 2003, www.lowermanhatten.info/news/tragedy_strikes_at-staten_80513.asp.

90. J. E. Brody, "Experts Offer Ways to Alleviate Stress," *Houston Chronicle*, April 20, 2003, p. 4E.

91. Ibid.

92. Ibid.

93. L. A. Mainiero and D. E. Gibson, "Managing Employee Trauma: Dealing with the Emotional Fallout from 9–11," *Academy of Management Executive* 17(3) (2003): 130–43.

94. Ibid.

95. C. Haberman, "As Opposed to Numbness, Pain Is Good," *New York Times*, October 21, 2003, p. C20.

96. M. A. Schuster, B. D. Stein, L. H. Jaycox, R. L. Collins, G. N. Marshall, M. N. Elliott, A. J. Zhou, D. E. Kanouse, J. L. Morrison, and S. H. Berry, "A National Survey of Stress Reactions after the September 11, 2001, Terrorist Attacks," *The New England Journal of Medicine* 345(20), November 15, 2001, pp. 1507–1512 "Feds Eye Engines in Air Crash," CNN.com/U.S, November 12, 2001, www.cnn.com/2001/US/11/12/newyork.crash.

97. "Tragedy Strikes at Staten Island Ferry Pier," LowerManhatten.info, October 16, 2003, www.lowerman-hatten.info/news/tragedy_strikes_at-staten_80513.asp.

98. C. Haberman, "As Opposed to Numbness, Pain Is Good," *New York Times*, October 21, 2003, p. C20.

99. S. Folkman and R. S. Lazarus, "An Analysis of Coping in a Middle-Aged Community Sample," *Journal of Health and Social Behavior* 21 (1980): 219–39; S. Folkman and R. S. Lazarus, "If It Changes It Must Be a Process: Study of Emotion and Coping During Three Stages of a College Examination," *Journal of Personality and Social Psychology* 48 (1985): 150–70; S. Folkman and R. S. Lazarus, "Coping as a Mediator of Emotion," *Journal of Personality and Social Psychology* 54 (1988): 466–75.

100. Folkman and Lazarus, "An Analysis of Coping in a Middle-Aged Community Sample"; Folkman and Lazarus, "If It Changes It Must Be a Process"; Folkman and Lazarus, "Coping as a Mediator of Emotion."

101. Ibid.

102. D. Dunn, "For Globetrotting Execs en Famille," *Business Week*, January 11, 1993, pp. 132–33.

103. A. Lakein, *How to Get Control of Your Time and Your Life* (New York: Peter H. Wyden, 1973); J. C. Quick and J. D. Quick, *Organizational Stress and Preventive Management* (New York: McGraw-Hill, 1984).

104. E. Alt Powell, "Time Management Can Produce Rewards," *The Atlanta Journal-Constitution ATC.com* (October 23, 2003) **www.ajc.com/business/ap/ap_s.../AP.V9597.AP-On-the-Money.htm.**

105. Ibid.

106. S. Shellenbarger, "Multitasking Makes You Stupid: Studies Show Pitfalls of Doing Too Much at Once," *Wall Street Journal*, February 27, 2003, p. B1.

107. Ibid.

108. Ibid.

109. W. L. French and C. H. Bell Jr., *Organizational Development: Behavioral Science Interventions for Organization Improvement* (Upper Saddle River, NJ: Prentice Hall, 1990).

110. S. Shellenbarger, "Work and Family: Men Find More Ways to Spend Time at Home," *Wall Street Journal*, February 12, 1992, p. B1.

111. S. Forster, "Companies Say Yoga Isn't a Stretch: Physical, Emotional Benefits Are Praised as More Firms Look to Cut Health Costs," *Wall Street Journal*, October 14, 2003, p. D4.

112. Ibid.

113. Ibid.

114. Quick and Quick, *Organizational Stress and Preventive Management.*

115. S. Begley, "Dalai Lama and MIT Together Investigate Value of Meditation," *Wall Street Journal*, September 19, 2003, p. B1.

116. Ibid.

117. S. Cohen and T. A. Wills, "Stress, Social Support, and the Buffering Hypothesis," *Psychological Bulletin* 98 (1985): 310–57; I. G. Sarason, H. M. Levine, R. B. Basham, and B. R. Sarason, "Assessing Social Support: The Social Support Questionnaire," *Journal of Personality and Social Psychology* 44 (1983): 127–39.

118. "Stress Busters."

119. B. Ash, "Companies Say Yes to Child-Care Services," *Bryan–College Station Eagle*, May 29, 1994, p. C5.

120. M. D. Fefer, "Babes in Work Land," *Fortune*, April 18, 1994, pp. 31–32.

121. S. Shellenbarger, "Firms Help Employees Work with Sick Kids," *Wall Street Journal*, May 11, 1994, p. B1.

122. "Work–Family Problems Get Their Own Managers," *Wall Street Journal*, April 14, 1992, p. B1.

123. "Training Workers to Be Flexible on Schedules," *Wall Street Journal*, February 10, 1993, p. 1; "Workplace Flexibility Is Seen as Key to Business Success," *Wall Street Journal*, November 23, 1993, p. A1.

124. "Training Workers to Be Flexible on Schedules."

125. J. Aley, "The Temp Biz Boom: Why It's Good," *Fortune*, October 16, 1995, pp. 53–55.

126. N. B. Kurland and D. E. Bailey, "Telework: The Advantages and Challenges of Working Here, There, Anywhere, and Anytime," *Organizational Dynamics* (Autumn 1999): 53–68.

127. Ibid.

128. P. J. Knight and J. Westbrook, "Comparing Employees in Traditional Job Structures vs. Telecommuting Jobs Using Herzberg's Hygienes & Motivators," *Engineering Management Journal* (March 1999): 15–20.

129. M. Igbaria and T. Guimaraes, "Exploring Differences in Employee Turnover Intentions and Its Determinants Among Telecommuters and Non-Telecommuters," *Journal of Management Information Systems* (Summer 1999): 147–64.

130. T. L. Dixon and J. Webster, "Family Structure and the Telecommuter's Quality of Life," *Journal of End User Computing* (Fall 1998): 42–49.

131. Kurland and Bailey, "Telework."

132. R. Eisenberger, P. Fasolo, and V. Davis-LaMastro, "Perceived Organizational Support and Employee Diligence, Commitment, and Innovation," *Journal of Applied Psychology* 75 (1990): 51–59; R. Eisenberger, R. Huntington, S. Hutchinson, and D. Sowa, "Perceived Organizational Support," *Journal of Applied Psychology* 71 (1986): 500–507; M. L. Ambrose, and M. Schminke, "Organization Structure as a Moderator of the Relationship Between Procedural Justice, Interactional Justice, Perceived Organizational Support, and Supervisory Trust," *Journal of Applied Psychology* 88 (2), (2003): 295–305.

133. D. N. Sull, "Managing By Commitments," *Harvard Business Review* (June 2003): 82–91.

134. J. M. George, T. F. Reed, K. A. Ballard, J. Colin, and J. Fielding, "Contact with AIDS Patients as a Source of Work-Related Distress: Effects of Organizational and Social Support," *Academy of Management Journal*, 35 (1996): 157–71.

135. B. Oliver, "How to Prevent Drug Abuse in Your Workplace," *HRMagazine* (December 1993): 78–81.

136. R. A. Wolfe and D. F. Parker, "Employee Health Management: Challenges and Opportunities," *Academy of Management Executive* 8 (2)(1994): 22–31.

137. U.S. Department of Health and Human Services, *1992 National Survey of Worksite Health Promotion Activities: A Summary Report* (Washington, DC: U.S. Department of Health and Human Services, 1992).

138. Wolfe and Parker, "Employee Health Management."

Chapter 10

1. "American Truck and SUV Sales Figures Thru September 2003," **Rockcrawler.com.**

2. F. Warner, "GM Goes Off-Road: Creating Hummer Meant Breaking the Old Rules—And Putting Together a New Team," *Fast Company* (February 2003): 40–42.

3. Ibid.

4. Ibid.

5. Ibid.

6. Ibid.

7. Ibid.

8. D. Welch, "Hummer: The Incredible Hulk," *Business Week Online*, March 24, 2003, **www.businessweek.com/ @@BDX8AIYQZNar3Qca/magazine/conte.../b3825 011.html.**

9. H. Sondak, M. Neale, and E. Mannix (Eds.), *Toward Phenomenology of Groups and Group Membership*, (Oxford: Elsevier Science, 2003); W. A. Kahn, Book Review of *Toward Phenomenology of Groups and Group Membership, Administrative Science Quarterly* (June 2003): 330–332.

10. H. Moon, D. E Conlon, S. E Humphrey, N. Quigley, C. E. Devers, and J. M. Nowakowski, "Group Decision Process and Incrementalism in Organizational Decision Making," *Organizational Behavior and Human Decision Processes* 92 (2003): 67–79.

11. B. Dumaine, "The Trouble with Teams," *Fortune*, September 5, 1994, pp. 86–92.

12. M. E. Shaw, *Group Dynamics*, 3rd ed. (New York: McGraw-Hill, 1981).

13. T. M. Mills, *The Sociology of Small Groups* (Upper Saddle River, NJ: Prentice Hall, 1967).

14. J. A. Pearce II and E. C. Ravlin, "The Design and Activation of Self-Regulating Work Groups," *Human Relations* 11 (1987): 751–82.

15. B. W. Tuckman, "Developmental Sequences in Small Groups," *Psychological Bulletin* 63 (1965): 384–99; B. W. Tuckman and M. C. Jensen, "Stages of Small Group Development," *Group and Organizational Studies* 2 (1977): 419–27.

16. R. G. LeFauve and A. C. Hax, "Managerial and Technological Innovations at Saturn Corporation," *MIT Management* (Spring 1992): 8–19.

17. R. S. Peterson and K. Jackson Behfar, "The Dynamic Relationship Between Performance Feedback, Trust, and Conflict in Groups: A Longitudinal Study," *Organizational Behavior and Human Decision Processes* 92 (2003): 102–12.

18. C. J. G. Gersick, "Time and Transition in Work Teams: Toward a New Model of Group Development," *Academy of Management Journal* 31 (1988): 9–41; C. J. G. Gersick, "Marking Time: Predictable Transitions in Task Groups," *Academy of Management Journal* 32 (1989): 274–309.

19. L. L. Thompson, *Making the Team: A Guide for Managers* (Upper Saddle River, NJ: Prentice Hall, 2000).

20. G. R. Jones, "Task Visibility, Free Riding, and Shirking: Explaining the Effect of Structure and Technology on Employee Behavior," *Academy of Management Review* 9 (1984): 684–95.

21. C. Gibson and F. Vermeulen, "A Healthy Divide: Subgroups as a Stimulus for Team Learning Behavior," *Administrative Science Quarterly* 48 (2003): 202–39.

22. Warner, "GM Goes Off-Road."

23. W. B. Swann, Jr., J. T. Polzer, D. C. Seyle, and S. J. Ko, "Finding Value in Diversity: Verification of Personal and Social Self-Views in Diverse Groups," *Academy of Management Review* 29 (1), (2004): 9–27.

24. F. Warner, "In a Word, Toyota Drives for Innovation," *Fast Company*, (August 2002): 36–38.

25. Ibid.

26. B. Bremner and C. Dawson, "Can Anything Stop Toyota? An Inside Look at How It's Reinventing the Auto Industry," *Business Week Online*, November 17, 2003, **www.businessweek.com:/print/premium/content/03_ 46/b3858001_mz001.htm?mz.**

27. Warner, "In a Word, Toyota Drives for Innovation."

28. "Into the Matrix," *Automotive Design & Production*, November 12, 2003, **www.autofieldguide.com/columns/gary/ 0102oncar.html.**

29. J. Stuart Bunderson and K. M. Sutcliffe, "When to Put the Brakes on Learning," *Harvard Business Review* (February 2003): 20–21.

30. T. C. Brown, "The Effect of Verbal Self-Guidance Training on Collective Efficacy and Team Performance," *Personnel Psychology* 56 (2003): 935–64.

31. A. Bandura, *Self-Efficacy: The Exercise of Control* (New York: W. H. Freeman and Company, 1997).

32. Ibid.

33. Ibid.

34. Ibid.

35. Ibid.

36. Ibid.

37. C. F. Bond Jr. and L. J. Titus, "Social Facilitation: A Meta-Analysis of 241 Studies," *Psychological Bulletin* 94 (1983): 265–92; Shaw, *Group Dynamics.*

38. Ibid.

39. B. Dumain, "Who Needs a Boss?" *Fortune*, May 7, 1990, pp. 52–60.

40. Ibid.

41. B. Burlington, "The Coolest Small Company in America," *Inc. Magazine* (January 2003): 64–74.

42. "Zingerman's Mail Order," **www.zingermans.com**, September 9, 2003, **www.zingerman.com/AboutUs.pasp.**

43. E. Levine, "Movable Feasts for the Holidays," *Business Week Online*, December 7, 1998, **www.businessweek.com/ @@JAsbxYQQBa@r3QcA/archives/ 1998/b36071553. arc.htm.**

44. Burlington, "The Coolest Small Company in America."

45. Ibid.

46. "Six Steps to Selecting Superior Cheese," **www.zingermans.com** (2003).

47. "A Guide to Getting Along: ZCoB Procedures for Dealing with Conflict or Dissatisfaction with a Co-Worker," *Zingerman's Staff Guide* (2002), **www.images.inc.com/freetools/zing_train/ zing_guide.pdf.**

48. "3 Steps to Great Finance," *Zingerman's Staff guide* (2002), **www.images.inccom/freetools/zing_train/zing_finance.pdf.**

49. Burlington, "The Coolest Small Company in America."

50. J. R. Hackman, "Group Influences on Individuals in Organizations." In M. D. Dunnette and L. M. Hough (Eds.), *Handbook of Industrial and Organizational Psychology*, 2nd ed., vol. 3 (Palo Alto, CA: Consulting Psychologists Press, 1992), 199–267.

51. Ibid.

52. D. C. Feldman, "The Development and Enforcement of Group Norms," *Academy of Management Review* 9 (1984): 47–53.

53. Hackman, "Group Influences on Individuals in Organizations."

54. E. P. Hollander, "Conformity, Status, and Idiosyncrasy Credit," *Psychological Review* 65 (1958): 117–27.

55. M. Dalton, "The Industrial Ratebuster: A Characterization," *Applied Anthropology* 7 (1948): 5–18.

56. Hackman, "Group Influences on Individuals in Organizations."

57. C. L. Jackson and J. A. LePine, "Peer Response to a Team's Weakest Link: A Test and Extension of LePine and Van Dyne's Model," *Journal of Applied Psychology* 88 (3), (2003): 459–75.

58. C. J. Nemeth and B. M. Staw, "The Trade-Offs of Social Control and Innovation in Groups and Organizations," *Advances in Experimental Social Psychology* 22 (1989): 175–210.

59. Ibid.

60. M. J. Grawitch, D. C. Munz, and T. J. Kramer, "Effects of Member Mood States on Creative Performance in Temporary Workgroups," *Group Dynamics: Theory, Research, and Practice* 7 (1), (2003): 41–54; M. J. Grawitch, D. C. Munz, E. K. Elliott, and A. Mathis, "Promoting Creativity in Temporary Problem-Solving Groups: The Effects of Positive Mood and Autonomy in Problem Definition on Idea-Generating Performance," *Group Dynamics: Theory, Research, and Practice* 7 (3), (2003): 200–13.

61. M. Williams and Y. Ono, "Japanese Cite Need for Bold Change, but Not at the Expense of 'Stability,'" *Wall Street Journal*, June 29, 1993, p. A10.

62. G. R. Jones, "Psychological Orientation and the Process of Organizational Socialization: An Interactionist Perspective," *Academy of Management Review* 8 (1983): 464–74.

63. J. Van Mannen and E. H. Schein, "Towards a Theory of Organizational Socialization." In B. M. Staw (Ed.), *Research in Organizational Behavior*, vol. 1 (Greenwich, CT: JAI Press, 1979), 209–64.

64. G. R. Jones, "Socialization Tactics, Self-Efficacy, and Newcomers' Adjustments to Organizations," *Academy of Management Review* 29 (1986): 262–79.

65. Ibid; Van Mannen and Schein, "Towards a Theory of Organizational Socialization."

66. www.intercotwest.com/disneyland; M. N. Martinez, "Disney Training Works Magic," *HRMagazine* (May 1992): 53–57.

Chapter 11

1. www.bedframes.com, 2004.

2. J. Bailey, "With Price Increases Rare, Small Firms Struggle to Survive," *Wall Street Journal*, September 4, 2001, p. B2.

3. R. T. King, "Jeans Therapy: Levi's Factory Employees Are Assigned to Teams and Moral Takes a Hit," *Wall Street Journal*, May 20, 1998, p. A1.

4. www.levistrauss.com, 2004, press release.

5. I. D. Steiner, *Group Process and Productivity* (New York: Academic Press, 1972).

6. R. A. Guzzo and G. P. Shea, "Group Performance and Intergroup Relations in Organizations." In M. D. Dunnette and L. M. Hough (Eds.), *Handbook of Industrial and Organizational Psychology*, 2nd ed., vol. 3 (Palo Alto, CA: Consulting Psychologists Press, 1992), 269–313; Steiner, *Group Process and Productivity*.

7. Guzzo and Shea, "Group Performance and Intergroup Relations in Organizations."

8. P. B. Paulus and H. C. Yang, "Idea Generation in Groups: A Basis for Creativity in Organizations," *Organizational Behavior and Human Decision Processes* (May 2000): 76–87.

9. L. Thompson and L. F. Brajkovich, "Improving the Creativity of Organizational Work Groups," *Academy of Management Executive* 17 (February 2003): 96–112.

10. C. Daniels, "This Man Wants to Help You. Seriously," *Fortune* (June 26, 2000): 327–33.

11. www.secondcity.com.

12. Daniels, "This Man Wants to Help You. Seriously."

13. Ibid., p. 328.

14. L. R. Offermann and R. K. Spiros, "The Science and Practice of Team Development: Improving the Link," *Academy of Management Journal* 44 (April 2001): 376–93.

15. P. C. Earley, "Social Loafing and Collectivism: A Comparison of the United States and the People's Republic of China," *Administrative Science Quarterly* 34 (1989): 565–81; J. M. George, "Extrinsic and Intrinsic Origins of Perceived Social Loafing in Organizations," *Academy of Management Journal* 35 (1992): 191–202; S. G. Harkins, B. Latane, and K. Williams, "Social Loafing: Allocating Effort or Taking It Easy," *Journal of Experimental Social Psychology* 16 (1980): 457–65; B. Latane, K. D. Williams, and S. Harkins, "Many Hands Make Light the Work: The Causes and Consequences of Social Loafing," *Journal of Personality and Social Psychology* 37 (1979): 822–32; J. A. Shepperd, "Productivity Loss in Performance Groups: A Motivation Analysis," *Psychological Bulletin* 113 (1993): 67–81.

16. George, "Extrinsic and Intrinsic Origins of Perceived Social Loafing in Organizations"; G. R. Jones, "Task Visibility, Free Riding, and Shirking: Explaining the Effect of Structure and Technology on Employee Behavior," *Academy of Management Review* 9 (1984): 684–95; K. Williams, S. Harkins, and B. Latane, "Identifiability as a Deterrent to Social Loafing: Two Cheering Experiments," *Journal of Personality and Social Psychology* 40 (1981): 303–11.

17. M. A. Brickner, S. G. Harkins, and T. M. Ostrom, "Effects of Personal Involvement: Thought-Provoking Implications for Social Loafing," *Journal of Personality and Social Psychology* 51 (1986): 763–69; S. G. Harkins and R. E. Petty, "The Effects of Task Difficulty and Task Uniqueness on Social Loafing," *Journal of Personality and Social Psychology* 43 (1982): 1214–29; N. L. Kerr and S. E. Bruun, "Dispensability of Member Effort and Group Motivation Losses: Free-Rider Effects," *Journal of Personality and Social Psychology* 44 (1983): 78–94.

18. N. L. Kerr, "Motivation Losses in Small Groups: A Social Dilemma Analysis," *Journal of Personality and Social Psychology* 45 (1983): 819–28.

19. J. M. Jackson and S. G. Harkins, "Equity in Effort: An Explanation of the Social Loafing Effect," *Journal of Personality and Social Psychology* 49 (1985): 1199–1206.

20. B. Latane, "Responsibility and Effort in Organizations." In P. S. Goodman (Ed.), *Designing Effective Work Groups* (San Francisco: Jossey-Bass, 1986); Latane, Williams, and Harkins, "Many Hands Make Light the Work"; Steiner, *Group Process and Productivity*.

21. M. E. Shaw, *Group Dynamics*, 3rd ed. (New York: McGraw-Hill, 1981).

22. K. Lovelace, D. L. Shapiro, and L. R. Weingart, "Maximizing Cross-Functional New Product Teams' Innovativeness and Constraint Adherence: A Conflict communications Perspective," *Academy of Management Journal* 44 (August 2001): 779–94.

23. S. Harkins and J. Jackson, "The Role of Evaluation in Eliminating Social Loafing," *Personality and Social Psychology Bulletin* 11 (1985): 457–65; N. L. Kerr and S. E. Bruun, "Ringelman Revisited: Alternative Explanations for the Social Loafing Effect," *Personality and Social Psychology Bulletin* 7 (1981): 224–31; Williams, Harkins, and Latane, "Identifiability as a Deterrent to Social Loafing."

24. Brickner, Harkins, and Ostrom, "Effects of Personal Involvement"; Harkins and Petty, "The Effects of Task Difficulty and Task Uniqueness on Social Loafing."

25. R. Rapaport, "To Build a Winning Team: An Interview with Head Coach Bill Walsh," *Harvard Business Review* (January–February 1993): 111–20.

26. Latane, "Responsibility and Effort in Organizations"; Latane, Williams, and Harkins, "Many Hands Make Light the Work"; Steiner, *Group Process and Productivity*.

27. J. D. Thompson, *Organizations in Action* (New York: McGraw-Hill, 1967).

28. G. Stewart and M. R. Barrick, "Team Structure and Performance: Assessing the Mediating Role of Intrateam Process and the Moderating Role of Task Type," *Academy of Management Journal* 43 (April 2001): 135–49.

29. Ibid.

30. Steiner, *Group Process and Productivity*.

31. G. S. Van Der Vegt, E. Van De Vliert, and A. Oosterhof, "Informational Dissimilarity and Organizational Citizenship Behavior: The Role of Intra-team Interdependence and Team Identification," *Academy of Management Journal* 46 (December 2003): 715–28.

32. L. Festinger, "Informal Social Communication," *Psychological Review*, 57 (1950): 271–82; Shaw, *Group Dynamics*.

33. D. Cartwright, "The Nature of Group Cohesiveness." In D. Cartwright and A. Zander (Eds.), *Group Dynamics*, 3rd ed. (New York: Harper & Row, 1968); L. Festinger, S. Schacter, and K. Black, *Social Pressures in Informal Groups* (New York: Harper & Row, 1950); Shaw, *Group Dynamics*.

34. D. A. Harrison, K. H. Price, J. H. Gavin, and A. T. Florey, "Time, Teams and Task Performance: Changing Effects of Surface- and Deep-Level Diversity on Group Functioning," *Academy of Management Journal* 45 (October 2002): 1029–46.

35. J. A. Chatman and F. J. Flynn, "The Influence of Demographic Heterogeneity on the Emergence and Consequences of Cooperative Norms in Work Teams," *Academy of Management Journal* 44 (October 2001): 956–75; A. E. Randel and K. S. Jaussi, "Functional Background Identity, Diversity, and Individual Performance in Cross-Functional Teams," *Academy of Management Journal* 46 (December 2003): 775.

36. B. Beersma, J. R. Hollenbeck, S. E. Humphrey, H. Moon, D. E. Conlon, and D. R. Ilgen, "Cooperation, Competition, and Team Performance: Toward a Contingency Approach," *Academy of Management Journal* 46 (October 2003): 591.

37. D. Knight, C. C. Durham, and A. Edwin, "The Relationship of Team Goals, Incentives, and Efficacy to Strategic Risk, Tactical Implementation, and Performance," *Academy of Management Journal* 44 (April 2001): 236–339.

38. J. S. Bunderson and K. M. Sutcliffe, "Comparing Alternative Conceptualizations of Functional Diversity in Management Teams: Process and Performance Effects," *Academy of Management Journal* 45 (October 2002): 875–94.

39. G. Chen and R. J. Klimoski, "The Impact of Expectations on Newcomer Performance in Teams as Moderated by Work Characteristics, Social Exchanges, and Empowerment," *Academy of Management Journal* 46 (October 2003): 591–608.

40. Shaw, *Group Dynamics*.

41. J. R. Hackman, "Group Influences on Individuals in Organizations." In Dunnette and Hough (Eds.), *Handbook of Industrial and Organizational Psychology*, 2nd ed., vol 2 (Palo Alto, CA: Consulting Psychologists Press, 1992), 199–267.

42. Shaw, *Group Dynamics*.

43. R. O. Crockett and S. Baker, "Suddenly, Mobile Phones Aren't Moving So Fast," *Business Week* (November 6, 2000): BusinessWeek Online; S. Baker, I. Resch, and R. O. Crockett, "Commentary: Nokia's Costly Stumble," *Business Week* (August 14, 2000): BusinessWeek Online.

44. **www.nokia.com**.

45. Ibid.

46. Ibid.

47. Ibid.

48. S. Finkelstein and D. C. Hambrick, "Top Management Team Tenure and Organizational Outcomes: The Moderating Role of Managerial Discretion," *Administrative Science Quarterly* 35 (1990): 484–503.

49. I. L. Janis, *Victims of Groupthink*, 2nd ed. (Boston: Houghton Mifflin, 1982).

50. C. J. Collins and K. D. Clark, "Strategic Human Resource Practices, Top Management Team Social Networks, and Firm Performance: The Role of Human Resource Practices in Creating Organizational Competitive Advantage," *Academy of Management Journal* 46 (December 2003): 740–52.

51. V. U. Druskat and J. V. Wheeler, "Managing from the Boundary: The Effective Leadership of Self-Managing Work Teams," *Academy of Management Journal* 46 (August 2003): 435–58.

52. J. A. Pearce II and E. C. Ravlin, "The Design and Activation of Self-Regulating Work Groups," *Human Relations* 11 (1987): 751–82.

53. A. R. Montebello and V. R. Buzzotta, "Work Teams That Work," *Training and Development* (March 1993): 59–64.

54. J. R. Hackman and G. R. Oldham, *Work Redesign* (Reading, MA: Addison-Wesley, 1980).

55. B. Dumain, "Who Needs a Boss?" *Fortune* (May 7, 1990): 52–60; Pearce and Ravlin, "The Design and Activation of Self-Regulating Work Groups."

56. A. B. Henley and K. H. Price, "Want a Better Team? Foster a Climate of Fairness," *Academy of Management Executive* 16 (August 2002): 153–55.

57. J. St. Bunderson, "Team Member Functional Background and Involvement in Management Teams: Direct Effects and the Moderating Role of Power Centralization," *Academy of Management Journal* 46 (August 2003): 458–75.

58. B. L. Kirkman and D. L. Shapiro, "The Impact of Cultural Values on Job Satisfaction and Organizational Commitment in Self-Managing Work Teams: The Mediating Role of Employee Resistance," *Academy of Management Journal* 44 (June 2001): 557–70.

59. Dumain, "Who Needs a Boss?"

60. T. D. Wall, N. J. Kemp, P. R. Jackson, and C. W. Clegg, "Outcomes of Autonomous Workgroups: A Long-Term Field Experiment," *Academy of Management Journal* 29 (1986): 280–304.

61. R. D. O'Keefe, J. A. Kernaghan, and A. H. Rubenstein, "Group Cohesiveness: A Factor in the Adoption of Innovations Among Scientific Work Groups," *Small Group Behavior* 6 (1975): 282–92; C. A. O'Reilly and K. H. Roberts, "Task Group Structure, Communication, and Effectiveness in Three Organizations," *Journal of Applied Psychology* 62 (1977): 674–81.

62. R. T. Keller, "Cross-Functional Project Groups in Research and New Product Development: Diversity, Communications, Job Stress, and Outcomes," *Academy of Management Journal* 44 (June 2001): 547–56.

63. J. B. White and O. Suris, "How a 'Skunk Works' Kept the Mustang Alive—on a Tight Budget," *Wall Street Journal*, September 21, 1993, pp. A1, A12.

64. Ibid.

65. B. L. Kirkman, B. Rosen, C. B. Gibson, P. E. Tesluk, and S. O. McPherson, "Five Challenges to Virtual Team Success: Lessons From Sabre, Inc.," *Academy of Management Executive* 16 (August 2002): 67–80.

66. J. Lipnack, "Virtual Teams," *Executive Excellence* 16(5) (May 1999): 14–15.

67. D. L. Duarte and N. T. Snyder, *Mastering Virtual Teams* (San Francisco: Jossey-Bass 1999); K. A. Karl, "Book Review: Mastering Virtual Teams," *Academy of Management Executive* (August 1999): 118–19.

68. Ibid.

69. B. Geber, "Virtual Teams," *Training* 32(4) (April 1995): 36–40; T. Finholt and L. S. Sproull, "Electronic Groups at Work," *Organizational Science* 1 (1990): 41–64.

70. B. L. Kirkman and D. L. Shapiro, "The Impact of Cultural Values on Job Satisfaction and Organizational Commitment in Self-Managing Work Teams."

71. G. R. Jones and J. M. George, "The Experience and Evolution of Trust: Implications for Cooperation and Teamwork," *Academy of Management Review* 23 (July 1998): 531–47.

72. Geber, "Virtual Teams."

73. E. J. Hill, B. C. Miller, S. P. Weiner, and J. Colihan, "Influences of the Virtual Office on Aspects of Work and Work/Life Balance," *Personnel Psychology* 31 (1998): 667–83; S. G. Strauss, "Technology, Group Process, and Group Outcomes: Testing the Connections in Computer-Mediated and Face-to-Face Groups," *Human–Computer Interaction* 12 (1997): 227–66; M. E. Warkentin, L. Sayeed, and R. Hightower, "Virtual Teams versus Face-to-Face Teams: An Exploratory Study of a Web-Based Conference System," *Decision Sciences* 28(4) (Fall 1997): 975–96.

74. Geber, "Virtual Teams."

75. www.hp.com, 2004.

76. Geber, "Virtual Teams."

77. Ibid.

78. Ibid.

Chapter 12

1. D. Hakim, "Type B Chief Guides GM on a Course to Revival," *New York Times*, November 25, 2001, p. 3.1.

2. Ibid.

3. www.ford.com, 2004.

4. B. Elgin, "Making Her Own Luck," *Business Week*, November 20, 2000, pp. EB48–EB56.

5. www.timewarner.com, 2004.

6. M. Peers, "Tuning Up; Unflamboyant CEO Parsons Calms Infighting, Cuts Debt," *Wall Street Journal*, December 11 2003, p. B.1.

7. J. L. Roberts, "Prime Time for Parsons," *Newsweek*, December 22, 2003, pp. 43–44.

8. G. Yukl, "Managerial Leadership: A Review of Theory and Research," *Journal of Management* 15 (1989): 251–89.

9. G. Yukl, *Leadership in Organizations*, 2nd ed. (New York: Academic Press, 1989).

10. W. Shen, "The Dynamics of the CEO–Board Relationship: An Evolutionary Perspective," *Academy of Management Review* 28 (July 2003): 466–77.

11. D. A. Waldman, G. G. Ramirez, R. J. House, and P. Puranam, "Does Leadership Matter? CEO Leadership Attributes and Profitability Under Conditions of Perceived Environmental Uncertainty," *Academy of Management Journal* 44 (February 2001): 134–44.

12. L. Coch and J. R. P. French, "Overcoming Resistance to Change," *Human Relations* 1 (1948): 512–32; G. Graen, F. Dansereau Jr., T. Minami, and J. Cashman, "Leadership Behaviors as Cues to Performance Evaluation," *Academy of Management Journal* 16 (1973): 611–23; G. Graen and S. Ginsburgh, "Job Resignation as a Function of Role Orientation and Leader Acceptance: A Longitudinal Investigation of Organizational Assimilation," *Organizational Behavior and Human Performance* 19 (1977): 1–17; R. J. House and M. L. Baetz, "Leadership: Some Empirical Generalizations and New Research Directions." In B. M. Staw and L. L. Cummings (Eds.), *Research in Organizational Behavior*, vol. 1 (Greenwich, CT: JAI Press, 1979): 341–423; N. R. F. Maier, *Problem Solving and Creativity in Individuals and Groups* (Belmont, CA: Brooks-Cole, 1970); K. N. Wexley, J. P. Singh, and G. A. Yukl, "Subordinate Personality as a Moderator of the Effects of Participation in Three Types of Appraisal Interviews," *Journal of Applied Psychology* 58 (1973): 54–59.

13. House and Baetz, "Leadership."

14. Yukl, "Managerial Leadership."

15. R. M. Stogdill, *Handbook of Leadership: A Survey of the Literature* (New York: Free Press, 1974) House and Baetz, "Leadership."

16. B. M. Bass, *Bass and Stogdill's Handbook of Leadership: Theory, Research, and Managerial Applications*, 3rd ed. (New York: Free Press, 1990); House and Baetz, "Leadership"; S. A. Kirpatrick and E. A. Locke, "Leadership: Do Traits Matter?" *Academy of Management Executive* 5(2) (1991): 48–60; G. Yukl, *Leadership in Organizations*; G. Yukl and D. D. Van Fleet, "Theory and Research on Leadership in Organizations." In M. D. Dunnette and L. M. Hough (Eds.), *Handbook of Industrial and Organizational Psychology*, 2nd ed., vol. 3 (Palo Alto, CA: Consulting Psychologists Press, 1992), 147–97.

17. E. A. Fleishman, "The Description of Supervisory Behavior," *Personnel Psychology* 37 (1953): 1–6; A. W. Halpin and B. J. Winer, "A Factorial Study of the Leader Behavior Descriptions," in R. M. Stogdill and A. E. Coons (Eds.), *Leader Behavior: Its Description and Measurement* (Columbus: Bureau of Business Research, Ohio State University, 1957).

18. E. A. Fleishman, "Performance Assessment Based on an Empirically Derived Task Taxonomy," *Human Factors* 9 (1967): 349–66.

19. D. Tscheulin, "Leader Behavior Measurement in German Industry," *Journal of Applied Psychology* 56 (1971): 28–31.

20. P. Nulty, "The Bounce Is Back at Goodyear," *Fortune* (September 7, 1992): 70–72.

21. G. G. Marcial, "Goldman & Schwab," *Business Week* (October 2, 2000): BusinessWeek Online; www.schwab.com.

22. "The Top 25 Managers—Managers to Watch"; "David S. Pottruck and Charles R. Schwab, Charles Schwab Corp.," *Business Week* (January 8, 2001): BusinessWeek Online.

23. Ibid.

24. E. A. Fleishman and E. F. Harris, "Patterns of Leadership Behavior Related to Employee Grievances and Turnover," *Personnel Psychology* 15 (1962): 43–56.

25. P. M. Podsakoff, W. D. Todor, R. A. Grover, and V. L. Huber, "Situational Moderators of Leader Reward and Punishment Behaviors: Fact or Fiction?" *Organizational Behavior and Human Performance* 34 (1984): 21–63; P. M. Podsakoff, W. D. Todor, and R. Skov, "Effects of Leader Contingent and Noncontingent Reward and Punishment Behaviors on Subordinate Performance and Satisfaction," *Academy of Management Journal* 25 (1982): 810–21.

26. G. Das, "Local Memoirs of a Global Manager," *Harvard Business Review* (March–April 1993): 38–47.

27. Podsakoff, Todor, Grover, and Huber, "Situational Moderators of Leader Reward and Punishment Behaviors"; Podsakoff, Todor, and Skov, "Effects of Leader Contingent and Noncontingent Reward and Punishment Behaviors on Subordinate Performance and Satisfaction."

28. E. A. Fleishman, *Leadership Opinion Questionnaire* (Chicago: Science Research Associates, 1960).

29. R. R. Blake and J. S. Mouton, *The New Managerial Grid* (Houston: Gulf, 1978).

30. P. Hersey and K. Blanchard, *Management of Organizational Behavior: Utilizing Human Resources* (Upper Saddle River, NJ: Prentice Hall, 1982).

31. F. E. Fiedler, *A Theory of Leadership Effectiveness* (New York: McGraw-Hill, 1967); F. E. Fiedler, "The Contingency Model and the Dynamics of the Leadership Process." In L. Berkowitz (Ed.), *Advances in Experimental Social Psychology* (New York: Academic Press, 1978).

32. M. Mofflet, "Culture Shock," *Wall Street Journal*, September 24, 1992, pp. R13–R14.

33. House and Baetz, "Leadership."

34. Ibid.; L. H. Peters, D. D. Hartke, and J. T. Pohlmann, "Fiedler's Contingency Theory of Leadership: An Application of the Meta-Analysis Procedures of Schmidt and Hunter," *Psychological Bulletin* 97 (1985): 274–85.

35. T. J. Maurer, H. R. Pierce, and L. M. Shore, "Perceived Beneficiary of Employee Development Activity: A Three-Dimensional Social Exchange Model," *Academy of Management Journal* 27 (July 2002): 432–45.

36. www.microosft.com, 2004; www.msn.com, 2004.

37. J. C. Wofford and L. Z. Liska, "Path-Goal Theories of Leadership: A Meta-Analysis," *Journal of Management* 19 (1993): 857–76.

38. V. H. Vroom and P. W. Yetton, *Leadership and Decision-Making* (Pittsburgh: University of Pittsburgh Press, 1973).

39. J. Templeman, "Bob Eaton Is No Lee Iacocca—But He Doesn't Need to Be," *Business Week* (November 9, 1992): 96.

40. V. U. Druskat and J. V. Wheeler, "Managing From the Boundary: The Effective Leadership of Self-Managing Work Teams," *Academy of Management Journal* 46 (August 2003): 435–58.

41. D. I. Jung and B. J. Avolio, "Effects of Leadership Style and Follower's Cultural Orientation on Performance in Group and Individual Task Conditions," *Academy of Management Journal* 42 (April 1999): 208–19.

42. R. M. Dienesch and R. C. Liden, "Leader–Member Exchange Model of Leadership: A Critique and Further Development," *Academy of Management Review* 11 (1986): 618–34; G. Graen, M. Novak, and P. Sommerkamp, "The Effects of Leader–Member Exchange and Job Design on Productivity and Satisfaction: Testing a Dual Attachment Model," *Organizational Behavior and Human Performance* 30 (1982): 109–31.

43. G. Graen and J. Cashman, "A Role-Making Model of Leadership in Formal Organizations: A Development Approach." In J. G. Hunt and L. L. Larson (Eds.), *Leadership Frontiers* (Kent, OH: Kent State University Press, 1975), 143–65.

44. C. A. Schriesheim, L. Neider, and T. A. Scandura, "Delegation and Leader–Member Exchange: Main Effects, Moderators, and Measurement Issues," *Academy of Management Journal* 41 (June 1998): 298–319.

45. M. Wakabayashi and G. B. Graen, "The Japanese Career Progress Study: A Seven-Year Follow-Up," *Journal of Applied Psychology* 69 (1984): 603–14.

46. H. J. Klein and J. S. Kim, "A Field Study of the Influence of Situational Constraints, Leader–Member Exchange, and Goals," *Academy of Management Journal* 41 (February 1998): 88–96.

47. W. E. McClane, "Implications of Member Role Differentiation: Analysis of a Key Concept in the LMX Model of Leadership," *Group and Organization Studies* 16 (1991): 102–13; Yukl, *Leadership in Organizations*; Yukl and Van Fleet, "Theory and Research on Leadership in Organizations."

48. J. R. Meindl, "On Leadership: An Alternative to the Conventional Wisdom." In B. M. Staw and L. L. Cummings (Eds.), *Research in Organizational Behavior*, vol. 12 (Greenwich, CT: JAI Press, 1990), 159–203.

49. S. Kerr and J. M. Jermier, "Substitutes for Leadership: Their Meaning and Measurement," *Organizational Behavior and Human Performance* 22 (1978): 375–403.

50. L. Killian, "California, Here We Come," *Forbes* (November 23, 1992): 146–47.

51. Ibid.

52. P. M. Podsakoff, B. P. Niehoff, S. B. MacKenzie, and M. L. Williams, "Do Substitutes for Leadership Really Substitute for Leadership? An Empirical Examination of Kerr and Jermier's Situational Leadership Model," *Organizational Behavior and Human Decision Processes* 54 (1993): 1–44.

53. R. J. Meindl, "On Leadership: An Alternative to the Conventional Wisdom," *Research in Organizational Behavior* 12 (1990): 159–203.

54. W. L. Gardner and B. J. Avolio, "The Charismatic Relationship: A Dramaturgical Perspective," *Academy of Management Journal* 23 (January 1998): 32–59.

55. B. M. Bass, *Leadership and Performance Beyond Expectations* (New York: Free Press, 1985).

56. J. E. Bono and T. A. Judge, "Self-Concordance at Work: Toward Understanding the Motivational Effects of Transformational Leaders," *Academy of Management Journal* 46 (October 2003): 554–72; Bass, *Bass and Stogdill's Handbook of Leadership*; Yukl and Van Fleet, "Theory and Research on Leadership in Organizations."

57. J. A. Conger and R. N. Kanungo, "Behavioral Dimensions of Charismatic Leadership." In J. A. Conger, R. N. Kanungo, and Associates, *Charismatic Leadership* (San Francisco: Jossey-Bass, 1988).

58. G. Chen and R. J. Klimoski, "The Impact of Expectations on Newcomer Performance in Teams as Mediated by Work Characteristics, Social Exchanges, and Empowerment," *Academy of Management Journal* 46 (October 2003): 591–608.

59. Ibid; D. A. Waldman, "CEO Charismatic Leadership: Levels-of-Management and Levels-of-Analysis Effects," *Academy of Management Journal* 24 (April 1999): 266–86.

60. J. C. Pastor, J. R. Meindl, and M. C. Mayo, "A Network Effects Model of Charisma Attributions," *Academy of Management Journal* 45 (April 2002): 410–21.

61. Bass, *Leadership and Performance Beyond Expectations*; Bass, *Bass and Stogdill's Handbook of Leadership*; Yukl and Van Fleet, "Theory and Research on Leadership in Organizations."

62. T. Dvir, D. Eden, B. Avolio, and B. Shamir, "Impact of Transformational Leadership on Follower Development and

Performance: A Field Experiment," *Academy of Management Journal* 45 (August 2003): 735–45.

63. Ibid.

64. C. Caldwell, R. Litz, and W. R. Nord, "Building Trust Through Effective Governance—Three Perspectives of Organizational Leadership," *Academy of Management Review* 28 (October 2003): 667–74.

65. N. Byrnes, "Avon: The New Calling," *Business Week* (September 18, 2000): 136–48; C. Hawn, "Tag Team," *Forbes* (January 11, 1999): 184–86; J. Pellet, "Ding-Dong Avon Stalling," *Chief Executive* (June 2000): 26–31; P. Sellers, "Big, Hairy, Audacious Goals Don't Work—Just Ask P&G," *Fortune* (April 3, 2000): 39–44.

66. Ibid.

67. www.avon.com, 2004.

68. Bass, *Leadership and Performance Beyond Expectations*.

69. Bass, *Bass and Stogdill's Handbook of Leadership*; B. M. Bass and B. J. Avolio, "Transformational Leadership: A Response to Critiques." In M. M. Chemers and R. Ayman (Eds.), *Leadership Theory and Research: Perspectives and Directions* (San Diego: Academic Press, 1993), 49–80; B. M. Bass, B. J. Avolio, and L. Goodheim, "Biography and the Assessment of Transformational Leadership at the World Class Level," *Journal of Management* 13 (1987): 7–20; J. J. Hater and B. M. Bass, "Superiors' Evaluations and Subordinates' Perceptions of Transformational and Transactional Leadership," *Journal of Applied Psychology* 73 (1988): 695–702; R. Pillai, "Crisis and the Emergence of Charismatic Leadership in Groups: An Experimental Investigation," *Journal of Applied Psychology* 26 (1996): 543–62; J. Seltzer and B. M. Bass, "Transformational Leadership: Beyond Initiation and Consideration," *Journal of Management* 16 (1990): 693–703; D. A. Waldman, B. M. Bass, and W. O. Einstein, "Effort, Performance, and Transformational Leadership in Industrial and Military Service," *Journal of Occupational Psychology* 60 (1987): 1–10.

70. R. Pillai, C. A. Schriesheim, and E. S. Williams, "Fairness Perceptions and Trust as Mediators for Transformational and Transactional Leadership: A Two-Sample Study," *Journal of Management* 25 (1999): 897–933.

71. J. M. George and K. Bettenhausen, "Understanding Prosocial Behavior, Sales Performance, and Turnover: A Group-Level Analysis in a Service Context," *Journal of Applied Psychology* 75 (1990): 698–709.

72. J. M. George, "Emotions and Leadership: The Role of Emotional Intelligence," *Human Relations* 53(8) (2000): 1027–55.

73. A. H. Eagly and B. T. Johnson, "Gender and Leadership Style: A Meta-Analysis," *Psychological Bulletin* 108 (1990): 233–56.

74. Ibid.

75. Ibid.

76. A. H. Eagly, M. G. Makhijani, and B. G. Klonsky, "Gender and the Evaluation of Leaders: A Meta-Analysis," *Psychological Bulletin* 111 (1992): 3–22.

77. R. Sharpe, "As Leaders, Women Rule," *Business Week* (November 20, 2000): 75–84.

78. P. Gogoi, "Teaching Men the Right Stuff," *Business Week* (November 20, 2000): 84.

Chapter 13

1. www.gucci.com, 2004.

2. A. Galloni, J. Carreyrou, and C. Rohwedder, "Stripped of Stars at Top, Will Gucci Still Be Gucci?" *Wall Street Journal*, November 5, 2003, pp. A.1, A.14.

3. C. Horyn, "Struggling to Design the Future at Gucci," *New York Times*, January 10, 2004, p. C.1.

4. R. A. Dahl, "The Concept of Power," *Behavioral Science* 2 (1957): 210–15; R. M. Emerson, "Power Dependence Relations," *American Sociological Review* 27 (1962): 31–41.

5. J. Pfeffer, *Power in Organizations* (Boston: Pitman, 1981).

6. A. M. Pettigrew, *The Politics of Organizational Decision Making* (London: Tavistock, 1973); R. H. Miles, *Macro Organizational Behavior* (Santa Monica, CA: Goodyear, 1980).

7. "Making Ends Meet," *The Economist*, April 7, 1993, p. 3.

8. S. K. Kearns, "When Goliaths Clash: Managing Executive Conflict to Build a More Dynamic Organization," *Academy of Management Executive* 17 (November 2003): 162–65.

9. J. G. March, "The Business Firm as a Coalition," *Journal of Politics* 24 (1962): 662–78; D. J. Vrendenburgh and J. G. Maurer, "A Process Framework of Organizational Politics," *Human Relations* 37 (1984): 47–66.

10. W. Shen and A. A. Cannella Jr., "Power Dynamics Within Top Management and Their Impacts on CEO Dismissal Followed by Inside Succession," *Academy of Management Journal* 45 (December 2002): 1195–1207.

11. P. H. Thornton, "The Rise of Corporation in a Craft Industry: Conflict and Conformity in Institutional Logics," *Academy of Management Journal* 45 (February 2002): 81–102.

12. This section draws heavily on J. R. P. French, Jr. and B. Raven, "The Bases of Social Power." In D. Cartwright (Ed.), *Studies in Social Power* (Ann Arbor: University of Michigan, Institute for Social Research, 1959), 150–67.

13. M. Weber, *The Theory of Economic and Social Organization* (New York: Free Press, 1947).

14. Ibid.

15. Pettigrew, *The Politics of Organizational Decision Making*; G. Yukl and C. M. Falbe, "Importance of Different Power Sources in Downward and Lateral Relations," *Journal of Applied Psychology* 76 (1991): 416–23.

16. J. A. Conger and R. N. Kanungo, "The Empowerment Process: Integrating Theory and Practice," *Academy of Management Review* 13 (1988): 471–81.

17. French and Raven, "The Bases of Social Power."

18. M. Weber, *Economy and Society* (Berkeley: University of California Press, 1978); H. M. Trice and J. M. Beyer, "Charisma and Its Routinization in Two Social Movement Organizations," *Research in Organizational Behavior* 8 (1986): 113–64.

19. B. M. Bass, "Leadership: Good, Better, Best," *Organizational Dynamics* 13 (1985): 26–40.

20. Weber, *Economy and Society*.

21. This section draws heavily on D. J. Hickson, C. R. Hinings, C. A. Lee, R. E. Schneck, and D. J. Pennings, "A Strategic Contingencies Theory of Intraorganizational Power," *Administrative Science Quarterly* 16 (1971): 216–27; and C. R. Hinings, D. J. Hickson, J. M. Pennings, and R. E. Schneck, "Structural Conditions of Interorganizational Power," *Administrative Science Quarterly* 19 (1974): 22–44.

22. Hickson, Hinings, Lee, Schneck, and Pennings, "A Strategic Contingencies Theory of Intraorganizational Power."

23. M. Gargiulo, "Two Step Leverage: Managing Constraint in Organizational Politics," *Administrative Science Quarterly* 38 (1993): 1–19.

24. M. M. Montoya-Weiss, A. P. Massey, and M. Song, "Getting It Together: Temporal Coordination and Conflict Management

in Global Virtual Teams," *Academy of Management Journal* 44 (December 2001): 1251–63.

25. Ibid.

26. M. Crozier, "Sources of Power of Lower Level Participants in Complex Organizations," *Administrative Science Quarterly* 7 (1962): 349–64.

27. T. Welbourne and C. O. Trevor, "The Roles of Departmental and Position Power in Job Evaluation," *Academy of Management Journal* 43 (August 2000): 761–72.

28. Ibid; J. D. Bunferson, "Team Member Functional Background and Involvement in Management Teams: Direct Effects and the Moderating Role of Power Centralization," *Academy of Management Journal* 46 (August 2003): 458–75.

29. A. M. Pettigrew, "Information Control as a Power Resource," *Sociology* 6 (1972): 187–204.

30. G. R. Salancik and J. Pfeffer, "The Bases and Uses of Power in Organizational Decision Making," *Administrative Science Quarterly* 19 (1974): 453–73; J. Pfeffer and G. R. Salancik, *The External Control of Organizations: A Resource Dependence View* (New York: Harper and Row, 1978).

31. K. S. Jehn and E. A. Mannix, "The Dynamic Nature of Conflict: A Longitudinal Study of Intragroup Conflict and Group Performance," *Academy of Management Journal* 44 (April 2000): 238–52.

32. D. A. Schuler, K. Rehbein, and R. D. Cramer, "Pursuing Strategic Advantage Through Political Means: A Multivariate Approach," *Academy of Management Journal* 45 (August 2000): 659–73.

33. T. Burns, "Micropolitics: Mechanisms of Institutional Change," *Administrative Science Quarterly* 6 (1961): 257–81.

34. E. Jennings, *The Mobile Manager* (New York: McGraw-Hill, 1967).

35. R. S. Meyers, "Managing with Power," *Academy of Management Executive* 6 (May 1992): 104–07.

36. M. D. Lord, "Constituency Building as the Foundation for Corporate Political Strategy," *Academy of Management Executive* 17 (February 2003): 112–25.

37. T. G. Pollock, H. M. Fischer, and J. B. Wade, "The Role of Power and Politics in the Repricing of Executive Options," *Academy of Management Journal* 45 (December 2002): 1172–83.

38. This discussion draws heavily on Pfeffer, *Power in Organizations*, Ch. 5.

39. Hickson, Hinings, Lee, Schneck, and Pennings, "A Strategic Contingencies Theory of Intraorganizational Power."

40. K. M. Eisenhardt and L. J. Bourgeois, III, "Politics of Strategic Decision Making in High-Velocity Environments: Toward a Midrange Theory," *Academy of Management Journal* 31 (December 1988): 737–71.

41. B. Townley, "The Role of Competing Rationalities in Institutional Change," *Academy of Management Journal*, 45 (February 2002): 163–80.

42. This section draws heavily on Pfeffer, *Power in Organizations*, Ch. 2.

43. G. Jones, "Kodak: We Push the Button, You Do the Rest." In C. W. L. Hill and G. R. Jones, *Strategic Management: An Integrated Approach*, 6th ed. (Boston: Houghton Mifflin, 2004).

44. **www.kodak.com**, 2004.

45. B. Gray and S. S. Ariss, "Politics and Strategic Change Across Organizational Life Cycles," *Academy of Management Review* 10 (October 1985): 707–24.

46. J. A. Litterer, "Conflict in Organizations: A Reexamination," *Academy of Management Journal* 9 (1966): 178–86; S. M. Schmidt and T. A. Kochan, "Conflict: Towards Conceptual Clarity," *Administrative Science Quarterly* 13 (1972): 359–70; Miles, *Macro Organizational Behavior*.

47. Miles, *Macro Organizational Behavior*.

48. S. P. Robbins, *Managing Organizational Conflict: A Nontraditional Approach* (Englewood Cliffs, NJ: Prentice-Hall, 1974); L. Coser, *The Functions of Social Conflict* (New York: Free Press, 1956).

49. A. C. Amason, "Distinguishing the Effects of Functional and Dysfunctional Conflict on Strategic Decision Making . . .," *Academy of Management Journal* 39 (February 1996): 123–49.

50. B. Kabanoff, "Equity, Equality, Power, and Conflict," *Academy of Management Review* 16 (April 1991): 416–42.

51. This discussion owes much to the seminal work of the following authors: Lou R. Pondy, "Organizational Conflict: Concepts and Models," *Administrative Science Quarterly* 2 (1967): 296–320; and R. E. Walton and J. M. Dutton, "The Management of Interdepartmental Conflict: A Model and Review," *Administrative Science Quarterly* 14 (1969): 62–73.

52. S. W. Floyd, "Strategizing Throughout the Organization: Managing Role Conflict in Strategic Renewal," *Academy of Management Review* 25 (January 2000): 154–78.

53. M. K. Duffy, J. D. Shaw, and E. M. Stark, "Performance and Satisfaction in Conflicted Interdependent Groups: When and How Does Self-Esteem Make a Difference?" *Academy of Management Journal* 43 (August 2000): 772–83.

54. M. Dalton, *Men Who Manage* (New York: Wiley, 1959); Walton and Dutton, "The Management of Interdepartmental Conflict."

55. Walton and Dutton, "The Management of Interdepartmental Conflict"; J. McCann and J. R. Galbraith, "Interdepartmental Relationships." In P. C. Nystrom and W. H. Starbuck (Eds.), *Handbook of Organizational Design* (New York: Oxford University Press, 1981).

56. R. E. Nelson, "The Strength of Strong Ties: Social Networks and Intergroup Conflict in Organizations," *Academy of Management Journal* 32 (June 1989): 377–402.

57. J. D. Thompson, *Organizations in Action* (New York: McGraw-Hill, 1967).

58. K. S. Jehn and E. A. Mannix, "The Dynamic Nature of Conflict: A Longitudinal Study of Intragroup Conflict and Group Performance," *Academy of Management Journal* 44 (April 2000): 238–52.

59. Walton and Dutton, "The Management of Interdepartmental Conflict," p. 65.

60. Ibid., p. 68.

61. Pondy, "Organizational Conflict," p. 300.

62. Ibid., p. 310.

63. S. W. Floyd, "Strategizing Throughout the Organization: Managing Role Conflict in Strategic Renewal," *Academy of Management Review* 25 (January 2000): 154–78.

64. G. Labianca, D. J. Brass, and B. Gray, "Social Networks and Perceptions of Intergroup Conflict: The Role of Negative Relationships and . . .," *Academy of Management Journal* 41 (February 1998): 55–68.

65. CIC Corp. Web site, **www.cicagency.com**.

66. B. Fannin, "CIC workers Ask Judge to Void Noncompliance Pact," *The Eagle*, October 23, 1997, p. 1.

67. P. S. Nugent, "Managing Conflict: Third-Party Interventions for Managers," *Academy of Management Executive* 16 (February 2002): 139–41.

68. J. Z. Rubin and B. R. Brown, *The Social Psychology of Bargaining and Negotiation* (New York: Academic Press, 1975).

69. J. F. Brett, "Stairways to Heaven: An Interlocking Self-Regulation Model of Negotiation," *Academy of Management Review* 24 (July 1999): 435–52.

70. J. T. Polzer, E. A. Mannix, and M. A. Neale, "Interest Alignment and Coalitions in Multiparty Negotiation," *Academy of Management Journal* 41 (February 1998): 42–55.

71. E. E. Neilsen, "Understanding and Managing Intergroup Conflict." In J. F. Veiga and J. N. Yanouzas (Eds.), *The Dynamics of Organizational Theory* (St. Paul, MN: West, 1979), 290–96; Miles, *Macro Organizational Behavior.*

72. T. L. Stanley, "When Push Comes to Shove: A Manager's Guide to Resolving Disputes," *Supervision* 64 (2003): 6.

73. P. S. Nugent, "Managing Conflict."

74. Neilsen, "Understanding and Managing Intergroup Conflict."

75. C. Bendersky, "Organizational Dispute Resolution Systems: A Complementarities Model," *Academy of Management Review* 28 (October 2003): 643–57.

76. R. E. Walton, "Third Party Roles in Interdepartmental Conflict," *Industrial Relations* 7 (1967): 29–43.

77. K. Thomas, "Conflict and Negotiation Processes in Organizations." In M. D. Dunnette and L. M. Hough (Eds.), *Handbook of Industrial and Organizational Psychology*, 2nd ed., vol 3 (Palo Alto, CA: Consulting Psychologists Press, 1992), 651–717.

78. R. L. Pinkley and G. B. Northcraft, "Conflict Frames of Reference: Implications for Dispute Processes and Outcomes," *Academy of Management Journal* 37 (February 1994): 193–206.

79. R. E. Walton and R. B. McKersie, *A Behavioral Theory of Labor Relations* (New York: McGraw-Hill, 1965).

80. Ibid.

Chapter 14

1. www.alteonwebsystems.com, 2000.

2. B. Riggs, "Smarter Networks," *Informationweek* (April 12, 1999): 6.

3. M. Borden, "When Big Growth Happens to Small Companies," *Fortune* (March 6, 2000) 385.

4. www.nortelnetworks.com, 2004.

5. L. W. Porter and K. H. Roberts, "Communication in Organizations." In M. D. Dunnette (Ed.), *Handbook of Industrial and Organizational Psychology* (Chicago: Rand McNally, 1976), 1553–89.

6. J. K. Barge and C. Oliver, "Working with Appreciation in Managerial Practice," *Academy of Management Review* 28 (January 2003): 124–43.

7. C. A. O'Reilly and L. R. Pondy, "Organizational Communication." In S. Kerr (Ed.), *Organizational Behavior* (Columbus, OH: Grid, 1979).

8. Ibid.

9. K. L. Ashcraft, "Perspectives on Organizational Communications: Finding Common Ground," *Academy of Management Review* 26 (October 2001): 666–69.

10. D. A. Hofmann and A. Stetzer, "The Role of Safety Climate and Communication in Accident Interpretation: Implications for Learning from Negative Events," *Academy of Management Journal* 41 (December 1998): 644–58.

11. N. Phillips and J. L. Brown, "Analyzing Communication in and Around Organizations: A Critical Hermeneutic Approach," *Academy of Management Journal* 36 (December 1993): 1547–77.

12. P. P. Le Breton, *Administrative Intelligence-Information Systems* (Boston: Houghton Mifflin, 1963); W. G. Scott and T. R. Mitchell, *Organization Theory* (Homewood, IL: Irwin, 1976).

13. R. Breeden, "Small Talk, Surfing the Net—At Work," *Wall Street Journal*, October 21, 2003, p. A24.

14. M. Conlin, "Employees, Surf at Your Own Risk," *Business Week* (June 12, 2000): 105–06.

15. Ibid.

16. L. Armstrong, "Someone to Watch Over You," *Business Week* (July 10, 2000): BusinessWeek Online.

17. "Internet Filters Curb Web Surfing," *Industrial Distribution* 92 (2003): 36.

18. Ibid.

19. Ibid.

20. O. W. Baskin and C. E. Aronoff, *Interpersonal Communication in Organizations* (Santa Monica, CA: Goodyear, 1989).

21. F. Fearing, "Toward a Psychological Theory of Human Communication," *Journal of Personality* 22 (1953–1954): 73–76; Scott and Mitchell, *Organization Theory.*

22. J. M. George, "Mood and Absence," *Journal of Applied Psychology* 74 (1989): 317–24; J. M. George, "State or Trait: Effects of Positive Mood on Prosocial Behaviors at Work," *Journal of Applied Psychology* 76 (1991): 299–307; J. M. George and A. P. Brief, "Feeling Good–Doing Good: A Conceptual Analysis of the Mood at Work–Organizational Spontaneity Relationship," *Psychological Bulletin* 112 (1992): 310–29.

23. S. Cohen and T. A. Wills, "Stress, Social Support, and the Buffering Hypothesis," *Psychological Bulletin* 98 (1985): 310–57; J. M. George, T. F. Reed, K. A. Ballard, J. Colin, and J. Fielding, "Contact with AIDS Patients as a Source of Work-Related Distress: Effects of Organizational and Social Support," *Academy of Management Journal* 36 (1993): 157–71.

24. V. Anand and C. C. Manz, "An Organizational Memory Approach to Information Management," *Academy of Management Review* 23 (October 1998): 796–810.

25. D. Krackhardt and J. R. Hanson, "Informal Networks: The Company," *Harvard Business Review* (July–August 1993): 104–11.

26. E. M. Rogers and R. Agarwala-Rogers, *Communication in Organizations* (New York: Free Press, 1976).

27. "Employers Struggle to Teach Their Employees Basic Communication Skills," *Wall Street Journal*, November 30, 1993, p. A1.

28. "Corporate Jargon: If You Don't Know the Inside Skinny, It Can Be a Jumble," *Wall Street Journal*, February 15, 1994, p. A1.

29. "Managing Your Boss," Harvard Business Review Video Series No. 4.

30. J. T. Malloy, *Dress for Success* (New York: Warner Books, 1975).

31. J. Sandberg, "People Are Hugging a Lot More Now and Seem to Like It," *Wall Street Journal*, March 15, 1993, pp. A1, A5.

32. J. Carey, "Getting Business to Think About the Unthinkable," *Business Week* (June 24, 1991): 104–06.

33. Briefings from the Editors, "The New Communications: Don't Fax Me, I'll Fax You," *Harvard Business Review* (March–April 1993): 8–9.

34. www.brownsteingroup.com, 2004.

35. "Ultimate Vision," *ADWEEK Eastern Edition* (November 10, 1997): 54.

36. www.brownsteingroup.com; "Pennsylvania," *ADWEEK Eastern Edition* (September 9, 1996): 57; H. Stout, "Self-

Evaluation Brings Change to a Family's Ad Agency," *Wall Street Journal*, January 6, 1998, p. B2.

37. H. Stout, "Self-Evaluation Brings Change to a Family's Ad Agency."

38. Ibid.

39. M. Anderson, "Renaissance Woman," *Adweek*, May 14, 2001, p. 5.

40. **www.walmart.com**, 2004.

41. N. Templin, "Companies Use TV to Reach Their Employees," *Wall Street Journal*, December 7, 1993, pp. B1, B16.

42. Baskin and Aronoff, *Interpersonal Communication in Organizations*.

43. A. Rossett and T. Bickham, "Diversity Training: Hope, Faith, and Cynicism," *Training* (January 1994): 41–45.

44. D. Tannen, "The Power of Talk," *Harvard Business Review* (September–October 1995): 138–48; D. Tannen, *Talking from 9 to 5* (New York: Avon Books, 1995).

45. Ibid.

46. Ibid.

47. R. L. Daft, R. H. Lengel, and L. K. Trevino, "Message Equivocality, Media Selection, and Manager Performance: Implications for Information Systems," *MIS Quarterly* 11 (1987): 355–66; R. L. Daft and R. H. Lengel, "Information Richness: A New Approach to Managerial Behavior and Organization Design." In B. M. Staw and L. L. Cummings (Eds.), *Research in Organizational Behavior* (Greenwich, CT: JAI Press, 1984).

48. R. L. Daft, *Organization Theory and Design* (New York: West, 1992).

49. J. D. Ford and L. W. Ford, "The Role of Conversations in Producing Intentional Change in Organizations," *Academy of Management Review* 20 (July 1995): 541–71.

50. Ibid.

51. S. P. Weisband and S. K. Schneider, "Computer-Mediated Communication and Social Information: Status Salience and Status Differences," *Academy of Management Journal* 38 (August 1995): 1124–52.

52. R. W. Collins, "Communications Policy and Information Technology: Promises, Problems and Prospects," *Academy of Management Review* 28 (October 2003): 673–76.

53. E. Licking, "Innovations," *Business Week* (November 6, 2000): BusinessWeek Online; International Editorials, "The Mobile Net Requires a New Ethos," *Business Week* (May 22, 2000): BusinessWeek Online.

54. Ibid.

55. Ibid.

56. R. W. Collins, "Communications Policy and Information Technology: Promises, Problems and Prospects."

57. Ibid.

58. Ibid.

59. A. L. Sprout, "The Internet Inside Your Company," *Fortune* (November 27, 1995): 161–68.

60. S. G. Straus and J. E. McGrath, "Does the Medium Matter? The Interaction of Task Type and Technology on Group Performance and Member Reactions," *Journal of Applied Psychology* 79 (1994): 87–97.

61. S. G. Straus, S. P. Weisband, and J. M. Wilson, "Human Resource Management Practices in the Networked Organization: Impacts of Electronic Communication Systems." In C. L. Cooper and D. M. Rousseau (Eds.), *Trends in Organizational Behavior*, vol. 5 (New York: John Wiley & Sons 1998), 127–54.

62. M. C. Boudreau, K. D. Loch, D. Robey, and D. Straud, "Going Global: Using Information Technology to Advance the Competitiveness of the Virtual Transnational Organization," *Academy of Management Executive* 12 (November 1998): 120–29.

63. F. Morring, "Culture Shock: NASA Considers a Test Flight to Validate Fixes Set by *Columbia* Board," *Aviation Week*, September 1, 2003, p. 22.

64. M. L. Wald, "Management Issues Looming in Shuttle Inquiry," *Wall Street Journal*, August 6, 2003, p. A11.

65. K. Chang and S. Coledad, "Some Recommended Changes Are Already Occurring," *New York Times*, August 27, 2003, p. A16.

Chapter 15

1. **www.nike.com**, 2004.

2. D. Shook, "Why Nike Is Dragging Its Feet," *Business Week* (March 19, 2001): 35–36.

3. B. Stone, "Nike's Short Game," *Newsweek* (January 26, 2004): pp. 40–41.

4. A. Grove, "How Intel Makes Spending Pay Off," *Fortune* (February 22, 1993): 56–61.

5. J. G. March and H. A. Simon, *Organizations* (New York: Wiley, 1958); H. A. Simon, *The New Science of Management Decision* (New York: Harper & Row, 1960).

6. March and Simon, *Organizations*.

7. Ibid., Simon, *The New Science of Management Decision*.

8. Ibid.

9. M. K. Stevenson, J. R. Busemeyer, and J. C. Naylor, "Judgment and Decision-Making Theory." In M. D. Dunnette and L. M. Hough (Eds.), *Handbook of Industrial and Organizational Psychology*, 2nd ed., vol. 1 (Palo Alto, CA: Consulting Psychologists Press, 1990), 283–374.

10. W. Edwards, "The Theory of Decision Making," *Psychological Bulletin* 51 (1954): 380–417; H. A. Simon, "A Behavioral Model of Rational Choice," *Quarterly Journal of Economics* 69 (1955): 99–118.

11. Ibid.

12. Edwards, "The Theory of Decision Making"; Stevenson, Busemeyer, and Naylor, "Judgment and Decsion-Making Theory."

13. Simon, "A Behavioral Model of Rational Choice."

14. March and Simon, *Organizations*.

15. Ibid.

16. Ibid.

17. Edwards, "The Theory of Decision Making"; March and Simon, *Organizations;* Simon "A Behavioral Model of Rational Choice."

18. March and Simon, *Organizations;* Simon, "A Behavioral Model of Rational Choice."

19. Stevenson, Busemeyer, and Naylor, "Judgment and Decision-Making Theory."

20. March and Simon, *Organizations;* Simon, "A Behavioral Model of Rationale Choice."

21. March and Simon, *Organizations*.

22. "Hoffman-La Roche and BASF Agree to Pay Record Criminal Fines for Participating in International Vitamin Cartel," U.S. Department of Justice News Release, Math 21, 1999.

23. J. R. Wilke and S. Warren, "Vitamin Firms Settle U.S. Charges. Agree to Pay $725 Million in Fines," *Wall Street Journal* (May 21, 1999): p. A3.

24. Simon, *The New Science of Management Decision.*

25. Ibid.

26. P. C. Nutt, "Why Decisions Fail," *Academy of Management Journal* 17 (February 2003): 130–33.

27. C. M. Fiol and E. J. O'Connor, "Waking Up! Mindfulness in the Face of Bandwagons," *Academy of Management Review* 28 (January 2003): 54–71.

28. P. C. Nutt, "Surprising but True: Half the Decisions in Organizations Fail," *Academy of Management Executive* 13 (November 1999): 75–91.

29. M. H. Bazerman, *Judgment in Managerial Decision Making* (New York: Wiley, 1994); D. Kahnman and A. Tversky, "Subjective Probability: A Judgment of Representativeness," *Cognitive Psychology* 3 (1972): 430–54; A. Tversky and D. Kahneman, "Judgment Under Uncertainty: Heuristics and Biases," *Science* 185 (1974): 1124–31.

30. Bazerman, *Judgment in Managerial Decision Making;* Tversky and Kahneman, "Judgment Under Uncertainty."

31. Ibid.

32. Ibid.

33. Bazerman, *Judgment in Managerial Decision Making.*

34. Ibid.; Tversky and Kahneman, "Judgment Under Uncertainty."

35. L. A. Burke and M. K. Miller, "Taking the Mystery Out of Intuitive Decision Making," *Academy of Management Executive* 13 (November 1999): 91–100.

36. Ibid.

37. Tversky and Kahneman, "Judgment Under Uncertainty."

38. B. M. Staw, "The Escalation of Commitment to a Course of Action," *Academy of Management Review* 6 (1981): 577–87; B. M. Staw and J. Ross, "Understanding Behavior in Escalating Situations," *Science* 246 (1986): 216–20.

39. Staw and Ross, "Understanding Behavior in Escalation Situations."

40. Ibid.

41. D. Kahneman and A. Tversky, "Prospect Theory: An Analysis of Decision Under Risk," *Econometrics* 47 (1979): 263–91; Staw and Ross, "Understanding Behavior in Escalation Situations."

42. S. B. Sitkin and L. R. Weingart, "Determinants of Risky Decision-Making Behavior: A Test of the Mediating Role of Risk Perceptions . . . ," *Academy of Management Journal* 38 (December 1995): 1573–93.

43. R. W. Collins, "Communications Policy and Information Technology: Promises, Problems and Prospects," *Academy of Management Review* 28 (October 2003): 673–76.

44. G. P. Huber, "A Theory of the Effects of Advanced Information Technologies on Organizational Design, Intelligence, and Decision Making," *Academy of Management Review* 15 (January 1990): 47–72.

45. www.sap.com, 2004.

46. P. S. Goodman and E. D. Darr, "Exchanging Best Practices Through Computer-Aided Systems," *Academy of Management Executive* 9 (May 1996): 7–20.

47. G. Jones, "SAP and the Enterprise Resource Planning Industry." In C. W. L. Hill and G. R. Jones, *Strategic Management: An Integrated Approach* (Boston: Houghton Mifflin, 2004).

48. Ibid.

49. Z. Schiller, "GE's Appliance Park: Rewire, or Pull the Plug?" *Business Week* (February 8, 1999): 30.

50. J. Martin, "Detroit's Designing Women," *Fortune* (October 18, 1993): 10–11.

51. M. Galen and A. T. Palmer, "White, Male, and Worried," *Business Week* (January 31, 1994): 50–55.

52. D. W. Johnson and F. P. Johnson, *Joining Together: Group Theory and Group Skills* (Boston: Allyn and Bacon, 1994); V. Villasenor, *Jury: The People vs. Juan Corona* (New York: Bantam, 1977).

53. M. Shaw, "A Comparison of Individuals and Small Groups in the Rational Solution of Complex Problems," *American Journal of Psychology* 44 (1932): 491–504; R. Ziller, "Group Size: A Determinant of the Quality and Stability of Group Decision," *Sociometery* 20 (1957): 165–73.

54. Schiller, "GE's Appliance Park."

55. Ibid.

56. I. L. Janis, *Groupthink,* 2nd ed. (Boston: Houghton Mifflin, 1982).

57. Ibid.

58. Ibid.

59. J. M. Darley and B. Latane, "Bystander Intervention in Emergencies: Diffusion of Responsibility," *Journal of Personality and Social Psychology* 8 (1968): 377–83; M. E. Shaw, *Group Dynamics* (New York: McGraw-Hill, 1981).

60. S. Moscovici and M. Zavalloni, "The Group as a Polarizer of Attitudes," *Journal of Personality and Social Psychology* 12 (1969): 125–35; Shaw, *Group Dynamics.*

61. M. A. Wallach, N. Kogan, and D. J. Bem, "Group Influence on Individual Risk Taking," *Journal of Abnormal and Social Psychology* 65 (1962): 75–86; M. A. Wallach, N. Kogan, and D. J. Bem, "Diffusion of Responsibility and Level of Risk Taking in Groups," *Journal of Abnormal and Social Psychology* 68 (1964): 263–74.

62. L. Festinger, "A Theory of Social Comparison Processes," *Human Relations* 7 (1954): 117–40.

63. A. Vinokur and E. Burnstein, "Effects of Partially Shared Persuasive Arguments on Group-Induced Shifts: A Group Problem-Solving Approach," *Journal of Personality and Social Psychology,* 29 (1974): 305–15; Shaw, *Group Dynamics.*

64. A. F. Osborn, *Applied Imagination* (New York: Scribners, 1957).

65. T. J. Bouchard Jr., J. Barsaloux, and G. Drauden, "Brainstorming Procedure, Group Size, and Sex as Determinants of the Problem-Solving Effectiveness of Groups and Individuals," *Journal of Applied Psychology* 59 (1974): 135–38.

66. M. Diehl and W. Stroebe, "Productivity Loss in Brainstorming Groups: Toward the Solution of a Riddle," *Journal of Personality and Social Psychology* 53 (1987): 497–509.

67. R. B. Gallupe, L. M. Bastianutti, and W. H. Cooper, "Unblocking Brainstorms," *Journal of Applied Psychology* 76 (1991): 137–42.

68. Ibid.

69. D. H. Gustafson, R. K. Shulka, A. Delbecq, and W. G. Walster, "A Comparative Study of Differences in Subjective Likelihood Estimates Made by Individual, Interacting Groups, Delphi Groups, and Nominal Groups," *Organizational Behavior and Human Performance* 9 (1973): 280–91.

70. N. Dalkey, *The Delphi Method: An Experimental Study of Group Decisions* (Santa Monica: CA: Rand Corporation, 1969).

71. S. M. Young, "A Framework for the Successful Adoption and Performance of Japanese Manufacturing Practices," *Academy of*

Management Review 17 (1992): 677–700; M. Walton, *The Deming Management Method* (New York: Perigee Books, 1990).

72. "How Does Service Drive the Service Company?" *Harvard Business Review* (November–December 1991): 146–58.

73. A. Gabor, "Rochester Focuses: A Community's Core Competences," *Harvard Business Review* (July–August 1991): 116–26.

74. W. M. Bulkeley, "Plexus Strategy: Smaller Runs of More Things," *Wall Street Journal,* October 8, 2003, pp. B1, B12.

75. www.plexus.com, 2004.

76. B. Hedberg, "How Organizations Learn and Unlearn." In W. H. Starbuck and P. C. Nystrom (Eds.), *Handbook of Organizational Design,* vol. 1 (New York: Oxford University Press, 1981), 1–27.

77. P. M. Senge, *The Fifth Discipline: The Art and Practice of the Learning Organization* (New York: Doubleday, 1990).

78. J. G. March, "Exploration and Exploitation in Organizational Learning" *Organizational Science* 2 (1991): 71–87.

79. M. J. Benner and M. L. Tushman, "Exploitation, Exploration, and Process Management: The Productivity Dilemma Revisited," *Academy of Management Review* 28 (April 2003): 238–57.

80. T. K. Lant and S. J. Mezias, "An Organizational Learning Model of Convergence and Reorientation," *Organizational Science* 5 (1992): 47–71.

81. M. Dodgson, "Organizational Learning: A Review of Some Literatures," *Organizational Studies* 14 (1993): 375–94.

82. A. S. Miner and S. J. Mezias, "Ugly Duckling No More: Pasts and Futures of Organizational Learning Research," *Organizational Science* 7 (1990): 88–99.

83. P. Senge, *The Fifth Discipline.*

84. P. M. Senge, "Taking Personal Change Seriously: The Impact of Organizational Learning on Management Practice," *Academy of Management Executive* 17 (May 2003): 47–51.

85. P. Senge, "The Leader's New Work: Building Learning Organizations," *Sloan Management Review* (Fall 1990): 7–23.

86. Miner and Mezias, "Ugly Ducking No More."

Chapter 16

1. www.sunlife.com, 2003.

2. www.sunlife.com, company history, 2003.

3. IT World Canada, Press Release, June 4, 2003.

4. G. R. Jones, *Organizational Theory, Design, and Change: Text and Cases* (Upper Saddle River, NJ: Prentice Hall, 2003).

5. J. Child, *Organization: A Guide for Managers and Administrators* (New York: Harper and Row, 1977).

6. P. R. Lawrence and J. W. Lorsch, *Organization and Environment* (Boston: Graduate School of Business Administration, Harvard University, 1967).

7. R. Duncan, "What Is the Right Organizational Design?" *Organizational Dynamics* (Winter 1979): 59–80.

8. T. Burns and G. R. Stalker, *The Management of Innovation* (London: Tavistock, 1966).

9. P. W. Beamish, "Sony's Yoshihide Nakamura on Structure and Decision Making," *Academy of Management Executive* 13 (1999): 12–17.

10. Jones, *Organizational Theory, Design, and Change,* Ch. 5; T. W. Malnight, "Emerging Structural Patterns within Multinational Corporations: Towards Process-Based Structures," *Academy of Management Journal* 44 (2001): 1187–2013.

11. G. DeSanctis, J. T. Glass, and I. M. Morris, "Organizational Designs for R&D," *Academy of Management Executive* 16 (2002): 55–67.

12. C. Perrow, *Organizational Analysis: A Sociological View* (Belmont, CA: Wadsworth, 1970).

13. J. Woodward, *Management and Technology* (London: Her Majesty's Stationery Office, 1958).

14. Ibid.

15. E. Gedajlovic and D. M. Shapiro, "Ownership Structure and Firm Profitability in Japan," *Academy of Management Journal* 45 (2002): 565–567.

16. P. K. Mills and G. Ungson, "Reassessing the Limits of Structural Empowerment: Organizational Constitution and Trust as Controls," *Academy of Management Review* 28 (2003): 143–54.

17. R. H. Hall, *Organizations: Structure and Process* (Englewood, Cliffs, NJ: Prentice-Hall, 1972); R. Miles, *Macro Organizational Behavior* (Santa Monica, CA: Goodyear, 1980).

18. www.dell.com, 2003.

19. Jones, *Organizational Theory, Design, and Change,* Ch. 6.

20. J. Child, *Organization: A Guide for Managers and Administrators* (New York: Harper and Row, 1977).

21. Jones, *Organizational Theory, Design, and Change,* Ch. 6.

22. D. Machalaba, "Burlington Northern Executives Retire, Raising Speculation About CEO Search," *Wall Street Journal,* June 2, 1994, p. B8.

23. L. Berton and M. Selz, "Peat Marwick Cuts U.S. Staff of Professionals," *Wall Street Journal,* June 2, 1994, p. A4.

24. M. V. Russo, "The Multidivisonal Structure as an Enabling Device: A Longitudinal Study of Discretionary Cash as a Strategic Resource," *Academy of Management Journal* 34 (1991): 718–34.

25. DeSanctis, Glass, and Morris, "Organizational Designs for R&D."

26. S. M. Davis and P. R. Lawrence, *Matrix* (Reading, MA: Addison-Wesley, 1977); J. R. Galbraith, "Matrix Organization Designs: How to Combine Functional and Project Forms," *Business Horizons* 14 (1971): 29–40.

27. L. R. Burns, "Matrix Management in Hospitals: Testing Theories of Matrix Structure and Development," *Administrative Science Quarterly* 34 (1989): 349–68.

28. S. M. Davis and P. R. Lawrence, "Problems of Matrix Organization," *Harvard Business Review* (May–June 1978): 131–42.

29. P. Blau, "A Formal Theory of Differentiation in Organizations," *American Sociological Review* 35 (1970): 684–95.

30. Ibid, pp. 201–18.

31. S. McCartney, "Airline Industry's Top-Ranked Woman Keeps Southwest's Small-Fry Spirit Alive," *Wall Street Journal,* November 30, 1995, p. B1.

32. P. M. Blau and R. A. Schoenherr, *The Structure of Organizations* (New York: Basic Books, 1971).

33. Jones, *Organizational Theory, Design, and Change.*

34. J. Galbraith, *Designing Complex Organizations* (Reading, MA: Addison-Wesley, 1973).

35. H. Mintzberg, *The Nature of Managerial Work* (New York: Harper and Row, 1973).

36. R. Parthasarthy and S. P. Sethi, "The Impact of Flexible Automation on Business Strategy and Organizational Structure," *Academy of Management Review* 17 (1992): 86–108.

37. www.daimlerchrysler.com, 2000.

38. "Man with a Plan," *Business Week* (October 4, 1999): 34–37.
39. K. Miller and J. Muller, "At the Wheel," *Newsweek* (November 16, 1998): 83–90.
40. www.daimlerchrysler.com, 2003.
41. H. Mintzberg, *The Structuring of Organizations* (Upper Saddle River, NJ: Prentice Hall, 1979), Ch. 1.
42. J. D. Thompson, *Organizations in Action* (New York: McGraw-Hill, 1967).
43. Elgin, "Running the Tightest Ships on the Net," *Business Week* (January 29, 2001): 125–26.
44. M. Rokeach, *The Nature of Human Values* (New York: Free Press, 1973).
45. T. Dewett and G. R. Jones, "The Role of Information Technology in the Organization: A Review, Model, and Assessment," *Journal of Management* 27 (2001): 313–46.
46. J. Child and R. G. McGrath, "Organizations Unfettered: Organizational Form in an Information Intensive Economy," *Academy of Management Journal* 44 (2001): 1135–49.
47. G. DeSanctis and P. Monge, "Introduction to the Special Issue: Communication Processes for Virtual Organizations," *Organization Science* 10 (1999): 693–703.
48. D. Constant, L. Sproul, and S. Kiesler, "The Kindness of Strangers: The Usefulness of Electronic Ties for Technical Advice," *Organization Science* 7 (1996): 119–35.
49. G. G. Dess and A. Rasheed, "The New, Corporate Architecture," *Academy of Management Executive* 9 (1995): 7–19.
50. J. Fulk and G. DeSanctis, "Electronic Communication and Changing Organizational Forms," *Organizational Science* 6 (1995): 337–49.
51. Y. P. Shao, S. Y. Liao, and H. Q. Wang, "A Model of Virtual Organizations," *Academy of Management Executive* 12 (1998): 120–28.
52. A. Williams, "Arthur Andersen-IT Initiatives Support Shifts in Business Strategy," *Informationweek* (September 11, 2000): 14–18.
53. T. Davenport and L. Prusak, *Information Ecology* (Oxford University Press, 1997).
54. www.accenture.com, 2003.
55. www.yahoo.com, 2003.
56. A. Grandori, "An Organizational Assessment of Interfirm Coordination Modes," *Organizational Studies* 18 (1997): 897–925.
57. www.nike.com, 2003.
58. G. S. Capowski, "Designing a Corporate Identity," *Management Review* (June 1993): 37–38.

Chapter 17

1. G. R. Jones, *Organizational Theory, Design, and Change* (Upper Saddle River, NJ: Prentice Hall, 2003).
2. www.3m.com, 2003.
3. www.3m.com, 2003.
4. G. M. Spreitzer and W. R. Nord, "Organizational Culture: Mapping the Terrain," *Academy of Management Review* 28, 3 (2003): 514–16 (book review); E. H. Schein, "Organizational Culture," *American Psychologist* (February 1990): 109–19.
5. G. R. Jones, "Transaction Costs, Property Rights, and Organizational Culture," *Administrative Science Quarterly* 28 (1983): 456–87; L. Smircich, "Concepts of Culture and Organizational Analysis," *Administrative Science Quarterly* 28 (1983): 339–58.
6. S. D. N. Cook and D. Yanow, "Culture and Organizational Learning," *Journal of Management Inquiry* 2 (1993): 373–90.
7. J. M. George and G. R. Jones, "Experiencing Work: Values, Attitudes, and Moods," *Human Relations* 50 (1997): 393–416; G. R. Jones and J. M. George, "The Experience and Evolution of Trust: Implications for Cooperation and Teamwork," *Academy of Management Review* 3 (1998): 531–46.
8. M. Rokeach, *The Nature of Human Values* (New York: The Free Press, 1973).
9. A. R. Jassawalla and H. C. Sashittal, "Cultures That Support the Product-Innovation Process," *Academy of Management Executive* 16 (2002): 42–55.
10. J. R. Detert, "A Framework for Linking Culture and Improvement Initiatives in Organizations," *Academy of Management Review* 25 (2000): 850–64.
11. M. J. Hatch, "The Dynamics of Organizational Culture," *Academy of Management Review* 7 (1993): 657–95.
12. D. M. Cable, L. Aiman-Smith, P. W. Mulvey, and J. R. Edwards, "The Sources and Accuracy of Job Applicants Beliefs about Organizational Culture," *Academy of Management Journal* 43 (2000): 1076–86.
13. P. L. Berger and T. Luckman, *The Social Construction of Reality* (Garden City, NY: Anchor Books, 1967).
14. E. H. Schein, "Culture: The Missing Concept in Organization Studies," *Administrative Science Quarterly* 41 (1996): 229–40.
15. A. Bianco, "Value Line: Too Lean, Too Mean," *Business Week* 16 (March 16, 1992): 104–06.
16. J. P. Walsh and G. R. Ungson, "Organizational Memory," *Academy of Management Review* 1 (1991): 57–91.
17. K. E. Weick, "Organizational Culture as a Source of High Reliability," *California Management Review* 9 (1984): 653–69.
18. A. Etzioni, *A Comparative Analysis of Organizations* (New York: The Free Press, 1975).
19. G. R. Jones, "Psychological Orientation and the Process of Organizational Socialization: An Interactionist Perspective," *Academy of Management Review* 8 (1983): 464–74.
20. C. Joinson, "The Best of Both Worlds," *HRMagazine* (September, 1999): 12–14.
21. J. Cone, "How Dell Does It," *Training & Development* (June 2000): 58–70.
22. A. Chen and M. Hicks, "Going Global? Avoid Culture Clashes," *PC Week* (April 3, 2000): 65.
23. H. M. Trice and J. M. Beyer, "Studying Organizational Culture Through Rites and Ceremonials," *Academy of Management Review* 9 (1984): 653–69.
24. H. M. Trice and J. M. Beyer, *The Cultures of Work Organizations* (Englewood Cliffs, NJ: Prentice Hall, 1993).
25. Trice and Beyer, "Studying Organizational Culture Through Rites and Ceremonials."
26. A. M. Pettigrew, "On Studying Organizational Cultures," *Administrative Science Quarterly* 24 (1979): 570–82.
27. www.walmart.com, 2003.
28. "Associates Keystone to Structure," *Chain Store Age* (December 1999): 17.
29. www.walmart.com, 2003.
30. M. Troy, "The Culture Remains the Constant," *Discount Store News* (June 8, 1998): 95–98.
31. S. Voros, "3D Management," *Management Review* (January 2000): 45–47.
32. M. Ramundo, "Service Awards Build Culture of Success," *Human Resources Magazine* (August 1992): 61–63.
33. "Neurosis, Arkansas-style," *Fortune* (April 17, 2000): 36.

34. H. M. Trice and J. M. Beyer, "Studying Organizational Cultures Through Rites and Ceremonials."

35. B. Schneider, "The People Make the Place," *Personnel Psychology* 40 (1987): 437–53.

36. J. E. Sheriden, "Organizational Culture and Employee Retention," *Academy of Management Journal* 35 (1992): 657–92.

37. E. H. Schein, "The Role of the Founder in Creating Organizational Culture," *Organizational Dynamics* 12 (1983): 13–28.

38. J. M. George, "Personality, Affect, and Behavior in Groups," *Journal of Applied Psychology* 75 (1990): 107–16.

39. E. Schein, *Organizational Culture and Leadership*, 2nd ed. (San Francisco: Jossey-Bass, 1992).

40. M. Hannan and J. Freeman, "Structural Inertia and Organizational Change," *American Sociological Review* 49 (1984): 149–64.

41. C. A. O'Reilly, J. Chatman, and D. F. Caldwell, "People and Organizational Culture: Assessing Person–Organizational Fit," *Academy of Management Journal* 34 (1991): 487–517.

42. George, "Personality, Affect, and Behavior in Groups"; D. Miller and J. M. Toulouse, "Chief Executive Personality and Corporate Strategy and Structure in Small Firms," *Management Science* 32 (1986): 1389–409.

43. T. M. Jones, "Ethical Decision Making by Individuals in Organizations: An Issue Contingent Model," *Academy of Management Review* 2 (1991): 366–95.

44. T. L. Beauchamp and N. E. Bowie (Eds.), *Ethical Theory and Business* (Englewood Cliffs, NJ: Prentice-Hall, 1979); A. MacIntyre, *After Virtue* (Notre Dame, IN: University of Notre Dame Press, 1981).

45. T. J. Peters and R. H. Waterman, Jr., *In Search of Excellence: Lessons from America's Best-Run Companies* (New York: Harper and Row, 1982).

46. B. Victor and J. B. Cullen, "The Organizational Bases of Ethical Work Climates," *Administrative Science Quarterly* 33 (1988): 101–25.

47. L. Kohlberg, "Stage and Sequence: The Cognitive-Development Approach to Socialization." In D. A. Goslin (Ed.), *Handbook of Socialization Theory and Research* (Chicago: Rand McNally, 1969), 347–80.

48. M. S. Frankel, "Professional Codes: Why, How, and with What Impact?" *Journal of Business Ethics* 8 (1989): 109–15.

49. J. Van Mannen and S. R. Barley, "Occupational Communities: Culture and Control in Organizations." in B. Staw and L. Cummings (Eds.), *Research in Organizational Behavior*, vol. 6 (Greenwich, CT: JAI Press, 1984), 287–365.

50. A. Sagie and D. Elizur, "Work Values: A Theoretical Overview and a Model of Their Affects," *Journal of Organizational Behavior* 17 (1996): 503–14.

51. G. R. Jones, "Transaction Costs, Property Rights, and Organizational Culture: An Exchange Perspective," *Administrative Science Quarterly* 28 (1983): 454–67.

52. www.bimba.com, 2003.

53. Ibid.

54. "ESOP Binges Change in Corporate Culture," *Employee Benefit Plan Review* (July 1992): 25–26.

55. C. Perrow, *Normal Accidents* (New York: Basic Books, 1984).

56. H. Mintzberg, *The Structuring of Organizational Structures* (Englewood Cliffs, NJ: Prentice Hall, 1979).

57. G. Kunda, *Engineering Culture* (Philadelphia: Temple University Press, 1992).

58. G. Hofstede, B. Neuijen, D. D. Ohayv, and G. Sanders, "Measuring Organizational Cultures: A Qualitative and Quantitative Study Across Twenty Cases," *Administrative Science Quarterly* 35 (1990): 286–316.

59. W. G. Ouchi, *Theory Z: How American Business Can Meet the Challenge of Japanese Management* (Reading, MA: Addison-Wesley, 1981).

60. G. Hofstede, "The Cultural Relativity of Organizational Practices and Theories," *Journal of International Business Studies* (Fall 1983): 75–89.

61. "Big-Company CEOs Exemplify Diversity," *HRMagazine* (August 1994): 25–26.

62. Hofstede, Neuijen, Ohayv, and Sanders, "Measuring Organizational Cultures."

63. G. Hofstede, "The Cultural Relativity of Organizational Practices and Theories."

64. www.corning.com, 2003; www.vitro.com, 2003.

65. A. DePalma, "It Takes More Than a Visa to Do Business in Mexico," *New York Times*, June 26, 1994, p. F5.

66. www.corning.com, 2003.

67. T. M. Jones, "Instrumental Stakeholder Theory: A Synthesis of Ethics and Economics," *Academy of Management Review* 20 (1995): 404–37.

68. J. Dobson, "Corporate Reputation: A Free Market Solution to Unethical Behavior," *Business and Society* 28 (1989): 1–5.

69. M. S. Baucus and J. P. Near, "Can Illegal Corporate Behavior Be Predicted? An Event History Analysis," *Academy of Management Journal* 34 (1991): 9–36.

70. J. B. Dozier and M. P. Miceli, "Potential Predictors of Whistle-Blowing: A Prosocial Behavior Perspective," *Academy of Management Review* 10 (1985): 823–36; J. P. Near and M. P. Miceli, "Retaliation Against Whistle-Blowers: Predictors and Effects," *Journal of Applied Psychology* 71 (1986): 137–45.

71. D. Collins, "Organizational Harm, Legal Consequences and Stakeholder Retaliation," *Journal of Business Ethics* 8 (1988): 1–13.

72. www.mci.com, 2003.

Chapter 18

1. J. P. Kotter, L. A. Schlesinger, and V. Sathe, *Organization* (Homewood, IL: Irwin, 1979), 487.

2. C. Argyris, R. Putman, and D. M. Smith, *Action Science* (San Francisco: Jossey-Bass, 1985).

3. R. M. Kanter, *The Change Masters: Innovation for Productivity in the American Corporation* (New York: Simon & Schuster, 1984).

4. C. W. L. Hill and G. R. Jones, *Strategic Management: An Integrated Approach*, 3rd ed. (Boston: Houghton Mifflin, 1995).

5. Ibid.

6. G. R. Jones, *Organizational Theory: Text and Cases* (Reading, MA: Addison-Wesley, 1995).

7. C. W. L. Hill, *International Business* (Chicago, IL: Irwin, 1994).

8. C. A. Bartlett and S. Ghoshal, *Managing Across Borders* (Boston: Harvard Business School Press, 1989).

9. C. K. Prahalad and Y. L. Doz, *The Multinational Mission: Balancing Local Demands and Global Vision* (New York: Free Press, 1987).

10. D. Jamieson and J. O'Mara, *Managing Workforce 2000: Gaining a Diversity Advantage* (San Francisco: Jossey-Bass, 1991).

11. T. H. Cox and S. Blake, "Managing Cultural Diversity: Implications for Organizational Competitiveness," *Academy of Management Executive* (August 1991): 49–52.

12. S. E. Jackson and Associates, *Diversity in the Workplace: Human Resource Initiatives* (New York: Guilford Press, 1992).

13. W. H. Shaw and V. Barry, *Moral Issues in Business*, 6th ed. (Belmont, CA: Wadsworth, 1995).

14. T. Donaldson, *Corporations and Morality* (Englewood Cliffs, NJ: Prentice-Hall, 1982).

15. "Nike Battles Backlash from Overseas Sweatshops," *Marketing News* (November 9, 1998): 14.

16. J. Laabs, "Nike Gives Indonesian Employees a Raise," *Workforce* (December 1998): 15–16.

17. W. Echikson, "It's Europe's Turn to Sweat About Sweatshops," *Business Week* (July 19, 1999): 96.

18. www.nike.com, 2003.

19. S. K. Piderit, "Rethinking Resistance and Recognizing Ambivalence: A Multidimensional View of Attitudes Toward an Organizational Change," *Academy of Management Review* 25, 4 (2000): 783–95.

20. M. Hannan and J. Freeman, "Structural Inertia and Organizational Change," *American Sociological Review* 49 (1989): 149–64.

21. L. E. Greiner, "Evolution and Revolution as Organizations Grow," *Harvard Business Review* (July–August 1972): 37–46.

22. R. M. Kanter, *When Giants Learn to Dance: Mastering the Challenges of Strategy* (New York: Simon and Schuster, 1989).

23. J. P. Kotter and L. A. Schlesinger, "Choosing Strategies for Change," *Harvard Business Review* (March–April 1979): 106–14.

24. T. Burns and G. M. Stalker, *The Management of Innovation* (London: Tavistock, 1961).

25. P. R. Lawrence and J. W. Lorsch, *Organization and Environment* (Boston: Harvard Business School Press, 1972).

26. R. Likert, *The Human Organization* (New York: McGraw-Hill, 1967).

27. C. Argyris, *Personality and Organization* (New York: Harper and Row, 1957).

28. This section draws heavily on K. Lewin, *Field Theory in Social Science* (New York: Harper and Row, 1951).

29. L. Chung-Ming and R. W. Woodman, "Understanding Organizational Change: A Schematic Perspective," *Academy of Management Journal* 38, 2 (1995): 537–55.

30. D. Miller, "Evolution and Revolution: A Quantum View of Structural Change in Organizations," *Journal of Management Studies* 19 (1982): 11–151; D. Miller, "Momentum and Revolution in Organizational Adaptation," *Academy of Management Journal* 2 (1980): 591–614.

31. C. E. Lindblom, "The Science of Muddling Through," *Public Administration Review* 19 (1959): 79–88; P. C. Nystrom and W. H. Starbuck, "To Avoid Organizational Crises, Unlearn," *Organizational Dynamics* 12 (1984): 53–65.

32. E. L. Trist, G. Higgins, H. Murray, and A. G. Pollock, *Organizational Choice* (London: Tavistock, 1965); J. C. Taylor, "The Human Side of Work: The Socio-Technical Approach to Work Design," *Personnel Review* 4 (1975): 17–22.

33. E. L. Trist and K. W. Bamforth, "Some Social and Psychological Consequences of the Long Wall Method of Coal Mining," *Human Relations* 4 (1951): 3–38; F. E. Emery and E. L. Trist, *Socio-Technical Systems* (London: Proceedings of the 6th Annual International Meeting of the Institute of Management Sciences, 1965), 92–93.

34. W. Edwards Deming, *Out of the Crisis* (Cambridge, MA: MIT Press, 1989); M. Walton, *The Deming Management Method* (New York: Perigee Books, 1990).

35. J. McHugh and B. Dale, "Quality Circles." In R. Wild (Ed.), *International Handbook of Production and Operations Research* (London: Cassel, 1989).

36. www.citigroup.com, 2003.

37. S. M. Young, "A Framework for the Successful Adoption and Performance of Japanese Manufacturing Techniques in the United States," *Academy of Management Review* 17 (1992): 677–700.

38. M. Hammer and J. Champy, *Reengineering the Corporation* (New York: HarperCollins, 1993).

39. A. M. Pettigrew, R. W. Woodman, and K. S. Cameron, "Studying Organizational Change and Development: Challenges for Future Research," *Academy of Management Journal* 44, 4 (2001): 697–714.

40. "Facts About Hallmark," www.hallmark.com, 2000.

41. J. Child and R. G. McGrath, "Organizations Unfettered: Organizational Form in an Information-Intensive Economy," *Organization Science*, 44, 6 (2001): 1135–49.

42. www.cypress.com, 2000.

43. www.microsoft.com, 2003.

44. W. McKinley, "Some Anticipated Consequences of Organizational Restructuring," *Academy of Management Review* 25, 4 (2000): 735–53.

45. Jones, *Organizational Theory*; R. A. Burgelman and M. A. Maidique, *Strategic Management of Technology and Innovation* (Homewood, IL: Irwin, 1988).

46. G. R. Jones and J. E. Butler, "Managing Internal Corporate Entrepreneurship: An Agency Theory Perspective," *Journal of Management* 18 (1992): 733–49.

47. E. Mansfield, J. Rapoport, J. Schnee, S. Wagner, and M. Hamburger, *Research and Innovation in the Modern Corporation* (New York: Norton, 1971).

48. K. J. Klein and J. Speer, "The Challenge of Innovation Implementation," *Academy of Management Review* 21, 4 (1996): 1055–71.

49. R. A. Burgelman, "Designs for Corporate Entrepreneurship in Established Firms," *California Management Review* 26 (1984): 154–66.

50. D. Frey, "Learning the Ropes: My Life as a Product Champion," *Harvard Business Review* (September–October 1991): 46–56.

51. Lewin, *Field Theory in Social Science*, pp. 172–74.

52. M. Crossan, "Altering Theories of Learning and Action: An Interview with Chris Argyris," *Academy of Management Executive* 17, 2 (2003): 40–47.

53. This section draws heavily on P. A. Clark, *Action Research and Organizational Change* (New York: Harper and Row, 1972); L. Brown, "Research Action: Organizational Feedback, Understanding and Change," *Journal of Applied Behavioral Research* 8 (1972): 697–711; N. Margulies and A. P Raia (Eds.), *Conceptual Foundations of Organizational Development* (New York: McGraw-Hill, 1978).

54. W. L. French and C. H. Bell, *Organizational Development* (Englewood Cliffs, NJ: Prentice-Hall, 1990).

55. L. Coch and J. R. P. French, "Overcoming Resistance to Change," *Human Relations* 1 (1948): 512–32.

56. French and Bell, *Organizational Development*.

57. Ibid.

58. www.lucent.com, 2003.

59. www.microsoft.com, 2003.

60. W. L. French, "A Checklist for Organizing and Implementing an OD Effort." In W. L. French, C. H. Bell, and R. A. Zawacki,

Organizational Development and Transformation (Homewood, IL: Irwin, 1994), 484–95.

61. Kotter, Schlesinger, and Sathe, *Organization*, p. 487.

62. W. G. Bennis, *Organizational Development: Its Nature, Origins, and Perspectives* (Reading, MA: Addison-Wesley, 1969).

63. Kotter and Schlesinger, "Choosing Strategies for Change."

64. S. Fox and Y. Amichai-Hamburger, "The Power of Emotional Appeals in Promoting Organizational Change Programs," *Academy of Management Executive* 15, 4 (2001): 84–95.

65. S. Myeong-Gu, "Overcoming Emotional Barriers, Political Obstacles, and Control Imperatives in the Action-Science Approach to Individual and Organizational Learning," *Academy of Management Learning and Education* 2, 1 (2003): 7–22.

66. E. H. Schein, *Organizational Psychology* (Englewood Cliffs, NJ: Prentice-Hall, 1980).

67. R. T. Golembiewski, "The Laboratory Approach to Organization Change: Schema of a Method." In Margulies and Raia (Eds.), *Conceptual Foundations of Organizational Development*, pp. 198–212.

68. E. H. Schein, *Process Consultation* (Reading, MA: Addison-Wesley, 1969).

69. M. Sashkin and W. Warner Burke, "Organization Development in the 1980s," *Journal of Management* 13 (1987): 393–417; D. Eden, "Team Development: Quasi-Experimental Confirmation Among Combat Companies," *Group and Organization Studies* 5 (1986): 133–46; K. P. DeMeuse and S. J. Liebowitz, "An Empirical Analysis of Team Building Research," *Group and Organization Studies* 6 (1981): 357–78.

70. French and Bell, *Organization Development*.

71. R. Beckhard, "The Confrontation Meeting," *Harvard Business Review* (March–April 1967): 159–65.

photo credits

name index

company index

subject index

Student Guidebook

to

Resources and Citation

Contents

AVOIDING PROBLEMS IN USING ONLINE SOURCES:

Using Online Sources

As you know, the Internet and computer technology have radically altered the way research is conducted and evaluated in our age today.

Without question, the chief difficulty in working with online sources is credibility. Many online sources are credible and make excellent sources for your essays. For example, your library may have specialized CD-ROM databases that contain thousands of articles and sources for certain academic areas. Examples of these are EconLit (for economics), Psych Articles (for psychology reports and studies), Lexis-Nexis (for newspaper articles and law journals), and ERIC (for education articles). Also, many academic Websites exist that collect useful links to guide your research—one of the best is The Voice of the Shuttle (*http://vos.ucsb.edu*).

Once you step outside these recommended parameters, you will find a host of questionable material on the Internet that may not be worth your time or, at worst, is full of false or erroneous information. Personal, as well as political or special interest, Websites often have no screening or referring devices and are not acceptable for use in your essays.

Evaluating Your Sources

Once you have found some possible sources of information, either in print or online, you should always read them carefully, noting any questions you may have, any doubts or ambiguities that you may discover in the work. Ask yourself questions:

- If facts and figures are presented, where did they come from?
- Are they the result of government or university studies?
- Could they be the results of biased or incomplete samples?

You are more of an authority than you may think—if the work leaves you with some doubt as to its reliability, then using it to back up your own arguments will leave your readers in doubt as well.

Authority

Careful reading can be your best clue to a writer's authority. Question your sources carefully:

- Does the author have first-hand knowledge or experience?
- Are arguments and supports presented logically and in an easy-to-follow order?

- Are facts and figures from reliable sources used to support the author's position when necessary?
- What kind of ethos, or personal authority, does the author present?
- Are the author's appeals based on logic (logos) or are they appeals to the reader's emotions (pathos)?

Some clues to the authority of a work can often be found outside the work itself. For print sources, the title page or book jacket gives important information: a university press such as Columbia University Press or Oxford University Press will probably wield more authority than a trade press targeted toward a more popular market. However, this will depend to a large extent on your topic. Sometimes the most authoritative source might be found in as unlikely a place as a comic book.

The author's credentials may include his or her own personal knowledge or experience, his or her education or demonstrated expertise, or may even reside in the presentation of the work itself, if it is logical and well-documented. Is the source cited in other works? Sometimes this can be a good clue to the authority of the source. Be careful, however; just because a work is referenced in other sources does not automatically grant it credibility, especially if the other sources have disputed the information it contains. If in doubt, check with your teacher or reference librarian.

The ease of publication on the Internet makes it possible for virtually anyone with the necessary technological skills to become a "published" author on the World Wide Web. It is often difficult to ascertain what the author's credentials may be, and there is usually no review or selection process for pages published on the Internet.

The World Wide Web (WWW) does have a kind of "book jacket" though—the domain name. The domain name is usually the first part of the Internet address (called the Uniform Resource Locator, or URL), and can provide some important clues to the location of the author (and, hence, perhaps to the authority of the author). For example, a document at *http://www.cas.usf.edu* resides on the World Wide Web server (*www*) for the College of Arts and Sciences (*cas*) at the University of South Florida (*usf*), an educational institution (*edu*). Generally, the last part of the domain name or Internet address gives valuable clues as to the type of site where the information resides:

.com   A commercial server or business

.org   an organization, often a non-profit

.edu   An educational institution

.gov   A government server

Outside of the United States, domain names may end with the abbreviation for the country of origin. *For example, http://www.unimelb.edu.au* is the World Wide Web server for the University of Melbourne, an educational institution in Australia. Some common abbreviations include:

.au   Australia

.ca   Canada

.jp   Japan

.uk   United Kingdom

.nz   New Zealand

Of course, many personal home pages can be found on University servers—some of little interest to anyone but the student and his or her friends—and many commercial sites may be maintained as a public service or may be used by scholars to provide useful and serious work. Just as with traditionally-published sources, then, your topic and your own critical reading skills will be your best judge.

The Modern Language Association (MLA) classifies online sources into several categories, including scholarly projects; professional sites; personal sites; online books and poems; articles in reference databases, journals, or magazines; and postings to electronic discussion lists. This classification is an attempt to help you to discern the reliability of a given source and may be useful in helping you to determine the source's authority. However, this *taxonomy* may be difficult to apply to the wide variety of information available online. Learning to read the parts of the *URL*, or Uniform Resource Locator, may provide a more reliable means of evaluating a potential source's authority and reliability.

The taxonomy of the URL breaks down into specific parts: the type of protocol used to access the resource, the domain name where the file resides, any directories and/or sub-directories, and the file name and type. URLs may not have some or all of these parts. It is important, however, when citing sources, that you include the entire URL as shown in the "Location" box in your browser.

Protocol	Domain	Directory	Sub-Directories	File	File Type
http://	www.cas.usf.edu	english	walker	mla	.html
http://	www.m-w.com				
http://	www.columbia.edu	acis	documentation/ghttp	search-info	.html

Timeliness

You will usually want to use the most recent sources you can find on a subject since these will not only reflect current trends and knowledge but will usually build upon (or refute) older work. Of course, this often depends on your subject—if you are trying to show how the sexual revolution of the 1960s affected marriage and divorce rates at the time, you may want to look at some magazine and journal articles or books written during that time period as well as at later works that look back on the period.

As you probably already know, journals and magazines are usually more recent sources than books simply because of the time involved in publication. Book publishing can be a time-consuming process and, often, by the time a book comes out in print, much of the information in it is already old news or out of date. You probably already look to indices of journals, magazines, and newspapers when you need to find more current information.

One of the distinct advantages of the Internet is the speed of publication—papers can be written and published on the same day. The Internet, then, can represent a source of up-to-the-minute information. Of course, being up-to-the-minute is not always the same thing as being authoritative. And, even on the Internet, sometimes Web pages are left to die, forgotten and seldom visited. Publication dates may have been omitted, so ascertaining how current a source is on the WWW may be difficult or impossible. Thus, although you want to look for current information, you also want to make sure that the work you use is reliable. This is a good reason why you should not rely on only one source for your research, either on the Internet or in print.

Relevance

There is no magic formula to determine how relevant a given source is to your topic. The best determiner, of course, is your own critical judgment.

▌ Does the information answer important questions that you have raised?

▌ Does it support your propositions or present counter-arguments that you need to address?

▌ Does it present examples or illustrate important points in your paper?

Do not include a source just because the information is interesting or just to add more titles to your Works Cited page. Above all, don't let your sources use you. You are conducting research to find answers, to find support, and to find illustrations of your thesis. Do not simply put together a paper that summarizes the research that others have done without having a point of your own. In determining how relevant a source is to your work, you must first determine what it can add to your own work. Of course, if it makes important points that you had not previously considered or convincingly disproves your own point of view, ethics will dictate that you acknowledge it in your work.

One important advantage that conducting online research may have is precisely that you will find sources of information that may not be included in library collections. Some of these may reflect points of view that need to be considered, whether or not they are "authoritative." If a Web search of your topic returns many sites that provide biased information, this might reflect a need to counter emotional appeals and misinformation that may have been widely disseminated in the popular presses.

Author's Purpose and Audience

During the course of your research, you will probably read many different sources on your topic, some of which will examine the same areas but will arrive at very different conclusions. Even facts and figures can be interpreted in many different ways (Is the glass half empty or half full?). Authors do not write in a vacuum; we all come to the work with our own biases, preconceptions, and objectives. The author's choice of what to include and what to exclude, of organization and emphasis, and of word choice and format all reflect the author's purpose and audience. Sometimes the author's bias or purpose is explicit—the thesis statement may clearly define what the author wants to prove. Sometimes, however, only careful reading will help you to discover the author's true purpose.

The choice of audience can be one key to discerning the author's biases. The choice to publish documents on the World Wide Web versus in-print publication, or to post to a public listserv or newsgroup rather than writing a letter to the editor of a print magazine or newspaper, for example, can sometimes provide clues since the audiences for print and for electronic publications are different. For instance, you can expect online audiences to have some knowledge of computers. An article written for a student newspaper on proposed tuition increases might present a different perspective than an article written for the University's Board of Trustees. Biases are not necessarily bad, but you do need to consider them in determining the value and credibility of your sources.

A Point to Remember

Scholarly writing is an ongoing conversation, something that becomes quite visible in electronic discussion lists and Web pages. But even in traditional print papers, giving proper credit to others for their words and ideas makes visible the thread of the conversation. Most student plagiarism is not intentional; poor note taking can often result in unintentional plagiarism. Students often do not realize that it is necessary to denote even one- or two-word quotations. Paraphrases and summaries, as well as direct quotations, must also be cited. No matter where your information comes from—books and articles, television, interviews and discussions, or electronic formats—make sure you give credit.

AVOIDING PROBLEMS IN USING SOURCES:
Avoiding Logical Fallacies

During the research writing process, both when selecting sources and using the information as support, writers must avoid logical fallacies. Since most writing in college courses is argumentative, the source materials that are used by students are also written arguments created by means of logical discussion. Therefore, writers must read their sources critically to analyze the arguments or points being made.

To be convincing to most readers, an argument must be valid. In order to validate a point, a writer must be clear, logical, and organized in his or her thinking. He must also provide adequate evidence to support the point being made and this is not an easy task. Since writing effective, valid arguments is not easy, many writers commit errors in their thinking that lead to fallacies in their writing. Logical fallacies are errors in argumentation. Here are common logical fallacies:

- Ad hominem argument: attacking the idea by attacking the person who holds the idea
- Bandwagon reasoning: claiming that an idea is valid since "everyone else does it"
- Hasty generalization: making a broad claim based on just a few occurrences
- Faulty cause and effect: claiming that one idea is the cause of another simply because one happened first in time
- Oversimplification: offering an easy solution to a complex problem

What Is Plagiarism?

Plagiarism is the failure to acknowledge your sources or the act of making it appear that someone else's work is your own. It often results from the unintentional failure to document sources accurately. All sources must be documented—not just print media, but interviews, broadcast media, and electronic sources as well. Internet or other electronic sources may need particular attention. Downloading information is so easy that it is equally easy for a writer to underestimate just how much he or she is relying on the electronic source. However, whether deliberate or not, plagiarism is a crime within the academic community and can result in serious consequences for the student writer and researcher.

Why should you care? Plagiarism is a form of dishonesty. The academic community relies upon the reciprocal exchange of ideas and information to further knowledge and research. Using information without acknowledging its source violates this process and cheats writers and researchers of the credit they deserve for their work and creativity.

Plagiarism can have even more dire consequences for students. A plagiarized paper can result in a failing grade in a course and, at some schools, disciplinary action ranging from suspension to expulsion. A record of such action may adversely affect professional opportunities in the future as well as graduate school admission.

▌ When to Document

Whenever you use information, facts, statistics, opinions, hypotheses, and ideas from outside sources, it is essential that you document them. Outside sources include:

- books
- Web sites
- periodicals
- newspapers
- material from electronic databases
- radio or television programs
- interviews
- speeches
- letters and correspondence, including e-mail

Your documentation must be thorough and correctly placed within the body of your paper and in the bibliography that follows your paper, according to the documentation style you are using. Common knowledge, such as widely known information about current events, famous people, geographical facts, or familiar history, normally does not need to be documented. However, if you are in doubt about whether information is common knowledge, the safest strategy is to provide documentation. Many instructors require that students document all information that they learn in their research.

Using Print and Electronic Sources

Most accidental occurrences of plagiarism involve problems with three techniques for using source information: quotation, paraphrase, and summary. These problems can occur with any kind of source— print materials (such as books and magazines), electronic sources (such as Web pages or CD-ROMs), images (from print or the Internet), interviews, and so on. The problems usually do not result from failing to credit a source but from failing to do so accurately. This section defines the three techniques for using sources and shows examples of plagiarism involving each. Because these three techniques figure prominently in the issue of plagiarism, we will revisit them throughout this tutorial.

Read the excerpt below from Gary J. Patronek's "The Problem of Animal Hoarding," originally published in *Municipal Lawyer* and later posted on the Internet. After reading it carefully, go to the reference site to learn more about the technique and to see an example of unintentional plagiarism.

Original Source

Although the stereotypical profile of a hoarder is an older, single female, living alone and known as the neighborhood "cat lady," in reality this behavior seems to cross all demographic and socioeconomic boundaries. As hoarders tend to be very secretive, many can lead a double life with a successful professional career—hoarding behavior has been discovered among doctors, nurses, public officials, college professors, and veterinarians, as well as among a broad spectrum of socioeconomically disadvantaged individuals. (Patronek, 2001, p. 1)

References

Patronek, G. J. (2001, May/June). The problem of animal hoarding. *Municipal Lawyer, 42*(3). Retrieved March 4, 2002, from *http://www.tufts.edu/vet/cfa/MunicipaLawyer.pdf*

Quotation

A quotation reproduces an actual part of a source to support a statement or idea or to provide an example. The length of a quotation can range from a word or phrase to several paragraphs.

Example of plagiarism:

According to Patronek (2001), the practice of animal hoarding can be found in a *broad spectrum of socioeconomically disadvantaged individuals.* Thus, agencies investigating reports of animal hoarding should be prepared to deal with people coming from a variety of backgrounds.

What's wrong?

Two things. First, the writer did not place quotation marks around the quotation (in italics). Second, the specific location, generally the page number of the citation, does not immediately follow the quotation.

Correction:

According to Patronek (2001), the practice of animal hoarding can be found in "a broad spectrum of socioeconomically disadvantaged individuals" (p. 1). Thus, agencies investigating reports of animal hoarding should be prepared to deal with people coming from a variety of backgrounds.

What's right?

The writer used quotation marks to indicate the beginning and end of the quotation. The page number follows immediately after the quotation. Unlike many Internet sources, this document does include page numbers. If you are quoting from an Internet document without page numbers, use other identifying information provided in it. For example, if the paragraphs are numbered, provide the paragraph number in your parenthetical citation, using either the paragraph symbol or the abbreviation para.: (Smith, 2001, ¶5) or (Smith, 2001, para. 5). In a document without numbered pages or paragraphs but with named subdivisions, the name of the subdivision may be used to identify the location of the quotation: (Perez, 2002, Findings section). If there are no page numbers, paragraph numbers, or named subdivisions, provide only the name of the author(s) and the date. If no author is identified, use a shortened form of the title.

Quotation Rules to Remember:

Regardless of the length of your quotation, to avoid plagiarism, observe these rules whenever you quote:

1. Copy the material from your source to your paper exactly as it appears in the original. Use ellipses, three spaced periods (. . .), to indicate where words or phrases have been omitted. Use square brackets ([ ]) to insert essential words not found in the original.

2. Enclose short quotations (under 40 words) in quotation marks.

3. Indent long quotations (40 words or longer) approximately ½ inch from the left margin. Begin the quotation on a new line and double-space throughout. Put the parenthetical citation (author, date, page number) after the period at the end of the quotation. Do not enclose the blocked quotation in quotation marks.

4. Provide clear attribution to your source so that your readers know the origin of the quotation.

5. Immediately follow each quotation by a citation indicating the specific source information required.

Paraphrase

A paraphrase is a restatement in your own words and sentence structure of specific ideas or information from a source. Paraphrase is useful when you want to capture certain ideas or details from a source but do not need or want to quote the author's actual words.

Example of plagiarism:

Although an animal hoarder is stereotypically thought of as an older, unmarried woman, living by herself and known as the neighborhood "cat lady," this behvior evidently crosses socioeconomic and demographic lines (Patronek, 2001, p. 1).

What's wrong?

The wording and sentence structure of the paraphrase are too close to the original.

Correction:

Animal hoarding may be practiced by a person of any age, gender, or socioeconomic background, not just by an older woman thought of as the local "cat lady" (Patronek, 2001, p. 1).

What's right?

The ideas from the source are conveyed in the writer's own words and sentence structure.

Paraphrase Rules to Remember:

To avoid plagiarizing when you paraphrase, be sure to follow these rules:

1. Use your own words and sentence structure. Your paraphrase must not duplicate the writer's words or phrases. If your paraphrase includes words "borrowed" from the original, you must use quotation marks within your paraphrase to indicate quoted material.

2. Introduce all paraphrases with clear attribution to your source so that your readers know the origin of your information.

3. Make sure your paraphrase is an accurate and objective restatement of the writer's specific ideas.

4. Immediately follow your paraphrase with a citation indicating the specific source of the information. Although the *Publication Manual of the American Psychological Association* states that authors are not required to provide a page or paragraph number with a paraphrase, it encourages authors to do so.

▎ Summary

Summary is a brief restatement in your own words of the main ideas in a source. Summary is used to convey the general meaning of the ideas in a source, without specific details or examples that may appear in the original. You can summarize a paragraph, a chapter, an Internet document, or even an entire book, depending on the needs of your paper.

Example of plagiarism:

According to Patronek (2001), not all animal hoarders fit the stereotypical profile of the neighborhood "cat lady" but can come from any demographic and socioeconomic group. Some hoarders are successful professionals including doctors, nurses, politicians, and teachers. Thus, agencies investigating reports of animal hoarding should be prepared to deal with people from a variety of backgrounds.

What's wrong?

Some of the writer's language remains too similar to the source. In addition, the writer's ideas are not distinguished from those in the source because the citation does not immediately follow the summary.

Correction:

According to Patronek (2001), animal hoarders can come from any demographic and socioeconomic group, including successful professionals (p. 1). Thus, agencies investigating reports of animal hoarding should be prepared to deal with people with a variety of backgrounds.

What's right?

The writer has separated his/her own ideas from the summarized ideas of the source by placing the citation immediately after the summary. As noted in the discussion of paraphrasing, the *Publication Manual of the American Psychological Association* states that authors are not required to provide a page or paragraph number with a paraphrase, but it encourages authors to do so. Providing the location of the summary of a portion of a document is equally desirable.

Summary Rules to Remember:

When summarizing, adhere to the following rules to avoid plagiarism:

1. Write the summary using your own words. If you "borrow" words or phrases from your source, you must use quotation marks within your summary to indicate quoted material.

2. Introduce all summaries with clear attribution to your source so that your readers know the origin of the information.

3. Make sure your summary is an accurate and objective restatement of the writer's main ideas.

4. Immediately follow your summary with a citation indicating the specific source of the information.

Avoiding Plagiarism

▌Seven Rules

This section takes an in-depth look at seven rules that will help you avoid unintentional plagiarism. It provides examples of problems that result when the rules are not followed, shows how to correct the problems, and offers practice exercises to help you develop accurate documentation skills. Remember that these rules apply equally to print and online documents.

1. **Provide clear attribution of outside sources; this can be done with parenthetical citations, lead-in or signal phrases, or a combination thereof.** Attributions may contain the name of the author and that individual's professional affiliation or the name of the organization that provided the information for your paper. Introductory phrases such as "Senator Johnson observes" or "According to the President's Initiative on Race" clearly identify your source and incorporate the information smoothly into your paper.

2. **Identify all words and phrases taken from sources by enclosing them within quotation marks,** unless those words or phrases are commonly used expressions or clichés.

3. **Follow all quotations, paraphrases, and summaries of outside sources with appropriate and complete citations**. Citations should immediately follow the material being quoted, paraphrased, or summarized. Information provided in your attribution, such as the name of the author, does not need to be repeated in the citation.

4. **Use your own words and sentence structure when you paraphrase.** A paraphrase should capture a specific idea from a source but must not duplicate the writer's phrases and words.

5. **Be certain that all summaries and paraphrases of your sources are accurate and objective.** You must clearly distinguish your own views and ideas from those of your sources.

6. **Include all print and retrievable electronic sources in the References page that follows the body of your paper.** Be sure that all the required information for each entry is accurate and complete. Personal communication, such as letters and e-mail, should be cited parenthetically but does not appear on the References page.

7. **Provide documentation for all visual images, charts, and graphs from printed or electronic sources.** Be certain to accurately record the URL for Internet sources so that your citation will be correct. Images, charts, and graphs require documentation whether they are "pasted" into your paper as illustrations or summarized within the text of your paper.

APA Style Guide

This style guide is based on the *Publication Manual of the American Psychological Association,* 5th edition, 2001.

Formatting References: In your papers, references should be double-spaced and the reference should be a hanging indent; the first line of each reference is set flush left and subsequent lines are indented.

▌ Citing Print Resources

Type of Source	Format of the Citation in the Reference List	Format of the Reference Citation in the Text of Your Document
Book with 1 to 2 authors	Bridges, E.M., & Hallinger, P. (1995). Implementing problem based learning in leadership and development. Eugene, OR: ERIC Clearinghouse of Educational Management.	(Bridges & Hallinger, 1995)
Book with 3 to 5 authors	Gordon, V.N., Habley, W.R., & Associates. (2000). Academic advising: A comprehensive handbook. San Francisco: Jossey-Bass.	(Gordon, Habley, & Associates, 2000) first citation (Gordon *et al.*, 2000) subsequent citations
Edited book	Rudestam, K.E., & Schoenholtz-Read, J. (Eds.). (2002). Handbook of online learning: Innovations in higher education and corporate training. Thousand Oaks, CA: Sage Publications.	(Rudestam & Schoenholtz-Read, 2002)
Chapter from a book	Masaro, D. (1992). Broadening the domain of the fuzzy logical model of perception. In H.L. Pick, Jr., P. van den Broek, & D.C. Knill (Eds.), Cognition: Conceptual and methodological issues (pp. 51–84). Washington, DC: American Psychological Association.	(Masaro, 1992)

(continued)

Type of Source	Format of the Citation in the Reference List	Format of the Reference Citation in the Text of Your Document
Journal article with 2 authors (paginated by issue)	Burbules, N.C., & Bruce, B.C. (1995). This is not a paper. Educational Researcher, 24(8), 12–18.	(Burbules & Bruce, 1995)
Journal article with 3 to 6 authors	Anderson, J.R., Reder, L.M., & Simon, H.A. (1996). Situated learning and education. Educational Researcher, 25(4), 5–11.	(Anderson, Reder, & Simon, 1996) first citation (Anderson *et al.*, 1996) subsequent citations
Magazine article	Lowry, T. (2003, November 17). ESPN's face-off over fees. Business Week, 66–68	(Lowry, 2003)
Encyclopedia article	Bergmann, P.G. (1993). Relativity. In the new encyclopaedia Britannica (Vol. 26, pp. 501–508). Chicago: Encyclopaedia Britannica.	(Bergmann, 1993)

Citing Electronic Resources

When using and citing Internet sources, you should observe the following two guidelines:

1. Direct readers as closely as possible to the information being cited; whenever possible, reference specific documents rather than home or menu pages.

2. Provide addresses that work.

Type of Source	Format of the Citation in the Reference List	Format of the Reference Citation in the Text of Your Document
Document available on university program or department Web site	McClintock, R. (1994). Educating America for the 21st Century: A Strategic Plan for Educational Leadership January 2000 through December 2004 Version 2.1. Retrieved November 28, 2003, from Columbia University, Institute for Learning Technologies Web site: *http://www.ilt.columbia.edu/publications/docs/ILTplan_new.html.*	(McClintock, 1994)
Electronic copy of a journal article, 3 to 5 authors, retrieved from database	Marriott, L. K., Hauss-Wegzyniak, B., Benton, R. S., Vraniak, P.D., & Wenk, G. L. (2002). Long-term estrogen therapy worsens the behavioral and neuropathological consequences of chronic brain inflammation [Electronic version]. *Behavioral Neuroscience, 116,* 902–911.	(Marriott, Hauss-Wegzyniak, Benton, Vraniak, & Wenk, 2002) first citation (Marriott *et al.,* 2002) subsequent citations
Internet articles based on a print source	Parrot, A. C. (1999). Does cigarette smoking *cause* stress? *American Psychologist, 54,* 817–820. Retrieved May 10, 2002, from *http://www.apa.org/journals/amp/amp5410817.html.*	(Parrot, 1999) first citation
Web Site	Microsoft. Investor Relations. Retrieved February 24, 2004, from *http://www.microsoft.com/msft.*	(Microsoft, 2004)